Oracle Business Intelligence 11g Developer's Guide

Mark Rittman

New York   Chicago   San Francisco
Lisbon   London   Madrid   Mexico City   Milan
New Delhi   San Juan   Seoul   Singapore   Sydney   Toronto

The McGraw·Hill Companies

Cataloging-in-Publication Data is on file with the Library of Congress

McGraw-Hill books are available at special quantity discounts to use as premiums and sales promotions, or for use in corporate training programs. To contact a representative, please e-mail us at bulksales@mcgraw-hill.com.

Oracle Business Intelligence 11*g* Developer's Guide

1234567890   DOC DOC   1098765432

ISBN   978-0-07-179874-7
MHID   0-07-179874-9

Sponsoring Editor Paul Carlstroem	**Technical Editors** Venkatakrishnan Janakiraman, Mike Durran	**Production Supervisor** George Anderson
Editorial Supervisor Jody McKenzie	**Copy Editors** Emily Rader, Bill McManus	**Composition** Cenveo Publisher Services
Project Manager Sandhya Gola, Cenveo Publisher Services	**Proofreader** Claire Splan	**Illustration** Cenveo Publisher Services
Acquisitions Coordinator Ryan Willard	**Indexer** Jack Lewis	**Art Director, Cover** Jeff Weeks

This book is of course dedicated to Janet, Scott, and Isabella, my wonderful family, who put up with my late nights, missing weekends, bad moods, and lack of attention while I put this book together. I've neglected you all over the past two years, and you'll get a lot more of my attention (whether you want it or not!) now. Also, I must thank my mother and father, who bought me my first video game (a Mattel Intellivision, back in 1980) and then, when I tried to reprogram it, bought me a Commodore Vic-20. Even at 3.5KB RAM and a 20 character–width screen, it was enough to start me on my life-long career in IT and computers.

About the Author

Mark Rittman is Technical Director and co-founder of Rittman Mead, an Oracle Gold Partner with offices in the UK, USA, India, and Australia. Rittman Mead provides consulting, implementation, training, and managed services for all of Oracle's BI, DW, and EPM products. Prior to co-founding the company, Mark worked for a number of high-profile clients in the UK, delivering business intelligence and data warehousing projects based on Oracle technology.

Mark is also an Oracle ACE Director specializing in business intelligence and middleware, writes a regular column on business intelligence for *Oracle Magazine,* and is a speaker at industry and user group events around the world. Mark also writes for the Rittman Mead Blog (http://www.rittmanmead.com/blog) and can be contacted on Twitter at @markrittman. Away from his professional life, Mark has two children, lives in Brighton, UK, and is still waiting for Tottenham Hotspur to finally win the English Premier League.

About the Technical Editors

Venkatakrishnan Janakiraman is the India Managing Director of Rittman Mead. He is an Oracle ACE and a well-known Oracle BI-EPM tools blogger. Venkat specializes in Oracle Business Intelligence and toolsets related to Enterprise Performance Management. Venkat has been a regular contributor to the Oracle BI community through his company, as well as personal blogs at www.rittmanmead.com/author/venkat/ and http://oraclebizint.wordpress.com. He has over nine years of related experience in Oracle Business Intelligence, and he can be contacted on Twitter at @krisvenkat.

Mike Durran joined Oracle in 1996 after completing a PhD in computational chemistry. He worked in Oracle consulting for four years, gaining experience with the complete data warehouse and business intelligence project life cycle.

After joining product development in 2000, Mike worked on the product management team for Discoverer until 2006 when he took on product management for Oracle BI Delivers, the component of Oracle BI Enterprise Edition responsible for proactive alerting and distribution of key business insight. More recently, Mike has been responsible for the infrastructure and life cycle aspects of the Oracle Exalytics In-Memory Machine.

Contents at a Glance

Contents

Foreword

Business Intelligence (BI), once limited to small groups of analysts and strategists, is now everywhere and central to everything successful organizations do. In fact, BI is so important and pervasive, it often is embedded into everyday business applications and processes, is touched by almost every employee, and is central to everything organizations do. End users—increasingly accustomed to rich, graphical, and intuitive interfaces from the likes of Facebook, Amazon, and Google—expect the same from their reporting and analytics systems. End users further expect to use BI on their mobile phones and tablets as easily as they do on their desktops and laptops.

Oracle Business Intelligence (OBI) is the industry's leading Business Intelligence platform and is designed to integrate wide ranges of data sources, applications, and technologies. The OBI 11g release, on which this book is based, introduces a host of new features including advanced visualizations, scorecards, key performance indicators, a process integration toolkit called the Action Framework, as well as Oracle BI Mobile for consuming analytics through mobile devices and tablets. In addition, Oracle BI 11g comes tightly integrated with Oracle Essbase and the Hyperion EPM Suite. Oracle BI 11g leverages Oracle Fusion Middleware and Oracle Enterprise Manager, providing enterprise-class infrastructure, security, and management for Oracle BI Applications.

This book provides comprehensive coverage of Oracle Business Intelligence from a number of perspectives: from initial installation and configuration, to the creation of rich, multi-source semantic models, to the presentation to users as simple-to-understand dimensional models. Once the model is in place, the book takes you through creating ad-hoc analyses, pixel-perfect published reports, and interactive scorecards. You are then shown how to secure the system, scale it out as demand increases, and manage it all using the same tools and technologies that used to manage the rest of your Oracle systems.

Oracle recently launched Oracle Exalytics In-Memory Machine, the industry's first integrated in-memory BI platform providing enterprise class speed-of-thought analytics. Oracle Exalytics is key to Oracle's BI strategy, and I'm pleased to see it not only referenced in the product architecture at the start of the book, but it is also given its own chapter.

Thanks to Mark and his team of technical editors and researchers. I hope you enjoy this book as much as I did.

Balaji Yelamanchili
Senior Vice President, Product Development
Analytics and Performance Management Products
Oracle Corporation

Acknowledgments

I'd like to put on record my thanks to Jon Mead, co-founder of Rittman Mead, and the rest of the team at Rittman Mead, who gave me the time, support, and encouragement to put the book together. Thank you to Jon, Venkat, Stewart, Gerry, Ashley, and Borkur, who covered for me on the management team while I was heads-down writing the book, and to the following colleagues who helped review the final draft of the book and provided invaluable feedback:

- Mike Vickers
- Michael Rainey
- James Coyle
- Adam Seed
- Ram Chaitanya
- Koen Vantome
- Chris Redgrave
- Daniel Adams
- Richard Yeardley
- Witold Kusnierz
- Borkur Steingrimsson
- Robin Moffatt
- Ragnar Wessels
- Jason Baer
- Gerry Williams

Thanks also to Venkat Janakiraman and Mike Durran, my technical editors, who of course are responsible for any remaining technical errors in this book … (!) Seriously, though, you both went above and beyond what was required and helped make sure the book is, hopefully, as useful and accurate as I hoped it would be.

This book wouldn't have happened without the support and guidance of the team at McGraw Hill, especially Paul Carlstroem, who had to talk me into writing the book in the first place, talk me out of quitting it at several points, and keep me going even when I thought I'd never complete it; Ryan Willard, who was so enthusiastic I couldn't bear to let her down, and Emily Rader who copyedited the book and helped make it all the more readable and consistent. Working with Paul, Ryan, and Emily showed me the value of working with a publisher like McGraw Hill, and the final quality of the end-product you're now reading bears testament to their professionalism and encouragement.

Another round of thanks is due to the Oracle user group community, including the UK Oracle User Group, Oracle Development Tools User Group, International Oracle Users Group, and the European Oracle Users Council, for having me as a guest at their conferences, allowing me to serve on their committees and boards, and generally promoting the interests of Oracle BI developers and customers around the world. In a similar vein, thanks also to the Oracle ACE Program, Oracle Technology Network, and Oracle Magazine for supporting my work in the Oracle community, publishing my articles and blog posts, and providing me with the platform that made this book possible.

Oracle Corporation provided invaluable assistance, early access to software, and technical briefings for this book. I'd like to thank Balaji Yelamanchili, Senior Vice President in charge of BI and EPM development within Oracle, who provided high-level sponsorship; Mike Durran, Adam Bloom, and Nick Tuson, who supported my work from the Oracle BI infrastructure development offices in Bristol, UK; and Matt Bedin, Alan Lee, Philippe Lions, and everyone else over in Redwood Shores, who answered all of my questions and helped review and fact-check the various chapters.

Finally, I just want to thank Graham Spicer, who gave me my first break in the world of Oracle BI and DW consulting, had faith in me when I started, and provided me with the encouragement and inspiration to start speaking and writing about Oracle Business Intelligence—Graham, without you, none of this would have happened.

Introduction

Oracle Business Intelligence 11*g* is Oracle Corporation's platform for delivering business intelligence across a complete range of data sources, applications, and business processes. It consists of a number of servers, query and analysis tools, plug-ins to popular third-party applications such as Microsoft Office, and tools for managing business metadata.

If your organization has recently licensed Oracle Business Intelligence to provide reporting, analysis, and dashboards across your organization—congratulations! You have made a wise decision. However, like most enterprise-class software products, Oracle Business Intelligence is a complex product that rewards those developers who take the time to learn how to correctly configure, build, and then deploy solutions built using it. By purchasing this book, you will gain a great introduction to the complexities of Oracle Business Intelligence, together with an invaluable reference for when you hit those tricky technical issues.

This book takes you through the complete life cycle for deploying Oracle Business Intelligence within your organization, and it is based on the 11*g* Release 1 (11.1.1.6) version of the product. The assumed audience for the book is developers who will be responsible for installing, configuring, and developing the initial business intelligence solution, who also need to know something about the internals of the product and how it has been put together.

What You Will Learn

With this book, you will learn how to perform the following tasks:

- Install Oracle Business Intelligence 11.1.1.6 on Microsoft Windows and Linux platforms
- Create an Oracle BI Repository using data sourced from a relational data mart

- Extend the repository to include data from multiple data sources, add calculations and drill paths, integrate detail-level and summary data, and understand more complex topics such as table sources, federation, and fragmentation

- Import metadata into the repository from Oracle Essbase, Oracle OLAP, and Microsoft Analysis Services databases, and integrate that data with relational and other data sources

- Manage and maintain the Oracle BI Server component, configuring features such as query caching, write back, usage tracking, and aggregate persistence

- Create analyses and dashboards, together with prompts and other dashboard objects

- Define key performance indicators and use them to create interactive scorecards

- Create production-quality reports and distribute them in PDF and other formats

- Create alerts and send them via e-mail, pager, or other delivery channels

- Embed business intelligence in your applications and business processes

- Define highly available systems with resilience, failover, and clustering

- Add row- and subject-level security to your reports, and integrate with external identity management systems such as Microsoft Active Directory

- Use Enterprise Manager to administer your BI infrastructure and learn how to script systems management tasks using JMX MBeans and the WebLogic Scripting Tool (WLST)

- Configure Oracle Exalytics In-Memory Machine after initial installation, and use the Summary Advisor to create in-memory aggregates to provide "speed-of-thought" analysis

What's in the Book

This book contains twelve chapters, starts with a product overview and installation steps, then covers topics from creating repositories through to deploying dashboards and making them secure. Each chapter contains detailed background and explanations for the concepts we are discussing, and has worked examples that you can try out yourself to practice key development techniques. This book is the product of three years of research, testing, and writing, and I hope covers the most important techniques you'll need to master to get the best out of Oracle Business Intelligence 11*g*.

Chapter 1: "Oracle Business Intelligence Overview and Architecture"

In this chapter, you'll learn about the capabilities and features within Oracle Business Intelligence, how the product is built on Oracle Fusion Middleware, and how components such as the Oracle BI Server, Oracle BI Presentation Server, and Oracle BI Scheduler work to deliver dashboards and reports to your users.

Chapter 2: "Installing and Upgrading Oracle Business Intelligence"

You'll explore the various installation scenarios for Oracle Business Intelligence and look at how metadata and dashboards from earlier releases can be upgraded to the 11*g* release. You'll also see how Oracle Business Intelligence can be extended and clustered over multiple servers, and how you can configure it to provide failover should a component fail.

Chapter 3: "Modeling Repositories Using Relational, File, and XML Sources"

In this chapter, you'll use the Oracle BI Administration tool to create a dimensional, semantic model over your data sources, starting with a simple Oracle Database data mart as your source and then extending it through vertical and horizontal federation techniques to cover additional sources of data. We will also look at creating calculations in the repository and at tools available to help you manage and work with the repository.

Chapter 4: "Creating Repositories from Oracle Essbase and Other OLAP Data Sources"

In this chapter, you'll learn how Oracle Essbase, Oracle OLAP, and Microsoft Analysis Services metadata can be imported into the repository, as well as how you can make best use of these multidimensional data sources, including combining them with relational tables and columns.·

Chapter 5: "Configuring and Maintaining the Oracle BI Server"

You'll learn how the Oracle BI Server component works and how you can work with features such as query caching, usage tracking, write back, and aggregate persistence.

Chapter 6: "Creating Analyses, Dashboards, KPIs and Scorecards"

You'll learn how to create ad-hoc analyses and display the results in the form of graphs, tables, pivot tables, and maps. You'll see how these analyses and other BI content can be added to interactive dashboards and then made interactive through prompts, sliders, and other controls. You'll also see how key performance indicators (KPIs) can be defined and how they can be used to create scorecards to help analyze the overall performance of your organization or department.

Chapter 7: "Actionable Intelligence"

In this chapter, you'll learn how to create actions, agents, and conditions, and use them to create proactive alerts that deliver information to relevant users when business events occur. You'll also see how Oracle Business Intelligence can integrate with business applications and business processes through Oracle Fusion Middleware using a feature called the Action Framework.

Chapter 8: "Security"

In this chapter, you'll learn about the security capabilities of Oracle Business Intelligence, how to create users, groups, and application roles, how to use them to apply catalog content and row-level filtering, and how to integrate with external directories such as Microsoft Active Directory.

Chapter 9: "Creating Published Reports"

You'll learn how to create pixel-perfect published reports using Oracle BI Publisher and how to distribute them via e-mail or other channels, or embed them in a dashboard.

Chapter 10: "Systems Management"

In this chapter, you'll learn how Oracle Enterprise Manager is used to provide systems management for Oracle Business Intelligence, how the various components stop and start, and how you can script systems management tasks using the WebLogic Scripting Tool (WLST).

Chapter 11: "Managing Change"

You'll learn about the various ways that teams can develop solutions using Oracle Business Intelligence and how project metadata is promoted through development, testing, and production environments. You'll see how version control works with the Oracle BI Repository and how large teams of developers can work collaboratively using the Multiuser Development Environment (MUDE).

Chapter 12: "Oracle Exalytics In-Memory Machine"

In this final chapter, you'll get a preview of the new Oracle Exalytics BI Machine, an engineered system from Oracle Corporation that combines optimized versions of Oracle Business Intelligence, Oracle Essbase, and Oracle TimesTen to deliver "speed-of-thought" analysis to users.

Intended Audience

This book is suitable for the following readers:

- Developers who need to create repositories against relational, OLAP, and other data sources, integrate BI with business processes and applications, and support business users creating analyses, dashboards, and reports

- Administrators and support staff who need to understand the systems management features of Oracle Business Intelligence, clustering and high-availability options, and how to support deployments into production

- Business users who need to create ad-hoc analyses, dashboards, reports, KPIs, scorecards, and other BI content

- Technical managers or consultants who need an overview of the capabilities and architecture of Oracle Business Intelligence

No prior knowledge of Oracle Business Intelligence is required for this book, but a basic understanding of databases, SQL, reporting, and analysis is assumed.

About the Examples, and Retrieving the Sample Data Set

The examples used in this book are based around a fictitious coffee shop and bakery store company called "Gourmet Coffee and Bakery Company" (GCBC), based in the United States, primarily in California and the Bay Area. In the examples and over the various chapters, we build up a repository, sourcing data from several database schemas, and go on to create dashboards, reports, scorecards, and other BI objects using this data.

All the SQL scripts, programs and other files used in this book can be downloaded from the Oracle Press web site, at www.OraclePressBooks.com, and require Oracle Database 11g Release 2. (Any edition, including the free XE edition, should be suitable.)

The files are contained in a Zip file. Once you've downloaded the Zip file, all files can be found in a folder called "Sample Data," together with a Microsoft Windows batch file that installs the data for you into your database. Note that you will need to have access to the SYS account's password (or amend the batch file to reference another account with DBA privileges) to install data in this way, as the script creates database accounts for various sets of data.

To install the sample data on an Oracle Database 11gR2 database, follow these steps:

1. Obtain and unzip the sample data to a suitable directory on your workstation that also has the Oracle database installed (for example c:\Sample_Data).

   (If you are installing the sample data on a server remote from your workstation and would normally connect to the database using a TNSNAMES connection string, edit the GCBC_Setup.bat file to add your database connection string when calling sql*plus.)

2. Open a command-line prompt and run the following two commands to install the sample data, substituting the password for your SYS account for *dba_password*:

   cd c:\Sample_Data

   GCBC_Setup.bat *dba_password*

3. The sample data should then be installed for you, automatically.

I hope you enjoy this book!

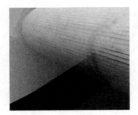

CHAPTER
1

Oracle Business Intelligence Overview and Architecture

racle Business Intelligence 11g Release 1 is a platform for delivering business intelligence across a wide range of data sources and to a wide range of audiences within the enterprise. You can consider it a "toolkit" in that, in itself, it does not come with any prebuilt reports, data, or other content, although as we will see later in this chapter, you can license content from Oracle Corporation and other providers that can be used with Oracle Business Intelligence.

Introducing Oracle Business Intelligence

As an end user, your first encounter with Oracle Business Intelligence would be when logging in to, and interacting with, a web-based dashboard such as that shown in Figure 1-1. Oracle Business Intelligence dashboards are made up of pages of analyses, displayed as tables, pivot tables, charts, gauges, or other views using data from potentially many sources. These can be interacted with, allowing the end user to, for example, start with a set of summarized figures and then progressively drill into more detail. Oracle Business Intelligence dashboards are typically highly graphical and provide a familiar, point-and-click environment for users to explore their data.

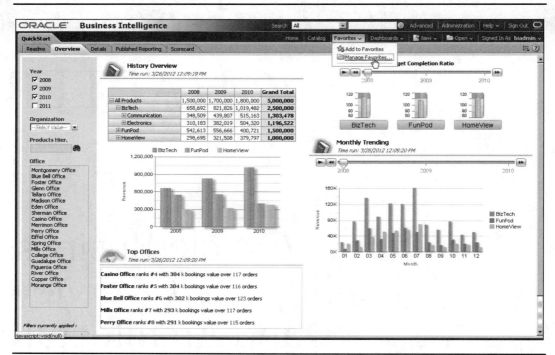

FIGURE 1-1. *An Oracle Business Intelligence dashboard*

For end users who wish to create their own reports, or those who wish to investigate their data in more detail, Oracle Business Intelligence allows users to create ad-hoc reports using data items taken from subject areas described using familiar business terms. Figure 1-2 shows a typical ad-hoc report, with a typical subject area made up of tables, columns, and hierarchies on the left-hand side of the screen that can be used to create table, chart, and other data views displayed on the right-hand side.

As well as providing an ad-hoc query environment suitable for data exploration, Oracle Business Intelligence also comes with tools for publishing reports in formats such as Adobe PDF and distributing them to large numbers of recipients through technologies such as e-mail. Analyses created using Oracle Business Intelligence can also be accessed through collaboration and office products such as Microsoft Outlook, Microsoft Word, Microsoft PowerPoint, and Microsoft Excel, or can be embedded directly into applications such as Oracle E-Business Suite, Siebel Customer Relationship Management (CRM), or in the new Fusion Applications from Oracle Corporation.

The 11.1.1.6 release of Oracle Business Intelligence 11g, on which the examples in this book are based, introduces new capabilities and visualization options, including the ability to create scorecards and key performance indicators, display data in the form of maps, and integrate with applications and business processes through a feature called the Action Framework. We will look at these capabilities in more detail in later chapters of this book.

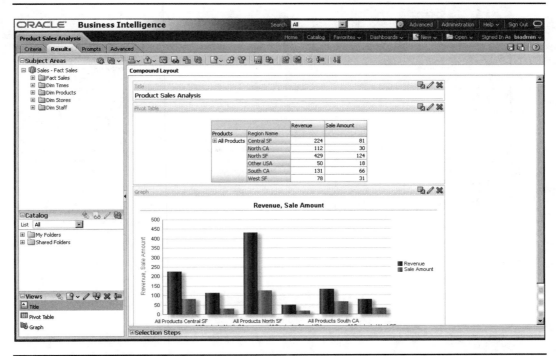

FIGURE 1-2.   *An Oracle Business Intelligence ad-hoc query*

The Development Toolkit

As developers, you have a number of tools within Oracle Business Intelligence that you can use to develop business intelligence solutions. The main tool that you will use is the Oracle Business Intelligence Administration tool, a Microsoft Windows–based tool that is used to define and then maintain the business metadata layer known as the Oracle BI Repository, used for creating reports and analyses. Several chapters of this book are devoted to this tool, and as a developer you will need to understand in detail the functionality of this tool and the Oracle BI Repository.

Figure 1-3 shows the Oracle Business Intelligence Administration tool, with a repository open for editing. The tool is also used for managing connection details through to data sources, defining security policies that control users' access to data, and performing a number of administration tasks such as defining variables, managing caching, and checking the status of the cluster.

From the 11*g* release of Oracle Business Intelligence, a number of systems administration tasks previously carried out using the Oracle Business Intelligence Administration tool are now performed using Oracle Enterprise Manager Fusion Middleware Control. These tasks include enabling and disabling caching, setting the cache size, and managing the status of the system components in a cluster.

Other tools for developers provided as part of Oracle Business Intelligence 11*g* Release 1 include the Catalog Manager, a Java application used for managing the catalog of reports, dashboards, and other business intelligence objects; Oracle Enterprise Manager Fusion Middleware Control,

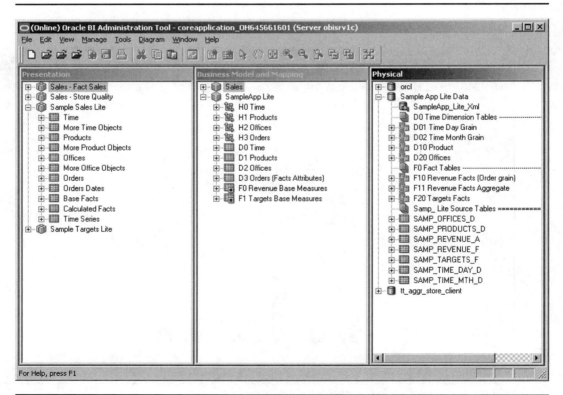

FIGURE 1-3. *The Oracle Business Intelligence Administration tool*

for administering the business intelligence platform; and Oracle WebLogic Server Administration Console, for controlling the functionality of the WebLogic Server application server.

Reports, analyses, and dashboards are created using web-based authoring tools that do not require any separate software to be installed on developers' desktops. Oracle Business Intelligence 11*g* Release 1 brings together all report-authoring tools into a single integrated environment using the same semantic model, and later chapters in this book will show you how easy it is to create compelling, interactive dashboards using these tools.

Platform Support

At the time of writing this book, Oracle Business Intelligence is at release 11.1.1.6 and can be installed on a number of Microsoft Windows, Linux, and Unix platforms, running on both 32-bit and 64-bit processors. Because the report and dashboard-authoring tools within Oracle Business Intelligence are mostly web-based, any operating system that supports these web browsers can be used to create reports. There are separate certifications for server and client tools within Oracle Business Intelligence, and you should refer to the Oracle Technology Network web site, and in particular the *System Requirements and Supported Platforms for Oracle Business Intelligence Suite Enterprise Edition 11gR1* document, to obtain the latest list of supported platforms and operating systems.

NOTE
The list of certified operating systems and platforms can change from release to release, and you should check the System Requirements and Supported Platforms for Oracle Business Intelligence Suite Enterprise Edition 11gR1 *document, available on the Oracle Technology Network web site (http://otn.oracle.com), for your particular version of Oracle Business Intelligence.*

How Does Oracle Business Intelligence Work?

So you now know that Oracle Business Intelligence comes with a number of end-user tools for developing and viewing reports, together with developer tools for administration, creating the semantic model, and maintaining the system. But how does Oracle Business Intelligence work, how does it access your various data sources, and what use does it make of other business intelligence systems such as data warehouses, online analytical processing (OLAP) servers such as Oracle Essbase, or data that might be of interest in your applications or company databases?

At a high level, Oracle Business Intelligence uses a four-tier architecture that provides access to your data through two main servers and a semantic model. Figure 1-4 shows a high-level schematic for Oracle Business Intelligence, with your data being accessed through two servers—the Oracle Business Intelligence (BI) Server and the Oracle BI Presentation Server—before it is presented to end users through a web browser.

Considering this four-tier architecture from the perspective of an end user requesting a dashboard of business information, the components within Oracle Business Intelligence perform the following high-level functions to return data to the user:

1. The web browser requests a dashboard of data, consisting of analyses, published reports, and other BI content.

2. This request is received by the Oracle BI Presentation Server, which translates requests for individual analyses and reports into logical SQL queries. These logical queries are then passed to the Oracle BI Server.

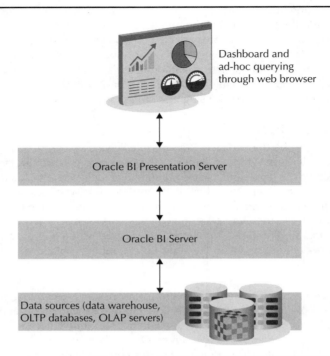

FIGURE 1-4. *High-level Oracle Business Intelligence schematic*

3. The Oracle BI Server takes these logical SQL queries, written against the semantic model contained in the Oracle BI Repository, and translates them into native SQL and MDX queries that are then sent to the underlying data sources.

4. The underlying data sources process the native SQL and MDX queries, and return results to the Oracle BI Server.

5. The Oracle BI Server returns a data result set to the Oracle BI Presentation Server. In instances where more than one data source is needed to satisfy the query, the BI Server is capable of combining multiple data sets into a single set of results.

6. Finally, the Oracle BI Presentation Server presents the results back to the end user, in the form of analyses, published reports, dashboards, and other BI content.

Unlike many other business intelligence tools that combine data presentation with query generation in a single server, Oracle Business Intelligence splits these functions into two separate servers:

■ **Oracle BI Server** This server provides simultaneous connectivity to heterogeneous data sources, a calculation and data federation engine, access to a semantic (metadata) model, and a security layer.

■ **Oracle BI Presentation Server** This server connects to the Oracle BI Server and provides users with a catalog of analyses, reports, and dashboards that they can use to analyze their data.

Oracle Business Intelligence 11*g* actually makes use of other servers to handle clustering, scheduling of reports, and other services; but, for now, consider these two servers the "core" of the Oracle Business Intelligence's functionality.

So Where Does the Data Come From?

As you will have seen from the above schematic, Oracle Business Intelligence does not itself hold data; instead, it uses a metadata layer to create a "virtual dimensional model" over one or more data sources and then generates SQL and MDX queries to retrieve data, on demand, from these data sources for presentation back to the user. As such, it leverages any investment you have made in data warehouse technology such as Oracle Database Enterprise Edition, or in OLAP technology such as Oracle Essbase, rather than replacing the need for them.

While Oracle Business Intelligence can optionally be configured to hold a cache of data to enable faster display of results, queries that it generates are otherwise sent directly to your underlying data sources. It follows, therefore, that your underlying data sources should be as optimized for queries as possible. Furthermore, the Oracle BI Server can also take advantage of any analytic functionality that is available on a particular data source to enable more efficient processing by "passing down" calculations to the underlying data source. Therefore, the recommended, optimal data source for Oracle Business Intelligence would be an enterprise data warehouse running on a database platform such as Oracle Database Enterprise Edition, potentially supplemented or enhanced by an OLAP server such as Oracle Essbase or the OLAP Option for the Oracle Database Enterprise Edition, to provide fast access to aggregated data.

However, Oracle Business Intelligence also has the ability to connect to more than one data source and "join together" results from each one into a single data set, giving you the ability to create "virtual" data warehouses made up of data taken in real time from separate databases, which can be departmental data warehouses, data marts, or even online transaction processing (OLTP) databases or nonrelational database sources such as OLAP servers, files, or sources such as Microsoft Excel spreadsheets. This ability to work with "federated" data sources gives you great flexibility in how you design your reporting system, allowing you to, for example, source the majority of your reporting data from a data warehouse but supplement it with data sourced in real time from a range of applications, file sources, and OLAP servers, as shown in Figure 1-5.

This approach becomes possible due to two key features provided by the Oracle BI Server:

■ The semantic model, which can create a metadata model over multiple data sources from different vendors, presenting users with a single, unified view over their data regardless of the data source

■ The ability of the BI Server to generate native, optimized queries for each data source and to combine the results returned into a single result set

So, it's clear that the BI Server and the semantic model that it uses are key to how Oracle Business Intelligence provides access to data. With this in mind, let's take a look at how the semantic model works and how it structures data so that it is optimized for querying.

The Oracle Business Intelligence Semantic Model

The Oracle Business Intelligence semantic model has three main objectives:

■ To represent your enterprise's data as a logical dimensional model

■ To map this logical dimensional model onto the data sources used by the enterprise

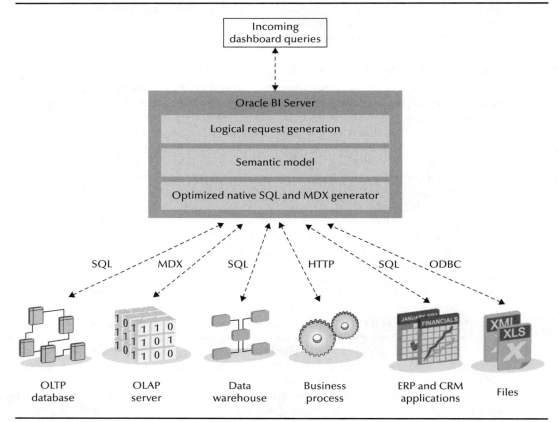

FIGURE 1-5. *The Oracle BI Server accessing heterogeneous data sources*

■ To provide personalized views over the logical dimensional model for subsets of users giving them access to just the data they need while preserving, "under the covers," a single unified business intelligence data model

Semantic models in the Oracle Business Intelligence repository therefore have three distinct layers:

■ **Physical layer** This layer contains metadata on the physical databases and other data sources that provide data for the semantic model.

■ **Business Model and Mapping layer** This layer contains the logical dimensional model defined for the business.

■ **Presentation layer** This layer provides personalized subsets of the logical dimensional model tailored for different audiences.

Data flows through the semantic model, as shown in Figure 1-6, from the Physical layer, through mappings into the Business Model and Mapping layer, and is eventually accessed by end

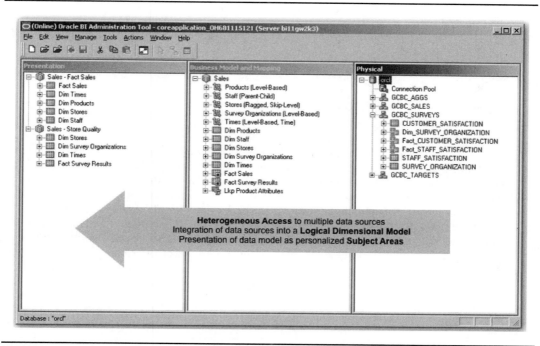

FIGURE 1-6. *The Oracle Business Intelligence semantic model*

users through the Presentation layer. The semantic model is defined and maintained using the Oracle Business Intelligence Administration tool and stored in the Oracle BI Repository, and Chapters 3 and 4 show you how semantic models can be created that access data from relational, OLAP, files, and other nonrelational sources.

Packaged Business Intelligence Solutions

The fact that Oracle Business Intelligence is, in effect, a toolkit that does not in itself provide any data or reports that you can use "out of the box" means that, realistically, you will need to spend a significant amount of time developing a solution before your users can start analyzing their data. In addition, because many organizations have standardized on packaged enterprise resource planning (ERP) systems such as Oracle E-Business Suite and PeopleSoft Enterprise or customer relationship management (CRM) suites such as Siebel CRM, the work you would be doing might essentially be "reinventing the wheel," as many organizations would have had requirements similar to yours in the past and created similar business intelligence solutions to deliver similar dashboards and reports.

Oracle Corporation, as well as third-party vendors such as Noetix, have addressed this opportunity by developing packaged sets of dashboards, data models, and data extraction routines that you can install, along with Oracle Business Intelligence, to provide dashboards and reports within days or weeks rather than the usual months that are required to create a custom solution. The Oracle Business Intelligence Applications, from Oracle Corporation, are a suite of packaged BI products built around Oracle Business Intelligence that provides applications such as the following:

- Financial Analytics
- Human Resources Analytics
- Project Analytics
- Procurement Analytics
- Supply Chain Analytics

In addition to these, it provides other, industry-specific "vertical" packaged applications for the financial services, pharmaceuticals, and other industries. Figure 1-7 shows the relationship between Oracle Business Intelligence Applications and Oracle Business Intelligence, and how data for this combined system is either accessed directly from application and database data sources, or through a prebuilt data warehouse fed by predefined data extraction routines.

These packaged business intelligence applications provide a prebuilt and extensible data warehouse; data extraction routines that provide preconfigured access to Oracle E-Business Suite, SAP, Oracle PeopleSoft, and Oracle Siebel applications; as well as content for use with Oracle Business Intelligence. As these data models and extraction routines are based on industry-standard tools and databases, they can be customized after installation; many customers use them as the starting point for their entire business intelligence solution, using the packaged data model and

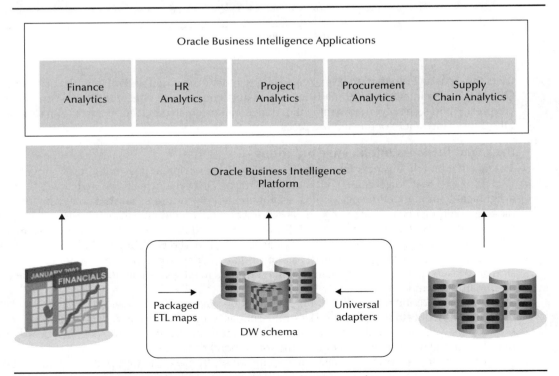

FIGURE 1-7.   *The Oracle Business Intelligence Applications architecture*

data extraction routines as the starting point, and then customizing and extending them to cover the full range of their enterprise data.

The use and deployment of packaged solutions is outside the scope of this book, which instead focuses on the Oracle Business Intelligence platform itself and the creation of custom solutions. However, once you are familiar with these topics you should take time to investigate these packaged solutions, which you may wish to deploy along with your custom development in order to bring down the total time, and cost, of your business intelligence deployment.

Oracle Exalytics In-Memory Machine

For customers looking for "speed-of-thought" analysis of very large sets of detail-level data, Oracle Exalytics In-Memory Machine is a combination of hardware and Oracle Business Intelligence software that uses an in-memory database cache and special management tools to manage the cache.

Figure 1-8 shows the architecture for Oracle Exalytics In-Memory Machine, which comes with Oracle Business Intelligence and Oracle Essbase installed on the Exalytics hardware device, along

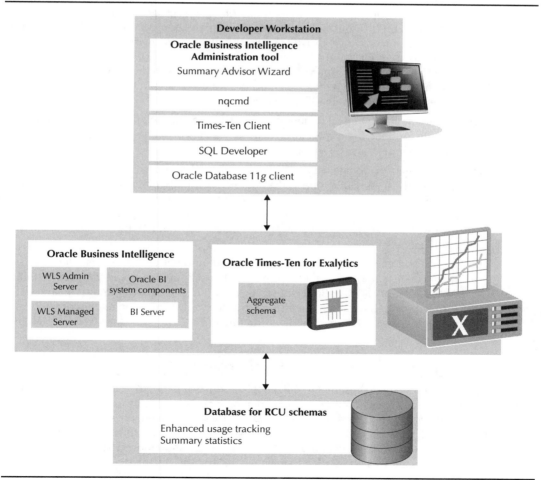

FIGURE 1-8. *Oracle Exalytics In-Memory Machine architecture*

with Oracle TimesTen for Exalytics as the in-memory database. Exalytics is typically used by those customers looking to interactively analyze large volumes of data in a very graphically rich environment and is sold as an "appliance" that you can add to your data center and connect, via InfiniBand to Oracle Exadata or via Ethernet, to your corporate databases and data warehouses.

We will look in more detail at Oracle Exalytics In-Memory Machine in the final chapter of this book, including how it is configured, how the in-memory cache is used, and the new visualization types that are enabled by this high-performance platform for your BI system.

What Does Oracle Business Intelligence "Not Do"?

When considering a new software tool, it's worth understanding also what it does "not do." While Oracle Business Intelligence is a suite of products that provides a wide range of analysis tools, data source adapters, and—with the Oracle Business Intelligence Applications—prebuilt content for a wide range of business applications, it is worth understanding what it is not:

- It is not a replacement for Microsoft Excel. Microsoft Excel provides a free-form environment for analyzing and reporting on data, is programmable, and places few restrictions on how data is presented, input, analyzed, and distributed. Oracle Business Intelligence, in contrast, provides a structured analysis environment based around a dimensional model, primarily providing analytical views of data through a web-based dashboard. Individual analyses can, however, be imported into Microsoft Excel, either through an export from the dashboard or through a plug-in to Microsoft Excel, and the BI Server can also act as an ODBC data source for Excel (and other clients).

- Because it uses a logical dimensional model for presenting data to users, it is not generally suitable for querying unstructured data, being better suited to reporting on transactional, data warehouse, and OLAP data sources.

- While it can report against the transactional databases used by applications such as Oracle E-Business Suite, due to the complexity and existing workload on these databases, repositories created directly against them are generally not recommended; instead, data from the transactional databases used by these applications is generally extracted into a data warehouse, or OLAP cube, and then queried from that location by Oracle Business Intelligence.

- Although it can access data in Oracle Essbase or other OLAP servers, Oracle Business Intelligence is not itself a multidimensional OLAP server; instead, it could be thought of as a relational OLAP (ROLAP) server, providing access to a dimensional model through (virtual) relational data structures, themselves mapped to either relational, file or multidimensional physical data structures.

A History of Oracle Business Intelligence

There have been several "business intelligence" products released by Oracle Corporation over the years, and you may have come to this book planning an upgrade from a previous generation of tools such as Oracle Discoverer or Oracle Reports. These tools were developed in-house by Oracle Corporation's developers and were designed to work primarily with Oracle's own database, application server, and security products. As Oracle Corporation moved from being solely focused on database technologies and started to make acquisitions in the middleware, applications, and infrastructure industry sectors, it became clear that it needed a "next-generation" business intelligence platform that did not have such a dependency on Oracle database technologies but that could still take advantage of them if, as is often the case, the customer had used Oracle technology for their data warehouse.

The acquisition of Siebel CRM Systems, Inc., though primarily for their Siebel CRM platform and their extensive customer base, presented Oracle with an opportunity to update their business intelligence platform through another, lesser-known product that Siebel offered; Siebel Analytics. Though well regarded in the industry, Siebel Analytics was not as well known as similar products from vendors such as Business Objects (now part of SAP) and Cognos (now part of IBM), but the Siebel Analytics platform met many of Oracle Corporation's requirements for a next-generation business intelligence platform in that it could access data from many different data sources, had an industry-leading metadata layer (the "semantic model"), very user-friendly dashboards and reporting tools, and also came ready-integrated with popular ERP and CRM systems such as SAP, Oracle E-Business Suite, PeopleSoft—and, of course, Siebel CRM—in a package called Siebel Business Analytics.

Oracle announced in 2005 that what was previously called Siebel Analytics would now be adopted by Oracle Corporation as their strategic business intelligence platform, and they renamed it Oracle Business Intelligence Enterprise Edition. The existing Oracle Discoverer and Oracle Reports tools would be packaged as Oracle Business Intelligence Standard Edition, and while customers would not be forced to upgrade from the older toolset to the new one, in time upgrade tools and services would be made available to make this process easier for those customers who chose to do so.

Siebel Analytics was itself, though, developed outside of Siebel CRM Systems, Inc., and was in fact originally developed by a technology startup out of Minneapolis, MN, called nQuire. Led by Larry Barbetta and a number of ex-Platinum Software engineers and product managers, nQuire released the nQuire Server, the predecessor to what eventually became the Oracle BI Server, back in the late 1990's as a stand-alone analytics and search server that featured connectivity to a wide range of data sources. The nQuire Query Server featured a metadata model (which eventually became the semantic model) that provided a virtual logical dimensional model over these data sources, and over time the nQuire Query Server was joined by nQuire Answers and nQuire Delivers, giving us the core of what is now Oracle Business Intelligence. nQuire was itself acquired by Siebel CRM Systems, Inc., in October 2001, and it developed the product further and licensed data models and data extraction routines from Informatica Corporation that now form the core of the Oracle Business Intelligence Applications. So while what you know as Oracle Business Intelligence may be a product that is only a few years old, the core of the product itself can be traced back to groundbreaking work done by the nQuire team back in the mid-1990's.

Oracle Product Release History

Shortly after Oracle Corporation acquired Siebel Systems, what was Siebel Analytics was renamed Oracle Business Intelligence Enterprise Edition, whilst Siebel Business Analytics was renamed Oracle BI Applications. The initial release of Oracle Business Intelligence was the 10*g* 10.1.3.2 version, with subsequent major releases of Oracle Business within the 10*g* timeline:

- **Oracle Business Intelligence 10.1.3.2**   First "Oracle-branded" release of Oracle Business Intelligence; introduced Oracle BI Publisher as a replacement for Actuate, a new Oracle "look and feel" with 64-bit support; time-series functions and features for multiuser development.

- **Oracle Business Intelligence 10.1.3.3.***x*   MS Office integration, support for metadata import through the Oracle Call Interface; support for embedded database functions; initial support for Oracle Essbase as a data source.

- **Oracle Business Intelligence 10.1.3.4.***x*   Integration with Hyperion Workspace; integration with Oracle Smart View and Oracle Smart Space; the introduction of a utility to upgrade Oracle Discoverer End-User Layers to Oracle Business Intelligence repositories.

In addition, at the time of writing this book there have been three major releases as part of the 11*g* Release 1 timeline:

- **Oracle Business Intelligence 11.1.1.3**   Initial 11*g* release, provided new "look and feel," support for KPIs and scorecards, the Action Framework, and other new features. Platform support limited to Microsoft Windows, Linux, and IBM AIX, with Oracle WebLogic Server as the sole JEE (Java Platform, Enterprise Edition) application server.

- **Oracle Business Intelligence 11.1.1.5**   Oracle Extension of platform support to HP/UX and Sun Solaris, introduction of iOS (Apple iPhone, Apple iPad) native clients, and restoration of data sources temporarily desupported in the 11.1.1.3 release.

- **Oracle Business Intelligence 11.1.1.6**   Support for the Exalytics In-Memory Machine platform and integration with version control tools. New visualization options and new certified data sources, including Oracle TimesTen.

In addition, there are three editions of Oracle Business Intelligence, the first two of which in the following list are within the scope of this book, and the third that is not:

- **Oracle Business Intelligence Enterprise Edition**   The full set of business intelligence tools and servers. This book will concern itself primarily with this edition.

- **Oracle Business Intelligence Standard Edition One**   "Departmental" or budget version of Oracle Business Intelligence that comes with certain restrictions on, for example, the number of allowable users and CPUs. Check with your Oracle representative or http://www.oracle.com for up-to-date details on this and other product packages.

- **Oracle Business Intelligence Standard Edition**   Somewhat confusingly, a different family of products altogether. This is a container for "legacy" Oracle Business Intelligence tools such as Oracle Discoverer and Oracle Reports. You can use upgrade tools to migrate Discoverer metadata to Oracle Business Intelligence Enterprise Edition and Standard Edition One; but, otherwise, this edition is outside the scope of this book.

Now that you know a little more about Oracle Business Intelligence's background and a little of its history, let's take a look in more detail at the individual products within the platform, its architecture, and how it works "under the covers."

Oracle Business Intelligence 11*g* Release 1 Architecture

Earlier in this chapter, we looked how the "heart" of Oracle Business Intelligence is the Oracle BI Server and the Oracle BI Presentation Server. The Oracle BI Server provides native, federated access to data sources, together with security, calculations, and data navigation. The Oracle BI

Presentation Server connects to the BI Server to obtain data, which it presents to users in the form of analyses, reports, and dashboards.

In addition to these two servers, there are three other servers that work with them to provide core Oracle Business Intelligence functionality:

- **Oracle BI Cluster Controller**   This server provides a central point of access for the Oracle BI Presentation Server when two or more BI Servers are working together in a cluster, together with load-balancing, failover, and other cluster services.

- **Oracle BI Java Host**   This server works alongside the BI Presentation Server to provide connectivity to Java tasks and the Java-based Oracle BI Publisher, as well as to support chart generation.

- **Oracle BI Scheduler**   This server is used to schedule and automate the production and distribution of analyses, as well as to automate workflow tasks based around business intelligence functionality.

These three servers, together with the Oracle BI Server and the Oracle BI Presentation Server, are known in Oracle Business Intelligence 11*g* Release 1 terminology as *system components,* and they run as services and servers directly on the host platform. They are operating system executables written in C-based languages.

To create the link between an end user's web browser and the dashboards, analyses, and reports provided by the Oracle BI Presentation Server, a Java application called the Oracle BI Analytics Plug-In runs in a Java application server and routes incoming requests through to the BI Presentation Server. (Currently, only Oracle WebLogic Server is supported, but later releases of Oracle Business Intelligence should support other application servers.) A simplified schematic of the Oracle Business Intelligence 11*g* system components, together with the Oracle BI Plug-In, is shown in Figure 1-9.

This basic, internal architecture has stayed consistent since the days of nQuire and Siebel Analytics and is still at the core of the 11*g* Release of Oracle Business Intelligence. It, together with two additional Java server applications for publishing reports and connecting to Microsoft office, is largely the architecture of the 10*g* release of Oracle Business Intelligence and would run fairly comfortably on a smaller server, desktop computer, or laptop. Because the product has been adopted within Oracle Corporation as their strategic business intelligence platform and, in particular, because it has been integrated over time into their wider Oracle Fusion Middleware platform due to customer requirements for BI to integrate into wider business processes and applications, these core components have been built on and enhanced with additional Java components to form the more complete architecture used in the 11*g* Release 1 version.

Oracle Business Intelligence 11*g* and Oracle Fusion Middleware

While the core components within Oracle Business Intelligence remain the Oracle BI Server and Oracle BI Presentation Server, supported by the Oracle BI Scheduler, Oracle Java Host, and Oracle BI Cluster Controller, these have been supplemented in the 11*g* Release 1 release by Java-based Oracle Fusion Middleware technologies based around the Oracle WebLogic Server application server (with plans to extend this to other non-WebLogic application servers in future releases). While the previous, 10*g* release of Oracle Business Intelligence made limited use of application server technology to, for example, host the Oracle BI Plug-In and Java-based applications

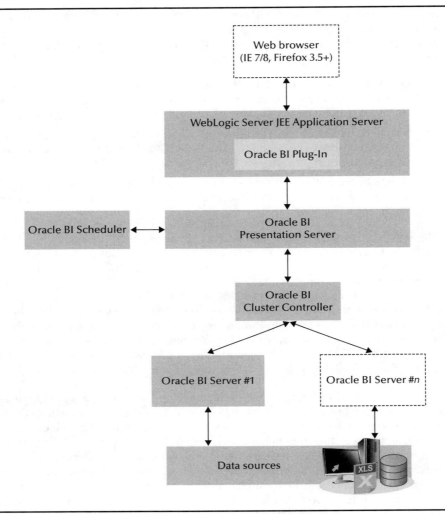

FIGURE 1-9. *Oracle Business Intelligence system components schematic*

such as Oracle BI Publisher and Oracle BI Office, the 11*g* release of Oracle Business Intelligence leverages Fusion Middleware and WebLogic technologies in areas such as the following:

■ *Security and authentication,* which are now delegated to Oracle Fusion Middleware 11*g,* with users and groups now held, by default, in the WebLogic Server LDAP directory rather than the Oracle BI Repository

■ *Systems administration,* now centralized using Oracle Enterprise Manager Fusion Middleware Control

- *Connectivity* to outside applications and processes through the Java-based Action Service, with security and credentials handled via Fusion Middleware's credential and policy stores

- *Administration scripting* using the Oracle WebLogic Scripting Tool and JMX MBeans (Java managed beans that provide the core administration functionality behind Oracle Enterprise Manager Fusion Middleware Control)

- *Process management* of the system components (BI Server, BI Presentation Server, and so on) through the Oracle Process Manager and Notification Server

- *High availability* through clustering of WebLogic Managed Servers within a WebLogic domain

Figure 1-10 shows the logical architecture for Oracle Business Intelligence 11*g* Release 1, which together is called an Oracle BI domain.

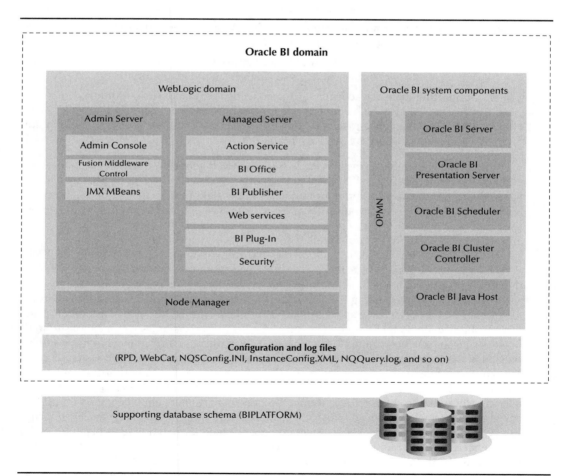

FIGURE 1-10.   *The Oracle Business Intelligence 11g logical architecture*

This logical architecture is made up of a number of components:

- **Oracle BI domain**   The complete set of Java and non-Java components that make up a single Oracle Business Intelligence environment
- **WebLogic domain**   Houses the Java components within the architecture
- **WebLogic Server Admin Server**   A JEE container (server) that contains a dedicated Java Virtual Machine used for monitoring and managing the system
- **WebLogic Server Managed Server**   Another dedicated JEE container that, in this case, is used to house the Java applications used by Oracle Business Intelligence
- **Java components**   Java applications such as the Oracle BI Analytics Plug-In, Oracle BI Publisher, the Action Service, and Oracle BI Office that work alongside the traditional system components described previously
- **System components**   The term now used for the original BI Server, BI Presentation Server, and other servers used in the core Oracle Business Intelligence architecture
- **WebLogic Server Administration Console**   An application that runs in the Admin Server and is used for controlling WebLogic Server
- **Oracle Enterprise Manager Fusion Middleware Control**   For managing the Oracle Business Intelligence system across a single or multiple cluster nodes
- **Supporting database schemas**   Created using the Oracle Fusion Middleware Repository Creation Utility, which contains relational tables used for storing additional Oracle Business Intelligence metadata (BIPLATFORM) and metadata used by Oracle Fusion Middleware's Metadata Services (MDS)

Note that it is possible to install Oracle Business Intelligence in a "simple" architecture configuration that does away with the WebLogic Managed Server and Node Manager, to reduce the software and memory footprint for laptop-style installations. This type of installation does, however, restrict you in how you can "scale out" your installation afterward, so it should only be used for demo or proof-of-concept scenarios. Chapter 2 details the various installation options and what these mean in terms of installed components on your server.

This distinction between Java components that are written in Java and managed by WebLogic Server, and System Components that run as operating system services and are written in C++, is due to the history of Oracle Business Intelligence. The core server components (system components, in 11g terminology) were written in C++, but most new development of distinct new functionality carried out by Oracle Corporation has been carried out in Java as part of Oracle Fusion Middleware. Rather than convert all of the legacy servers to Java applications from C++, however, these have been "lifted" into the new 11g architecture but allowed to run stand-alone, outside of the Oracle WebLogic Server domain structure, and are now called system components. This approach is actually common to many Oracle Fusion Middleware products that need to combine long-standing C-based server products with more recent, Java-based applications, and allows both sets of products to benefit from the same management and integration infrastructure based around Oracle Enterprise Manager Fusion Middleware Control and Oracle WebLogic Server.

While the distinction between system components and Java components becomes obvious to experienced Oracle Business Intelligence developers, both types of components are managed at a system level by the same application: Oracle Enterprise Manager Fusion Middleware Control. While each component and type of component has its own unique configuration tools, Fusion

Middleware Control provides a centralized, web-based console for controlling the business intelligence system.

In addition to the Java and system components, two additional servers are used to control and monitor the running of these component categories:

- **WebLogic Server Node Manager**   This server is used to start, stop, restart, and monitor the Managed Server, or multiple Managed Servers if WebLogic Server is running clustered (not available for "Simple" install types, which do not need to stop and start any Managed Servers).

- **Oracle Process Manager and Notification Server (OPMN)**   This server performs a similar role for the system components—stopping, starting, and restarting them, and reporting their status to monitoring applications.

Let's now take a look at some of these components in detail.

The Oracle BI Domain
The Oracle BI domain is the overall container for all Java and non-Java (in most cases, C++) applications and servers that make up a single Oracle Business Intelligence environment, together with the repositories, catalogs, and configuration files that these components use. An Oracle BI domain contains a single WebLogic domain (containing an Administration Server and one or more Managed Servers), and a typical customer may have several Oracle BI domains, for example:

- A development Oracle BI domain
- A test/QA Oracle BI domain
- A production Oracle BI domain

Each Oracle BI domain requires its own separate installation, with, in general, its own binaries and configuration files, though it is possible to share a single WebLogic Server installation among multiple domains, to aid patching and management.

The WebLogic Domain
A WebLogic domain is the basic administrative unit for a WebLogic installation. In the context of Oracle Business Intelligence 11*g*, each Oracle BI domain contains a single WebLogic domain, which in turn contains a single Administration Server and one or more Managed Servers (optionally clustered), containing the Oracle Business Intelligence Java components.

The Oracle WebLogic Server Administration Server
Every WebLogic domain contains a single Administration Server, which you use to configure, and then manage, all other server instances and resources in the domain. In terms of Oracle Business Intelligence 11*g*, the Administration Server is the first component that you start when starting an Oracle BI domain, and the Managed Servers (via the Node Manager) contact the Administration Server as they start up, to obtain their configuration information.

You work with the Administration Server either graphically, through the Administration Console Java application that runs in the Administration Server JVM, or from the command line. Once you have successfully set up and configured your Oracle BI domain, you rarely interact with the Administration Server except when you configure security and when you stop, start, and restart the Oracle BI domain.

The Oracle WebLogic Server Managed Server(s)

While it is possible to install the Oracle Business Intelligence Java components directly into the Administration Server (and this is what happens when you choose the Simple Install option described in Chapter 2), generally Java applications such as these are installed into a separate WebLogic Server Managed Server. In a WebLogic domain, servers other than the Administration Server are referred to as *Managed Servers,* which refer to the Administration Server to obtain their configuration information. Each Managed Server is based around its own Java Virtual Machine, and typically each host running Oracle Business Intelligence will have a single WebLogic Server Managed Server installed on it that can take advantage of the full resources of the host.

Two or more Managed Servers can optionally be configured as a cluster. This is distinct and separate to the clustering used by Oracle Business Intelligence's system components (the BI Server, the Presentation Server, and the Java Host), although these two types of clustering are often used together in a scaled-out Oracle BI domain. Chapter 13 goes into clustering, high-availability, and scale-out of the Oracle BI domain in more detail.

The Oracle WebLogic Server Node Manager

As your Oracle BI domain may be spread over several hosts and several locations, Oracle Business Intelligence uses another WebLogic component called Node Manager to manage the Managed Servers that you have configured for your domain. Node Manager is a Java utility, separate from the Administration Server, that Oracle Business Intelligence uses to start up, shut down, and restart Managed Servers across hosts and locations.

Node Manager, along with Oracle Process Manager and Notifications Server, is one of the few services that has to be running on a Microsoft Windows–based environment for your domain to start successfully, and under Linux/Unix, you would need to ensure the Node Manager service is running before you attempt to start your Managed Servers. Beyond ensuring that it is running, though, you do not generally have to interact with this WebLogic utility.

Java Components

Most new functionality added to Oracle Business Intelligence since the original Siebel and nQuire days has been added as Java-based applications, or "Java components." Java components are installed into the WebLogic server Managed Server and Administration Server, and those installed in the Managed Server can be clustered through standard WebLogic clustering. Compared to the non-Java system components, Java components apart from Oracle BI Publisher generally do not require much maintenance and do not, for example, require the same level of stopping, starting, and restarting due to configuration changes that system components require.

The following Java components are installed as part of Oracle Business Intelligence 11*g* Release 1.

The Oracle BI Analytics Plug-In   As the Oracle BI Presentation Server system component cannot, in itself, communicate over the Internet with a web browser, the Oracle BI Analytics Plug-In runs as an application in the Managed Server; receives requests for dashboards, analyses, and other BI content; and routes it to the Presentation Server. The Oracle BI Analytics Plug-In handles requests such as these via HTTP and HTTPS, and performs a similar role for web service requests via the Simple Object Access Protocol (SOAP).

Oracle BI Publisher   Oracle BI Publisher is a report authoring, publishing, and distribution server that was initially developed separately from Oracle Business Intelligence as a reporting platform for Oracle E-Business Suite. With the 10.1.3.2 release of Oracle Business Intelligence,

Oracle replaced Actuate, which until then, with Oracle BI Publisher, performed a similar role for Siebel Analytics and across other Siebel products. As a Java-based application, it was installed into a Java application server rather than running as an operating system service.

Oracle BI Publisher runs as a Java component in the Managed Server, and reports can be authored and viewed either stand-alone through a Java-based front-end or integrated into Oracle BI Presentation Services dashboards. If installed and configured together with Oracle Business Intelligence, Oracle BI Publisher shares security with the rest of your business intelligence deployment and stores report and data model definitions in the same catalog.

Oracle BI Office   Oracle Business Intelligence comes with a plug-in to Microsoft Office 2003, 2007, and Oracle Office that allows analyses to be embedded in spreadsheets and other office documents. The Oracle BI Office Java component provides connectivity between these office tools and Oracle Business Intelligence, allowing these tools to act as a client for Oracle Business Intelligence and reuse the security that you have applied to your business intelligence objects.

Oracle BI Action Services   Oracle BI Action Services is part of the Action Framework (detailed in Chapter 7 which covers the wider topic of "Actionable Intelligence") and is used when invoking external web services and processes. Oracle BI Action Services contains a set of web services that provides directories of external services that users can browse, as well as call from their analyses, dashboards, and agents.

Oracle BI Security Services   Previous releases of Oracle Business Intelligence had authentication and authorization provided directly by the Oracle BI Server system component, which could connect to external directories such as Microsoft Active Directory and Oracle Internet Directory to authenticate users against existing enterprise security systems. The 11*g* release of Oracle Business Intelligence instead delegates this process to an Oracle Fusion Middleware service called Oracle Platform Security Services, and Oracle BI Security Services acts as the interface between it and the Oracle BI Server system component.

Oracle Real-Time Decisions   Oracle Real-Time Decisions is an optional component of Oracle Business Intelligence that provides automated decision making based on data mining–style models that it creates. Oracle Real-Time Decisions was originally developed by a company called Sigma Dynamics, which in turn licensed the technology to Siebel Systems, Inc., for use within Siebel CRM. Sigma Dynamics itself was later acquired by Oracle Corporation, shortly after it acquired Siebel Systems.

Oracle Real-Time Decisions consists of a server element, installed as a Java component within the Managed Server, and client tools that can be downloaded from the Oracle Technology Network. Oracle Real-Time Decisions is outside the scope of this book; however, you may wish to research it if you need to add a real-time, self-learning, decision-making process to your CRM or other applications.

Oracle BI SOA Services   In addition to calling external services and processes through the Action Framework and Oracle BI Action Services, BI objects such as analyses, conditions, and agents can also be invoked by external applications through Oracle BI Service-Oriented Architecture (SOA). Oracle BI SOA Services provide a web service framework for invoking analyses, conditions, and agents from Business Process Execution Language (BPEL) processes, giving applications the ability to connect to business intelligence functionality to add intelligence and analytics to your applications.

Administrative Components   While most of the Java components used by Oracle Business Intelligence run in the Managed Server, some run in the Administration Server instead. The Managed Server Java components are directly related to business intelligence functionality, while the ones that run in the Administration Server are used for administering the system. These include the Oracle WebLogic Server Administration Console and Oracle Enterprise Manager Fusion Middleware Control, and Java JMX Mbeans used for programmatic access for managing the domain.

System Components

The system components are the "core" of Oracle Business Intelligence and consist of C++ and J2SE (Java 2 Platform, Standard Edition) components that provide the central functionality of Oracle Business Intelligence. They were largely developed by nQuire and Siebel prior to the Siebel acquisition and have been enhanced over time by developers at Oracle Corporation.

The Oracle BI Server   The Oracle BI Server provides several areas of functionality for Oracle Business Intelligence:

- It receives incoming logical SQL queries from the Oracle BI Presentation Server (and other clients via the Oracle BI ODBC Client), and through the semantic model turns these into one or more physical SQL and MDX queries, which are sent to the underlying data sources.

- It provides the connectivity through to these data sources, through OCI, ODBC, Essbase Client, and other native adapters.

- It provides load-balancing data to the Oracle BI Cluster Controller, to enable Oracle Business Intelligence to be run in a scaled-out, highly available configuration.

- It applies row-level and subject-area security for data described using the semantic model.

- It can maintain a data cache, storing the results of previously executed queries locally to avoid unnecessary round trips to the underlying data sources.

- Where user queries require data from more than one data source, it can join results returned from each data source together and also apply calculations and analytics to the resulting data set.

As such, the Oracle BI Server performs the role of an extra, "analytic" server that sits over your data warehouse and data sources, providing additional integration features, an additional layer of calculation and analysis, and data security, before passing it to the Oracle BI Presentation Server for display as dashboards, analyses, and reports.

Figure 1-11 shows a diagram of the internal architecture of the Oracle BI Server, made up of a number of logical components.

The key components within the BI Server logical architecture include

- **Logical SQL/ODBC interface and business model**   This receives from the client tool requests for information against a logical business model (semantic model).

- **Navigator**   This takes these logical requests and, using the information in the semantic model, turns these into individual physical requests to be sent to the underlying data sources.

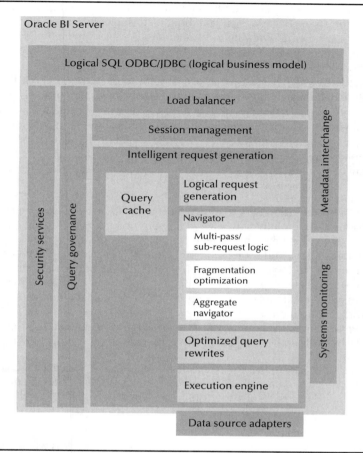

FIGURE 1-11.   *The Oracle BI Server logical architecture*

- **Optimized query rewrite engine**   This takes these physical requests and the BI Server's knowledge of the calculation capabilities of the underlying data sources, passes function requests to these sources where possible and, where not, rewrites the query to obtain the basic data set and has the BI Server perform the calculations instead.

- **Execution engine**   This passes these physical queries to the underlying data sources and collects the results back.

- **Cache management**   This stores the results of previous queries to avoid future round trips to the underlying data sources for the same queries.

- **Security services**   This applies row-level and subject-area security to the logical business model (semantic model).

- **Query governance**   This applies limits to the number of rows returned by queries and the times that users can access data.

Business intelligence systems built using Oracle Business Intelligence can use the features of the BI Server to varying degrees. A system built on a single, integrated data warehouse as a dimensional "star schema" with built-in summaries, indexes, and derived calculations may end up using very little of the BI Server's capabilities, perhaps using it only to provide load balancing, connection pooling, and row and subject-area security over the data.

Other systems, where data is spread over several source systems and is not naturally organized into a dimensional model, where aggregations, calculations, and other analytics need to be applied post-query, may use more of these features. The way you use the BI Server will depend on the nature of your data and how much additional processing is required after data retrieval takes place, but you will find that the BI Server provides a very powerful additional analytic layer to your business intelligence system, providing some functionality faster and more flexibly than if you tried to implement everything in extraction, transformation, and loading (ETL) processes or tried to materialize all calculations or aggregations in advance.

The Oracle BI Presentation Server   In contrast to the Oracle BI Server, the Oracle BI Presentation Server performs a more traditional role within your architecture—that of a presentation and visualization server that takes incoming data and renders results in the form of dashboards, analyses, reports, alerts, and scorecards. The Oracle BI Presentation Server receives requests for BI content through the Oracle BI Plug-In, installed in a JEE application server (WebLogic Server as of Oracle Business Intelligence 11.1.1.6), and then communicates with the Oracle BI Server via ODBC to authenticate incoming users, pass to it logical SQL queries, and then receive results back for rendering on the users' screens.

The BI Presentation Server also performs a number of additional roles in support of its role in providing dashboards and other visualizations for users:

- In a similar way to the BI Server, the Presentation Server caches its output (tables and pivot tables of data, charts, and other graphics) so that when the user switches between dashboard pages, results are displayed immediately rather than the user having to wait while the analysis is rerun.

- The BI Presentation Server also caches the repository metadata provided by the BI Server so that users can quickly select between subject area items when creating analyses.

- The BI Presentation Server also maintains its own repository, called the "catalog," which stores definitions of analyses, dashboards, alerts, and other BI content.

- The BI Presentation Server also provides two SOAP interfaces that can be used by external applications to request the output of analyses, alerts, and conditions and integrate them into standards-based portals and other applications. One of these SOAP interfaces, Oracle Business Intelligence Web Services for SOA , provides a simplified API for executing analyses and other BI objects typically used by other SOA processes such as BPEL workflows, while the older Oracle Business Intelligence Session-Based Web Services also found in the 10g release provide a more fine-grained API that is more suited for programmatic use.

While the 11g version of the Oracle BI Server supports OLAP analysis against any data source, more granular caching, and a wider range of hierarchy types, the BI Presentation Server also had a number of significant changes compared to the previous 10g release, including the following:

■ It no longer maintains its own set of users and groups (referred to as "webgroups" in the 10*g* release); instead, it uses the same users and application roles as the BI Server, and these are defined using Oracle Fusion Middleware 11*g*. These webgroups are, however, still available for backward-compatibility purposes when upgrading systems from the 10*g* version to 11*g*.

■ The BI Presentation Server now uses the underlying data source to calculate as many totals and subtotals as possible, rather than calculating them itself after the main data set has been returned from the source database.

While developers would benefit from having a close knowledge of the workings of the Oracle BI Server, the BI Presentation Server generally does not require a large amount of understanding or maintenance. There are some tasks and configuration changes that you may wish to apply over time (detailed in later chapters of this book), but for the most part the BI Presentation Server can be considered a "black box" that does its required job without much intervention on your part.

The Oracle BI Cluster Controller   The Oracle BI Cluster Controller provides load-balancing and query-routing functionality in a clustered Oracle BI Server environment. While the BI Cluster Controller was an optional server in the 10*g* version of Oracle Business Intelligence, it assumes a more significant role in the 11*g* version, as clustering is enabled by default, albeit with a single BI Server node.

As discussed earlier in this chapter, when the BI Cluster Controller is used (by default in 11*g* installations, but optional in 10*g* ones), it is the Cluster Controller rather than the BI Server itself that the BI Presentation Server communicates with to pass requests and receive results back. Of the BI Servers it is responsible for, the BI Cluster Controller maintains a record of which ones are actually online and available for queries, and routes requests to them on a round-robin basis. Individual BI Server components contain load-balancing functionality that reports their current load to the BI Cluster Controller, and the BI Cluster Controller treats the BI Server components under its control as "active-active" resources, meaning that all available BI Servers are used if available, with failover happening dynamically as BI Server resources become unavailable and then available again.

In contrast, the BI Cluster Controller (along with the BI Scheduler) is considered an "active-passive" resource; if the primary BI Cluster Controller becomes unavailable, a secondary BI Cluster Controller is then activated (if previously configured for this role), and user queries use the secondary controller for subsequent queries. Only primary and secondary BI Cluster Controllers can be configured (in contrast to BI Servers, BI Presentation Servers, and Java Hosts, which effectively have no limit to how many you can configure actively in a cluster), and the secondary controller only becomes active if the primary one becomes unavailable.

The Oracle BI Scheduler   The Oracle BI Scheduler is enabled by default in Oracle Business Intelligence 11*g* and provides the ability to schedule analyses, agents, and other BI content to be delivered to users via a number of channels. For clustering purposes, the Oracle BI Scheduler (like the Oracle BI Cluster Controller) is considered "active-passive," with a secondary BI Scheduler often defined to provide backup and failover if the primary one becomes unavailable.

The BI Scheduler stores details of job executions in relational tables within the supporting database schema, although definitions of the jobs themselves are held in the Oracle BI Presentation Server Catalog. Note that the BI Scheduler is not included in the Standard Edition One license for Oracle Business Intelligence.

The Oracle BI Java Host   The Oracle BI Java Host is a component that you can generally leave to work in the background. As a developer, you do not usually interact with this component, but it works in the background with other components to provide support for Java tasks. In particular, it provides or supports the following functionality with Oracle Business Intelligence 11*g*:

- Graph generation
- SVG rendering
- Java task support for the Oracle BI Scheduler
- Oracle BI Publisher
- Advanced reporting
- URL Connect (issues an HTTP request to another component)
- Integration Service calls (used by the Oracle BI Server to execute Java code)
- Authentication to external systems such as Hyperion Financial Management and Hyperion Shared Services

In general, your only interactions with the Oracle BI Java Hosts are first to ensure that it is running and, second, to configure additional clustered BI Java Hosts to work in "active-active" mode with the default one, to provide failover and load balancing.

Oracle Process Manager and Notification Server   Oracle Process Manager and Notification Server (OPMN) is a standard piece of Oracle Fusion Middleware Technology used to stop, start, and monitor the status of Oracle Business Intelligence system components across a network. It is used by Oracle Fusion Middleware Control, and by yourself manually from the command line, to control the status of the BI Server, BI Presentation Server, and other system components. It works alongside the WebLogic Server Node Manager, which performs a similar role for the Java components.

OPMN is used by Oracle Business Intelligence because key servers such as the BI Server and BI Presentation Server aren't written in Java and can't have their status controlled by the usual Java-based management servers found within Oracle Fusion Middleware. OPMN provides a server for managing the status of non-Java components and is used by Fusion Middleware Control to provide the interface between the Java-based Enterprise Manager JEE application and the operating system executables that make up the Oracle Business Intelligence system components. When you view the status of the BI Server, BI Presentation Server, or other system components in the Fusion Middleware Control management screens, it is OPMN that is being used to report back their status and pass on your requests to stop, start, and resume them.

Supporting Database Schema   The supporting database schema is a set of database tables that can be installed via the Oracle Fusion Middleware Repository Creation Utility into an Oracle, Microsoft SQL Server, or IBM DB/2 database. The database schema, typically called BIPLATFORM and accompanied by another one called Metadata Services (MDS) that contains metadata used by Oracle Fusion Middleware, contains tables that support the following system and Java components:

- Oracle BI Scheduler
- Oracle BI Publisher
- Oracle BI Server (usage tracking and other functions)
- Oracle Scorecard and Strategy Management

If you use a tool such as Oracle SQL*Developer or Oracle SQL*Plus to look at the contents of this schema, you will also note that there are other tables to support products such as Oracle Real-Time Decisions, Oracle Calculation Manager, and Oracle Essbase; however, you can ignore these tables, and they are outside the scope of this book.

So now you understand a little more about the architecture of Oracle Business Intelligence, and we will return to the topic of this architecture, and management of the various components, in later chapters of this book. For now, though, let's move on to what is probably the single most important topic that you need to understand as a developer: creating repositories against relational data sources.

CHAPTER
2

Installation and Upgrading Oracle Business Intelligence

he first chapter of this book provided an overview of Oracle Business Intelligence and took you through the architecture of the product platform. In this chapter, we will look at how you install Oracle Business Intelligence into Microsoft Windows, Linux, and other platforms, and how you upgrade existing installations of both the 10*g* and 11*g* versions of the product up to the latest release. Before we start the installation or upgrade, though, let's take a quick look at what preparations you need to make for your environment.

Preparing for the Installation

Oracle Business Intelligence 11*g* has a number of hardware and software prerequisites, including software that you need to install into your environment before you start the installation. As this list of supported hardware and operating system software changes from release to release, you should check the *System Requirements and Supported Platforms for Oracle Business Intelligence Suite Enterprise Edition 11gR1* document available on the Oracle Technology Network web site for the latest certifications, at the time of writing found at http://www.oracle.com/technetwork/middleware/ias/downloads/fusion-certification-100350.html and located within the "Oracle Business Intelligence" section.

In addition to ensuring that you have adequate hardware and the correct operating system version installed, there are a number of Microsoft Windows and Linux- or Unix-specific preinstallation tasks that you will need to carry out, and you will also need to ensure that a suitable database server is available to host the supporting database schemas.

Note that in subsequent chapters of this book we refer to where you have installed Oracle Business Intelligence on your server's file system as [*middleware_home*]; for example:

[*middleware_home*]\Oracle_BI1

This would equate to the following file system location on a Microsoft Windows–based system if you had installed Oracle Business Intelligence to c:\Middleware:

c:\Middleware\Oracle_BI1

Note also that, for Microsoft Windows Server environments, the configuration of the desktop Start menu can change depending on how you have configured the Start menu properties. For all examples in this and later chapters, it is assumed that the Windows Server 2003 classic Start menu has been chosen for your system. (Right-click the Start menu on your desktop taskbar, and then select Properties. In the Taskbar And Start Menu Properties dialog box, select the Start Menu tab and then choose Classic Start Menu.) If you are using the default, "new-style" Start menu, you may have to alter some of the walkthrough instructions to reference the correct menu item location in your Start menu.

Microsoft Windows–Specific Preinstallation Tasks

Before you install Oracle Business Intelligence into a Microsoft Windows environment, if the server does not have a permanent, static IP address but rather an IP address provided automatically through a DHCP server, you should install the Microsoft Loopback Adapter and configure that to have a permanent static IP address instead. If you are in this situation and do not have the loopback adapter configured for your environment, the installation may fail or you may subsequently encounter connectivity problems among the business intelligence components.

Most problems encountered when installing Oracle Business Intelligence 11*g* on Microsoft Windows can be traced back to not having installed or properly configured the loopback adapter, and you should therefore ensure that the following steps are carried out before you start the installation process.

Installing the Microsoft Loopback Adapter with Microsoft Windows Server 2003

To install the Microsoft Loopback Adapter using either the 32- or 64-bit version of Microsoft Windows Server 2003, follow these steps, which assume that you have one other network adapter already installed that connects you to your corporate network or the Internet (or adjust the network adapter naming in the steps if this is not the case):

1. Log into your Microsoft Windows Server 2003 using an account with administrator privileges.

2. Select Start to bring up the Windows Start menu; then select Settings | Control Panel.

3. When the Control Panel window is displayed, double-click the Add Hardware icon to display the Add Hardware Wizard.

4. Click Next to progress past the opening screen in the wizard, and when asked "Is the hardware connected?" select the radio button for "Yes, I have already connected the hardware."

5. The wizard will then present you with a list of already installed hardware. Scroll to the bottom of the list, select Add A New Hardware Device, and click Next.

6. On the next screen of the wizard, select the "Install the hardware that I manually select from a list (Advanced)" radio button, and then click Next.

7. From the list of common hardware types displayed on the next screen of the wizard, select Network Adapters from the list and click Next.

8. On the Select Network Adapter screen, select Microsoft in the Manufacturer list and Microsoft Loopback Adapter in the Network Adapter list; then click Next.

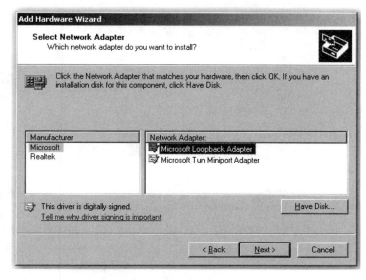

9. Click Next and then Finish to compete the installation.

Now that the loopback adapter is installed, you need to give it a static IP address. To do this, follow these steps:

1. Select Start to bring up the Windows Start menu; then select Settings | Control Panel.

2. From the list of icons in the Control Panel window, select Network Connections.

3. Within the Network Connections window, there should be a new network adapter listed called Local Area Connection 2. (The number may differ if you have more than one physical network adapter installed.) This network adapter will be labeled as using the Microsoft Loopback Adapter, and there should be a message stating that it has limited or no connectivity.

4. Double-click this new network adapter icon, and when the Local Area Network Connection 2 Status dialog box is shown, click the Properties button.

5. With the Properties dialog box displayed, ensure that the General tab is selected and then double-click the Internet Protocol (TCP/IP) entry, so that you can set the static IP address for the network adapter.

6. With the Internet Protocol (TCP/IP) Properties dialog box shown, select the "Use the following IP address" radio button and enter the following details:

   IP address: **10.10.10.10**
   Subnet mask: **255.255.255.0**

Leave all other values blank, or at their default value.

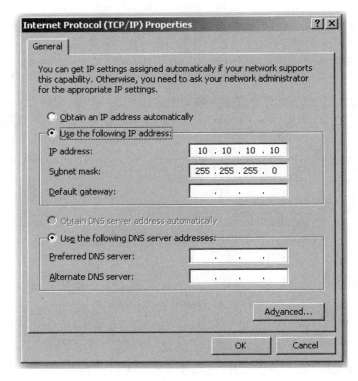

7. Click OK and then OK again to close the various dialog boxes. When you view the Local Area Connection 2 icon within the Network Connections window now, you should see that its status has changed to Connected.

Installing the Microsoft Loopback Adapter with Microsoft Windows Server 2008

To install the Microsoft Loopback Adapter using the 32- or 64-bit version of Microsoft Windows Server 2008, follow these steps, which assume that you have one other network adapter already installed that connects you to your corporate network or the Internet (or adjust the network adapter naming in the steps if this is not the case):

1. Log into Microsoft Windows Server 2008 using an administrator account.

2. Select Start to bring up the Windows Start menu, and in the search box at the bottom of the screen, type **Device Manager**.

3. When the Device Manager dialog box is shown, right-click the machine name at the top of the device list and select Add Legacy Hardware.

4. The Add Hardware Wizard will then be displayed. Click Next, select the "Install the hardware that I manually select from a list (Advanced)" radio button on the next screen, and then click Next to proceed.

5. Click Next to have the wizard search for new hardware, and then click Next when it does not find the loopback adapter. When the list of common hardware types is then shown on the subsequent screen, select Network Adapters and click Next.

6. At the Select Network Adapter screen, select Microsoft in the Manufacturer list and Microsoft Loopback Adapter in the Network Adapter list.

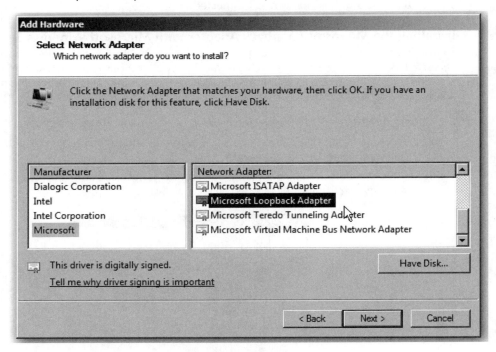

7. Click Next and then Finish to complete the installation.

Now that the loopback adapter is installed, you need to give it a static IP address. To do this, follow these steps:

1. Select Start to bring up the Windows Start menu, and in the search box at the bottom of the menu, type **Network and Sharing Center**.

2. With the Network And Sharing Center dialog box open, locate and click the link for your new network adapter. (It usually will be called Local Area Network Connection 2 and will appear within the View Your Active Networks section.)

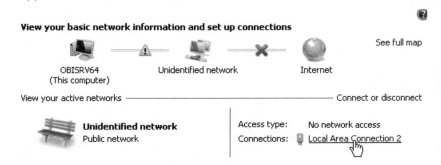

3. The Local Area Network Connection 2 Status dialog box will then be displayed. Click the Properties button at the bottom of the dialog box to display the Properties dialog box, and then, with the Networking tab selected, double-click the Internet Protocol Version 4 (TCP/IPv4) entry.

4. In the Internet Protocol Version 4 (TCP/IPv4) Properties dialog box that appears, select the "Use the following IP address" radio button and enter the following details:

IP address: **10.10.10.10**
Subnet mask: **255.255.255.0**

Leave the remaining entries in the dialog box blank, or at their default value.

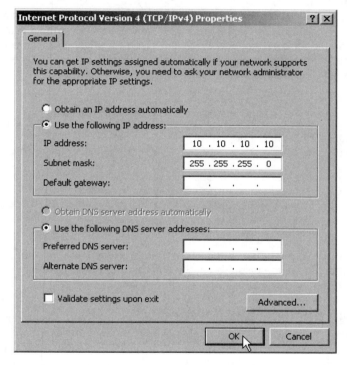

5. Click OK, and OK again; then click Close to close the various dialog boxes.

Linux- and Unix-Specific Preinstallation Tasks

When installing Oracle Business Intelligence into a Linux or Unix environment, there are a number of preinstallation tasks that you should carry out to ensure a successful installation. The tasks outlined in this section are specific to Oracle Linux 5, so you should check the product documentation for any steps specific to other Linux or Unix versions.

Required Packages and Operating System Changes

As with other Oracle products that can be installed on Linux and Unix platforms, Oracle Business Intelligence has specific requirements for packages and other operating system changes that need to be applied prior to the installation. As these packages and changes can vary from operating system to operating system, and version to version, you should check the *System Requirements and Supported Platforms for Oracle Business Intelligence Suite Enterprise Edition 11gR1* document available as part of the product documentation on the Oracle Technology Network web site before performing the installation. As a guideline, though, if you have configured your operating system such that you can install the 11g release of Oracle Database Server or Client, you will normally be able to install Oracle Business Intelligence without any further configuration; if not, the Universal Installer will warn you or stop you from performing the installation if your host environment does not meet the installation prerequisites.

Network Settings
Unlike Microsoft Windows–based installations, you do not need to install a separate loopback adapter before installing Oracle Business Intelligence. Instead, using a text editor, edit the /etc/ hosts file so that it contains the following entries (substituting your own host name for obisrvlnx64, as appropriate), which then ensure that requests made to your machine's host name are directed to the pre-installed loopback adapter:

```
127.0.0.1               obisrvlnx64
127.0.0.1               localhost.localdomain localhost
```

To check that your host name now resolves back to the loopback IP address, use the /bin/ping utility to check connectivity. The results of this check should look like this:

```
[root@obisrvlnx64 ~]# ping obisrvlnx64
PING obisrvlnx64 (127.0.0.1) 56(84) bytes of data.
64 bytes from obisrvlnx64 (127.0.0.1): icmp_seq=1 ttl=64 time=0.027 ms
64 bytes from obisrvlnx64 (127.0.0.1): icmp_seq=2 ttl=64 time=0.038 ms
64 bytes from obisrvlnx64 (127.0.0.1): icmp_seq=3 ttl=64 time=0.052 ms
```

In general, Unix and Linux systems take their machine name from this hosts file entry, so if you see the machine name displayed at the command prompt like this, you can usually be reasonably confident that the host name will resolve properly.

Database Server Requirements
Before you can successfully install Oracle Business Intelligence 11g, you have to run the Repository Creation Utility, a component of Oracle Fusion Middleware 11g, which creates supporting database schemas and tables that are used to hold application metadata. You cannot install Oracle Business Intelligence until you have successfully carried out this step, and therefore you will need database administrator access to a supported database type before you start the product installation.

As of Oracle Business Intelligence 11g, here are the supported database types for these schemas:

- Oracle Database
- Microsoft SQL Server
- IBM DB/2
- Oracle Database enabled for edition-based redefinition
- MySQL Database

However, as with the hardware and software requirements outlined earlier in this chapter, you should check the *System Requirements and Supported Platforms for Oracle Business Intelligence Suite Enterprise Edition 11gR1* document on the Oracle Technology Network web site for up-to-date details and certifications, including specific versions of each product that are supported by the Repository Creation Utility.

When creating an Oracle database for use with Oracle Business Intelligence, ensure that you select Unicode (AL32UTF8) as the database character set, for maximum compatibility. Non-Unicode database character sets will usually work without issue, but future functionality or wider use of Oracle Fusion Middleware may require the Unicode character set.

Because the Repository Creation Utility creates database accounts, data files, and other system-level database artifacts, you will need a database administrator to enter their credentials when you use this utility. Because of this, you might wish to make it the responsibility of a database administrator to run the Repository Creation Utility, with your assistance. Once these database accounts are used, you can then perform the main installation using the database accounts that were created for you by the Repository Creation Utility.

Creating the Supporting Database Schemas

The Repository Creation Utility simplifies the installation of database schemas and tables that Oracle Business Intelligence requires to hold its data and metadata. Because the Repository Creation Utility is designed to be used across all Oracle Fusion Middleware products, when you come to use it you will see that there are options to install schemas for many different products; however, when you are installing just Oracle Business Intelligence, there are only two schemas that you need to be concerned with.

What Schemas Are Created During the Installation Process?

When used along with an Oracle Business Intelligence installation, the Repository Creation Utility installs two schemas that are required by the product.

The BIPLATFORM schema contains tables used by Oracle Business Intelligence, along with other products such as Oracle Real-Time Decisions. In general, you do not need to concern yourself with the contents of these tables except to ensure that they are adequately backed up each day, and you should not manually alter their contents except when directed to by this book or by Oracle Support.

The MDS schema (for Metadata Services) contains metadata tables used by Oracle Fusion Middleware and Oracle Business Intelligence, and again should not be manually altered or accessed except under the direction of Oracle Support.

Running the Repository Creation Utility to Create Repository Schemas

Once you have ensured that you have a suitable database available, together with the username and password for a database administrator account, follow the steps listed in this section to run the Repository Creation Utility.

Note that you can use the Microsoft Windows version of the Repository Creation Utility to connect to a Unix or Linux server running your repository database, as long as the version of the Repository Creation Utility that you are running is correct for the version of Oracle Business Intelligence that you are installing. Running this utility natively on Windows is sometimes easier to do than running it on a Unix or Linux server, so it's useful to bear this in mind.

Once you have obtained a copy of the Repository Creation Utility, unzip the download files and, using either the command line or a utility such as Windows Explorer, open the \BIN directory within the downloaded files. Locate the rcu.bat (Microsoft Windows) or rcu.sh (Unix/ Linux) file and either start it from the command line, or double-click it to execute it from the file system explorer window:

1. Once the Repository Creation Utility starts, click Next to proceed past the Welcome screen.

2. Select the Create radio button to create new repository schema components in your database.

3. At the Database Connection Details screen, select your database type from the options in the drop-down list. Then, for your particular database type, enter the connection details for a DBA user, for example:

   Database Type: Oracle Database
   Host Name: obisrv
   Port: 1521
   Service Name: orcl
   Username: SYS
   Password: *password*
   Role: SYSDBA

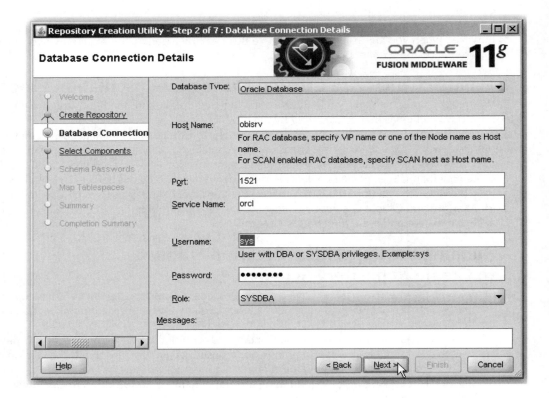

Click Next, and the Repository Creation Utility will then check prerequisites before proceeding to the next screen. If any issues are raised by these checks, resolve the issues before proceeding to the next stage.

4. At the Select Components screen, shown in Figure 2-1, first enter a prefix into the Create A New Prefix text box (for example, DEV or PROD), ensuring that only alphanumeric characters are used. This prefix allows a single database to contain metadata schemas for several business intelligence domains.

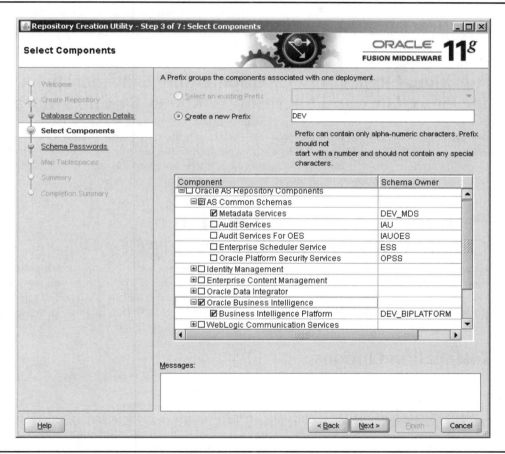

FIGURE 2-1. *Selecting the Business Intelligence schema option*

Then select the Oracle Business Intelligence check box; when you select this option, the Metadata Services check box automatically will be selected for you as well, as this schema is also required for Oracle Business Intelligence 11g. Click Next to proceed, and again resolve any issues raised by the next prerequisite check before proceeding further.

5. At the Schema Passwords screen, enter either a single password that will be used for all schemas being created by the Repository Creation Utility, or enter separate passwords for each schema. Click Next to proceed to the next screen.

6. At the Map Tablespaces screen, either accept the default tablespace and temporary tablespace settings or select alternative ones from the drop-down lists, and then click Next to proceed to the Creating Tablespaces dialog box. At this point, any new tablespaces and temporary tablespaces will be created in the target database. Click OK.

7. At the summary screen, click the Create button to create the repository schemas. Once the creation process completes, click the Close button to exit the Repository Creation Utility.

Additional Repository Creation Utility Considerations for Linux/Unix and Microsoft Windows 64-Bit Platforms

The process of running the Repository Creation Utility under Linux or Unix is the same as under Microsoft Windows, apart from the process used to start the utility itself. Make sure, however, that when you use the Repository Creation Utility you choose the version that is correct for the operating system you're using and the version that corresponds to the version of Oracle Business Intelligence you are subsequently going to install.

Performing a New Installation of Oracle Business Intelligence 11g

Once you have created the required repository schemas for Oracle Business Intelligence, you can then install the software itself. When you install Oracle Business Intelligence, you are given three options that affect what software is copied to your server and how it is configured, and you can perform additional Client Tools installations after the main installation to allow developers to work away from the main server.

Installation Options

When installing Oracle Business Intelligence 11g, the Universal Installer provided with the download gives you options for three different installation types:

- **Simple Install** This installation type asks you fewer configuration questions at the start, and then installs a single-server topology that simplifies configuration and management and requires fewer server resources to run but cannot be scaled out to additional nodes and servers after this initial installation.

- **Enterprise Install** This option allows you either to create a new BI system or scale out an existing BI system, provides access to the full set of installation parameters, installs the full server topology (including separate Administration and Managed Servers), and allows you to add additional servers to an existing installation.
- **Software Only Install** This installation is used when you have an existing application server to install to. It installs only the Oracle Business Intelligence software into this application server and requires you to run a separate configuration step after the installation to create the WebLogic Server domain. This installation type is also used for patch upgrades between releases of Oracle Business Intelligence 11*g*.

In addition, a separately downloadable Client Tools installer allows you to install the Windows-only Oracle BI Administration tool to a client PC, along with the ODBC driver required for it to connect to the Oracle BI Server. Note also that the 11.1.1.6 release of Oracle Business Intelligence allows you to download the Client Tools installer from the Oracle Business Intelligence home page using the Download BI Desktop Tools menu under the Getting Started section, avoiding the need for a separate software download from the Oracle web site.

Using the Simple Install Option

The Simple Install option is typically used when you wish to create a demonstration or prototype installation of Oracle Business Intelligence, typically on a laptop or desktop PC that has 4GB or less of RAM available.

Unlike the Enterprise Install option that installs both a WebLogic Administration Server and a Managed Server, along with the Node Manager, the Simple Install option does away with the Managed Server and Node Manager and installs all Java components into the Administration Server, saving you memory and disk space at the cost of not being able to add Managed Servers after the installation.

This installation type also presents you with fewer installation parameters and settings, making it ideal for quick installations for demonstration purposes but giving you fewer options around the installation locations, naming of components, and so on.

Performing a Simple Installation Using Microsoft Windows Server 2003 32-Bit Edition

To perform a simple installation of Oracle Business Intelligence 11.1.1.6, follow these steps:

1. Ensure that you have carried out the required previous step of using the Repository Creation Utility to create the required repository schemas.
2. Download the software from the Oracle Technology Network, and unzip the downloaded files to create a single installation directory called bishiphome, containing five subdirectories named Disk1 to Disk5.
3. Open the Disk1 directory, and then double-click the setup.exe executable file to start the Universal Installer.

4. The Universal Installer will then present you with a Welcome message. Click Next to proceed to the first screen of the installer wizard.

5. At the Install Software Updates screen, either enter your My Oracle Support (formerly Metalink) username and password to search for product updates or select the Skip Software Updates radio button to proceed without downloading updates; then click Next to proceed.

6. At the Select Installation Type screen, select the Simple Install radio button, as shown in Figure 2-2, and click Next to proceed.

7. The Prerequisite Checks screen will then check that your operating system certification, service pack level, and amount of physical memory are correct for this installation. If any checks do not have a check mark in the Status column beside them and you can fix the issue immediately, do so and then click the Retry button or close the installer and fix the issue before starting the installation process again. Click Next to proceed to the next screen.

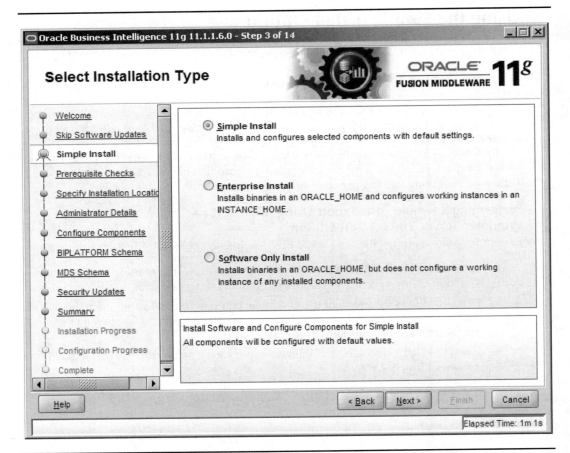

FIGURE 2-2.   *Selecting the Simple Install type*

8. At the Specify Installation Location screen, click the Browse button to navigate to the file system location where the Oracle Business Intelligence software should be installed.

Ensure that you pick a directory on a local hard disk rather than a network share, and try to have the installation path as close to the root of your file system as possible (for example, c:\Oracle\Middleware) because unzip utilities that you may use afterward to import sample data into your environment can encounter issues with file paths that are too long. Click Next to proceed to the next screen.

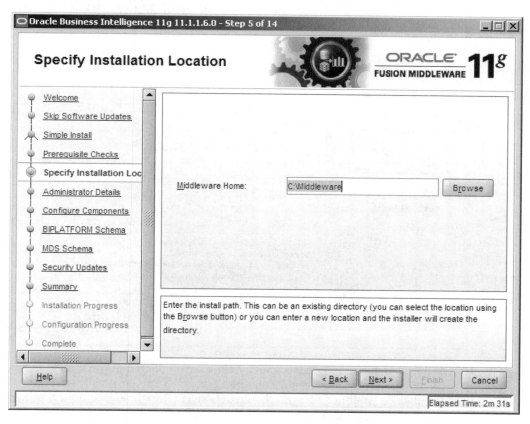

9. At the Administrator Details screen, enter the username and password for the administrator account for your system, including a mixture of numbers and letters (for example, weblogic/welcome1). This account replaces the "Administrator" account found in previous releases of Oracle Business Intelligence and also acts as the administrator account for WebLogic Server and Oracle Fusion Middleware.

Write the details of this account down safely, as you will need it to log into Oracle Business Intelligence after the installation, and to perform administrative functions. Once these details are entered, click Next to proceed.

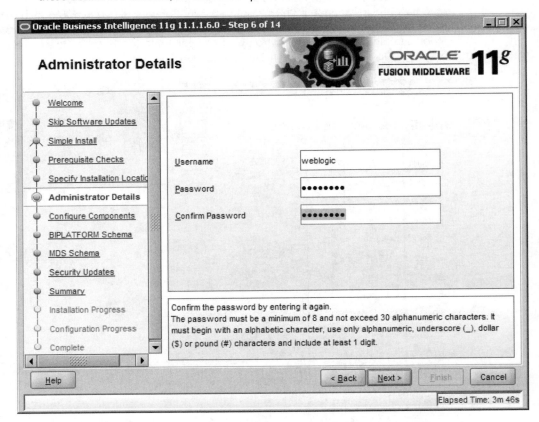

10. At the Configure Components screen, select the products that you wish to install. Selecting Business Intelligence Enterprise Edition will automatically select Business Intelligence Publisher, and you should only select Real-Time Decisions if you wish to evaluate the product or you have purchased the additional license required for its use. (A license for Business Intelligence Publisher is automatically included in the Business Intelligence Enterprise Edition license.)

CAUTION
If you don't configure these components here, you can't then go back and configure them after the installation.

Once your products are selected, click Next to proceed.

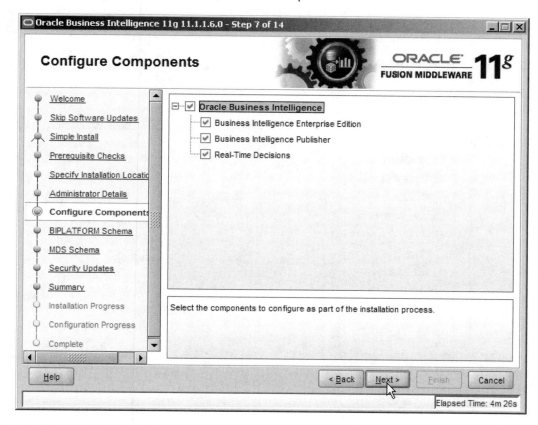

11. The BIPLATFORM Schema screen will then be displayed. Using the entries on this screen, select the database type for your repository schema database from the Database Type drop-down box, and then enter the connection details into the rest of the dialog box, using the JDBC format for the connect string; for example:

Database Type: Oracle Database
Connect String: obisrv:1521:orcl
BIPLATFORM Schema Username: DEV_BIPLATFORM
BIPLATFORM Schema Password: *password*

Once these details are entered, click Next to proceed.

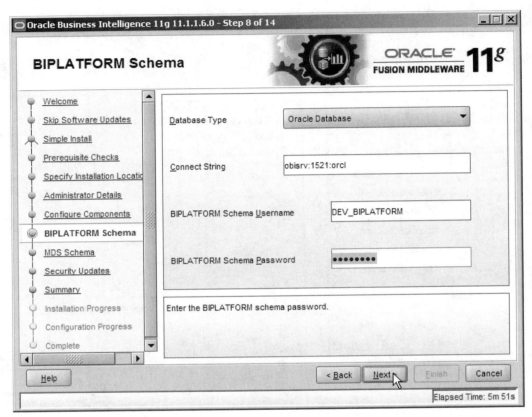

12. At the MDS Schema screen, either confirm the default details that specify the same database connection as the BIPLATFORM schema or alter these details if you are planning to reuse an existing MDS schema elsewhere in your Oracle Fusion Middleware deployment. Click Next to continue.

NOTE
This MDS schema should be the same version number as the version of Oracle Business Intelligence that you are installing, and if you are upgrading from an earlier 11g release of Oracle Business Intelligence, see the section of this chapter titled "Upgrading from Oracle Business Intelligence 10g," rather than following these instructions.

13. At the Specify Security Updates screen, again enter your My Oracle Support credentials if you wish to be automatically notified of security and other updates to the products you install. Click Next to continue.

14. At the Summary screen, check the installation details that you have entered, and then click Install to begin the installation of your products.

15. The installation will then proceed in two parts. First, your products will be installed by copying binary files and configuration templates to your server or PC. While this copying takes place, the installer will advise you of progress and any issues, as shown in Figure 2-3.

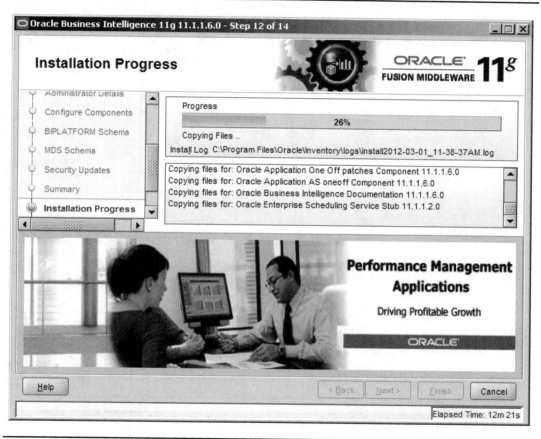

FIGURE 2-3.   *The Installation Progress screen in the Universal Installer*

16. After the installation completes, the Universal Installer will then start the configuration stage of the installation. The Configuration Progress screen, shown in Figure 2-4, will then detail these configuration steps, which should not require any intervention from you if everything progresses correctly.

Check the progress of this configuration, and if any steps fail, follow any instructions provided by the installer and restart the affected stage in the process. Once complete, click Next to proceed to the final screen of the installer.

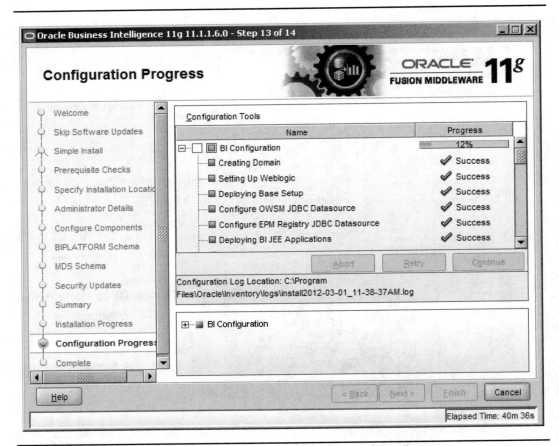

FIGURE 2-4.   *The Configuration Progress screen in the Universal Installer*

17. Once the configuration stage has completed successfully, click Finish to close the Universal Installer. After a minute or so, your web browser will open a new window and will display the Business Intelligence sign-in screen.

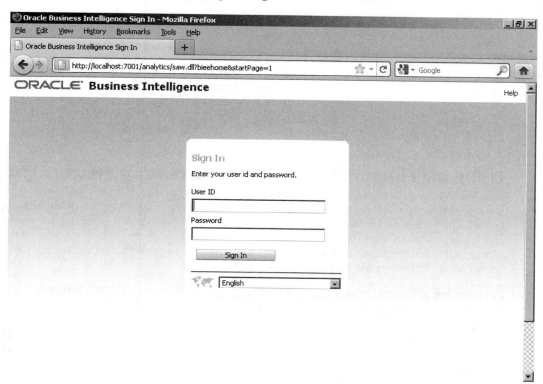

NOTE
For the Simple Install type only, the port number that you use to connect to Oracle Business Intelligence is by default 7001, rather than 9704, as all components are installed in the same WebLogic Administration Server rather than a separate Managed Server.

Simple Install Considerations on Other Platforms

In addition to installing Oracle Business Intelligence using the Simple Install option on Microsoft Windows 32-bit platforms, you can use the same installation option for 64-bit Windows systems, as well as for 32- and 64-bit Linux and Unix platforms, as per the "Supported Systems and Configurations" document available on the Oracle Technology Network.

When installing on 64-bit Microsoft Windows systems, download and unzip the 64-bit installation files, and then run the setup.exe installer file within the Disk1 directory. The installer will install the 64-bit version of the Oracle Business Intelligence files, including the 64-bit Java JVM, automatically for you.

For Linux 32-bit and 64-bit simple installations, unzip the downloaded files as before, but execute the ./runInstaller.sh script rather than setup.exe to start the Universal Installer, like this:

```
cd bishiphome/Disk1
./runInstaller
```

NOTE
You must install Oracle Business Intelligence using a non-root user, such as an account that you have created for performing Oracle software installations. After the main part of the installation completes, though, you may need to run a script as the root user to configure the Oracle Inventory if this is the first Oracle software installation on that server.

Using the Enterprise Install – Create New BI System Option

Installing a new BI system using the Enterprise Install option follows the same pattern as a simple installation but asks you more questions in order to allow more customization of the installed system. The Enterprise Install option also installs the full WebLogic Server topology for your system, giving you a single Administration Server, along with a Managed Server and Node Manager. You can extend this system over additional physical servers later on through the Enterprise Install – Scale Out BI System option, detailed later in this book.

Performing an Enterprise Installation Using Oracle Linux 5 64-Bit Edition

As with the Simple Install option, the installation steps when using the Universal Installer are almost identical across platforms and across 32- and 64-bit versions. For the following installation example, we will use the Microsoft Windows Server 2003 32-bit platform to illustrate the steps that differ between the Simple and Enterprise installation processes; however, as detailed in the following section, there are no significant differences between this and the same installation type on other platforms, including those based around Linux or Unix.

To perform an Enterprise Install – Create New BI System installation on the Microsoft Windows Server 2003 32-bit platform, follow these steps:

1. Ensure that you have carried out the required previous step of using the Repository Creation Utility to create the required repository schemas.

2. Download the software from the Oracle Technology Network, and unzip the downloaded files to create a single installation directory called bishiphome, containing five subdirectories named Disk1 through to Disk5.

3. Open the Disk1 directory, and then double-click the setup.exe executable file to start the Universal Installer.

4. The Universal Installer will then present you with a Welcome message. Click Next to proceed to the first screen of the installer wizard.

5. At the Install Software Updates screen, either enter your My Oracle Support (formerly Metalink) username and password to search for product updates or select the Skip Software Updates radio button to proceed without downloading updates; then click Next to proceed.

6. At the Select Installation Type screen, select Enterprise Install as the installation type, as shown in Figure 2-5.

7. The Prerequisite Checks screen will then check your host environment for the correct packages, libraries, memory, and other prerequisites. If any of these checks fail, correct the issue and then either click the Retry button to recheck the prerequisites, or exit the installer and restart it again once the issues are resolved; otherwise, click Next to proceed to the next screen.

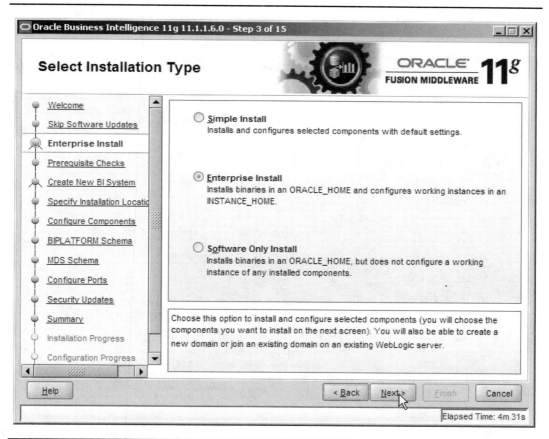

FIGURE 2-5. *Selecting the Enterprise Install type*

TIP
Generally, if you have prepared a Linux or Unix environment for an Oracle Database 11g installation, it will pass the prerequisite checks for Oracle Business Intelligence 11g.

Click Next to proceed to the next screen.

8. At the Create Or Scale Out BI System screen, shown in Figure 2-6, select Create New BI System, enter the username in the User Name field, and enter the user password that should be used for the system administrator account in the User Password field; then confirm or change the name of the custom WebLogic Server domain name that will be created for Oracle Business Intelligence. (Generally, you would leave this domain name at the default value.) Once complete, click Next to proceed to the next screen.

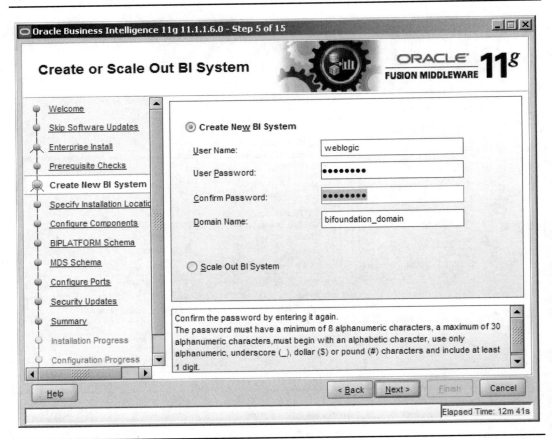

FIGURE 2-6. *Selecting the option to create a new BI system*

9. On the Specify Installation Location screen, click the Browse button to navigate to a directory into which you wish to install Oracle Business Intelligence; if possible, use the default file system location, as many scripts from Oracle and other providers point to default installation locations. Once this directory is selected, the dependent locations will be automatically populated for you, along with the name of the Oracle instance. Either leave these values at their default or alter them if you need to customize their values.

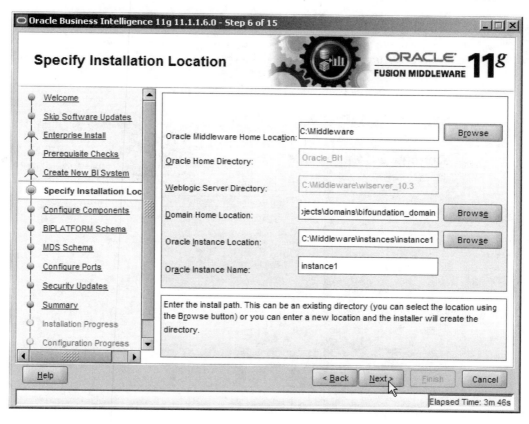

10. At the Configure Components screen, select the products that you wish to install. Selecting Business Intelligence Enterprise Edition will automatically select Business Intelligence Publisher, and you should only select Real-Time Decisions if you wish to evaluate the product or you have purchased the additional license required for its use. (A license for Business Intelligence Publisher is automatically included in the Business Intelligence Enterprise Edition license.)

CAUTION
If you choose not to configure these components here, you can't go back and configure them after the installation.

Once your products are selected, click Next to proceed.

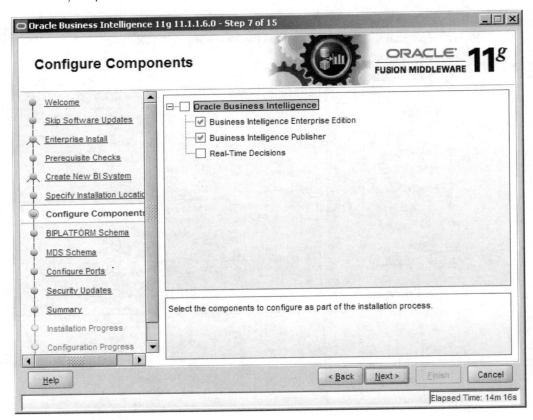

11.   The BIPLATFORM Schema screen will then be displayed. Using the entries on this screen, select the database type for your repository schema database from the Database Type drop-down box, and then enter the connection details into the rest of the dialog box, using the JDBC format for the connect string; for example:

Database Type: Oracle Database
Connect String: obisrv:1521:orcl
BIPLATFORM Schema Username: DEV_BIPLATFORM
BIPLATFORM Schema Password: *password*

Once these details are entered, click Next to proceed.

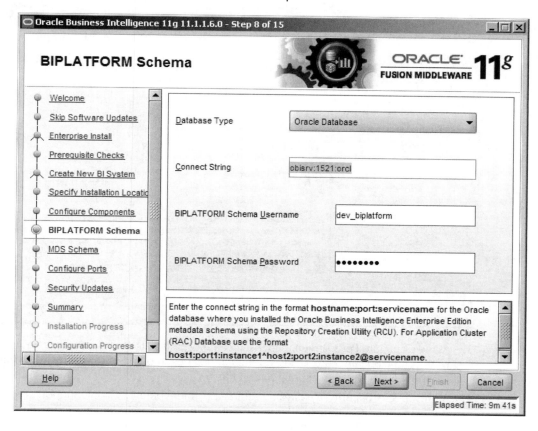

12. The MDS Schema screen will then be displayed, with the connection details prepopulated for you based on the settings you chose for the BIPLATFORM schema. Check that these details are correct, amend them if you have installed the MDS schema in a different location, and then click Next to continue.

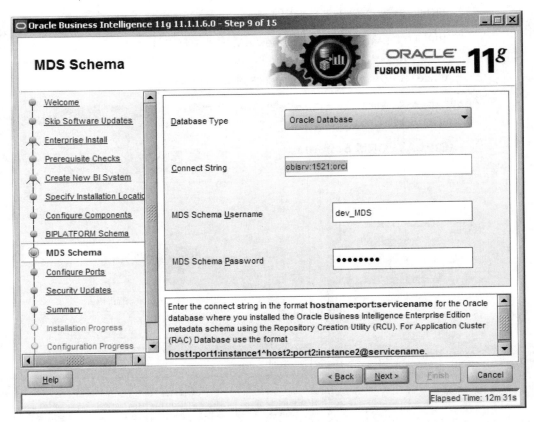

13. At the Configure Ports screen, either select the default Auto Port Configuration radio button or select the Specify Ports Using Configuration File radio button to specify individual component ports using a configuration file.

14. At the Specify Security Updates screen, again enter your My Oracle Support credentials if you wish to be automatically notified of security and other updates to the products you install. Click Next to continue.

15. At the Summary screen, check the installation details that you have entered and click Install to begin the installation of your products.

16. The installation will then proceed in two parts. First, your products will be installed by copying binary files and configuration templates to your server or PC. While this copying takes place, the installer will advise you of progress (see Figure 2-3, shown earlier in the chapter) and any issues.

17. After the installation completes, the Universal Installer will then start the configuration stage of the installation. The Configuration Progress screen (shown previously in Figure 2-4) will then detail these configuration steps, which should not require any intervention from you if everything progresses correctly.

    Check the progress of this configuration, and if any steps fail, follow any instructions provided by the installer and restart the affected stage in the process. Once complete, click Next to proceed to the final screen of the installer.

18. Once the configuration stage has completed successfully, click Finish to close the Universal Installer. After a minute or so, your web browser will open a new window and will display the Business Intelligence sign-in screen.

Enterprise Installation Considerations for Other Platforms

Apart from using ./runInstaller rather than setup.exe to start the Universal Installer, there are no differences between Linux/Unix and Microsoft Windows–based platforms, and between 32- and 64-bit installations when performing an enterprise installation of Oracle Business Intelligence.

Using the Software Only Install Option

The Software Only Install option is used when you have an existing installation of WebLogic Server on a host server that you wish to install Oracle Business Intelligence into, when you wish to share a single Oracle WebLogic installation between two Oracle BI domains, or when configuring Oracle Business Intelligence with the Enterprise Deployment Guide (EDG) high-availability topology. It can also be used when you have an existing installation of Oracle Business Intelligence that you wish to upgrade using a patch upgrade, and details of this scenario are detailed later in this chapter.

For now, though, we will concentrate on the main usage of the Software Only Install option, which is to install Oracle Business Intelligence into an exiting WebLogic Server installation.

When you perform a software-only installation, there are four stages to the installation:

1. Before the installation, obtain and install a supported version of Oracle WebLogic Server. See the "System Requirements and Certification" document on the Oracle Technology Network web site for WebLogic Server versions that are compatible with your version of Oracle Business Intelligence.

2. Run the Repository Creation Utility to create the required supporting database schemas.

3. Perform the software-only installation on the host server. When the installer starts, point it to your existing WebLogic Server installation.

4. Use the Oracle Business Intelligence Configuration utility to create the WebLogic Server domain and Oracle instance.

Software Prerequisites

To perform a software-only installation, you will need the following Oracle software available for your particular platform:

■ A supported database server, such as Oracle Database 11*g*, to hold the required supporting database schemas

■ The Repository Creation Utility, to create the required supporting database schemas

■ Oracle WebLogic Server, using a version compatible with your release of Oracle Business Intelligence

■ Oracle Business Intelligence 11g

To prepare your environment for the software-only installation, follow the steps outlined in the sections titled "Preparing for the Installation" and "Creating the Supporting Database Schemas," earlier in this chapter. Once these steps have been carried out, do the following to perform a software-only installation.

Performing a Software-Only Installation Using Microsoft Windows Server 2003 32-Bit Edition

If you have not yet installed WebLogic Server, follow these steps to perform this install:

1. Obtain the WebLogic Server installer, and double-click it to open it.

2. When the installer Welcome screen displays, click Next to continue.

3. At the Choose Middleware Home Directory screen, select the Create A New Middleware Home option and click the Browse button to navigate to a new directory folder (for example, c:\Oracle\Middleware). Click Next to continue.

4. At the Register For Security Updates screen, enter your My Oracle Support credentials if you have them, and click Next to proceed.

5. At the Choose Install Type screen, select Typical and click Next to proceed.

6. At the Product Installation Directories screen, click Next to accept the default locations.

7. When the Choose Shortcut Location screen is shown, leave the selection at the default value and click Next to proceed.

8. The Installation Summary screen will then be displayed. Click Next to start the installation.

9. When the WebLogic Server installation process completes, the Installation Complete screen will be displayed. Uncheck the Run Quickstart check box and click Done to complete the process.

Once WebLogic Server is installed, you can begin the software-only installation process, which goes as follows:

1. Obtain and unzip the installation files for Oracle Business Intelligence 11g so that you have a main folder that contains five subfolders named Disk1 to Disk5.

2. Open the Disk1 folder and double-click the setup.exe file to start the Universal Installer.

3. When the Universal Installer starts, it will begin by displaying the Welcome screen. Click Next to start the installation process.

4. At the Install Software Updates screen, enter your My Oracle Support details, if you have them, to download and install updates to your particular version of Oracle Business Intelligence, or select the Skip Software Updates radio button if you do not have these details. Once done, click Next to proceed.

5. At the Select Installation Type screen, select the Software Only Install option, as shown in Figure 2-7, and then click Next to proceed.

6. The Prerequisite Checks screen will then be displayed. Check that all prerequisites are met, and then click Next to proceed to the next screen. If any checks do not have a check mark in the Status column beside them, close the installer, correct the issue, and then start the installation process again. Click Next to proceed to the next screen. You can also just click Retry if you are able to fix the issue without exiting the installer.

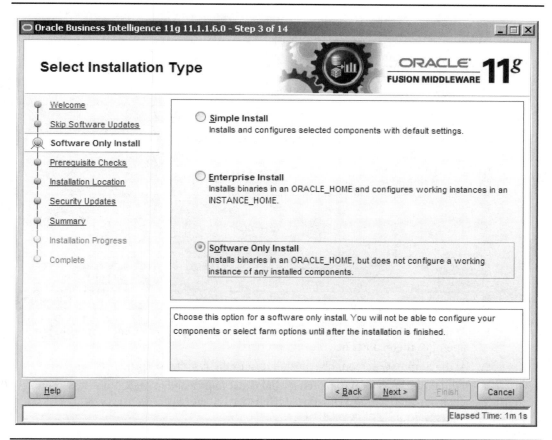

FIGURE 2-7. *Selecting the Software Only Install option*

7. At the Specify Installation Location screen, click the Browse button to navigate to where you have installed Oracle WebLogic Server, and leave the Oracle Home Directory name at the default. Click Next to proceed.

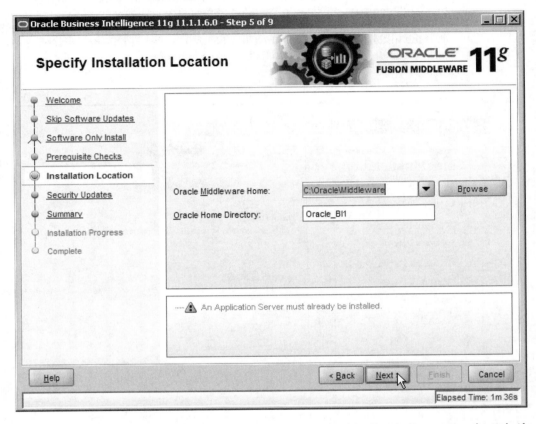

8. At the Specify Security Updates screen, again enter your My Oracle Support credentials if you have them, and click Next to proceed.

9. At the Summary screen, click Install to start the installation process.

10. When the installation completes, click Next to proceed to the Complete screen, and then click Finish to exit the Universal Installer.

Running the Oracle Business Intelligence Configuration Utility

Performing a software-only installation copies the binary file and configuration templates to your host server but does not in itself create the WebLogic Server domain or the Oracle instance containing your system components. To create these two items, you need to run the Oracle Business Intelligence Configuration utility, which will have been installed as part of the software-only installation.

When you run the Configuration utility, you will be presented with three options:

- **Create New BI System**   This is the usual option to select; it creates a new WebLogic Server domain and Oracle instance.

- **Scale Out BI System**   This option adds an additional WebLogic Managed Server to an existing enterprise installation of Oracle Business Intelligence.

- **Extend BI System**   This option takes an existing empty WebLogic Server domain, extends it to include business intelligence components, and then creates an accompanying Oracle instance for the system components.

NOTE
You cannot currently use this option with a WebLogic domain that already contains other products such as Oracle EPM Suite or Oracle Identity Management.

To use the Oracle Business Intelligence configuration utility, perform the following steps:

1. Navigate to the [*middleware_home*]\Oracle_BI1\bin directory on the host server where you installed Oracle Business Intelligence, and double-click the config.bat file to start the configuration utility.

2. The Configuration utility will then display the Welcome screen. Click Next to proceed.

3. The utility will then perform its prerequisite checks. Once all checks have passed successfully, click Next to proceed.

4. At the Create, Scale Out Or Extend screen, select Create New BI System to configure an existing WebLogic Server installation that has no WebLogic Server domains already configured or business intelligence products already installed. Select Extend BI System to configure an already-existing, empty WebLogic Server domain for use with Oracle Business Intelligence; the Scale Out BI System option is covered later in this book.

    For this example, we will use the Create New BI System option. Once selected, enter the username in the User Name field and the user password that you wish to use for your

WebLogic Server installation in the User Password field; then accept the default domain name, and click Next to proceed.

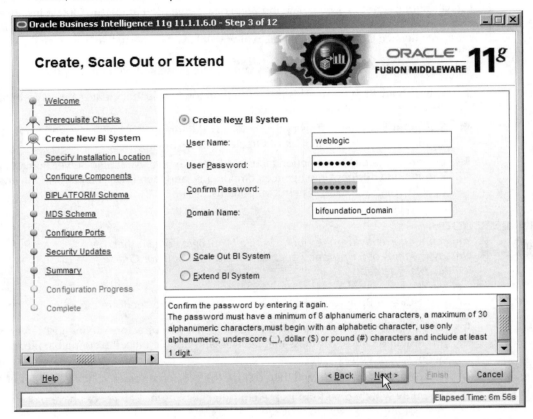

5. At the Specify Installation Location screen, accept the default file system locations or change them to your required values. Click Next to proceed.

6. At the Configure Components screen, select the components that you wish to configure. If you select Business Intelligence Enterprise Edition, Business Intelligence Publisher will be selected as well. Once selected, click Next to proceed.

7. At the BIPLATFORM Schema screen, enter the connection details to the database account into which you installed the BIPLATFORM supporting schema using the Repository Creation Utility. Click Next to proceed, and then do the same for the MDS schema also created using the Repository Creation Utility.

8. At the Configure Ports screen, either select Auto Port Configuration or click the Browse button to select a staticports.ini file containing port assignments for your system. Click Next to continue.

9. At the Security Updates screen, enter your My Oracle Support credentials if you wish to be automatically notified of security and other updates to the products you install. Click Next to continue.

10. At the Summary screen, check the configuration details that you have entered and click Configure to begin the configuration of your products.

11. The Configuration Progress screen will then be displayed, showing you the progress of the WebLogic Server domain and the Oracle instance.

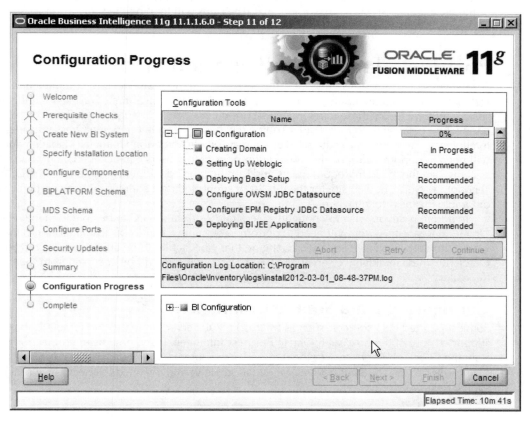

12. Once the Configuration process completes, click Next and then click Finish to exit the configuration utility. Your default web browser should then open at the Oracle Business Intelligence web site, where you can use the WebLogic Server username and user password you entered earlier to log in.

Software-Only Installation Considerations for Other Platforms

As with regular simple and enterprise installations of Oracle Business Intelligence, there are no differences between the 32- and 64-bit software-only installation processes when using Microsoft Windows–based servers.

When running a software-only installation on Unix- or Linux-based platforms, start the Universal Installer using the ./runInstaller script rather than setup.exe, and start the configuration utility using config.sh rather than config.bat. The steps will then be the same as for Microsoft Windows–based installations and configurations.

Post-Installation Configuration Steps

For all types of installations, there are steps that you will normally need to complete after the installation to configure connections to source databases. While Oracle Business Intelligence ships with Oracle Database and Oracle Essbase clients, you will need to configure these with the connection details for your particular source databases. In addition, while Oracle Business Intelligence can connect to data sources such as Oracle Hyperion Financial Management, you will need to perform additional configuration steps before users can access data from these systems. See the "System Requirements and Certification" document available on the Oracle Technology Network web site for the full list of supported data sources for your particular version of Oracle Business Intelligence.

In addition, if you wish to configure a separate workstation PC to be able to manage the Oracle BI Repository, you will need to perform a separate Client Tools installation into the workstation environment, and then configure that workstation to be able to connect to your Oracle Business Intelligence server and the data sources that will be accessed from the Oracle BI Repository.

Configuring Data Source Connectivity

Some supported data sources, such as Microsoft SQL Server, Teradata, and Oracle Essbase, are supported "out of the box" with Oracle Business Intelligence and only need connections created from the Oracle BI Repository to the required data source. Others, such as Oracle Database, have client software installed but need a configuration file to allow named connections through to source data.

Configuring Oracle Database Access

Oracle Business Intelligence comes with preinstalled Oracle Client software, but this client has not been configured with a TNSNAMES.ORA file so that you can access Oracle databases using an Oracle Net connect string.

To configure TNSNAMES access, follow these steps:

1. Within your Oracle Business Intelligence installation, navigate to the [*middleware_ home*]\Oracle_BI1\network\admin directory.

2. Copy into this directory to a TNSNAMES.ORA file that contains the connections to your source Oracle databases, which should be obtained from another server or workstation that accesses these databases. A typical TNSNAMES.ORA file would have contents like this:

```
# tnsnames.ora Network Configuration File: C:\app\product\11.2.0\
dbhome_1\network\admin\tnsnames.ora
# Generated by Oracle configuration tools.
ORACLR_CONNECTION_DATA =
  (DESCRIPTION =
    (ADDRESS_LIST =
      (ADDRESS = (PROTOCOL = IPC)(KEY = EXTPROC1521))
    )
    (CONNECT_DATA =
      (SID = CLRExtProc)
      (PRESENTATION = RO)
    )
  )
ORCL =
  (DESCRIPTION =
    (ADDRESS = (PROTOCOL = TCP)(HOST = obisrv)(PORT = 1521))
    (CONNECT_DATA =
      (SERVER = DEDICATED)
      (SERVICE_NAME = orcl)
    )
  )
```

3. If either Oracle Business Intelligence or the Oracle BI Administration tool is currently running, restart it to pick up the contents of this file. From that point on, you should be able to access your Oracle Database servers using the connection strings within the TNSNAMES.ORA file.

Installing Oracle Business Intelligence Client Tools

For situations where you wish to install the Oracle BI Administration tool on a workstation separate from the main Oracle Business Intelligence installation, a separate Client Tools download is available on the Oracle Technology Network web site and on the home page of the Oracle Business Intelligence web site for the 11.1.1.6 release. This installer installs the Oracle BI Administration tool and the ODBC client files for Oracle Business Intelligence, together with the Catalog Manager and Job Manager utilities. (The Catalog Manager is not included in Client Tools installations prior to 11.1.1.6.)

This Client Tools installer is available for Microsoft Windows–based platforms only and is available in both 32- and 64-bit versions.

Installing the Client Tools on Microsoft Windows 32-Bit Edition

To install the Oracle BI Administrator tool together with the Oracle Business Intelligence ODBC drivers, Catalog Manager, and Job Manager on a stand-alone workstation PC, follow these steps:

1. Either download the Client Tools installer from the Oracle web site and unzip the downloaded archive files to obtain the biee_client_install.exe installer file or download them directly from the Get Started | Download BI Desktop Tools menu on the Oracle Business Intelligence home page (11.1.1.6 and higher).

2. Double-click the biee_client_install.exe file to start the Installer application.

3. The installer will then start and display the Introduction screen. Click Next to proceed.

4. At the Choose Install Folder screen, enter the path to the installation directory that you wish to use, or accept the default value. Click Next to continue.

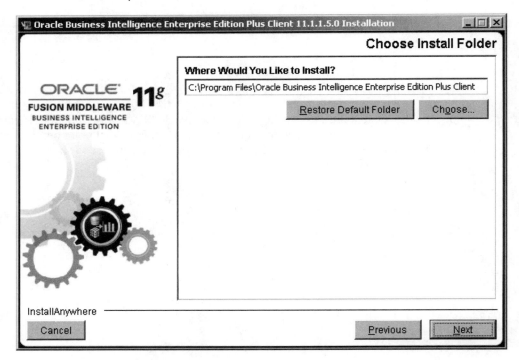

5. At the Choose Shortcut Folder screen, select where you would like the installer to create product icons and select the Create Icons For All Users check box if you would like these icon shortcuts to be available for all users, not just yourself. Click Next to continue.

6. At the Pre-Installation Summary screen, review the installation details and then click Install to start the Client Tools installation.

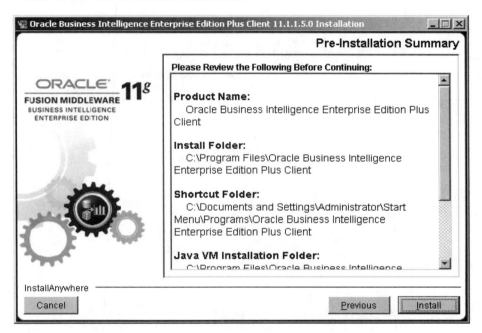

7. The installer will then install the Client Tools on your workstation. Microsoft Visual C++ Redistributable may be installed as part of the process and may ask you to restart your computer. Do not click to restart at this point, as this will cancel the rest of the installation process. When the installation process has completed, the Install Complete screen will display. Click Done to close the installer.

8. The installer will then automatically open the ODBC Data Source Administrator dialog box on the workstation so that you can configure the ODBC connection that the Oracle BI Administration tool will use to connect to your server installation of Oracle Business Intelligence.

9. With the ODBC Data Source Administrator dialog box open, select the System DSN tab and click the Add button to start creating the ODBC data source.

10. From the New Data Source dialog box, select the Oracle BI Server driver from the list, and click Finish to select it.

11. The Oracle BI Server DSN Configuration dialog box will then be displayed. Using the dialog box, enter the connection details to your main Oracle BI host server using the following values (substituting your own host server name and description for obisrv1a

and entering details of your secondary cluster controller if you have scaled out your
Oracle Business Intelligence installation):

```
Name: obisrv1a
Description: OBI11g Server
Clustered DSN: (Select this check box.)
Primary Controller: obisrv1a                    Port: 9706
Secondary Controller:                           Port: 9706
```

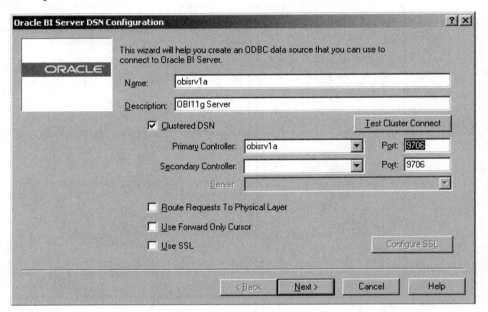

12. Leave all other values at the default and click the Test Cluster Connect button to test the
    connection. Ensure that the Test Connect Successful message is displayed, click OK, and
    then click Next to proceed to the next screen.

13. At the next Oracle BI Server DSN Configuration screen, leave all values blank and click
    Next to proceed.

14. At the final Oracle BI Server DSN Configuration screen, click Finish to close the dialog box
    and create the System DSN; then click OK to close the ODBC Data Source Administrator
    dialog box.

15. You can now test the connection between the Oracle BI Administration tool that you have
    just installed and your main Oracle BI installation. Select Start to bring up the Windows
    Start menu; then select Oracle Business Intelligence Enterprise Edition Plus Client |
    Administration to start the client.

16. Once the Oracle BI Administration tool starts, select File | Open | Online to connect
    your Oracle BI Repository online. When the Open dialog box displays, type in the
    username and password for an administrative user (for example, the one you used when
    installing Oracle Business Intelligence) and the password for the online repository. If the
    connection to your Oracle BI host server was set up correctly, you should now see your
    repository open online the Oracle BI Administration tool main window.

Configuring Stand-Alone Client Tools for Oracle Database Access   If you wish to connect your workstation installation of the Oracle BI Administration tool to an Oracle Database using a local machine (rather than remote server) connection, or indeed any source database that requires a separate client installation, you will need to perform this installation before you can connect to those databases, and configure the client installation to connect to your source databases through the TNSNAMES.ORA file. (Similar steps may be required for other database types, such as Microsoft SQL Server or IBM DB/2.)

To configure a separate Oracle Client installation for use with the stand-alone Oracle BI Administration tool, follow these steps, which are based on an Oracle Database 11*g* Release 2 client installation:

1. Download the Oracle Client installer files from the Oracle web site, ensuring that you download the 32-bit client installer. Unzip the downloaded archive file and navigate to the client directory within the unzipped file system.

2. Within the client directory, double-click the setup.exe file to start the Universal Installer.

3. Using the Universal Installer, when the Select Installation Type screen is shown, select the Runtime option and click Next.

4. At the Select Product Languages screen, select any required available languages and click Next to proceed.

5. At the Specify Installation Location screen, select your Oracle base and software location directory paths, and click Next to proceed.

6. Click Next to perform prerequisite checks, and then click Finish to perform the Oracle Client installation.

7. Next, you will use the Oracle Net Configuration Assistant that has been installed along with the main Oracle Client installation to create the TNSNAMES.ORA file that will be required to connect to your source Oracle databases. Select Start to bring up the Windows Start menu; then select Programs | Oracle – OraClient11g_home1 | Configuration And Migration Tools | Net Configuration Assistant.

8. Using the Net Configuration Assistant, select Local Net Service Name Configuration from the Welcome screen and click Next.

9. At the Net Service Name Configuration screen, select Add and click Next.

10. At the Service Name screen, enter the Service Name for the database that you wish to connect to (for example, orcl) and click Next.

11. At the Select Protocols screen, select the protocol (for example, TCP) that is used by the database that you want to access, and click Next.

12. At the TCP/IP Protocol screen, enter the host name (for example, obisrv1a) and either leave the port number at the default 1521 or select the Use Another Port Number radio button to enter a different Oracle Net port number. Click Next to proceed.

13. At the Test screen, select "Yes, perform a test" and click Next.

14. At the Connecting screen, click the Change Login button to alter the username and password to the database account that contains the data you wish to access from the Oracle BI Administration tool. Click OK and then check that the dialog box shows the message Connecting… Test Successful before clicking Next to continue.

15. Click Next, confirm the net service name (TNSNAME) that you wish to use for this connection, and click Next to proceed.

16. At the Another Net Service Name screen, either select Yes if you wish to configure more Oracle Net Service name connections, or leave the selected value at No, click Next, then Next again, and then Finish to exit the Oracle Net Configuration Assistant.

17. Now you have to configure the bi-init.cmd startup script used by the BI Administration tool to connect to the new Oracle Client installation. To do this, use a text editor tool able to handle Unix line breaks (such as Microsoft WordPad) and open the bi-init.cmd file located in the following directory:

    [*BI Administration Tool Install Directory*]\oraclebi\orahome\bifoundation\server\bin

18. With the bi-init.cmd file open, edit the line that by default reads

    ```
    set ORACLE_HOME=[BI Administration Tool Install Directory]
    ```

    to instead reference the location of the Oracle Client installation, like this:

    ```
    set ORACLE_HOME=[Oracle Client Install Directory]
    ```

    For example:

    ```
    set ORACLE_HOME=C:\app\product\11.2.0\client_1
    ```

19. Finally, close any Oracle BI Administrator tool sessions that may be open, and then reopen the BI Administrator tool. From this point forward, you should be able to connect locally from your workstation to any configured Oracle Database source.

Configuring Stand-Alone Client Tools for Oracle Essbase Access

While the full installation of Oracle Business Intelligence has an Oracle Essbase client preinstalled, the stand-alone installation of Oracle Business Intelligence tools does not. This means that if you want to connect offline to Essbase sources using a stand-alone installation, you will need to download the Essbase client software separately, and configure the Administration Tool startup script to reference where the Essbase client software is installed.

To configure Oracle Essbase access for a stand-alone Oracle BI Administrator installation, first download, unzip, and assemble the Oracle EPM Suite installer files that you require, and then follow these steps (based on Oracle EPM Suite / Essbase 11.1.2 for Microsoft Windows 32-bit edition):

1. From within the downloaded Oracle EPM installer files, run the installTool.cmd batch file from the root of the install directory.

2. The Enterprise Performance Management Installer will then start. When prompted, select the language for the installer (for example, English).

3. At the Welcome screen, check that all prerequisites are met and then click Next to proceed.

4. At the Destination screen, click the Browse button to select a Middleware Home installation directory for your Essbase client files. Ensure that you do not select a directory already used by an Oracle Middleware product, such as Oracle Business Intelligence.

5. At the Installation Type screen, select Choose Components By Tier, and click Next.

6. At the Product Selection screen, deselect all components except for Essbase Client.

7. Click Next and then Next again to install the Essbase Client software onto your workstation. Once the installation process completes successfully, click Finish to close the installer.

NOTE
See the System Requirements and Supported Platforms for Oracle Business Intelligence Suite Enterprise Edition 11gR1 *document available on the Oracle Technology Network web site for the most up-to-date list of which Essbase server and client versions can be used with Oracle Business Intelligence.*

Now that the Essbase Client software is installed, you need to configure the startup script used by the Oracle BI Administration tool to reference the Essbase Client install location:

1. Using Windows Explorer, navigate to the following directory on the workstation you wish to configure:

   [*BI Administration Tool Install Directory*]\oraclebi\orahome\bifoundation\server\bin

   Within this directory, open the bi-init.cmd file for editing, using a text editor that can handle Unix line breaks, such as Microsoft WordPad.

2. Within the bi-init.cmd file, add the following entry, substituting your Essbase client path for the values below, into the file:

   ```
   set ESSBASEPATH=
   C:\Oracle\Middleware\EPMSystem11R1\products\Essbase\EssbaseClient
   ```

   Then, within the same bi-init.cmd file, edit the PATH variable assignment so that it includes the %ESSBASEPATH%\bin directory; for example:

   ```
   set PATH=%ORACLE_HOME%\bifoundation\server\bin;
   %ORACLE_HOME%\bifoundation\web\bin;%ORACLE_HOME%\bin;
   C:\Program Files\Oracle Business Intelligence Enterprise Edition Plus
   Client\jre\bin;%windir%;%windir%\system32;%ESSBASEPATH%\bin;%PATH%
   ```

3. Save the amended bi-init.cmd file, and then restart the BI Administration tool and connect to an Essbase data source to check connectivity.

Installing the Client Tools on Microsoft Windows 64-Bit Edition

For versions of Oracle Business Intelligence 11g prior to the 11.1.1.6 release, the installer for the Oracle BI Client Tools is a 32-bit application, but it will install into a Microsoft Windows 64-bit environment with no problems. However, because it is a 32-bit application, you should install a 32-bit Oracle Client onto the 64-bit Windows Server environment or you may hit issues connecting to your Oracle data source. You should also use the same approach for any other database client installation software that you need to install, such as the Oracle Essbase Client.

From the 11.1.1.6 version of Oracle Business Intelligence 11g onwards, both 64-bit and 32-bit versions of the Oracle BI Client Tools installer are shipped along with the main product installation. For these versions and when working with 64-bit environments, you should of course install the 64-bit version of these tools, along with the corresponding 64-bit versions of any database client tools.

Upgrading from Oracle Business Intelligence 10*g*

If you have developed a system using the earlier, 10*g* release of Oracle Business Intelligence, you can upgrade it to work with Oracle Business Intelligence 11*g*. Much of the process is automated through the use of a tool called the Upgrade Assistant that comes with Oracle Business Intelligence 11*g*, though you may need to perform some pre- and post-upgrade configuration tasks yourself. As with any upgrade between two major releases of a software product, you need to plan carefully for the upgrade and then test thoroughly once the upgrade has taken place; but Oracle Corporation has put a lot of thought and effort into the upgrade process, and considerable guidance is available both within this chapter and in the official product documentation.

So, if you are planning to upgrade your current installation of Oracle Business Intelligence 10*g* to 11*g*, at a high-level, how does the process work?

Overview of the Upgrade Process

When you upgrade an existing Oracle Business Intelligence 10*g* installation to 11*g*, you leave the current 10*g* system in place; copy the repository, catalog, and other metadata to the new 11*g* environment; and then use an included tool called the Upgrade Assistant to convert this metadata to the new 11*g* standard. The Upgrade Assistant also copies data from your existing scheduler schemas into the equivalent 11*g* repository schema, and upgrades your 10*g* security model to use the updated model, based around Oracle Fusion Middleware and the WebLogic application server.

All of your existing Oracle Business Intelligence 10*g* installation is left untouched during the upgrade process, so you can test out the upgrade and gradually put it into production while leaving your existing system working normally. While you can install the new 11*g* version of Oracle Business Intelligence onto the same physical environment as your 10*g* installation, in general this is not recommended, and instead you should commission a new server or environment suited to the increased requirements of Oracle Business Intelligence 11*g*, and migrate your metadata and system into this new installation.

When Oracle Corporation launched the 11*g* release of Oracle Business Intelligence, it was also made available as part of a wider BI software license package called Oracle BI Foundation, that added Oracle Scorecard and Strategy Management and Oracle BI Mobile, along with Oracle Essbase server for multi-dimensional OLAP analysis. If you have a support and upgrade contract with Oracle Corporation, you will be able to upgrade your 10*g* version of Oracle Business Intelligence to the 11*g* release at no further cost, but if you wish to take advantage of new functionality provided by the additional products within Oracle BI Foundation, you may need to purchases licenses and support for them if you wish to use them in a production environment.

Similarly, while Oracle Business Intelligence 11*g* comes with an embedded, limited-use license for Oracle WebLogic Server that replaces Oracle Containers for Java (OC4J) license that came with the 10*g* release, you will need to purchase the full Oracle WebLogic Server Enterprise Edition license if you intend to cluster or "scale out" your installation over additional servers.

Planning for the Upgrade

While as you will see in a moment, the Upgrade Assistant automates much of the upgrade process, you still do need to think carefully about the wider implications of the upgrade to this newer release, and the opportunities that it presents to you.

Oracle Business Intelligence 11*g* has a number of new features that you may wish to take advantage of, and it also reimplements areas of functionality previously provided by the 10*g* release, but in different ways. You will need to think about how you will test the upgraded system to confirm that it is functionally equivalent to your previous system, and you might want to "spring clean" your 10*g* system to remove redundant or invalid content that does not need to be upgraded.

Some aspects of your 10*g* system will not be automatically upgraded, and you will need to reimplement features such as clustering, Single Sign-On, and other system configurations on the new 11*g* system. While your existing initialization blocks, webgroups, and other security artifacts will be upgraded and work as before with the 11*g* system, security as a whole has changed significantly in the 11*g* release, and Oracle recommends that you rework your security setup to take advantage of new functionality.

A typical upgrade plan to take you from the 10*g* release of Oracle Business Intelligence to the 11*g* release will include the following steps:

1.   Review your existing Oracle Business Intelligence 10*g* metadata and system to remove redundant, invalid, or otherwise unrequired content prior to the upgrade.

2.   Install the latest release of Oracle Business Intelligence 11*g* on a new test server, and verify that the installation is working correctly.

3.   Develop a test plan to enable you to verify that the upgraded system is functionally equivalent to your old system and that key reports, dashboards, and scheduled jobs are working as expected.

4.   Copy the file metadata from your 10*g* system over to the new 11*g* test environment, and store it in a temporary folder.

5.   Use the Upgrade Assistant to automatically upgrade and upload your 10*g* metadata to the new 11*g* test system, and upgrade and copy the contents of your 10*g* scheduler database schemas to the new 11*g* BIPLATFORM schema.

NOTE
*If users and groups from the repository do not need to be automatically moved into the embedded LDAP server that comes with Oracle Business Intelligence 11*g*, you can instead use the bieerpdmigrateutil.exe utility to migrate just the repository to the 11*g* format, leaving you to migrate and rework security separately.*

6.   Perform manual configuration changes to the 11*g* test system, such as enabling or disabling caching, and other parameter changes.

7.   Validate the new 11*g* test system to confirm that upgraded metadata, reports, and dashboards work as expected.

8.   Perform any manual upgrades, such as reimplementation of style sheets and custom scripts, to the new 11*g* test system.

9.   Once you are happy that the upgraded test 11*g* system works as planned, migrate it into production, make it available to users, and decommission the 10*g* system.

TIP
In addition to reading the contents of this chapter, you should also review carefully the "Planning to Upgrade from Oracle BI 10g to BI 11g" section of the Oracle® Fusion Middleware Upgrade Guide for Oracle Business Intelligence 11g Release 1 (11.1.1) *within the product documentation. It contains many details, tips, and exceptions that you will wish to consider when performing the upgrade; these cannot be included in this book for reasons of space. In particular, read carefully the sections on understanding the upgrade of repository metadata and Presentation Catalog metadata, and understanding the security upgrade process.*

To minimize the amount of things that are changing when performing an upgrade, you should plan to upgrade only between equivalent operating systems and architectures, performing any such migrations only once the upgrade has successfully taken place. For example, if you currently deploy Oracle Business Intelligence 10g on a Microsoft Windows 32-bit platform, perform the upgrade to an equivalent Microsoft Windows 32-bit environment rather than trying to incorporate a move to a 64-bit Linux environment, because otherwise you will not know whether problems you hit are due to the upgrade itself or the move to a new type of environment.

Finally, try not to reuse the same host server for both the 10g and 11g systems, as you may hit resource issues, and you will also need to be extremely careful about port assignments, which can potentially complicate what can already be a complicated process.

What Is Automatically Upgraded?

The Upgrade Assistant, a utility that is installed alongside Oracle Business Intelligence 11g when you use the Universal Installer, automatically upgrades the following metadata items for you:

- The Oracle Business Intelligence Repository (RPD) file
- The Web Catalog (referred to as the Presentation Catalog in 11g)
- The Oracle BI Publisher Repository
- The Oracle BI Delivers scheduler schema
- The Oracle BI Publisher scheduler schema

You can run the Upgrade Assistant multiple times to upgrade additional repository files, web catalogs, and other metadata items beyond those used for your primary system. In addition, command-line tools are available to perform scripted upgrades if this approach is more appropriate.

As well as upgrading the presentation, business model and mapping, and physical layer objects within the Oracle BI Repository, the Upgrade Assistant also migrates the users and groups within the repository into the LDAP directory used by Oracle Business Intelligence 11g. In addition, as Oracle Business Intelligence 11g uses application roles rather than LDAP groups to assign permissions to, equivalent roles are created for the groups, which are then automatically mapped together.

You should be aware that the Upgrade Assistant not only upgrades your 10g metadata and security arrangements to the 11g format, but it also places this new metadata online in the 11g system. At the end of the upgrade process, you should have a functioning 11g system, albeit one that needs testing and may require additional post-upgrade configuration. You should not, therefore, upgrade 10g metadata into an 11g system that is already being used for reporting and analysis, unless this is intended and you wish to replace the repository and Presentation Catalog currently being used, and merge the 10g users and groups into the 11g LDAP server.

What Has to Be Manually Upgraded?

Any changes that you have made within the NQSConfig.INI configuration file, the instanceconfig .xml configuration file, or any other configuration file used by Oracle Business Intelligence 10g, will need to be manually reapplied, if appropriate, within your new Oracle Business Intelligence 11g system. Some of these changes will need to be applied using Oracle Fusion Middleware Control or through Weblogic Scripting Tool (WLST) scripts, while others will need to be manually entered into the relevant configuration file. In addition, some settings have changed across releases, particularly settings in the BI Presentation Server instanceconfig.xml file, and your 10g settings will therefore need to be checked for correctness before being applied into the 11g version of this configuration file.

Custom JavaScript scripts and other user interface customizations and extensions that you have applied to your 10g dashboards and requests will need to be reapplied, or reworked, for use in your 11g system if you wish to bring them over to the new, upgraded environment. In some cases however, customizations that you needed to add to your 10g environment may now be standard product functionality in the 11g release, and you should check the relevant sections in this book, as well as the product documentation, to determine what actually needs to be re-implemented. When considering this, bear in mind that the steps required to customize the "look and feel" of Oracle Business Intelligence have in addition changed considerably with the 11g release, and you should make sure you consult the product documentation before planning any re-implemented user interface customizations.

The Upgrade Assistant is designed to upgrade single-node Oracle Business Intelligence 10g systems to 11g, and therefore, if you wish to cluster and extend your 11g system over several host servers or add additional system components to each server, you will need to perform this scale-out or scale-up after the upgrade takes place. If you extend your BI system over more than a single host server, you may need to upgrade your Oracle WebLogic Server license from the bundled limited-use Standard Edition license to a paid-for Enterprise Edition license, as the Standard Edition license precludes WebLogic clustering, which is a prerequisite for scaling out your 11g system.

How Upgrades Affect Security and Permissions

One of the most significantly changed areas of functionality between the 11g and 10g versions of Oracle Business Intelligence is security. While at a functional level, the upgraded system will have the same users and groupings of users compared to the 10g system, permissions and privileges in Oracle Business Intelligence 11g are assigned to application roles rather than groups, and the groups that you bring across from the 10g version are related to these roles through mappings. In addition to the introduction of application roles, users and groups are no longer held within the repository RPD file but are instead copied into an embedded LDAP server within the Oracle WebLogic application server.

Oracle Business Intelligence 10g systems often make use of web catalog groups to assign permissions and privileges to dashboard users , and while these are still supported for backwards-compatibility, they should not be used in new implementations. Instead, the same application roles used to assign permissions and privileges in the Oracle BI repository are also available for use within the 11g Presentation Catalog, simplifying administration and removing the need to maintain two sets of group definitions.

In addition, while initialization blocks can still be used to authenticate and authorize users against external LDAP servers, during or after the upgrade you should consider moving to Oracle Fusion Middleware–based security, which is the preferred way to connect to LDAP servers and other identity stores with Oracle Business Intelligence 11*g*. The topic of security is covered in a lot more detail later in Chapter 8 of this book, which you should at least take a quick look at before starting an upgrade from the 10*g* release of Oracle Business Intelligence.

Performing Upgrade Testing

Unless you are upgrading a development or personal "sandbox" Oracle Business Intelligence 10*g* system to 11*g*, you will want to put in place a comprehensive test plan to ensure that your new system performs as expected. Typically, as you will see in the next section of this chapter, you will use the Upgrade Assistant in stages to upgrade separate parts of your 10*g* metadata, and you should note the expected results and perform appropriate tests after each stage.

In addition, you may wish to copy your existing 10*g* system into a test environment, perhaps only copying across a representative subset of this system, and perform a test upgrade on this before attempting the full upgrade. It is also important to understand that there may be visual differences between dashboards and analyses created using the 11*g* version of Oracle Business Intelligence compared to earlier versions, and any testing that you carry out should concentrate on confirming functional equivalence rather than on identifying cosmetic differences between the two.

Using the Upgrade Assistant

The Upgrade Assistant ships with Oracle Business Intelligence 11*g* and can be found at [*middleware_home*]/Oracle_BI1/bin. Versions exist for both Microsoft Windows and Unix/Linux platforms, and it provides an interactive, graphical user interface for stepping through the upgrade process.

Before you start the upgrade, ensure that the Oracle WebLogic Server Administration Server, and the Managed Server, if installed, are running and available before you start the upgrade. In addition, if you are upgrading the 10*g* Delivers schema and/or the 10*g* BI Publisher schema, ensure that the database(s) holding these schemas are running and can be connected to from the server that you will run the Upgrade Assistant from.

You run the Upgrade Assistant on the server that hosts your installation of Oracle Business Intelligence 11*g*. Copy across the repository (RPD) file, web catalog, and BI Publisher repository directory from 10*g* installation to a temporary folder on the 11*g* server, and you are then ready to start the Upgrade Assistant.

To start the upgrade assistant on a Microsoft Windows platform, navigate to the [*middleware_home*]\Oracle_BI1\bin directory and double-click the ua.bat file. To start the Upgrade Assistant on a Unix or Linux platform, change the directory to [*middleware_home*]/Oracle_BI1/bin using the command-line terminal and run the ua command, like this:

```
cd /u01/app/middleware/Oracle_BI1/bin
./ua
```

In the following examples, we will look at the Upgrade Assistant that ships with Oracle Business Intelligence 11g for Microsoft Windows 32-bit. However, the procedure and steps will be the same with any version of the utility. When the Upgrade Assistant starts, you are presented with a Welcome message, and you should click Next to continue.

The Upgrade Assistant will then present you with the Specify Operation screen, which gives you the following list of options:

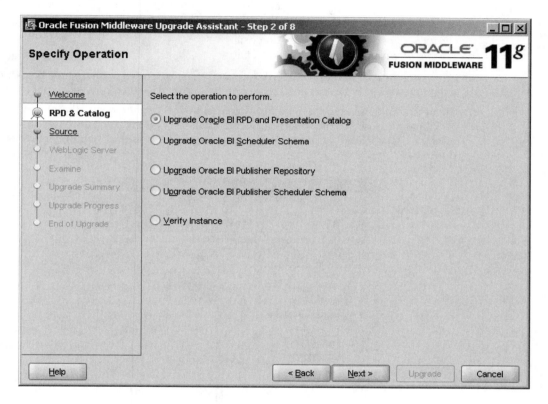

- Upgrade Oracle BI RPD and Presentation Catalog
- Upgrade Oracle BI Scheduler Schema
- Upgrade Oracle BI Publisher Repository
- Upgrade Oracle BI Publisher Scheduler Schema
- Verify Instance

You can use the first four options in any order, and then verify the instance once you have completed some or all of the steps. For now, though, we will start with the upgrade of the repository (RPD) and web catalog.

Upgrading the 10*g* Repository (RPD) and 10*g* Web Catalog (Presentation Catalog)

To upgrade an existing Oracle Business Intelligence 10*g* repository (RPD) and web catalog, follow these steps, which use the paint repository and web catalog that come with most installations of Oracle Business Intelligence 10*g* as the example:

1. On the original Oracle Business Intelligence 10*g* server, locate on the file system the repository (RPD) file and web catalog directory that you wish to upgrade. You can normally find these files in the following locations, respectively:

   [*install_home*]\OracleBI\server\Repository
   [*install_home*]\OracleBIData\web\catalog

   Within the [*install_home*]\OracleBIData \web\catalog directory, there may be a directory called deliveries. If there is not, create one now, and leave the contents empty.

2. Create an empty directory on the file system of this server, and copy all of the files into it, so that the contents of the directory contain the RPD file; the top-level web catalog directory with shared, system, and user directories underneath it; and the deliveries directory.

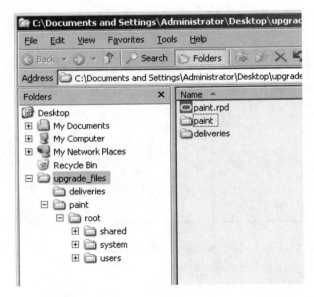

   Now, using an archiving tool such as Winzip, create an archive file of the contents of this directory, and transfer this archive file to the new server running Oracle Business Intelligence 11*g*.

3. Unzip the contents of the archive file on the server running Oracle Business Intelligence 11*g,* so that the contents of the folder are available for use by the Upgrade Assistant. Start the Upgrade Assistant using either [*middleware_home*]\Oracle_BI1\bin\ua.bat, for Microsoft Windows–based systems, or [*middleware_home*]/Oracle_BI1/bin/ua for Unix- and Linux-based systems.

4. Once the Upgrade Assistant starts, click Next to proceed to the Specify Operation screen, and then select the Upgrade Oracle BI RPD And Presentation Catalog option.

5. At the Specify Source Details screen, select the Upgrade Repository (RPD) check box and click the Browse button to navigate to the folder containing your 10*g* metadata. Select the repository (RPD) file to update and click OK.

   Back at the Specify Source Details screen, enter the administrator name in the Administrator User Name field, and in the Administrator Password field, enter a password for the 10*g* repository (RPD) file (typically, Administrator/Administrator). Then, in the Password field, enter a password that will be used to encrypt the new 11*g*-format repository (RPD) file.

6. To upgrade an accompanying web catalog, select the Upgrade Catalog check box and click the Browse button to locate the 10g catalog file top directory that you copied across in the archive file. The Catalog Deliveries Directory path will automatically be populated for you.

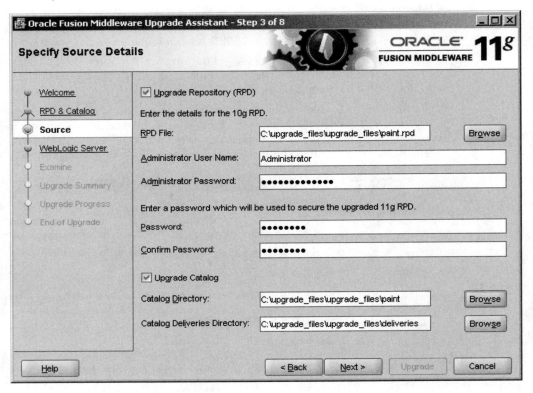

Click Next to proceed.

7. At the Specify WebLogic Server screen, ensure that your Oracle WebLogic Administration Server is running and available, and enter the port (normally 7001) and the username and password for an administration user for this server.

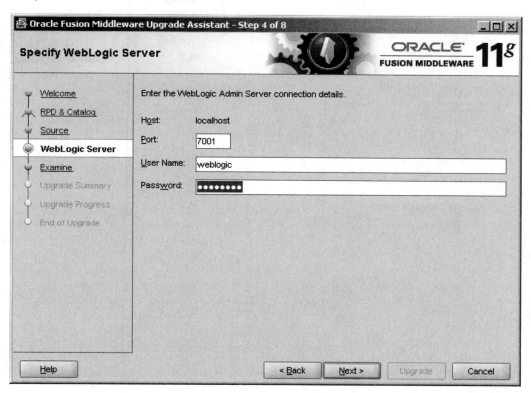

8. At the Examining Components screen, check that the Status column reports the progress as succeeded, and click Next to proceed.

9. At the Upgrade Summary screen, click the Upgrade button to start the upgrade process, and then Upgrading Components screen shown next will then display the progress of the upgrade.

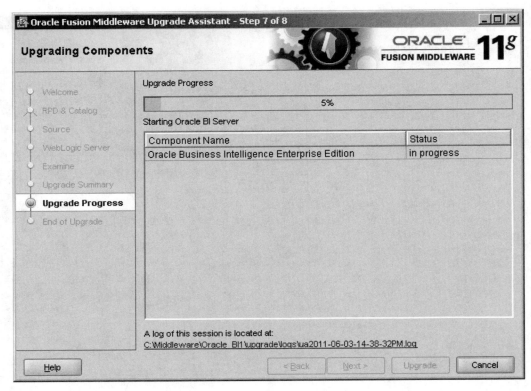

10. Once the process completes successfully, click Next to view the Upgrade Success screen, review the list of tasks that you need to carry out after the upgrade, and click the Close button to exit the Upgrade Assistant.

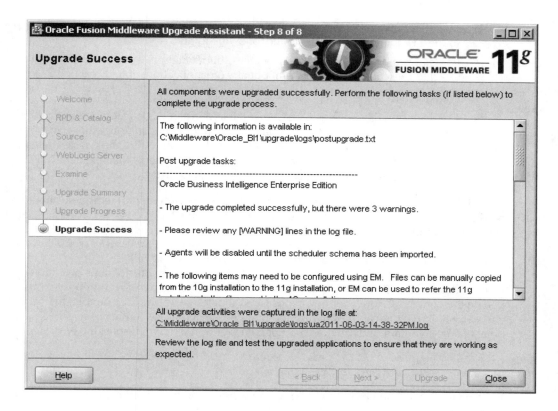

What Happens During the RPD and Catalog Upgrade? When you click the Upgrade button, the Upgrade Assistant does a number of things:

- It upgrades the repository (RPD) file from the 10*g* format to the 11*g* format and uses the password you supplied to encrypt the file. You can perform the same task yourself from the command line using the following utility if you wish to upgrade other RPD files after this migration:

  [*middleware_home*]\Oracle_BI1\bifoundation\server\bin\obieerpdmigrateutil.exe

- This repository file is then copied to the following directory, and a sequence number is appended to the filename:

  [*middleware_home*]\\instances\instance1\bifoundation\OracleBIServerComponent\ coreapplication_obis1\repository

■ A similar process then is performed for the catalog directory structure, which is upgraded to the 11g format and copied to the following folder:

[*middleware_home*]\\instances\instance1\bifoundation\
OracleBIPresentationServicesComponent\coreapplication_obips1\catalog

Unlike the RPD file, though, these files are not encrypted.

■ Configuration files such as NQSConfig.INI and instanceconfig.xml are updated with the details of this new RPD file and catalog, and other configuration settings and credential store entries are updated with these new details as well. All of these tasks are carried out on behalf of the Upgrade Assistant by the Oracle BI Systems Management API using the JMX MBeans in the WebLogic Server Administration Server.

While simple RPD files and web catalogs will upgrade with no problems, you should read the product documentation, particularly the "Understanding the Upgrade of Repository Metadata" and "Understanding Oracle BI Presentation Catalog Upgrade" sections of the *Oracle® Fusion Middleware Upgrade Guide for Oracle Business Intelligence 11g Release 1 (11.1.1),* in order to understand differences and new features introduced with the 11g release.

In particular, Oracle Business Intelligence 11g imposes tighter restrictions on validity checks when validating the Oracle BI Repository, and you may need to revisit your repository model and update the contents before your new repository validates correctly. For example, the consistency checker within the Oracle BI Administration tool no longer allows trailing spaces in repository object names, and if it finds any in your upgraded repository it will display the error message:

```
[38126] 'Logical Table' '"Sales Model"."Dim Customers "'
has name with leading or trailing space(s).
```

To resolve this issue and remove the error, you would need to edit the name of the repository object and remove any trailing spaces.

The two error messages below are typical of those shown when a logical column does not map to either a column in a logical table source, or derived using a formula based on some other logical columns. To resolve this issue, either remove that particular logical column from the logical table definition, map it to it's correct column source, or give it a value of 0 or equivalent so that is has a valid definition.

```
[38012] Logical column Dim_Staff.Staff_DOB does not have
a physical data type mapping, nor is it a derived column.

[38001] Logical column Dim_Staff.Staff_DO has no physical
data source mapping.
```

The 11g version of Oracle Business Intelligence has in many cases different physical database feature settings compared to those found in the 10g release, and the feature settings that came across from your 10g system's repository as part of the upgrade may no longer be the default ones for those physical databases in the 11g release. When this happens, you will see the following type of warning message when using the consistency checker:

```
[39028] The features in Database 'oracle' do not match
the defaults. This can cause query problems.
```

Unless you have deliberately changed your database settings from the default for a particular reason, you can get rid of this warning by just resetting your physical databases' feature settings in the upgraded repository to the new default values.

Another new warning that can sometimes be raised when checking the consistency of an 11g repository happens when none of the columns in a logical table source definition are actually used in the logical table into which it is mapped, giving you the following warning message when performing a consistency check:

```
[39057] There are physical tables mapped in Logical Table
Source ""Sales Model"."Dim Products"."Product Details""
that are not used in any column mappings or expressions.
```

The 10g release of Oracle Business Intelligence also had looser rules about creating joins between physical tables that connected aggregated fact table sources to lower-level dimension sources using non-unique column values. Creating such joins gave you flexibility when modelling source objects but sometimes led to situations where measures were double-counted, as these joins ended-up returned more than one row from the dimension table when normally only one should be.

When the consistency checker detects this type of join in an 11g repository, you will see a warning message like this:

```
[39059] Logical dimension table Dim_Times has a source
DAYS_D at level Daily that joins to a higher level fact
source MONTHS_SUM.MTHLY_SUM
```

You can ignore this warning if you wish, but if possible you should try and amend your physical model so that your dimension source table has a unique key and only returns one row per member when joined to the fact table, giving more predictable results and removing the warning message from subsequent consistency checks.

Other warnings and errors may be displayed when you come to validate your upgraded repository, and you should check the "Understanding the Upgrade of Repository Metadata" section of the *Oracle® Fusion Middleware Upgrade Guide for Oracle Business Intelligence 11g Release 1 (11.1.1)* for more examples of warnings and errors, and how they should be resolved.

There are also some changes to how Presentation Catalog items are stored and validated, and content that was valid with the 10g release may need to be either updated or removed before you make your upgraded system available to users. Navigations between requests in Oracle Business Intelligence 10g are converted to inline actions in your upgraded 11g catalog, for example, and the behavior of calculations and pivot tables may change compared to how they worked on your original system. You should plan for several iterations of this process before the upgrade can be considered complete, and anything you can do to remove unused or invalid content prior to the upgrade will make the process quicker and less error-prone. See the "Understanding Oracle BI Presentation Catalog Upgrade" section of the *Oracle® Fusion Middleware Upgrade Guide for Oracle Business Intelligence 11g Release 1 (11.1.1),* for full details of the changes for your particular release.

Finally, you should note that iBots (called *Agents* in Oracle Business Intelligence 11g) will not work again until you have upgraded the Oracle BI Delivers (Scheduler) schema, the steps for which are also detailed later on in this chapter.

Upgrading the 10*g* BI Publisher Repository
To upgrade the BI Publisher repository, follow these steps:

1. In the same way as was described for the web catalog upgrade in the previous section, copy the BI Publisher repository file system from your 10*g* system, usually found at [*install_home*]\OracleBI \xmlpxXMLP, to a temporary directory elsewhere on that server, which should then be archived and transferred over to where you have installed your new Oracle Business Intelligence 11*g* system.

2. Start the Upgrade Assistant, as detailed before, and click Next to proceed to the Specify Operation screen.

3. At the Specify Operation screen, select the Upgrade Oracle BI Publisher Repository option, and click Next to proceed.

4. At the Specify Source Details screen, select the Upgrade 10*g* BI Publisher Repository Directory check box and click the Browse button to navigate to and select the repository files that you copied across from the 10*g* system. Click Next to proceed.

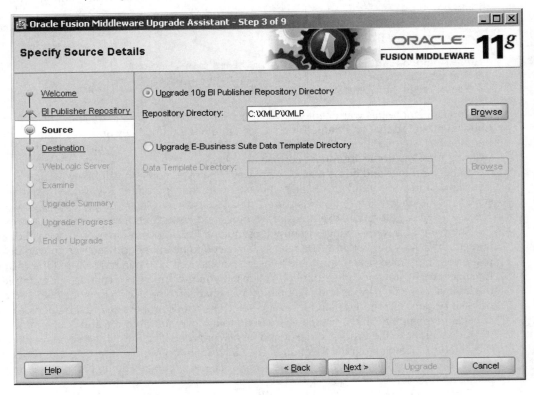

5. At the Specify Destination Details screen, click the Browse button to navigate to the file system directory that you would like the upgraded files to be copied to. Usually, this is the following directory:

    [*middleware_home*]\\user_projects\domains\bifoundation_domain\config\bipublisher\ repository

    However, you can, in fact, choose any directory you wish, as long is it is accessible to the Oracle Business Intelligence 11*g* installation. Click Next to proceed.

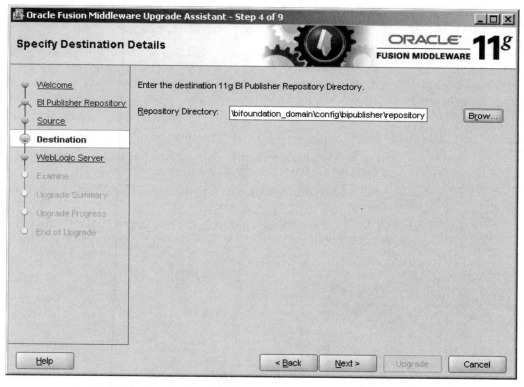

6. At the Specify WebLogic Server screen, enter the connection details for the Oracle WebLogic Server Administration Server, which should be running when you then click Next to proceed.

7. At the Examining Components screen, check that the Status column shows the progress as succeeded; then click Next, and then Upgrade, to begin the upgrade process.

8. Once the upgrade completes, click Next to review any upgrade notes, and then click Close to close the Upgrade Assistant.

What Happens During the BI Publisher Upgrade?   When you run the Upgrade Assistant to upgrade your Oracle BI Publisher repository, the Upgrade Assistant copies the reports within your 10g repository to the destination location and upgrades them to the 11g format. As part of this process, it splits your 10g report files into separate report and data model definition files because Oracle BI Publisher 11g treats the report definition and the data model definition as two separate metadata objects.

When you install Oracle Business Intelligence Publisher 11g as an integrated part of Oracle Business Intelligence 11g, it normally holds its report definitions in the same Presentation Catalog as regular analyses, dashboards, and other catalog objects. If you wish to copy your upgraded BI Publisher report definitions into the Presentation Catalog, there is one further, one-off step you need to perform to accomplish this:

1. Log into Oracle Business Intelligence 11g using an administrator username and password.

2. At the home page, click the Administration link in the header area, and at the Administration page click the Manage BI Publisher link.

3. At the BI Publisher Administration page, click the Server Configuration link in the System Maintenance list.

4. Within the Catalog area, click the Upload To BI Presentation Catalog button to upload the contents of the BI Publisher stand-alone repository to the Presentation Catalog.

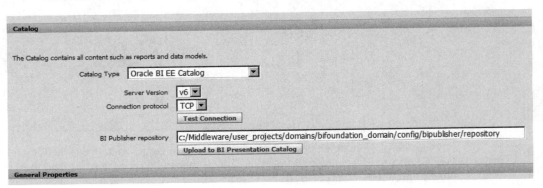

After this upload step, you will find the uploaded folders, report definitions, and data model definitions in the root of the Shared Folders directory. Use the Catalog page or the Catalog Manager utility to move these directories and change their permissions if required.

The Upgrade Assistant will preserve the configuration settings and, in particular, the security model that you used for your 10*g* version of BI Publisher. At the BI Publisher Administration page, click the Security Configuration link under the Security Center heading to change this security model if required. If your 10*g* installation of Oracle BI Publisher was configured to use Oracle BI Server security as the security model, you will also need to edit the xmlp-server-config.xml file, found in the Admin\Configuration file of the upgraded repository, to reference the correct server name for the BI Server and Presentation Services, as the Upgrade Assistant will leave the old 10*g* BI Server and Presentation Server references in this file.

NOTE
*As with Presentation Catalog content, you can only use 10*g *BI Publisher reports with BI Publisher 11*g *if they have been through this upgrade process. However, templates created with the BI Publisher Desktop utility will work across both versions. See the "Understanding BI Publisher Upgrade" section within the* Oracle® Fusion Middleware Upgrade Guide for Oracle Business Intelligence 11g Release 1 (11.1.1) *product documentation for full details of the changes between Oracle BI Publisher 10*g *and 11*g.

Upgrading the 10*g* Delivers (Scheduler) and 10*g* BI Publisher Schemas

Compared to upgrading the repository files, upgrading the Delivers (Scheduler) and BI Publisher Scheduler database schemas is a relatively straightforward process, though you will need network connectivity to both the 10*g* and 11*g* database schemas to perform the upgrade.

To upgrade the 10*g* Delivers (Scheduler) schema to the 11*g* format and move its contents in the BIPLATFORM schema created using the Repository Creation Utility, follow these steps:

1. Start the Upgrade Assistant using either [*middleware_home*]\Oracle_BI1\bin\ua.bat for Microsoft Windows–based systems or [*middleware_home*]/Oracle_BI1/bin/ua for Unix- and Linux-based systems.

2. Once the Upgrade Assistant starts, click Next to proceed to the Specify Operation screen; then select the Upgrade Oracle BI Scheduler Schema option, and click Next to proceed.

3. At the Specify Source Database screen, enter the following details, changing the specifics to match your source system's Oracle BI Delivers schema credentials and database name and connection details:

    Database Type: Oracle
    Connect String: obi10gsrv:1521/orcl
    Source Schema: S_NQ_JOB
    Password: *password*
    DBA User Name: SYS AS SYSDBA
    DBA Password: *password*

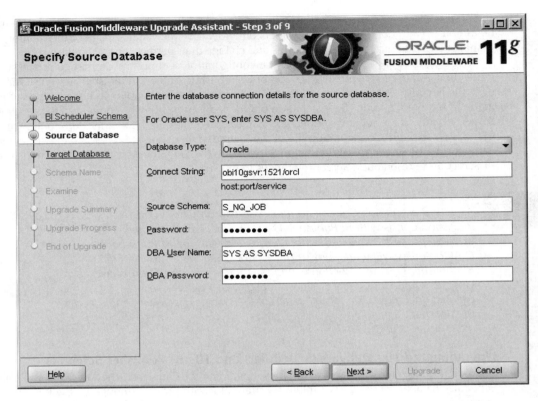

Click Next to continue.

4. At the Specify Target Database screen, enter the connection details for the BIPLATFORM schema that you would have created previously using the Repository Creation Assistant, together with a DBA username and password for the target database; for example:

   Target Database Type: Oracle
   Connect String: localhost:1521/orcl
   DBA User Name: SYS AS SYSDBA
   DBA Password: *password*

5. At the Specify Schema Name screen, select the BIPLATFORM schema name that corresponds to the Oracle Business Intelligence 11g system you are upgrading to, and enter the password. Click Next to proceed.

6. At the Examining Components screen, check that the Status column reports that both status values are succeeded, click Next, and then click Upgrade to perform the upgrade. Once complete, click Close to close the Upgrade Assistant.

The process for upgrading the BI Publisher 10g schema to the 11g format is virtually identical to that for upgrading the Delivers (Scheduler) schema. When you start the Upgrade Assistant, at the Specify Operation screen, select Upgrade Oracle BI Publisher Scheduler Schema, and then provided the source and target database connections before starting the upgrade process.

Verifying the Instance

Once you have completed all of the upgrade steps, you can use the Upgrade Assistant to verify that you now have a valid upgraded system. Note that this is a very high-level check, and you should still perform your own post-upgrade testing after this process.

To run the verification check, follow these steps:

1. Start the Upgrade Assistant using either [*middleware_home*]\Oracle_BI1\bin\ua.bat for Microsoft Windows–based systems or [*middleware_home*]/Oracle_BI1/bin/ua for Unix- and Linux-based systems.

2. Once the Upgrade Assistant starts, click Next to proceed to the Specify Operation screen; then select the Verify Instance option and click Next to proceed.

3. At the Specify WebLogic Server screen, enter the connection details for the Oracle WebLogic Server Administration Server, which should be running at this point. Click Next to proceed.

4. At the Specify Ports screen, click Verify to run the verification checks. Once complete, click Next and then click Close to close the Upgrade Assistant.

CAUTION
If you perform an upgrade using the Upgrade Assistant and the upgrade fails, you will normally leave your Oracle Business Intelligence 11g system in an incomplete state and will have to re-create the Oracle instance using the configuration utility before it can become usable again. Because of this, it is important that you take a backup of your 11g system before the upgrade takes place, in case such an issue should occur.

Post-Upgrade Configuration Tasks

Once you have successfully completed the upgrade from Oracle Business Intelligence 10*g* to 11*g*, your new 11*g* system will be using the same default configuration settings that it had when you first installed it. Query caching, for example, will be enabled by default, but you may wish to disable this feature for your system. If your 10*g* system was scaled out over several physical servers, your new 11*g* system will exist on just a single server. Single Sign-On and SSL will be disabled, and features such as usage tracking will need to be enabled and configured before you can make use of them.

Since Oracle Business Intelligence 11*g*, many configuration settings are now managed through Oracle Fusion Middleware Control, and you will need to log into this web application and reapply settings that you wish to reinstate for your new, upgraded system. Other settings that have not yet migrated to Fusion Middleware Control will need to be configured directly in their respective configuration files. If you wish to scale out, or scale up, your business intelligence installation, Fusion Middleware Control and the Universal Installer will need to be used to put in place your required configuration. These tasks are covered in more detail in later chapters, but in the following sections we will highlight those tasks most commonly carried out after the upgrade has taken place.

Applying Configuration Changes Using Oracle Fusion Middleware Control

Most of the configuration settings that you want to access will be available from the Oracle Fusion Middleware Control web site. When you use Fusion Middleware Control to make a configuration change to your system, it automatically applies those changes to all the servers within your BI cluster, which at this initial stage is not all that relevant, but later on can be very useful if you scale out your system over several physical servers.

To log into Fusion Middleware Control, use your web browser to navigate to http://[*host_name*]:7001/em, where [*host_name*] is the host name of the Oracle Business Intelligence 11*g* server that contains your upgraded 10g metadata. When the login page is displayed, enter the username and password of an administrative user.

The use of Fusion Middleware Control is covered in more detail in Chapter 12, but settings that you can configure using this tool include the following:

- Enabling and disabling the query cache, and setting the maximum size of the cache and number of entries

- Settings having to do with the maximum number of rows that can be returned by an analysis or the maximum number of rows that can be downloaded to Microsoft Excel

- The number of BI Servers, Presentation Servers, and other system components that are installed on this initial server and other servers to which you may scale out your system

- Specifying new repositories or Presentation Catalogs, or making existing catalogs or repositories shared

If you are looking to make a configuration change, check to see if you can make it using Fusion Middleware Control first, even if you made the change in your 10*g* system by directly editing a configuration file. Oracle Business Intelligence is gradually moving toward a goal where all configuration settings are managed through Fusion Middleware Control, and only settings that explicitly are not managed by Fusion Middleware Control should be altered by directly editing a configuration file, as we shall see in the next section.

Applying Configuration Changes Using Configuration Files

While Oracle's long-term aim is to move as many configuration settings as possible to Fusion Middleware Control, some settings in the meantime will still need to be configured directly within configuration files. When editing configuration settings in these files, check first that they are not now managed by Fusion Middleware Control, as any changes that you make directly in the file will be automatically overwritten later on by the system. You can tell whether a setting is managed now by Fusion Middleware Control, as it will have a comment to that effect in the file; for example, query cache settings in the NQSConfig.INI file are managed in this way:

```
####################################################################
#
#   Query Result Cache Section
#
####################################################################
[CACHE]
ENABLE = YES;  # This Configuration setting is managed by
Oracle Business Intelligence Enterprise Manager
```

Not all settings are managed by Fusion Middleware Control, however, and there are some key settings, detailed in Chapter 5 on BI Server Administration and Chapter 10 on Systems Administration, that you will have to manage manually using the following configuration files and others:

- BI Server configuration settings:

  [*middleware_home*]/instances/instance1/config/OracleBIServerComponent/ coreapplication_obis1/NQSConfig.INI

- BI Presentation Server configuration settings:

  [*middleware_home*]/instances/instance1/config/OracleBIPresentationServerComponent/ coreapplication_obips1/instanceconfig.xml

- BI Java Host configuration settings:

  [*middleware_home*]/instances/instance1/config/OracleBIJavaHostComponent/ coreapplication_obijh1/config.xml

Remember that, if you subsequently scale out or scale up your system by adding additional servers to your cluster or additional system components to a server, you will have to apply any such changes to every instance of these configuration files in your system as detailed in the "Clustering and Scaling Out Your System" section that follows later in this chapter.

Settings that you may need to to alter directly by editing configuration files include the following:

- **Oracle BI Server**   Query cache settings that are not managed through Fusion Middleware Control; date and time display formats; whether inaccessible columns are projected as NULL; maximum session limits; whether user and role GUIDs are updated; and whether usage tracking is enabled and configured.

- **Oracle BI Presentation Server**   Whether user and role GUIDs are updated. (See Chapter 11 for details on GUIDs and why you might want to update them.)

- **Oracle BI Java Host**   Enabling certain point-to-point Single Sign-On settings or enabling access to data sources such as Oracle Hyperion Financial Management.

Data Source Configuration

As detailed earlier in this chapter, while Oracle Business Intelligence 11*g* comes with built-in clients for Oracle Database and Oracle Essbase, if you need to access a remote Oracle database you will need to create a new TNSNAMES.ORA file within [*middleware_home*]/Oracle_BI1/ network/admin that contains connection details for any databases that you wish to access.

Similarly, you may need to create or update ODBC data source connections or other client configurations to access the data sources that your 10*g* system connected to.

Security and External Directories

When you upgrade your repository (RPD) file using the Upgrade Assistant, any users and groups within your repository file are copied into the embedded LDAP server that Oracle Business Intelligence now uses to hold these details. Corresponding application roles are created for these groups, and the existing Administrator user is placed in the BIAdministrators LDAP group and thereby granted the BIAdministrator application role.

Any initialization blocks that were contained within your 10*g* repository file will function as before when upgraded to 11*g*, and if you use this feature to authenticate users against an external LDAP directory and then to establish what RPD groups to assign them to, these features will still work. You may, however, over time wish to transition to the Fusion Middleware security model, detailed in Chapter 11, to take advantage of the additional capabilities that it provides.

In addition, if you had implemented Single Sign-On (SSO) or Secure Sockets Layer (SSL) security for your 10*g* system, you will need to reimplement these features using the Fusion Middleware security model to have them in your upgraded system. See Chapter 11 for more details.

Implementing New Features

Once you have completed the transition to your new Oracle Business Intelligence 11*g* system and confirmed that like-for-like functionality is working as expected, you may then wish to start implementing some of the new features and capabilities of the 11*g* system, including the following:

- Using hierarchical columns in your analyses for OLAP-style analysis
- Implementing key performance indicators and scorecards
- Adding maps and spatial analysis to your analyses
- Adding actions and links to external applications or business processes
- Other new features introduced with Oracle Business Intelligence 11*g*

See later chapters in this book for details on how these new features are implemented and used.

Clustering and Scaling Out Your System

When you upgrade your Oracle Business Intelligence 10*g* system to 11*g*, your new system will have a single node with either a single WebLogic Server Administration Server, if you chose the Simple Install option, or a WebLogic Server Administration Server, Managed Server, and Node Manager, if you chose the Enterprise Install option. This single node will start off with a single instance of each of the system component types, such as the BI Server and BI Presentation Server. Your previous Oracle Business Intelligence 10*g* system may, however, have been clustered over more than one server, with perhaps one server being used for the BI Server and another for the BI Presentation Server.

If you wish to extend your BI system over more than one physical server (referred to as "scaling out" your system) or add additional system components to individual servers (referred to as "scaling up"), you can do so easily, as even single-node Oracle Business Intelligence 11*g* has clustering enabled and set up during the installation process. If you wish to scale out over more than one server, you will need to use the Universal Installer to first extend your WebLogic domain to this additional server and then use Fusion Middleware Control to add new system components to this new server. If you wish just to add more system components to your existing server to add resilience and additional capacity, you can do so now using Fusion Middleware Control.

Be aware, though, that scaling out and extending your WebLogic domain to an additional server will require the Enterprise Edition license for WebLogic Server, which you will have to obtain from Oracle because the bundled WebLogic license provided with Oracle Business Intelligence is only the Standard Edition that does not include the clustering capability required for this operation.

To extend, or scale out your Oracle Business Intelligence domain to an additional server, you will need to first do the following:

- Install just the operating system and any prerequisites for an Oracle Business Intelligence installation on the new server, but don't run the Repository Creation Assistant or create any additional BISHIPHOME or MDS schemas.

- Ensure that both servers can contact each other over your network and resolve each other's machine names. (You may need to place entries in each server's "hosts" files to make this possible.)

- Obtain some shared disk storage that each server can mount, and read and write to, for the shared Oracle BI Repository and catalog that you will need to configure.

- Provision and configure a load balancer and virtual IP address that users will connect to initially, and then send their queries to either one of the two servers in your scaled-out cluster.

Configuring Shared Locations for the Repository and Catalog   Every Oracle BI instance has a single active repository and catalog that are used at any one time by the BI Server and BI Presentation Server components in the instance, respectively. Each BI Server component has its own copy of the repository (RPD) file, but when you have more than one BI Server component provisioned you should also configure a shared network location for a shared, central copy of the repository file that holds the master copy of repositories edited in online mode and that is read by each BI Server component when it restarts, in order to synchronize its local copy with this master copy.

Similarly, when you have just a single Oracle BI Presentation Server component, the catalog directory and files are stored locally. Because there is no facility for catalog synchronization, however, if you have more than one BI Presentation Server component configured, you will need to set up a second shared network location, copy the catalog files to that location, and then configure the instance and all of its BI Presentation Server components to use this single, shared catalog instead.

Before you start the scale-out installation, then, let's go through the process of setting up a shared location for the catalog and repository, as you'll need this to be in place before you fully configure the installation on your new server. To set up these shared locations, follow these steps:

1. Configure shared network locations and directories for the repository (RPD file) and catalog. In this example, the repository will be stored on the \\fileserver\RPD shared network drive, and the catalog will be stored on the //fileserver/catalog shared network drive.

2. Log into Oracle Fusion Middleware Control at http://[*machine_name*]:7001/em (for example, http://obisrv:7001/em), and log in using the username and password for an administrative user. Using the navigation tree on the left-hand side of the page once you connect, select Business Intelligence | coreapplication.

3. Select the Deployment tab and then the Repository subtab; then click Lock And Edit Configuration.

4. Navigate to the BI Server Repository section and check the Share Repository check box. When the RPD Publishing Directory text box becomes active, type in the location of the shared directory (for example, //fileserver/RPD) and click Apply.

5. Click the Activate Changes button to active this configuration change, select the Availability tab and then the Processes subtab; then select the BI Servers row in the Processes table and click the Restart Selected button to start using the shared repository location.

   Now, whenever you edit your repository online, the master copy will be stored in this shared location and other BI Server components will use it to update themselves with any changes made online.

6. To set the shared location for the catalog, use FTP or a file system copy tool to copy to this new location all of the contents of the active catalog folder, which is normally found here:

   [*middleware_home*]/instances/instance/bifoundation/
   OracleBIPresentationServicesComponent/coreapplication_obips1/catalog

7. Then switch back to the Repository subtab under the Deployment tab, and again click Lock And Edit Configuration. Navigate to the BI Presentation Catalog area and type in the path to your network directory (for example, //fileserver/catalog). Once done, click Apply and then click Activate Changes; then use the Processes subtab under the Availability tab to restart the BI Presentation Servers component category to start using this shared catalog location.

8. Once complete, log into the Oracle Business Intelligence web site and run some analyses and dashboards to check that the changeover has worked correctly and that you can still access your BI content.

Now that you have set up the required shared locations, let's move on to the scale-out installation.

Performing the Scale-Out Installation onto a Second Server   Once you have configured your shared repository and catalog, follow these steps to scale out and extend your system to the second and any subsequent servers in your cluster:

1. On the server that you will be scaling out to, locate the downloaded software files and then the bishiphome folder containing five subdirectories named Disk1 to Disk5.

2. Open the Disk1 directory and then double-click the setup.exe executable file to start the Universal Installer.

3. The Universal Installer will then present you with a Welcome message. Click Next to proceed to the first screen of the installer wizard.

4. At the Install Software Updates screen, either enter your My Oracle Support (formerly Metalink) username and password to search for product updates, or select the Skip Software Updates radio button to proceed without downloading updates; then click Next to proceed.

5. At the Select Installation Type screen, previously shown in Figure 2-5, select Enterprise Install as the installation type.

6. The Prerequisite Checks screen will then check your host environment for the correct packages, libraries, memory, and other prerequisites. If any of these checks fail, correct the issue and then either click the Retry button to recheck the prerequisites or exit the installer and restart it again once the issues are resolved; otherwise, click Next to proceed to the next screen.

TIP
Generally, if you have prepared a Linux or Unix environment for an Oracle Database 11g installation, it will pass the prerequisite checks for Oracle Business Intelligence 11g.

Click Next to proceed to the next screen.

7.   At the Create Or Scale Out BI System screen, select Scale Out BI System. Then, when prompted, enter the connection details for the primary server in your cluster, which would normally be the one that you first installed Oracle Business Intelligence into. Enter the connection details; for example:

Host Name: obisrv
Port: 7001
User Name: weblogic
User Password: *password*

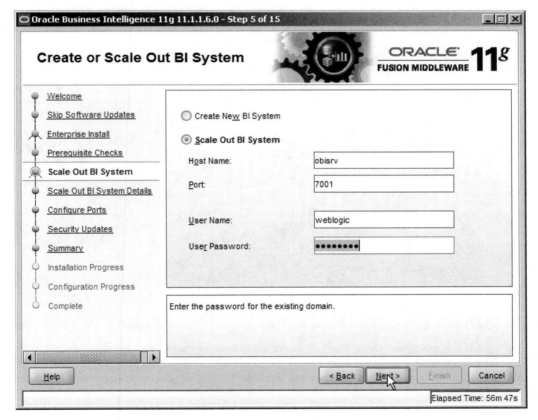

8.   At the Scale Out BI System Details screen, review the settings and click Next to proceed.

9.   Similarly, at the Configure Ports screen, click Next to accept the default Auto Port Configuration choice and continue.

10. At the Specify Security Updates screen, either enter your details for your support account or click Next to continue.

11. Finally, at the Summary screen, click Install to start the scale-out installation.

    The scale-out operation will then begin and will start by copying across and installing the program files for this server's installation of the software. Once the installation has completed, the Configuration Progress screen will be displayed and will show you the progress of scaling out the domain to this additional server.

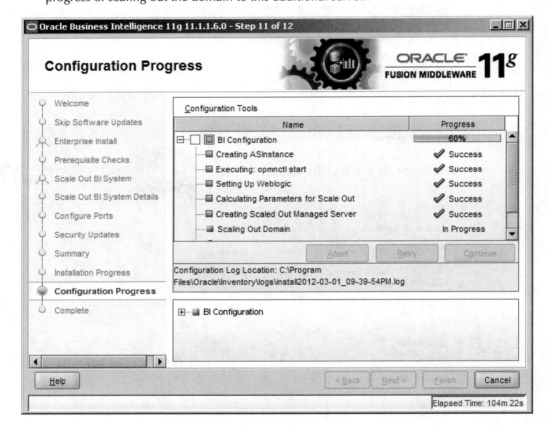

12. Once the process completes, click Next, and then click Finish to close the dialog box.

At this point, the default web browser on the scaled-out server will open, with the login page for Fusion Middleware Control open. Type in the username and password for an administration user, and then navigate to the Business Intelligence | coreapplication entry in the navigation tree menu.

Although a new WebLogic Server Managed Server will have been added to this scaled-out server by default, there will be no system components deployed on it, so you will need to use the "scale-up" feature to add them to it. This is something you can also do for existing servers if you want to add more BI Server, BI Presentation Server, or Java Host components to them to increase resilience or make better use of overall resources.

If you have more than one BI Server or BI Presentation Server component in your Oracle BI Domain, though, you should configure the domain to use shared locations for the Oracle BI Repository and catalog, respectively. When you configure a shared location for the Oracle BI Repository, each BI Server component keeps its own local copy of the repository but references the shared location to keep its copy synchronized with the overall domain; when you configure a shared catalog location, each BI Presentation Server component uses that shared catalog instead of a local copy so that new analyses, dashboards, and other BI objects are available to all BI Presentation Servers at all times.

To add system components to this new server or add additional system components to an existing server, follow these steps:

1. With Fusion Middleware Control open and the coreapplication module selected, select the Capacity Management tab and then the Scaleability subtab. You should see both hosts in the cluster now listed, with the new, scaled-out host showing zero BI Servers, Presentation Servers, or Java Hosts.

2. Click the Lock And Edit Configuration button to lock the domain configuration. Then, using the controls to the right of each of these component types, increase the number of components to the value you require; for example, 1 or 2 of each component type.

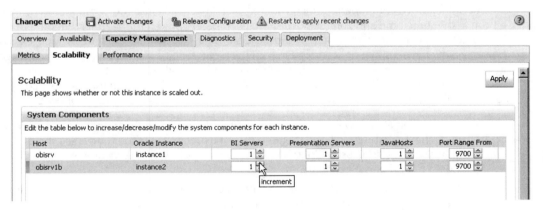

3. Once done, click the Activate Changes button to apply the changes, and then switch to the Processes subtab under the Availability tab to bring the new system components online. Click the Restart All button and then wait until all of the new system components

restart successfully. Once complete, you will see these newly provisioned components running within the overall Oracle BI instance, with their server locations listed alongside.

Change Center:	🔑 Lock and Edit Configuration						

Overview	**Availability**	Capacity Management	Diagnostics	Security	Deployment

Processes	Failover

Processes

▶ Start All	■ Stop All	🔄 Restart All		▶ Start Selected	■ Stop Selected	🔄 Restart Selected	

Name	Status	Host	Port	Oracle Instance	N
⊟ 🗗 BI Presentation Services	⬆				
🗗 coreapplication_obips1	⬆	obisrv	9710	instance1	
🗗 coreapplication_obips1	⬆	obisrv1b	9710	instance2	
⊟ 🗗 BI Servers	⬆				
🗗 coreapplication_obis1	⬆	obisrv	9703	instance1	
🗗 coreapplication_obis1	⬆	obisrv1b	9703	instance2	
⊞ 🗗 BI Schedulers	⬆				
⊞ 🗗 BI Cluster Controllers	⬆				
⊟ 🗗 BI JavaHosts	⬆				
🗗 coreapplication_obijh1	⬆	obisrv	9810	instance1	
🗗 coreapplication_obijh1	⬆	obisrv1b	9810	instance2	

All of the above components are considered "active-active" clustered components, as they can all run at the same time and can take over from each other without further intervention if one fails. The Oracle BI Scheduler and Oracle BI Cluster Controller components are termed "active-passive," however, which means that only one instance of them can run at a single time. Another is designated as the secondary instance, and it automatically starts and then takes over if the first one fails.

To add a secondary Oracle BI Scheduler as well as Oracle BI Cluster Controller system components to your scaled-out server, therefore providing more resilience for your system, follow these steps:

1. With Fusion Middleware Control still open and the coreapplication module selected, click the Availability tab and then the Failover subtab. You should now see the BI Scheduler and BI Cluster Controller components listed, with a recommended action of Configure Primary/Secondary.

2. To configure secondary BI Scheduler and BI Cluster Controller components, first click the Lock And Edit Configuration button to lock the domain for editing. Then navigate to the Primary/Secondary Configuration area and select the second, scaled-out host as the secondary host/instance. Once done, click Apply to save the changes. The Potential Single Points of Failure message will now read "No problems; all components have a backup."

3. To activate these changes, click the Activate Changes button; then switch to the Processes subtab under the Availability tab and click the Restart All button.

You will then see your new BI Scheduler and BI Cluster Controller processes listed but inactive, as they are secondary and will only be used if the primary ones fail.

Now that you have your Oracle Business Intelligence system installed and configured, let's continue on and create your first repository.

CHAPTER
3

Modeling Repositories
Using Relational, File,
and XML Sources

hen working on a project using Oracle Business Intelligence, the single most important thing that you need to get right is the Oracle BI Server Repository, or "repository" for short. The repository defines the data that your users work with, its relationship to your various data sources, and the calculations and analyses that your users can produce. A well-designed repository reflects the way that users think about their data and the organization of your company, and makes it easy for them to quickly find the information they are looking for. In contrast, a poorly constructed repository will not make sense to users, will not accurately reflect the way you do business, and will actively work against your users rather than help them find the numbers that they need.

This chapter is probably the most important one in this book, and I would recommend that you read and understand it before progressing too far with other topics. It will outline the basics of the repository, explain how you plan its design, and then take you through a number of scenarios that illustrate different aspects of repository modeling. As we progress through the scenarios, I will explain some of the more complex topics as we go along, explaining why we need to make use of more advanced features, and in the process hopefully show you some of the remarkable capabilities of the Oracle Business Intelligence Repository, and the Oracle BI Server that it is used with.

To start, though, let's first look at what the Oracle Business Intelligence Repository is, how it is stored, what products use it, and how it relates to other metadata stores such as the Oracle BI Presentation Catalog.

What Is the Oracle Business Intelligence Repository?

The Oracle Business Intelligence Repository is a metadata store that holds the logical dimensional models that users work with when creating their analyses and reports. The repository presents itself to users as one or more subject areas, made up of tables, columns, and hierarchies, which are then mapped internally within the repository to the underlying data sources that provide data for your reports.

The repository is primarily used by the Oracle BI Server, which uses it to translate incoming logical SQL requests into physical SQL, MDX, and other queries against underlying data sources. Figure 3-1 shows at a conceptual level the flow of data through the repository, with users selecting data items from one or more subject areas that are subsets of a wider, integrated logical data model. This data model contains mapping instructions so that the BI Server can make the necessary physical SQL and MDX queries to provide data for the requested user query.

The Oracle BI Repository is used alongside another metadata store within Oracle Business Intelligence, and that is the Oracle BI Presentation Server Catalog. The Oracle BI Presentation Server Catalog, or "catalog" for short, contains definitions of analyses, dashboards, agents, conditions, scorecards, and other BI objects that users create in order to analyze their data. As such, then, an Oracle Business Intelligence system can be thought of as containing three layers of data and metadata, listed here and shown in Figure 3-2:

- The Oracle BI Presentation Server Catalog, containing the report definitions
- The Oracle BI Server Repository, containing the logical dimensional model used to populate the reports
- The underlying databases, OLAP cubes, and other data sources that actually contain the data

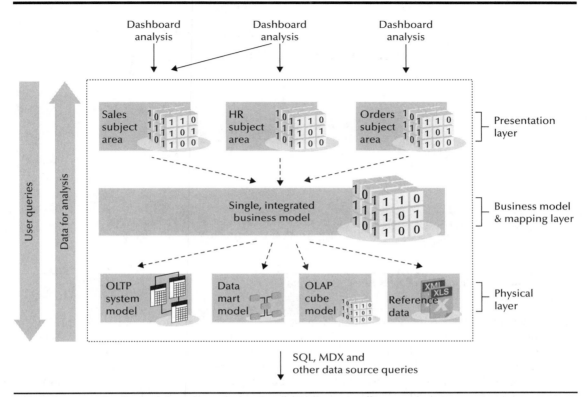

FIGURE 3-1. *The flow of data through the Oracle Business Intelligence repository*

The main user of metadata from the Oracle BI Repository is Oracle BI Answers, the analysis editor and ad-hoc query component within the Oracle Business Intelligence web site.

Other users of this metadata include Oracle BI Publisher, which allows report developers to create reports using data from the repository, and third-party reporting tools, which can work with the repository through the Oracle BI ODBC client.

The repository is traditionally stored in a single, binary file within the middleware home directory structure, which is typically at

[*middleware_home*]\instances\instance1\bifoundation\OracleBIServerComponent\ coreapplication_obis1\repository

with the file having an ".rpd" suffix, such as the SampleAppLite.rpd that ships with every installation of Oracle Business Intelligence 11*g*.

This file is encrypted using a password, and like any operating system file, while it can be read by many processes in parallel, only one can write to it at any one time. This, as you will see, has implications for team development because you will need to serialize write access to this file using one means or another.

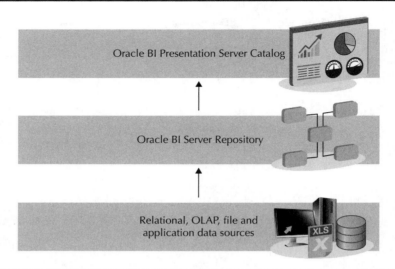

FIGURE 3-2. *Oracle Business Intelligence data layers*

With the 11.1.1.6 release of Oracle Business Intelligence, a new storage format for the repository was introduced, called MDS XML Documents. This storage format is primarily used when integrating Oracle Business Intelligence with source-control systems, as it breaks the repository down into individual XML files that can be checked in and checked out of source control. In this chapter, we assume that you will be using the traditional, RPD file-based format, and we cover the new MDS XML format, along with source control, in Chapter 11.

Repositories in either storage format can be accessed either offline or, for RPD file-based storage only, online. Offline access is when you are directly connecting to the repository file through, for example, the Oracle BI Administration tool, and in this case only one developer can access the file at one time in this way. Repositories can also be accessed online, which involves the BI Server itself connecting to the repository through an ODBC connection, with subsequent, potentially multiple, connections to the repository then being routed through the BI Server. You will see the differences between offline and online access to the repository later in this chapter.

An Oracle Business Intelligence Repository Modeling Primer

So, before we get into the details of how you model the Oracle Business Intelligence repository, let's take some time to look into the makeup of the repository in more detail. We'll start by looking at the three layers that make up the repository, what those layers contain, what they are used for, and what other information is held in the repository. Taking a step back for a moment, we'll look at some of the concepts around the dimensional model on which much of the repository is based, and then we'll take a look at various strategies you can use to create an effective repository.

The Three-Layer Repository Architecture

The Oracle Business Intelligence repository is made up of three layers of metadata, which build on each other to create a "semantic model" that describes in business terminology the data coming from your source databases:

- **Physical layer**   This layer describes the physical databases, schemas, tables, columns, joins, and keys that make up your relational data stores, and similar metadata for OLAP and other nonrelational sources.

- **Business model and mapping layer**   This layer contains definitions of one or more business models, made up of logical tables, columns, and dimensions, together with table sources that contain mappings among the logical objects in the business model and physical objects in the physical layer.

- **Presentation layer**   This layer contains one or more subject areas made up of presentation tables, columns, hierarchies, and folders.

Figure 3-3 shows these three layers, as displayed in the Oracle BI Administration tool. The physical layer is on the right-most side, with the business model and mapping layer in the middle and the presentation layer on the far left.

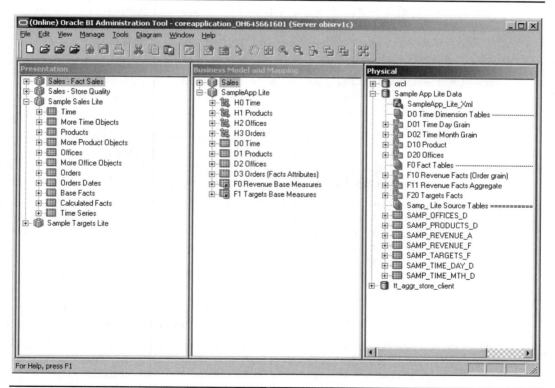

FIGURE 3-3.   *The repository as viewed in the Oracle BI Administration tool*

All of this metadata is held in the repository, which is generally built and administered through the Oracle BI Administration tool. Let's take a look in more detail at the three metadata layers within the repository using this tool.

The Physical Layer

The physical later is where details of the physical data sources that provide data for your reports are held. Typically, you use the Import Metadata function within the BI Administration tool to read in table and object metadata from your source databases into this layer, which you can then enhance by adding, removing, or correcting key and join definitions, and adding table aliases to improve manageability. Later on, you will map the physical table columns within this layer to the logical columns within the business model and mapping layer through objects called logical table sources that hold sets of these mappings.

Data Sources defined within the physical layer can be one of three main types:

- **Relational data sources**   These are sources that present their metadata using relational structures such as tables, columns, joins, and keys.

- **Multidimensional data sources**   This is a special type of data source recognized by Oracle Business Intelligence that, at the time of writing, is used for Oracle Essbase, Microsoft Analysis Services, and SAP B/W data sources (with Oracle OLAP slated for inclusion in this list in a subsequent release).

- **File, XML, ADF, and other non-database data sources**   In addition to data sources from relational and OLAP sources, Oracle Business Intelligence can import metadata from nonrelational sources such as files, XML sources, and Oracle Application Development Framework (ADF) sources.

Relational and relational-like data sources in the physical layer, such as those shown in Figure 3-4, have the following objects associated with them; however, not all relational-like sources implement all object types:

- **Database**   This is the overall container for the metadata relating to a physical database. It contains the definition of what type of database holds the data (for example, vendor, name, or version), together with a list of features that the database is capable of providing and that the BI Server can therefore make use of when creating queries for this database type.

- **Connection pool**   Connections to databases are made through connection pools, which aggregate individual sessions and aid scalability. Connection pool definitions include username, password, and other connection details, together with settings for the number of concurrent connections, the call interface to use, details of any scripts to run once the connection is made, and other specifics about how the BI Server physically connects to the underlying data source. This also removes the need for individual uses to have a database account.

- **Physical display folder**   This is an optional way of grouping collections of physical objects in order to help with organizing and sorting your metadata.

- **Physical schema**   Some relational databases (Oracle Database, for example) organize their physical tables into schemas to provide a physical separation between different application data sets. Physical schemas can be set up within databases to mirror this organization and to provide schema name suffixes for physical tables when accessing data through a superuser-type account.

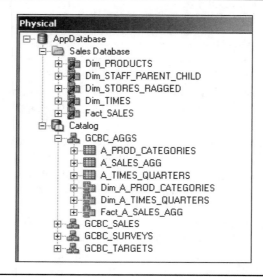

FIGURE 3-4. *A physical database definition based on relational data*

- **Physical catalog** Physical catalogs are optional objects that are used to group sets of schemas or, in the case of databases such as Microsoft SQL Server, to group physical tables directly. Whether you use physical schemas or physical catalogs usually comes down to the type of database server you are using and the way data has been set up within it. If in doubt, consult with your database administrator to determine the best way to structure your data in the Oracle Business Intelligence physical layer.

- **Physical table** Physical tables represent the actual tables of data within your source database. They can either be configured as physical tables, select tables (analogous to a database view but defined within the repository rather than the database data dictionary), or stored proc (procedure) tables, typically used for Microsoft SQL Server data sources and which take their data from the output of a stored procedure.

- **Alias table** Alias tables are variants on physical tables and are used to create alternative names for the same physical database object. This feature is useful if you wish to provide more descriptive names for your database objects while preserving their physical names in the repository, or for situations where the same table plays many "roles," such as to provide order dates, shipping dates, payment dates, and so on, through alternative join relationships.

- **Physical column** Physical columns are held within physical or alias tables, and they represent the actual columns that store data within the tables in your physical database.

In addition to implementing database and connection pool physical layer objects, multidimensional data sources implement their own special physical layer objects that distinguish

OLAP data sources from regular relational ones, an example of which is shown in Figure 3-5. Following is a list of these data sources:

- **Database**   This is the container for all the cube tables, physical cube dimensions, and other objects that make up a multidimensional data source. In Oracle Essbase terms, a database would correspond to a physical Essbase server.

- **Physical catalog**   This is a container for one or more cube tables. In Oracle Essbase terms, each catalog would correspond to an Essbase application.

- **Cube table**   A cube table contains the physical cube columns, physical cube dimensions, and other objects that together in Oracle Essbase terms would be considered a database containing a database outline.

- **Physical cube column**   These are individual data elements (either measures or columns derived from hierarchy levels) that will go on to form the logical columns in the business model and mapping layer.

- **Physical cube dimension**   This is contained with the cube table and represents the dimensions that are used to organize the measures in the cube table.

- **Physical hierarchy**   One or more physical hierarch may be contained within each cube dimension and represent individual roll-ups such as day-month-year or day-period-financial year.

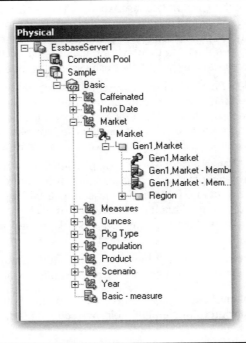

FIGURE 3-5.   *A physical database definition based on a multidimensional data source*

In this chapter, we will focus on relational data sources, along with flat file and XML data sources. In the following chapter we will cover the additional things you need to know when working with multidimensional data sources, such as Oracle Essbase and Microsoft Analysis Services.

Physical Joins and Keys   In addition to the actual tables, columns, dimensions, and other data dictionary objects that you find in the physical layer, you will need to define keys and table joins, or what in the world of database administrators is called "constraints." You can either import these from the source database, along with the table and column definitions, or create them yourself manually (or, most often, do a bit of both).

Key definitions (and the alias, stored proc, and select table variants) are created within physical tables, and they define the identifier column for the table (that is, the "primary key"). This does not have to be the same primary key column that the underlying database uses, but you must ensure that it uniquely identifies each row and that there are no duplicate values within the associated column; otherwise, the BI Server may return unexpected or incorrect results for a query.

If you have created your underlying data sources yourself or you can be absolutely sure that their primary key definitions are correct, then you can probably just import your key definitions along with your table and column definitions; if, however, these key definitions do not exist or you are not sure they are correct, you can choose not to automatically import them and can instead create them yourself manually after the initial metadata import.

Keys are primarily used when creating physical or complex joins from a master-level table (for example, one containing dimensional data) to a table containing detail-level data (typically, data containing facts and measures). These joins tell the BI Server how to retrieve data from more than one table—and again, they can either be automatically imported from the underlying database (by reading the foreign key information in the database data dictionary) or you can create them yourself manually.

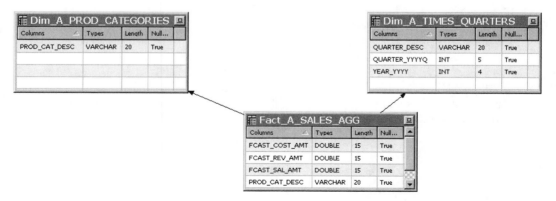

Correctly and efficiently setting up keys and joins in your physical layer is probably one of the most important tasks you will undertake as an Oracle Business Intelligence developer, and we will explore several scenarios involving different types of keys and joins later in this chapter. Note that, unlike tools such as Oracle Discoverer, joins can only be set up by an administrator; and if there is more than one possible join path between two physical tables, these have to be resolved in advance by the administrator rather than giving the user the ability to select between them when creating the query.

Table Aliases and Physical Display Folders   Aliases are physical layer metadata objects that represent alternative names for a single physical table. You create them typically for two reasons:

- To add additional usage information to the physical object names in your repository; for example, a physical table called DAY might be aliased to Dim_DAY to indicate that it contains dimensional-type data. Adding this additional information makes it easier to understand the purpose of the physical tables in your repository.

- To allow a table to be joined to more than once. For example, where an ORDERS table contains multiple foreign key references to a DAY table to represent order date, ship date, payment date, and return date, you will need to create aliases such as Dim_DAY_Order_Date and Dim_DAY_Ship_Date for each "role" that the table performs.

To organize sets of physical objects into groups, you can also define physical display folders under the main database definition, into which you can place sets of physical objects.

Physical display folders are particularly useful if your naming standard is always to work with aliased table names and you want to place these aliases in a display folder to keep them separate from your physical table names.

Database Definitions   When defining a new database in the physical layer, you can select from a number of database servers from different vendors to correspond with how your data is stored.

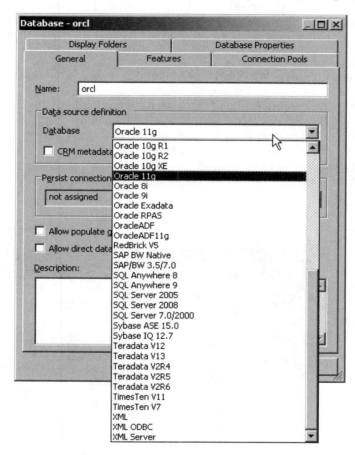

Check the *System Requirements and Supported Platforms for Oracle Business Intelligence Suite Enterprise Edition 11gR1* document for the full list of databases supported for your particular release.

When you select a particular database type as you are defining or importing new database metadata into the physical layer, you are in effect selecting two things: first, the call interface such as Oracle OCI, ODBC, or other native database network protocols that the BI Server will use to retrieve data and database metadata, and second, a default list of database capabilities that the BI Server will use subsequently when constructing physical database queries.

Database Capabilities   As you will have seen from the list in the preceding illustration, Oracle Business Intelligence supports a wide range of databases from a wide range of software companies. Each database will tend to support a set of core features by virtue of supporting SQL or MDX as a query language, but then each vendor will innovate by extending its database's capabilities and adding new functions and capabilities to their dialect of SQL or MDX.

When you select a particular database and version for your physical database settings, a default set of capabilities are provided for you, as shown in Figure 3-6.

Normally, you will not need to amend this feature list beyond the defaults, but if your database vendor brings out a new version that can still be connected to by the existing protocol, or if you are accessing an unspecified data source through the generic ODBC database type, you can amend this list to reflect the correct set of features for your database.

Refreshing and Updating Physical Layer Metadata Typically, you create your initial physical layer database metadata using the Import Metadata feature within the Oracle BI Administrator tool and then make manual amendments to this metadata to add or correct keys or joins, and to add aliases, display folders, and the like. If, after this initial metadata import, your underlying database schema changes, you can reimport your physical database metadata and it will update the physical model. Alternatively, you can add or remove tables, columns, or other objects yourself from the physical layer, although you will need to ensure that any changes you make correctly reflect the physical database structures in your database.

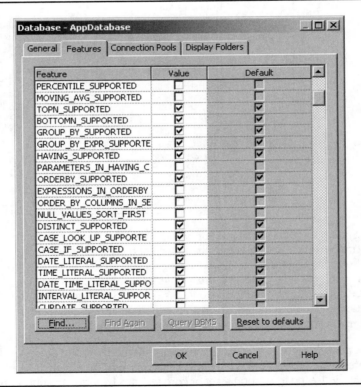

FIGURE 3-6. *The default features list for an Oracle 11g database*

The Business Model and Mapping Layer

The business model and mapping layer, usually the middle layer when viewing the semantic model using the Oracle BI Administration tool, performs two functions:

- It defines the logical, dimensional business model for your BI system.
- It maps the logical columns within this business model to the physical columns in the physical layer of the semantic model.

Your semantic model can contain multiple business models within this layer, something that typically happens when you want to report across multiple source systems but your data sets are not well integrated. Your long-term objective, though, should be to have a single, integrated (or "conformed") business model so that users can easily create analyses that span multiple subject areas using common dimensions. Figure 3-7 shows a typical business model containing two fact tables and conformed dimensions that, in turn, map to a larger number of source databases. Such a model would make it possible for users to query across both sets of fact measures using dimensions that are common to both.

Each business model defined within the business model and mapping layer contains some or all of the following repository objects:

- **Business models** The business model is the container for a set of logical tables, logical columns, logical table sources, and logical dimensions. Business models can map to more than one physical data source, and data mapped into the business model can come from data sources at differing levels of detail (or "granularity").

- **Logical display folders** As with the physical layer of the semantic model, logical objects within a business model can be organized into logical display folders. Logical display folders are useful when you have large amounts of objects within a business model and you wish to organize them to make navigating the business model easier and more efficient.

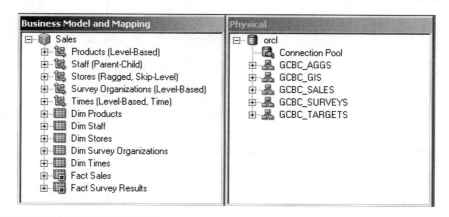

FIGURE 3-7. *A business model and corresponding physical model*

- **Logical tables** These are "virtual" tables that represent the data set that users will use to create their analyses, sourced from a single physical table or a set of tables, and either through direct mappings or through SQL expressions. They can be categorized into three types: facts—logical tables containing measures such as profit, revenue, cost, and margin; dimensions—logical tables containing reference data by which measures are analyzed, such as customers, products, times, and stores; and lookups—new with the 11*g* release of Oracle Business Intelligence.

- **Logical columns** Logical tables, whether used for facts or dimensional data, are made up of one or more logical columns. Logical columns are the "building blocks" of logical tables, and each one is either mapped to one or more physical columns, inheriting their data types, or is derived from an expression based on other logical columns.

- **Logical dimensions** Logical dimension (not to be confused with logical tables containing dimension, or reference, data) define the drill paths, or "hierarchies," within your logical tables. Logical dimensions contain either level-based hierarchies (which themselves can either be balanced, ragged, and/or skip-level) or parent-child hierarchies, where the hierarchical relationship between data items is determined by member ID and parent ID columns.

- **Logical table sources** A logical table source is a mapping that maps logical columns either directly to physical columns or indirectly through an SQL expression. Figure 3-8 shows a typical logical table source that maps logical columns within a logical dimension table to physical columns held in multiple linked physical tables, either directly or through SQL expressions.

For simple business models with a single physical data source, a logical table might be mapped 1:1 with a corresponding physical table in your database. For more complex models, you might map data in from aggregate or summary tables, and you might source certain logical columns from additional sources such as files, OLAP cubes, or other databases. Logical tables represent a way for semantic model designers to create a simplified, dimensional view of the

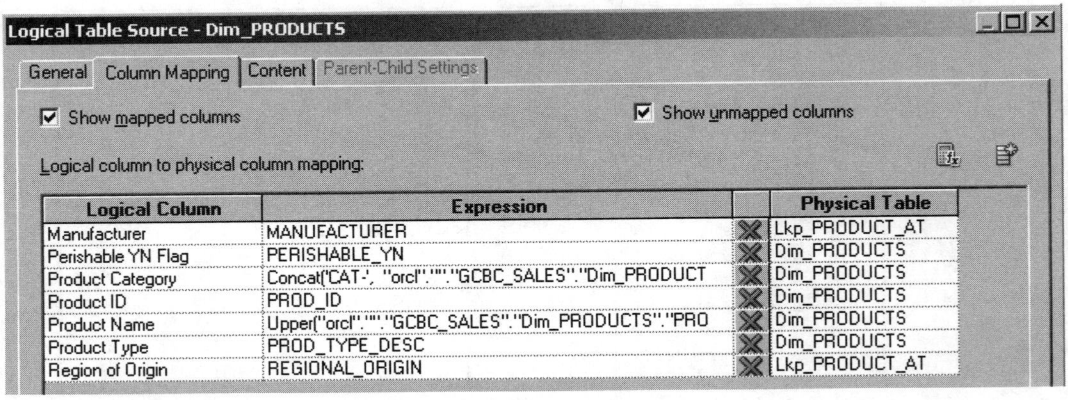

FIGURE 3-8. *A logical table source mapping*

FIGURE 3-9. *A logical table with multiple logical table source mappings*

organization's data even when that data might be stored in more complex, normalized database schemas. As such, along with the rest of the business model, you can think of them as an "abstraction layer" over your organization's physical data sources.

Logical tables typically contain a single logical table source when you first develop them, but as you map in additional sources of data for the logical table, typically you will end up creating more than one. For example, in Figure 3-9, a logical fact table has three logical table source mappings associated with it that provide data at a detailed, aggregated level and data for logical columns that are sourced from a separate database.

When a user's analysis requests data from this logical table, the Oracle BI Server will use one or several of these logical table sources when sending physical SQL queries to source databases, depending on which of the logical columns were used in the analysis and the level of aggregation requested.

Logical Keys and Joins   Like physical tables, logical tables have keys and joins. Each logical table containing dimensional data must have a logical key, which usually (but not always) corresponds to the primary key in the associated physical table.

Logical joins are like physical joins, but they do not specify any logical columns to join on. Instead, the Oracle BI Server determines which particular physical column to join the underlying physical tables on based on the particular logical table sources that are being used to access the underlying data sources or, in the case of multidimensional sources, uses other methods to return data from the fact and dimension. Logical joins are the way that you tell the BI Server that a particular dimension joins to a particular fact, and if users request data from both, the data can be returned. Conversely, not declaring a logical join between fact and dimension logical tables, even if they are physically joined in the database, will prevent the user from reporting on columns from two tables.

This allows the Oracle BI Server to handle data sources for a logical table that might hold aggregated data and not, therefore, join on detail-level dimension keys. It also allows the BI Server to work with sources that provide compatible data but that might themselves be joined on different physical columns (or that, as in the case of data sources such as Oracle Essbase, do not feature "columns" or "joins" in the same sense as relational data).

The Presentation Layer

While it is best practice to have as few separate business models in your semantic model as possible and try to integrate as much of your source data into a single business model, presenting this full data set to users would probably overwhelm them. In addition, you might want to separate your business model into subject area–orientated data sets, which users can still combine together since you've done the hard work in creating links between them. This, together with the ability to further alter the naming and organization of tables to suit particular audiences, is the purpose of the third layer in the semantic model: the presentation layer.

At its simplest, the presentation layer could just be a 1:1 reflection of what is in your business model and mapping layer. More usually, though, the presentation layer contains subject areas for each of the fact tables in the business model and mapping layer, with each subject area also containing copies of the dimension tables that link to each fact table. Figure 3-10 shows a presentation layer containing two subject areas that, in turn, both map back to a single business model in the business model and mapping layer.

The analysis editor allows report developers (where allowed by their security settings) to include more than one subject area in an analysis, as long as they all originate from the same business model. By creating presentation layer subject areas in this way, you can break your otherwise integrated business model into small, "easily digested" chunks of data customized for particular groups of report consumers in your organization.

A presentation layer within the semantic model can contain the following repository objects, as shown in Figure 3-11:

- **Subject areas** A container for presentation tables and other objects within the presentation layer is a subject area. Subject areas are analogous to databases, or data marts, and are selected by users when creating analyses in order to work with a particular selection of tables and columns. A subject area can contain a single fact table together with associated dimension tables, or it can contain multiple facts and dimensions. Indeed, a subject area can contain any selection of tables sourced from a single business model, but it is important to ensure that tables included have some relationship to each other; otherwise, users may select combinations of tables for their reports that cannot be joined together.

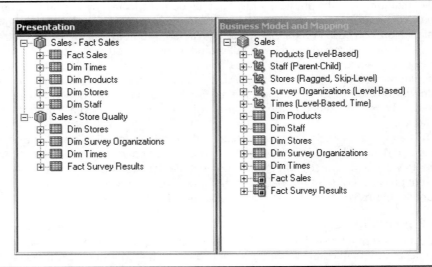

FIGURE 3-10. *Presentation layer subject areas and their corresponding business model*

FIGURE 3-11. *A presentation subject area in more detail*

- **Presentation tables**   These are containers for presentation columns and presentation hierarchies. In many cases, presentation tables are derived in their entirety from corresponding logical tables in the business model and mapping layer, but in fact you can drag-and-drop columns from any logical table within the same business model into a presentation table. You still need to be careful, however, that column selections made by users will result in a valid SQL query.

- **Presentation columns**   These are columns within presentation tables, which are usually created when you drag-and-drop logical columns from a business model into presentation tables. Presentation columns in Oracle Business Intelligence 11*g* can be either *attribute columns,* which contain columns from dimension logical tables and to which the Oracle BI Server applies a GROUP BY and DISTINCT clause, or *measure columns,* which typically are numeric columns from a fact logical table to which the Oracle BI Server applies an aggregate function (for example, SUM ()).

- **Presentation hierarchies**   These are new with the 11*g* release of Oracle Business Intelligence and are created when you drag-and-drop logical dimensions from the business model and mapping layer into a presentation table. Separate presentation hierarchies are created for every hierarchy within a logical dimension, and when included in an analysis they create a new type of column called a *hierarchical column* that can be used alongside attribute and measure columns when analyzing data.

Other Information Stored in the Oracle BI Repository

In addition to the three-layer semantic model, the Oracle BI Repository contains other information used by the Oracle BI Server to define and manage variables, manage row-level and subject area security within the semantic model, and define subsets of the repository that can be checked out by developers to enable multiuser development.

Variables and Initialization Blocks

Variables can be defined within the repository that can then be referenced in expressions and filters. These variables are defined using the Oracle BI Administration tool and initialized once when the Oracle BI Server process starts, when a user logs into the dashboard, or to a set schedule defined by the administrator.

Oracle BI Server variables can be one of two types:

- **Repository variables**   These have the same value systemwide and are either initialized on system startup or have their values set by a database lookup on a predefined schedule.

- **Session variables**   These are private to each user session and are generally set when a new user session is created, although in the 11*g* release of Oracle Business Intelligence this initialization can be deferred until the variable is first accessed.

The process that sets the value of dynamic repository variables, and all session variables, is called an *initialization* (or "*init*") *block*. Initialization blocks read from a data source and use the results to populate the variable, and like variables are defined using the Variable Manager within the Oracle BI Administration tool.

Row and Subject Area Security Settings

The Security Manager within the Oracle BI Administration tool is used for managing object permissions, row-level data filters, and query limits that can be applied to application roles and individual user accounts. Together with the Oracle BI Administration tool's ability to define access rights to objects at any level in the presentation layer, security can be defined at row level and subject area level for all data in the repository, or responsibility for such filtering can be delegated to the source database through technologies such as Oracle's Virtual Private Database.

Oracle BI Server variables, and the security settings that make the best use of them, are described in more detail in Chapter 8.

Projects

The Oracle BI Repository is in most cases stored in a single, monolithic file, and therefore Oracle has had to develop a special process for handling concurrent editing of the file. One such process is the Multiuser Development Environment (MUDE), which allows developers to check out subsets of the repository, called *projects,* that are edited separately and then checked back into the main repository. These projects are defined using the Project Manager and are pointers to business models, subject areas, variables, users, initialization blocks and application roles that can then either be manually exported as a project (a subset repository file) or automatically exported using MUDE.

Projects and multiuser development are described in more detail in Chapter 11.

Identifying the Logical Dimensional Model

When defining the data layer for your Oracle Business Intelligence 11*g* system, you need to think in terms of the "model" that will be required to support the range of queries your users will require, rather than individual data sets to support individual reports. This is often termed a "model first" approach and ensures that users can write queries that go across a range of subject areas and measures. The key to this is getting the right design for the business model and mapping layer within your semantic model.

As you will have seen from the overview of the semantic model, while data can be sourced for the physical layer from any number of database types and designs, the business model and mapping layer is designed around a logical dimensional model that, at a minimum, contains a single fact and single dimension with a join between them. The logical tables within a business model are organized into *star schemas,* a database design approach popularized by Ralph Kimball in the book *The Data Warehouse Lifecycle Toolkit*. Figure 3-12 shows a typical star

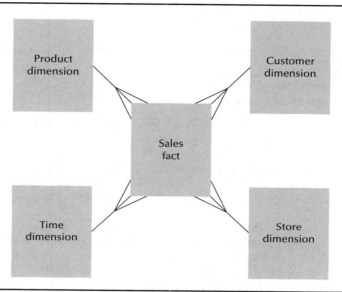

FIGURE 3-12.   *A star schema*

schema, with a sales fact table in the center linked to product, times, customer, and store dimensions.

In addition to star schemas, Oracle Business Intelligence supports the more normalized version of this data model type, called a *snowflake schema*. Snowflake schemas are sometimes used by customers with large data sets looking to minimize the storage required for their data warehouse, or in cases where their schema has lots of hierarchies and levels that can be built easily from snowflake-dimension "building blocks."

Each dimension has one or more hierarchies that define the hierarchical relationship between columns in the table and a key that defines the unique reference for table rows. The fact table contains one or more measures, and while in the business model and mapping layer there is no need to include dimension keys in the logical fact table, these keys are derived by the Oracle BI Server at query time through logical table source mappings back to the physical layer of the semantic model.

If you're lucky enough to be creating a semantic model where your data source is a single data warehouse or an Essbase OLAP cube, creating the logical dimensional model will be as easy as dragging and dropping the whole schema from the physical layer over to the business model and mapping layer. If, however, your source database is in third-normal form (a common data modeling approach for transactional systems that minimizes duplicate storage of data at the cost of a highly fragmented and complex data model, defined in more detail at http://en.wikipedia.org/wiki/Third_normal_form) or is an enterprise data warehouse or operational data store organized in a normalized fashion, how do you go about identifying what goes where in the logical dimensional model?

Overview of a Dimensional Model

A dimension model divides data into two main categories:

- **Fact tables**   These contain either numbers or dimension keys (references to dimension table IDs).
- **Dimension tables**   These are containers for reference data that are used to analyze, or "slice and dice," the measures in the fact table.

Fact tables can themselves contain reference data (usually called "degenerate dimensions" in this context) but from a purist point of view should only contain measures and keys. Dimension tables can also contain numbers (for example, the square footage of a store), but only when they are used to make selections from the dimension. Within the dimension table, columns are referred to as "attributes," which contain values referred to as "members." Columns within the fact table containing values are called "measures," with the values they contain referred to as "measure values."

Dimension tables within a dimensional model usually contain one or more hierarchies. Within Oracle Business Intelligence 11g, these hierarchies are either level based or parent-child based (value based), and these hierarchies define how data is aggregated within the fact table. When defining a dimension, you generally have to work out whether it will be level based or parent-child based. If it is level based, you also have to know what the levels are, and if parent-child based, which column will provide the member ID and which will provide the parent ID. In the case of level-based hierarchies, you then need to organize the various levels into the hierarchy itself, while for parent-child hierarchies the data itself will define the hierarchy (through a recursive relationship in the data).

Fact tables are perhaps easier to define, although as we will see later on, there is the additional question of how many fact tables to use and how to source them. You will, however, need to choose a default aggregation method for each measure (for example, sum or average) and decide to which dimension each fact table joins. So how do we go about identifying the facts and dimensions and, in Oracle Business Intelligence 11g, candidates for lookup tables?

Identifying Facts

Your source database, if not already a dimensional data warehouse, will typically be a transactional database designed along the principal of third-normal form modeling. *Third-normal form modeling* is a design approach where data is stored just once, in the most space-efficient manner and in a way that makes transactions as efficient as possible to process. Your task as a dimensional modeler is to identify those data items within this data model that will provide the "facts" for your business model.

Candidates for facts are typically data items that record events, and business processes within your organization. For example, if you are an insurance company, your main business processes are likely to be the following:

- Selling insurance policies
- Placing them on risk
- Processing claims
- Paying commission to salespeople

Similarly, in the examples used in this book, a retail chain selling food and beverages is likely to run the following key business processes:

- Baking cakes and manufacturing sandwiches
- Selling food and beverages in the stores
- Paying its staff and suppliers
- Monitoring quality and running "mystery shopper" exercises

These activities and business processes will form the most likely candidates for the fact tables in your logical model. Each process will be associated with measures and metrics (how many sandwiches you sold, how many claims were made), and interviews with potential users of your business intelligence system should help you focus on what facts and measures you should have in your model.

Identifying Dimensions

While it would be useful to know the total number of claims or sandwiches your organization has handled over all the years you have been in business, it's usually more useful to be able to break this total figure down by customer type, region, year, and so on. Then, once you start thinking about year, for example, you realize that it would also be useful to break this figure down by quarter, month, and sometimes day. It would also be useful to analyze data by other calendars (or "hierarchies") such as fiscal, academic, or taxation.

The things that you break facts and measures down by are your dimensions. Dimension tables are typically organized by theme, such as customer, product, store, or time, with each dimension typically containing a number of levels and hierarchies. Within your logical dimensional model, fact tables contain the numbers you wish to analyze, while dimensions contain the reference data you analyze these numbers by. If you keep your model as simple as that, you won't go far wrong.

Identifying Columns

Your source database will typically have hundreds of columns, some of which users are interested in for reporting on and some of which they aren't. The temptation, when you aren't sure which are which, is to include them all in the logical model and then, through a process of "natural selection," monitor which ones are used and which ones you can safely discard. Instead, focus on bringing into your model just those columns that are needed, which for the fact table are those containing your measures, and in the dimension tables are those which either form the dimension unique key or those that will be required by users to make dimension member selections. If in doubt, leave them out initially, and you can easily add them in once you have a better handle on your users' requirements.

Identifying Lookup Tables

A new feature in the 11*g* release of Oracle Business Intelligence is the ability to create a third type of table in the business model and mapping layer, called a *lookup table*. Lookup tables contain IDs and reference data that can be accessed by the LOOKUP function also introduced with 11*g*, and they are typically used to include data in an analysis that needs to be accessed outside of the usual grouping and aggregation that takes place in a query, such as in the following cases, for example:

- You wish to perform a currency conversion after the main aggregation has taken place in a query.
- You need to access data stored in a physical column with a CLOB data type that cannot be included in a GROUP BY clause.

In most cases, you would use the new LOOKUP function within a logical table source mapping to reference such data directly from the physical layer in your semantic model, but when the lookup data you wish to reference is held in a separate database to your main data set, a lookup table can bring this data directly into your business model where its original source is not relevant.

You would therefore plan for lookup tables in your logical model when your requirement fits this narrow set of circumstances but the lookup data is held in a source database that cannot easily be joined to within a single logical table source.

What Tools Do I Use to Build the Repository?

In general, you would use the Oracle BI Administration tool to build the repository, which ships as part of every installation of Oracle Business Intelligence or can be installed stand-alone, downloaded from the home page on the Oracle Business Intelligence web site. The Oracle BI Administration tool lets you import source table metadata into the semantic model and then use this metadata to build out the business model and mapping layer and then the presentation layer. You can also use it to manage variables, security (row-based and subject area security), and caching, as well as perform other administrative functions. This book focuses entirely on the Oracle BI Administration tool as the tool to create the repository, as this is by far the most common method used by developers.

Historically, another tool that you might consider is Oracle Warehouse Builder (OWB). OWB ships as part of the Oracle Database and provides data loading, data modeling, and data warehouse lifecycle functionality for developers looking to create an Oracle-based data warehouse. OWB does, however, come with functionality for creating a "first-cut" Oracle Business Intelligence semantic model, deriving the repository from the dimensional metadata contained in a Warehouse Builder project. Figure 3-13 shows Warehouse Builder deriving metadata from a warehouse project for use as an Oracle Business Intelligence repository.

Using OWB is certainly an interesting idea, as it allows you to trace metadata lineage from derived business intelligence repository information right back to the original source database, and comes with version control, change management, and other project lifecycle tools. It does not, however, replace the Oracle BI Administration tool, as it has no features for managing variables, caching, projects, and other repository information; and repositories created by Warehouse Builder and subsequently amended outside of the tool cannot then be reimported back into OWB.

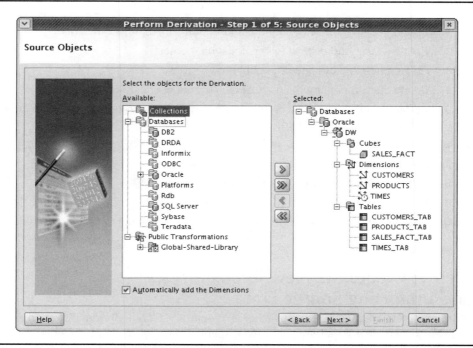

FIGURE 3-13.   *Using Warehouse Builder to derive a repository*

Moreover, Warehouse Builder is no longer on Oracle's strategic data integration roadmap; customers will eventually need to move to its replacement, Oracle Data Integrator, and there are no plans to introduce similar functionality in this tool. As such, while Warehouse Builder may be a useful option for repository creation if you already use the tool extensively, it is probably not worth investing time in if you use other methods to populate your supporting data warehouse.

Example: Creating the Oracle BI Repository

Now that you know the basics and have the sample data installed, how do you go about creating a new repository from scratch? The following steps outline the basic process for creating a new repository, and later on in this chapter we will look at more complex scenarios such as integrating (or "federating") separate data sources, working with complex hierarchies, integrating historic and real-time data, and adding time-series and other advanced analytics. For now, though, let's walk through the basic process of creating a repository against a single Oracle data warehouse data source.

At a high level, the ten steps to create a new repository are as follows:

1. Create the new repository offline, and import source object metadata.
2. Create aliases and display folders for source objects.
3. Create physical keys and physical joins.
4. Create the business model, logical tables, and logical columns.
5. Add logical keys and logical joins, and configure the column to be sorted by another column's values if required.
6. Define logical dimensions and hierarchies.
7. Define calculations and other derived columns.
8. Publish a business model as one or more subject areas.
9. Perform a consistency check for errors and warnings.
10. Publish the repository online so that it becomes available to users.

Let's now take a look at these steps in more detail.

Step 1: Create the New Repository and Importing Source Data

Your first step in creating a new repository is to open the Oracle BI Administration tool and select the option to create a new, blank repository. Using this option will display a dialog box asking if you wish to import source data, and you will also be prompted to set a repository password. Make a note of this password, as there is no way to recover it if the password is lost.

In the following example, we will create a new repository called GCBC_Repository.rpd and import database metadata into it, with the repository file being stored in a working area on the workstation PC.

1. Select Start to bring up the Windows Start menu; then select Programs | Oracle Business Intelligence | BI Administration. When the BI Administration tool opens, select File | New Repository to start creating the new repository.

2. In the Create New Repository dialog box, enter the following values:

   Create Repository: Binary
   Name: **GCBC_Repository.rpd**
   Location: **c:\biee_workarea**
   Import Metadata: Yes
   Repository Password: **welcome1**
   Retype Password: **welcome1**

NOTE
Ensure that the directory specified under Location actually exists; otherwise, you will not be able to proceed to the next screen.

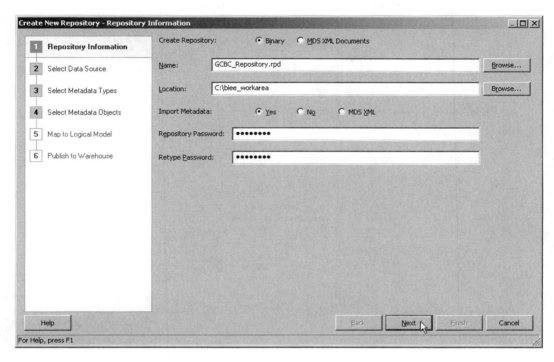

3. In the Create New Repository – Select Data Source dialog box that appears, select the connection type for your source database from the Connection Type drop-down list, and then enter the connection details; for example:

   Connection Type: Oracle OCI10g/11g
   Data Source Name: **orcl**
   User Name: **gcbc_sales**
   Password: ***password***

NOTE
For Oracle sources, the data source name should be the Oracle Net (TNSNAMES) connection name to your database. See Chapter 2 for details on how to configure the embedded Oracle Client software within Oracle Business Intelligence to recognize this connection name.

4. In the Create New Repository – Select Metadata Types dialog box, select the metadata types (database object types) that you wish to import (for example, table, keys, and foreign keys).

   You will be shown a listing of all of the database objects that your database username has SELECT privileges for. For this example, we use the dialog box to select the PRODUCTS, SALES, and TIMES tables from within the GCBC_SALES schema.

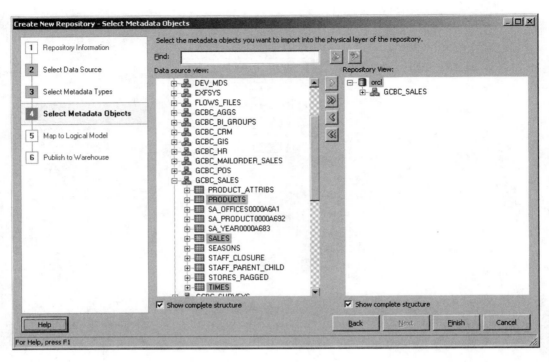

5. After initially selecting the metadata objects to import, the Connection Pool dialog box will be shown. For now, just click Finish to close this dialog box, and we will look in more detail at the connection pool settings in a moment.

If you look within the physical layer of your new semantic model and expand the database node, you will see your newly imported source data.

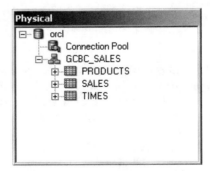

You now have the basic set of tables imported into the physical layer of your semantic model. Now you can enhance this physical model by creating aliases for the physical tables and then placing them in a separate display folder.

Step 2: Create Aliases for Imported Table Names, and Physical Display Folders to Organize Them

Aliases are alternative names for a physical layer object that can be used to make the names more descriptive or to distinguish between roles for an object. In this example, we will create aliases for our imported tables to make it clear what role the table plays, as a form of "naming standard" to make it easier for other people to understand our model.

1. Within the physical layer, locate the database that you have just imported. Right-click the first of the tables and select New Object | Alias. Use the Physical Table dialog box to give the alias a name; for example, for a physical table called PRODUCTS that holds product dimension information, call the new alias Dim_PRODUCTS.

2. Repeat this for the other physical tables, using the following alias prefixes:

    Dim_: Source table used for dimension information
    Fact_: Source table used for fact (measure) information
    Lkp_: Source table used for lookup information

    If a table is used for multiple roles, for example, a table containing dates or times, create an alias for each role that it plays, such as Dim_TIMES_Order_Date, Dim_TIMES_Ship_ DATE, and so on. If a source table contains both dimension and fact information, create an alias for each of these roles, such as Dim_ORDERS and Fact_ORDERS. Do this for every table in the physical schema.

3. Once all the aliases are created, right-click the physical database item orcl, and select New Object | Physical Display Folder. Give the folder a name (for example, GCBC Sales), and then drag-and-drop the aliases you just created into this new folder.

4. Dragging and dropping the aliases into the display folder copies them there rather than moving them. To display only these aliases within this folder, from the menu select Tools | Options, and then select the Repository tab. Select the "Show tables and dimensions only under display folders" check box and click OK; then return to the physical layer. Expand the database entry, and you will see that the aliases are shown now only under the display folder. Going forward, you will only work with these aliases and not the physical tables you initially imported.

Now that you have renamed and simplified your physical model, you can create or check the primary and foreign keys.

Step 3: Create Primary and Foreign Keys in the Physical Model

If your database source has primary and foreign keys defined, and you are confident that these keys are valid, then you can import them into the physical layer as part of the metadata import process. If you are not sure that these keys are correct, or if they would not be valid when used within the Oracle BI Repository (for example, recursive joins or multiple joins between two tables), you can create them yourself manually.

NOTE
Only create keys on physical tables that will be used for dimension logical table sources. Physical tables used for fact table sources do not need keys; instead, you create joins from them to the physical dimension tables, joining to the keys that you created for them.

To manually create keys (primary keys) and joins (foreign keys), take the following steps:

1. To create keys on physical layer tables and alias tables, locate the table or alias in the physical layer and right-click it. Select Properties, and then select the Keys tab. With the Keys tab selected, use the Key Name column to name the key (use something descriptive, such as Dim_PRODUCTS_Key), and then use the Columns drop-down menu to select the column on which the key will be created.

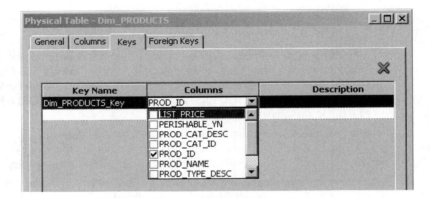

2. To create joins (foreign keys) in your physical layer, you can either create them using the table properties dialog box as with keys, or you can use the Physical Diagram view to create them graphically. To create joins using the table properties dialog box, select a physical table containing fact data, right-click it, and select Properties; then select the Foreign Keys tab and click the Add button to display the Physical Foreign Key dialog box. Use the dialog box to select the dimension table and column you wish to join to, as well as the fact table column that joins to them, and click OK to save the join.

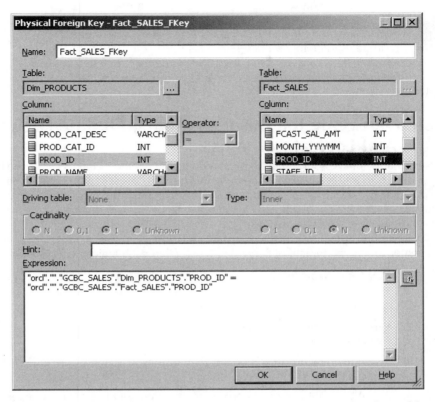

3. Alternatively, to create joins using the Physical Diagram view, using the physical layer to locate the tables or aliases you wish to join, CTRL-click them to select them all, and then right-click and select Physical Diagram | Selected Object(s) Only. When the Physical Diagram view is then displayed, starting with the fact table and with the New Join button selected, click the fact table and then draw lines (joins) to the dimension tables, selecting the columns to join on when the Physical Join dialog box is shown. Repeat this step until the SALES fact table is joined to the TIMES and PRODUCTS dimension tables.

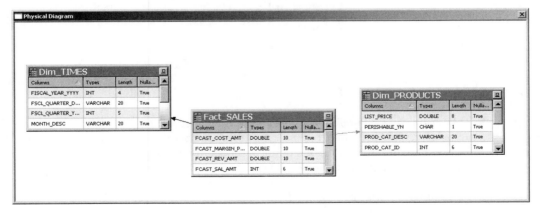

NOTE
When creating the physical joins, give them a descriptive name such as Sales_Fact_to_Product_Dim_FK so that you can identify the purpose of the join if it is referenced in a warning or error raised when using the Consistency Checker, detailed later on in this chapter.

Step 4: Create the Business Model, Outline Logical Tables, and Add Logical Columns

Now that you have your initial physical model, you can now start to create the business model to go with it. Your objectives when creating this business model are to create a dimensional model consisting of fact tables containing measures, together with dimension tables containing attributes, to which you will add calculations, hierarchies, and other information that users will find useful when creating analyses.

To start this process, create empty fact and dimension logical tables, and then join them together so that the Oracle BI Server knows whether each logical table is a fact or dimension:

1. Using the Oracle BI Administration tool, locate the business model and mapping layer in the semantic model. Move the mouse pointer to an area away from any other objects (for your first model, there should be none), right-click and select New Business Model.

2. When the Business Model dialog box is shown, type in the name of the new model (for example, Sales).

3. When the new business model is then displayed, right-click it and select New Object | Logical Table).

4. At the Logical Table dialog box, enter the name of the logical table (for example, Fact Sales). Now repeat steps 3 and 4 to create the remaining logical tables in your business model, starting with the fact tables and then moving on to the dimension tables.

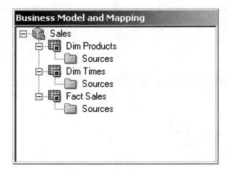

5. Now you can start adding columns to the logical tables you just created. Starting with the fact table, locate the column in the physical layer that you wish to map across, and then drag-and-drop it from the physical model into the logical fact table. Notice how within the Sources folder in your logical fact table you now have an entry with the same name as the source table. When adding columns to the fact table, only drag the measure (numeric) columns across, not the dimension ID columns, as the Oracle BI Server takes

care of the join for you in the background based on the keys and joins you set up in the physical layer of the semantic model. Make sure you drag across the dimension key columns, though, as you will need these later on to create your logical table keys. In some situations, you might need to source columns for a logical table from more than one physical table. Later on in this chapter, we will take a look at a number of situations where this is the case, and how you model this in the repository.

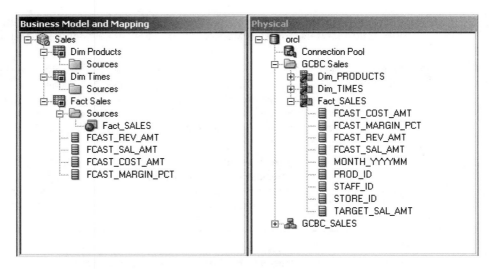

6. Once you have added all of the columns to your logical model, rename them so that they use regular business names rather than the system names that were used in the source database. For example, you might want to rename the incoming logical column FCAST_SAL_AMOUNT to Amount Sold so that users are better aware of the meaning of the column. To rename a column, either select it and then single-click it to open the name for editing or right-click the logical column and select Rename.

NOTE
Never rename columns in the physical layer unless the name has also changed in the underlying database, as doing so may cause errors when the Oracle BI Server tries to access the database source.

7. Finally, you need to set the default aggregation rule for the measure columns in your logical fact table. To do this, double-click each measure column in the fact table to display the Logical Column dialog box, select the Aggregation tab, and then select the required aggregation type from the Default Aggregation Rule drop-down list. Alternatively, if you wish to set the same default aggregation rule for a set of logical columns, CTRL-click all of the logical columns to select them, and then right-click and select Set Aggregation. When the Aggregation dialog box is displayed, select the default aggregation that you wish to apply to the logical columns. You can also uncheck the All Columns The Same check box if you wish to set different default aggregation types for the columns that you selected.

Step 5: Create Logical Keys and Logical Joins

In the business model and mapping layer, you need to ensure that all logical tables used for dimension data have suitable keys defined for them. If you have already created keys in the physical layer, these keys will come across when you drag the relevant physical column into a logical table. If you do not have physical keys defined yet, though, or you wish to create a logical key using a different column, follow the steps below to create them.

1. Right-click the logical table that you wish to create the logical key for, and select Properties; then use the Keys tab to create the logical key, naming it and selecting the relevant logical column.

2. Now CTRL-select all of the logical tables that you have just created; then right-click them and select Business Model Diagram | Selected Table(s) Only. When the Business Model diagram opens, with the New Join button selected, join the fact table to the dimension tables, starting with the fact table. As these are logical joins, you do not need to specify the columns on which the join takes place, as this will be determined by the Oracle BI Server at query run time.

You now have a basic business model, made up of a logical fact table and one or more logical dimensions. Check that your business model looks similar to Figure 3-14, with a pound or hash (#) icon over the fact table; if the pound or hash sign is over the dimension tables instead, you have created your logical joins the wrong way round.

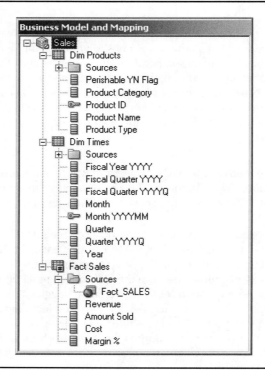

FIGURE 3-14. *An initial logical business model*

3. To change the order in which columns are listed within a logical table, right-click it and select Properties (or just double-click the logical table to display the Properties dialog box), ensure that the General tab is selected, click the logical column you wish to move, and then use the Move Up and Move Down arrow buttons.

4. Similarly, if you wish to sort one logical column using the values in another (for example, sort a column containing months in the format Feb-2010 by a column containing months in the format 201002), double-click the logical column to display the Logical Column dialog box. Then, using the Set button next to the Sort Order Column area, select the column you wish to sort this one by.

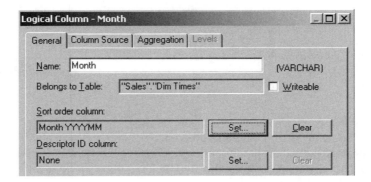

Step 6: Define Logical Dimensions and Hierarchies

An optional, but recommended, next step is to create the logical dimensions and hierarchies (or "drill paths") within your business model. The term "logical dimension" can be confusing because you have, of course, just created logical tables holding dimension information in the previous steps, but these logical dimensions are additional metadata elements that help users navigate through the hierarchies in your data. To create simple, balanced, level-based hierarchies (we will get into the more complex ones later on), follow these steps:

1. Using the Oracle BI Administration tool within the business model and mapping layer, right-click the business model for which you wish to create a logical dimension. Select New Object | Logical Dimension | Dimension With Level-Based Hierarchy.

NOTE
If the option to create a logical dimension is not shown, check that you have created logical joins between your logical tables, as this option only becomes available when you have logical dimension tables identified that do not otherwise have logical dimensions defined for them.

2. When the Logical Dimension dialog box is shown, type in the dimension name (for example, Products). Ignore the other options on this dialog box for the moment, and we will look in detail at these later on in this chapter.

3. Now you will create the levels in the level-based hierarchy for this logical dimension. Select the logical dimension that you have just created, right-click it, select New Object | Logical Level, and the Logical Level dialog box will be shown. This first level will be the "grand total" level for your dimension's hierarchy, so name it All *<Dimension Name>* (for example, All Products), and select the Grand Total Level check box.

4. Right-click this grand total level and select New Object | Child Level. Using the Logical Level dialog box, type in the name of the level, and then when the dialog box closes, right-click this level and repeat this step, creating levels under each other to form the level-based hierarchy.

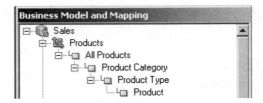

5. Now that you have created the levels, the next step is to associate logical columns with the levels. To do this, drag-and-drop columns from the logical table associated with the dimension onto the relevant level, and then right-click the column and select New Logical Level Key…. Repeat this step for all of the levels in the logical dimension apart from the grand total level.

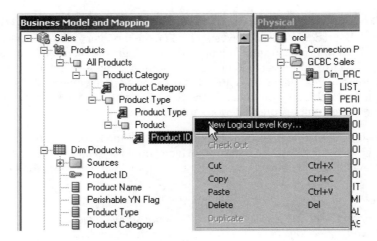

Ensure that each logical column that you set as a logical level key does, in fact, contain unique values; otherwise, the Oracle BI Server may provide incorrect results for a query. In cases where you have an ID and a descriptive value for a dimension level (for example, Product ID and Product Name), if just the ID is unique, drag both values into the logical level but set just the ID as the level key. If both the ID column and the descriptive column are unique, you can set both columns as level keys, and then select the descriptive column for display during drill-down by right-clicking the logical level, selecting the Keys tab, and checking the Use For Display check box for just the key containing the descriptive column. This will be used when drilling down in the front end as the column to be displayed.

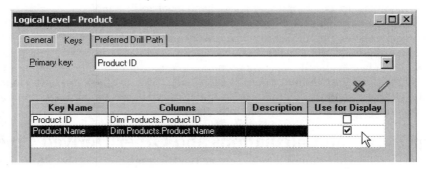

Some dimensions can contain more than one hierarchy. For example, a logical time dimension may need to aggregate data through a calendar hierarchy and a fiscal hierarchy. In these situations, all of the hierarchies will share a common top (grand total) and bottom (leaf) level, but in between they will contain their own levels organized into alternate hierarchies. To create a dimension with two alternative hierarchies, follow these steps:

1. Create the new logical dimension as before, and create a grand total level directly under the logical dimension, naming it, for example, All Times. Ensure you select the Grand Total Level check box when you create the level. (Note that it is not mandatory to create a grand total level, but it is considered "best practice.")

2. Start by creating the first hierarchy. Right-click the grand total level and create, one by one, the child levels under it, until you reach the bottom (leaf) level.

3. Now return to the grand total level, right-click it, and select New Object | Child Level. Continue now creating the levels under this alternative hierarchy, until you reach the level just above the leaf level.

4. To join this alternative hierarchy back to the main one at the leaf level, right-click the last level you created in the alternative hierarchy and select New Object | Shared Level As Child. Then select the leaf (bottom) level from the list of levels so that this alternative hierarchy is then joined back to the main one, at the leaf level.

5. Then, as before, drag-and-drop the logical columns from the related logical table onto the levels, and create the logical level keys. You will only need to add the logical column for the leaf level once, even though it is displayed as part of two separate hierarchies under the logical dimension.

You may have noticed when creating your logical levels a setting labeled "Number of elements at this level." Best practice is for you to enter into this setting the number of unique values (members) in the column designed as the level key. Providing this value is optional, but when it is present it helps the BI Server determine the most optimal execution plan for a query. You can either enter the number in manually or populate the values automatically when the repository is open in online mode by right-clicking the logical dimension and selecting Estimate Levels, which causes the BI Administration tool to run a series of queries on the source database(s) to count the number of distinct values at each level. Note that the values used in this setting need only be estimates, and you do not need to update them unless the number of unique values in the associated logical column change significantly.

Step 7: Define Calculations and Other Derived Columns

In addition to logical columns that you create by dragging and dropping physical columns into the logical table, you can create additional ones by deriving their values from other logical columns in the business model. For example, you could create a logical column for profit by subtracting costs from revenue. We will cover the different types of calculations you can create in the business model and mapping layer in more detail later on, but to create a basic derived logical column, follow these steps:

1. Right-click the logical table for which you wish to create the new logical column, and select New Object | Logical Column.

2. When the Logical Column dialog box is shown, ensure the General tab is selected and then type in the name for the column (for example, Profit).

3. Next, click the Column Source tab, and select the "Derived from existing columns using an expression" radio button. Then click the Edit Expression button to the left of this radio button to display the Expression Builder dialog box.

4. Using the dialog box, use the Category panel to select the Logical Tables entry, and then use the Logical Tables panel to select the fact table containing your measures. With the fact table selected, select from the Columns panel the first measure in your expression, and then use the list of operators on the bottom right-hand side of the dialog box to select the operator (for example, a minus operator: –). Then, to complete the expression, repeat this step to select the second measure.

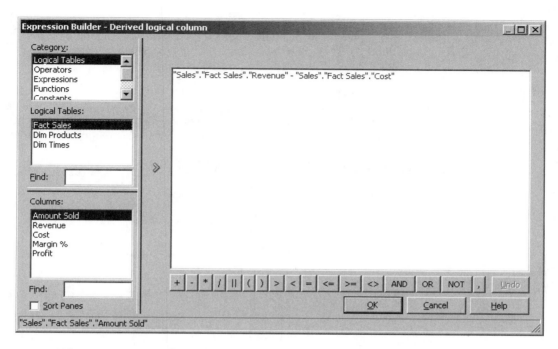

5. When you return to the Logical Column dialog box, your expression will be listed in the bottom panel of the dialog box, and the logical column will be calculated at query time using the expression you used as its column source.

Step 8: Publish the Business Model as Subject Areas

Now that you have a business model ready for querying, you should publish it to the presentation layer of the repository so that it can be used in analyses. You can either publish the business model automatically, creating separate subject areas for each fact table and its associated dimensions, or you can create a custom subject area by dragging and dropping individual logical tables and columns into the presentation layer.

To automatically publish subject areas based on the fact tables in your business model, right-click a business model in the business model and mapping layer of the semantic model and select Create Subject Areas For Logical Stars And Snowflakes. This will then create a separate subject area in the presentation layer for each fact table in your business model.

To create a custom subject area based on tables in a single business model, follow these steps:

1. Using the Oracle BI Administration tool, right-click anywhere that is empty in the presentation layer and select New Subject Area.

2. When the Subject Area dialog box is shown, type in the name of the subject area. Leave the other options at the default, and we will look in more detail later in this chapter at what they are for.

3. Drag-and-drop the logical tables and logical columns that you wish to add to the subject area from where they are in the business model and mapping layer. Double-click the presentation column or table to rename it, and use the Properties dialog box for the presentation table if you wish to change the ordering of the columns.

Notice how when you drag-and-drop a logical table from the business model over to the presentation layer, it also brings across any logical dimensions associated with the logical table. If the logical dimension has more than one hierarchy, each hierarchy will become its own presentation hierarchy, allowing users to select which hierarchy they wish to use when creating an analysis.

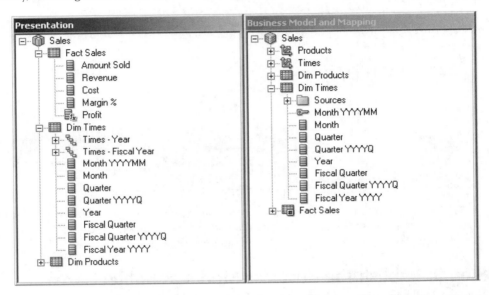

Having a presentation layer separate to the business model gives us an opportunity to create a further level of abstraction away from the underlying data. We can, for example, split an existing logical table into two or more presentation tables, or create presentation tables that contain columns taken from more than one logical table. (Be careful, though, not to create presentation tables that combine columns from logical tables that need to be joined via a fact table before they can be displayed together.)

You can also "nest" one set of presentation tables within another to create a set of subfolders under a master folder. In an example where you have a fact table containing both based (physically mapped) and derived (calculated) measures, to place each set of measures in their own folder, follow these steps:

1. Navigate to the presentation layer within your semantic model and locate the subject area that you wish to work with.

2. Right-click the subject area and select New Presentation Table.

3. When the Presentation Table dialog box is shown, enter a name for the new presentation table (for example, Base Facts), and within the Description area, type in -> (a minus sign, followed by a greater-than sign). Repeat this step for any other subfolders that you wish to create.

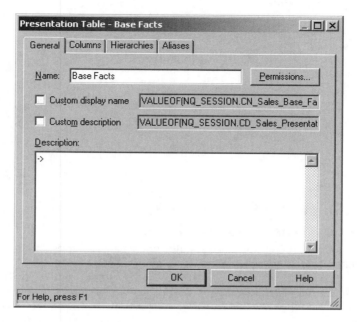

4. Drag-and-drop the columns that you wish to add to these subfolders, either from the existing presentation table containing them in the subject area or from the corresponding business model if you have not already dragged them to the presentation layer.

5. Finally, double-click the subject area you are working within the presentation layer, select the Presentation Tables tab, and use the Move Up and Move Down buttons to place the two subfolders under the presentation table that you wish to nest them under.

When you return to the main presentation layer view in the semantic model, you will see just these two subfolders listed under the main folder. However, when you place the repository online and view the list of folders within Oracle BI Answers, you will see folders nested and with presentation columns listed under each subfolder.

NOTE
This can also be done by putting a dash (–) in the name of the presentation table (for example, – Base Facts).

Step 9: Check the Repository for Consistency Warnings and Errors

At this point, it would probably be a good idea to check your repository for errors and violations of best practices. To do this, you use the Consistency Check Manager.

You can either use the Consistency Check Manager automatically, as you save changes to your repository, or manually, for either a single object in the repository or the whole repository.

To use the consistency checker as part of a repository save, with the Oracle BI Administrator tool open select File | Save and answer Yes to whether you wish to check global consistency. The Consistency Check Manager dialog box will then be shown, and you can select whether to display warnings, errors, or best practices violations. Once you have resolved any issues, you can then save the repository to the file system.

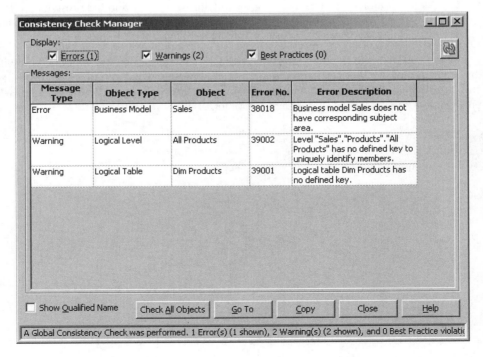

To check consistency manually, again with the Oracle BI Administrator tool open, either select a single object, right-click it and select Check Consistency, or select File | Check Global Consistency from the menu to check all objects in the repository. If you receive the message "Consistency check didn't find any errors, warnings or best practice violations," you are free to move on to the last stage of the process. If not, either resolve the issue and recheck the repository as before or mark the business model as unavailable and come back and resolve any issues later on.

When you are first creating a repository, though, you may well end up with warnings or errors reported by the consistency checker. Here are examples of some common warnings and errors, and how to resolve them:

- **[39002] Level "Sales"."Products"."All Products" has no defined key to uniquely identify members.** If you get this warning for a level in a logical dimension hierarchy that is the grand total (topmost) level, you have forgotten to check the Grand Total Level check box for it. Go back and select this box, and the warning will go away. If the level referenced in the warning is not the grand total level, though, this means that you have forgotten to define the logical level key for it. Double-click the warning in the consistency checker to go straight to this level, and then set the key to remove the warning.

- **[39001] Logical table Dim Products has no defined key.** This means that while you have defined a logical table as a dimension table, you haven't created the table key for it. Double-click the warning row in the consistency checker, and use the Keys tab to set the logical key.

- **[38018] Business model Sales does not have corresponding subject area.** This error is shown when you have defined a business area but not yet a corresponding subject area in the presentation layer for it. Create the subject area as you would do normally, and the error will go away.

Step 10: Publish the Repository as the Default, Online Repository

So far you have been working "offline" with this repository. This means that the Oracle BI Administration tool is connected to the repository file directly, and only you are able to make changes to it. It also means that nobody can run analyses using it, as it has not yet been uploaded to the Oracle BI Server and placed "online," ready for queries.

To place the repository online, you have to use Oracle Enterprise Manager Fusion Middleware Control to deploy the repository file to the Oracle BI Server file system, activate the changes, and then restart the Oracle BI Server component. To do this, follow these steps:

1. Using your web browser, navigate to the URL where Fusion Middleware Control is located (for example, http://obisrv1:7001/em).

2. When prompted, enter the username and password for an administrator account (typically, the account details you used when installing Oracle Business Intelligence Enterprise Edition (OBIEE); for example, weblogic/welcome1).

3. When the Fusion Middleware Control home page is displayed, navigate to the Business Intelligence folder on the left-hand side under the Farm_bifoundation_domain menu. Open the Business Intelligence folder and click the coreapplication entry within it.

4. A set of tabs and subtabs will then be shown on the right-hand side of the screen. Click the Deployment tab and then the Repository subtab. Click the Lock And Edit Configuration button at the top of the screen to lock the system configuration for editing. No other administrator will be able to make configuration changes until you either activate your changes or release the configuration.

5. Navigate to the Upload BI Server Repository section, and click the Browse button to locate your repository file on your workstation. Then enter the Repository Password under the Repository File section, and enter it again in the Confirm Password section.

NOTE
Be sure to enter the password correctly because while the two passwords are checked as matching at this point, they have not been checked as to whether they are valid for the repository that you have selected. If they are invalid, you will still be able to proceed to complete the rest of these steps, but the Oracle BI Server will not restart at the end and you will need to repeat these steps again.

6. Locate and click the Apply button on the right-hand side of the screen (you may have to scroll up to see it), and then click the Activate Changes button on the top of the screen.

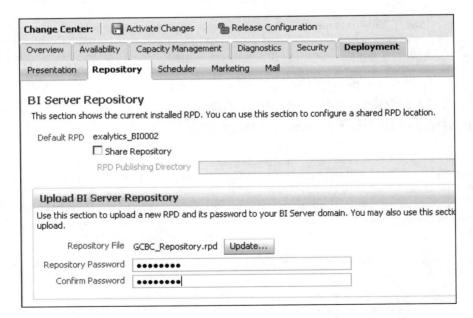

NOTE
Be sure to click the Apply button before the Activate button, as otherwise the activation will not include your changes, and you will not know this until the whole process has completed and your repository has not been uploaded and made active.

7. You should then receive the message "Activate Changes – Completed Successfully."

8. Using the two rows of tabs at the top of the screen, select the Capacity Management tab and then the Availability tab. Within the System Components Availability area, locate the Oracle BI Servers folder, select it, and click the Restart Selected button. Click Yes when you see the "Are you sure you want to restart the selected component?" message, and then wait for the restart process to complete.

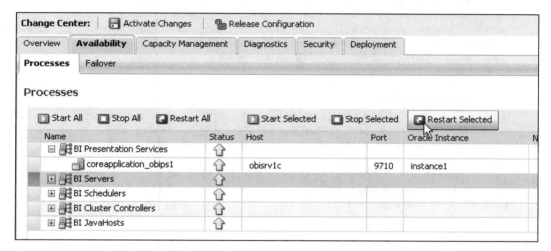

9. After a few minutes, you should then see the message "Restart Selected – Completed Successfully." If you receive an error message, repeat steps 3–9, but check carefully that you have entered the correct password; and if the process fails again, use the Consistency Check Manager on the offline repository to check that there are no errors that are stopping the Oracle BI Server from starting with this repository online.

Congratulations! Your repository is now online and ready for use. Now that you know the basics, let's take a look in more detail at what else you can do with the repository.

Calculations and Formulas

In the repository creation steps detailed earlier in this chapter, we outlined briefly the way in which you can create additional logical columns that are based on calculations involving other logical columns. In fact, you can create a range of calculations involving both logical and physical columns, which gives you the ability as a developer to considerably enhance your repository by adding calculations and derivations that may be of use to report developers, and to also ensure that all report developers use a consistent definition of derived measures: a "single version of the truth."

Before we start looking at the range of calculations available, though, let's take a moment to think about how the repository and the Oracle BI Server handle calculations.

How the Oracle BI Server Performs Calculations

You can define calculations, or "formulas," in several places within Oracle Business Intelligence; if the calculation is only needed for a specific analysis, you can define it in the analysis criteria; if it will be used across many analyses and by many developers, you can define it directly in the repository instead. If you define the calculation in the repository, you can either base it on logical columns in a business model or you can work directly with source columns and tables in the semantic model physical layer.

However you define your calculations, though, the same process takes place when the BI Server calculates your data: where possible, the BI Server takes your calculations and converts them into database-specific SQL functions ("function push-down"), and where the database lacks the capability to do the calculation directly or when the data used in the calculation comes from more than one physical database, the BI Server requests the raw data and performs the calculation itself ("functional compensation").

Function Push-Down

The Oracle BI Server uses a form of query language called "logical SQL." Logical SQL is very much like regular Oracle, Microsoft, and other dialects of SQL, except that in most cases it does not require GROUP BY, ORDER BY, or aggregation functions because these are instead defined as part of the business model definition in the repository. Logical SQL lets you focus on the data retrieval parts of SQL without worrying about joins, ordering, or default aggregations.

So that a common set of functions can be provided for all data in the semantic model, regardless of the data source, the BI Server converts logical SQL functions used in the repository and in analyses into the specific SQL and MDX functions used by each underlying, supported data source.

For example, a logical column that requests rank of sales would use the logical SQL function RANK (*column_name*), which would be translated into RANK () OVER (ORDER BY...) when pushed down to an Oracle, Microsoft SQL Server, or IBM database. Whether or not the Oracle BI Server can perform this function push-down is determined by the database type and version you select for the physical database, as well as what capabilities that database has been configured for. You can display these by right-clicking a physical database in the semantic model and selecting the Features tab, as shown in Figure 3-15.

Functional Compensation

If the source database had less functionality, though (such as a Microsoft Access database), the BI Server "compensates" for this by just requesting the raw information from the source database, and the BI Server then performs the additional calculations in memory.

Taking this approach allows Oracle Business Intelligence to provide the same calculation capabilities regardless of the data source, so users can create analyses spanning different source database types without worrying which sources support which types of calculations. All of this happens transparently to the end user, though as a developer you need to be aware of the extra

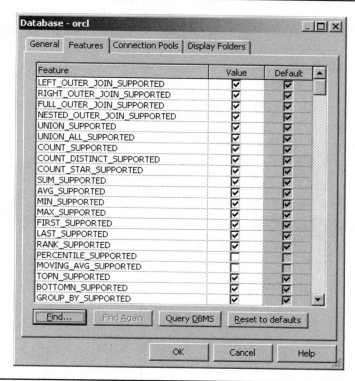

FIGURE 3-15. *Displaying physical database features*

load this can place on both the source database (which potentially has to return a larger set of raw data to the BI Server) and the BI Server (which has to perform what can be quite complex calculations).

Logical and Physical Calculations

For calculations defined in the repository, you can use either logical columns or columns from the physical layer of the semantic model in your expression. You use logical columns when you define the calculation as part of a logical column's properties, and you use physical columns when you define the calculation within a logical table source mapping. Regardless of where you create the calculation, it will still get pushed down to the underlying data source (where the data source supports it), but if more than one column is used in the calculation, the results might get aggregated differently, as logical calculations are carried out following aggregation, while physical calculations are performed prior to aggregation.

NOTE
This aggregation behavior is only for measure columns in fact tables. For dimensional calculations, in some cases the logical calculations will get pushed to the grain of the query, before aggregation.

Example: Comparing the Aggregation Outcome
of Logical and Physical Column Calculations

As an example, consider a situation where you wish to calculate the percentage margin for sales
of bread assortments. The repository has physical columns for revenue and profit, and you
calculate margin by dividing profit by revenue, like this:

	Revenue	Profit	Margin %
Transaction #1	26.95	4.95	0.18367347
Transaction #2	29.95	14.95	0.49916528
Transaction #3	29.95 80.85	9.95	0.33222037

The revenue and profit figures are modeled as physical columns in the physical layer of the
semantic model, and logical columns are directly mapped to their corresponding physical ones,
with a default aggregation rule of Sum.

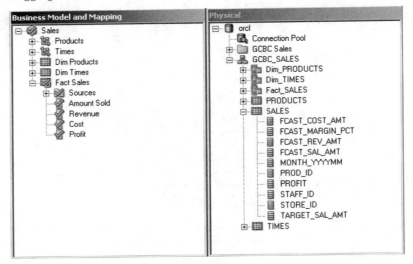

Should you now wish to calculate the average percentage margin for these sales as a new
logical column, there are two ways in which you could derive the calculation: you could base the
calculation on the revenue and profit logical column in the logical layer (a "post-aggregation"
calculation), or you could define the calculation directly in the logical table source mapping,
based on the physical columns (a "pre-aggregation" calculation), and depending on which route
you take, you'll potentially get different numbers returned.

In this example, to create the logical column using a logical calculation, you would do the
following:

1. Using the Oracle BI Administration tool, right-click the fact table and select New Object |
   Logical Column.

2. Using the Logical Column dialog box, select the General tab and give the column a
   name; for example, Avg. Margin % (Logical).

3. Click the Column Source tab for this new column, and select "Derived from existing
   columns using an expression" as the column source type.

4. Click the Edit Expression button to the right of this label. Then, using the Expression Builder dialog box, enter the expression for the column source, such as ("Sales"."Fact Sales"."Profit" / "Sales"."Fact Sales"."Revenue") * 100.

5. Close the dialog box and copy the new logical column to the presentation layer of the semantic model. Finally, save the repository, ensure it is online, and then create a test analysis to view the results.

For the preceding data set, the average percentage margin for sales of bread assortments is reported as 34.37, which has been calculated in the following way:

sum (*all revenue*) / sum (*all profit*) = % margin

You now create a second percentage margin logical column, but this time you'll use a physical calculation to perform it. To do this, follow these steps:

1. Using the Oracle BI Administration tool, right-click the fact table, and select New Object | Logical Column.

2. Using the Logical Column dialog box, select the General tab and give the column a name; for example, Avg. Margin % (Physical).

3. Click the Column Source tab for this new column, and select "Derived from physical mappings" as the column source type.

4. Click the logical table source mapping under this option to select it, and click the Edit button to edit the table source mapping and ensure that the Show Unmapped Columns check box is selected.

5. With the Logical Table Source dialog box open, click the blank area next to the new logical column, and click the Edit Expression button.

6. Using the Expression Builder dialog box, create the calculation; for example:

```
("orcl".."GCBC_SALES"."Fact_SALES"."PROFIT" /
"orcl".."GCBC_SALES"."Fact_SALES"."REV_AMT")
* 100
```

7. As this is a physical calculation derived using column mappings, you will need to set the default aggregation type for the column. With the Logical Column dialog box still open, switch to the Aggregation tab and set the default aggregation rule to Avg.

8. Again, close the dialog box and copy the new logical column to the presentation layer of the semantic model. Then save the repository, ensure it is online, and create a test analysis to view the results of this second query.

This time, the average percentage margin reported back is 33.84. So why do the two numbers differ?

Title			
Table			

Revenue	Profit	Avg. Margin % (Logical)	Avg Margin % (Physical)
86.85	29.85	34.37	33.84

It has to do with where the percentage margin calculation is done. The logical calculation sums up all the revenue figures and all the profit figures, and then calculates the percentage margin based on dividing one total by another. The physical calculation, however, calculates the percentage margin at a line level, and then averages these figures, giving a different overall total to the logical calculation. So when you create calculations like these in your business model, make sure that you do them consistently; also be aware that percentages and other calculations can come out differently depending on the point at which you aggregate your data.

A Guide to Repository Functions

So what type of calculations and functions can you make use of in your repository? Oracle Business Intelligence provides you with a set of logical SQL functions that it translates into the equivalent physical SQL and MDX functions used by each supported data source. Where a data source does not have an equivalent function (because the logical SQL function is unique to Oracle Business Intelligence or because the data source does not support more advanced calculations), the BI Server requests the basic data set required to perform the calculation and does the calculation itself.

A comprehensive guide to logical SQL functions can be found in the online product documentation, and many of them will be familiar to you through working with Oracle, Microsoft, and other databases, as well as tools such as Microsoft Excel. However, a few are specific to Oracle Business Intelligence, and others may have a different syntax than what you are used to, so it is worth reviewing them at a high level if you are new to the platform.

NOTE
Not all logical SQL functions are available for use within the repository. See later chapters for functions that can be accessed when creating analyses using Oracle BI Answers, and see the product documentation for a full logical SQL reference guide.

Mathematical, String, and Calendar/Time Functions

Logical SQL contains the usual set of mathematical (ABS, COS, LOG, MOD, TRUNCATE, and so on) and string (CONCAT, LOCATE, equivalent to INSTR in Oracle, SQL, LENGTH, ASCII, and so on) functions found in most physical databases. You may find that the function names differ or that the syntax differs slightly from what you are used to with your particular physical database, but most logical function names are reasonably obvious, and the online documentation details the syntax should you need clarification.

Logical SQL has a number of functions used for returning the current date and time, and for manipulating date/time data types and converting to and from them. The syntax for these differs from most physical database platforms, though, and functions in this category that are worth noting include the following:

- **CURRENT_DATE, CURRENT_TIME, and CURRENT_TIMESTAMP (*integer*)**   These are for returning the current date, time, or timestamp (with a specified number of digits of precision), based on the system clock.

- **DAYNAME (*dateExpr*), DAYOFWEEK (*dateExpr*), MONTHOFQUARTER (*dateExpr*), DAYOFQUARTER (*dateExpr*), MONTHNAME (*dateExpr*), SECOND (*timeExpr*), and YEAR (*dateExpr*)**   These and other similar functions are used to extract elements of a date, time, or timestamp for use in a calculation.

- **TIMESTAMPADD (*interval, intExpr, timestamp*) and TIMESTAMPDIFF (*interval, timestamp1, timestamp2*)** These are for adding a specified number of days, months, seconds, or other intervals to a timestamp, or for calculating the number of intervals between two timestamps.

Conversion Functions

Logical SQL comes with a number of conversion functions for converting between data types, dealing with missing values, or performing Oracle BI–specific functions such as making use of variables or switching between columns:

- **IFNULL (*expr, value*)** This provides a value should the column contain a NULL (a missing value) and is equivalent to Oracle's NVL and other similar functions; for example, IFNULL (*company_name*, 'Allied Bakers').

- **CAST (*expr* | NULL as *data_type*)** This converts between two different data types, converting, for example, string columns into dates using the expression CAST (*commence_date* AS DATE).

- **VALUEOF (*variable_name*)** This is unique to logical SQL and allows a calculation to reference the value held in a repository variable; for example, VALUEOF (NQSESSION. *home_store*) accesses the value contained within the repository session variable *home_ store,* which would typically be set using an initialization block at the start of a new user session. There are various variable name formats that you need to use, depending on the type of repository variable being used, all of which are detailed later in this book.

- **INDEXCOL (*integer, expr_list*)** This returns the column or expression in *expr_list,* starting with 0 for the first entry in the list, based on the integer value passed to the function. This function can be useful, for example, when you wish to dynamically select a column from a list based on a value in a variable, allowing a single function to make use of a set of columns with the particular column selected at query time. For example, consider a situation where you wish to display data in either US dollars or UK pounds, based on the currency code set for a user. For users who wish to display values in US dollars, the session variable *PREF_CURRENCY* is set to 0, while for UK pounds it is set to 1. You could then use the INDEXCOL function to display the correct currency amount based on this variable:

  INDEXCOL (VALUEOF(NQ_SESSION.*pref_currency*), *usd_amount, gbp_amount*)

- **CHOOSE (*expr1, expr2, expr3 ... exprN*)** This performs a similar function to INDEXCOL but selects the column to be returned based on the first one in the list that the user has permissions to view, rather than an index value. For example, if four columns are defined that contain product data at total, category, type, and *product_name* level, and users are only given permission to access those columns appropriate to their role, the following function would return the first column in the list that the user had permission to view:

  CHOOSE (*product_total, product_category, product_type, product_name*)

  This function is again useful for displaying one particular column for a user based on the user's role, this time based on security permissions rather than an index value stored in a variable.

Aggregate and Running Aggregate Functions

Logical SQL has a number of aggregate and running aggregate functions equivalent to analytic functions found in databases such as Oracle Database. A subset of these, detailed here, are available for use within the Oracle BI Repository, while others, detailed in a later chapter, are available within Oracle BI Answers when you create an analysis:

- **RANK (*numExpr*), TOPN (*numExpr, integer*), MAX (*numExpr*), NTILE (*numExpr, numTimes*), and PERCENTILE (*numExpr*)** These and others are standard aggregation functions and are typically translated to the equivalent analytic functions on the source database platform (where supported).

- **MAVG (*numExpr, integer*), RSUM (*numExpr*)** These and other moving and rolling aggregation functions also typically translate to analytic functions on the source database.

Time-Series Functions

Logical SQL has three time-series functions that allow you to calculate the value of a measure a set number of periods ago, up to a particular period, or between two arbitrary periods. All of these functions require you to create a "time dimension," a logical dimension based on your own calendar table that has one or more chronological keys defined.

A chronological key has to satisfy three requirements:

- The members (values) in it must be sequential, with their own natural order and with members equally spaced out.

- The member list must be complete (that is, no missing months, days, and so on).

The Oracle BI Server then uses chronological keys to generate mathematically correct time period predictions, working out, for example, that January, 2011 plus two periods would equal March, 2011. Ideally, you will create chronological keys for each level in the time dimension, but you can get by with just a chronological key at the bottom (leaf) level. If you perform a time-series calculation at a hierarchy level that does not contain a chronological key, however, the BI Server is forced to aggregate up from the next level down that does have such a key, which can cause performance problems.

Earlier in this chapter we looked at how a logical dimension with a basic, balanced level-based hierarchy was set up. Time dimensions are a variation on these types of dimension but with additional metadata to assist with time-based calculations. Having a time dimension is a prerequisite for performing time-series functions, so to set one up, follow these steps:

1. Ensure that you have a logical table within a business model that contains calendar data columns (months, days, years, quarters, and so on), and that you have not previously associated with a logical dimension.

2. Using the Oracle BI Administration tool, navigate to the business model within the business model and mapping layer that contains the calendar logical table, right-click the business model, and select New Object | Logical Dimension | Dimension With Level-Based Hierarchy.

3. When the Logical Dimension dialog box is shown, type in the name (for example, Times), and within the Structure section, select the Time check box.

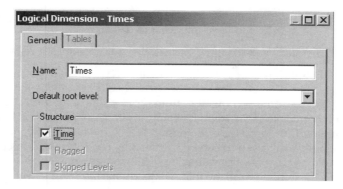

4. Now create the levels within the hierarchy as you would do for a regular level-based logical dimension, creating logical level keys for each level as usual. A typical hierarchy for a time dimension would contain levels for all times, years, quarters, months, and days.

5. As you have created a time dimension, you now have to designate at least one of the logical level keys as a chronological key, each of which must pass the three tests described earlier. To define a chronological key, double-click the level for which you wish to define the key, and when the Logical Level dialog box is shown, select the Keys tab. Locate the key in the key list that you wish to designate as the chronological key, and select the Chronological Key check box for it. You may have to scroll over to the right to see this check box.

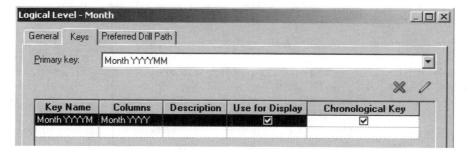

6. Repeat step 5 for any other chronological keys you wish to create for the time dimension.

Once you have defined at least one time dimension, you can then make use of Oracle Business Intelligence's time-series functions in your business model. These functions are listed here:

■ **AGO (*expr, time_dimension_level, periodoffset*)**   This is used for calculating the value of a measure a set number of time dimension levels (periods) ago. For example, this would calculate the value for revenue, one month ago:

Ago ("Sales"."Fact Sales"."Revenue" , "Sales"."Times"."Month" , 1)

Substitute other time dimension levels (ideally with chronological keys defined for them) and numbers of offset periods for other time-offset calculations.

■ **TODATE (*expr, time_dimension_level*)**   This is used for calculating the period to date value for a measure; for example, year to date:

TODATE ("Sales"."Fact Sales"."Revenue" , "Sales"."Times"."Year")

■ **PERIODROLLING (*measure, x, y [,hierarchy]*)**   This is a new time-series function introduced with the 11*g* release of Oracle Business Intelligence. It can be used to calculate the value of a measure from offset *x* to offset *y*, with *x* typically being a negative figure to indicate the past, and *y* being a number of periods on from *x*, potentially into the future. The period (time dimension level) type is either inferred from the period used in the analysis, or it can be specified by use of the AGGREGATE AT function. For example, to calculate the value of revenue for the previous month, the current month, and the next month, use the following formula:

PERIODROLLING ("Sales"."Fact Sales"."Revenue", -1, 1)

The keyword UNBOUND can be used to specify all periods that are available, that is, to the current period. For example, to calculate the value of revenue for the previous six months to now (assuming no data exists beyond the current period), use the following formula:

PERIODROLLING ("Sales"."Fact Sales"."Revenue", -6, UNBOUND)

The optional hierarchy clause can be used to specify a particular hierarchy if the logical dimension has more than one (for example, Times – Fiscal Year). For situations where you wish to directly specify the dimension level to which to apply the PERIODROLLING function, rather than infer it from the grain of the analysis, the AGGREGATE AT function can be embedded within the PERIODROLLING function, like this:

PERIODROLLING (AGGREGATE("Sales"."Fact Sales"."Revenue" AT *quarter*), -2, UNBOUND)

Care should be taken with the use of time-series functions, as the Oracle BI Server can generate quite complex and expensive SQL to return values using these functions. Because regular database SQL cannot normally return data from two time periods simultaneously using a single WHERE clause, the Oracle BI Server typically generates two or more queries to retrieve data for all time periods, the result sets for which it then either joins together internally in memory, or has the source database join if it has the capability to do so.

If you plan to make extensive use of time-series functions, consider using a multidimensional database such as Oracle Essbase, which supports time-series functions natively and can perform such calculations using far fewer database and system resources.

Evaluate (Database) Functions

While logical SQL comes with a large number of functions, including ones not normally found in physical database SQL, you may have a particular function that is unique to your particular database platform (or indeed one that you have written yourself) that you wish to make use of. Evaluate, or database, functions allow you to call native database SQL functions, along with any required parameters, and use them either to return a scalar (single) value, return an aggregatable value, make use of a database analytic function, or return a Boolean value for use in a query predicate:

■ **EVALUATE (*'db_function(%1...%N)'* [AS *data_type*] [, *column1, columnN*])**   This is typically used with logical table attribute (dimension) columns to apply functions to modify the column value. For example, the following would return the third to the fifth characters contained within the *product_category* column when used with an Oracle database:

EVALUATE ('SUBSTR(%1,%2,%3)', "Dim Products"."Product Category", 3, 5)

The first parameter in the EVALUATE function represents the database function name (either built in, or user-defined), followed by placeholders for the function parameters. The remaining parameters are then substituted for these placeholders when pushing the function down to the underlying physical database.

■ **EVALUATE_AGGR('*db_agg_function*(%1...%N)' [AS *data_type*] [, *column1*, *column*N)** This is typically used with fact table measures, and it returns a value that has been aggregated and can be used along with a GROUP BY clause. Measures defined using EVALUATE_AGGR must have their default aggregation rule set to Evaluate_Aggr so that the Oracle BI Server knows that an external function provides aggregation for this measure. Therefore, when modeling the repository, this function can only be used with physical columns within a logical table source mapping and cannot be used with a logical column expression.

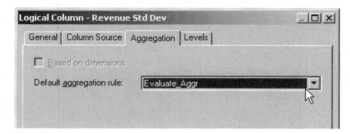

For example, the following function uses the Oracle Database STDDEV built-in function to calculate the standard deviation for the revenue measure:

Evaluate_Aggr ('STDDEV(%1)', "orcl"."
"."GCBC_SALES"."Fact_SALES"."FCAST_REV_AMT")

■ **EVALUATE_ANALYTIC ('*db_function*(%1...%N)' [AS *data_type*] [, *column1*, *column*N])** This is used for calling database analytic functions; for example, the following calculation returns the dense rank based on the revenue measure:

EVALUATE_ANALYTIC ('dense_rank() over(order by %1)' AS INT,
("Sales"."Fact Sales"."Revenue")

■ **EVALUATE_PREDICATE ('*db_function*(%1...%N)', [, *column1*, *column*N)** This is typically used within an analysis filter or within a logical table source filter clause, and it returns a Boolean value based on an expression evaluation. Its most common use is when handling data from an Oracle OLAP source, using database views over multidimensional objects in an analytic workspace.

Lookup Functions

A new type of function introduced with the 11*g* release of Oracle Business Intelligence is the lookup function. Lookups are a concept familiar to most BI and data loading developers, and typically they involve retrieving a descriptive value for a given ID value. You can do this fairly simply in the Oracle BI Repository by editing a logical table source mapping using the Add (+) button to add the physical tables to the table source mapping, and then using lookup columns provided by the new mapped physical table to populate corresponding ones in the logical table.

The lookup function introduced with Oracle Business Intelligence 11g is for a different scenario, though, in which, for one reason or another, you wish to isolate one part of a query from the main part.

There are two types of lookup functions that you can use in Oracle Business Intelligence 11g:

- **LOOKUP (DENSE (*lookupColumn, commaSepExprs*))**   This is used for lookups where you can be certain that a lookup value will be returned for every input value (equivalent to an inner join in SQL).

- **LOOKUP (SPARSE (*lookupColumn, alternateColumn, commaSepExprs*))**   This is where you cannot be certain that you will always get a lookup value returned (equivalent to a left outer join in SQL).

The LOOKUP function can also be used with both physical columns and logical columns when used in conjunction with a logical table designed as a lookup table. Lookup tables are just like regular logical tables; however, by designating them as lookup you remove the need for them either to play the role of fact tables (with other tables joining to them) or dimension tables (which join directly to fact tables).

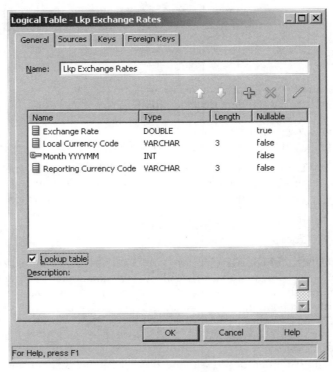

To explain how the LOOKUP function works, let's take a look at an example of the lookup function in use, where we wish to perform a currency conversion.

When converting currency measures in a fact table from a base currency to a reporting currency, a common approach is to create an exchange rate table in the physical layer, join this table to the physical table containing the fact table measures in the logical fact table source, drag the exchange rate to the logical fact table, and then multiply the base currency with it to obtain the reporting currency amount. This converts base currency to reporting currency successfully, but it has the disadvantage of including the join to the exchange rate physical table into the main SQL GROUP BY clause, giving you a physical SQL query looking like this log file excerpt:

```
WITH
SAWITH0 AS (select distinct T1114.EXCH_RATE as c1,
      T1128.PROD_CAT_DESC as c2,
      T1173.MONTH_YYYYMM as c3
from
      GCBC_SALES.TIMES T1173,
      GCBC_SALES.PRODUCTS T1128,
      GCBC_MAILORDER_SALES.EXCHANGE_RATES T1114,
      GCBC_MAILORDER_SALES.UK_MAILORDER_SALES T1120
where  ( T1114.MONTH_YYYYMM = T1120.MONTH_YYYYMM ...
```

If it were possible instead to perform the main aggregation of the query as one step, and then apply the exchange rates to the final, aggregated data set, your query might perform better and use fewer database resources. This would be where you could use a dense lookup function. By retrieving the exchange rate from either the physical exchange rate table or from a logical lookup table, let's say you use an expression such as the following, where the Lkp_EXCHANGE_RATES table contains a single exchange rate between the base currency and the reporting currency, keyed on the month and year:

```
LOOKUP (DENSE     "orcl".."GCBC_MAILORDER_SALES"
   ."Lkp_EXCHANGE_RATES"."EXCH_RATE" ,
"orcl".."GCBC_MAILORDER_SALES"
."Fact_UK_MAILORDER_SALES"."MONTH_YYYYMM" )
```

This would instead result in a physical SQL query looking like the following excerpt:

```
WITH
SAWITH0 AS (select sum(T1120.LOC_REV_AMT) as c1,
      T1128.PROD_CAT_DESC as c2,
      T1173.MONTH_YYYYMM as c3
from
      GCBC_SALES.TIMES T1173,
      GCBC_SALES.PRODUCTS T1128,
      GCBC_MAILORDER_SALES.UK_MAILORDER_SALES T1120
where  ( T1120.MONTH_YYYYMM = T1173.MONTH_YYYYMM
  and  T1120.PROD_ID = T1128.PROD_ID )
group by T1128.PROD_CAT_DESC, T1173.MONTH_YYYYMM),
...
SAWITH2 AS (select T1114.EXCH_RATE as c1,
      T1114.MONTH_YYYYMM as c2
from
      GCBC_MAILORDER_SALES.EXCHANGE_RATES T1114),
```

As you will see, the access to the exchange rate table has now moved outside of the main GROUP BY in the SQL query, potentially improving the efficiency of the query.

System Functions

In some situations you may wish to include the user's login details in a query, perhaps to help filter the data returned by the database. In others, you might want to return the name of the default subject area. To do this, you can use the two following system functions that do not have any arguments:

- **USER**   This returns the login name for a user.
- **DATABASE**   This returns then name of the default subject area.

Hierarchy Functions

There are also a number of functions introduced with the 11g release of Oracle Business Intelligence that you cannot normally access through the repository or through your own analyses in Oracle BI Answers but that are used by various parts of Oracle Business Intelligence to traverse hierarchies, create hierarchical groups, and perform aggregations. These include ISLEAF, ISPARENT, and ISDESCENDENT, and more details on these are included in the product documentation; however, you would not normally use them yourself in a column definition or Oracle BI Answers analysis.

The Calculation Wizard

In addition to creating calculations manually, you can also use the Calculation Wizard to automatically create calculations based on two measures and to create standard sets of derived measures. The Calculation Wizard is typically used in conjunction with time dimensions and time-series calculations, where your repository already contains time and date-offset measures and you now wish to generate standard derivations such as change and percentage change.

To see how the Calculation Wizard is used in practice, let's walk through a simple example.

Example: The Calculation Wizard in Use

The existing business model with which we will use the Calculation Wizard has a fact table containing four measures: Revenue, Cost, Sale Amount, and Sale Amount Month Ago. The Sale Amount Month Ago measure was defined using the AGO time-series function, and we will now use the Calculation Wizard to create standard derivations based on it and on the Sale Amount measure:

1. To start using the Calculation Wizard, right-click the first logical column fact table measure (in this case, Sale Amount) and select Calculation Wizard.

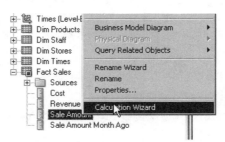

2. The Calculation Wizard – Introduction dialog box will then be shown. Click Next to proceed.

3. The Calculation Wizard – Select Columns dialog box will then be shown. For every column you select, the Calculation Wizard will then create a set of derived measures, comparing them to the original logical column fact table measure. Select the measure(s) that you wish to compare against the first measure (for example, Sale Amount Month Ago), and click Next to proceed.

4. The Calculation Wizard – New Calculations dialog box will then be shown.

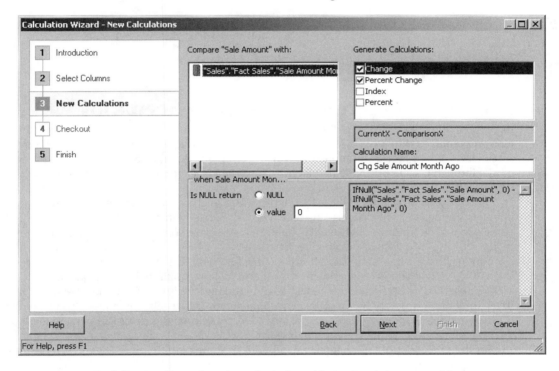

From the following list, select the calculations (derivations) that you wish to create:

■ **Change**   This subtracts the second column from the first (for example, Sale Amount – Sale Amount Month Ago).

■ **Percent Change**   This subtracts the second column from the first and shows the value as a percentage; for example: (100.0 * (Sale Amount – Sale Amount Month Ago) / Sale Amount Month Ago).

■ **Index**   This divides the first column by the second; for example: (1.0 * Sale Amount / Sale Amount Target).

■ **Percent**   This divides the first column by the second and expresses the result as a percentage; for example: (100 * (Sale Amount / Sale Amount Target)).

5. Each of the preceding calculation types has special cases, such as when one of the two numbers is missing, null, or above or below a certain value. For each calculation, click it and use the panel on the left-hand side of the wizard to specify any special handling for it.

6. Click Next, and then click Finish to complete the wizard. New calculations to match your selections and special handling instructions will then be created in your business model.

Advanced Repository Modeling Scenarios

In the preceding example, you have modeled a repository based on a single data source that is already organized dimensionally. This is a "best case" scenario where your data is probably in a single data mart or a data warehouse and all you are really doing is exposing this dimensional model through Oracle Business Intelligence's metadata layer so that you can analyze it in a dashboard.

Most projects aren't as simple as that, though. You might want to combine data from more than one data source, and some of this data may not be organized dimensionally in a star schema. To make queries run faster, your DBAs may have pre-aggregated some of your data into summary tables, and you may wish to incorporate these summary tables into your repository model.

You may have a transactional data source that you wish to use alongside your data warehouse in analyses so that you can combine historical and real-time data in the same query. Your hierarchies may not be simple, balanced, level-based hierarchies; instead, they may be organized in a parent-child (value-based) fashion or with ragged or skip levels. You might also want to create business models with more than one fact table and create analyses across all of them even when they do not necessarily share the same dimensionality.

For the remainder of this chapter, we will look at some of these more advanced repository modeling concepts and see how the Oracle BI Administrator tool can work with more complex relational data structures.

Repository Development Tools and Concepts

Before we get on to more advanced concepts such as federation, fragmentation, and aggregates, though, it's worth taking a moment to look at a few Oracle BI Administration tool concepts that are often misunderstood by beginners. We'll start by looking at a concept more or less unique to Oracle Business Intelligence and something that confuses a lot of beginners: logical table sources.

Logical Table Sources

When you create your first logical table in the business model and mapping layer, once you start dragging and dropping physical columns into your various logical tables, you may notice that entries start appearing in the Sources folder under your logical table. For simple business models that map to a single dimensional physical database, each folder may contain a single entry, but more complex models sourced from multiple physical tables may result in many entries within the Sources folder, each one representing a different possible data source for your logical table. So what do these entries represent?

Each entry within the Sources folder represents a logical table source. A logical table source is a set of mappings between logical columns in your business model and physical columns in the physical layer of the semantic model. When you drag-and-drop columns from the physical layer to a logical table, the Oracle BI Administration tool automatically creates the logical table source for you, or you can create it yourself if you wish to create these mappings manually. In cases where the physical tables you wish to map into the logical table are in fact part of a physical database already mapped into the logical table via an existing logical table source, in most cases you should extend the existing logical table source by editing it and adding it to the existing logical table source mapping, but in some instances you will actually want to create whole new logical table sources.

As an example, suppose that you have created a logical table called Fact Sales that is primarily sourced from a physical (alias) table called Fact_SALES, within a physical database and schema called orcl.GCBC_SALES. You create the outline (empty) logical table in the business model and mapping layer and then add the columns by dragging and dropping physical columns from the corresponding physical table to the logical Fact Sales table. If you double-click the single entry under the Fact Sales Sources folder and select the Column Mapping tab, you'll see that it contains the column mappings between these two metadata layers, as shown in Figure 3-16.

It is, however, possible to create more than one logical table source mapping for a logical table. This situation occurs when, as described in more detail later in this chapter, you wish to

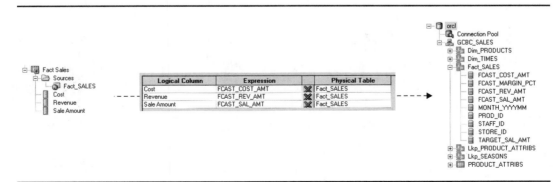

FIGURE 3-16.   *A single logical table source mapping*

add additional logical columns to a logical table that are sourced from a second, separate physical database, and you cannot of course just join these two tables together using a traditional SQL join clause.

Instead, the Oracle BI Server will need to generate a second, separate physical SQL query to obtain data from this second database's table, and the BI Server then needs to join together the two sets of returned queries before presenting the results back to the user using an Oracle BI Server capability called "horizontal federation."

Another reason that a logical table might have more than one logical table source is if the same set of logical columns can be sourced from physical databases containing data of differing levels of granularity. For example, the initial physical data source that you map in may be at the lowest level of detail, such as with transaction-level data, while a second source may contain the same data but pre-aggregated into a summary table or OLAP cube. In this case, the summary-level table source would need to be configured to be used only by the Oracle BI Server when the user requested an analysis at an appropriate level of aggregation using a feature known as "vertical federation." Figure 3-17 shows how these three sets of logical table source column mappings then provide the Oracle BI Server with three possible physical SQL statements that could be used to return data for a logical table, with the Oracle BI Server choosing which ones to use based on the particular columns requested and the level of detail requested by the analysis.

As mentioned, logical table sources can be configured to be used only when an analysis requests data at a particular level of detail or aggregation, and this setting is controlled by editing the table source properties and selecting the Content tab. This ability requires you to define logical dimensions in your business model, and if this logical table source provides the only

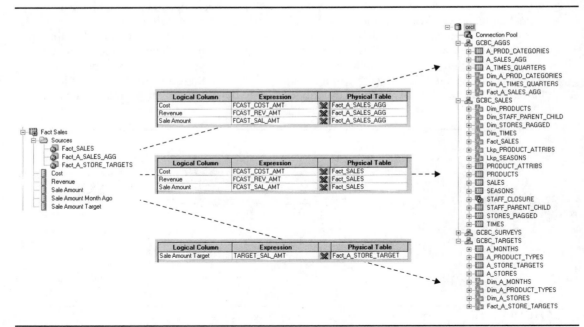

FIGURE 3-17. *Three logical table source mappings for a logical table*

source for a particular column and the user requests the column at a more detailed level of granularity, the Oracle BI Server will return a NULL or an error for the column, depending on what fact measures are chosen.

Typically, though, another table source will provide data at this lower level of detail, and the Oracle BI Server will switch to this other table source when the user requires data at the lower level of detail.

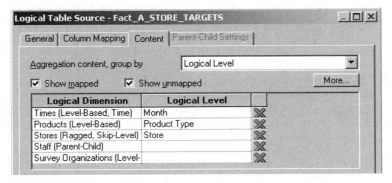

In addition to containing direct logical column to physical column mappings, logical table source mappings can contain transformations (expressions) that use the same logical SQL syntax used in logical column definitions. These transformations are often called "physical calculations" and are performed before column data is aggregated, as opposed to after column aggregation, as is the case with logical column calculations. See the section titled "Logical and Physical Calculations" within the wider "How the Oracle BI Server Performs Calculations" section for more details on this topic.

Online and Offline Repository Development

In the repository development example used in the "Creating the Oracle BI Repository" section earlier in this chapter, you worked offline with the repository file. That example described a situation where the Oracle BI Administration tool was connected directly to a repository (RPD) file and any changes you made to the repository were visible to you only and saved to the repository when you saved and closed the file. If you open a repository file offline, but the repository is also the online, default repository for your Oracle BI Server, the offline repository will open in read-only mode only.

To open a repository offline, start the Oracle BI Administration tool from the Windows Start menu. In the Administration tool, select File | Open | Offline, and then select the repository file to open.

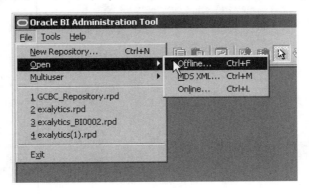

When you open a repository offline in this way, you are opening the repository in the traditional binary format. You can, however, save and then open the repository in the MDX XML format, which is typically used when checking a repository in, and out, of a source control system. MDX XML format repositories, and integration with source control systems, are covered in detail in Chapter 11.

After you have selected the repository file to open, you are then prompted to enter the repository password. The repository password secures the repository file, is set when you first create the repository, and can be changed after you have successfully opened the repository file from the Oracle BI Administration menu when the repository is accessed offline (File | Change Password).

Note that, unlike the 10*g* release of Oracle Business Intelligence, you should not open repository files directly by double-clicking them to open them directly within the Oracle BI Administration tool, as this bypasses a script that the Oracle BI Administration tool requires to configure various environment variables and will stop you from accessing physical database sources. Instead, always start the Oracle BI Administration tool from the Windows Start menu or run the script itself manually by calling the following command-line script (amending path names for your particular environment):

```
C:\WINDOWS\system32\cmd.exe "/cC:\Middleware\instances\instance1\
   bifoundation\OracleBIApplication\coreapplication\setup\bi-init.cmd
coreapplication_obis1 2 && C:\Middleware\Oracle_BI1\bifoundation\server\bin\
AdminTool.exe"
```

In addition to offline repository development, you can also connect online to a repository file. In this case, you connect to the repository not directly to the file, but through an ODBC connection to the Oracle BI Server, which in turn connects you to the default, online repository for that Oracle BI Server. When you work with a repository file online, you check in and check out repository objects as you work with them, and changes that you save are visible to users once the Oracle BI Presentation Server's copy of the repository has been refreshed and are visible to other developers after they reconnect online to the repository.

To connect to a repository online, open the Oracle BI Administration tool and select File | Open | Online from the application menu. You will then be presented with the Open Online dialog box, into which you should enter the repository password and the connection details for an account that has been granted the BI Administrator application role (or a comparable role if you have created additional application policies).

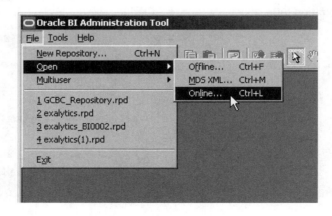

When you connect to a repository online, other developers can also be connected online and edit the same repository, checking in and checking out objects as they are edited. Oracle Corporation states that best practice is for only a single developer to be working online with each repository, as concurrent editing can cause performance issues for both developers and users, although the 11*g* release of Oracle Business Intelligence does support up to five developers working online at the same time (as opposed to a single developer in Oracle Business Intelligence 10*g*). However, be careful when editing a repository online because while the Oracle BI Administration tool tries to stop you from saving an invalid repository, if you do manage to do so it may bring down the Oracle BI server and stop other developers and users from working.

Editing a repository online does, however, give you access to a few functions that are not available when working offline:

- Managing scheduled jobs
- Managing user sessions
- Managing the query cache
- Managing clustered servers

Example: Uploading a Repository to the Oracle BI Domain   To upload a repository and place it online, use Oracle Enterprise Manager Fusion Middleware Control to perform the following steps:

1. Ensure that you have saved any offline changes to the repository and that you have used the Consistency Check Manager to ensure that there is at least one subject area in the repository that is valid and available for querying.

2. Using your web browser, navigate to Fusion Middleware Control using the URL http:// [*machine_name*]:7001/em. For example:

   ```
   http://obisrv1:7001/em
   ```

   Then enter the username and password of an account that has been assigned the BIAdministrator application role or a role with equivalent permissions.

3. When the Fusion Middleware Control website opens, navigate to the Farm_bifoundation_ domain menu on the left-hand side of the screen, open the Business Intelligence folder, and click the coreapplication menu entry. Then, when the coreapplication screen opens, click the Deployment | Repository tab and subtab to open the BI Server Repository screen.

4. Click the Lock And Configuration button within the Change Center area to lock the configuration of your Oracle BI Domain.

5. Click the Browse button within the Upload BI Server Repository area of the screen and navigate to the location on the file system when you have saved your offline repository. Double-click the repository file to select it, and then enter the repository password twice in the area under the repository file name.

6. Click the Apply button to record the selection of the repository file. Then click the Activate Changes button, and Fusion Middleware Control will upload the repository to the Oracle BI Server file system area and edit the internal configuration file (NQSConfig.INI) that references the file location.

| Change Center: | 🔒 Activate Changes | 🔄 Release Configuration |

| Overview | Availability | Capacity Management | Diagnostics | Security | **Deployment** |

| Presentation | **Repository** | Scheduler | Marketing | Mail |

BI Server Repository

This section shows the current installed RPD. You can use this section to configure a shared RPD location.

Default RPD   exalytics_BI0002

☐ Share Repository

RPD Publishing Directory [＿＿＿＿＿＿＿＿＿＿＿＿＿]

Upload BI Server Repository

Use this section to upload a new RPD and its password to your BI Server domain. You may also use this sectio upload.

Repository File   GCBC_Repository.rpd   [Update...]

Repository Password   [••••••••]

Confirm Password   [••••••••]

Note that this configuration file and others used by the BI Server component are described in more detail in Chapter 5.

7. To make the Oracle BI Server start using your new repository, switch to the Availability | Processes tab and subtab within Fusion Middleware Control and navigate to the BI Servers folder. Select the folder by clicking the box to the left of the folder name, and click the Restart Selected button. Click Yes when prompted, and then check that the activity completes successfully.

NOTE
If the restart of the BI Server components does not complete successfully, check the log files for the failure reason. In most cases, it is because you did not enter the correct repository password or the repository is invalid and cannot be brought online.

Administration Tool Utilities

There are a number of utilities that are available to you from the Tools | Utilities menu in the Oracle BI Administration tool. These are discussed next.

Replace Column or Table in Logical Table Source   Changes to the tables and columns in your physical data sources may require you to update the logical table source mappings in your semantic model to accurately reflect these changes. This update may be required because you are moving from one source database schema to another, or you may be switching database types and require your mappings now to point to this new source.

The Replace Column or Table in Logical Table Source utility works in the following way:

1. Using the Oracle BI Administration menu, select Tools | Utilities | Replace Column Or Table In Logical Table Source.

2. Then select whether you wish to change an individual physical column or a complete physical table.

3. Select the physical column or physical table that you wish to change from, as well as the one you wish to change to.

4. Review the list of physical columns that will be affected by the change.

5. Review the list of logical table sources that will be updated by the change.

6. Click Finish to complete the process and make the changes.

Once complete, any logical table sources that reference your original physical column or physical table will reference the new ones instead.

Oracle BI Event Tables   The Oracle BI Server query cache, when enabled, stores the results of analyses and uses these to return results quicker to subsequent analyses. For BI systems that are sourced from a data warehouse or other data source loaded using an ETL (extract, transform, load) process, the query cache can significantly improve the performance of queries by minimizing round-trips to the database data source.

One drawback with the query cache, though, is that it is not aware of when the underlying data source has been updated, potentially leaving its cached results out of date, or "stale." To address this issue, there are several ways in which the query cache can be invalidated or "flushed," one of which is the event polling table.

Starting with the 11g release of Oracle Business Intelligence, the event polling table is automatically created for you as S_NQ_EPT within the BIPLATFORM schema set up by the Repository Creation Utility. The Oracle BI Event Tables tool allows you to register this table with the repository so that the Oracle BI Server can then start polling it to see which tables need to have their entry in the query cache flushed. (Note that there are several other ways to manage cache entries, detailed later in this book.)

To use the Oracle BI Event Polling Tables tool, do the following:

1. Using the Oracle BI Administration tool, use the Import Metadata Wizard (File | Import Metadata) to import the S_NQ_EPT table into the semantic model physical layer from the BIPLATFORM schema (for example, DEV_BIPLATFORM).

2. Select Tools | Utilities | Oracle BI Event Tables from the menu.

3. Use the Oracle BI Event Tables dialog box to select the S_NQ_EPT table from the list of physical tables.

4. Use the "Polling Frequency every … minutes" text box to enter the number of minutes that the Oracle BI Server should wait between checks on the entries in this table.

5. Choose File | Save to save your changes. This configuration change will take effect as soon as you save the repository if it is running online, or whenever you upload the repository and take it online, if it is currently offline.

See Chapter 5 for more details on query caching.

Externalize Strings   For BI systems that are used by users in different regions, it can be useful to display table, column, subject area, and hierarchy names from the presentation layer in the user's particular language. The externalize strings feature allows the administration to select particular presentation layer objects and then either store names or descriptions for these objects in an external file, which you can then populate with versions of these names and descriptions in particular languages.

Setting up the externalize strings feature requires two steps:

1. First, select the presentation layer objects for which you wish to externalize names or descriptions by right-clicking the object in the Oracle BI Administration presentation layer and selecting either Externalize Display Names | Generate Custom Names or Externalize Descriptions | Generate Custom Descriptions. Nothing will be displayed on the screen when you make these selections, but the list of objects you have selected will be recorded by the Oracle BI Administration tool for use later.

2. Once you have marked the presentation layer objects that you wish to externalize strings for, run the Externalize Strings utility by selecting Tools | Utilities | Externalize Strings from the Oracle BI Administration menu. When the Externalize Strings dialog box is shown, select those subject areas that you wish to externalize into a file (you can select them all or just single ones, with each one being externalized into a separate file), and then click Save to save the externalized strings files.

Rename Wizard   When you create logical columns in your business model by dragging and dropping physical columns, your logical columns inherit the physical column names. Physical column names are often restricted by the source database to uppercase letters and may use underscores (_) and other characters in the place of spaces. If you wish to replace these system-generated logical column names with more user-friendly ones, you can either manually edit them yourself or you can use the Rename Wizard to automatically rename them using rules that you specify so that you can change, for example, a logical column name imported from your physical layer as PRODUCT_NAME to instead be called Product Name.

To use the Rename Wizard, follow these steps:

1. Using the Oracle BI Administration menu, select Tools | Utilities | Rename Wizard.

2. Using the Rename Wizard – Select Objects dialog box, select either the presentation layer objects or business model and mapping layer objects that you wish to rename. Click the Add button to add just the selected object, or the Add Hierarchy button to add the object plus all its dependent (child) objects.

3. On the Rename Wizard – Select Types screen, check or uncheck those object types contained in the object set you selected that you wish to rename.

4. On the Rename Wizard – Select Rules screen, create the rules that you wish to apply to your selected objects; for example, you may wish to capitalize all first letters, change letters to lowercase, add spaces, or replace one character with another. Click the Up and Down buttons to change the sequence in which the rules are applied.

5. Click Next to review the changes that will be applied, and then click Finish to make the changes.

Update Physical Layer   The tables, columns, and other objects in your source databases may have changed or been removed since you performed your initial metadata import. The Update Physical Layer utility performs a check on the physical databases listed in the physical layer of the semantic model and can update tables and column definitions that have changed, as well as remove tables from the physical layer that are no longer present in the source database. Note that this utility does not alter table keys in your physical layer, nor does it add tables or columns that are not in the semantic model but are now present in the source database.

To run the Update Physical Layer Wizard, do the following:

1. From the Oracle BI Administration menu, select Tools | Utilities | Update Physical Layer.

2. There will normally now be a short pause while all the source databases are scanned. The Update Physical Layer Wizard will then be displayed, and the Select Connection Pool screen will be displayed if you have more than one connection pool defined in your physical layer. Use this screen to select which connections to use to connect to your source databases.

3. The Update screen will then be displayed. Every object that is present in the physical layer but changed or missing in the source database will then be displayed. Select the check box for each item you wish to update.

4. The Checkout screen will then confirm the action to perform on each physical layer object. Click Back to return to the previous screen and amend your choice of objects to update, or click Finish to perform the selected actions.

The Update Physical Layer Wizard relies on your connection pool names staying constant between your initial metadata import and your physical model now. It looks for objects within the same connection pool name, with the same object name, and checks to see if the object still exists in the source database or if the data type or length has changed. As an alternative to this utility, you can select File | Import Metadata from the Oracle BI Administration menu and reimport your source database metadata, but doing so will automatically overwrite any objects that have changed since import and will not prompt you to confirm these changes before making them.

Repository Documentation   Given that there are three layers of object metadata in the repository, it is useful to be able to generate a "lineage" report that shows how each presentation layer object is sourced through the repository model, and equally how the removal or change of a physical layer object could affect downstream objects in the repository. The Repository Documentation utility goes some way to providing this lineage information, though it does not extend to Oracle BI Presentation Server objects and really requires you to load this information into a database to make much use of it.

To generate this repository documentation, take the following steps:

1. From the Oracle BI Administration menu, select Tools | Utilities | Repository Documentation.

2. When prompted, select a file system location and document format to output to.

The Repository Documentation utility will then generate a file that, for each presentation layer object, lists the presentation table, business model and mapping layer table and column, any derivations, and the same for the corresponding physical layer objects and derivations. You can then load this information into a relational database to track the lineage of your objects and any changes to them over the development lifecycle.

Generate Metadata Dictionary   The Generate Metadata Dictionary utility generates a set of files that can be hosted in the Oracle Business Intelligence environment and can provide more information to users on the data in their BI system. Generating and integrating the metadata dictionary is a two-stage process; first, you use the Generate Metadata Dictionary utility to create the dictionary, and then you configure the Oracle BI Presentation Server to make use of it.

For example, consider a situation where you have a repository called GCBCRepository.rpd that is currently deployed as the online, default repository, for which you wish to generate a metadata dictionary. To create a metadata dictionary for this repository, follow these steps:

1. Before you start, use your web browser to navigate to Fusion Middleware Control using, for example, the URL http://obisrv1:7001/em and log in using the Weblogic administration username and password. Then navigate to the coreapplication entry in the Business Intelligence folder in the left-hand menu and select Deployment | Repository from the tabs and subtabs. Within the BI Server Repository section, make a note of the name of the default, online repository; for example, this may be called GCBCRepository_BI0031.

2. Using the Oracle BI Administration tool, open a copy of that same repository file offline (using file system tools if necessary to make a copy first), and then select Tools | Utilities | Generate Metadata Dictionary.

3. When prompted, enter a location to save the metadata dictionary files to, such as c:\files.

4. Locate the created folder structure within the directory that you specified. The folder created by the utility should be named the same as your repository, without the .rpd suffix; in this example, it would be named c:\files\GCBCRepository.

   Rename this subfolder to match the currently deployed name of the repository, as noted in the first step. In this example, the folder would therefore be renamed to C:\files\ GCBCRepository_BI0031. Copy the contents of this renamed folder to the analyticsRes folder under your Oracle Business Intelligence installation so that the dictionary files are located here:

   C:\Middleware\instances\instance1\bifoundation\
   OracleBIPresentationServicesComponent\coreapplication_obips1\analyticsRes\
   GCBCRepository_BI0031

5. Next, you need to deploy the analyticsRes folder within the WebLogic Server Admin Console. To do this, using your web browser, navigate to http://obisrv1:7001/console (changing the host name for your particular installation) and log in using the Weblogic

administration user account and password. Then navigate to the Deployments entry under the Domain Structure menu, click this entry, and then click the Lock And Edit Configuration button. To deploy the analyticsRes folder, within the Summary Of Deployments area, click the Install button. Then, using the directory browser, navigate to the area in the file system in which the analyticsRes folder resides, and click the radio button to the side of it to select it. Then click Next, select "Install this deployment as an application," and click Next again. Under the Clusters section, select bi_server1 as the deployment location. Finally, in the Source Accessibility section on the next screen, select "I will make the deployment accessible from the following location," click Next, and then click Finish.

6. On the left-hand side of the Administration Console screen, click the Activate Changes button. Once the changes are confirmed as activated, return to the Deployments entry under the Domain Structure menu on the left-hand side of the screen, and select the check box to the left of the analyticsRes entry that now exists. Locate the Start button above all of the deployment entries, click it, and select Servicing All Requests. When prompted, click Yes to start deployments, and then check that the state of the service is now listed as Active.

7. You can now check that your metadata dictionary is available by calling it though a URL. Use your web browser again, this time to access the dictionary, using in this example the following URL:

http://obisrv1:9704/analyticsRes/GCBCRepository/TreeIndex.xml

The Top Level Repository Objects screen in the metadata repository should now show in your browser.

8. Next, you need to configure the Oracle BI Presentation Server to make use of this dictionary file. To do this, using a text editor, open the instanceconfig.xml file typically found in the following location:

C:\Middleware\instances\instance1\config\OracleBIPresentationServicesComponent\ coreapplication_obips1

Add the following text just before the </ServerInstance> tag at the end of the file:

```
<SubjectAreaMetadata><DictionaryURLPrefix>
http://localhost:9704/analyticsRes/</DictionaryURLPrefix>
<!--CollateSubjectAreaNames>true</CollateSubjectAreaNames-->
</SubjectAreaMetadata>
```

Save the file once you have made this change.

9. Use your web browser to navigate to Fusion Middleware Control, using, for example, the URL http://obisrv1:7001/em and log in using the Weblogic administration username and password. Then, navigate to the coreapplication entry in the Business Intelligence folder in the left-hand menu and select Capacity Management | Availability from the tabs and subtabs. With the Availability tab showing, select the Presentation Servers entry and click the Restart Selected button to restart the Oracle BI Presentation Server.

10. Now when you create an analysis you will see an Open Metadata Dictionary icon above the subject areas available for your criteria.

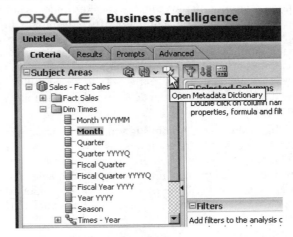

When you select a subject area column or other object and click the Open Metadata Dictionary button, your web browser will display a metadata report for the object in question.

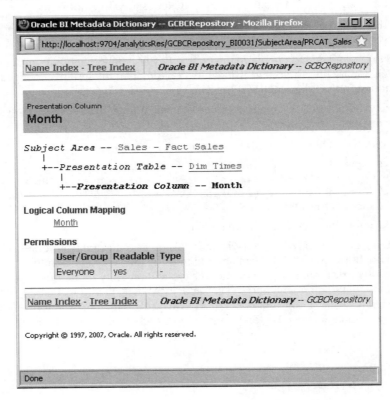

Remove Unused Physical Objects   The Remove Unused Physical Objects utility can be used to remove physical tables, views, and other objects from the semantic model if they are no longer present in the underlying data source. Removing unused objects can be useful, as it reduces the size of the repository file and consequently reduces the memory usage of the Oracle BI Server.

To use this utility, do the following:

1.   Using the Oracle BI Administration tool, open your repository online or offline, and then select Tools | Utilities | Remove Unused Physical Objects.

2.   The Oracle BI Administration tool will then scan your data sources, as defined through the physical layer of the Oracle BI Repository, and present you a list of candidate objects to be removed.

3.   Select the check box for any objects you wish to remove, and click the Yes button to remove them from the repository.

Aggregate Persistence   The Aggregate Persistence Wizard can automate the production and population of aggregate (summary) tables, which are then automatically mapped into your semantic model using the vertical federation feature described later in this chapter. Aggregate tables can improve the response time of your analyses through precomputing common aggregations, and the Oracle BI Server will automatically make use of them when the analysis requests the appropriate level of aggregation.

The Aggregate Persistence Wizard creates physical database tables, along with scripts, to create indexes and then populate these tables. As with the parent-child relationship table created by the Parent-Child Relationship Table Wizard, you run the table creation script first and then rerun the population script every time the underlying data changes. As such, it is best suited to scenarios where you control the loading of data into your system (for example, a data warehouse) and can therefore trigger the calling of the aggregate table refresh routine after each data load.

If you are using a database such as Oracle Database 10g Enterprise Edition or higher, you might also want to consider having the database create your aggregate tables for you, in the form of materialized views, which the database will then automatically use through a feature called query rewrite. The Aggregate Persistence Wizard is therefore particularly well suited to situations such as the following:

- You are not able, or allowed, to create materialized views (or equivalent) in your source database.

- You wish to store the aggregates in a separate database to your main data set, potentially using a different database type.

- You are using, for example, the Standard Edition of the Oracle Database, and advanced features such as materialized views are not available to you.

- You wish to create aggregate tables for logical fact table mapping to multiple source databases but store the aggregates in a single location.

To use the Aggregate Persistence Wizard, follow these steps:

1.   Using the Oracle BI Administration tool, open your repository either online or offline. Then, select Tools | Utilities | Aggregate Persistence from the application menu.

2.   At the Aggregate Persistence – Select File Location dialog box, enter a complete path and file to which the aggregate persistence scripts will be saved. Select the "Generate DDL in

a separate file" check box if you wish to generate the table creation script separate to the table population script (normally they are combined into one), for example, if you wish to amend this script before running it.

3. At the Aggregate Persistence – Select Business Measures dialog box, select the business model, and then the fact table measures that you wish to aggregate.

4. At the Aggregate Persistence – Select Levels dialog box, select the logical dimension levels at which you wish to aggregate these measures. Select the Use Surrogate Key? check box only if the primary key for the logical level is a noninteger or extends over several columns.

5. At the Aggregate Persistence – Select Connection Pool dialog box, select the physical database, catalog/schema, and connection pool that connect to the physical database where you wish to create the aggregate tables.

6. Click Next and then click Finish to create the aggregate table scripts.

At this point, while the scripts have been generated, you need to actually execute them to create the aggregate tables and map them into the semantic model. Unlike the parent-child relationship table scripts that you execute through your database command-line utility, the scripts generated by this utility are executed by the Oracle BI Server so that it can also use them to automatically map the tables into your repository's physical layer.

To run the script(s), you need to use the nqcmd.exe utility, which can normally be found within your Oracle BI installation, typically in the following location:

C:\Middleware\Oracle_BI1\bifoundation\server\bin\nqcmd.exe

Before you run this command, though, you must run the initialization command file, bi-init.cmd, typically found here:

C:\Middleware\instances\instance1\bifoundation\OracleBIApplication\coreapplication\setup\bi-init.cmd

The nqcmd.exe utility is run from the command shell launched from this command file.

The repository to which you wish to deploy the aggregates needs to be online when you run this utility. To run nqcmd.exe, you must supply five parameters:

- The *ODBC DSN name* for the connection to the BI Server hosting the repository (for example, coreapplication_OH1094451294)

- A *username* and *password* (for example, weblogic/welcome1) that connects to Oracle Business Intelligence and that has the BIAdministrator (or equivalent) application role granted to it

- The *name of the input file,* which will be the name of the file just generated by the Aggregate Persistence utility

- The *name of an output file* to which to output the results of the command

You should also enable query logging for this user so that you can see if any queries have failed or exited abnormally.

For example, to run the nqcmd.exe utility for your script, you might run the following command:

```
C:\Middleware\Oracle_BI1\bifoundation\server\bin\nqcmd.exe -d coreapplica-
tion_OH1094451294 -u weblogic -p welcome1 -s c:\files\agg_wiz.txt -o c:\files\
agg_wiz_output.txt
```

Your aggregate tables will then be generated and automatically mapped in your semantic model.

Advanced Repository Modeling Concepts

In the "Creating a Repository" example in this chapter, we looked at creating a simple business model from a single data source that was organized into a star schema with simple, balanced, level-based hierarchies. This is the most straightforward type of data source to model against, and if possible you should work closely with the data warehousing team within your organization to ensure that the data source for your BI system is a single, conformed, dimensional model, as this makes your job easier and also maximizes the performance of your system.

Real life often is not as simple as this, though, and you may instead have more than one dimensional data source to work with (for example, a set of departmental or country data marts), or you may need to integrate data with differing levels of granularity. Luckily for you, Oracle Business Intelligence 11*g* comes with a range of features for integrating disparate data sources into a single semantic model, together with features for integrating historic data as well as real-time data and handling more complex hierarchy types than simple, balanced, level-based hierarchies.

Ragged and Skip-Level Hierarchies

So far in this chapter, we have modeled simple, level-based balanced hierarchies for our logical dimensions. A *level-based* hierarchy is one that has distinct, named levels within the hierarchy (for example, Product Category, Product Type, and Product Name), and *balanced* refers to the fact that each branch of the hierarchy descends to the same level and each member has a parent at the level immediately above it in the hierarchy.

In some situations, though, this may not be the case. Consider a situation where a store network has to be modeled, which has the following named levels:

- All Stores, the grand total level
- Regions
- Stores
- Concessions

In our store network, however, the following special situations occur:

- Only certain stores are responsible for concessions, meaning that some branches of the hierarchy have a *leaf* member at the concession level, while some stop at the branch level.
- One concession is so large that it reports directly into the regional office.
- Both stores and concessions can have sales recorded against them.

When the hierarchy has leaf members at differing levels, we call this a *ragged hierarchy*. When members miss a level when linking to their parent, this is called a *skip-level hierarchy*. Figure 3-18 shows a typical ragged and a typical skip-level hierarchy, based on our store network.

Oracle Business Intelligence 11*g* allows you to create logical dimensions with both ragged and skip-level hierarchies, though care should be taken with these as they can have performance implications in some cases.

In the example in Figure 3-19, a physical table called STORES_RAGGED has been defined that contains columns for each level in the hierarchy, together with a surrogate (synthetic) key that links the table to a fact table called SALES. Figure 3-19 shows the table, as displayed in Oracle SQL*Developer, with the columns that we will use for the logical dimension.

Note how some rows feature concession IDs and descriptions that are null; these represent either stores with no concessions linked to them or a single record for a store that does have a concession for the purposes of recording sales specifically against the store. One other row features a concession but not a store; this is a skip-level member and represents a concession that reports directly into the regional office. Finally, if you are working with ragged and/or skip-level hierarchies, you will need to ensure that all of the levels for your hierarchy are contained in a single table, rather than in normalized, snowflaked tables, as the ID columns that would normally contain level keys may in fact contain NULL values and are therefore not valid as keys.

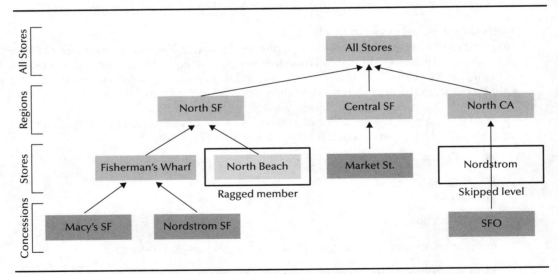

FIGURE 3-18. *A ragged and a skip-level hierarchy*

	CONCESSION_ID	CONCESSION_NAME	STORE_ID	STORE_NAME	REGION_ID	REGION_NAME	STORE_PK
1	(null)	(null)	3	Geary Street	1	Central SF	3
2	(null)	(null)	1	Market Street	1	Central SF	1
3	(null)	(null)	4	North Beach	2	North SF	4
4	(null)	(null)	5	Taylor Street	2	North SF	5
5	(null)	(null)	2	Fishermans Wharf	3	North SF	2
6	102	SFO	(null)	(null)	3	North CA	10
7	(null)	(null)	6	Walnut Creek	3	North CA	6
8	(null)	(null)	11	San Diego	4	South CA	11
9	(null)	(null)	9	Santa Clara	4	South CA	9
10	(null)	(null)	7	Anaheim	4	South CA	7
11	(null)	(null)	8	Los Angeles	4	South CA	8
12	(null)	(null)	14	Embarcadero	5	East SF	14
13	(null)	(null)	15	10th Avenue	6	West SF	15
14	(null)	(null)	16	Haight Street	6	West SF	16
15	(null)	(null)	12	Chicago	7	Other USA	12
16	(null)	(null)	13	New York	7	Other USA	13
17	100	Nordstroms, SF	2	Fishermans Wharf	2	North SF	17
18	101	Macys, SF	2	Fishermans Wharf	2	North SF	18
19	103	Macys, NY	13	New York	7	Other USA	19

FIGURE 3-19. *A relational table used as the source for a ragged/skip-level hierarchy*

To create a ragged and skip-level hierarchy that uses this physical table as a source, follow these steps, which are the same as for creating a balanced, level-based hierarchy, apart from marking the hierarchy as ragged and/or skip-level:

1. Using the Oracle BI Administration tool, ensure that the physical table containing the data for your ragged/skip-level hierarchy is present in the physical layer of the semantic model, that the table is aliased, and that you have defined a key for the physical table (based on the STORE_PK column in the example we are using). Then, using this key, create a physical join between this table and the fact table it is associated with.

2. Within your business model, create a logical table to correspond with the physical dimension table, ensure that you have defined a logical key for it, and create a join between this logical table and your logical fact table. So far, this process has been identical to how you would prepare your business model for a regular balanced, level-based hierarchy.

3. To create the logical dimension that will contain the ragged and skip-level hierarchy, right-click the business model containing the logical table you just created and select New Object | Logical Dimension | Dimension With Level-Based Hierarchy.

4. When the Logical Dimension dialog box is shown, within the Structure area select the Ragged check box if the hierarchy is ragged and the Skipped Levels check box if the hierarchy features skip levels. Note that you can select both of these boxes if required, but these options are grayed out and unavailable if you first select the Time check box, as time dimensions must have balanced hierarchies.

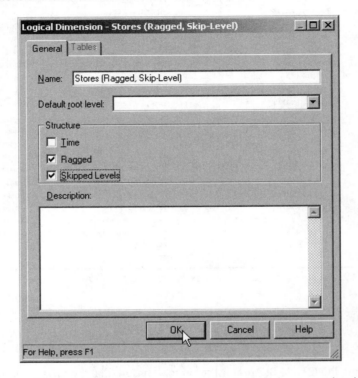

5. Now, as you did for the balanced hierarchy earlier in this chapter, right-click the new logical dimension and select New Object | Logical Level. This will be your grand total level, so name it appropriately and select the Grand Total Level check box.

6. Now, as with balanced, level-based hierarchies, right-click the grand total level and select New Object | Child Level. Name the level, enter the estimated number of distinct members at this level, and then repeat this step to create the remainder of the level, down to the concession level in the case of our example.

7. Drag-and-drop columns from the dimension logical table onto the levels that you just created, right-click them, and select New Logical Level Key to create the level keys.

8. Finally, drag-and-drop the logical dimension table (not the hierarchy) to your corresponding subject area in the presentation layer. Your hierarchy and logical table are now ready for use within an analysis.

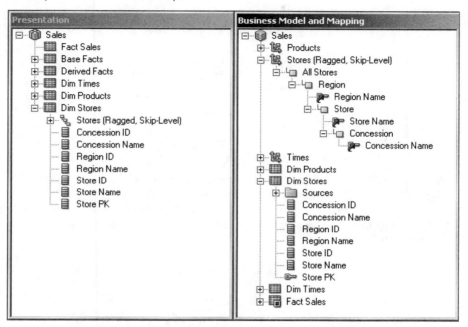

Performance Implications of Ragged and Skip-Level Hierarchies With the steps for creating a ragged and/or skip-level hierarchy so similar to those used for a balanced, level-based hierarchy, as well as the fact that the ragged and skip-level settings work fine for hierarchies that are in fact balanced, you might conclude that the safest option when creating level-based hierarchies is to mark all level-based hierarchies this way. There are, however, performance implications when using ragged and skip-level hierarchies in combination with another new feature in Oracle Business Intelligence 11*g* called hierarchical columns.

For example, consider a situation where you have created an analysis using the Products logical dimension defined earlier in this chapter, along with the Amount Sold measure. Using a pivot table view, the user can drill-down from the top of the product hierarchy (All Products) down to the next level, in this case Product Category.

Title	

Pivot Table	

Products	Amount Sold
⊟ All Products	350
⊞ Bread	286
⊞ Drinks	2
⊞ Gifts	13
⊞ Snacks	10

If you have query logging (described later in this chapter in the section "How Does the Oracle BI Server Handle Vertically Federated Data?") enabled for this account and you examine the physical SQL generated for the analysis, an excerpt of the SQL would look like this:

```
WITH
SAWITH0 AS (select distinct sum(T71.FCAST_SAL_AMT) as c1
from
      SALES T71 /* Fact_SALES */ ),
SAWITH1 AS (select sum(T71.FCAST_SAL_AMT) as c1,
      T52.PROD_CAT_DESC as c2
from
      PRODUCTS T52 /* Dim_PRODUCTS */ ,
      SALES T71 /* Fact_SALES */
where  ( T52.PROD_ID = T71.FCAST_COST_AMT )
group by T52.PROD_CAT_DESC),...
```

Note how only those columns required for the query are included in the WHERE clause and only a regular GROUP BY is used to provide the aggregation.

If we now create a similar analysis involving the ragged and skip-level hierarchy, the resulting pivot table would look the same, as there are no ragged members or skip levels at this point in the hierarchy.

Stores (Ragged, Skip-Level)	Amount Sold
⊟ All Stores	350
⊞ Central SF	81
⊞ North CA	30
⊞ North SF	124
⊞ Other USA	18
⊞ South CA	66
⊞ West SF	31

However, if you examine the physical SQL generated by the query, you will note how, in this instance, all of the levels and therefore columns in the hierarchy are included in the query and how GROUPING_ID / GROUPING_SETS has been used to provide the aggregations:

```
WITH
SACOMMON26514 AS (select sum(T71.FCAST_SAL_AMT) as c1,
      max(T414.REGION_NAME) as c2,
      max(T414.CONCESSION_NAME) as c3,
      max(T414.STORE_NAME) as c4,
      T414.REGION_NAME as c5,
      T414.STORE_NAME as c6,
      T414.CONCESSION_NAME as c7,
      grouping_id(T414.REGION_NAME,
      T414.STORE_NAME,
      T414.CONCESSION_NAME) as c8
```

```
from
     STORES_RAGGED T414 /* Dim_STORES_RAGGED */ ,
     SALES T71 /* Fact_SALES */
where   ( T71.STORE_ID = T414.STORE_PK )
group by grouping sets (
     (),
     (T414.REGION_NAME),
     (T414.STORE_NAME, T414.REGION_NAME),
     (T414.CONCESSION_NAME, T414.STORE_NAME, T414.REGION_NAME))),
...
```

GROUPING_ID and GROUPING_SETS are used across all level-based hierarchies when hierarchical columns are used in a pivot table and when the analysis requires subtotals and totals across multiple hierarchies in levels. They are used much earlier in ragged and skip-level hierarchies, however, because for the following reasons the Oracle BI Presentation Server has to consider more than just the immediate levels selected for analysis:

- A member being displayed may in fact be a ragged member, and the Presentation Server will need to indicate that no more drilling to detail can be performed on that branch of the hierarchy.
- A particular hierarchy branch may feature a skip level, and therefore members from the lower levels in the hierarchy may need to be displayed if its parent is skipped in the level being displayed.

This means that, in practice, when an analysis uses a ragged or skip-level hierarchy, all of the levels and columns for a query will be included in the physical SQL to retrieve that hierarchy's columns from the database, and results will be aggregated across all of these levels to deal with these situations. Therefore, you may find that queries using ragged and skip-level hierarchies generate more expensive database queries than those with balanced, level-based hierarchies, so you should reserve use of this feature for those logical dimensions that actually feature ragged or skip-level hierarchies.

Parent-Child Hierarchies

In addition to supporting ragged and skip-level hierarchies, the 11*g* release of Oracle Business Intelligence now also supports parent-child, or value-based, hierarchies. Instead of having the hierarchy defined by separate columns in the database, one for each level, parent-child hierarchies define the hierarchy through a member ID and a parent ID, with the parent ID recursively joining back to the member ID.

Consider a situation where we have a STAFF_PARENT_CHILD table in the physical layer of the semantic model, as shown in Figure 3-20, that features five columns:

- **STAFF ID** This is the key for the table and ID for individual staff members.
- **STAFF_NAME** This is the descriptive column for the staff member.
- **STAFF_GENDER and STAFF_DOB** These are attributes for the staff member.
- **MANAGER_ID** This is a column that references the STAFF_ID column and contains the staff ID for the staff member's manager.

STAFF_DOB	STAFF_GENDER	STAFF_NAME	STAFF_ID	MANAGER_ID
1	01-DEC-40	M	Pierre Houdan	1	(null)
2	10-JAN-72	F	Diana Daves	2	45
3	12-OCT-80	M	Jose Nigro	3	46
4	28-MAY-81	F	Doris Lines	4	45
5	14-SEP-87	M	Antony Bogart	5	46
6	19-JUL-87	M	Earl Hodson	6	46
7	16-DEC-78	M	Walter Bridgeman	7	47
8	14-AUG-71	F	Kara Grossman	8	48
9	15-APR-87	M	Hasty Gonzales	9	48
10	11-SEP-88	M	Adam Rumph	10	48
11	04-NOV-55	F	Edith Lofton	11	47
12	29-JUL-84	M	Larry Nolen	12	48
13	16-DEC-78	F	Cassandra Barry	13	51
14	22-DEC-76	M	Russell Durkee	14	51
15	18-FEB-80	M	Douglas Bader	15	49
16	01-DEC-82	F	Mildred Butters	16	50
17	03-JAN-90	M	Geoff Blowe	17	2
18	03-OCT-89	M	Archie Krigbaum	18	3
19	23-APR-87	M	Malcom Doig	19	4
20	25-APR-87	M	Vernice Kennebeck	20	4
21	23-SEP-87	M	Archie Toto	21	5
22	01-MAR-89	M	Alton Mutu	22	5

FIGURE 3-20.   *The source table for a parent-child hierarchy*

This type of table and hierarchy can be modeled within the Oracle Business Intelligence 11*g* semantic model. To assist with using it in analyses, a parent-child relationship table, or "closure" table, is generated for you by the Oracle BI Administration tool when defining the hierarchy. This parent-child relationship table then has to be maintained by you, using a supplied SQL script whenever the underlying data in the dimension physical table changes.

To create a logical dimension with a parent-child hierarchy, follow these steps:

1.   Using the Oracle BI Administration tool, select File | Import Metadata to import the physical table metadata for the source table into the semantic model, create an alias for it (for example, Dim_STAFF_PARENT_CHILD) and create a table key. Ensure that there is no foreign key defined for this physical table from the Parent ID to the Member ID column, as this may raise warnings from the consistency checker. Then, using the dimension table key, create a physical join between this table and the fact table it is associated with.

2. Within your business model, create a logical table to correspond with the physical dimension table, ensure that you have defined a logical key for it, and create a join between this logical table and your logical fact table. So far, this process has been identical to how you would prepare your business model for a regular balanced, level-based hierarchy.

3. To create the logical dimension that will contain the parent-child hierarchy, right-click the business model containing the logical table you just created, and select New Object | Logical Dimension | Dimension With Parent-Child Hierarchy.

4. The Logical Dimension dialog box will then be shown. Check and update if necessary the name chosen for the hierarchy, and check that the Member Key column is set to the primary key for the logical table (the default setting). Then, using the Browse button next to the Parent Column text box, select the parent ID (for example, Manager ID) for this parent-child hierarchy.

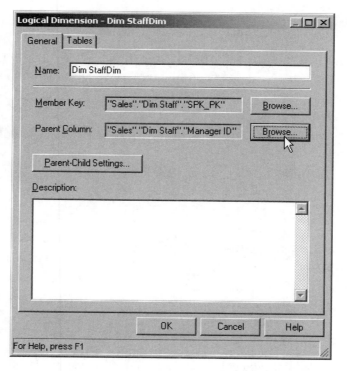

5. With the Logical Dimension dialog box still open, click the Parent-Child Settings button to create the parent-child relationship table. The Parent-Child Relationship Table Settings dialog box will then be displayed.

6. With the Parent-Child Relationship Table Settings dialog box open, highlight the row for your logical table and click the Create Parent-Child Relationship Table button to the right of it (the middle button in the list of buttons, with a "new table" icon).

7. The Generate Parent-Child Relationship Table Wizard will then open. Type in a name and file system location for the DDL Script To Create Parent-Child Relationship Table and DDL Script To Populate Parent-Child Relationship Table settings. Note that the wizard will not let you progress to the next screen unless the file system directory you specify actually exists.

8. On the next screen of the wizard, type in a name for the table (for example, STAFF_CLOSURE) and select the connection pool that corresponds with the physical database that you intend to store the parent-child relationship table in. Once the wizard completes, this physical database within your semantic model will be updated to include the parent-child relationship table that you are now creating.

9. Review the scripts that the wizard will create for you, and click the Finish button to create the scripts and place them in the file system location you specified. You will then return to the Parent-Child Relationship Table Settings dialog box. Click OK to return to the Logical Dimension dialog box, and click OK again to return to the main Oracle BI Administration screen.

10. Now you have to run the two scripts generated by the previous steps. To do this, start a command-line prompt for your database so that you can run the scripts. For example, if you are using an Oracle database, select Run from your Windows Start menu, type in **cmd.exe**, and then enter the following commands (assuming that you have saved the scripts to the c:\files directory, you have chosen to store the closure table in the GCBC_SALES/password schema, and your TNSNAMES net service name is "ORCL":

```
cd c:\files
sqlplus gcbc_sales/password@orcl
@create_closure_table.sql
@pop_closure_table.sql
commit;
```

11. Drag-and-drop the logical dimension table to the subject area within your presentation layer containing the other data for your business model. Save your repository, and use the consistency checker to ensure that there are no warnings or errors for the repository.

If you take a look at the logical dimension created by the Oracle BI Administration tool, you will notice that it has two levels within the hierarchy, one for the grand total level and one for the detail level, containing all of the keys and attributes for the logical dimension table. The presentation hierarchy within the subject area presentation table has just a single entry to show that when it is to be included in an analysis you work with just a single object that recursively drills into itself.

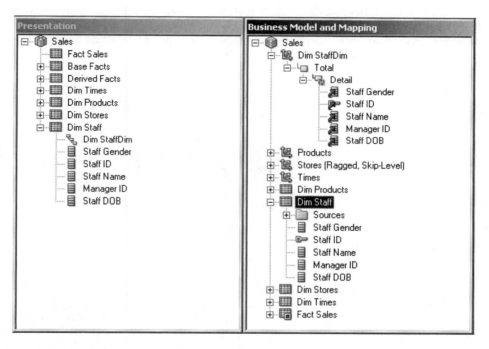

Showing the Member Description Rather Than the Member ID in a Parent-Child Hierarchical Column If you were to now publish your repository online and query the hierarchy in an analysis, you will notice that, as the STAFF_ID and MANAGER_ID columns were used for the member ID and parent ID for the parent-child hierarchy, it's actually the STAFF_ID that is shown in the hierarchical column member description, rather than the staff member's name. To ensure that the hierarchical column shows the descriptive column rather than the ID column, follow these steps:

1. Using the Oracle BI Administration tool, navigate to the presentation hierarchy that you wish to switch from ID to descriptive column display. Double-click the column to open the Presentation Hierarchy Properties dialog box, and select the Display Columns tab.

2. Click the existing column listed within the Name section (for example, Staff ID), and click the Delete button to remove it from the list.

3. Click the Add button to open the Browse dialog box, and then expand the subject area listing on the left-hand panel to locate the column you wish to display instead of the ID (for example, Staff Name).

4. Click OK to close the dialog box, and then save your changes to the repository.

Your parent-child hierarchical column will now use the descriptive column for a dimension member rather than the ID column next time you take the repository online and refresh the Oracle BI Presentation server's cached copy of its metadata.

Altering the Aggregation Properties of a Parent-Child Hierarchy If you view a parent-child hierarchy through a hierarchical column in an analysis, along with a fact table measure, you may notice that, by default, values are not aggregated up the hierarchy, so measure values shown against each member in the hierarchy actually represent the total for that member, rather than that member and all its descendents.

Title		

Pivot Table		

Staff	Amount Sold
⊟ Pierre Houdan	53
⊟ Adrian Boles	8
⊞ Walter Bridgeman	20
⊞ Alison Chisel	37
⊞ Jon James	20
⊞ Lacey Laxson	11
Pete Sims	26
⊞ Ronald Koeman	15

This is not, however, the behavior for level-based hierarchies, where each member's total is equal to the sum of the lower-most leaf levels in the hierarchy that roll up (aggregate) into that member. The reason for this is due to how the parent-child relationship table is included into the physical layer when it is created by the Oracle BI Administration tool.

If you select the dimension table, fact table, and parent-child relationship table within the physical model, right-click them and select Physical Diagram | Selected Object(s) Only, you will see that the parent-child relationship table is not, by default, joined to either the dimension table or the fact table. Instead, the fact table joins to the dimension table only, or in this instance the STAFF_ID column, which is why the Oracle BI Server only includes values for that particular staff member when calculating the total for each staff member.

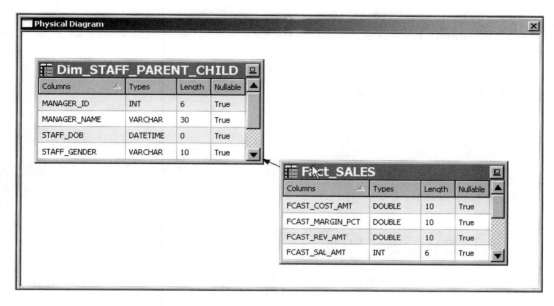

To ensure that the Oracle BI Server includes the dimension member's descendents in its total, and therefore that values aggregate up the hierarchy, you have to modify the physical layer joins to include the parent-child relationship table. To do this, follow these steps:

1. Using the Oracle BI Administration tool, open your repository offline and then navigate to the physical layer of the semantic model; then, right-click the physical dimension table, fact table, and parent-child relationship table for your parent-child hierarchy, and select Physical Diagram | Selected Object(s) Only.

2. With the Physical Diagram screen open, check that the physical dimension table joins directly to the physical fact table and that the parent-child relationship table is not included in the join (as per the previous screenshot).

3. Click the join between the physical dimension table and physical fact table, and then right-click and select Delete.

4. With the New Join button selected, draw a join starting at the fact table and ending at the parent-child relationship table. When prompted to specify the join columns, select the MEMBER_KEY column from the parent-child relationship table and the dimension key column (for example, STAFF_ID) from the fact table.

5. Repeat step 4, but this time create a join between the parent-child relationship table and the dimension table, joining the key column from the dimension table (for example, STAFF_ID) to the ANCESTOR_KEY column in the parent-child relationship table. Your physical diagram should now look like this:

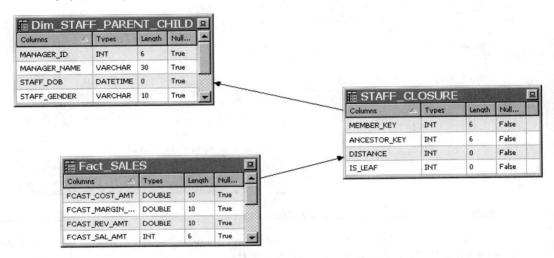

6. As there is now no direct link between the dimension physical table and the fact physical table, you will need to include the parent-child relationship table in the logical table source used by the parent-child hierarchy's logical table. To do this, navigate to the business model and mapping layer in the semantic model, locate the parent-child dimension's logical table, expand the Sources folder, and double-click the table source to edit it.

7. With the Logical Table Source dialog box open, select the General tab to display the list of mapped tables (currently just the physical dimension table). Click the Add button, and then select the parent-child relationship table to add it to the table list.

8. To save the repository, select File | Save. The Consistency Check Manager dialog box will then be displayed and will show a warning that the logical table source you just edited contains columns not used in any column mappings. You can ignore this warning, as it just refers to the parent-child relationship table that you needed to map in to create the link between the fact and dimension table sources.

9. Click Close to close this dialog box, save your repository to the file system, and then use Fusion Middleware Control to make this repository the default, online repository.

If you then display the parent-child hierarchical column in an analysis, along with a measure, you will see that the total for each member now includes aggregated values for that member's descendants added to the value associated with that individual member.

	Amount Sold
Staff	
⊟ Pierre Houdan	350
⊟ Adrian Boles	60
⊞ Walter Bridgeman	52
⊞ Alison Chisel	53
⊞ Jon James	63
⊞ Lacey Laxson	80
Pete Sims	26
⊞ Ronald Koeman	15

Displaying Hierarchy Members When No Measure Values Are Associated (Left Outer Joins)   If you display any type of hierarchical column in an analysis on its own, all of the members will be displayed when you drill into the analysis. If, however, you include measures from a fact table into the analysis criteria, only those members with corresponding values in the fact table will be displayed, due to the inner join that is created by default between the two tables in the business model and mapping layer of the semantic model.

If you change this logical join to a left outer join instead, all rows from the logical dimension table will be returned when you include the hierarchy in an analysis, even if there is no fact table data associated with the measure. Make this change with caution, though, as it will affect all analyses that use this dimension table and can cause existing analyses to return incorrect or different data than before.

To alter your business model to use a left outer join between a dimension and a fact table, follow these steps:

1. With your repository open in the Oracle BI Administration tool, navigate to the business model containing the logical dimension and fact table. Locate the two tables, right-click them, and select Business Model Diagram | Selected Tables Only.

2. The Business Model Diagram screen will then be displayed. Double-click the join between the two tables to display the Logical Join dialog box. Within the Logical Join dialog box, locate the Type drop-down list. Change the selected value from Inner to Left Outer, and click OK to save the change. Save your repository as usual, and then take your repository online, using Fusion Middleware Control if you have been working offline with it.

When you next query the hierarchy, you will see that dimension members are displayed regardless of whether fact table data is associated with them.

Staff	Amount Sold △▽
⊟ Pierre Houdan	350
⊞ Adrian Boles	60
⊞ Alison Chisel	53
⊟ Hector Nunez	
⊟ Mildred Butters	
Ashly Loerm	
⊞ Jon James	63
⊞ Lacey Laxson	80
Pete Sims	26
⊞ Ronald Koeman	15

Horizontal Federation (Cross-Database Modeling)

Horizontal federation describes a capability of Oracle Business Intelligence to combine two or more data sources, at the same level of granularity, into a single business model. As long as each data source shares at least one conformed (jointly used) dimension, and therefore one dimension key, you can combine the data sources based on their shared columns and present the data to users as a single business model, allowing them to create analyses that span multiple subject areas.

In the example earlier in this chapter, we have a physical schema called GCBC_SALES that contains a physical table containing fact data and four others containing dimension data for stores, staff, products, and times. In a typical horizontal federation scenario, we have another source of facts, this time on quality assurance and store/customer surveys, that shares the Store and Times dimensions with our other fact data, but that has one other dimension, Survey Organization, that is unique to it.

In this instance, where we have two fact tables but they are not of exactly the same dimensionality, it is best if we model the two fact sources as two separate fact tables in the business model, and these can subsequently be combined into a single analysis when just the shared dimensions are used in the analysis criteria; this is to avoid potential situations where, if facts of differing dimensionality were included in the same logical fact table, the user might not be aware of their different dimensionality and then have problems including them all in an analysis along with all the dimensions.

Later on in this section, we will look at when it is possible to combine all incoming facts into a single logical fact table, what happens when the Oracle BI Server combines data from more than one logical fact table, and how you can include facts into the same analysis when they have differing dimensionality. For now, though, let's look at what happens when each incoming physical fact table leads to its own logical fact table.

Example: Horizontal Federation by Creating Multiple Logical Fact Tables   In the situation just described, we have an existing sales fact table dimensioned by products, time, stores, and staff, and an additional fact table containing customer satisfaction survey data, this time dimensioned by time and store, and a new dimension, survey organization. As the new incoming physical data source contains facts with an additional dimension, we will include the new data in the same logical business model but create a new, separate fact table for the survey data.

Using this situation as the scenario to horizontally federate the data, follow these steps:

1. Using the Oracle BI Administration tool, either connecting online or offline to your data, open the repository that contains the existing business model. Then, select File | Import Metadata from the menu and import the new physical objects into the semantic model. Create aliases and physical display folders for the new objects as required.

2. For any new physical tables or aliases that provide dimension data, create physical keys on these tables and join them to new physical fact tables also brought in as part of this import. In the screenshot shown here, the GCBC_SURVEYS physical schema contains the new physical fact table, CUSTOMER_SATISFACTION, along with a new dimension fact table, SURVEY_ORGANIZATION. Both of these tables have been aliased and also copied into physical display folders. Going forward, only these aliases in the display folders will be used for the federation.

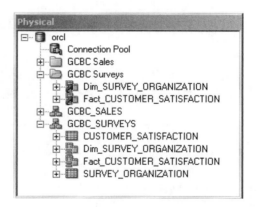

3. To enable the new objects to be included in the same logical business model, and therefore for the end user to be able to include facts from the new fact table into analyses with facts from the existing fact table, foreign key links now need to be created between the new physical objects and the existing ones in the physical layer. Within the physical layer of the semantic model, CTRL-click the new fact table and its corresponding new dimension table, as well as the dimension tables or aliases that this fact table will also join to. Right-click these objects and select Physical Diagram | Selected Object(s) Only to bring up the Physical Diagram screen.

4. Using the Join button in the Physical Diagram screen, create joins between the dimension tables and the fact table, joining both of those dimension objects that come from the new data source and those from the other data source you wish to federate the data with.

If both sources come from the same physical database, the Oracle BI Server will most likely issue a single SQL statement at query time to cover both sources, while if they come from different physical databases, the BI Server will probably issue two or more physical SQL queries and join the results together in-memory.

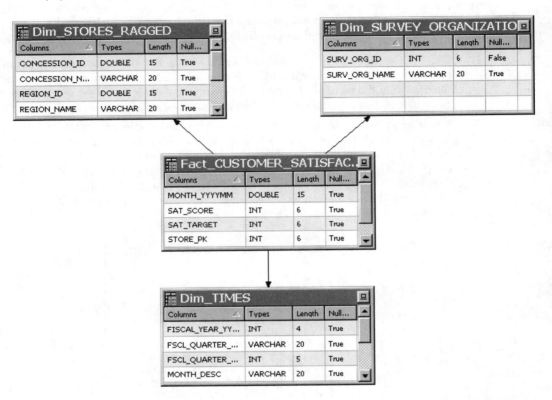

5. Close the Physical Diagram screen, and then navigate to the business model and mapping layer in the semantic model. Locate the existing business model that you wish to extend to include the new fact table, right-click it, and select New Object | Logical Table. Create the empty logical table for your fact table, and then repeat this for any new logical tables to contain dimension data.

6. Drag-and-drop any physical columns from the physical layer onto these new logical tables, create the logical key on any new logical dimension tables, and use the Business Model Diagram view to create the logical join between the new logical fact table and the logical dimension tables that it joins to. Define the default aggregation for each of the new fact table measures, and set any other properties for your new object as you would for any other new business model.

7. Create any new logical dimensions for the new logical fact tables, and add the logical levels and keys as appropriate. Your logical model, with the new logical fact table and any new logical dimension tables, should now look like this screenshot:

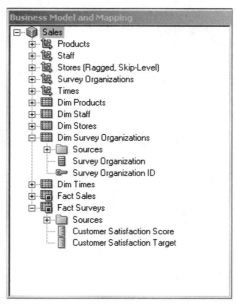

8. Finally, publish the new fact table and any dimension tables to the presentation layer of the semantic model, either by dragging and dropping the new objects into an existing subject area or by creating a new subject area for this new fact table, plus all of the dimensions that it joins to (the preferred option in Oracle Business Intelligence 11*g*, as multiple subject areas can now be included in a single analysis criteria, as long as they map back to a single business model).

Example: Horizontal Federation into the Same Logical Fact Table   In the preceding example, the incoming fact table (CUSTOMER_SATISFACTION) had an additional dimension table (SURVEY_ORGANIZATION) that wasn't shared with the existing fact table in the business model, so it made sense to create a new logical fact table for its measures. In some situations, though, additional source data that you wish to horizontally federate shares all the same dimensions as an existing logical fact table, and therefore you may wish to incorporate its measures into the existing logical table.

As an example, consider a situation where the data source providing survey information detailed in the preceding section also has another fact table containing staff satisfaction survey data. This new fact table source shares the same dimensionality as the customer satisfaction fact table, and therefore we wish to incorporate its measures into the same logical fact table that contains the other survey measures. To do this, follow these steps:

1. As with the example in the preceding section, use the Oracle BI Administration tool to import the new physical fact table into the semantic model, and alias the table as appropriate. In this example, the new fact table is called STAFF_SATISFACTION and

exists in the same GCBC_SURVEYS physical schema as the CUSTOMER_SATISFACTION table imported earlier.

2. Using the physical layer of the semantic model, join this new fact table to the existing physical dimension tables that it connects to using the Physical Diagram screen. Do not join the new fact table to any other fact tables, though. (You should generally never join facts to facts; only connect them through shared dimension tables.)

3. Drag-and-drop the measures from the new physical fact table into the logical fact table that you wish to place them in. Rename them as necessary, and note how the logical fact table now has an additional logical table source; we will look into the reason for this in a moment.

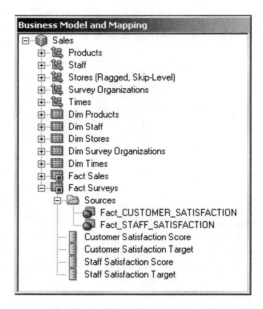

4. Define the default aggregation for these new measures, and then drag-and-drop them into the corresponding subject area in the presentation layer to make them available for users to query.

What Happens When We Join Two Fact Tables? So what happens when we include measures from more than one logical fact table in an analysis? How does the Oracle BI Server generate the physical SQL for such an analysis, and also, does this change when we include, as with the last example, measures from two physical fact tables into the same logical fact?

Let's first take a look at what happens when we include measures from two different logical fact tables in the same analysis; only shared dimensions are used in the analysis, and both physical sources point to different physical schemas but come from the same physical database. Figure 3-21 shows the relationship between the two logical fact tables and the two dimension tables that join them.

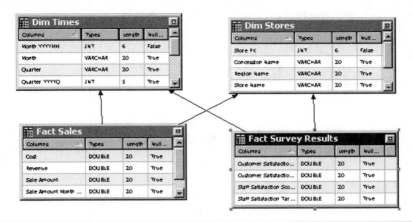

FIGURE 3-21.   *Relationship between logical fact and dimension tables*

When measures from the two fact tables are included in an analysis, along with attributes from one or more of the logical dimensions, the Oracle BI Server internally generates two logical queries, one for each of the fact tables. This is to avoid what is called a "fan trap" error, where SQL would otherwise double-count measures from the fact tables when joining through a common dimension. Where possible, though, the Oracle BI Server will try to join these two logical queries together into a single physical SQL, using what is called *subquery factoring*. The physical Oracle Database 11*g* Enterprise Edition SQL shown here, resulting from a query against the business model in the preceding section, shows how this would look in practice:

```
WITH
SAWITH0 AS (select avg(T616.SAT_SCORE) as c1,
     T414.REGION_NAME as c2,
     T62.MONTH_YYYYMM as c3
from
     GCBC_SALES.STORES_RAGGED T414 /* Dim_STORES_RAGGED */ ,
     GCBC_SALES.TIMES T62 /* Dim_TIMES */ ,
     GCBC_SURVEYS.CUSTOMER_SATISFACTION T616 /* Fact_CUSTOMER_SATISFACTION */
where  ( T62.MONTH_YYYYMM = T616.MONTH_YYYYMM
and T414.STORE_PK = T616.STORE_PK )
group by T62.MONTH_YYYYMM, T414.REGION_NAME),
SAWITH1 AS (select sum(T71.FCAST_SAL_AMT) as c1,
     T414.REGION_NAME as c2,
     T62.MONTH_YYYYMM as c3
from
     GCBC_SALES.STORES_RAGGED T414 /* Dim_STORES_RAGGED */ ,
     GCBC_SALES.TIMES T62 /* Dim_TIMES */ ,
     GCBC_SALES.SALES T71 /* Fact_SALES */
where  ( T62.MONTH_YYYYMM = T71.MONTH_YYYYMM
```

```
and T71.STORE_ID = T414.STORE_PK )
group by T62.MONTH_YYYYMM, T414.REGION_NAME),
SAWITH2 AS (select D1.c1 as c1,
     D1.c2 as c2,
     D1.c3 as c3,
     D1.c4 as c4,
     D1.c5 as c5
from
     (select 0 as c1,
                 case  when D2.c2 is not null then D2.c2
                 when D1.c2 is not null then D1.c2 end
                 as c2,
                 case  when D1.c3 is not null then D1.c3
                 when D2.c3 is not null then D2.c3 end
                 as c3,
                 D1.c1 as c4,
                 D2.c1 as c5,
                 ROW_NUMBER() OVER (PARTITION BY case
                 when D1.c3 is not null then D1.c3
                 when D2.c3 is not null then D2.c3 end ,
                 case  when D2.c2 is not null then D2.c2
                 when D1.c2 is not null then D1.c2 end
                 ORDER BY
                 case  when D1.c3 is not null then D1.c3
                 when D2.c3 is not null then D2.c3 end  ASC,
                 case  when D2.c2 is not null then D2.c2
                 when D1.c2 is not null then D1.c2 end  ASC) as c6
         from
                 SAWITH0 D1 full outer join
                 SAWITH1 D2 On D1.c3 = D2.c3
                 and nvl(D1.c2 , 'q') = nvl(D2.c2 , 'q')
                 and nvl(D1.c2 , 'z') = nvl(D2.c2 , 'z')
     ) D1
where  ( D1.c6 = 1 ) )
select D1.c1 as c1,
     D1.c2 as c2,
     D1.c3 as c3,
     D1.c4 as c4,
     D1.c5 as c5
from
     SAWITH2 D1
order by c1, c2, c3 NULLS FIRST
```

Notice the two WITH blocks at the start of the query (this is subquery factoring) and the full outer join at the end of the query, where the Oracle BI Server realizes that it can "push" the joining of these two separate logical queries into a single physical SQL statement; if we were working with a database such as Microsoft Access or mySQL, where subquery factoring is not available, two separate physical SQL queries would have been issued and the Oracle BI Server would perform a full outer join, or *stitch join,* in its memory instead.

A similar situation would occur if it was just a dimension table that was being horizontally federated from a new physical data source; if the new data source came from the same physical database as the rest of the user's analysis, the Oracle BI Server would push the join down to the physical database, by including it and the full set of tables in the physical SQL. If, however, the new physical dimension table came from a different database, two separate queries would be issued for the two data sources and the Oracle BI Server would join the resulting data sets in memory before passing the results back to the Oracle BI Presentation Server.

Example: Joining Facts of Differing Dimensionality   In the example we have been using so far, the new logical fact table shares two dimensions with the existing logical fact table (products and times) but has one specific to itself (survey organizations). In turn, the existing logical fact table has two other dimensions (staff and products) that are not used by the new logical fact table.

So what happens if we include measures from both logical fact tables in one analysis and one of the dimensions not shared by both fact tables? In this case, the measures that are not dimensioned by one of the logical dimension tables really should not be shown in the results, as they cannot be "broken down" by the extra dimension, and therefore no valid results should be shown for them. The following screenshot shows this happening in practice:

This is logically correct, as there is no way of displaying the Staff Satisfaction Score broken down by Product Category because data is not stored to this level of detail in the source database. If you take a look at an excerpt of the physical SQL generated for this query, you will see that the Oracle BI Server uses the CAST(NULL) function to return nulls for results from the fact table in question:

```
select distinct 0 as c1,
      D1.c2 as c2,
      cast(NULL as   DOUBLE PRECISION  ) as c3,
      D1.c1 as c4
from
      SAWITH0 D1
```

What if, however, you specifically still want to return results from this fact table, even if an unconfirmed dimension is included in the analysis criteria? Well, this approach is not really advisable because, as you will see, it returns repeated values for the measure in question, but if you understand how the results will look, these are the steps you should carry out:

1. Ensure that all of the logical dimension tables that you will include in the query have logical dimensions and hierarchies defined for them, as we have with the Dim Products logical table and its corresponding logical dimension.

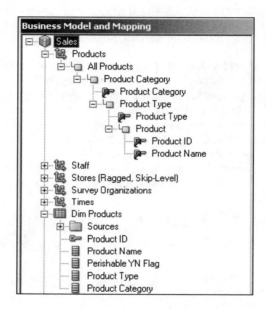

2. Within the business model, locate the logical columns that you wish to display values for even when the unconfirmed dimension is included in the analysis. Double-click the logical column to display the logical column Properties dialog box, and then select the Levels tab.

3. With the Levels tab selected for those dimensions that do not ordinarily join to the logical fact table containing the logical column (Product, in this example), set the Logical Level to the grand total level for that logical dimension's hierarchy.

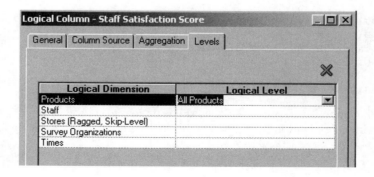

4. Save your repository in the normal way, and check the repository's consistency as usual.

5. Now rerun the analysis that you created earlier and note how, for the column you just changed, values now appear for the measure, but these are in fact repeated across all of the rows from the unconfirmed dimension.

Product Category	Amount Sold	Staff Satisfaction Score
Bread	286	45.18
Drinks	2	45.18
Gifts	13	45.18
Snacks	10	45.18

Vertical Federation (Aggregates)

In addition to joining together physical data sources at the same level of detail (granularity), Oracle Business Intelligence 11*g* can also create single logical data sets out of data stored at different levels of granularity. For example:

- Detail-level data may be stored in a relational database such as Oracle Database 11*g*, while summary-level data may be held in an OLAP server such as Oracle Essbase.

- Detail-level data may be stored in an Oracle database, while summary tables may be held in another Oracle database.

- Data for sales, for example, may come from an invoicing system that stores some measures solely at detail level, while other measures apply only at the whole-invoice level.

Oracle Business Intelligence 11*g* can bring these sources of differing granularity together using a feature called *vertical federation*. A common use case for this is handling summary-level data, which may be created using an ETL process or may have been generated automatically using the Aggregate Persistence Wizard. In Chapter 4, we will look at how you might use vertical federation to bring together detail-level relational data and summary-level OLAP server data, but for now let us take a closer look at vertically federating detail and summary-level relational data.

Vertical federation relies on your having defined logical dimensions and logical hierarchies to accompany the logical tables in your business model. You use these logical dimensions and hierarchies to tell the semantic model at which level of detail a new logical table source applies, and the Oracle BI Server will then switch to this new logical table source once an analysis requests data aggregated to the appropriate level.

For a logical table source, you define the level of detail at which the Oracle BI Server should use it by setting the logical level for the source in the logical table source Properties dialog box. In the following example, the Oracle BI Server will start making use of the table source once the analysis requests data at the Product Category and Quarter logical levels, and will use a more detailed logical table source for its columns up until that point.

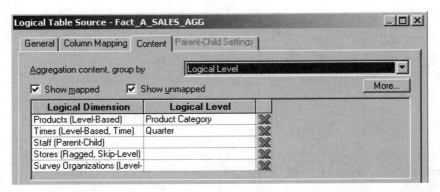

This type of repository modeling is useful when, for example, you cannot use database-specific features such as Oracle materialized views to handle pre-aggregation at the physical database level or where you wish to store aggregated values in a different physical database than the one storing your detail-level data. In addition, as previously mentioned and as covered in Chapter 4, it is also a useful technique for when you wish to combine relational and multidimensional data sources into a single business model.

To see how this works in practice, let's work through an example where we map some aggregate tables into an existing logical business model and configure the new logical table sources so that the Oracle BI Server uses them when analyses request the required level of aggregation.

Example: Vertical Federation Using Relational Data Sources   In this scenario, we have a semantic model containing a single logical fact table that contains sales data that is then dimensioned by product, store, times, and staff logical dimension tables. We now wish to introduce a second data source, this time containing summary-level data for this same logical fact table, which we intend to map in using the vertical federation feature.

At the start of the process, the business model and corresponding physical layer looks as in the following screenshot. Note the existing detail-level logical table sources under each logical table's Sources folder and the single physical schema holding their corresponding physical table sources.

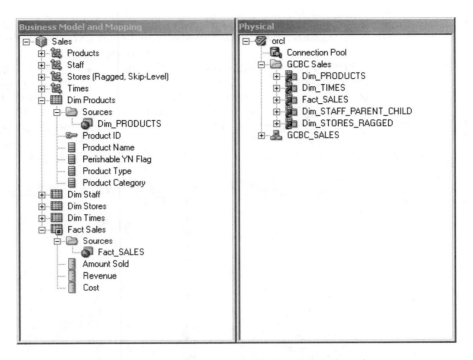

To incorporate the aggregated data using vertical federation, follow these steps:

1. Using the Oracle BI Administration tool, connect to the aggregated data source, for example, the GCBC_AGGS schema that comes with the sample data that accompanies this book. Import the objects into the physical layer of the semantic mode and then alias the tables as required, and then create keys and foreign key joins between just the tables in this physical schema. In the example we are using, three tables are imported: A_PROD_CATEGORIES, which contains product category data; A_TIMES_QUARTERS, which contains quarters and year information; and A_SALES_AGG, which contains sales data aggregated to the product category and quarters levels.

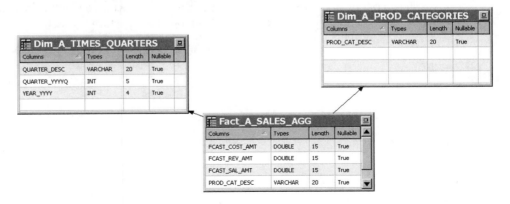

2. Unlike horizontal federation, you do not create physical foreign key joins between the new physical data source tables and the existing ones. Instead, you define the links between the detail- and aggregate-level data sources by creating additional table sources for individual logical columns within your business model. Starting with the aggregated physical dimension tables, locate a physical column that has a corresponding logical column in the business model you wish to vertically federate into. For example, the Dim_A_PROD_CATEGORIES alias table (based on the A_PROD_CATEGORIES physical table) has a physical column called PROD_CAT_DESC that corresponds to the Dim Products Product Category logical column in our business model. Drag-and-drop this physical column onto the corresponding logical column to create the join.

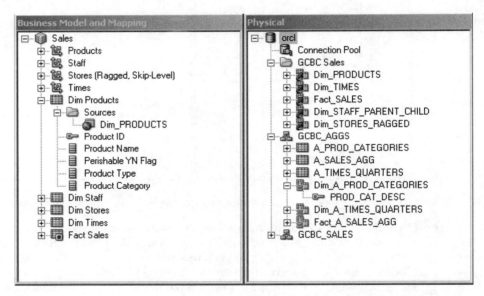

3. If you now navigate to the logical table and column that you just dragged the aggregate-level physical column to, you will notice two things: first, a new logical table source has been added to the Sources folder for this logical table, and second, if you double-click the logical column and select the Column Source tab, you will see that this logical column now has two possible table sources that can be used to return values for it.

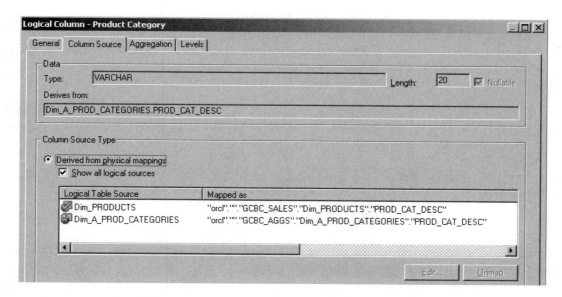

4. Now you should set the logical level for the logical table source created by your previous mapping step. Navigate to the Sources folder under the logical table you just mapped the physical column into and double-click the logical table source that corresponds to your aggregated data source. With the Logical Table Source dialog box open, select the Content tab. For a dimension logical table, only one logical dimension should be listed under this tab, which will correspond to this logical table. Use the Logical Level drop-down list to select the hierarchy level that this source should be used at (for example, Product Category).

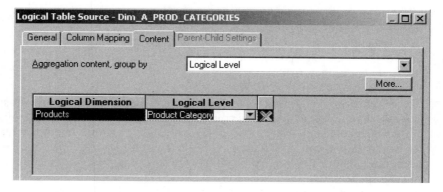

5. Repeat step 4 for any other columns in the incoming aggregated table source, and then do the same for any other dimension physical tables in the new data source.

6. Now do this for the physical fact table in the presentation layer, mapping in the aggregated physical columns to connect to the existing logical columns in your logical fact table. When setting the aggregation level for the logical fact table aggregated table source, you will need to specify levels for all of the relevant dimensions, and some of the dimension levels will need to be left blank if the aggregated source does not contain aggregate data for these dimensions.

7. Once complete, save your repository and check its consistency. As you have not created any new logical columns, you do not need to make any further changes to the presentation layer of your repository.

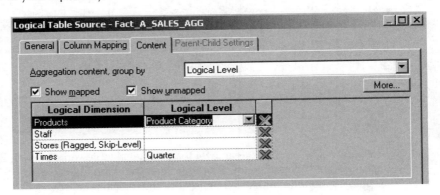

NOTE
When performing a consistency check, you may get an error along the lines of "Table Dim Products is functionally dependent upon level Product Category, but a more detailed child level has associated columns from that same table or a more detailed table." If so, check to see whether the dragging and dropping of your aggregate-level physical column onto the logical table has created an additional logical key at the aggregate level. If it has, delete the extra key and recheck consistency.

Other variations on this process include mapping a new column from the aggregated data source, which provides an additional column for the logical table but only applies at this aggregated level of detail. This is, in fact, a combination of vertical and horizontal federation, which would require you to take steps similar to the preceding example, but you would need to create a new, additional logical column and corresponding presentation column for the new aggregate-only measure.

Once complete, your semantic model, with aggregated data sources mapped in, should look similar to that shown in Figure 3-22.

How Does the Oracle BI Server Handle Vertically Federated Data?   So what happens when you create a vertically federated semantic model and the Oracle BI Server has to switch between the detail-level and aggregated data sources?

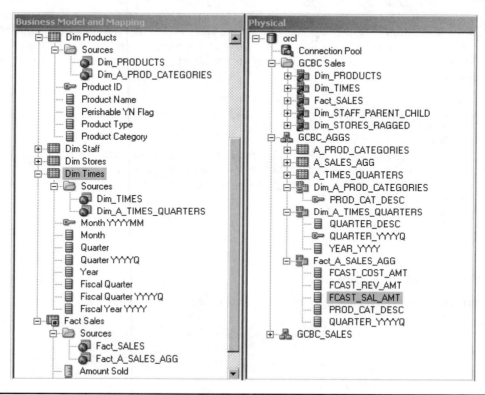

FIGURE 3-22.   *Vertically federated semantic model*

To show what happens, let's take the example that we used in the previous section ("Vertical Federation Using Relational Data Sources") and enable query logging to see the SQL that is generated for the query. To enable query logging, use the Oracle BI Administration tool and select File | Manage Identity, with the repository open in online mode, and create an analysis that lists the amount sold by product category.

Product Category	Amount Sold
Bread	852.00
Drinks	1548.00
Gifts	126.00
Snacks	1068.00

Taking a look at the corresponding entry in the query log file, you can see that the Oracle BI Server used the aggregate tables imported from the GCBC_AGGS schema referenced in the previous section's example to return data for the analysis. This is because the semantic model maps the corresponding logical table sources in at this level of aggregation, and the Oracle BI Server therefore assumes that it will return data more efficiently than the alternative, detail-level table source.

```
WITH
SAWITH0 AS (select sum(T926.FCAST_SAL_AMT) as c1,
     T924.PROD_CAT_DESC as c2
from
     GCBC_AGGS.A_PROD_CATEGORIES T924 /* Dim_A_PROD_CATEGORIES */ ,
     GCBC_AGGS.A_SALES_AGG T926 /* Fact_A_SALES_AGG */
where  ( T924.PROD_CAT_DESC = T926.PROD_CAT_DESC )
group by T924.PROD_CAT_DESC)
select distinct 0 as c1,
     D1.c2 as c2,
     D1.c1 as c3
from
     SAWITH0 D1
order by c2
```

However, if you now click the Product Category column to drill down, like this,

Product Category	Product Type	Amount Sold
Bread	Bread Assortments	235.00
	Rounds & Loaves	50.00
	Speciality Breads	1.00
Drinks	Hot Drinks	2.00
Gifts	Bread Clubs	7.00
	Gifts & Baskets	6.00
Snacks	Sandwiches	10.00

and check the corresponding query log entry, you will see that the Oracle BI Server now switches to the detail-level table sources, pointing to the GCBC_SALES physical schema in our example data set:

```
WITH
SAWITH0 AS (select sum(T71.FCAST_SAL_AMT) as c1,
     T52.PROD_CAT_DESC as c2,
     T52.PROD_TYPE_DESC as c3
from
     GCBC_SALES.PRODUCTS T52 /* Dim_PRODUCTS */ ,
     GCBC_SALES.SALES T71 /* Fact_SALES */
where  ( T52.PROD_ID = T71.FCAST_COST_AMT )
group by T52.PROD_CAT_DESC, T52.PROD_TYPE_DESC)
```

```
select distinct 0 as c1,
     D1.c2 as c2,
     D1.c3 as c3,
     D1.c1 as c4
from
     SAWITH0 D1
order by c2, c3
```

In this way, the Oracle BI Server picks the most efficient table sources to satisfy a query, based on the logical levels at which you mapped them into the business model, all transparently to the end user.

Fragmentation

Fragmentation is the name for another repository feature for Oracle Business Intelligence that makes it possible to combine specific multiple table sources for a particular logical table, all at the same level of detail, with each *fragment* providing a particular discreet range of values.

For example, a logical table containing sales transactions may have two logical table sources defined for it, one that provides transactions up until midnight yesterday (perhaps from a data warehouse) and another that provides today's transaction (from, for example, an operational system).

To set up fragmentation, you need to consider the following:

- Each fragmented table source requires an expression that defines the range of values that it provides; for example, you may define a fragmentation clause that specifies that the table source provides values from 01-JAN-2010 until 31-DEC-2011.

- This fragmentation clause may reference a repository variable so it could specify that it provides values up until midnight yesterday, for example.

- Fragmented logical table sources must have valid physical joins to appropriate fact or dimension physical tables so that if the Oracle BI Server switches to using the fragment it can still join to appropriate physical fact and dimension table sources.

Fragmentation is defined using the Logical Table Source properties dialog box, under the Content tab, as shown in Figure 3-23.

To specify the range of values that the fragmented table source provides, use the Expression Builder to specify the required expression, and select the "This source should be combined with other sources at this level" check box.

You can also make reference to a repository variable within the fragmentation clause, allowing you to set up fragmentation so that, for example, a historical fragment provides data up until yesterday, while the current fragment provides real-time data for today only.

Example: Using Fragmentation to Combine Current and Historical Data   To see how fragmentation works in practice, let's work through an example related to the ones we have used earlier in this chapter but where the fact table data is split over two physical tables, each of which holds a subset of the total fact data. The source schema contains a shared set of physical dimension tables, and the two fact tables are split as follows:

- SALES_CURRENT holds measure values from July, 2010 onward.
- SALES_HISTORIC holds measure values prior to July, 2010.

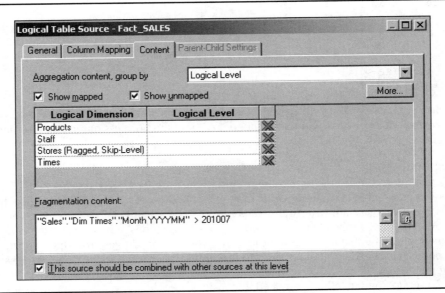

FIGURE 3-23. *Setting the fragmentation clause for a logical table source*

All of these physical tables have been aliased in the physical layer of the semantic model, and we now wish to combine these two fact table sources together into a single logical table using the federation feature of the Oracle BI Server.

The physical model at the start of the process looks like this, with both of the physical fact tables joining to both of the physical dimension tables:

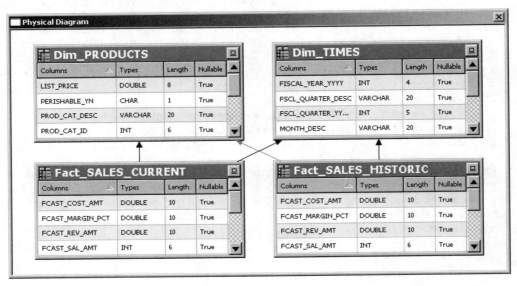

To set up fragmentation in this scenario, follow these steps:

1. First, using the business model and mapping layer, define the outline business model and logical tables that will hold your data. Create a single logical fact table for the measures (for example, Fact Sales) and logical dimension tables for the dimension attributes (for example, Dim Products and Dim Times).

2. Using the physical layer of the semantic model, select one of the logical fact table source tables (in this example, Fact_SALES_HISTORIC, the alias for the SALES_HISTORIC physical table), and drag-and-drop the measure columns into the logical fact table that you just created. Rename the columns as appropriate, and then expand the Sources folder under the logical fact table. You will see a new logical table source listed, named after the physical fact table that you just dragged the columns from.

3. Repeat step 2 to create the columns for the logical dimension tables so that each table in the business model has logical columns defined and a corresponding logical table source. Create logical keys for the dimension tables and use the Business Model Diagram tool to create logical joins between the logical dimension tables and the logical fact table, as you would do with a normal business model.

4. Double-click the logical table source for the logical fact table to display the Logical Table Source properties dialog box. Click the Content tab and locate the Fragmentation Content section headed. Click the Expression Builder button and use the Expression Builder dialog box to create a suitable expression that defines the scope of the data this initial table source contains; in this example, the initial table source provides data up to June, 2010, so the expression becomes "Sales - Fragmented"."Dim Times"."Month YYYYMM" <= 201006. Then select the check box under this text area that reads "This source should be combined with other sources at this level."

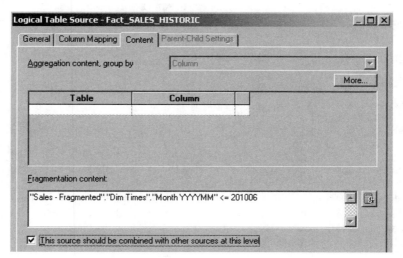

5. Now you can create the second logical table source for the fact table, which this time references the second physical fact table that in this example contains measure data from July, 2010 onward. To do this, navigate to the second physical fact table in the physical layer and drag-and-drop its measure columns on top of the existing logical ones in the logical fact table so that a second logical table source is added under the Sources folder.

As with the previous logical table source, use the Content tab under the Logical Table Source dialog box to set the fragmentation content for the table source; in this example, it will be set to "Sales - Fragmented"."Dim Times"."Month YYYYMM" > 201006. Ensure that the "This source should be combined with other sources at this level" check box is selected, and then close the dialog box.

NOTE
Ensure that there are no gaps or overlaps between the ranges covered by all of the table sources in your fragmented tables.

6. This completes the process of working with fragmentation. Create your presentation layer objects as usual, save and check the consistency of your repository, and then take it online to see the effect of the fragmentation clause in action.

Now, when you create an analysis using this business model and restrict, for example, the criteria to show only data for May, 2010, the Oracle BI Server uses just the Fact_SALES_HISTORIC logical table source and the corresponding physical table to satisfy the query, like this:

```
WITH
SAWITH0 AS (select distinct sum(T71.FCAST_REV_AMT) as c1
from
     TIMES T82 /* Dim_TIMES */ ,
     SALES_HISTORIC T71 /* Fact_SALES_HISTORIC */
where  ( T71.MONTH_YYYYMM = T82.MONTH_YYYYMM
and T71.MONTH_YYYYMM = 201006
and T82.MONTH_YYYYMM = 201006 ) )
select distinct 0 as c1,
     D1.c1 as c2
from
     SAWITH0 D1
```

If the user queried a date that corresponded to the other physical fact table, a similar query would be issued but would reference the other physical fact table instead.

However, if you create an analysis that requests data that spans both physical fact tables, you will see both tables used in the physical SQL query, with a UNION ALL clause to combine the two sets of data:

```
WITH
SAWITH0 AS ((select T71.FCAST_REV_AMT as c2
from
     TIMES T82 /* Dim_TIMES */ ,
     SALES_HISTORIC T71 /* Fact_SALES_HISTORIC */
where  ( T71.MONTH_YYYYMM = T82.MONTH_YYYYMM
and T71.MONTH_YYYYMM between 201006 and 201010
and T82.MONTH_YYYYMM between 201006 and 201010 )
union all
select T60.FCAST_REV_AMT as c2
from
     TIMES T82 /* Dim_TIMES */ ,
     SALES_CURRENT T60 /* Fact_SALES_CURRENT */
where  ( T60.MONTH_YYYYMM = T82.MONTH_YYYYMM
and T60.MONTH_YYYYMM between 201006 and 201010
and T82.MONTH_YYYYMM between 201006 and 201010 ) )),
SAWITH1 AS (select distinct sum(D3.c2) as c1
from
     SAWITH0 D3)
select distinct 0 as c1,
     D2.c1 as c2
from
     SAWITH1 D2
```

Finally, in this particular example, a common set of physical dimension tables were able to be used for both of the physical fact tables because they held all of the dimension member details referenced by both fact tables. Often, though, each fragmented physical fact table will come with its own set of reference dimension tables, and you will therefore have to model both sets in the physical layer of the semantic layer and make sure that both sets of physical fact tables have the correct join to their respective physical dimension tables. This would mean that not only would the logical fact table in the business model have two logical table sources, but the logical dimension tables would also need two as well, adding to the complexity of your repository model.

Double Columns

Double columns, or descriptor ID support, describes a feature within Oracle Business Intelligence 11*g* where an ID column can be assigned to a descriptive column. This can sometimes be useful to help the underlying data source optimize its query and also provides the ability to see the ID in the front end without giving the users direct access to the ID column.

For example, you might assign an ID column to a descriptive column if the underlying physical table is partitioned on the ID column and you wish for the ID to be used in the query predicate rather than the descriptive column. As another example, you might want to create multiple language translation columns for a dimension attribute column but have each of them use a common ID column if used in a query.

To specify the descriptor ID column for another logical column, do the following:

1. Using the Oracle BI Administration tool, open your repository either offline or online.

2. Navigate to the business model and mapping layer and locate the descriptive logical column that you wish to designate an ID column for (for example, Product Name).

3. Double-click the column to display the Logical Column dialog box. Locate the Descriptor ID Column area and click the Set button. Pressing this button displays the Browse dialog box, which you can then use to select the column you wish to use as the descriptor ID column (for example, Product ID).

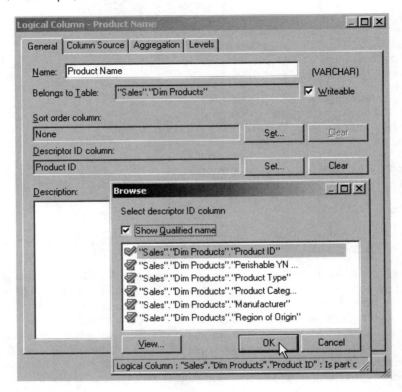

4. Close the dialog box and save your repository as usual.

With this example, if the Product Name logical column is used as the filter (predicate) in an analysis, the Oracle BI Server will substitute the Product ID column instead, generating, for example, the following excerpt of SQL:

```
WITH
SAWITH0 AS (select sum(T117.REV_AMT) as c1,
     T107.PROD_CAT_DESC as c2,
     T107.PROD_ID as c3
from
     GCBC_SALES.PRODUCTS T107,
     GCBC_SALES.SALES T117
where  ( T107.PROD_ID = T117.PROD_ID and (T107.PROD_ID in (12, 17, 31)) )
```

Existing analyses that filter on the Product Name column do not need to be changed, as the Oracle BI Server will substitute the descriptor ID column in any filters automatically.

Until now in this chapter, we have looked at importing and then modeling data sourced from relational data sources. In some cases, though, you may wish to report against data from sources such as Microsoft Excel spreadsheets, text files, or XML documents either on networked file systems or accessed over the Internet.

In the next section, we will look at how file and XML sources are accessed and how you create physical models that can then be used along with other physical models to create the business model and presentation layers in your Oracle BI Repository. As official support for these sources varies by type, we will also look at the restrictions and limitations in working with these sources so you can make a decision as to whether to access them directly from the repository or copy their data into relational or multidimensional databases and access them from there instead.

Overview of File and XML Source Support

Each type of file, XML, and Oracle ADF source has different requirements in terms of access methods, and you will need to perform different steps and work with differing levels of support depending on the source type you work with. In this section, we will look at each source type in turn, and to what extent each source is officially supported, and see how the process differs from working with relational and multidimensional sources.

What File, XML, and Oracle ADF Sources Can You Use with Oracle Business Intelligence?

Oracle Business Intelligence directly supports a number of relational and multidimensional data sources, the most up-to-date list of which you can find in the *System Requirements and Supported Platforms for Oracle Business Intelligence Suite Enterprise Edition 11gR1* document available on the Oracle Technology Network web site. If you wish to access a relational or other database source that is not on this list, you can usually provide access to them through the Oracle BI Server's support for ODBC access. You can also use this ODBC access to obtain file sources with suitable ODBC drivers that you need, such as Microsoft Excel and text file sources.

Oracle Business Intelligence does directly support access to XML sources, through either an XML ODBC driver or through a feature called the XML Gateway. Such XML access is particularly useful for demonstration purposes where you want to store sample data in an XML document (removing the need for a database to be available) or if you want to report against XML data made available over the Internet, possibly from a web service.

Oracle ADF projects created with Oracle JDeveloper 11.1.1.4 onward can be used as data sources for Oracle Business Intelligence repositories from version 11.1.1.5 onward. To enable this data access, you need to import various libraries into the WebLogic domain that contains your deployed ADF application, and the metadata import utility that comes with the Oracle BI Administration tool reads the ADF metadata and uses it to create a physical model that maps to your ADF business components. The Oracle BI Server then either accesses the underlying data used by the ADF application through these business components, or you can configure an SQL Bypass database within the repository that takes the SQL queries used by the ADF business components and uses it to access the underlying relational data directly, giving the BI Server the ability to "push down" more database functions to improve query performance.

For each of these data source types, the rest of this chapter will describe the steps to configure access, the detailed list of source types that can be accessed, and how you would then go on to model these sources in the physical layer of your Oracle BI Repository.

Supported vs. Unsupported Sources

When working with file, XML, and ADF data sources, it is important to understand the distinction between *supported* and *compatible* data sources, and this is discussed in this section.

The *System Requirements and Supported Platforms for Oracle Business Intelligence Suite Enterprise Edition 11gR1* document available on the Oracle Technology Network web site details the current officially supported data sources that you can use with Oracle Business Intelligence. This list includes sources such as the Oracle Database, Microsoft SQL Server, Teradata, Oracle Essbase, XML, and Oracle ADF. The Oracle BI Server has been certified to work with these sources, which are typically accessed through native drivers and are included in testing whenever a new release of Oracle Business Intelligence is made available.

Other sources, such as file sources or unsupported database sources such as Microsoft Access, may well be compatible with Oracle Business Intelligence because of its ability to access data through Open Database Connectivity (ODBC), a standard software interface for accessing databases. ODBC drivers exist for most data sources that you might want to access, including file sources such as comma-separated or fixed-width files, but these are not officially supported by Oracle and you may need to perform additional configuration steps before they can be reliably accessed. In addition, as these sources are not supported and not tested for, you may experience unusual results or not be able to gain access at all.

Even for supported sources such as XML or ADF, you might also want to consider copying your data into a relational or multidimensional database, or loading your data into a data warehouse alongside your other reporting data in order to get the best query performance. File sources in particular are not designed for large numbers of concurrent users and should only really be considered for data that is rarely accessed or is being mapped into the repository only for testing or prototyping purposes.

How Does This Differ from Relational and OLAP Sources?

While each of the sources outlined in this chapter have their own metadata import and physical modeling steps, once you have set up the physical database model, they are then used in the repository just like any other data source.

Because of the abstraction between physical, business model and mapping, and presentation layers in the Oracle BI Repository, physical models created from these sources can then be used to create, or add to, business models that are otherwise sourced from relational and multidimensional sources, with the Oracle BI Server generating the appropriate physical queries against all sources in order to return a combined data set to the user.

As such, then, we will just focus on importing metadata from these sources and creating the physical layer of the repository, as the steps to create the rest of the repository layers is then the same as with any other source type.

Modeling File Sources, Including Microsoft Excel

We will start by looking at what is probably the most common type of source other than relational and multidimensional ones: accessing data from files.

Overview

When creating an Oracle BI Repository that sources data from across the enterprise, best practice is to source that data from a single enterprise data warehouse or an OLAP cube that combines data together into a single data source. Creating data warehouses or OLAP cubes can be a time-consuming process, though, and in some situations you might want to make data available that is held in a file, either as a tactical solution or as a way of gauging demand for a new source of data before formally incorporating it into a data warehouse.

Using ODBC to Import File Sources

When you access file sources through the Oracle BI Repository, you do so using ODBC drivers, either provided for you as part of your operating system installation through your Oracle Business Intelligence installation or through drivers that you obtain and install yourself.

A typical installation of Microsoft Windows Server 2003, for example, comes with a number of default ODBC drivers that you can use to access data held in Microsoft Access, Microsoft Excel, and fixed-width and comma-separated files. In addition, when you install Oracle Business Intelligence on a server, you also gain access to ODBC drivers provided by DataDirect, including drivers for sources such as MySQL, PostgreSQL, and XML, which can be used on both Microsoft Windows–based systems and on Linux-/Unix-based systems after following some additional configuration steps.

When you use ODBC to access data sources, you need to perform two steps to import the data into the Oracle BI Repository:

1. Set up the ODBC connection to your data, either through graphical tools provided by your operating system or through text-based configuration files.

2. When the connections are set up, import the metadata into your repository.

Additional steps may be required if you are performing the metadata import on a workstation where just the Oracle Business Intelligence client tools are installed, particularly if you need to copy source files between workstation and server.

Finally, although supported sources such as the Oracle Database can also be accessed via ODBC drivers, you should always, when possible, access them through native drivers such as Oracle Call Interface (OCI). Native drivers, where available and supported, generally provide superior performance to ODBC drivers and are the default setting when you import these sources through the Oracle BI Administrator tool's Import Metadata feature.

Restrictions and Limitations

As mentioned before, while you can import and work with file sources such as Microsoft Excel and Microsoft Access using Oracle Business Intelligence, they are not considered "supported" sources by Oracle, and you may experience unexpected results or need to perform additional configuration steps to make them work as expected.

In addition, as file sources are not typically designed to support large numbers of concurrent users, you should be aware of potential performance issues with these sources and consider using features such as query caching (detailed in Chapter 6) to minimize any impact.

Types of File Sources Compatible with Oracle Business Intelligence

While any file source that has a compatible ODBC driver is, in theory, accessible by Oracle Business Intelligence, several sources are more commonly used with this product and are known to work well. These sources include

- Microsoft Excel workbooks
- Microsoft Access databases
- Comma- and tab-delimited text files using the .csv and .tab file extensions
- Fixed-width files using the .txt and .asc file extensions

Files containing XML data will be covered later in this chapter.

Microsoft Excel   Data held in Microsoft Excel worksheets can be accessed via the Microsoft Excel driver that ships with most installations of Microsoft Windows. If your installation of Oracle Business Intelligence is running on a Linux or Unix server, you would normally need to convert the Excel file to a CSV (comma-separated values) file and access it through one of the DataDirect ODBC drivers provided by Oracle or obtain a Microsoft Excel ODBC driver for Linux/Unix and configure it separately.

Once you have set up your ODBC connectivity, you configure your Microsoft Excel worksheet to behave like a relational database by setting up named ranges in your worksheets, each one of which is treated as a relational table by the ODBC driver. Then, when you import your Microsoft Excel workbook metadata into the Oracle BI Repository, each named range/"table" becomes a physical table, which can have keys and joins created for it and data types adjusted to match the data types used by your other physical sources.

Microsoft Access   Though not covered in detail in this chapter, Microsoft Access database support is similar to Microsoft Excel support in that you would use the default ODBC drivers that ship with most Microsoft Windows operation system installations or convert to a more compatible format if your Oracle Business Intelligence installation is running on a Linux or Unix platform. Once your ODBC connection is set up, because Microsoft Access is itself a relational database, it behaves just like any other relational source, albeit with no formal support and the need to adjust the default physical database settings depending on which version of Access you are using.

CSV (Comma-Separated Values) and Flat Files   Access to file sources such as fixed-width files, and comma- and tab-delimited files is provided through the Microsoft ODBC drivers that ship with most installations of Microsoft Windows and the DataDirect ODBC drivers that ship with Oracle Business Intelligence for Windows and Unix/Linux.

If you want to access data from a file, the most compatible and straightforward way to access such data is by using these standard, open file formats, along with XML.

Setting Up Connectivity and Importing File Metadata Using ODBC Drivers

Before you can access file data through ODBC drivers, you need to first ensure that you have access to the required drivers, and second, create the ODBC connection to your file data source. For Microsoft Windows–based systems, this is fairly straightforward, as the ODBC drivers you need are usually included with your Microsoft Windows operating system, while for Unix/Linux systems, a bit more configuration may be required before you can get started.

In addition, as with any file source, you may need to copy some files around if you are performing the metadata import on a workstation but the files will eventually reside on the Oracle Business Intelligence Server.

Using ODBC with Microsoft Windows–Based Systems

In the following examples, we will first set up an ODBC connection on the Oracle Business Intelligence Server to a directory containing a CSV file and a fixed-width (TXT) file. Then we will look at the steps that you will need to perform if you wish to access data in a Microsoft Excel workbook, using the Microsoft Excel ODBC driver available on Microsoft Windows–based systems.

Example: Accessing CSV and Fixed-Width Files using ODBC   To set up an ODBC connection to the directory containing the CSV and fixed-width files and then use this connection to define the format of the two files, using Windows Server 2003 where the Oracle BI Administration tool is on the same server, follow these steps:

1. Copy the CSV and TXT files to a location on the server file system that is accessible to Oracle Business Intelligence (for example, c:\source_files\products.csv and c:\source_files\sales.txt).

2. Select Start to bring up the Windows Start menu; then select Settings | Control Panel | Administrative Tools | Data Sources (ODBC).

3. When the ODBC Data Source Administrator dialog box opens, select the System DSN tab and click Add to create the new data source.

4. From the list of drivers, select Microsoft Text Driver (*.txt, *.csv) and click Finish.

5. The ODBC Text Setup dialog box will then be displayed. At the Data Source Name text field, type in a name for the source (for example, Source Files) and optionally a description. Uncheck the Use Current Directory check box and click the Select Directory button to browse to the directory location containing your files.

   Then, in the Database Directory text box, enter the full path and name of the CSV file, and select Comma as the default table type. Finally, select the Column Names In First Line check box if the first line in your file contains the column names (recommended).

6. With the ODBC Text Setup dialog box still open, click the Options button to display the Files area. You will now use this area to define the formats of the two files.

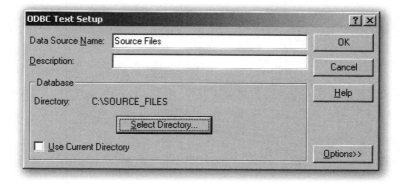

7. Click the Define Format button to start the definition of the CSV file's format. When the Define Text Format dialog box is displayed, use the Tables list on the left-hand side to select the file you wish to define (for example, products.csv).

8. As this CSV file contains column names in the first row, select the Column Name Header check box, ensure that CSV Delimited is selected as the format, and click the Guess button next to the empty Columns list on the right to read the column names into the definition. Change any column widths as required, and then click OK to save the definition.

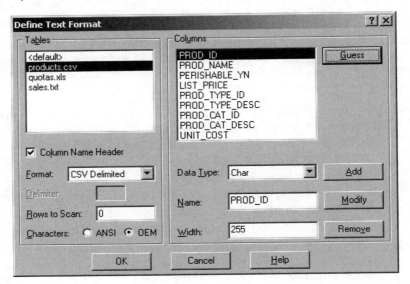

You may receive an error message that states, "Failed to save table attributes of (null) into (null)." This is a known issue with Microsoft ODBC drivers and can be safely ignored.

9. To now define the format of the SALES.txt file, which is a fixed-width file, click the Define Format button again, and this time select SALES.txt from the list on the left-hand side of the dialog box; then select Fixed-Length as the format.

10. As fixed-width files do not have delimiter characters to separate out columns, you will now need to manually add column definitions for each of the columns in your file. For example, this file has two fields within it, one for PROD_ID that is seven characters long and one for SAL_AMT that is also seven characters long. Because both fields need to be

in numeric format, enter the following values, pressing the Add button at the end of each column definition:

Name	Data Type	Width
PROD_ID	Integer	7
SAL_AMT	Float	7

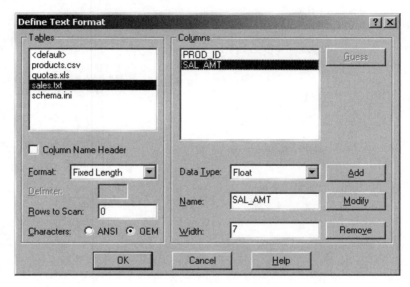

11. Click OK once the table definition is complete, and then click OK again to close the dialog box and return to the ODBC Data Source Administrator dialog box. Click OK to close it.

12. To test that your new ODBC connection works as expected, first open the Oracle BI Administration tool and create a new, empty repository.

13. Next, select File | Import Metadata and select ODBC 3.5 as the connection type. From the list of connections, select the one that you just created and enter a dummy username and password (for example, dummy/dummy) into the User Name and Password text boxes.

14. At the Import Metadata – Select Metadata Types screen, click Next to display the Import Metadata – Select Metadata Objects screen, and your files should then appear as tables in the Data Source View area.

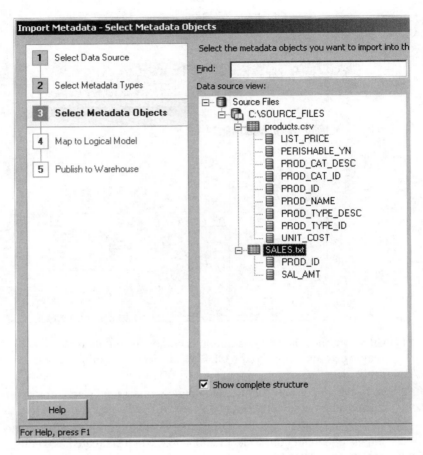

15. Click the Import All button to the right of this source file listing to add your files to the Repository View area, and then click Finish to complete the import.

16. Finally, to check that the ODBC connectivity works, right-click one of the imported tables in the physical layer and select View Data. A screen should then open that displays the contents of the file for you.

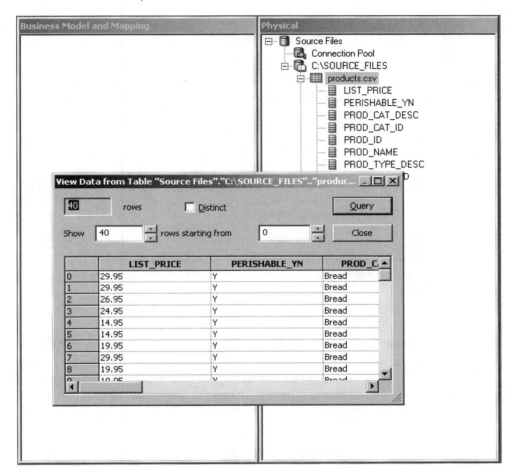

Example: Accessing Microsoft Excel Workbook Files using ODBC   You can easily create an ODBC connection to a Microsoft Excel workbook if your Oracle Business Intelligence Server is running on a Microsoft Windows–based server, as all Microsoft installations come with an Excel ODBC driver that you can use for this purpose. To use this feature, you will need to define named ranges in your Excel worksheets that will then be treated as tables by the Excel ODBC driver, and Oracle Business Intelligence will then allow you to import these "tables" into the repository physical layer.

In the example we will use now, consider a situation where we have a file called quotas.xls containing three sets of data that we wish to use in an Oracle BI Repository, created using Microsoft Excel 2003 and contained within the sample data that accompanies this book:

■ QUOTAS data, held in cells A1 > C16

■ MONTHS data, held in cells E1 > G4

■ CATEGORIES data, held in cells E6 > E11

Ensure that each of these data sets has column names defined at the top of each data column.

For each of these worksheets within the spreadsheet file, a named range has previously been defined within the spreadsheet to define data sets that will be imported as physical tables when you use the Import Metadata feature in the Oracle BI Administration tool. To create named ranged in other Microsoft Excel worksheets, first highlight the range you wish to name and then select Insert | Name | Define from the Microsoft Excel application menu to bring up the relevant dialog box, and once the definitions are complete, save the file.

For the following example, we will use the quotas.xml file that comes with the sample data, and use the following steps to first create an ODBC connection to the file, and then import its metadata into the Oracle BI Repository.

1. Copy the XLS file to a location on the server file system that is accessible to Oracle Business Intelligence (for example, c:\source_files\quotas.xls).

2. Select Start to bring up the Windows Start menu; then select Settings | Control Panel | Administrative Tools | Data Sources (ODBC).

3. When the ODBC Data Source Administrator dialog box opens, select the System DSN tab and then click Add to create the new data source.

4. From the list of drivers, select Microsoft Excel Driver (*.xls) and click Finish.

5. The ODBC Microsoft Excel Setup dialog box will then be displayed. At the Data Source Name text field, type in a name for the source (for example, Quotas XLS) and optionally a description. Use the Version drop-down menu to select the correct Excel version, and then click the Select Workbook button to browse and select the Excel workbook that you wish to make available.

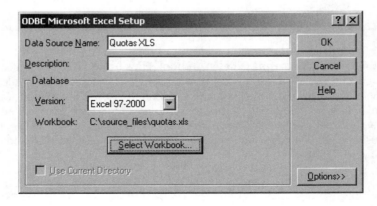

Click OK when complete, and then click OK again to close the ODBC Data Source Administrator dialog box.

6.   To test that this connection works as expected, as with the file sources, use the Oracle BI Administrator to create a new repository. When the repository is open for editing, select File | Import Metadata, and then leave the Connection Type selection as ODBC 3.5.

Your new Excel data source should then appear in the DSN list; select it and click Next. Click Next again to proceed to the Import Metadata – Select Metadata Objects dialog box.

7.   Each of the named ranges should then be displayed in the Data Source View area, with each named range represented as a table with columns named after the column names you put at the top of each range of data.

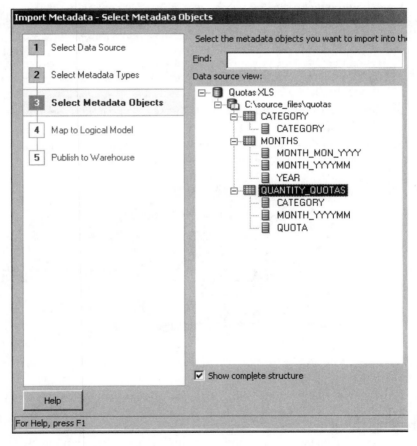

8.   Use the Import All button to add your files to the Repository View area, and then click Finish to complete the import.

9.   Finally, to check that the ODBC connectivity works, right-click one of the imported tables in the physical layer and select View Data. A screen should then open that displays the contents of the file for you.

Creating the Physical Model

Once you have imported the metadata for your file sources into your repository, you can fine-tune the physical model that has been created for you, to add keys and joins, amend data types, and adjust the database feature settings as appropriate.

Defining Table Keys

As physical tables created from file sources do not normally come with key definitions, you will need to create these manually after performing the metadata import.

Physical tables created from file sources do not usually have keys automatically created for them based on the file metadata. Therefore, you will need to review each of the physical tables created during the import, identify if keys are needed, and create them manually.

Keys should only be created for physical tables that contain dimension-related data, and they must be created only on columns that contain unique (nonrepeating) values. To create a key for a physical table based on the products.csv file imported earlier, follow these steps:

1. Using the Oracle BI Administration tool and with the repository open for editing, locate the physical table that you wish to create the key for, and double-click it to display the Properties dialog box.

2. Select the Keys tab and click inside the Key Name field. Type in a key name (for example PROD_KEY).

3. Click within the Columns field and use the drop-down menu to select the column to create the key for (for example, PROD_ID).

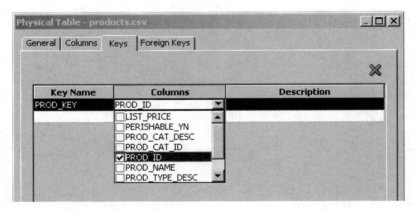

4. Click OK to close the dialog box.

Creating Physical Joins

As with keys, the metadata you import from file sources does not normally include joins (foreign keys) between tables, and you will therefore need to create these yourself manually. Joins are created from physical tables containing fact data to tables containing dimension data, and you would normally create them after creating keys for the dimension tables.

To create a physical join between the physical tables created from the SALES.TXT and products.csv file imported earlier, follow these steps:

1. Using the Oracle BI Administration tool and with the repository open for editing, locate the physical tables that you wish to join, CTRL-click them to select them all, and then right-click and select Physical Diagram | Selected Object(s) Only.

2. With the Physical Diagram screen open, locate the New Join button in the toolbar, and then draw a line to connect the fact table (SALES.txt) to the dimension table (products.csv).

SALES.txt

Columns	Types	Length	Nullable	
PROD_ID	INT	10	True	
SAL_AMT	DOUBLE	15	True	

products.csv

Columns	Types	Length	Nullable	
PROD_ID	INT	0	True	
PROD_NAME	VARCHAR	255	True	
PERISHABLE_YN	VARCHAR	255	True	
LIST_PRICE	VARCHAR	255	True	

3. When the Physical Foreign Key dialog box is then shown, ensure that the correct columns are listed in the expression, and click OK to close the dialog box.

4. If you receive the error message "[nQSError: 22024] A Comparison is being carried out between noncompatible data types," click OK, click Cancel, and use the steps in the next section to amend the data type of the affected column to match the one you are joining to.

Amending Imported Column Data Types

Sometimes when you try to create joins between columns in two physical tables, you find that the data type that has been automatically assigned to a physical column needs to be changed to be compatible with the data type of another column.

For example, in the product.csv physical table that was imported previously in this chapter, all of the physical columns have been set to a default data type of VARCHAR(255). This presents a problem when the PROD_ID column within this table needs to be joined to the PROD_ID column in the SALES.txt physical table, which has a data type of INT.

SALES.txt

Columns △	Types	Length	Nullable	
PROD_ID	INT	10	True	
SAL_AMT	DOUBLE	15	True	

products.csv

Columns △	Types	Length	Nullable	
PROD_ID	VARCHAR	255	True	
PROD_NAME	VARCHAR	255	True	
PERISHABLE_YN	VARCHAR	255	True	
LIST_PRICE	VARCHAR	255	True	

In these situations, it usually makes sense to amend the data types for your imported physical table to make them compatible with other columns and also to make them suitable for numeric analysis, for example. To amend the data type for an imported physical column, follow these steps:

1. Using the Oracle BI Administration tool and with the repository open for editing, locate the physical table that contains the columns that you wish to amend, and double-click it to display the Properties dialog box.

2. Select the Columns tab, and then click the column you wish to update (for example, PROD_ID). Click the Edit (pencil) button to open the column for editing.

3. With the Physical Column dialog box open, use the Type drop-down menu to change the data type to one that is more appropriate (for example, INT). Note that you should only change a data type where this is appropriate for the values in the column; do not, for example, set a column's data type to INT if it contains numeric data.

4. Click OK twice to close the Physical Column and Table dialog boxes.

Amending Physical Database Properties

Finally, depending on the ODBC source that you are using, the default set of database features assigned to your physical database may need to be altered. For example, file sources do not support the "count distinct" SQL function, and therefore the COUNT_DISTINCT_SUPPORTED feature will need to be disabled for these source types; otherwise, unexpected errors may occur.

To view the list of database features set up for your physical database after the metadata import, locate the physical database in your repository (usually named after the ODBC DSN name), double-click it, and select the Features tab. You will see that, by default, COUNT_ DISTINCT_SUPPORTED is enabled for file sources.

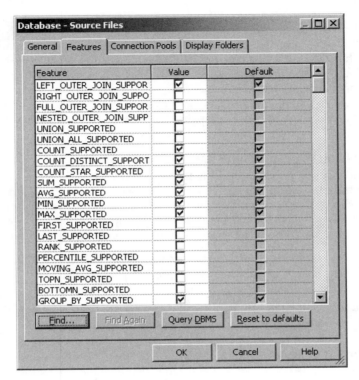

To set this to the correct value, either uncheck the Value check box for this property, or to set all values to the correct value, click the Query DBMS button, which will query the ODBC driver and set the values correctly. Click OK after setting the values, and save your repository afterward.

Now that your physical model is set up, you can use the tables made available by it within the rest of your repository, mapping them as sources into your business model along with tables sourced from relational and multidimensional sources.

Modeling XML Sources

Data sources based on XML documents, unlike file sources, are fully supported by Oracle Business Intelligence and can be used to source data from external web servers or to provide sample data without the need for a separate database server.

Like file sources, you will still get better query performance if you can colocate all of your data in a single data warehouse or OLAP cube, but there are many use cases where working with XML data directly makes sense, and this section of the chapter will outline the options and steps required to work with data from XML sources.

Overview

Extensible Markup Language (XML) is a topic that by itself would probably fill a book as big as this one, and therefore it is assumed that you have a basic knowledge of XML already and understand the key concepts. In this section of the chapter, we will start by looking at why you might want to bring XML data into your Oracle BI Repository and look at the various types of scenarios where XML data might be used with Oracle Business Intelligence.

We will then look at limitations you will need to bear in mind when working with XML data, as well as the two main methods Oracle Business Intelligence uses to access data of this type. Finally, we will go through the steps required to import XML metadata into your repository and how you can set up the physical layer in the repository to connect your XML data together and to other sources.

Why Might You Want to Model XML Sources?

XML is a widely used format for creating structured documents, and it can be used as a data source for physical tables in your repository. XML documents can be stored locally on file systems, or you can access them over the Internet from a web server, which may in turn store them statically or generate them dynamically on demand.

There are two main use cases for working the XML data in Oracle Business Intelligence:

- You may have one or more XML documents on the server file system that you wish to use as a data source, possibly as part of a prototyping exercise or as a means of mapping in additional data generated as a static document by another application.

- You may want to read in dynamically created data in XML format, generated by an application or web service available on the Internet.

Restrictions and Limitations

Not every type of XML document scenario can be handled by Oracle Business Intelligence. XML documents that embed references to other XML documents (other than XML schema documents) cannot be used, nor can XML documents be used if they use element and attribute inheritance contained within a Microsoft XML schema. Finally, XML documents that use element types of a mixed content model cannot be used; see the *Oracle® Fusion Middleware Metadata Repository Builder's Guide for Oracle Business Intelligence Enterprise Edition 11g Release 1 (11.1.1)* for more details on XML document restrictions.

In addition, data accessed from XML documents is handled in a similar way to cached relational and multidimensional data in that the Oracle BI Server's copy of the data is refreshed to a schedule that you determine when configuring the physical repository objects. As such, by default, XML data is read once and then stays static unless you configure a refresh schedule to keep the Oracle BI Server's copy up to date. Details of how to configure this refresh schedule are provided in the following examples.

XML Source Access Methods

You can access XML data in the following types of documents:

- Static XML documents served from a local or networked file system location (for example, c:\xmlfiles\BUDGETS.xml)

- Static XML documents accessed over the Internet using a URL (for example, http://www.rittmanmead.com/xml/SAMP_XML_REVENUE_F.xml)

- Dynamic XML documents accessed over the Internet using a URL (for example, http://www.rittmanmead.com/xmljsp/revenue.jsp)
- An HTML file that contains tables, defined by <table> and </table> tags

Typically, you would access these documents through the XML Gateway that comes with the Oracle BI Server in the same way that you access Oracle Essbase data via the Essbase gateway and Oracle Database data via the Oracle OCI8i or OracleOCI10g gateway.

Alternatively, you can access XML data via an XML ODBC driver, though as Oracle Business Intelligence does not ship with such a driver by default and you would therefore need to license and install such a driver yourself, most developers use the XML Gateway instead.

Using the XML Gateway   The XML Gateway used by Oracle Business Intelligence converts your XML documents into a tabular structure, basing the table name on the name of the file (without the file suffix, typically .XML) and creating rows and columns out of the second and third-level elements in the XML tree.

For example, consider a situation where the following XML document named SAMP_PRODUCTS_D.xml is a data source for the XML Gateway:

```xml
<?xml version="1.0" encoding="UTF-8"?>
<Table Name="SAMP_PRODUCTS_D">
    <SAMP_PRODUCTS_D>
        <PROD_KEY>8</PROD_KEY>
        <PROD_DSC>V5x Flip Phone</PROD_DSC>
        <ATTRIBUTE_2>Red</ATTRIBUTE_2>
        <ATTRIBUTE_1>Size 10</ATTRIBUTE_1>
        <TYPE>Cell Phones</TYPE>
        <LOB>Communication</LOB>
        <BRAND>BizTech</BRAND>
        <SEQUENCE>1</SEQUENCE>
        <BRAND_KEY>10001</BRAND_KEY>
        <LOB_KEY>1001</LOB_KEY>
        <TYPE_KEY>101</TYPE_KEY>
    </SAMP_PRODUCTS_D>
    <SAMP_PRODUCTS_D>
    <PROD_KEY>9</PROD_KEY>
        <PROD_DSC>Touch-Screen T5</PROD_DSC>
        <ATTRIBUTE_2>Blue</ATTRIBUTE_2>
        <ATTRIBUTE_1>Size 25</ATTRIBUTE_1>
        <TYPE>Smart Phones</TYPE>
        <LOB>Communication</LOB>
        <BRAND>BizTech</BRAND>
        <SEQUENCE>3</SEQUENCE>
        <BRAND_KEY>10001</BRAND_KEY>
        <LOB_KEY>1001</LOB_KEY>
        <TYPE_KEY>102</TYPE_KEY>
    </SAMP_PRODUCTS_D>
```

The XML Gateway would import this document as a table called SAMP_PRODUCTS_D with columns named ATTRIBUTE_1, BRAND, BRAND_KEY, PROD_KEY, and so on.

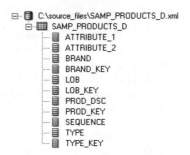

Your XML document should follow this format, and you should use XSLT or a similar technology to transform your XML to this format if it is not in that format already. Your XML document can also reference a separate XML schema document if you wish to define the data types of each element as other than the default STRING type.

Using XML ODBC   As an alternative to the XML Gateway that ships with Oracle Business Intelligence, you can also obtain and install an XML ODBC driver and use that to connect to an XML data source. Most XML ODBC drivers are commercial and require a license fee, though, and you will need to obtain the drivers yourself.

Once you have obtained and installed the drivers, though, consult their documentation for how they interpret XML documents and present them to calling applications, such as Oracle Business Intelligence, as table-and-column structures.

Setting Up Connectivity to XML Sources

To test connectivity to XML data sources, we will use the XML sample data that comes with the SampleAppLite sample application that ships with all installations of Oracle Business Intelligence. You can usually find this XML data, in the form of the following XML files, at [*middleware_home*]\\ instances\instance1\bifoundation\OracleBIServerComponent\coreapplication_obis1\sample\ SampleAppFiles\Data\:

SAMP_OFFICES_D.xml
SAMP_PRODUCTS_D.xml
SAMP_REVENUE_A.xml
SAMP_REVENUE_F.xml
SAMP_TARGETS_F.xml
SAMP_TIME_DAY_D.xml
SAMP_TIME_MTH_D.xml

Example: Accessing XML Data through the XML Gateway

In the following examples, we will set up connectivity to these files using the following XML Gateway methods:

- By connecting to a directory of static XML documents
- By connecting to a web server via a URL to a single static XML document

Accessing a dynamic XML file from a web server via a URL would involve the same process as the second step, so it will not be detailed separately.

To import a set of XML documents into the Oracle BI Repository from a location on a local or networked file system using the XML Gateway, follow these steps:

1. Using the Oracle BI Administrator tool, open your repository and then select File | Import Metadata.

2. The Import Metadata – Select Data Source screen will then be shown. On this screen, select either Remove Server or Local Machine as the import type, and then, using the Connection Type drop-down menu, select XML.

3. Then, with the same screen still open, click the Browse button to locate a single XML document or enter the directory path to a directory of XML files if you wish to import all files from a directory. Leave the User Name and Password fields blank, and then click Next to proceed.

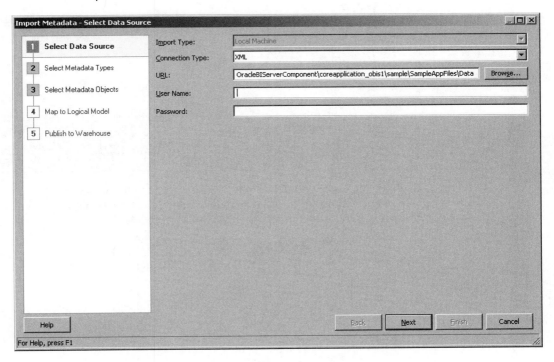

4. At the Import Metadata – Select Metadata Types screen, click Next, and your XML files will be listed on the Import Metadata – Select Metadata Objects screen. If you entered the location of a directory in the earlier step, all of the valid XML files in that directory will be listed for import, while if you only select a single XML file, just that file will

be listed. Select which files you wish to import into the repository, and then click Finish to complete the import.

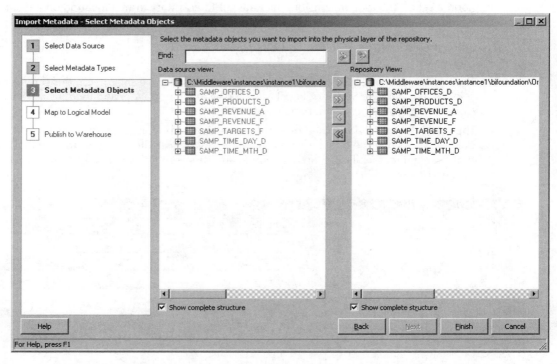

5. Within the physical layer of your Oracle BI Repository, you will now see the XML files for which you imported metadata listed as individual physical tables with columns that correspond to the third-level elements in your XML documents.

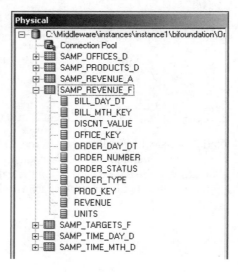

If the XML document that you wish to import metadata for exists on the Internet, either as a dynamically created XML feed or as a static XML document, you would follow the same steps as the previous example, except that you would enter a web URL into the Import Metadata – Select Data Source screen when using the Import Metadata Wizard.

For example, if you wished to import the metadata for an XML document located at http://www.rittmanmead.com/xml/SAMP_XML_REVENUE_F.xml, you would follow these steps:

1. Using the Oracle BI Administrator tool, open your repository and select File | Import Metadata.

2. The Import Metadata – Select Data Source screen will then be shown. On this screen, select either Remove Server or Local Machine as the import type, and then, using the Connection Type drop-down menu, select XML.

3. With the same screen still open, enter the following values into the URL, User Name, and Password fields:

   URL: **http://www.rittmanmead.com/xml/SAMP_XML_REVENUE_F.xml**
   Username: [*leave blank, unless web server uses Basic Authentication*]
   Password: [*leave blank, unless web server uses Basic Authentication*]

Import Type:	Local Machine
Connection Type:	XML
URL:	http://www.rittmanmead.com/xml/SAMP_XML_REVENUE_F.xml Browse...
User Name:	
Password:	

4. The rest of the steps for the XML document metadata import would be the same as with an XML document stored on a local or networked file system, as detailed previously.

Because you cannot reference a directory of files using this method, accessing XML documents via an Internet URL will only work for a single document. If you wish to access more than one XML document in this way, you will have to repeat the import process for each file.

Example: Accessing XML Data through XML_ODBC

If you wish to use the XML ODBC approach to working with XML documents, you will need to license and install suitable ODBC drivers before accessing your data, as these drivers do not ship with Oracle Business Intelligence and they do not get installed automatically as part of a Microsoft Windows installation. Once you have these drivers, follow these steps to use them to import XML document metadata into your repository:

1. Using the Oracle BI Administrator tool, open your repository and then select File | Import Metadata.

2. The Import Metadata – Select Data Source screen will then be shown. On this screen, select either Remove Server or Local Machine as the import type, and then, using

the Connection Type drop-down menu, select ODBC 3.5 as the connection type and select your ODBC DSN from the list displayed. Type in a username and password as appropriate, click Next, and then click Next again to proceed.

3. At the Import Metadata – Select Metadata Objects screen, select the database objects that you would like to import, and then click Finish to complete the import.

Creating the Physical Model

Once you have successfully imported your XML document metadata into the repository, you will need to perform additional steps to define keys, create joins between physical tables, and, in some cases, amend settings for your connection pool. This is because, unlike relational or multidimensional sources, keys and joins are not defined within the XML document, and you will need to define how often the Oracle BI Server retrieves new data from your documents.

Defining Table Keys

As with relational sources, you will need to define physical keys within the physical tables that hold dimension-related data. To create keys within these tables, follow these steps:

1. Using the Oracle BI Administration tool and with the repository open for editing, locate the physical table that you wish to create the key for, and double-click it to display the Properties dialog box.

2. Select the Keys tab. Click inside the Key Name field, and type in a key name (for example, PROD_KEY).

3. Click within the Columns field, and use the drop-down menu to select the column to create the key for (for example PROD_KEY).

4. Click OK to close the dialog box.

Creating Physical Joins

Similarly, you will need to create physical joins between the physical tables containing fact-related data in your physical model and those containing dimension-related data. To do this, follow these steps:

1. Using the Oracle BI Administration tool and with the repository open for editing, locate the physical tables that you wish to join, CTRL-click them to select them all, and then right-click and select Physical Diagram | Selected Object(s) Only.

2. With the Physical Diagram screen open, locate the New Join button in the toolbar, and then draw a line to connect the fact table (for example, SAMP_REVENUE_F) to the dimension table (for example, SAMP_PRODUCTS_D).

3. When the Physical Foreign Key dialog box is then shown, ensure that the correct columns are listed in the expression, and click OK to close the dialog box.

4. Repeat these steps for any other dimension-related physical tables in your model until you have joined the fact table to every related dimension table in your model.

Amending Physical Database and Connection Pool Properties

While you can leave most physical database and connection pool settings at their default after an XML document metadata import, one setting that you will need to consider is the URL refresh interval setting within the connection pool.

The Oracle BI Server treats XML sources similarly to cached database sources in that it uses a consistent copy of its data until the copy is refreshed. How often this data is refreshed is determined by the URL refresh interval setting, which you can adjust by double-clicking the connection pool used by your physical database and selecting the XML tab.

By default, this setting is set to infinite, which means that data will never be refreshed, even if you update the data in the XML document. If you set this to another value, such as 10 minutes, the data will be refreshed according to the following rules:

- If the data source points to a web location, the document will be reread and the BI Server's data copy will be updated according to this schedule.

- If the data source points to a static XML document on a file system, the data copy will be reread according to the schedule, as long as the file itself has been updated in the meantime.

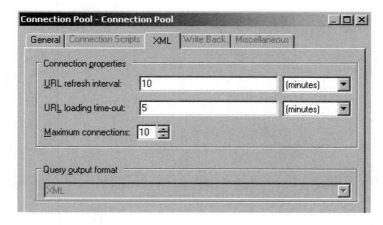

Similarly, the URL loading timeout setting on the same dialog box can be used to set how long the BI Server waits for an Internet-accessed XML document to return values before giving up with a timeout error.

CHAPTER
4

Creating Repositories from Oracle Essbase and Other OLAP Data Sources

n addition to creating repositories that source their data from relational databases such as the Oracle Database, you can also import metadata from online analytical processing (OLAP) servers such as Oracle Essbase, Microsoft Analysis Services, and the OLAP Option to Oracle Database, which store their data in multidimensional databases. In this chapter, we will look at how data from these multidimensional data sources can be imported and modeled in your repository, combined with other data, and then presented to users for analysis on their dashboards.

Overview of Oracle Business Intelligence Support for Multidimensional Data Sources

Oracle Business Intelligence, through the Oracle BI Server and the Oracle BI Administration tool, allows you to import metadata from, and then create business models against, data held in multidimensional OLAP databases such as Oracle Essbase and Microsoft Analysis Services. OLAP data sources are modeled, in a similar way to relational databases, in the physical layer of the Oracle BI Repository. You can then create business models that source data from OLAP data sources along with other types of data sources in the business model and mapping layer.

While OLAP data sources have their own physical object types in the physical layer of the repository, once you map them into the business model and mapping layer and then make them available for querying through the presentation layer, they are indistinguishable to end users from regular relational and other data sources, although analyses created using them hopefully should return data faster. There are some modeling concepts that are used in particular with OLAP data sources, such as external aggregation and the EVALUATE and EVALUATE_AGGR clause, but once you have imported the metadata for your OLAP data source into the physical layer of the repository, it behaves in most cases just like any other non-OLAP data source.

One particular benefit of working with OLAP data sources has to do with the additional dimensional metadata contained with the OLAP data dictionary as compared to non-OLAP sources. When you import an OLAP data source such as Oracle Essbase or Oracle OLAP into the physical layer of the repository, creating the business model and mapping layer and then the presentation layer is usually just a case of dragging and dropping the physical database into the business model and mapping layer, and from there into the presentation layer. The BI Administration tool then creates the logical joins, logical dimensions, and hierarchies based on the metadata imported from the source OLAP database.

Once you have imported your OLAP data source into the repository, you can report on it in isolation or you can combine it with relational or other non-OLAP data using the vertical and horizontal federation techniques initially described in Chapter 3. In addition, you can enhance the business model derived from the OLAP data source using Oracle Business Intelligence functions such as time-series functions, or you can leverage native functions and calculations provided by the OLAP server.

Supported OLAP Data Sources

At the time of this writing, the following OLAP servers were supported by the 11.1.1.6 release of Oracle Business Intelligence 11*g*:

- Oracle Essbase
- The OLAP Option to Oracle Database

- SAP Business Information Warehouse (SAP BW)
- Microsoft Analysis Services

For the most recent list of supported OLAP servers, including the particular version numbers that are supported, see the *System Requirements and Supported Platforms for Oracle Business Intelligence Suite Enterprise Edition 11gR1* document, part of the product documentation set updated for each release of Oracle Business Intelligence.

How the Oracle BI Server Accesses OLAP Data Sources

When you execute an analysis using Oracle Business Intelligence, the Oracle BI Presentation Server sends a request for data to the Oracle BI Server, which then uses the semantic model held within the Oracle BI Repository to identify the physical data sources that need to be accessed to satisfy this request. The Oracle BI Server then generates queries against these data sources, using the native query language and call interface best suited to that data source, as shown in Figure 4-1.

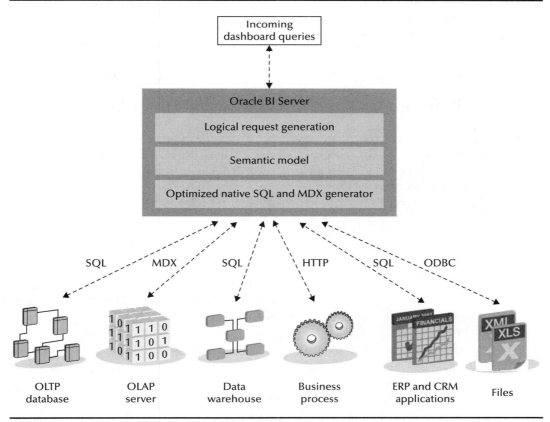

FIGURE 4-1. *The Oracle BI Server generating native queries*

For supported relational database sources such as the Oracle Database, the Oracle BI Server generates SQL requests using the syntax and specific capabilities of the Oracle Database. Similarly, for sources such as Microsoft SQL Server and Teradata, SQL requests that use the particular capabilities of those data sources are generated, with those capabilities being determined by features selected by the repository administrator for each particular physical database.

For OLAP data sources, in all cases except for Oracle OLAP, these data sources are accessed via Multidimensional Expressions (MDX) queries, rather than SQL queries. MDX, like SQL, is a declarative language, but it is optimized for working with multidimensional data sets and is the standard query language for most modern OLAP servers. In order to access data held in OLAP servers such as Oracle Essbase and Microsoft Analysis Services, the Oracle BI Server generates MDX queries and converts the returned multidimensional data set into a relational rows-and-columns data set that it then combines as required with other data requested by the user before returning it to the Oracle BI Presentation Server for display to the user.

In the case of Oracle OLAP, instead of using MDX to access its multidimensional data set, it uses a built-in Oracle conversion function called OLAP_TABLE, which in turn converts OLAP data into relational rows and columns. To retrieve data from an Oracle OLAP data source, the Oracle BI Server generates a special type of SQL query that uses the OLAP_TABLE function, relying on the Oracle Database to perform the multidimensional-to-relational data set conversion.

All of this process is handled automatically by the Oracle BI Server, so that the end user does not need to be aware of what data sources are relational, what ones are multidimensional, and what ones are sourced from files or other data source types. However, as an administrator, you need to be aware of the nuances and differences among the different data source types, and this chapter will outline what you need to know about working with OLAP data sources.

Multidimensional-Specific Repository Metadata Objects

When working with multidimensional OLAP data sources within an Oracle BI Repository, there are specific metadata objects that are used only with these types of sources. These metadata objects are found only within the physical layer of the repository, as once you model these sources in the business model and mapping layer and presentation layer of the repository, they behave just like any other data source.

Multidimensional data sources that are accessed via MDX queries, such as Oracle Essbase and Microsoft Analysis Services, have their own specific physical layer objects that contain properties specific to this type of data source. Figure 4-2 shows a typical Oracle Essbase physical database definition within the physical layer of the Oracle BI Repository.

The physical repository object types used by these types of OLAP servers are listed here:

- **Database**   This is the container for all the cube tables, physical cube dimensions, and other objects that make up a multidimensional data source. In Oracle Essbase terms, a database would correspond to a physical Essbase server.

- **Physical catalog**   This is a container for one or more cube tables. In Oracle Essbase terms, each catalog would correspond to an Essbase application.

- **Cube table**   A cube table contains the physical cube columns, physical cube dimensions, and other objects that together, in Oracle Essbase terms, would be considered a database containing a database outline.

- **Physical cube column**   A physical cube column is analogous to a regular physical database column, and holds measure or attribute values that then go on to become sources for logical columns in the business model and mapping layer of the repository.

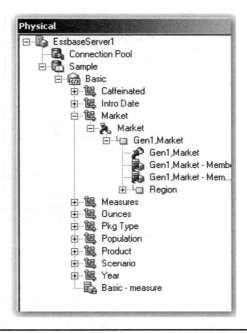

FIGURE 4-2. *An Oracle Essbase multidimensional database definition*

- **Physical cube dimension**   The cube dimension is contained with the cube table and represents the dimensions used to organize the measures in the cube table.

- **Physical hierarchy**   One or more physical hierarchies may be contained within each cube dimension and represent individual roll-ups such as day-month-year or day-period–financial year.

Because they are accessed via SQL queries and the OLAP_TABLE function, Oracle OLAP database definitions have their own specific physical object types that are distinct from the ones used by MDX-accessible OLAP servers, as shown in Figure 4-3. These object types have their own Oracle OLAP–specific properties that reflect the particular way that multidimensional data is held within an Oracle Database server, and are listed here:

- **Oracle OLAP analytic workspace**   This is the container for the Oracle OLAP dimensions, levels, cubes, and columns within an Oracle OLAP database definition. An Oracle OLAP analytic workspace corresponds with analytic workspaces that you create within the Oracle Database in that they are multidimensional stores of data held within multidimensional data types stored in relational tables.

- **Oracle OLAP dimension**   An Oracle OLAP dimension contains Oracle OLAP Columns, and level-based and value-based Oracle OLAP hierarchies that organize these columns for aggregation purposes.

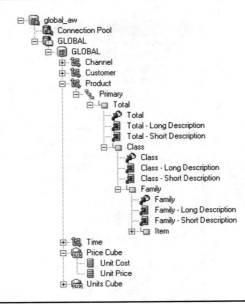

FIGURE 4-3. *An Oracle OLAP multidimensional database definition*

NOTE
Oracle Business Intelligence does not support dimensions that have no hierarchies, and if you try to import such a dimension into the Oracle BI Repository, you will receive an error message.

- **Level-based Oracle OLAP hierarchy** Level-based hierarchies are made up of one or more Oracle OLAP levels, which are arranged into a hierarchy to define how data is aggregated, or "rolled up," within the dimension.

- **Value-based Oracle OLAP hierarchy** Oracle OLAP and Oracle Business Intelligence support value-based hierarchies that use member and parent ID values to define how data is aggregated.

NOTE
Unlike Essbase data sources, you cannot change the definition of an Oracle OLAP hierarchy from level based to value based (or vice versa) within the Oracle BI Repository, as this is determined solely within the Oracle OLAP analytic workspace definition.

- **Oracle OLAP level** Level-based Oracle OLAP hierarchies are made up of one or more Oracle OLAP levels, which define the individual aggregation steps in a level-based hierarchy and have level keys defined that map to one of the Oracle OLAP columns within the level.

- **Oracle OLAP column** Oracle OLAP columns are contained within Oracle OLAP levels; therefore, they hold attribute data or are contained within Oracle OLAP cube objects, and they contain measure data. Oracle OLAP columns have their own data types and hold the actual attribute and measure data that you will display in your analyses.

- **Oracle OLAP cube** An Oracle OLAP cube is a container for Oracle OLAP columns containing measures that share the same dimensionality. Oracle OLAP cube objects have properties to define whether they are sparse or dense and whether they are fully or partially materialized.

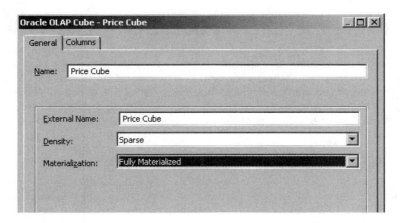

For Oracle OLAP 10*g* cubes, setting the Density option to Sparse and the Materialization option to Fully Materialized causes the Oracle BI Server to use the "loop optimized" access method to retrieve cube data. This is a more efficient access method for this type of cube, assuming that your physical analytic workspace cube has these storage options applied. For Oracle OLAP 11*g* cubes, though, this optimization happens automatically, and therefore you will see that these options are not set (and should not be set) when you import your cube metadata.

Automatic Creation of Business Models

One of the benefits of working with multidimensional data sources with the Oracle BI Administration tool is its automatic creation of metadata for the business model and mapping layer and presentation layer, once you have imported the physical database model into the repository.

When you import a multidimensional database definition to an Oracle BI repository, as well as importing attribute and measure information, you are also importing definitions of dimensions, hierarchies, and levels—information that you normally have to manually determine and then add to your business model for relational sources. Because this information is already present within your physical database model, you can automatically create a full business model definition corresponding to your OLAP data source by dragging and dropping your physical model into the business model and mapping layer of the Oracle BI Repository, and you can then drag this business model into the presentation layer of the repository to create the corresponding subject area. Business models and subject areas created in this way can subsequently be amended or combined with other business models and subject areas, should you wish to create a repository that spans both relational, multidimensional, and other sources.

The flip side of this capability, though, is that it is actually quite difficult to manually create physical database definitions for multidimensional data sources or amend existing physical database definitions once they have been imported.

TIP
It is recommended that you always use the Import Metadata feature within the Oracle BI Administration tool to create multidimensional database definitions within the Oracle BI Repository rather than try to create the definition yourself manually.

Pass-Through Security for Data and Metadata Filters

As with any data source, you can either use the OLAP server to implement data security, use filters defined in the Oracle BI Repository, or do a combination of the two. For example, Oracle Essbase has the concept of filters and metafilters, which restrict access to data based on policies defined in the Essbase outline. If you wish to make use of these security settings, you would configure the connection pool settings either to pass through the user ID and password of the logged-in user or use one of a set of shared credentials used to grant access to subsets of data.

NOTE
If you do make use of Essbase security by passing user credentials in the connection pool settings for the Essbase database, this may limit your use of agents, for example, that rely on the impersonation feature to execute the agent using the credentials of the subscriber rather than the agent author. When you pass username and password credentials to Essbase or any other data source in this way for individual users, the Oracle BI Scheduler will not have access to the user's password, will not therefore be able to authenticate, and no data will be returned.

Similarly, for Oracle OLAP and other multidimensional data sources, you can either have filters and other access restrictions imposed by the Oracle BI Repository, or you can pass through sets of credentials that will then be used by the OLAP server to apply its own filters and restrictions.

Generally, when deciding whether to apply filters, either at the physical database level or instead within the Oracle BI Repository, your decision is determined by the degree to which data is integrated across sources within the repository. If you are sourcing your repository business model from just a single source, it often makes sense to leverage database-level filters if they are already present through the :USER and :PASSWORD session variables, which can be used to pass through the logged-in users' credentials to the underlying database server. If your business model is sourced from lots of individual data sources, it usually makes sense to build your filtering and access restrictions at the repository level so that they can be applied across all subject areas.

One particular consideration with OLAP server data sources is whether applying filters at the OLAP server level will result in more efficient queries than if you used the BI Server to filter your data. In the case of filtering hierarchical column members, in particular, it may be considerably more efficient to create filters at the OLAP server level and then just pass through the users' credentials in the connection pool; therefore, you should carefully analyze your source data, and likely usage and filtering scenarios, before deciding where to place your filters.

In the following sections, for each covered data source, we will look at how database-level filtering works and also how you can apply filters at the repository level that can apply across all data sources.

Leveraging OLAP Functions and Analytics

Multidimensional OLAP servers such as Oracle Essbase and Oracle OLAP come with powerful analytic, calculation, and forecasting capabilities that you may wish to make use of in your business intelligence project. For example, Oracle Essbase comes with MDX functions that allow you to, for example, allocate data among child dimension members according to a formula or calculate values offset by a time period or for a period to date.

There are also many equivalent functions within the Oracle BI SQL syntax, and for most supported relational sources the Oracle BI Server will translate Oracle BI function syntax to the supported databases's function syntax for you automatically (a feature often referred to as "function push-down"). However, for multidimensional data sources, this function push-down happens in far fewer cases, and only the most basic functions (SUM and AVERAGE, for example) are pushed down to the multidimensional server, in most cases because MDX does not support a particular function, such as most string functions. (For Essbase sources, time-series functions are also pushed down to the Essbase server,)

Because of this, if you wish to make use of these capabilities, you will often have to use the EVALUATE and EVALUATE_AGGR Oracle BI functions to instead pass down a native MDX function to the multidimensional server. Use of these functions, along with details of what Oracle BI functions are actually pushed down to the supported multidimensional database servers, is detailed later in this chapter.

Federation of OLAP, Relational, and Other Sources

Apart from being able to report and analyze multidimensional data using the rich dashboards, pivot tables, charts, maps, and other visualizations provided by Oracle Business Intelligence, the major reason that users access multidimensional data sets from Oracle Business Intelligence is to combine this data with other, usually relational, data sets within their organization. Combining separate source data sets into a single business model is referred to as "data federation" and can be categorized as follows:

- **Vertical federation**   This is where typically aggregated multidimensional data is combined with detail-level relational or file-based data sets.

- **Horizontal federation**   This is where data at the same level of detail is combined into a single data model.

Often, business models that are based on federated data actually use combinations of vertical and horizontal federation to perhaps combine aggregated OLAP data and transaction-level relational data, with relational descriptive data used to enhance the OLAP data. Figure 4-4 shows a typical analysis sourced from relational, file, and multidimensional data sources. In the background, as each level of detail is accessed, the Oracle BI Server will generate the appropriate SQL, MDX, or other queries to retrieve data from the appropriate sources.

Federating data sources is one of the strengths of Oracle Business Intelligence, and it is a reasonably straightforward process to enable. You will need to be conscious of performance issues when combining data sources if the Oracle BI Server is required to combine data sets before returning them to the Oracle BI Presentation Server. There are techniques, such as the use of the

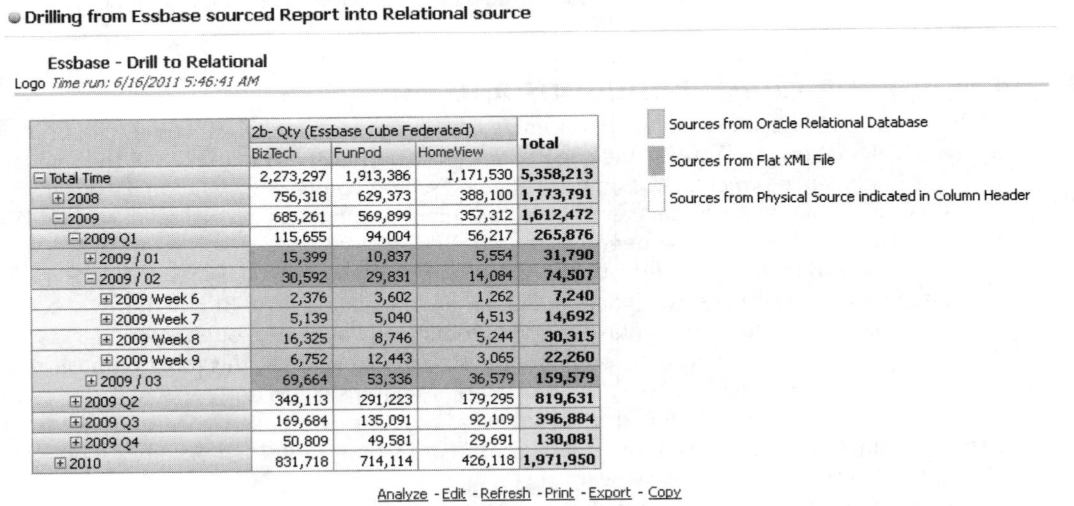

● Drilling from Essbase sourced Report into Relational source

Essbase - Drill to Relational
Logo *Time run: 6/16/2011 5:46:41 AM*

	2b- Qty (Essbase Cube Federated)			Total
	BizTech	FunPod	HomeView	
⊟ Total Time	2,273,297	1,913,386	1,171,530	**5,358,213**
⊞ 2008	756,318	629,373	388,100	**1,773,791**
⊟ 2009	685,261	569,899	357,312	**1,612,472**
⊟ 2009 Q1	115,655	94,004	56,217	**265,876**
⊞ 2009 / 01	15,399	10,837	5,554	**31,790**
⊟ 2009 / 02	30,592	29,831	14,084	**74,507**
⊞ 2009 Week 6	2,376	3,602	1,262	**7,240**
⊞ 2009 Week 7	5,139	5,040	4,513	**14,692**
⊞ 2009 Week 8	16,325	8,746	5,244	**30,315**
⊞ 2009 Week 9	6,752	12,443	3,065	**22,260**
⊞ 2009 / 03	69,664	53,336	36,579	**159,579**
⊞ 2009 Q2	349,113	291,223	179,295	**819,631**
⊞ 2009 Q3	169,684	135,091	92,109	**396,884**
⊞ 2009 Q4	50,809	49,581	29,691	**130,081**
⊞ 2010	831,718	714,114	426,118	**1,971,950**

Sources from Oracle Relational Database

Sources from Flat XML File

Sources from Physical Source indicated in Column Header

Analyze - Edit - Refresh - Print - Export - Copy

FIGURE 4-4. *An analysis using Essbase, relational, and XML Sources*

LOOKUP function, that can make this type of modeling more efficient. We will look at this topic in more detail later in this chapter once we have covered the specifics of handling each type of multidimensional data source.

End-User Analysis Features for OLAP Data

Once you have modeled your multidimensional data sources in the Oracle BI Repository, you will want to analyze them using the various analysis views available within Oracle Business Intelligence.

Typically, data sourced from multidimensional sources is analyzed using pivot table views and a combination of hierarchical, attribute, and measure subject area column types. Figure 4-5 shows a typical pivot table using two of these features, where the user is displaying OLAP data aggregated across several dimensions, with subtotals generated at various levels.

Once a basic pivot table analysis has been created, as well as filtering data in the analysis criteria, you can also perform post-aggregation modeling of the data using a feature called "selection steps." Selection steps, combined with such OLAP-friendly features as hierarchical prompts, allow you to create a rich analytic query environment for users comparable to those provided by dedicated OLAP query clients, as shown in Figure 4-6.

More details on how pivot tables, together with selection steps, hierarchical prompts, and other query features are used, are provided in Chapter 7. You should note, however, that while these types of analyses and views work very well with multidimensional data sources, they provide the same functionality for all supported data sources, albeit with perhaps not as good a query response time.

	Total Time								
		2008						2009	2010
			2008 Q1	2008 Q2	2008 Q3	2008 Q4			
Michele Lombardo	50,000,000	16,500,000	2,707,686	8,109,716	4,338,844	1,343,754		15,000,000	18,500,000
Aurelio Miranda	2,300,000	710,044	138,906	336,189	185,834	49,115		721,245	868,710
Helen Mayes	9,460,000	3,062,284	477,583	1,521,364	792,458	270,879		2,932,022	3,465,694
Monica Velasquez	17,090,000	5,758,674	998,025	2,776,321	1,505,513	478,814		5,016,544	6,314,782
Paul Atkinson	4,220,000	1,411,440	197,886	708,334	388,131	117,088		1,203,576	1,604,983
Sophie Bergman	16,820,000	5,522,214	888,371	2,753,103	1,460,874	419,865		5,108,525	6,189,261
Peter Marzec	7,733,719	2,568,351	413,510	1,252,386	681,519	220,937		2,336,205	2,829,164
Russell Wolin	9,086,281	2,953,863	474,862	1,500,717	779,356	198,929		2,772,320	3,360,098

Edit - Refresh - Export - Copy

FIGURE 4-5. *A pivot table view using hierarchical and measure columns*

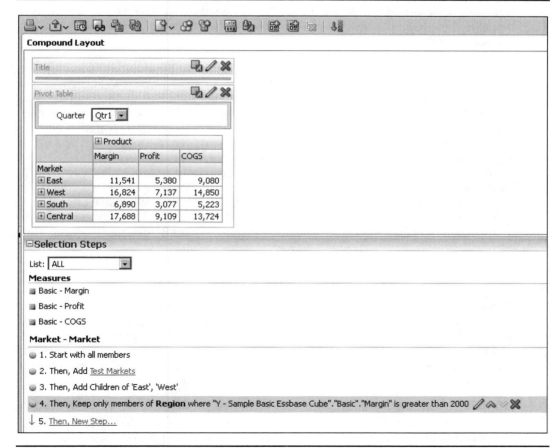

FIGURE 4-6. *A pivot table view using selection steps*

Creating Repositories from Oracle Essbase Data Sources

So now that you understand the theory and principles behind accessing multidimensional data sources, we will take a look at a number of supported multidimensional database servers and how their data models are imported into the Oracle BI Repository. We will start first with Oracle Essbase, perhaps the most commonly used multidimensional database server with Oracle Business Intelligence, and then look at accessing Microsoft Analysis Services and the OLAP Option for the Oracle Database.

Connecting to Oracle Essbase

In terms of development effort within Oracle, probably the best supported and most fully featured multidimensional data source is Oracle Essbase. Oracle Essbase, acquired as part of the Hyperion acquisition back in 2007, is Oracle's strategic multidimensional OLAP server that powers many of Oracle's performance management tools and is embedded in products such as the Oracle Fusion Applications. As such, if you do not currently use a multidimensional OLAP server but wish to choose one that has the maximum compatibility with Oracle Business Intelligence, Oracle Essbase would be a wise choice.

Setting Up Essbase Client Connectivity

The full installation of Oracle Business Intelligence 11g ships with an embedded Oracle Essbase client installation, which it uses to connect to local or remote Essbase servers from the Oracle Business Intelligence installation. While the 11.1.1.3 release of Oracle Business Intelligence required you to perform some post-installation configuration of the client before it could be used (see the product documentation for more details), versions from release 11.1.1.5 upward do not require any configuration and connect to Essbase "out of the box."

If, however, you have installed just the Client Tools installation for Oracle Business Intelligence, it does not itself come with an Essbase client installation. If you wish to make use of local (rather than remote server) connections to an Oracle Essbase data source using the stand-alone installation of the Oracle BI Administration tool, you will need to follow the instructions in Chapter 2 to install the Essbase Client and configure the Oracle BI Administration tool to make use of it.

Finally, because Oracle Business Intelligence connects to Oracle Essbase via the Essbase Client, rather than through Oracle Provider Services (a mid-tier Hyperion product that provides high availability and clustering for Essbase databases), you cannot connect directly to an Essbase cluster using this technique. Instead, you will need to connect to individual host servers using the Essbase client but replace the host name in the database connection pool details with a session variable, the value of which you will need to alter through an initialization block as you move from Essbase host server to Essbase host server. As such, Oracle Business Intelligence is best suited to accessing Essbase data sources where the Essbase server is not clustered, unless you wish to develop and maintain your own clustering system that does not use Provider Services.

Example: Using the Metadata Import Wizard to Import Oracle Essbase Metadata

To import the metadata from an Oracle Essbase database into the Oracle BI Repository using the Oracle BI Administration tool, ensure that you are accessing a supported Essbase version, that you have network connectivity either from the workstation you are working from or from the server hosting Oracle Business Intelligence, and then follow these steps:

1. Click Start to bring up the Windows Start menu and select Programs | Oracle Business Intelligence | Oracle BI Administration.

2. When the Oracle BI Administration tool opens, either connect online or offline to your repository, or create a new repository to hold your Essbase data. (See Chapter 3 for more on accessing repositories.)

3. From the Oracle BI Administration menu, select File | Import Metadata.

4. At the Import Metadata – Select Data Source screen, select either Local Machine or Remote Machine from the Import Type drop-down menu (which will be preset to Local Machine if accessing your repository offline) and select Essbase as the connection type.

5. After selecting Essbase as the connection type, enter the Essbase server, username, and password details into the text boxes; for example:

   Essbase Server: demo.us.oracle.com
   User Name: admin
   Password: *password*

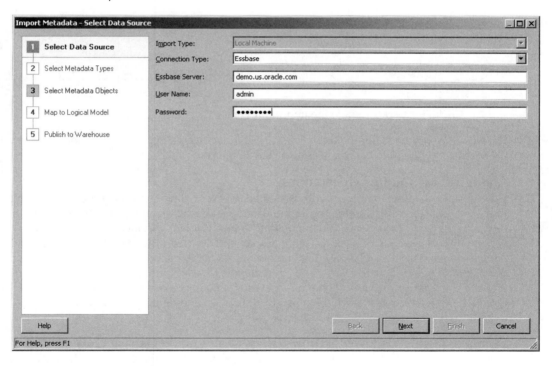

Click Next to proceed to the next screen.

6. At the Import Metadata – Select Metadata Objects screen, use the Data Source View panel to select the Essbase server, applications, or databases that you wish to import into the repository by selecting them and using the arrow buttons to move them to the

Repository View panel on the right. In the example here, we are importing the Sample .Basic Essbase database, which comes by default with most Essbase installations:

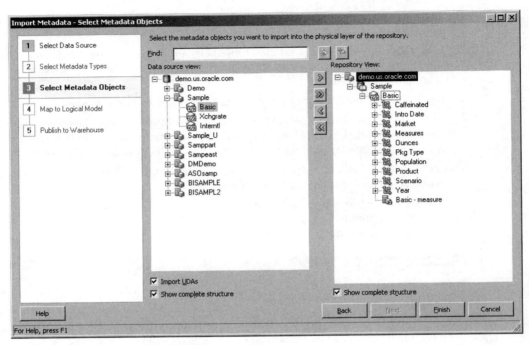

7. Click Finish to complete the import process.

Now that you have imported the Essbase outline metadata into your repository, you can view the results and fine-tune the physical database definition.

About Essbase Outline Generations

When you import metadata from your Essbase database outline into Oracle Business Intelligence, the Oracle BI Administration tool bases the names for the cube columns that it creates on the hierarchy generation names within the outline. If you have not specifically named these generations, default names such as Gen3, Market will be used instead of more business-friendly names such as Market or Country. You can alter these default names later on when you map your physical model in to the business model and mapping layer of the repository, but it is good practice to edit your Essbase outline to name your generations before importing them into the Oracle BI Repository, as this will save you work later on and reduce the risk of misnaming columns later on.

Example: Configuring Generation Names in an Oracle Essbase Outline

In this example, we will access the Demo.Basic sample Essbase database, which, unlike the Sample.Basic database, does not have generation names set by default. To set or amend the generation names within such an Essbase outline using Essbase Administration Services, follow these steps:

1. Log into Essbase Administration Services using a suitable username and password.

2. Using the Enterprise View tree menu on the left-hand side of the screen, expand the Essbase Servers node, locate the Essbase Server that contains the application you are interested in, and within that application locate the database that you intend to import into the Oracle BI Repository. In this example, we will use the Demo.Basic database that comes with most Essbase installations.

3. Use the plus sign (+) to the left of the database name to expand the tree menu, and display the Outline, Linked Reporting Objects, and other metadata items under the database node. Double-click the Outline object to display the database outline on the right-hand side of the screen.

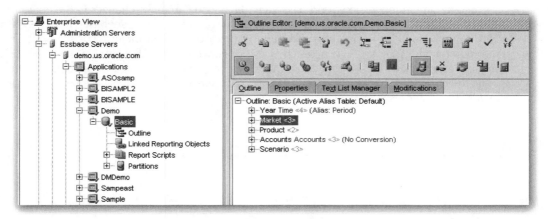

4. Within the Outline tab, right-click one of the dimensions (for example, Market) and select Generations from the menu that is displayed.

5. The Define Generations dialog box will then be displayed. Using this dialog box, enter names for the generations (analogous to hierarchy levels but starting from the top of the hierarchy rather than the bottom). The names that you enter here will become the physical cube column names when you import the Essbase outline information into the Oracle BI Repository.

6. Once you have completed naming the generations for the first of the outline dimensions, use the Dimensions drop-down menu to enter names for the other dimension generations. Once you have finished, click OK, and then click Save to save your outline changes.

Viewing and Amending the Physical Model

Figure 4-7 shows the Essbase physical database definition for the Sample.Basic Essbase database using the default settings after a metadata import. Contained within the physical database you can see the regular and attribute dimensions brought through from the Essbase database, together with a single measure called Basic – Measure, named after the database that it is contained within.

Once the initial metadata import has taken place, you can make changes to the definition such as altering dimension hierarchies to be value based rather than level based (or vice versa), create columns for alias values, create columns for user-defined attributes (UDAs), convert nested dimension members into a single hierarchy view, or convert the measure or account hierarchy into a single measure view. These changes are independent of the underlying Essbase data structure, though the changes you make may well change or influence the MDX that is sent by the Oracle BI Server to the Essbase server.

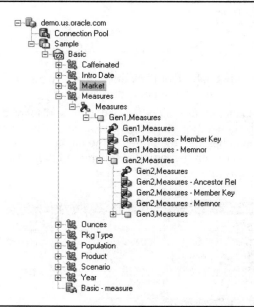

FIGURE 4-7. *An Essbase physical database featuring a measure hierarchy*

Converting Level-Based Hierarchies to Value-Based Hierarchies

Chapter 3 describes a new feature in the 11g release of Oracle Business Intelligence where logical dimension hierarchies can be designated as value based, or parent-child, rather than the traditional level-based approach. When you designate a hierarchy as value based, there are no levels defined, and instead the hierarchy is defined by member ID and parent ID relationships with a single "detail" level.

As Essbase internally defines all hierarchies as value based or parent-child anyway, you may wish to change the hierarchy type of one or more of your physical hierarchies from Unbalanced (or any other level-based hierarchy type) to Value. This can bring advantages in terms of searching and filtering members in a hierarchy, and it will allow you to avoid having to reimport your Essbase outline metadata into the repository if you add additional generations to your hierarchy.

If you edit the properties of an Essbase physical hierarchy object to designate it as parent-child from the default level based (balanced, unbalanced, or ragged), when you drag-and-drop the database definition into the business model and mapping layer of your repository, the Administration tool will create the logical dimension hierarchy as parent-child and there will no longer be individual logical columns for the generations, or levels, in your Essbase hierarchy. Thereafter, if your Essbase outline changes and additional generations are added, you will not need to reimport the outline to reflect the changes in your repository.

Note, however, that there are some limitations when working with value-based hierarchies, both in terms of Essbase and in general. First, while this will mean you avoid having to completely reimport your physical model if additional generations are added to your Essbase Block Storage Option (BSO) database's outline, it will not help you if a whole hierarchy or dimension is then added. (The Essbase Aggregate Storage Option, or ASO, value-based hierarchies still have this issue, unfortunately, because of the way that data is stored with the Essbase ASO database structure.)

Moreover, if you designate your hierarchies as value based, you cannot then combine your Essbase data with other, detail-level data sets using vertical federation, as there are no longer any "levels" to which to designate the granularity of each source. Therefore, value-based hierarchies work best when you are analyzing Essbase data in isolation and you do not intend to combine the data at the business model level with other data of lesser or greater granularity.

Example: Converting Level-Based Essbase Physical Hierarchies to Value-Based

With these limitations in mind, let's switch now to the Sample.Basic Essbase database that you imported earlier on using the Import Metadata Wizard, and then follow these steps to convert the Market physical hierarchy object from level based to value based:

1. With the Oracle BI Administration tool open and your repository open online or offline, navigate to the physical database (for example, demo.us.oracle.com) that contains your Essbase application and database.

2. Expand the application name and then database name, and then locate the physical dimension that contains your hierarchy (for example, Market).

3. Within this physical dimension, you will find one or more physical hierarchy objects. In this example, the physical hierarchy object is also called Market. Right-click this object and select Properties.

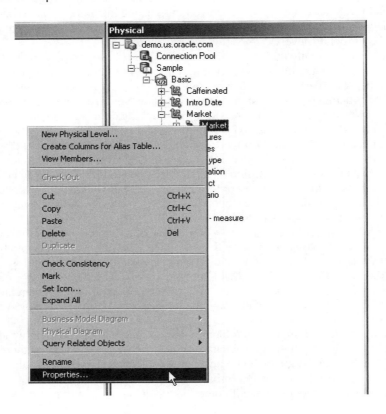

4. The Physical Hierarchy dialog box will then be shown. By default, the Hierarchy Type drop-down list will have Unbalanced selected. Use this drop-down list to select Value; then click OK to close the dialog box.

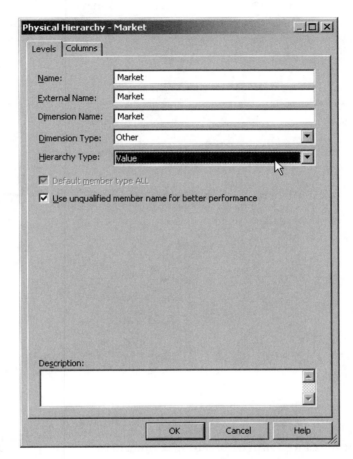

The "Use unqualified member name for better performance" check box is checked by default and should be left at this default value wherever possible. Most Essbase databases have unique member names across individual dimensions, indeed across all dimensions, and have to be specifically enabled for handling nonunique member names. Both Essbase and Oracle Business Intelligence can generate simpler and more efficient MDX queries if nonunique member names are disabled (the default), and you should only deselect this setting if you are sure that this feature has indeed been enabled in your Essbase database.

5. When you return to the main BI Administration tool view of the physical model, you will see that the individual levels/generations within your physical hierarchy have now been replaced by a single level that contains physical cube columns for the parent key, the member, the member key, and the "memnor" column, used for outline (hierarchy) sorting.

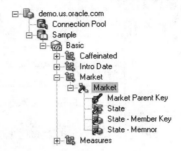

Later on, if then you drag-and-drop your Essbase database into the business model and mapping layer of the repository, you will see that the logical dimension hierarchy created for this Essbase hierarchy will similarly feature a parent-child hierarchy.

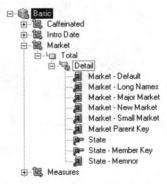

Converting Measure Dimensions to Flat Measures

By default, when you import an Essbase outline into the physical layer of the Oracle BI Repository, the dimension that you have designed as your accounts, or measure, dimension will be imported as a regular, level-based physical dimension just like all of the other dimensions in the outline. Your physical database in the repository will also feature a single measure, named after the database name with "- measure" as the suffix, as shown previously in Figure 4-7, replicating the functionality of an Essbase database where measures themselves are a dimension with members for values such as Profit, Margin, % Margin, and so forth.

Earlier releases of Oracle Business Intelligence did not have this ability to properly model the Essbase measure dimension as a hierarchy; instead they "flattened" this hierarchy so that it was removed, and each measure dimension member became a separate measure in the physical model. While this can be useful in some types of situations, described in a moment, it could also lead to fact tables with thousands of individual members, because in the Essbase database the

	Measures				Inventory	Ratios
		Profit				
			Margin	Total Expenses		
	Basic - measure	Basic - measure	Basic - measure	Basic - measure	Basic - measure	Basic - measure
Quarter						
Qtr1	24,703	24,703	52,943	28,240	117,405	55
Qtr2	27,107	27,107	56,317	29,210	119,143	55
Qtr3	27,912	27,912	57,872	29,960	143,458	55
Qtr4	25,800	25,800	54,387	28,587	141,850	55

FIGURE 4-8. *Analyzing an Essbase source using a measure hierarchy*

corresponding measure dimension had thousands of members (accounts) organized into a chart with an accounts-style hierarchy.

If you wish to analyze your Essbase data in isolation, replicating as much of the native behavior of Essbase-specific client tools, keeping your physical database this way would make sense. To pick a particular measure to display in an analysis, you would select this single measure in your analysis criteria. Then you would use filters, selection steps, or drilling into hierarchical columns to choose the measure dimension members that you would like to see on the screen or calculate new measure values based on existing ones, as shown in Figure 4-8.

If, however, you wish to create calculations in the repository or in an analysis, it is sometimes easier if this measure dimension is instead turned in a flattened list of individual measures, which then can be selected individually and have calculations based on them. Often, when modeling Essbase sources, you might want to create two physical database representations of your Essbase database, one with a measure hierarchy and one with flattened measures, to suit the different types of analysis your users may wish to perform.

NOTE
You can actually represent both a flattened set of measures and a measure hierarchy in the same physical model by using the FILTER function described in Chapter 3 to create individual derived measures based on filtering the measure dimension to return specific measure names. Doing this still generates optimal MDX, though it can be more involved to set up and maintain, particularly if new measure dimension members are subsequently added to your Essbase database. Make sure, though, that the relevant dimension is marked as being an accounts/measure dimension in the Essbase outline; otherwise, you may encounter issues accessing more than a single filter measure in the same analysis.

Example: Converting a Physical Essbase Database Definition to Use Flattened Measures

In this example, we will use the Oracle BI Administration tool to duplicate the physical database representing the Sample.Basic Essbase data source and convert this second physical database to use flattened measures:

1. Using the Oracle BI Administration tool and with your repository open, locate within the physical layer of your repository the physical database object that contains your physical database. (In the example we are using, this is called demo.us.oracle.com.) Right-click this physical database object and select Duplicate.

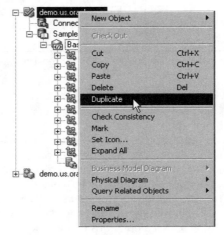

2. Your physical layer in the repository should now have an additional database containing a duplicate of your Essbase-sourced physical database, with a "#1" as a suffix (or similar, depending on how many duplicates you have created).

3. Within this new duplicated physical database, navigate to the cube table (in our case, called Basic) that contains your physical dimensions, hierarchies, and measure. To configure this cube table to use a flattened list of measures, right-click it and select Convert Measure Dimension To Flat Measures.

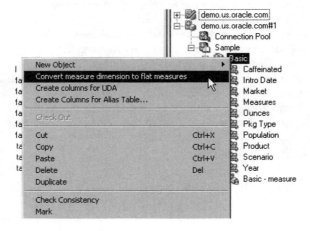

4. Click the plus sign (+) next to the cube table that you just converted, to show the objects within it. You will now see that the measure dimension has been removed and that you now have a listing of individual measures, one for each member in the measure dimension within your database.

5. Once you have confirmed that the conversion has taken place as expected, check in your changes if you are working online, and then save your repository.

6. Now, when you drag-and-drop your physical database or cube table to the business model and mapping layer of the repository, instead of having a logical fact table containing a single measure, you will instead see a single fact table containing one measure for every member in your Essbase measure hierarchy.

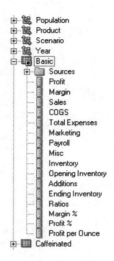

If you subsequently wish to create derived logical columns based on these measures, you can select the particular measure (for example, Inventory or COGS) on which you wish to base the calculation, without having to separately reference the measure dimension.

Working with User-Defined Attributes

When working with Essbase sources, there are additional elements of Essbase outline metadata that you may wish to make available in your physical model for use later on in the business and presentation models you create off of it.

User-defined attributes (UDAs) are textual strings that can be associated with members in Essbase dimensions, and they are used often in Essbase applications to apply filters and selections from data. When you first import an Essbase outline into the physical layer of the repository using the Import Metadata Wizard, by default any UDAs that are imported are set up as properties for the associated physical dimension, but you can convert these after the import to their own individual columns.

As an example, the Sample.Basic Essbase database has a dimension called Market that has three UDAs: Major Market to indicate, or "tag," dimension members that represent major markets;

Small Market; and New Market. Any member in the dimension can have one or more of these UDAs applied to it.

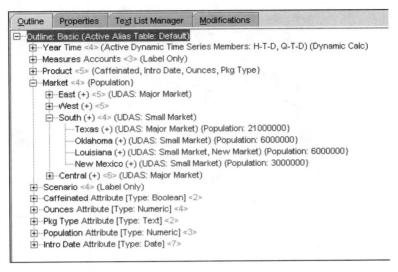

When you import this Essbase database's outline into the Oracle BI Repository, the Import Metadata wizard gives you the option to import UDAs at the same time, with the Import UDAs check box selected by default.

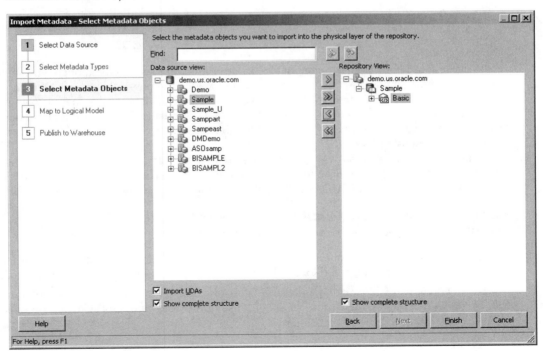

Then, when you view the properties for the physical dimension that contained the UDAs after the import, you will see these UDAs listed as physical dimension properties.

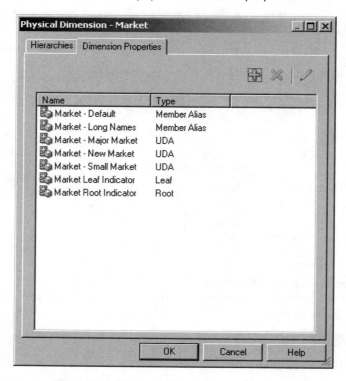

If you wish to filter dimension member selections based on these UDAs, though, you should really create separate physical cube columns for them within the physical layer, which then become logical and subject area columns that you can filter against using the analysis criteria. (If you do not create these physical columns, as of the 11.1.1.6 release the Administration tool will automatically create corresponding UDA logical and subject area columns for only the topmost level in each dimension hierarchy.)

When you do this, a physical UDA column is created for every generation in the associated dimension hierarchy, so if you have three UDAs in the dimension and three generations in the hierarchy, creating all possible UDAs will involve creating nine separate new cube columns.

Example: Creating Physical Cube Columns for Essbase UDAs

To create physical cube columns for UDAs in this way, follow these steps:

1. Using the Oracle BI Administration tool, open your repository, navigate to the physical layer of the repository, and locate the physical database containing your Essbase data.

2. To convert all UDAs within a physical cube table to their own physical cube columns, right-click the required cube column (for example, Basic) and select Create Columns For UDA.

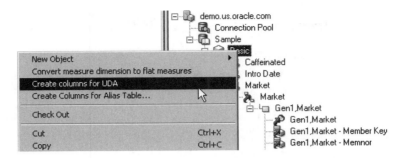

3. To create one or more individual physical cube columns for UDAs within a particular dimension, right-click the physical dimension, select Create Columns For UDA, and then select All UDAs or select the individual UDA that you wish to create the column for.

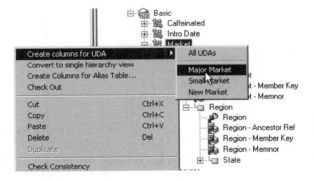

4. When you then drag-and-drop the physical cube table or database over to the business model and mapping layer of the repository, you will see that, for each generation in the hierarchy, separate logical columns have been created for each UDA that you configured in this way. For example, if you created a column for the Major Market UDA, you will see three corresponding logical columns in the logical table corresponding to that Essbase dimension, named Gen1, Market – Major Market; Region – Major Market; and State – Major Market.

5. To filter members in a logical dimension table using one of these UDA values, include within your analysis the attribute or hierarchical column that you are interested in, and then create a filter against the associated UDA column, testing for "1" if you want to

return members that have that UDA associated with them, and "0" if you want to return members that do not have that UDA associated with them.

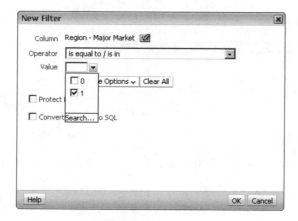

Working with Aliases

Members within Essbase dimensions have a property called Name that generally contains a descriptive value that would, in turn, be suitable for displaying in an analysis. For example, in the Sample.Basic Essbase database provided with most Essbase installations, the Market dimension has members with Name property values such as East, West, and North; and when you import this dimension into the Oracle BI Repository and create logical and subject area tables based off of it, markets will be displayed using these descriptive values.

In some cases, though, instead of having a descriptive value contained within it, this Name property instead has an ID or another value that you don't necessarily want to be displayed to users when they create analyses. The Product dimension within the Essbase Sample.Basic database has this issue so that if you import this dimension into your Oracle BI Repository and report against it, product IDs will be displayed rather than readable product names.

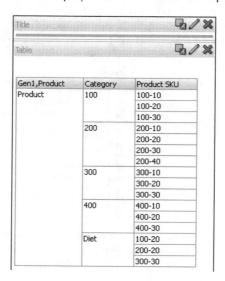

If, as you are using a tool such as Essbase Administration Services, you look at the outline properties for such a dimension, you will see that in addition to the Name property there are values under an Aliases heading.

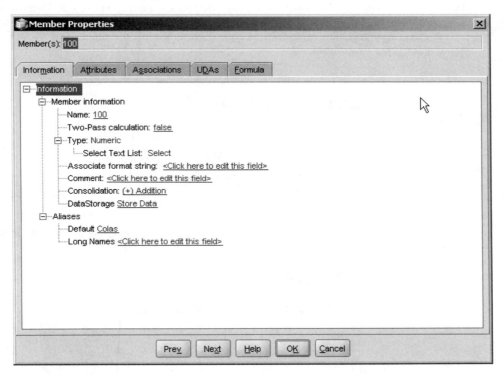

Aliases are alternate names for Essbase dimension members that allow developers to create additional, alternative labels for dimension members in order to allow member names to be displayed in different languages or to use more descriptive terms, for example. These aliases are stored internally within Essbase in what are called "alias tables."

When you import an Essbase outline into the Oracle BI Repository, by default only the Name property is brought into the repository, not the aliases. In most cases this is not a problem because the name property is descriptive and can be used in analyses. In some cases, though, such as in the case of the Product dimension, you really need to bring the aliases into the repository and use those instead when you include the dimension in an analysis.

Example: Creating Physical Cube Columns for Essbase Alias Tables

To import alias tables into your physical database model, follow these steps:

1. Using the Oracle BI Administration tool, navigate to either the physical database that contains your Essbase data or to the particular physical dimension within the database that you wish to create alias columns for. Then right-click the object and select Create Columns For Alias Table.

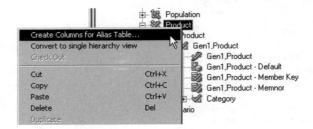

2. When the Select An Alias dialog box is shown, select the alias table that you wish to import (for example, Default), and click Create to create the corresponding physical cube column.

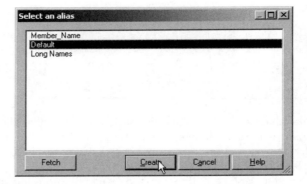

3. The Essbase cube table object in the physical layer of the repository, which corresponds to the Essbase database, has a property that determines which value to display for members. To view this property setting, double-click the Essbase cube table object that represents your Essbase database and select the General tab. Locate the Display Column settings and note how the display column can be set to use either the member name or an alias.

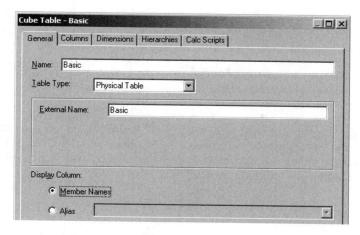

If you wanted to switch your cube table to always use the alias for display columns rather than the member name, you could use this setting to change the default value. However, this choice will then apply across all dimensions, and in the case of the Sample.Basic Essbase database, all of the other dimensions apart from Product have blank values for their two alias tables. Therefore, in this instance, you should leave the Member Names radio button selected and make use of your new alias column in a different way, which we will describe later on.

4.   To bring in other alias tables, repeat this process, selecting the other required aliases at the relevant point. If you are importing aliases for a physical database model that has already been used to create a corresponding business model, you can drag-and-drop these new columns into the relevant business model, as well as subject area columns, as required, and make use of them in analyses. If you have not yet created your business model, these additional physical cube columns come across to the business model along with the other cube columns when you automatically create your business model.

Now that you have created and fine-tuned the physical model of your Essbase database, you can create the business model that corresponds with it.

Creating the Business Model

Compared to creating the physical model of your Essbase database, creating the business model is very simple and straightforward, as the Oracle BI Administration tool does most of the work for you. Using the dimensional metadata that you imported from your Essbase database into the physical model, simply dragging and dropping your physical model into the business model and mapping layer of the Oracle BI Repository automatically creates the logical tables, logical joins, and logical dimensions corresponding to your physical model. This makes Essbase and other supported multidimensional sources some of the easiest source types to model in the repository.

Of course, just as with relational and other data sources, you can model your Essbase source in the business model and mapping layer manually or make manual amendments to automatically derived models after you first create them. Manually creating a business model against Essbase or other multidimensional sources completely from scratch is not recommended, however, because it is a complicated process involving a lot of manual work that, in reality, isn't needed. In the example in this section, we will look at the automatic business model creation process and at what fine-tuning and post-creation additions are made. Then, later on in this chapter, we will consider in detail one situation where manual manipulation of this metadata is required, which is when we combine OLAP and non-OLAP data using vertical and horizontal federation techniques.

Example: Creating a Business Model from an Essbase-derived Physical Model

To create a business model from an Essbase source modeled in the physical layer of your Oracle BI Repository, follow these steps:

1. Within the physical layer of your Oracle BI Repository, locate the Essbase database model that you wish to create a corresponding business model for. Within the physical model, locate the cube table (called Basic from the Sample.Basic example Essbase database, in the example we are using here) that you wish to create the business model for.

2. With this cube table selected, drag-and-drop it into the business model and mapping layer of the repository. Click the plus sign (+) next to the newly created business model to view the logical tables, columns, and dimensions that the Oracle BI Administration tool has automatically derived for you from the corresponding metadata in the physical layer.

Your initial business model has now been created for you. Using this new business model, expand the various logical tables and logical dimensions to view the metadata that has been created. Logical tables are created for each dimension in the Essbase physical model, and logical dimensions together with either level- or value-based hierarchies are also created, depending on what type of hierarchy settings you have set for your physical hierarchies after you imported them from the Essbase source.

If you chose to create separate physical columns for UDA values after the initial metadata import, you will see separate logical columns for these UDA values in the new business model.

Similarly, if you created additional alias columns in the physical layer, you will notice that there are corresponding logical columns for these values in the new business model. Unless you amended the Display Column setting in the cube table properties in the physical layer, in order to set a table-wide cube preference for using an alias for member names rather than the default member name setting, you will need to perform an additional step detailed later in this section for these aliases to be used when displaying the dimension members in an analysis.

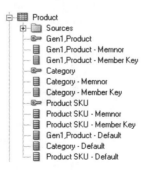

In addition, depending on whether you left your account (measure) hierarchy at the default settings after the initial metadata import or chose to use the "Convert Measure Dimension To Flat Measures" option, your business model will have a single fact table named after the cube table it was associated with, with either a single measure or individual, separate measures for each member of the Essbase database's accounts dimension.

In general, and particularly if you intend to analyze your Essbase source in isolation, you do not need to perform any further steps to fine-tune this business model. However, as we will see in a moment, particular settings and configurations in your Essbase metadata might require you to make some changes before publishing your Essbase source as a subject area in the presentation layer of the repository.

Multiple Hierarchies

If you have an Essbase database that features multiple hierarchies within a single dimension, you can import and model these correctly in the Oracle BI Repository. For this feature to be available, your Essbase database must be created with the Aggregate Storage Option (ASO) and have multiple hierarchies enabled in the outline.

For example, the ASOSamp.Sample Essbase database provided with most Essbase installations has several dimensions that have multiple hierarchies enabled for them, including the Time dimension, which has hierarchies for YTD, MTD, and QTD.

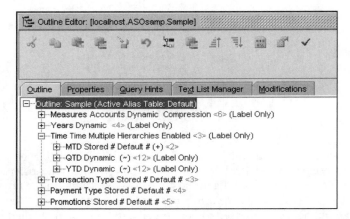

When you initially import this database into the physical layer of your repository, you will see that a single physical dimension has been created in this case for the Time dimension in the Essbase database, and this dimension has three physical hierarchies contained within it.

Then, when you drag-and-drop the cube table containing this dimension and multiple hierarchies into the business model and mapping layer, you will see that each of the hierarchies has been modeled as two objects; a logical table and a corresponding logical dimension.

End users will then be able to query these as if they were separate dimensions and hierarchies. Should you wish to, you can nest these separate hierarchies in an enclosing subject area table to indicate their relationship to each other, as discussed later in this chapter in the section, "Nesting Multiple Hierarchies and Attribute Dimensions."

Attribute Hierarchies

Another feature of Essbase databases that you might wish to consider is attribute dimensions. Attribute dimensions are a special type of dimension within Essbase that are used to describe members of an associated dimension and are stored in such a way that they take up little space in the database. For end users looking to analyze Essbase cubes, they will want to be able to make selections from attribute dimensions just like any other dimension, but it would be helpful to be able to see the association between the attribute dimension and its related regular dimension.

When you import an Essbase database outline into the Oracle BI Repository physical layer, for example, the Population attribute dimension in the Sample.Basic sample Essbase database, the attribute dimensions are represented in almost the same way in the physical model as regular dimensions, except that they have their Dimension Type property in the associated physical hierarchy set to Attribute Dimension.

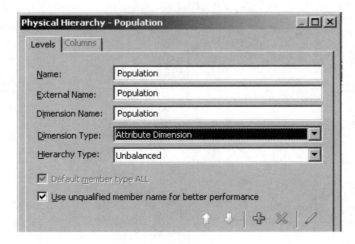

When you drag-and-drop your cube table into the business model and mapping layer, the Oracle BI Administration tool creates logical tables and logical dimensions for attribute dimensions in just the same way as regular dimensions.

When you come to publish your business model as a subject area in the presentation layer of the repository, as with multiple hierarchies you can use the "nesting" feature within presentation tables to identify these attribute dimensions with their associated regular dimensions. See the upcoming section, "Nesting Multiple Hierarchies and Attribute Dimensions," for more details.

Essbase-Specific Aggregation Settings

When you create the business model for an Essbase-source physical model, depending on whether you have kept the measure (account) hierarchy in place or flattened it into a set of individual measures, the BI Administration tool will create a logical table for your fact data with either a single measure or multiple measures within it. Normally, when you create a logical table containing measure columns within it, you then have to define the default aggregation rule for each column as, for example, Sum, Count Distinct, or Min. You do this using the Aggregation tab within the Logical Column dialog box for each measure column. (Right-click a measure column within a logical fact table and select Properties.)

For measures sourced from Essbase sources, though, you will find that this setting has been preset to External Aggregation.

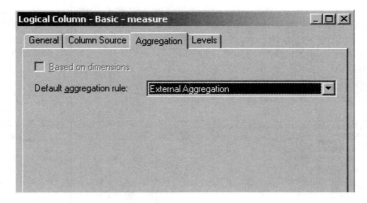

External aggregation means that the Oracle BI Server will expect the source database, in this case Essbase, to aggregate the data for you. You can override this setting using either the BI Administration tool or the Edit Formula link in the analysis editor, but this is not recommended because you will lose the benefit of Essbase having, in most cases, precalculated the aggregate value for this measure according to the definition of the database outline.

In the vast majority of cases, therefore, you should leave this setting at its default value and only change it within the analysis editor for a particular analysis, understanding that in this case the BI Server will need to aggregate the data for you, potentially retrieving unaggregated, detail-level records onto the BI Server that it then needs to aggregate itself, often returning data a lot slower than would normally be the case.

Example: Setting Display Properties for Hierarchical Columns

If you want your aliases to be displayed by default when using hierarchical columns in an analysis, then you must amend your logical dimension. By default, the member names are set to the display key for each of the levels, and you will need to change this to use the alias column for display. To do this, follow these steps:

1. Open the Logical Level Properties for the logical dimension.

2. Switch to the Keys tab.

3. Alter the existing Display Key setting, which is set by default to Member Names, to instead use Alias Columns.

4. Repeat step 3 for every logical level in the logical dimension.

Creating the Subject Area

Now that you have created the physical and business models for your Essbase data, you can publish it as a subject area to the presentation layer so that users can start creating analyses using this data. Like creating business models, creating subject areas is very straightforward once you have performed the initial import, as most of the work will have been done for you automatically by the BI Administration tool.

To create a subject area for your business model, drag-and-drop the business model from the business model and mapping layer into the presentation layer of the Oracle BI Repository, and the subject area will be created for you automatically.

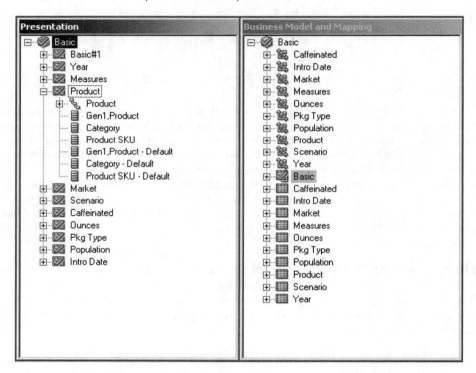

Although the majority of the work will have been automatically done for you, there are a couple of fine-tuning changes you may wish to make depending on the underlying Essbase database.

Nesting Multiple Hierarchies and Attribute Dimensions

Earlier we looked at the situation where an ASO Essbase database could have multiple hierarchies enabled for one or more dimensions. When you import this database's metadata into the physical and then the business model and mapping layer of the Oracle BI Repository, each of the separate hierarchies within the multiple hierarchy-enabled dimension is created as its own logical table and logical dimension (YTD, MTD, and QTD, in the example we used earlier based on the ASOSamp.Sample Essbase database), and there is no longer any separate table or dimension within the business model for the Essbase dimension that contained the multiple hierarchies (in our case, Time).

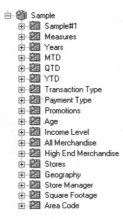

If you wish, you can leave your subject area this way, with each presentation table being independent and separate from the other hierarchies associated with the same Essbase dimension. Alternatively, you can use the ability within the presentation layer to "nest" presentation tables to create a parent presentation table, which in this example we will call Time. That parent presentation table then contains the other presentation tables associated with the attribute dimensions. To create such a table, follow these steps:

Example: Creating Nested Presentation Tables for Essbase Attribute Dimensions

1. Within the presentation layer of the Oracle BI Repository, navigate to the subject area that corresponds to your Essbase source. Right-click it and select New Presentation Table.

2. Using the Presentation Table dialog box with the General tab selected, enter a name (for example, Time) into the Name text field. Click OK to close the dialog box.

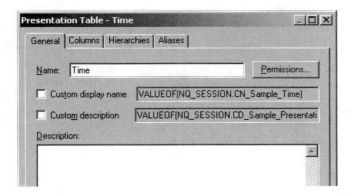

3. By default, the new presentation table that you have just created will be listed at the bottom of the existing set of presentation tables, within your subject area. To nest within this table the presentation tables that you want to contain in it, you need to move it so

that it is listed before the other tables. To do so, navigate to the subject area that contains your presentation tables, and double-click it to display the Subject Area dialog box.

4. When the Subject Area dialog box is shown, click the Presentation Tables tab to display the list of presentation tables within the subject area. Click the new table that you have just created to select it, and then use the Move Up and Move Down buttons to position the table that you have just created above the ones that you wish to nest within it. Click OK to close the dialog box when you have positioned the new table correctly.

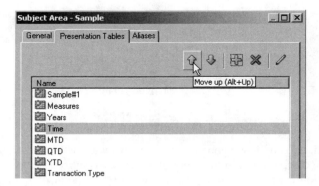

Now, double-click the first of the presentation tables that contains your multiple hierarchies to display the Presentation Table dialog box. Then, within the Description area on the General tab, type –> (a minus sign, followed by a greater than sign) as the description. This is a special description that instructs Oracle BI Answers to nest this presentation table within the one above it.

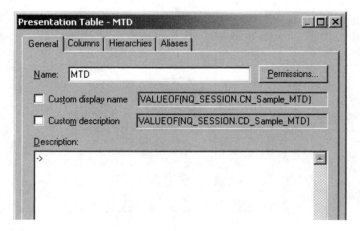

5. Repeat step 4 for any other presentation tables containing hierarchies you wish to nest within the main presentation table, so that, in our example, all of the YTD, MTD, and QTD presentation tables have this description set for them.

6. At this point, your subject area within the Oracle BI Repository will not look any different than before, as the nesting is only visible when displayed in the analysis editor. When you save your repository and upload it to Fusion Middleware Control for users to access, you will, however, find that your multiple hierarchy tables are now nested within the presentation table that indicates their common dimension so that their relationship to each other is made clearer.

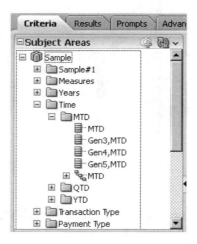

Similarly, you can nest attribute dimension presentation tables within the presentation table holding the associated, regular dimension. In this instance, you will not need to create a new presentation table to nest the attribute dimension presentation table within, as it will already have been created for the associated, regular dimension.

Instead, just use the Presentation Tables tab in the Subject Area dialog box, along with the Move Up and Move Down buttons, to re-order the presentation tables so that any tables associated with attribute dimensions are listed under their corresponding parent regular dimension tables. Then, edit the properties of the attribute dimension presentation table so that its description is set to ->, as in the preceding example.

In the following screenshot, based on the subject area derived from the Sample.Basic Essbase database, the Caffeinated, Ounces, and Pkg Type attribute dimension presentation tables have been nested within the Product presentation table to show that they are attribute dimensions that can further classify members in the main Product dimension.

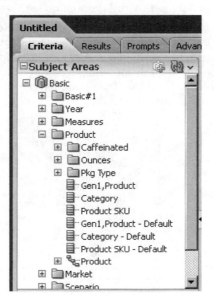

Leveraging Essbase Security and Filters

Data filters and metaread filters, which you define using Essbase Administration Services and other tools, are respected by Oracle Business Intelligence and can be used to filter access to data and metadata (dimensions and dimension members) in your Essbase database.

When you perform the initial import of Essbase database metadata into the Oracle BI Repository, you generally use an Essbase administrator account (for example, admin) to perform the import. After this initial import, you can, however, replace the account details in the connection pool settings with details of another, more restricted account or replace them with repository or session variables in order to pass through specific credentials for a user.

While leveraging filters and metaread filters in the Essbase database has the advantage of pushing data security down to the source level, you might want to consider using the row and subject area security described in Chapter 11 to create access rules that apply across whole business models and subject areas, particularly if your business models and subject areas are sourced from multiple data sources. In this section, though, we will explain how Essbase filters and metaread filters are accessed, and what effect these have on the analyses that your users may create.

Leveraging Essbase Data Filters

Consider a situation where, using the Sample.Basic Essbase database that we imported earlier, you first define a data filter using Essbase Administration Services that restricts access within the Market dimension to only the West member and its descendants, removing access to other regions such as East, South, North, and their descendants using the filter clause @IDESCENDANTS("West").

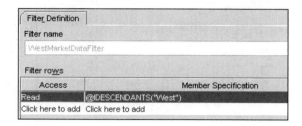

Assume that you have also created a new user in Shared Services called westuser1 that has been granted access to the Sample.Basic database only and has had this filter applied to their account.

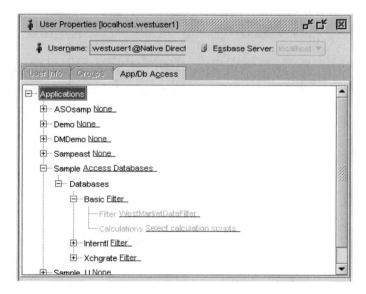

While users will be able to browse the metadata for any member in any dimension in the database with this filter in place, they will only be able to see data (measure values) for those Market dimension members from the West member downward through its descendants.

Now, if you edit the Oracle BI Repository that references this Essbase database and edit the connection pool settings for the physical database corresponding to this database, replacing the default Essbase administrator credentials with the westuser1 username and password, your connection will now make use of this data filter.

When you now create an analysis using the subject area derived from this data source and the user credentials that have the data filter applied to them, you will see that if you just include the dimension in the analysis (either the whole hierarchy or columns based off of this dimension), the members that are displayed will not be affected by this filter, which is for data (measures) only.

However, if you add a measure into the analysis criteria, the list of members in the restricted dimension is then limited to those allowed by the data filter, a restriction that is applied by the Essbase server in the background.

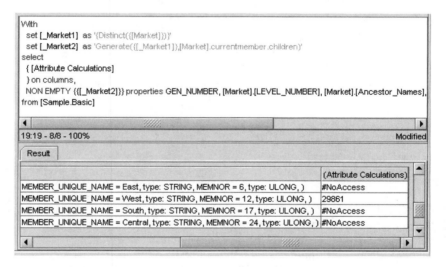

So how does this work? When you try to access data in an Essbase database that a data filter then restricts you from viewing, the result set returned by the Essbase server will include the special value #NoAccess to indicate that the user is not allowed to see the value concerned.

Oracle Business Intelligence is aware of this feature, and when it encounters #NoAccess values, it removes the data item from the analysis results, just as if it were a relational source that you were accessing and it restricted the data set it returned to you.

What if you not only wanted data items associated with dimension members not to be returned to users, but you didn't even want the user to see the dimension members? In that case, you would use an Essbase metaread filter.

Leveraging Essbase Metaread Filters

Essbase *metaread filters,* unlike data filters, stop users from accessing members in dimensions rather than just the data items they reference. They are defined in the same way as data filters, using a tool such as Essbase Administration Services, and in the following screenshot an Essbase metaread filter has been defined that, as with the preceding data filter example, restricts access to just the West member within the Sample.Basic Market dimension. However, this filter, being a metaread filter, will stop users who have it applied to them from actually seeing any members within this dimension not explicitly allowed by the metaread filter.

Now, if this user's credentials are used in the connection pool settings for the Essbase physical database model, users will not even see the dimension members that are hidden from them through the metaread filter, even if they include only dimension members in the analysis criteria.

CAUTION
When using Essbase filters and metaread filters to restrict access to data at the Essbase server level, be careful when also using query caching (detailed in Chapter 5) in conjunction with this feature, as the cache manager within the Oracle BI Server will not by itself be aware of this additional filtering that takes place at the source database level. If you intend to use caching, Essbase filters, and metaread filters together, consider enabling the virtual private database feature detailed in Chapter 6 to ensure that cache entries are private to each user; otherwise, incorrect results may be returned in your analyses.

Managing Changes to Essbase Metadata

Over the lifetime of your BI application, the structure of your Essbase database may change, and, if so, you will need to reflect these changes in your Oracle BI Repository. Some changes to the Essbase database outline require no work on your part, whereas others may require you to update your repository model to be in sync with your Essbase outline.

Typical changes that your Essbase outline may encounter are as follows:

- **Adding or removing members from a dimension but keeping the same number of generations** These actions require no change to your Oracle BI Repository.

- **Adding or removing members that result in additional generations being added or removed from the outline** These actions require changes to your Oracle BI Repository because you have to add or remove physical cube columns and physical levels and then reflect these changes in the business model and mapping layer and presentation layer, as well as in analyses that filter on presentation columns based on the subject area columns derived from these hierarchies, which may no longer be valid.

- **Adding or removing dimensions** These actions require changes to the Oracle BI Repository because you have to add or remove physical dimensions, hierarchies, and dependent objects and then reflect these changes in the business model and mapping layer and presentation layer.

- **Adding or removing UDAs, aliases, or other member properties** These actions require changes to reflect these new properties in the physical layer and add them to the business model and mapping layer and presentation layer.

You can reimport your Essbase outline metadata into the Oracle BI Repository in the same way as for other data sources. The import process will detect new and changed metadata items and will reflect these changes in the physical layer of your Oracle BI Repository. Depending on the changes, you may then need to feed them through to the other layers in the repository so that end users can work with updated subject areas that reflect the changed Essbase outline.

In the following two sections, we will look at the three scenarios outlined in the preceding list that require you to reimport and then update your repository to reflect changes in your Essbase outline. We will start with adding and removing generations, then adding and removing whole dimensions from your physical model, and finally updating your repository model to reflect new or changed member attributes.

Example: Adding New Generations from an Essbase Outline

Hierarchies within Essbase database outlines are organized into generations and levels. Generations start from the top of the hierarchy, with generation 1 being the dimension name itself, whereas levels start from the bottom, leaf level. When you import your Essbase outline metadata into the Oracle BI Repository using the Oracle BI Administration tool, the generations within your outline define physical levels within your Oracle BI Repository physical layer, with each level then having a number of cube columns depending on the keys, aliases, and properties used by the dimension members within that generation.

If you subsequently add new members or remove members from your Essbase outline, or alter the parentage of existing members, you may end up creating, or removing, generations from the Essbase hierarchy. Because generations correspond with levels and sets of physical cube columns in your Oracle BI Repository, you will then need to reflect these changes in order to be in sync with your Essbase database.

In the following example, consider a situation where an Essbase database called Sample.Basic2, a copy of the standard Sample.Basic database, has previously been imported into the Oracle BI Repository and a business model and subject areas have been created based off of the initial physical model. The Scenario dimension within this Essbase outline has subsequently been updated to add two new members, Initial Budget and Revised Budget, as children to the Budget member, which creates a new generation compared to the previous outline.

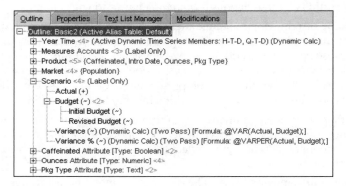

To update your Oracle BI Repository with this additional generation, follow these steps:

1. Using the Oracle BI Administration tool, open your repository either online or offline.

2. From the Oracle BI Administration menu, select File | Import Metadata.

3. When the Import Metadata dialog box is shown, select Essbase as the connection type, and enter the Essbase server, username, and password details to connect to your Essbase server.

NOTE
These should be the same details that you originally used when importing your Essbase metadata; otherwise, the Oracle BI Administration tool will create a fresh physical model during the import rather than update your existing one.

4. At the Import Metadata – Select Metadata Objects screen, click the Essbase database, application, or host that you wish to import from within the Data Source View area, and use the arrow button to add it to the Repository View area on the right-hand side of the screen.

5. When you select an existing Essbase database, application, or server that has already previously been imported into the repository, a warning message will be shown, telling you that the object you wish to import already exists. Click OK to continue and update the existing model in your repository.

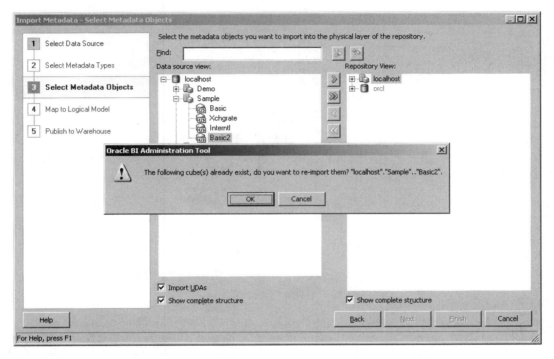

6. Click Finish to complete the metadata import. If you are working with your repository online, you will be prompted to check out affected objects. Click the Check Out button to allow this to take place.

7. Once the import of metadata has completed, you will be returned to the main repository view within the Oracle BI Administration tool. Navigate to the physical layer within the repository view and use the plus (+) signs next to the dimension that has been updated in the corresponding Essbase database (in this case, Scenario). Navigate down the hierarchy

until you see the new level within it that corresponds to the new generation in the
Essbase outline.

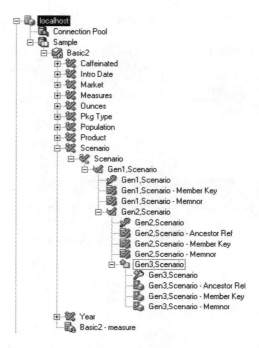

8. Now that the physical layer of your repository has been updated, you can update
   the business model and mapping layer. To do this, select the physical cube columns
   within the new physical level in your physical model and drag-and-drop them into the
   corresponding logical table within the business model and mapping layer to add new

logical columns to the logical table. Again, if working with your repository online, check out the affected objects when prompted.

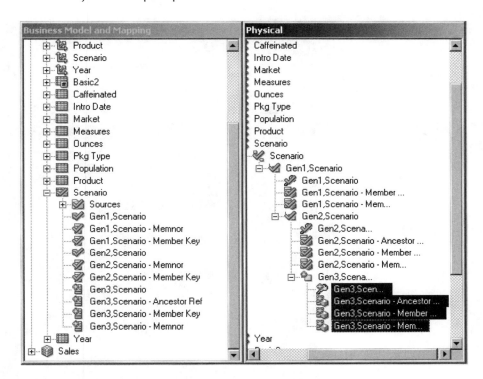

Alternatively, if your previous metadata import removed a physical level from the physical model, together with its corresponding physical cube columns, delete the corresponding logical columns from the logical table associated with the physical dimension that contained the physical level.

9. The logical key used by the logical table that you just added logical columns to needs to be updated to reference the key column for this new level. To do so, right-click the logical table that contains your new columns (in this example, Scenario) and select Properties. Then, when the Logical Table properties dialog box is shown, select the Keys tab and edit

the definition of the existing key to reference the new key column introduced in step 8 (in this example, Gen3, Scenario).

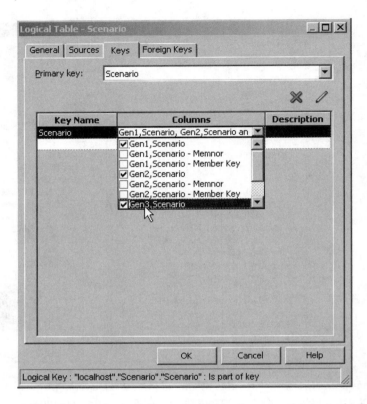

10. Next, you will update the logical dimension that references this logical table, which up until now only references the previous set of levels. To do this, again within the business model and mapping layer, locate the logical dimension that you wish to update, navigate to the bottom logical level of the hierarchy, right-click it, and select New Object | Child

Level. If working online, check out the affected object. If removing a level rather than adding one, delete this level instead.

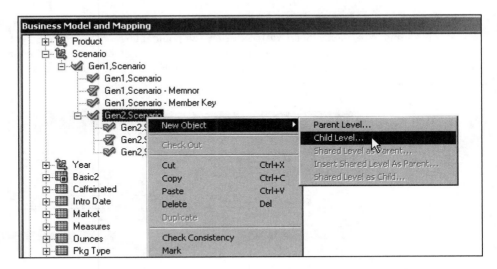

11. At the Logical Level dialog box, name the level as appropriate (for example, Gen3, Scenario) and click OK to close the dialog box.

12. Within the logical table that contains the new logical columns you created when dragging and dropping the physical cube columns from the physical model, drag-and-drop the key column (for example, Gen3, Scenario) and the Member Key column (for example, Gen3, Scenario – Member Key) from the logical table onto the new logical level you created in step 11. Do not drag-and-drop the Memnor or Ancestor Ref columns into the logical dimension, as they are not required for display in hierarchies or drill-down and can sometimes cause issues when used in a manual update of an Essbase-derived logical dimension.

13. Now you need to define the logical level keys for this new logical level. To do so, first right-click the Member Key column for this new level (in this example, Gen3, Scenario – Member Key) and select New Logical Level Key. When the Logical Level Key dialog box is shown, deselect the Use For Display check box.

14. Repeat this process for the other column in the logical level, which in the example would be Gen3, Scenario. Create the new logical level key, but this time do not deselect the Use For Display check box; instead, leave it at its default setting.

15. To double-check your settings, double-click the logical level that you are working with (in this case, Gen3, Scenario) to display the Logical Level dialog box. Select the Keys tab and ensure that the primary key is set to the Member Key column, but note that, when listed in the keys listing, this column has the Use For Display check box deselected. Click OK to close this dialog box.

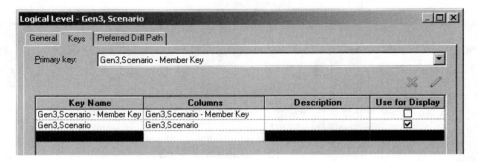

16. Next, you need to edit the content level setting for the logical table sources used by your dimension and associated fact table. To do this, locate the logical table containing your dimension columns (in this case, Scenario), expand the Sources folder, and double-click the logical table source contained within it, which in this instance would be called Basic2, based on the cube table name created during the Essbase metadata import.

    With the Logical Table Source dialog box open, select the Content tab and use the drop-down list to set the content level for your source to the new generation that you have created during this process (in this example, Gen3, Scenario).

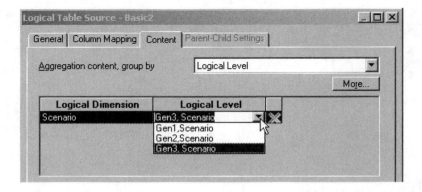

Repeat this for the logical table source used by your fact table (in this instance, also called Basic2), setting the content level for the Scenario logical dimension to the new lowest level (in this case Gen3, Scenario).

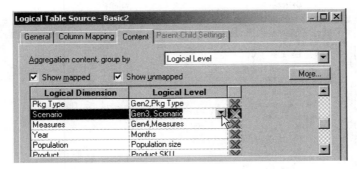

Performing these two steps tells the Oracle BI Server that scenario data is now available at a new, lower level of detail than before, corresponding to the new generation in your Essbase outline.

17. Now that you have updated your business model, you can complete the task by updating the corresponding subject area. Using the Oracle BI Administration tool, locate the subject area that corresponds with your business model, navigate to the presentation table containing the affected dimension columns (in this case, called Scenario), and then drag-and-drop the Gen3, Scenario logical column into this presentation table.

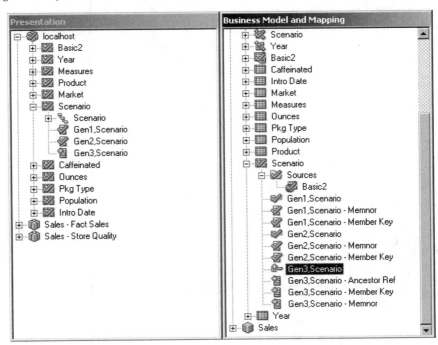

18. To update the presentation hierarchy within this presentation table, delete the existing one, and then drag-and-drop the relevant logical dimension into the presentation table to replace it.

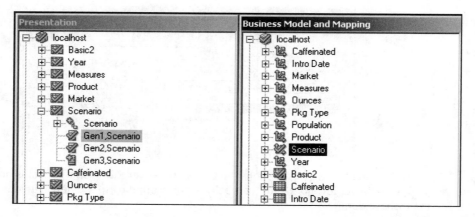

19. Finally, to check that your editing has left you with a valid repository, select File | Check Global Consistency. If you get any warnings or errors, fix them before proceeding. Once complete, select File | Save to save your repository, restart the Oracle BI Server using Fusion Middleware Control, and create analyses to check that your new members and generation are displayed correctly, both on their own and with a measure associated with them.

NOTE
If you do not have any data associated with your new members, your analysis will not allow you to drill them down but will put a plus (+) next to the parent member to indicate that members do exist below it in the hierarchy.

	Basic2 - measure
Scenario	
⊟ Scenario	105522.00
Actual	105522.00
⊞ Budget	129380.00
Variance	-23858.00
Variance %	-18.44

Example: Adding New Dimensions from an Essbase Outline

In addition to adding new generations to an existing dimension hierarchy, you may wish to add a whole new dimension, and its hierarchy or hierarchies, to your Oracle BI Repository. This scenario is less common than adding new dimensions to an existing Essbase database and is a fairly major operation. Often you will just be presented with a new database, complete with the new dimension, rather than updating an existing one.

For scenarios where this does happen, though, follow these steps. For this example, we have first removed the Population attribute dimension from Sample.Basic3 (a copy of the Sample.Basic Essbase database) and imported it into the Oracle BI Repository, creating a corresponding business model and subject area for the Essbase database:

1. Using the Oracle BI Administration tool, open your repository either online or offline.

2. Connect to your Essbase database source by selecting File | Import Metadata. When prompted, enter the connection details for your Essbase source, making sure that you use the same hostname, username, and password that you used when first importing the Essbase database outline.

3. At the Import Metadata – Select Metadata Objects screen, select the database that you wish to reimport metadata for. When you select an existing database, click OK when the warning appears that says the cube(s) already exist. Click Finish to complete the import, and in the Check Out Objects dialog box click the Check Out button if you are accessing your repository online.

4. If you now take a look at the physical model of your Essbase database in the physical layer of the Oracle BI Repository, you will see the new dimension and hierarchy listed within the cube table corresponding to your Essbase database.

NOTE
If you have set any of your level-based hierarchies in the physical model to any hierarchy type other than Unbalanced, this reimport will reset the hierarchy type back to Unbalanced. You should go back and change any such hierarchies to your preferred hierarchy type after such a reimport. This does not affect hierarchies you have set to a hierarchy type of Value.

5. Now you should introduce this new hierarchy and dimension into your business model. To do this, drag-and-drop the new physical dimension into the business model and mapping layer of your repository, dropping it on top of the corresponding business model. Doing so will add a new logical table and a new logical dimension to your business model, both named after the physical dimension in your physical model.

6. Create a logical join between the new logical table and the fact table within the business model. Select and then right-click both logical tables, select Business Model Diagram | Selected Table(s) Only, and then use the Business Model Diagram View area to join the existing logical fact table to your new logical dimension table.

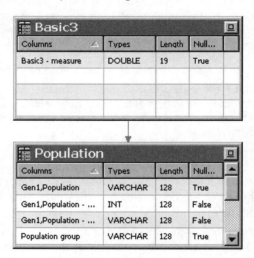

Basic3				
Columns △	Types	Length	Null...	
Basic3 - measure	DOUBLE	19	True	

Population				
Columns △	Types	Length	Null...	
Gen1,Population	VARCHAR	128	True	
Gen1,Population - ...	INT	128	False	
Gen1,Population - ...	VARCHAR	128	False	
Population group	VARCHAR	128	True	

7. Next, you should edit the logical table source used by the logical fact table to reference the correct detail level from the new logical dimension. To do this, navigate to the logical fact table within your business model, expand the Sources folder, and double-click the logical table source that maps to your Essbase physical model. With the Logical Table Source

dialog box open, select the Content tab and set the logical level for the logical dimension that you just imported to the lowest detail level (in this example, Population Size).

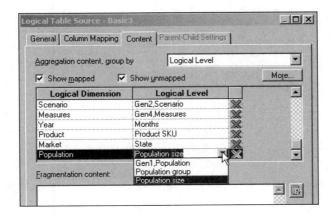

8. Finally, drag-and-drop the logical table containing your new dimension to the presentation layer of the repository, dropping it on top of the existing subject area. Select File | Check Global Consistency to check that there are no errors, and then save your repository when complete. Your new dimension will then be available for selection by users in their analyses.

Example: Adding New UDAs and Aliases from an Essbase Outline

Like adding new generations and dimensions, adding new UDAs and aliases to an existing Essbase-derived physical model is straightforward and involves reimporting the outline by selecting File | Import Metadata and dragging and dropping any new physical cube columns, first into the business model and then into the subject area so that they are available for use by users in their analyses.

NOTE
Only UDA columns are automatically imported; alias columns will need to be re-created manually by right-clicking the physical cube table and selecting Create Columns For Alias Table.

As before, though, note that this reimport will reset any level-based hierarchies to a hierarchy type of Unbalanced unless you have previously set them to Value. To restore your settings, edit the hierarchy properties and select the hierarchy type you require.

Querying Essbase Data—MDX Considerations

A basic principle of Oracle Business Intelligence is that the Oracle BI Server provides the same calculation functionality across all supported data sources. Regardless of whether you have your source data stored in an Essbase database, an Oracle Database, or an XML file, you can still use the same functions within the Oracle BI Administration tool or in an analysis, and the Oracle BI Server will either "push down" or "function-ship" the function to the equivalent native database function or request just the measure data and perform the calculation itself.

Surprisingly, given the calculation capability of the Essbase server, very few calculations in Oracle Business Intelligence are function-shipped down to the Essbase database, with the BI Server, in most cases, performing all the calculations. It is only in the case of time-series functions that these are function-shipped to the Essbase database, as we shall see in the following examples.

Consider a situation where you have imported the outline for an Essbase database into your repository and used the option to flatten the measure hierarchy into a flat list of measures. In the following example, the Sample.Basic Essbase database has been imported into the repository in this way, and an analysis has been created that adds together the Opening Inventory and Additions measures to create a derived measure for this calculation.

Region	Opening Inventory	Additions	Opening Inventory + Additions
East	25,744	92,887	118,631
West	38,751	153,802	192,553
South	15,285	46,231	61,516
Central	37,625	136,854	174,479

If this analysis were written against a relational database source, the SQL query generated by the BI Server would push the addition function into the SQL so that the database engine could perform the calculation. For Essbase and other multidimensional sources, though, the MDX statement generated by the BI Server requests just the base measure values, and the BI Server performs the calculation instead, as shown in the following MDX example taken from the nqquery.log file:

```
With
  set [_Market2]  as '[Market].Generations(2).members'
select
  { [Measures].[Additions],
    [Measures].[Opening Inventory]
  } on columns,
  NON EMPTY {{[_Market2]}} properties GEN_NUMBER, [Market].[MEMBER_UNIQUE_NAME],
[Market].[Memnor] on rows
from [Sample.Basic]
```

Similarly, if you use an aggregate function such as Rank() in one of your analyses, this will not be function-shipped down to the equivalent MDX function. The following example shows a list of market regions and their total sales, with a Rank() function applied in the analysis criteria, which for Oracle relational and similar sources would normally be function-shipped to a RANK analytic function.

Region	Sales	RANK(Sales)
East	87,398	3
West	132,931	1
South	50,846	4
Central	129,680	2

As with the simple calculation, the MDX sent to the Essbase server only requests the measure value and does not pass down a request for the RANK MDX function:

```
With
   set [_Market2]   as '[Market].Generations(2).members'
select
   { [Measures].[Sales]
   } on columns,
   NON EMPTY {{[_Market2]}} properties GEN_NUMBER, [Market].[MEMBER_UNIQUE_
NAME],
[Market].[Memnor] on rows
from [Sample.Basic]
```

The exception to this situation is time-series functions. In the following example, sales values for four different quarters are time-shifted by one quarter using the AGO function.

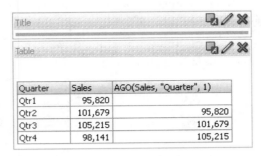

Quarter	Sales	AGO(Sales, "Quarter", 1)
Qtr1	95,820	
Qtr2	101,679	95,820
Qtr3	105,215	101,679
Qtr4	98,141	105,215

The MDX for this query, as generated by the Oracle BI Server, does in fact use the MDX ParallelPeriod function, like this:

```
With
   set [_Year2]   as '[Year].Generations(2).members'
     member [Measures].[_MSCM1] as '(ParallelPeriod([Year].[Quarter], 1, [Year].
currentmember), [Measures].[Sales])'
select
   { [Measures].[Sales],
```

```
    [Measures].[_MSCM1]
  } on columns,
  NON EMPTY {{[_Year2]}} properties GEN_NUMBER,
[Year].[MEMBER_UNIQUE_NAME], [Year].[Memnor] on rows
from [Sample.Basic]
```

In most cases, this lack of push-down to the Essbase server does not cause issues, as the main benefit in using Essbase as a data source is the pre-aggregation of data. In some cases, however, you may wish to make use of MDX functions provided by Essbase because, for example, having the BI Server perform a calculation is inefficient and retrieves excessive amounts of data from Essbase to then perform the calculation. In this case, you can use the EVALUATE and EVALUATE_ AGGR functions first mentioned in Chapter 3 to make use of native MDX function capabilities in the Essbase database.

Using EVALUATE and EVALUATE_AGGR to Leverage Essbase MDX Functions

If you want to make use of a native MDX function in your analysis or in the definition of a logical column in the Oracle BI Repository, you can use the EVALUATE and EVALUATE_AGGR Oracle BI functions to pass the request through to the Essbase server.

EVALUATE is typically used to return attribute values for a dimension member and can be used in analyses or to provide derived values to add to a dimension logical table, though you cannot subsequently drill through to more detail-level attributes when using this feature. EVALUATE_AGGR, on the other hand, is used to return values for measures that typically are aggregated in analyses. When you use either of these functions, you pass through the name of the MDX function together with placeholders for the arguments, and then pass values through for the arguments as references to physical or presentation layer objects or columns in your analyses.

Using EVALUATE with Essbase Sources   To illustrate how EVALUATE and EVALUATE_AGGR can be used for Essbase sources, let us first consider a situation where you wish to display the count of child members under a particular member. In this example, we will display the count of cities under each region in the Market dimension for the Sample.Basic Essbase database.

In this case, the MDX function that we wish to use is COUNT. COUNT takes a single parameter, the name of a dimension member, and we will use a reference to the current member in the analysis to return the number of children under each member.

Region	EVALUATE('count(%1.dimension.currentmember.children)', Gen1,Market)
East	5.0
West	5.0
South	4.0
Central	6.0

The expression to use the MDX COUNT function in this example is as follows:

```
EVALUATE('count(%1.dimension.currentmember.children)',"Market"."Gen1,Market")
```

In this example, *%1* is a placeholder and is substituted with the first value after the expression, in this case a reference to the Gen1, Market level in the Essbase database.

The .dimension.currentmember.children expression is MDX notation for the child members for the member that is being referenced, and the level reference plus this "children of" reference is then passed to the COUNT function. Each MDX function used by Essbase has similar syntax and sets of parameters, and you should consult the Essbase documentation for the full list of available functions.

When you then take a look at the MDX generated by the Oracle BI Server for this query, you can see the MDX function request being pushed down to the Essbase server:

```
With
  set [_Market2]  as '[Market].Generations(2).members'
  member [Measures].[_MSCM1] as 'count([Market].Generations(1).
    dimension.currentmember.children)'
select
  {[Measures].[_MSCM1]} on columns,
  {{[_Market2]}} properties GEN_NUMBER, [Market].[Memnor] on rows
from [Sample.Basic]
```

As you can see, you will need to know MDX and know how functions are used in MDX to get the best out of this feature. As such, you may wish to use it only in exceptional situations and have the BI Server perform other calculations itself before it returns values to you.

Example: Using EVALUATE_AGGR with Essbase Sources   To illustrate how EVALUATE_AGGR can be used to return measure values, consider a situation where you wish to use the AVG MDX function to return the average sales value for the children of a particular dimension member within the Market dimension. Instead of defining this calculation in an analysis, we will define it as a logical column in the repository business model. (You could also use this function directly in the analysis editor, should you require it for only a single analysis, for example.) To create a new logical column using the EVALUATE_AGGR function, follow these steps:

1. Using the Oracle BI Administration tool, open your repository either online or offline. Navigate to the fact table within your business model, right-click it, and select New Object | Logical Column.

2. When the Logical Column dialog box is shown, name the column (for example, Avg. Sales for Child Measures) and then click the Column Sources tab. Within the Column Source Type area, select the "Derived from physical mappings" radio button, select the logical table source, and click the Edit button.

3. With the Column Mapping tab selected, ensure that you have selected the expression for the new column, and click the Edit Expression button (which looks like a calculator).

4. With the Expression Builder dialog box open, enter the expression, for example:

Evaluate_Aggr('AVG(Market.currentmember.children, %1)',
"localhost"."Sample".""."Basic"."Sales")

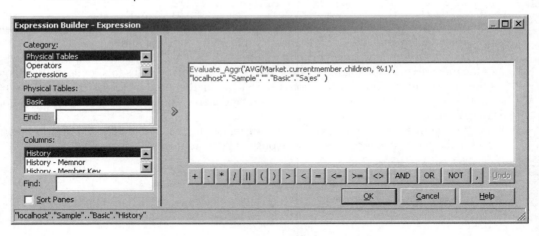

5. Close the Expression Builder dialog box and then the Logical Column dialog box. Then, double-click this new logical column to display the Logical Column dialog box again, and select the Aggregation tab. In the Default Aggregation Rule drop-down box, select Evaluate_Aggr.

6. Finally, drag-and-drop this new logical column into the presentation layer subject area, adding it to the existing presentation fact table.

Now, when you use this presentation column in an analysis, the BI Server will push down the AVG MDX function to the Essbase server, allowing you to display the average sales amount for each Market dimension member.

Region	Avg. Sales for Child Members
East	17,480
West	26,586
South	12,712
Central	21,613

If you examine the query sent to the Essbase server, you will see your MDX function being used:

```
With
  set [_Market2]  as '[Market].Generations(2).members'
  member [Measures].[_MSCM1] as
    'AVG(Market.currentmember.children,
  [Measures].[Sales])', SOLVE_ORDER = 101
select
```

```
{ [Measures].[_MSCM1]
} on columns,
  NON EMPTY {{[_Market2]}} properties GEN_NUMBER, [Market].[MEMBER_UNIQUE_
NAME],
    [Market].[Memnor] on rows
from [Sample.Basic]
```

If you want to produce a particular analysis that uses an MDX function, though, this technique can be useful when the Oracle BI Server would otherwise only request basic data from the Essbase database.

Hierarchical Columns and Selection Steps

One of the new features within analyses in Oracle Business Intelligence 11*g* is *hierarchical columns*. Hierarchical columns, detailed in Chapter 7, work alongside the traditional attribute and measure columns and allow you to drag-and-drop an entire dimension hierarchy into your analysis criteria, giving you the ability to drill into and explore a whole hierarchy within a single column. Hierarchical columns are particularly suited to working with multidimensional data sources because they allow you to easily visualize and manipulate the data hierarchies that provide structure to your data sets.

When you analyze data using a hierarchical column, the Oracle BI Server generates what are termed *logical SQL queries* that provide subtotals and groupings of your data at different levels of analysis. For modern relational data sources such as Oracle Database, the BI Server then combines these separate logical SQL queries into a single physical SQL query that uses the WITH clause (known as *subquery factoring*) to combine what would otherwise be lots of separate SQL statements into a single one.

For multidimensional data sources such as Oracle Essbase, the BI Server cannot perform this final step of combining separate logical queries into a single MDX statement, so you may experience high numbers of separate MDX queries being sent to your Essbase server when you use hierarchical columns in your analyses, particularly when you include more than one and drill into several levels of detail.

NOTE
*The number of MDX queries generated by the BI Server for a given analysis has been reducing over the various Oracle Business Intelligence 11*g *releases, for example, for queries that use both selection steps and pivot table views from the 11.1.1.6 release onwards. Make sure that you are on the latest release and patchset for Oracle Business Intelligence 11*g *when using Essbase sources, and be prepared to apply one-off patches from Oracle Support to address specific MDX generation issues that arise from time to time.*

For example, consider a situation where you are querying a subject area that is sourced from Sample.Basic to show sales figures for all regions and for all states within the Central region.

	Profit
Market	
⊟ Market	105,522
⊞ East	24,161
⊞ West	29,861
⊞ South	13,238
⊟ Central	38,262
Illinois	12,577
Ohio	4,384
Wisconsin	3,547
Missouri	1,466
Iowa	9,061
Colorado	7,227

In this instance, if you were to enable level 2 query logging and examine the nqquery.log file, you would see six separate MDX queries generated for this particular analysis. (See Chapter 5 for more on query logging.)

Three of the queries would return members at the grand total, region, and state levels, with sales figures aggregated for each member at the correct level:

```
With
   set [_Market1]  as '[Market].Generations(1).members'
select
   { [Measures].[Sales]
   } on columns,
   NON EMPTY {{[_Market1]}} properties GEN_NUMBER, [Market].[MEMBER_UNIQUE_
NAME], [Market].[Memnor],
[Market].[LEVEL_NUMBER] on rows
from [Sample.Basic]

With
   set [_Market1]  as '{Distinct({[Market]})}'
   set [_Market2]  as 'Generate({[_Market1]},[Market].currentmember.children)'
select
   { [Measures].[Sales]
   } on columns,
   NON EMPTY {{[_Market2]}} properties GEN_NUMBER,
[Market].[LEVEL_NUMBER], [Market].[Ancestor_Names], [Market].[MEMBER_UNIQUE_
NAME], [Market].[Memnor] on rows
from [Sample.Basic]
```

```
With
  set [_Market2]  as '{Distinct({[West]})}'
  set [_Market3]  as 'Generate({[_Market2]},[Market].currentmember.children)'
select
  { [Measures].[Sales]
  } on columns,
  NON EMPTY {{[_Market3]}} properties GEN_NUMBER,
[Market].[LEVEL_NUMBER], [Market].[Ancestor_Names], [Market].[MEMBER_UNIQUE_
NAME], [Market].[Memnor] on rows
from [Sample.Basic]
```

The remaining three would return metadata values that are used when joining these three data sets together and sorting the output in outline order:

```
With
  set [_Axis1Set] as '{Distinct({[Market]})}'
select
  {} on columns, {[_Axis1Set]} properties GEN_NUMBER, [Market].[MEMBER_UNIQUE_
NAME],
[Market].[Memnor] on rows
from [Sample.Basic]

With
  set [_Axis1Set] as '{[Market].Generations(1).members}'
select
  {} on columns, {[_Axis1Set]} properties GEN_NUMBER, [Market].[MEMBER_UNIQUE_
NAME],
[Market].[Memnor] on rows
from [Sample.Basic]

With
  set [_Axis1Set] as '{Distinct({[West]})}'
select
  {} on columns, {[_Axis1Set]} properties GEN_NUMBER, [Market].[Ancestor_
Names],
[Market].[MEMBER_UNIQUE_NAME],
[Market].[Memnor] on rows
from [Sample.Basic]
```

The Oracle BI Server would then take the returned values from each of these individual MDX statements and "stitch together" the results in memory before returning the complete data set to the Oracle BI Presentation Server to display in the analysis results.

For an individual analysis, when we analyze data like this using a single hierarchical column, we get two separate physical MDX queries for each level of indentation we create in the hierarchy. The number of individual MDX queries is increased significantly, though, when we combine more than one hierarchical column in a single analysis, particularly when both hierarchies are drilled into.

Take, for example, the same analysis as earlier, but this time with the Year hierarchy displayed on the pivot table columns, with the user then drilling into the Year and Quarter levels.

| | Profit | | | | |
| | ⊟ Year | | | | |
Market		⊞ Qtr1	⊞ Qtr2	⊞ Qtr3	⊞ Qtr4
⊟ Market	105,522	24,703	27,107	27,912	25,800
⊞ East	24,161	5,380	6,499	6,346	5,936
⊞ West	29,861	7,137	7,515	7,939	7,270
⊞ South	13,238	3,077	3,267	3,515	3,379
⊟ Central	38,262	9,109	9,826	10,112	9,215
Illinois	12,577	2,855	3,298	3,453	2,971
Ohio	4,384	1,103	1,092	1,077	1,112
Wisconsin	3,547	913	900	956	778
Missouri	1,466	399	388	294	385
Iowa	9,061	2,036	2,336	2,511	2,178
Colorado	7,227	1,803	1,812	1,821	1,791

In this instance, 24 separate physical MDX statements will be sent to the Essbase server, a number that rises to around 60 if we drill further into the Year hierarchy. So what is the impact of these high numbers of separate queries sent to the Essbase server for what ostensibly seems a fairly simple query?

The major impact of these high numbers of individual queries is on concurrency. If you have sized your system based on *X* number of users running *Y* queries per hour, you may find that *Y x 50* queries are actually being sent to the Essbase server, which may have the effect of increasing response time or limiting the total number of users you can support at any one time. In addition, while each individual MDX query is relatively simple, you are also putting more load on the Oracle BI Server system component within your Oracle Business Intelligence installation, as it has to stitch together each set of MDX result sets before returning them to the end user through the Oracle BI Presentation Server. You can help mitigate this situation by taking these actions:

■ Use hierarchical columns in your analysis only when you really need to; if attribute columns (regular column types in the dimension presentation tables) can be used instead, do so because they require only a single MDX query to return their values.

■ If you have to use hierarchical columns, consider using just one in an analysis, replacing the other with one or more attribute columns.

■ If you use more than one hierarchical column, try to keep the levels of drilling to the minimum.

■ Make sure you are on the latest release and patchset for Oracle Business Intelligence 11g to benefit from the latest MDX query optimizations from Product Development.

If all else fails, size your Essbase server to expect between 10 and 50 MDX queries per analysis, as this is the number of MDX queries you can expect for a typical pivot table query using two or more hierarchical columns. If you create analyses that use multidimensional sources, you should try to ensure that caching and subquery caching are enabled for this data source so that as many subtotals as possible are retrieved from the query cache as possible rather than sent as MDX queries to the OLAP server. Caching is discussed in detail in Chapter 5.

Selection steps, also new in Oracle Business Intelligence 11g, allow you to create post-query and aggregation selections, groupings, and calculations on the results of an analysis. Using this feature, you could, for example, create two selection steps per dimension hierarchy to limit the displayed values to those over a certain value and group together dimension members to create new calculations or groupings.

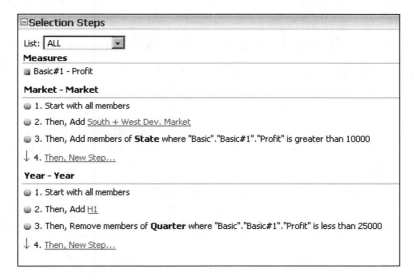

Using the analysis described before, this would typically result in a revised pivot table output that applied these selection steps after the main query runs.

	Profit				
	Year				H1
		Qtr2	Qtr3	Qtr4	
Market					
Market	105,522	27,107	27,912	25,800	51,810
East	24,161	6,499	6,346	5,936	11,879
West	29,861	7,515	7,939	7,270	14,652
California	12,964	3,288	3,593	2,954	6,417
South	13,238	3,267	3,515	3,379	6,344
Central	38,262	9,826	10,112	9,215	18,935
Illinois	12,577	3,298	3,453	2,971	6,153
Ohio	4,384	1,092	1,077	1,112	2,195
Wisconsin	3,547	900	956	778	1,813
Missouri	1,466	388	294	385	787
Iowa	9,061	2,336	2,511	2,178	4,372
Colorado	7,227	1,812	1,821	1,791	3,615

Looking at the query log output for this revised query, the number of individual MDX queries generated has risen from 24, without selection steps applied, to 40 with them applied. In fact, the number of MDX queries added through the use of selection steps is the product of the number of steps per hierarchy, meaning that the number increases exponentially the more hierarchies you apply selection steps to and the more selection steps you add to each hierarchy. As such, to minimize the effect of this, you should try to limit your use of selection steps where possible using filters instead, and where you do use them keep them to the minimum number of hierarchies and the minimum number of steps per hierarchy. See Chapter 6 for more on selection steps.

Creating Repositories from Microsoft Analysis Services Data Sources

Apart from the process of importing Microsoft Analysis Services cube metadata into the Oracle BI Repository, working with Microsoft Analysis Services cubes within Oracle Business Intelligence is mostly the same as working with Essbase sources. As with Essbase databases, once you import your Analysis Services metadata into the repository physical layer, you can then automatically create business models and subject areas by dragging and dropping the cube definition between the various layers. Working with Analysis Services sources is actually simpler than working with Essbase, as there are no source-specific features such as UDAs and aliases to work with, and you can still leverage native MDX functions through the EVALUATE and EVALUATE_AGGR functions.

Because working with Analysis Services sources is so similar to working with Essbase sources, this section of the chapter will mainly outline the differences between the two sources, with the main detail being about how to create physical, business, and presentation models detailed in the Essbase section earlier in the chapter. We will start, though, with the import process, which is where the main differences between support for the two database types is most apparent.

Connecting to Microsoft Analysis Services

Oracle Business Intelligence connects to Microsoft Analysis Services through the XML for Analysis (XMLA) specification, a web-based protocol that accesses Analysis Services cubes through web service calls. As such, you do not need to install specific drivers on your Oracle Business Intelligence server to access Analysis Services, but you will need to configure the server running Microsoft Analysis Services to provide XMLA access to your Analysis Services cubes before you can access them from the Oracle BI Administration tool.

At the time of this writing, Oracle Business Intelligence supports Microsoft Analysis Services 2000, 2005, and 2008, though you should refer to the *System Requirements and Supported Platforms for Oracle Business Intelligence Suite Enterprise Edition 11gR1* document on the Oracle Technology Network web site for up-to-date details. Setting up XMLA access for your Microsoft Analysis Services cube is outside the scope of this book, as it can vary from platform to platform and version to version, but it generally involves installing and configuring Microsoft Internet

Information Services on either the server running Microsoft Analysis Services or a server that has connectivity to Microsoft Analysis Services, and then creating a virtual directory that exposes one or more DLLs that provide the XMLA functionality.

You may also need to amend the default settings for your XMLA provider to handle the high numbers of MDX queries sent from the BI Server to the Analysis Services engine. For example, if you are using Microsoft Windows Server 2003, you should add the lines in bold in the following excerpt to your msmdpump.ini configuration file and adjust the amounts upward if you receive "service unavailable" errors when executing queries:

```
<ConfigurationSettings>
    <ServerName>localhost</ServerName>
    <SessionTimeout>3600</SessionTimeout>
    <ConnectionPoolSize>100</ConnectionPoolSize>
    <MinThreadPoolSize>250</MinThreadPoolSize>
    <MaxThreadPoolSize>500</MaxThreadPoolSize>
    <MaxThreadsPerClient>200</MaxThreadsPerClient>
</ConfigurationSettings>
```

Consult your Microsoft Analysis Services and Windows Server documentation for full details on how to configure XMLA access for your particular source environment.

Example: Using the Metadata Import Wizard to Import Microsoft SQL Server Analysis Services Metadata Using the Metadata Import Wizard

Once you have set up and tested XMLA access to your Microsoft Analysis Services cube, you can use the Oracle BI Administration tool to connect to, and import the metadata for, your Analysis Services cube. In the following example, we will use as the source data for our repository the Adventureworks_DW cube that is available as sample data for Microsoft SQL Server 2005 Analysis Services (SSAS):

1. Using the Oracle BI Administration tool, either create a new repository (File | New Repository) or open an existing repository either online or offline.

2. From the application menu, select File | Import Metadata.

3. At the Import Metadata – Select Data Source screen, select XMLA as the connection type, and then enter the following details:

   URL: [*URL for your XMLA provider for SSAS*]; for example:
   　　http://msas-server/olap/msmdpump.dll
   Provider Type: [Analysis Services 2000 or 2005/2008]
   User Name: [*username for your SSAS server*]
   Password: [*password for your SSAS server*]
   Target Database: [*dummy value—ignored*]

Once your details are entered, click Next to proceed.

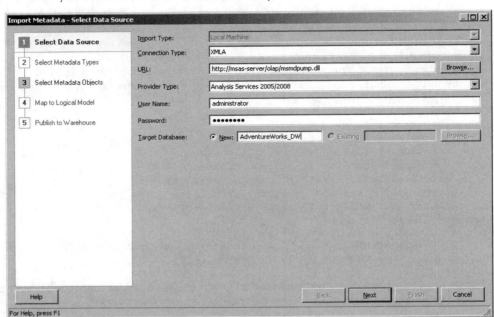

4. At the Import Metadata – Select Metadata Objects screen, select the cubes that you wish to import metadata for from the Data Source View area, and use the arrow buttons to move the selection to the Repository View area. Click Finish to close the screen and start the import.

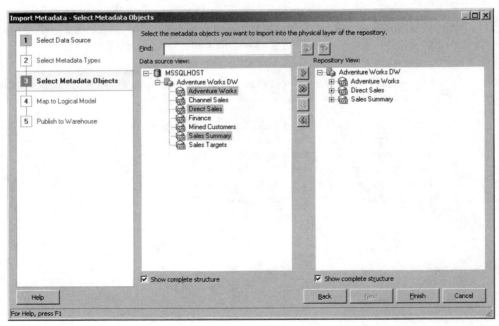

5. After the import has completed, the physical layer of your Oracle BI Repository will contain metadata objects representing the cubes, dimensions, members, and measures imported from your Analysis Services database.

Creating the Physical Model

Like an Essbase-derived physical model, a physical model based on a Microsoft Analysis Services database will have a number of multidimensional-specific metadata objects within it.

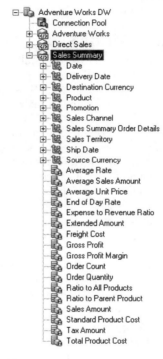

- **A database object** This represents the Analysis Services server, which contains one or more cube tables.

- **One or more connection pools** These contain the connection details through to your Analysis Services server.

- **One or more cube tables** This is analogous to a cube in Analysis Services.

- **One or more physical dimensions** One or more physical dimensions contain one or more physical hierarchies.

- **Physical levels** These are contained within the physical hierarchies, and define the different aggregation levels in your hierarchies

- **Physical cube columns** These represent either dimension member attributes (for example, name, key, or sort order) or measures (for example, profit, sales, or inventory).

For more details on these multidimensional-specific metadata objects, see the Essbase section earlier in this chapter.

As with Essbase sources, you can set the hierarchy type for individual physical hierarchies from the Analysis Services default of Fully Balanced to either Unbalanced, Ragged Balanced, Network, or Value. However, the import process should set the hierarchy type correctly for each imported hierarchy, and therefore you should only change this hierarchy type setting if your underlying data structures have changed and you wish to update your physical model to reflect this.

Unlike Essbase data sources, Analysis Services cubes generally always have flattened lists of measures, and therefore there are no options presented to you to flatten your measure hierarchy, nor are there options to create alias or UDA columns because Analysis Services does not support these Essbase-specific metadata features.

Creating the Business Model

The process for creating a business model from an Analysis Services–sourced physical model is the same as with Essbase sources. Drag-and-drop the required cube table from the physical layer into the business model and mapping layer, and the BI Administration tool will automatically create a subject area together with logical dimensions, tables, joins, and columns to represent your Analysis Services cube.

One step that you might wish to consider, after the initial creation of your business model, is to trim the number of logical dimensions and logical tables in your business model. Analysis Services cubes typically have many more hierarchies within each dimension (a feature called *multiple hierarchies*), and the Oracle BI Administration tool will create a separate logical table and logical dimension for each of these hierarchies.

For example, the Sales Summary cube within the Adventure Works DW sample Analysis Services database has ten dimensions, each of which has several hierarchies within it, such that when a corresponding business model is created there are around 100 logical dimensions and logical tables.

If you do not need to have all of these available for users to query, you can either delete them from the business model or make them easier to navigate by nesting them within a main dimension presentation table in the presentation layer, using the technique outlined in the "Nesting Multiple Hierarchies and Attribute Dimensions" section earlier in this chapter.

Creating the Subject Area

Like creating a business model from an Analysis Services–sourced physical model, creating a corresponding subject area for an Analysis Services–sourced business model is the same as for Essbase sources, and simply involves dragging and dropping the business model from the business model and mapping layer of the repository into the presentation layer. Presentation tables, presentation hierarchies, and presentation columns are then created for the logical tables, logical hierarchies, and logical columns in your business model.

Once you have created your subject area, select File | Check Global Consistency to validate your repository, and then select File | Save to save your changes. If you are working offline, use Fusion Middleware Control to upload your repository and take it online, and then your users will be able to query your Analysis Services data. All of the features available when using Essbase sources, such as hierarchical columns, selection steps, the various views, filters, and other analyses features, will be available for them to use, as shown in Figure 4-9.

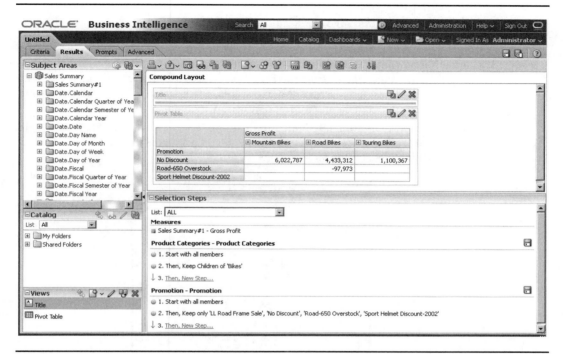

FIGURE 4-9. *Analyzing Analysis Services data*

Managing Changes to Microsoft Analysis Services Metadata

As the underlying Analysis Services database evolves, individual cubes may have dimensions, levels, members, and measures added to and removed from them. To keep your physical model and the derived business and subject areas in sync with the physical Analysis Services database, you can reimport and update your physical model using the BI Administration tool. Subsequently, and as detailed earlier in the chapter in the corresponding section for Essbase sources, you can then use this updated physical model to introduce the appropriate changes into your business model and subject area.

Example: Reimporting Microsoft SQL Server Analysis Services Metadata

To reimport your Analysis Services database metadata and update your physical model, follow these steps:

1. With your repository open, select File | Import Metadata.

2. At the Import Metadata – Select Data Source screen, select XMLA as the connection type, and then enter the following details:

   URL: [*URL for your XMLA provider for SSAS*]; for example:
         http://msas-server/olap/msmdpump.dll
   Provider Type: [*Analysis Services 2000 or 2005/2008*]
   User Name: [*username for your SSAS server*]

Password: [*password for your SSAS server*]
Target Database: [*dummy value—ignored*]

Once your details are entered, click Next to proceed.

3. At the Import Metadata – Select Metadata Objects screen, select the cubes that you wish to update the metadata for from the Data Source View area, and use the arrow buttons to move the selection to the Repository View area. Click Finish to close the screen and start the reimport of metadata and import of any new metadata.

4. After the import has completed, the physical layer of your Oracle BI Repository will contain updated metadata objects, which you can distinguish when working in online mode by highlights on the various object icons.

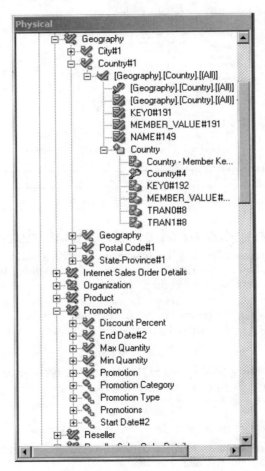

Once your reimport of metadata is complete, follow the steps outlined earlier in this chapter (see "Adding or removing members that result in additional generations being added or removed from the outline" and "Adding or removing dimensions in the section titled "Managing Changes to Essbase Metadata") to introduce new levels and dimensions into the corresponding business model and subject area in your repository.

Querying Microsoft Analysis Services Data—MDX Considerations

Compared to analyses that source their data from relational sources, you have to pay particular attention to the way the Oracle BI Server generates physical MDX queries when working with multidimensional sources. If you use hierarchical columns and/or selection steps, the BI Server may end up generating large numbers of MDX queries to produce the totals and subtotals required for your analysis. In addition, very few Oracle Business Intelligence functions are shipped down to the Analysis Services server, meaning that you may wish to make use of the EVALUATE and EVALUATE_AGGR functions to make use of native MDX functionality.

Pivot Table Views with Hierarchical Columns and/or Selection Steps

As with Essbase sources, analyses created using hierarchical columns and/or selection steps result in MDX queries being generated for each level, or subtotal, in the query. When the BI Server receives a request for an analysis using hierarchical columns, where the user has drilled into various levels in the hierarchy, the BI Server generates separate logical SQL queries for each set of subtotals. For relational sources, it normally combines these subtotals back into a single physical SQL query using a feature mentioned earlier in the chapter called subquery factoring. For sources that use MDX as the query language, though, the BI Server cannot combine these logical queries into one physical MDX statement and instead generates one or more separate MDX statements for each subtotal.

As an example, using the Sales Summary cube within the Adventure Works DW sample Analysis Services database, an analysis that breaks down gross profit by the Date.Calendar hierarchy would produce a number of totals and subtotals.

Date.Calendar	Gross Profit
⊟ All Periods	12,551,366
⊞ CY 2001	1,640,533
⊟ CY 2002	2,970,252
⊟ H1 CY 2002	1,193,388
⊞ Q1 CY 2002	870,708
⊞ Q2 CY 2002	322,680
⊞ H2 CY 2002	1,776,864
⊞ CY 2003	3,904,175
⊞ CY 2004	4,036,406

This, in turn, would lead to the BI Server generating four separate MDX queries, one for each level of indentation in the hierarchical column:

```
With
  member [Measures].[Date_Calendar_(All)
    - Member KeyAnc] as '([Date.Calendar].Currentmember)
    .properties("MEMBER_UNIQUE_NAME") '
  set [Date.Calendar1]  as '{[Date.Calendar].[(All)].members}'
```

```
set [Axis1Set] as '{[Date.Calendar1]}'
select
  {[measures].[Date_Calendar_(All)
    - Member KeyAnc],[Measures].[Gross Profit]} on columns,
  NONEMPTY({[Axis1Set]},{[Measures].[Gross Profit]}) on rows
from
  [Sales Summary]

With
  member [Measures].[Date.Calendar(All)Anc] as 'ancestor([Date.Calendar]
.Currentmember,
  [Date.Calendar].[(All)]).name'
  member [Measures].[Date_Calendar_(All) - Member KeyAnc] as 'ancestor([Date
.Calendar].Currentmember,
  [Date.Calendar].[(All)]).properties("MEMBER_UNIQUE_NAME")'
  member [Measures].[Calendar Year - Member KeyAnc] as '([Date.Calendar]
.Currentmember).properties("MEMBER_UNIQUE_NAME")'
    set [Date.Calendar1]  as '{[Date].[Calendar].[All Periods]}'
  set [Date.Calendar2]  as 'Generate({[Date.Calendar1]}
  ,Descendants([Date.Calendar].currentmember
  ,[Date.Calendar].[Calendar Year],SELF), ALL) '
set [Axis1Set] as '{[Date.Calendar2]}'
select
  {[measures].[Date.Calendar(All)Anc]
  ,[measures].[Date_Calendar_(All)
    - Member KeyAnc],[measures].[Calendar Year - Member KeyAnc],
  [Measures].[Gross Profit]} on columns,
  NONEMPTY({[Axis1Set]},{[Measures].[Gross Profit]}) on rows
from
  [Sales Summary]

With
  member [Measures].[Date.Calendar(All)Anc] as       'ancestor([Date.Calendar]
.Currentmember
  ,[Date.Calendar].[(All)]).name'
  member [Measures].[Date_Calendar_(All) - Member KeyAnc] as       'ancestor([Date
.Calendar].Currentmember
  ,[Date.Calendar].[(All)]).properties("MEMBER_UNIQUE_NAME") '
  member [Measures].[Calendar YearAnc] as 'ancestor([Date.Calendar].Currentmember
  ,[Date.Calendar].[Calendar Year]).name'
  member [Measures].[Calendar Year - Member KeyAnc] as 'ancestor([Date.Calendar]
.Currentmember
  ,[Date.Calendar].[Calendar Year]).properties("MEMBER_UNIQUE_NAME") '
  member [Measures].[Calendar Semester - Member KeyAnc] as '([Date.Calendar]
.Currentmember).properties("MEMBER_UNIQUE_NAME") '
    set [Date.Calendar2]  as '{[Date].[Calendar].[Calendar Year].&[2002]}'
  set [Date.Calendar3]  as 'Generate({[Date.Calendar2]}
  ,Descendants([Date.Calendar].currentmember
  ,[Date.Calendar].[Calendar Semester],SELF), ALL) '
set [Axis1Set] as '{[Date.Calendar3]}'
select
  {[measures].[Date.Calendar(All)Anc]
  ,[measures].[Date_Calendar_(All) - Member KeyAnc]
  ,[measures].[Calendar YearAnc]
  ,[measures].[Calendar Year - Member KeyAnc]
  ,[measures].[Calendar Semester - Member KeyAnc]
```

```
  ,[Measures].[Gross Profit]} on columns,
  NONEMPTY({[Axis1Set]},{[Measures].[Gross Profit]}) on rows
from
  [Sales Summary]

With
  member [Measures].[Date.Calendar(All)Anc] as 'ancestor([Date.Calendar].Currentmember
  ,[Date.Calendar].[(All)]).name'
  member [Measures].[Date_Calendar_(All) - Member KeyAnc] as 'ancestor([Date
.Calendar].Currentmember
  ,[Date.Calendar].[(All)]).properties("MEMBER_UNIQUE_NAME") '
  member [Measures].[Calendar YearAnc] as 'ancestor([Date.Calendar].Currentmember
  ,[Date.Calendar].[Calendar Year]).name'
  member [Measures].[Calendar Year - Member KeyAnc] as 'ancestor([Date.Calendar]
.Currentmember
  ,[Date.Calendar].[Calendar Year]).properties("MEMBER_UNIQUE_NAME") '
  member [Measures].[Calendar SemesterAnc] as 'ancestor([Date.Calendar].Currentmember
  ,[Date.Calendar].[Calendar Semester]).name'
  member [Measures].[Calendar Semester - Member KeyAnc] as 'ancestor([Date.Calendar]
.Currentmember
  ,[Date.Calendar].[Calendar Semester]).properties("MEMBER_UNIQUE_NAME") '
  member [Measures].[Calendar Quarter - Member KeyAnc] as '([Date.Calendar]
.Currentmember).properties("MEMBER_UNIQUE_NAME") '
    set [Date.Calendar3]  as '{[Date].[Calendar].[Calendar Semester].&[2002]&[1]}'
  set [Date.Calendar4]  as 'Generate({[Date.Calendar3]}
  ,Descendants([Date.Calendar].currentmember
  ,[Date.Calendar].[Calendar Quarter],SELF), ALL) '
set [Axis1Set] as '{[Date.Calendar4]}'
select
  {[measures].[Date.Calendar(All)Anc]
  ,[measures].[Date_Calendar_(All) - Member KeyAnc]
  ,[measures].[Calendar YearAnc]
  ,[measures].[Calendar Year - Member KeyAnc]
  ,[measures].[Calendar SemesterAnc]
  ,[measures].[Calendar Semester - Member KeyAnc]
  ,[measures].[Calendar Quarter - Member KeyAnc]
  ,[Measures].[Gross Profit]} on columns,
  NONEMPTY({[Axis1Set]},{[Measures].[Gross Profit]}) on rows
from
  [Sales Summary]
```

This actually amounts to fewer MDX queries than would be generated if you were running a similar query against Oracle Essbase, because the BI Server does not need to generate separate queries for each indentation to obtain the sort order for each member, but it is still four times as many MDX queries as you might ordinarily have expected to be produced.

It's a similar story for analyses that use more than one hierarchical column or analyses that use selection steps. (See the section, "Hierarchical Columns and Selection Steps" earlier in the Essbase part of this chapter, for more on what happens here.) Take, for example, an analysis that breaks down profit figures by the Date.Calendar and Promotions hierarchies, drilling into each by a couple of levels:

Title   🔲 ✏ ✖

Sample MSAS Query

Pivot Table   🔲 ✏ ✖

	Gross Profit						
	⊟ All Periods	⊞ CY 2001	⊟ CY 2002	⊞ H1 CY 2002	⊞ H2 CY 2002	⊞ CY 2003	⊞ CY 2004
Promotions							
⊟ All Promotions	12,551,366	1,640,533	2,970,252	1,193,388	1,776,864	3,904,175	4,036,406
⊞ No Discount	13,501,872	1,639,449	3,557,023	1,812,079	1,744,944	4,450,257	3,855,144
⊟ Reseller	-950,506	1,084	-586,771	-618,691	31,921	-546,081	181,262
⊞ Discontinued Product	-709,354		-617,514	-617,514			-91,840
⊞ Excess Inventory	-97,973		-97,973		-97,973		
⊞ New Product	-807,630					-807,630	
⊞ Seasonal Discount	823		621		621	202	
⊞ Volume Discount	663,628	1,084	128,095	-1,178	129,273	261,347	273,103

In this instance, 19 separate MDX queries would be sent to Analysis Services, which is less than would be sent to Essbase because separate queries to retrieve sort order would not be required, but probably there would be more than you would expect. As with Essbase sources, to minimize the number of MDX queries generated you should follow these guidelines:

- Use hierarchical columns in your analysis only when you really need to; if attribute columns (regular column types in the dimension presentation tables) can be used instead, do so, because they require only a single MDX query to return their values.

- If you have to use hierarchical columns, consider using just one in an analysis, replacing the other with one or more attribute columns.

- If you use more than one hierarchical column, try to keep the levels of drilling to the minimum.

- If all else fails, size your Analysis Services server to expect between 5 and 30 MDX queries per analysis, as this is the amount of MDX queries you can expect for a typical pivot table query using two or more hierarchical columns.

Using EVALUATE and EVALUATE_AGGR to Leverage Analysis Services MDX Functions

When users create analyses that use formulas to calculate derived values for columns, in general these are function-shipped down to the underlying database so that, for example, a request for Rank(Sales) within your analysis criteria is shipped down to the equivalent analytic function within the Oracle database. For multidimensional sources, however, only time-series functions are shipped down to the equivalent MDX function, with all other functions (including simple additions and subtractions, all the way through to TopN and Rank functions) performed instead by the Oracle BI Server.

In most cases, you will not notice this as the bulk of the "heavy lifting" in such an analysis as the retrieval and aggregation of the base data, but there may be some circumstances where such an approach becomes inefficient or you may wish to take advantage of a particular MDX function in your query.

In this case, as with Essbase sources, you can use two special Oracle Business Intelligence functions to make use of native Analysis Services functions:

- **EVALUATE**   This function returns single values, typically as attributes for a dimension member.
- **EVALUATE_AGGR**   This function returns measure values that will be aggregated as part of an analysis results set.

The use of EVALUATE and EVALUATE_AGGR for Analysis Services sources works the same way as for Essbase sources and is described in more detail earlier in this chapter in the section, "Using EVALUATE and EVALUATE_AGGR to Leverage Essbase MDX Functions."

Creating Repositories from Oracle OLAP Data Sources

In addition to supporting MDX-based sources such as Oracle Essbase and Microsoft Analysis Services, Oracle Business Intelligence supports queries against the OLAP Option to Oracle Database 10g Release 2 and 11g Releases 1 and 2. The OLAP Option is an embedded OLAP server available as an option to the Enterprise Edition of the Oracle Database. It provides full multidimensional data types and calculations, but unlike Essbase and Analysis Services it uses SQL rather than MDX as its query language. OLAP data is held in *analytic workspaces,* which are binary data types held within regular Oracle tables and tablespaces.

Oracle OLAP appeals to customers and developers who already have large investments in Oracle Database technology and wish to leverage the scalability and reliability of the Oracle Database while providing full OLAP functionality to their end users.

Connecting to Oracle OLAP

Support for Oracle OLAP as a data source was provided from the 11.1.1.5 release of Oracle Business Intelligence, and you should check the *System Requirements and Supported Platforms for Oracle Business Intelligence Suite Enterprise Edition 11gR1* document on the Oracle Technology Network web site for the latest supported configurations.

Oracle Business Intelligence connects to Oracle OLAP through the Java Host system component, which it uses first to retrieve cube metadata and later on to access the actual cube data. If you connect to Oracle OLAP from an installation of the Oracle Business Intelligence Administration tool on the same host server as Oracle Business Intelligence, you will not need to carry out any configuration tasks before importing metadata into the Oracle BI Repository. If you wish to use a stand-alone client installation of the BI Administration tool, away from the server running Oracle Business Intelligence, you will need to configure your Java Host environment variable before starting the import, a task that is detailed in the following section.

Your Oracle OLAP cube can be on any Oracle Database server that is accessible to your Oracle Business Intelligence installation, and your Oracle BI Administration tool if you are working on a remote workstation.

Example: Setting Up Oracle OLAP Client Connectivity

If you are using Oracle Business Intelligence on the Microsoft Windows platform and are working with the Oracle BI Administration tool on that same server, you do not need to perform any additional tasks to set up connectivity to Oracle OLAP.

If you are working with a separate client installation of the Oracle BI Administration tool, which does not itself come with the Java Host system component that is used for Oracle OLAP connectivity, you will need to perform the following steps to configure the BI Administration tool to connect to the Java Host installation on your main Oracle Business Intelligence installation.

1. On the host machine on which you have the stand-alone installation of Oracle Business Intelligence, use Windows Explorer to navigate to the following directory:

   [*Oracle Business Intelligence Enterprise Edition Plus Client Home*]\oraclebi\orainst\ config\OracleBIServerComponent\coreapplication

   Then open the NQSConfig.INI file with a text editor such as Notepad.exe.

2. At the end of the file will be a configuration setting for Java Host, which should look like this:

   ```
   ###################################################
   #
   #   Javahost Section
   ###################################################
   [JAVAHOST]
   #JAVAHOST_HOSTNAME_OR_IP_ADDRESSES =
   "<machine-name1>":<port_number1>,<machine-name2>:<port_number2>;
   ```

3. Add under this line a copy of the Java Host configuration setting (with the commenting out removed) and the IP address or hostname, together with the port number of the Java Host instance on your Oracle Business Intelligence server. For example:

   ```
   JAVAHOST_HOSTNAME_OR_IP_ADDRESSES = "obisrv1a:9810";
   ```

4. Your NQSConfig.INI file section should now look like this:

   ```
   ###################################################
   #
   #   Javahost Section
   #
   ###################################################
   [JAVAHOST]
   #JAVAHOST_HOSTNAME_OR_IP_ADDRESSES =
   "<machine-name1>":<port_number1>,<machine-name2>:<port_number2>;
   JAVAHOST_HOSTNAME_OR_IP_ADDRESSES = "obisrv1a:9810";
   ```

When you then follow the instructions in the next step to import Oracle OLAP metadata into the Oracle BI Repository, your stand-alone BI Administration tool will connect correctly to your Java Host installation and will import your metadata via your Oracle Business Intelligence server.

Example: Using the Metadata Import Wizard to Import OLAP Metadata

To import metadata from your Oracle OLAP cube into the Oracle BI Repository, follow these steps:

1. With your repository open either online or offline, select File | Import Metadata.

2. At the Import Metadata – Select Data Source screen, select and enter the following settings, using the *host:port:sid* connection settings for the Oracle database containing your Oracle OLAP analytic workspace and user account details for an account containing your Oracle OLAP analytic workspace:

   Connection Type: Oracle OLAP
   Data Source Name: [*host:port:sid*] (for example, localhost:1521:orcl)
   User Name: [*username for your Oracle Database*]
   Password: [*password for your Oracle Database*]
   Target Database: [*Enter details for a new physical database or select* Existing *for an existing physical database.*]

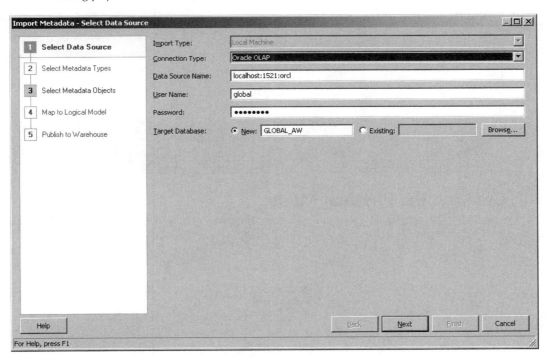

3. At the Import Metadata – Select Metadata Objects screen, select the Oracle OLAP analytic workspace objects you wish to import into the Oracle BI Repository and copy them from the Data Source View area into the Repository View area. Click Finish to complete the import.

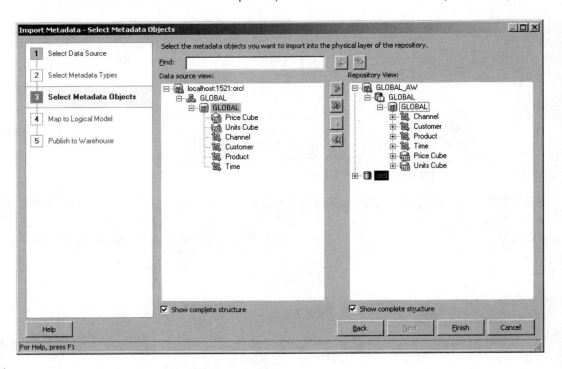

Creating the Physical Model

After you complete the metadata import from the Oracle OLAP data source, your initial physical model can be found in the physical layer of the Oracle BI Repository.

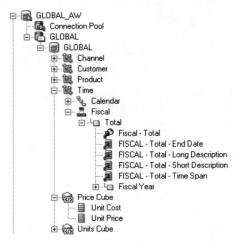

As with physical models sourced from Oracle Essbase and Microsoft Analysis Services, the import process creates special multidimensional physical layer metadata objects for your data source. In fact, for Oracle OLAP cubes, there are metadata types unique to this data source:

- **Database and catalog**   These are common to all data sources and relate to the database name and schema name that contain the Oracle OLAP analytic workspace.

- **Oracle OLAP analytic workspace**   This equates to cube tables for Essbase and Analysis Services sources, and corresponds to the analytic workspace containing your dimensions, hierarchies, levels, and measures.

- **Oracle OLAP dimension**   This equates to Essbase and Analysis Services physical dimensions, and is a container for hierarchies, levels, and columns.

- **Oracle OLAP level-based hierarchy**   This is for holding level-based hierarchies containing levels and columns.

- **Oracle OLAP value-based hierarchy**   This is for holding value-based hierarchies and columns.

- **Oracle OLAP column**   This contains either dimension attributes or measure values.

- **Oracle OLAP cube**   This is a container for columns containing measures.

Oracle Business Intelligence uses these different physical layer metadata objects because of the different way that Oracle OLAP data is stored and accessed compared to the MDX-based access used for Analysis Services and Essbase. Once they are created, though, you work with them in much the same way as you would for Essbase and Analysis Services sources, including being able to drag-and-drop the whole cube into the business model and mapping layer to automatically create a business model, complete with dimensions, hierarchies, facts, and joins.

Oracle OLAP-Specific Physical Model Enhancements

Directly after you import your Oracle OLAP metadata into the physical layer of your repository, you should double-click the connection pool for your physical model. Then, using the General tab, edit the data source name to remove the *host:port:sid* connection settings and replace them instead with the Oracle Net (TNSNAMES) connection settings for your Oracle database.

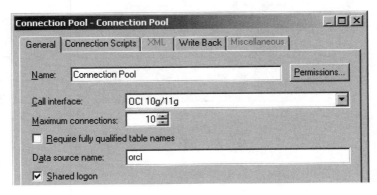

Apart from this change, in general and unlike with Essbase sources you do not edit or change the metadata for Oracle OLAP–sourced physical models after the first import, as most significant changes (changing a level-based hierarchy to a value-based hierarchy, for example) have to be carried out in the analytic workspace itself. Ragged, skip-level, and time-based hierarchies will be detected during the metadata import process, and you should not normally have to manually change these values after the initial import.

Settings that you might need to change for Oracle OLAP 10*g* cubes, though, are the Density and Materialization Settings. To edit these settings, navigate to your Oracle OLAP Cube object in the physical layer and double-click it to view the General tab.

For Oracle OLAP cubes sourced from an Oracle OLAP 11*g* cube, these settings are left blank and are handled automatically for you by the Oracle Database. For Oracle OLAP 10*g* cubes that are sparse and fully materialized, you should set these values to Sparse and Fully Materialized to take advantage of the Oracle OLAP loop clause to skip empty cells and improve the performance of your queries.

Creating the Business Model

As with other multidimensionally sourced physical models in the Oracle BI Repository, creating a business model based off of your physical model is as simple as dragging and dropping the Oracle OLAP Analytic Workspace object from the physical layer into the business model and mapping layer of your repository. When you do this, the Oracle BI Administration tool will automatically create a business model complete with logical tables, logical dimensions, logical levels, logical columns, and logical joins based on the dimensional metadata in the physical model.

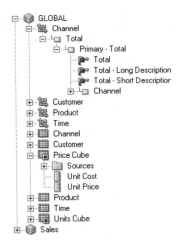

As with Oracle OLAP–sourced physical models, you do not generally have to change or fine-tune business models created from Oracle OLAP data, except to add further calculations or merge the data with other data sources, as described later in this chapter.

Creating the Subject Area

To create a subject area for an Oracle OLAP–sourced business model, just drag-and-drop the business model into the presentation layer of the repository. A corresponding subject area, along with presentation tables, hierarchies, and columns, will be created for your Oracle OLAP data source.

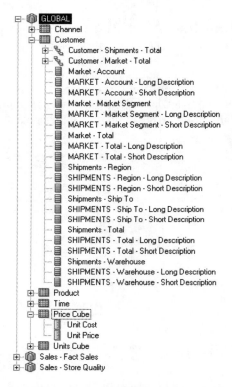

Each hierarchy within logical dimensions in the business model will be converted to its own separate presentation hierarchy in the subject area, and you will also notice the long descriptions, short descriptions, and member name attributes represented as presentation columns within the presentation tables. Logical columns used for measures will automatically have their default aggregation method settings set within the business model, and you will see that these logical columns are indicated as measures within the fact table presentation tables.

One change that you may wish to make to the presentation hierarchies within your subject area is to remove the redundant "total" level that is usually created for each hierarchy. With Oracle OLAP analytic workspaces, it is common to have a specific "total" level for each hierarchy, but the import process into the repository creates another total level. In the example of the Channel dimension in the Global sample analytic workspace, this leaves you with two total levels in the hierarchy.

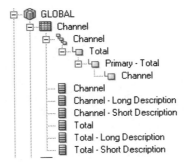

If you then include this presentation hierarchy in an analysis, your users will need to drill through two "total" levels to get to the levels they are looking for.

If you want to remove one of the redundant "total" levels from the hierarchy, you are best to remove the one added by the Oracle BI Administration tool (Total, rather than the Total Channel one that was imported from Oracle OLAP), as this does not relate to a specific stored aggregation in the Oracle OLAP cube. To remove it, delete the existing presentation hierarchy in the subject area, and then just drag-and-drop the Primary Total logical level from the logical dimension into the presentation table so that a presentation hierarchy that starts from this level and misses the Total level above it is created.

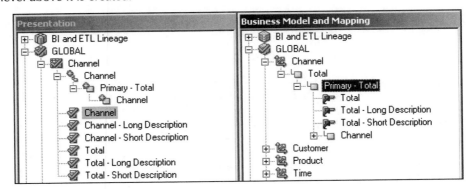

Finally, repeat this process for the other presentation hierarchies in your subject area, removing the additional total level from each one of them. Then, when you include these hierarchies in your analyses, you will not see the redundant additional total levels within them.

Managing Changes to Oracle OLAP Metadata

Unlike metadata sourced from Oracle Essbase and Microsoft Analysis Services, you cannot at this point reimport Oracle OLAP metadata into the repository to reflect changes in your source data model. If your underlying data model does change, you will have to manually apply changes to the physical model (and make sure these are valid and accurately reflect the underlying Oracle OLAP data model) or delete and then reimport the physical object metadata.

If you manually update your physical object metadata, you can then apply these changes and new metadata objects to the business model and to subject area that you have derived for it. If you have deleted and then reimported your physical model, though, you will generally have to delete and then re-create the business model and subject area, as the previous logical table source mappings will have been invalidated by the physical model replacement.

Querying Oracle OLAP Data—OLAP_TABLE and OLAP DML Considerations

Unlike Oracle Essbase–based and Microsoft Analysis Services–based sources, Oracle Business Intelligence obtains data from Oracle OLAP not through MDX queries but through SQL statements that use the OLAP_TABLE function. The primary query interface for Oracle OLAP is SQL, and the Oracle database interfaces between the relational SQL query language and the multidimensional Oracle OLAP engine through this OLAP_TABLE function, a built-in Oracle table function that passes parameters to the OLAP engine and translates the returned multidimensional data set into the relational row-and-column output that a SQL query would expect.

All of this happens "under the covers" through the Oracle BI Server and the Oracle BI Repository, though it does have some impact in terms of functions you can use within your repository and in your analysis criteria. To explain the basics, though, let's take a look at a simple analysis that returns the list of product families without any reference to measures or any other dimensions.

If you have previously enabled query logging at level 2 or above for the user running the analysis and you examine the entries in the nqquery.log file for this analysis, you will see that the BI Server has written the physical query using the OLAP_TABLE function to access the underlying analytic workspace data:

```
WITH
SAWITH0 AS (select distinct family_product_long_descripti1 as c1
from
      (select *
          from table(olap_table('GLOBAL.GLOBAL duration session', '', '',
              'dimension product_id as varchar2(100) from PRODUCT with ' ||
              ' attribute product_level as varchar2(100)
                  from PRODUCT_LEVELREL ' ||
              ' hierarchy PRODUCT_PARENTREL
                  (PRODUCT_HIERLIST ''PRIMARY'') ' ||
              '   inhierarchy PRODUCT_INHIER ' ||
              '   familyrel family_product_long_descripti1
                  as varchar2(100) from ' ||
              '   PRODUCT_FAMILYREL(PRODUCT_LEVELLIST ''FAMILY'') ' ||
              '   label PRODUCT_LONG_DESCRIPTION ' ||
              'row2cell r2c '
          ))
          where product_level = 'FAMILY'
      ))
select distinct 0 as c1,
      D1.c1 as c2
from
      SAWITH0 D1
order by c2
```

If you take this analysis and then add a measure to it, you can see how the SQL and OLAP_ TABLE changes when you start to reference measures. The following example adds the Profit measure to the previous analysis:

Family - Long Description	Profit
Accessories	8,162,817
CD/DVD	19,765,631
Desktop PCs	17,151,377
Documentation	3,092,104
Memory	5,742,324
Modems/Fax	7,164,215
Monitors	4,330,199
Operating Systems	6,677,016
Portable PCs	10,222,282

Now you will see that the OLAP_TABLE function call has to reference all of the dimensions in the analytic workspace, as well as the measure:

```
WITH
SAWITH0 AS
     (select case when count(*) > 1 then null
        else max(units_cube_profit) end as c1,
      family_product_long_descripti1 as c2,
      family_product as c3
from
     (select *
          from table(olap_table('GLOBAL.GLOBAL duration session', '', '',
             'measure units_cube_profit from UNITS_CUBE_PROFIT ' ||
             'dimension channel_id as varchar2(100) from CHANNEL with ' ||
             ' attribute channel_level as varchar2(100)
                from CHANNEL_LEVELREL ' ||
             ' hierarchy CHANNEL_PARENTREL
                (CHANNEL_HIERLIST ''PRIMARY'') ' ||
             ' inhierarchy CHANNEL_INHIER ' ||
             'dimension customer_id as varchar2(100)
                from CUSTOMER with ' ||
             ' attribute customer_level as varchar2(100)
                from CUSTOMER_LEVELREL ' ||
             ' hierarchy
                CUSTOMER_PARENTREL(CUSTOMER_HIERLIST ''SHIPMENTS'') ' ||
             ' inhierarchy CUSTOMER_INHIER ' ||
             'dimension product_id as varchar2(100) from PRODUCT with ' ||
             ' attribute product_level as varchar2(100)
                from PRODUCT_LEVELREL ' ||
             ' hierarchy
                PRODUCT_PARENTREL(PRODUCT_HIERLIST ''PRIMARY'') ' ||
             ' inhierarchy PRODUCT_INHIER ' ||
             ' familyrel family_product as varchar2(100) from ' ||
             ' PRODUCT_FAMILYREL(PRODUCT_LEVELLIST ''FAMILY'') ' ||
             ' label PRODUCT ' ||
             ' familyrel family_product_long_descripti1
                as varchar2(100) from ' ||
             ' PRODUCT_FAMILYREL(PRODUCT_LEVELLIST ''FAMILY'') ' ||
             ' label PRODUCT_LONG_DESCRIPTION ' ||
             'dimension time_id as varchar2(100) from TIME with ' ||
             ' attribute time_level as varchar2(100)
                from TIME_LEVELREL ' ||
             ' hierarchy TIME_PARENTREL(TIME_HIERLIST ''CALENDAR'') ' ||
             ' inhierarchy TIME_INHIER ' ||
             'loop optimized ' ||
             'row2cell r2c '
          ))
          where channel_level = 'TOTAL'
          and customer_level = 'TOTAL'
          and product_level = 'FAMILY'
```

```
           and time_level = 'TOTAL'
           and (units_cube_profit is not null)
     )
where  ( 1 = 1 )
group by family_product_long_descripti1, family_product),
SAWITH1 AS (select distinct 0 as c1,
     D1.c2 as c2,
     D1.c1 as c3,
     D1.c3 as c4
from
     SAWITH0 D1)
select D1.c1 as c1,
     D1.c2 as c2,
     D1.c3 as c3
from
     SAWITH1 D1
order by c1, c2
```

Toward the end of the query you will see the references to CHANNEL_LEVEL, PRODUCT_LEVEL, and so on, which are used to reference the correct levels when retrieving data from the cube. Notice also how the OLAP_TABLE function also automatically makes use of the loop optimized clause, an import performance enhancer for sparse Oracle OLAP cubes, because we are using an Oracle OLAP 11*g* cube.

If you start to add filters to your analysis, such as in this example where we filter on the product family being in Memory and Modems/Fax:

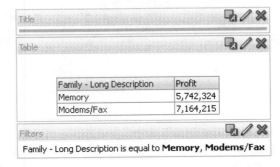

you will see this filter being pushed into the SELECT statement that surrounds the OLAP_TABLE call, as shown in the following SQL excerpt:

```
'       inhierarchy TIME_INHIER ' ||
               'loop optimized ' ||
               'row2cell r2c '
          ))
          where channel_level = 'TOTAL'
          and customer_level = 'TOTAL'
          and product_level = 'FAMILY'
          and time_level = 'TOTAL'
          and (units_cube_profit is not null)
     )
```

```
where  ( family_product_long_descripti1 in ('Memory', 'Modems/Fax') )
group by family_product_long_descripti1, family_product),
SAWITH1 AS (select distinct 0 as c1,
     D1.c2 as c2,
     D1.c1 as c3,
     D1.c3 as c4
from
     SAWITH0 D1)
select D1.c1 as c1,
     D1.c2 as c2,
     D1.c3 as c3
from
     SAWITH1 D1
order by c1, c2
```

Finally, if you were to create an analysis that used hierarchical columns (unlike the situation you have with MDX-based sources in which multiple MDX queries are sent for all of the subtotals in your pivot table), a single SQL statement with OLAP_TABLE calls within the subqueries will be sent instead.

Product	Profit			
	Total Channel			
		Catalog	Direct Sales	Internet
Total Product	82,307,964	50,030,914	5,314,409	26,962,641
Hardware	64,376,027	40,179,074	4,142,116	20,054,836
Software/Other	17,931,937	9,851,840	1,172,292	6,907,805
Accessories	8,162,817	4,461,288	493,495	3,208,034
Documentation	3,092,104	2,058,448	252,787	780,869
Operating Systems	6,677,016	3,332,104	426,010	2,918,902

How does this affect functions and calculations you may create within your analysis? EVALUATE and EVALUATE_AGGR, as described for Essbase and Microsoft Analysis Services sources earlier in this chapter, do work but require you to use the OLAP_EXPRESSION Oracle Database function to wrap OLAP DML function calls rather than the MDX function calls you would use with MDX-based sources. Features like time-series functions may work but may need different handling than MDX-based sources. You should be aware that, because Oracle OLAP does not use the same MDX functionality as other multidimensional sources when all end-user features are present, you should test carefully any functions or other modeling features in case these are not yet present for Oracle OLAP sources.

Combining OLAP and Relational Data in Business Models

One of the most common uses for multidimensional data within Oracle Business Intelligence is to combine it with existing relational, file, or other data that exists in the Oracle BI Repository. For example, you may have aggregated data and stored it in an Oracle OLAP analytic workspace and you wish to combine this with the detail-level transaction data already mapped into your repository to allow users to seamlessly drill from aggregated data in the Oracle OLAP cube down to the detail-level data in your Oracle database. This technique is usually referred to as "vertical federation" because you are federating (joining) data across differing, "vertical" levels of detail.

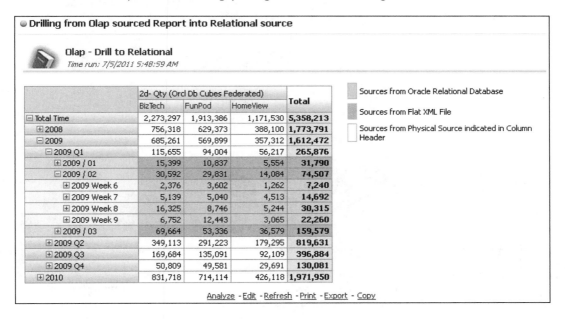

Another common use case is to combine measures sourced from relational and multidimensional sources into a single logical fact table. You could, for example, source "quantity" data from your Oracle database and "revenue" data from an Essbase cube. Depending on whether the user requests one or both of the measures, the Oracle BI Server will generate SQL, MDX, or a combination of the two queries in response to the analysis. This is often referred to as "horizontal federation," as data is combined across rather than "up and down" the business model.

Products Hierarchy	1b- Revenue (Essbase Cube Only)	2a- Qty (Orcl Db Tables Only)	20b - Unit Price (Essb Cube/Orcl Db)
⊟ Total Products	15,000,000	1,612,472	9.30
⊞ BizTech	6,302,087	685,261	9.20
⊞ FunPod	5,160,340	569,899	9.05
⊞ HomeView	3,537,573	357,312	9.90
Grand Total	15,000,000	1,612,472	9.30

Finally, you may wish to supplement numeric data held in an Essbase or other multidimensional cube with descriptive data from a relational or other data source. While this can be achieved using a similar technique as that used for horizontal federation, it can often make sense to perform this lookup "post-aggregation" using the LOOKUP function.

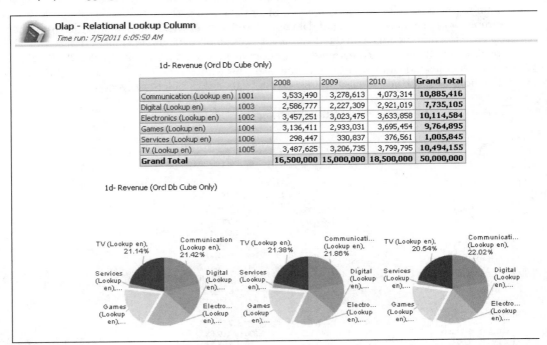

While horizontal and vertical federation can be used for all sources, not just relational and multidimensional combined, they are two of the most common ways that multidimensional data is used in the context of Oracle Business Intelligence. So how do these techniques work?

Vertical Federation of OLAP and Relational Data

When you combine detail-level relational or file data with summary-level multidimensional data within your repository, both data sources are mapped into common logical table structures but are demarcated through logical dimension content-level mappings. When an analysis is created against such a logical table, the BI Server will select between the available logical table sources based on which one of these content-level mappings it believes will return data most efficiently.

For example, consider a situation where we have a subset of the GCBC_SALES physical model described in Chapter 3 that contains relationally sourced sales data for an organization. This model has then been used to create a business model and subject area based around two dimensions, Products and Time, and a Sales fact table containing various metrics on product sales.

This data goes down to the month and product level, and it is the most detailed sales information we have in the repository.

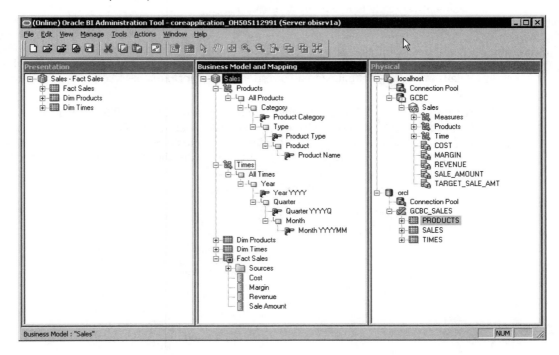

We now have an additional source of data, the same data set summarized to the Product Type and Quarter level, which is held in an Essbase database. What we would like to do is to map this additional source of data into the repository such that the BI Server, when presented with an analysis that is at the Quarter and/or Product Type level, uses the Essbase source but if asked to display data in more detail reverts to the relational source.

For this vertical federation technique to work, there are certain prerequisites you will have to meet:

■   The hierarchies you wish to integrate have to be balanced, level-based hierarchies. Value-based or ragged/skip-level hierarchies will not work, as there will not be consistent values at each level in the hierarchy to join the two data sources together.

■   Member names have to be consistent across the two sources.

■   You may need to transform your relational dimension member names to, for example, add level and hierarchy prefixes to match the more strict naming rules that Essbase has around uniqueness.

■   You may also find it useful to create named generations for your Essbase hierarchies to make matching the resulting physical cube columns with their relational counterparts easier.

■   When working with Essbase sources, make sure that you convert the measure hierarchy to a flat list of measures to correspond with the measure logical columns in the logical fact table you wish to map to.

Example: Combining OLAP and Relational Data using Vertical Federation

With these prerequisites met, follow these steps to combine your relational and multidimensional data into a single, vertically federated business model:

1. The starting point for these steps is an Oracle BI Repository with physical models for your detail-level relational data set (GCBC_SALES) and your summarized Oracle Essbase data set (GCBC.Sales), together with a business model initially sourced exclusively from the detail-level relational data and a corresponding subject area based off of the business area.

2. The business model should have logical dimensions defined for all of the logical tables that you intend to map your summary-level OLAP data set to. In the example we are using, we have a Product dimension with a single hierarchy All Products > Category > Product, and a Time dimension with the hierarchy All Times > Year > Quarter > Month.

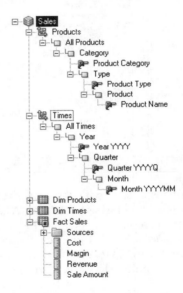

3. The first dimension we will vertically federate is Time. To do this, navigate to the physical cube column in the Essbase physical model that you wish to map to an existing logical column (for example, the Year physical cube column under the Year physical level), and then drag-and-drop it on top of its corresponding logical column in the business model (in this case, the Year YYYY column in the Dim Times logical table). Repeat this for the remaining physical cube columns you want to match up, which in this example is only the Quarter physical column in the Quarter physical level.

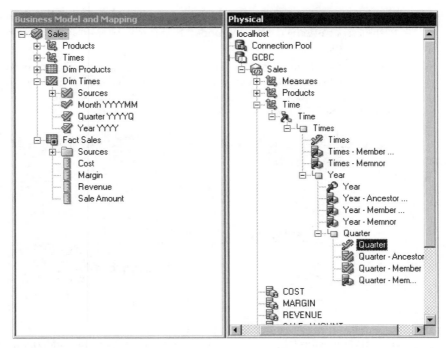

4. If you now expand the Sources folder within the logical table that you just mapped your OLAP columns to, you should see a new logical table source mapping has been added, which contains the mappings for your logical columns back to the Essbase source.

5. If you then double-click the logical table source that relates to the multidimensional Essbase source and select the Column Mapping tab in the Logical Table Source dialog box, you will see mappings for the logical columns that have a corresponding source in the Essbase source.

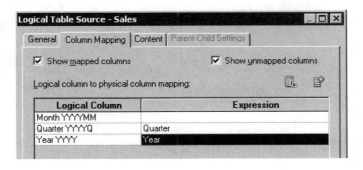

In this example, only the Quarter YYYYQ and Year YYYY logical column have mappings to the Essbase-derived physical model, as this is the lowest level of detail that the Essbase database goes down to.

6. Now you need to tell the Oracle BI Server at which level in the corresponding logical dimension it should begin using this source. To do this, click the Content tab in the same dialog box, and for the logical dimension select the logical level at which the lowest level of data in the OLAP source is stored (in this case, Quarter).

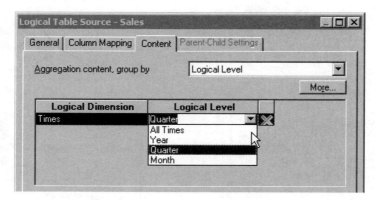

7. Repeat this process for the other dimension logical tables. In this example, the other logical dimension table is Products, and we would map the Category and Type physical cube columns from the Essbase physical model to the Product Category and Product Type logical columns within the Products logical table, and then edit the logical table source properties to set the content level to Type.

8. The next step is to map the measure physical cube columns from the Essbase physical model into the logical fact table's measure logical columns. As with the dimensions, drag-and-drop the physical cube columns onto their corresponding measure logical columns, and when you come to set the content level for the new logical table source, select the correct logical levels for the logical dimensions that define your new source. In our example, this means setting the logical level for the Products logical dimension to Type and the logical level for the Times logical dimension to Quarter.

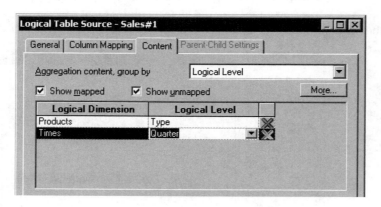

9. You are now ready to try out your new business model. Save your model and check its consistency, upload your repository if required, and refresh the metadata used by the BI Presentation Server.

Before you test your updated repository, open your repository online using the Oracle BI Administration tool and set the query logging level for your user to 2 or higher. To do this, select Manage | Identity, then select Action | Set Online User Filter, entering a wildcard (*) if required, double-click the required user, and set the logging level to 2.

Start your testing by creating an analysis using the top-most level from one of your vertically federated dimensions, and include with it one of your measures. In this example, we will use the Product Category attribute column along with the Revenue measure.

Product Category	Revenue
Bread	521
Drinks	202
Gifts	132
Snacks	170

If you then examine the nqquery.log file, you will see that an MDX query has been sent to the Essbase source. This is because the BI Server looks at the two logical sources mapped into the fact and dimension logical tables and determines that both would satisfy the query, but that because the Essbase-derived one is mapped in at a higher level of detail, it would return results faster:

```
With
  set [_Products2]  as '[Products].Generations(2).members'
select
  { [Measures].[REVENUE]
  } on columns,
  NON EMPTY {{[_Products2]}} properties GEN_NUMBER on rows
from [GCBC.Sales]
```

You would see similar behavior for all columns that can be sourced from the Essbase database until such time as you drill down to a column that can only be sourced from the relational logical table source.

Product Category	Product Type	Product Name	Revenue
Bread	Rounds & Loaves	Bread Bowls	60
		Sandwich Rolls	20
		Sourdough Loaves	224
		Sourdough Rounds	30

When this happens, you will see in the nqquery.log file that the BI Server has switched to using SQL queries against the relational source, as shown here:

```
WITH
SAWITH0 AS (select sum(T3919.FCAST_REV_AMT) as c1,
     T3908.PROD_CAT_DESC as c2,
     T3908.PROD_NAME as c3,
     T3908.PROD_TYPE_DESC as c4
from
     PRODUCTS T3908,
     SALES T3919
where  ( T3908.PROD_CAT_DESC = 'Bread'
and T3908.PROD_ID = T3919.PROD_ID
and T3908.PROD_TYPE_DESC = 'Rounds & Loaves' )
group by T3908.PROD_CAT_DESC, T3908.PROD_NAME, T3908.PROD_TYPE_DESC)
select distinct 0 as c1,
     D1.c2 as c2,
     D1.c3 as c3,
     D1.c4 as c4,
     D1.c1 as c5
from
     SAWITH0 D1
order by c2, c4, c3
```

Finally, if instead of attribute columns you use hierarchical columns in your analysis, you will see the BI Server typically using a mixture of MDX queries and SQL queries for the various subqueries resulting from your analysis, depending on the level of detail you drill into in your pivot table.

Horizontal Federation of OLAP and Relational Data

In addition to combining detail- and summary-level data to create alternate sources for fact table measures, you can also configure your business model so that some measures come from relational sources (for example, historical or actuals data) while others come from OLAP sources (for example, budget or forecast data).

Typically, the data coming from the OLAP source is of a different level of granularity than the relationally sourced data, so you can either make its measures available in their own specific logical fact table or you can combine them with the detail-level measures in a single logical fact table, the choice of which is up to you and your users' requirements. In the following example, we use the same initial logical model and table mapping used in the previous example, and we have a set of measures that are solely sourced from a relational database (Margin, Revenue, Cost, and Sale Amount) and a new measure that is being provided, at summary-level, from an Essbase source (Sale Amount Target). Depending, then, on whether the user selects just the relationally sourced measures, the Essbase-sourced one, or both, the BI Server will generate SQL, MDX, or both types of queries to provide data for the analysis.

Example: Combining OLAP and Relational Data using Horizontal Federation

Follow these steps to combine relationally and multidimensionally-sourced measures using the horizontal federation feature:

1. The repository we are working with has an existing business model that is sourced entirely from a relational physical model. The new column we wish to add to this model is held within another physical layer model, sourced from Essbase with the column named TARGET_SALE_AMOUNT.

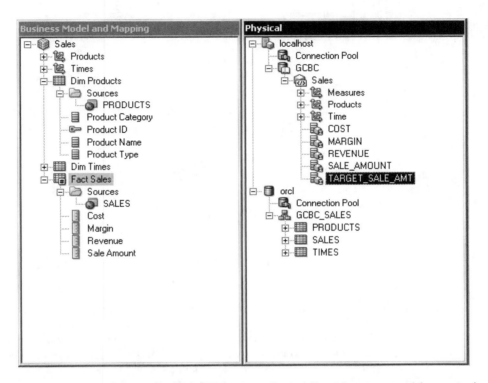

2. The first step in this horizontal federation is actually to follow the steps used for vertical federation: all of the relevant dimension physical cube columns provided by the Essbase source (the Category and Type cube columns from the Product physical dimension and the Quarter and Year cube columns from the Time physical dimension) need to be mapped into their relevant logical dimension tables in the business model, and their new logical table sources need to have assigned the correct logical dimension content level. See the preceding section on vertical federation for the full set of steps for how to perform this mapping.

3. If, as is the case in this example, the Essbase source also provides aggregated values for the logical table measures, you can map these in as you did with the vertical federation example in the preceding section. In many cases, though, the new Essbase source will provide a different set of measures than those provided by the relational, detail-level source, so this step is optional.

4. For the new physical cube column (TARGET_SALE_AMOUNT, in this example), drag-and-drop it onto the logical fact table in the business model. This will add a new logical column of the same name, which you can edit to fit with the naming standards already in use in the logical table.

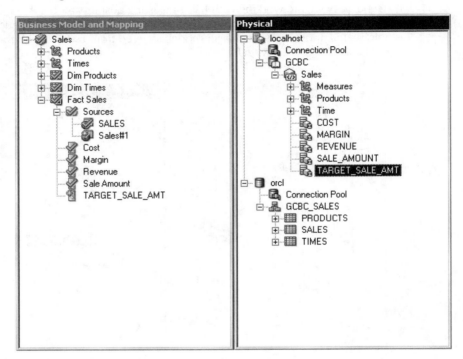

5. Adding this new logical column from the new Essbase source will create a new logical table source under the fact logical table. Double-click this table source to view it, and if you have mapped in only this Essbase physical cube column, then it alone will be listed when you select the Column Mapping tab. Click the Content tab to set the logical level for the logical dimensions that are linked to the logical fact table and to the levels of detail provided by the new Essbase source. (In our example, these would be set to Type and Quarter.)

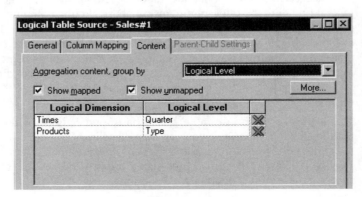

6. Finally, drag-and-drop the new logical column from the business model to the subject area fact table so that it is then available for users to query. Save your repository, and if working online check in any changes, upload the repository, and refresh any Presentation Server metadata before making it available for end users to query.

Now, when your users query your subject area fact table, if they select only measures that are sourced from the relational data source, only SQL queries will be issued by the BI Server. Similarly, if only the new Essbase-sourced column is used and the user requests the correct level of detail, only an MDX query will be issued. If, however, both types of columns are requested, the BI Server will generate both SQL and MDX queries, and the results will be "stitched together" in the BI Server's memory before being returned to users in their analysis results.

Product Category	Sale Amount	Target Sale Amount
Bread	71	77
Drinks	172	154
Gifts	18	15
Snacks	89	77

Looking at the output in the nqquery.log file, you will see the two types of queries being generated, as shown here, plus the additional steps where the BI Server joins the two result sets together (not included in the following excerpt):

```
select T3908.PROD_CAT_DESC as c1,
     sum(T3919.FCAST_SAL_AMT) as c2
from
     PRODUCTS T3908,
     SALES T3919
where   ( T3908.PROD_ID = T3919.PROD_ID )
group by T3908.PROD_CAT_DESC
order by c1

With
  set [_Products2]  as '[Products].Generations(2).members'
select
  { [Measures].[TARGET_SALE_AMT]
  } on columns,
  NON EMPTY {{[_Products2]}} properties GEN_NUMBER on rows
from [GCBC.Sales]
```

Note, however, that if you drill down in the analysis below the level supported by the Essbase source, the column that is solely sourced from this source will display a NULL value. This is because the source does not support that level of detail, and the value at the higher level cannot be broken down (or "allocated") down to the required level of detail. It is because of this that some repository modelers keep measures such as the one you just added, which are at a different level of detail (or "granularity") in their own logical fact table, along with measures of the same granularity, although as you will have seen from this example, this is not mandatory.

Adding Attributes to OLAP Data Using Lookups

One final use case that is often used when combining relational and multidimensional data sources is supplementing OLAP-sourced measures with descriptive data from a relational database. Most OLAP servers do not allow you to hold large amounts of descriptive data in their OLAP cubes, and it may well be the case that your descriptive data sits elsewhere anyway, perhaps in a transactional application or in a content management system.

While you can use the horizontal federation technique to add descriptive data to a business model otherwise sourced from a multidimensional database, this approach often does not perform well, as large amounts of data have to be combined for this to work. Instead, the new LOOKUP function provided with Oracle Business Intelligence 11*g* allows us to retrieve descriptive lookup data post-aggregation, an approach that can be much more efficient.

Example: Using the LOOKUP function to enhance OLAP-sourced Business Models

In this example, we have a repository build, this time directly from the Essbase data source used earlier in these examples, that provides product, category, and type basic member information for the Product dimension.

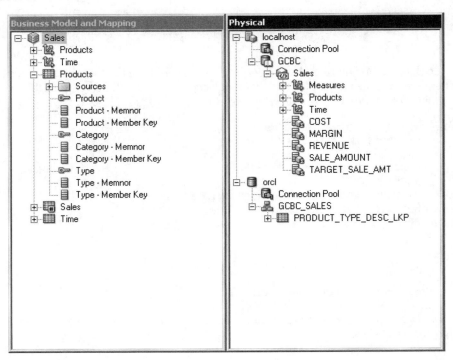

In addition to the Essbase data source, the physical layer of the repository contains a relational source that provides a single lookup table that we will use to provide more descriptive names for product types. Chapter 3 explains the new LOOKUP function, and in this instance, we will use this function, along with a logical lookup table, to add these descriptions to the business model:

1.   Navigate to the physical model of the repository and double-click the physical table that contains your lookup data (in this case, PRODUCT_TYPE_DESC_LKP). When the Physical Table dialog box is shown, click the Keys tab and create a key for the table, if one is not already present.

2.   Now, because the lookup table will be coming from a different physical database model to the data that currently populates the business model (an Essbase database), you will need to create a logical lookup table in the business model to hold the lookup data from this table. To do so, right-click the business model and select New Object | Logical Table, give the table a name (for example, Product Type Lkp), and then drag-and-drop the physical columns into this new logical table. Rename the columns as appropriate, and check that this new logical table has inherited the table key from the physical table you mapped into it.

3.   To designate this new logical table as a lookup table, double-click it again, and on the main General tab of the Logical Table dialog box, select the Lookup Table check box.

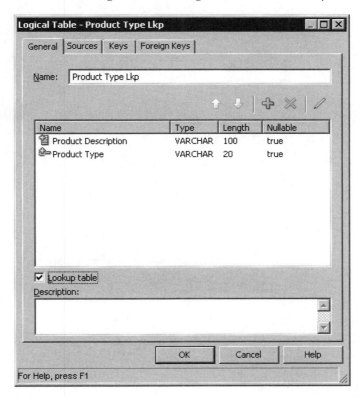

Now you can use the LOOKUP function to retrieve your product type description. To do so, right-click the logical table containing your dimension attributes (in this example,

Products) and select New Object | Logical Column. Name the column (for example, Product Type Description) and then switch to the Column Source tab to define the lookup expression. Select the "Derived from existing columns using an expression" radio button, and then use the Expression Editor to enter the following expression:

```
Lookup(DENSE   "Sales"."Product Type Lkp"."Product
Description" ,   "Sales"."Products"."Type" )
```

where DENSE signifies that the function will always return a lookup value, the first parameter is the column to be returned from the logical lookup table, and the second value is the logical column that will be used to return keyed values from the lookup table so that values in the two columns will match and provide a valid lookup. If more complex lookups are required, multiple key values can be passed using this function. Alternatively, use a SPARSE lookup if you believe that values will not always be returned, which in addition to requiring the input column for the key match also requires an extra parameter that provides the default return value when no match takes place.

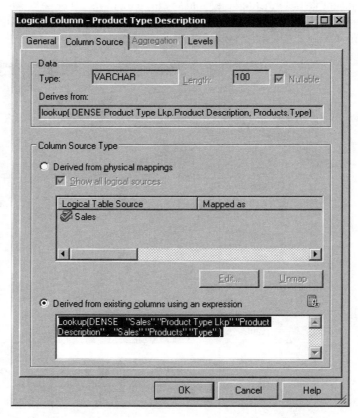

4. Finally, drag-and-drop the new logical column containing the description to the corresponding subject area in the presentation layer of the repository. Your repository is now ready for querying by users.

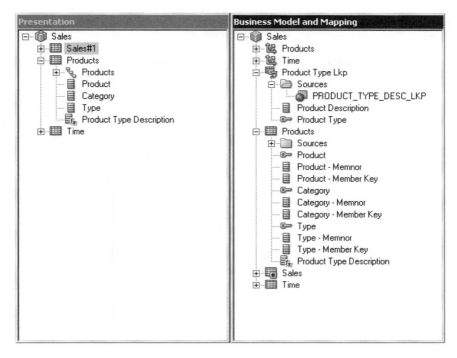

Now, when users create analyses that include both the member short details and these new descriptive details, the BI Server will generate an MDX query to return the aggregated measure data along with basic member details and send a separate SQL query to the database holding the lookup table, joining the two data sets together in the BI Server's memory before returning the combined results back to the user.

SALE_AMOUNT	Type	Product Type Description
63	Cold Drinks	Sodas, juices, water
109	Hot Drinks	Coffee, specialitity teas, hot chocolate
10	Gifts & Baskets	Breads in baskets
8	Bread Clubs	Collectable breads
7	Seasonal Breads	Challah breads, Easter loaves etc
49	Rounds & Loaves	Batch loaves, sourdough bowls etc
8	Bread Assortments	Table breads, rolls etc
7	Speciality Breads	Santa Breads etc
2	Accompaniments	Various accompanyments such as oils
26	Sandwiches	Chicken salad, tuna, pastrami
61	Soup	Clam chowder, tomato, minestrone

So that concludes our look at repository modeling for the Oracle BI Server; let's take a look now at some administration tasks you might need to perform using this component before deploying your system to end users.

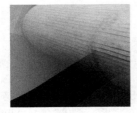

CHAPTER
5

Configuring
and Maintaining the
Oracle BI Server

o far in this book, we have looked at the overall architecture of Oracle Business Intelligence, and in the last couple of chapters we've examined the Oracle BI Repository that serves as the data access layer for your dashboards and analyses. Before we move on to other areas of functionality within Oracle Business Intelligence, we will take another look at the Oracle BI Server component that makes use of the Oracle BI Repository and list any configuration steps that you might need to perform with it.

Configuring the Oracle BI Server

Chapter 1 of this book looked in detail at the architecture of the Oracle BI Server and described the various components that are contained within it, including components that process and parse incoming SQL statements, store and retrieve query results in cache, and generate physical SQL and MDX statements to retrieve data from various data sources. You can think of the Oracle BI Server as a piece of "analytic middleware" that provides a unified, enhanced data layer over your various data sources and allows users to query this data using an overall logical dimensional model made up of business data items and hierarchies.

While in most cases the Oracle BI Server will work "out of the box" with little to no additional configuration needed (except, of course, to create the Oracle BI Repository metadata layer described in Chapters 3 and 4), there are additional configuration options available that may be useful for some customers. In this chapter, therefore, we will look at these additional configuration options and explain how you use Oracle Enterprise Manager Fusion Middleware Control and other tools to work with them.

Configuration Settings Handled by Fusion Middleware Control

Many configuration settings for the Oracle BI Server are handled by Oracle Enterprise Manager Fusion Middleware Control (or "Fusion Middleware Control" for short), and Oracle's long-term strategy is to expose all configuration settings via Fusion Middleware Control's web console or via the configuration JMX MBeans and the WebLogic Scripting Tool (WLST). These settings, described in more detail in Chapter 10, include

- Configuring which repository file is online and available for queries
- Configuring the location of the Oracle BI Presentation Services catalog
- Increasing and decreasing the number of system components (BI Servers, BI Presentation Servers, BI Java Hosts, BI Schedulers, and BI Cluster Controllers) present on each physical server
- Enabling and disabling the query cache, as well as configuring global cache and the size of the cache file
- Configuring how many rows can be returned in analyses

For a full list of the Oracle BI Server settings managed through Fusion Middleware Control and WLST, together with instructions on how to use Fusion Middleware Control to set their values, refer to Chapter 10.

Manually Configured Settings

Although the long-term strategy for Oracle Business Intelligence is to expose all configuration settings through Fusion Middleware Control, configuration JMX MBeans, and WLST, at the time of writing this book (with the current version of Oracle Business Intelligence being 11.1.1.6), some configuration settings still need to be set using configuration files within the Oracle Business Intelligence file system. For the Oracle BI Server, the file that configures these settings is the NQSConfig.INI file, and copies of this file are created for every additional BI Server component that you provision on your server. At the time of this writing, therefore, this file still contains some significant configuration settings, including the following:

- For systems upgraded from releases version 11.1.1.6, setting whether usage tracking and summary statistics are enabled or disabled, as well as how usage tracking and summary statistics data is recorded and stored. (For new systems from release 11.1.1.6 onward, this setting is instead controlled through a JMX MBean attribute property and should not be manually altered in this configuration file.)
- Fine-tuning configuration settings for caching.
- Sorting order and sorting locale for the BI Server.
- Time and date display format.
- Whether Globally Unique Identifiers (GUIDs) are updated when a user logs into the dashboard.

You can view which configuration settings are still managed through this file by opening it with a text editor and seeing which configuration settings do not have the following comment after them:

```
# This Configuration setting is managed by Oracle Business Intelligence
Enterprise Manager
```

To change the values of these settings, follow these steps:

1. With a text editor, open the NQSConfig.INI file usually found at [*middleware_home*]\ instances\instance1\config\OracleBIServerComponent\coreapplication_obis1\ NQSConfig.INI.

2. Locate the setting you wish to change, and update the setting to the value you wish to set.

3. Save the file and close the text editor.

4. Repeat this for every other BI Server component that you have provisioned within your instance; for example, if you have provisioned a second BI Server component on the same host, you should edit the NQSConfig.INI configuration file. Ensure that you set the same configuration value for each file and that you repeat this step for any other hosts within your cluster.

5. Using Fusion Middleware Control, log on as an administrator. Select Business Intelligence and then coreapplication from the navigation tree menu; then select the Capacity Management tab and the Scalability subtab. Using this screen, restart all of your Oracle BI Server system components so that changes in the configuration files will be picked up.

Additional BI Server Functions and Management Tasks

In addition to changing configuration settings for the Oracle BI Server through Fusion Middleware Control and manually by editing the NQSConfig.INI file, there are a number of more involved configuration tasks that you can perform with the Oracle BI Server—configuring and managing the query cache, setting up usage tracking, creating aggregates through the Aggregate Persistence Wizard, and enabling write back.

Configuring and Managing the Query Cache

Chapter 10 details how you enable, disable, and set high-level configuration settings for the query cache, the feature within the Oracle BI Server that stores and then retrieves query results locally to the BI Server component to avoid unnecessary data retrievals from data sources. In addition to this high-level configuration, you can set a number of more detailed settings for the query cache using the NQSConfig.INI file, including the following:

- DATA_STORAGE_PATHS
- MAX_ROWS_PER_CACHE_ENTRY
- POPULATE_AGGREGATE_ROLLUP_HITS
- USE_ADVANCED_HIT_DETECTION

Configuring these settings, however, is only part of the work involved in managing the query cache. Because the cache does not keep track of whether the underlying data sources used to populate the cache have been updated, you have to put in place what is called a "cache management strategy" to remove all entries from (or "flush") the cache after each data source is refreshed, and you can also load (or "seed") the cache with data before users access their dashboards in order to ensure that as many queries as possible are served from the cache. We will look in more detail in this chapter, therefore, at how you manage the cache to seed and flush it.

Setting Up Usage Tracking

Usage tracking is an optional feature provided by the Oracle BI Server to record the usage of analyses and dashboards by users of your system so that you can understand which parts of the system are being used and which are not. Usage tracking is particularly useful if you wish to monitor the performance of your system, as you can see the trend over time for individual analyses and establish whether performance is increasing or decreasing over time. It can also help you establish whether parts of your repository and catalog are being underutilized, which may point to issues in how they have been set up or made available to users.

Usage tracking is not enabled by default, and it requires you to perform a number of tasks before it becomes operational. These tasks include configuring the NQSConfig.INI configuration file to enable the feature, either by directly editing the file or enabling it from the 11.1.1.6 release through a configuration JMX MBean.

NOTE
Usage tracking data, along with an additional summary statistics table populated through a similar process, are also used by the Oracle Exalytics In-Memory Machine's Summary Advisor feature to help recommend aggregates based on previous query activity.

Using the Aggregate Persistence Wizard

Although the Aggregate Persistence Wizard is more of a feature of the Oracle BI Administration tool than a set of configuration settings in the NQSConfig.INI file, it does require you to perform some scripting tasks and is similar in operation to management of the BI Server's query cache. This wizard creates definitions of aggregates that are then processed by the BI Server to create aggregate tables in a relational database or in the Oracle TimesTen in-memory database that are then mapped into your Oracle BI Repository to improve the performance of queries.

In this chapter, we will look at the operation of the Aggregate Persistence Wizard and how you manage aggregates that it creates for you, updating them as data in your underlying data sources changes.

Setting Up Write Back

Write back is a feature within the Oracle BI Server that allows analyses to write values back to an underlying relational data source such as the Oracle Database or Microsoft SQL Server. Write back is not enabled by default and has to be configured through write back templates to write back to the database on a column-by-column basis.

Managing the Oracle BI Server Query Cache

The Oracle BI Server query cache can improve the performance of analyses that request commonly used data items. When the query cache is enabled, results generated by analyses are stored in the cache and are then available for use by other analyses requesting the same data or data that could be at least partly satisfied or derived from data stored in the cache.

The query cache has to be actively managed, though, as it does not know when data in the cache is out of date or stale compared to data in the source systems, and you might want to control settings to determine how big the cache can get, how many entries it can store, and how hard the BI Server should search the cache to find results that can be useful to a query. In addition, you might also want to "pre-seed" the cache with commonly used results in advance of your users running their daily dashboards so that all queries run as fast as possible right from the start.

Overview of the BI Server Query Cache

Before looking at how the query cache is managed, it is worth taking a few moments to understand how the query cache works and where it fits into the overall architecture of the Oracle BI Server.

How Does Query Caching Work?

The Oracle BI Server query cache has three main elements within its architecture:

- Cache storage space
- Cache metadata
- Cache detection in query compilation

The Oracle BI Server query cache is one of the components of the Oracle BI Server logical architecture. (Figure 1-11 in Chapter 1 provides a diagram showing the structure of this architecture.)

When enabled, the query cache stores, within limits that you define, the results generated by analyses and other BI objects so that subsequent analyses that retrieve results from the cache will not have to wait while the underlying database is queried for those results. Using the query cache should be faster than querying the underlying data source because the cache is stored locally and already contains results that are precomputed, prejoined, and prefiltered.

The contents of the query cache are stored in a set of files on the Oracle BI Server file system, with each BI Server component having its own query cache and set of cache files. When you scale-out or scale-up your Oracle BI installation so that you have more than one BI Server component in your Oracle BI instance, you can also enable a *global cache* that can be accessed by all BI Servers in the cluster.

NOTE
You can move your BI Server's cache files to a solid state disk (SSD) if you have one, giving you potentially faster access to these files and even faster queries.

When deciding whether results stored in the cache can be used to satisfy a user's query, the Oracle BI Server query cache follows a series of rules to try to maximize the chance of achieving

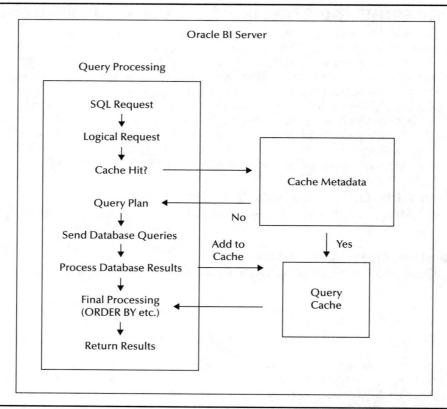

FIGURE 5-1. *Query Processing Stages within the BI Server, and interaction with the Query Results Cache*

a *cache hit*. You can also influence these rules by changing settings in the NQSConfig.INI file to, for example, tell the BI Server to spend more time searching the cache than is enabled by default.

Here are the steps (diagrammed in Figure 5-1) that Cache Services performs when processing a query sent to the Oracle BI Server:

1. When the BI Server receives a logical SQL query via the ODBC client, it parses the SQL statement, and if query caching is enabled, the cache detection in query compilation feature then uses cache metadata to determine whether the data it requires can be satisfied by the query cache or derived from data held in the query cache.

2. If it can, the required data is retrieved from the query cache and then passed to the final stage where ordering, sorting, and generation of additional derived data is performed before being passed back to the calling application.

3. If the cache cannot provide the required data, a query plan is generated, queries are issued to the relevant data sources, and the returned data is processed to create the combined data set. If query caching is enabled, the results of this processing are then stored in the cache so that subsequent queries can make use of it.

4. As with queries returned from the cache, these results are then ordered, sorted and otherwise finally processed, and then returned to the calling application.

The Oracle BI Server query cache uses a number of rules, or factors, to determine whether data stored in the cache can be used to satisfy a query. In addition, the 11*g* release of Oracle Business Intelligence introduced the ability to store the results of subrequests in the cache to improve the performance of OLAP-style queries generated when using hierarchical columns in analyses. Analyses using hierarchical columns, particularly those that use pivot tables and selection steps, frequently generate large numbers of totals and subtotals that are satisfied through SQL subqueries, and this new capability allows the BI Server query cache to reuse the results of these subqueries across a wider range of subsequent analyses.

The query cache can be used to satisfy queries at the same, or higher, levels of aggregation as data stored in the cache, and the cache will also be used if the BI Server could derive the data it requires based on data held in the cache. The following factors, or rules, are used by the query cache to determine whether a cache hit takes place:

- All of the columns in the SELECT list of the query either have to be present in the cached query or should be derivable (computable) from these columns.

- The WHERE clause must be equivalent to that used in the cached query or a subset of those in the cached query.

- To avoid potential issues with dimensions having multiple logical table sources, queries that return values only from a dimension must be an exact match of the projected (returned) columns.

- Queries with certain types of "special functions," such as time-series functions or external aggregation functions, must be an exact match both in terms of the columns selected and the filters used.

- The incoming query must use the same full set of logical tables that the cached query used in order to avoid the problem in which missing a join to a table would alter the number of rows returned.

■ If the query uses session variables, the values of those variables must match those of the cached query; if you're using the Virtual Private Database feature to implement row-level security in your underlying database, the values of those variables' must match those for the particular user running the query.

■ The values of any session variables referenced in the incoming SQL must match those used in the cached query; in addition, if you have defined a physical database as using the Virtual Private Database (database-managed row-level security), the value of session variables used in the cached query that are security sensitive need to match those that are defined for the current user in order to prevent results for another user from inadvertently being provided for this user.

■ The incoming cached query needs to have equivalent join conditions.

■ Queries must contain compatible aggregation levels; they must either be the same as each other, or the cached query must be aggregated at a level that can then be rolled up to provide correct results for the incoming query.

■ Any use of ORDER BY in the incoming query needs to use columns that are in the SELECT list for the query; otherwise, there will be a cache miss.

In addition, you can enable the advanced hit detection feature by setting the ADVANCED_HIT_ DETECTION parameter in the NQSConfig.INI file, which together with the MAX_SUBEXPR_SEARCH_ DEPTH parameter then uses an expanded search for cache hits at the cost of more processing work for the BI Server. Both of these parameters are described in more detail in the next section.

In general, when query caching is enabled, all query results are added to the cache to be made available for subsequent queries, except in the following circumstances:

■ The query includes a column that it would not make sense to include in a query cache, such as CURRENT_TIMESTAMP, CURRENT_TIME, RAND, POPULATE, or a parameter marker.

■ The query uses a physical table marked as non-cacheable in the repository.

■ The query is itself satisfied from the query cache, except when the POPULATE_ AGGREGATE_ROLLUP_HITS query caching parameter has been set to YES and the query is an aggregation of data returned by the cache.

■ The query's result set would be too big to store in the cache, as defined by the DATA_ STORAGE_PATHS and MAX_ROWS_PER_CACHE_ENTRY parameters described later in this chapter.

■ The query is cancelled, either by the user or through a time-out.

Special considerations apply when you are using query caching in a clustered environment. When you have more than one Oracle BI Server clustered within your Oracle BI Domain, each BI Server stores and retrieves query results from its own local cache but can also make use of a global cache that is stored on a shared file system.

This global cache can only be populated, however, by "seeding it" using agents. Therefore, you may encounter a situation where your overall system has processed a query from a user with the results stored in the local cache for one BI Server component, but a subsequent query that matches the previous one does not benefit from the cache because it is processed by another BI Server component that does not have these results stored in its own cache.

We will look at strategies for managing caching in a clustered environment in the next section of this chapter.

When Should You Use the Query Cache?

A typical scenario that would make good use of the query cache would be a BI system that has many users running similar queries against a data warehouse data source refreshed once a day. In this instance, the cache would be purged at the start of each day; then, as users run their dashboard queries, commonly used results sets would be stored in the cache and used instead of repeated requests to the underlying data warehouse for what is essentially the same data.

Similarly, a scenario that would not be a good fit for query caching would be one in which the dashboard is querying a constantly changing transactional database and in which each user's queries are largely unique and do not return similar data. In this scenario, caching would cause problems because data in the cache would soon be out of data (or "stale") compared to data in the underlying database, and very few cache hits would occur anyway since most queries are unique.

In general, systems are suitable for query caching when the following rules are true:

- Data is loaded into the database rather infrequently (once an hour at most), and the data load process can include a call at the end to purge the query cache so that all new cache hits take place against the updated data set. A data warehouse extract, load, and transform (ETL) process is a good example of this type of data load.

- Users typically request the same or very similar data, maximizing the chances of cache hits.

Conversely, systems are not suitable for caching when the following rules are true:

- The underlying database changes frequently, such as with a transactional line-of-business system or a data warehouse loaded constantly in real time.

- Users typically run queries that have little commonality with other users, such as large, one-time data warehouse queries or very precise lookups of individual customer, product, or other information.

What Other Caches Does Oracle Business Intelligence Use?

In addition to the Oracle BI Server query cache, a number of other caches are typically in operation when you run queries through an Oracle Business Intelligence system. These include

- The Oracle BI Presentation Services cache, which stores the results of queries and uses them, for example, to avoid round-trips to the BI Server when you switch between screens on a dashboard

- The cache in your web browser, which may store images and files locally to avoid round-trips to the web server used by Oracle Business Intelligence

While the Presentation Services cache can be configured through settings in the instanceconfig .xml file, it generally does not need managing, and default settings are usually appropriate for most configurations. If you need to change any of the Presentation Server cache settings, you will need to add an entry within the <ServerInstance></ServerInstance> tags in this file using a text editor, where you can set the following parameters:

- **MaxEntries**   The minimum value is 3 and the default value is 500, but you may want to increase to up to 1000 for systems under heavy load.

- **MaxExpireMinutes**   The default value is 60 minutes.

- **MinExpireMinutes**   The default value is 10 minutes.

- **MinUserExpireMinutes**   The default value is 10 minutes.

Set these parameters using XML nested elements like this:

```
<ServerInstance>
  <Cache>
    <Query>
      <MaxEntries>100</MaxEntries>
      <MaxExpireMinutes>60</MaxExpireMinutes>
      <MinExpireMinutes>10</MinExpireMinutes>
      <MinUserExpireMinutes>10</MinUserExpireMinutes>
    </Query>
  </Cache>
<ServerInstance>
```

If you add entries for these settings in the instanceconfig.xml file, ensure that you replicate the entries across all BI Presentation Server components in the BI instance and that you restart all Presentation Server components to register the new settings. Again, however, it is rare that you will need to do this or that you will get benefit from amending these values from their default settings.

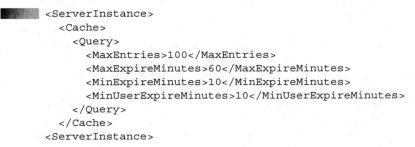

NOTE
In addition to these caches, it is also possible to set Oracle HTTP Server to cache static files used in your Oracle Business Intelligence system. For details on how to set up and configure Oracle HTTP Server to cache static files, see the Oracle® Fusion Middleware System Administrator's Guide for Oracle Business Intelligence Enterprise Edition 11g Release 1 *in the product documentation.*

What Are the Drawbacks of Using Query Caching?

Query caching can bring some significant benefits for your BI system, but it does have significant costs that you need to bear in mind.

Query caching provides the following benefits:

- It can significantly improve the performance of analyses, dashboards, and other BI objects by retrieving content from local files rather than waiting for one or more databases to retrieve results.

- It can reduce network traffic by accessing data locally rather than making round-trips to remote databases.

- It can reduce the workload on your source databases by removing the need to retrieve the same data repeatedly.

- It can reduce the work required by the BI Server, which otherwise may have to combine data sets from different sources and apply post-retrieval processing.

Following are the drawbacks associated with query caching:

- The cache has to be actively managed; at a minimum, you need to purge it every time you load your source databases, and often, seeding and purging separate parts of the cache as data from different sources gets refreshed.

■ The cache takes up space on your file system, and you may need to move the cache to a fast disk (SSD or RAM) to get the full benefit.

■ Queries to seed the cache may put an additional load on your source database and may require time at the end of your data load (ETL) process to perform the seeding.

■ Retrieving data from the cache will place additional CPU and I/O load on the server hosting the cache entries.

In general, caching is worth implementing if your circumstances make it feasible, namely if your data is loaded on a regular schedule and your users run queries that are similar or identical to each other. However, you need to understand how the query cache is administered and managed, and the next section of this chapter will outline how these tasks are performed.

Managing the Query Cache

There are three areas involved in managing and administering the query cache:

■ Enabling, disabling, and fine-tuning the running of the query cache

■ Purging the cache to remove entries that may well be stale

■ Actively seeding the cache to "preload" it with frequently accessed data

We will now take a look at these three areas in turn.

Enabling, Disabling, and Setting Parameters for the Query Cache

Enabling, disabling, and setting parameters for the query cache is largely performed using Fusion Middleware Control, with some settings only available through the NQSConfig.INI configuration file.

Enabling and Disabling the Query Cache   The Oracle BI Server query cache is enabled by default on new Oracle Business Intelligence systems, and it is enabled and disabled through Fusion Middleware Control or through WLST and the Oracle BI Systems Management API.

To enable or disable the query cache using Fusion Middleware Control, follow these steps:

1. Using your web browser, navigate to the Fusion Middleware Control web site, at http:// [server_name]:7001/em, and log in using an administrator username and password.

2. Using the navigation menu tree on the left-hand side of the screen, select Business Intelligence and then coreapplication. Then select the Capacity Management tab and finally the Performance subtab.

3. The Performance subtab will now show the current settings for the cache, including whether or not it is enabled, the maximum cache entry size, and the maximum number of cache entries, together with details of the global cache if it has been enabled.

4. To change any of these cache settings (for example, to disable the query cache), click the Lock And Edit Configuration button, and then make your configuration change.

5. Once complete, either click the Apply button and then the Activate Changes button to save the configuration changes or click the Release Configuration button to release any changes and make the system available for other administrators to make changes.

6. If you do activate your changes, you will need to restart all of the BI Server components within your Oracle BI Domain before the new cache settings will be recognized. To do this, select the Capacity Management tab and then the Availability subtab, highlight the BI Servers row, and then click the Restart Selected button to restart all of your BI Server components.

Setting Cache Parameters in the NQSConfig.INI file   While Fusion Middleware Control provides access to the main configuration settings for the query cache (namely whether caching is enabled or disabled, the maximum size of a cache entry, and the maximum number of cache entries, along with the location of the global cache and the global cache size), a number of query cache settings still have to be managed through the NQSConfig.ini file, the main configuration file for the Oracle BI Server typically found at [*middleware_home*]\instances\instance1\config\OracleBIServerComponent\ coreapplication_obis1. The settings you manage through this file are as follows:

- **DATA_STORAGE_PATHS**   This setting defines the directories that will be used to store the cache files and the maximum size that they can reach. If possible, you should update this parameter to point to a fast disk, such as an SSD disk, to make cache retrieval times as fast as possible.

- **MAX_ROWS_PER_CACHE_ENTRY**   This setting determines, per query, the maximum number of rows that the query can have to be allowed in the cache. This setting defaults to 100000 and is a useful way to ensure that a single query does not fill up the entire cache.

- **POPULATE_AGGREGATE_ROLLUP_HITS**   This setting is set to NO by default and is responsible for the fact that queries that themselves are satisfied from the cache and then aggregate that data are not stored in the cache. If you set this to YES, queries that roll up data from the cache will themselves be stored in the cache after the query completes. In most cases, it is best to leave this parameter at the default setting.

- **USE_ADVANCED_HIT_DETECTION** This setting is similarly set to NO by default, but you may wish to set it to YES if you know that results are actually in the cache but that the cache retrieval process does not use them. Setting this value to YES tells the BI Server to spend more time looking for cache hits at the expense of additional CPU overhead and more time spent on cache retrieval.

- **MAX_SUBEXPR_SEARCH_DEPTH** This setting has a default value of 7 and tells the BI Server how many subexpressions in a function the BI Server should go down through to get a cache hit. Again, you may wish to amend this value if your users are creating particularly complex formulas and you are not getting the cache hits that you require.

- **DISABLE_SUBREQUEST_CACHING** This setting is set to NO by default and enables the query cache to cache the results of subqueries typically generated when you use hierarchical columns in analysis. In general, you should leave this parameter at its default value unless you are using subqueries extensively, filling the cache but experiencing little reuse of queries.

To change these parameters, edit the NQSConfig.INI file for each of the BI Server components in your Oracle BI Domain, making sure you set the same values for each component. When you have completed your edits, use Fusion Middleware Control to restart your BI Server components and pick up the new parameter values.

NOTE
Unlike settings managed centrally through Fusion Middleware Control, manually edited settings such as these will need to be added by yourself to any additional NQSConfig.INI configuration files created for BI Server components following a horizontal or vertical scale-out.

Configuring the Global Cache If, as described in Chapter 2, you add new BI Server components to your Oracle BI Domain, each of these components maintains its own local query cache. When a BI Server component within the cluster processes a query and caching is enabled, it adds the results to its local cache so that it can use them for similar queries in the future. However, the entries it places in its local cache are not available for use by other BI Server components in the cluster; if a similar query is then received by one of the other clustered BI Servers, it will have to retrieve the results separately from the source database and then place the results in its own cache directory.

To address this issue, you can define a global cache that then becomes available to all BI Servers in the cluster. When you define such a global cache, entries in the cache are periodically copied to all local query caches in the cluster so that all BI Servers can benefit from the cached results. However, a significant limitation in the global cache is that the only way you can get results into it is to perform specific seeding actions, usually by running an agent whose destination is defined as the global cache; normal queries run by individual BI Server components do not get copied to the global cache and therefore cannot be distributed to the other BI Server components. We will look at how the global cache is seeded later in this section.

To enable the global cache, use Fusion Middleware Control to set the following parameter values:

- The location of the global cache, which should be a network share available to all of the BI Server components in the cluster
- The size of the global cache

To set these parameters, use the same approach as detailed in the preceding section for general cache settings.

In addition to these two high-level parameters, you can also set the following global cache settings within the NQSConfig.INI file:

- **MAX_GLOBAL_CACHE_ENTRIES**   This setting determines the maximum number of entries that can be stored in the global cache.

- **CACHE_POLL_SECONDS**   This setting determines how frequently each BI Server component polls the global cache to copy down any new global cache entries to its own local query cache.

- **CLUSTER_AWARE_CACHE_LOGGING**   This setting is normally set to NO and should only be set to YES for debugging purposes.

We will look at how the global cache is seeded and purged in the upcoming sections "Purging the Query Cache" and "Seeding the Query Cache."

Viewing Cache Statistics   Once you have enabled the query cache, you can view which queries have been placed into the cache and how often they have been used by using the Oracle BI Administrator tool in online mode. To view cache statistics, follow these steps:

1. Start the Oracle BI Administrator tool and select File | Open | Online.

2. Enter the connection details for your Oracle BI Repository, and then select Manage | Cache.

3. The Cache Manager dialog box will then open. Use this dialog box to view the cache entries for each BI Server within the cluster and to see which physical tables have had their data cached.

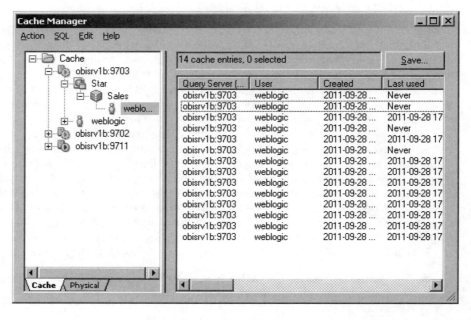

You can also use this dialog box to purge the entire cache, individual entries, or entries for individual physical tables. We will look at this process in a moment.

Purging the Query Cache

Once you have enabled query caching, each BI Server component will start adding entries to its local caches as users run dashboards and analyses. This process is automatic, and you do not need to do anything to make it happen. What you do need to do, though, is periodically clear out, or *purge,* these caches because the data within them becomes stale.

Typically, you will run a simple ODBC command to purge the entire cache at the end of your data warehouse load process. However, there are many ways that you can purge the cache, and one of them may be more appropriate than another for your particular source system.

Configuring Cache Persistence Times for Individual Physical Objects You can set, at an individual physical object level, cache persistence times for each object; you can also define individual physical objects as non-cacheable should you wish. This type of cache management approach may be appropriate for transactional or frequently updated source systems, though you need to be careful that your data does not become inconsistent due to some physical tables returning up-to-date data and some returning potentially stale data.

To set cache persistence times for individual physical objects or to disallow caching completely for them, open your repository using the Oracle BI Administration tool and navigate to the physical object you wish to configure. Double-click the object and select the General tab. Then, using the Cacheable and Cache Persistence settings, you can determine whether the object is cached and, if it is, for how long.

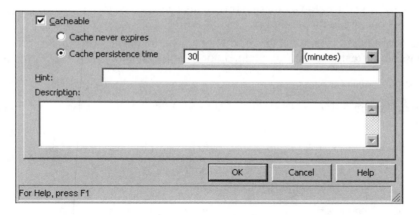

If you set a cache persistence time, entries in the cache for this object are purged according to the timetable. For example, if you have a fact table that is loaded once per hour, you might set the cache persistence time for 59 minutes so that cache entries for this table are removed within the hour.

Purging the Cache Using the Oracle BI Administrator Tool For testing purposes, you can purge the cache using the Oracle BI Administrator tool, either entirely or for individual queries or physical objects. You have to perform this step manually, so it is not really suitable for purging the cache on a regular schedule, but it can be useful when testing caching and wanting to manually clear cache entries.

To purge the cache using the Oracle BI Administrator tool, open your repository online and select Manage | Cache. Using the Cache Manager dialog box, you can do one of the following:

- Select the Cache tab at the bottom, and then right-click an individual cache entry and select Purge.
- Use the Physical tab at the bottom, select an individual physical object, schema, database, or BI Server component, and select Edit | Purge to remove all entries that involve those objects.

Purging the Cache Using ODBC Procedures   If you want to programmatically purge the cache rather than purge it manually, probably the easiest way to do that is to use ODBC procedures provided with the product for performing this task. Oracle Business Intelligence ships with four ODBC procedures that you can use to purge local query caches for an individual BI Server component:

- **SAPurgeCacheByQuery**   This can be used to purge the cache for a given logical SQL query.
- **SAPurgeCacheByTable**   This performs a similar task for a given physical table, as defined in the physical layer of the repository.
- **SAPurgeAllCache**   This removes all cache entries for a given BI Server component.
- **SAPurgeCacheByDatabase**   This clears all cache entries for a given physical database, as defined in the repository.

For example, to clear the entire cache for a given BI Server component, you would create a script using a text editor that contained, for example, the following ODBC procedure call:

```
Call SAPurgeAllCache();
```

To purge entries for just the GCBC_SALES.STORES_RAGGED physical table within the orcl physical database, you would use the following ODBC call syntax:

```
callSAPurgeCacheByTable(physical_database, physical_catalog,
physical_schema, physical_table);
```

For example, save this command into a text file:

```
callSAPurgeCacheByTable('orcl',,'GCBC_SALES','STORES_RAGGED');
```

Then pass it to the nqcmd utility, which can usually be found at [*middleware_home*]\Oracle_BI1\bifoundation\server\bin, using the following parameters:

```
nqcmd -d [data_source_name] - u username -p password -s script_name
```

Note that the *data_source_name* parameter is the name of the ODBC data source that connects the workstation or server that you are running the script on to the server running Oracle Business Intelligence. For example:

```
nqcmd -d coreapplication_OH1572096352 -u weblogic -p welcome1
-s c:\temp\purge_all_cache.txt
```

One limitation of this cache management approach is that, if you have a number of BI Server components arranged into a cluster, the command will only be processed by the BI Server component that the Cluster Controller passes your query to; therefore, to ensure that cache purging commands are processed by all BI Server components in the domain, you will need to define separate ODBC connections for each BI Server that connects directly to the BI Server component and not the cluster controller, and then run the ODBC procedure calls using these "direct" connections, targeting each BI Server component in turn.

Purging the Cache Using Event Polling Tables   Another way to purge the cache programmatically is to use a cache polling table. The cache polling table feature allows you to define and then register a table in a predefined format, which is then polled on a regular basis to detect records signifying physical table updates. To make use of a cache polling table, you need to perform the following tasks:

1. Either create a new cache polling table using a script or use the cache polling table created for you as part of the BIPLATFORM schema created by the Repository Creation Utility before you installed Oracle Business Intelligence.

2. Import metadata for the cache polling table into the physical layer of your repository.

3. Register the cache polling table with the repository, as well as the frequency at which it will be polled.

4. Add entries to the cache polling table as you update tables in your physical data sources.

The cache polling table has a predefined set of columns and is precreated for you in the BIPLATFORM schema as S_NQ_EPT (for "event polling table"). The format of the table is as follows:

Column Name	Data Type	Purpose
UPDATE_TYPE	NUMBER	Set to 1 for update. (Other values may be used in future releases.)
UPDATE_TS	DATE	Date and time of the update.
DATABASE_NAME	VARCHAR2(120)	Physical database name, as defined in the repository.
CATALOG_NAME	VARCHAR2(120)	Physical catalog name (if appropriate), as defined in the repository.
SCHEMA_NAME	VARCHAR2(120)	Physical schema name (if appropriate), as defined in the repository.
TABLE_NAME	VARCHAR2(120)	Physical table name, as defined in the repository.
OTHER_RESERVED	VARCHAR2(120)	Must be set to NULL. (Other values may be used in future releases.)

If you wish to use a table other than S_NQ_EPT for your event polling table (perhaps for testing purposes), you can create it using a script and register it instead of S_NQ_EPT. Once you have created and registered the table, you should add entries to it for every source table that is updated; then cache entries for that table will be purged according to the schedule you set.

To import the metadata for the S_NQ_EPT table into a repository and register it for polling, follow these steps:

1. Start the Oracle BI Administration tool and open your repository either online or offline.

2. Select File | Import | Metadata, and enter the connection details to the database that contains your cache polling table; for example:

    Import Type: Remote Server
    Connection Type: OCI 10g/11g
    Data Source Name: *orcl*
    User Name: *DEV_BIPLATFORM*
    Password: *password*

3. When prompted, select the S_NQ_EPT table within your BIPLATFORM schema and import its metadata into the physical layer of your repository.

4. Check in your changes if you are working online, and then save your repository. The cache polling table will then be listed in the physical layer of your repository.

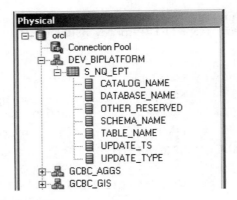

5. To register this table as this repository's cache polling table, select Tools | Utilities | Oracle BI Event Tables, and then click the Execute button. The Oracle BI Event Tables dialog box will then be displayed.

6. Select your table from the Tables list on the left-hand side and add it to the Event Tables list on the right. Then enter a frequency, in minutes, for how often this table should be polled, and click OK to close the dialog box. Finally, save the repository to start polling the table.

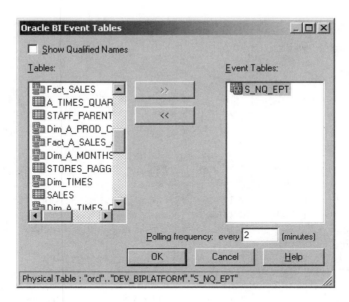

If you are working with a single BI Server component within your Oracle BI Domain, these steps will be sufficient to make use of your polling table. However, if you are working in an environment with more than one Oracle BI Server component in the domain, you will need to take additional steps so that all of the BI Server components start polling this table.

NOTE
When you save changes to an online repository in a clustered environment, the changes only apply to the repository to which your Oracle BI Administration Server was connected. If you have defined a shared repository for your domain, you will need to use Fusion Middleware Control to restart all of the nonmaster BI Servers in your domain in order to synchronize them with this shared repository and pick up the polling table definition. If, however, you have not defined a shared repository, you will need to copy the repository that you updated to a temporary directory and upload it again to the Oracle BI Domain using Fusion Middleware Control in order to distribute the changes to each of the BI Server components.

Now, to add entries to the cache polling table (for example, to add an event to register the update of the orcl.GCBC_SALES.STORES_RAGGED table), you would use an SQL INSERT statement such as this:

```
insert into s_nq_ept (update_type
,       update_ts
, database_name
, schema_name
, table_name)
values (1
```

```
,to_date('2011-09-28 20:45:00','YYYY-MM-DD HH24:MI:SS')
, 'orcl'
,'GCBC_SALES','STORES_RAGGED');

commit;
```

Then, when the cache polling frequency is reached, all cache queries for the BI Server component that processes the purge activity will be cleared. Like the ODBC procedure approach, though, in a clustered environment only the BI Server component that processes the purge will have its cache entries purged.

Purging the Global Cache   Unlike the local caches used by each BI Server component, the global cache does not have a specific process that you can use to purge it. However, because the global cache files are not locked by any BI Server process while running, you can safely delete these files from the global cache directory when you wish to purge them. Ensure that you do not delete the NQS_CLUSTER_CACHE_SPACE.DES file within this directory, though, as this is used by the global cache process.

Seeding the Query Cache

If you wish to place entries into the query cache in advance of users running queries so that these queries benefit from the cache right from the start, you will need to seed it. For the local query cache used by each BI Server component, this process is optional, as queries executed by users will eventually seed the cache anyway; but for the global cache, this is the only way to get entries into it.

Using Agents to Seed the Cache   To seed entries in the local cache, you should create an agent and schedule it as described in Chapter 8. Seeding performed in this way will only add entries to the local cache of the BI Server that executed the query on behalf of the agent. While this will be fine if you only have a single BI Server component in your Oracle BI Domain, for domains that have more than one BI Server component, you will need to perform additional steps to seed the global cache.

To create an agent that seeds the global cache, follow these steps:

1. Using Fusion Middleware Control, ensure that the global cache is enabled.

2. Log into the Oracle Business Intelligence web site, and then create an analysis that represents the query you wish to add to the global cache. Save it to the Shared Folders area of the catalog so that it can be accessed by the agent you will now create.

3. Use the Catalog view to locate the analysis you just created, and then use the menu next to the object to select Schedule.

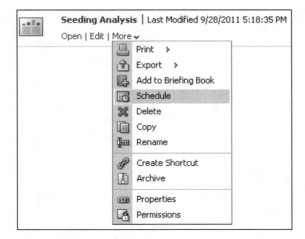

4. Use the Schedule tab to set the schedule for the agent and the General tab to select which user to run the agent as.

5. Click the Condition tab and ensure that a condition is defined that, by default, runs the agent if the analysis returns more than one row. Keep this condition, as it is a requirement for a global cache seeding agent.

6. Click the Delivery Content tab, and ensure that Conditional Analysis is selected as the content type. Again, this is a requirement for global cache seeding.

7. Click the Destinations tab, deselect all of the user destinations, and select the Oracle BI Server Cache (For Seeding Purposes) check box.

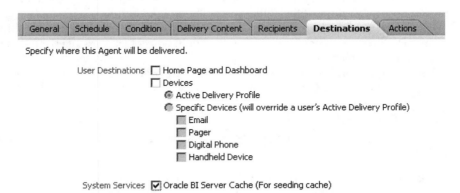

When you select the option to seed the cache in this way, the previous cache entry for the associated analysis will be cleared automatically, and the agent will not appear on the user's dashboard as an alert.

8. Save the cache to the catalog, and then click the Run Agent Now button to execute the agent now, as a test.

Shortly after the agent executes, you will see the cache entries appear as files in the global cache directory. Then, after a period defined by CACHE_POLL_SECONDS in the NQSConfig.INI file for each BI Server component in the cluster, these cache entries will be copied down to each BI Server's cache directory and made available to each BI Server.

NOTE
The main difference between agents that seed the global query cache and regular agents, is that agents used to seed the global cache do not then appear in the Alerts section of your dashboard.

Usage Tracking

Usage tracking is an optional feature that you can make use of to keep track of which analyses and dashboards are being used by users so that you can monitor the performance of these queries and deal with any performance issues that may start to arise over time.

Usage tracking is also a prerequisite for the Summary Advisor and Summary Statistics features introduced with the 11.1.1.6 release of Oracle Business Intelligence to support the Oracle Exalytics In-Memory Machine. The Oracle Exalytics In-Memory Machine uses usage tracking to recommend summaries that may improve the performance of some queries. See Chapter 12 for more details on the Summary Advisor and Summary Statistics features that it uses.

Overview of Usage Tracking

Usage tracking can run in one of two modes; one mode writes usage tracking data to a file and is not recommended because these file writes can cause a bottleneck for your system. The second, recommended mode for usage tracking is to use what is called *direct insertion,* where the usage tracking data is written instead to a table called S_NQ_ACCT that is created for you when you use the Repository Creation Utility at the start of the product installation process.

When you enable usage tracking with the direct insertion option, the Oracle BI Server records in this table every analysis, dashboard, and other BI object that is executed through the BI Server, along with the number of rows returned, details of the user that ran the query, and the time the query took to run. By building up usage tracking data over time, you can see which of your analyses and other BI objects are the most popular, as well as keep track of their performance over time.

Setting Up Usage Tracking

How you enable usage tracking depends on which version of Oracle Business Intelligence 11g you are using:

- With the 11.1.1.6 release of Oracle Business Intelligence, the settings in the NQSConfig .INI file that relate to usage tracking are now managed by a JMX MBean unless you have upgraded to this system using an in-place upgrade from an earlier release.

- For earlier releases of Oracle Business Intelligence and for 11.1.1.6 installations that have been upgraded from earlier releases, you will need to edit the NQSConfig.INI file manually for each BI Server component in your Oracle BI instance.

In addition to enabling usage tracking in the BI Server's configuration file, you also have to import metadata for the S_NQ_ACCT table into your repository so that the BI Server can write tracking entries to this table as users run queries through the system. Let's look at what this involves first, and then move on to the usage tracking configuration process.

Creating Usage Tracking Tables

The S_NQ_ACCT table required for usage tracking will already be installed into the BIPLATFORM schema created by the Repository Creation Utility. If you wish, you can create your own table to hold usage tracking data within this or another database schema, as long as you follow the same table and column structure as this table. Unless you have a particular reason to do so, though, you should generally use this predefined table to hold this data.

Importing Usage Tracking Tables into the Repository

To have the BI Server start adding entries to the usage tracking table, you have to first import the usage tracking table's metadata into the repository. To do so, follow these steps:

1. Using the Oracle BI Administration tool, open your repository either online or offline, enter the repository password, and then select File | Import | Metadata to start the import process.

2. Enter the connection details to the BIPLATFORM schema that contains the S_NQ_ACCT table; for example:

   Import Type: Remote Server
   Connection Type: OCI 10g/11g
   Data Source Name: *orcl*
   User Name: *DEV_BIPLATFORM*
   Password: *password*

3. When prompted, select the S_NQ_ACCT table within your BIPLATFORM schema and import its metadata into the physical layer of your repository.

4. Check in your changes if you are working online, and then save your repository. The S_NQ_ACCT table will then be listed in the physical layer of your repository.

As with the cache polling table mentioned in the section "Purging the Cache Using Event Polling Tables," to have these changes distributed to other BI Server components in your domain, you will either need to make use of a shared repository and then restart each BI Server component to pick up the changes or upload this repository back to the domain to ensure that each BI Server component has the usage tracking table registered in its copy of the repository file.

Example: Manually Configuring the NQSConfig.INI File for Usage Tracking

For systems running Oracle Business Intelligence 11.1.1.3 or 11.1.1.5, or running 11.1.1.6 but having upgraded from an earlier release, you now have to manually edit the NQSConfig.INI file to tell the BI Server component to use direct insertion usage tracking and where the NQSConfig.INI file is located. If you have added additional BI Server system components to your BI instance through the vertical scale-out technique described in Chapter 2, you will need to perform this task for every BI Server component in the BI instance.

To do this, once the S_NQ_ACCT usage tracking table has been imported into the repository, make a note of the physical database, catalog (if used), and schema that it is registered under in the repository, and then open the NQSConfig.INI file with a text editor.

Within this file, you will find a section on usage tracking, with the following default settings (comments section removed to save space):

```
[USAGE_TRACKING]
ENABLE = NO;
#=========================================================
DIRECT_INSERT = YES;
#=========================================================
#  Parameters used for inserting data into a table
    (i.e. DIRECT_INSERT = YES).
#
PHYSICAL_TABLE_NAME = "<Database>"."<Catalog>"."<Schema>"."<Table>";
    # Or "<Database>"."<Schema>"."<Table>" ;
CONNECTION_POOL = "<Database>"."<Connection Pool>";
BUFFER_SIZE = 250 MB;
BUFFER_TIME_LIMIT_SECONDS = 5;
NUM_INSERT_THREADS = 5;
MAX_INSERTS_PER_TRANSACTION = 1;
#
```

While you can configure usage tracking to write tracking data to a file (DIRECT_INSERT=NO in the preceding file), in practice this can cause contention issues and may slow down your system. In the following steps, we will configure usage tracking to write to the S_NQ_ACCT table registered a moment ago, and this is the usual method of configuring usage tracking:

1. Using a text editor, change the ENABLE=NO entry to read as follows:

   ```
   [USAGE_TRACKING]
   ENABLE = YES;
   ```

2. Update the physical table name and connection pool settings to point to your S_NQ_ACCT table; for example, if your S_NQ_ACCT table is held in a physical database called orcl and in a schema called BIPLATFORM, as shown here.

   Your entry should read as follows:

   ```
   PHYSICAL_TABLE_NAME = "orcl"."DEV_BIPLATFORM"."S_NQ_ACCT";
   ```

3. If this physical table accesses data through a connection pool called Connection Pool, the CONNECTION_POOL setting should read as follows:

   ```
   CONNECTION_POOL = "orcl"."Connection Pool";
   ```

4. Once complete, save the file and restart your BI Server components. If you have more than one BI Server component in your Oracle BI Domain, make the same changes in each BI Server's NQSConfig.INI file and restart each BI Server before proceeding further. The remaining settings within this section in the NQSConfig.INI do not normally need to be changed and can be left at the default.

5. Using the Oracle Business Intelligence web site, create an analysis and run it so that entries start getting added to the usage tracking table. Then, with the Oracle BI

Administration tool open, right-click the S_NQ_ACCT table and select View Data to see the entries that have now been created in this table.

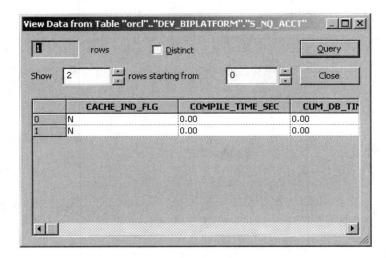

If you do not see entries appearing in this file, for each BI Server component check the nqserver.log file found at [*instance_home*]\diagnostics\logs\OracleBIServerComponent\ coreapplication_obisn\nqquery.log, where you should see a message at the end of the log file indicating what the issue is. (Usually it is that you have not referenced the S_NQ_ACCT table correctly in the NQSConfig.INI file, or if you have, you have not imported its metadata into the repository.)

Example: Automatically Configuring the NQSConfig.INI File for Usage Tracking Using the System MBean Browser

For installations of Oracle Business Intelligence using the 11.1.1.6 release of the product that have not been upgraded from a previous release (that is, fresh installations of the product), you should use the System MBean browser, described in more detail in Chapter 10, to configure your system and automatically add the required entries to the NQSConfig.INI file. If you have added additional BI Server components to your BI instance using vertical scale-out, this process will automatically add the correct settings for each BI Server in the instance.

NOTE
As with all system configuration settings managed through Fusion Middleware Control, you should not manually edit these settings using a text editor; otherwise, any changes you make will be overwritten by the managed settings next time you restart your system.

To use the System MBean Browser to configure your usage tracking settings, follow these steps:

1. Using your web browser, log into Fusion Middleware Control using the credentials of an administrative user.

2. When the Fusion Middleware Control home page opens, expand the WebLogic Domain folder in the left-hand navigation tree menu and drill down until you see an entry for AdminServer under the bifoundation_domain heading. Right-click this entry and select System MBean Browser.

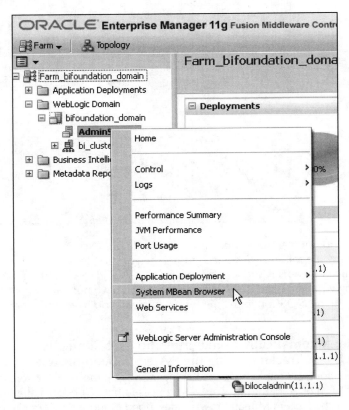

3. With the System MBean Browser, navigate to Application Defined MBeans > oracle.biee .admin > Domain: bifoundation_domain.

4. You will need to lock the domain so that other administrators cannot make configuration changes while you perform these steps. To do this, expand the BIDomain folder, select the BIDomain MBean (where *group*=Service), and then select the Operations tab. To lock the domain, click the Lock link, as shown in the next illustration, and then click the Invoke and Return buttons when prompted.

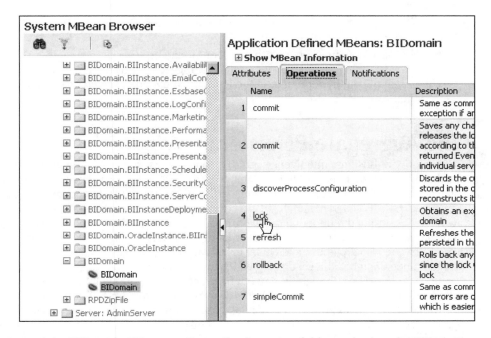

5. Expand the BIDomain.BIInstance.ServerConfiguration folder and select the BIDomain .BIInstance.ServerConfiguration MBean. Ensure that the Attributes tab is selected, and then you will see a number of attribute names, descriptions, and values displayed in a table. Check that the UsageTrackingCentrallyManaged parameter's value is set to true; if it is set to false, then usage tracking needs to be configured as described previously, by manually editing the NQSConfig.INI file, or you can set it to true and manage it as described in the next few steps.

6. Using this table, set the following parameters using the values appropriate for your system; for example:

UsageTrackingConnectionPool: *"orcl"."Connection Pool"*
UsageTrackingDirectInsert: true
UsageTrackingEnabled: true
UsageTrackingPhysicalTableName: *"orcl"."DEV_BIPLATFORM"."S_NQ_ACCT"*

17	UsageTrackingCentrallyManaged	Centrally manage Usage Tracking attributes	RW	true	▾
18	UsageTrackingConnectionPool	Connection Pool for Usage Tracking Table	RW	"orcl"."Connection Pool"	
19	UsageTrackingDirectInsert	Direct Inserts on the Usage Tracking table	RW	true	▾
20	UsageTrackingEnabled	Enable Usage Tracking	RW	true	▾
21	UsageTrackingPhysicalTableName	Physical Usage Tracking table in RPD	RW	"orcl"."DEV_BIPLATFORM"."S_NQ_ACCT"	

When you have finished, click Apply to save your changes.

7. To commit your changes and release the lock on the domain, return to the BIDomain MBean (where *group*=Service) under oracle.biee.admin, Domain: bifoundation_domain,

BIDomain. Select the Operations tab and click the top-most Commit link. Once done, click Invoke and then Return.

8. You have now finished with the System MBean browser. To restart your Oracle BI instance and start using the new configuration settings, click Business Intelligence, select the coreapplication menu item in the left-hand menu tree, select the Overview tab, and click the Restart All button.

The Aggregate Persistence Wizard

The majority of business intelligence projects source most, if not all, of their data from relational database sources such as the Oracle Database. To improve the performance of queries that require aggregated data, databases such as Oracle Database allow you to precompute these aggregates in advance in objects called materialized views, and use these to answer user queries that require these aggregations. Using the underlying database sources to create these precomputed aggregations is considered good practice, as the database handles the automatic rewriting of queries to use these aggregates and also provides incremental refresh mechanisms that keep the summaries synchronized with the underlying detail-level data on which they are based.

In some situations, though, it may not be practical or desirable to create materialized views or other summary structures within your source databases, or you may not have the ability or knowledge to create them within these databases. For example, you may not be allowed to create summaries in a transactional database, but you may have access to a separate database, possibly of a different type, in which you can create precomputed summaries. Also, you may not have the time or experience to set up summaries in your database and ideally would look to Oracle Business Intelligence to help set up and maintain these summaries. For both of these examples, the Aggregate Persistence Wizard, part of the Oracle BI Administration tool, will be useful.

Overview of Aggregate Handling in the BI Server

In Chapter 3, we looked at how the Oracle BI Repository could have more than one logical table source mapped into a logical table and how these table sources could represent data of the same granularity as other data in the table (what we call *horizontal federation*) or represent data at higher or lower levels of aggregation to other data in the table (*vertical federation*).

For example, in the repository developed during this chapter, the Dim Products logical table has three table sources that provide product data at different levels of aggregation.

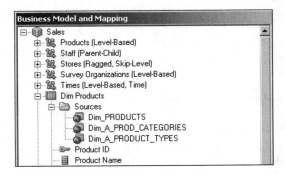

These table sources are listed here:

- **Dim_PRODUCTS** This logical table source provides data at the lowest level of detail for products (for example, product line information).

- **Dim_A_PROD_CATEGORIES** This logical table source is at the product category grain and is used to join to an aggregate fact table also at the product category grain.

- **Dim_A_PRODUCT_TYPES** This logical table source is stored at the product type grain and joins to an aggregated fact table also at this level of granularity.

For each logical table source, the granularity of its data is defined using the Content tab in the Logical Table Source dialog box, where, in the example of the Dim_A_PROD_CATEGORIES logical table source, it is defined as being at the Product Category level in the associated Products (Level-Based) logical dimension.

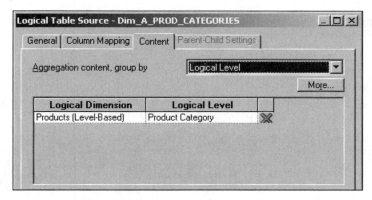

Aggregated table sources such as these are useful in that they allow you to map into the repository sources of data that are at different levels of granularity to the detail-level sources that you initially map in. You might introduce these types of sources because they represent precomputed aggregates that the BI Server will make use of when queries are received at these levels of aggregation, or they may present targets or other data that is only available at a summarized level.

However, creating and populating aggregate tables can be a time-consuming task, as can mapping them in to the repository correctly. To address this issue, the Aggregate Persistence Wizard automates the process of defining, creating, populating, and mapping aggregates within the Oracle BI Administration tool.

Creating Aggregates with the Aggregate Persistence Wizard

The Aggregate Persistence Wizard helps you perform four tasks associated with managing aggregate sources in the Oracle BI Repository:

- It provides the ability to define an aggregate based on objects already defined within the repository.

- It provides a script that can be run to create the aggregate tables, either in the same database that provides your detail-level data or in another database mapped into the physical layer of your repository (restricted to Oracle Database, Microsoft SQL Server, and IBM/DB2 sources).

■ It provides a second script that populates these aggregate tables with summarized data.

■ It maps these new aggregate logical table sources into your repository so that the Oracle BI Server can start making use of them.

Let's take a look at how the process works by creating a set of aggregates to precalculate sales by year and product category in a more simplified repository, GCBC Repository – No Aggs.rpd, which contains only detail-level data.

Example: Creating the Aggregate Definition

To create a new aggregate using the Aggregate Persistence Wizard, follow these steps:

1. Using the Oracle BI Administration tool, open your repository either online or offline, and enter the repository password. For this example, we will use the GCBC Repository – No Aggs.rpd repository file, which has the password welcome1.

2. From the application menu, select Tools | Utilities | Aggregate Persistence, and then click the Execute button to launch the Aggregate Persistence Wizard.

3. The Aggregate Persistence – Select File Location screen will then be displayed, and you will use it to define the location and name of the script(s) that will be used to create the aggregate tables. In the Name text box, enter the name of the script (for example, create_ aggs.txt). In the Location text box, enter the location for the script (for example, c:\temp). Leave the "Generate DDL in a separate file" check box unselected.

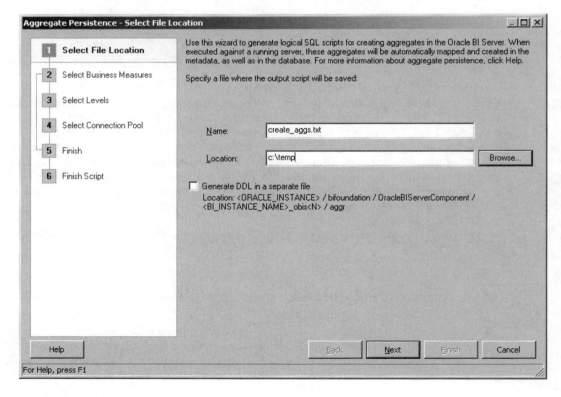

4. The Aggregate Persistence – Select Business Measures screen is used first to select the business model and, second, the actual measures that you wish to aggregate. In this example, select Sales as the business model and then Revenue and Sale Amount (under Fact Sales) as the measures, and click Next to proceed.

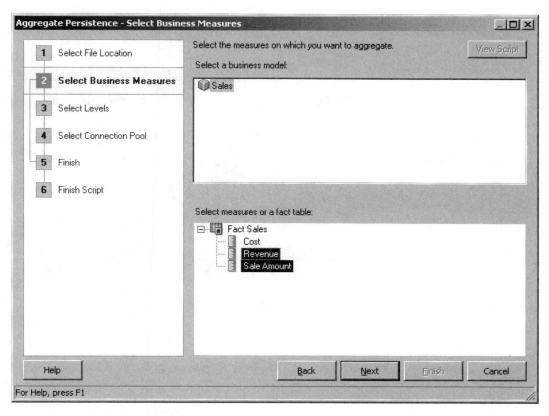

5. Using the Aggregate Persistence – Select Levels screen, select those dimension hierarchy levels that you wish to aggregate the measure by; for example, in this case, you would select the Year level from the Times (Level-Based, Time) logical dimension and the Product Category level from the Products (Level-Based) logical dimension.

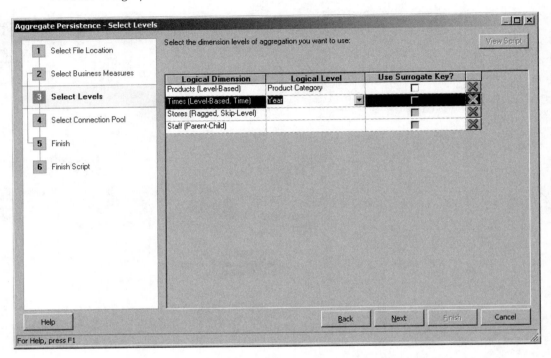

You do not have to select levels from every dimension, and if your logical tables have large and complex primary keys, you should check the Use Surrogate Key? check box to create separate surrogate keys for the generated aggregate tables, which could improve the performance of your queries, potentially at the expense of longer load times. Note also that if you select a logical level from a ragged or skip-level hierarchy, the dimension and level will be dropped from the aggregate later on, as they cannot be used for creating aggregate tables.

6. The Aggregate Persistence – Select Connection Pool screen is used to select where the aggregates will be created. This can be any Microsoft SQL Server, Oracle Database, or IBM/DB2 database that you are allowed to create tables in, and you can alter the name of the generated aggregate fact table as appropriate. Click Next once you have specified your target database.

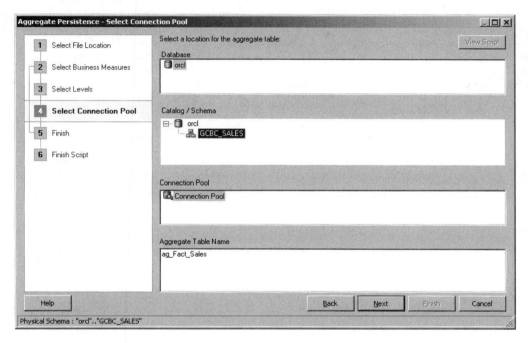

7. The Aggregate Persistence – Finish screen will then be displayed. A preview of the script that it will generate will be displayed, and you can then select whether to create a new aggregate or finish the process. Click the Next button to proceed, note the location of the file(s) that the wizard will create, and then click Finish to close the screen.

Example: Running the Aggregate Persistence
Wizard Script to Initially Create the Aggregates

In the preceding example, a single script called create_aggs.txt was created by the wizard in the specified directory. If you chose the option to create DDL in a separate file, a second script (with a _DDL suffix) would also be created, which when executed would generate an SQL DDL script to create the aggregate tables separately. For now, though, we will run this single script, which will both create and populate the aggregate tables for you. If you open this script with a text editor, you will see, for example, the following commands:

```
create aggregates
"ag_Fact_Sales"
for "Sales"."Fact Sales"("Revenue","Sale Amount")
at levels ("Sales"."Products (Level-Based)"."Product Category"
, "Sales"."Times (Level-Based, Time)"."Year")
```

```
using connection pool "orcl"."Connection Pool"
in "orcl".."GCBC_SALES";
```

To run this script, you use the nqcmd.exe command-line utility, available in both Windows and Unix/Linux installations, which you may also have used for running the cache-purging ODCB procedures detailed earlier in this chapter. It provides a command-line interface to the Oracle BI Server ODBC client. Using this command-line utility, we can pass commands to the Oracle BI Server, including commands for creating and populating tables.

To run the script that the Aggregate Persistence Wizard created for you, start a command-line session on your workstation or server, and then use the nqcmd.exe utility in this way:

```
nqcmd.exe - d [ODBC connection to BI Server] - u [administration username]
- p [administration password] - s [path and name of script from Aggregate
Persistence Wizard]
```

For example, to run this script, you might follow these steps:

1. Ensure that the repository for which you wish to create aggregates is the default, online repository for your Oracle BI Domain and that your Oracle BI Domain has been started.

2. Start a command-line session and change directories to where the nqcmd.exe utility is located; for example:

```
cd c:\middleware\Oracle_BI1\bifoundation\server\bin
```

3. Run the command using the parameters mentioned above; for example:

```
nqcmd -d coreapplication_OH1572096352 -u weblogic -p welcome1 -s
c:\temp\create_aggs.txt
```

4. When the nqcmd.exe utility runs, it will output the status of the process as it creates the aggregates. For example, creating the aggregates above, the nqcmd.exe might output the following:

```
-------------------------------------------------------
            Oracle BI ODBC Client
            Copyright (c) 1997-2011 Oracle Corporation, All rights reserved
-------------------------------------------------------
sql script file is utf8
create aggregates
"ag_Fact_Sales"
for "Sales"."Fact Sales"("Revenue","Sale Amount")
at levels ("Sales"."Products (Level-Based)"."Product Category"
, "Sales"."Times
(Level-Based, Time)"."Year")
using connection pool "orcl"."Connection Pool"
in "orcl".."GCBC_SALES"
create aggregates
"ag_Fact_Sales"
for "Sales"."Fact Sales"("Revenue","Sale Amount")
```

```
at levels ("Sales"."Products (Level-Based)"."Product Category"
, "Sales"."Times
(Level-Based, Time)"."Year")
using connection pool "orcl"."Connection Pool"
in "orcl".."GCBC_SALES"
Statement execute succeeded
Processed: 1 queries
```

This would indicate that the script has executed correctly, with no errors. If you see an error indication in the output, check the nqserver.log and NQSQuery.log files for your BI Server component for the reason for the error, which is usually due either to the repository not being available online or tables required for the aggregation process not being available.

Viewing Aggregate Definitions in the Repository and in the Target Database

Once you have run the script to create and initially populate your aggregates, you can open the Oracle BI Repository online using the Oracle BI Administration tool to see the new aggregate definitions created by the script. To do this, open your repository online and navigate to the physical layer of the repository. The aggregate tables created by the wizard and script will be prefixed and will use a different icon than the regular physical tables in the physical layer of your Oracle BI Repository.

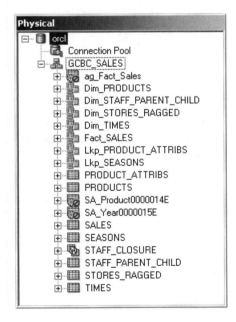

Similarly, if you navigate to the business model and mapping layer of the repository, you will see new logical table sources, mapped in at the correct level of detail, for the logical tables that you created the aggregates for.

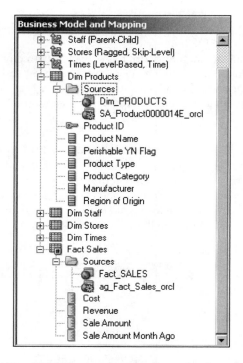

If you then use a tool such as SQL*Plus or SQL*Developer for the Oracle Database, or equivalent tools for Microsoft SQL Server or IBM/DB2, you will see the equivalent tables, together with indexes, created and populated in the target database.

Refreshing Aggregates Created by the Aggregate Persistence Wizard

To refresh these aggregates after their initial creation so that they reflect changes in your detail-level tables, you can rerun the script created by the Aggregate Persistence Wizard after first inserting an extra command to delete the aggregate tables. You can run this script from the command line as before, or you can use a scheduling tool capable of running command-line scripts to run it to a schedule for you.

To add the additional command to delete system-generated aggregates before re-creating them, add the following command to the script generated by the wizard:

```
delete aggregates;
```

Then it will read like this, for example:

```
delete aggregates;
create aggregates
"ag_Fact_Sales"
for "Sales"."Fact Sales"("Revenue","Sale Amount")
```

```
at levels ("Sales"."Products (Level-Based)"."Product Category"
, "Sales"."Times (Level-Based, Time)"."Year")
using connection pool "orcl"."Connection Pool"
in "orcl".."GCBC_SALES";
```

When you then rerun this script, the BI Server will first delete all existing system-generated aggregates and then re-create them according to your specification.

Working with Write Back

The final administration task for the Oracle BI Server we will cover in this chapter is enabling and configuring write back. Write back is a feature that allows users to type values into the dashboard and then copy them back to the underlying source database to, for example, enter quota information, update reference data details, or adjust figures used in a "what-if" planning exercise. By using write back, users can in a limited form interact with the underlying database in a way that is strictly controlled by the administrator.

How Is Write Back Configured and Performed?

To configure an analysis to use write back, there are some "global" tasks that need to be carried out to enable write back on your system and for a particular user or application role. Also, there are some analysis-specific tasks that enable write back for a particular table view column or set of columns.

To enable write back for your system and repository, you will need to carry out the following tasks, as the system administrator:

1. To enable write back globally across your system, add a setting to the instanceconfig.xml file that contains the settings for the Oracle BI Presentation Server.

2. Edit the repository to enable direct database requests for the user or application role that will use write back for a particular physical database source.

3. Set the presentation columns that will use write back as read/write, rather than as read-only, their default setting.

4. Restart your Oracle BI Domain to pick up the new settings for the Oracle BI Presentation Server and Oracle BI Server components.

Once write back is enabled for your system and repository, you can configure the analysis and the write back template it will use:

1. Create the analysis that will make use of write back and make a note of the order of columns in the analysis criteria.

2. Create the write back template to include an SQL INSERT statement (optional) and an UPDATE statement.

3. Edit the analysis created previously to reference the write back template that you just created, and enable write back for the columns and table view.

4. Test the write back feature to ensure that it works and that values are written back to the source database.

The write back template is an XML document usually stored in the [*middleware_home*]\
instances\instance1\bifoundation\OracleBIPresentationServicesComponent\coreapplication_
obips1\analyticsRes\customMessages directory on your Oracle BI installation. (You may need to
create the customMessages directory if it does not already exist.) A typical write back template
would look like this:

```
<?xml version="1.0" encoding="utf-8" ?>
<WebMessageTablesxmlns:sawm="com.siebel.analytics.web/message/v1">
<WebMessageTablelang="en-us" system="WriteBack" table="Messages">
<WebMessage name="wb_product">
<XML>
<writeBackconnectionPool="Sample Relational Connection">
<insert></insert>
<update>
UPDATE SAMP_PRODUCTS_D SET ATTRIBUTE_1='@2' WHERE PROD_DSC='@1'
</update>
</writeBack>
</XML>
</WebMessage>
<WebMessage name="wb_order">
<XML>
<writeBackconnectionPool="Sample Relational Connection">
<insert></insert>
<update>
UPDATE SAMP_ORDER_COMMENTS SET COMMENTS='@2' WHERE ORDER_NUMBER=@1
</update>
</writeBack>
</XML>
</WebMessage>
</WebMessageTable>
</WebMessageTables>
```

A typical write back template contains one or more separate write back definitions, which are
labeled using the <WebMessage name="[*label name*]"> tag. When the Oracle BI Presentation
Server is restarted, it reads all of the write back template files in the customMessages folder, and
these then become available to you when enabling write back for a particular analysis. The
template contains the SQL INSERT and UPDATE statements that implement the write back
function for a given analysis using substitution variables that allow you to reference columns in
the analysis criteria and pass them back to the database using these statements.

To enable write back for the analysis, you need to enable the feature in two places. First you
will enable the feature for the columns in the analysis criteria that will use write back by editing
their column properties, as shown in the next illustration.

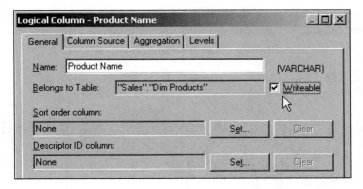

Then you edit the properties for the table view in the analysis to enable write back and to reference one of the template labels in the write back XML document, like this:

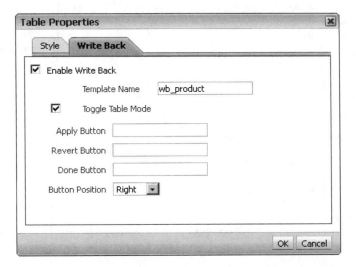

Later on in this section, we will walk through, step by step, the process of enabling write back for an analysis. First, though, let's take a look at the restrictions to write back and limitations to its use.

Write Back Limitations

There are a number of limitations that apply to write back that you need to consider when using this feature:

- The use of write back is limited to relational database sources that can be updated or written to using SQL INSERT and UPDATE statements (or related statements such as MERGE).

- Write back templates can only be used with table views in an analysis, and each column should contain a single value.

- Numeric columns in the analysis should contain only numbers (as opposed to commas, periods, and $ or £ currency signs), and text columns should contain string data only.

- Oracle BI Presentation Services performs only minimal checking of data, such as to check that you have entered numbers into a numeric field. Any checks for logically invalid or out-of-range values will need to be enforced by constraints on the underlying database table and columns.

Example: Configuring Write Back to a Relational Data Source

In the following example, we will set up write back to allow the user to amend the names of products in the GCBC_SALES.PRODUCTS table. This table is contained within the same GCBC Repository – No Aggs.rpd repository file that we used earlier in the chapter.

The first step is to add an entry to the instanceconfig.xml file to enable write back, and then we will configure the repository file as required for this feature:

1. Using a text editor, open the instanceconfig.xml file usually found at [*middleware_home*]\ instances\instance1\config\OracleBIPresentationServicesComponent\coreapplication_ obips1. (Note that if you have added additional BI Presentation Server components to this host or to other hosts in your cluster, you will have to edit their instanceconfig.xml files in their corresponding locations as well.)

2. Within the file, locate the <serverInstance> section and add the following tag under the <DSN></DSN> section:

```
<LightWriteback>true</LightWriteback>
```

The start of the file will then read like this:

```
<?xml version="1.0" encoding="UTF-8" standalone="no"?>
<!-- Oracle Business Intelligence Presentation Services
   Configuration File -->
<WebConfigxmlns="oracle.bi.presentation.services/config/v1.1">
<ServerInstance>
<!--This Configuration setting is managed by
   Oracle Business Intelligence Enterprise Manager-->
<CatalogPath>
C:\Middleware\instances\instance1/bifoundation/
 OracleBIPresentationServicesComponent/coreapplication_obips1/
catalog/GCBC
</CatalogPath>
<DSN>coreapplication_OH1572096352</DSN>
<LightWriteback>true</LightWriteback>
<Logging>
```

3. Open your repository file either online or offline using the Oracle BI Administration tool. Enter the repository password, and then view the contents of the repository prior to editing.

4. Locate the logical table that you wish to enable write back for (in this example, the Dim Products table within the Sales business model). Double-click each logical column that you wish to enable write back for (in this example, the Product Name logical column). When the Logical Column dialog box is shown, ensure that the General tab is selected and select the Writeable check box.

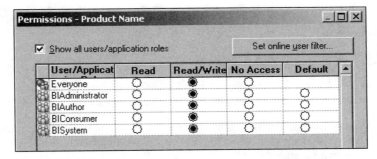

5. Locate the corresponding presentation column in the presentation layer of the repository and double-click it to display the Presentation Column dialog box. When the dialog box is displayed, ensure that the General tab is selected and click the Permissions button. Then, with the Permissions dialog box open, change the permission for all roles to Read/Write rather than the default Read, or make this change just for particular users or application roles.

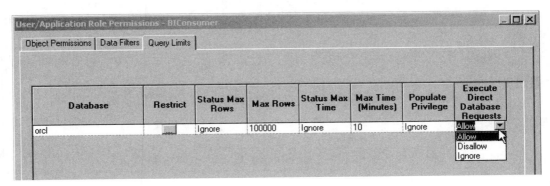

6. Select Manage | Identity from the BI Administration tool menu. With the Identity Manager dialog box open, double-click the user or application role (for example, BI Consumer) that you will enable write back for, and then click the Permissions button. Then, when the User/Application Role Permissions dialog box is shown, click the Query Limits tab. For the physical database that you will be writing back to, select Allow from the drop-down box in the Execute Direct Database Requests column.

7. Save your repository, and make sure that it is uploaded to the Oracle BI Domain and running as the default online repository. Then, using Fusion Middleware Control, select the Capacity Management tab and then the Availability subtab to restart all of the system components in your Oracle BI Domain in order to pick up the changes to the repository and instanceconfig.xml file.

8. If query caching is enabled, either disable it completely by selecting the Capacity Management tab and the Performance subtab and then uncheck the Cache Enabled check box, or disable it for the individual physical table that you are writing back to by unchecking the Cacheable setting on the General tab for the physical table's settings in the Oracle BI Repository. It is important that you do this; otherwise, your write back–enabled columns in the analysis you create will always show the cached original value for a column rather than any changes you have made using write back.

9. Next, you need to complete the configuration of your system to enable write back. Log into the Oracle Business Intelligence web site and select Administration from the list of links at the top of the page. With the Administration page open, click the Manage Privileges link.

10. When the Manage Privileges screen is displayed, scroll to the bottom to reveal the Write Back settings and change the Write Back To Database and Manage Write Back settings to, for example, grant to the user or application role the ability to use this feature.

View View Selector	Add/Edit View SelectorView	BI Author Role
Write Back	Write Back to Database	Authenticated User
	Manage Write Back	BI Administrator Role, BI Author Role

Now that you have enabled write back at the system level, you can create the analysis that will use the write back feature and create the write back template that the analysis will make use of:

1. With the Oracle Business Intelligence web site open, log in as a user with permission to use write back and create the analysis that will make use of this feature. For example, create an analysis that lists the product ID and product name from the Dim Products presentation table.

2. With the Criteria tab selected, click the column that you wish to allow write back for (in this case, Product Name), and from the menu that appears next to the column, select Column Properties.

3. When the Column Properties dialog box is shown, select the Write Back tab, and then select the Enable Write Back check box. If this check box is grayed out, go back and check the previous steps, as it probably indicates you have missed one of the previous configuration steps or applied a step incorrectly.

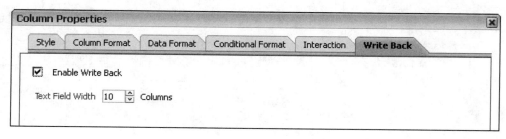

Make a note of the position of the column in the criteria that you wish to enable write back for; for example, if your criteria consists of the Product ID and then the Product Name column, then Product ID is column #1 and Product Name is column #2.

4. Save the analysis to the catalog so that you can come back to it later to complete the write back configuration.

5. You will now create the write back template for this query. Using a text editor, create an XML document such as the following one, which enables updates to be made to the PRODUCTS.PROD_NAME database column:

```
<?xml version="1.0" encoding="utf-8" ?>
<WebMessageTablesxmlns:sawm="com.siebel.analytics.web/message/v1">
<WebMessageTablelang="en-us" system="WriteBack" table="Messages">
<WebMessage name="wb_product_name">
<XML>
<writeBackconnectionPool="Connection Pool">
<insert> </insert>
<update>
UPDATE PRODUCTS SET PROD_NAME='@2' WHERE PROD_ID=@1
</update>
</writeBack>
</XML>
</WebMessage>
</WebMessageTable>
</WebMessageTables>
```

Note that the WebMessage Name element is how you will refer to this write back template in the next step; the connection pool name is the connection pool that connects to your data source. (You may choose to create a separate connection pool solely for write back use to minimize contention on your connections.) The included update statement uses @1 and @2 placeholders to reference the first and second columns in the analysis criteria. (For columns that are character data types, remember to put single quotes around the column placeholder.)

6. Save the template file, using any name that you wish, to the [*middleware_home*]\ instances\instance1\bifoundation\OracleBIPresentationServicesComponent\ coreapplication_obips1\analyticsRes\customMessages directory on your Oracle Business Intelligence installation (creating the customMessages directory if required), and copy it to the corresponding folders of any other Presentation Services components you may have configured. Once complete, use Fusion Middleware Control to restart your Oracle BI Presentation Services components so that they read in the template files you have created.

7. Using the Oracle Business Intelligence web site, log in and open the analysis you created earlier. Select the Results tab, and then click the Edit View button for the tabular analysis on the results page. Click the Table View Properties button for the view, select the Write Back tab, and then select the Enable Write Back check box. In the Template Name text box,

enter the name from the <WebMessage name="wb_product_name"> element in the Write Back template file (for example, wb_product_name), like this:

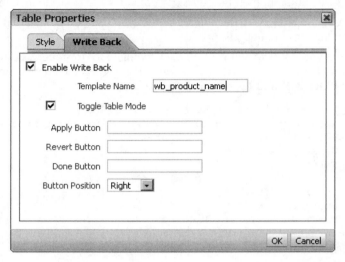

Once you have finished, save your analysis, and you are then ready to test out your write back configuration.

8. The table view in your analysis should now have an Update button at the bottom. Click this button to open the table for editing, whereupon you will then see Revert, Apply, and Done buttons.

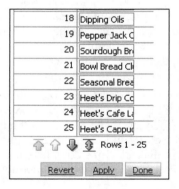

Now test the write back feature. Edit one of the values, and then click the Apply button to test that write back is working correctly.

9. Click Done to save your changes to the database.

If the changes are applied to your target database correctly (that is, no error messages are displayed when you click Apply), you have now successfully set up write back.

CHAPTER
6

Creating Analyses, Dashboards, KPIs, and Scorecards

o far in this book, we have spent all of our time looking at the installation, configuration, and administration of the infrastructure supporting Oracle Business Intelligence, including the steps required to create and maintain the repository layer that describes the data available for reporting against. Now, finally, we will take a look at how you can actually create analyses, dashboards, scorecards, and other interactive reports using all of the infrastructure and business metadata that you've been learning how to use.

Oracle Business Intelligence comes with a range of powerful, intuitive, and visually compelling tools for creating reports, ad-hoc analyses, dashboards, and other types of visualization that you can access either through a web browser, a mobile device such as the Apple iPhone or iPad, or productivity tools such as Microsoft Office. In this chapter, we will first go through an overview of the user interface for reporting and analysis, and then look in detail at how analyses and dashboards are created for use with these devices.

An Introduction to Analyses, Dashboards, and Interactive Reporting

The main way in which users query the data sources mapped into your business intelligence system and create reports and web pages that show data in the form of tables, pivot tables, graphs, and other visualizations is to create analyses that are then embedded in dashboards. Dashboards provide a means to display one or more analyses around a theme such as sales, procurement and spending, and customers, displaying data and graphics to help users understand the data they are working with.

What Are Analyses and Dashboards?

An *analysis* in Oracle Business Intelligence is a report that uses a common set of selected columns, calculations, and filters, and displays the report results in one or more tables, pivot tables, graphs, or other visualizations.

An analysis is made up of the following components:

- **Analysis criteria** This criteria defines the data items used in the report.
- **Analysis results** These results are displayed in the form of one or more views.
- **Optional prompts** These prompts are used to prefilter the data provided to the analysis.

Figure 6-1 shows typical analysis criteria, with a number of subject area columns selected, along with filters and a calculated column (or *formula*) added to the column selection.

Every analysis has one or more views associated with the analysis results, with each view using all, a subset, or derivations based off of the analysis criteria. For example, you might define a Table view listing sales for a particular product brand, along with one or more graph views that show sales broken down by brand and by time period.

Typically, these views are then organized into a display through the use of a *Compound Layout view,* which takes one or more views and organizes them vertically and horizontally next to each other. Figure 6-2 shows a typical analysis Compound Layout view, with a table and graph view organized so that they are displayed alongside each other.

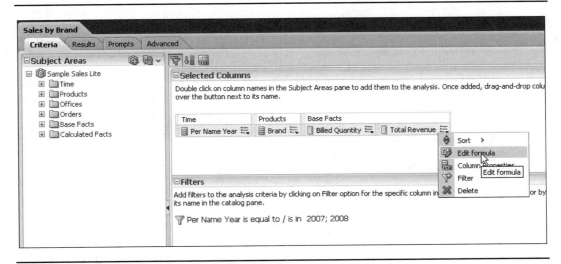

FIGURE 6-1. *Analysis criteria*

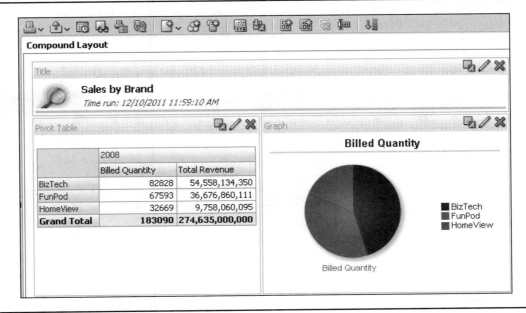

FIGURE 6-2. *An analysis Compound Layout view*

The views in analyses are typically interactive so that you can click bars in a bar chart to drill into product categories or navigate up and down a hierarchy in a pivot table. Actions, described in detail in Chapter 7, can be associated with analysis columns, allowing you to assign right-click contextual menu items to views that navigate to related reports, invoke a business process, or take the user to a screen in a related transactional system.

Although analyses can be viewed and interacted with in the Oracle BI analysis editor (called Oracle Answers in previous versions of Oracle Business Intelligence), you would typically deliver analyses to users by embedding them in a dashboard. *Dashboards* typically bring together a number of analyses, along with prompts and other data selection tools, and are displayed in the user's web browser or on a mobile device such as an Apple iPad. Figure 6-3 shows a typical dashboard, taken from the sample application that comes with every installation of Oracle Business Intelligence.

Compared to Published Reporting

In addition to creating analyses, which are typically embedded in a dashboard and used interactively, you can create another type of visualization in Oracle Business Intelligence called a published report. Created using another Oracle tool called Oracle BI Publisher, *published reports* are similar to analyses in that they can take their data from the Oracle BI Repository and display results in the form of tables, pivot tables, and charts; but they are primarily used for reports that need to be printed and/or distributed rather than embedded in a dashboard.

Published reports are described in detail in Chapter 10, which provides some typical examples of their use. For now, though, consider analyses as the reporting method you use when you want to publish highly interactive tables and graphs of data that users will interact with and use to explore their data, while published reports are typically used when you want to publish data outside of the dashboard with a high degree of control over the report layout.

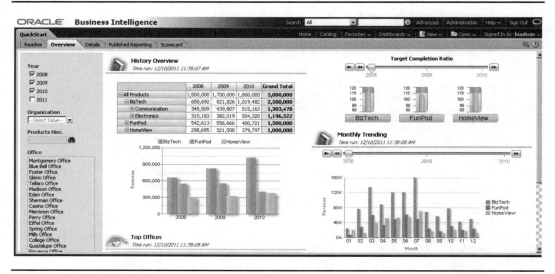

FIGURE 6-3. *An Oracle Business Intelligence dashboard*

Access Through Mobile Devices and Microsoft Office

More and more these days, professionals are using mobile devices such as the Apple iPad and Apple iPhone to access their business applications away from the office. Using WiFi and cellular connections, devices such as these can connect securely to business applications, display data and information using high-fidelity color screens, and provide communication and collaboration tools to allow users to share and comment on information of interest.

Dashboards and published reports created using Oracle Business Intelligence can be displayed on mobile devices using a product called Oracle Business Intelligence Mobile, part of the Oracle Business Intelligence Foundation product family that also includes Oracle Business Intelligence. Dashboards and reports can be displayed on mobile devices, with no formatting required, by a user interface optimized for mobile platforms.

Figure 6-4 shows a dashboard displayed using an Apple iPhone. It shows the same Pivot Table views you would see if you viewed the dashboard through a web browser.

Scorecards and Key Performance Indicators

Another new option for visualizing and analyzing data introduced with the 11*g* release of Oracle Business Intelligence is the ability to display data in the form of key performance indicators (KPIs) and scorecards. KPIs are another form of visualization that take actual and target measures sourced from the Oracle BI Repository, along with dimensions such as product, customer, and time, and couple them with thresholds and KPI states to provide the building blocks for KPI watchlists and scorecards. Figure 6-5 shows a typical scorecard, showing KPIs organized into a hierarchy that reflects the breakdown of objectives for an organization.

FIGURE 6-4. *A dashboard displayed on the Apple iPhone mobile device*

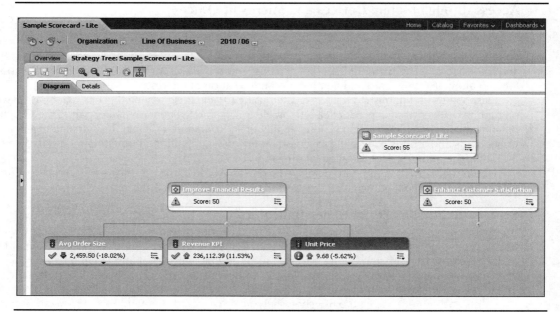

FIGURE 6-5. *A scorecard showing a hierarchy of objectives and KPIs*

Scorecards and KPIs, like published reports, can be displayed stand-alone or embedded in a dashboard, sharing parameters and prompts with analyses. Like Oracle BI Mobile, however, scorecards and KPIs are part of a separate product within Oracle BI Foundation that may have license implications if you are upgrading from previous releases of Oracle Business Intelligence. KPIs and scorecards are described in more detail in Chapter 9.

An Initial Look Around the Oracle Business Intelligence Web Site

Now that you have a better understanding of the types of visualizations that you can create using Oracle Business Intelligence, let's take a look at the main user interface that you are presented with when logging into the Oracle Business Intelligence web site. Using this user interface, you can analyze data held in dashboards; create your own analyses, dashboards, and other BI visualizations; and perform administration tasks related to reporting and analysis.

The Home Page

When you first log into the Oracle Business Intelligence web site, you are typically presented with the Home page, which provides fast access to recently used dashboards and analyses, as well as menu items used to create objects such as analyses, dashboards, conditions, and published reports.

To open the Home page, use a web browser to navigate to the URL http://[*server_name*]:*port*/ analytics; for example, http://obisrv:9704/analytics—the port number may be different depending on how your system is set up. Once you have successfully logged in, you will be presented with the Home page, as shown in Figure 6-6.

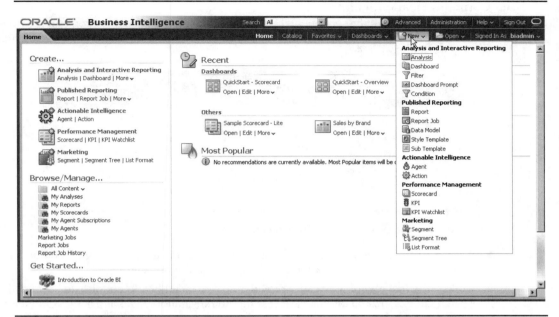

FIGURE 6-6. *The BI Home page*

The Home page contains a number of distinct sections:

■ **Header section** Common to all of the pages in the Oracle Business Intelligence web site, the header includes links to administration and search functions, as well as a drop-down menu that provides links for creating various BI objects.

■ **Create** This section includes links for creating objects such as analyses, dashboards, and scorecards. The links correspond to the drop-down menu items in the header areas.

■ **Browse/Manage** This section displays the Catalog page with a predefined search for a particular object type.

■ **Getting Started** This section provides links for downloading the client installation of the BI Administration tool, plug-ins for Microsoft Office, and links to documentation and introductory guides.

■ **Recent** This section show icons for recently accessed dashboards and KPIs, as well as other recently accessed catalog content.

■ **Most Popular** This section is populated after the system has been used for a while and shows the most popular catalog content accessed by users within roles that you have been granted.

You can return to the Home page at any time by clicking the Home link at the top of every Business Intelligence web site page.

The Common Header Section

As mentioned in the preceding section, at the top of each page is a header section that provides common links to application resources. Let's take a moment to look at this common header area and some of the functions it provides.

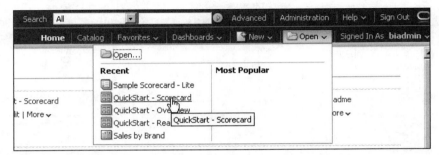

The header section provides the following facilities:

■ **Search** This feature can be used for searching either the entire catalog or a particular catalog object type such as a scorecard, an analysis, or an action.

■ **Links** The first row of the header provides an Advanced link to perform an advanced search, an Administration link to access the Administration page, and a Sign Out link to sign out of the web site. The first part of the second row of the header contains Home and Catalog links to access the Home and Catalog pages.

■ **Drop-down menus** New in the 11.1.1.6 release is a Favorites drop-down menu, providing one-click access to BI objects that you have marked elsewhere as "favorites." Other drop-down menus on the header are the Help menu that provides a link to access online Help, the Dashboards menu for opening a particular dashboard, the New menu for creating new catalog objects scoped by object permissions and catalog privileges, and the Open menu for opening existing catalog content.

■ **A link to the My Account dialog box** This dialog box provides access to settings associated with your account and is accessed by clicking a link in the Signed In As drop-down menu next to your login name at the end of the second row of the header.

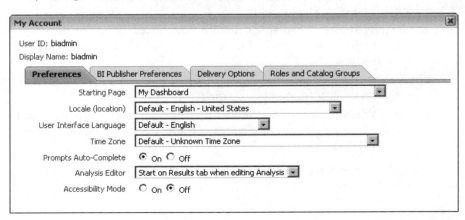

The Dashboard Interface

Once you have selected a dashboard from the Home page, either through the Dashboard drop-down menu or by clicking it in a catalog view, the dashboard interface will open. A dashboard, shown in the following illustration, typically contains one or more analyses, along with dashboard prompts and other objects that provide filtering and navigation.

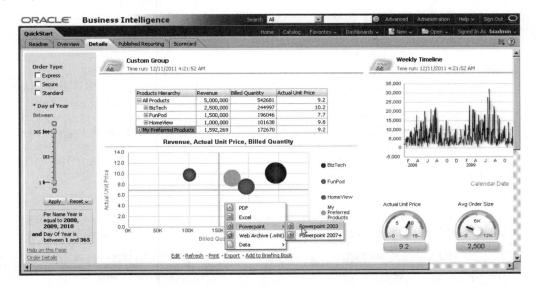

Dashboards contain a range of content, including:

- A set of analyses, arranged into columns and sections
- Dashboard prompts in the form of check boxes, sliders, and other controls
- Apply and Reset buttons, as well as menu items for resetting all parameter values or saving them as a set of personalized values.
- Analysis-level menu items (shown in the following illustration) for printing, exporting, and refreshing views

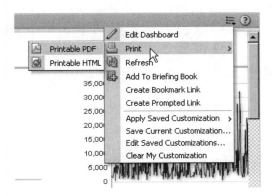

■ Tabs at the top of the dashboard page that allow you to switch among different dashboard pages

Dashboards are typically defined by administrators or "authors" and consumed by users who may apply and save customizations, for example, to display data just for a particular region or time period. Dashboards that are published and then shared in this way are typically "locked down" so that individual end users cannot alter the layout and choice of analyses, but you can enable a feature where users have their own "My Dashboard" personal workspace that they can customize as they wish.

The Analysis Editor

The building blocks of dashboards are analyses, and the Business Intelligence web site includes the full analysis editor, which allows you to author analyses prior to publishing them in a dashboard.

The analysis editor (called Oracle Answers in previous releases but in this release subsumed into the wider Oracle Business Intelligence web site) was described at a high level earlier in this chapter and is the focus of much of the rest of this chapter. It provides features for selecting data items, creating calculation and filtering data, and then presenting data in one or more views such as tables, pivot tables, and graphs.

The Catalog Page

The Catalog page, accessed either from the header section or by clicking one of the Browse/Manage links on the Home page, lists out catalog items and provides menu items for managing them.

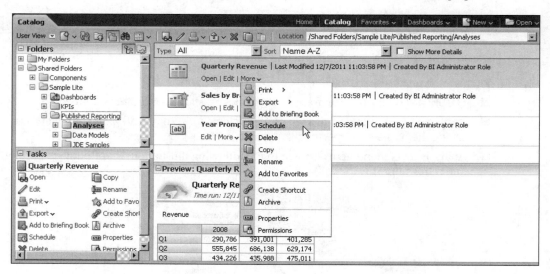

The Catalog page is divided into a number of sections:

■ **Panels** On the left-hand side of the page are panels—a Folders panel to show the folders and objects within the catalog, and a Tasks panel for tasks that can be performed on catalog objects selected in the main catalog section.

- **Main catalog view** In the top right-hand side of the page is the main catalog view, which lists folders and catalog objects. It provides Open and Edit links for opening and editing the object, as well as options for performing other tasks such as scheduling, adding to favorites, and viewing properties.

- **Preview section** By default minimized and disabled, when the Preview section is enabled it provides a preview of the default view associated with the selected object.

On the Catalog page, at the top of the page just below the common header section, there is also a graphical toolbar for performing tasks on a selected catalog object.

The Presentation Services Administration Page

Similar to the way in which the administrative menu items are provided for the BI Server component in the BI Administration tool, the Oracle Business Intelligence web site has an Administration page for performing administration tasks. It is accessed from the Administration link in the common header section.

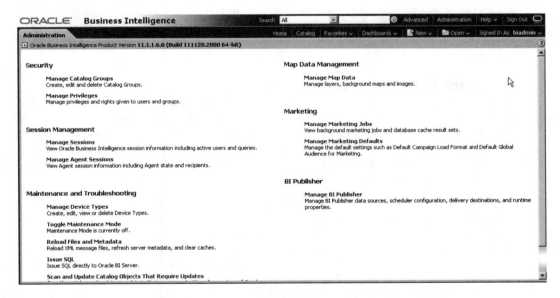

These administration tasks are grouped into several categories:

- **Security** This section is used for administering catalog object permissions as well as privileges assigned to users and groups, such as to create new analyses or execute an agent.

- **Session Management** This section is used to view details of all current sessions associated with the Presentation Server and all agents currently being executed on behalf of users and roles.

- **Maintenance and Troubleshooting** This section is used for tasks such as reloading the Presentation Server's copy of the repository metadata and enabling and disabling "maintenance mode" that stops users from adding or changing catalog content while it is being backed up or migrated.

- **Map Data Management**   This section is for creating and maintaining links between catalog content and geospatial data sets.

- **Marketing**   This section is for managing the settings for the marketing component (not covered in this book and typically licensed separately as part of a Siebel CRM implementation).

- **BI Publisher**   This section is for managing BI Publisher, the Java component that provides the published reporting feature, which will be described in more detail in Chapter 10.

Now that you know your way around the Business Intelligence web site interface, let's start looking at what's involved in creating an analysis.

Creating Analyses

Analyses are the foundation for your business intelligence dashboard, and they present data to users in the form of interactive tables, pivot tables, graphs, maps, and other visualizations. In this section of the chapter, we will use the sample data provided with this book together with the GCBC Repository – Final.rpd that accompanies it to see how the criteria for an analysis is built up, and the results turned into a number of interactive visualizations such as tables, pivot tables and charts.

Defining the Analysis Criteria

First we will look at creating the criteria for an analysis. The criteria defines the total set of source columns for an analysis, which can either be selected directly from columns in a subject area, or calculated using combinations of subject area columns and formulas. An analysis criteria can either return all rows for a particular set of columns, or you can create filters that restrict the result set to just a subset of the total source rows. Let's start off then by creating a new analysis, and then adding some subject area columns to its criteria.

Creating a New Analysis, and Selecting Subject Area Columns for the Analysis Criteria

To start creating an analysis, you first have to select one or more columns from subject areas and add them to the analysis criteria. Subject areas are defined in the Oracle BI Repository, and they contain attribute, measure, and hierarchy column types. You can combine subject areas together when they are both sourced from the same underlying repository business model.

Let's create analysis criteria sourced from the GCBC Repository – Final.rpd repository within the sample data files provided with this book. Then we will look in more detail at these different column types.

To begin creating criteria for an analysis, follow these steps:

1.   With the Oracle Business Intelligence web site open in your browser, select New | Analysis. Alternatively, with the Home page open, click the Analysis link under the Create section.

2.   You will be presented with a list of available subject areas and, depending on the roles assigned to the user, the option to create an analysis using a direct database request or a simple logical SQL query. We will come back to the second and third options later in this chapter; but for now, select one of the subject areas (for example, Sales – Fact Sales).

3. The analysis editor will then be displayed, if not already open. On the left-hand side are two panels, the topmost showing the list of subject areas and their tables and columns available for adding to the criteria.

4. To add columns to the criteria, either drag-and-drop them from the Subject Areas panel to the Selected Columns area on the right or double-click them. In this example, we will add the following subject area columns to the Selected Columns area:

Dim Products.Product Type
Dim Stores.Stores
Dim Staff.Staff
Dim Times.Quarter

Fact Sales.Sale Amount
Fact Sales.Revenue
Fact Sales.Cost

The list of columns in the Selected Columns area should now look like the following illustration.

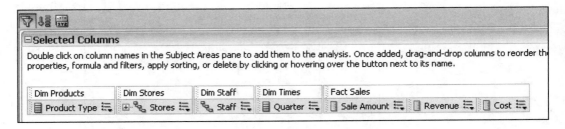

At this point it would probably make sense to save your analysis. To do so, click the Save Analysis button on the right-hand side of the screen and then use the Save As dialog box to save the analysis definition to the catalog. We will look into this topic more later in the chapter, but if you save the analysis to the My Folders area of the catalog, only you will be able to see and access it, whereas if you save it to the Shared Folders area, others will generally be able to see and run the analysis.

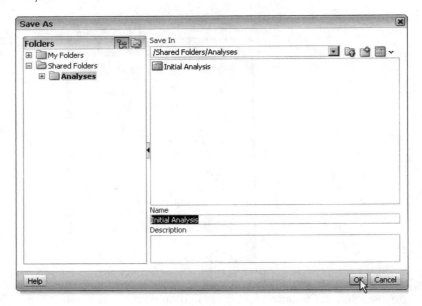

You may have noticed that the subject area columns in your criteria have different icons and come from both fact (measure) and dimension tables. Let's take a moment to look at these different column types and how you work with them.

Attribute and Measure Columns   Subject area columns that
are sourced from presentation columns in the Oracle BI
Repository are either attribute or measure columns. *Attribute
columns* contain information on dimension attributes or keys,
such as product descriptions, customer names, or time periods.
They are generally held in subject area tables that relate to
dimensions. Attribute columns do not have aggregation rules
such as Sum or Average associated with them, but they are
often used to help filter data returned by the analysis. You can
identify attribute columns by their light blue icon, which looks
like a stack of levels.

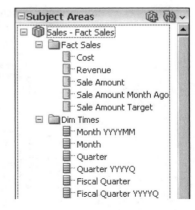

  Measure columns, similarly, are usually found within
subject area tables containing fact or measure data, and they
can be identified by their yellow "ruler," or measure, icons.
Measure columns will always have an aggregation rule associated with them, though you can
change this or temporarily remove it for a particular analysis if you want to. As with attribute
columns, you can apply filters to measure columns, for example, in order to return data only for
products selling over a certain amount.

Hierarchical Columns   Hierarchical columns correspond to presentation hierarchies in the
Oracle BI Repository and represent a whole dimension hierarchy in your source data. When you
add a hierarchical column to your analysis, users can then explore their
data by drilling within a single column using hierarchies that can be
balanced, ragged, or skip-level and can be sourced from both level-based
and value-based (parent-child) hierarchies. Filters, however, cannot be
applied to hierarchical columns; instead, you must use selection steps
(see the "Selection Steps" section later in this chapter) to restrict or modify
their values.

Adding Additional Subject Areas to the Criteria   When you first created your analysis, you
were prompted to select a single subject area from which you would then go on to select subject
area tables and columns. You can, however, add additional subject areas to your analysis criteria,
as long as the subject areas you select share a common underlying business model in the Oracle
BI Repository.

  To add an additional subject area to the criteria defined in the previous steps, do the
following:

1. With the analysis open for editing, locate and click the Add / Remove Subject Areas
    button at the top of the Subject Areas panel.

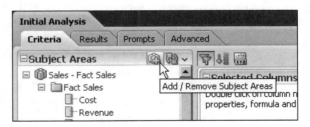

2. When prompted, select the check box for every other subject area that you would like to add to the criteria; in this instance, you can select the Sales – Store Quality subject area, as it shares the same underlying business model as the Sales – Fact Sales subject area.

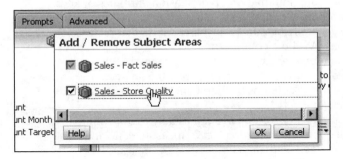

3. Click OK to close the dialog box. In the Subject Areas panel, you will now see the additional subject areas listed.

TIP
When you go on to select subject area columns from the additional subject areas, make sure that any columns selected are compatible with the ones already selected. The reason for this is that there must always be a valid join path between columns in the criteria, as they may be sourced from separate database schemas and physical servers. (This compatibility requirement is necessary for all column selections in the criteria.)

Filters

If you now click the Results tab in the analysis editor, you will see data returned for all of the columns in your criteria, restricted by any join conditions in your source data set or mandatory filters defined in the repository. If you want to apply your own filters, though, you can do so using the Criteria tab.

To apply a filter to an attribute column such as the Dim Products.Product Type column, follow these steps:

1. With the analysis open for editing and the Criteria tab selected, hover your mouse pointer over the menu icon to the right of the column you wish to filter. When the column menu is displayed, click the Filter menu item.

   Alternatively, if the column is not listed in the Selected Columns area, ensure that the Show / Hide Filters pane button above the Selected Columns area is selected, and then click the "Create a filter for the current subject area" button. Clicking this button allows you to

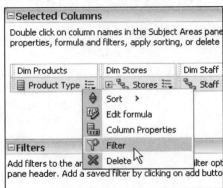

create a filter for the analysis using a subject area column not necessarily listed in the Selected Columns area.

2. The New Filter dialog box will now be displayed. To filter the Dim Products.Product Types column to return only Hot Drinks, Rounds & Loaves, and Sandwiches, select "is equal to / is in" as the operator and click either the "Open to pick values" button or the Search button to select the required values.

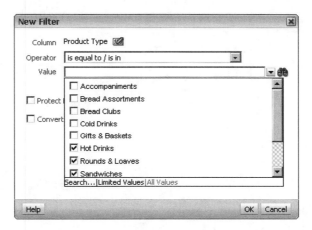

3. Click OK to save the filter definition.

Instead of filtering on an exact set of values, you can use the operator selection to filter instead on ranges of values, values above and below certain values, and other selection criteria. Similarly, you can use filters along with measure columns to return only rows where sales are above a certain level or are in the top ten values for profit, for example.

A special type of operator you can use when creating filters is "is prompted." This operator selection initially leaves the column unfiltered but "listens" for any dashboard prompts that use this subject area column, filtering the column on whatever the dashboard prompt is set to. We will look in more detail at dashboard prompts and the "is prompted" operator later in this chapter.

Referencing Variables in Filters   In Chapter 3 of this book, we looked at how you could define variables within the Oracle BI Repository that could contain, for example, the value for the current month, a list of products or regions that you were responsible for, or a static value that contains the name of the main store for your company. Later on, we will also look at how you can define variables for use within dashboards and analyses so that you can, for example, set a variable value based on a prompt selection and pass it to an analysis or a published report.

You can also reference variable values in filters, filtering the values returned by an analysis by the current month, for example. Let's do this now using a repository variable called CURRENT_ QUARTER, defined previously in the Oracle BI Repository using the Oracle BI Administration tool.

1. With the analysis open for editing and the Criteria tab selected, open the New Filter or the Edit Filter dialog box for the column you wish to filter.

2. Select the operator for the filter (for example, "is equal to / is in") and then click the Add More Options button to display the list of variable types that can be used in the filter.

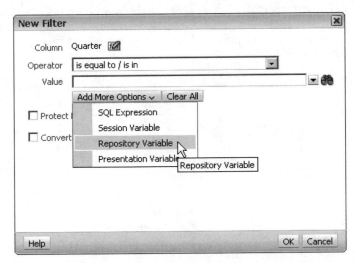

3. To filter against the CURRENT_QUARTER repository variable, select Repository Variable from the list of options. The New Filter or the Edit Filter dialog box will then change to add an entry for Repository Variable.

4. Type in the name of the variable, and then click OK to close the dialog box. Repeat this for other variable types to reference them in the filter definition instead.

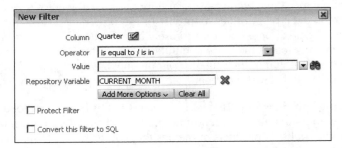

If you have the Filters pane enabled, you will see this variable referenced along with any other filters defined for your analysis criteria.

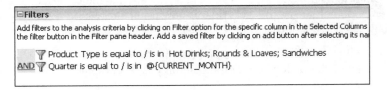

NOTE
Repository variables are referenced using an "at" (@) sign before them; other variable types have a different notation, which we will look at later in the chapter.

Protecting Filters   The Protect Filter check box in the New Filter and Edit Filter dialog boxes is used to protect the filter value from being overridden by dashboard prompts on a dashboard page or by a user who uses a Navigate To BI Content action to navigate to a linked report.

For example, consider a situation where you have created analysis criteria that contain Dim Products.Product Category and Fact Sales.Revenue columns, have placed a filter on the Product Category column to restrict rows to just Drinks and Gifts, and have not used the Protect Filter option.

Now you create a dashboard prompt (described in more detail later in this chapter) that is based on the same Dim Products.Product Category column. When you include the prompt and the analysis on a dashboard, even though you did not set the analysis filter on the Product Category column to "is prompted," the analysis still uses the prompt's column value selection rather than the filter values you "hard-coded" into the analysis.

How can you correct this behavior? The answer is to protect the filter. To do so, open the analysis and switch to the Criteria tab, click the Edit link next to the filter in the Filters pane, and when the Edit Filter dialog box is shown, select the Protect Filter check box and click OK to close the dialog box.

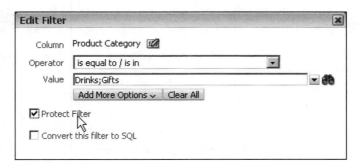

Now, when you use the dashboard prompt on the dashboard and alter the selection of product categories, the values in the analysis filter stay protected and static. Protecting filters in this way can be particularly useful when you add multiple filter conditions to a column using And and Or, though you should be careful to ensure that filter protection is used on all filters associated with the column.

Converting a Filter to SQL   Sometimes it is easier to define a filter using an SQL statement than it is to try to construct it using the Filter dialog box. For example, you may wish to create a complex filter condition using a string or other function, which may be difficult to do using the regular Filter dialog box.

For example, you may have analysis criteria that includes the Dim Stores.Region Name and Fact Sales.Revenue columns and wish to apply a filter that returns regions beginning with the substring "North":

```
left("Dim Stores.Region Name",5) = 'North'
```

To test for this condition, you could create a filter using an SQL WHERE clause by following these steps:

1. Create a new analysis and add the columns (for example, Dim Stores.Region Name and Fact Sales.Revenue) to the analysis criteria.

2. Hover your mouse pointer over the menu to the right of the column you wish to filter (in this case, Dim Stores.Region Name). When the menu is displayed, click Filter.

3. When the New Filter dialog box opens, select the Convert This Filter To SQL check box, and click OK.

4. The Advanced SQL Filter dialog box will be shown. Using the dialog box, edit the initial SQL clause to reflect the logical SQL that you wish to use (for example, the SQL WHERE clause preceding this list).

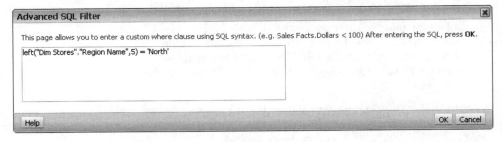

5. Click OK to close the dialog box. Note now that in the Filters pane the filter condition is shown using logical SQL.

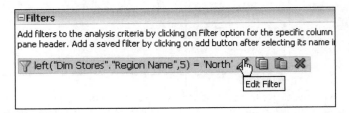

If you click the Edit Filter button now, the Advanced SQL Filter dialog box is shown, rather than the normal Edit Filter dialog box.

6. Click the Results tab to see the results of the analysis. Your filter condition, expressed using logical SQL, should now be applied.

Filtering Hierarchical Columns　Earlier in this chapter we looked at the three subject area column types that are available in Oracle Business Intelligence: measure columns, attribute columns, and hierarchical columns. As we have just seen, you can filter attribute and measure columns by applying filter conditions to the column, but if you try to do that now with a hierarchical column, where is the option to apply a filter?

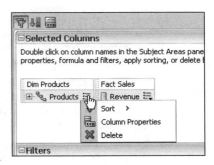

The reason that there is no option to apply a filter condition to a hierarchical column is that this column type typically encompasses several presentation columns; in the example of the Dim Products.Products hierarchical column shown in the preceding illustration, this brings together the Dim Products.Product Category, Product Type, and Product Name presentation columns, whereas a filter needs to refer to just a single subject area column.

If you want to filter values shown in a hierarchical column, then, you have two options:

- You can use the selection steps feature to filter the results of the hierarchical column query post-aggregation (described in more detail later in this chapter).

- You can add filters to the query that references the columns included in the hierarchical column.

To use the second approach and add a filter reference to columns that are referenced in the hierarchical column (in this case, to filter results to include only the Drinks and Snacks product categories), follow these steps:

1. Create an analysis that includes the hierarchical column of choice (in this case Dim Products.Products) and any measures that you require (in this case, Fact Sales.Revenue).

2. To see which subject area columns are included in the hierarchical column, select the Criteria tab and navigate to the Subject Areas pane, locate the hierarchy, and click the plus (+) icon next to the hierarchy name to see the columns that it includes. These are the columns that you should place filters on to restrict values being returned for the hierarchy.

3. In this instance, you are going to restrict the hierarchy values to only those products that have either Drinks and Snacks recorded as their product category. Because the Dim Products.Product Category column is not included in the analysis criteria and you do not really want to display this column as an attribute column in the analysis results, you will now add it as just a filter reference.

To do this, ensure that the Filters pane is shown at the bottom of the Criteria screen. (If it is not, click the Show/Hide Filters Pane button just above the Selected Columns pane.) Then click the "Create a filter for the current subject area" button. A list of columns currently in the Selected Columns list will be displayed, which at this point is just the Revenue column, the only other nonhierarchical column in the list.

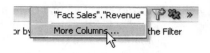

4. To create a filter against a column not included in the Selected Columns list, click the More Columns menu item. The Select Columns dialog box will be shown, and you can now use it to select another column to filter on (in this case, the Dim Products.Product Category column).

5. Click OK, and then use the New Filter dialog box to create the filter condition you require (in this case, "is equal to / is in Drinks; Snacks").

Now, when you switch to the Results tab, you will see that the hierarchy includes only those products whose categories match the filter you have just applied. Later on, we will take a look at selection steps and how you can use these as an alternative way to filter data in hierarchies.

	Revenue
Products	
⊟ All Products	3859.05
⊞ Drinks	1821.69
⊟ Snacks	2037.36
⊞ Accompaniments	4.99
⊞ Sandwiches	58.91
⊞ Soup	105.88

Sorting

When your analyses display data to users, often they will want to see it sorted in a particular order (for example with greatest values first or by customer name). Users can apply this sorting in individual analysis views or you can specify sort rules in the analysis criteria, which then applies as the default for all views based off of it.

To apply sorting to a column or set of columns, follow these steps:

1. With the analysis editor open and the Criteria tab selected, navigate to the Selected Items pane. In this example, the selected items list includes the Dim Products.Product Category, the Dim Products.Product Type, and the Fact Sales. Revenue columns.

2. To sort all the analysis results by a single column, hover your mouse pointer over the column menu and select Sort | Sort Ascending or Sort Descending. Once done, switch to the Results tab to see the sorted results.

3. To sort by multiple columns, use the Sort menu again, but this time select Add Ascending Sort or Add Descending Sort. Starting in this way with the first column to sort by, you can add additional columns that are then used as additional sort instructions.

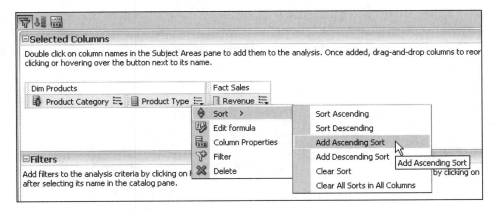

4. To clear sort instructions, use the Clear Sort or Clear Sort In All Columns menu item.

NOTE
If you want to sort one column (for example, date in "Apr-2010" format) by another (for example, "201004"), you can do so by defining the sort order column for a logical column in the Oracle BI Repository. Refer to Chapter 3 to see how this is done.

Calculations

In Chapter 3, we looked at how you could define calculations in the Oracle BI Repository that would then be available to all users who have permission to use the column. In addition to defining these "shared" calculations, you can also define calculations, or column formulas, in the analysis criteria.

The syntax and range of calculations available to you within an analysis is more or less the same as when working with the repository, apart from a small number of calculation types that apply to one or the other situation only. As with repository calculations, calculations in analyses are organized into the following groupings:

Aggregate, running aggregate, and time-series functions
String functions
Math functions
Calendar date/time functions
Conversion functions
Database functions
System functions

More details on the different calculation types can be found in Chapter 3, and in a moment we will look at a couple of particular calculation types that you might find useful (or tricky) to use in analyses. To create a calculation in the analysis criteria, though, follow these steps:

1. To add a calculation to an existing analysis criteria, ensure that the analysis editor is open with the Criteria tab selected. Using the Subject Areas pane on the left-hand side of the screen, add a column to the Selected Columns area; if you are performing a mathematical calculation, add a measure, while if you are performing a string or date

function on an attribute column, add one of those so that you start with the correct default aggregation setting for the column.

2. With your mouse pointer, hover over the menu for the column and select Edit Formula.

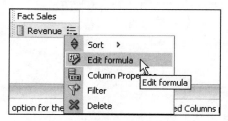

3. The Edit Column Formula dialog box will open, and you can use this dialog box to alter the default source (formula) for your column, change the aggregation rule if required, and alter the column name.

Let's now take a look at the Edit Column Formula dialog box in more detail.

The Edit Column Formula Dialog Box   Calculations, or formulas, are defined in an analysis using the Edit Column Formula dialog box. Starting with the default formula for a column, you can alter this formula to reference other columns, operators, variables, and other objects; remove the existing column reference if required; and alter the folder heading and column heading to better reflect the values in the column.

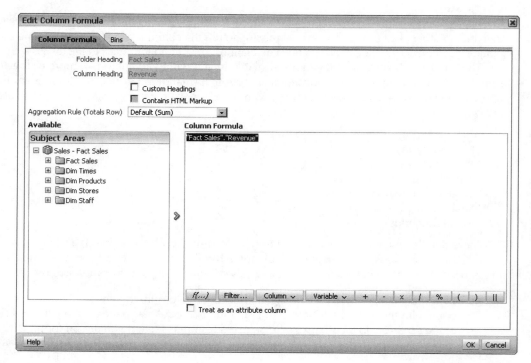

The Edit Column Formula dialog box has a number of sections:

- **Column Formula** On the right-hand side of the screen, there is a section for the column formula itself, initially set to the subject area column for this particular column, but you can edit it and add to it using the other parts of this dialog box.

- **Subject Areas** This section lists out the subject area columns that you can reference in your formula. As with the same pane in the analysis editor, measures are shown as yellow "ruler" icons, while attributes are shown as light blue, stacked "level" icons.

- **Custom headings** A check box at the top of the dialog box allows you to enable custom headings. If you enable them, you will be able to edit the folder heading (that is, the table name) and column heading, as well as specify whether HTML markup should be displayed as HTML or as markup code.

- **Available functions** A section under the Column Formula area gives you access to the list of available functions, including the filter function, other columns currently in the selection criteria, variables, and operators.

For example, consider a situation where you want to alter the formula of the Fact Sales.Revenue column to instead provide the rank of sales using the Rank function. To do this, you would follow these steps:

1. With the analysis editor open and the Criteria tab selected, add a measure column to the Selected Columns area (for example, Fact Sales.Revenue). Then, using the menu next to the column, select Edit Column Formula.

2. The column currently returns the revenue measure from the Oracle BI Repository. To apply a rank function to it, first double-click the existing Column Formula to select it, and then click the *f(...)* button at the bottom of the dialog box.

3. When the Insert Function dialog box is shown, select Functions | Aggregate | Rank from the Insert Function dialog box. Click OK to close the dialog box.

4. When you return to the Edit Column Formula dialog box, your previous formula should now be wrapped within the function you selected.

5. To alter the name of the column to better reflect its new purpose, select the Custom Headings check box and change the column heading to read **Sales Rank**.

6. Add an attribute column to the Selected Columns pane (for example, Dim Products. Product Category). Now when you click the Results tab, you will see that the revenue measure displays the rank of sales for product categories instead.

Setting the Aggregation Rule for a Column Total Row With Table and Pivot Table view types, you can choose to include grand totals and subtotals in the view in order to total sales by product category or by region, for example. When these totals are requested, by default the aggregation method used by the column aggregates the totals, with the Presentation Server using logical SQL functions such as REPORT_SUM, REPORT_AVG, and REPORT_AGGREGATE to request the report-level aggregates.

In some circumstances, you might want to alter the aggregation rule used for totals to select MIN or MAX, for example, instead of the standard Default (Sum) or equivalent for the aggregation method used by the repository column. Also, in some cases, you might want to give additional instructions to the Presentation Server to tell it to use the aggregation rule for the column in the repository (Server Determined) or its best estimate for what the rule should be based on the data in the report (Server Complex Aggregate).

To alter the aggregation method for a measure in the analysis criteria, use the Edit Column Formula menu item to view the Edit Column Formula dialog box, and then change the Aggregation Rule (Totals Row) drop-down menu value to the aggregation method you require. Changing these values, along with choices you make regarding views (pivot tables, tables, and so on), causes the logical SQL generated by the Presentation Server to be altered to use different logical SQL functions to perform the aggregation, which may be more appropriate for your report than the default aggregation method.

Binning   *Binning* is a technique where you can group results into "bins" of 10, 10–100, 100–500, 500, and above that are displayed instead of the actual column value. Binning can be used for both measure and attribute columns, and you can define the bins using the usual set of operators.

For example, consider a situation in which you wish to report on revenue from products. Each of the products in your inventory has a revenue figure associated with it, but you wish to report instead on revenue broken down into four groupings:

- Products with total revenue up to $10
- Products with revenue between $10 and $25
- Products with revenue from $25 up to and including $100
- Products with revenue in excess of $100

When the data is then displayed in the analysis, the actual revenue figures will be replaced with the name of the bin that the figure fell into.

To do this, you would use the binning feature in the analysis editor, like this:

1. Create a new analysis and include the columns that you wish to display and to bin (for example, Dim Products.Product Name and Fact Sales.Revenue, with the latter being the column whose values you wish to bin).

2. Navigate to the Selected Columns pane, hover your mouse pointer over the Fact Sales .Revenue column, and select Edit Formula from the column menu.

3. With the Edit Column Formula dialog box shown, click the Bins tab.

4. You will now add the four bins. To start this process, click the Add Bin button on the bottom left-hand corner, and then when the New Filter dialog box is shown, create the filter condition for the first bin, which in this case is "Revenue is less than 10". When prompted to enter the bin name, type in **Revenue up to $10**.

5. Repeat step 4 for the next two bins, defining them as **Revenue between $10 and $25** and **Revenue between $25 and $100**.

6. To create the bin for the remaining values, select the "Create a bin for all other values" check box and call the bin **Revenue above $100**. Your binning definition should now look as it does in the next illustration.

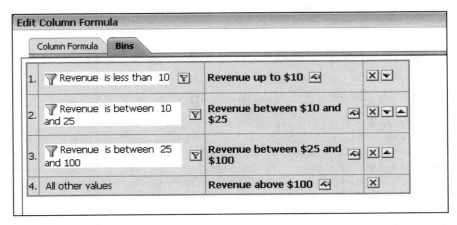

7. When you click OK and then click the Results tab to display the analysis results, you will see the column formula replaced by the name of the bin that the value fell into.

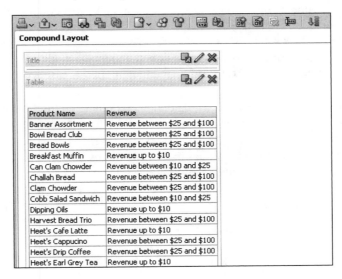

Adding Formula Filters At the bottom of the Edit Column Formula dialog box is a button labeled Filter. This button allows you to filter the values returned by a column based on a filter condition; for example, you might want to show revenue for a particular product category in one column and for a different category in another. Similarly, for Essbase sources, you might want to show revenue for a forecast scenario and margin for an actual scenario. Filters on column formulas let you create this type of report.

To show how formula filters work, let's take an example where you wish to create an analysis where one measure is filtered on a particular filter value, while another is filtered on a different filter value. In this example, you will create an analysis that contains the following three subject area columns:

■ **Month**   Returns all months in the data set, along with their year
■ **Revenue**   Returns revenue for all stores
■ **Sale Amount**   Returns the amount of sold items for all stores

Normally, analyses that use the Revenue and Sale Amount measures in the criteria will return the sum (or other default aggregation) for those measures filtered by whatever filter session may have been defined for the analysis, as a whole. However, we will now use the formula filter function to filter the Revenue measure to only return values for the Revenue measure for stores in the North CA region, and to filter the Sale Amount Measure to only return values for stores in the North SF region. The analysis itself, however, will not have any filter conditions applied and will return rows based on all rows in the dataset, giving us a result set that covers the full range of months in the data set.

To create this example, follow these steps:

1. Using the analysis editor, create a new analysis that contains the columns you require (for example, the Dim Times.Month, Fact Sales.Revenue, and Fact Sales.Sale Amount columns from the Sales – Fact Sales subject area).

2. With the Criteria tab selected, navigate to the Selected Columns pane, and for the first column select the Edit Formula menu item. In this case, you select the Fact Sales.Revenue column for editing.

3. With the Edit Column Formula dialog box open and the Column Formula tab selected, click the Filter button under the Column Formula area.

4. The Insert Filter dialog box will be shown. In this instance, we wish to filter the revenue measure by North CA values in the Dim Stores.Region column, so locate that column in the Subject Areas pane and double-click it to select it.

5. The New Filter dialog box will be shown. Use the dialog box to create the filter "Region Name is equal to / is in North CA." The Insert Filter dialog box will now show your filter condition.

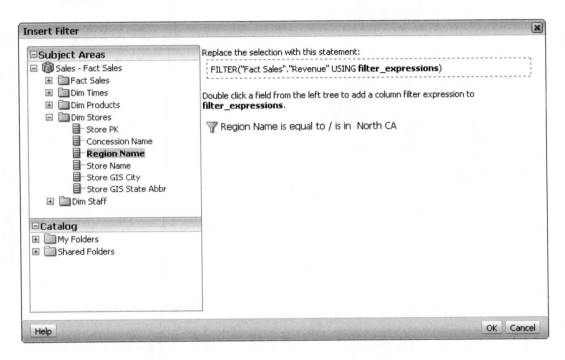

6. Click OK to return back to the Edit Column Formula dialog box, which will now show your column formula with the filter condition applied. To make the contents of this column clearer, select the Custom Headings check box and change the column name to **Revenue in North CA Region**.

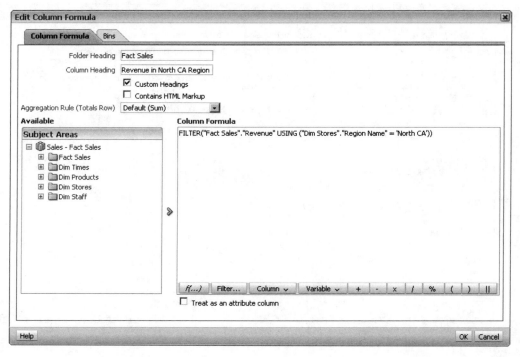

7. To add the filter condition for the other column, repeat the process, but this time create the filter condition as "Region Name is equal to / is in North SF" and alter the column name to **Sale Amount in North SF Region**.

8. Now when you display the results of the analysis, only values for the regions specified in the filter will be included in the column values.

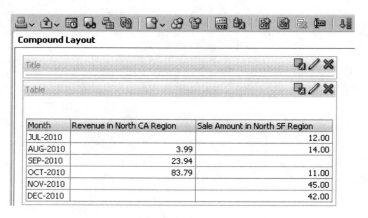

Month	Revenue in North CA Region	Sale Amount in North SF Region
JUL-2010		12.00
AUG-2010	3.99	14.00
SEP-2010	23.94	
OCT-2010	83.79	11.00
NOV-2010		45.00
DEC-2010		42.00

Setting Column Properties

Columns in an analysis criteria have properties, such as their style, their format, and what happens when you click them in the analysis results. Like setting the formula or a filter for a column, you set a column's properties by using the column menu in the Selected Columns pane. When you choose Column Properties in this pane, as shown here:

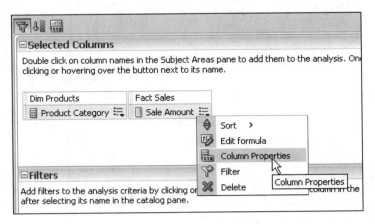

the Column Properties dialog box is displayed.

Properties for a column are organized into the following groupings:

- **Style**   This tab is for setting the font family, size, color, and effects for the column, as well as the styling for the cell and border.

- **Column Format**   You use this tab to set the folder (table) and column heading for the column, as well as choose whether to suppress or repeat recurring values.

- **Data Format**   Here is where you override the default format to use currency, percentage, or other formats instead.

- **Conditional Format**   This tab is for conditionally formatting a column based on one or more filter conditions.

- **Interaction**   Use this tab to define what happens when a user clicks on a column value.

■ **Write Back**   This tab, described in more detail in Chapter 5, is for configuring how users can write values (such as budget or quota figures) back to a data source.

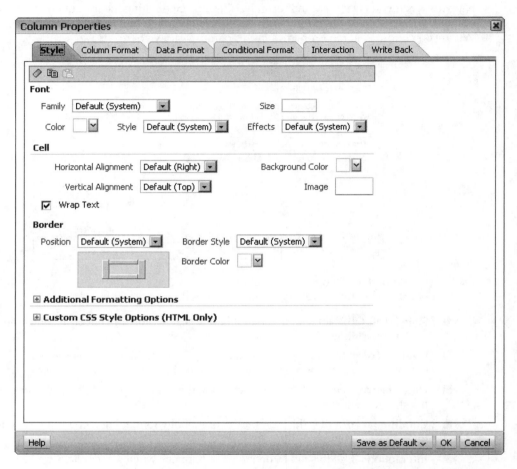

Most of these properties are self-explanatory, but let's take a look at the Conditional Format and Interaction tabs, which may not be obvious when you first look at them.

Column Conditional Formatting   The Style tab of the Column Properties dialog box allows you to define the font, color, size, and other visual aspects of a column, giving you the ability to color the column's values red, change the font, put a border around the cell, and so on. The Conditional Formatting tab allows you to do this and more based on conditions you define against this or other columns in the analysis criteria.

For example, consider a situation where you have three columns in an analysis criteria:

Region Name
Amount Sold
Amount Sold Performance to Target

You now wish to create an analysis that displays the amount sold column in white with a red background if the value is less than 20 and displays the performance-to-target value as a set of stars, with one star for less than zero, two stars for 0–10 percent, three stars for 10–25 percent, and so on.

To do this, you will use the conditional formatting feature in the analysis editor.

1. Using the analysis editor, create a new analysis that includes the columns you require (for example, Dim Stores.Region Name, Fact Sales.Sale Amount, and Fact Sales.Sale Amount Target).

2. Use the Edit Column Formula dialog box to alter the formula of the Fact Sales.Sale Amount Target column to instead show performance to target, using the following formula:

   ```
   (("Fact Sales"."Sale Amount" - "Fact Sales"."Sale Amount Target" ) /
   "Fact Sales"."Sale Amount Target" ) *100
   ```

3. Use the Custom Headings check box to enable a custom heading for the column, and call it **Performance to Target**.

4. Now you can start conditionally formatting the two measure columns. Begin by hovering your mouse pointer over the Fact Sales.Sale Amount column and select Column Properties when the menu appears. When the Column Properties dialog box is shown, click the Conditional Formatting tab.

5. Click the Add Condition button to add the column condition, and when prompted, select the Sale Amount column to base the condition on. When the New Condition dialog box is shown, create the condition "Sale Amount is less than 20" and then click OK to close the dialog box.

6. You will now be shown the Edit Format dialog box. Use this dialog box to set the cell background color to red and the font color to white, and then click OK to close the dialog box and return to the Column Properties dialog box, which should now look like the following illustration:

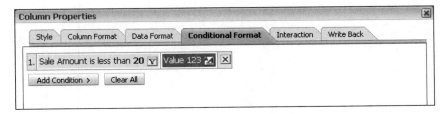

7. Click OK to return to the analysis editor.

8. For the performance-to-target measure, we will use a set of images to replace the column values based on filter conditions. To start defining this formatting, select the Column Properties menu item for the column in the Selected Columns pane, and when the Column Properties dialog box is shown, select the Conditional Format tab again.

9. Now you can start to define the filter conditions. Start by defining the first condition, which in this example should be **Performance to Target is less than 0**. Then, when the Edit Format dialog box is shown, this time click the Image button, which initially will be blank, like this:

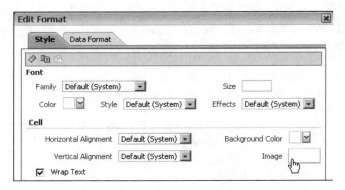

10. The Graphics dialog box will then be shown. You can use this to select an image to display when this condition is met; in this example, first select the horizontal stars image, and then when the set of images are displayed, select the one with a single filled-in blue star to the left.

11. Finally, using the Image Placement drop-down menu, select the Images Only option to replace the measure value with the image rather than displaying it to the left or right of the measure value. Click OK to close this dialog box, and then OK again to close the Edit Format dialog box.

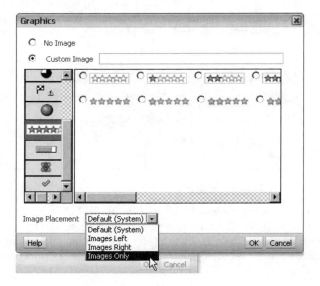

12. Repeat steps 9–11 to create filter conditions for the other images so that in the end the Conditional Format tab of the Column Properties dialog box looks like the following illustration:

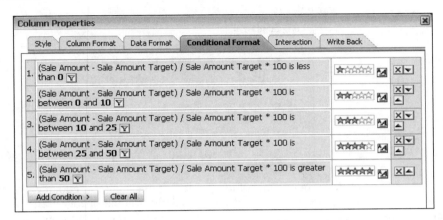

Now when you view the analysis results, you will see the figures in the Sale Amount column highlighted in red and those in the Performance to Target column shown as a set of stars, with five stars signifying the best performance.

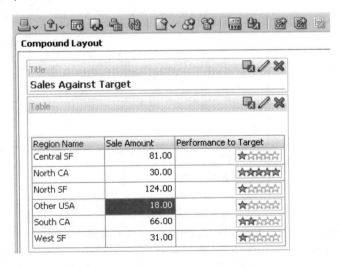

Configuring Interaction for Columns   When you create an analysis and include an attribute column or hierarchical column in the view, if the column is part of a hierarchy when the user clicks on the column, by default the view then shows the next level of detail down. This is termed "drilling to detail" and is the default behavior or "interaction" for columns and column headings.

For example, if you click a region such as North SF in an analysis view, by default the view will then display the stores within this region, with revenue aggregated by these stores.

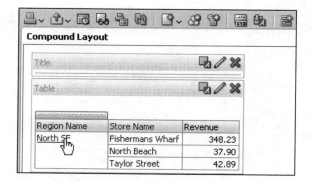

When you click an individual column value like this, a filter is added to the analysis that filters on this particular value, whereas if you click the column header itself, the values for that column are preserved but the next level down is added to the analysis criteria.

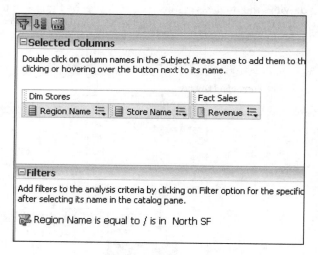

Combining Analysis Results Using Set Operations

Sometimes you might want to combine into a single analysis results set two or more queries joined together by a set operation. For example, you might want to query one set of product data and then use the Minus set operation to remove from it another set of product data from a different location. When you combine data sets in this way, the combined columns create a new, separate column governed by the chosen set operation.

The following set operations are available for use in combining one or more sets of result columns:

- ■ **Union** This set operation combines the two sets and removes duplicates.
- ■ **Union All** This combines the two data sets but leaves duplicate rows found in both sets.

■ **Intersect**   This returns just those rows that can be found in both sets.

■ **Minus**   This returns rows from the first set that are not found in the second.

These set operations can be combined if you add a third or more result sets to the set operation. Columns that you combine in this way must have some commonality, such as matching data types, and each result set must return the same number of columns in the same order as the other result sets.

For example, to add a second set of result columns to an analysis using a set operation, such as to remove products that have been returned from a set of product sales data, follow these steps:

1.   Create an analysis as normal, and add columns to the Selected Columns pane. In this example, the columns we will add are Dim Products.Product Name and Fact Sales.Revenue.

2.   With the first set of columns added to the Selected Columns pane, click the "Combine results based on union, intersection, and difference operations" button, which initially prompts you to select a subject area.

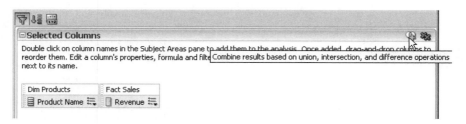

3.   You can now select the subject area that contains the columns you wish to add to the analysis using a set operation.

Once you do this, the Selected Columns pane will change to show Set Operations. Within the Result Columns area, your second subject area will now be highlighted, and you can switch between editing the result columns you just added and the ones that were already in the analysis criteria by clicking the result set name in this area.

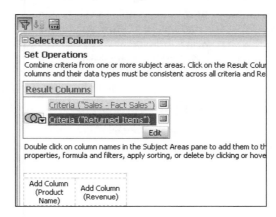

4. Below the Result Columns area, there are two column spaces where you can add columns from this new subject area to match the ones from the previous subject area. Starting with the first column space (which in this example equates to the Product Name column in the initial result set), navigate to the Subject Areas pane and double-click the new column that will correspond to this.

5. Repeat step 4 for the other columns until you have selected a set of columns that matches the other result set.

6. Use the drop-down menu in the Result Columns area to select the set operation that you wish to use to combine the two result sets.

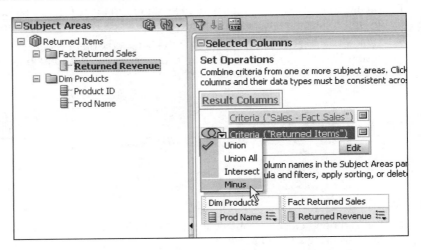

Now, when you switch to the Results tab, the analysis will display the result of combining the two result sets using the set operation.

Creating Analysis Views

Now that you have seen how the criteria for an analysis is specified, let us take a look at the different types of views that you can create to display your data. Each analysis can have one or more views associated with it, which are typically combined into the compound layout and then displayed, along with other analyses, in the dashboard.

Let's start then with the most basic of views, the Table view. This is the default view that is created for you when you define an analysis using only attribute and measure columns.

Table Views

Table views show one or more columns organized into a table, with optional totals and subtotals. Tables are particularly good for showing tabular lists of measures in simple lists, and you can add interactivity by configuring table prompts and sections, as well as adding navigation actions to columns so that users can link to other related analyses.

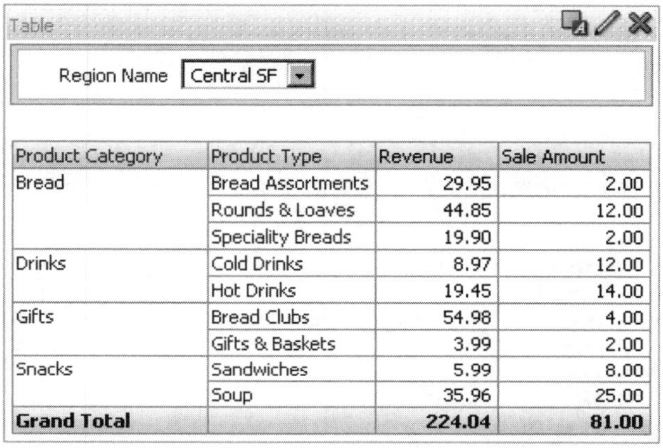

Product Category	Product Type	Revenue	Sale Amount
Bread	Bread Assortments	29.95	2.00
	Rounds & Loaves	44.85	12.00
	Speciality Breads	19.90	2.00
Drinks	Cold Drinks	8.97	12.00
	Hot Drinks	19.45	14.00
Gifts	Bread Clubs	54.98	4.00
	Gifts & Baskets	3.99	2.00
Snacks	Sandwiches	5.99	8.00
	Soup	35.96	25.00
Grand Total		**224.04**	**81.00**

Table — Region Name: Central SF

A Table view is added to your analysis by default when you include just attribute and measure columns in your analysis criteria. If you include a hierarchical column in your criteria, a pivot table is added instead.

To show how Table views work, let's start by working with the default Table view that is provided for us when adding some attribute and measure columns to an analysis, and then we will add totals and subtotals to see how these work.

Working with the Default Table View   In this example, we are working with a Table view that is added for you by default when you select the following columns from the Sales – Fact Sales subject area:

Dim Products.Product Name
Dim Products.Manufacturer
Dim Products.Perishable YN Flag
Fact Sales.Revenue
Fact Sales.Sale Amount

After adding these columns to the analysis criteria, click the Results tab to see the default views for the analysis. One of these, below the Title view, is the Table view, which by default shows the first 25 rows returned by the analysis. To display the next 25 rows or display all rows up to a maximum of 500, click the Next 25 Rows button or the Display Maximum (500) Rows Per Page button at the bottom of the Table view.

Product Name	Manufacturer	Perishable YN Flag	Revenue	Sale Amount
Banner Assortment		Y	29.95	2.00
Bowl Bread Club		Y	49.98	2.00
Bread Bowls		Y	59.90	3.00
Breakfast Muffin	Harringtons	Y	6.99	1.00
Can Clam Chowder		N	11.98	6.00
Challah Bread		Y	25.90	3.00
Clam Chowder		Y	89.90	55.00
Cobb Salad Sandwich		Y	11.98	12.00
Dipping Oils		N	3.99	2.00
Harvest Bread Trio		Y	29.95	4.00
Heet's Cafe Latte	Heet's Coffee Co.	N	7.98	3.00
Heet's Cappucino	Heet's Coffee Co.	N	79.80	54.00
Heet's Drip Coffee	Heet's Coffee Co.	N	41.88	46.00
Heet's Earl Grey Tea	Heet's Coffee Co.	N	4.98	3.00
Heet's Tea	Heet's Coffee Co.	N	4.98	3.00
Holiday Bread Trio		Y	26.95	2.00
Mineral Water		N	20.93	29.00
Minestrone		Y	7.99	5.00
North Beach Sandwich		Y	11.98	3.00
Panettone	Gusieppe Inc.	Y	13.90	4.00
Pepper Jack Cheese		N	5.99	2.00
Raisin Baguette		Y	4.99	2.00
Salt Beef Sandwich		Y	27.96	10.00
Sandwich Rolls		Y	19.95	3.00
Seasonal Bread Club		N	29.99	3.00

Rows 1 - 25

Display maximum (500) rows per page

Within the Table view, you can reorder the columns and apply sort orders to them. To move a column around within the view, hover your mouse pointer over the header column to display the grab bar, and then use this bar to reposition the column. To sort a column either high to low or low to high, use the two arrow controls that appear on the header when you hover your mouse pointer in this area.

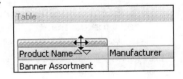

In addition to sorting and reordering columns, you can right-click a table cell to bring up a menu that allows you to create groups and calculated items for that column, as described in more detail in a moment. This menu also allows you to create selection steps (described in more detail in the "Selection Steps" section later in this chapter) to add or remove members from the result set or perform other actions on the data in the table.

Product Name	Manufacturer	Perishable YN Flag	Revenue	Sale Amount
Banner Assortment		Y	29.95	2.00
Bowl Bread Club		Y	49.98	2.00
Bread Bowls		Y	59.90	3.00
Breakfast Muffin	Harrington	Y	6.99	1.00
Can Clam Chowder		Keep Only	11.98	6.00
Challah Bread		Remove	25.90	3.00
Clam Chowder			89.90	55.00
Cobb Salad Sandwich		Create Group...	11.98	12.00
Dipping Oils		Create Calculated Item...	3.99	2.00
Harvest Bread Trio			29.95	4.00
Heet's Cafe Latte	Heet's Cof	Manufacturer ⟩	⇅ Sort Column ⟩	
Heet's Cappucino	Heet's Coffee Co.	N	Keep Only ⟩	
Heet's Drip Coffee	Heet's Coffee Co.	N	Remove ⟩	
Heet's Earl G	Top X ⟩		Based on Revenue...	
Heet's Tea	Bottom X ⟩		Based on Sale Amount...	
Holiday Bread	Members where Revenue is greater than ⟩			
Mineral Wate	Members where Revenue is less than ⟩		Show Subtotal ⟩	
Minestrone	Members where Sale Amount is greater than ⟩		Remove All Steps	
North Beach	Members where Sale Amount is less than ⟩		Show Row level Grand Total ⟩	
Panettone	Specific Members...			
Pepper Jack	Based on a Custom Condition...		Exclude column	
Raisin Baguet			Hide Column	
Salt Beef San			Move Column ⟩	
Sandwich Rolls		Y		
Seasonal Bread Club		N		

⬆ ⬆ ⬇ ⬇ Rows 1 - 25

You can also use this menu to add totals, subtotals, other controls, or even to exclude certain columns, or you can edit the Table view layout instead.

Editing the Table View Layout Every view within the analysis results screen has three controls in the top right-hand corner of the view:

- ■ **Format Container** This is for editing the alignment, borders, padding, and other settings for the view.
- ■ **Edit View** This is for editing the layout of the view.
- ■ **Remove View from Compound Layout** The compound layout is discussed in the upcoming section of this chapter titled "The Compound Layout View."

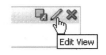

To make changes other than sort order or ordering of columns to a Table view, you will need to edit the view layout by clicking the Edit View button. When you do so, the pane changes to show a preview of the view in the top half of the window and the Layout pane in the bottom half.

If you wish, you can move the Layout pane up and down the screen to create more room to edit the layout. To do this, click and then drag the Layout pane header with your mouse pointer.

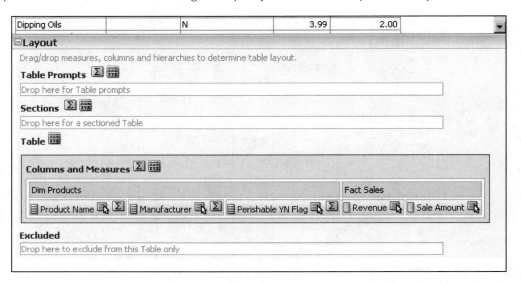

Using the Layout pane, you can make the following changes to the Table view:

■ Drag one or more columns into the Table Prompts area to add drop-down lists of products, customers, or other dimension attributes that will then be used to filter the Table view.

■ Drag one or more columns into the Sections area to create repeating sets of Table views, one per value in the column(s).

■ Reorder the columns.

■ Drag one or more columns into the Excluded area to leave the column in the criteria but exclude it from this particular view.

Every column in the Layout pane also has a menu available for it that can be accessed by hovering your mouse pointer over the More Options icon to the right of the column. This column menu contains options for formatting the column, duplicating it in the view, and setting the aggregation rule. For attribute columns, there is an option for creating calculated members based on values from that particular column.

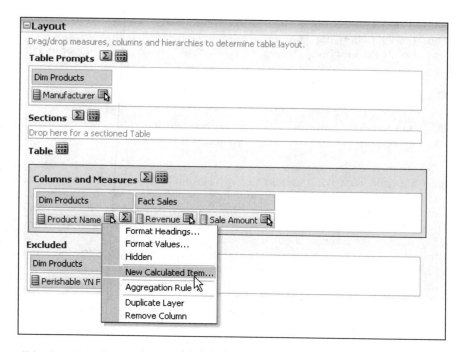

We will look at calculated items and another feature called *groups* in a moment.

Finally, at the top of the pane, above the preview of the layout, is a toolbar with a set of buttons for setting properties for the Table view.

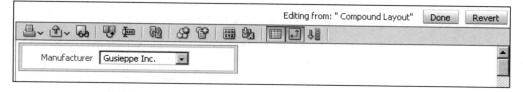

These buttons include

- Buttons to print, export, refresh, and preview the analysis and individual view
- Buttons to rename and duplicate the view
- Two buttons to create new calculated items and groups
- A Table Properties button for configuring where the paging controls are for the view, how many rows are displayed on each page, configuring master-detail events (described later in this chapter), and configuring write back for columns (described in Chapter 5)
- A button to allow you to import formatting from another analysis so that you can use a single analysis as a "template" for this analysis's column formatting

Calculated Items and Groups   In addition to displaying the members in a dimension that are sourced from the underlying data source modified by any filters that are applied to the column, you can also create your own, custom members based on selections of members and one or more functions. There are two ways in which you can create these custom members:

- You can create a *calculated item,* which allows you to define a new dimension member and specify the way in which dimension members are aggregated.
- You can create a *group,* a selection of members that inherits the aggregation function of the measure column with which the group is displayed.

In addition, when you create a group using the hierarchical column type, the group becomes drillable, allowing you to drill into detail for the group and for members within the group.

Groups and calculated items that are defined as part of a view are referred to as *inline objects* and only exist as part of the view. If you define a calculated item or group as part of a set of selection steps, though, the item or group can be saved to the catalog as a named object and then reused or referenced in other calculated item or group definitions.

For example, you can create a calculated item called San Francisco Stores that adds together sales from all stores in the San Francisco region, and you can create a group that combines these stores but allows you to "drill into" the grouping, showing the individual stores underneath regions, as well as concessions underneath stores.

As another example, we will use another column, Dim Products.Product Name, to create two such custom members:

- A calculated member (item) called Heets Products that adds together sales of all hot beverage products from the supplier called Heets
- A group called Sourdough Products that creates a grouping of sourdough products that will inherit whatever aggregation settings are used for measures displayed alongside it

To create the Heets Products calculated item, follow these steps:

1. With the analysis open for editing and the Results tab selected, navigate to the Table view and click the Edit View button to display the Layout pane.

2. To start defining the calculated item, hover your mouse pointer over the More Options button for the Product Name column in the layout and then select New Calculated Item from the menu or click the New Calculated Item button in the toolbar.

3. The New Calculated Item dialog box will then be displayed. If you selected the More Options | New Calculated Item option for a specific column, that column will be selected and greyed out in the dialog box; otherwise, you can use the drop-down menu next to the Values From item to select the column to base the calculated item on.

   Using this dialog box, enter a name into the Display Label text box, and then start adding member names from the Available pane to the Selected pane by either using the set of operators at the bottom of this pane to define how the members are combined or selecting one of the functions from the Function drop-down menu to use Sum, Average, or other predefined functions.

For example, to create the Heets Products calculated item that adds together all products from Heets, select or enter the following values into the New Calculated Item dialog box:

Display Label: Heets Products
Values From: Dim Products.Product Name
Function: Sum
Selected: Heets Cafe Latte, Heets Cappucino, Heets Drip Coffee, Heets Earl
       Grey Tea, Heets Tea

By default, the calculated item will be displayed as well as the individual members that you based the calculation on, but this could lead to double counting in your view. To remove these items and just show the calculated item, select the "Remove calculated item members from view" check box.

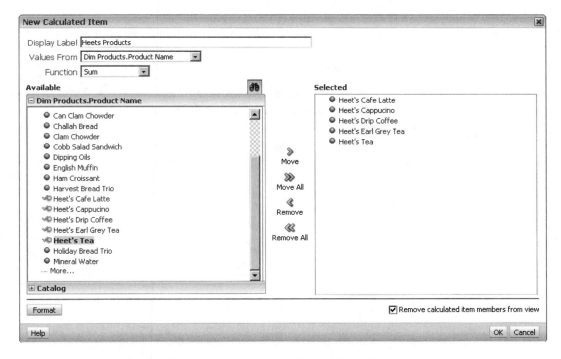

Now when you display the view, the calculated item will be listed alongside the other dimension members, with its constituent members either displayed alongside it or removed from the view, depending on the option you chose in the previous step.

Product Name	Revenue	Sale Amount
Tropics Apple Juice	8.97	5.00
Tropics Orange Juice	17.94	19.00
Turkey Bread	39.90	6.00
Vegetable Soup	7.99	1.00
Heets Products	139.62	109.00

Rows 26 - 30 (end)

Next, we will create the Sourdough Products group, which, unlike the calculated item, preserves and displays the hierarchy on which the group is based. To create a group that brings together all of the sourdough products, follow these steps:

1. Open the analysis for editing, switch to the Results tab, and click the Edit View button on the Table view.

2. Using the toolbar at the top of the view editor, click the New Group button to display the New Group dialog box.

3. Using this dialog box, you can name the group using the Display Label setting, select a column from the Values From drop-down menu, and add members from the Available pane to the Selected pane. Select or enter the following values to create the group:

   Display Label: Sourdough Products
   Values From: Dim Products.Product Name
   Selected: Sourdough Bread Club, Sourdough Loaves, Sourdough Rounds, Sourdough Sampler

   Click OK to create the group.

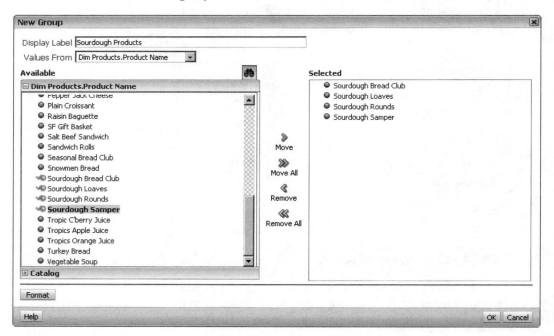

Again, when you now include this group in an analysis, it will be displayed alongside the other members, but this time it will inherit the aggregation rule for the measure it is displayed next to.

If you were to create a group using a hierarchical column, you would be able to drill on any members included in the group. Let's create another group now, but this time let's base it on the Dim Stores.Stores hierarchical column, and we'll use it to define a set of test regions and stores that we will display alongside other regions and stores in the stores hierarchy:

1. Create a new analysis, and add a hierarchical column and measure to the hierarchy (for example, Dim Stores.Stores and Fact Sales.Revenue).

2. Switch to the Results tab. By default, a Pivot Table view will have been created for you because you included a hierarchical column in the analysis criteria. To create a new Table view, using the Views pane in the bottom left-hand corner, select New View | Table. You can use this menu to add any new view to an analysis.

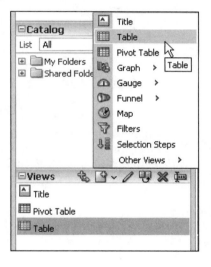

3. The new Table view will now open in the Edit View mode. To add the group, click the New Group button at the top of the view area to display the New Group dialog box.

4. Enter **Test Market** as the display label, and use the hierarchy shown in the Available pane to select the following members:

   East SF
   Fishermans Wharf
   Haight Street
   10th Avenue

5. Click OK to close the dialog box and create the new group.

Now when you view the new group in the Table view, you will see the group name and also be able to drill into the hierarchy under it, including any members that are descendants of the members you added to the group.

Stores	Revenue
⊟ All Stores	1024.61
⊞ Central SF	224.04
⊞ North CA	111.72
⊞ North SF	429.02
⊞ Other USA	50.38
⊞ South CA	131.19
⊞ West SF	78.26
⊟ Test Market	426.49
⊟ Fishermans Wharf	348.23
Macys, SF	17.94
Nordstroms, SF	22.46
10th Avenue	52.84
Haight Street	25.42

TIP
To edit a group once it has been created, right-click the group within a view to display a menu that includes an option for collapsing the hierarchy if working with a group from a hierarchical column, as well as options for editing, viewing, and deleting the group definition.

Adding Totals and Subtotals

Something you will often want to do when displaying data in a Table view is add a grand total, and sometimes subtotals, to the view. How the totals are arrived at is determined by the Aggregation Rule settings for the measure columns in your analysis criteria, though you can override this setting per individual view.

Totals and subtotals can be generated for attribute columns in the main part of the Table view, in the Table Prompts area, and in the Sections area. To determine whether a total or subtotal is displayed for a column in a particular position in the view, use the Edit View button to display the Layout pane, and look for the Sum icon (Σ) next to column names. When you hover your mouse pointer over these icons, a menu is displayed typically giving you options for displaying no total (None), for displaying the total After the column, and for formatting the total labels and values.

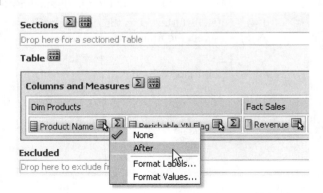

In this example, we will display revenue and sale amount values for products grouped by manufacturer by selecting the following columns for the analysis:

Dim Products.Product Name
Dim Products.Manufacturer
Fact Sales.Revenue
Fact Sales.Sale Amount

We will filter the Manufacturer column to remove all values that are null (Manufacturer is not null) and then reorder the columns in the view so that the Manufacturer column is listed before the Product Name column. This will allow us to subtotal on Manufacturer.

To create totals and subtotals for the view in this way, follow these steps:

1. Create a new analysis as before, and add the columns to the analysis criteria. Switch to the Results tab, and click the Edit View button for the Table view that was created for you.

2. Open the Layout pane and navigate to the Table element within the layout editor. Reorder the columns in the Table view so that the columns you wish to subtotal on are on the left-hand side of the column list.

3. To add a grand total to the table, hover your mouse pointer over the Totals icon next to the Columns and Measures label, and select After from the menu that appears.

4. To subtotal on the manufacturer name, click the Totals icon next to the Manufacturer column and select After again.

5. Click the Done button at the top right-hand side of the screen to return to the previous window.

Now, when you look at the table, it is subtotaled on the Manufacturer column, and a grand total has been added at the end.

Manufacturer	Product Name	Revenue	Sale Amount
Gusieppe Inc.	Panettone	13.90	4.00
Gusieppe Inc. Total		**13.90**	**4.00**
Harringtons	Breakfast Muffin	6.99	1.00
Harringtons Total		**6.99**	**1.00**
Heet's Coffee Co.	Heet's Cafe Latte	7.98	3.00
	Heet's Cappucino	79.80	54.00
	Heet's Drip Coffee	41.88	46.00
	Heet's Earl Grey Tea	4.98	3.00
	Heet's Tea	4.98	3.00
Heet's Coffee Co. Total		**139.62**	**109.00**
Tropico	Tropic C'berry Juice	14.95	10.00
	Tropics Apple Juice	8.97	5.00
	Tropics Orange Juice	17.94	19.00
Tropico Total		**41.86**	**34.00**
Grand Total		**202.37**	**148.00**

NOTE
The aggregation rule used for totals is generally the same as for the columns that are being totaled, though you can override this by using the Edit Formula menu item for a column in the analysis criteria. Alternatively, you can override this aggregation rule by clicking the More Options button next to a measure column in the Layout pane and selecting a new rule from the Aggregation Rule menu item that is then displayed among other menu items.

Title Views

If you have just been working with the Table view in the previous section in this chapter, you may have noticed another view just above the Table view, called the Title view. By default empty, this view allows you to define a title plus an icon for the analysis to help users identify it when viewing it in a dashboard.

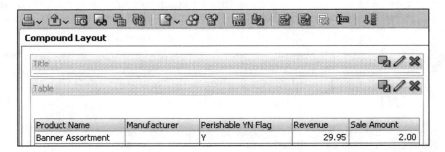

As with the Table view, the Title view has three controls at the top right-hand corner. You should click one of these, Edit View, to define the title. When you click this control, a dialog box is shown that allows you to define different aspects of the Title view:

- The title text, which by default is the saved named of the analysis that you can override with your own title text if you wish
- An optional logo, typically taken from a set of predefined logos that you can access for your own analysis titles
- An optional subtitle
- Whether or not the started time for the analysis is displayed
- A Help URL for a document providing help on this analysis

To use a logo for your Title view, you would typically use one of the predefined logos, shown in Figure 6-7, which are stored in two locations on your Oracle Business Intelligence server:

- [*middleware_home*]/Oracle_BI1/bifoundation/web/app/res/s_blafp/images
- [*middleware_home*]/user_projects/domains/bifoundation_domain/servers/bi_server1/ tmp/_WL_user/analytics_11.1.1/[*folder_name*]/war/res/s_blafp/images

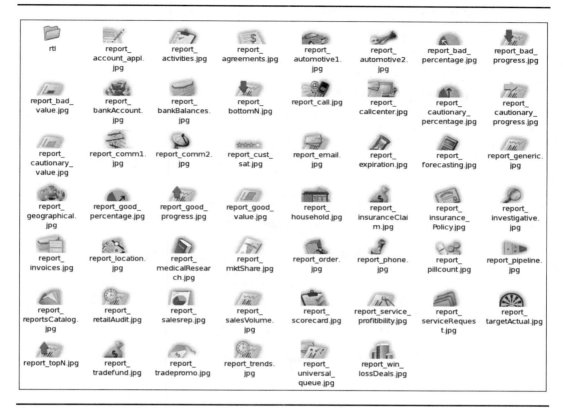

FIGURE 6-7. *Title view logos*

The first of these folders is the original location for the images, and the second is where they are copied to when your Oracle BI domain is created during installation. If you wish, you can add more images to this list, such as to add your own logos or copy them to the second of the two folders, as this is where the Oracle Business Intelligence web site will look when you reference them in the Title view definitions. If you want to create your own directories on the Oracle Business Intelligence server to hold image files or help files for the Help URL setting, you will need to create them within the AnalyticsRes directory and expose this directory using the web server that you have configured for use with Oracle Business Intelligence.

Unfortunately, the Logo text box in these settings does not provide a graphical "picker" for selecting a particular logo, so you will have to reference them using the address format fmap:images/[*image_filename*] (for example, fmap:images/report_generic.jpg). You can use the image list shown previously in Figure 6-7 to find the correct filename for the logo you want to use.

Let's now define a Title view for the analysis that features the Table view we created in the previous section. We'll use a logo from this folder and other settings available for this view:

1. Open the analysis for editing and switch to the Results tab. Locate the Title view and click the Edit View button to open the view for editing.

2. Select or enter the following values as settings for the Title view:

Title: Product Report
Display Saved Name: [*unselected*]
Logo: fmap:images/report_forecasting.jpg
Subtitle: A sample product report
Started Time: Display date and time

As you type in the settings, a preview of the Title view will be created, showing you the view as you create it.

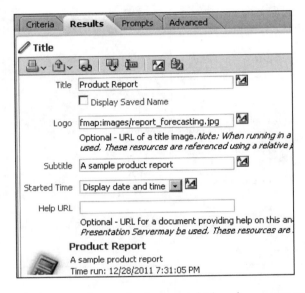

3. Once complete, click the Done button in the top right-hand corner to return to the previous page.

You will now be able to see your Title view above the Table view in your analysis, which uses the title text, subtitle, and logo specified in the view settings.

The Compound Layout View

If you have been working through this chapter and you created a table and Title view for your analysis, you may be wondering what the Compound Layout title above your views is referring to. The *compound layout* is a composition layout view that lets you arrange one or more other views together for display on a dashboard. Each analysis comes with an initial compound layout containing a Title view and either a table or a Pivot Table view that you can amend, add to, or leave as is.

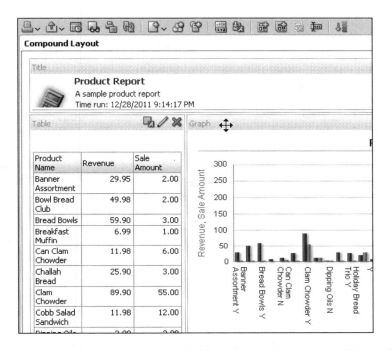

By default, when you add an analysis to a dashboard, it is the compound layout for the analysis that is displayed, though you can change this setting so that an individual view such as a chart or pivot table is displayed instead. The advantage of using the compound layout is that you can include several views in the layout, such as the Title and Table view, or you can position a table and a chart together to display data in two ways.

We will look at charts in more detail later on, but for now, let's look at how you might create a chart view to go with your Table view and include both of them, together with the Title view, in your compound layout:

1. Using either the Title and Table view created previously in this chapter or a Title and Table view created for a new analysis, ensure that the analysis is open for editing and that the Results tab is selected so that these views are displayed in the default compound layout for your analysis.

2. Now add a new view to the analysis. To do this, using the Views pane at the bottom left-hand corner of the screen, select New View | Graph | Bar | Default (Vertical). The graph view will then be created and opened in edit mode; click Done to close it with its default settings used.

3. When you create a new view in this way, it is listed in the Views pane but not included by default in the compound layout, and therefore it wouldn't be displayed if you included the view in a dashboard. To add the new graph view to the compound layout, you can either drag-and-drop the view from the Views pane onto the compound layout or select the view in this pane and click the Add View button.

Typically, the new view will be added to the compound layout under the existing view; you can reposition it by dragging it to wherever else you want it to appear, such as next to the table rather than under it.

4. If you want to include the graph view but remove the Table view, from the compound layout, click the Remove View From Compound Layout button at the top of the view you wish to remove. This will remove the view from the compound layout but not from the analysis. (To remove the view from the analysis, select the view within the Views pane and click the Remove View From Analysis button.)

5. If you would like to see a preview of how the compound layout will look if displayed in a dashboard, locate the "Show how results will look on a dashboard" button. A preview of the currently selected view (in this case, the compound layout) will then be displayed so you can see how users would see it when viewing your analysis.

6. Finally, you can actually create more than one compound layout, and you can select from each of them when displaying the analysis in a dashboard. First you might want to rename the existing compound layout; to do so, click the Rename View button on the topmost toolbar in the analysis editor and give the compound layout a new name (for example, Table and Graph Compound Layout).

   Using the same toolbar, either click the Create Compound Layout button or the Duplicate Compound Layout button to create either a new, empty one or a copy of the existing compound layout that you can then amend.

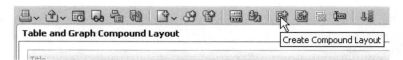

7. This second compound layout will then be displayed as a second tab within the view editing area for you to work with, and you can rename it to something more meaningful if you wish.

Now that you understand the basics of Table, Title, and Compound Layout views, let's take a look at something more complex: the Pivot Table view.

Pivot Table Views

So far, we have looked at Table views, which are useful for displaying lists of data with totals and subtotals. When you are analyzing data, though, often it is useful to be able to break down and total numbers over more than one dimension, and a Pivot Table view is ideal for this.

Pivot Table views allow you to display measures across two or more dimensions. For example, you can break down sales by product and geography, with the ability to page through years of data. Pivot Table views also provide lots of options for totaling and subtotaling, as well as displaying measures as percentages and in other ways, to help users understand the meaning behind sets of data. Pivot Table views are also ideal for use alongside hierarchical columns, giving users lots of ways to drill into and explore the hierarchies in their data sets.

Pivot Table					

Quarter Q3-2010 ▼

Products	Central SF		North SF	
	Sale Amount	Revenue	Sale Amount	Revenue
⊟ All Products	20.00	100.0%	26.00	100.0%
⊞ Bread			6.00	43.0%
⊟ Drinks	6.00	9.7%	17.00	27.0%
⊞ Cold Drinks	2.00	42.8%	2.00	11.1%
⊞ Hot Drinks	4.00	57.2%	15.00	88.9%
⊞ Gifts	6.00	82.0%	3.00	30.1%
⊞ Snacks	8.00	8.3%		

Pivot Table views share all of the capabilities of Table views, including the ability to add totals and subtotals, prompts and sections, right-click dimension members to create selection steps, and have some of their own unique capabilities such as the ability to graph the contents of the pivot table. What differentiates pivot tables from regular tables, though, is the display of dimension attributes across both rows and columns, making pivot tables particularly suitable for "OLAP-style" analysis.

The best way, however, to show how Pivot Table views can be used is to work through an example where we progressively add features from the pivot table to show how it typically might be used, using columns from the Sales – Fact Sales subject area.

Creating the Basic Pivot Table

To create a basic Pivot Table view and arrange two dimensions into rows and columns, follow these steps:

1. Create a new analysis (New | Analysis from the Oracle Business Intelligence web site menu) and select the subject area on which you will initially base the analysis (for example, Sales – Fact Sales).

2. Add the columns to the analysis criteria that you wish to base the Pivot Table view on; in this example, we will start with the following columns:

    Dim Products.Products (a hierarchical column)
    Dim Stores.Stores (another hierarchical column)
    Fact Sales.Revenue

3. Click the Results tab to view the analysis results. Since you have added at least one hierarchical column to the criteria, the compound layout will feature a Title view and a Pivot Table view instead of the Table view you saw earlier in this chapter.

4. By default, the Pivot Table view will show all of the dimension attributes and hierarchies in the rows area and the measures in the columns area. To break down the revenue

measure by the stores hierarchy, drag-and-drop the All Stores object in the rows area so that it is placed under the Revenue measure.

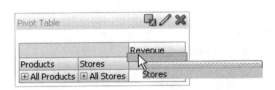 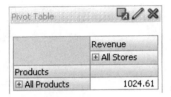

5. You can also add additional columns to the pivot table after you have first created it. To add the Sale Amount measure to the pivot table, double-click it within the Fact Sales subject area folder to add it to the measures area in the pivot table.

At this point, your pivot table will show the total for the two measures, with products on the rows (the Y axis) and stores on the columns (the X axis).

Swapping Rows and Columns, and Drilling into Hierarchies   Now that you have added your initial dimensions and measures to the Pivot Table view, you can start to drill into the dimension hierarchies, rearrange the dimensions, and so on.

For example, you might want to swap the row and column dimensions so that, in this example, Products are displayed as columns in the pivot table and Stores are shown as rows. To swap pivot table dimensions, hover your mouse pointer over the first dimension to show the grab bar, and then drop it onto the dimension you wish to swap it with. Your Pivot Table view will then update to show the new rows and columns arrangement.

You can also drill into the hierarchies within the dimensions. For attribute columns, clicking an attribute that is part of a hierarchy will filter the attribute column on that value and add to the pivot table the column that is directly below that in the hierarchy. If, instead, you click the attribute column header, the next column below it in the hierarchy will be added, but no filter will be placed on the column you clicked.

When creating pivot tables, you can choose whether to use attribute or hierarchical columns based on the type of analysis that users will want to perform. When working with complex hierarchies, particularly ones featuring ragged or skip-levels, hierarchical columns are usually more appropriate, though they do create more "expensive" queries compared to pivot tables that contain attribute columns because of the larger amount of subtotals that hierarchical columns generate.

If you have more than one measure in your pivot table, you will usually want to arrange the columns area of the pivot table so that measures are displayed under the dimension rather than above it. In the following illustration, the measure labels have been moved under the Stores dimension so that each store in the hierarchy has the two measures displayed under it. In this way, it is easy to read the sale amount and revenue for each member in the dimension.

Pivot Table				
	⊟ All Stores			
			⊞ Central SF	
	Sale Amount	Revenue	Sale Amount	Revenue
Products				
⊟ All Products	350.00	1024.61	81.00	224.04
⊞ Bread	852.00	6246.00	16.00	94.70
⊟ Drinks	1548.00	1821.69	26.00	28.42
⊞ Cold Drinks	63.00	62.79	12.00	8.97
⊟ Hot Drinks	109.00	139.62	14.00	19.45
Heet's Cafe Latte	3.00	7.98		
Heet's Cappucino	54.00	79.80	12.00	15.96
Heet's Drip Coffee	46.00	41.88	2.00	3.49

Pivot Table Prompts and Sections   As with Table views, you can add (pivot) table prompts and sections to your Pivot Table view to provide filtering against a particular dimension attribute and to split the pivot table into individual sections, again based on one or more attribute values.

In the following example, we will take the Pivot Table view created before and first add the Dim Times.Quarter attribute as a pivot table prompt. Then we will move it to the Sections area to see how this changes the view:

1. Create a Pivot Table view as before, with the Dim Products.Products, Dim Stores.Stores, and Fact Sales.Revenue columns, and arrange the view so that Products are on the rows and Stores are on the columns. Drill into the Products hierarchy so that the first level below the grand total level, product category, is shown in the Pivot Table view.

2. We will now start by adding the Dim Times.Quarter attribute to the view. To do this, locate the column in the Subject Areas pane and double-click it to add it to the rows area by default.

3. You can either move this new column to the Pivot Table Prompts area by clicking the Edit View control as we did earlier with the Table view, or you can just drag-and-drop it into the area yourself from where it was added into the pivot table. To do this, click the attribute column header so that the grab bar is displayed, and then drag it above the pivot table until you see you see the Pivot Table Prompts marker displayed. Let go at this point, and the column will now become a drop-down list that filters the rest of the pivot table.

4. If you wish, you can add more than one column to the Pivot Table Prompts area by either repeating the preceding steps to first add it to the pivot table and then moving it to the prompts area afterward, or you can just drag the column from the Subject Areas pane onto the Pivot Table Prompts area to add it as an additional drop-down list next to the first one.

5. Move the Quarter column from the Pivot Table Prompts area to the Sections area. Again, you can do this using the Edit View button and the layout editor, or you can just drag the column from one area to the other, and the view will then adjust itself to show the new layout.

Note how moving the column to the Sections area creates a separate pivot table for each section.

Graphing Pivot Table Results   One of the features unique to Pivot Table views is the ability to graph the contents of the pivot table. This differs from adding a graph view to the analysis in that the graph view will generally reflect the results of the analysis, while graphing the pivot table itself will reflect the pivot table prompt filters applied and will break the graph into whatever sections are defined for the view.

Adding a pivot table graph requires you to edit the layout of the pivot table, as the button to enable this is in the toolbar, which is only shown in edit mode for the view. In the following example, we will create a new analysis that initially starts with just the Dim Stores.Stores and Fact Sales.Revenue columns, and then we will introduce the Dim Times.Quarter column as a pivot table prompt and see how it affects the graph:

1. Create a new analysis using the Sales – Fact Sales subject area, and include the Dim Stores.Stores and Fact Sales.Revenue columns in the criteria.

2. Switch to the Results tab and check that a Pivot Table view has been created. Drill into the Stores hierarchy to show the regions level.

3. Click the Edit View button to display the Layout pane and the toolbar for the Pivot Table view.

4. To create the graph, locate the Graph Pivoted Results button in the toolbar and click it. Initially, the graph will be displayed to the right of the pivot table, though you can change this by using the Position drop-down menu that now appears in the toolbar above the pivot table and graph.

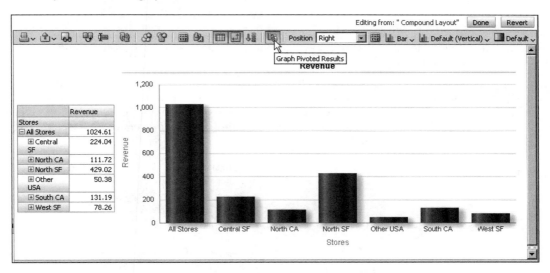

5. Drag-and-drop the Dim Times.Quarter column from the Subject Areas pane onto the Pivot Table Prompts area in the Layout pane.

See how the graph changes to reflect the filter values you select for the prompt, which may differ from filter values that are applied in the overall analysis criteria. If you add sections to the view, additional graphs will be created for each of the sections you define.

Showing Measures as Percentages and Indexes, and Altering Aggregation Rules   Another useful feature in Pivot Table views is the ability to display measure values as percentages and index values of the overall column total. To do this, it is often useful to be able to duplicate the column concerned in the view to show the measure as both its value and one of these additional measure view types.

In this example, we will use the same Dim Stores.Stores and Fact Sales.Revenue columns used in the previous example, and we will show the revenue measure as both percentage and index values, as well as the original value.

1. With the analysis open for editing, switch to the Results tab and click the Edit View button for the Pivot Table view to display the Layout pane.

2. Within the Pivot Table area, you should see a section called Measures, with your Revenue measure shown within it. To duplicate this measure, click the More Options button next to the measure and select Duplicate Layer from the menu that is displayed.

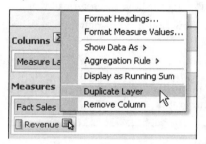

3. Repeat step 2 so that you now have three measures all with the same name in the Measures area.

4. To set the second measure so that it displays its value as a percentage of the overall total for this column, hover your mouse pointer over the second column in the list, and from the menu that is displayed select Show Data As | Percent Of | Column. Other settings are available for this percentage option if required, such as percent of row, section, page, and row or column parent.

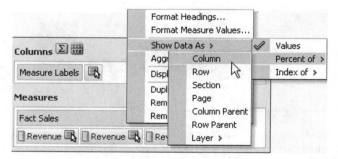

5. Repeat step 4 for the third column, this time setting the value as Show Data As | Index Of | Column. If you now look in the preview section of the view editor, you should see the three columns displaying their values in these three different ways.

6. It would probably make more sense now to rename the two additional columns to reflect the way their values are being displayed. To do this, locate within the Layout pane the first of the measures that you changed in this way and select Format Headings from the More Options menu.

7. With the Edit Format dialog box now open, type a more appropriate name into the Caption text box, such as Revenue (%). Repeat this step for the other measure, again renaming the measure (for example, Revenue (Index)).

8. Click the Done button to close the view editor, and check that the pivot table now shows the renamed columns displaying their values in the way that you configured them a moment ago.

Pivot Table			
	Revenue	Revenue (%)	Revenue (Index)
Stores			
⊟ All Stores	1024.61	100.0%	1.00
⊞ Central SF	224.04	21.9%	0.22
⊞ North CA	111.72	10.9%	0.11
⊞ North SF	429.02	41.9%	0.42
⊞ Other USA	50.38	4.9%	0.05
⊞ South CA	131.19	12.8%	0.13
⊞ West SF	78.26	7.6%	0.08

Nesting Hierarchies and Attributes   So far we have worked with a single dimension in each of the rows and columns in the Pivot Table view. We can, however, "nest" dimensions within these areas, allowing us to break down measures, for example, by products and then by staff, using any combination of attribute and hierarchical columns.

		Revenue		
		⊞ All Stores		
		JUL-2010	AUG-2010	SEP-2010
Products	Staff			
⊟ All Products	⊞ Pierre Houdan			2.49
⊞ Bread	⊞ Pierre Houdan			
⊞ Drinks	⊟ Pierre Houdan			2.49
	⊞ Adrian Boles		7.97	
	⊞ Alison Chisel			3.99
	⊞ Jon James	3.49	2.99	3.99
	⊞ Lacey Laxson			
	Pete Sims		11.97	
	⊞ Ronald Koeman	3.49	6.98	2.49
⊞ Snacks	⊞ Pierre Houdan			

To nest dimensions within each other in a Pivot Table view, you can do one of the following:

■ Drag-and-drop the hierarchical or attribute column into the preferred location on the Pivot Table view.

■ Double-click the column to add it by default to the rows area, nested behind the existing row items, and then move it yourself to the required area.

■ Double-click it to add it and click the Edit View button to open the Layout pane to move the column to the required area in the Pivot Table.

CAUTION
Depending on the size of your data set and the type of database
that is providing your data, nesting dimensions can create very
complicated database queries due to the need to create subtotals at
all levels, especially when using hierarchical columns.

Sorting and Totaling   Just like Table views, Pivot Table views can have totals displayed at the bottoms and ends of rows and columns, and totals can be configured for sections and pivot table prompts.

To show how totaling works with a Pivot Table view, we will work with an analysis that includes the following columns in the following positions:

- Dim Stores.Stores hierarchical column on the rows
- Dim Products.Product Category attribute column on the columns
- Fact Sales.Revenue column in the measures
- Dim Times.Quarter attribute column in the Pivot Table Prompts area
- Dim Times.Month attribute column in the Sections area

With no totaling added, the view will show Quarter as a drop-down menu at the top of the view, sections for each month, and sales for each individual store when you drill into the Stores hierarchy.

To add totaling to the view, click the Edit View button and open the Layout pane. Start by adding totals to the rows and columns by locating the Totals icon and selecting either Before, After, At The Beginning, or At The End for the total location.

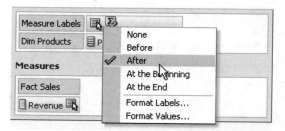

Now when you look at each pivot table within each section of the view, you will see totals where you have added them for rows and columns.

Quarter Q3-2010 ▼

JUL-2010

	Revenue				Revenue Total
	Bread	Drinks	Gifts	Snacks	
Stores					
⊟ All Stores	14.95	14.96	84.97		**114.88**
⊞ Central SF		3.99	54.98		**58.97**
Market Street		3.99	54.98		**58.97**
⊞ North SF	14.95	10.97	29.99		**55.91**
⊞ Fishermans Wharf	14.95		29.99		**44.94**
North Beach		3.49			**3.49**
Taylor Street		7.48			**7.48**
Grand Total	**14.95**	**14.96**	**84.97**		**114.88**

You can also add totals to the pivot table prompts and sections. When you do so, the view adds an additional prompt value, or section, for all values to show the pivot table at the grand total level.

In the same way as you can for Table views, you can sort rows and columns in Pivot Table views by ascending or descending values. To do so, hover your mouse pointer over the dimension member you wish to sort by, and use the left or right arrow buttons to sort the corresponding rows or columns by their values.

Adding Selection Steps and Other Right-Click Menu Actions   As an analysis author, when you create a Pivot Table view, you typically use filters in the analysis criteria to restrict returned dimension members to a particular year, product group, or geography, and use other features such as calculated items or groups, sorting, and totals to format the data in a way that is suitable for use by end users. Another powerful feature of Oracle Business Intelligence is the ability for users to right-click a pivot table you give them and make their own customizations and further manipulate the data after it is initially returned as results by the analysis.

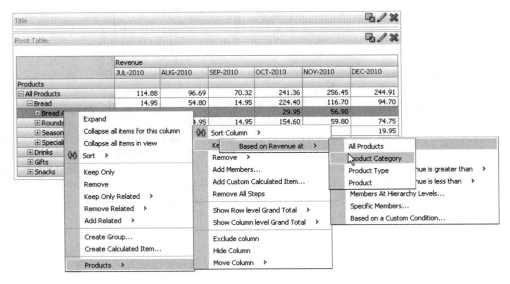

When you right-click a dimension member in a Pivot Table view (or in a Table view), a menu is displayed whose contents vary depending on whether the column is hierarchical or not. This menu is divided into four sections:

- A section for drilling, sorting, and collapsing the hierarchy or column values
- A section for keeping and removing dimension members from the results set using the selection steps feature
- A section for creating calculated items and groups
- A section for applying similar steps to the whole column, not just the selected value

We will look in more detail at selection steps in the next section of this chapter, but for now let's work through a simple example to show how keeping and removing members from the result set works. We will use a simple Pivot Table view showing the Dim Products.Products hierarchical column on the rows and the Dim Times.Month attribute column on the column, with Fact Sales .Revenue as the measure:

1. Create the analysis as described above and drill into the products hierarchy so that your pivot table looks similar to the following illustration.

Pivot Table						
	Revenue					
	JUL-2010	AUG-2010	SEP-2010	OCT-2010	NOV-2010	DEC-2010
Products						
⊟ All Products	114.88	96.69	70.32	241.36	256.45	244.91
⊟ Bread	14.95	54.80	14.95	224.40	116.70	94.70
⊞ Bread Assortments				29.95	56.90	
⊞ Rounds & Loaves	14.95	14.95	14.95	154.60	59.80	74.75
⊞ Seasonal Breads		19.95		19.95		19.95
⊞ Speciality Breads		19.90		19.90		
⊞ Drinks	14.96	29.91	27.42	10.97	45.87	73.28
⊞ Gifts	84.97		15.97		5.99	24.99
⊞ Snacks		11.98	11.98	5.99	87.89	51.94

2. At the moment, the pivot table shows all products and all months in the data set, as no filters have been applied to the analysis criteria. Now, though, we wish to exclude the Snacks product category from the results. To do so, right-click Snacks in the pivot table and select Remove from the menu that is displayed.

   When the resulting pivot table is redisplayed, Snacks and all products types and products that are part of this category are removed from the results set. You can use similar actions to keep only a particular dimension member, or if the column is a hierarchical column you can keep or remove members based on their hierarchical relationship to this column.

3. Now we wish to keep only those months where total revenue is greater than 100, which will exclude Aug-2010 and Sep-2010 when the rule is applied.

To apply this rule, right-click any of the Month column values, and from the menu select Month | Keep Only | Members Where Revenue Is Greater Than | A Value. When the Value dialog box is shown, type in **100**, and the rule will be applied to the data.

4. Next, create a custom group for the Products hierarchy to reflect a number of products that are about to go on promotion. First, expand the Products hierarchy so that the following products are visible:

Challah Bread
Panettone
Can Clam Chowder

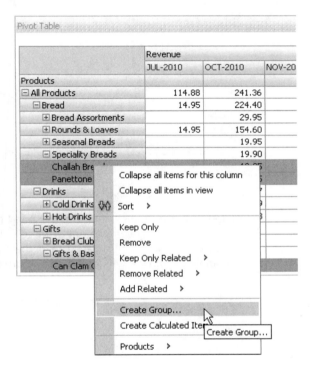

Hold down the CTRL key on your keyboard, select each of these dimension members, and then right-click and select Create Group from the menu that is displayed. When prompted, name the group **Promotion Products**, and you should then see the new group with a total and the products displayed under it in the Products hierarchy.

5. Now add row-level totals across the pivot table so that sales of each product are totaled across all months. To do so, right-click any one of the Month attribute columns and select Month | Show Column Level Grand Total | After Values.

Your final pivot table should look as in the following illustration.

	Revenue				Revenue
Products	JUL-2010	OCT-2010	NOV-2010	DEC-2010	
⊟ All Products	114.88	241.36	256.45	244.91	**857.60**
⊟ Bread	14.95	224.40	116.70	94.70	**450.75**
⊞ Bread Assortments		29.95	56.90		**86.85**
⊞ Rounds & Loaves	14.95	154.60	59.80	74.75	**304.10**
⊞ Seasonal Breads		19.95		19.95	**39.90**
⊟ Speciality Breads		19.90			**19.90**
Challah Bread		12.95			**12.95**
Panettone		6.95			**6.95**
⊟ Drinks	14.96	10.97	45.87	73.28	**145.08**
⊞ Cold Drinks		2.99	11.96	35.88	**50.83**
⊞ Hot Drinks	14.96	7.98	33.91	37.40	**94.25**
⊟ Gifts	84.97		5.99	24.99	**115.95**
⊞ Bread Clubs	84.97			24.99	**109.96**
⊟ Gifts & Baskets			5.99		**5.99**
Can Clam Chowder			5.99		**5.99**
⊟ Promotion Products		19.90	5.99		**25.89**
Can Clam Chowder			5.99		**5.99**
Challah Bread		12.95			**12.95**
Panettone		6.95			**6.95**

Once you have completed all of these steps, locate and expand the Selection Steps pane, below the compound layout that you have been working with, to see all of the steps that you have specified allocated to their respective dimensions. Each one of these steps is applied to the results set after it is returned by the analysis, and we will look next in more detail at what else you can do with selection steps.

⊟**Selection Steps**

List: [ALL ▼]

Measures

■ Fact Sales - Revenue

Dim Products – Products

◉ 1. Start with all members

◉ 2. Then, Remove 'Snacks'

◉ 3. Then, Add Promotion Products

↓ 4. Then, New Step...

Dim Times – Month

◉ 1. Start with all members

◉ 2. Then, Keep only members of "Dim Times"."Month" where "Sales - Fact Sales"."Fact Sales"."Revenue" is greater than 100

↓ 3. Then, New Step...

Selection Steps

Selection steps are as a set of options that become available when you right-click a Table or Pivot Table view in your analysis results. Let's take a look in more detail now at this feature and how it differs from and complements the filters feature.

What Are Selection Steps?   *Selection steps* are sets of instructions that limit, manipulate, or add to the results displayed in an analysis view. They are applied after the results are aggregated, unlike filters, which limit data down before results are returned to the user and work at the detail level. Selection steps, though, do not affect the totals displayed in the view because they work at the presentation level only, and any dimension members you remove from the analysis results are removed only from the lists of members displayed in analysis rows and columns.

Selection steps can be defined for attribute and hierarchical column types but not for measure columns. Attribute and hierarchical columns can reference measures in selection step definitions, however, such as to keep only those products selling more than target.

TIP
Having the selection steps feature makes it possible for end users to further manipulate data sets to add, remove, or keep certain dimension members and create new calculated items or groups for custom aggregations. You can also use selection steps to create analyses that previously would have taken several separate analyses to create, and you can filter and select members from hierarchical columns based on parentage, siblings, ancestors, and other hierarchical relationships.

How Do I Define Selection Steps for My Analysis?   When you create a new view for your analysis results, a set of default selection steps are created for each dimension in the criteria, with the selection steps returning all members. Subsequently, either you or the end user (if you permit this action) can apply selection steps to the results shown in the view to, for example, remove certain dimension members, create a new calculated item, and keep only those products that are the descendants of a particular product category.

These selection steps can be defined by the author in the analysis editor by clicking the Edit View button for the view, showing the Selection Steps pane, and then adding one or more selection steps to the initial one that returns all members.

Alternatively, either the analysis author or the end user of the analysis can right-click Table and Pivot Table views to add selection steps to either the selected member or the entire dimension. Note that you can restrict a user's ability to perform right-click actions, including using selection steps, by using the Analysis Properties button displayed above the Selected

Columns area when the Criteria tab is selected, which displays the Analysis Properties dialog box as shown in the illustration below.

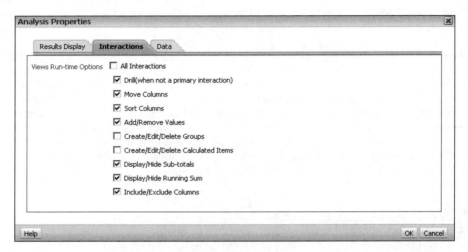

How Can I View the Selection Steps Defined for My Analysis? You can view what selection steps have been added to an analysis view within the analysis editor, or you can add a special type of view called a Selection Steps view to the analysis that lists what steps have been defined for each dimension.

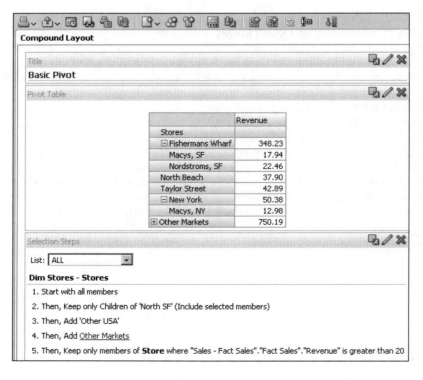

To view and work with selection steps in the analysis editor Results tab, click the Edit View button and then, when the view is opened for editing, locate and maximize the Selection Steps pane under the view.

To add a Selection Steps view to an analysis compound layout, ensure the Results tab is selected and then navigate to the Views pane, then select New View | Selection Steps. When the new view is listed in the Views pane, click it and click the Add View button to add it to the compound layout.

To see how selection steps are used in practice and how they complement filters that you might add to the analysis criteria, let's look at two examples using the Sales – Fact Sales subject area.

Example 1: Using Selection Steps to Refine the Results of an Analysis   In this first example, imagine that you are an analyst responsible for sales in the Central SF region and who has recently put together a promotion on lunch items at the bakery stores that you are responsible for. You are only interested in reporting against large-selling products, and another analyst has special responsibilities for bread items, the biggest selling product in your stores.

An analysis has been created by your BI team that, for all stores in San Francisco, shows sales of products over all time by region. (That is, there is a filter to return only those regions in the San Francisco area.) You now wish to use the selection steps feature in Oracle Business Intelligence to take this report and customize it to give you the information you need.

The analysis author has defined an initial view against the analysis results that has then been saved to the catalog and deployed on a dashboard. Note that to see the filters applied to an analysis alongside the view, you would select New View | Filters from the Views pane in the same way that you would add a Selection Steps view.

Compound Layout

Title

Pivot Table

Products△▽	Revenue		
	Central SF	North SF	West SF
⊟ All Products	224.04	429.02	78.26
⊟ Bread	94.70	239.35	41.85
⊞ Bread Assortments	29.95	56.90	
⊞ Rounds & Loaves	44.85	149.55	14.95
⊟ Seasonal Breads		19.95	19.95
Snowmen Bread		19.95	
Turkey Bread			19.95
⊟ Speciality Breads	19.90	12.95	6.95
Challah Bread	12.95	12.95	
Panettone	6.95		6.95
⊞ Drinks	28.42	80.76	27.42
⊞ Gifts	58.97	54.98	
⊞ Snacks	41.95	53.93	8.99

Filters

Region Name is equal to **Central SF, East SF, North SF, West SF**

Now, to create the particular analysis view that you require, you will need to implement the following changes to the report using selection steps:

- Create a new grouping made up of the Drinks and Snacks product categories, and call these **Lunchtime Products**. This gives you a separate custom aggregation of these two product categories that you can report on separately and drill into the product hierarchy.

- Show the Seasonal Breads and Speciality Breads types with just their totals and remove the detail of the products underneath, as these are handled by another analyst.

- Create a new, calculated member for the Regions attribute, combining Central and West SF into a new member called **Other SF**, removing the two regions from the view at the same time.

- Remove from the view all products whose revenue across all regions is less than $20.

To implement selection steps such as these using the initial analysis Pivot Table view given to the user, follow these steps:

1. Adding the Selection Steps view to the analysis would need to be carried out by the analysis author, assuming that the end user does not have the required privileges to edit and change analyses.

   To do this, the analysis author should open the analysis for editing. With the Results tab selected, select New View | Selection Steps to create the Selection Steps view.

2. With the new view opened for editing, click Done to return to the previous screen, and then to add it to the compound layout, click it within the Views pane, and select Add View.

3. Save the analysis back to the catalog, and the dashboard will then automatically show the updated version when the user next views the page. (We will look at dashboards in more detail later in this chapter.)

   The user can now view the analysis in the dashboard. At first, the analysis looks just like the analysis editor Results page, except that there is now an extra view in the compound layout to show the selection steps that have been applied. We will now start to manipulate the Pivot Table view within the analysis to return just the data that the analyst requires, without having to actually edit the analysis definition.

4. The first selection step that you will apply is to create the custom group to aggregate drinks and snacks product categories. To do this, hold down the CTRL key and select the Drinks and Snacks categories in the analysis; then right-click and select Create Group.

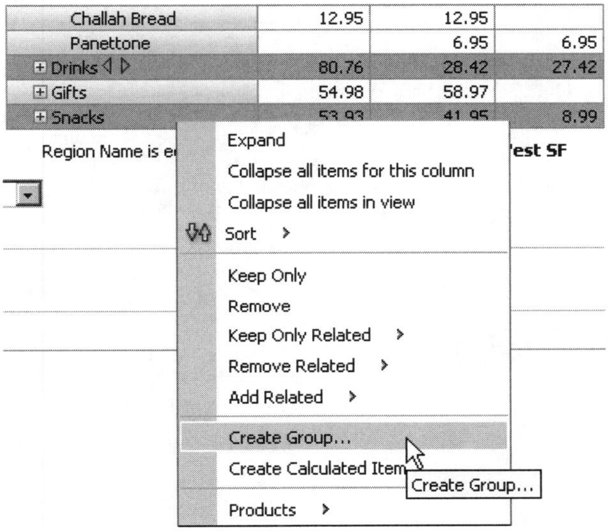

Challah Bread	12.95	12.95	
Panettone		6.95	6.95
⊞ Drinks ◁ ▷	80.76	28.42	27.42
⊞ Gifts	54.98	58.97	
⊞ Snacks	53.93	41.95	8.99

Region Name is e[...]   'est SF

Expand
Collapse all items for this column
Collapse all items in view
Sort   ›

Keep Only
Remove
Keep Only Related   ›
Remove Related   ›
Add Related   ›

Create Group...
Create Calculated Item   Create Group...

Products   ›

5. In the New Group dialog box, type in **Lunchtime Products** as the Display Label and click OK to close the dialog box.

   The new group will then be added to the end of the Products hierarchy but will not affect the overall total for products as it is a display-only hierarchy. Underneath the Pivot Table view, you will see this new selection step added to the set of selection steps for this dimension.

6. Next you need to remove the "children" under the Speciality Breads and Seasonal Breads product types, which are a number of bread products that you do not wish to see the detail for. As selection steps manipulate only the members that are shown in the view, not the totals, the totals for these bread product types will not be affected and will still be shown.

To do this, hold down the CTRL key and select the Seasonal Breads and Speciality Breads product types; then right-click and select Remove Related | Children. The Pivot Table view will now still show the Seasonal Breads and Speciality Breads totals, but now you will not be able to drill into the products that make up these totals.

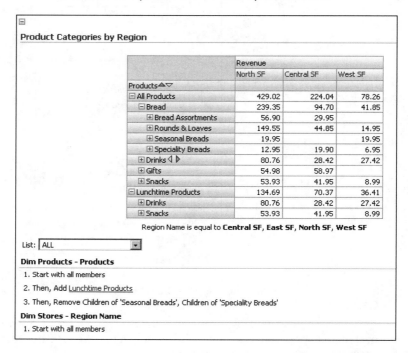

7. Now, as you are only responsible for the North SF region, you want to combine Central and West SF into a single, calculated member that you will then use to replace the individual regions in the Stores dimension. To do this, you will use the calculated item feature within selection steps.

   To create the calculated item, CTRL-click the Central SF and West SF members in the columns area of the Pivot Table view (which will actually select all of the rows in those columns, not just the column headers), right-click, and select Create Calculated Item.

8. When the New Calculated Item dialog box is shown, type in **Other SF** as the Display Label, and select Sum as the function. Finally, select the "Remove calculated item members from view" check box to remove the Central and West SF members from the view, and replace them with this new calculated member, or calculated *item*, in Oracle Business Intelligence terminology.

   Now, when you view the pivot table, the two regions that you just specified will have been replaced by the new calculated member, which contains the sum of the two previous members.

9. Remove from the view (but not from the totals) all products selling less than $20 across all regions in the view. To perform this final step, right-click any product (for example,

Banner Assortment in the bottom level of the Products hierarchy), select Products | Remove | Members Where Revenue Is Less Than | A Value At | Products, and when prompted, type in **20** as the value. Now, all products whose sales across all regions total less than 20 will be removed from the view.

Product Categories by Region

Products △▽	Revenue	
	Central SF	Other SF
⊟ All Products	224.04	507.28
⊟ Bread	94.70	281.20
⊟ Bread Assortments	29.95	56.90
Banner Assortment	29.95	0.00
Harvest Bread Trio		29.95
Holiday Bread Trio		26.95
⊞ Rounds & Loaves	44.85	164.50
⊞ Seasonal Breads		39.90
⊞ Speciality Breads	19.90	19.90
⊞ Drinks	28.42	108.18
⊞ Gifts	58.97	54.98
⊞ Snacks	41.95	62.92
⊟ Lunchtime Products	70.37	171.10
⊞ Drinks	28.42	108.18
⊞ Snacks	41.95	62.92

Region Name is equal to **Central SF, East SF, North SF, West SF**

List: ALL ▼

Dim Products - Products

1. Start with all members
2. Then, Add Lunchtime Products
3. Then, Remove Children of 'Seasonal Breads', Children of 'Speciality Breads'
4. Then, Remove members of **Product** where "Sales - Fact Sales"."Fact Sales"."Revenue" is less than 20

Dim Stores - Region Name

1. Start with all members
2. Then, Add Other SF

Finally, while the changes you have made to this analysis view within the dashboard cannot be saved back to the catalog as part of the analysis definition, you can save them as a dashboard customization instead and reapply them either on demand or as the default when you view this dashboard again. See the section "Enabling Dashboard Customizations" later in this chapter, for more on saving and applying dashboard customizations.

Example 2: Using Selection Steps to Make Hierarchical Selections of Members Another typical use of selection steps is to make selections of dimension members, based on the dimension hierarchy, when working with hierarchical columns. Filters that you create for your analysis criteria cannot be applied to hierarchical columns, though you can include a filter on one of the attribute columns included in the hierarchy to restrict returned values for a particular level in a hierarchy.

Selection steps, though, give you full access to the dimension hierarchy when making selections. This is particularly useful to users of OLAP databases such as Essbase or Oracle OLAP who are used to working exclusively with hierarchies when creating dimension member selections. Note, however, that, as long as you have defined a column in the subject area as a hierarchical column, you can still make hierarchical member selections using selection steps, regardless of the data source type, even if your data source is a relational database such as Oracle Database.

When you create selection steps using a hierarchical column, you can either keep, remove, or add dimension members:

- **Keep** This option removes all members in the hierarchy besides the selected members, together with their descendants.

- **Remove** This option removes the selected members, plus their descendants.

- **Add** This option adds back in the members that you specify, as long as they were in the original result set returned by the analysis view.

When specifying members to add through their hierarchical relationships, you can reference the following relationship types:

- **Children** This selects all of the members directly below that member in the hierarchy (the "children").

- **Parents** This selects the member above this member in the hierarchy (its "parent").

- **Siblings** This selects those dimension members at the same level in the hierarchy as this member (that is, members that share the same parent, or "siblings").

- **Descendants** This selects all members that descend from this member (this is, children, children of children, and so on).

- **Ancestors** This selects those members from whom the selected member is descended.

- **Leaves** This selects those dimension members who are descended from this member and are at the lowest ("leaf") level of the hierarchy.

Note also that, when making a hierarchical member selection, you can specify whether the dimension member you click is also included in the selection, as well as make member selections by their hierarchy level and family relationships.

Apart from making selections through hierarchical relationships and levels, another advantage that selection steps has for OLAP-style analysis is the ability to select members for display through a hierarchical picker. This allows you to drill into the hierarchy and select members in that way rather than having to remember which level a member can be found at and then placing a filter on that level. In the following scenario, we will see some of these features in action, again using the Sales – Fact Sales subject area.

In this scenario, you are a manager responsible for all stores outside of San Francisco with some responsibility for concessions that run in stores and are attached to local stores. You are considering placing some products on promotion and are particularly interested in looking at the top five products sold by the Fishermans Wharf store in San Francisco, which is the company's "flagship" store.

Before the introduction of selection steps, this type of analysis would have required you to create two separate analyses to return the data you required, one of which would have returned the top five products for the Fishermans Wharf store, which would then have acted as the filter values for a second analysis that showed sales for the stores you were interested in. Typically referred to as "multipass" queries, these are much easier to set up with selection steps.

In the next example, you will create an initial analysis and a Pivot Table view that includes the Store and Product hierarchical columns, along with the Revenue measure, so that the Pivot Table view at the start looks like the illustration below.

Then, you will use selection steps to alter the result set in the following way:
   To do this, you will need to implement the following:

- In addition to the default All Stores member, include just the North CA, South CA, and Other USA members, plus their descendants.

- Remove concessions from the remaining members, as you will add these back in later as their own custom group.

- Create a new calculated item (member) called San Francisco to sum the total of the North SF, East SF, Central SF, and West SF regions, and then save this calculated item to the catalog so you can reuse it later on.

- Create a new group called All Concessions and include in it all of the members at the Concession level across the company.

Then, for the products dimension, you will do the following:

■ Keep only the leaf members (that is, products, another way of selecting members from the lowest Product level in this balanced hierarchy).

■ From those products, keep only the ones that are in the top five products by revenue for the Fishermans Wharf store.

To create these steps, you would therefore do the following, which uses a variety of different ways to create selection steps to show the different creation options:

1. Starting with the initial Pivot Table view described earlier, ensure that the Results tab is selected and that the Selection Steps pane is visible.

2. Within the Selection Steps pane, locate the Dim Stores – Stores area and click the Then, New Step link under the initial step that selects all members.

3. The first step you will add will retain just the North CA, South CA, and Other USA regions and will remove the other regions from the view but preserve the correct total at the All Stores level.

   With the menu that appears when you click the Then, New Step link, choose the Select Members item. The New Member Step dialog box will then be displayed. Drill into the Dim Stores.Store hierarchy and, using the Move button, add the North CA, South CA, and Other USA members to the Selected area.

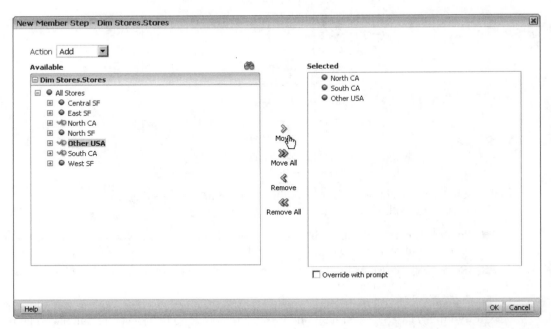

4. Remove concessions from any members that remain in the Stores hierarchy. To do so, right-click any member in the hierarchy and select Stores | Remove | Members At Hierarchy Levels. When the Select Levels dialog box is shown, click the Concession level and click OK.

5. Create a new calculated item (member) to show revenue for stores in the San Francisco region. This time you will create the selection step by clicking the New Calculated Item button in the toolbar above the view to display the New Calculated Item dialog box. Using this dialog box, select or enter the following values:

   Display Label: San Francisco
   Values From: Dim Stores.Stores
   Function: Sum
   Selected members: Central SF, East SF, West SF, North SF
   Remove calculated item members from view: [*selected*]

6. The final change you will make to the Stores dimension is to create the All Concessions group. To do this, click the New Group button in the toolbar and enter the following values into the New Group dialog box using the Stores hierarchy to locate the Nordstroms, SF, and Macys SF concessions that have Fishermans Wharf as their parent, the Macys NY concession that has New York as its parent, and the SFO concession that has the North CA region as its parent:

   Display Label: All Concessions
   Values From: Dim Stores.Stores
   Selected members: Nordstroms SF, Macys SF, Macys NY, SFO

   When you then view the dimension in the Pivot Table view, note how the group can be drilled into from the All Concessions level, while the calculated item is just a total that cannot be drilled into further.

7. As this calculated item and group may be useful in other analyses, you can add it to the catalog by clicking the link containing the calculated item or group name in the Selection Steps view, and then select Save Calc Item or Save Group from the menu that appears.

   Then, in future, when you wish to use this calculated item or group in a selection step for its respective dimension hierarchies, click the Then, New Step link and select Add Groups Or Calculated Items | Select Existing Groups or Calculated Items and navigate to the item in the catalog to add it to your list of selection steps.

8. Replace the contents of the Products dimension with just the lowest level product members. To do this, right-click any member in the Products dimension and select Keep Only Related | Leaves.

   As you did not keep members using the Including Selected menu option when applying the selection step, only the leaf members (products) will be retained, removing even the All Products member.

9. Now, to retain only those products that were in the top five for the Fishermans Wharf branch, you can create another selection step by using the Selection Steps pane or right-clicking the Pivot Table view.

   In this instance, we will use the right-click method. Right-click one of the members in the Products dimension and select Products | Keep Only | Based On A Custom Condition.

10. When the New Condition Step dialog box is shown, click the Condition Type drop-down menu to display the list of condition templates grouped into three types: Exception, Top/ Bottom, and Match.

11. To create the condition we require, select the "Top 10 based on X" condition template, and the dialog box will then change to give you all of the options for this template. Start by setting the "top 5 products" part of the condition by selecting or entering the following values:

Condition Type: Top 10 based on X
Action: Keep only Product
Operator: is top
Rank: 5

The measure that you wish to use in this condition is the Revenue measure, but you only want to consider revenue for the Fishermans Wharf store, not all stores. To do this, select these values:

Measure: Fact Sales.Revenue
Dim Stores.Stores member: Fishermans Wharf

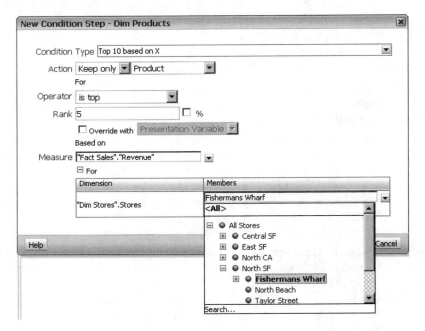

12. To remind yourself what selection steps have been applied to the view, add the Selection Steps view to the compound layout. In the Views pane, select New View | Selection Steps, and then click Done to close the view editor.

13. With the new Selection Steps view selected in the Views panel, click the Add View button to add it to the compound layout. Your final compound layout should then look as in the following illustration.

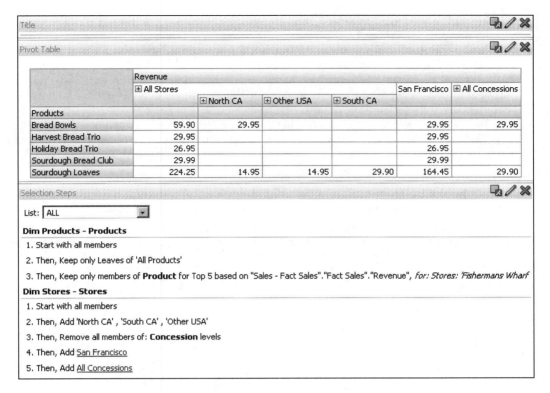

As you can see, selection steps give you some powerful ways to manipulate the result set returned by an analysis. You can add and remove members, create custom members and aggregates, and filter members based on conditions that you define in the analysis editor or that users define by right-clicking the analysis view in a dashboard. Now though, let's move on from tables and pivot tables and start looking at some of the graphical ways that you can present data to users.

Graph Views

Graphs are one of the most effective ways of communicating information on the dashboards you develop for users because you can quickly show the relationship between measures and dimension attributes in a visual, easy-to-understand way. A line chart that shows sales increasing or decreasing over time, or a pie chart that shows how customers break down by type or geography, is often a more effective way of communicating the meaning behind data than lists of numbers.

Oracle Business Intelligence provides a number of graph types that you can add to your analysis, along with maps, funnel views, and gauge views. Some graph types can work with just a single measure and dimension, while others work best with two or more measures. All graph types have a similar set of controls for allocating dimensions to axes and for enabling features such as 3-D displays and graph sizes. You can use graph views to replace Table and Pivot Table views in an analysis compound layout or display them beside Table and Pivot Table views, or you can use the View Selector view described later in this chapter to allow users to switch between a graph and a Table or Pivot Table view.

Graph views, like Table and Pivot Table views, are added to an analysis using the Results tab in the analysis editor and are typically included in the compound layout along with a Title view before being added to a dashboard. You can use selection steps to further manipulate the results returned by the analysis in the same way as for Table, Pivot Table, and other views, and graphs also will respond to actions such as drilling, navigation actions, and invocation actions if you have defined these in the repository and analysis criteria.

Let's start by creating a simple bar chart graph view, and then later on we'll look in more detail at the different types of graphs available to you within the analysis editor and how you can configure the various graphing options.

To create a simple bar chart graph using the Dim Products.Product Category, Dim Times.Month, and Fact Sales.Sale Amount and Sale Amount Target columns from the Sales – Fact Sales subject area, follow these steps:

1. Create a new analysis and include the columns in the criteria. Once the columns have been added to the Selected Columns area, click the Results tab, which initially will display a Title view and Table view within the compound layout.

2. To add a new graph view directly into the compound layout, click the New View button in the Compound Layout toolbar. When you click this button, you can select between the different view types; in this instance, select New View | Graph | Bar | Default (Vertical).

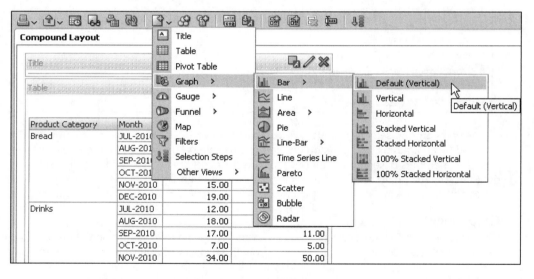

Alternatively, you can click the New View button within the Views pane, select the view as before, close its "edit" mode, and then use the Add View button within the same pane to add the view into the compound layout.

3. Your graph should now be added to the compound layout, below the existing Table view. Delete the Table view from the compound layout by using the Remove View From Compound Layout button on the top right-hand side of the Table view, leaving just the Graph view under the Title view.

4. Initially, this bar graph will probably show both the Sale Amount and Sale Amount Target measures, as well as both the Product and Times dimensions in the X axis. While showing actual and target measures as bars next to each other makes sense, you probably would want to show just one of the dimensions in the X axis.

To edit the graph view to make this change, click the Edit View button at the top right-hand corner of the view to open the view in edit mode.

5. The graph view will now typically display a preview in the top half of the pane, with the Layout pane underneath it. (The Selection Steps pane is typically displayed under these two, initially minimized.)

In the Layout pane, there are areas for graph prompts and sections, which perform a role similar to Table and Pivot Table views. Under these sections is an area that changes for each graph type and allows you to specify which measures and dimension columns are used in the bars, for this graph type, and for other X and Y axis data elements in other graph types.

To display only Product Category in the X axis and to also allow the end user to filter the graph on just particular months, click the Months item in the Group By (Horizontal Axis) area and move it into the Graph Prompts area. Now the graph shows only Products as the bars and has a drop-down menu for Month at the top of the view.

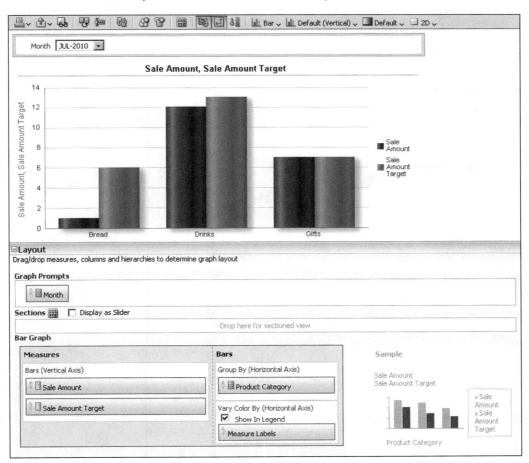

6. Click the Done button to close the view editor, and you will see the graph view in the compound layout, ready for you to save the analysis to the catalog and then include it in a dashboard page.

Now that you know the basics of creating a graph view, one of the most important decisions you will make is choosing which type of graph to use. Some types of graphs are better suited to displaying data in a time series, such as sales over time, while others are better for comparing two or more measures or comparing data on items that are not part of a series. Let's take a look now at the types of graphs available within the analysis editor and what types of data and scenarios they are best suited to showing.

Choosing Between Graph Types   Oracle Business Intelligence provides a number of graph types that you can use to create views of the results returned by your analyses. You can see a listing of all the graph types by selecting New View | Graph from the Results page in the analysis editor. The graph types include the following:

- **Bar**
- **Line**
- **Area**
- **Pie**
- **Line-bar**
- **Time-series line**
- **Pareto**
- **Scatter**
- **Bubble**
- **Radar**

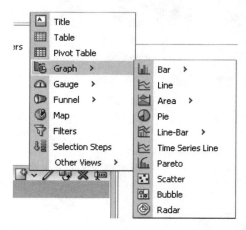

So how do you select an appropriate graph type for the data you are displaying in your analysis? In fact, certain types of graphs are more suited to certain types of analyses.

For example, line graphs are good at displaying changes and progressions in values over time. If you wanted to show how sales and revenue have progressed over the last six months, a line chart, possibly showing different lines for different product dimension members, regions, or actual and target measures, would be a good way of showing the trend of data over time.

Similarly, bar graphs are useful for showing values for a dimension where the members are not in a series. For example, you might want to show store sales in a graph, and because stores are not naturally in a series (unlike days, for example) a horizontal or vertical bar chart would make most sense for this data set.

Pie graphs are great for showing how a measure breaks down into proportions, for example showing how total sales break down by product category or by type of customer. By choosing line, bar, and pie charts correctly, you will communicate the message from your data to your users far more effectively.

Oracle Business Intelligence also provides some variants on these graph types. Stacked bar charts, for example, are useful for showing how a measure, such as revenue by a set of region names, also breaks down within each region by product category, giving you an extra dimension to your view.

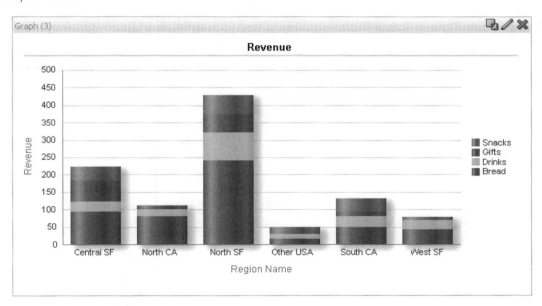

A variation, the 100 percent stacked bar graph, like a pie graph is useful for showing how a measure in total is broken down by another dimension, such as total sales for each region broken down by product category.

Area graphs (and their variation, 100 percent area graphs) are good for showing how a measure such as revenue changes over time. They include a breakdown within the measure to show how the measure's value has changed proportionately over a period of time.

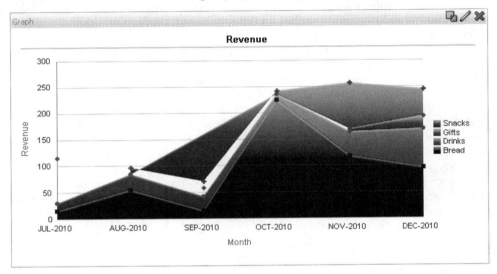

Other types of graphs you might want to use include pareto, scatter, and line-bar graphs. Pareto graphs shows how a measure breaks down into components and how those components combine over time, for example, to make up the final total. Scatter graphs show the values for two independent variables in a scattered "cluster" and are useful for observing relationships and trends in large data sets. Line-bar graphs show two or more measures over a series such as time but with one measure (for example, Sale Amount) shown as a set of bars and another (for example, Sale Amount Target) shown as a line. The following illustration shows an example of a line-bar graph.

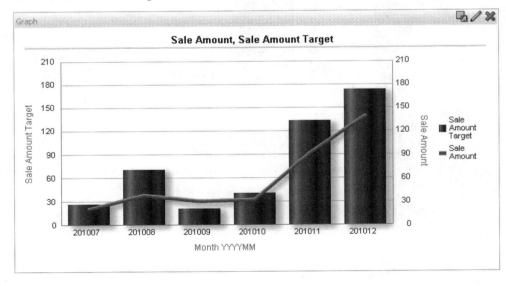

Graphs can be set via the toolbar at the top of the graph view editor as either two-dimensional or three-dimensional, and this variety of styles can be useful. Be careful, though, not to make the style of the graph too visually distracting; otherwise, you will take away from the message the graph is meant to provide.

Enabling Section Sliders   If you have a data set that has a time or date element, or any other dimension that is part of a series, you might want to consider adding a slider to the graph view to allow the user to "play" the graph along this series. For example, you might want to show how regional revenue breaks down by product type using a slider that allows the user to animate the graph and see how the proportions change over time.

To enable a slider for your graph view, you will need to add the dimension attribute to the Sections section in the Layout pane for the graph view and select the Display As Slider check box.

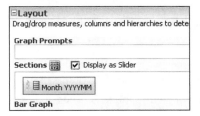

Now when the graph view is displayed, instead of the Sections setting causing a number of separate graphs to be displayed, a single graph is shown with a slider at the top. Either the slider can be moved manually by the user or the Play and Return buttons can be used to animate through the time series.

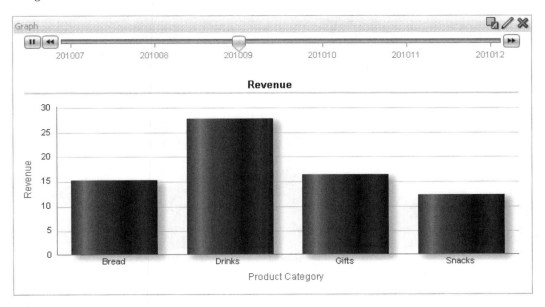

Setting Graph and Analysis Properties   Graph views, like all views within the analysis editor, have property values that you can update or change. For example, you can use the Graph Properties dialog box to change the canvas height and width, decide whether the user can zoom and scroll into the data set or whether the graph is animated on display, and the scale, titles and labels for the graph.

To access the Graph Properties dialog box, click the Edit View control when the graph view is shown in the analysis editor Results page, and then locate and click the Edit Graph Properties button in the view toolbar.

The **Graph Properties** dialog box has tabs for

- **General**   This tab is for setting canvas height and width, animation settings, and zoom and scroll settings.
- **Style**   This tab is for setting the style of the plot area, legends, canvas, and borders.
- **Scale**   This tab is for setting the axis limits, axis scale, and scale markers.
- **Titles and Labels**   This tab is for setting the graph title, axis titles, and various labels.

In addition to properties dialog boxes for each type of view, you can also edit the values of properties for the analysis as a whole by using the Analysis Properties button and dialog box that is shown when you return back to the Compound Layout view in the Results page.

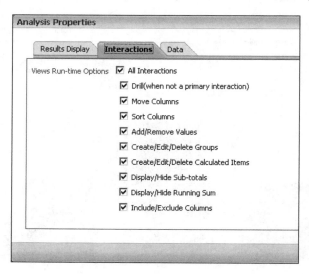

Using this dialog box, among other settings you can determine whether a user can create totals and subtotals, custom groups, swap around rows and columns, and perform other interactions on the analysis results once the analysis is published to a dashboard.

Gauge Views

Gauges are a special type of graph that can be used to show a measure against a target, with thresholds defined to categorize performance into bands such as "below target," "on target," and "above target." Although technically a type of graph, gauges have many settings and visual styles that are unique to it and therefore they have their own view type within the analysis editor—the Gauge view.

When you define a Gauge view, there are a couple of key decisions you will have to make to determine how the gauge displays its status, apart from whether it will be shown as a set of dials, bars, or bulbs:

- Will you allow the Gauge view to choose the start and end values for the gauge range, or should the view determine these values dynamically?

- Will you allow the view to dynamically set the threshold limits for the standard red, yellow, and green states, or will you customize the limits and/or the states?

- Do you want the gauge to display values as the default percentage to target (0–100 percent) based on either the dynamic range or a range you specify, or do you want it to display the actual measure values?

Typically, you would want to provide your own settings for these aspects of the Gauge view; therefore, let's take a look at an example where we wish to turn the Table view shown in the following illustration into a set of gauges showing performance to target for sales of product categories by region.

In this example, we would like to:

- Display a set of gauges showing % as a percentage, with the % as a gauge prompt.
- Run the gauge scale from 0–250 and display it as a percentage.
- Set the gauge states to be Under Target (for values up to 100 percent), On Target (for values between 100 percent and 200 percent), and Above Target (for values above 200 percent).
- Initially display the gauges as dials but also create a version that uses horizontal bars instead.

To create the analysis that will use the Gauge view, the following columns and column formulas will be selected for the analysis criteria and are taken from the Sales – Fact Sales subject area:

- Dim Stores.Region Name
- Dim Products.Product Category

■ Fact Sales.Sale Amount vs. Target %, defined as follows:

```
((("Fact Sales"."Sale Amount"-"Fact Sales"."Sale Amount Target")/
"Fact Sales"."Sale Amount Target")+1)*100
```

Once the analysis criteria are created, switch to the Results tab in the analysis editor and then follow these steps to create this gauge:

1. The Compound Layout view for the analysis should contain a Title and a Table view. To create the gauge, select New View | Gauge | Default (Dial) from the Views pane.

2. The Gauge view will now open it edit mode. There will be three panes visible on the right-hand side of the analysis editor: a preview of the gauge, the Layout pane, and a Settings pane, which allows you to define the thresholds and states for the Gauge view.

3. By default, the Gauge view will create gauges for every combination of dimension in the criteria; in our instance, we want the Dim Stores.Region Name column to be displayed as a gauge prompt, so locate this column in the Gauge Rows area and drag-and-drop it onto the Gauge Prompts area.

   The preview of the gauge should now show a dashboard prompt and gauges for the different product categories that have data recorded against them for the particular region selected in the gauge prompt.

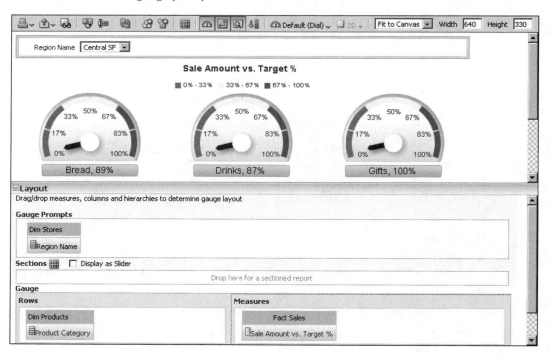

4. When they are first created, gauges display measure values as percentages against a dynamically determined range of values. For our gauges, though, we wish to define the range as being from 0 percent to 300 percent, and to change the gauge to use this range

you need to edit the Gauge view properties. To do so, locate the Edit Gauge Properties button above the gauge preview and click it.

Edit gauge properties

5. When the Gauge Properties dialog box is shown, click the Scale tab. To manually define the start and end range of the gauge scale, select the Specify radio button within the Scale And Limits area, and then enter the values **0** and **250** in the Maximum and Minimum fields, respectively.

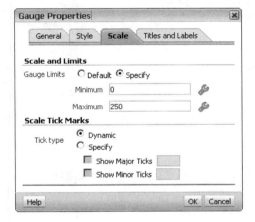

6. Similarly, to have the Gauge view show actual values on the scale rather than the default 0 to 100 percent, click the Titles and Labels tab and then click the icon next to the Scale Labels label.

7. When the Scale Labels dialog box is displayed, select the Display Options tab and change the Scale Labels setting to Actual Value to display the scale labels as amounts rather than percentages; then click the Number Format tab and set the Treat Numbers As setting to Percentage.

8. When you close the properties dialog box, the gauge will show the correct scale and scale label format, but the thresholds that define the statuses are not the exact values you wish to use, and the statuses do not have a name yet. To define the statuses and the thresholds between them, locate the Settings pane below the Layout pane and expand it so that you can see its contents.

   By default, the Gauge view has three statuses corresponding to green, yellow, and red colors. You can add additional statuses to this list by clicking the Add Thresholds button under the list of existing thresholds, but for now we will stay with the default three statuses.

9. Give names to the three default statuses. Click the menu icon next to the Status definition and select the Specify Label option. Enter **Above Target**, **On Target**, and **Under Target** as the three status names.

By default, the threshold limits between statuses are set dynamically to divide the scale by the number of statuses. (This may also be defined dynamically, but in our case we have set it manually.) We wish to set the thresholds differently because stopping the scale at 250 makes each threshold an odd number, so use the menu icons next to the Threshold text boxes to set the thresholds to 100 (between the red and yellow statuses) and 200 (between the yellow and green statuses).

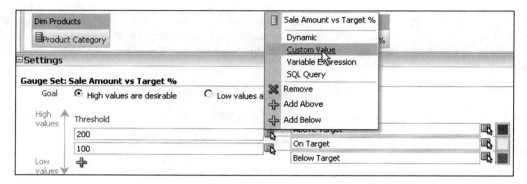

10. Click Done to close the view editor, and then click the Add View button in the Views pane to add the view to the compound layout after first removing the default Table view from the layout using its Remove View From Compound Layout button.

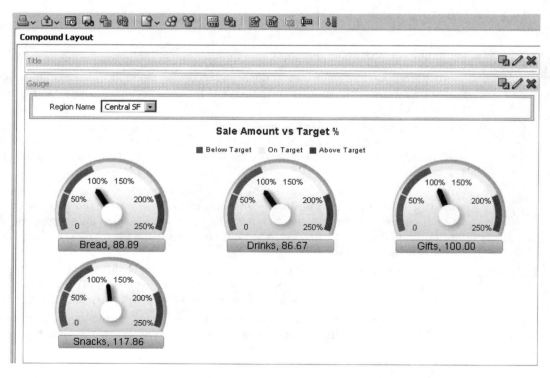

NOTE
You can change the Gauge view to display the gauges as bar (vertical or horizontal) or bulb gauges by clicking the Edit View button again and then selecting the gauge type from the drop-down menu in the view toolbar.

Now let's look at another type of visualization available within Oracle Business Intelligence: the funnel view.

Funnel Views

A *Funnel view* is a specialized type of graph used to show performance across a process or set of steps. For example, your organization may have a sales process where opportunities are first established, a proposal is then written, negotiation takes place, and then sometimes an order is received. As not every inquiry will result in a proposal and not every proposal will in the end result in a sale, the process can be visualized as a "funnel" with large numbers of inquiries coming in one end and a progressively smaller set of resulting proposals, negotiations, and eventual sales.

Funnel views require a minimum of one dimension for the stages in the process and two measures, one for the count at each stage and one for each stage's target. When you then come to display the measures in the funnel chart, each measure is categorized by a set of statuses with settings and thresholds that you can define in the view editor.

For example, consider a situation where stores in the organization start selling catering services to local businesses and consumers in the area. To track sales performance, each store has a sales process that involves four stages:

- Receive an inquiry over the phone, or in person at the store
- Provide a quote, with not every inquiry being suitable for a quote
- Receive the preliminary order from the customer, which can be cancelled
- Deliver the goods, which is considered a completed sale

Each store has a target for each of these stages, and it records the number of inquiries, quotes, orders, and deliveries in a set of tables that have been imported into the Oracle BI Repository and exposed as a subject area (Fact – Sales Catering) in the catalog. You now wish to create a Funnel view that uses the stages in the sales process (the Catering Sale Stage Name column in the following list) to create the sections in the funnel. You will use Store Name as a prompt so that users can switch between stores and see where bottlenecks and problems might be occurring in the sales process.

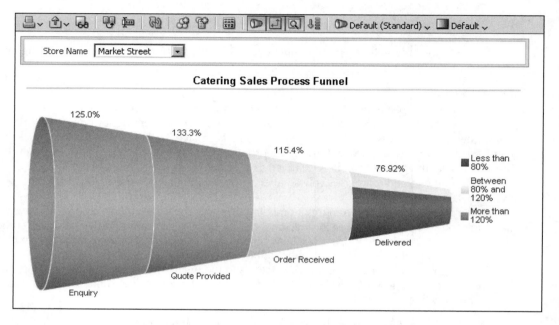

To create the analysis that will create a Funnel view like this, the following columns from the Sales – Catering Sales subject area have been added to the analysis criteria:

Dim Catering Sales Stage.Catering Sale Stage Name
Dim Stores.Store Name
Fact Catering Sales.Number
Fact Catering Sales.Target

To create the Funnel view based on this type of criteria, follow these steps:

1. With the analysis editor open and the columns from the preceding list added to the criteria, click the Results tab to show the analysis results. By default, the compound layout will contain a Title and a Table view.

2. To add the Funnel view, navigate to the Views pane and select New View | Funnel | Default (Standard). The Funnel view will then be displayed on the right-hand side of the screen, open for editing.

3. As with the Gauge view, the Funnel view has two panes below the view preview pane, one for the layout and one for the settings. Use the Layout pane to ensure that the dimension attribute representing the business process (in this case, Dim Catering Sales

Stage.Catering Sale Stage Name) is placed in the Stage area and that the Actual and Target areas have the measures representing the actual amounts (in this case, Fact Catering Sales. Number) and the target amount (in this case, Fact Catering Sales.Target) placed on them.

In this example, the additional dimension attribute, Dim Stores.Store Name, is moved to the Graph Prompts area so that store names will then be displayed as a drop-down menu at the top of the view.

4. In the same way as for Gauge views, you can use the Settings pane to define the statuses of each process step (set by default to green, yellow, and red) and the threshold values that separate each status.

5. Once complete, click Done to close the view editor, and then add the new view to the compound layout by selecting the Funnel view in the Views pane and clicking the Add View button.

Column Selector and View Selector Views

Column Selector and View Selector views are a special type of view found under the New View | Other Views menu in the Views pane. They do not display data themselves but instead amend or switch between other views. Using a Column Selector view, you can change the column that is selected for a particular position in the analysis criteria, while a View Selector view allows the user to switch between table, graph, and other types of views to display data in the way that they prefer.

For example, consider a situation where you want to display revenue information for a particular product category but you think the end user might also be interested in viewing sale amount or event sale amount vs. target information instead. Using a Column Selector view, you can provide a drop-down menu with different measures that the user can choose to display instead of your original choice:

1. Start by creating an analysis using columns from the Sales – Fact Sales subject area. Create the analysis using New | Analysis, and select the following columns for the criteria:

    Dim Products.Product Category
    Fact Sales.Revenue

2. Click the Results tab to see the Title and Table views that are created for you, by default, in the compound layout.

3. You now wish to add the ability for the user to switch the Fact Sales.Revenue measure for either the Sale Amount measure or a calculated measure called Fact Sales.Amount Sold vs. Target %. To do so, navigate to the Views pane and select New View | Other Views | Column Selector.

4. The Column Selector view will now open in edit mode. For any column you wish to make available for changing by the end user, select the Include Selector check box under the column name.

To make the Revenue column changeable, select the check box under it, and then locate and double-click the Fact Sales.Amount Sold column in the Subject Areas pane to add it to the list.

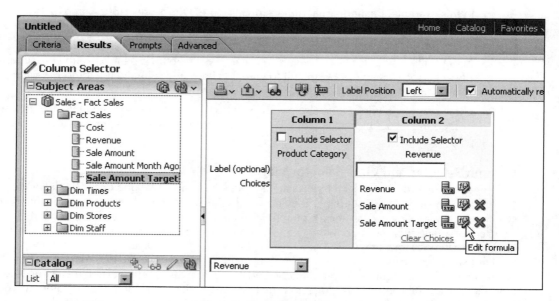

5. To add the Sale Amount vs. Target % measure to this column's list, you should first locate and then double-click the Fact Sales.Sale Amount Target column to add it, and then click the Edit Formula button to edit the formula so that the formula reads as follows:

```
((("Fact Sales"."Sale Amount"-"Fact Sales"."Sale Amount Target")/
"Fact Sales"."Sale Amount Target")+1)*100
```

6. Then edit the column heading so it reads **Sale Amount vs. Target %**. Once complete, click Done to close the view editor.

7. To add the column selector to your compound layout, locate it within the view listing in the Views pane and click the Add View button, moving the view to between the Table and Title views once it has been added, initially by default, under the existing Title view.

You will now be able to use the Column Selector view to change the column that is displayed for that particular position in the criteria by using the drop-down menu in the view.

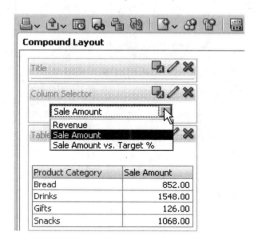

If you then switch back to the Criteria tab in the analysis editor, you will see that the column name in that position has now changed to Column Group (default: Revenue) to reflect this change.

As another example, consider a situation where you wish to create an analysis that shows revenue figures for regions initially in a table, but you also want to allow the user to change the view so that the measure is displayed either as a bar chart or a pie chart that shows the breakdown of revenue across all regions. To do this, you will use the View Selector view:

1. Create a new analysis using the Dim Stores.Region Name and Fact Sales.Revenue measures from the Sales – Fact Sales subject area. Once complete, switch to the Results tab to see the initial results of the analysis, displayed as a Title and a Table view.

2. Use the New View | Graph | Bar | Default (Vertical) menu option in the Views pane to add a new bar graph to the analysis. Click Done once the view editor opens to accept the default view settings.

3. Repeat step 2, but this time use the New View menu to add a pie graph to the analysis, again accepting the default settings once the view editor opens and clicking Done to close the editor afterward.

4. To define the View Selector view, select New View | Other Views | View Selector from the Views pane to open a new View Selector view for editing. Using the Available Views list, add the Table, Graph, and Graph:2 views to the Views Included list, and enter **Select Preferred View** as the caption.

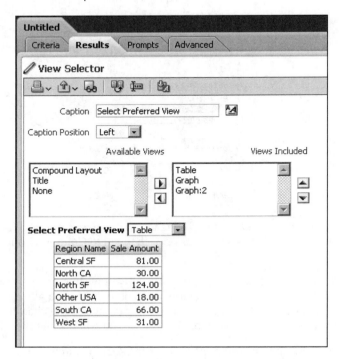

5. Unlike the Column Selector view, which is added to the compound layout along with any existing views, the View Selector view replaces all of these views in the compound layout (except the Title view, which remains).

   To add the View Selector view to the compound layout, click the Remove View From Compound Layout button above the existing Title view in the compound layout, and then use the Add View button in the Views pane to add the new View Selector view to the layout in its place.

6. You might have noticed that the bar and pie graph views are listed as Graph and Graph:2 in the list of views in the View Selector drop-down menu. To rename these views to more meaningful names, select each one in turn in the Views pane, click the Rename View button, and enter your preferred view name into the dialog box.

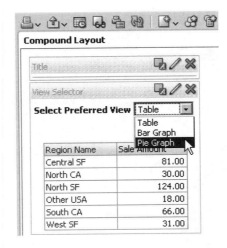

When you now look at your view results, the View Selector view will allow users to switch between the views that you have provided using the view names that you specified in the last step of the preceding list.

Map Views

Almost every data set used in business intelligence applications includes an element of geographic data, in the same way that most business intelligence data sets include dates, times, and measures.

Customers and suppliers, for example, are located in cities, regions, and countries, while sales and other business activities take place in different towns, cities, or company locations. Since maps are one of the most effective ways that geographic data can be displayed, showing your business intelligence data in the form of maps such as the one shown in Figure 6-8 can be a very effective way to visualize your data.

Map views are another type of view that you can add to your analyses, and they allow you to display the results of your data in the form of maps, with overlays in the form of charts, icons, and text. Before you can make use of map views in your analysis, though, you must first source some spatial data and configure it for use with Oracle MapViewer, another part of Oracle Fusion Middleware that comes preinstalled as part of Oracle Business Intelligence. Oracle MapViewer is responsible for rendering the maps that you can then include with your analyses.

In this part of the chapter, we will first look at how Oracle Business Intelligence takes the data from your repository and turns it into a map view, as well as how you can go about obtaining some suitable mapping spatial data for use with Oracle MapViewer. Then we will look at how you configure MapViewer to work with your repository data and how you can create analyses that include map views in their results.

Obtaining Mapping Data and Configuring Oracle MapViewer   Although mapping is built into Oracle Business Intelligence in the form of Oracle MapViewer and the map view type that makes use of MapViewer, you first need to obtain some spatial data in the Oracle MapViewer format before you can render maps using map views. Note that map views in Oracle Business Intelligence require you to have an Oracle database to hold this spatial data because Oracle MapViewer, on which the feature is built, works only with Oracle spatial data sources.

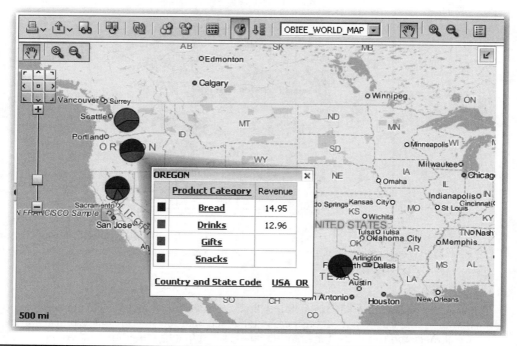

FIGURE 6-8. *An example map view*

The most common source of data in this format is Navteq, a company that has various partnering agreements with Oracle Corporation and that provides a set of mapping spatial data on the Oracle Technology Network web site that can be downloaded for free once you agree to their licensing terms. Other spatial data sets can be obtained from Navteq and from other vendors, but for the examples in this part of the chapter, we will use the free Navteq spatial data set that, at the time of writing, can be downloaded from http://www.oracle.com/technetwork/middleware/bi-foundation/obiee-samples-167534.html.

To install the Navteq spatial data set into an Oracle database, follow these steps:

1. On the database that holds your other source data, create a new user account to hold the Navteq data set, amending the connection details as appropriate:

```
sqlplus system/password@orcl
create user obiee_navteq identified by password;
grant connect, resource to obiee_navteq;
exit
```

2. Use the Oracle import (imp) utility to import the database export file provided as part of the Navteq download into this database account's schema, again amending filenames as appropriate:

```
imp obiee_navteq/password file=c:\temp\obiee_navteq.dmp
```

3. Run the following commands on your database server to register the map layers, tiles, and other spatial elements that are now in the obiee_navteq schema:

```
sqlplus obiee_navteq/password
insert into user_sdo_maps select * from my_maps;
insert into user_sdo_themes select * from my_themes;
insert into user_sdo_styles select * from my_styles;
insert into user_sdo_cached_maps select * from my_tile_cache;
commit;
exit
```

Next, you need to configure Oracle MapViewer to make use of this new mapping spatial data. Oracle MapViewer is another Java application that is installed along with Oracle Business Intelligence in the WebLogic application server, and you will now need to use MapViewer's web-based administration interface to register this new database schema and make its spatial data available for rendering as maps.

To configure Oracle MapViewer for use with Oracle Business Intelligence, follow these steps:

1. Using your web browser, navigate to the Oracle MapViewer web site, typically found at http://[*machine_name*]:port/mapviewer; for example:

    http://obisrv1:9704/mapviewer

2. When the Oracle MapViewer web site is displayed, locate the Admin icon in the top right-hand corner of the screen and click it. When prompted for a username and password, enter the same ones that you would normally use to log into Oracle Business Intelligence as an administrator (for example, weblogic/welcome1).

3. The first configuration step you will need to perform is to register a data source, which will point to the obiee_navteq schema that you created in the previous steps. (Other spatial data sources that you set up subsequently will need their own data sources created in the same way.)

    To create the data source, click the Configuration link on the left-hand side of the page. When the configuration page opens, a text box will display an XML file that defines the configuration for this installation of Oracle MapViewer.

    To add the data source to this file, scroll to the end of it and within the section named Predefined Data Sources but just before the </MapperConfig> section, add the following XML snippet to define the data source, changing the jdbc_host, jdbc_sid, and jdbc_port values appropriately for your source database:

```
<map_data_source name="obiee_navteq"
jdbc_host="localhost"
jdbc_sid="orcl"
jdbc_port="1521"
jdbc_user="obiee_navteq"
jdbc_password="!password"
jdbc_mode="thin"
number_of_mappers="3"
allow_jdbc_theme_based_foi="false"
 />
```

NOTE
The exclamation mark (!) in front of the password is mandatory and tells MapViewer to encrypt the password in this file when restarting.

4. Click the Save & Restart button to restart MapViewer and start using the new data source.

5. To check that the data source has been registered correctly, click the Datasources link on the left-hand side of the page. Your new data source will then be listed above a section to create a dynamic data source.

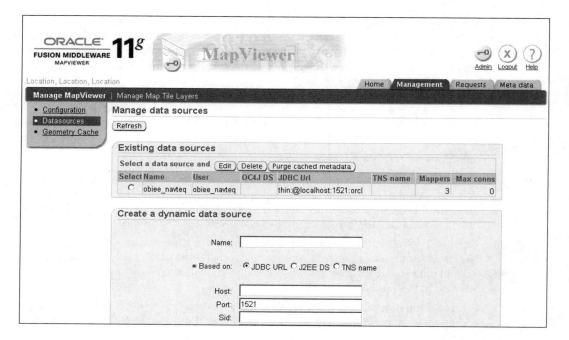

NOTE
Data sources created using this form will persist only while this particular instance of MapViewer is running and would be lost when you next restart the server running MapViewer and Oracle Business Intelligence, while data sources created in the configuration XML file persist between server reboots.

6. To see the maps (or *map tile layers,* in Oracle MapViewer terminology) that are provided by this data set, click the Manage Map Tile Layers link at the top of the page. For the Navteq data set we are using, there are a number of map tile layers that we could use, and in the following examples we will be focusing on two, OBIEE_SF_MAP1 and OBIEE_WORLD_MAP.

Now that we have imported the spatial data required for map rendering and have configured Oracle MapViewer so that it is aware of this spatial data, let's move on to Oracle Business Intelligence to configure the catalog and repository for map views.

Configuring the Catalog and Repository for Mapping   The mapping spatial data that you have imported into your Oracle database provides a number of "layers" that correspond to cities, regions, countries, other boundaries, and points of interest on a map. Each layer is typically represented by a table or set of tables with keys such as city or state names.

In the example using the Navteq sample data that was obtained and installed in the previous steps, there are actually a number of tables that provide these map layers. These tables have been set up especially for use with Oracle Business Intelligence:

OBIEE_CITY
OBIEE_COUNTRY
OBIEE_ISO_COUNTRY_STATE_CITY
OBIEE_STATE
OBIEE_STREETS
OBIEE_STREET_GEOMETRIES

Two of these tables, OBIEE_CITY and OBIEE_STATE, contain layer data that we can match to the stores and regions held in the Dim Stores logical table in the GCBC Repository and the Sales – Fact Sales and Sales – Fact Store Quality subject areas in the corresponding catalog.

Taking a look at the OBIEE_CITY and OBIEE_STATE layer tables in the Navteq data set, we can see two columns (OBIEE_CITY.CITY_NAME and OBIEE_STATE.STATE_ABBRV) containing city names and state name abbreviations that we can use with our store dimension:

```
SQL> select table_name from user_tables where table_name like 'OBIEE%';
TABLE_NAME
------------------------------
OBIEE_CITY
OBIEE_COUNTRY
OBIEE_ISO_COUNTRY_STATE_CITY
OBIEE_STATE
OBIEE_STREETS
OBIEE_STREET_GEOMETRIES
6 rows selected.
SQL> describe obiee_city
 Name                                      Null?    Type
 ----------------------------------------- -------- ----------------
 ISO_COUNTRY_CODE                                   VARCHAR2(3)
 CITY_NAME                                          VARCHAR2(255 CHAR)
 POPULATION                                         NUMBER(10)
 GEOMETRY                                           MDSYS.SDO_GEOMETRY
 DISPLAY_NAME                                       VARCHAR2(255 CHAR)
 STATE_PROVINCE_ABBRV                               VARCHAR2(255)
 STATE_PROVINCE                                     VARCHAR2(255)
 CTRY_CD3_CITY                                      VARCHAR2(255)
 CTRY_CD3_STATE_NAME_CITY                           VARCHAR2(255)
 CTRY_CD3_STATE_ABBRV_CITY                          VARCHAR2(255)
SQL> describe obiee_state
```

```
Name                                 Null?      Type
------------------------------------ --------   --------
STATE_NAME                                      VARCHAR2(255 CHAR)
ISO_COUNTRY_CODE                                VARCHAR2(5)
SQKM                                            NUMBER(11)
GEOMETRY                                        MDSYS.SDO_GEOMETRY
STATE_ABBRV                                     VARCHAR2(5 CHAR)
STATE_NAME_INITCAP                              VARCHAR2(255)
ISO_CTRY_CD_STATE_NAME                          VARCHAR2(255)
ISO_CTRY_CD_STATE_NAME_INITCAP                  VARCHAR2(255)
ISO_CTRY_CD_STATE_ABBRV                         VARCHAR2(40)
ISO_COUNTRY_CODE2                               VARCHAR2(2)
```

Note that, in most other cases, mapping data such as this will not set up tables specifically for Oracle Business Intelligence, but there will be tables containing similar layer data and layer keys that you can use. Consult your provider of spatial data for the details for your data set.

So far in this book and chapter, we have used the Dim Stores.Store Name and Dim Stores .Region Name logical and subject area columns for most of our analyses. However, the repository and catalog also contain four additional columns that were added to correspond with the OBIEE_ CITY.CITY_NAME and OBIEE_STATE.STATE_ABBRV columns provided with the mapping data set, and that we will then need to use when displaying analysis results as a map view:

- **Dim Stores.Store GIS City** This is the city name that corresponds to the store name, capitalized to match the values in the OBIEE_CITY.CITY_NAME spatial data set column.

- **Dim Stores.Store GIS State Abbr** This is the ISO country code, together with the state code, again capitalized to match the values in the OBIEE_STATE.STATE_ABBRV spatial data set column.

- **Dim Stores.Latitude** This is the latitude of each individual store.

- **Dim Stores.Longitude** This is the longitude of each individual store.

Now that you have a source of map data, and columns in your repository that correspond with layer keys in the map data, you will need to perform one more administration task to link your repository columns to the layer keys in the mapping spatial data set. For the current example, this means that the following steps will need to be carried out:

- The Dim Stores.Store GIS Name subject area columns will need to be linked to the OBIEE_CITY.CITY_NAME column in the spatial data set.

- The Dim Stores.Store GIS State Abbr subject area columns will need to be linked to the OBIEE_CITY.STATE_ABBRV column in the spatial data set.

TIP
The latitude and longitude columns in your subject area and repository do not need to be linked to corresponding spatial data columns, as the MapViewer software can plot points of interest using latitude and longitude data directly.

To create these links, use the Administration page on the Oracle Business Intelligence web site as follows:

1. Log into the Oracle Business Intelligence web site using the username and password of an administration user (for example, weblogic/welcome1).

2. Using the common header area at the top of the page, click the Administration link; when the Administration page is displayed, click the Manage Map Data link under the Map Data Management heading.

3. The Manage Map Data page will then be displayed, with tabs for Layers, Background Maps, and Images. Ensuring that you have performed the steps detailed earlier to register your spatial data set as an Oracle MapViewer data source, select the Layers tab and click the Import Layers button to the right of the tabs.

4. When the Import Layers dialog box is displayed, import the spatial data map layers that you wish to use in your map views, which in this instance are OBIEE_CITY and OBIEE_STATE2, by selecting them and then clicking the OK button to close the dialog box.

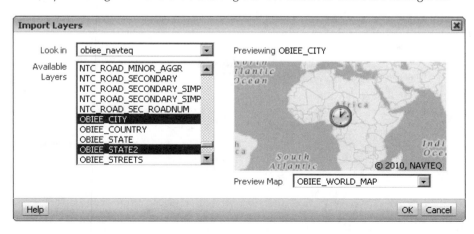

5. The Layers tab on the Manage Map Data page will now list the layers you have selected. To connect each layer's key column to the corresponding subject area columns in your catalog, select each layer in turn and click the Edit Layers button to the right of the tabs. Start by clicking this button for the OBIEE_CITY layer.

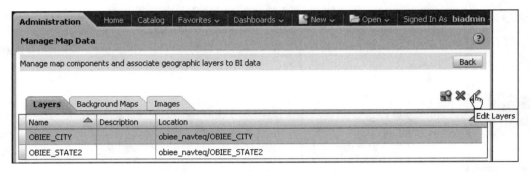

6. In the Edit Layer dialog box that appears, navigate to the BI Associations area of the dialog box and use the Layer Key drop-down menu to check the spatial data set columns that can be used to provide key values for this layer. For this example, select CITY_NAME as the Layer Key for the OBIEE_CITY layer.

7. Click the BI Key Columns button to open the Select Subject Area dialog box to start mapping the BI Key columns. Start by selecting Sales – Fact Sales.

8. In the Select BI Key Columns dialog box that appears, select the subject area column that matches the layer key column. In this case, select the Dim Stores.Store GIS City column and use the Move button to move it to the Selected Columns area.

9. If, as in this case, there is more than one subject area that has columns that map to this layer key, repeat steps 7 and 8, this time selecting the other subject area(s) that contain the relevant columns.

10. In this example, the Sales – Store Quality subject area also features this table and subject area column, so select this subject area now and map its Store GIS City column to the layer key so that your Edit Layer dialog box now features two subject area columns and two BI Keys.

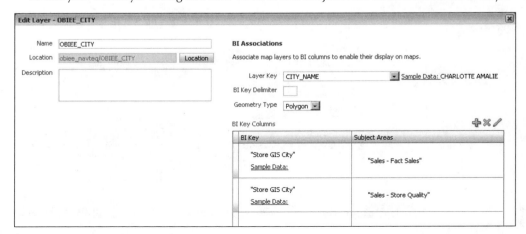

11. Repeat steps 5–10 to define the mapping between the OBIEE_STATE2 layer and the Dim Stores.GIS Stores State Abbr subject area columns in both the Sales – Fact Sales and the Sales – Store Quality subject areas.

    Now both layers have BI Key columns mapped to them, and we can move on to the next tab to define the background maps.

NOTE
Background maps are the canvases onto which you overlay layers.
They can be provided as part of the Navteq sample spatial data, or
you can use third-party services such as Google Maps or Bing Maps.

12. To define the background maps that map views will be able to make use of (we will use the OBIEE_WORLD_MAP and OBIEE_SF_MAP_1 maps provided as part of the Navteq sample data), click the Background Maps tab on the Manage Map Data page, and then click the Import Background Maps button. Select the two background maps from the resulting dialog box.

13. At this point, you have selected some map layers, mapped those layers to subject area columns, and selected some background maps on which to display the layers. Now you need to define which layers are shown at which zoom level on the background maps you have chosen.

    For each of the background maps listed under the Background Maps tab, you can specify, for example, that the OBIEE_STATE layer is displayed only when the OBIEE_SF_MAP1 background map is zoomed out to the maximum. Similarly, if you had lots of customers displayed on a city- or town-level layer, you might decide to display this layer only if the map was zoomed in.

    By default, each background map needs to have layers added to it, so click the first background map in the list and click the Edit Background Map button.

14. To add layers to the map, click the plus (+) button above the list of zoom levels; in this example, select the OBIEE_SF_MAP1 background map first, and then add the OBIEE_ CITY and OBIEE_STATE2 layers to the list.

15. To select which layers are displayed at which map zoom level, click the boxes in the table so that they are colored gray, with gray indicating that the layer is displayed at that level. Once done, click OK to close the dialog box.

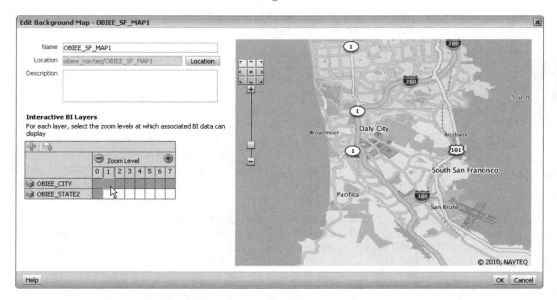

16. Repeat steps 12–15 for any other background maps that you have imported (for example, the OBIEE_WORLD_MAP background map). If you wish to make each layer viewable at all zoom levels in the map, click the far left-hand box once, and then click the far right-hand box, and all boxes in the dialog box will be automatically selected for you. Click OK once you have completed this task.

17. If you wish to use a set of custom images (icons) provided with the mapping spatial data for points of interest on your map (for example, stores), click the Images tab and then click the Import Images button. Select any images you wish to import, and they will then be available to you when you design your map view.

You are now ready to start creating your map views. Remember, though, that these setup steps apply only to the current catalog, so if you create a new catalog or swap another catalog for the one you have been using, you will need to complete these steps again.

Creating Map Views   On a business intelligence system that is deployed out to end users, all of the previous steps for importing spatial data, as well as those for configuring the repository and catalog to access this data, will have been carried out beforehand by the systems administrator. When users then come to create analyses, they will be able to display their analysis results in the form of map views, as long as they select columns that are defined as BI Keys that match to your layer keys.

Like any other view, Map views are accessed using the New View | Map menu item in the Views panel under the Results tab. As shown in Figure 6-9, the map view editor provides a preview of the map, a Selection Steps pane at the bottom of the screen, a toolbar at the top with buttons for setting map properties, adding a legend, creating groups and calculated items, and so

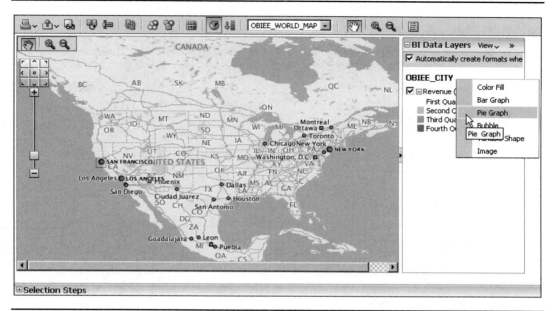

FIGURE 6-9. *The map view editor*

forth. On the right-hand side of the screen is a panel called BI Data Layers for defining the layers that are placed on your selected background map.

Using the BI Data Layers panel, you can define your city layer as showing cities with pie charts that indicate how sales break down for each city by product category. Each city would have a pie chart placed next to it, with a legend that allows the user to see the individual product category values for that city. Other layers might shade states, for example, by their revenue amount quartile, while others might plot actual store locations by their latitude and longitude coordinates. Each store that you click and each category in the product category segments is "clickable" like any other data object in a view type, and we will see later on in this chapter how you can link maps to other views to create a fully interactive reporting environment.

For now, though, let us walk through two map view scenarios where we use the two background maps and the map view layers imported in the previous steps to create the following two maps:

- A map of the San Francisco region, where most of our stores are based, showing revenue for each store
- A map of the world, centered on the U.S., showing the breakdown of revenue by product category for each city in which we operate

In the first map, then, we will be analyzing retail data for stores in the organization. Most of our stores are in the San Francisco bay area, and we will now create a map view that places each store in its correct location, along with a legend and store icon that will be colored red, amber, or green, depending on how well the store is performing.

To create the first map view, follow these steps:

1. From the common header menu, select New | Analysis.

2. When prompted, select the Sales – Fact Sales subject area, and choose the following columns for your analysis from the Subject Areas panel on the left-hand side of the screen:

   Dim Stores.Store Name
   Dim Stores.Latitude
   Dim Stores.Longitude
   Fact Sales.Revenue

3. Hover your mouse pointer over the Dim Stores.MetroCity column in the Selected Columns areas on the right-hand side of the screen, and select Filter from the menu. Use the New Filter dialog box to create the following filter:

   Store GIS City is equal to / is in SAN FRANCISCO

4. Switch to the Results tab and check that a list of store locations in San Francisco, along with revenue figures, is displayed.

5. Now create your map view. To do this, navigate to the Views panel in the bottom left-hand side of the screen, and select New View | Map. When the map view is displayed, ensure that OBIEE_SF_MAP1 is displayed as the map name. (If it is not, change it using the drop-down menu.)

6. The new map view will now be open for editing. On the right-hand side of the map view is a panel that lets you define map formats. Delete the existing map format that is displayed by default (a thematic format based on the OBIEE_CITY layer).

7. Using the Add New Map Formats button, add an image map format using a custom point layer. This will allow you to place icons on the map based on latitude and longitude coordinates.

8. In the Image (Custom Point Layer) dialog box that appears, select or enter the following settings to place the branches on the map:

   X (e.g. longitude): Longitude
   Y (e.g. latitude): Latitude
   ToolTips: Longitude, Latitude, Revenue
   Vary Image By: Revenue
   Bin Type: Percentile Binning
   Bins: 3

9. Now, using the Select Image dialog box, select the red, yellow, and then green circles (traffic lights) for the 0–33%, 33%–66%, and 66%–100% bins.

10. Click Done to save this map definition, and then use the Add View button to add this new view to the compound layout, removing the Table view from the layout beforehand. Now you can use the pan and zoom buttons on the left-hand side of the map to locate downtown San Francisco and see store locations.

11. Click Done to save this map definition. Then use the pan and zoom buttons on the left-hand side of the map to locate downtown San Francisco.

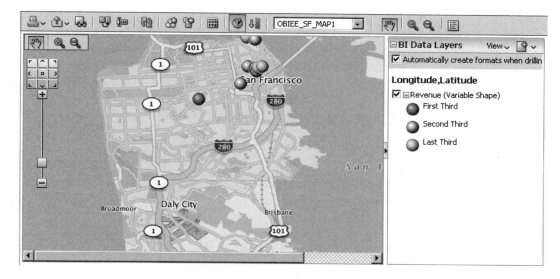

12. If you wish to alter properties of the map view, for example, to change the size of the map canvas, click the Map Properties button in the toolbar that is shown when the view is in edit mode, as it is now. To change the canvas size, ensure that the Canvas tab is selected and change the Canvas Size drop-down menu item from Default to Custom. Click the Tools, Interaction and Labels tab of this dialog box to change other map property settings.

In the previous example, we placed shapes on the map based on latitude and longitude values that were returned alongside one of the BI Key columns in the analysis results. One of the limitations of this approach is that you cannot display other BI visualizations such as charts or thematic shading alongside these coordinate plots.

In the next example, then, we will look at plotting stores and adding pie charts using the OBIEE_WORLD_MAP that you imported in the previous section, "Configuring the Catalog and Repository for Mapping." When creating the map view, we will display a larger-scale continental map of the U.S. and place pie charts over states in which the company operates, with the pie charts showing the breakdown of sales across product categories.

To create this type of map, follow these steps:

1. Select New | Analysis from the Oracle Business Intelligence menu at the top of the screen, and then select Sales – Fact Sales as the subject area.

2. Using the Subject Areas panel on the left-hand side of the screen, choose the following columns to add them to the Selected Columns area:

Dim Stores.Store GIS State Abbr
Dim Products.Product Category
Fact Sales.Revenue

Switch to the Results tab and check that a list of states, together with product categories and revenue amounts, are shown.

3. To create the map, locate the Views panel and click the New View button. Select Map from the list of views, and ensure that the OBIEE_WORLD_MAP is selected.

4. As with the previous map view, navigate to the Map Formats panel and remove the default map format. Use the Add New Map Formats button, but this time select Pie Graph from the list of formats. Then, when prompted, select OBIEE_STATE2 from the list of map layers available.

5. In the Pie Graph dialog box that appears, use the following settings for the pie graph:

   ToolTips: Store GIS State Abbr;Revenue
   Slice Size: Revenue
   Graph Size: 10
   Slices: Product Category

6. Click OK to save the settings, and then click Done to close the Edit View dialog box that you are then returned to.

Now, when you add the map view to the analysis compound layout using the Add View button, you will see pie charts overlaying each of the states in your data set. You can click the charts to display a legend that responds to clicks to drill further down into the dimension hierarchy.

For now, let's leave map views, though we will come back to them later on in this chapter when we look at master-detail linking. Until then, let's finish off the remainder of the view types, looking now at views that allow you to display moving tickers, legends, filter values, and other items of text on your dashboard page.

Static Text, Narrative, Ticker, Legend, and Filter Views

Another set of view types that you can add to analyses are ones to provide additional information to the user, for example explanatory text or details on what filters have been applied to the analysis results. As these types of views perform similar types of functions, we will look at them now and see the different ways they can be used to provide additional context for an analysis.

In addition to the Selection Steps view type that we looked at earlier in this chapter, there are five view types you can use to add additional textual information to your analysis results:

- **Static Text**   This view is for adding to the results static text that does not include elements of the analysis result set.

- **Narrative**   This view is for displaying text that includes data from the analysis results, with one row of text being displayed for each row of returned data.

- **Ticker**   This view displays text along with data from the results in the form of a moving ticker-tape display.

- **Legend**   This view is for displaying legends to explain the meaning behind the conditional formatting in views.

- **Filter**   This view displays the filters that have been applied to the analysis results.

To see how these view types work, let's create a new analysis using the Sales – Fact Sales subject area that uses the following columns:

Dim Products.Product Category
Fact Sales.Revenue

For the Fact Sales.Revenue measure, use the conditional formatting feature to color the background of each column cell green if the revenue amount is above 5000, and red if it is below 1000. Then switch to the Results tab in the analysis editor to see the initial Table and Title views that have been added to the compound layout, which should look like the following illustration.

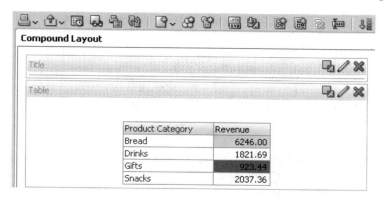

We'll use this particular analysis to illustrate all of these different textual views, adding new views to the Result tab as we go along. Let's start now by looking at Static Text views.

Static Text Views   Static Text views are for adding text to the analysis such as help messages or additional information about the results. For example, you might want to add some boilerplate text to your analysis to advise users where to find out additional information about the sales department, including a hyperlink to an internal intranet page.

To add a Static Text view like this to your analysis, follow these steps:

1.   With the analysis editor open and the Results tab selected, select New View | Other Views | Static Text from the Views pane in the bottom left-hand corner of the screen.

2. A new Static Text view will then open in edit mode. Within this view editing panel, you will see a large text box with controls at the top for setting text to bold, italic, and underline. Using this text box, enter the following text:

```
For more information on our sales activity,[br/] contact administration
on 650 230 2321 or see our <a href="http://gcbc.com/intranet">intranet
page</a>.
```

3. To add the [br/] text, click the Line Break button.

4. As this text contains HTML markup, select the Contains HTML Markup check box above the text. Note that you, as the analysis developer, will need to ensure that you have the "Save Content with HTML Markup" privilege (granted by default to administrative users).

5. Click Done to close the view editor.

Now when you click the Add View button to add the view to the compound layout, the static text that you have entered will be displayed alongside or under the Table view, adding more context to the data being displayed.

Narrative Text Views   While Static Text views can be used for displaying blocks of "boilerplate" text, Narrative views display text alongside data from your analysis results. As your results often span several rows of data, the Narrative view also displays over multiple rows, though you can restrict the view to show only a subset of the total number of result rows.

Narrative views are typically used to display data from an analysis result set in a more "verbose" way; for example, you might wish to create a section of your dashboard that presents sales of product categories in the form of a news report, with an introductory bit of text and details on sales figures, as well as details on where to get further information. Let's create such a Narrative view to replace the current table of data:

1. Using the same analysis criteria defined at the start of this section ("Static Text, Narrative, Ticker, Legend, and Filter Views"), click the Results tab and click the Remove View From Compound Layout button to temporarily remove the Table view from the compound layout.

2. To create the Narrative view, in the Views pane select New View | Other Views | Narrative.

3. In addition to having the same text-editing buttons at the top as the Static Text view editor, the Narrative view editor has four boxes for entering text for the view:

   ■ **Prefix**   This box is for entering text that appears once, at the top of the view.

   ■ **Narrative**   This box is for entering text and column substitution variables that are displayed once per row of data in your analysis results (or less, if you choose to limit the rows used). To reference one of the columns of data in your analysis results, use the variables @1 for the first column, @2 for the second, and so on.

   ■ **Row Separator**   This box is for entering text (for example, a line break) used to separate the narrative text rows.

   ■ **Postfix**   This box is for entering text that is displayed once only at the end of the view.

To create the required Narrative view text, enter the following values into these boxes, using the bold [b] and line break [br/] buttons where necessary:

Prefix: [b]Here are the results for product categories.[/b][br/][br/]
Narrative: The "@1" product category made $@2 in revenue.
Row Separator: [br/]
Postfix: [br/][br/]Further details on our products can be found
        <a href="http://gcbc.com/products">here</a>.

Now, because the text contains HTML markup, select the Contains HTML Markup check box. Note that you will need to be granted the "Save Content with HTML Markup" privilege to be able to save this type of analysis to the catalog, a privilege only granted by default to administrative users (i.e., granted the BI Administrator application role, as described in Chapter 8 of this book).

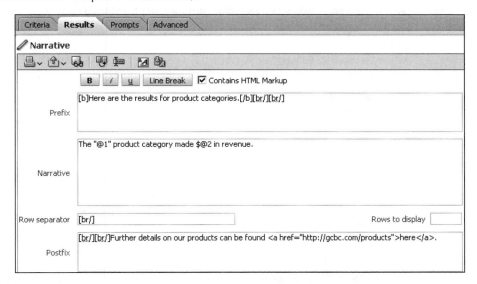

4. Click Done to close the view editor and then add the view to the compound layout.

You will see the text you have entered included in the rows of data returned by the analysis, along with the prefix and postfix text that you specified.

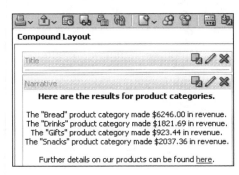

Ticker Views   Ticker views are like Narrative views in that multiple rows of data in your analysis results turn into multiple sets of text output in the view. Unlike Narrative views, though, which display text statically on the screen with rows typically separated by line breaks, Ticker views scroll the view output across the screen, similar to ticker-tape displays.

Consider a situation in which you wish to display a rolling ticker-tape display of sales data at the top of a dashboard, with an opening message, revenue figures for product categories scrolling across the screen, and a closing message displayed at the end. Let's create this type of view now using the Ticker view type:

1. Continuing with the same analysis used in the previous two examples (defined earlier at "Static Text, Narrative, Ticker, Legend, and Filter Views"), create a new Ticker view by selecting New View | Other Views | Ticker from the Views panel in the Results tab.

2. The Ticker view editor now presents you with a set of text boxes that are similar to those used by the Narrative view, except that they already contain some HTML markup text that provides the ticker functionality.

   Using the following values below, type the text into the text boxes and select the option values to create a ticker that scrolls across the page. Note that @1 refers to the first column in the analysis results, @2 refers to the second column, and so on.

   Behavior: Scroll
   Direction: Left
   Width: 420
   Height: *[leave blank]*
   Beginning Text: <table class="TickerTable"><tr><td><table
               class="TickerGroup"><tr><td>Breaking sales data from our
               revenue team ...
   Row Format: Revenue figures for @1 category were $@2 ...
   Row Separator: </td></tr></table><td><table class="TickerGroup"><tr><td>
   Column Separator: </td></tr><tr><td>
   Ending Text: Check back later for updated revenue
               figures!</td></tr></table></td></tr></table>

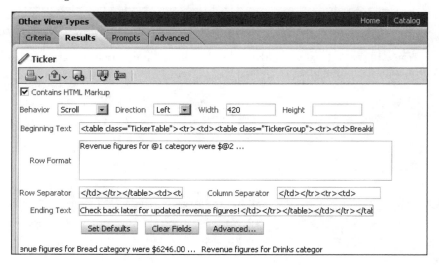

3. Click Done to close the view editor, and then use the Add View button to add this new view to the compound layout.

Legend Views   Legend views are different from Narrative and Ticker views in that they don't display data but instead are typically used to provide legends for Table or Pivot Table views featuring conditional formatting.

For example, in the analysis that we created in the previous examples (see "Static Text, Narrative, Ticker, Legend, and Filter Views" for the analysis definition), the Fact Sales.Revenue measure was conditionally formatted to show a red background if revenue was below $500 and a green background if it was above $5000, to indicate below- and above-target figures. However, these conditional formatting rules may not be clear to all users, so let's create a Legend view to add to the Table view in the compound layout to make this formatting more clear.

1. With the analysis editor open and with the same columns listed in the analysis criteria as used in the previous examples in this section, and which feature the conditional formatting settings mentioned a moment ago, click the Results tab to display the default Table and Title views in the compound layout.

2. To create the Legend view, select New View | Other Views | Legend from the Views pane in the bottom left-hand corner.

3. In the Legend view editor that appears, enter a title for the legend (for example, Table Key) in the Title text box.

4. Create the first caption for the legend, indicating what values with a green background signify. The Items area will already have text boxes for you to type the first legend details into. To create the legend element for above-target revenue, enter the following details:

   Caption: Above Target
   Sample Text: $6000
   Format Text: Background color green (to match the analysis conditional
                           formatting)

5. Click the Add Caption button to add another caption line to the editor. Repeat the process from step 4 to create the next caption, indicating what values with a red background signify. Enter the following details, which will create the legend element for below-target revenue:

   Caption: Below Target
   Sample Text: $500
   Format Text: Background color red (again, to match analysis conditional
                           formatting)

6. The view editor will show a preview of the legend, which should look like the following illustration.

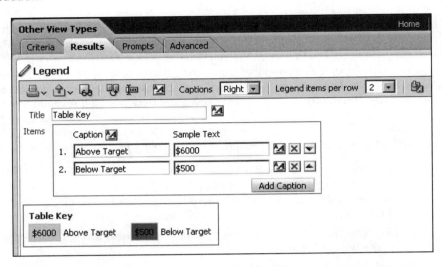

7. Click Done to close the editor, and then click the Add View button to add the Legend view to the compound layout next to the existing Table view.

Filter Views Like the Selection Steps views we looked at earlier in this chapter, which allow you inform users about the underlying selection steps that have been applied to the analysis criteria, you can use Filter views to inform users about the underlying filters that have been applied to the criteria. You or they cannot use these views to create or amend existing filters, but they are useful for dynamically listing the applied filters for an analysis.

To add a Filter view to your analysis results, select New View | Filters from the Views pane, and then add the view by clicking the Add View button, typically positioning it below the main view in your analysis.

Master-Detail Events

So far you have seen that individual analysis views allow you to set up interaction within them by defining hierarchies in your data and adding table prompts to let users filter the displayed values by a dimension attribute. You can also define actions, described in detail in Chapter 7, that allow users to navigate to related analyses, dashboards, or BI objects or interact with external services or applications.

Another type of interaction you can define links two or more analyses within the same dashboard page, with selections made in one analysis immediately filtering values in the others. For example, one analysis on your dashboard might display revenue by product category, and when you click on one of the individual product categories in that analysis' views, other analyses that are linked to it then filter their results on that product category.

These types of interaction are defined through what are termed "Master-Detail" events, and setting one up involves two separate steps:

1. For the "master" analysis that will send the master-detail events, edit the column properties for the relevant column to set the interaction for the primary value to send master-detail events, and specify a channel for the events.

2. For the analysis views that will respond to the events, set the view properties to listen to master-detail events on that channel.

More than one channel can be used on a dashboard page, and more than one view can listen on a channel. Using master-detail events, you can set up highly interactive dashboards where users can click charts and other views, and then see their selections reflected immediately in the other views on the page.

Let's look now at creating an example master-detail event interaction, by setting up a simple example that filters a Table view based on pie chart segments clicked in another view.

Using Master-Detail Events to Link Chart and Table Views In this example, we will create the following two analyses and then link them together using master-detail events:

■ An analysis containing a pie chart that breaks revenue down by product category

■ An analysis that features a Table view of store sales against target, with a table prompt for product category that also responds to changes (events) in the selected pie chart segment in the other analysis

Because you need to display both analyses on the screen at the same time, you will create a simple dashboard to hold the results. We will look in much more detail at dashboards later in this chapter, so don't worry if the dashboard editing interface is unfamiliar at this stage. To create the two analyses, follow these steps:

1. Create the first analysis using the Sales – Fact Sales subject area, and select the Dim Products.Product Category and Fact Sales.Revenue columns for the analysis criteria.

2. With the Criteria tab selected, you will now configure the Dim Products.Product Category column to send master-detail events when clicked on. To do this, begin by hovering your mouse pointer over the Dim Products.Product Category column in the Selected Columns area, select Column Properties from the menu that appears, and then click the Interaction tab.

3. For the Value setting, select Send Master-Detail Events from the Primary Interaction drop-down menu and type in a channel name (in this example, **MD1**) to distinguish these events from others that you might set up for subsequent analyses. Once complete, click OK to close the dialog box and return to the Criteria tab for the analysis editor.

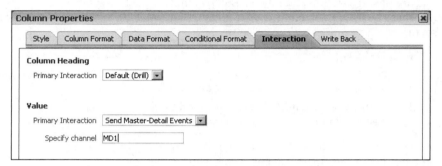

4. Now switch to the Results tab and select New View | Graph | Pie to add a pie chart to your results. Use the default values for the graph, click Done, and then edit the Compound Layout view so that only the title and graph views are displayed.

5. Save this analysis to the catalog in one of the shared folders so that you can add it to a dashboard later on.

6. Now you can create the detail-level analysis that will respond to events raised by the master analysis. Using the analysis editor, create a new analysis using the Sales – Fact Sales subject area, and this time include the following subject area columns in the analysis criteria:

Dim Products.Product Category
Dim Stores.Store Name
Fact Sales.Sale Amount
Fact Sales.Sale Amount Target

7. Switch back to the Results tab, and click the Edit View button for the Table view that has been automatically created for you.

8. For a Table view to respond to events from another analysis, the column that corresponds to the one sending the events needs to be moved into the table prompts area of the view. To do this, drag-and-drop the column into the Table Prompts area of the Layout pane so that your table now contains only the store attribute and measures, while Product Category is now a drop-down menu prompt.

9. Now configure this Table view to listen for the events raised by the other analysis. With the view editor open, click the Table View Properties button. Then, with the Style tab selected, select the Listen For Master-Detail Events check box and type in the channel name, in this case **MD1**, which you specified for the other analysis.

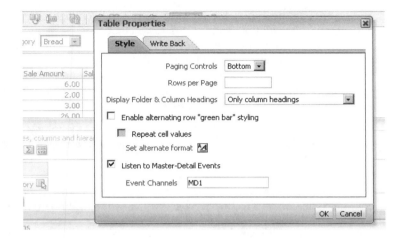

Once you have finished, click OK, and then click Done to close the view editor. Save the analysis to the catalog, again to a shared folder.

10. Now that you have the two analyses set up and saved into the catalog, you can test the master-detail event settings by placing both analyses into a new dashboard page. To start this process, select New | Dashboard from the common header menu and when prompted give the dashboard a name, making sure the Add Content Now radio button is selected.

11. When the dashboard editor page is displayed, locate the two analyses that you have just created in the folders within the Catalog pane. Drag-and-drop the two analyses onto the dashboard canvas so that they are next to each other, with the master analysis on the left and the detailed one on the right. Click Save to save the dashboard to the catalog, and then click Run to run it.

Now, when you click any of the product category values in the pie chart legend, the selected value in the Table view's table prompt will change to reflect what you have selected.

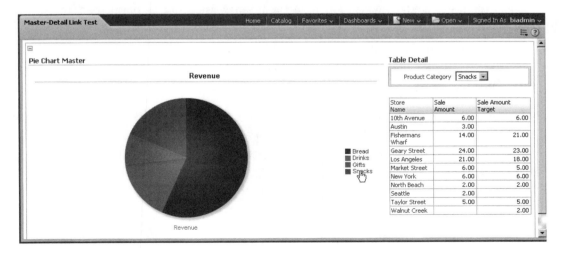

Notice, though, how the table prompt's values only change when you click the chart legend, not the actual pie chart slices. Given that it's most likely that users will click the slices, it's a good idea to configure the analyses to use this event as well. The way to do this is to set the measure column used in the pie chart to also send master-detail events, using the same channel as you used before, and you'll do this in the next step.

12. Open the original analysis that contains the pie chart, and with the Criteria tab selected, select the Column Properties menu item for the measure column.

13. With the Column Properties dialog box shown, select the Interaction tab, and as you did before, for the Value setting select Send Master-Detail Events from the Primary Interaction drop-down menu.

14. When you enter the value in the Specify Channel text box, be sure to enter the same value (in this case, **MD1**) as you used when configuring the Dim Products.Product Category column. Once done, save the analysis and view the dashboard again.

Now, when you click the pie chart segments, the Table view filter value will reflect your selection.

Analysis Prompts

So far in this chapter, we have looked at creating the criteria for your analyses and then creating views that display the results of those analyses in the form of tables, pivot tables, graphs, and other visualizations. You may have noticed that the analysis editor has two other tabs that you can click: one labeled Prompts and another labeled Advanced. Let's take a look now at what the Prompts tab is for.

Prompts can either be embedded within an analysis definition or created stand-alone, and they are used for applying filters to an analysis result set. When embedded in an analysis definition, the prompt is displayed before the results are returned, making this approach more suitable when you do not want to display any data until the user has applied a filter condition. Stand-alone prompts, by contrast, are typically considered optional and generally are used to alter the default values returned by an analysis. They can be used to filter several analyses at once.

Prompts created using the Prompts tab in the analysis editor are considered "embedded prompts" and by default can be created as one of three types:

- **Column**   This is the most common type of prompt.
- **Variable**   This prompt is used for setting the value of a presentation variable.
- **Image**   This type of prompt allows the user to select values via an HTML image map.

In addition to these prompt types, another one becomes available if you perform some steps to configure it:

- **Currency**   This prompt allows users to choose the currency symbol that is displayed when currency values are shown in a measure column.

Let's take a look now at column and currency prompts, and we'll take a look at variable prompts later on in the chapter when we look in more detail at the whole topic of variables. Image prompts are less commonly used but you can find details on how they are configured in the *Oracle® Fusion Middleware User's Guide for Oracle Business Intelligence Enterprise Edition 11g Release 1* product documentation.

Creating Column Prompts

Column prompts allow users to select one or more column values in order to filter the results of an analysis. The prompt can be created against all types of columns and will be displayed in place of the analysis results initially, with the results then being displayed after the prompt values have been selected.

For example, consider a situation in which you wish to prompt the user to select some stores, regions, and concessions, along with some product categories, before you display the results of the analysis to the user. Store selections should be shown in the store hierarchy, whereas product categories will be displayed as a simple list. Using the Sales – Fact Sales subject area, follow these steps to create this type of prompt:

1. Using the analysis editor, create a new analysis using the Sales – Fact Sales subject area.

2. With the Criteria tab selected, select the following subject area columns and add them to the Selected Columns area:

    Dim Stores.Stores (a hierarchical column)
    Dim Products.Product Category
    Fact Sales.Revenue

3. Click the Prompts tab to create the prompts. The Definition area lists any existing inline prompts defined for this analysis, and at this stage the list will be empty. To create a new inline column prompt for the Dim Stores.Stores hierarchical column, select New | Column Prompt | "Dim Stores.Stores".

4. In the New Prompt dialog box that appears, click the plus (+) sign next to the Options label and ensure that the "Enable user to select multiple values" check box is selected by default. If you want to force users to select a value, select the "Require user input" check box; otherwise, leave it at its default, unselected value.

5. Then, using the Default Selection drop-down menu, select Specific Values and use the Select Values button (the green "+" icon to the right of the Default Selection drop-down menu) in order to add the following region and stores to the default selection:

North SF
Fishermans Wharf
North Beach
Taylor Street

6. Now create a second column prompt, this time for the Dim Products.Product Category column. This time, though, do not select the "Require user input" check box, and do not provide a default selection of column values.

7. Under the Definition area of the New Prompt page you will see a preview of the prompts that you have just defined. By default, the prompts are shown on top of each other. To display them on a single line, click the Row-Based Layout button above the prompt definition.

8. Switch back to the Results tab, and click the "Show how results will look on a Dashboard" button.

When the analysis is then previewed, you will first be prompted to select values for the two prompts. When you do so and then click the OK button, the analysis will be displayed using the prompt values you provided as a filter.

Creating Currency Prompts

Another type of prompt that you can define can be used to select from currency symbols to display alongside measures in analysis views. Note that currency prompts do not in themselves perform actual currency conversions, but they are useful for display purposes when displaying currency amounts in views

Before you can use currency prompts, though, you need to perform some initial configuration to define what currencies are listed as being available for selection. There are actually quite a few options for creating this list statically (with a set of values that apply to all users) or dynamically (determined individually for users via a database lookup), but for now we will look at a more simple example of how you can use this feature. See the "Configuring Currency Options" section in the *Oracle Fusion Middleware System Administrator's Guide for Oracle Business Intelligence Enterprise Edition 11*g *Release 1* for more details on this topic.

In this example, we wish to configure Oracle Business Intelligence so that users can select from US dollars, British pounds, or euros as their currency symbol. To do this, first you have to configure the userprefs_currencies.xml file, which you can usually find in the [*middleware_ home*]/instances/instance1/config/OracleBIPresentationServicesComponent/coreapplication_ obips1 directory:

1. Using a text editor, open the userprefs_currencies.xml file.

2. Within this file are a set of default entries that have been commented out. The documentation describes a large number of settings that you can work with in this file, but to create your very simple example, you will need to add the following entries to this file between the <Config></Config> entries:

    ```
    <UserCurrencyPreferences currencyTagMappingType="static">
    <UserCurrencyPreference sessionVarValue="gc1" currencyTag="int:USD" />
    <UserCurrencyPreference sessionVarValue="gc2" currencyTag="int:GBP" />
    <UserCurrencyPreference sessionVarValue="gc3" currencyTag="int:euro-1"
    />
    </UserCurrencyPreferences>
    ```

    In these entries, the sessionVarValue entry specifies a unique value that will be passed to the PREFERRED_CURRENCY session variable, while the currencyTag value refers to a set of currency entries in the currencies.xml file usually found at [*middleware_home*]/ Oracle_BI1/bifoundation/web/display.

3. Once done, save the file and then use Fusion Middleware Control to restart your BI Presentation Services system components.

4. Create a new analysis containing the Dim Products.Product Category and Fact Sales .Revenue columns as the analysis criteria. When the Fact Sales.Revenue column is displayed in the Selected Columns area, hover your mouse pointer over the column and select Column Properties from the menu that is displayed.

5. With the Column Properties dialog box shown, select the Data Format tab, and then select the Override Default Data Format check box. Select Currency as the Treat Numbers As setting. When prompted, select User's Preferred Currency as the currency symbol. Click OK to close the dialog box.

6. Now you can click the Prompts tab to set up the currency prompt. Click this tab, and select New | Currency Prompt from the menu at the top of the Definition area. When the New Prompt dialog box is shown, enter a label for the prompt (for example, Select Currency), and then click OK to close the dialog box.

7. You can see a preview of the currency prompt under the Definition area of the screen. If you are happy with it, save the analysis and then try out the prompt, which will ask you to select a currency before displaying the analysis results with that currency symbol displayed alongside the measure.

NOTE
If you have configured more than one BI Presentation Server component, you will have to repeat these steps for each of the components.

We will look at creating stand-alone, named prompts later on in this chapter. For now, though, let's start looking at how you can publish your analyses in the form of a dashboard.

Creating Dashboards

So far in this chapter we have looked at creating individual analyses using the analysis editor. Although you can provide the analysis editor to users to view their data, the best way to present the results of analyses to them is in the form of a dashboard. Dashboards can combine multiple analyses from the same or different data sources, and you can include objects such as dashboard prompts, folder listings, action links, and other interactive elements to create a web-based business intelligence application.

As with analyses, dashboards have their own editor that you can access from the Home page or through the common header menu. In this section of the chapter, we will look at how you can create dashboards that contain analyses and other BI objects, starting with single-page dashboards and then, later on, adding additional pages and scoping sections to particular application roles.

Creating a Simple Dashboard

To start creating your first dashboard, you can either use the task-based links on the Home page of the Oracle Business Intelligence web site, or you can select New | Dashboard from the menu in the common header area.

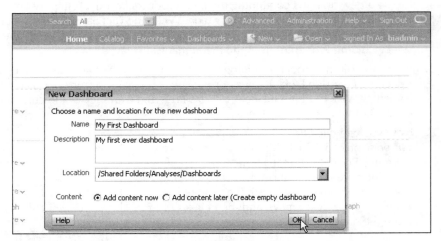

When you first create a dashboard, you are prompted for a name, a description, and a catalog location, as well as to decide whether you wish to start adding content now or later on. Note that for the dashboard you create to appear in the list of dashboards accessed from the Dashboards menu in the common header area, you must save it to a top-level sub-folder within the Shared Folders area in the catalog, such as /Shared Folders/Sales/Dashboards.

If you save the dashboard to the /My Folders area or to a subfolder under a top-level folder (for example, /Shared Folders/Sales/Products/Dashboards), the dashboard will not then appear in the Dashboards menu, as only you can access it. Note also that if you select a top-level sub-folder under Shared Folders that does not already have a /Dashboards subfolder under it (for example, /Shared Folders/Sales), a /Dashboards subfolders will automatically be created under it for you when you save your dashboard. See the section "Managing the Catalog," within the wider "Managing the Catalog and Oracle BI Presentation Services" section later in this chapter, for more information about the catalog structure and recommendation for where to save shared and private dashboards, analyses, and other BI objects.

In most cases, each user will have their own private "scratchpad" dashboard called "My Dashboard" already created for them and located with their My Folders catalog area. Objects saved by a user in this part of the catalog cannot normally be accessed by other users, and are a useful place for users to save analyses and other BI objects that are only for their use. As such, you should encourage users to use My Dashboard as their personal "working area" dashboard rather than creating ones in the shared area of the catalog.

After you have specified your dashboard details, depending on whether you chose the Add Content Now or Add Content Later button, the dashboard will either be opened, ready for editing, or will just have been created for you in the catalog.

Dashboards that have already been created and saved into the catalog can either be opened for editing directly from the Oracle Business Intelligence web site's Catalog page, or by selecting the option to edit the dashboard when viewing it on the screen. To edit a dashboard that you are currently viewing, select the Page Options menu in the top right-hand side of the screen, and then select Edit Dashboard from the list of options displayed, as shown in the illustration below.

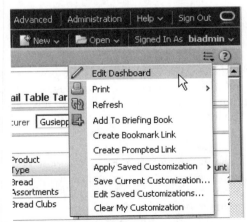

Note that, like all options for creating or editing BI objects in the catalog, whether you have this ability has to do with the privileges assigned to your user account or the application roles that you have been granted. If you are signed is as an administrator, you will generally always have these privileges.

Example: Creating a New Dashboard, and Adding Content To It

In the following example, we will create a dashboard for our company, which we will save into a new top-level sub-folder under the main Shared Folders area in the catalog. We will call the dashboard "GCBC Corporate", and initially add to it two analyses and a BI Publisher report, arranged into columns and sections.

To create this dashboard, follow these steps;

1. With the Oracle Business Intelligence web site open, select New | Dashboard from the common header menu. Alternatively, ensure that the Home page is open and click the Dashboard link under the Create section on the left-hand side of the page.

2. When the New Dashboard dialog box is shown, select or enter the following values to create a new dashboard in a new top-level shared folder called GCBC Corporate, and leave the dashboard open for editing afterward:

Name: Corporate Dashboard
Description: Company-wide dashboard for GCBC Corporation
Location: /Shared Folders/GCBC Corporate/Dashboards
Content: Add content now

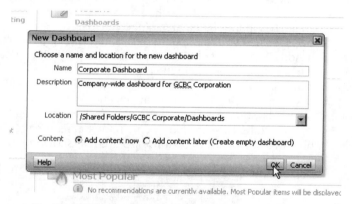

To create the specified catalog location, the /Shared Folders/GCBC Corporate folder, you will need to use the Browse Catalog option presented when you click the Location drop-down menu, and then the Select Location dialog box. A subfolder called /Dashboards will then be automatically created for you under this new folder, into which you can save your new dashboard.

NOTE
The dashboard will now be created and then opened for editing. You will see that the dashboard editor has three panes, two of which are on the left-hand side and are labeled Dashboard Objects and Catalog, and a third that is on the right-hand side, takes up most of the page, and is where you drag-and-drop dashboard and catalog objects to.

Dashboard pages can be divided up into columns and sections, with a column typically containing one or more sections that, in turn, contain analyses and other BI objects and can be displayed vertically (the default) or horizontally.

3. Start by dragging and dropping a Column object from the Dashboard Objects pane onto the main pane, and then a second one so that this pane now shows two columns next to each other, as shown in the following illustration.

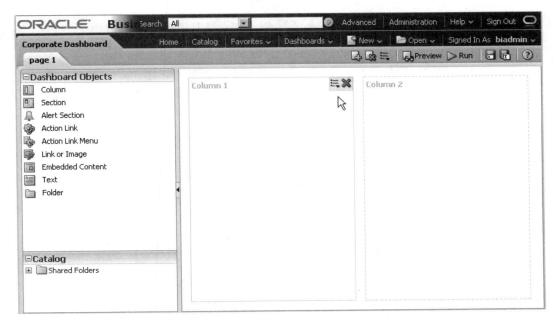

4. Using the Dashboard Objects pane again, drag-and-drop a Section object onto the Column 1 object on the dashboard so that it is now shown inside the column.

5. Drag-and-drop two analyses into the section within Column1, using the Catalog pane in the bottom left-hand corner of the page.

CAUTION
If, as in this case, your dashboard is saved into the Shared Folders area, you need to make sure that any analyses you drop onto the dashboard are also stored in the Shared Folders area; otherwise, only you will be able to view these analyses when the dashboard is actually used.

6. Now you can preview the dashboard. To do so, click the Save button in the toolbar at the top of the page and click the Run button. You will see the dashboard displayed on screen, with one analysis displayed on top of the other.

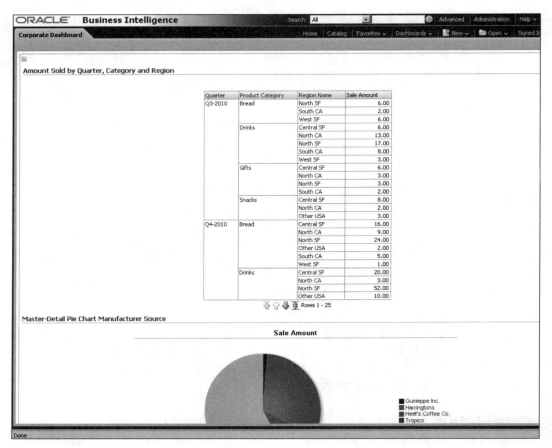

You may have noticed that, even though you specified two columns, your analyses have stretched right across the page, as the other column contained no sections or objects to display.

7. Next, add a BI Publisher report to the dashboard and arrange the dashboard so that your columns are actually displayed as rows, with one row at the top containing the two analyses and a second row underneath, which will contain the BI Publisher report. To do this, start by opening the dashboard page again for editing by selecting Edit Dashboard from the Page Options menu at the top of the page.

8. Hover your mouse pointer at the top of Section 1 within Column 1 so that a toolbar containing four buttons is displayed. Click the Horizontal Layout button so that the two analyses are now displayed next to each other rather than on top of each other.

9. Drag-and-drop the BI Publisher report onto the Column 2 column by dragging it from the Catalog pane onto the main dashboard pane. Notice how the dashboard editor automatically adds a new section to the column to contain the report.

10. Drag-and-drop the Column 2 object itself so that it is shown under the Column 1 object rather than next to it. Your final dashboard layout should look as shown in the following illustration.

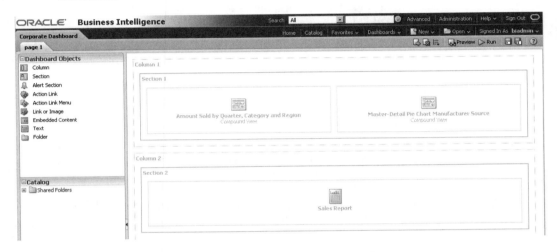

11. Once complete, click the Save button again and then click Run.

You should now see the final dashboard, with your analyses arranged in a row at the top of the page and your BI Publisher report shown under it.

Adding Embedded Content, Text, and Folders

In addition to adding analyses and reports to your dashboard, you can add other content, including plain text, catalog folder displays, and even embedded content from other web sites.

In the following examples, we will add additional content of the type to the dashboard page you just created. This content will include

- The Oracle Fusion Middleware 11*g* web site front page included as embedded content
- A text message at the top of the page directing users to the company support helpline
- A folder view to replace one of the analyses, displaying the contents of the Shared Folders area

Adding Embedded Web Site Content   To add content from another web site into your dashboard, use the Embedded Content object from the Dashboard Objects pane in the dashboard editor. When you include embedded content like this, you can specify a URL, together with width and height sizing, as well as whether scroll bars are shown in cases where the embedded web page is wider or taller than the space you have allowed.

To add content such as this, follow these steps:

1. Open the dashboard editor by selecting Edit Dashboard from the Page Options menu.
2. Drag-and-drop a new Column and/or Section object from the Dashboard Objects pane to where you would like the embedded content to be placed.
3. Drag-and-drop an Embedded Content object into this column and/or section. To specify the web site URL and other settings, hover your mouse pointer over the Embedded Content object and click the Properties button.
4. In the Embedded Content Properties dialog box that opens, enter the following details to display the Fusion Middleware 11*g* home page in this section, replacing [*machine_name*] with the server name for your server.

   URL: http://[*machine_name*]:7001
   Width: 1200px
   Height: 500px
   Hide Scroll Bars: [*unselected*]

5. Click OK to close the dialog box, and then click Save and then Run to display the embedded content within your dashboard page.

Adding Text   Similarly, text can be added to your dashboard page to add help instructions, comments, or other useful text. For example, to add a text message above the external content that we just added in the previous example, follow these steps:

1. With the dashboard open for editing, drag-and-drop a Text object from the Dashboard Objects pane into the same section as the Embedded Content object is held in so that it will display just above the embedded content.
2. To set the text, click the Properties button for the Text object, and when the Text Properties dialog box is shown, enter the following text into the text box:

   GCBC are not responsible for the content of external web sites. For more information, contact the <a href="http://gcbc.com/support">support team</a>.

3. Select the Contains HTML Markup check box to ensure that the hyperlink within this text is displayed correctly. When complete, click the Preview button to see how the text will look, and then click OK to close the dialog box.
4. Click Save and then Run to see the new text.

Adding Folder Views   Rather than including every analysis that you have developed in your dashboard, you can instead include a folder view that allows users to select their own analysis or other BI object to view. Folder views, therefore, are a great way to provide access to a catalog of reports without cluttering up your dashboard.

To add a folder view to your dashboard, follow these steps:

1. With the dashboard editor open, drag-and-drop a Folder View object from the Dashboard Objects pane onto your dashboard layout.

2. To specify which folder is then displayed, click the Properties button for the Folder View object that you have just added.

3. In the Folder Properties dialog box that is shown, use the Browse button and check boxes to select the following values to display an expanded view of the Shared Folders area and present an RSS link that allows the user to subscribe to the folder listing in their RSS newsreader:

   Folder: /Shared Folders
   Expand: [*selected*]
   Show RSS Link: [*selected*]

4. Click OK to close the dialog box, and then click Save and Run to see the folder view in your dashboard.

Your dashboard and Folder View object should now look as in the following illustration.

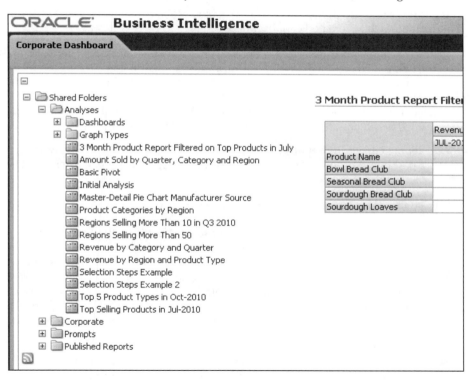

Adding Action Links, Action Link Menus, Report Links, and Alert Sections

Oracle Business Intelligence gives you the ability to create within the catalog objects called *actions*, which are instructions on how to invoke external web pages or business processes, other analyses or objects in the catalog, and are typically linked to columns on an analysis to provide additional functionality beyond that normally provided with an analysis view. Along with *agents*, processes that run in the background to detect business events, raise alerts, and distribute

BI content, these two features described in detail in Chapter 7 of this book give you the ability to create dashboards and business intelligence applications that interact and integrate with your enterprise applications and business processes.

Actions and agents are linked to analyses and dashboards through three features:

- **Action links**   One or more actions can be associated with a particular subject area column in an analysis criteria, with the available actions for a column then displayed as a contextual menu when the user hovers their mouse pointer over the column. Linking actions to a particular column is done through an action link, an instruction to the view to display a particular action with an optional condition attached to determine when the action link should be displayed.

- **Action link menus**   While individual actions can also be added to a dashboard page (to, for example, navigate to a different dashboard page or analysis), you can also add menus of them using the action link menu feature.

- **Alert sections**   These are dashboard objects that display for a user alerts raised by agents that they have created or subscribed to.

Chapter 7 of this book describes actions, agents and other elements that make up what is called the "Action Framework" for Oracle Business Intelligence 11*g*, so take a look there if you would like some background to these features. For now though, we'll concentrate on how these actions and agents can be added to dashboards through the features listed above.

As well as action links and action link menus, though, there is also one other type of link that can be added to the dashboard to help the user interact with its content:

- **Report Links**   Report links are options you can enable for each analysis that you add to a dashboard page, and enable features such as downloading to Microsoft Excel, printing the analysis view or opening it for editing in the analysis editor.

Let's go through an example now, to see how some of these features work.

Adding Action Links, Action Link Menus, and Report Links to the Dashboard

Consider a situation where you are working with the dashboard and analyses defined earlier in the "Creating a Simple Dashboard" example, or your own dashboard and analyses. You wish now to add some additional links and menu items to the dashboard to provide additional functionality for users, and to create navigation paths to other, related content. Note that this example assumes that your dashboard, analyses, and actions are already defined and concentrates on creating the links; see Chapter 7 for details on creation actions if you do not already have such objects defined.

In this example, you will:

- Create an action link that will be placed under an existing analysis in the dashboard that will be displayed conditionally and take the user to a related analysis when they click on it.

- Create an action link menu also placed on the dashboard, displaying a list of action links that the user can select from to invoke related functionality.

- Configure the report links for an analysis to enable export, editing, and refreshing of the analysis from the dashboard.

To create these links, follow these steps:

1. We will start by adding an action link that displays a link to a dashboard when the number of products without a manufacturer recorded for them is more than 50 percent of total products. This test has been defined as a condition that has previously been stored in the catalog. (See Chapter 7 for more details on conditions.)

   To begin, open your dashboard for editing so that the dashboard editor is displayed. Decide which analysis will have the link placed under it; in this example, we will use an analysis that shows sales broken down by product manufacturer as a pie chart view. Note that for this approach to work, you will need to arrange your sections vertically and also typically create more than one column per page so that your BI content generally flows down, rather than across and down the page.

2. Locate the Action Link object in the Dashboard Objects area, and then drag-and-drop it so that it is placed under the analysis but within the same section. This ensures that the link text is displayed right underneath the analysis.

3. To display the Action Link Properties dialog box, click the Properties button for the Action Link object that you just added to the page. Then, since this action that we'll associate with the action link already exists in the catalog, click the Select Action button to browse the catalog and select it.

4. Type some text into the Link Text text box, which will be displayed as the link on the page. For example, you could enter the text, "More than 50% of products do not have a manufacturer recorded. Click here for the Product Strategy dashboard."

5. Select the Open Link In New Window check box, and then select the Conditionally radio button for the Show Link setting. Doing this adds a section to the dialog box for defining or selecting a condition.

6. Next, either create a new condition (see Chapter 7 on how to create conditions) or select an existing one from the catalog using the Select Condition button so that the dialog box looks like the following illustration.

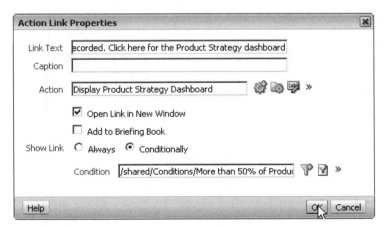

7. Click OK, click Save, and then click Run to view the dashboard. If the condition is met, you will see a link under the analysis to the BI object that you have specified in the action link details.

Action link menus are similar to action links except that they are displayed in menu form and can contain multiple action links. For example, to add an action link menu elsewhere on the dashboard, follow these steps:

1. With the dashboard page open for editing, drag-and-drop an Action Link Menu object from the Dashboard Objects pane onto the dashboard editing pane. Typically, action link menus are placed in their own sections, as they do not specifically relate to a single analysis or BI object.

2. Navigate to where you have added the action link menu item to the dashboard layout, and then click the Properties button that appears when you hover your mouse pointer over the right-hand corner of the object in the dashboard editor.

3. In the Action Link Menu Properties dialog box that is displayed when you press the Properties button, click the Add button to add individual action links to this action link menu. Add the links you wish to see in the menu, and enter a title for the menu label (for example, Other Actions).

4. Click OK, click Save, and then click Run to view the action link menu in the dashboard.

The following illustration shows the action link you created earlier and the action link menu on the dashboard.

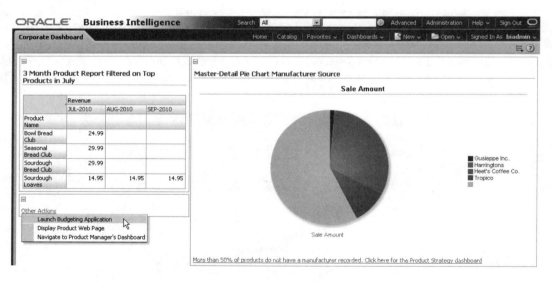

Finally, let's now override the default, page-level report links for an analysis already added to the dashboard and instead enable the Refresh, Export, and Edit links for it.

1. With the dashboard page open for editing, hover your mouse pointer over any analysis already included in the dashboard layout, and when the Properties button is displayed in the right-hand corner, click on it to display a menu of options.

2.   When this menu is displayed, it shows a number of options that you can select from:

■   **Display Results**   Use this option to display the results, either embedded in a section (the default) or as a link that opens either in the dashboard or on a separate page.

■   **Report Links**   Use this to set report links.

■   **Show View**   This option allows you to change the displayed view from the default Compound Layout view to one of the other views. (Note, however, that you will not see the analysis title if you choose anything other than the compound layout.)

■   **Rename**   This lets you rename the view.

■   **Edit Analysis**   This option opens the analysis for editing.

Click the Report Links option to display the Report Links dialog box.

3.   To change the settings inherited from the page, click the Customize radio button. Then, using the check boxes, select the links that you wish to display under the analysis. In this example, we will select the Export, Edit, and Refresh links.

4.   Click OK, click Save, and then click Close to view your dashboard and see the links displayed under the analysis.

Creating Dashboards with Multiple Pages, Conditional Display, and Section-Level Permissions

So far, our dashboard has consisted of a single page, with all content visible to all users and application roles. You can, however, create multiple pages for your dashboard, as well as set rules for which users and roles can see each page and each section within the page.

By default, each dashboard has a single page when you first create it. To add additional pages which then appear as tabs at the top of the dashboard, select Page Options | Edit Dashboard if the dashboard is already being displayed; if not, click the Edit link next to the dashboard in the Catalog view. Once the dashboard editor is opened, you can add new pages and set other dashboard settings by using the Add Dashboard Page and Remove Dashboard Page buttons in the toolbar.

Thereafter, you can rename or reorder pages by selecting the Dashboard Properties menu option from the Tools menu.

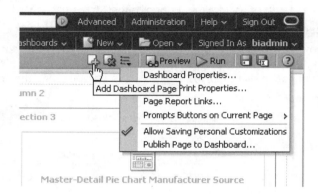

We'll walk through some of these functions now, starting with using the two buttons to add and remove pages from the dashboard.

Adding New Pages to the Dashboard and Setting Dashboard Properties

You can add more pages to your dashboard, or delete ones you've created previously, using the Add Dashboard Page and Remove Dashboard Page buttons in the toolbar at the top right-hand corner of the dashboard editor, as shown in the illustration below.

When you add a dashboard page, you are prompted for a Page Name and Page Description, and you can create as many pages in a dashboard as you like (within reason, considering usability). In the following illustration, two additional pages have been added to the dashboard and named Products and Stores.

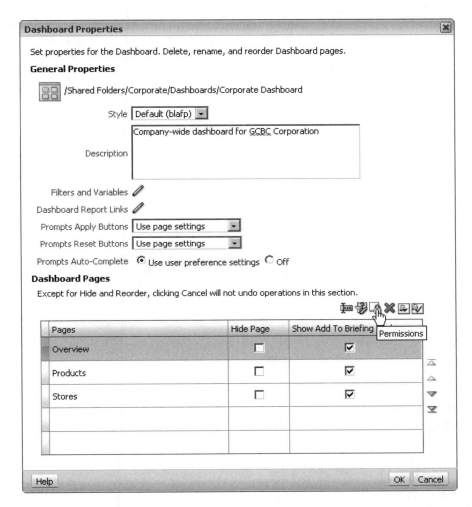

By default, new dashboard pages are given names such as "page 1" and "page 2". To change the name of a dashboard page either after it is first created or later on, you can select Tools | Dashboard Properties from the toolbar to open the Dashboard Properties dialog box.

Using this dialog box, you can edit existing page names and reorder them, set dashboard-wide defaults for prompts, reset and apply buttons, and set permissions for pages so that they are only visible to certain application roles.

Dashboard and Section Permissions and Conditions In addition to whole dashboard pages being scoped to certain application roles, you can also configure sections within the dashboard page to be visible only to certain application roles. To do this, open the dashboard page using the dashboard editor, and then hover your mouse pointer over the section you wish to restrict access to; then, you can select one of the following options:

- **Condition** This is used to set a condition such as whether to display the section or not.
- **Permissions** This is used to restrict access to the section to particular application roles.

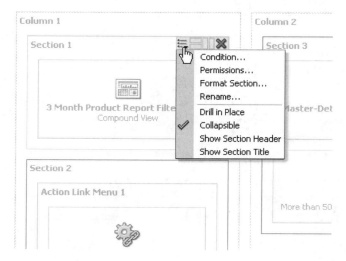

By using these two features, you can conditionally display information on your dashboard based on events that happen in your source systems or data being within certain ranges.

You can also create general-purpose dashboards that contain information suitable for lots of different types of users, and then for certain users display only those sections that are relevant based on their application role grants.

Enabling Dashboard Customizations

When you publish analyses and other BI objects to a dashboard, changes users make to the layout of an analysis, selection of prompt values, and so on are not generally saved when the users leave the dashboard. This ensures that every user who opens the dashboard sees it in its original format and does not have to "undo" the changes made by the previous user.

If, however, you would like to give users the ability to save their dashboard customizations and recall them later without affecting the view of the dashboard seen by other users, you can do this by selecting Allow Saving Personal Customizations from the Tools menu on the dashboard editor. (This setting is actually enabled by default, so all dashboard pages generally can be customized in this way unless you turn this feature off.)

When this feature is enabled, users can save and recall their customizations by following these steps:

1. In this example, we are working with a simple Pivot Table view published within a dashboard, with the Allow Saving Personal Customizations setting enabled for the dashboard. The end user logs in and selects the dashboard page for display.

2. The end user then manipulates the Pivot Table view, performing the following customizations:

    ■ Swaps the X and Y axes of the pivot table (Stores and Products)

    ■ Adds column- and row-level totals

    ■ Removes one of the members from the Products dimension, thereby adding a new selection step to the analysis

3. To save these customizations, the end user selects Page Options | Save Current Customization, which displays a dialog box of the same name. The end user then enters a name for the customization so they can recall it later, decide whether it is available just for them or for other users, and whether it becomes the default setting for when they open this page in the future.

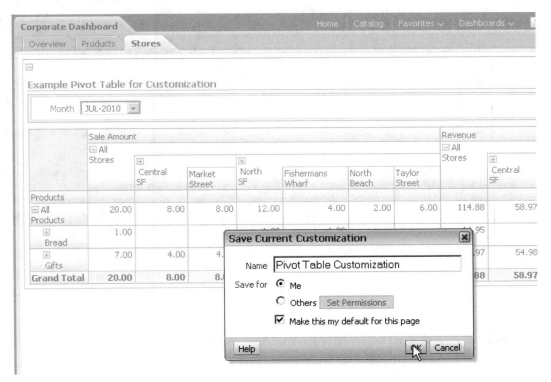

4. If the end user selected the "Make this my default for this page" check box, they will see these customizations automatically when they open the dashboard page again. Otherwise, to apply the customizations to the standard page layout, they would select Page Options | Apply Saved Customization | *customization name*.

We're now at the point where you have seen most of the features involving analyses, dashboards, and dashboard pages. Let's take a look now at some features that complement and work with dashboards and analyses, such as named prompts and named filters, and we'll also take a look at how variables can be used with dashboard pages, analyses, and other BI objects.

Dashboard Prompts, Presentation Variables, Saved Filters, and Other Dashboard Additions

Earlier in this chapter, we looked at analyses and how you could define *inline* prompts that were used to restrict the data that was subsequently returned by the analysis. You probably have noticed by now that many features of analyses, such as actions and conditions, can be defined as part of the analysis or stored separately in the catalog as a *named* item. Prompts and also filters, as we will see in a moment, can be defined inline or named, and we will start therefore by looking at how named—or dashboard—prompts are put together.

Dashboard Prompts

Dashboard prompts are prompts saved in the catalog that are then added to dashboards. They pass filter values to one or more analyses or other BI objects. Also referred to as *named* prompts, dashboard prompts typically have a number of advantages over inline prompts:

- They allow filter values to be passed to more than one analysis or other BI object, giving you the ability to filter several objects at the same time.

- They are typically used after all analyses on the dashboard have returned their initial values, giving users the ability to see default values and then use the prompts to change the displayed values.

- There are a number of different prompt types that are not available for inline prompts, such as radio buttons, check boxes, slider values, and so on.

Dashboard prompts can also have their initial values set by reference to repository or presentation variables or SQL queries, and can also set the value for presentation variables when the user selects a value. In addition, prompts can be defined against all types of columns including hierarchical columns, allowing users to select filter values by reference to a dimension hierarchy if present.

Creating and making use of dashboard prompts is a two-stage process:

1. You define the prompt and specify how it will be displayed: as a choice list, a set of radio buttons, a slider, a date picker, and so on.

2. You configure individual BI objects such as analyses to respond to changes in the dashboard prompt's selected values.

Let's take a look now at how dashboard prompts are created, and then later on we'll see how they can then be used to pass filter values to objects on the dashboard.

Creating a Dashboard Prompt

To create a dashboard prompt, either select New | Dashboard Prompt from the common header area menu, or click the Home page of the Oracle Business Intelligence web site and select Analysis And Interactive Reporting | More | Dashboard Prompt under the Create header. You will be asked to select the subject area from which you will select a column to base the prompt on, and then the dashboard prompt editor will open with the prompt ready for editing.

Using the dashboard prompt page, as with the Prompt tab in the analysis editor, you can create three types of prompts immediately:

- **Column** This prompt is based on either a subject area column or an expression.

- ■ **Image**   This prompt uses an HTML image map.
- ■ **Variable**   This prompt sets the value of a presentation variable.

Once you have configured the Oracle BI Presentation Server, you can create a fourth type of prompt:

- ■ **Currency**   This prompt allows the end user to select the currency symbol displayed in their reports.

In addition, when creating your prompt you can select from a number of different user input types, some of which are only available for certain types of columns and data types:

- ■ **Text field**   This is for typing values in directly.
- ■ **Choice list**   This is a drop-down list of values with a search box at the top, displayed as a list of values for attribute columns and a hierarchical list of dimension members for hierarchical columns.
- ■ **Check box**   This is for selecting one or more values.
- ■ **Radio button**   This is for selecting one value from a set of values.
- ■ **List box**   This is for selecting one or more values from a list.
- ■ **Slider**   This is available only for numeric fields, for selecting a value using a slider, and for an optional spinbox.

To show how dashboard prompts work in practice, we'll use a scenario where we wish to create a dashboard page for analyzing product sales. In this dashboard, there are two analyses that we will connect to a number of prompts:

- ■ An analysis showing revenue by product name and a store hierarchy in a pivot table
- ■ An analysis showing store performance against target in a table, with a custom measure called Sale Amount vs. Target %

We will create four dashboard prompts that we will later connect to these analyses:

- ■ A prompt for the month, which will be linked to both analyses. It will default to the current month by reference to a session variable and will filter the analyses to show a particular month's data.
- ■ A prompt for the store hierarchy to allow us to select which stores are displayed in the pivot table.
- ■ A prompt for sale amount percentage to target, which we will have to derive from the Fact Sales.Amount Sold and Amount Sold Target columns. The prompt will be shown in the form of a slider and used to filter the Table view.
- ■ A prompt that combines product category and manufacturers, filtering the list of types by the categories that have been selected. One will be shown in list form and the other in check box form.

Creating a Simple Column Prompt with a Default Value   Let's start by creating a column prompt on the Dim Times.Month column and set its default value to the current month:

1. With the Oracle Business Intelligence web site open, select New | Dashboard Prompt. When prompted, select the Sales – Fact Sales subject area to base the prompt on.

2. The dashboard prompt editor will now open. To create the prompt based on the Dim Times.Month column, click the New button in the top-right hand corner of the editor and select New | Column Prompt. When the Select Column dialog box is shown, locate and select the Dim Times.Month column, and then click OK.

3. The New Prompt dialog box will then be displayed. Select or enter the following values for the settings:

   Label: Month
   Description: Choice list prompt for month, defaulting to current month and year
   Operator: is equal to / is in
   User Input: Choice List

4. To set the default value for the prompt, click the plus (+) sign next to the Options label to display more of the dialog box. Locate the Default Selection setting and click the drop-down menu next to it to show the following options:

   ■ **None**   This option configures the prompt to have no default value.

   ■ **Specific Values**   This option allows you to select one or more of the column values as the default value.

   ■ **Variable Expression**   This option allows you to specify a variable or expression containing a variable.

   ■ **Server Variable**   This option is for referencing a specific repository or session variable.

   ■ **SQL Results**   This option allows you to specify a logical SQL query to return a set of values.

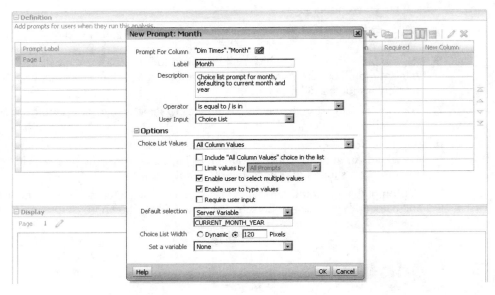

5. Set the prompt to the current month. Use the Server Variable option to set the prompt to the value held in the CURRENT_MONTH_YEAR server variable defined in Chapter 5 by selecting the following values in the Options area:

    Default Selection: Server Variable
    (*variable name*): CURRENT_MONTH_YEAR

6. Click OK to close the dialog box. The new prompt will now be previewed for you, below the prompt list.

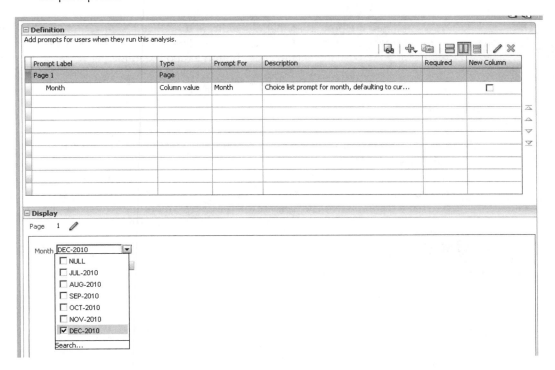

7. Click Save to save the prompt to the catalog so that you can use it later on when you add it to the dashboard.

Creating a Prompt Using a Hierarchical Column   In this example, we will create another column prompt but this time base it on a hierarchical column. When you create a prompt on a hierarchical column, the user is presented with a hierarchy member picker that allows them to select values by the dimension hierarchy. Let's use this to create a prompt that allows users to select members from the Dim Stores.Stores hierarchical column:

1. Using the Oracle Business Intelligence web site common header menu, select New | Dashboard Prompt. When the list of subject areas is displayed, select the Sales – Fact Sales subject area.

2. When the dashboard prompt editor is displayed, Select New | Column Prompt. In the New Column Prompt dialog box, select the Dim Stores.Stores column. Click OK to close the dialog box.

3. When the New Prompt dialog box is shown, select the following values to define the basic prompt settings:

   Label: Stores
   Description: Stores Hierarchical Prompt
   User Input: Choice List

4. Now configure the prompt so that it defaults to the All Stores and San Francisco region-level members. To set the default values, select Specific Values for the Default selection setting, and then use the Select Values button to add the following values to the list:

   All Stores
   North SF
   East SF
   Central SF

5. Ensure that the "Enable user to select multiple values" check box is selected, and click OK to close the dialog box.

6. Preview the prompt at the bottom of the dashboard prompt editor screen, and once you have done so, save the prompt to the catalog. When you preview the prompt, you will see that it displays the list of dimension members according to its hierarchy and uses the default values that you specified when you defined the prompt.

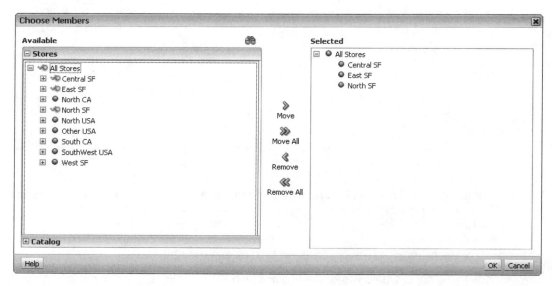

Next we will create another column prompt, but this time we will base the values on an expression rather than just a column value.

Creating a Prompt Based on an Expression

In this example, we will create a prompt that is based on an expression that calculates the percentage to target for the Fact Sales.Sale Amount measure, which we will use later on to filter the values returned in an analysis. We will start by selecting the Fact Sales.Sale Amount measure to base the prompt on but then amend it by altering the column formula to use an expression.

In addition, because we will want to use this prompt to filter all values below the amount selected by the user instead of creating it with the "Is equal to / is in" operator, we will instead use the "Is greater than or equal to" one instead.

To create this prompt, follow these steps:

1. Create the new prompt by selecting New | Dashboard Prompt from the Oracle Business Intelligence web site menu. When prompted to select a subject area, select Sales – Fact Sales.

2. When the dashboard editor opens, select New | Column Prompt. In the Select Column dialog box, navigate to and select the Fact Sales.Amount Sold column. Then click OK to close the dialog box.

3. In the New Prompt dialog box, create the prompt using a slider to set the values and define the comparison operator as "is greater than or equal to" by selecting or entering these settings:

   Label: Sale Amount vs. Target %
   Description: Slider prompt that allows user to select a percentage to target for
                Sale Amount vs. Target
   Operator: Is greater than or equal to
   User Input: Slider

   The Options area will then automatically open to present more options for the slider control. Do not touch these options for the moment, though.

4. When we created the prompt, we specified the Sale Amount measure as the prompt column; however, what we really want to do is to set this to an expression:

   ```
   (("Fact Sales"."Sale Amount"/"Fact Sales"."Sale Amount Target")/
   "Fact Sales"."Sale Amount Target")*100
   ```

   To do this, click the Edit Expression button to the right of the column name in the Prompt For Column area, and use the expression editor to create this expression. Then click OK to close the Expression Editor dialog box.

5. Now you can set the Option settings for the prompt. Use the following settings for these options:

   * Lower Limit: -100
   * Upper Limit: +200
   Show Spinbox: [*selected*]
   Compress Values: [*unselected*]
   Default Selection: 0

6. Leave all other values at the default, and click OK to close the dialog box.

7. You can now preview the slider control. Once you have done so, click Save to save the prompt to the catalog.

Later on, we will see how you can connect this control to an analysis and use it to filter out all stores that have fallen below a certain performance-to-target percentage.

Creating Prompts That Cascade Their Values to Other Prompts   Finally, we will create a prompt containing two columns, where the second column's available values are limited by the selection made for the first column. This feature is sometimes called "cascading prompts." In this example, product categories will be shown in a list, and when selections are made in this list, a corresponding set of manufacturers will be displayed, filtered by the product categories that have been selected. Note that this filtering will happen only when you publish the prompt to a dashboard, not when you view it in the preview area of the dashboard prompt editor.

To create a cascading prompt such as this, follow these steps:

1. With the Oracle Business Intelligence web site open, select New | Dashboard Prompt. When prompted to select a subject area, select Sales – Fact Sales.

2. When the dashboard prompt editor opens, create the first column prompt by selecting New | Column Prompt. Then, in the Select Column dialog box, select the Dim Products. Product Category column.

3. When the Edit Prompt dialog box opens for this column, change the User Input selection to List Box, and then click OK to close the dialog box.

4. With the dashboard prompt editor still open, add a second column prompt by selecting New | Column Prompt again. In the Select Column dialog box, this time select the Dim Products.Product Type column, and then click OK to close the dialog box.

5. When the Edit Prompt dialog box is displayed for this column, change the User Input selection to Check Boxes and expand the Options area.

6. To configure this prompt to restrict its values to those that correspond to the selection made in the other prompt, select the Limit Values By check box and select Product Category as the prompt to filter on. Then click OK to close the dialog box.

7. You will now see both columns listed in the Display area under the listing of columns. In this preview mode, the linking of the two prompts does not automatically take effect, but when you publish the prompt to a dashboard in a moment, you will see it working.

8. Click Save to save the prompt to the catalog.

Now that you have defined a number of prompts and saved them to the catalog, let's combine them with some analyses on a dashboard to see how they work.

Configuring Analyses to Respond to Dashboard Prompts

Analyses, as you have seen earlier in this chapter, can have filters defined in their criteria that restrict the rows returned to the user. These filters can have a number of different operators assigned to them, such as "is in/is equal to", "is greater than", or "is in top". If you want an analysis to react to changes in a dashboard prompt, you would place a filter on that column as you would do normally, but instead of selecting one of the normal operators you would select a special one: "is prompted".

The "is prompted" operator will filter on whatever values of the same column name or expression are passed by dashboard prompts on either the same page or the same dashboard, depending on how the prompt has been scoped. Multiple analyses can be configured in this way so that, for example, all analyses on a dashboard page can be filtered on the same dashboard prompt setting.

Other BI objects also can be configured to respond to dashboard prompt values, either directly or through presentation variables. We will see some examples of these later in the chapter.

When analysis criteria contain a hierarchical column, the columns cannot be filtered in the normal way; instead, you would set up one or more selection steps for the analysis that would be linked to the dashboard prompt values.

To see how this works, consider a situation where you have the two analyses mentioned earlier:

■ An analysis showing revenue by product name and store hierarchy in a pivot table

■ An analysis showing store performance against target in a table, with a custom measure called Sale Amount vs. Target %

We'll now include these analyses on a dashboard page, along with the prompts we defined earlier, so that:

■ The store hierarchy prompt filters the first analysis through a selection step

■ This same analysis is also filtered by the product category and manufacturer prompt

■ The second analysis is filtered by the amount sold vs. target filter, showing just those stores exceeding the filter value

■ Both analyses are filtered by the month and year filter

Configuring the Analyses and Adding Them to the Dashboard with the Prompts   In this
example, we will be configuring an analysis containing a Pivot Table view that contains the
following columns in the analysis criteria:

Dim Stores.Stores (a hierarchical column)
Dim Products.Product Name (an attribute column)
Fact Sales. Revenue (a measure column)

At the start of the process, the analysis you create will have no filters currently applied and
saved into the catalog ready for including on a dashboard page.

We will now configure this analysis to respond to changes in the prompts we have set up and
include the analysis and the prompts on a dashboard page. We will start by adding an "is prompted"
filter to this analysis' criteria to respond to changes in the prompt that includes the Dim Products
.Product Category and Dim Products.Manufacturer columns. As this particular analysis does not
have these columns already in the criteria, we will create a filter using the "Create a filter for the
current Subject area" button in the Filters pane under the Selected Columns Pane:

1.   To add the first filter, click the "Create a filter for the current Subject area" button, and
     when prompted, select More Columns.

2.   Then, in the Select Column dialog box that appears, select the Dim Products.Product
     Category column and click OK to display the New Filter dialog box.

3.   Change the Operator to "is prompted", and then click the OK button to close the dialog box.

4.   Repeat this process to add a second filter to the analysis criteria, this time basing it on the
     Dim Products.Manufacturer column. Create this filter using the "is prompted" operator
     again so that the Filters area of your analysis criteria looks as shown in the following
     illustration.

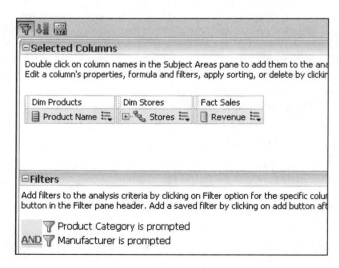

5.   Create another filter using the "is prompted" operator, but this time base it on the Dim
     Times.Month column.

6. Configure the analysis to filter the Dim Stores.Stores hierarchical column. To do this, switch to the Results tab in the analysis editor and navigate to the Selection Steps pane, where you will find a section showing the heading Dim Stores – Stores, with a single step under it labeled "1. Start with all members".

7. To add the filter, click the Edit button that appears when you hover your mouse pointer over the step. This will display the Edit Member Step dialog box.

8. To have the selection step respond to the dashboard prompt values, change the Action setting to "Start with all members", and then select the Override With Prompt check box. Only one step per dimension can have this value set, but when you set it, the values selected in the prompt will replace the default values set here.

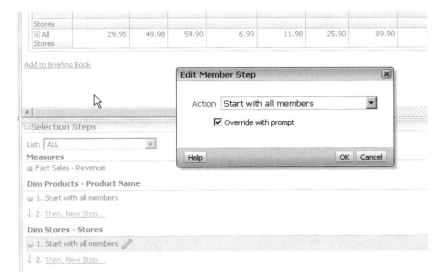

9. Click OK to close the dialog box and save the step.

10. At this point you might want to include Filter and Selection Steps views into the compound layout so that you can see the filter values that have been applied to the analysis. To do so, with the Results tab still selected, click the New View button in the Compound Layout toolbar and select Filters first, and then Selection Steps. Once completed, save your analysis back to the catalog.

11. Now add the analysis and the associated prompts to the dashboard page. Either create a new dashboard (New | Dashboard) or open an existing one; in this example, open the Corporate Dashboard created earlier and switch to the Stores page within it.

12. Within this dashboard page, remove any existing sections or columns that might already exist within it. Then add two columns, arranged so that one is to the right of the other. Within the first column, add four sections.

13. Within these sections, add each of the prompts, one by one, so that each prompt is in its own section. Then, in the right-hand column, add two sections and drop the analysis that you have just been editing into the section. Once this is done, click Save and then Run on the dashboard editor toolbar.

14. You will now see the prompts and the analysis on the dashboard. Try changing some of the prompt values, check that the analysis responds to these changes, and check that the Filter and Selection Steps views that you added display the filter criteria.

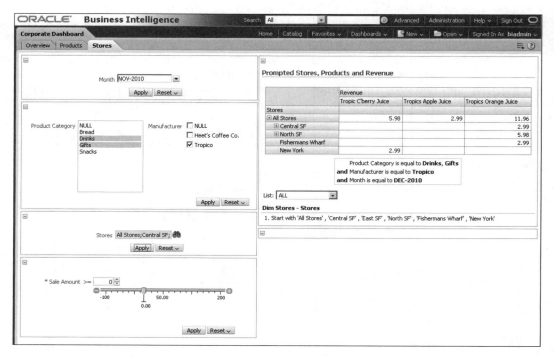

15. Open the second analysis for editing and click the Criteria tab. Locate the "Fact Sales .Sale Amount vs. Target %" measure, which is based on the expression used in the corresponding prompt, and create a filter for it using the "is prompted" operator.

16. Add a second filter, this time on the Dim Times.Months column, adding it using the Filters pane since the column does not currently exist in the analysis criteria.

17. As with the previous analysis, add a Filter view to the compound layout (but not a Selection Steps view, as we will not be using these for this analysis) and save the analysis back to the catalog.

18. Add this second analysis to the dashboard page that contains the prompts and the other analysis. You should see both analyses now reacting to changes in the Months prompt, with this second analysis returning store details only for those stores that have met or exceeded their target.

19. Once complete, save this dashboard, as we will use it again in a moment when we look at removing the Reset and Apply buttons from these prompts.

Disabling and Enabling Apply and Reset Buttons for Prompts   If you have a very fast source database, have used caching extensively, or are using Oracle Exalytics as the hardware platform for your BI application, then you may want to disable the Apply and/or Reset buttons that are displayed alongside each prompt.

Removing the Apply button causes the dashboard to refresh whenever a value is selected, which provides instantaneous feedback to users but is very demanding on the underlying source database. Therefore, use this feature only if you are sure that your data sources can handle the increased load from this feature. If you remove the Apply button, you might also want to remove the Reset button as well, to remove all buttons from the prompt and dashboard. Whether to remove the Apply and/or Reset buttons can be specified per prompt, and this can be overridden for each page of the dashboard.

To remove or restore the Apply and Reset buttons for an individual dashboard prompt, open the prompt for editing and select the page that contains the individual column or other prompts. Click the Edit button for the page, and then either select or deselect the Show Apply Button or Show Reset Button check boxes.

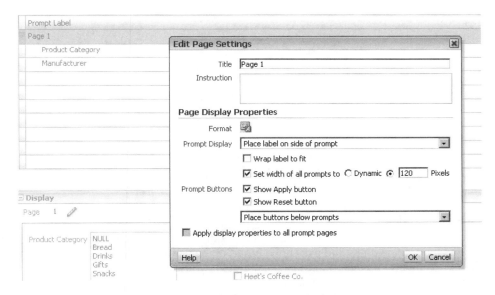

Similarly, to show or hide the Apply or Reset buttons for all prompts on a dashboard page, open the dashboard page for editing, select Tools | Prompts Button On Current Page, and then select the Apply Buttons option or the Reset Buttons option. For the Apply Buttons option, you will be presented with three options:

Use Prompt Setting
Show All Apply Buttons
Hide All Apply Buttons

If you have chosen to hide the Apply and/or Reset buttons for one or more prompts, the values in analyses with filters linked with these prompts will change whenever you specify a new value, and with our example analyses and filters will look similar to the dashboard in the following illustration.

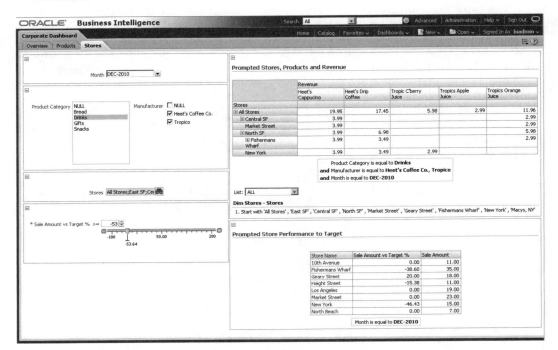

Saved Filters

So far in this chapter we have looked at filters defined as part of analysis criteria. These filters are referred to as *inline* filters and exist only as part of the analysis definition. If you anticipate that a filter might be useful beyond just this filter, though, you can define the filter as a *named* or *saved* filter and store it into the catalog for later use.

You can create saved filters in one of two ways:

■ By creating the filter using the New | Filter option in the common header menu or selecting Create | More | Filter from the left-hand side of the Home page

■ By extracting one or more *inline* filters already defined in analysis criteria and turning them into named, saved filters that you then store in the catalog for use elsewhere

When you first save a filter object to the catalog, you will be prompted to save it to a special folder called Subject Area Contents, either under My Folders or Shared Folders depending on whether you chose your private area of the catalog or the shared area. This special folder is the default location for objects such as filters, and other "minor" objects such as groups, and is the recommended place to store them so as to keep them all in a common area.

When you then want to use this saved filter later on in an analysis criteria, you can either include it through a *reference*, or by copying its definition into the analysis' own definition. Including it as a reference only means that just a pointer to the filter definition is included in the analysis definition, allowing the analysis to use updated definitions of the filter if you update them in the future. Copying the filter definition into the analysis definition "freezes" the filter definition at that point in time, protecting it from subsequent changes to the filter or even its deletion from the catalog.

To show how saved filters work, let's look at two scenarios using the Sales – Fact Sales subject area:

- ■ First we will define a saved filter just for our own use and save it into the My Folders area of the catalog; then we will create a new analysis and add the shared filter to the analysis criteria.

- ■ Then we will take an existing analysis within the Shared Folders area of the catalog and extract its filters into a new saved filter, which we will then again save to the Shared Folders area of the catalog for later use.

Follow the steps below to create a new saved filter, save it into your private area of the catalog, and then use it in analysis definition.

1. Using the Oracle Business Intelligence web site, log in and create a new analysis (New | Analysis). When prompted, select Sales – Fact Sales as the subject area.

2. Add the following columns to the analysis criteria:

   Dim Products.Product Category
   Dim Times.Month
   Fact Sales.Revenue

3. Create the following filter on the Dim Products.Product Category column:

   Dim Products.Product Category is equal to / is in Drinks
   Dim Times.Month is prompted

4. Save the analysis to the Shared Folders area of your catalog (for example, /Shared Folders/ Analyses), and call the analysis **Product Category Sales**.

5. Create your first shared filter, which will filter analyses so that only stores within the three San Francisco regions will be returned. To do this, select New | Filter from the common header menu, and when the filter editor is displayed, locate and double-click the Dim Stores.Region Name column in the Subject Area pane.

6. In the New Filter dialog box that appears for this column, select the following values:

   Column: Region Name
   Operator: is equal to / is in
   Value: Central SF, East SF, North SF

7. Click OK to close the dialog box.

8. Click Save to save the filter to the catalog. When you do so, by default the Save As dialog box displays the My Folders/Subject Area Contents folder, which is a special location for storing filters, groups, and other named objects in order to separate them from regular BI objects. Name the shared filter **Only Include San Francisco Regions** and click OK to close the dialog box.

9. To now test out this shared filter, create a new analysis (New | Analysis) and include the following columns within the analysis criteria:

    Dim Products.Product Category
    Fact Sales.Revenue

10. To add the shared filter to the analysis criteria, navigate to the Catalog pane in the bottom left-hand corner of the page and locate the filter in the set of catalog folders. With the filter selected, click the Add More Options button.

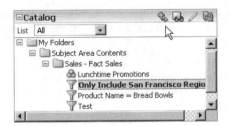

11. The Apply Saved Filter dialog box will then be displayed, confirming the contents of the filter and giving you options for clearing all existing filters before applying it and for applying the contents of the filter instead of a reference. For this example, leave both check boxes unselected and click OK to close the dialog box and add the filter to your analysis.

12. Once complete, click the Results tab to see the filter being applied to your analysis results.

Now, let's take a look at the second example, which instead of defining the filter directly extracts one from a filter used in an analysis, saving this inline filter definition as a named, saved filter. For this example, use the same analysis definition that you created in the previous example. To create a named filter in this way, follow these steps:

1. Using the Oracle Business Intelligence web site menu, open the analysis that you created previously (Open | Open | /Shared Folders/Analyses/Product Category Sales).

2. With the Criteria tab selected, navigate to the Filters pane, where you should see two filters listed. To save these filters as a shared filter in the catalog, locate the More Options button at the top right-hand side of the pane, click it, and then click the Save Filters button.

3. In the Save As dialog box that is shown, navigate to the Shared Folders area, click the Show Folder Tree button in the Folders area, and then click the Shared Folders folder, followed by a subfolder (for example, GCBC Corporate) when it is displayed. Notice also how there is a check box at the bottom of the dialog box that allows you (by default) to replace the filters in the analysis with a reference to the shared filter.

4. With the Shared Folders/GCBC Corporate folder selected, type in **Product Category = Drinks and Month Prompted** as the filter name. Click OK to save the filter, and you will be prompted to save the filter into a subfolder called Subject Area Contents; this is similar to the My Folders subfolder of the same name in that it is a recommended subfolder used to keep your catalog organized. Select the recommended option and click OK to close the dialog box.

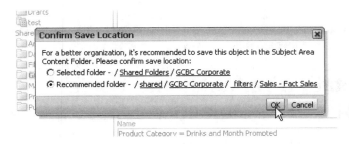

The shared filter will now be saved to the catalog, and if you selected the option to replace these filters with a reference to the saved filter, the analysis criteria will be updated accordingly.

Managing Favorites

If you have a particular analysis, dashboard, or other BI object that you would like to access quickly from the catalog, you can add it as a favorite. Once objects are added as favorites, you can access them quickly from the Favorites menu in the Oracle Business Intelligence web site common header area, and organize sets of favorites into folders to create categories and subcategories.

Adding Objects as Favorites

To add a particular analysis, dashboard, or other BI object as a favorite, you use one of two methods:

- Locate the object in the Catalog page or the Home page on the Oracle Business Intelligence web site, and select More | Add to Favorites from the menu for this object.

- With the object open for editing, select Favorites | Add to Favorites from the common header area.

Favorites that you add are personal to you and are not visible to other users or roles. Each user's list of favorites are also recorded in the catalog alongside other settings such as your delivery profile (described in detail in Chapter 7), list of delivery devices, and so on, so if your administrator creates a new catalog or restores an old one from a backup, your favorites may no longer be accessible.

Organizing Your Favorites into Categories and Subcategories

Favorites can be organized in categories and subcategories (for example, Useful Dashboards or Product Analyses). To organize your favorites in this way, select Favorites | Manage Favorites from the web site menu.

When you select this option, the Manage Favorites dialog box will be displayed. Using this dialog box, you can create new category folders, move favorites in and out of these folders, and rename them or sort them in different ways.

Presentation Variables and Using Variables in BI Objects

Earlier on in this chapter in the section headed "Referencing Variables in Filters," we looked at how repository variables, defined in the Oracle BI Repository using the Oracle BI Administration tool, can be used to provide values for filters and calculations used by analyses. There are in fact two types of these repository variables, detailed in the list below:

- **Repository variables** These contain the same value for all users of the system.
- **Session variables** These are initialized at the start of a user session and contain values for just that session.

In addition to these types of variables, you can also define variables within Oracle BI Presentation Services. Known as *presentation variables,* these are useful when, for example:

- You want to display the value selected in a prompt elsewhere in the analysis results, such as in the Title view.
- You want to pass values from one analysis to another or from one prompt to many analyses.
- You want to create a filter based on a prompt value, but the columns you are filtering on are in different subject areas and don't necessarily have the same column name as that used in the filter.
- You want to create a prompt based on a set of arbitrary values and then use this to filter a report or add to a column formula expression.

Together with request variables, which are session variables that have their value temporarily overridden for a particular analysis result set, presentation variables provide flexibility in creating filters and links between analyses, and allow you to take the values selected in prompts and use them flexibly within your analysis definitions.

Creating and Populating Presentation Variables

Presentation variables are defined and populated through prompts, either created inline as part of an analysis definition or named through a dashboard prompt. Their values persist for as long as the user stays logged into the dashboard, with values being private to each user in the same way as session variables. To create a presentation variable, you just specify its name within the prompt setup dialog box, and the variable is automatically created for you.

Defining Presentation Variables Using a Column Prompt

The most common way to define and then populate a presentation variable is to do so through either an inline or a named (dashboard) prompt. When you do so, the prompt is created with a text data type, though you can alter this to be a number, date, time, or date and time data type if you wish.

When the prompt is first used within a user session, the presentation variable will be created and populated with the value selected by the user with the prompt. The presentation variable will use the default text data type and will contain the same value until the prompt is used again.

You could also define the variable in the same way if using an inline prompt within an analysis, which would present the same options and same dialog box once you had chosen to create your prompt based off of the selected column.

Defining Presentation Variables Using a Variable Prompt

The other way to define and populate a presentation variable is to use a variable prompt.

Unlike column prompts that are tied to a particular column source, *variable prompts* allow you to define prompts that populate a presentation variable of any allowed data type and can source their data from a number of different sources. Variable prompts are a more flexible way of defining prompts when the simplicity of using a column prompt doesn't meet your requirements.

Defining Request Variables Using Prompts

Request variables, which are nonsecurity-sensitive session variables with their values temporarily overridden, are defined in a similar way as presentation variables. You can either create a column prompt or a variable prompt, which you then configure in your preferred way to present a set of prompt values. Then you specify that the prompt sets the value of a variable, which in this instance would be a request rather than a presentation variable.

When the prompt is used and a query references the relevant session variable, the prompt and the request variable override this session variable's value for the duration of the analysis execution, temporarily overriding the value of the session variable to, for example, display results for an alternate region or show staff data for a different division than the user is normally assigned to by a session variable initialization block.

Referencing Presentation Variables and Other Variable Types in Analyses and Other BI Objects

Once you have used a prompt to configure your presentation variable with a set of potential values, you will then want to reference it within an analysis or other BI object. Similarly, you may wish to reference the value of a session, repository, or request variable in an analysis, for example, to filter the results or highlight certain rows in a Table view output.

Referencing variables within Oracle Business Intelligence can be a tricky task, as the syntax used for each variable type often varies depending on the context in which it is being used. Session and repository variables, for example, are referenced using a different syntax than presentation variables, and the syntax for all types varies depending on whether you are referencing the variables within a dialog box, a view, or a column expression. Let's take a look now at the overall rules for variable referencing, and later on we'll walk through a scenario where each of these variable types is used in a dashboard to pass around values set through a set of prompts.

Referencing Variables in Dialog Boxes

The easiest way to reference any type of variable is in the dialog boxes presented (for example, when you define a prompt or a column filter).

In these cases, the dialog box will tell you which type of variable can be used at this point (not all variable types can be used in all situations), and all you need to do is select the variable type and enter its name. If the BI object then needs to prefix the variable name (to add, for example, NQ_SESSION. in front of a session variable name), it will do this for you automatically.

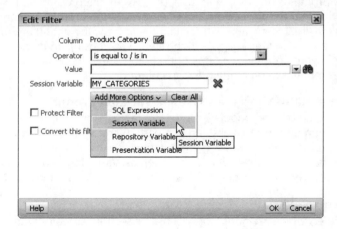

In the example in the next illustration, the New Filter dialog box used to add the NQ_SESSION session variable has also added the correct syntax around a subsequent presentation variable reference.

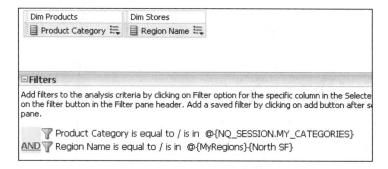

Adding variable references in this way is relatively straightforward because the dialog box does the hard work for you.

Referencing Variables in Views

Referencing variables in view definitions is more complicated, as you must use the correct syntax for the type of variable you are using. To reference presentation, request, session, or repository variables within a view definition, use the syntax forms shown here:

■ Presentation or request variables:

@{variables.*variablename*}{*default value*}

For example:

@{variables.MyRegion}{North SF}

■ Session variables:

@{biServer.variables['NQSESSION.*variablename*']

For example:

@{biServer.variables['NQSESSION.home_store']

■ Repository variables

@{biServer.variables[*variablename*]

For example:

@{biServer.variables[current_month]

Other variations on these syntax forms, for example, to scope the presentation variable reference to a particular analysis, dashboard page, or dashboard when it is used in multiple places, can be found in the "What Is the Syntax for Referencing Variables?" section of the *Oracle® Fusion Middleware User's Guide for Oracle Business Intelligence Enterprise Edition 11g Release 1*.

Referencing Variables in Expressions

For referencing these types of variables within an expression, different syntax forms apply:

■ Presentation or request variables:

@{*variablename*}{*default value*}

For example:

`@{MyRegion}{North SF}`

■ Session variables:

VALUEOF(NQ_SESSION."*variablename*")

Note the double quotes around the session variable name. For example:

`VALUEOF(NQ_SESSION."SalesRegion")`

■ Repository variables

VALUEOF("*variablename*")

Again, note the double quotes around the session variable name. For example:

`VALUEOF("current_month")`

As with referencing variables in view definitions, other variations on these syntax forms can be found in the product documentation. For now, though, let's work through a few examples of variables in use in a dashboard to see in practice how they are created, populated, and referenced.

Examples of Variables in Use on a Dashboard

In the following examples, we will look at using prompts and variables to add interactivity to a dashboard page, passing values from various prompts to filter the results displayed by an analysis. The scenario we will be looking at is one in which a user wishes to analyze sales data across regions and quarters, and wants to compare actual sales data with some arbitrary target figures that display the variance between the two.

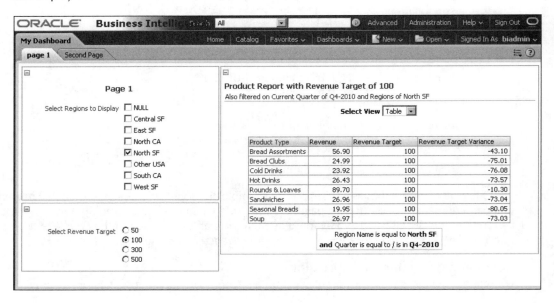

To accomplish this, we will create:

- A *column prompt* that creates and populates a presentation variable, which we will then use in a column filter within the analysis

- A *variable prompt,* which we will use to create a numeric presentation variable that we'll then use in some column expressions

- A *repository variable* containing the current quarter that we'll use to filter the analysis results

- A *Title view* of the analysis that will reference these variables to show the parameters that have been passed to the analysis

Let's start with the first example, where we'll define a presentation variable and use it in a column filter.

Example 1: Creating Presentation Variables Using Column Prompts and Column Filters

To create a presentation variable using a column prompt and then use the prompt to filter the results of an analysis, follow these steps:

1. Using the Oracle Business Intelligence menu, select New | Dashboard Prompt. When prompted to select a subject area, select Sales – Fact Sales.

2. The dashboard prompt editor will then open. Select New | Column Prompt, and when the Select Column dialog box is shown, select Dim Stores.Region Name.

3. The New Prompt dialog box will then be displayed. In this example, we will create the prompt as using check boxes for the value selection, and we'll allow the user to select more than one region as the parameter value. Expanding the Options area to display the remaining settings, select or enter the following values to define the prompt and create the presentation variable that we'll use in a moment to create the analysis filter:

   Prompt for Column: Dim Stores.Region Name
   Label: Select Regions to Display
   Operator: is equal to / is in
   User Input: Check Boxes
   Default Value: North SF
   Set a variable: Presentation Variable
                   MyRegions

4. Close the dialog box, and then save the prompt to the catalog.

5. To create the analysis that we will be filtering using these variables and prompts, use the Oracle Business Intelligence web site menu and select New | Analysis.

6. When prompted, select Sales – Fact Sales as the subject area, and then select the following subject area columns to add to the analysis criteria:

   Dim Products.Product Type
   Fact Sales.Revenue

7. Use the Filters pane to add a new filter to the analysis and select the Dim Stores.Region Name as the column to filter on.

8. To reference the MyRegions presentation variable in the filter definition, click the Add More Options button and select Presentation Variable as the variable type. Then enter the following values to reference the variable:

   Variable Expr: MyRegions
   (*default*): North SF

9. Close the dialog box, and then switch to the Results tab to see the default Title and Table views within the default compound layout.

10. In the Compound Layout toolbar, select Add View | Filter to add a Filter view to the compound layout so that you can see the filter values that are being applied to the analysis results. Save the analysis to the catalog.

11. Now create a new dashboard to hold the prompt and analysis, and test that the filtering works. Select New | Dashboard from the Oracle Business Intelligence web site menu, name the dashboard, and select the Add Content Now option.

12. Add the prompt and the analysis to the dashboard, and then save and run the dashboard page. You should now see values that you select in the prompt being used to filter the analysis results, with the filter values being displayed in the Filter view in the analysis compound layout.

TIP
In this example, you didn't really need to pass the prompt value via a presentation variable to filter the analyses data, as you could just have used an "is prompted" filter instead. This technique would be useful, though, if you wanted to use a prompt with analyses from different subject areas on the same dashboard, where the column name containing regions differed across subject areas.

In the next example, the prompting we are going to use could only be performed through the use of a presentation variable, as the set of target values that we will be specifying do not exist in any subject area column in our system.

Example 2: Creating Presentation Variables Using Variable Prompts and Expressions

In this next example, we'll create another prompt for the dashboard that this time will display radio button options for four different revenue target amounts.

The selected target amount will then be displayed in the analysis Table view, next to the revenue measure, with another measure then added to calculate the difference between the revenue and target amounts.

This requirement will necessitate a variable prompt, as there are no existing columns in the subject area that contain target values and these particular target amounts. Therefore, we will create a variable prompt to populate a presentation variable for the target amount, and then use the presentation variable in some column expressions:

1. Using the Oracle Business Intelligence web site menu, select New | Dashboard Prompt. When prompted to select a subject area, select Sales – Fact Sales.

2. In the dashboard prompt page, create a new variable prompt by selecting New | Variable Prompt.

3. In the New Prompt dialog box, start by selecting or entering the following values for the dialog box settings:

   Prompt for: Presentation Variable
              MyTarget
   Label: Select Revenue Target
   User Input: Radio Buttons

4. Once you select Radio Buttons as the Input Type, a section appears for you to enter the radio button values. Select Custom Values from the Radio Buttons Values drop-down list, and then use the Select Values button to add the four target values to this list:

   50
   100
   300
   500

5. Now, to set the default value for the prompt and set the data type for the presentation variable to numeric, click the Options button at the bottom of the dialog box and select or enter these values:

   Variable Data Type: Number
   Default selection: Specific Custom Value
                    100

6. Click OK to close the dialog box, and then save the prompt to the catalog.

7. Now, to add target and variance information to the analysis, we can use the presentation variable that we've just created. First, open the analysis for editing, and add the Fact Sales.Revenue measure back into the analysis criteria twice so that we can use the column's formula to reference the presentation variable.

8. Hover your mouse pointer over the first of the two new columns in the Selected Columns area, and select Edit Formula to bring up the Edit Column Formula dialog box.

9. Initially, this column formula will be the column name that you clicked to add the column to the selected columns area. To change it to reference the MyTarget presentation variable instead, delete the existing entry and then select Variable | Presentation from the buttons at the bottom of the dialog box. Enter the following values when the Insert Variable dialog box is shown:

   Variable Expression: MyTarget
   Default Value: 0

10. Click OK to close the dialog box. The expression within the main part of the dialog box should now read @{MyTarget}{0}.

11. Select the Custom Headings check box and enter **Revenue Target** as the Column Heading value. Click OK to close the dialog box.

12. Repeat step 11 for the second of the new columns, but this time enter **Revenue Target Variance** as the Column Heading value and set the formula to the expression **"Fact Sales"."Revenue"-@{MyTarget}{0}** so that the value of the variable is deducted from the revenue measure, giving the variance.

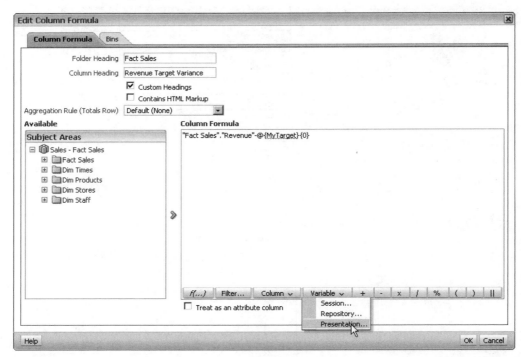

13.   Once complete, click OK to close the dialog box.

14.   To test the new prompt and the updated analysis, open the dashboard that you created earlier for editing and add the new prompt onto the dashboard layout. You should see now that when you change the selected radio button setting for the revenue target, these changes are reflected in the analysis results, with the value of the MyTarget presentation variable being used to show the target value and variance to target.

Example 3: Filtering an Analysis Using a Repository Variable

Similar to the first example (see "Example 1: Creating Presentation Variables Using Column Prompts and Column Filters"), you can also reference repository and session variables in expressions, view definitions, and column filters.

If, for example, you had previously defined a repository variable called CURRENT_QUARTER in the Oracle BI Repository and you wanted to use this to filter values in the Dim Times.Quarter column, you could do so using the Filters pane in the Criteria tab of the analysis editor.

When defining the filter, instead of selecting Presentation as the variable type, you would instead select Repository (or Session if you are using a session variable instead). When the Insert Variable dialog box is then displayed, you would type in the name of the variable but not a default value, as default values for these types of variables are defined within the Oracle BI Administration tool when you create the variable in the first place.

As with the presentation variable example, the dialog box takes care of referencing the variable for you correctly, and you would then see the variable referenced in the correct way when you close the dialog box and view the filter definitions in the Filters pane.

Example 4: Referencing Variables in a View Definition

The final way that we will reference variables in these examples is in the definition of a view. For example, you might want to display the values passed in the prompts in the Title view for the analysis so that users can see that the analysis is filtered on a particular set of regions, quarters, or other parameter values.

In this example, we will amend the Title view for the analysis defined earlier to reference the three variables in the previous examples:

- The MyRegions presentation variable using the syntax @{*variablename*}
- The MyTarget presentation variable using the syntax @{*variablename*}
- The CURRENT_QUARTER repository variable using the syntax @{biServer.variables .*variablename*}

To use these variables in the analysis Title view, follow these steps:

1.   Open the analysis for editing and select the Results tab to show the default compound layout. Navigate to the Title view and click the Edit View button.

2.   Use the MyTarget variable in the Title setting and the other variables in the Subtitle setting. Type in the following to set these values:

Title: Product Report with Revenue Target of @{MyTarget}
Subtitle: Also filtered on Current Quarter of @{biServer.variables.CURRENT_QUARTER} and Regions of @{MyRegions}

3. Close the Edit View page and save the analysis. Ensure that all of the prompts have been added to the dashboard page that you have been working with earlier, and then change some of the prompt settings so that their values are passed through to the analysis.

| Home | Catalog | Favorites ∨ | Dashboards ∨ | New ∨ | Open ∨ | Signed In As **biadmin** ∨ |

Product Report with Revenue Target of 100
Also filtered on Current Quarter of Q4-2010 and Regions of North SF

Select View Table ▾

Product Type	Revenue	Revenue Target	Revenue Target Variance △▽
Bread Assortments	56.90	100	-43.10
Bread Clubs	24.99	100	-75.01
Cold Drinks	23.92	100	-76.08
Hot Drinks	26.43	100	-73.57
Rounds & Loaves	89.70	100	-10.30
Sandwiches	26.96	100	-73.04
Seasonal Breads	19.95	100	-80.05
Soup	26.97	100	-73.03

Region Name is equal to **North SF**
and Quarter is equal to / is in **Q4-2010**

The references that you have made to these variables should now reflect in the analysis, both in the filter values used on the analysis results and in the filter and Title views, which will now display the variable values.

Managing the Catalog and Oracle BI Presentation Services

So far in this chapter, if you have followed along with the examples, you will have created a number of analyses, dashboards, and other BI objects, and you will have saved them at various points into the catalog. You may be aware that there are two broad areas that make up the catalog: the My Folders area, which is private to your user account, and the Shared Folders area, which unsurprisingly is shared among all users.

But how should you structure folders within the catalog, and how can you manage things such as permissions to access folders and individual objects, or indeed to access whole areas of functionality such as the analysis editor or the scorecard editor, which we'll be looking at later on in this chapter?

In this section, then, we'll look at two very important areas of administration for an Oracle Business Intelligence developer: how to organize the catalog and set up proper permissions and access, and how to manage privileges and other settings within Oracle BI Presentation Services so that the right users get access to the right areas of functionality.

Managing the Catalog

The catalog is divided into two main areas:

- A set of user folders, called My Folders, which are private to each user and listed in each user's view of the catalog
- A common folder, called Shared Folders, that is accessible to all users

Typically, users create analyses, dashboards, and other BI objects that are for their own, exclusive use within the My Folders area. They put objects that they want to share within their organization in the Shared Folders area. Within each of these top-level folders, further subfolders are then created to organize catalog objects by subject area and type of object.

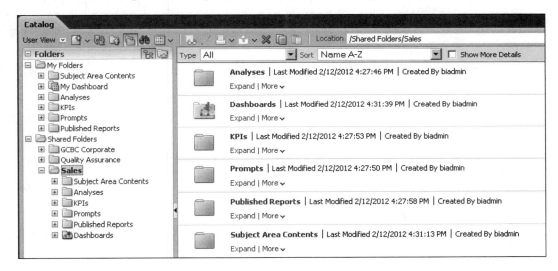

Let's take a look now in more detail at what these folders typically contain.

Personal Folders ("My Folders")

The My Folders area within the catalog is your personal view into your user folder within the catalog. When you log into the Oracle Business Intelligence web site for the first time, the system creates a user folder for you, only accessible to you, and it is this folder that is presented to you as the My Folders folder when you then view the contents of the catalog.

Typically, users would then create subfolders within the My Folders directory to hold the various types of catalog objects that they do not (at this point) wish to make available to everyone else in the organization. Permissions are set up on this folder so that only you have access to its contents, and this restriction also applies to administrators.

However, permission restrictions on catalog objects only apply when the catalog is accessed online, such as through the Catalog page on the Oracle Business Intelligence web site. We'll look later at how you can access the catalog offline, something that an administrator might want to do to get around permission restrictions.

Shared Folders

The Shared Folders area is where you store catalog objects that you want others in the organization to have access to. By default, objects stored in the Shared Folders area are readable and executable by any user granted the BIConsumer role so that other users can run your analyses but can't alter or delete them.

Group Folders   Folders created directly under the Shared Folders top-level folder are significant within the catalog, and they are often termed group folders. *Group folders* typically correspond to functional areas such as sales, marketing, operations, and so on, and are where you save new dashboards in order for them to be available from the Dashboards menu in the common header area.

   Within each group folder, you would typically create subfolders for catalog object types, with a folder called Subject Area Contents being automatically created for you within each group folder when you save objects such as shared filters or groups to the catalog. Most organizations then create application roles to correspond to these group folders that are then used to restrict access to the folders. In this case, users have access to the folders only if they are granted that role.

"Gold Standard" Group Folders   Typically, organizations make each functional area responsible for its own group folder within the Shared Folders area, which may then contain dashboards that are used exclusively within that area. Sometimes, though, you might want to create dashboards that span multiple functional areas, and you might also want to "certify" certain analyses and other catalog objects as being "gold standard" reports that have been signed off as providing agreed metrics for the business.

   When this is the case, it is often common to create another group folder within the Shared Folders area for these gold-standard reports, with change management used to control how catalog objects from other parts of the catalog are promoted into this area. Sometimes these gold-standard reports are actually created and maintained by the IT department and are overwritten and replaced when new releases of the BI system are made, unlike other user-maintained parts of the Shared Folders area which you should generally leave unchanged from release to release.

   With those guidelines in mind, how might you structure and manage the catalog in an enterprise situation, where multiple sets of users wish to store objects in the catalog in a secure way, and in a way that does not lead to hundreds of analyses and other catalog objects being stored in an uncontrolled fashion? Let's look at a typical solution now.

How to Structure the Catalog for an Enterprise BI Deployment

The catalog design approach we'll look at in this section makes the following assumptions:

- Users will be allowed to save reports to their My Folders area, and while they are stored there, no other users will have access to them.
- There are three functional areas within the organization that wish to use Oracle Business Intelligence: Sales, Quality Assurance, and Operations. Application roles will be defined and granted to users, and those users will be required to have full access to the group folders created for these areas.
- Within each group folder, subfolders will be created for catalog object types, with the standard Subject Area Contents folder used within each group for minor catalog objects.

■   A gold-standard group folder will also be created that will be used for certified catalog objects across the organization.

■   No catalog objects will be maintained in the production catalog by the IT department, and any objects IT does create will be for testing purposes only and stored in development or test catalogs.

To meet these objectives, a catalog structure should be created in the production catalog along the following lines, with each set of catalog type subfolders created under each group folder:

```
+- My Folders
+- Shared Folders
+-- Sales
+--- Analyses
+--- Prompts
+--- Published Reports
+--- KPIs
+--- Scorecards
+--- Agents
+--- Actions
+-- Quality Assurance
...
```

Dashboards that are for shared use should be created within these group folders, and the Subject Area Contents folder used for storing minor objects will be created automatically when a user first tries to store a filter, group, or other relevant object within each group folder.

In addition to these function-based group folders, the gold-standard group folder should also be created within the Shared Folders area so that the directory structure then looks like this (with the other group folders minimized, for clarity):

```
+- My Folders
+- Shared Folders
+-- Sales
+-- Quality Assurance
+-- Operations
+-- Corporate
+--- Analyses
+--- Prompts
+--- Published Reports
+--- KPIs
+--- Scorecards
+--- Agents
+--- Actions
```

The following rules will then be applied to placing objects into these folders:

■   If users wish to promote their own personal objects in their My Folders area into the relevant Shared Folders group folder, they will need to move the objects themselves and ensure that permissions are set correctly to grant access to the relevant group.

- Objects promoted from functional area group folders into the gold-standard Corporate folder have to be controlled via a change request, with the relevant team within the organization certifying that numbers in the analyses are the "one version of the truth."

- Each group-level folder will have access restricted to just the relevant functional area, with subfolders under these folders inheriting these permissions.

Now that we have a basic structure and set of rules, how do we go about actually managing catalog objects, both in terms of physically moving and copying them, as well as managing their permissions and properties? Let's discuss this next.

Managing Catalog Objects and Their Permissions and Properties

If your role involves administering the catalog, there are two main tasks that you will need to be able to perform:

- Creating catalog folders, and then moving, deleting, renaming, and altering properties for catalog objects within these folders

- Managing permissions for catalog objects, including group folders under the main Shared Folders area

In addition to these two tasks, you may also have to manage the development lifecycle for the catalog, such as moving development and test catalog objects into the production catalog or across different catalogs. This is, however, a topic in itself and is dealt with, along with managing repository objects over the development lifecycle, in Chapter 11.

Creating, Moving, Deleting, Renaming, and Managing Properties for Catalog Objects

Typically, you would create catalog folders and then manipulate catalog objects within these folders using the Catalog page within the Oracle Business Intelligence web site. To access the Catalog page, log into the Oracle Business Intelligence web site and select the Catalog link from the list of menu items at the top of the page.

To create a new catalog subfolder, navigate to the Folders pane in the top left-hand corner of the page and select the folder that you wish to create this subfolder under (for example, Shared Folders or a group folder under this). Then select New | Folder from the Catalog page toolbar, and the subfolder will inherit the permissions of the folder under which it was created.

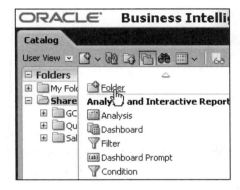

To move, rename, archive, unarchive, or alter the permissions for a folder or individual catalog object, locate it in the Catalog main pane and select the More link to see the list of actions that your user account is permitted to perform.

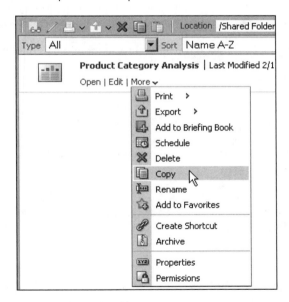

To move an individual catalog object from one catalog to another, use the Archive and Unarchive options to save an XML definition of the object to the workstation file system and then copy it to the other catalog. To move an object between two locations in the same catalog, copy the object, delete its current definition, and then locate the required folder in the catalog view and select Paste to copy the object definition to the new location.

Alternatively, you might want to use the Catalog Manager utility described in a moment, particularly if you are looking to move multiple objects or you need to access the object offline to get around access restrictions.

Managing Permissions   The default security configuration for the catalog is as follows:

- If you save an object to the My Folders area, only you can access it.
- If you save an object to the Shared Folders area, others can access it and execute the object, but only you are able to delete or amend it.

There are, by default, three application roles defined within Oracle Business Intelligence that govern what you can do within the catalog:

- **BIConsumer**   This role allows you to execute existing analyses, published reports, and agents, and schedule existing published report for distribution.
- **BIAuthor**   This role allows you to create new catalog objects such as analyses, published reports, and prompts.
- **BIAdministrator**   This role allows you to create new catalog folders, as well as move or otherwise administer catalog objects, including changing their access permissions.

Each of these roles inherits the capabilities of the role below it, so the BIAdministrator role inherits the capabilities of the BIAuthor role, which inherits the capabilities of the BIConsumer role.

In addition, typically you would want to create individual, functional area–specific application roles to control access to the group folders you create under the Shared Folders area so that an administrative user for the Sales group folder would have the following application roles granted:

BIAdministrator
BISales

Additionally, an administrator for the QA group would have these application roles granted:

BIAdministrator
BI QA

However, an end user who only needs to access objects in the Sales folder to execute them might be granted the following roles:

BIConsumer
BISales

Application roles, and LDAP groups that map to them, are defined in the Oracle WebLogic Server Administration Console and Oracle Enterprise Manager Fusion Middleware Control web applications, with the process described in detail in Chapter 8. Once you have defined these additional application roles and thereafter wish to restrict access to group folders based on them, follow these steps, which alter the permissions on an example QA and Sales set of group folders:

1. To create an initial group folder that will have access restricted to members of a particular application role (for example, a QA group folder), log in as a user that has been granted the BIAdministrator role and click the Catalog link to display the Catalog page.

2. Locate the Folders pane and click the Shared Folders folder to select it; then select New | Folder from the Catalog toolbar. When the New Folder dialog box is shown, type in the name (in this case, **QA**).

3. With the folder now listed in the main catalog view, select More | Permissions. By default, the Permission dialog box will show the BIAdministrator role having full access and the BIConsumer role having Custom access. If you click the Edit Custom Permissions button, the BIConsumer role will show a number of permissions, including Read, Traverse, and Schedule Publisher Report.

4. To restrict access to this folder to just users granted the BI QA role, select the BIConsumer role in the list and click the Delete Selected Users/Roles button.

5. Click the Add Users/Roles button, and when the Add Application Roles, Catalog Groups And Users dialog box is shown, click the Search button to locate the role that you wish to grant access to (in this case the BI QA role).

6. Use the Set Permission To drop-down menu to select Custom, and then click OK to close the dialog box.

7. Use the Edit Custom Permission button to set the permissions for this role to those that were originally granted to the default BIConsumer role:

   Read
   Traverse
   Run Publisher Report
   Schedule Publisher Report
   View Publisher Output

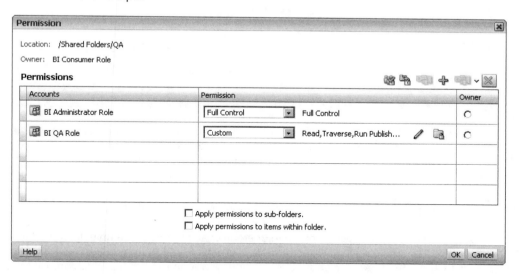

8. As you may have seen from the dialog box, users granted the BIAdministrator role will still have full control of and access to this folder. If you wish to remove this permission from this role, you will need to create special administrator roles just for these group folders, remove the default BIAdministrator role from this permission list, and replace it with these special administrator roles.

9. Now, any further subfolders that you create under this group folder will inherit the same permissions as their parent folder. You can amend these permissions if you wish, but this

inheritance helps you preserve the same permission scheme throughout the folder and its subfolders. In the same way, any objects such as analyses, prompts, and KPIs that you store in these folders will inherit the same permissions.

10. Similarly, if you have already defined a group folder, such as Sales, under your main Shared Folders area, you can retrospectively change its permissions and then propagate this change to all of its subfolders.

    To do so, log in as a user with the BIAdministrator role and select More | Permissions from the menu next to the folder name in the catalog panel. Then go through the same steps as before, removing the BIConsumer role from the list of roles in the Permission dialog box, and add the role that you wish to grant access to.

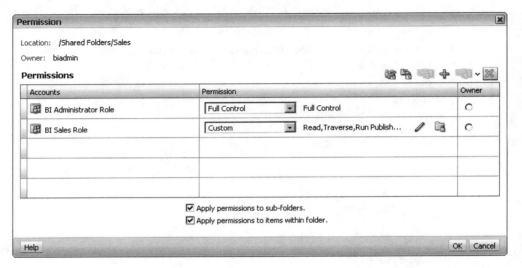

11. To ensure that all subfolders under this existing group folder also have the same permissions assigned, select the "Apply permissions to sub-folders" check box. Similarly, if the folder already contains items other than other folders, select the "Apply permissions to items within folder" check box before clicking the OK button.

Accessing the Catalog Offline Using Catalog Manager   While the Catalog page on the Oracle Business Intelligence web site is useful for maintaining individual objects in the catalog, sometimes you may wish to work with more than one object at a time, for example, to amend the permissions of more than one object at a time or move a group of objects from one folder to another.

In addition, there may be situations where you wish to bypass permissions on the catalog to access, such as individual users' reports in their My Folders directory, and move them into the Shared Folders area. In this case, the Catalog Manager utility can be used either in online or offline mode to access and manage the catalog.

When you use the Catalog Manager to access the catalog in online mode, you connect through a network connection to the catalog in the same way that the Catalog page in the Oracle Business Intelligence web site connects to the catalog. All permissions on folders and other objects are enforced, but you can use a Windows Explorer–like graphical interface to interact with objects in the catalog.

If you access the catalog in offline mode, you will need to be able to connect to an offline file system copy of the catalog typically on the same workstation as the catalog manager utility. Working offline, though, allows you to manipulate catalog objects without permissions being applied, which can be useful if you cannot otherwise gain access to catalog objects that you otherwise need to work with. See the *"Configuring and Managing the Oracle BI Presentation Catalog"* section within the *Oracle® Fusion Middleware System Administrator's Guide for Oracle Business Intelligence Enterprise Edition 11g Release 1* for more information on the Catalog Manager utility.

Administering Oracle BI Presentation Services

In addition to having links for the Home page, Catalog page, Favorites, and Dashboards, the common header area in the Oracle Business Intelligence also has a link for Administration.

Clicking this link takes you to the Administration page for the Oracle BI Presentation Server, which then presents you with a number of administration areas under various headings:

- **Security**   This area is for managing Presentation Server privileges and for creating and maintaining catalog groups.
- **Session Management**   Use this section for viewing details about user sessions and those created by agent executions.
- **Maintenance and Troubleshooting**   This is for performing various maintenance tasks.
- **Map Data Management**   This area is described earlier in this chapter.
- **Marketing**   Use this section for managing the Marketing feature within Oracle Business Intelligence.
- **BI Publisher**   This is for managing BI Publisher options.

Map Data Management was covered previously in this chapter in the "Map Views" section, and BI Publisher administration is described later in this book in Chapter 9. Let's take a look, though, at the other options listed on this page and how you use them to administer your Oracle BI Presentation Server environment.

Managing BI Presentation Server Security

The Administration page provides two links for managing BI Presentation Server security: one for managing groups and one for managing privileges.

Managing Catalog Groups   Catalog groups are provided in Oracle Business Intelligence 11g for backward compatibility with previous releases and should not be used for new implementations. Catalog groups have been replaced in this release with application roles, and to create the equivalent of a catalog group you should instead create an application role with a corresponding group folder under the Shared Folders folder.

If you use this link to create and maintain catalog groups, you will see the groups are listed alongside application roles when you come to assign permissions to folders and catalog objects. Therefore, you should only use this link if an upgrade from a previous release has automatically created catalog groups for you, and over time you should plan to move these catalog groups to application roles and retire the catalog groups from your application.

Managing Privileges   Managing privileges is all about controlling which Presentation Server features your users and application roles have access to. By default, the BIAdministrator role has access to most (but not all) BI Presentation Server features, while the BIAuthor role has the ability to create analyses and other catalog objects but not perform administration tasks.

Access	Access to Dashboards	BI Consumer Role
	Access to Answers	BI Author Role
	Access to BI Composer	BI Author Role
	Access to Delivers	BI Author Role
	Access to Briefing Books	BI Consumer Role
	Access to Mobile	BI Consumer Role
	Access to Administration	BI Administrator Role
	Access to Segments	BI Consumer Role
	Access to Segment Trees	BI Author Role
	Access to List Formats	BI Author Role
	Access to Metadata Dictionary	BI Author Role
	Access to Oracle BI for Microsoft Office	BI Consumer Role
	Access to Oracle BI Client Installer	BI Consumer Role
	Access to KPI Builder	BI Author Role
	Access to Scorecard	BI Consumer Role
Actions	Create Navigate Actions	BI Consumer Role
	Create Invoke Actions	BI Author Role
	Save Actions containing embedded HTML	BI Administrator Role

The BIConsumer role, by contrast, generally has privileges only to execute existing catalog content. However, by using this link and the subsequent Manage Privileges page, you can amend these privileges. Be careful, though, not to significantly change the purpose of any of these roles, creating instead new roles with appropriate naming if you wish to create new types of users with elevated privileges in certain areas.

A common reason that you might want to access this feature is to grant the privilege to perform database write back or execute direct database requests to a particular application role. These privileges are listed on this page, are disabled by default for all application roles, and will need to be explicitly enabled, even for the BIAdministrator role, before you can make use of these features.

If your organization has not licensed the Oracle Scorecard and Strategy Management component of Oracle Business Intelligence Foundation, which is described in the upcoming section "Creating KPIs and Scorecards," you might also want to deny access to this feature to all roles within your system in order to ensure that you do not inadvertently use features that your organization is not licensed for.

Session Management

If you wish to see SQL and other details of currently running user sessions, you can open the nqquery.log file (normally found at [*middleware_home*]/instances/instance1/diagnostics/ OracleBIServerComponent/coreapplication_obis1/) using a text editor to see varying amounts of detail, depending on the log level you have selected for users.

Opening log files on the server is not always practical, though; instead you can use the Manage Sessions and Manage Agent Sessions links on the Administration page to view details of currently connected sessions. To do this, click the Manage Sessions link to see a listing of current sessions and the queries they are running.

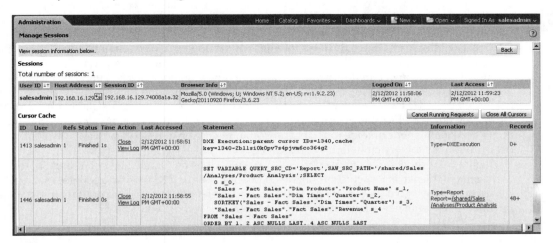

To view the individual nqquery.log entries for each of the queries that are executing, click the View Log link. If query logging has been enabled for that particular user, you will see the entries in the nqquery.log file for that particular query. If logging has not been enabled for that user, you will instead receive a No Log Found error message. Similarly, you can click the Manage Agent Sessions link to see a listing of currently executing agents, with details of the job and instance ID and a link to view the agent definition.

Maintenance and Troubleshooting

Using the Maintenance and Troubleshooting area of the Administration page, you can use the following links on the page to perform administration tasks:

- **Manage Device Types**   You can use this link to manage device types used by agents as delivery targets for analyses and other BI objects.

- **Toggle Maintenance Mode**   This can be used to set the catalog as "read only" temporarily while you copy the catalog to another location, or make a backup copy.

- **Reload Files and Metadata**   This is for refreshing the BI Presentation Server's cached copy of the Oracle BI Repository after online changes have been made to it, and for clearing caches.

- **Issue SQL**   Select this to directly issue logical SQL queries to the BI Server. It is useful for debugging and testing purposes.

■ **Scan and Update Catalog Objects That Require Updates** Choose this after a patch migration from one release of Oracle Business Intelligence 11g to another (for example, version 11.1.1.3 to 11.1.1.5 or 11.1.1.6).

Creating KPIs and Scorecards

Until this point, we have been creating analyses, agents, prompts, and other BI objects that display data to users in the form of measures, dimension attributes, and hierarchies. To a database developer, such terms are commonplace and familiar, and are not too far removed from the underlying database structures in your data sources. Business users, however, do not talk in terms of measures, attributes, and hierarchies; they typically think in terms of objectives, key performance indicators (KPIs), and the state of the initiatives they are working on.

The 11g release of Oracle Business Intelligence introduced a new feature that addresses the needs of business-oriented end users, called Oracle Scorecard and Strategy Management. Using this new feature, you can define in your catalog such new object types as KPIs and scorecards, allowing you to create catalog metadata that conveys more meaning to business-orientated users because it provides more "context" than just simple tables and columns of data. Dashboards that clearly reference hierarchies of corporate objectives, linked to KPIs such as sales performance to quota and quality performance to target can communicate, in a very visual way, how your organization is progressing in terms of its strategy and goals.

Figure 6-10 shows an example dashboard page built using Oracle Scorecard and Strategy Management, displaying a scorecard made up of objectives and KPIs organized into a strategy tree.

So how do we go about creating these KPIs and scorecards, and where does their metadata fit in with the rest of the catalog metadata that we've been working with so far?

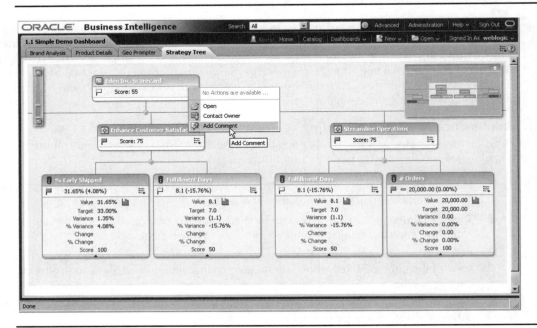

FIGURE 6-10. *A strategy tree within a dashboard page*

Overview of KPIs and Scorecards

Oracle Scorecard and Strategy Management is a new component within Oracle BI Foundation that is embedded directly into the Oracle Business Intelligence web site. It stores its metadata in the catalog, similar to how Oracle BI Publisher is a separate application to Oracle Business Intelligence but is integrated into its user interface. Using Oracle Scorecard and Strategy Management, you can define key performance indicators (KPIs), KPI watchlists, and scorecards and embed them in your dashboard pages.

What Are KPIs?

Key performance indicators (KPIs) are catalog objects that bring together existing pieces of catalog metadata and make them into something more meaningful to business users. The set of KPIs that you define for your project are completely up to you, but examples of KPIs that you might create include

- Sales performance to quota
- Products returned to target
- Cost-to-income ratio
- Average revenue per FTE (full-time equivalent)

KPIs bring together several bits of catalog metadata to create something that potentially has more meaning and impact for end users:

- They bring together sets of actual and target measures.
- These measures are then linked to dimensions, allowing you to slice and dice them.
- The relationship between the actual and target measures is then used to set a status for the KPI, such as on target, above target, or below target, which is then used instead of percentages and numbers.
- The KPIs can also have supporting documents and catalog objects associated with them.

 # Employees | Last Modified 7/8/2011 4:24:30 PM | Created By Paulo Rodney
Open | Edit | More ⌄

 # Orders | Last Modified 7/8/2011 4:25:01 PM | Created By Paulo Rodney
Open | Edit | More ⌄

% Early Shipped | Last Modified 7/8/2011 4:25:57 PM | Created By Paulo Rodney
Open | Edit | More ⌄

Attrition Rate | Last Modified 7/8/2011 4:27:05 PM | Created By Paulo Rodney
Open | Edit | More ⌄

Avg Order Size | Last Modified 7/8/2011 4:26:36 PM | Created By Paulo Rodney
Open | Edit | More ⌄

Avg Revenue per FTE | Last Modified 7/8/2011 4:26:51 PM | Created By Paulo Rodney
This KPI tracks the Average revenu per FTE.
Open | Edit | More ⌄

Billed Qty | Last Modified 6/29/2011 2:08:52 PM | Created By Paulo Rodney
This KPI tracks the Billed Quantity again the Target Quantity Measure.
Open | Edit | More ⌄

Once you define a set of KPIs in the catalog, you can use them in various ways; you can view them in the form of an analysis to see how the KPI's state varies across its dimensions, or you can create conditions based on the KPI state that can then be used as part of agents or to drive other conditional behavior.

The primary uses for KPIs, though, are in conjunction with two other new catalog object types that you can create with Oracle Scorecard and Strategy Management: KPI watchlists and scorecards.

What Are KPI Watchlists?

KPI watchlists take sets of KPIs and organize them into lists of related items, which you can then drop onto dashboard pages and use as a way of quickly understanding the status of your organization's main drivers. KPI watchlists can have prompts associated with them so users can vary the point of view they are using to analyze the KPIs and can communicate with KPI owners to find out the background for the information they are looking at.

KPI Watchlist - Functional Example KPIs

Objects ∨   View ∨   Summary: ⭐⭐⭐⭐⭐ 4 Stars (2) ⭐⭐⭐⭐⭐ 3 Stars (1) ⭐⭐⭐⭐⭐

Label	Status	Trend	Actual	Target	Variance	% Variance
Basic 5 State KPI	⭐⭐⭐⭐⭐		50,000,000.00 USD	54,000,000.00 USD	4,000,000.00 USD	7.41%
Basic 5 State KPI - Pinned to Biztech	⭐⭐⭐⭐⭐		21,000,000.00 USD	22,310,000.00 USD	1,310,000.00 USD	5.87%
Basic 5 State KPI - Pinned to FunPod	⭐⭐⭐⭐⭐		17,500,000.00 USD	20,522,000.00 USD	3,022,000.00 USD	14.73%
Basic 5 State KPI - Pinned to HomeView	⭐⭐⭐⭐⭐		11,500,000.00 USD	11,168,000.00 USD	(332,000.00 USD)	-2.97%
KPI with Self-Sustaining target	✓	⬆	20,000	13,233	(6,767)	-51.14%
KPI with Self-Sustaining target 2	✓	▭	50,000,000	50,000,000	0	0.00%
KPI with Self-Sustaining target 3	✗	⬇	1,525,598 USD	8,390,787 USD	6,865,189 USD	81.82%

KPI watchlists are an effective way to bring together sets of related KPIs and present them to users in a simple-to-understand way. If you want to use KPIs to try and communicate how an organization is performing against an overall strategy, one that perhaps has many facets or perspectives to it, then the other way to make use of KPIs is in the form of a scorecard.

What Are Scorecards?

Scorecards are catalog objects that take KPIs and use them to show progress against an overall strategy, expressed in terms of overall objectives and the initiatives that support them.

For example, your company strategy might be to be the best restaurant chain in the San Francisco Bay area, which you will achieve through the twin objectives of being the most financially successful chain and being the one with the best customer service ratings. To measure progress against these objectives, individual KPIs such as profit to target, revenue per FTE, and customer service ratings to target can be used to objectively measure how close you are to achieving your strategy. Scorecard visualizations such as strategy trees and cause-and-effect maps can then be used to graphically show the relationship between objectives and the state of their associated KPIs.

Scorecards, KPIs, and KPI watchlists are a very effective way of communicating your overall strategy to users, and as they use the same underlying catalog metadata as the analyses that you have created for more detailed analysis of your data, you can link them all together to provide a coherent, joined-up view of your business's performance with appropriate levels of detail and focus for all types of users within your organization.

Oracle Scorecard and Strategy Management Licensing

Oracle Scorecard and Strategy Management, like Oracle BI Mobile, which we'll look at in the next section of this chapter, is not included in the basic Oracle Business Intelligence Enterprise Edition Plus license but is licensed separately, either on its own or as part of the wider Oracle Business Intelligence Foundation package.

Therefore, although you will see links and menu items for KPIs, KPI watchlists, and scorecards on the Oracle Business Intelligence web site, bear in mind that if you have just upgraded from an earlier release of Oracle Business Intelligence and not licensed this product separately or as part of Oracle Business Intelligence Foundation, you will need to speak to your Oracle representative before you can use it in a production situation.

Creating KPIs

Now that we have seen an overview of what Oracle Scorecard and Strategy Management is all about, let's take a look at a scenario where we can see them in action. In this scenario, your organization has recently completed a review of strategy and used this to define some objectives and KPIs that you would like to use Oracle Business Intelligence to help communicate.

As hinted at earlier, your organization, the Gourmet Coffee and Bakery Company, wishes to become the most successful bakery and coffee shop chain in the country, and to do this it has decided on two objectives:

■ To be as financially successful as it can be

■ To have the best customer service and staff loyalty in the industry

To measure progress against these objectives, it has identified four key performance indicators that it needs to monitor:

■ **Sales to target**   With each store having its own monthly targets

■ **Margin to target**   With a constant margin target of 30 percent for the business

■ **Customer service survey ratings vs. target**   With each store having its own monthly target

■ **Staff satisfaction survey ratings vs. target**   With each store having its own target per period

The first two KPIs use subject area tables from the Sales – Fact Sales subject area, whereas the second two use tables from the Sales – Store Quality subject area. Let's start by creating these KPIs within the Oracle Business Intelligence catalog, and then later on we'll use them to create a KPI watchlist and a scorecard.

Creating an Example Set of KPIs

To create KPIs within the catalog, you use the KPI editor within the Oracle Business Intelligence web site, which takes you through the various stages in defining the KPI. Let's start off with the sales to target KPI, and then we'll create the other three KPIs in turn.

1. To create the first KPI, select New | KPI from the Oracle Business Intelligence web site menu. You will then be prompted to select a subject area; for this first KPI, select Sales – Fact Sales.

2. The KPI editor will then open, at the General Properties page, where you can select the actual and target values for the KPI, and enable trending if you wish. In this first example,

there are measures already within the catalog that we can use for the actual and target values, so enter the following values for this page:

Description: Sales Amount vs. Target KPI
Business Owner: [*leave at default*]
Actual Value: "Fact Sales"."Sale Amount"
Target Value: "Fact Sales"."Sale Amount Target"

Later on we will set one of these values to a calculation, but for now, use the actual and target measures in the catalog to set the actual and target values.

3. Under these settings you should see a check box labeled Enable Trending. Trending uses a time dimension object within your subject area to show how the KPI is trending compared to a prior period, and should be enabled if possible in order to show the maximum amount of context to the end user.

   Select this check box, and then select or enter the following values to enable trending against the Month level in this subject area's corresponding time dimension.

   Enable trending: [*selected*]
   Compare to prior: "Dim Times"."Month YYYYMM"
   Tolerance: 2
         % Change

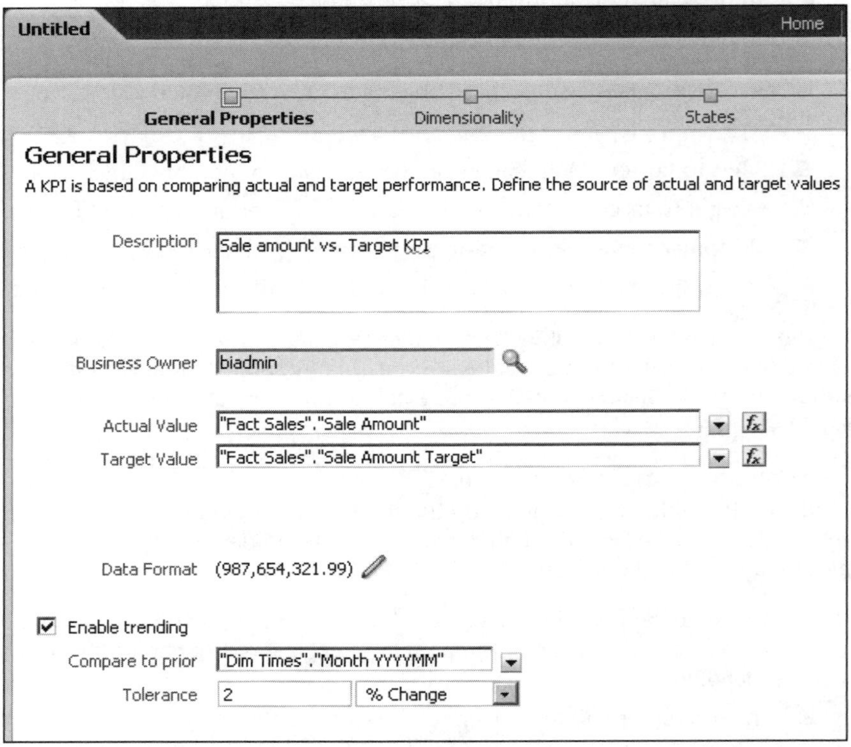

4. Note that the value selected for "Compare to prior" is a subject area attribute column associated with a level in a time dimension, not the time dimension level itself. We'll see the effect of this trending setting later on in the example, when we place this KPI on a KPI watchlist. For now, click Next to proceed to the next step in the KPI editor.

5. The Dimensionality page will then open. This KPI, along with all of the other KPIs, will be dimensioned by the Dim Stores.Stores and Dim Times.Times - Year hierarchical columns, though you could use regular dimension attribute columns instead of hierarchies if you wish (or a combination of both column types).

   Click the Add button, and select the following values to dimension your KPI by these dimension hierarchies:

   Dimension: Dim Times.Times – Year   Value: <is prompted>
   Dimension: Dim Stores.Stores   Value: <is prompted>

	Untitled				Home	Catalog	Favorites ⌄	Dashboards ⌄

General Properties	**Dimensionality**	States	Related Documents	Custo

Dimensionality
Define dimension values for the KPI or allow each dimension to be prompted by the user.

Define KPI value for

Dimension	Value
Dim Times.Times - Year	<is prompted> ▼
Dim Stores.Stores	<is prompted> ▼

[Add...] [Remove]

NOTE
Setting the dimension columns to <is prompted> rather than a specific dimension member allows the user to change the dimension point of view through a prompt on the dashboard within the constraints of what data their security profile allows them to see. You would, however, set these dimension settings to a specific value if you wanted to, for example, "pin" time to a particular period or stores to a specific region.

6. Click Next to proceed to the next page in the KPI editor.

7. The States page will now be displayed. This page is probably the most important step in defining the KPI, as it determines how the various states that the KPI can have are defined.

A KPI in Oracle Business Intelligence can have one of three goals:

■ **High values are desirable.** This goal is used for measure to target–style KPIs where you want the actual values to be as large as possible compared to the target values.

■ **Low values are desirable.** This goal is used for costs to income–style KPIs where the opposite is true and the actual values need to be as small as possible compared to the target values.

■ **Target value is desirable.** This goal is used, for example, in actual to target risk–style KPIs where you have a target risk percentage and you want the actual risk recorded to be as close as possible to this, with both higher and lower actual risk amounts being equally worse, as one indicates not taking enough risk (and therefore lowering return), whereas the other indicates taking too much risk (and therefore potentially losing too much money).

In this example, as we are defining a measure to target–style KPI, so from the Goal drop-down box, select High Values Are Desirable.

Using the rest of the dialog box, you can set the various states that the KPI can have and fine-tune the threshold levels between each state. By default, every KPI has three states, which correspond to green (OK), yellow (Warning), and red (Critical). You can use this dialog box to add extra states, change the state's names and colors, change the threshold levels, and associate actions with each state.

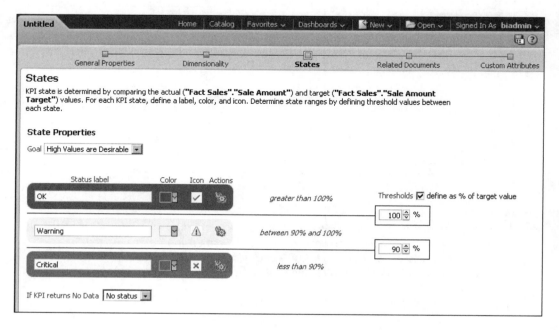

For this KPI, though, leave the states at their default settings, which define the threshold points as less than 90% for the critical state, between 90% and 100% for the Warning state, and greater than 100% for the OK state.

8. Click Next to move on to the next page of the KPI editor.

9. Using the Related Documents and Custom Attributes pages, you can link the KPI to other catalog objects or to external web pages and also associate other measures in the catalog with this KPI. For now, though, just click the Finish button and save the KPI to the catalog using the name **Sale Amount vs. Target**.

10. Repeat the preceding steps to create three more KPIs, using the same Dim Stores.Stores and Dim Times.Time – Year dimensions, the same trending settings, and the same state definitions so that you have a set of KPIs you can use with the KPI watchlist and scorecard you'll be creating later on in this section.

KPI Name	Subject Area	Actual Value	Target Value
Margin vs. Target	Sales – Fact Sales	(("Fact Sales"."Revenue"-"Fact Sales"."Cost")/"Fact Sales"."Revenue")*100	30
Customer Satisfaction vs. Target	Sales – Store Quality	Fact Survey Results.Customer Satisfaction Score	Fact Survey Results.Customer Satisfaction Target
Staff Satisfaction vs. Target	Sales – Store Quality	Fact Survey Results.Staff Satisfaction Score	Fact Survey Results.Staff Satisfaction Target

11. When you finish defining these KPIs, you should then be able to view them within the catalog and also within the Home page on the Oracle Business Intelligence web site. In the following illustration, the four KPIs are listed in the Home page Recent area and are ready for us to analyze and embed in KPI watchlists and scorecards.

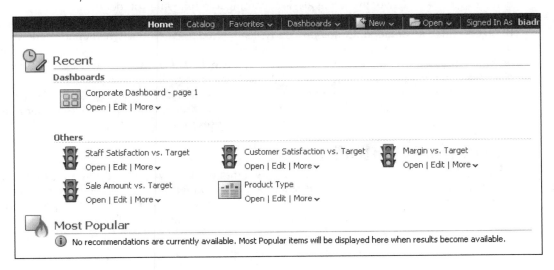

Analyzing KPIs and Using Them for Conditions   Now that you have defined some KPIs, what can you do with them apart from using them in KPI watchlists and scorecards? Two things that you can do right away are to analyze the KPI based on its dimension settings and use it to create a condition.

To analyze a KPI, select Open from the menu links next to the KPI in the catalog view. Opening the KPI will display it in the form of an analysis, and you can drill into the dimensions that you have defined for it to see how its states vary over the dimension members. In the following illustration, you can see the states for the Sale Amount vs. Target that we defined a moment ago varying across the stores and times hierarchies.

| Sale Amount vs. Target | | | | | | Home | Catalog | Favorites ∨ |

Sale Amount vs. Target

Times - Year	Stores	Actual	Target	Status	Variance	% Variance
⊟ All Times	⊞ All Stores	350.00	463.00	✘	(113.00)	-24.41
⊞	East SF					
⊞ 2010	⊟ All Stores	1,050.00	463.00	✓	587.00	126.78
	⊞ Central SF	75.00	82.00	⚠	(7.00)	-8.54
	⊞ North CA	26.00	5.00	✓	21.00	420.00
	⊞ North SF	113.00	249.00	✘	(136.00)	-54.62
	North USA	19.00				
	⊞ Other USA	18.00	28.00	✘	(10.00)	-35.71
	⊞ South CA	62.00	64.00	⚠	(2.00)	-3.13
	SouthWest USA	6.00				
	⊞ West SF	31.00	35.00	✘	(4.00)	-11.43

Refresh - Print - Export

Similarly, you can select More | Create Agent for an individual KPI to create a new agent definition that will deliver the KPI analysis according to a schedule you define.

Agents are described in more detail in Chapter 7 of this book, which also describes a type of BI object called a *condition*. *Conditions* are typically used to determine whether an agent distributes a report or invokes an *action*, and return Boolean true or false values based typically on the number of rows returned by an analysis. You can, however, use KPIs to determine the outcome of a condition, testing for a particular KPI state and returning Boolean true or false values depending on whether the required state was detected, making it possible to drive a piece of workflow or conditionally display part of a dashboard based on the state of one of your KPIs.

Now let's take a look at one of the most common uses for KPIs: creating a KPI watchlist.

Creating KPI Watchlists

KPI watchlists take sets of KPIs and organize them into a list showing the current state of the KPI, actual and target values, variance, and other indicators. Dimension controls at the top of the KPI watchlist allow the user to vary the point of view where KPI dimensions are set to "is prompted" and messages can be sent to the KPI owner to request clarification or feedback on a particular KPI.

Let's take the four KPIs created in the previous section and create a KPI watchlist to display their states and values. Later on, we'll embed the KPI watchlist in a dashboard page and use prompts to vary the dimension member point of view.

Creating an Example KPI Watchlist

The following example uses the four KPIs created in the previous example. Two of the KPIs use the Fact – Sales Fact catalog subject area, while the other two use the Fact – Store Quality subject area.

1. Using the Oracle Business Intelligence web site menu, select New | KPI Watchlist.

2. The KPI Watchlist editor will then open with a blank area to add KPIs to. Navigate to the Catalog pane on the left-hand side and use the catalog folder structure to locate the Sale Amount vs. Target KPI that you created earlier. Drag-and-drop it into the main watchlist area, and the KPI editor will display the Add KPI dialog box once to complete the drop.

3. The Add KPI dialog box allows you to select a particular dimension member value for each of the KPI dimensions or leave them as Use Point-of-View if you want the user to be able to vary the member selection.

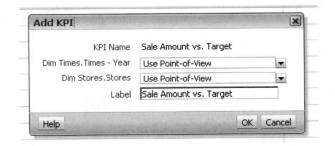

Leave these values at their default Use Point-of-View setting, and leave the Label value at its default setting. Then click OK to close the dialog box and add the KPI to the watchlist area.

4. Drag-and-drop the remaining three KPIs onto the watchlist, again accepting the default values when the Add KPI dialog box is shown. You should then have four KPIs listed on the watchlist.

5. By default, the dimension selections are set to "all members"; that is, all time periods and all stores. To show KPI values for a particular month and store, use the dimension drop-down prompts to select the following values:

Sales – Fact Sales.Dim Stores.Stores: Fishermans Wharf
Sales – Fact Sales.Dim Times.Times – Year: 201012
Sales – Store Quality.Dim Stores.Stores: Fishermans Wharf
Sales – Store Quality.Dim Times.Times – Year: 201010

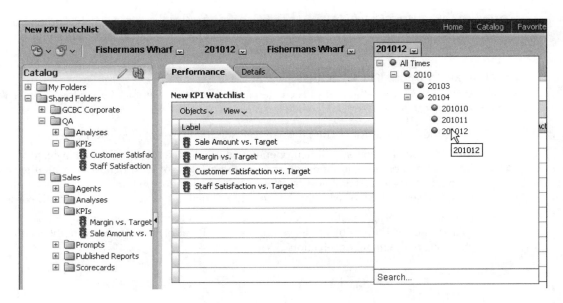

Note that, although the two dimension hierarchies (Store, and Times – Year) are logically the same, because they come from two different catalog subject areas, they are listed twice in the point of view selector and have to be set separately.

6. Now that you have selected a particular time period, the trend calculations in the KPI Watchlist will become active. You will be able to see the trend upward or downward for each KPI, relative to the previous month's status, as well as actual and target values, variance, and so on.

   By right-clicking individual KPIs, you can display a menu of actions that you can perform on the KPI.

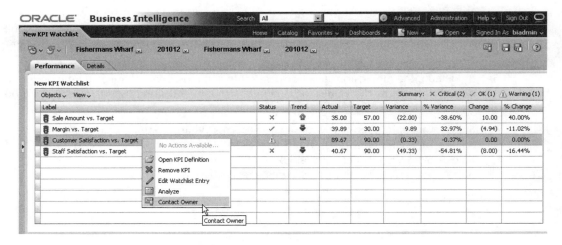

For example, you can open the KPI definition for exiting, or analyze the KPI in the same way as if you clicked on the Open link for the KPI in the catalog view. Contact Owner brings up a dialog box where you can send a message to the owner of KPI, with the message being delivered by the email server registered by the system administrator for general agent use using the email address registered in the system by the KPI owner.

7. Once complete, save the final KPI watchlist to the catalog.

Embedding KPI Watchlists in Dashboards

So far, we have analyzed the KPI watchlist from within the KPI Watchlist editor, but usually you'll want to include the watchlist in a dashboard page, along with some prompts so that users can vary the dimension hierarchy point of view. Prompts are described in more detail earlier in this chapter, but in this example we'll create prompts using hierarchical columns rather than the attribute columns we've used so far in this chapter so that these match with the hierarchical columns we used to define the dimensionality of the various KPIs.

To embed a KPI watchlist in a dashboard page and connect it to a set of prompts, follow these steps:

1. Start by creating named (dashboard) prompts for each of the dimensions used in the KPI definitions. Then open the Oracle Business Intelligence web site and select New | Dashboard Prompt from the menu. When prompted, select Sales – Fact Sales as the subject area.

2. When the dashboard prompt editor is displayed, select New Prompt | Column Prompt from the editor toolbar.

3. When the Select Column dialog box is displayed, select the first hierarchical column that was used in the KPI definition (for example, Dim Times.Times – Year), and click OK to close the dialog box. Then, when the New Prompt dialog box is shown, click OK to use the default values and close the dialog box.

4. Once done, click Save to save the prompt to the catalog, and then repeat these steps to create the remaining three prompts that you'll need to use for the dimensions used by your KPIs.

5. Now you can add the KPI watchlist and the prompts to a dashboard page. Either open an existing dashboard page or create a new one (New | Dashboard) so that you have the dashboard editor open and the Dashboard Objects pane available on the left-hand side of the page.

6. Add two Column objects to the main dashboard page layout, and then drag-and-drop the four prompts onto one of the columns. Next, drag-and-drop the KPI watchlist onto the other column so that the Dimension Pinnings dialog box is shown. Click OK to leave these set to the default Not Pinned value so that they get their values from the prompts you have added to the page.

NOTE
At the time of writing, the 11.1.1.6 release allows pinning for only one of the subject areas referenced in a KPI watchlist, even if there are two or more subject areas referenced. Check the My Oracle Support web site for a patch if this issue affects you.

7. Save the dashboard, and then click Run to execute it.

You will now be able to change the dimension points of view by selecting values in the prompts you have just created.

Creating Scorecards

In the "What Are Scorecards?" section of this chapter, we mentioned scorecards as being an effective way to communicate the strategy being implemented by an organization. By defining things such as objectives and initiatives, and using KPIs to measure progress against these, you can use documents such as strategy trees, strategy maps, and cause-and-effect maps to show progress against your strategy in a very visual way.

Scorecards, of course, are not a new idea, and in fact there is much theory and writing around the scorecard concept. Before we get into the mechanics of how scorecards are implemented using Oracle Business Intelligence, let's take a look at this theory.

The Theory of Balanced Scorecards

Balanced scorecards first became popular with the writings of Kaplan and Norton, who proposed the idea in the first edition of their bestselling book, *The Balanced Scorecard: Translating Strategy into Action*. *Balanced scorecards* are a way of defining objectives and linking them together to show how, for example, one set of objectives can be broken down into sub-objectives, which all together help define the aims of an organization. The balanced element of this comes from the idea that for an organization to succeed it has to adopt a balanced approach to business, making sure that quality and customer care are as much of a priority as the traditional financial objectives of an organization.

The scorecard element of Oracle Scorecard and Strategy Management implements many of the aspects of Kaplan and Norton's theories, so let's take a look now at the components that make up an Oracle scorecard.

Scorecard Components

Scorecards within Oracle Scorecard and Strategy Management are created using the scorecard editor, and they have a number of components you can define:

- **Objectives**   These are the primary aims of the organization, such as to improve customer satisfaction or financial performance. Objectives can be nested so that the financial performance objective can break down into objectives around reducing costs, increasing revenues, or improving stockholder returns.

- **Initiatives**   These are projects and other programs that are being run in support of the objectives. Implementing a new IT system, for example, would not be an objective of the organization, but it would be an initiative that is in support of potentially multiple objectives.

- **Perspectives**   These are ways of categorizing objectives and initiatives; for example, you might categorize objectives as being financial, customer, internal process, or learning and growth perspectives (the standard perspectives proposed by Kaplan and Norton), or you might define your own that are more appropriate for your organization.

- **Key performance indicators (KPIs)**   These are used to assess progress against your objectives and initiatives.

- **Scorecard documents**   These are the various visualizations that you can use to display objectives, initiatives, and KPIs.

Initiatives are considered optional when working with Oracle scorecards, though they can be useful to help illustrate how efforts within the organization are feeding into objectives and overall strategy. All of these components, along with the overall scorecard, are defined within Oracle Business Intelligence in the scorecard editor.

The Scorecard Editor

The scorecard editor is actually part of Oracle Scorecard and Strategy Management, but it is embedded within the main Oracle Business Intelligence web site. You can use it to define and edit scorecards, as well as to analyze scorecards that you have already created, though in most cases you would embed individual scorecard documents in a dashboard page, as you would with KPI watchlists.

Figure 6-11 shows the scorecard editor, which like the dashboard editor and the analysis editor has a number of panes down the left-hand side and a main pane that contains the design of the scorecard.

Working around the editor from the left-hand side, these panes are

- **Strategy** This pane is for defining the hierarchy of objectives and previewing them as a strategy tree or a cause-and-effect map.

- **Initiatives** Use this pane for defining initiatives and linking them to objectives.

- **Scorecard Documents** Here you can define documents such as strategy trees and strategy maps. (We'll look at the full range of documents in a moment.)

- **Perspectives** You can use this pane for editing and adding to the default set of perspectives.

- **Catalog** This pane is for selecting KPIs and other objects to add to the scorecard.

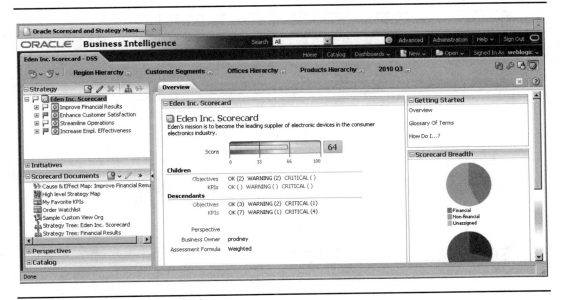

FIGURE 6-11. *The scorecard editor*

- **Dimension member selectors** This is across the top and is for analyzing scorecards and changing the dimension member point of view.
- **The main scorecard editor** This pane is in the main part of the page and is for viewing the details of the scorecard objects you create.

Scorecard Documents

Once you have defined your objectives, initiatives, KPIs, and the relationships between them, you can visualize your scorecard through a number of scorecard document types such as the strategy map document, which is embedded in a dashboard page. An example of a strategy map document is shown in Figure 6-12.

These document types include

- **Cause-and-effect maps** These let you illustrate the cause-and-effect relationships of an objective or KPI.
- **Strategy maps** These show how objectives and the KPIs that measure their progress are aligned by perspectives. They also indicate cause-and-effect relationships between objectives and KPIs.
- **Strategy trees** These show an objective and its supporting child objectives and KPIs hierarchically in a tree diagram.
- **Custom views** These allow you to drop individual objectives onto a canvas background that you design.

Now that you know the basics about what's in a scorecard, read on to learn the process that you have to follow to create one.

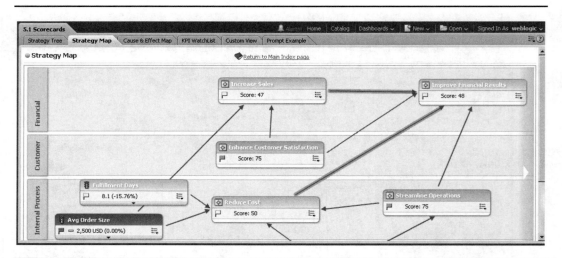

FIGURE 6-12. *A strategy map*

Workflow for Creating a Scorecard Scorecards are quite a big area within Oracle Business Intelligence, and this section of the chapter can only serve as an introduction to the topic. At a high level, though, the steps you will need to define and then use a scorecard are as follows:

1. Within your organization, identify and define your objectives, initiatives, and the key performance indicators that you will use to measure progress against them.

2. Within Oracle Business Intelligence, create KPIs and store them in the catalog.

3. Create the new scorecard using the scorecard editor, and select the perspectives that you will be using to categorize objectives and initiatives.

4. Define the objectives and organize them into the required hierarchy.

5. Define your initiatives and organize them into a hierarchy. Where appropriate, link these initiatives to your objectives.

6. Assign your KPIs to these objectives and initiatives.

7. For your objectives and initiatives, assign actions and other settings such as narratives, descriptions, and so on.

8. Create your scorecard documents.

9. Publish the scorecard documents into dashboard pages, linking them to prompts as appropriate.

Before you do that, though, there's one small piece of administration you need to carry out so that scorecard annotations can be saved to a database.

Configuring the Oracle BI Repository to Connect to the Annotations Database Schema
When users analyze scorecard documents, they can leave comments on objectives for particular combinations of dimension members. For example, if an objective of Improve Financial Performance were showing as "critical" for a particular month and store, a comment could be attached to the objective explaining why performance was poor that month or asking for additional information. When you add these comments to the scorecard document, they are persisted in a set of tables in the BIPLATFORM schema created by the Repository Creation Utility when you install Oracle Business Intelligence (described in detail Chapter 2 of this book).

Before this comment persistence can be used, though, you need to configure a connection in your Oracle BI Repository to this schema that Presentation Services will then use in order to write annotation elements to the relevant tables. This connection must use specific physical database and physical connection pool names, as Presentation Services looks for these particular names in the physical layer of the repository when attempting to save an annotation. Note that when you come to configure this connection, only the physical database and connection pool settings need to be defined—Presentation Services uses these to locate your BIPLATFORM schema and then knows automatically which tables are used to store annotations.

To create this connection, follow these steps, ensuring that the database name and connection pool name are specified exactly as in the steps:

1. Using the Oracle BI Administration tool, open your repository online (File | Open | Online).

2. Navigate to the physical layer of the repository and create a new physical database entry by right-clicking and selecting New Database.

3. When the Database dialog box is displayed, name the database **BSC** and select the database type of the database for which you used the Repository Creation Utility to create the BIPLATFORM schema when you first installed Oracle Business Intelligence.

4. Right-click the BSC database that you just created and select New Object | Connection Pool.

5. In the Connection Pool dialog box, name the connection pool **BSC** and then select or enter the connection details to the database that holds your BIPLATFORM schema; for example:

Name: BSC
Data Source Name: orcl
Shared logon: DEV1_BIPLATFORM
Password: welcome1

6. Select File | Save to save the repository. If you ever use a different repository with your system, make sure you re-create this database and connection pool entry if you want to ensure that your scorecard comments and annotations are persisted.

Creating an Example Scorecard

Let's start now with creating a scorecard. To recap the scorecard scenario we went through at the start of this section of the chapter, we are creating a scorecard for the Gourmet Coffee and Bakery Company that wishes to become the most successful bakery and coffee shop chain in the country. To do this, they have decided on two company objectives:

■ To be as financially successful as they can be

■ To have the best customer service and staff loyalty in the industry

To measure progress against these objectives, they have identified four key performance indicators that they need to monitor:

■ **Sales to target**   With each store having its own monthly targets

■ **Margin to target**   With a constant margin target of 30 percent for the business

■ **Customer service survey ratings vs. target**   With each store having its own monthly target

■ **Staff satisfaction survey ratings vs. target**   With each store having its own target per period

We'll begin by defining the objectives, and we'll then add some example initiatives afterward to show how they fit into the scorecard model.

Defining the Objectives   To define the two objectives identified a moment ago and create the initial scorecard, follow these steps:

1. With the Oracle Business Intelligence web site open, select New | Scorecard, and in the New Scorecard dialog box, select or enter the following values:

Name: GCBC Scorecard
Description: Scorecard for the GCBC Corporation
Location: /Shared Folders/GCBC Corporate
Use Default Perspectives: [*selected*]

2. Click OK to close the dialog box and open the scorecard editor.

3. Navigate to the Strategy pane in the top left-hand corner of the scorecard editor. You will see an existing entry in there, named after the scorecard.

4. To rename it to just GCBC so that this becomes the name of the top-most entry in your strategy tree documents, double-click it to open it in the main editor area. Then rename it **GCBC** and click the Save button just above where you overtyped the objective name.

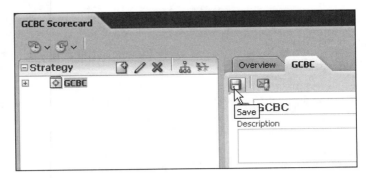

5. Now you can add the first of the two objectives. Within the Strategy pane, right-click the GCBC objective and select Create Objective.

6. The new objective will open on the right-hand side of the page. Rename the objective to **Improve Financial Performance**, and then select Financial as the perspective type lower down in the dialog box. Click Save to save the objective.

7. Repeat step 6 by again right-clicking the GCBC objective in the Strategy pane and this time calling the objective **Maintain Quality**. Select Customer as the perspective. Click Save when you are finished.

If you now view the contents of the Strategy pane, you will see your two new objectives listed under the main GCBC objective. We'll leave these objectives for now, but we'll come back to them later after we've assigned some KPIs to them.

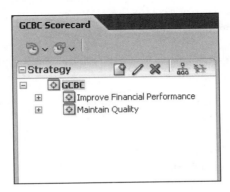

Defining the Initiatives   Initiatives aren't mandatory when creating a scorecard, but if there are projects going on within your organization in support of your objectives, it's useful to record them in the scorecard definition. If you have KPIs that manage progress against these initiatives, you can also assign them to these initiatives to show progress.

We'll now add an initiative called Refurbish branches, which (at least in the short term) has a negative effect on financial performance, but in the long term it has a positive effect on customer and staff satisfaction.

1. Using the scorecard editor, navigate to the Initiatives pane and click the Create Initiative button.

2. When the new initiative opens in the main area, rename it **Refurbish Branches** and click the Save button.

3. To record the relationship this has with the two objectives you created a moment ago, scroll down within the Initiative Linkage dialog box until you find the Related Items area. Then drag the Improve Financial Performance objective into this area, and when the Objective Linkage dialog box is shown, select the following values:

   Initiative: Refurbish Branches
   Objective: Improve Financial Performance
   Strength: Weak
   Proportionality: Inverse

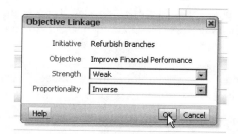

4. Repeat step 3, this time adding the Maintain Quality objective to the Related Items area and setting the strength to Strong and the proportionality to Direct. Once complete, click Save to save the initiative details.

Assigning KPIs to Objectives   Now we can add the relevant KPIs to the objectives created earlier on. To do so, follow these steps:

1. Either select the Improve Financial Performance objective in the tab listing at the top of the screen if the objective is still open for editing, or double-click it in the Strategy section to open it for editing.

2. With the objective open for editing, drag-and-drop the following two KPIs from the Catalog pane into the Objectives and KPIs section:

   Amount Sold vs. Target
   Margin vs. Target

3. When prompted by the Add KPI dialog box, click OK to accept the default values and allow the KPI point of view to be varied by the scorecard editor or prompts on the dashboard.

4. Repeat step 3 for the other objective, Maintain Quality, dragging and dropping the following KPIs into the Objectives and KPIs section:

    Customer Satisfaction vs. Target
    Staff Satisfaction vs. Target

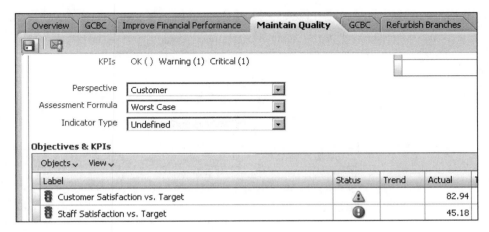

5. Once complete, make sure you save all of your objective definitions.

Determining How Objective and Initiative States Are Defined   If you now view your objectives in the Strategy pane, you will see that the KPIs you assigned to them are now showing states, and these states are causing the objectives to have their own state. As you will see at this point, the overall status of the top-level GCBC objective is critical, as are the objectives under it.

To see why this is the case, follow these steps:

1. Open the Improve Financial Performance objective again, and scroll down to just above where the KPIs are listed. You will see three drop-down menu settings:

    Perspective: Financial
    Assessment Formula: Worst Case
    Indicator Type: Undefined

2. The Perspective setting we looked at earlier and the Indicator Type setting can be changed to Leading or Lagging. It's the Assessment Formula setting that's determining our overall objective state, though, with the current Worst Case setting telling the scorecard to take the single worst KPI state assigned to the objective and use that to set the overall objective's state. You can change this setting to one of the following values:

Worst Case
Best Case
Most Frequent Worst Case
Most Frequent Best Case
Weighted

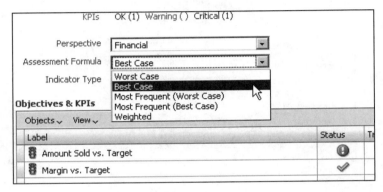

Let's change this now to Best Case, save the objective, and then view the overall state of the objectives in the Strategy pane. You'll see that this objective now has an OK status, but overall the topmost objective is still shown as critical. Why do you think this is?

3. To find out why, double-click the overall GCBC objective and view the Assessment Formula setting for it. Again, it's set to Worst Case, and the critical status of the Maintain Quality objective is causing this objective's status still to be reported as critical.

4. For our company, although financial and customer objectives are both important, in reality financial objectives are more important, so let's use the Weighted option to reflect this. Select Weighted for the Assessment Formula, and then edit the weighting values next to each of the objectives so that Improve Financial Performance is weighted 75%, while the other objective is weighted 25%.

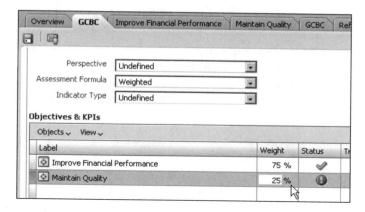

5. Save the objective, and you should now see the overall GCBC objective in the Strategy pane showing OK as the state, since the OK state in the financial objective now has greater weighting than the state of the customer objective.

Now that we have defined the objectives for our scorecard, and fine-tuned the way in which the objectives' statuses are defined, let's perform one last configuration task, to assign actions to the Improve Financial Performance objective.

Linking Actions to Objectives   In Chapter 7, we will look in detail at a feature called actionable intelligence, and in particular at a catalog object type called an action. *Actions* are metadata objects that define navigation paths to analyses or other objects, or invoke external processes such as workflows or web services. At a simple level, though, we can use actions to set up links between BI objects such as objectives and analyses in the catalog so that, for example, those objectives can provide links to supporting analyses depending on the current state of the action.

In this example, we have two analyses defined in the catalog:

- Finance High-Level Breakdown
- Finance Exceptional Items Analysis

We will configure the scorecard so that if the Improve Financial Performance objective has a status of OK or Warning, we will provide an action link that allows the user to see the Finance High-Level Breakdown analysis. If the objective has a status of Critical, though, we will set this link to change so that it takes the user to the Finance Exceptional Items analysis, as this is a more appropriate analysis for when the finance situation is concerning.

To associate these analyses through action links with this objective, follow these steps:

1. With the scorecard editor open, double-click the Improve Financial Performance objective in the Strategy pane to open it for editing.

2. Scroll down to the Analytics area in the objective dialog box and locate the currently empty Actions area.

3. To add the first action link, click the New Row button to display the Action Link dialog box and select OK as the State Equals setting. Click the New Action button next to the Action setting to select Navigate to BI Content, and then use the Browse button to select the required analysis.

4. Change the Link Text value to read **Display High-Level Breakdown of Numbers**, and click OK to close the dialog box.

5. Repeat steps 3 and 4 to select the Warning value for State Equals, selecting the same action type and analysis, and entering the same Link Text value.

6. Create a third entry in this list for the Critical setting for State Equals, but this time link to the other analysis, Finance Exceptional Items Analysis, giving the link text an appropriate value.

All three action links should now be displayed in the Actions list, as shown in the following illustration.

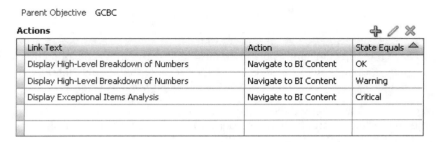

Parent Objective   GCBC

Actions   + / ✖

Link Text	Action	State Equals △
Display High-Level Breakdown of Numbers	Navigate to BI Content	OK
Display High-Level Breakdown of Numbers	Navigate to BI Content	Warning
Display Exceptional Items Analysis	Navigate to BI Content	Critical

Creating the Strategy Tree Document   We're now at the point where we can create some scorecard documents so that we can start to visualize the relationship between our objectives, initiatives, and KPIs. Let's start with a strategy tree, the most commonly used scorecard visualization.

1. With the scorecard editor open, navigate to the Scorecard Documents pane and select Create | Create Strategy Tree.

2. A new strategy tree document will open in the main area of the editor. To display individual KPIs associated with each objective, click the little circle button under each objective.

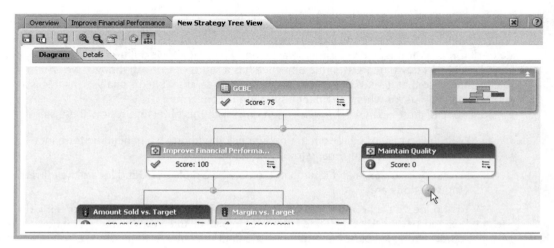

3. Because you will use this strategy tree document in a dashboard page in a moment, click the Save button to save the document to the catalog.

Other scorecard documents can be created using the Create menu in the Scorecard Documents pane; for now, though, let's use the scorecard editor to analyze the scorecard.

Analyzing the Scorecard from Within the Scorecard Editor and from Within a Dashboard Page   Now that you have created the scorecard, you can analyze it either from within the scorecard editor using the dimension drop-down menus at the top of the page, or you can embed individual scorecard documents within a dashboard page in the same way you do with KPI watchlists, using prompts to control the values used by the various KPI dimension settings.

Accessing Dashboards and Reports Using Mobile Devices

So far we have looked at accessing your business intelligence data through a web browser on your desktop PC or laptop. There are, however, several tools you can use to access data in your Oracle Business Intelligence system:

- A desktop or laptop web browser, as we have done so far
- Microsoft Office, using Oracle BI Office
- Briefing Books, another feature for offline access of your data
- Oracle BI Mobile

Oracle BI Mobile is a part of Oracle BI Foundation, and it allows you to access your analyses, dashboards, alerts, and published reports using mobile devices such as the Apple iPad and Apple iPhone. Let's take a look now at what you can do with Oracle BI Mobile and how you can use it to access your analytics "on the move."

Overview of Mobile Access Using the iPad and iPhone

Oracle BI Mobile is a feature within Oracle BI Foundation that provides client access to Oracle Business Intelligence through iPhone Operating System (iOS) devices such as the Apple iPad and Apple iPhone. Dashboards and other BI objects developed for desktop web browsers will display with no changes required using Oracle BI Mobile, allowing you and your users to access BI information on the road using their mobile devices.

To use Oracle BI Mobile, your users download the Oracle Business Intelligence application from the Apple iTunes Store and then connect to your Oracle Business Intelligence system over the Internet or through secure networks set up using a virtual private network (VPN). Users working with Oracle BI Mobile can view existing catalog content but cannot create their own, making it effectively a read-only solution for end users.

How Does It Work?

The Oracle BI Mobile application, shown in its Apple iPad form in Figure 6-13, is a "hybrid" mobile application that uses a native iOS application to connect to Oracle Business Intelligence with a built-in web browser that renders analyses, dashboards, and other objects so they will display with no modification in your mobile device.

Apple iOS devices do not use Adobe Flash, the technology that Oracle Business Intelligence uses to display charts and other visualizations in desktop web browsers, so the Oracle BI Mobile application displays charts and other data in a format compatible with these devices. Because Flash is not used, though, you do not get the full range of chart drilling and other interaction types. However, you can still navigate between dashboards, browse the catalog, and use prompts, for example.

Licensing

Although you can download the Oracle Business Intelligence application from the iTunes Store for free, you do need to have the Oracle BI Mobile license to use this feature. Licensable separately or bundled as part of Oracle Business Intelligence Foundation, you need to have this license in place for the number of users who will be accessing your system via mobile devices or on a per-CPU basis before using this feature in production.

Prerequisites

No specific setup of Oracle Business Intelligence is required to enable mobile access, although if your system is generally only available on your internal company network, you may wish to put in place a VPN server so that users on the public Internet can connect to your network and then access your Oracle Business Intelligence installation.

FIGURE 6-13. *Oracle BI Mobile on an Apple iPad device*

Configuring an Apple iPad for Oracle BI Mobile

Let's now go through the process required to set up an Apple iPad to connect to an Oracle Business Intelligence system so that you can try out Oracle BI Mobile. The steps required to set up an Apple iPhone or iPod Touch would be more or less the same, but see *Oracle® Fusion Middleware User's Guide for Oracle Business Intelligence Mobile 11***g** *Release 1* for full details for your particular device.

To set up an Apple iPad for Oracle BI Mobile, follow these steps:

1. Start the Oracle Business Intelligence Mobile application, and if it is the first time that you have used it, tap Accept to accept the end user license agreement.

2. The application then displays the list of available Oracle Business Intelligence servers. The first time you use the mobile application, tap the + sign (next to Add Server) to add your server to the list.

3. In the Server Settings dialog box, select or enter the following details:

   Name: The name you will assign to this server (for example, SampleApp)
   Host: The hostname or IP address for the server (for example, obisrv1)
   Port: The port number for the server. Initially set to 80, this should typically
   be changed to 7001 or 9704 if you have not enabled SSL, or 443 if you
   have enabled SSL.
   SSL: Secure Sockets Layer. Initially set to ON, you should select OFF unless
   you have enabled SSL on your server.
   SSO: Single sign on. By default set to OFF, only set to ON if your server has
   single-sign on enabled.
   Username: Your username on the server (for example, asmith)
   Password: Your password on the server (for example, welcome1)
   Save Password: Select ON to save your password on your iPad, or OFF if it is a
   shared device and you want to enter your password each time
   you connect to the server.
   Device Locale: Select ON if you wish to pass the mobile device's locale settings
   to the Business Intelligence Server. Leave at OFF if you want to
   use the default locale for your login credentials.
   Analytics Path: Leave this at the default value of /analytics/saw.dll.
   Publisher Path: Leave this at the default value of /xmlpserver.

4. When you've entered the server setting information, tap Save to save your details, and then when you return to the list of servers screen, tap Login to connect using these details.

The first time you connect to the business intelligence server, a small set of files will be downloaded to your mobile device, and you can then start analyzing your BI content from your Apple iPad, iPhone, or iPod Touch.

Analyzing Data Using the iPad and iPhone

Now that you have configured your Apple iPad to access your Oracle Business Intelligence system, let's walk through a scenario where you are using the Sample App that comes with every installation of Oracle Business Intelligence to update yourself on your business's performance while having your early-morning coffee.

After having configured your iPad for connecting to Oracle Business Intelligence, you can click the Home button in the top left-hand corner of the iPad screen and select from the Favorites list the Brand Analysis dashboard to display a dashboard containing graphs, pivot tables, a ticker, and some prompts.

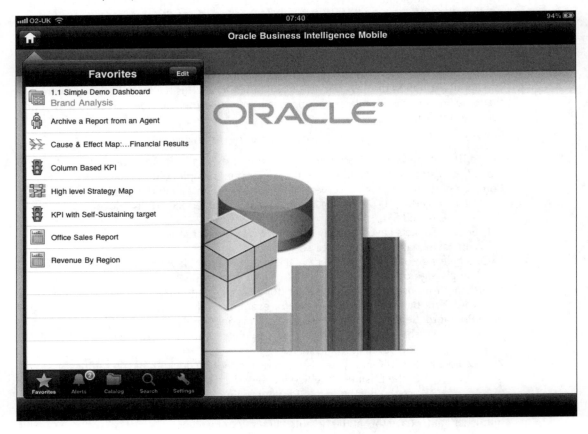

TIP
You can add any dashboard to the Favorites list by clicking the Favorites button at the bottom of the iPad screen at any time.

To switch to another page within this dashboard, you click the arrow at the top of the page to display a drop-down menu listing all the pages (tabs) on this particular dashboard.

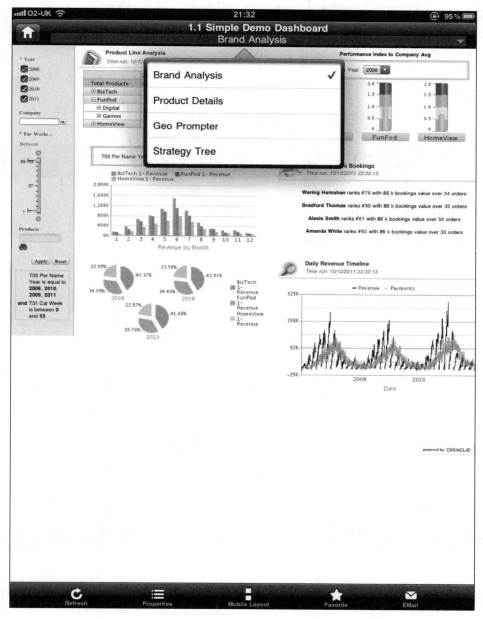

Just as you can with dashboards on your laptop or desktop, you can interact with tables, prompts, and other objects on the screen to further explore your data. For example, you can tap EMail at the bottom of the screen to send someone a link to that page, and you can tap Refresh at any time to update your view of the data.

NOTE
Oracle Business Intelligence Mobile requires a connection with your Oracle Business Intelligence server, either through a WiFi connection or a cellular network.

So far we have been accessing whole dashboards of data using Oracle BI Mobile, but we can also access individual analyses or published reports through the mobile interface. In addition, you can select Alerts on the Favorites list to see a list of alerts and delivered reports that have been sent to you, and this offers a useful way to keep yourself apprised about events of interest within your organization while you're away from the office.

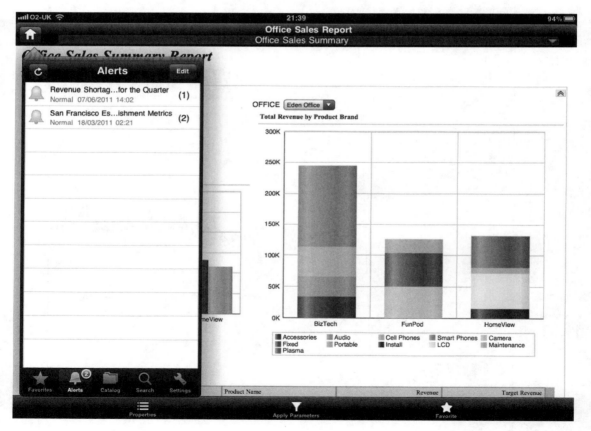

With Oracle Business Intelligence Mobile, you can access your business intelligence content on the road, in a café, or wherever else you may be when you need that information.

So with this look at Oracle BI Mobile we've now completed the chapter on creating analyses, dashboards, scorecards, and KPIs. In the next chapter, we'll look at how they can be integrated with external applications and processes using the agents, actions, and conditions that were mentioned several times in this past chapter, using a feature called *actionable intelligence*.

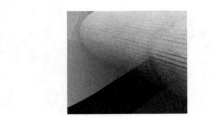

CHAPTER
7

Actionable Intelligence

ypically, when someone analyzes their data using a dashboard or report and sees something of interest that they want to act on, they have to make a note about it and perhaps investigate it later on, when they are back at their desk and have access to all their applications. If they want to initiate a workflow or start a business process, they have to log on to another application, pick up the phone, or send an e-mail, involving themselves in more work and raising the risk of the action not being taken at all.

Similarly, while dashboards can display business information in a meaningful and interesting way, it is not always possible to hunt through every page, every analysis, and every report to find out if something you are monitoring now requires you to take action. Wouldn't it be great if your business intelligence system could alert you when something happens that needs your attention, so you can spend your time spotting opportunities and solving problems rather than monitoring thousands of reports?

Actionable intelligence is the term used by Oracle to describe a set of features provided by the Oracle Business Intelligence 11*g* Action Framework. The Action Framework uses catalog objects called *agents*, *actions*, and *conditions* to help you create multi-step workflows that can "sense and detect" events of interest to end users, present them with information to help them make a decision, and then give them the option to take action on what they've decided to do, right from the dashboard, in what could be called a closed-loop BI system.

As a practical example of how actionable intelligence can be implemented, you could create a BI system that notifies a sales representative about an "out of stock" situation on a key inventory item by an alert sent to the sales representative's mobile phone by an agent that runs every hour to check stock levels. This situation would require the sales representative's immediate attention because, if left unaddressed, some key accounts would not be able to order that key inventory item. The sales representative would read the alert, review all of the orders currently outstanding for that product, and realize that the order management system needs to be adjusted to prioritize the product's delivery. The sales representative would therefore initiate an "action" that calls a workflow process, ensuring that new stock arrives in the distribution center later that week. All of this would take place on the sales representative's mobile phone, and the situation could be rectified within minutes, avoiding thousands of dollars of lost orders and several unhappy customers.

In this chapter, we will first take an overall look at the Actionable Intelligence concept, and how the Action Framework within Oracle Business Intelligence 11*g* uses actions, agents and workflows to create these "sense and detect" workflows. We will look at how navigation actions and invocation actions make it possible to link your dashboard and analyses to external applications and business processes, and we will see how agents provide the workflow and automation features that drive these features and also allow you to distribute reports and information to users via multiple channels. Let's start though by taking a high-level view of what actionable intelligence is.

What Is Actionable Intelligence and the Action Framework?

Before we get into the details of how we work with the Action Framework, it's worth taking a moment to understand, at a high level, how actionable intelligence works within Oracle Business Intelligence 11*g* and how users and developers interact with actions and agents when you add them to your dashboards.

Actions

The Action Framework is the overall term for the part of Oracle Business Intelligence that provides actions, agents, and conditions together with capabilities to connect to external processes and applications. Actions, a part of the Action Framework, are catalog objects that define interactions with these outside processes and can be linked, via action links, to columns and KPIs in your analyses and scorecards.

From an end user's perspective, actions usually take the form of menu items called *action links* that appear next to column values in analyses, enabling the user to invoke an external business process, navigate to a related report, display a related web page, or take some other action related to the data in their report.

Amount Due	Days Overdue		Action
700	26		Click to take Action
2,712	61		Click to take Action
1,832	39		Click to take Action
3,157	34		Click to take Action
1,263	45		Click to take Action
1,509	70		Click to ~~take Action~~
			Search for company news
3,743	80		Click to Initiate Credit Hold
1,619	24		Click to take Action
			Initiate Credit Hold
1,385	32		Click to take Action

Actions can be made available from table views, pivot tables, charts, scorecards, and other BI objects, and can also be invoked by agents, which are like workflow processes with "sensors" running in the background that are configured to detect events by running analyses to test for conditions. Action links can even be made conditional so that different actions are presented to the user depending on the values displayed in the report.

Developers can create actions that either navigate to content or invoke some form of functionality, for example to initiate a business process in an external application. Actions can be used to execute business processes through invoking a web service, which in turn might start a human workflow task through a BPEL process, all using standard-based interfaces provided by middleware platforms such as Oracle Fusion Middleware.

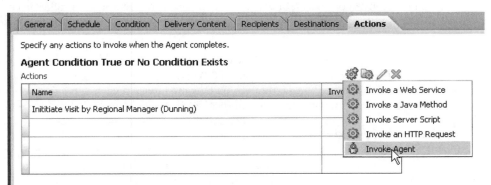

Actions are stored in the Presentation Server catalog, and while many actions do not require any prior configuration, some require you to set up connections and security settings so that your business intelligence system can connect securely and seamlessly to outside systems.

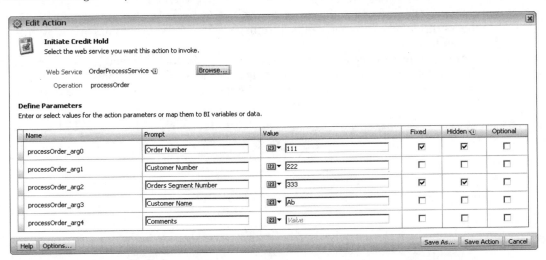

Let's take a look at actions now in more detail, starting by looking at how actions and the Action Framework are implemented as part of Oracle Business Intelligence's component architecture.

Component Architecture

Actionable intelligence is supported by server-side Java integration components that run within Oracle WebLogic Server, and user interface and metadata features provided by the Oracle BI Presentation Server system component, that also provides the dashboard, analyses, and other visual elements provided to the end user.

- **Oracle BI Presentation Server system component**   This stores the definition of actions, action links, and action link menus in the Presentation Server catalog and displays actions as part of analyses and dashboards through the user's web browser.

- **Oracle BI Action Services Java component**   This is part of the bimiddleware JEE application that is deployed on the WebLogic Managed Server for Enterprise installations of Oracle Business Intelligence, and on the Administration Server for installations using the Simple Install type.

Not all actions use the Action Services Java component, for example, actions to invoke other analyses or dashboards, or actions to navigate to EPM components such as Hyperion Financial Reporting reports. Those that do use it though, such as the Invoke a Web Service action, use the Action Service as an intermediate process that receives instructions to invoke a service from the Oracle BI Presentation Server, calls the service, and then passes the results back to the Presentation Server, for display in the users' analysis or dashboard.

Oracle Business Intelligence uses a configuration file called ActionFrameworkConfig.xml. This file contains several elements that you manually create and edit to define how the Action Framework works, including registries of available services, location aliases to help when you move systems from development to production, and details of how services are secured so that your system can pass credentials and connect to each system securely.

Away from the back-end infrastructure, developers and end users working with the Action Framework have access to three types of BI metadata objects in the Presentation Server catalog:

- **Actions**   These are named objects that reference another BI object, web page, or external report to navigate to, or an operation, function, or process to invoke. Actions can be secured and scoped to particular users or application roles and are stored in the catalog alongside dashboards, analyses, conditions, KPIs, and other BI objects.

- **Action links**   These are how you tie individual actions to specific analysis columns, scorecard objectives, KPI states, or other BI contents. When clicked, action links run the associated action.

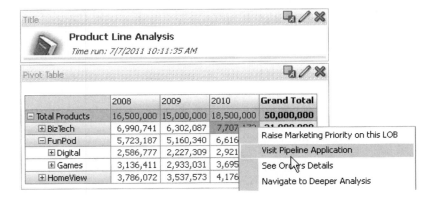

- **Action link menus**   These are collections of action links that you add to a dashboard page, enabling users to select from a list of actions after analyzing the data on their dashboard.

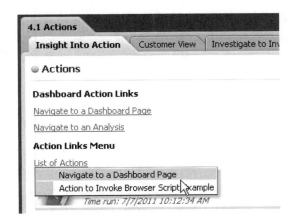

Depending on what services you access through the Action Framework, Oracle Fusion Middleware security can also be involved in the process, providing the capability to store credentials that you will need to access internal services, and interfacing with the security systems used by web services and other external applications and processes.

Types of Actions

A number of action types are available to use with Oracle Business Intelligence. They can be categorized as either navigation actions, which navigate to content such as analyses or other web pages, or invocation actions, which launch a business process or workflow.

Navigation Actions   Two navigation actions are available by default:

■ **Navigate to BI Content**   This action is used to link one analysis or dashboard to another one, to provide drill-through or drill-down functionality between reports.

■ **Navigate to a Web Page**   This action is used to launch a web page and, optionally, pass parameters in the URL string.

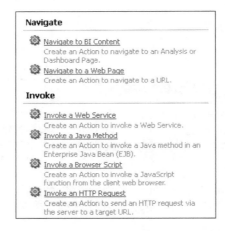

Other navigation actions can be added if you configure the Action Framework to enable them:

■ **Navigate to EPM Content**   This action is used to link an analysis or dashboard to an EPM report, currently limited to Hyperion Financial Reporting, and, optionally, to pass parameters to set the report's "point of view."

■ **Navigate to E-Business Suite**   This action is used to navigate to a particular screen in Oracle E-Business Suite.

■ **Navigate to Siebel CRM**   This action is used to navigate to a particular screen in Oracle's Siebel CRM system.

Invocation Actions   Four invocation actions are available by default:

■ **Invoke a Web Service**   This action is used to invoke individual web services or workflows through technologies such as Business Process Execution Language (BPEL).

■ **Invoke a Java Method**   This action is used to create actions to invoke Java methods in an Enterprise Java Bean.

- **Invoke a Browser Script** This action is used to run JavaScript to, for example, collect and then forward parameters to a web site.
- **Invoke an HTTP Request** This action is typically used for GET/POST interactions with a web-based service.

There are also two invocation actions that you can define through the Action Framework that, instead of appearing on the dashboard menu, are invoked through the Oracle BI Scheduler:

- **Invoke a Server Script** This action is used to run VBScript or JavaScript scripts on a Microsoft Windows server to, for example, archive log files or perform some other action.
- **Invoke an Agent** This action is used to chain agents together as part of a workflow.

Another form of invocation action is run from the Java Host system component:

- **Java Jobs** This action is used to run custom Java programs at the end of an agent execution, through the Java Host component.

Later in this chapter, we will look at each type of action and explore, in depth, how it is configured and used in a business intelligence application. Some actions require little or no setup before you can use them, while others, as you will see, require some knowledge of technologies such as service-oriented architecture, web services, Java, and security.

Agents and Conditions

Agents and conditions also have their own server-side elements, as well as metadata objects that you create in the Presentation Server catalog:

- **Agents** These are objects that you create in the Presentation Server catalog that automate the running of analyses, typically to check for conditions and deliver alerts to subscribed users. In previous releases of Oracle Business Intelligence, agents were called iBots.
- **Conditions** These are objects that use analyses or KPIs to test for conditions and return a Boolean value, which is typically used by agents to determine whether to raise an alert or distribute a report.

Agents can be defined to run immediately, to run on demand, or to run on a schedule (either once or on a regular basis by using the Oracle BI Scheduler system component). Agents can be configured to test for a condition at startup and then carry out their assigned task only if the condition is met (or not met). Agents can deliver content such as analyses or dashboards to users via their chosen distribution channel.

Behind the scenes, the BI Server system component connects to the Oracle BI Presentation Server component and is capable of "impersonating" the user who has subscribed to the agent, allowing it to run with the data and system privileges of that user. To do this, credentials are stored in the credential store, part of Oracle Fusion Middleware security, to allow impersonation to take place and for the various system components to securely communicate together.

Introduction to the Action Framework

Now that you understand conceptually how actionable intelligence works within Oracle Business Intelligence 11g and the roles of the Action Framework, agents, and components, this section explains how the Action Framework is implemented through actions, action links, and action link menus. For this example, we will use a different set of sample data to that used elsewhere in the book, the Sample Application ("SampleApp") for Oracle Business Intelligence 11g that can be downloaded from the Oracle Technology Network. At the time of writing, the current version of SampleApp is v107 and can be downloaded from http://www.oracle.com/technetwork/middleware/bi-foundation/obiee-samples-167534.html; SampleApp is, however, updated from release to release of Oracle Business Intelligence and you should download the version that matches your product version.

In this section, we will also look at the structure and content of the Action Framework configuration file, see how actions interact with Oracle Fusion Middleware security, and see how the Action Framework relates to another integration technology within Oracle Business Intelligence; Oracle BI Services for SOA.

Creating Actions, Actions Links, and Action Link Menus

Apart from the specific configuration actions you may have to take for certain action types, the process of creating and using actions is similar across all action types. The process varies in how you choose the action target. You may need to select the action target from the Presentation Server catalog, select it from a registry, or enter it as a URL or other web address. Once your target is selected, though, parameters are defined in a common way and your action is either stored in "named" form in the catalog or is defined "inline" as part of another BI object's definition.

Once the action itself is defined, using it as part of an analysis, dashboard, scorecard, or other BI object involves the same process regardless of the action type. So, before we get into the specifics of configuring and working with each type of action, let's take a high-level look at how actions are created, how they are then associated with columns in an analysis, and then made available to end users in a dashboard.

Example: Creating an Action and Using as an Action Link in an Analysis

The following steps show a simple example of creating an action to navigate to the Oracle Technology Network web site. We will create the navigation using the Navigate to Web Page action type, save it to the catalog, and then associate it with a column in an analysis so that it displays conditionally, depending on values for that column in each row of the analysis view.

Actions are created from the Oracle BI web application, using either the list of shortcuts on the left-hand side of the home page or the common header menu at the top of every screen.

1. To create an action using the menu, for example, ensure that you are logged in as a user with the ability to create actions and then select New | Action. As you can see here, Action is listed in the menu along with Agent under the Actionable Intelligence heading.

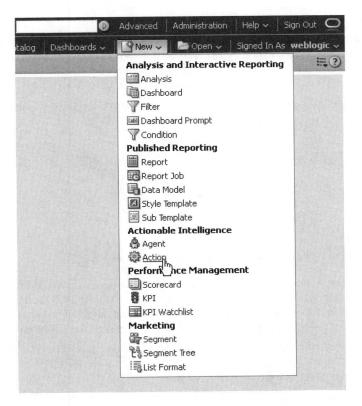

2.   After selecting New | Action, you are presented with the following menu of action types that you can select from. You can add to this list of default, out-of-the-box selections by configuring additional action types such as Navigate to EPM Content or Invoke a Server Script. (We will look at how to configure these additional actions later in this chapter.)

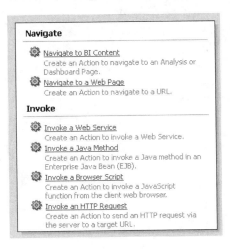

3. Using the Action menu, select Navigate To A Web Page.

4. This type of action requires a URL to navigate to, and also allows you to pass parameters to the web page, which in turn can be mapped to columns in an analysis. For now, though, in the New Action dialog box, just enter the URL for the Oracle Business Intelligence on the OTN web site, which at the time of writing is

    http://www.oracle.com/technetwork/middleware/bi-enterprise-edition/overview/index.html

    and then click Save Action.

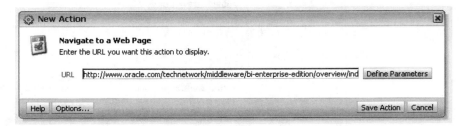

5. The Save Action dialog box that opens allows you to save the action definition into the Presentation Server catalog. Save the action to your required location (remember to save the action to a shared location if you want to make it available to other people) and then click OK to close the dialog box. You have now completed the definition of this simple action.

6. To try out your new action, either create a new analysis or open an existing one. In this example, we will use a simple analysis that lists product categories and sales, and displays the results in the form of a table view.

7. Associate with this analysis the action you created previously. To do so, with the analysis open for editing, select the Criteria tab and, for the column that you wish to attach the action to, select the Column Properties menu item.

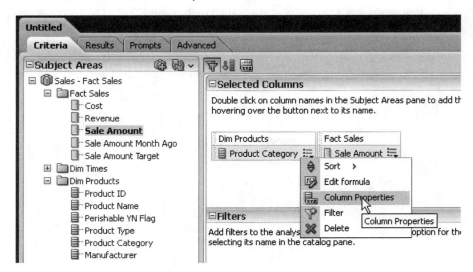

8. In the Column Properties dialog box, select the Interaction tab. You can then use this tab to select the Action Links option for the column heading or for individual values in the column. In this example, select Action Links from the Primary Interaction drop-down list under Value, and leave the Column Heading setting at the default (Drill).

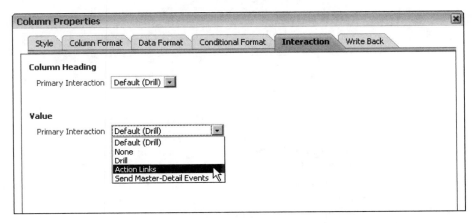

9. In the Action Links table that is displayed, you can define one or more action links that are either displayed for all values or displayed depending on a condition being satisfied. Click the Add Action Link button to start creating your first action link.

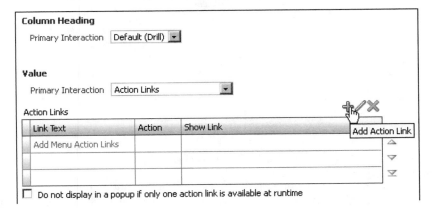

10. In the New Action Link dialog box, enter a name for the action (for example, Display Oracle BI Website), and then either click the Create New Action button to create a new, "inline" action definition that will exist only within this analysis, or click the Select Existing Action button to choose the "named" action you created earlier.

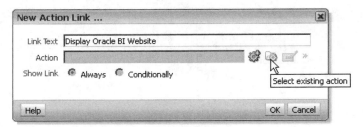

11. In the Select Action dialog box, navigate to, and then select, the action you wish to add as an action link to the analysis.

12. Back in the New Action Link dialog box, you are given the option to show the link always or conditionally. If you select the Always option, the action link will be displayed for all rows in the analysis. In this instance, though, select Conditionally so that the action link will be displayed only for certain rows, depending on the value displayed in this column.

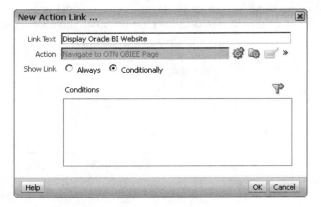

13. Click the New Condition (the filter icon) button and either select a column name from the list that is displayed or select More Columns if you wish to base the condition on another column in the subject area. In this example, select Sale Amount as the column to base the condition on.

14. In the New Condition dialog box, create a condition (for example, Sale Amount is greater than 1000) to define when the action link will be displayed, and then click OK to close the dialog box.

15. Your action link definition is now complete. Click OK to save it, and then use the Action Links list on the Interaction tab to define any other action links that you would like to associate with this analysis column.

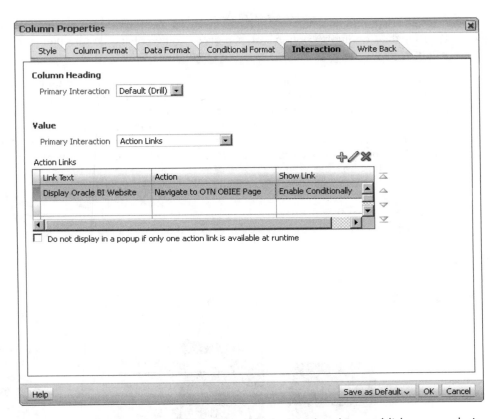

16. Try out your new action and action link. Switch to the Results tab, or publish your analysis to a dashboard, and then look at the column in the analysis view that uses the action link. In this example, where the Product Category value for a particular row is greater than 100, the action link is displayed and you can use it to navigate to the Oracle Technology Network web site. Where values are less than or equal to 100, no action link is displayed because of the condition that you added to it.

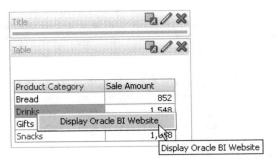

17. When the action link is displayed, click it, which will navigate you to the web page as defined in the action.

Any column in the analysis can have none, one, or more than one action associated with it. By using the Conditional option, you can display different actions for different column values. So where else can you use actions, then, apart from analyses?

Where Can I Use Action Links?   When you associate an analysis column with an action in the form of an action link, the action link becomes available for use by any appropriate view that you define for the analysis. The previous example used a table view, but you could use a pivot table view, map view, gauge view, or chart view, and the action link would also be available if you clicked the column value in the view. The following screenshot captures a bar chart showing the action link when we click a product category that meets the condition we defined earlier for this particular action link.

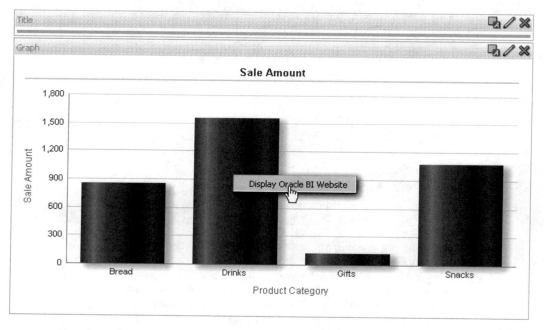

In addition to adding action links to analyses, you can also add them to dashboard pages, scorecard objectives, scorecard initiatives, and KPIs. For example, KPIs have "states" rather than values, and you can associate specific action links with specific KPI states, giving users the ability to display relevant information or invoke a business process depending on the state the KPI is in.

Some types of actions (such as Invoke a Server Script and Java Jobs) cannot be added as action links to an analysis, dashboard, or other object on the screen, but instead must be invoked by the BI Scheduler using an agent. Other types, such as those to invoke web services, browser scripts, HTTP requests, or other agents, can be either added as action links or invoked through an agent. See the more detailed explanations of each action type later in this chapter for more details.

Action Link Menus   When you add action links to an analysis, scorecard objective, or other BI object, you can add more than one of those links to the object by using the action link table that you saw in the previous section. When you add action links to a dashboard page, you can either add individual action links to the page or explicitly add another object, called an *action link menu*, which gives you the same table of action links to work with.

To illustrate how this works, consider a situation where you have a new dashboard page that you wish to add actions to. In this instance, when you open the dashboard page for editing, the Dashboard Objects panel on the left-hand side has menu entries for both Action Link and Action Link Menu.

If you drag-and-drop an Action Link dashboard object onto the dashboard canvas, you will be prompted by the Action Link Properties dialog box to define, or select, an individual action that will then be displayed as a single link on the dashboard page. This is often useful when you want to add individual links to the page to annotate an analysis, or provide links to external applications or web sites (equivalent to the "guided navigation" feature in earlier releases of Oracle Business Intelligence).

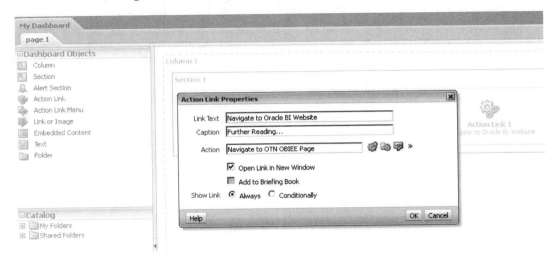

If you add an Action Link Menu dashboard object to the dashboard page, though, you will then be presented with the same table of action link settings that you see when defining sets of action links for analyses. When you then go to display this action link menu on the dashboard, you will see a menu of actions that users can select between (shown next), each of which, like regular action links, can be made conditional on either the results of an analysis or the state of a KPI.

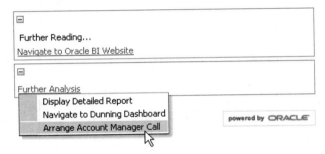

Actions, Configuration, and Security

While some action types are available for use "out of the box" with a default Oracle Business Intelligence installation, others require you to perform upfront configuration tasks before they become available to users. In some cases, these configuration steps are optional, but you may need them if the service you wish to link to requires either authentication or encrypted or signed communications.

The main configuration file for the Action Framework is called ActionFrameworkConfig.xml and can be found by default at

[*middleware_home*]/user_projects/domains/bifoundation_domain/config/fmwconfig/
biinstances/coreapplication/

Only certain types of actions need to use the configuration file, but those that do can use it to define target registry entries, security policy settings, and other configuration details that are required to set up the more "advanced" types of actions. For example, you may use this file to set up a list of web service operations that developers can use when creating Invoke a Web Service actions, avoiding the need for them to remember specific WSDL URL addresses and allowing you to set up in the background the required security policies that these services require.

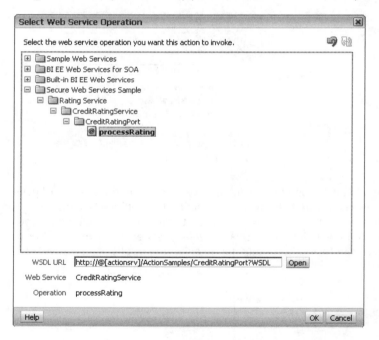

The following action types do not use the ActionFrameworkConfig.XML file at all. The Navigate to BI Content actions simply use the built-in dialog boxes to allow you to browse and target existing BI content or link to external web pages or web sites.

- Navigate to BI Content
- Navigate to a Web Page

- Invoke an HTTP Request
- Invoke an Agent

Two more action types are configured through other settings and configuration files, detailed later in this chapter:

- Invoke a Server Script
- Java Jobs

The action types listed in the following table also use the ActionFrameworkConfig.XML file to some extent. For those action types, the table details whether use of the file is mandatory or optional; whether registry entries in this file are mandatory or optional for this type; whether further credentials are needed; and whether the action type can implement security policies (a feature that is explained in the next section).

Action Type	Requires Configuration Entry?	Supports Registries?	Additional Credentials Required?	Policy Enabled?
Navigate to EPM Content	Yes (Registry)	Yes (Mandatory)	Yes	No
Navigate to E-Business Suite	Yes	No	No (Requires Oracle E-Business Suite security integration)	No
Navigate to Siebel CRM	Yes	No	No (Requires Siebel CRM integration)	No
Invoke a Web Service	No	Yes (Optional)	No (Optional)	Yes
Invoke a Browser Script	No	No (Browse for navigation targets enabled by default)	No	No

Later in this chapter, we will look in turn at how this configuration file is set up for each of these action types, but for now, let's take a quick look at an example ActionFrameworkConfig.xml file to see how it is structured. Later on, we'll look at how actions work with secured services and applications by passing user credentials and access tokens, and how you can secure actions themselves so that only authorized users can make use of them.

An Example ActionFrameworkConfig.xml File

As mentioned earlier, Oracle Business Intelligence comes with a template ActionFrameworkConfig .xml file, which contains a minimal set of configuration entries. If you would like to see a more complete ActionFrameworkConfig.xml file that contains examples of configuration entries for different types of action, the SampleApp mentioned earlier and used for the examples in this chapter has a more complete configuration file that you can examine. Let's use this file now to illustrate various settings and sections within this file.

Aliases Section The first section of this ActionFrameworkConfig.XML file defines a set of *aliases*, names for servers that will subsequently be referenced elsewhere in this configuration file.

Aliases are useful in situations where the absolute location of a target service may change over time, either because the service itself moves or because you have different services that you use in development, test, or other environments. By using aliases, you avoid the situation where absolute target references are used either later in this file or in action definitions. The Action Framework uses this alias list at run time to convert your references to these servers into their actual host name, URL or IP address.

The aliases section in the file is defined by the <aliases></aliases> tags:

```
<?xml version="1.0" encoding="UTF-8"?>
<obi-action-config xmlns:xsi="http://www.w3.org/2001/XMLSchema-instance" xsi:n
oNamespaceSchemaLocation="afconfig.xsd">
    <aliases>
        <location-alias>
            <alias>actionsrv</alias>
            <actual>localhost:7001</actual>
        </location-alias>
        <location-alias>
            <alias>biserver</alias>
            <actual>
    http://localhost:7001/analytics/saw.dll?WSDL
            </actual>
        </location-alias>
    </aliases>
```

In this example, two location aliases have been defined; the first points to the WebLogic Server hosting the action service, and the second points to the location of the Oracle BI session-based web services. Your configuration file may have different entries here, depending on which services and targets you wish to make available to developers and users.

Registries Section   The registries section is where the actual list of services available to users and developers is defined, for those services that are configured through this file. A typical ActionFrameworkConfig.xml file contains multiple entries for registries, enclosed by <registry> </registry> tags, one for each set of web services accessed, EPM server providing financial reports, Enterprise Java Bean (EJB), or other Action Framework target.

The following example shows a sample registry entry for a secure web service that provides credit rating services:

```
<registry>
        <id>reg2</id>
        <name>Secure Web Services Sample</name>
        <content-type>webservices</content-type>
        <provider-class>oracle.bi.action.registry.wsil.WSILRegistry</
provider-class>
        <description></description>
        <location>
        <path>
    http://localhost:7001/ActionSamples/secure.wsil
        </path>
        </location>
```

```
    <service-access>
        <path>/Secure Web Services Sample/Rating Service/CreditRating-
Service/CreditRatingPort/processRating</path>
        <policy>SAMLPolicy</policy>
        <propagateIdentity>true</propagateIdentity>
    </service-access>
</registry>
```

The <registry></registry> entry itself contains a number of elements that define how the service is registered and accessed:

- **id, name, and description** These provide an ID and label for the entry, and a header for when the target services' entries are displayed on the Registry dialog box.

- **content-type and provider-class** These refer, respectively, to a setting defined later in the file and a setting chosen from a predefined list, and provide background information on the category of service that the registry entry is based on.

- **location** This points to the location of the service and may reference one of the aliases defined in the previous section.

- **service-access** This optional element is used to specify the authentication required to access this particular service. We will look at the security aspect of this part of the file in a moment.

Actions that make use of this configuration file use this to record settings that are appropriate to each action type, and when the service being called is secured, uses Oracle Fusion Middleware's standard-based security framework to gain access. With secured services in particular, you need to have a basic understanding of Oracle Fusion Middleware security, and in particular how web services are secured and identity established before looking into this area much further.

Content Types Section The content types section is standard and should not be modified beyond the following settings. You do not have to worry about this section other than to make sure that it is included in the file.

```
<content-types>
    <content-type>
        <typename>webservices</typename>
        <displayname>
        Web Services and BPEL Processes
        </displayname>
        <actionType>WebServiceActionType</actionType>
    </content-type>
    <content-type>
        <typename>psft</typename>
        <displayname>
        PeopleSoft Applications
        </displayname>
        <actionType>URLActionType</actionType>
    </content-type>
    <content-type>
```

```
        <typename>epm</typename>
        <displayname>
        Hyperion Applications
      </displayname>
        <actionType>
        URLActionType
      </actionType>
    </content-type>
    <content-type>
        <typename>misc</typename>
        <displayname>
        Mixed Services
        </displayname>
        <actionType>URLActionType</actionType>
    </content-type>
    <content-type>
        <typename>java</typename>
        <displayname>
        Java Actions
        </displayname>
        <actionType>JavaActionType</actionType>
    </content-type>
</content-types>
```

Accounts Section   Most web services and other external systems that you will target as part of the Action Framework will require you to authenticate before granting access. Instead of storing usernames and passwords in plain text in this file, it contains an accounts section that refers to entries in the Oracle Fusion Middleware credential store, using a credential key and credential map:

```
<accounts>
        <account>
            <name>wsil.browsing</name>
            <description>Account for BI WS for SOA</description>
            <adminonly>false</adminonly>
            <credentialkey>wsil.browsing</credentialkey>
            <credentialmap>oracle.bi.enterprise</credentialmap>
        </account>
        <account>
            <name>WLSJNDI</name>
            <description>Account used to access WLS JNDI.
            </description>
            <adminonly>false</adminonly>
            <credentialkey>JNDIUser</credentialkey>
            <credentialmap>oracle.bi.actions</credentialmap>
        </account>
        <account>
            <name>EPM</name>
            description>Account used to connect to EPM.</description>
            <adminonly>false</adminonly>
            <credentialkey>EPM</credentialkey>
```

```
<credentialmap>oracle.bi.actions</credentialmap>
</account>
</accounts>
```

We will look at the role of the credential store, along with credential keys and maps, a bit later in the chapter.

Policies Section   The policies section is used by web service action types only. It describes the location of Oracle Web Service Manager client policy files used to access secured web services. In the following example, the policies section specifies two policy files, one for using Security Assertion Markup Language (SAML) tokens and one for the oracle/wss_username_token_policy type:

```
<policies>
    <policy>
        <name>SAMLPolicy</name>
        <policyfile>ActionsSAMLPolicy.xml</policyfile>
    </policy>
    <policy>
        <name>wss_username_token_policy</name>
        <policyfile>wss_username_token_policy.xml</policyfile>
    </policy>
</policies>
```

Proxy, E-Business Suite, and Siebel Sections   Finally, proxy settings for enabling access to external services via a proxy server can be defined in the file, and two sets of tags, <ebusinesssuiteconfig> </ebusinesssuiteconfig> and <siebelcrmconfig></siebelcrmconfig>, can be added to turn on support for E-Business Suite and Siebel CRM action types:

```
    <!-- Uncomment this element to enable support for using proxy settings to
enable browsing/invocation
    of external web services when running behind a firewall
        <proxy>
            <host>@proxy.host@</host>
            <port>@proxy.port@</port>
            <userid>@proxy.user@</userid>
            <password>@proxy.password@</password>
            <nonProxyHosts>localhost|*.oracle.com|@proxy.nonProxyHosts@
            </nonProxyHosts>
        </proxy>
    -->
<ebusinesssuiteconfig>
        <visible>true</visible>
</ebusinesssuiteconfig>
</obi-action-config>
```

Actions and Security

At this point, you're probably feeling fairly confident about the web service settings and other registry settings you can add to the ActionFrameworkConfig.xml file, but you might be a bit confused about all the security settings that relate to web services. So, before we start to dig into the details of each action type, let's go through a quick primer on web service security and other security as provided by Oracle Fusion Middleware and define some terms that we'll use later in the chapter when describing how each type of action type is configured.

Actions interact with Oracle BI security in a number of ways, both internally to the Presentation Server catalog and externally, in terms of how external services and applications are accessed. The following list sets out the different ways that actions can be secured, both in terms of restricting who can use an action through and giving actions a way to authenticate themselves when accessing secured external resources.

- **Oracle BI EE privileges**   These privileges, as controlled through the Oracle BI Presentation Server Administration screen, control whether users or application roles have the right to access action features and functionality, such as the ability to create or use actions. These are the same types of privileges that control whether a user or application role can use Oracle BI Answers, schedule an agent, or perform other dashboard functionality.

- **Oracle BI Presentation Catalog permissions**   These permissions are granted to individual actions or folders of actions and control whether the user or application role can read, write, execute, or delete actions. These are the same types of permissions that you manage for analyses, dashboards, or other BI objects.

- **Oracle BI EE credentials**   These credentials are particular to actions and the Action Framework and are used to set up authentication and authorization between actions and the services and applications they interact with. Because most external services require some sort of authentication before you can use them, this is an important aspect of working with the Action Framework and requires some understanding of how web services are secured in enterprise applications.

As explained in Chapter 1, Oracle Business Intelligence is part of a wider middleware product family called Oracle Fusion Middleware. This benefits you as a developer in that Oracle has already built enterprise-level security into its middleware tools, in the form of a product called Oracle Platform Security Services, described in more detail in Chapter 8. You can therefore use features such as the credential store and Oracle Web Services Manager (OWSM) to provide this secured access to the external systems you wish to use with the Action Framework, all in a way that is standards based and interfaces easily with the authentication requirements of your target services.

The Credential Store   Some web services, such as those you might access on the Internet that perform currency conversion or return ZIP codes for a given address, are available for use by the public and do not require authentication before they are used. Others, such as the applications and services used by your organization, are secured and require some sort of authentication before you can use them.

Rather than store the usernames and passwords required to access these services in plain-text files, Oracle Business Intelligence uses a feature called the credential store to hold these credentials, in an encrypted form and accessible through credential keys and credential maps. Credential maps can be thought of as groupings of credential keys, and the two are used together to retrieve a particular set of credentials.

You can access the credential store either through Fusion Middleware Control or by writing scripts that access it using WebLogic Scripting Tool (WLST). When you create an entry in the credential store—for example, to store details of a user with administration privileges that you can use to access Oracle BI Web Services for SOA—you select a credential map, enter a new key used for accessing the credentials, and enter the username and password you want to store against the credential map and key.

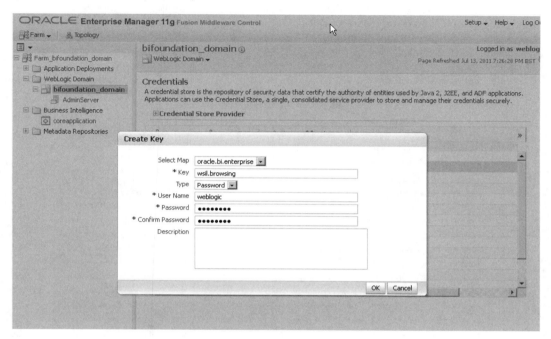

Once you have created an entry in the credential store, you then reference it in the <accounts> </accounts> section of the ActionFrameworkConfig.xml file when you want to define the "gateway account" to access a particular web service, like this:

```
<account>
          <name>wsil.browsing</name>
          <description>Account for BI WS for SOA</description>
          <adminonly>false</adminonly>
          <credentialkey>wsil.browsing</credentialkey>
          <credentialmap>oracle.bi.enterprise</credentialmap>
   </account>
```

This approach, while secure and standards based, does have a number of limitations. Every user that uses this action will use the same credentials to access the service, which may be an issue if you want to pass the actual logged-in user's details to the service you are calling.

In addition, your organization may use features such as SAML, which uses tokens to authenticate between trusted systems and allows you to thereafter pass through the details of the calling user, or use technologies such as Single Sign-On (SSO), which requires a different approach to authentication. Because of this, you will probably need to start looking into the world of policies, key stores, message protection, and OWSM.

Policies   Oracle Business Intelligence, through the OWSM component within Oracle Fusion Middleware, comes with a number of policies that describe ways in which two systems can authenticate, trust, and pass messages between each other. These policies range from simple ones that merely pass usernames and passwords to the target system, to advanced ones that protect messages through encryption, signing, and exchanging of tokens. To see the list of available policies in Fusion Middleware Control, expand Farm_bifoundation_domain in the navigation tree menu, expand WebLogic Domain, right-click bifoundation_domain to display the contextual menu and then select Web Services | Policies to display the list of policies, as shown next.

Web Services Policies ?   Web Services Assertion Templates

This page allows you to create a new policy, make changes to an existing policy, make a copy of a policy, and delete a policy. Policies can be imported into the data store from a file, and policies can be exported to a file.

Category [Security ▾]   Applies To [Service Endpoints ▾]   Name [   ]

⚑ Create	⚑ Create Like	👓 View	✏ Edit	✂ Delete		⬇ Import From File	⬆ Export To File	Generate Clie
Name					Enabled	Attachment Count	Description	View Full Description
oracle/wss11_saml_or_username_token_with_message_proce					✔	3	This policy enforces messa...	∞
oracle/wss11_saml_token_with_message_protection_service_					✔	1	This policy enforces messa...	∞
oracle/wss11_sts_issued_saml_hok_with_message_protection					✔	0	This policy authenticates ...	∞
oracle/wss11_username_token_with_message_protection_ser					✔	0	This policy enforces messa...	∞
oracle/wss11_x509_token_with_message_protection_service_					✔	0	This policy enforces messa...	∞
oracle/wss_http_token_over_ssl_service_policy					✔	0	This policy extracts the c...	∞
oracle/wss_http_token_service_policy					✔	0	This policy uses the crede...	∞
oracle/wss_saml20_token_bearer_over_ssl_service_policy					✔	0	This policy authenticates ...	∞
oracle/wss_saml20_token_over_ssl_service_policy					✔	0	This policy authenticates ...	∞
oracle/wss_saml_or_username_token_over_ssl_service_policy					✔	0	This policy authenticates ...	∞
oracle/wss_saml_or_username_token_service_policy					✔	3	This policy authenticates ...	∞
oracle/wss_saml_token_bearer_over_ssl_service_policy					✔	0	This policy authenticates ...	∞
oracle/wss_saml_token_over_ssl_service_policy					✔	0	This policy authenticates ...	∞
oracle/wss_sts_issued_saml_bearer_token_over_ssl_service_					✔	0	This policy authenticates ...	∞
oracle/wss_username_token_over_ssl_service_policy					✔	0	This policy uses the crede...	∞
oracle/wss_username_token_service_policy					✔	4	This policy uses the crede...	∞

For web services that only require a username and a password, selecting the appropriate policy and referencing it in the ActionFrameworkConfig.xml file is about as much security configuration as you will need to perform. For services that use digital signatures, encryption, and tokens to secure access, you have to delve one final level deeper and start to look at message protection and key stores.

Message Protection, Key Stores, and SAML/X509   As previously mentioned, one drawback of using just a single, common username and password held in the credential store to access a web service, is that you can't then pass the actual end users' credentials across and apply security based on that. Web services secured in that way provide the same levels of access to any users that have been granted access to it, and you would need to restrict access to the action that calls the service through catalog permissions if you only wanted a particular group of users to be able to make use of it.

For situations where you want to be able to gain access to a secured web service, but also then pass across a set of user credentials in order to apply further security rules, many organizations use certificate-based systems such as SAML and X509 to establish trust between two systems and encrypt communications using public/private keys. Oracle Business Intelligence, through Oracle Fusion Middleware (on which it is built), can make full use of security such as this. We will explore how you work with such configurations later in this chapter.

Action Types

Now that you understand the principles behind the Action Framework and recognize some of the complexity you may encounter when working with web services and other secured services, let's now step through each of the action types, starting with the less-complex navigation actions and then tackling the more-complex invocation actions.

Navigation Actions

Navigation actions are used to define links to other analyses, dashboards, or BI objects, to other web pages, or to applications such as Oracle E-Business Suite or Oracle Hyperion Enterprise Performance Management Suite (or Oracle EPM Suite for short). They differ from invocation actions in that they do not execute any processes or return any data, but instead provide a means for the user to navigate to related content.

You can use navigation actions to link two analyses together, automatically filtering one report on the value you clicked in the other. If you have developed reports in the Oracle EPM Suite's Financial Reporting application, you can create action links that navigate to these reports, automatically passing across parameters and optionally passing across their credentials if you have separately configured SSO between Oracle Business Intelligence and Oracle EPM Suite.

If your organization uses Oracle E-Business Suite or Siebel CRM, you can use navigation actions to set up links from analyses and other BI content that display screens in those applications, passing across the context so that they are taken directly into the account, product, or customer details that are being referred to in their analyses.

Navigating to BI Content

Navigate to BI Content actions are probably the simplest and most commonly used action types within Oracle Business Intelligence. They are based on a feature that was actually present in the 10*g* and earlier releases of the product, in the form of request navigations. To set up this type of action, you just need an analysis, dashboard, or other BI object to navigate to. Optionally, you can configure this BI object to be automatically filtered on the value the user clicks to trigger the action.

To show how Navigate to BI Content actions work, let's start with a simple example that shows how you can link two analyses together and automatically pass a parameter from one to the other.

Example: Navigating to an Analysis or Dashboard In this example, consider a situation where you have previously created an analysis that will now become the target for this navigation action. The analysis lists all the products that the company sells, along with some sales figures and product attributes.

Product Name	Product Type	Manufacturer	Revenue	Sale Amount
Banner Assortment	Bread Assortments		30	2
Bowl Bread Club	Bread Clubs		50	2
Bread Bowls	Rounds & Loaves		60	3
Breakfast Muffin	Sandwiches	Harringtons	7	1
Can Clam Chowder	Gifts & Baskets		12	6
Challah Bread	Speciality Breads		26	3
Clam Chowder	Soup		90	55
Cobb Salad Sandwich	Sandwiches		12	12
Dipping Oils	Gifts & Baskets		4	2
Harvest Bread Trio	Bread Assortments		30	4
Heet's Cafe Latte	Hot Drinks	Heet's Coffee Co.	8	3
Heet's Cappucino	Hot Drinks	Heet's Coffee Co.	80	54
Heet's Drip Coffee	Hot Drinks	Heet's Coffee Co.	42	46
Heet's Earl Grey Tea	Hot Drinks	Heet's Coffee Co.	5	3
Heet's Tea	Hot Drinks	Heet's Coffee Co.	5	3

The analysis has previously been saved to the catalog in a shared folder, so that it can be accessed by other users or, as in this case, an action.

To create a navigation action that will then display this analysis when used in an action link, follow these steps:

1. Create the navigation action by selecting New | Action from the application menu and then clicking Navigate to BI Content in the list of actions.

2. In the Select BI Content For Action dialog box, navigate to and then select the analysis that you wish to use as the action target, which in this example is the analysis you just saved to the catalog.

3. In the New Action dialog box confirming the BI content that the action will navigate to, click the Save Action button to save the action to the Presentation Server catalog.

4. You now can use the newly created action as an action link. In this example, we have a different analysis that displays the breakdown of sales by product category, in the form of a pie chart.

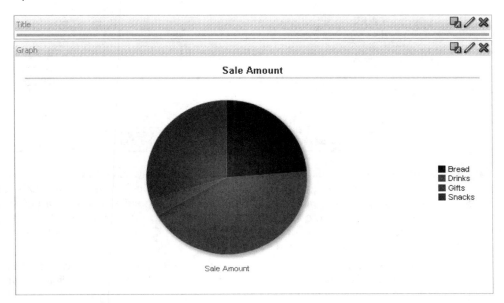

To start creating the action link, open the analysis for editing and select the Criteria tab. In the Selected Columns area, hover your mouse pointer over the column that you wish to create the action link for (in this case, Product Category), and select Column Properties.

5. In the Column Properties dialog box, select the Interaction tab. Set the Primary Interaction field under either Column Heading or Value to Action Links. If you want to pass the selected value for a particular column as a parameter, make sure you set the Primary Interaction field under Value to Action Links, as this adds the action link to individual column values in the analysis rather than to the overall column header.

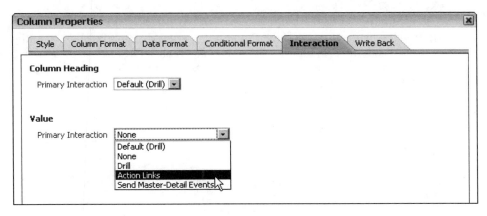

6. Once you set either of these primary interaction types to Action Links, a table of (initially empty) action links is then displayed in the dialog box. Click the Add Action button to add your first action link to this table.

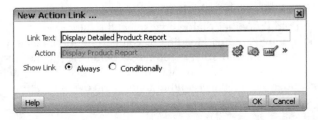

7. The New Action Link dialog box is displayed. If you wanted to create an action "inline," equivalent to the request navigation feature in Oracle Business Intelligence 10*g*, you would click the Create New Action button and define the action as part of the analysis definition. If you were to create your action inline and then wanted to save it in the catalog as a named action so that it can be reused, you would select More | Save Action to extract the definition and save it to the catalog.

    In this example, because we have already created our action (known as a "named" action), instead click the Select Existing Action button and use the Select Action dialog box to select the action you created before. Back in the New Action Link dialog box, enter a label for the action link in the Link Text field, and then click OK to close the dialog box.

8. On the Interaction tab of the Column Properties dialog box, add any further action links you wish to create for this column, and then click OK to close the dialog box. When you now display the analysis results and click one of the pie chart segments, you will see the action link displayed.

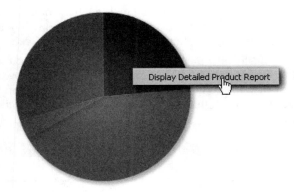

Sale Amount

9. When you have just a single action link defined for a column, you may wish to disable
    the link menu and have the action performed automatically when the column is clicked.
    To do so, display the Interaction tab for the column and select the "Do not display in a
    popup if only one action link is available at runtime" check box.

Action Links			
Link Text	Action	Show Link	
Display Detailed Product Report	Display Product Report	Always Enabled	

☑ Do not display in a popup if only one action link is available at runtime

10. Similarly, to make the action link conditional on the value displayed in each row of
     the analysis, select Conditionally for Show Link when defining the action link, and use
     the filter button to define a condition on the selected column, on another column in the
     analysis, or on another column in the subject area.

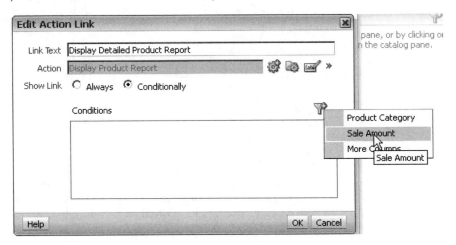

11. If you now test the action link, you will see that when you select it, you navigate to the target analysis defined in the action. However, you will notice that the analysis does not, by default, limit the products to just those that you clicked in the original report.

12. To automatically filter the target analysis on the value clicked in the calling report, open the target analysis for editing and select the Criteria tab to show the Selected Columns area. Then, create a filter on the column that you wish to filter on (in this case, Product Category, to match the column that has the action link associated with it in the other analysis.)

13. In the New Filter dialog box, select Is Prompted as the operator.

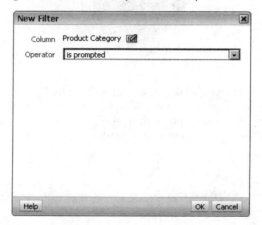

Now, whenever this analysis is called from another analysis that passes a Product Category value through an action link, this value will be used to filter the report.

Product Report

Product Category is equal to / is in **Bread**

Product Name	Product Type	Manufacturer	Revenue	Sale Amount
Banner Assortment	Bread Assortments		30	2
Bread Bowls	Rounds & Loaves		60	3
Challah Bread	Speciality Breads		26	3
Harvest Bread Trio	Bread Assortments		30	4
Holiday Bread Trio	Bread Assortments		27	2
Panettone	Speciality Breads	Gusieppe Inc.	14	4
Sandwich Rolls	Rounds & Loaves		20	3
Snowmen Bread	Seasonal Breads		20	1
Sourdough Loaves	Rounds & Loaves		224	38
Sourdough Rounds	Rounds & Loaves		30	5
Turkey Bread	Seasonal Breads		40	6

Add to Briefing Book

Using this method, you can set up navigation between one analysis and another, passing the value that was clicked as a parameter to the target report. But what if you are using a pivot table view, and you want to pass parameter values for more than one dimension? Let's take a look at this more complicated scenario in the next example.

Example: Navigating from Pivot Table Analyses   In the previous example, we set up a Navigate to BI Content action that filtered the target analysis on the column value clicked in the calling analysis. The calling analysis actually used a table view so that each row in the view had a value for Product Category, and this value was then automatically passed by the action to the target report and used for filtering.

Consider a situation, though, where you have created an analysis that uses a pivot table view, with regions and product categories on the axes and revenue figures in the pivot table cells. You now wish to create an action link that calls another analysis, which in turn breaks down the revenue figure for the selected region and product category in the form of a table.

Title						
Product Region Crosstab						

Pivot Table						
	Revenue					
	Central SF	North CA	North SF	Other USA	South CA	West SF
Product Category						
Bread	95	80	239	15	50	42
Drinks	28	21	81	13	31	27
Gifts	59	6		Display Sales Breakdown		
Snacks	42	5	54	22	38	9

In this situation, you do not want the value in the cell to be passed through to the target analysis; instead, you want the "point of view," the combination of the X and Y axis values (in this case, Drinks and North SF for product category and region, respectively), to be passed to the target analysis. So how do you do this?

In reality, it is quite simple. You would define the action and the action link, as you would for any other Navigate to BI Content action, but instead of creating just a single Is Prompted filter on the target analysis, you would create one for each of the columns listed in the Columns, Rows, Sections, or Prompts in the calling analysis, and the currently selected value for each would be passed to the target application automatically, as part of the Navigate to BI Content action function.

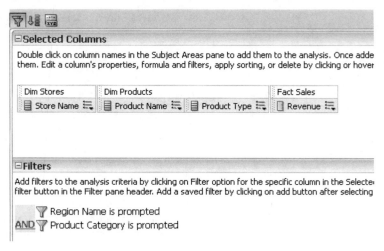

Then, when the target analysis is displayed through the action link, you can see the filter values being passed across and applied to the analysis criteria.

Store Product Breakdown

Region Name is equal to / is in **North SF**
and Product Category is equal to / is in **Drinks**

Store Name	Product Name	Product Type	Revenue
Fishermans Wharf	Heet's Cappucino	Hot Drinks	12
	Heet's Drip Coffee	Hot Drinks	7
	Heet's Earl Grey Tea	Hot Drinks	2
	Heet's Tea	Hot Drinks	2
	Mineral Water	Cold Drinks	12
	Tropic C'berry Juice	Cold Drinks	3
	Tropics Orange Juice	Cold Drinks	9
North Beach	Heet's Cappucino	Hot Drinks	4
	Heet's Drip Coffee	Hot Drinks	7
	Tropics Orange Juice	Cold Drinks	3
Taylor Street	Heet's Cafe Latte	Hot Drinks	4
	Heet's Cappucino	Hot Drinks	8
	Heet's Drip Coffee	Hot Drinks	7

Add to Briefing Book

This behavior is, in fact, common to all analyses views, not just pivot tables. When you click a column value to use an action link to navigate to another BI object, all of the column values for that row, or for that pivot table point of view, are passed to the target analysis.

Title

Product Region Crosstab

Pivot Table

Products	Revenue ⊟ All Stores	⊞ Central SF	⊞ North CA	⊞ North SF	⊞ Other USA	⊞ South CA	⊞ West SF
⊟ All Products	1,025	224	112	429	50	131	78
⊞ Bread	6,246	95	80	239	15	50	42
⊟ Drinks	1,822	28	2*			31	27
⊞ Cold Drinks	63	9		Display Sales Breakdown		9	12
⊞ Hot Drinks	140	19	21	54	Display Sales Breakdown		15
⊞ Gifts	923	59	6	55		12	
⊞ Snacks	2,037	42	5	54	22	38	9

Note, however, that this functionality is currently limited to attribute columns, and you cannot pass the selected values of a hierarchical column as parameters through a Navigate to BI Content action (the Override with Prompt setting available with selection steps works only with dashboard prompts, not Navigate to BI Content actions).

Navigating to a Web Page

The other type of navigation action that is available "out of the box" with Oracle Business Intelligence is the ability to navigate to a web page, optionally passing parameters to the page so that, for example, it can look up details of a product from an online product catalog. Although security and authentication is limited in this scenario (any logon details will need to be passed in the web site URL), it can be a useful way of displaying additional information for a user to provide background to some data.

Example: Displaying a Google Map   As an example of how to use the Navigate to a Web Page action, consider a situation where you wish to display the approximate location of a store using a service such as Google Maps. While Oracle Business Intelligence has built-in capabilities for displaying maps in analyses, this feature does require configuration and does not always have the same information on locations and neighborhoods that a commercial service makes available, for free.

You can access Google Maps at http://maps.google.com. You can pass one or more parameters to Google Maps to, for example, search for a particular location and display it centered on the map. To display a Google map for the Fisherman's Wharf area of San Francisco, for example, you would use the URL http://maps.google.com/?q=Fisherman's%20Wharf, which would display a map in the browser window as if you had typed the search term into the application search box.

To create a Navigate to a Web Page action that can display a Google map for a given search term, follow these steps:

1. From the menu at the top of the Oracle Business Intelligence home page, select New | Action. When the list of actions is displayed, select Navigate To A Web Page.

2. In the New Action dialog box, type in the URL for the web page that you would like to link to (in this example, http://maps.google.com/?q=).

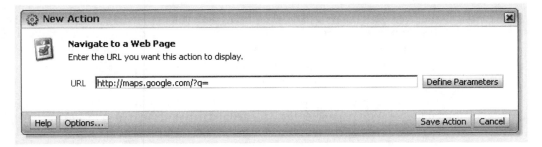

3. Because this URL uses a parameter (the ?q= after the main part of the web address), click the Define Parameters button to display a table of parameters, which will have a single parameter already displayed in the list based on the parameter list in your entered URL. You will also see that the original URL you typed in has now been updated to reference this first parameter, so that the web address in the URL area is now http://maps.google .com/?q=@{1}. In this instance, the @{1} refers to the parameter named 1 in the parameter list, which you can leave as is or change to a more meaningful name such as location.

4. Change the parameter name in the parameter list to **location**. The URL will be updated to use this new parameter name, as shown next. Note also how you can configure each

parameter to be either fixed (unchangeable), hidden or optional, settings that would then be applied every time this action was used in an action link. For now, leave these choices at their default values, and once you are happy with the parameter setup, click Save Action to close the dialog box and save the action, giving it a name such as Display Google Map.

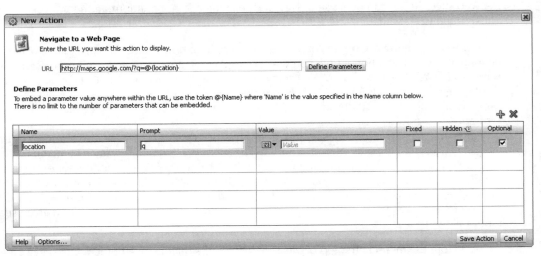

5. To use the action, create or open an analysis or other BI object that contains a column referencing a geographic location, such as a city, state, or country. With the analysis open for editing, select the Criteria tab and, for the column you wish to associate the action with, select the Column Properties menu item.

6. In the Column Properties dialog box, click the Interaction tab and select Action Links in the Primary Interaction drop-down list under Value. When the Action Links table is displayed, click the Add Action button.

7. In the New Action Link dialog box, click the Select Existing Action button and then select the action you created earlier that navigates to a Google map.

8. Because this action uses a parameter, the Edit Parameter Mapping dialog box opens. To map the location parameter that you defined earlier to a column in your analysis, select Column Value from the drop-down list under the Value heading.

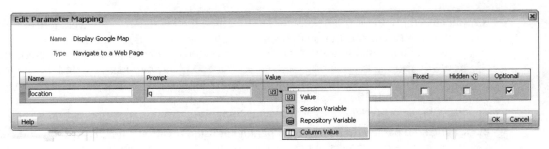

9. When you select Column Value as the value to map to the parameter, the drop-down menu shown next appears to the right of this setting, allowing you to choose the actual column that maps into the parameter. Select the appropriate column (in this example, "Dim Stores"."Store Name") to complete the mapping.

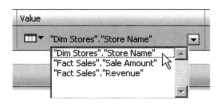

10. As when you created the action initially, you can select whether the parameter is fixed (displayed, but not changeable), hidden or optional, and (optionally) you can change the Prompt message that is displayed if the value is visible to the user. Click OK when you have completed the parameter definition, which returns you to the New Action Link dialog box.

11. If required, select Conditionally for Show Link to set a condition for the action link to be displayed, give the action link a name (for example, Display Google Map for this Location), and then click OK to close the dialog box and click OK again to return to the application.

12. Test your new action link by displaying the analysis results and then selecting the action link that displays the map. When selected, depending on the settings you have chosen, you will be prompted to view, or amend, the prompt value, and then the map will be displayed based on the column value you mapped into the search parameter.

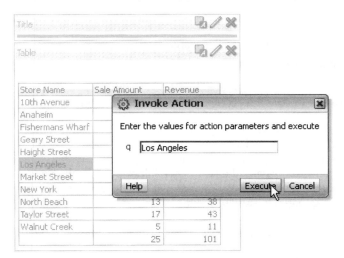

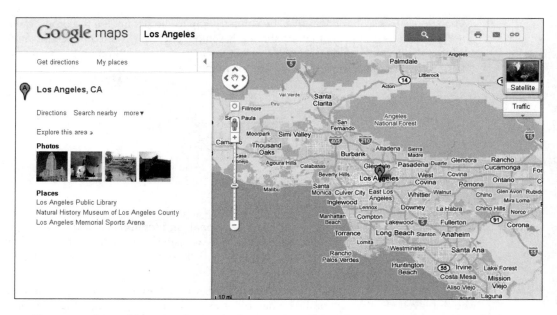

The example used here has just a single parameter, but, of course, you can use multiple parameters when you create actions to link to web sites. Google Maps, for example, has an API that allows you to specify the zoom level for a map, the size of the map, and so on, with a typical URL looking like this:

http://maps.google.com/maps/api/staticmap?center=Boston&zoom=14&size=400x400&sensor= false

This API call to Google Maps uses the following parameters (among others):

- **center**   Used to pass the search term to the API call and center the map on the location
- **zoom**   Used to set the zoom level of the map
- **size**   Used to set the size in pixels (X and Y) of the map
- **sensor**   Used to specify whether the device calling has a location sensor

To make use of this API, you would create another Navigate to a Web Page action and type in the preceding URL, including all the parameters. Then, when you click the Define Parameters button, each parameter will be extracted from the URL, with the parameter names used to create the parameter prompts and the parameter values used for the default parameter value, which you can then change or remove as required. Each URL parameter will then, as with the previous example, be updated to use the @{} format in order to be substituted with your column or other values at runtime.

In this example, the sensor parameter is really of interest only to the API and is not relevant in this context, so the Hidden or Fixed options can be chosen. Similarly, the size parameter could be fixed, but not hidden, depending on your requirements.

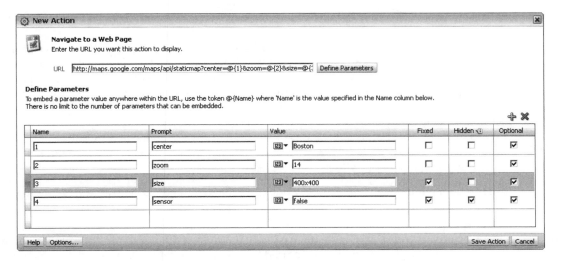

Then, when you use this action as an action link for an analysis or other BI object, with the action link open for editing and the Edit Parameters option selected, you would map a column to the center parameter to pass the location to be mapped, as shown next. In this case, you would also pass a value to the zoom parameter to set the zoom level. Based on the parameter settings chosen in the preceding screenshot, the size parameter would be visible but fixed, while the sensor parameter, because it was set to be hidden, would not be listed at all.

Navigating to EPM Content

If your organization uses Oracle's Enterprise Performance Management suite of products and has developed reports using Hyperion Financial Reporting, you can register your EPM server with the Action Framework and allow users to create actions that navigate to individual reports. Using action parameters, you can pass column values from your analysis to Hyperion Financial Reporting, allowing you to "drill through" from a particular cell or column value and use that to set the "point of view" in your Financial Reporting report.

Unlike actions that navigate to web services or other BI content, Navigate to EPM Content actions do not, in themselves, pass user credentials to the Hyperion Financial Reporting application. If you wish to provide SSO between Oracle Business Intelligence and Hyperion Financial Reporting, you will therefore have to set up SSO between these applications beforehand, using the steps outlined in Chapter 11.

In the following example, we will set up an action that provides navigation to a Hyperion Financial Reporting report, shown in Figure 7-1, created using the Oracle Essbase Demo.Basic sample database. The action we create will pass a value for the Year dimension, which will then be used to filter this report for a particular Year dimension member value.

The version of Hyperion Financial Reporting that is used in this example is 11.1.2. While Oracle does not officially certify any particular release of Hyperion Financial Reporting for use with Oracle Business Intelligence, most recent releases of the product should work with this feature.

To set up a Navigate to EPM Content action, you need to perform two configuration tasks before you can create these actions:

1. Configure the ActionFrameworkConfig.xml file to tell the Action Framework where your EPM Server is located, and which credentials to use when connecting to it.

2. Set up an entry in the credential store, accessible via a credential key and credential map, that contains the username and password for an EPM administrator. This set of username and password credentials is then used to browse the EPM workspace catalog to review the list of reports that can be used as action targets.

Example: Configuring the ActionFrameworkConfig.xml File   To configure the ActionFrameworkConfig.xml file to enable the Navigate to EPM Content action type, you need to create three entries:

- A registry entry that points to the location of the EPM server
- If not added already, a <content-type> for EPM content
- An account entry that points to an entry in the credential store that contains the administration username and password for the EPM server, to allow the action service to browse the list of available reports

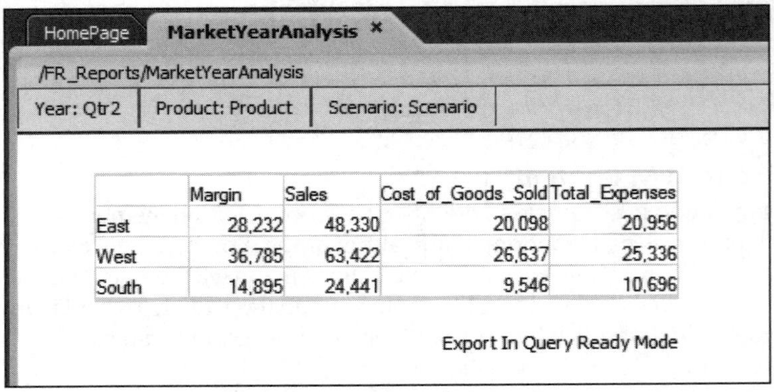

FIGURE 7-1. *A sample Hyperion Financial Reporting report*

To create the registry entry for an EPM installation at version 11.1.2 or higher, add the following entry within the tags, changing the server host name in the <path></path> element as required:

```
<registry>
        <id></id>
        <name>Hyperion Directory Provider</name>
        <content-type>epm</content-type>
        <provider-class>
        oracle.bi.action.registry.epm.HDPRegistry</provider-class>
        <description>Hyperion Financial Reports Registry
        </description>
        <location>
    <path>http://epmserver:19000/raframework/browse/listxml</path>
                        </location>
        <service-access>
            <account>EPM</account>
                    <propagateIdentity>false</propagateIdentity>
        </service-access>
</registry>
```

Be sure to include the <propagateIdentity></propagateIdentity> element, as this is a requirement of the action service—though the need for it is not included in the product documentation (at least at version 11.1.1.5 of the product; later releases may remove the need for this element or alternatively add the requirement for it into the documentation). Also, for EPM Suite installations prior to version 11.1.2, use the following <path></path> value, again amending the host name as appropriate:

```
<path>http://epmserver:19000/workspace/browse/listXML</path>
```

The preceding registry entry references a content-type entry that is not in the ActionFrameworkConfig.xml file by default, as well as an account entry that you need to add to match an entry you will put in the credential store later on.

To add the content-type entry to this file, if it is not already present, add the following XML snippet between the <content-types></content-types> tags:

```
<content-type>
        <typename>epm</typename>
        <displayname>Hyperion Applications</displayname>
        <actionType>URLActionType</actionType>
        </content-type>
```

Finally, add an entry within the <accounts></accounts> tags to reference the credential store entry you will create in a moment. Be sure to note the credentialkey and credentialmap entries, as you will use these in the next section when creating the credential store entry.

```
<account>
        <name>EPM</name>
        <description>Account used to connect to EPM.</description>
        <adminonly>false</adminonly>                    <credentialkey>EPM</
credentialkey>
        <credentialmap>oracle.bi.actions</credentialmap>
    </account>
```

Once completed, save the file and move on to the credential store entry.

Example: Configuring the Credential Store   When a user creates a Navigate to EPM Content action, they are presented with a list of reports that are available from EPM servers that you have configured the Action Framework to browse. Because these EPM servers require an administration username and password to access this report list, the Action Framework has to store these credentials somewhere to pass to the EPM server as required.

These credentials are stored in the credential store, and you label them with a credential key and credential map so that they can be accessed via the account entry you previously put in the ActionFrameworkConfig.xml file. You have to create credential store entries for each EPM server that you wish to access via this action type, and you need to update the entries if the administration username or password changes on the EPM server.

To create these entries, you can either use Fusion Middleware Control or script the addition using WebLogic Scripting Tool (WLST), a utility explained in more detail in Chapter 10.

To add the entry using Fusion Middleware Control, follow these steps:

1. Log into the Fusion Middleware Control web site and enter the username and password for an administration user.

2. Using the navigation tree menu on the left-hand side, expand Farm_bifoundation_domain, expand WebLogic Domain, right-click bifoundation_domain, and select Security | Credentials.

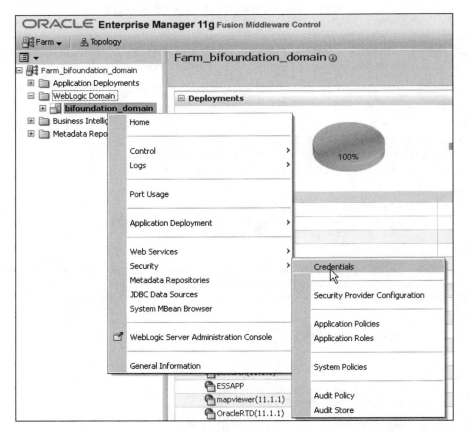

3. If the list of credential folders (otherwise known as credential maps) on the Credentials screen does not yet include one called oracle.bi.actions, click the Create Map button and create it using the Create Map dialog box. Click OK to close the dialog box.

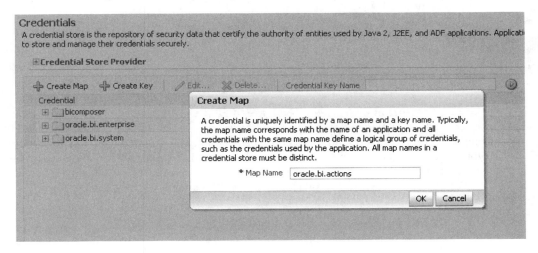

4. Click the Create Key button and enter and select the following details to create the credential key entry:

Select Map: oracle.bi.actions
Key: EPM [*to match the account entry in the file earlier*]
Type: Password
User Name: admin [*replace with EPM Suite administrator username*]
Password: welcome1 [*replace with EPM Suite administrator password*]
Confirm Password: welcome1
Description: EPM Administrator credentials for catalog browsing

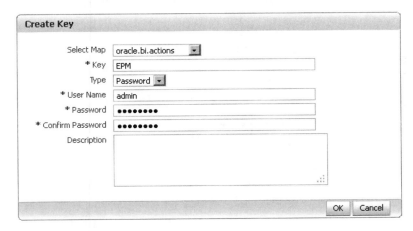

5. To now have Oracle Business Intelligence use the new credential and the new entries in the ActionFrameworkConfig.xml file, restart the WebLogic Managed Server (or the Administration Server, if using the Simple Install type). You will then be able to start using this new action type.

NOTE
You will also have to stop and start the Managed Server to pick up any new folders, or new reports, that have been added to the EPM Workspace catalog since the last restart of this server.

Example: Creating and Using the Navigate to EPM Content Action   Once you have completed the two mandatory setup steps detailed earlier, you can use the Navigate to EPM Content action type in your analyses and other BI content. Ensure that you have one or more Hyperion Financial Reporting reports available in your EPM Suite system, and then follow these steps to create an action. In this example, we will create an action that allows the user to pass a value for the Year dimension to the Financial Reporting report as an action parameter, which we will assign to an analysis column later on.

1. Log into the Oracle Business Intelligence web site and select New | Action from the application menu.

2. From the list of actions, select Navigate To EPM Content from the list. If this action type is not listed, go back and check the configuration steps that you performed beforehand.

3. In the "Select the Hyperion Resource you want this action to invoke" dialog box, a list of folders appears under the heading Hyperion Directory Provider (determined by the <registry><name></name></registry> entry that you previously added to the ActionFrameworkConfig.xml file). Navigate through the folder list and locate the report that you wish to use as the target for the action, and then press OK. In this example, we will use the HTML view of the FR_Reports/MarketYearAnalysis report stored in this catalog.

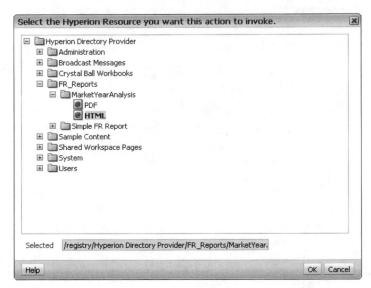

4. In the New Action dialog box, the parameters used by Hyperion Financial Reporting to establish a connection and retrieve a report are shown. These will not change for a particular report, so you can select the Hidden check box for these parameters so that users do not have to see or configure them.

5. If you wish to pass a parameter value to the Financial Reporting report (for this example, the ID of a Year dimension member), click the Add Parameter button and enter the following values in the dialog box:

   Name: Year [*amend as appropriate*]
   Prompt: **Enter value for year**
   Value: [*leave blank*]
   Fixed: [*leave unchecked*]
   Hidden: [*leave unchecked*]
   Optional: Yes [*amend as appropriate*]

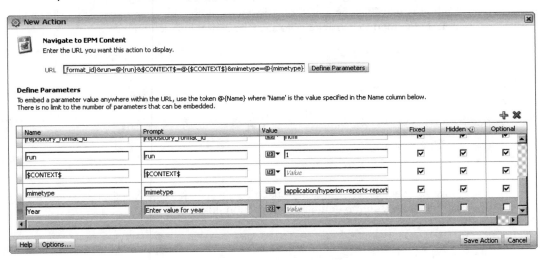

6. After creating any additional parameters, you need to amend the URL to include an extra parameter setting that references the new action parameter you defined. To do this, add the reference in the following format:

   &attribute=[*Dimension Name*].id.@{*parameter name*}

   For example, to pass the Year parameter and use it to set the member ID for the Year dimension in the Essbase Demo.Basic cube, you would add the following to the end of the URL generated for you by the action:

   ```
   &attribute=Year.id.@{Year}
   ```

   Your full URL, for this report and EPM Server, would look like this:

   ```
   http://epmserver:19000/workspace/index.jsp?module=@{module}&repository_
   path=@{repository_path}&elementType=@{elementType}&repository_name=@
   {repository_name}&repository_format_id=@{repository_format_id}&run=@
   {run}&$CONTEXT$=@{$CONTEXT$}&mimetype=@{mimetype}&attribute=Year.id.@
   {Year}
   ```

Repeat this step for any other parameters you wish to pass to the report. For example, if you were to also define a Market parameter, the end of your URL would look like this:

```
&attribute=Year.id.@{Year}&attribute=Market.id.@{Market}
```

Once completed, click Save Action to save your action to the catalog.

7. To test your action, create a suitable analysis that includes the dimension for which you wish to pass values to the Financial Reporting report. With the analysis open for editing, select the Criteria tab, and then click the Column Properties menu entry to open the Column Properties dialog box and select the Interaction tab, in the same way as when you define other action links.

8. Set the Primary Interaction field for Value to Action Links and then click the Add Action Link button to select the action that you just created. Once selected, you will be prompted by the Edit Parameter Mapping dialog box, shown next, to provide a value for any additional parameters you have defined. For the parameter value mapping, select Column Value as the value type, and then select the column (for example, the "Year".Year hierarchy column) to map to it. Click OK to save the action link definition.

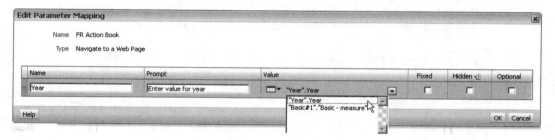

9. Now you can test your new action. To do so, switch to the Results tab, select a year value, and click the column containing the action link.

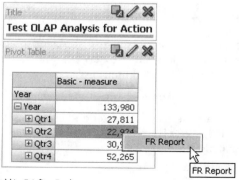

If you have created any additional parameters, the Invoke Action dialog box appears, prompting you to view, or amend, the parameter values. Then, click Execute, and the Financial Reporting report will run, as shown next, with your parameter being used to set the relevant dimension member setting. If you have not enabled SSO between

Oracle Business Intelligence and EPM Suite, you will be prompted to log into Hyperion Workspace before the report is displayed.

Navigating to Oracle E-Business Suite and Siebel CRM

If you have set up security integration between Oracle Business Intelligence and Oracle E-Business Suite or Siebel CRM, you can enable Navigate to E-Business Suite and Navigate to Siebel CRM action types. Integration between Oracle Business Intelligence and these products is not detailed in this book, but you can find full details in the *Oracle Fusion Middleware Integrator's Guide for Oracle Business Intelligence Enterprise Edition* manual, as part of the online Oracle Business Intelligence documentation set.

Configuring ActionFrameworkConfig.xml for Navigate to E-Business Suite and Navigate to Siebel CRM Action Types   Most of the integration between Oracle Business Intelligence and these products is performed elsewhere in the product. To enable Navigate to E-Business Suite and Navigate to Siebel CRM actions, you have to add two short XML snippets to the ActionFrameworkConfig.xml file and then enter details of what you want to navigate to when creating the action.

To enable the Navigate to E-Business Suite action type, add the following XML to the ActionFrameworkConfig.xml file:

```
<ebusinesssuiteconfig>
        <visible>true</visible>
</ebusinesssuiteconfig>
```

To enable the Navigate to Siebel CRM action type, add the following XML entry:

```
<siebelcrmconfig>
    <visible>true</visible>
</siebelcrmconfig>
```

Restart the WebLogic Managed Server to pick up the changes to this file, and then, when you select New | Action from the Oracle Business Intelligence web site menu, the two new action type are available in the actions menu.

Creating Actions Using Navigate to E-Business Suite and Navigate to Siebel CRM   When you create an action using the Navigate to E-Business Suite action type or Navigate to Siebel CRM action type, you are prompted to enter details to specify the application functionality you wish to target.

When creating a Navigate to E-Business Suite action, two default parameters are provided for you:

- **FunctionCode**   Use this parameter to specify the E-Business Suite function that you wish to target; for example, GLXIQJRN.

- **ConnectionPool**   Use this parameter to specify the repository connection pool that connects to the E-Business Suite database.

You can either "hard-code" these values as fixed parameter values when defining the action or leave them to be mapped to column values or session variables when the corresponding action link is created.

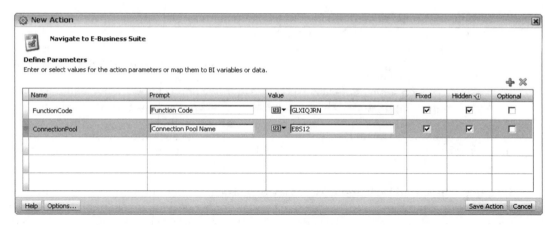

Similarly, when you create an action using the Navigate to Siebel CRM action type, you are prompted to provide values for View, Applet, and Pass Value. See the Siebel CRM product documentation for guidance on values to pass to this action type.

Invocation Actions

In addition to navigation actions, the other category of actions that you can create using Oracle Business Intelligence is *invocation* actions. Invocation actions execute a web service, process, or other activity that, in some cases, returns results to the Action Framework to process and present back to the user.

In this section, we will look at creating invocation actions to invoke a web service, invoke server-side and browser scripts, invoke Java methods, and invoke HTTP requests. All of these actions require external processes to invoke, and the sample data that comes with this book includes setup instructions so that you can re-create these examples yourself.

To start this section, we will take a look at what is probably the most commonly used invocation action: invoking a web service.

Invoking a Web Service

Web services are commonly used by organizations to provide encapsulated, abstracted business services over the Internet that can be consumed by applications and other services. Web services have gained in popularity over the years because they use a common format to describe their capabilities (WSDL, or Web Services Description Language), are platform- and system-independent, and allow applications and processes to communicate over widely used Internet protocols.

Oracle Business Intelligence developers typically use web services in their applications in several ways:

- To provide source data for part of a repository, through ADF View Objects
- To provide validation for credit cards or other customer information
- To provide background information or quotes for stocks
- To provide access to a business process that is made available through an action link on a dashboard, analysis, or other BI object

Depending on the organization and the requirements for security, some web services may be unsecured and publically available on the Internet or a company intranet, or they may require usernames, passwords, or other access tokens before they can be used. Web service use with Oracle Business Intelligence, because of the types of web services and how they are secured, can get somewhat complicated, especially if you do not have prior experience with this technology. To explain how web services are accessed through the Action Framework, we will start with a simple example, then progressively introduce more concepts to show how you can interact with web services of all types.

To start with, let's look at how you might access a credit card validation service, available unsecured and for free on the Internet, to enable you to check the validity of a given customer's credit card number.

Invoking Unsecured Web Services   Many organizations offer free web services on the Internet, for educational purposes or to provide free services for the developer community. One such web service is offered at the CDYNE Developer Wiki. This web service checks the validity of credit card numbers using the Luhn checksum algorithm. The URL for this service is http://wiki.cdyne .com/index.php/Credit_Card_Verification, with the web service itself available at https://ws.cdyne .com/creditcardverify/luhnchecker.asmx?wsdl.

NOTE
By the time you read this book, this service may have been altered or removed, but the principal applies to any unsecured web service that is accessed by SOAP and returns values to the calling application.

This web service requires a single parameter, CardNumber, which is a credit card number that you would like to check using the Luhn checksum algorithm (note that it does not check with the relevant credit card company; it only checks that the number is valid). The response payload for this web service returns two values, CardType and CardValid, using this XML format:

```
HTTP/1.1 200 OK
Content-Type: text/xml; charset=utf-8
Content-Length: length
<?xml version="1.0" encoding="utf-8"?>
<soap:Envelope xmlns:xsi="http://www.w3.org/2001/XMLSchema-instance"
xmlns:xsd="http://www.w3.org/2001/XMLSchema" xmlns:soap="http://schemas.xml-
soap.org/soap/envelope/">
  <soap:Body>
    <CheckCCResponse xmlns="http://ws.cdyne.com/">
      <CheckCCResult>
        <CardType>string</CardType>
        <CardValid>boolean</CardValid>
      </CheckCCResult>
    </CheckCCResponse>
  </soap:Body>
</soap:Envelope>
```

The two values within this XML response that we want to return to the user can be extracted using the following XPath expressions:

- **CardType**   Body/CheckCCResponse/CheckCCResult/CardType
- **CardValid**   Body/CheckCCResponse/CheckCCResult/CardValid

Because this web service is unsecured and available for free use on the Internet, it demonstrates how simple accessing web services via actions can be. This first example will pass the WSDL URL to the action as we create it, rather than enter the service into the Action Framework registry. We will parse and return the service results to the user, using the preceding XPath expressions.

To create an action that calls a public, unsecured web service that returns response data to the client, follow these steps:

1. From the Oracle Business Intelligence application menu, select New | Action. From the list of actions displayed, select Invoke A Web Service.

2. In the Select Web Service Operation dialog box, enter the URL https://ws.cdyne.com/ creditcardverify/luhnchecker.asmx?wsdl into the WSDL URL text box, then click Open to parse the WSDL file and display the available list of services.

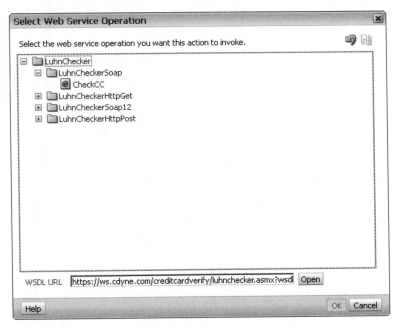

3. Within the list of services, expand the LuhnChecker folder and the LunhcheckerSoap folder and then select the CheckCC service. Click OK to use this service for the action.

4. The New Action dialog box is displayed with a single parameter for the credit card number that has to be sent along with the service call. Leave all of the options at their default values for the moment so that their values can be customized by the report developer when he or she creates the action link.

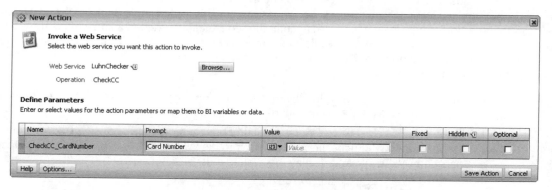

5. To parse and display the response from the web service for the user, click the Options button.

6. In the Action Options dialog box, select the Action Results tab. Within the XPath Results table, enter the following values (click the Add XPath Expression button to add the second row to the table):

Name: 1
XPath Expression: Body/CheckCCResponse/CheckCCResult/CardType
Name: 2
XPath Expression: Body/CheckCCResponse/CheckCCResult/CardValid

Within the Dialog Text area, type **The card type is @{1} and the status is @{2}**, which references the names in the XPath Results table.

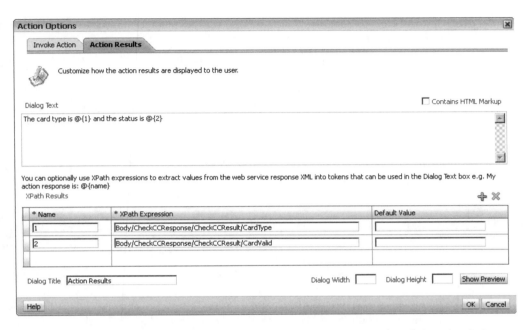

7. To indicate that the user should be prompted to run the action and to define the dialog box title and execute button text with which to prompt the user, or to set other options, select the Invoke Action tab. Otherwise, click OK, and then click Save to save the new action to the Presentation Server catalog.

8. To use this new action as an action link, create or open an analysis that contains or uses credit card numbers. In the following example, we are using a simple tabular report that lists the name, credit card number, and sale amount of customers who have bought products from our company.

9. To add the action as an action link to the analysis, select Column Properties for the column you wish to add the action link to.

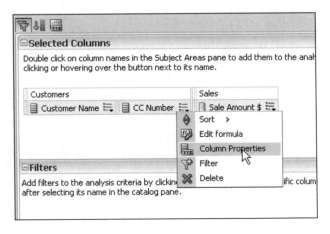

10. In the Column Properties dialog box, select the Interaction tab and select Action Links in the Primary Interaction drop-down list under Value.

11. When the Action Links table is displayed, click the Add Action Link button to display the New Action Link dialog box. Type **Check Credit Card Validity...** in the Link Text field, and click the Select Existing Action button to select the action you created a moment ago.

12. In the Edit Parameter Mapping dialog box, use the Value drop-down menu to select Column Value, and then use the right-hand drop-down menu to select the column to map to the parameter (for example, "Customers"."CC Number").

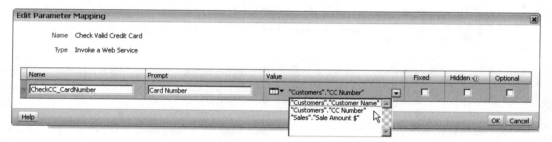

Either leave the Fixed, Hidden, and Optional check boxes at their default values or select the options you would like to use, then press OK to close this dialog.

13. You will now have been returned to the New Action Link dialog box. If you would like the action link to be displayed conditionally, using this dialog select Conditionally and add a condition; otherwise, just click OK to save the action link definition. Click OK to close the Column Properties dialog box, and save your analysis when complete.

14. You can now test your new action. With the analysis open, switch to the Results tab, and then click one of the credit card numbers to display the action link.

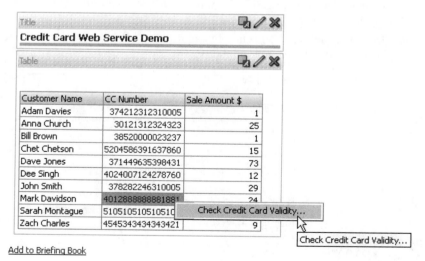

15. When you click the action link, the Invoke Action dialog box is shown. Depending on the options you chose when creating the action link, the credit card number may be editable, and may be optional. Click Execute to invoke the web service.

16. After the web service completes its execution, the Action Results dialog box is shown, which parses the response using the XPath expressions you specified earlier and presents the results to the end user.

Now that you know how to call a simple, unsecured web service, and how to parse the response to return information to the user, let's take a look at a slightly more involved example, where the web service requires a set of username and password credentials when using its services.

Invoking Secured Web Services Using Simple Usernames and Passwords   Most web services that you will want to access are secured in some way. To enable access to such secured services, you will need to make configuration entries in the ActionFrameworkConfig.xml file, to include details of the service and details on how credentials, certificates, and key stores are used to authenticate yourself to the service.

The simplest form of security is where the service requires a single set of username and password credentials, which all users who access the service will use. For more secure communication, you might also want to consider setting up certificates and key stores so that each person passes their own credentials to a web service.

In this next example, we will use the built-in Oracle BI Web Services for SOA that comes with Oracle Business Intelligence to illustrate how username and password credentials can be passed to a web service. In this example, we will store a single set of username and password credentials in the credential store. Every person that connects to this service will connect using the same credentials.

When you start to look at secured web services, you need to be aware of a feature called *policies*. Policies are used by web services to advertise their rules (or *policies*) around security, quality of service, and so on that web service consumers must then adhere to if they wish to make use of them. Policies for a particular web service are set up by the creator of that service, and when you therefore need to configure the Action Framework to work with such a web service, you will need to find out what policies that web service uses.

In general, two types of polices can be attached to web services:

■ **WebLogic Web Service policies** These are provided by WebLogic Server and are managed from the WebLogic Server Administration Console.

■ **Oracle Web Services Manager (OWSM) policies** These are managed from Fusion Middleware Control.

Oracle's recommendation is to use OWSM policies where possible. These policies are used by the OBIEE Web Services for SOA that we are now working with.

OBIEE Web Services for SOA comes with three services:

■ **ExecuteAgent** This is for running an agent.

■ **ExecuteAnalysis** This is for running an analysis.

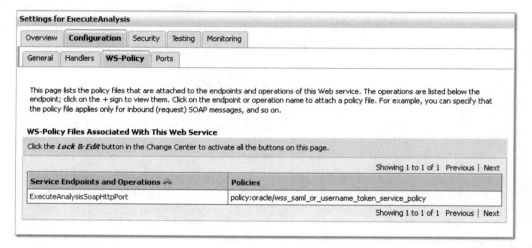

■ **ExecuteCondition** This is for executing a condition and returning a Boolean value.

Each of these services is secured using the "policy:oracle/wss_username_token_service_policy" security policy. This means that we first have to create in the credential store a credential key to hold a suitable username and password to access these services, and then enter details of the service into the ActionFrameworkConfig.xml file to allow the services to be accessed and to connect them to the entry in the credential store.

OBIEE Web Services for SOA also automatically creates and keeps updated a Web Services Inspection Language (WSIL) document that provides endpoints for every agent, analysis, and condition in a particular web catalog. If you register this WSIL document, rather than the WSDL document that just describes each individual service, your users will be able to pick from individual agents, analyses, and conditions when creating actions against this service.

When retrieving credentials to gain access to a secured web service, the Action Framework expects the credential key that you specified in the ActionFrameworkConfig.xml file to be within a credential map called oracle.bi.actions. If this credential map does not exist in your credential store, you will need to create it before storing the credential there. When we do this in a moment, we will store the credential using the credential key wsil.browsing, though you could name it however you wish, as long as you make sure the ActionFrameworkConfig.xml file reflects the name you choose.

In addition to this credential, if you are accessing Oracle BI Web Services for SOA on your own server or workstation and you have not previously used or configured this service, you also need to set up a separate credential store entry for use by the web service itself. By default, this web service is not active and it requires you to place an entry in the oracle.bi.enterprise credential map folder, also called wsil.browsing, where you need to enter the name and password for an administrative user within your Weblogic domain. In this instance though, the name wsil.browsing is mandatory as this is the credential key name that the web service automatically looks for when authenticating itself on startup.

In the following example then, we will make use of this web service via an Invoke a Web Service action, first creating a new administrative user for use by the web service and also by our action, and then we'll create the two credential store entries so that the service can start, and we can then access it in the required, secured, way. Then, we'll go on to configure the ActionFrameworkConfig.xml file and start making use of the service.

1. Create a new username and password that will be used by Oracle BI Web Services for SOA, and also by the action for authenticating against this secured web service. To do this, log into the WebLogic Server Administration Console using an administration user account, and select Security Realms from the navigation tree on the left.

2. In the list of realms, select myrealm, and then select the Users And Groups tab. When the list of users is displayed, click New and create a new user called obiee_ws_browse with a password of welcome1 (for example, the name is arbitrary).

3. This new user needs to be part of the BIAdministrators LDAP group. With the Users And Groups tab still selected, click the new user to display the General tab, and then select the Groups tab. Use the arrow key to add the obiee_ws_browse user to the BIAdministrators group, and then click Save to save the definition.

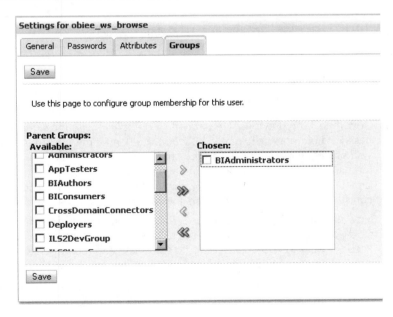

4. Add this new user's details to the credential store. We will need to do this twice, once using the oracle.bi.enterprise map for use by the web service, and then again under the oracle.bi.actions map for use by the Action Framework when connecting to the web service. Using your web browser, open the Fusion Middleware Control web site and log in using an administration username and password. Using the navigation tree menu on the left of the screen, expand Farm_bifoundation_domain, expand WebLogic Domain, right-click the bifoundation_domain entry, and select Security | Credentials to display the Credential Store Provider list.

5. Starting with the credentials required by the web service itself, if the oracle.bi.enterprise credential folder (credential map) entry is not present, click the Create Map button to create it in the Create Map dialog box. After you create it, or if it already exists, click the Create Key button and create the following credential key:

Select Map: oracle.bi.enterprise
Key: wsil.browsing
Type: Password
User Name: oracle_ws_browse
Password: welcome1
Confirm Password: welcome1

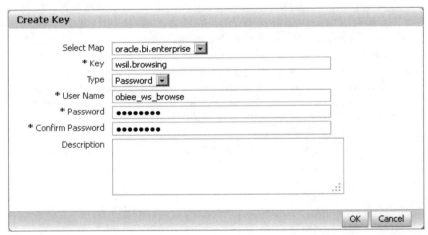

6. Now repeat the previous step to create a credential with the same key, type, username and password but under the oracle.bi.actions credential map. You should now have added the wsil.browsing credential key to the credential store twice, once under the oracle.bi.actions map and once under the oracle.bi.enterprise map. Once you have done so, restart your Oracle Business Intelligence system so that the Oracle BI Web Services for SOA service can start using the new credentials to provide browse (WSIL) access to the catalog.

7. Now that you have set up a user account and entered its details into the credential store, you can configure the ActionFrameworkConfig.xml file to register the OBIEE Web Services for SOA service. To do so, locate and then open for editing the ActionFrameworkConfig.xml file, which by default is located at:

[*middleware_home*]\user_projects\domains\bifoundation_domain\config\fmwconfig\
biinstances\coreapplication\ActionFrameworkConfig.xml.

8. With the file open for editing, add the following entry within the <registries></registries> tags:

```
<registry>
          <id>reg1b</id>
          <name>BI EE Web Services for SOA</name>
          <content-type>webservices</content-type>
          <provider-class>oracle.bi.action.registry.wsil.WSILRegistry</
provider-class>
          <description></description>
          <location>
<path>http://localhost:7001/biservices/inspection?wsil</path>
          </location>
            <service-access>
               <account>wsil.browsing</account>
               <policy>wss_username_token_policy</policy>
              <propagateIdentity>false</propagateIdentity>
            </service-access>
</registry>
```

Within this registry entry there are three elements that are of additional interest to us:

- ■ **provider-class**   This specifies a WSILRegistry class so that the Action Framework knows that it will be browsing a WSIL document, rather than a WSDL document, to list available services.

- ■ **account**   This specifies an account entry (which we will create in a moment) that references the wsil.browsing credential key created in the previous steps.

- ■ **path**   This specifies the URL for the WSIL file provided by the service, listing all the agents, analyses, and conditions in the catalog.

- ■ **policy**   This specifies a policy entry (which we will also create in a moment) that references the security policy used by this particular service.

9. Within the <content-types></content-types> section, if there is not an entry already for webservices, add it like this:

```
<content-type>
          <typename>webservices</typename>
          <displayname>Web Services and BPEL Processes</displayname>
          <actionType>WebServiceActionType</actionType>
      </content-type>
```

10. Now you need to add an entry that corresponds to the wsil.browsing account entry you made in the <registry> section. This entry references the credential key you specified earlier when adding the browsing user details to the credential store, and assumes that the key is stored under the oracle.bi.actions credential map. The Action Framework will use these credentials when browsing the WSIL document and executing the services the document points to. Within the <accounts></accounts> section, add the following entry:

```
<account>
          <name>wsil.browsing</name>
          <description>Account for BI WS for SOA</description>
          <adminonly>false</adminonly>
```

```
<credentialkey>wsil.browsing</credentialkey>
<credentialmap>oracle.bi.enterprise</credentialmap>
    </account>
```

11. Similarly, you now need to add the following entry within the <policies></policies> section to reference a policy XML definition file we will create in a moment. This policy corresponds with the "policy:oracle/wss_username_token_service_policy" security policy that OBIEE Web Services for SOA uses to control access to its services.

```
<policy>
        <name>wss_username_token_policy</name>
        <policyfile>wss_username_token_policy.xml</policyfile>
    </policy>
```

Once you have made this last entry, save and close the ActionFrameworkConfig.xml file.

12. The policy entry you added to the configuration file in the last step references an XML file that you also need to create, and then save into a specific location in the application file system. Using a text editor, create a file called **wss_username_token_policy.xml** and add the following XML to it:

```
<?xml version="1.0" encoding="UTF-8"?>
<oracle-webservice-clients>
<webservice-client>
<port-info>
<policy-references>
<policy-reference uri="oracle/log_policy" category="management"/>
<policy-reference uri="oracle/wss_username_token_client_policy"
category="security"/>
</policy-references>
</port-info>
</webservice-client>
</oracle-webservice-clients>
```

Save this file to the following location:

[*middleware_home*]\user_projects\domains\bifoundation_domain\config\fmwconfig\ biinstances\coreapplication\wss_username_token_policy.xml

13. Now that you have completed the configuration tasks, stop and start the WebLogic Managed Server (or Administration Server, if using the Simple Install type).

14. You can now test your new action, which is secured through passing a common username and password to the service along with the request. To do this, log into the Oracle Business Intelligence web site and select New | Action. From the list of actions, select Invoke A Web Service. You will then be presented with a list of all the shared analyses, agents, and other BI objects in the catalog.

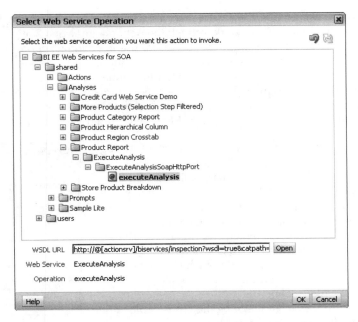

To create an action, select one of the endpoints corresponding to the object you wish to run, and then save the action to the catalog. This type of action is particularly useful in conjunction with agents, as it allows you to create action links that can schedule agents to run immediately from the dashboard.

So, through the preceding example, you have seen how you can use policies to enable username and password credentials to be passed to a web service so that access can be restricted to only those consumers that have the relevant credentials. But this approach is limited in three ways: messages between Oracle Business Intelligence and the web service are sent in plain text rather than encrypted; by default, only a single set of username and password credentials is required; and the messages are not digitally signed, so you can't be sure of their integrity.

An alternative to this type of policy is to use one that is instead SAML-based using digital certificates to authenticate clients requiring access to a service. The server providing the web service maintains a key store that records all of the certificates in use, so this type of communication is very secure; only clients with trusted certificates are allowed to use the service, and all messages are encrypted and digitally signed. This approach also has the advantage that it can pass the username of the invoking user to the web service, allowing it to run with the credentials of the user rather than with those of an administrator account.

Full details of SAML and its associated key stores, certificates, and other artifacts are outside the scope of this book. Consult the Oracle Fusion Middleware product documentation, together with the Oracle Business Intelligence documentation, for more details on this feature.

Invoking a Java Method

Another way that an action can call external functionality is through invocation of a Java method, embedded in an EJB session bean. In previous releases of Oracle Business Intelligence, calling Java method functionality was limited to doing so through Oracle Delivers and the Java Host system component, but in the 11g release, you can register Enterprise Java Beans and present them for use as action links.

To use a Java method within an Enterprise Java Bean, you have to register an application server with the Action Framework through the ActionFrameworkConfig.xml file. This registration then exposes the EJBs present on that server for use in defining actions. This feature is especially useful for tasks such as external application integration through Java APIs (for example, Oracle Essbase) or for accessing file system or other functionality.

In the following example, based on the Action Framework Sample Application content available to download separately from the Oracle Technology Network web site, we will look at the steps required to register an EJB that archives BI content from the catalog to a file system.

Example: Using a Java Method to Archive a Catalog Object   In this example, we will use the ActionSamples EJB provided as part of the Oracle Business Intelligence 11.1.1.5 or 11.1.1.6 Sample Application, together with Oracle JDeveloper 11.1.2, which are both downloadable from the Oracle Technology Network. The Enterprise Archive (EAR) file provided as part of this download includes an EJB providing two Java methods, one of which we will use in this example to demonstrate archiving a catalog object to the file system.

When the EAR file containing the EJB is deployed to your application server, a module called ActionSamplesEJB.jar appears in the WebLogic Server Administration Console Deployments screen, as shown next. It is this EJB module that we will access through the Action Framework.

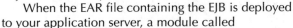

Deployments

	Name ⌃	State	Health	Type	Deployment Order
Install	Update	Delete	Start ⌄	Stop ⌄	Showing 1 to 67 of 67 Previous | Next

	Name ⌃	State	Health	Type	Deployment Order
☐	⊟ 📦 ActionSamples	Active	✔ OK	Enterprise Application	100
	⊟ Modules				
	🔘 ActionSamples			Web Application	
	📄 ActionSamplesEJB.jar			EJB Module	
	⊟ EJBs				
	📄 HelloworldSession			EJB	

Before you start this example, ensure that you have deployed the Sample Application and that you can see the EJB Module present, and working correctly, through the WebLogic Server Administration Console. To register the application server (in this example, the same WebLogic Server that is running Oracle Business Intelligence), follow these steps:

1. Open the ActionFrameworkConfig.xml file for editing, the default location for which is

   [*middleware_home*]\user_projects\domains\bifoundation_domain\config\fmwconfig\ biinstances\coreapplication\ActionFrameworkConfig.xml

2. Add the following entry within the <registries></registries> tags:

```
<registry>
                <id>reg03</id>
                <name>Sample EJBs</name>
                <content-type>java</content-type>
                <provider-class>oracle.bi.action.registry.java.EJBRegistry</
provider-class>
                <description>Custom Java classes which can be invoked as ac-
tion targets</description>
                <location>
                     <path/>
                </location>
                <custom-config>
                    <ejb-targets>
                        <appserver>
                            <context-factory>weblogic.jndi.WLInitialCon-
textFactory</context-factory>
                            <jndi-url>t3://localhost:7001</jndi-url>
                            <server-name>localhost</server-name>
                            <account>WLSJNDI</account>
                            <ejb-exclude>mgmt</ejb-exclude>
                            <ejb-exclude>
                            PopulationServiceBean</ejb-exclude>
                        </appserver>
                        <ejb-app>
                            <server>localhost</server>
                            <app-context>ActionSamplesEJB</app-context>
                        </ejb-app>
                    </ejb-targets>
                </custom-config>
</registry>
```

Within this registry entry, the appserver element tells the Action Framework which application server to connect to, to obtain the list of EJBs that will then be used to create the registry. Individual EBJs do not need to be listed here, although selected ones can be removed through the ejb-exclude element.

NOTE
For EBJs to be usable with the Action Framework, they must include the actionframework-common.jar file, which provides communication between the Action Framework and any input parameters that the Java methods within the EJB may provide. This file normally can be found in a subdirectory under the [middleware_home]\user_projects\ domains\bifoundation_domain\servers\bi_server1\tmp_WL_user\ bimiddleware_11.1.1\ folder (the name will vary by your installation and is based under a temporary folder name).

3. The preceding registry entry also references an account element, which in this case points to an entry called WLSJNDI. This entry will reference a credential store entry that will be used to authenticate with the application server. If you do not have a corresponding entry in your ActionFrameworkConfig.xml file within the <accounts></accounts> element, create one now, using this format:

```
<account>
              <name>WLSJNDI</name>
              <description>Account used to access WLS JNDI.</description>
              <adminonly>false</adminonly>
              <credentialkey>JNDIUser</credentialkey>
</account>
```

Once complete, save the ActionFrameworkConfig.xml file.

4. The accounts entry you made in the ActionFrameworkConfig.xml file references an entry that you need to add to the credential store, within the oracle.bi.actions credential map. To do this, open the Fusion Middleware Control web site and log in using an administrator username and password. Then, using the navigation tree menu on the left of the screen, expand Farm_bifoundation_domain, expand WebLogic Domain, right-click the bifoundation_domain entry, and select Security | Credentials to display the Credential Store Provider list.

5. If the oracle.bi.actions credential folder (credential map) entry is not present, click the Create Map button to create it. Then, click the Create Key button and create the following credential key:

Select Map: oracle.bi.actions
Key: JNDIUser
Type: Password
User Name: weblogic
Password: welcome1
Confirm Password: welcome1

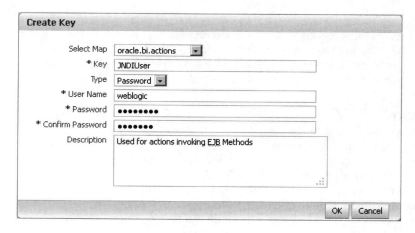

The username and password should correspond to a user account on the application server hosting the EJBs—an account that has the ability to access the EJBs. In this case, the application server hosting the EJBs is the same one that hosts Oracle Business Intelligence, but this does not have to be the case, particularly as the WebLogic Server embedded license that comes with Oracle Business Intelligence does not allow you to install your own applications into the WebLogic Server that hosts Oracle Business Intelligence (without your first purchasing a full-use license).

6. Once you have created this entry, stop and start the WebLogic Managed Server hosting Oracle Business Intelligence (or the Administration Server, if using the Simple Install type).

7. You can now try out the new Invoke a Java Method action, using the EJBs found on the application server you have just registered with the Action Framework. To do so, log into the Oracle Business Intelligence web site and select New | Action from the application menu. When the list of action types is displayed, select Invoke A Java Method from the list.

8. In the Select Java Method dialog box, expand the folder list to select the Java method that you would like to use; in this example, select the ArchiveReport method, and then click OK.

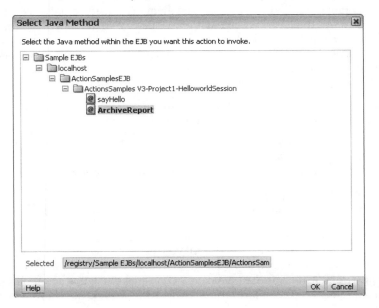

9. The list of parameters provided by the Java method is then presented to you using the New Action dialog box. As with any other action, you can provide Prompt labels and default values for the parameters using this dialog box, and you can select whether the parameter value is Fixed, Hidden, or Optional.

10. When you use the action—for example, as an action link on a dashboard—it will prompt you, in this case, to enter the filesystem location for the archive file and select the catalog object to be archived. Clicking the Execute button will then invoke the Java method, in this case archiving the catalog object to the file system.

Invoking a Browser Script Action

Browser Script actions can be used to execute arbitrary JavaScript functions to, for example, gather a set of parameter values and concatenate them into a URL, or raise events in an application that Oracle Business Intelligence content is embedded in. To use these types of actions, you need to be able to create functions and other code in JavaScript, and to understand how scripts are held within Oracle Business Intelligence and interact with the Action Framework.

All of the browser script actions that you set up need to be stored in a single JavaScript file called userscripts.js, which you can find at:

[*middleware_home*]\user_projects\domains\bifoundation_domain\servers*XXX*\tmp_WL_ user\analytics_11.1.1*YYY*\war\res\b_mozilla\actions

where *XXX* is either AdminServer or bi_server1, depending on whether you have a simple installation or enterprise installation, and *YYY* is a unique directory name defined during your install (for example, silp1v). By default, this file has the following entries:

```
USERSCRIPT=function(){};
USERSCRIPT.parameter=function(b,a,c){this.name=b;this.prompt=a;this.value=c};
```

These two functions set up a method of reading parameters from the action that you set up, and thus should be left in the file even if you add your own functions to it.

All JavaScript functions that you add to this file should be prefixed with USERSCRIPT; for example, USERSCRIPT.display_amazon_photo. By adding this common prefix, you avoid any naming clashes with other JavaScript functions that Oracle may have added to the product, and you keep to the naming standard used in all other installations.

Example: Searching the Twitter Stream for a Given Value In the following example, we will create a browser script action that searches the Twitter "stream" for a value passed using your action. To search Twitter (a web-based "micro-blogging" service) for a value, you use the following URL format:

http://www.twitter.com/#1/search/[*search_term*]

where [*search_term*] is the term you wish to use (for example, Exadata).

NOTE
This URL format may in time be changed by Twitter, so you should verify that it is still correct before attempting the example.

Optionally, you can include /realtime/ in front of the search term to return the most recent results from the Twitter stream rather than the most commonly read results, or you can include /links/ in front of the search term to return results with hyperlinks included. We will use JavaScript together with a browser script action to construct the correct URL to call the Twitter search, and then create an action link in an analysis to allow the user to search Twitter for messages about a selected column value.

The JavaScript that you need to add to the userscripts.js file comes in two parts and builds on the parameter object already defined in that file to pass values to your function. The first part is a JavaScript function that actually creates the URL based on the parameters that are passed, and then calls the window.open() method to open a new browser window using this URL. The conditional logic is included within the function so that we do not try and add a blank search option to the URL, which could cause the search to fail.

```
USERSCRIPT.searchTwitter = function (params)
{

    if (params.search_option == "realtime" || params.search_option == "links")

    {
        var twitterURL = "http://twitter.com/#!/search/"
                        + params.search_option
                        + "/"
                        + params.search_term;

    }

    else

    {
        var twitterURL = "http://twitter.com/#!/search/"
                        + params.search_term;

    }

    window.open(twitterURL,"searchTwitter");
};
```

The second function is optional unless you want your function to be listed in a menu for the user to select from, in which case it is required. The .publish suffix is detected by the Action Framework and, together with the parameter definition that it includes, determines how the browser script action is presented to the user when a new action is created. If you do not include this .publish function, the action is still available, but the user will have to type in the name manually together with the required parameter definitions.

```
USERSCRIPT.searchTwitter.publish =
{
    parameters:[
        new USERSCRIPT.parameter("search_term" , "Twitter Search Term" , ""),
        new USERSCRIPT.parameter("search_option" , "Option (realtime, links)"
, "")
    ]
};
```

Once complete, the full userscripts.js file, together with the function entries added at the start of the file by Oracle, should look like this:

```
USERSCRIPT=function(){};USERSCRIPT.parameter=function(b,a,c){this.name=b;this.
prompt=a;this.value=c};
USERSCRIPT.searchTwitter = function (params)
{

    if (params.search_option == "realtime" || params.search_option == "links")

    {
        var twitterURL = "http://twitter.com/#!/search/"
                    + params.search_option
                    + "/"
                    + params.search_term;

    }

    else

    {
        var twitterURL = "http://twitter.com/#!/search/"
                    + params.search_term;

    }

    window.open(twitterURL,"searchTwitter");
};
USERSCRIPT.searchTwitter.publish =
{
    parameters:[
        new USERSCRIPT.parameter("search_term" , "Twitter Search Term" , ""),
        new USERSCRIPT.parameter("search_option" , "Option (realtime, links)"
, "")
    ]
};
```

To create this browser script action, follow these steps:

1. Using a text editor, open the userscripts.js file at the location:

    [*middleware_home*]\user_projects\domains\bifoundation_domain\servers*XXX*\tmp_
    WL_user\analytics_11.1.1*YYY*\war\res\b_mozilla\actions

    where *XXX* is either AdminServer or bi_server1, depending on whether you have a simple
    installation or enterprise installation, and *YYY* is a unique directory name defined during
    your install (for example, silp1v).

2. Add to the end of this file the two JavaScript functions that implement the browser script
    action, remembering to preserve any existing functions that either you, or Oracle, have
    added to this file:

```
USERSCRIPT=function(){};USERSCRIPT.parameter=function(b,a,c){this.
name=b;this.prompt=a;this.value=c};
USERSCRIPT.searchTwitter = function (params)
{

    if (params.search_option == "realtime" || params.search_option ==
"links")

    {
        var twitterURL = "http://twitter.com/#!/search/"
                        + params.search_option
                        + "/"
                        + params.search_term;

    }

    else

    {
        var twitterURL = "http://twitter.com/#!/search/"
                        + params.search_term;

    }

    window.open(twitterURL,"searchTwitter");
};
USERSCRIPT.searchTwitter.publish =
{
    parameters:[
        new USERSCRIPT.parameter("search_term" , "Twitter Search Term"
, ""),
        new USERSCRIPT.parameter("search_option" , "Option (realtime,
links)" , "")
    ]
};
```

3. Save the file, and then clear the cache for your web browser and any web browsers that will be using this new action. To clear the cache using Mozilla Firefox 5.0, select Tools | Clear Recent History. To clear the browser cache for Microsoft Internet Explorer 8, select Tools | Delete Browsing History. Once you have cleared the browser cache, close and then reopen the browser. This step is required because your web browser caches copies of the userscripts.js file, and you will need to remove it from the cache to pick up your new functions.

4. You can now use your new browser script action. To test it, create for an analysis an inline action that will allow the user to search Twitter for mentions of a product type.

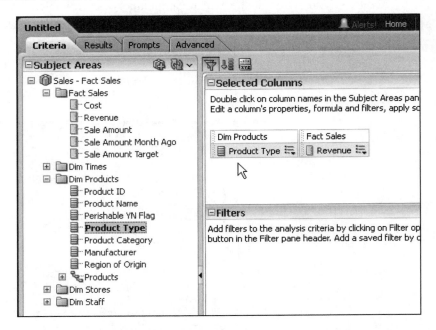

To create the inline action, open the drop-down menu next to the column that you wish to add the action link to (in this example, Product Type) and select Column Properties.

5. On the Interaction tab of the Column Properties dialog box, select Action Links in the Primary Interaction field under Value.

6. To add the action link, click the Add Action Link button. In the New Action Link dialog box, select Invoke A Browser Script from the Create A New Action drop-down menu.

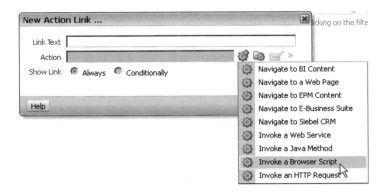

NOTE
This browser script action could in fact be created as a separate, named action, but we are creating it as an inline action to show how these types of actions are defined.

7. In the Create New Action dialog box, click the Browse button to select your new JavaScript function. If it does not appear in the list in the Select Script Function dialog box, shown next, make sure you have cleared your browser cache, restart your browser, and, just to be sure, restart Presentation Services in case it is caching your old content.

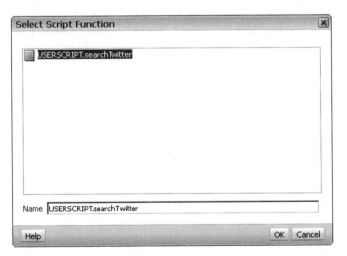

8. After selecting the function, the list of parameters should be automatically listed in the Create New Action dialog box. Use the Value column to map the search_term parameter to a column value, and either provide a default value for the search_option parameter or select the Optional check box and leave it to the user to provide a value (or leave it blank).

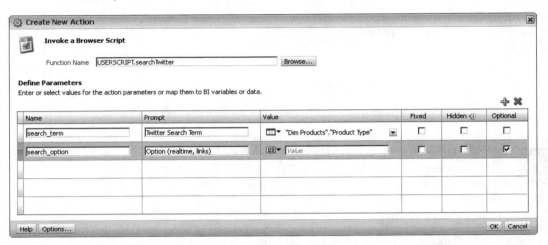

9. Once you have defined the new inline action, click OK to return to the New Action Link dialog box. Add a value in the Link Text field (for example, Search Twitter...) and then click OK to close the dialog box.

10. To test out the new browser script action, view the analysis results and click the action link that you just created. You will then be prompted for the search term, and the option value if required. Depending on the values you enter, a new browser window will then open that displays the results of the Twitter search.

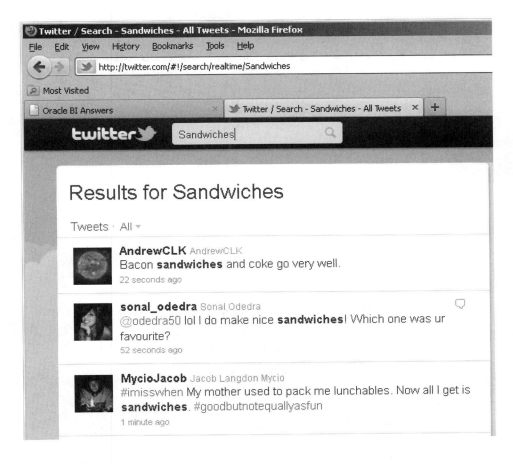

Invoking an HTTP Request

The final action type that we will cover in this chapter is Invoke an HTTP Request. This type of action is used for calling a web page or service, where parameters are passed either through GET or POST methods. Web sites often use GET and POST methods to pass variables between pages, and while this is not the most secure of methods, it can be useful as a way of integrating with a web site that does not use web services, JavaScript, or other more modern methods.

When you call a web page using the GET method, the value of a variable is included in the URL, in the format http://www.example.com?variable=value. If you use the POST method, however, the value is passed as part of a form submission and is not visible in the URL. Any scripting language such as PHP, ASP, Perl, or JSP can read the values being passed across and can perform an action based on them and your request.

One limitation of this type of action is that, while you can pass values to it, you cannot process the returned values to display to the user or to pass to an agent or other process. As such, these types of actions are typically used to integrate with web-based services using GET and POST to perform services and initiate processes or workflows.

Example: Invoking a Restock Request via an HTTP Request and GET/POST

In this example, we will see how an Invoke an HTTP Request action can be used to request a product restock via a web site service. In this example, requests to restock products can be made by calling a URL and either sending a product ID via the following HTTP GET method:

http://www.gcbc-products.com/restock?prod_id=[*product_id_number*]

or a POST method that uses the variable name prod_id = [*product_id_number*]

NOTE
This service is for illustration only and is not a real publically available web service; it will not return values when you call it using the action link in this example.

To create this browser script action, follow these steps:

1. Log into the Oracle Business Intelligence web site, and select New | Action from the application menu. When the list of action types is displayed, select Invoke An HTTP Request.

2. In the New Action dialog box, type in the URL for the HTTP request, including the parameter if you wish the parameter list to be automatically populated. For example, to call the service that we are using for this example, type in the following URL:

http://www.gcbc-products.com/restock?prod_id=

New Action

Invoke an HTTP Request
Enter the URL you want this action to invoke.

URL http://www.gcbc-products.com/restock?prod_id=@{1}   ▼ Define Parameters
Request GET ▼

Define Parameters
To embed a parameter value anywhere within the URL, use the token @{Name} where 'Name' is the value specified in the Name column below.
There is no limit to the number of parameters that can be embedded.

Name	Prompt	Value	Fixed	Hidden	Optional
1	prod_id	123 ▼ Value	☐	☐	☐

Help   Options...   Save Action   Cancel

3. Click the Define Parameters button to parse the URL and extract the parameters out of it, replacing them with placeholder values. Select the Fixed, Hidden, or Optional check boxes as required, select POST as the Request setting if you would like to remove the parameter from the URL and send it via the POST method instead, and click Save Action to save the action to the catalog.

4. To test the action, create an analysis that features product information and product IDs. Add the action as an action link to one of the columns, as described earlier in this chapter. When adding the action, map a column containing the product ID to the parameter value. Then, when you select the action link when viewing the analysis results, the action will call the web page and pass the product ID value as an HTTP request, using either GET or POST.

Creating Agents and Conditions

In addition to defining actions, which enable you to initiate a process or navigate to an application based on insight gained from a dashboard, the actionable intelligence feature within Oracle Business Intelligence also allows you to define tests, or *conditions*, which you can use to check for particular business situations, and *agents*, which can use conditions to determine, for example, whether to distribute a report or execute a workflow according to a schedule, raising alerts or initiating actions based on your instructions.

Introduced earlier in the chapter as part of the Action Framework, in conjunction with actions, agents and conditions give you the ability to create closed-loop BI systems that detect situations of interest, bring them to your attention, and then optionally take action on them, the results of which will then be checked over by the same or other agents at a later date.

Overview of Agents and Conditions

Agents (called iBots in earlier releases of Oracle Business Intelligence) are processes that you create to deliver content, provide alerts, publish data, and provide other automation tasks to support your business intelligence system. Together with conditions, they are used to deliver analyses, dashboards, or other content to one or more users. In the following two sections we'll take a closer look at these other features within the Action Framework.

Agents

Agents are defined within the Presentation Server catalog and can be configured to run immediately, on demand, or on a predefined schedule. Agents can either execute unconditionally or can test for a condition before proceeding to distribute whatever content you have designated as the "payload."

Agents are typically defined by an administrator responsible for the analyses, dashboards, and other BI objects within a particular department of the organization. Agents can be configured to execute with the permissions and data visibility of the agent author, or they can be made available for subscription and run using the credentials of the subscriber or with the author's permission. As part of the agent's execution, it can deliver analyses or other BI content to the subscriber's e-mail account, to a pager or other device, or as alerts that appear on the user's dashboard.

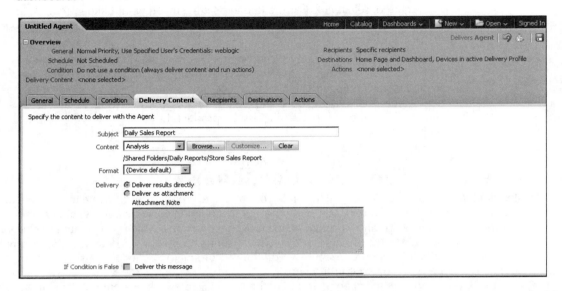

Agents should be thought of primarily as a means to automate the business intelligence process, distributing reports and checking for conditions in the background to save users from having to dig through dozens of reports and dashboards each day to perform daily checks. Agents use the Oracle BI Scheduler component to run according to a schedule, and they can also make use of agents (including two agent types, Server Script agents and Java Job agents that are only available for use with agents) to perform activities such as archiving files, invoking web services, and initiating business processes.

Conditions

You can configure agents to either execute unconditionally or to test for a defined condition before executing. As with actions, you can define conditions either as part of the agent definition (referred to as *inline* conditions) or as stand-alone Presentation Server catalog objects and reuse them across several agents (referred to as *named* conditions). Again, the same as with actions, an inline condition can be converted to a named agent and then reused by other agents.

A condition uses either the results of an analysis or the status of a KPI to determine whether the condition has been met or not. For a condition based on an analysis, you can define whether the condition is true or not based on whether one or more rows were returned by the analysis. For a condition based on a KPI, the condition outcome will be determined by whether or not the KPI has the status that you select.

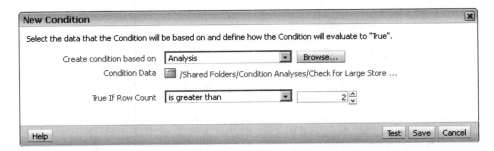

Similar to the "guided analytics" feature included in earlier releases of Oracle Business Intelligence, conditions can also be used in dashboards to, for example, determine for a particular user or role whether to display a particular section or link in a shared dashboard.

The Oracle BI Scheduler

When you schedule an agent for execution, including scheduling it for immediate execution, it is the Oracle BI Scheduler system component that actually runs the agent. The Oracle BI Scheduler component, like other system components such as the Oracle BI Server, Oracle BI Presentation Server, and Oracle BI Java Host, is controlled and configured using Fusion Middleware Control and can be clustered for high availability across multiple servers, with one Oracle BI Scheduler being designated the primary scheduler and a second, for failover purposes, becoming the secondary scheduler.

You can view which agents are currently executing on your system by logging into the Oracle Business Intelligence web site as an administrative user and then clicking the Administration link at the top of the screen. On the Administration screen that is displayed, you can click the Manage Agent Sessions link to view details of all currently executing agents.

The Oracle BI Scheduler has its own client utility for viewing and monitoring the execution of agent jobs, and stores metadata on scheduled tasks in database tables within the BIPLATFORM schema, which are installed for you automatically by the Repository Creation Utility before you install Oracle Business Intelligence. Unlike earlier releases of Oracle Business Intelligence, you do not have to perform any post-installation tasks before using the scheduler, and it should be available for use with all Oracle Business Intelligence Enterprise Edition systems.

NOTE
As with all of the actionable intelligence features within Oracle Business Intelligence, agents and conditions are not available as part of the license for Oracle Business Intelligence Standard Edition One.

Creating an Agent

To illustrate how an agent is created, consider a situation where each of the regional sales managers within a company needs to be notified when a store within their responsibility has sold less than their target sales amount. The requirement is for regional sales managers to be sent a report only when one or more of their stores has met this condition, and this report should be sent to them via e-mail and appear as an alert on their BI dashboard. Finally, there is a requirement for one or other business processes to be carried out depending on the status of the agent, which we will look at toward the end of the example.

Defining Basic Agent Settings

Before we create the agent itself, we need to determine whether or not the agent should deliver an analysis or other BI object as part of the execution. If so, we first need to define the BI object and store it in the Presentation Server catalog, typically in the Shared area if the agent is going to be made available to other users for subscription.

In this example, the analysis delivered by the agent lists stores, their actual sales figure, and their target sales figure, as shown next. Conditional formatting has been used to highlight in red those stores that have not met their sales target.

Store Name	Sale Amount	Sale Amount Target	Variance
10th Avenue	20.00	22.00	-2.00
Anaheim	8.00	7.00	1.00
Fishermans Wharf	94.00	216.00	-122.00
Geary Street	35.00	34.00	1.00
Haight Street	11.00	13.00	-2.00
Los Angeles	58.00	57.00	1.00
Market Street	46.00	48.00	-2.00
New York	18.00	28.00	-10.00
North Beach	13.00	13.00	0.00
Taylor Street	17.00	20.00	-3.00
Walnut Creek	5.00	5.00	0.00

Later on, we will look at how we can configure this analysis to be delivered conditionally, but for now, follow these steps to define the basic analysis, making it available for subscription and having it use the subscribers' view of the data:

1. Log into the Oracle Business Intelligence web site and select New | Agent from the application menu. The Untitled Agent (New Agent) screen that is displayed includes the following seven tabs, which contain the configuration details that you may define for the agent:

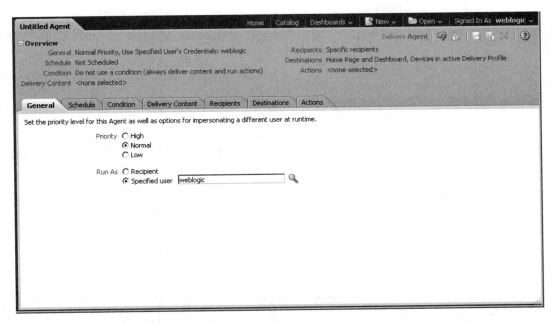

- **General**   This tab is used to define the priority for the agent and whether it runs using the credentials of the agent author or as a specific user (usually the superuser or agent author).
- **Schedule**   This tab defines the agent schedule, including the frequency, when the schedule starts, how often it re-runs, and when the schedule ends.
- **Condition**   This tab lets you select an analysis, or a KPI, to be tested against before executing the rest of the agent.
- **Delivery Content**   This tab is used to select the analysis, dashboard, or briefing book that the agent will deliver to the selected recipients.
- **Recipients**   This tab defines the users, roles, e-mail addresses, or catalog groups (deprecated; included for backward compatibility only) that the delivery content will be sent to.
- **Destinations**   This tab lets you define where the results of the agent will be delivered. The destination is usually what the recipients define as their "active delivery profile," but you can override this for particular agents.
- **Actions**   This tab is used for "chaining" other agents to this one, either to create a multistep, automated process or to select actions such as invoking a BPEL process via a web service based on the outcome of the agent condition.

On the General tab, select the Priority setting (High, Normal, or Low) for the agent and select Recipient as the Run As choice to specify that the agent runs using the subscriber's credentials and data visibility. The Priority setting can be used to select from multiple devices that a user has registered for deliveries, so that, for example, the user can be contacted via pager for urgent deliveries but via e-mail for normal or low-priority deliveries.

2. Click the Schedule tab to select the agent schedule. If, for example, the agent is to run at 8 A.M. each day, with no repeat during the day and no fixed end date, select the following values (and leave the other settings at their default values):

Enabled: Checked
Frequency: Daily Every 1 Days
Start: [*start date*; for example, 08/02/2011 08:00:00 AM]
End: No end date

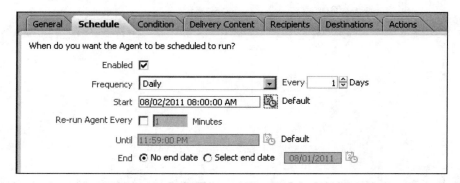

3. On the Condition tab, leave the values at their default settings at this stage. We will set the condition for the agent in the next section of the chapter.

4. On the Delivery Content tab, enter a subject for the delivery message (for example, Daily Sales Report), and then click the Browse button to select for delivery the analysis you created earlier.

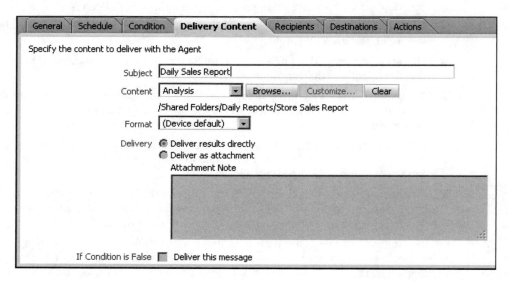

5.   If you want to change the delivery format from the default for the user's specified device, select a different format from the Format drop-down menu. If you make a change, select one of the two delivery radio buttons to specify whether the results are sent directly or as an attachment.

6.   On the Recipients tab, select which recipients (other than the subscriber to the agent) will receive the agent output. Recipients can be other users, other application roles, or other catalog groups, or you can click the Add Email Recipients button to specify individual e-mail addresses (which do not have to belong to registered users of Oracle Business Intelligence) to send the output to.

7.   On the Destinations tab, for the User Destinations settings, specify whether the agent output is delivered to the home page and dashboard (in the form of an alert) and whether it is sent to the active delivery profile for the user or to a specific device whose choice overrides their default profile.

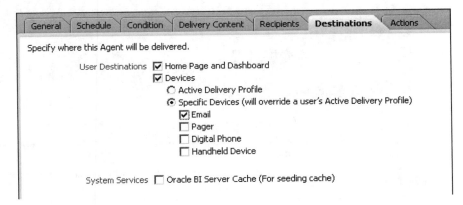

The Oracle BI Server Cache (For Seeding Cache) option is used for a special situation where an administrator wishes to pre-seed the query cache with the results of commonly used analyses and dashboards, typically before the start of each day and in order to have such reports run near-instantaneously. Using this option is the only way to pre-seed the global cache used when your Oracle Business Intelligence system has been clustered, and should normally be used only when this outcome is required. Leave this check box deselected in this example.

8. The Actions tab is used for selecting agents that execute for each row of the agent output data, based on whether the condition is met (or there is no condition) or is not met. Leave the settings on this tab at their default values, and we will come back to these later on.

9. Click Save to save this basic agent definition to the catalog. Make sure that you save it to the Shared Folders area in the catalog in order to make it available for other users to subscribe to.

To test the agent before the date and time of its scheduled execution, either click the Run Agent Now button on the agent definition screen or select the Run menu link under the agent definition when viewed in the catalog.

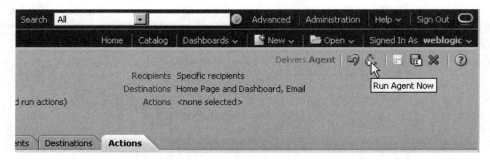

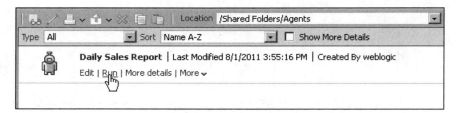

After the agent schedule completes, you will see an entry in the Alerts section of the user's home page, as long as the Home Page and Dashboard option was one of the selected options on the Destinations tab. Clicking the link for the alert will display details of the agent execution, along with a link to display the agent payload. Clicking the Clear option will remove the alert from the dashboard until the agent runs again.

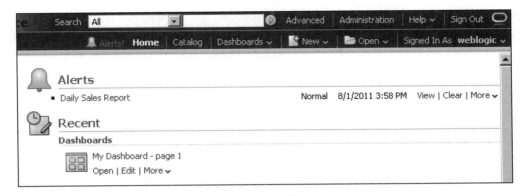

Now that you have seen how a basic agent is defined, let's take a look at some more options that you can use with this feature.

Managing Delivering Profiles for Users

In the previous example, when selecting destinations for the agent, you had the option on the Destinations tab to select the Active Delivery Profile for the recipient. This profile is a set of choices that users can make to determine how they receive the output of agents. You can choose whether to use this profile or override it for a particular agent.

Users can set their active delivery profile from the menu area in the Oracle Business Intelligence web site by selecting My Account from the drop-down menu next to their logged-in name.

When the My Account dialog box is shown, click the Delivery Options tab to set the delivery profile for the user. Using this tab, you can define one or more delivery profiles (for example, Regular Days and Holidays), which can have different devices associated with them. For example, for your Regular Days profile, you may choose to define a work e-mail address, while for the Holidays profile, you may use a pager or a mobile device.

To define such a profile, follow these steps:

1. With the My Account dialog box open, select the Delivery Options tab.

2. To first register your devices, use the Devices drop-down menu to select your device type (for example, Email), and then click the Create Device button to enter your device details

in the Create Device dialog box. Repeat this for each device type you wish to register (for example, pager, mobile device, phone, or handheld).

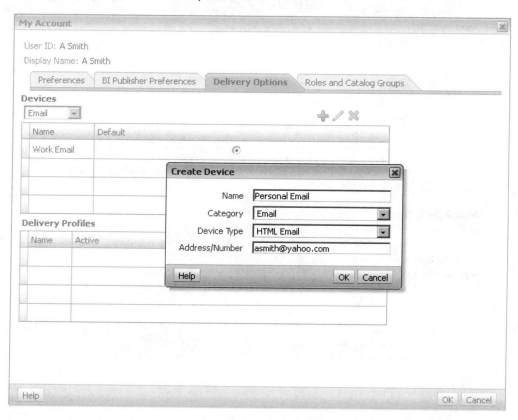

3. To assign devices to profiles, first create a profile (for example, Regular Days) by clicking the Create Delivery Profile button next to the Delivery Profiles table. In the Create Delivery Profile dialog box, enter a name for the profile and then select which of the devices you have registered should be used for high-, medium-, and low-priority agent deliveries. Repeat this step for all of the delivery profiles you wish to create.

Create Delivery Profile ☒

Name [Regular Days]

Device Priorities

Device	High	Normal	Low
Blackberry	☑	☐	☐
Personal Email	☐	☐	☐
Personal Pager	☐	☐	☐
Work Email	☐	☑	☑

Help   OK   Cancel

4. Select one of your delivery profiles to be the default. If you wish to change this choice, you can do so from here again in the future—for example, if you go on holiday and wish to set the Holidays profile to be active over this period.

Delivery Profiles ✚ ✐ ✖

Name	Active
Holidays	○
Regular Days	⊙

Automatically Generating System Delivery Devices and Profiles Using the SA_SYSTEM Subject Area In addition to having your users set up their own delivery devices and profiles, you might want to automatically register devices for them and create profiles. You can do this through one of two approaches:

- You can use the SA_SYSTEM subject area to store devices for users in a database table and automatically use these to populate their profiles.

- You can retrieve e-mail addresses from your LDAP server and use them to populate the e-mail device details for users in their profiles, but you can do this only if you are not already using the SA System subject area.

In previous releases of Oracle Business Intelligence, the approach of using the SA_SYSTEM subject area was generally used, as it allowed the administrator to automatically populate e-mail, cell phone, pager, and other device types for users so that alerts could be sent via these different types of mobile devices.

Nowadays, because most end users have mobile devices that can read HTML e-mails (and, consequently, they do not use pagers and handheld PCs), it is most common to use the second approach and automatically populate an e-mail address for the user from their LDAP directory record. The SA_SYSTEM subject area approach should generally no longer be used unless absolutely necessary. To see how the two approaches work, though, let's first look at creating the SA System subject area:

1. In a database such as Oracle Database, create a table using a script such as this:

```
CREATE TABLE SA_SYSTEM
(
EMAIL VARCHAR2(100),
EMAIL_PRIORITY VARCHAR2(10) DEFAULT 'HNL',
EMAIL_TYPE VARCHAR2(50) DEFAULT 'html',
CELL_PHONE VARCHAR2(40),
CELL_PHONE_PRIORITY VARCHAR2(20),
PAGER VARCHAR2(20),
PAGER_PRIORITY VARCHAR2(30),
HANDHELD VARCHAR2(20),
HANDHELD_PRIORITY VARCHAR2(30),
TIMEZONE VARCHAR2(100),
GROUP_NAME VARCHAR2(20),
LOGON VARCHAR2(50) NOT NULL,
DISPLAY_NAME VARCHAR2(100),
LOCALE VARCHAR2(20) DEFAULT 'en',
LANGUAGE VARCHAR2(20) DEFAULT 'en'
)
```

   The name of the table is not important (though it is good practice to keep it at SA_SYSTEM, so other administrators will know what it is for). The table must, however, have the full set of columns within it, ideally with default values set for the "priority" fields and appropriate values for the locale and language fields based on your country and locale.

2. Using the Oracle BI Administrator tool, import this table into the physical layer. This table can be either in its own physical database model or in a model used by other tables from your source data. See Chapter 3 for more information on importing table metadata into your repository.

3. Drag-and-drop the physical table into the business model and mapping layer of your repository. Business models must have at least one fact table and one dimension table, so you need to create a dummy dimension table within the business model to satisfy this rule. To do this, create a new logical table within this business model called LOGON, and drag-and-drop the LOGON physical column into this new logical table. Create a logical key for this new logical table based on the LOGON column, and create a logical join between the two tables so that the LOGON table is designated as the logical dimension table and the SA_SYSTEM table is designated as the fact table.

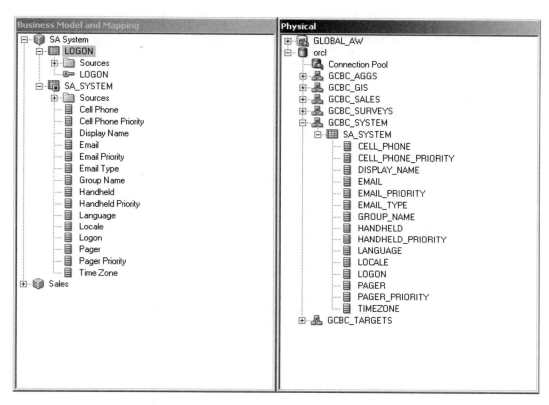

4. Drag-and-drop the SA SYSTEM business model into the presentation layer of your repository and delete the dummy LOGON presentation table, leaving just the SA_SYSTEM table. Rename the columns in the table so that they exactly match the following list:

Cell Phone
Cell Phone Priority
Display Name
Email
Email Priority
Email Type
Group Name
Handheld
Handheld Priority
Language
Locale
Logon
Pager
Pager Priority
Time Zone

5. Once complete, check your repository for consistency errors, and then save it.

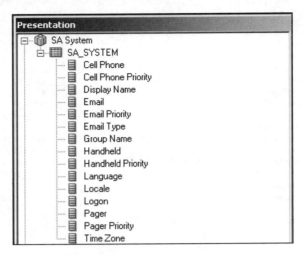

6. Now you can insert some entries into this table, to provide device information for your users. For example, if you have these four users in your system,

weblogic
Mr A Smith
Mr B Jones
Mr C Peters

you could use the following SQL commands to add entries to the SA_SYSTEM table for these users, like this:

```
insert into sa_system (email, logon) values ('admin@gcbc.com','weblogic');
insert into sa_system (email, logon) values ('asmith@gcbc.com','A Smith');
insert into sa_system (email, logon) values ('bjones@gcbc.com','B Jones');
insert into sa_system (email, logon) values ('cpeters@gcbc.com','C Peters');
commit;
```

These SQL commands will add to the table a single e-mail address for each user, which inherits the default e-mail priority of "HNL" (High, Normal, and Low) and default e-mail type of "html" defined for those columns. You can add additional rows to this table for the same users, to register additional e-mail accounts with different priorities, but these will all be registered using the "System Email" label, making it difficult for users to distinguish between e-mail accounts when maintaining their profile. If you have more than one e-mail account to register for users, it is best to use this approach to register a single main, default account, and have users register their own additional accounts manually via the My Account dialog box previously mentioned.

7.   Using Fusion Middleware Control, restart the BI Presentation Server component, and then log in as one of the users in your system. You should then see on the Delivery Options tab of the My Account dialog box entries for System Email and System Profile, plus other system-registered devices for any other entries you add to the table row for that user.

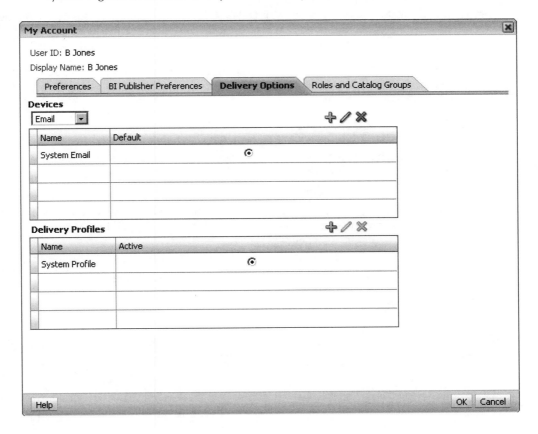

Users can then add further devices and profiles manually using this screen, if they wish to define other devices and profiles other than the default one you set up for them.

Automatically Generating E-mail Addresses and System Profile Using an LDAP Attribute

Instead of using the SA_SYSTEM subject area, you may want to automatically populate a user's profile with an e-mail attribute in your LDAP server. If you use this approach, you cannot combine it with the SA_SYSTEM subject area, although users can subsequently add their own additional devices and profile. This approach can be used to populate only the e-mail address for a user, not the pager, handheld, or other device types.

Note that this feature does not work with the 11.1.1.5 release of Oracle Business Intelligence because of a bug; therefore, you need to use either release 11.1.1.6 or higher or release 11.1.1.3.

To populate a user's e-mail address using the LDAP mail attribute, follow these steps:

1. Log into the WebLogic Server Administration Console (http://[*hostname*]:7001/console) as a WebLogic administration user, and select Security Realms in the navigation tree menu on the left side of the screen.

2. Under the list of security realms, click the myrealm link.

3. Within the Settings for myrealm area, click the Users and Groups tab.

4. Either create a new user or locate the user for which you wish to enter a new e-mail address. Click that user in the list to open their details for editing.

5. In the Settings For *User* dialog box, click the Attributes tab.

6. Scroll through the list of attributes until you locate the mail attribute. Click within the Value column and type in the e-mail address, if it is not already there.

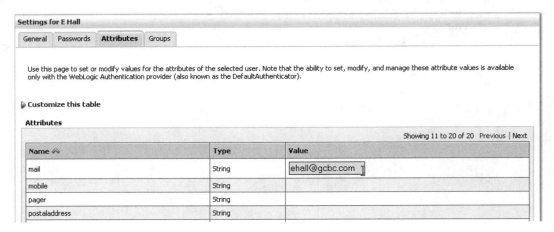

Ensure that the change was saved, and then either repeat for other users or log out.

Now ask a user to log into the Oracle Business Intelligence web site and select My Account | [*account name*] from the drop-down menu at the top-right side of the screen. When they select the Delivery Options tab in the My Account dialog box, their e-mail address should be configured as System Email, and a default System Profile should be created for them.

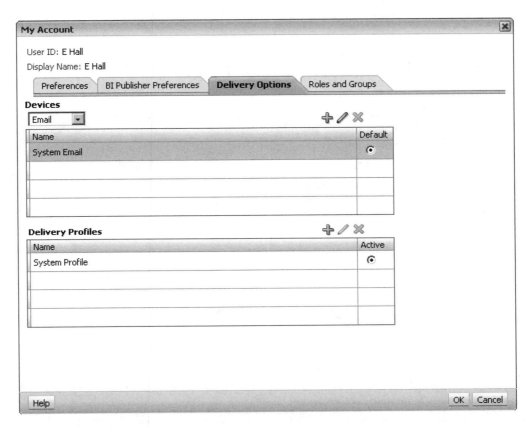

After you configure this default e-mail address, the user is free to add additional devices or profiles to their account, as long as you do not use the SA_SYSTEM subject area to do this.

Adding Conditional Execution to the Agent

The agent we defined earlier executes unconditionally, every time it is run. You can also define agents to execute conditionally so that, for example, you are sent a report on underperforming stores only if a certain number of stores actually underperform. In this way, your users can "manage by exception," only being sent reports and alerts when a situation of interest has arisen.

To make an agent execution conditional, you need to assign a condition to it. You can do this either by using a named condition, as described in the "Creating Conditions" section later in this chapter, or by defining the condition inline as part of the agent definition, as described next.

In the example used earlier in the chapter, a store sales report is delivered through an agent to regional sales managers, with stores that are performing below target highlighted with a red background. We would now like to amend this agent so that the report is sent only to the manager when one or more stores have performed below the target.

To define the condition for the agent, you need either a KPI or an analysis, to base the condition on. In the example we used earlier, stores are listed along with their sale amount and target amount, and we will use this analysis as the starting point to define the condition. To create such an agent, follow these steps:

1. Create or obtain an analysis that lists the data items that you want to create the condition on. In this example, we have an analysis that lists stores along with their actual and target sales amounts.

2. To make this analysis useful as the basis of a condition, with the analysis open for editing, switch to the Criteria tab and add a filter to return only those stores that have sold less than their target amount.

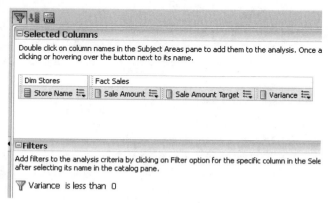

Now when you view the analysis results, only those stores that have fallen short of their target will be displayed. Save this analysis to the catalog, typically in a shared folder called Condition Analyses.

3. To update your agent to use this analysis as a condition, open the agent for editing, and click the Condition tab. Click the Use A Condition radio button, and click the Create button to create the condition.

4. In the Create Condition dialog box, select Analysis from the Create Condition Based On drop-down menu, or select KPI if you wish to base the condition on the state of a KPI. Then, click the Browse button to select the analysis you created a moment ago, and use the up and down arrows to select the number of rows that the condition needs to return True.

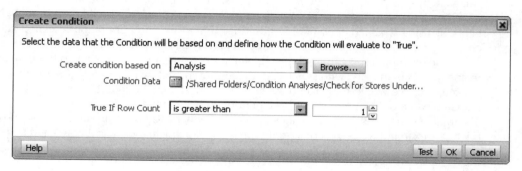

5. Click the Test button to test your condition with the current set of source data, and then click OK to close the dialog box.

6. Your agent now will execute conditionally based on the Boolean result returned by this inline condition. If you wish to convert the inline condition into a named condition, as described later in this chapter, click the Save To Catalog button.

Subscribing to Agents

In addition to using your own agents, you can also subscribe to other agents, and other users can subscribe to your agents, depending on the permissions to assign to the agent.

To make an agent available for subscription, open the agent for editing and click the Recipients tab. At the bottom of the screen is the Publish For Subscription area, with two check boxes:

■ Publish Agent for subscription
■ Allow subscribers to customize Agent

The second check box is used when the analysis that is delivered by the agent has an Is Prompted filter applied to the analysis criteria; if you enable this option, the user can change the filter value to one of their own—for example, to select just the products or customers that they would like the agent to report on.

Under these two check boxes is a list of agent subscribers, which will be updated with a list of users, application roles and catalog groups that have subscribed to the agent.

As an example, if you wish to publish the agent that you defined in the previous section so that it is available for subscription, select the Publish Agent For Subscription check box and then save the agent.

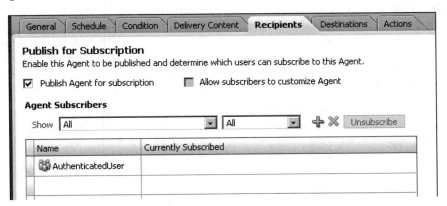

Then, when another user who is able to view the agent in the catalog wishes to subscribe to the agent, they can select Subscribe from the More drop-down menu next to the agent in the catalog view. They can later select Unsubscribe from the same menu if they wish to unsubscribe from it.

If a user then wishes to view a list of the agents they are subscribed to, they can select the My Agent Subscriptions entry under Browse/Manage on their home page, and you can view a list of the users, roles, and groups subscribed to your agent by viewing the Destinations tab in the agent details screen.

Monitoring Agent Executions

If an administrator wishes to see which agent sessions are currently running, or see a history of past agent executions, there are two options available to them.

From the Oracle Business Intelligence Administration screen (click the Administration link), select Manage Agent Sessions to see details of those agent sessions that are currently running. To view past agent executions, along with other scheduled jobs, you will have to use the Job Manager utility, as described next, which provides a graphical interface for the Oracle BI Scheduler component.

Using the Job Manager Utility to Manage the Oracle BI Scheduler   Job Manager is a Java utility that is available only on Windows installations of Oracle Business Intelligence. You can use the Job Manager to view the history of past scheduler jobs, including scheduled agent executions. It uses tables stored in the BIPLATFORM schema set up during installation by the Repository Creation Utility, and can also be used to create scheduled jobs to perform tasks such as cache purging and Java job actions.

To start the Job Manager, from the Windows Start menu, select Start | Programs | Oracle Business Intelligence | Job Manager. When the Job Manager starts, select File | Open Scheduler Connection and then either enter the connection details for a specific scheduler or choose to connect through the Oracle BI Cluster Controller component to have it select the active scheduler for you. For the login credentials, use the details of an administrator account (for example, weblogic/welcome1).

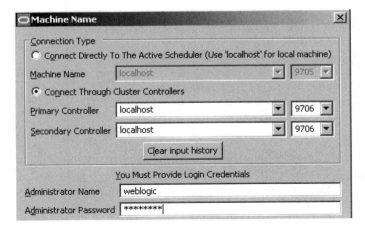

Using the Job Manager, you can view the history of all jobs that are recorded in the Oracle BI Scheduler tables, broken down by status, by user, by instance ID, and by job ID. You can also create new jobs, to create, for example, scheduled tasks that clear log files, clear the query cache, or perform other systems management tasks.

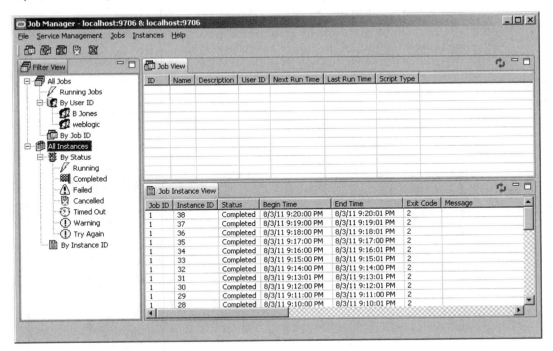

Adding Actions to the Agent

In addition to delivering analyses, dashboard pages, or briefing books to users, agents can also call actions at the end of their processing, including calling web services, calling server scripts, or even calling other agents. Actions are called for each row in the output, and you can select different actions for different agent condition statuses.

Consider the example agent defined earlier that delivers a report on underperforming stores when one or more stores have underperformed. This agent has been defined to use a condition to test for underperforming stores, and the agent is subscribed to by a set of regional sales managers, each of whom has a certain group of stores that they manage.

You now wish to assign actions to this agent, to perform one of two tasks per store based on the condition used by the agent:

- If the agent condition equates to True, you want a BPEL web service to be called that arranges for a meeting with the store manager, to discuss performance.

- If the agent condition equates to False (that is, no stores within the region are underperforming), you wish to call a further agent that checks that store quality is within target.

To configure your agent for this scenario, follow these steps:

1. Open the agent for editing, and select the Agents tab.

2. Within the Agent Condition True Or No Condition Exists section, either click the Add New Action button to create a new, inline action, or click the Add Existing Action button to select an action from the catalog.

3. If you would like the action to execute for every row in the analysis that is being delivered by the agent, select the Invoke Per Row check box.

NOTE
If your analysis details those stores, for example, that have exceeded their target as well as those that have fallen short, this action will be invoked for those stores as well.

General	Schedule	Condition	Delivery Content	Recipients	Destinations	**Actions**

Specify any actions to invoke when the Agent completes.

Agent Condition True or No Condition Exists

Actions

Name	Invoke per Row
Arrange Manager Meeting (BPEL)	☑

4. If you wish to define an action for when the agent condition is False, click the same buttons in the Agent Condition Is False area. To add, for example, an action that then calls another agent, select Invoke An Agent as the action type and then, in the New Action dialog box, select the agent to run, and for whom the agent will execute.

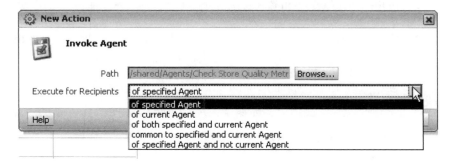

For any action types other than Invoke an Agent, you can select whether the action runs for all rows or just once. For Invoke an Agent action types, the agent will run only once, based on the settings defined in the previous step.

Creating Conditions

The examples used in the previous section used conditions to conditionally execute agents. These conditions were based on the output of analyses or KPI states, and were defined as part of the agent definition, creating what are termed *inline conditions*.

Conditions can, however, like actions, be created as named objects and stored in the Presentation Server catalog, to be reused by many agents and in other places in the BI system. The process of creating *named conditions* is almost identical to the process of creating inline conditions, except that the condition is created from the common header menu using New | Condition rather than as part of an agent definition.

In addition to being based on the output of an analysis, conditions can also be based on the state of a KPI. To create a named condition based on the state of a KPI, follow these steps:

1. Select New | Condition.

2. In the New Condition dialog box, select KPI from the Create Condition Based On dropdown menu.

3. Click the Browse button and select the KPI that you wish to use with the condition.

4. You will then be prompted to set values for KPI dimensions where the KPI value was not pinned during its definition. Provide values for all dimensions, select which KPI state will equate to True for the condition, and then test the condition before saving it to the catalog.

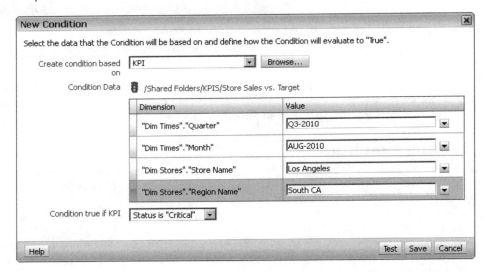

As you saw in the previous section, conditions are typically used as part of agent definitions to make the execution conditional on values in your source systems. You can also use conditions in other places, though, including in dashboards, to make the display of sections conditional, and when adding action link and action link menus to a dashboard page.

To use conditions to conditionally display sections and action links in a dashboard, follow these steps:

1. Using the Oracle Business Intelligence web site, log in and open a dashboard for editing (for example, My Dashboard).

2. Using the Dashboard Objects panel on the left-hand side of the screen, drag-and-drop a Section object onto the dashboard.

3. Hover your mouse pointer over the Properties menu button for the section and select the Condition menu item.

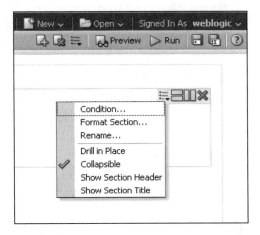

4. In the Section Condition dialog box, click either the New Condition button or the Select Condition button to either create a new, inline condition or select an existing, named condition. Use the arrow button to the right of these buttons to test, edit, remove, or save an inline condition defined as part of this process.

The section that you have defined this condition for will now display only if the condition equates to True.

5. To make an action link or action link menu display conditionally, similarly add a new Action Link or Action Link Menu item to the dashboard from the Dashboard Objects panel. To set the condition, click the Properties button for the action link or action link menu, and in the Properties dialog box, select Conditionally for the Show Link radio button.

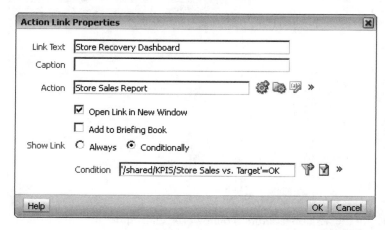

Then, as before, click either the New Condition button or the Select Condition button to define a new condition or select an existing one from the catalog.

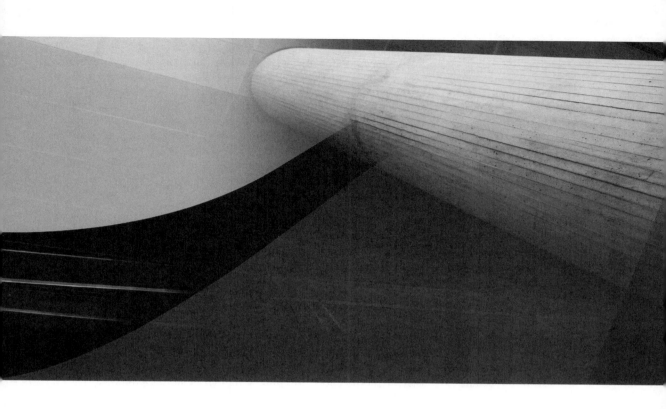

CHAPTER
8

Security

o far in this book we have looked at ways to make as much of your organization's data available to as many people as possible, in ways that make it easy for them to access and discover the information that is relevant to them. As we all know, though, in some cases you do not want certain people to see sensitive data that is not appropriate for them, and often you will want to restrict and simplify the data available to users so that they are not overwhelmed by the amount of information available. To do this, we need to have a way to control which information is available to users and groups within the organization, for security and privacy reasons and to prevent users from spending a lot of time searching through irrelevant data and subject areas.

In addition, users do not want to have to remember many individual usernames and passwords to access their systems and, instead, ideally prefer to have a single logon that accesses their business intelligence dashboards as well as their general line-of-business applications. This means that, as an Oracle Business Intelligence developer, you typically will need to connect your BI infrastructure to a corporate "directory" server so that the usernames and passwords used to access dashboards are the same as those used to access users' desktops and business applications.

In this chapter, we look at two main areas concerning security. First, we look at what most end users think of in terms of security, which is controlling access to subject areas and data items within their business intelligence data set. To do this, we also look at variables, something touched on in Chapter 6 in the discussion of presentation variables to pass values from prompts to analyses and dashboards; in this case, they are created in the repository and are typically used for session-based security. Then we look at the more complex topic of Oracle Business Intelligence's security infrastructure, how to create application roles and apply them within the repository and catalog, and how to connect to external directory servers such as Microsoft Active Directory.

An Overview of Oracle Business Intelligence Security

Security within the context of Oracle Business Intelligence normally comprises four functional areas:

- Creating row-level data filters, which are applied to data "in the background" to restrict the scope of data that users see in an analysis or report
- Controlling access to columns, tables, or entire subject areas within the repository
- Restrictions and controls over which parts of the application you can access; for example, whether a user has the ability to create or edit analyses
- Controlling who has access to which reports, dashboards, and other BI objects within your system

When you first connect into Oracle Business Intelligence as an administrative user after installing the product on your laptop or workstation, none of these areas typically affect you, as you can access all functionality and all data with no restrictions. However, when you deploy Oracle Business Intelligence on customer sites, they usually want to restrict the view of data available to end users and control which functions those end users can access within the application, allowing some users to create new catalog content while allowing others to view it only on the dashboard.

Restricting which data is available to which users, in terms of the rows of data displayed in reports and the subject areas that can be accessed, is referred to in security as *authorization*. As you will see later on in this chapter, you can automatically configure user accounts such that users can see only certain subsets of data through a number of means, including dynamically loaded session variables that contain authorization lists and application roles that can be granted to users so that they can access subject areas in the repository and catalog.

A topic that typically goes hand in hand with authorization and row-level security is setting up and using server-side variables. Like the presentation variables discussed earlier in this book, server-side repository and session variables hold values that you can use to filter or otherwise control or customize the data presented to users.

In the context of security, repository and session variables can be used, for example, to retrieve the list of products, or stores, that a user is allowed to see at the start of a user session so that row-level filtering can then be applied automatically to show only the data they are allowed to see. We look at how you set up and populate repository and session variables later in this chapter and how they can be used to control the data that users see in their reports and dashboards.

In addition to authorization, you typically need to verify that those who log into a system really are who they say they are: this is *authentication*. This can be as simple as checking a username and password stored in the embedded LDAP (Lightweight Directory Access Protocol) server that comes as part of Oracle Business Intelligence or configuring Oracle's Business Intelligence's underlying middleware infrastructure to use external authentication and authorization providers such as Microsoft Active Directory. Much of the effort in setting up security in the Oracle Business Intelligence system is devoted to row-level and subject area authorization, so we look at these two topics first in this chapter.

Authentication and authorization for your business intelligence system are, however, just two aspects of identity administration. In a typical Oracle Business Intelligence project, other identity administration tasks that you will need to perform include

- Administering users and groups in the embedded LDAP server and mapping these through to application roles administered in Oracle Fusion Middleware

- Working with the application roles and application policies that Oracle Business Intelligence uses to assign permissions and privileges to users, as well as the default security configuration shipped with Oracle Business Intelligence

- Connecting Oracle Business Intelligence to external directories, such as Microsoft Active Directory, as well as configuring Oracle Business Intelligence and the underlying Oracle Fusion Middleware infrastructure to work with custom authenticators and authorization schemes

That said, security is one of the most complex topics involved in developing and administering an Oracle Business Intelligence system. It is easy to get sidetracked in Fusion Middleware infrastructure configuration and the many places where you can configure optional and mandatory filters on data. Therefore, we begin this topic by looking at the aspect of security that is most immediately usable and has the most immediate impact on end users: configuring row-level security for your reports and analyses.

Configuring Row-Level Security

Apart from ensuring that all users have their own logon and password (something that we cover in more detail later in this chapter), the first aspect of "security" that most organizations wish to put in place for their business intelligence system is usually row-level security, in which groups of users have access to shared reports but each group sees different data and totals in each report depending on its area of responsibility.

This row-level security can be added by the author of a report or analysis when creating it by adding additional filters to the report that restrict the data shown based on a user's group membership. Ideally, this row-level filtering of data occurs automatically and in the background so that report writers can write general-purpose reports that are automatically filtered according to end users' areas of responsibility.

For example, in the following two dashboard illustrations, the user on the left has responsibility for stores in the South California region and sees only these stores when viewing his dashboards even if no other filters have been applied. The user on the right, by contrast, has responsibility for stores in the North California region, and his reports show just those stores, even with no filters applied by the report writer.

User "Isangelo" sees stores in South CA   User "sfrancesco" sees stores in North CA

Row-level security can be set up in Oracle Business Intelligence in two main ways:

- You can define filters that are applied to users or roles in the Oracle BI Repository, usually based on repository or session variable values set for users when they log into the dashboard.

- You can define row-level security in the source database, using a feature such as Virtual Private Database in the Oracle Database, and configure Oracle Business Intelligence to pass on the users' credentials to the database and ensure that caching becomes private to each user, as the BI Server will not otherwise know that the database will provide different results for different users even if it processes the same query for them.

This second approach is not covered in this book, but details of how it can be set up are in the product documentation and depend on the type of source database you are using. For now, however, let us go through the first, most common option now, where we configure row-level security using the Oracle BI Server and the Oracle BI Repository.

Row-Level Security Using the BI Server and the Oracle BI Repository

To set up row-level security using the Oracle BI Server and Oracle BI Repository, you can use the User/Application Role Permissions dialog box in the Oracle BI Administration tool to apply data filters that are applied to particular users and roles, which can be displayed by selecting Manage | Identity | Role | Permissions from the application menu.

For example, you might have an application role in your system that, when applied to a user, allows that user to see stores in the San Francisco area, as shown in the following illustration.

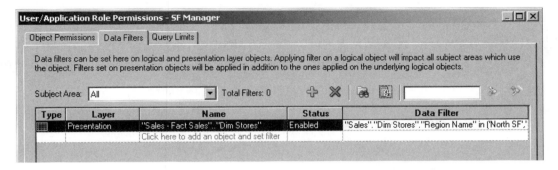

If a user had more than one such role granted to him or her, then the regions that this user could view in reports would increase along with the roles. But, in practice, granting row-level security access in this way is impractical, as you need one role for each set of rows to which you want to grant access.

What if, instead, you could just create a generic "manager" role or assume that all users in your system with a role such as BIConsumer or BIAuthor need to have this security applied and then create and populate some sort of variable that was assigned at the time of logging in, which would dynamically filter rows of data based on a database lookup of regions that the user or role was allowed to see? Using repository and session variables, you can do precisely this, which we look at now, before getting into more details on row-level security.

Defining Repository and Session Variables for Use with Row-Level Security

Earlier in this book, we looked at Presentation Server variables, which are primarily used for capturing the values set in prompts and then passing them on to other BI objects, such as analyses and BI Publisher reports, so that that they can be used in filters or displayed in report headings. You can also, however, define variables for use in the Oracle BI Repository, which can be referenced in analyses and reports as well, but can also be used to automatically filter in the background data returned by these reports.

Two main types of variables are defined in the Oracle BI Repository:

- **Repository** These can be either static or dynamically refreshed to a schedule and hold the same value for all users.

- **Session** These are initialized for users each time they log into the BI Server and hold values specific for them.

Both types of variables are defined in the Variable Manager dialog box in the Oracle BI Administration tool (Manage | Variables). Session variables, which can hold different values for different users and are initialized, typically, using database lookups, are particularly useful for row-level security.

Example: Defining Static and Dynamic Repository Variables   Repository variables are defined using the Oracle BI Administration tool and have their values initialized either when the repository is updated online (for static repository variables), when the BI Server component is restarted, or on a schedule (for dynamic repository variables).

Let's start by defining a static repository variable to hold the name of our company's flagship store, which involves the fewest steps to set up. Then we use this static repository variable to filter values in an analysis:

1. Using the Oracle BI Administration tool, open the repository either online or offline and select Manage | Variables.

2. The Variable Manager dialog box will be displayed. On the left-hand side is a panel with a tree navigation menu; click the Repository | Variables | Static entry, and then right-click in the right-hand panel and select New Repository Variable.

3. The Static Repository Variable dialog box will be displayed. Enter or select the following values to define the variable:

   Name: FLAGSHIP_STORE
   Type: Static
   Default Initializer: 'Fishermans Wharf'
   Description: Flagship store name

4. Click OK to close the dialog box and then select Action | Close from the Variable Manager dialog box to close that dialog box. Finally, save the repository online by selecting File | Save from the application menu.

5. Now create an analysis that will be filtered by this static repository value. Log into the Oracle BI web site and create a new analysis using the Sales – Fact Sales subject area. Add the Dim Stores.Store Name, Fact Sales.Revenue, and Fact Sales.Sale Amount columns to the analysis criteria.

6. To use the variable in a filter, click the "Create a filter for the current subject area" button in the Filters pane, and select the Dim Stores.Store Name column to base the filter on. To reference the variable, click the Add More Options button, and select Repository Variable from the drop-down menu.

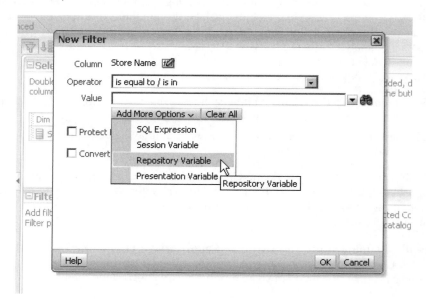

7. When prompted for the variable name, type it in (for example, FLAGSHIP_STORE). When you then display the analysis results by clicking the Results tab, the values returned will be filtered by the value assigned to this variable.

With static repository variables, the value assigned to the variable changes only if and when you alter the Default Initializer value for it in the repository and save this repository online. If you want the value to change automatically, for example to hold the current month for a variable called CURRENT_MONTH_YEAR, you need to use a *dynamic repository variable* instead.

Dynamic repository variables are created in a similar way to static ones, except that in addition to defining a default initializer, you also create an initialization block (or "init block"), which assigns the variable a value using a database lookup and a predefined schedule.

When you assign a value to a dynamic repository variable through a database lookup, you do so using a connection pool defined in the physical database layer of your repository. To do so, if you have only a single connection pool defined for your physical database, you need to create a second one for use by this and subsequent initialization blocks in order to separate this type of database activity from regular activity to retrieve data for reports and analyses. To create such an additional connection pool setting, follow these steps:

1. Using the Oracle BI Administration tool, open your repository online.

2. Navigate to the physical layer of your repository and locate the physical database that will contain the tables that will provide the data for the variable value assignment. (Note that this table could be a virtual table, such as DUAL for the Oracle Database, which will still require you to specify a physical database to process the SQL query.)

3. In that database, locate the existing connection pool setting, right-click it, and select Copy. Then select the physical database, right-click it, and select Paste to create a duplicate of the original connection pool.

Alternatively, if you wish to create a connection pool that uses a specific, different set of connection settings for initialization blocks, create a new connection pool here, rather than copying an existing one.

4. Give the new connection pool a distinct name (for example, init_blocks_cp). After you are done, save your repository.

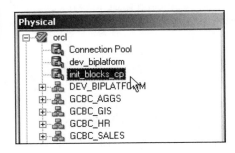

Now you can create your dynamic repository variable, which will populate a variable called CURRENT_MONTH_YEAR with the current month and year, based on an SQL expression executed every day:

1. Using the Oracle BI Administration tool and with the repository open online, select Manage | Variables from the application menu.

2. Using the Variable Manager dialog box, select Repository | Variables | Dynamic, right-click in the right-hand panel, and select New Repository Variable.

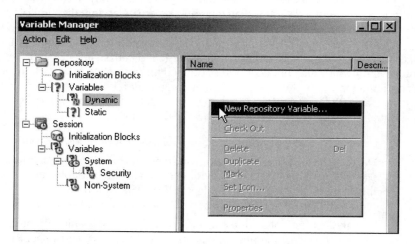

3. The Dynamic Repository Variable dialog box is displayed. Enter or select the following values to define the variable's settings:

   Name: CURRENT_MONTH_YEAR
   Type: Dynamic
   Default Initializer: 'DEC-2010'

4. At this point, you have defined the variable and its initial value. To have the variable automatically refresh, you need to define an associated initialization block for it. To do so, click the New button next to the Initialization Block drop-down menu, to start the definition process.

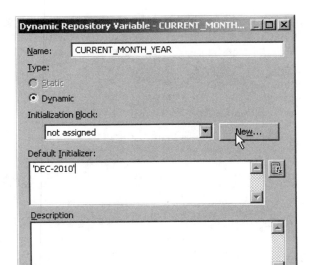

5. The Repository Variable Initialization Block dialog box is displayed. Type in or select the following values to define the basics settings:

    Name: GET_CURRENT_MONTH_YEAR
    Start on: [*enter a date and time; for example,* Wednesday, March 21, 2012, 12:00:00 AM]
    Refresh Interval: 1(days)

    This instructs the repository to use the default initializer for now and give the variable a new value on the starting date, refreshing it every day after that at the beginning of the day.

6. To define the SQL expression that will be used to refresh the variable according to this schedule, click the Edit Data Source button in the Data Source area, like this:

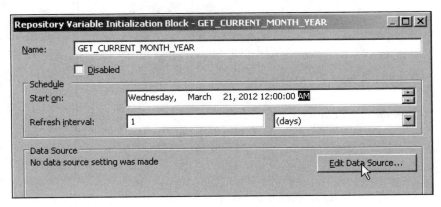

7. The Repository Variable Initialization Block Data Source dialog box is displayed, which allows you to type in an SQL expression to populate the variable associated with the initialization block. To define the required SQL expression, select or enter the following values:

   Data Source Type: Database
   Default initialization string: [*selected*]
   SQL Expression: SELECT TO_CHAR(SYSDATE, 'MON-YYYY') FROM DUAL
   Connection Pool: [*connection pool you created earlier; for example,* init_blocks_cp]

8. Click Test to check that your SQL and connection work correctly, and click OK to close the dialog box.

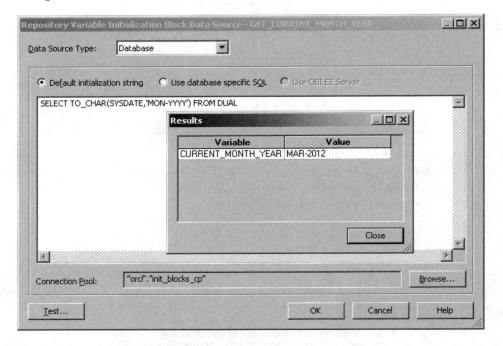

9. When you then return to the Repository Variable Initialization Block dialog box, the Data Targets section should be preset to use the variable that you have been creating and for which you created this initialization block. Click OK and then OK again to close all the dialog boxes, and save the repository online.

10. Now you can use this variable in an analysis filter, in the same way as the static repository variable defined before. When you first save the variable, the dynamic repository variable is automatically refreshed using the initialization block and as per your schedule after that. Repository variables are particularly useful for creating "constant" values that are set once and never changed or, as in the last example, refreshed to a schedule so that users can automatically filter data based on the current date or period.

For what most developers think of as row-level security, though, in which users or groups see a different view of the data based on their requirements, we need to have a way to define variables that can hold different values for each user. For that, we need to define another type of repository variable: a *session* variable.

Session Variables Session variables are defined in the same way as repository variables, using the Variable Manager dialog box and an initialization block to set the variable's value. With a session variable, though, the variable value is initialized every time the user logs into the Oracle Business Intelligence web site, and the value assigned at that point is specific to that particular user. Also, you can delay the execution of the variable's initialization block until the variable's value is first requested (rather than automatically when the user logs in), and you can override the value of a session variable for the particular execution of an analysis using a *request* variable (as long as that variable is not set with the "used for security" option, which stops their value from being overridden in this way).

Session variables are defined using the Variable Manager dialog box and can be system or non-system session variables. System session variables (and their subtype, security system variables) use reserved variable names that set, for example, the group or roles assigned to a user. Non-system session variables, by contrast, use names defined by you as the developer and can be used, as we will see in the next example, to hold a value or list of values that you can then use to configure row-level security.

Using security system session variables to configure group membership and authenticate users against external LDAP servers such as Microsoft Activity Directory is, however, a feature in Oracle Business Intelligence primarily for backward compatibility with systems upgraded from earlier releases of the product. In the examples in the rest of this chapter, we use the Oracle Fusion Middleware–based security tools that now ship with Oracle Business Intelligence to perform authentication and authorization tasks and use session variables and initialization blocks mainly to perform row-level security filtering.

Example: Configuring Row-Level Security Using Non-System Session Variables
In the next example, we set up row-based security for users of our system who have the BIConsumer role granted to them—in other words, all users of the system apart from administrators, who do not have restrictions like this applied to them. This row-based security ensures that only stores that are within a user's assigned region will be displayed in reports and analyses, even without the application of any filters by the user or the report author.

To set up this row-based security, a session variable called REGION is configured to retrieve, from a database, the region to which a user is assigned. This variable is used to create a mandatory data filter for all users with the BIConsumer role, filtering data in reports to only those stores in their region.

Two database tables have been created in the GCBC_HR schema, one of which contains a list of users and their descriptions (name), with the other containing a list of users and the region to which they are assigned. In this example, each user is assigned to one, and only one, region, but the example that follows shows how we can handle scenarios in which users are assigned to more than one group.

STAFF_LOGINS

Columns	Types	Length	Nullable
LOGIN_NAME	VARCHAR	20	False
STAFF_DESC	VARCHAR	20	True

STAFF_REGIONS

Columns	Types	Length	Nullable
LOGIN_NAME	VARCHAR	20	False
REGION	VARCHAR	20	False

After the tables have been created and populated with user and region details, they are imported into the physical layer of the repository so that other developers are aware of their presence.

To set up row-level security using this session variable, this role, and these tables, follow these steps:

1. We first define the session variable that holds the region name that the user is allowed to see. Using the Oracle BI Administrator tool with the repository open online, select Manage | Variables to open the Variable Manager dialog box.

2. In the navigation tree on the left-hand side of the Variable Manager dialog box, select Session | Variables, right-click in the area on the right, and select New Session Variable.

3. With the Session Variable dialog box open, type **REGION** into the Name text box and then click the New button next to the Initialization Block area, which currently has "not assigned" as its setting.

4. The Session Variable Initialization Block dialog box is displayed. Type **GET_REGION_ SESS_VAR** into the Name text box, and click the Edit Data Source button to bring up the Session Variable Initialization Block Data Source dialog box.

5. Using this dialog box, type in or select the following values:

   Data Source Type: Database
   Default initialization string: [*selected*]
   SQL Expression: `select r.region from gcbc_hr.staff_logins l,`
   `gcbc_hr.staff_regions r wherel.login_name =`
   `r.login_name and l.login_name = 'VALUEOF(NQSESSION.USER)'`
   Connection Pool: [*connection pool you created earlier; for example,* init_blocks_cp]

NOTE
The VALUEOF(NQ_SESSION.USER) used in the SQL expression will substitute the log-in name of the user for whom the initialization block is running.

6. If your repository is open offline, you can click Test to check that your SQL and connection work correctly.

7. After this process is completed, click OK to close the dialog box; the Session Variable Initialization Block dialog box should look as in the following illustration.

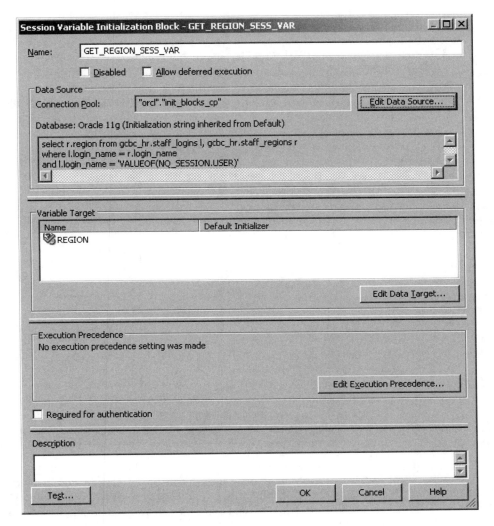

8. Using the Oracle BI Administrator tool with the repository open online, select Manage | Identity from the application menu.

9. The Identity Manager dialog box is displayed. Click the Application Role tab on the right-hand side, and double-click the role you wish to assign to the row-level security settings—in this case, BIConsumer, to apply the rule to all users of the system.

10. In the Application Role dialog box that is displayed, click the Permissions button to open the User/Application Role Permissions dialog box.

11. Click the Add button to bring up the Browse dialog box and select the table to which you wish to apply the filter.

12. In this instance, we can set up the filter in a couple of different ways:

■ The Region column that corresponds to the filter is in the Dim Stores table, which means that if you wanted to apply the filter when any column from this table is included in an analysis, you would double-click this particular table to select it for the filter condition.

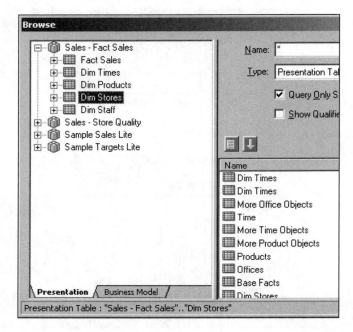

■ You could also place the same filter on any fact tables that use this dimension, such as Fact Sales, to ensure that if a user selects only measures from the fact table, the filter is still applied. Adding this second filter ensures that grand totals shown to users always reflect the scope of data that they can see, something that you may or may not wish to do for your particular reports.

NOTE
You can place the filter on either a presentation table or a business model table. If you choose the former and you have several subject areas based on the same business model, only the table from that particular presentation layer subject area will be subject to the filter.

If, however, you click the Business Model tab and select a business model table, every subject area that contains presentation tables derived from that business model table will have the filter applied.

13. After double-clicking a table, you are returned to the User/Application Role Permissions dialog box to define the actual filter expression.

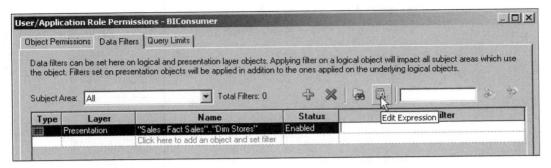

14. Select the Data Filters tab, and then click the Edit Expression button to bring up the Expression Builder – Security Filter dialog box.

15. Set the following filter, which references the session variable defined earlier using the syntax VALUEOF(NQ_SESSION.*variablename*):

```
"Sales"."DimStores"."Region Name" = VALUEOF(NQ_SESSION.REGION)
```

16. Click OK to close the dialog box, and then click OK in the other dialog boxes to return to the Identity Manager dialog box. To close that final dialog box, select Action | Close.

When users who log in have entries in this table, they can see that queries that reference the Dim Stores table (in this case), or any fact table associated with this dimension table if you have set up the data filter against the Fact Sales fact table, return only the data for the region assigned to the user.

But what happens if, as is the case in many organizations, users are allowed to see data from more than one region, and the corresponding SQL expression used above ended up returning more than one row per user? In that case, we use a variation on session variables called a *row-wise initialized* session variable.

Example: Row-Level Security with Multivalue Variables (Row-Wise Initialization) Suppose that you have a situation in which, instead of having each user allowed to see only one row in the STAFF_REGIONS table and therefore the SQL expression in the initialization block returns only a single row, the table contains more than one row per staff member, signifying that users can see more than one region in their reports. For example, in the following illustration, the user sfrancesco has four regions assigned to him, which would cause the initialization block to return an error if he tried to log in, because it would be unable to assign the required single value to the REGION session variable.

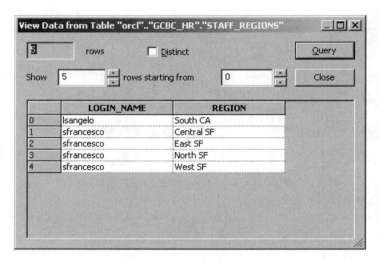

To handle this type of situation, "multivalue" variables can be defined, using a process called *row-wise initialization*. In this scenario, the session variable is defined entirely through an initialization block, which sets up the variable automatically and stores multiple values in the form of a single value but with your actual values concatenated using semicolons (;).

To define a row-wise initialized variable, follow these steps:

1. Using the Oracle BI Administration tool with the repository online, select Manage | Variables as before. This time, however, do not create the variable first; instead, select Session | Initialization Blocks in the Variable Manager navigation tree, right-click on the right-hand panel, and select New Initialization Block.

2. Unlike regular session variables that are defined as specific objects in the repository, row-wise initialized session variables are defined as part of an SQL statement in an initialization block. This SQL statement returns two columns, the first of which sets the variable name and the second of which gives it its value. When more than one row is returned for a particular variable, the initialization block concatenates their values using the semicolon (;) value mentioned earlier.

   In the Session Variable Initialization Block dialog box, type in a name for the initialization block (for example, GET_REGIONS_ROWWISE_SESS_VAR), and click the Edit Data Source button to bring up the Session Variable Initialization Block Data Source dialog box.

3. As before, select the following values to define the data source for the initialization block:
   Data Source Type: Database
   Default initialization string: [*selected*]
   Connection Pool: [*connection pool you created earlier; for example,* init_blocks_cp]

When you type in the SQL, though, you define the variable as part of the SQL expression by adding it as a value in the first column returned by the query, like this:

```
select 'REGIONS', r.region
from gcbc_hr.staff_logins l, gcbc_hr.staff_regions r
where l.login_name = r.login_name
and l.login_name = 'VALUEOF(NQ_SESSION.USER)'
```

The literal values—'REGIONS', in this case—define the row-wise variables as part of the initialization block definition.

4. Click OK to close this dialog box and return to the Session Variable Initialization Block dialog box.

5. In the previous example, you see the variable name listed in the Variable Target area. To assign this initialization block to the row-wise variable we just defined in the SQL statement, click the Edit Data Target button, and when the Session Variable Initialization Block Variable Target dialog box is shown, select the Row-Wise Initialization check box.

Your final Session Variable Initialization Block dialog box should now look like the following illustration.

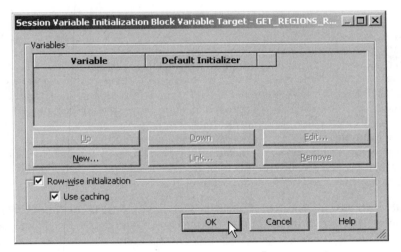

6. To reference the row-wise session variable in a filter, for example, in the mandatory filter we applied to the BIConsumer role, you reference it in the same way as with a regular variable:

```
"Sales"."DimStores"."Region "Name" = "VALUEOF(NQ_SESSION."REGIONS")
```

Now any users with more than one region assigned should receive the correct values in their analyses.

Apart from setting up variables designed to hold more than one value, you might also find this approach useful in initializing and setting the values for all session variables, as it allows you to set the values for multiple variables with a single SQL statement. In this instance, you would create a database table containing the variable name, the value you wish to set for it, and the username to set it for, and use a single initialization block to read this table and set all session variable values for the user who has just logged in.

These examples show how variables, defined in the repository and of various types, can be used along with application roles to enforce row-level security through the Identity Manager utility in the Oracle BI Administration tool. But row-level security is defined in one other area, and it is not one that you might notice without any clues.

Example: Configuring Row-Level Security Through Logical Table Source "Content" Settings

Although most row-level security in repositories is configured using the Identity Manager, you might also find it applied in logical table source definitions in the business model and mapping layer of your repository. This technique is often used in the Oracle BI Applications repository and to apply row-level security across all users of this logical table, not just those with a particular role granted.

To see where these settings are held, open your repository online or offline using the Oracle BI Administration tool and navigate to a logical table source in the business model and mapping layer. Double-click the table source to display the Logical Table Source dialog box, and select the Content tab. This dialog box includes a section where you can add an SQL WHERE clause to limit the rows returned by the table source; in most cases, this section is empty, as shown in the following illustration.

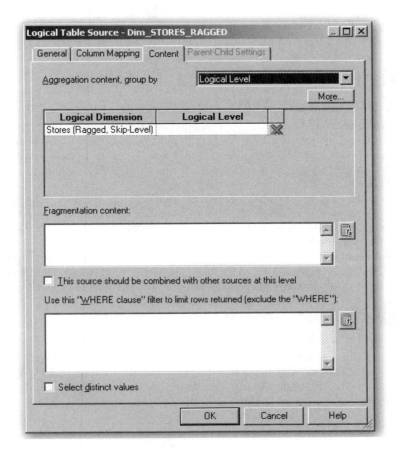

If this section is populated, it is usually used to restrict rows from being returned that are not relevant to the BI application; for example, to remove all stores whose STORE_NAME is NULL. You can, however, reference session or other repository variable types in the WHERE clause here, and any restriction so applied will apply to all users regardless of the role granted.

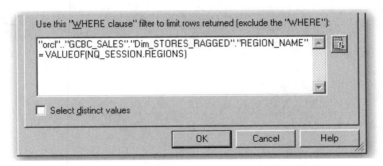

CAUTION
Care should be taken in using this feature, as the filtering is "hidden" in a table source definition and might not be obvious to administrators who subsequently take responsibility for your repository.

Configuring Subject Area, Catalog, and Functional Area Security

In the previous section of this chapter, we looked at restricting the rows of data that users could see in reports and analyses. But what if you wanted to stop people from seeing entire subject areas, or just individual tables or columns within a subject area, or certain catalog objects or folders? What if you wanted to restrict them to using dashboards but not the analysis editor, for example? Let us look at these two scenarios.

You have a choice of two different main approaches to restricting access to a particular subject area or to certain tables or columns in a subject area: the first involves restricting access to data at the repository (RPD) level, and the second is at the catalog, Presentation Services, level. Repository-level subject area restrictions can be as broad as an entire subject area or as narrow as individual presentation tables or columns. Catalog-level security works only at the entire subject area level, though you might want to use this approach sometimes even for repository-level restrictions. Let's walk through a scenario to see which approach works best and when.

Example: Subject Area Security Through the Oracle BI Repository

Consider a situation in which you have a repository with two subject areas, both of which map back to a single business model. The first, Sales – Fact Sales contains sales data on stores and products, while the second, Sales – Quality Assurance, contains survey results from your store network. In general, everyone in the organization can see the sales data, while only quality assurance managers can see the survey data.

To facilitate this, you create a group in your LDAP server and a corresponding application role, which you grant to users who perform this role. (We discuss how you create LDAP groups and application roles later in this chapter.)

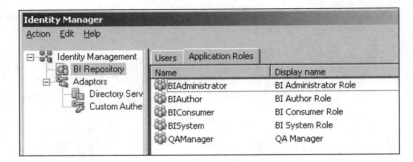

Unlike the application roles that come precreated with Oracle Business Intelligence (which you will read about later in the section "The Default Security Profile"), QA Manager is a special type of role that is used only to grant access to objects; users who are granted this role are also typically granted more general roles, such as BIAuthor or BIConsumer, which will give them more general access to system functionality.

For now, we want to set up our system so that only users granted the QA Manager role will have access to the data in the Sales – Store Quality subject area shown in the following repository illustration.

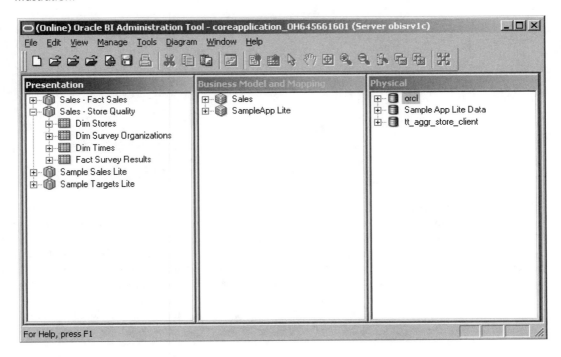

You can do this as follows:

1. Double-click the Sales – Store Quality subject area in the presentation layer of the repository, which will display the Subject Area dialog box. With the General tab selected, click the Permissions button.

2. The Permissions dialog box for this presentation layer object appears. Change the permissions of the BIAuthor and BIConsumer roles from the Default value (read/write) to No Access and set the permissions for the QA Manager role to Read/Write. Now only

users who have been granted this role will be able to view data from this subject area in their analyses.

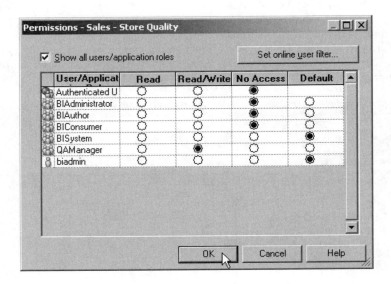

If you now create an analysis using tables and columns from this subject area and make it available to a user who was not granted the required application role, the analysis will execute as normal but will exclude these tables and columns from the results set.

You can take this type of security down to the individual presentation table and column level so that, for example, you could create an HR Manager role that is the only one, apart from administrators, who can see the "Date of Birth" column for staff, as shown in the following illustration.

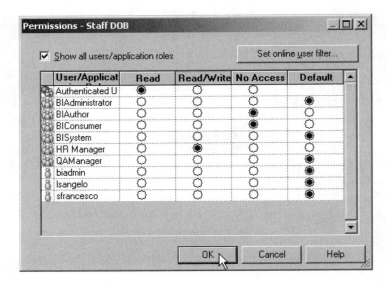

If a user who has been granted the HR Manager role tries to create or access an analysis using this column, the results display as normal. If, however, a user not granted this role tries to access the same analysis, the results omit this particular column, as shown in the following illustrations.

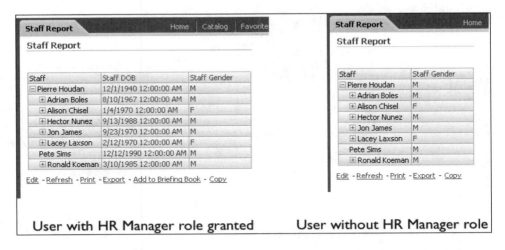

If a user who has been granted the HR Manager role tries to create or access an analysis using this column, the results display as normal. If, however, a user not granted this role tries to access the same analysis, the results omit this particular column, as shown in the following illustrations.

Subject Area Security Using Presentation Server Catalog Privileges

When you configure subject area security using the Oracle BI Repository, you prevent users from accessing certain data items completely. But what if, instead of restricting data access completely, you want to create a situation in which users cannot create their own analyses using sensitive data but can view analyses and dashboards created by others who do have the required permissions?

Let's remove the subject area restriction currently in the repository for the Sales – Store Quality subject area so that its security permissions now appear as in the following illustration.

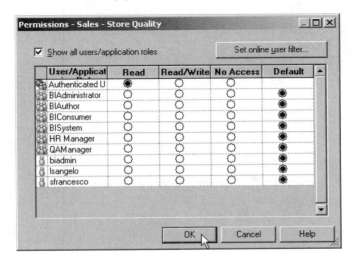

At this point, all users granted one of these roles can access data from this subject area. Now let's move to the Administration page on the Oracle Business Intelligence web site, which has a link under the Security heading called Manage Privileges. By clicking this link, you can control access to individual subject areas using the analysis editor interface. As you can see, all users with the BIAuthor role can access all subject areas.

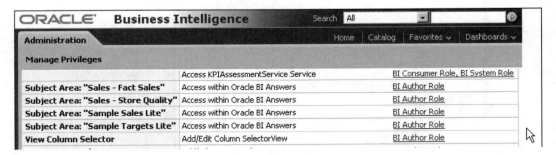

If, however, you want to configure your system so that only users with the QA Manager role can create new analyses using the Sales – Store Quality subject area, along with users granted the BIAdministrator role and the system account BISystem, you should click the existing BI Author Role link and change the settings as listed here so that they appear as shown in the illustration following the list:

■   The BIAuthor role is removed from the list.

■   The QA Manager role is added, with the granted permission.

■   The BIAdministrator and BISystem roles are also added with this permission.

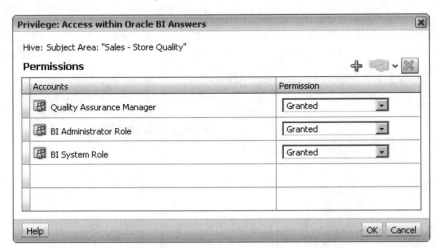

When setting these permissions, you may have noticed that another setting is available: Denied. If you set the BIAuthor permission to Denied, you would explicitly deny access to this subject area to any users with the BIAuthor role, even those who also have the QA Manager role, and this is something you probably do not want to do.

However, if explicitly denying access to a particular subject area to a group of users is what you want to do, this is the setting to use. For the moment, though, you only want to remove this role's default ability to use this subject area, so remove it from the list.

In addition, you must also explicitly add the BI Administrator and BI System roles to the dialog box because normally they would inherit the permissions of the BI Author role, so you would not need to list them separately. Because we removed this role from the permission list, we need to add them in their own right.

Now when users granted the QA Manager role log in, they can see the subject area when they create a new analysis or add an additional subject area to an existing analysis. Users not granted this role, however, will not see this subject area as an option when they create a new analysis, and if they try to edit an existing analysis that uses it, they will receive an error message indicating that they do not have access privileges for that particular subject area.

The difference between this approach and setting permissions at the repository level is that users can still access analyses and dashboards created using columns from this subject area, which gives you the option of sharing analyses with those who use these columns, if you wish to.

So, the choice of how you enable subject area security depends on your objective:

■ If you want to ensure that only users granted a particular role can see this subject area's data, down to the table and column level, set the restrictions using the repository-level permissions approach.

■ If you only want to restrict users' ability to create and edit analyses in a particular subject area, but you do not mind if they view a shared analysis that includes this data, then set the restrictions at the catalog/Presentation Services level.

The approach of using catalog permissions can also be used to control access to aspects of Presentation Server functionality so that, for example, you can remove the right to use the analysis editor from a particular application role. We look at an example of this in the next section of this chapter.

Finally, you can set permissions on individual catalog objects, including folders of objects. The default permissions on objects can be altered to grant or deny access to individual users, application roles, or catalog groups (a deprecated way of organizing users now replaced by application roles but maintained for backwards-compatibility purposes) using either:

- The Home page, or Catalog page, on the Oracle Business Intelligence web site
- The Catalog Manager standalone Java utility.

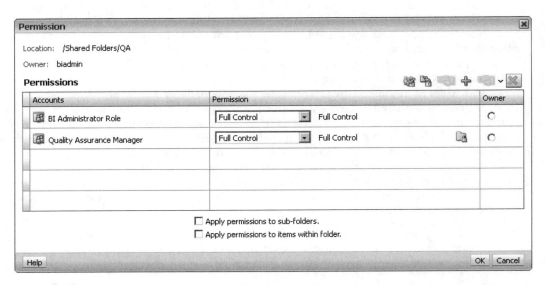

Now that we understand how to control access to data items in the repository and the catalog, let us take a look at the infrastructure that underpins Oracle Business Intelligence and see how users, LDAP groups, and application roles are related.

Understanding Oracle Business Intelligence Security Infrastructure, Application Roles, and Application Policies

Oracle Business Intelligence, as we have seen earlier in this chapter, has to authenticate users when they log into the dashboard, authorize them to use aspects of the application, and have a location to administer and store the role assignments, permissions, and other elements of security that are required for an Oracle BI domain. Oracle Business Intelligence does this by leveraging the security infrastructure of Oracle Fusion Middleware, the platform on which it is built.

Figure 8-1 shows the overall security infrastructure for Oracle Business intelligence, with end users connecting to applications that are hosted in the Oracle WebLogic Server JEE environment, which in turn connect to the Oracle BI Presentation Server and Oracle BI Server. The Oracle BI Server then authenticates users through the Security Service hosted in the WebLogic Server, which uses a feature called Oracle Platform Security Services to connect to embedded and external authenticators and directory services.

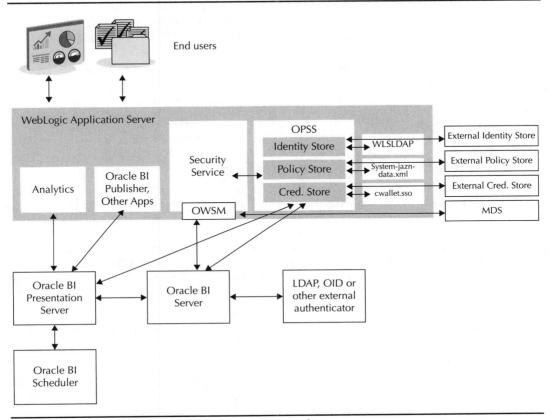

FIGURE 8-1. *Oracle Business Intelligence security infrastructure*

When end users navigate to the Oracle Business Intelligence web site and enter in their username and password in order to view a dashboard at a high level, this is the process that takes place:

1. Users enter their usernames and passwords into the analytics application (http://obisrv1:9704/analytics) that runs on WebLogic and is displayed in their browser.

2. The User ID and password are then sent to Oracle BI Presentation Services.

3. Oracle BI Presentation Services uses these credentials as part of the ODBC connection string that it uses to connect to the Oracle BI Server.

4. The Oracle BI Server calls the Security Service (bimiddleware) to authenticate these user credentials.

5. The Security Service calls Oracle Platform Security Services (OPSS), to authenticate users against the embedded LDAP server or whatever external directory has been connected to OPSS, and to establish which LDAP groups, application roles, and application policies have been granted to the users.

6. Finally, the Security Service passes this information back to the Oracle BI Server, and the BI session is considered authenticated.

OPSS, thus, is central to the entire authentication, authorization, and security process. Let's explore which services OPSS provides and how it facilitates the connection between Oracle Business Intelligence security infrastructure and your organization's security arrangements.

Oracle Platform Security Services

Because organizations typically have diverse security requirements, Oracle Fusion Middleware, on which Oracle Business Intelligence is built, uses a security abstraction layer called Oracle Platform Security Services (OPSS) to connect to companies' various authenticators and other security frameworks. Instead of having Fusion Middleware, and therefore Oracle Business Intelligence, connect directly to directory servers such as Microsoft Active Directory, it connects via OPSS, which has a standard interface over this directory through a "provider."

Figure 8-2 shows an overview of OPSS and how it uses providers to extend connectivity to these services.

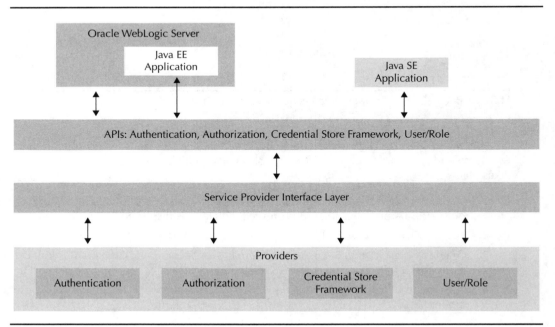

FIGURE 8-2. *Oracle Platform Security Services*

At a high level, OPSS provides three abstracted services for OBIEE and for other Fusion Middleware–based applications:

- **Identity store**   By default this is set to use an embedded WebLogic Server LDAP server, but it can be configured to connect to Microsoft Active Directory, for example.

- **Policy store**   This contains details of application roles, application policies, and the permissions they use, which by default are stored in a file called system-jazn-data.xml but can be redirected to an LDAP or file-based policy store.

- **Credential store**   This replaces the external one that OBIEE 10*g* used, which contains the usernames, passwords, and other credentials that system services require. It can be externalized if required.

When an application such as Oracle BI Publisher or the "analytics" application that you use to connect to Oracle BI Presentation Services connects to OPSS, it does so through a set of application programming interfaces (APIs) that provide access to these services. These APIs cover areas such as authentication, authorization, and the storage and retrieval of credentials, which in turn communicate through a service provider interface layer to a series of providers.

Providers, as we will see later in this chapter, define the connection to authentication services such as Oracle Internet Directory and Microsoft Active Directory, and Oracle Business Intelligence ships with a set of preconfigured providers and security artifacts that we refer to as the *default security configuration*.

Application Roles and Policies

In Oracle Business Intelligence, you can set permissions on catalog and repository objects so that only authorized users can access them. Although you can configure individual user accounts to access such objects, it is much more practical to divide users into groups and then configure these objects with permissions for these groups.

Oracle Fusion Middleware handles the separation of users into groups through a feature called *application roles*. If, for example, you want to restrict human resources–related data to a particular group of users, you could create an application role for this purpose, assign permissions and privileges to this role, and grant the role to a set of users. Similarly, if you want to grant certain application privileges to a set of users, such as the ability to edit the repository and restart the BI Server component, you could assign these privileges to an application role and then grant the role to the relevant users.

Application roles are a concept that is specific to Oracle Fusion Middleware, but your corporate user directory probably uses groups to assemble sets of users doing a similar job. Although introducing the additional concept of application roles can initially seem a bit confusing and might appear to create more work for you as an administrator, it creates extra flexibility into your security setup and has the welcome effect of separating the administration of your Oracle BI domain security from the administration of your corporate LDAP directory.

With all this in mind, one of your most important administration tasks when setting up your Oracle Business Intelligence system is to map your LDAP directory groups into the application role structure that you set up for your Oracle Business Intelligence system so that, for example, a member of your administrator group in your corporate LDAP server is automatically granted an equivalent role when logging into Oracle Business Intelligence.

We will look at how this process works, and the default set of application roles with which Oracle Business Intelligence ships, in a moment.

The Default Security Profile

Oracle Fusion Middleware, through OPSS, can connect to a wide range of authentication and other security services, such as Microsoft Active Directory and other types of directory servers used by organizations.

However, when you first install and configure your system, you will need a default set of services that you can use immediately so that you can start registering users and allocating them to security groups. To make this possible, Oracle Business Intelligence ships with a *default security configuration,* which gives you a starting point for your system security.

Oracle Business Intelligence uses the following default security providers:

- For authentication and authorization, it stores users and groups in an embedded LDAP server running on the WebLogic server.

- For storing credentials for use by the BI Server, for example, when connecting to the Oracle BI Repository, it uses a file-based credential store on the WebLogic Server.

- Similarly, for storing details of application roles and policies (more on these in a moment), it uses a file-based policy store, also held on the WebLogic server.

It also ships with, among others, three application roles that you can grant to new and existing users:

- **BIConsumer**   This is a base-level role that grants the user access to existing analyses, dashboards, and agents and allows them to run or schedule existing BI Publisher reports but not create any new ones.

- **BIAuthor**   This is a role that is also recursively granted the BIConsumer role, which also allows users to create new analyses, dashboards, and other BI objects.

- **BIAdministrator**   This role is recursively granted the BIAuthor (and therefore BIConsumer) roles, which allows the user to administer all parts of the system, including modifying catalog permissions and privileges.

To accompany these roles, the built-in LDAP server comes with three groups that are assigned these roles and that have almost the same name as the roles, but with the LDAP group names in the plural, whereas the application role names are singular:

BIConsumers
BIAuthors
BIAdministrators

When you create or administer users for your system, these users typically are defined in an LDAP server, which also holds the groups named above. Internally, in the policy store within Oracle Fusion Middleware, these groups are then mapped to their corresponding application roles so that users that you assign to an LDAP group are automatically granted the relevant application role, as shown in Figure 8-3.

You can, however, map completely differently named LDAP groups into application roles, which is why this arrangement was put in place. Your LDAP server might have a set of LDAP groups set up that can be broadly categorized as administrators, "power users," and "report consumers," and you might have several groups that fit into these categories. By obtaining the means with which to map these disparate groups into the more controlled set of application roles that your Oracle BI domain requires, you can deal with the reality of your corporate directory structure while working with a more suitable set of user groupings in your Oracle BI domain.

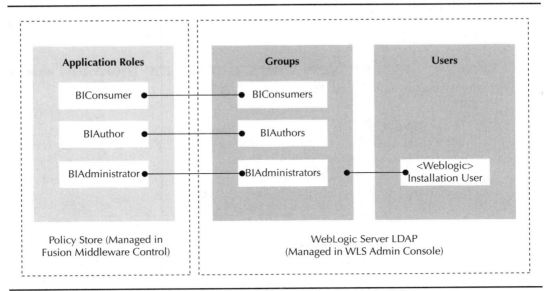

FIGURE 8-3. *Application role to LDAP group mapping, using the default security configuration*

Similarly, you can extend this initial set of application roles to create ones for controlling access to data or controlling access to dashboard functionality, or you can configure OPSS so that alternative policy stores, such as Oracle Internet Directory, are used instead of the default ones provided as part of your installation.

Now that you know the theory behind Oracle Business Intelligence's security infrastructure, we are going to look at your three remaining tasks as an Oracle Business Intelligence security administrator:

■ Creating users and groups in the embedded WebLogic LDAP server and assigning them to the default LDAP groups and application roles

■ Creating new application roles and assigning users (through LDAP groups) to them, and also working with another OPSS feature called *application policies*

■ Connecting OPSS to alternative authentication and authorization providers, such as Microsoft Active Directory

Let's begin by looking at how new users and groups are created in the embedded LDAP server.

Working with Users and Groups in the Embedded LDAP Server

When you install Oracle Business Intelligence, the installer asks you to enter the username and password for an administrative user, which you then use to log into Fusion Middleware Control, the dashboard, and other components to perform administrative tasks. However, you should create separate, regular user accounts for your application users so that they have their own usernames and passwords, and you can control their level of access.

To add new users to your system and assign them to groups (which, as we will see, are later mapped to application roles), you use the web-based Oracle WebLogic Administration Console, which contains various features for managing the embedded LDAP server.

Example: Creating New Users and Adding them to Groups

To create a new user, in this case called *auser* and assigned to the BI Authors LDAP group, follow these steps:

1. Using your web browser, navigate to the Oracle WebLogic Server Administration Console at http://[*machine name*]:7001/console and log in as a user with administrative privileges (for example, weblogic/welcome1).

2. When the Administration Console home page appears, click the Security Realms menu item in the Domain Structure navigation tree menu.

3. When the Summary Of Security Realms page appears, click the myrealm link, the default "container" for security settings for your system.

4. The Settings For Myrealm screen will appear. Click the Users And Groups tab to start creating the new user.

5. Click the New button and then enter or select the details for the new user; for example:

Name: auser
Description: Mr Andrew User
Provider: DefaultAuthenticator
Password: welcome1
Confirm Password: welcome1

The DefaultAuthenticator selected for the Provider setting is referring to the embedded LDAP server, which is the default provider of authentication for a newly configured system.

We will see later how you can supplement this by connecting to other authentication providers, such as Microsoft Active Directory. For now, click OK to create the new user and close this page.

6. To add this user to one of the LDAP groups in your LDAP directory, and therefore grant the user the corresponding application role, click the user in the list of users displayed on the page to which you return and click the Groups tab.

7. Select an LDAP group, for example, BIAuthors, from the Parent Groups Available pane and move it to the Chosen pane. After this is done, click OK to complete the process.

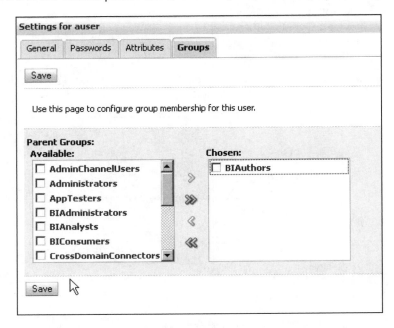

To delete users or amend their details so that, for example, they are now allocated to a new LDAP group, use this feature within the Oracle WebLogic Administration Console. As we will see later, only users held within the embedded WebLogic LDAP server can be administered in this way.

Managing Application Roles and Policies

Now that you have created a new user and added him or her to the BIAuthors LDAP group, this user has also been granted the BIAuthor application role behind the scenes, as this role has been granted to the BIAuthors LDAP group in the OPSS's policy store as part of the default security configuration.

To check this, and see how application roles and policies are administered, you can view their details using Fusion Middleware Control in the following way:

1. Using your web browser, log into Fusion Middleware Control using the URL http://[*machine_name*]:7001/em and enter the username and password of an administrative user (for example, weblogic/welcome1).

2. When the Fusion Middleware Control home page is displayed, navigate to the Business Intelligence | coreapplication menu item and right-click it. When the right-click menu is displayed, select Security | Application Roles.

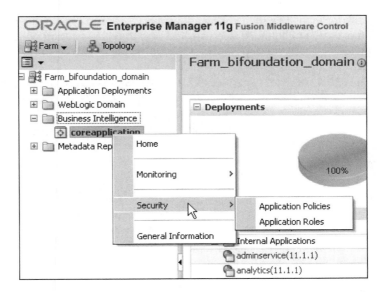

3. In the Application Roles page that is displayed, locate the BIAuthor application role in the list at the bottom of the page, click it to select it, and click the Edit button.

4. After the application role details are displayed, you will see two other objects that have been granted this role. One is the BIAuthors LDAP group, and the other is the BIAdministrator application role, so this object inherits the permissions and privileges of this role.

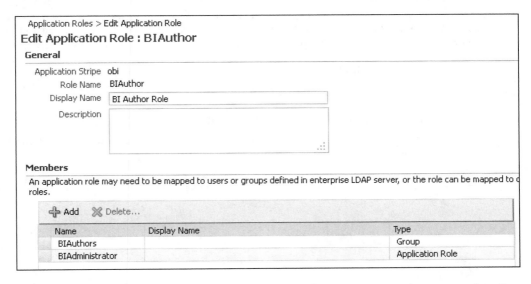

With application roles, as seen in the previous steps, as long as you map them correctly using the preceding dialog box, users assigned to LDAP groups will automatically be granted the relevant application roles according to these mappings. As an administrator, though, you are responsible for managing the existing application roles and creating new ones, and in some circumstances you might need to create and work with application policies. The next two sections of this chapter provide an overview of what this involves.

Example: Creating and Managing Application Roles

Earlier in this chapter, we looked at two new application roles, QA Manager and HR Manager, which we used to control access to subject areas in the catalog. These application roles, unlike the BIAdministrator, BIAuthor, and BIConsumer application roles that ship with OBIEE 11g, do not have privileges assigned to them, but we use them to grant access to subject areas, display sections of dashboards, or provide access to catalog objects.

To create an application role for this type of access control, you must perform the following administration steps in Fusion Middleware Control and the Oracle WebLogic Administration Console:

1. Create the application role, using Fusion Middleware Control.

2. Create a matching LDAP group using the Oracle WebLogic Administration Console or identify in Fusion Middleware Control which existing LDAP groups you want to map to the application role.

3. In Fusion Middleware Control, grant the role to this LDAP group.

4. Using the Administration Console, add your users to the relevant LDAP groups.

5. Launch the Oracle BI Administration tool and refresh its view of the current application roles in your policy store.

In the next example, we create the two application roles that were used in the subject area security examples earlier in this chapter. The first role, QA Manager, maps back to a single LDAP group that we need to create for this purpose; the second role, HR Manager, maps to three separate HR manager LDAP groups that will be granted this application role:

1. Using Fusion Middleware Control (http://[*machine_name*]:7001/em), log in as an administrative user and select Business Intelligence | coreapplication from the navigation tree menu.

2. With coreapplication selected, right-click it and select Security | Application Roles.

3. A list of application roles is displayed. To create a new application role called QA Manager, click the Create button.

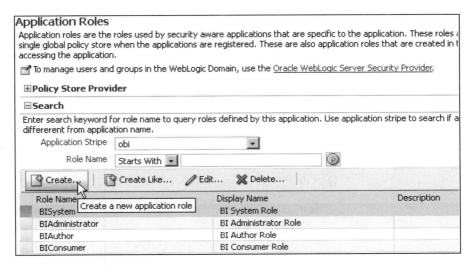

4. The Create Application Role page is displayed. Enter the following details to define the application role:

Name: QA Manager
Description: Quality Assurance Manager

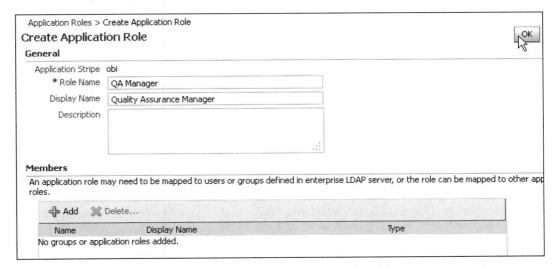

5. Click OK to create the role.

6. Create the corresponding LDAP group and assign any required users to the group. To start this process, using your web browser navigate to the WebLogic Server Administration Console (http://[machine_name]:7001/console), log in as an administrative user, and select Security Realms | myrealm from the application menu.

7. After the Settings For Myrealm page is displayed, click the Users and Groups tab, and select the Groups subtab after it is displayed. Create the new group using the plural version of the application role name you used earlier (that is, **QA Managers**). Finally, add any required users to this LDAP group and exit the Oracle WebLogic Server Administration Console.

8. Log back into Fusion Middleware Control and launch the Application Roles page again. Click the new QA Manager application role that you created earlier and click the Edit button.

9. To grant this new application role to its corresponding LDAP group, in the Members section click the Add button, and then select the LDAP group from the Searched Principals group. After this process is completed, you should see the LDAP group listed as one of the members granted this application role.

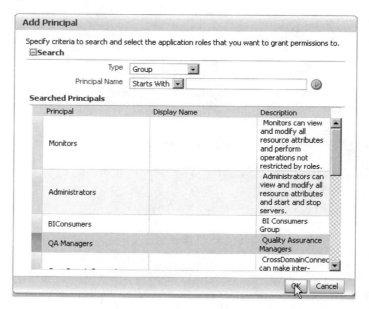

At this point, you can repeat the process to create other, similar application roles that can, for example, map more than one LDAP group into the role. An example of this is when a single application role, HR Manager, has three LDAP groups: Northern HR Managers, Western HR Managers, and Central HR Managers, mapped to it in its Members listing. For now, let's look at another situation, in which we want to add a new application role to the existing BIConsumer, BIAuthor, and BIAdministrator roles.

Creating Additional Application Roles

By default, Oracle Business Intelligence ships with three application roles that you assign to users of your system:

■   **BIConsumer**   This is the base-level role that grants the user access to existing analyses, dashboards, and agents and allows them to run or schedule existing BI Publisher reports but not create any new ones.

- **BIAuthor**   This is a role that is also recursively granted the BIConsumer role, which also allows users to create new analyses, dashboards, and other BI objects.
- **BIAdministrator**   This role is recursively granted the BIAuthor (and therefore BIConsumer) roles, which allows the user to administer all parts of the system, including modification of catalog permissions and privileges.

In some cases, you might want to add another role to this list to fit between the BIConsumer and BIAuthor roles, called BIAnalyst, which allows users to create and edit analyses but not create new dashboards.

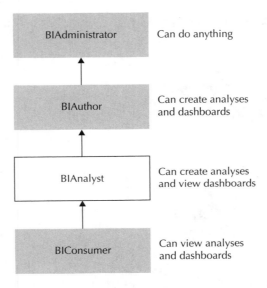

The requirement for this type of additional application role often arises when users need to be able to create new analyses but someone else publishes those to dashboards. To create and configure this application role, after first creating a matching LDAP group that you add users to and map to it, you must do two things:

- Create the role and reconfigure the inheritance hierarchy in the policy store so that it inherits the permissions of the BIConsumer role, and the BIAuthor role in turn inherits its permissions.
- Reconfigure Presentation Server catalog privileges so that the new BIAnalyst role becomes the lowest-level role that can access the analysis editor, with the existing BIAuthor role then inheriting this privilege.

Example: Creating the BIAnalyst Application Role   To create this additional BIAnalyst application role, you can either create a new role from scratch or base it on an existing one such as BIAuthor, as we will do now:

1. Using Fusion Middleware Control, log on as an administrative user and select Business Intelligence | coreapplication | Security | Application Roles.

2. After the list of application roles is displayed, select the BIAuthor role and click the Create Like button. After the Create Application Role Like page is displayed, enter the details for the new role, called BIAnalyst, and a suitable description.

3. In the Members section, remove the existing BIAuthors group from the Members list and replace it with the LDAP group that you created to map to this role (in this case, BIAnalysts). Remove the BIAdministrator role from the Members list and replace it with the BIAuthor role so that the correct role in the hierarchy inherits this new role's permissions and privileges.

Application Roles > Create Application Role

Create Application Role Like : BIAuthor

General

Application Stripe	obi
* Role Name	BIAnalyst
Display Name	BI Analyst Role
Description	

Members

An application role may need to be mapped to users or groups defined in enterprise LDAP server, or the role can be mapped to roles.

+ Add   ✗ Delete...

Name	Display Name	Type
BIAnalysts		Group
BIAuthor		Application Role

4. Click OK to close the dialog box and create the new application role.

5. Edit the BIConsumer application role, remove the BIAuthor role from its list of members, and replace it with the new BIAnalyst role. This action places the new BIAnalyst role midway between the BIConsumer and BIAuthor roles in the role hierarchy so that each role is granted the correct roles under it in the role hierarchy shown in the illustration preceding this list, and it is an important step in assigning catalog privileges.

6. Catalog privileges in Oracle BI Presentation Services are currently configured such that only users granted the BIAuthor role can create analyses. To alter this so that users granted this new BIAnalyst role can also create analyses, log on to the Oracle Business Intelligence web site (typically http://[machine_name]:9704/analytics) as an administrative user, click the Administration link, and then click the Manage Privileges link in the Administration page.

7. In the Access category, locate the Access To Answers item, and click the BI Author Role link next to it. After the Privilege: Access To Answers dialog box is displayed, remove the BI Author role currently listed and replace it with BI Analyst, which you should assign the Granted permission.

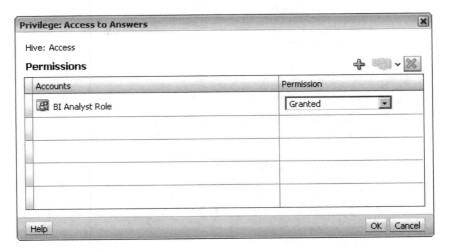

8. This new role has the right to use Answers (the legacy name for the analysis editor), and, as the BIAuthor role inherits (has been granted) the BIAnalyst role, it gains this privilege as well.

9. You can test the new role by creating a user and assigning it to an LDAP group that corresponds to the BIAnalyst role, and logging in as that user. You should see that this user can now create new analyses but cannot create dashboards or any other BI content.

This takes us through looking at creating and working with application roles, but what about application policies, the other entry under the Security menu that you see when you right-click coreapplication in Fusion Middleware Control? What are they?

Creating and Managing Application Policies

Application policies, like application roles, are held in the policy store administered and accessed through OPSS. You can access the existing list of application policies by logging into Fusion Middleware Control, selecting Business Intelligence | coreapplication, right-clicking it, and selecting Security | Application Policies.

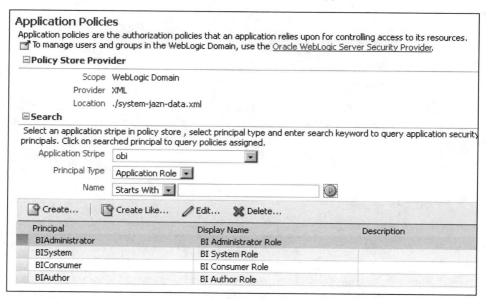

After selecting obi as the application stripe and clicking the Search Application Security Grants button, you will see a list of the existing application policies in your policy store. Each one, by default, is named after the application role to which it applies.

What is an application policy? Select the BIAuthor principal and click the Edit button, and let's take a look.

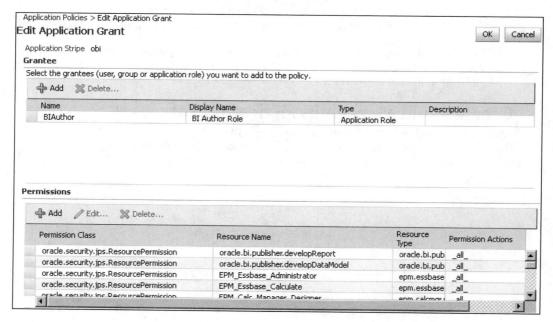

Application policies are sets of Java permissions associated with a principal, in this case an application role. The BIAuthor application policy, for example, allows the user to develop reports and data models with BI Publisher, access Oracle Essbase administration and calculation functions, and perform other report-authoring tasks. Application policy permission classes do not explicitly cover privileges such as accessing the analysis editor, creating dashboards, or using other areas of repository or Presentation Server functionality that are controlled by permissions set in the Oracle BI Administration tool or the Administration page in Presentation Services.

Functional area privileges and permissions in OBIEE 11*g* are controlled in two places:

- For applications written in Java, such as BI Publisher, Financial Reporting, and Real-Time Decisions, you control their use by using application policies.

- For the C++ "legacy" components such as the BI Server and BI Presentation Server, you control them with their own built-in privileges and permissions.

When do you use application policies? In reality, not very often, as the permissions they work with are outside the usual catalog and repository permissions, but one example might be when you wish to create a new application policy that grants permissions to author Oracle BI Publisher reports and data models as the BIAuthor does, but leaves out the Essbase permissions that this role normally includes.

Example: Creating a New Application Policy

In this example, we would like the BIAnalyst role that we created a moment ago to have permissions to create BI Publisher reports and data models but not have any of the Essbase permissions that would normally be associated with the BIAuthor role on which it was based. To set this up, you must:

- Create an application policy based on the BIAuthor one and grant it to the BIAnalyst role.

- Remove the permission classes from this new application policy that relate to Oracle Essbase.

To do this, follow these steps:

1. With the Application Policies page open in Fusion Middleware Control, select the BIAuthor principal and click the Create Like button.

2. On the Create Application Grant Like Grant To : BIAuthor page, click the Add button in the Grantee section and select the BIAnalyst role.

3. In the Permissions area, select the following permission classes by resource name and click the Delete button to remove them from this application policy:

    EPM_Essbase_Administrator
    EPM_Essbase_Calculate
    EPM_Calc_Manager_Designer
    oracle.epm.financialreporting.editBatch
    oracle.epm.financialreporting.editBook
    oracle.epm.financialreporting.editReport
    oracle.epm.essbasestudio.cpadmin

After this process is complete, your application policy should look as in the following illustration.

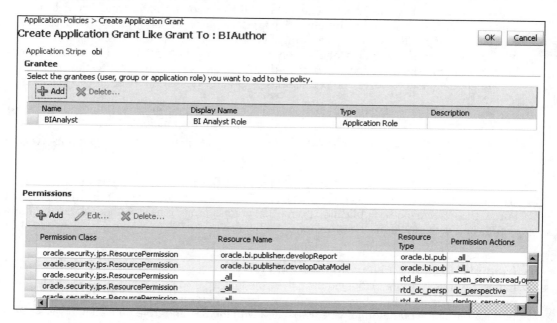

4. Click OK after you have finished.

Now, when users with this corresponding application role try to use Essbase administrative or authoring features, they will be denied as per the application policy that you have assigned to this role.

Connecting to External Directories and Other Sources for Authentication and Authorization

In this section in this chapter, we look at two common tasks that an OBIEE 11g administrator might have to perform:

■ Connecting the system to an external directory server, in this case Microsoft Active Directory, so users can log into the dashboard using their Windows Active Directory username and password, and retrieve group membership as an alternative to the default authenticator

■ Connecting the system to an external set of database tables that contain the group membership for users authenticated through Active Directory, to provide an alternative authorization scheme

Although OBIEE 11g comes with the embedded WebLogic LDAP server to hold users and groups, this is intended only for test and development purposes and has license restrictions that allow you to use it only to hold user and group details for Oracle Business Intelligence. In production environments, you will typically want to connect Oracle Business Intelligence to your existing corporate directory, allowing you to use user and group details that you already hold.

To make this possible, Oracle Business Intelligence uses OPSS as its security abstraction layer, connecting to external directories such as Active Directory. Not every type of authentication provider available through OPSS can be used with Oracle Business Intelligence, but using the LDAP server support within OPSS and Oracle Fusion Middleware you can connect Oracle Business Intelligence to LDAP servers such as:

Oracle Internet Directory
Oracle Virtual Directory
Microsoft Active Directory
OpenLDAP
Sun Java System Directory Server
eDirectory 8.8

You should check the documentation for the version of Oracle Business Intelligence you are using, as different versions support different sets of external directories, and support increases with each release of the product.

When you connect to external directories, as mentioned earlier in this chapter, you need to consider two security aspects:

- *Authentication,* the process of validating a User ID and password and consequently setting the USER session variable in the Oracle BI session.

- *Authorization,* the process of discovering which groups the user is a member of and then deriving which application roles (and associated permissions) the user should be granted. This sets the ROLES session variable in the Oracle BI session.

Historically, in earlier releases of Oracle Business Intelligence, you connected to external directories for authentication and authorization through initialization blocks, instructions to the Oracle BI Server defined in the Oracle BI Administration tool that are executed at the start of a user session and that set the USER and GROUP (and therefore ROLES) session variables.

Although this method is still available in the current release of Oracle Business Intelligence to provide backward compatibility and to support security integration with Oracle E-Business Suite, in general you should use the system of providers and authenticators provided as part of Oracle Fusion Middleware, in which:

- *Authentication* is via OPSS, which in turn uses the WebLogic authentication mechanism (authenticators defined in the WebLogic Security Realm). The resulting authenticated User ID is used to set the USER session variable.

- *Authorization* is via OPSS to retrieve group membership via WebLogic authenticators. This works together with the policy store to derive a list of application roles for the user and the groups assigned to that user. This list of application roles is used to set the ROLES session variable.

Let's look now at how OPSS and the WebLogic authentication mechanism can be used to configure alternative or additional authentication and authorization mechanisms.

Example: Configuring Oracle Business Intelligence to Connect to Microsoft Active Directory

In the following example, we will use an Active Directory server running on the host pdc.gcbc.com, that in turn contains three users:

- **ADBISystemUser** This is used by OBIEE as the principal to connect to the Active Directory server and is a "regular" user account; that is, it's not an administrator account within Active Directory.

- **Anne Administrator** This is a user on Active Directory who wants to have administration rights in the Presentation Server and BI Server.

- **AD User** This is another user who only wants to be able to create analyses and dashboards.

These users are organized into three groups in the Active Directory server:

- **ADBIAdministrators** These are analogous to the BIAdministrators group in the WLS LDAP server.

- **ADBIAuthors** These are analogous to the BIAuthors group in the WLS LDAP Server.

- **ADBIConsumers** These are analogous to the BIConsumers group in the WLS LDAP server.

Note that these groups are for example only, and not mandatory.

Configuring connections to corporate directory servers can be complicated, and the specifics of each connection will depend on the server and its particular configuration options. Also, the complexity of the task will depend on whether you intend to replace the embedded LDAP server with this external directory, using it to host the system account used by Oracle Business Intelligence to connect to its internal components, or whether the external directory will be used in addition to the existing embedded LDAP server.

For the definitive setup steps to configure security connectivity to any particular directory server, you should always consult the Oracle product documentation together with up-to-date release and technical notes on My Oracle Support (http://support.oracle.com), where you will always find the most complete and error-checked examples that are currently available.

That said, in the following example, we go through a minimal set of steps used to connect an additional, external directory to OPSS and use it to authenticate users from that directory in addition to the existing ones in the embedded LDAP server. If you wish to replace the embedded LDAP server, consult the *Oracle® Fusion Middleware Security Guide for Oracle Business Intelligence Enterprise Edition 11g Release 1*, part of the product documentation, for full instructions.

Looking first at the Active Directory Users and Computers dialog box on the Microsoft Windows server, you can see the list of users we are interested in on the left-hand screen and the list of groups on the right-hand screen.

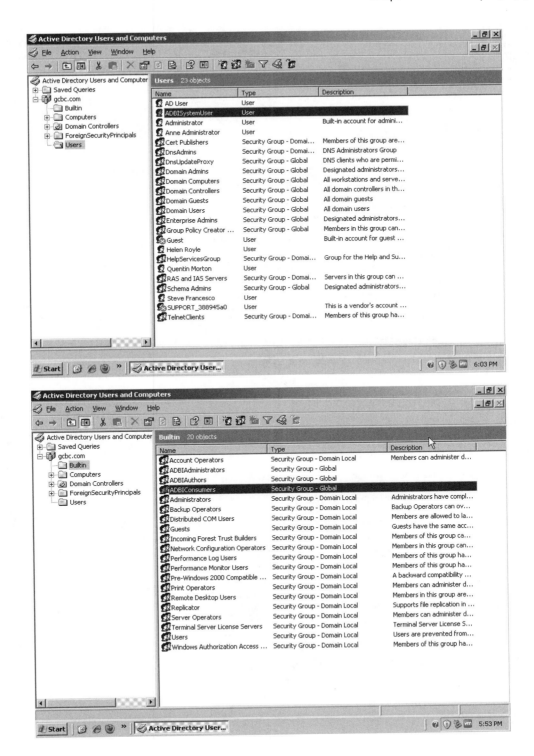

When we connect the Active Directory server to OPSS, all the users in the directory, subject to any additional filters and the base level specified during the provider setup, are available to us in Oracle Business Intelligence, and we can map the groups within it to application roles so that its users are properly authorized in our system.

Let's now enter the Oracle WebLogic Server Administration Console (http://[*machine_name*]:7001/console) and start configuring the system for Active Directory integration:

1. Log into the Oracle WebLogic Server Administration Console as an administrative user (for example, biadmin/welcome1).

2. After the Administration Console home page is displayed, click the Security Realms menu item on the left-hand side and then myrealm after the link is displayed.

3. To alter the domain configuration, click the Lock And Edit button. Then click the Providers tab in the Settings For Myrealm page.

4. Active Directory integration is achieved through registering a new authentication provider, using the Active Directory provider type. To register this, click the New button under the Authentication Providers label.

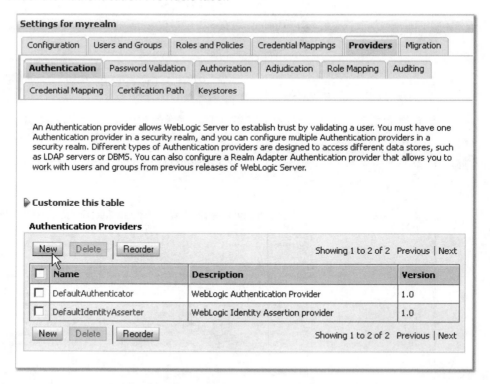

5. The Create a New Authentication Provider page is displayed. Type in or select the following values to create your provider:

    Name: ADProvider
    Type: ActiveDirectoryAuthenticator

6. Click OK to create the provider.

7. Click the new authentication provider in the list, and then after the Settings For ADProvider page is displayed, set the control flag to SUFFICIENT and click Save.

8. Click the Provider Specific tab, and select or enter the following details for your Active Directory installation, amending the settings as appropriate for your Active Directory server; for example:

Host: pdc.gcbc.com
Port: 389
Principal: CN=ADBISystemUser, CN=Users, DC=gcbc, DC=com
Credential: Welcome1
Confirm Credential: Welcome1
User Base DN: CN=Users, DC=gcbc, DC=com
User Name Attribute: cn
User Object Class: user
Group Base DN: CN=Builtin, DC=gcbc, DC=com
GUID Attribute: objectguid

9. Click Save to save and close the page.

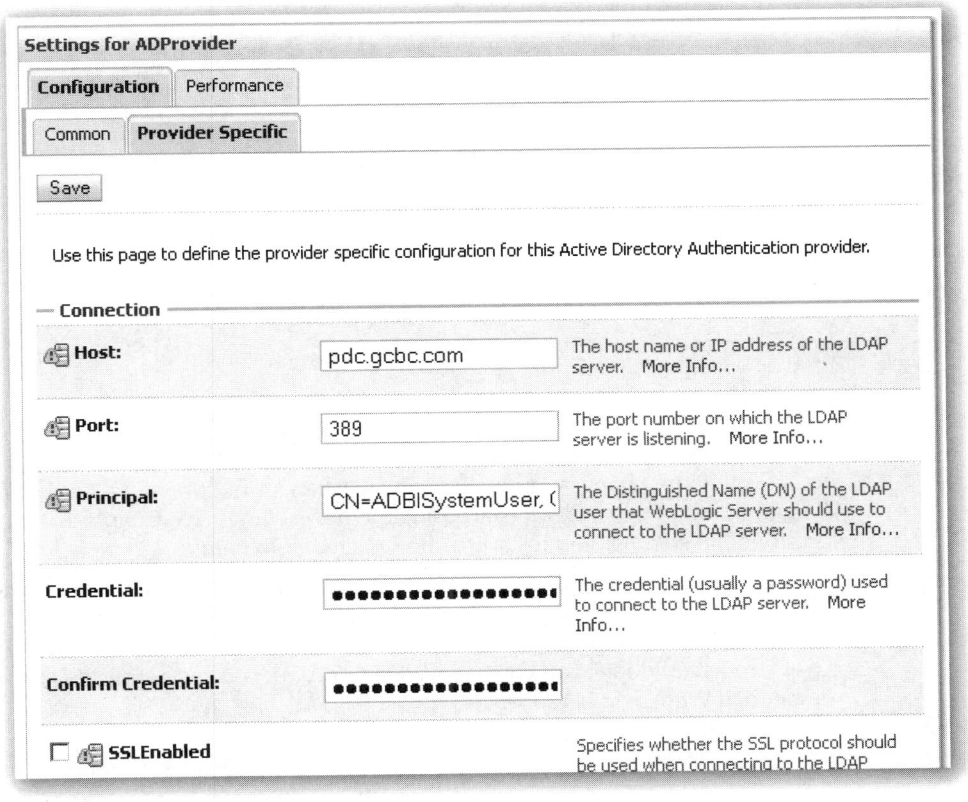

NOTE
In situations in which your User Name Attribute is sAMAccountName rather than cn, see the section after this one for details on how you will also need to configure the username attributes used by Fusion Middleware's identity store to provide log-in details for Presentation Services.

10. Return to the list of providers, and click the DefaultAuthenticator one. With the Configuration | Common subtab selected, set the control flag to OPTIONAL, and click Save.

11. With the list of authentication providers displayed, click the Reorder button and change the order of the providers so that ADProvider is first, followed by DefaultAuthenticator and DefaultIdentityAsserter.

12. To activate these changes, press the Activate Changes button, and then restart your entire Oracle BI domain in order to start using the new settings (see Chapter 10 for full details on stopping, starting, and restarting the Oracle BI Domain).

13. After you restart your system, you should now be able to see the new users and groups in the Oracle WebLogic Administration Console. To do this, once logged into the Administration Console and then select Security Realms | myrealm | Users and Groups | Users. You should then see your Active Directory users listed alongside the ones from the embedded WebLogic LDAP server.

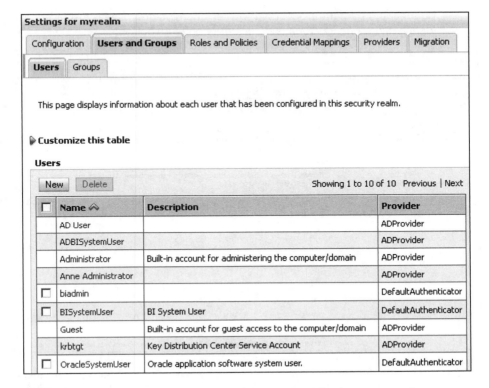

Similarly, you should see your Active Directory groups under the Groups tab.

NOTE
You cannot edit these externally provided users and groups from within the Oracle WebLogic Administration Console, nor can you create new external users or groups here. To do that, you must use Active Directory's own console and tools.

14. Next, switch to Fusion Middleware Control, first to configure Fusion Middleware's Oracle Platform Security Services to accept users and groups from both WLS LDAP and Active Directory when logging into the dashboard, and then to map the Active Directory groups to their equivalent application roles.

    Log into Fusion Middleware Control, and select the WebLogic Domain | bifoundation_ domain menu item on the left. Right-click it and select Security | Security Provider

Configuration. After the Security Provider Configuration page is displayed, expand the
Identity Store Provider area and click the Configure button.

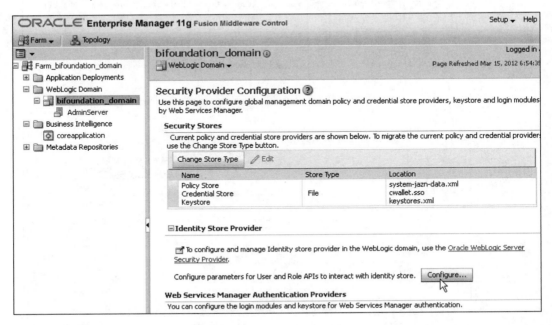

15. The Identity Store Configuration page is displayed. Click the Add button next to the
Custom Properties area, and add a new custom property with these settings:

Property Name: virtualize
Value: true

NOTE
*Setting this property allows OPSS to use more than one authentication
provider for your system, in this case using the embedded LDAP server
and Microsoft Active Directory.*

16. Click OK to close the page after you are finished.

17. While still in Fusion Middleware Control, right-click the Business Intelligence |
coreapplication entry in the left-hand side menu, and select Security | Application Roles.
As you may have done with the application role settings in one of the previous examples
in this chapter, edit the BIAdministrator, BIAuthor, and BIConsumer application roles so
that the new Active Directory groups are listed as members.

⬆ **coreapplication** ⓘ   Logge

⊕ Business Intelligence Instance ▼   Page Refreshed Mar 15, 2012 7

Application Roles > Edit Application Role

Edit Application Role : BIAdministrator

General

Application Stripe	obi
Role Name	BIAdministrator
Display Name	BI Administrator Role
Description	

Members

An application role may need to be mapped to users or groups defined in enterprise LDAP server, or the role can b
other application roles.

➕ Add   ✖ Delete...

Name	Display Name	Type
BIAdministrators		Group
ADBIAdministrators		Group

NOTE
Doing this ensures that the Active Directory users obtain the same type of Presentation Server and repository privileges as WLS LDAP users, but they will not have administration access to the Oracle WebLogic Administration Console or Fusion Middleware Control.

You should now be able to log in as one of the Active Directory users, and see the roles granted to that user through their membership of corresponding groups in Active Directory.

If an Active Directory user who is named Anne Administrator and is assigned to the ADBIAdministrator group logs in, she will be able to administer the Presentation Server permissions and privileges, but she will not be able to log into Fusion Middleware Control to change the repository, for example.

Note that, in cases in which the User Name Attribute for your Active Directory server is set to sAMAccountName, for example, rather than cn, as in the preceding example, you must perform an additional set of steps to map Active Directory's user attribute details to the ones used by Oracle Business Intelligence.

Example: Mapping Login Attributes for Active Directory Integration When the sAMAccountName Username Attribute Is Used

In the following example, we will map the sAMAccountName attribute used in Microsoft Active Directory to the user attributes used by Oracle BI Presentation Services to authenticate dashboard users. This step is required when your Active Directory installation uses sAMAccountName as the

User Name attribute, rather than the LDAP standard of cn. To map this Active Directory attribute using Fusion Middleware Control, follow these steps:

1. Log into Fusion Middleware Control using administrative credentials (for example, biadmin/welcome1).

2. Using the navigation tree menu on the left, expand the WebLogic Domain directory and right-click the bifoundation_domain menu option. From the menu that is displayed, select Security | Security Provider Configuration.

3. Expand the Identity Store Provider area and click the Configure button.

4. To map the Active Directory attributes to OBI's user attributes, add two entries as follows:

   Property Name: user.login.attr
   Value: sAMAccountName
   Property Name: username.attr
   Value: sAMAccountName

5. After this process is completed, click OK to close the dialog box.

Note that, as with any other Oracle Fusion Middleware task, you can also perform this configuration through WLST scripting; for more details on WLST, see Chapter 10 of this book and the *Oracle® Fusion Middleware Application Security Guide 11g Release 1*.

Example: Using Database Tables for User Authorization

In the previous example, we saw how we can use LDAP servers such as Microsoft Active Directory to provide user details and their group membership for our Oracle BI domain. In cases in which the LDAP group setup does not match the roles that we wish to use for our Oracle BI domain, we can use the mapping facility in Fusion Middleware Control to define the roles we want, and map groups to them as appropriate. For most customer scenarios, using the LDAP server to provide both user details and group membership will be the correct solution, one that has the virtue of simplicity because only a single external directory solution is connected to Oracle Business Intelligence and the Fusion Middleware platform. If this describes your situation, you can skip the next example in this chapter.

In some cases, you might not wish to use your LDAP server to provide group membership for your users, because it was never intended for this purpose or because you have an existing system, perhaps a set of tables in a database that provide details of which users belong to which BI group.

In this situation, you can use another type of authenticator (BISQLGroupProvider) introduced with the 11.1.1.6 release of Oracle Business Intelligence (and via a patch for the earlier, 11.1.1.5 release) that supports authorization via SQL queries against database tables. This provider does not and will not authenticate end-user credentials and serves only to add any external group memberships held in a database table to an authenticated user's identity, such as those provided by the default LDAP authenticator or the Microsoft Active Directory LDAP server that we set up earlier in the previous set of examples.

You should also note that this authenticator is new and requires a fair amount of manual configuration, and releases after the 11.1.1.6 version might make this authenticator redundant or provide an easier way to configure it. If, however, you do wish to use database tables to provide details of group membership and, as recommended, OPSS (rather than the deprecated initialization blocks approach) to do this, you should use this authenticator.

To use the new BISQLGroupProvider authenticator, you must first create two database tables using the following definition (or the equivalent DDL for non-Oracle databases):

```
CREATE TABLE GROUPS
(    G_NAME VARCHAR2(50 BYTE) NOT NULL ENABLE,
     G_DESCRIPTION VARCHAR2(50 BYTE),
      CONSTRAINT GROUPS_PK PRIMARY KEY (G_NAME)
  );
CREATE TABLE GROUPMEMBERS
(    G_MEMBER VARCHAR2(50 BYTE) NOT NULL ENABLE,
     G_NAME VARCHAR2(50 BYTE) NOT NULL ENABLE,
      CONSTRAINT GROUPMEMBERS_PK PRIMARY KEY (G_MEMBER, G_NAME),
      CONSTRAINT GROUP_FK FOREIGN KEY (G_NAME)
       REFERENCES GROUPS (G_NAME) ENABLE
  );
```

Although using these table and column names is not mandatory, it is best if you can keep to these, as otherwise the SQL used by default by the authenticator and detailed in a moment in the example will have to be changed to reflect your actual table and column names.

GROUPS	G_NAME = G_NAME	**GROUPMEMBERS**
G_NAME G_DESCRIPTION	⟷	G_MEMBER G_NAME

To use this provider, you must perform the following steps:

1. Install the provider library files in the correct WebLogic server file system location.

2. Configure a data source in WebLogic that the provider will use to connect to the schema and tables just described.

3. Configure a BISQLGroupProvider with the SQL SELECT statements required to access these tables.

4. Reorder your authentication providers, and if you have not already done so, enable the virtualized identity store adapter (as we did in a previous example).

5. Configure a database adapter so that the identity store APIs can map your groups into application roles.

In this example, Microsoft Active Directory has previously been configured, as per the previous example, as an additional authentication provider for our Oracle Business Intelligence system. This additional directory contains a number of users, and these users are then referenced in the preceding tables, along with a set of groups and group membership, in anticipation of the use of this SQL database group provider.

Before using the BISQLGroupProvider, you must install it by performing one of the following two steps, depending on whether you are using release 11.1.1.5 (which requires a patch to be installed) or 11.1.1.6 (which does not, but does require some additional steps before this provider can be used):

■ If you are using the 11.1.1.5 release, apply the patch associated with Bug 11667221 / ARU 14523400.

■ If you are using the 11.1.1.6 release, copy the BISecurityProviders.jar file from [*middleware_home*]/Oracle_BI1/bifoundation/security/providers to [*middleware_home*]/wlserver_10.3/server/lib/mbeantypes, and then restart the Administration Server.

At the time of writing, the 11.1.1.6 release of Oracle Business Intelligence was the most current. If you are using a subsequent release, check your product documentation for up-to-date information on this provider, which might or might not require any special configuration.

After it is installed, to make use of this provider and obtain group membership from these database tables, follow these steps, which use an Oracle database as the data source but can be modified by you to use other database sources supported as WebLogic Server JDBC data sources:

1. First, configure the data source and BISQLGroupProvider. To do this, use your web browser to navigate to the Oracle WebLogic Administration Console (http://[*machine_name*]:7001/console), and then click the Lock And Edit button.

2. From the left-hand menu, select Services | Data Sources. Then, from the Data Sources list, select New | Generic Data Source.

3. On the Create a New JDBC Data Source page, enter or select the following details:

    Name: BIDatabaseGroupsDS
    JNDI Name: jdbc/BIDatabaseGroupsDS
    Database Type: Oracle (*for example*)

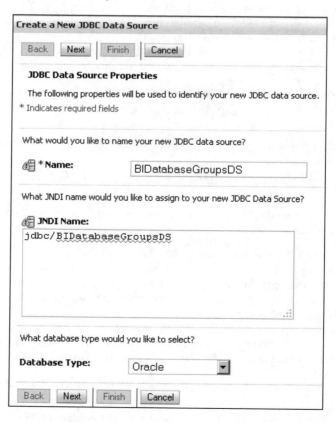

4. On the following page, select the database driver (for Oracle database sources, use Oracle's Driver (Thin) for Service Connections, versions 9.0.1 and later) and then on the

Connection Properties page, select or enter the connection details to your schema and database; for example:

Database Name: orcl
Host Name: obisrv1c
Port: 1521
Database User Name: gcbc_bi_groups
Password: *password*
Confirm Password: *password*

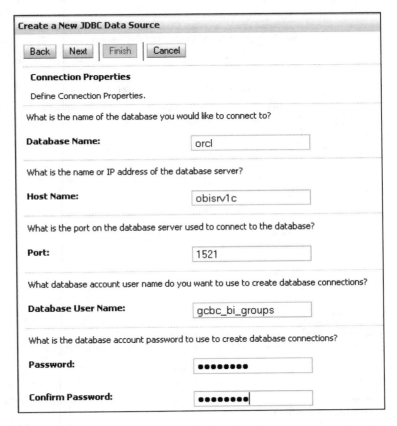

5. Test the connection on the next page, and deploy the data source to AdminServer (the Administration Server within your WebLogic domain) for Simple Install types, and AdminServer and BI_Server1 (the Managed Server) for Enterprise Install types, any other Managed Servers that you may have added to your cluster).

6. Click Finish, and then click the Activate Changes button.

Next you will create a BISQLGroupProvider against this JDBC data source. This provider uses SQL SELECT statements to retrieve group membership details for users and comes with a default set of SELECT statements that reference the tables that we created earlier on. If you need to use tables other than the ones that we created earlier to hold your user and group details, you will have to amend these SQL SELECT statements appropriately.

1. Start by clicking the Lock & Edit button to start editing the domain configuration. Select Security Realm | myrealm | Providers from the menus and tabs. With the Providers tab selected, click the New button to create a new authentication provider. Finally, when prompted, select or enter the following values:

   Name: MySQLGroupProvider
   Type: BISQLGroupProvider

2. Click OK to close the page and then click the new MySQLGroupProvider authentication provider to display its settings page. Select the Provider Specific tab and type in the name of the JDBC data source that you created earlier (**jdbc/BIDatabaseGroupsDS**).

3. If you are using the default set of tables for user and group settings, the SQL settings for this provider will not need to be changed. If you altered the table or column names, update the SQL commands to reflect your actual database structure. After this process is completed, click Save.

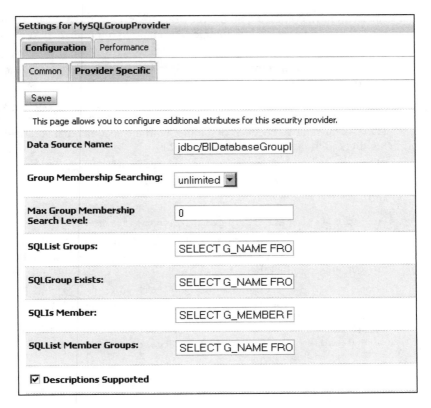

4. Return to the list of providers and reorder them so that the new MySQLGroupProvider is at the top of the list.

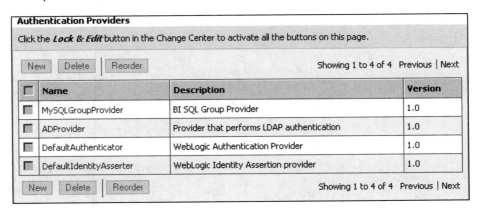

5. If you have not done so already, set the virtualized=true flag in the Identity Store Provider settings in Fusion Middleware Control; see the steps to set this property in the previous Active Directory integration example for full details on how to perform this task and thereby enable multiple authenticators for your system.

6. After you have completed all the previous steps, click the Activate Changes button and stop, then restart your entire Oracle BI domain to reinitialize all servers and components within your Oracle BI domain.

7. Now create an XML template file that is in turn used by the identity store APIs to map groups provided by this provider to the application roles in your system.

To create this file, use a text editor to save a new file called bi_sql_groups_adapter_template.xml, and type in the following details, substituting your own organization's LDAP details in two sections of the file, with the sections that you need to change highlighted in bold in the following code:

```
<param "name="ReplaceAttribute"value="uniquemember=
{cn=%uniquemember%,cn=Users,dc=gcbc,dc=com}"/>
```

and

```
<objectClass "name="groupofuniquenames" rdn="cn">
```

In addition, if you have used different database table names and columns in the default GROUPS and GROUPMEMBERS detailed earlier, you must adjust the SQL statements in the XML file to reflect them:

```
<?xml version = '1.0' encoding = 'UTF-8'?>
<adaptersschvers="303" version="1" xmlns="http://www.octetstring.com/
schemas/Adapters"
xmlns:adapters="http://www.w3.org/2001/XMLSchema-instance">
    <dataBase id="directoryType" version="0">
      <root>%ROOT%</root>
      <active>true</active>
      <serverType>directoryType</serverType>
      <routing>
          <critical>true</critical>
          <priority>50</priority>
          <inclusionFilter/>
          <exclusionFilter/>
          <plugin/>
          <retrieve/>
          <store/>
          <visible>Yes</visible>
          <levels>-1</levels>
          <bind>true</bind>
          <bind-adapters/>
          <views/>
          <dnpattern/>
      </routing>
      <pluginChains xmlns="http://xmlns.oracle.com/iam/management/ovd/
config/plugins">
          <plugins>
             <plugin>
                <name>VirtualAttribute</name>
<class>oracle.ods.virtualization.engine.chain.plugins.virtualattr.
VirtualAttributePlugin</class><initParams>
                <param name="ReplaceAttribute"
```

```
        value="uniquemember={cn=%uniquemember%,cn=Users,dc=gcbc,dc=com}"/>
                    </initParams>
                </plugin>
            </plugins>
            <default>
                <plugin name="VirtualAttribute"/>
            </default>
            <add/>
            <bind/>
            <delete/>
            <get/>
            <modify/>
            <rename/>
        </pluginChains>
        <driver>oracle.jdbc.driver.OracleDriver</driver>
        <url>%URL%</url>
        <user>%USER%</user>
        <password>%PASSWORD%</password>
        <ignoreObjectClassOnModify>false</ignoreObjectClassOnModify>
        <includeInheritedObjectClasses>true</includeInheritedObjectClass-
es>
        <maxConnections>10</maxConnections>
        <mapping>
<joins/>
            <objectClass name="groupofuniquenames" rdn="cn">
<attributeldap="cn" table="GROUPMEMBERS" field="G_NAME" type=""/>
                <attributeldap="description" table="GROUPMEMBERS"
                field="G_NAME" type=""/>
                <attributeldap="uniquemember" table="GROUPMEMBERS"
field="G_MEMBER" type=""/>
            </objectClass>
        </mapping>
        <useCaseInsensitiveSearch>true</useCaseInsensitiveSearch>
        <connectionWaitTimeout>10</connectionWaitTimeout>
        <oracleNetConnectTimeout>0</oracleNetConnectTimeout>
        <validateConnection>false</validateConnection>
    </dataBase>
</adapters>
```

8. After this process is completed, copy the template file into [*middleware_home*]/oracle_ common/modules/oracle.ovd_11.1.1/templates/.

9. Open a command-prompt session in the server running Oracle Business Intelligence, and enter the following commands, adjusting for your environment and LDAP settings, to configure the adapter using the template file that you have just created. The following commands are for a Microsoft Windows–based environment:

```
cd c:\Middleware\oracle_common\bin
set ORACLE_HOME=c:\Middleware\Oracle_BI1
set WL_HOME=c:\Middleware\wlserver_10.3
set JAVA_HOME=c:\Middleware\jdk160_24
```

```
libovdadapterconfig -adapterNamebiSQLGroupAdapter -adapterTemplate
bi_sql_groups_adapter_template.xml -host localhost -port 7001
-userNamebiadmin -domainPath c:\Middleware\user_projects\domains\bi-
foundation_domain
-dataStore DB -root cn=Users,DC=gcbc,DC=com -contextName default
-dataSourceJNDINamejdbc/BIDatabaseGroupsDS
```

10. When prompted, enter the password for the Oracle WebLogic Administration Server. After this step is completed, you should see the following message:

```
Adapter created successfully: biSQLGroupAdapter
```

   You might also see the warning message "WARNING: BISQLGROUPSPROVIDER: CONNECTION POOL NOT USABLE," which is expected and can be ignored.

11. Restart the entire Oracle BI domain. During the restart, you will see an error message saying that the connection pool you just created is unusable. This is expected and will not cause a problem.

   If you do run across any issues in setting up this provider, please review technical note 1428008.1 on the My Oracle Support web site (http://support.oracle.com, for which a valid Oracle support contract is required for access), which has full details on how the provider is configured and how to deal with any errors that might arise during its configuration and deployment.

12. After you have successfully configured the provider, navigate to Fusion Middleware Control using your web browser, log in as an administrative user, and create a matching role for one of your new database-defined groups. You should see the new groups when you add a group to the application role; if not, check the console output for the WebLogic Server for diagnostic messages.

13. Now test the new roles and groups. Restart your Oracle BI domain, log in as one of the users with groups in the database tables, and then view the list of roles assigned to the user. You should see your new roles, corresponding to the group settings in the database tables, assigned to the user (in this case, the HR Manager role).

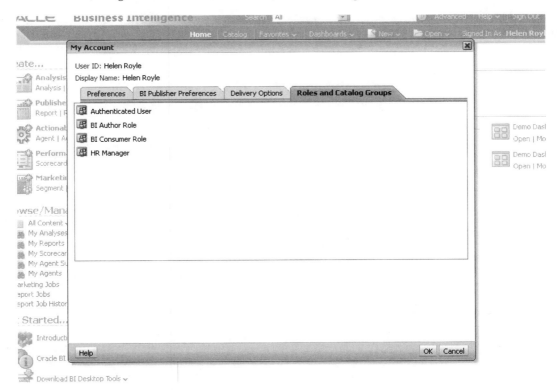

That concludes our look at security in Oracle Business Intelligence. You might need to perform other tasks relating to security in your system, such as enabling Secure Sockets Layer (SSL) communication between components or connecting your system to Single Sign-On server, for which you should consult the product documentation that comes with Oracle Business Intelligence.

For now, let's move on to our next topic: creating published reports using Oracle BI Publisher.

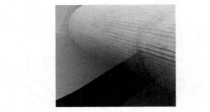

CHAPTER
9

Creating Published Reports

n Chapter 6, we looked at creating analyses and dashboards using Oracle Business Intelligence. Reports created in this way are designed to be used by data analysts who wish to analyze, in a web-based online environment, data in the form of tables, pivot tables, graphs, and charts, typically published in the form of dashboards accessed through a web browser.

But suppose that instead of accessing reports through a browser, you wish to publish them in PDF, Microsoft Excel, or other formats and send them out to users via e-mail or other channels. Suppose you want to have complete control over the layout, including images, logos, and other content in your report, or add paragraphs of text to give some context to your numbers. For this sort of reporting requirement, Oracle Business Intelligence includes a tool called Oracle BI Publisher, which allows you to create print-quality, distributed reports aimed at consumers of data rather than data analysts.

In this chapter, we will look at Oracle BI Publisher and understand what features it provides, how you develop reports using it, and why you would want to use it on a project. We will look at the concept of BI Publisher data models and the range of data sources they support, and we'll look at how reports are created and then delivered via email and other channels as well as through a dashboard.

Let's start though by taking a look at what Oracle BI Publisher actually does.

Introduction to Oracle BI Publisher

Oracle BI Publisher is used to author and then publish print-quality reports from a number of data sources. BI Publisher is integrated with Oracle Business Intelligence, and is also available for use as a stand-alone tool or integrated into products such as Oracle E-Business Suite and Oracle PeopleSoft. You can also integrate the "engine" within BI Publisher with your own applications created using tools such as Oracle JDeveloper and Oracle Application Server.

In the context of Oracle Business Intelligence, BI Publisher is generally used to create highly formatted reports, using data sourced from both the Oracle BI Repository and other data sources. The reports are then distributed to users via e-mail and other channels. BI Publisher complements the more "structured," data analysis–style reports created using Oracle Answers by providing a means to add blocks of text, images, and other content to reports, and to create reports in the form of letters, brochures, and other print-style output.

ORACLE CUST

ORACLE

Eato
for E
Worl

Customer Profi

Vision Operations
5645 Main Street
Jacksonville, FL 32209-1234
US

Dear Sirs/Madam,

According to our records as of Thur

CORPORATE

Eaton Brazil
Valinhos, Brazil

Your CAD balance is 31,500.00 ma

Industry
Industrial Manuf
Geographies
LAD
Oracle Products
- Enterprise Edi
- Oracle Financ
- Oracle Manufa
- Oracle Human
Management Sy
- Procurement
- iSupplier Port
- Purchasing Int
Key Benefits
- Integrated ERP
result in a comp
information base
- Model ERP im
serves as a ben
plants
- Streamlined p
process reduces
time and costs
- E-commerce Web site
provides reseller network with
quick, inexpensive access to
products
- Online storefront expedites
service to specialty automotive
manufacturers via seamless
integration with ERP and CRM
applications
Improved communication with
headquarters and quality of
information supports significant
export business

Your USD balance is 3,365,647.81

Invoice Number	Date
502444	Dec 6, 2003
502445	Dec 6, 2003

Invoice Number	Date
10019903	Nov 18, 2003
10020178	Nov 20, 2003
10020219	Nov 21, 2003
502394	Nov 22, 2003
10020280	Nov 24, 2003
10020310	Nov 25, 2003
10020319	Nov 26, 2003
234	Dec 2, 2003

computer," explained Oswaldo Luiz Agostinho, IT manager for the transmissions division at Eaton Brazil. "We needed to improve data integration across functions and our financial management capabilities. We researched packaged ERP applications available."

High-Level Project Goals
- Consolidate data from ERP applications and external systems
- Streamline business processes to improve operational efficiencies

- Implement robust and comprehensive financial application
- Transition from proprietary mainframe to flexible, integrated environment

Why Oracle?
"In addition to Oracle Financials, Oracle suggested that we consider a manufacturing system and showed us how we could have a completely integrated ERP environment based on a flexible, internet-based

Private and Confidential

W-2 Wage and Tax Statement 2010

a Employee's social security number: 888-88-8888
OMB No. 1545-0008

b Employer identification number (EIN): 00-5763965

c Employer's name, address, and ZIP code:
ABC Corporation
8356 Main Street
Suite A
Chicago, IL 85439

d Control number: 000008953 JRM

e Employee's first name and initial / Last name:
Jane Smith
8943 Elm Street
Naperville, IL 85433

1	Wages, tips, other compensation	$50,000.00
2	Federal income tax withheld	$7,000.00
3	Social security wages	$50,000.00
4	Social security tax withheld	$3,000.00
5	Medicare wages and tips	$50,000.00
6	Medicare tax withheld	$700.00
7	Social security tips	
8	Allocated tips	
9	Advance EIC payment	$1,000.00
10	Dependent care benefits	
11	Nonqualified plans	
12a C		$8.00
12b D		$90.00
12c V		$4,000.00

15 State	16 State wages, tips, etc.	17 State income tax	18 Local wages, tips, etc.	19 Local income tax	20 Locality name
IL 01-656239 1	$50,000.00	$1,500.00	$50,000.00	$700.00	Naperville

Copy B—To Be Filed With Employee's FEDERAL Tax Return.
This information is being furnished to the Internal Revenue Service.

Department of the Treasury—Internal Revenue Service

In addition to creating print-quality reports typically distributed via e-mail, BI Publisher also has the ability to create online, dashboard-style reports with a very similar look and feel to the analyses created within Oracle BI dashboards. In fact, since the 11*g* release of Oracle BI Publisher, reports created with this tool use the same graphing engine used within regular BI analyses, allowing you to seamlessly integrate BI Publisher reports within regular dashboards. BI Publisher, in this context, gives you the extra capability to access data sources outside of the

Oracle BI Repository, a feature that is useful, for example, if you want to access data from a transactional database that is not suitable for mapping into a logical dimensional model.

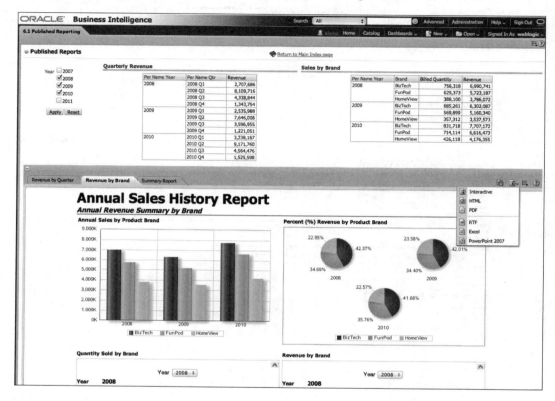

Creating reports in BI Publisher typically can be helpful when you need more control over the layout of a report, or you wish to, for example, create a single report definition and "burst" the report so that individual pages are sent to managers within the company. As you will see in a moment, though, BI Publisher also comes with its own authoring environment and means of accessing data sources, which may make it more appropriate than the regular analysis editor in Oracle BI for certain types of reports.

Oracle BI Publisher Data Model Editor

A key difference between reports created using Oracle BI Publisher and those created using the analysis editor in Oracle Business Intelligence is that you use a separate Data Model Editor to prepare and format data, which has access to a range of data source types, including:

- The Oracle BI Repository
- The output of Oracle BI analyses
- SQL queries
- MDX queries

- XML from web services
- Microsoft Excel files
- LDAP queries
- XML over HTTP
- ADF view objects

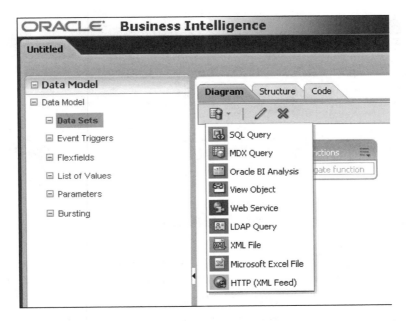

Using the Data Model Editor, you select from a range of data source types and then construct queries to return data for your report. Data from different sources can be combined, for example, when they share common data items, allowing you to combine transactional data from an Oracle database with lookup data from a Microsoft Excel spreadsheet. All data returned from these sources is converted internally by BI Publisher into XML documents, which are then rendered in combination with a template to create the required report output.

Oracle BI Publisher Online Layout Editor

Once you have created a suitable data model for your report, the BI Publisher Online Layout Editor gives you a Microsoft Office–style authoring environment for laying out your report elements. Using a familiar ribbon-style toolbar, you can select from data items to add to your template, select from a range of report objects, such as tables, pivot tables, charts, and gauges, and add paragraphs of text and images.

As such, the Online Layout Editor, shown next, is particularly suited to users who wish to lay out reports in the form of documents, using an environment similar to the office productivity tools that they use daily.

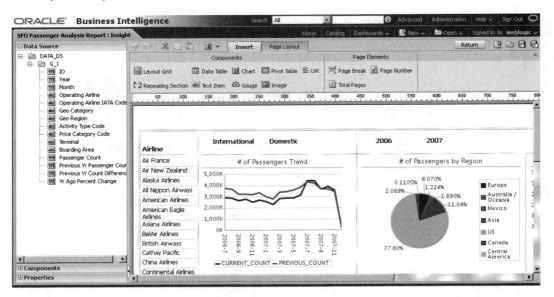

In addition to creating templates using the Online Layout Editor, you can also author templates in Rich Text Format (RTF), Microsoft Excel, and Adobe PDF format, each of which gives you additional options in terms of programmability, control over the output format, and ability to use predefined forms such as those provided by government agencies.

How Does Oracle BI Publisher Generate Reports?

Under the covers, BI Publisher combines data extracted from report data sources and combines it, at runtime, with a report template to provide report output in the form of PDFs, Excel spreadsheets, and dynamic HTML. Figure 9-1 shows how source data, templates, and optional translation files are brought together by the BI Publisher engine to produce report output in many formats.

Templates take the data items provided by a data model and arrange them, in the form of tables, pivot tables, graphs, and free-form text, into a report layout. Developers can create more than one template for each data model, giving you the ability to define a single data query and produce several report outputs based on it, for different types of report consumers and even in different languages.

Oracle BI Publisher is based on an Oracle product originally called Oracle XML Publisher, which was so named because the reporting engine within the product converted all data sources to XML before rendering in the form of a report. You will see these XML underpinnings when you create data models and work with your data, and these roots in XML data also make it easy for BI Publisher to create reports against XML, web service, and other data sources created from middleware applications.

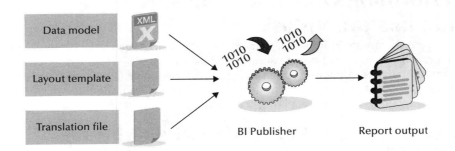

FIGURE 9-1.   *BI Publisher data flow*

Oracle BI Publisher Features Covered in This Chapter

Oracle BI Publisher is a fully featured reporting and publishing tool, and would itself warrant a whole book to cover all of its features. As we have only one chapter to cover its features, we will instead concentrate on the features most relevant to Oracle Business Intelligence developers:

- Creating data models against Oracle BI Repository, Oracle BI Answers, SQL query, and file data sources
- Creating templates using the Online Layout Editor, to create dashboard and printed-style reports
- Analyzing data using the Interactive Viewer, either stand-alone or with reports embedded in dashboards
- Setting up schedules to distribute reports to users in PDF, and other formats

For other uses of Oracle BI Publisher, you might want to consult the product documentation on the Oracle Technology Network web site (http://otn.oracle.com). Topics that we will not cover in this chapter include:

- Creating data models based on ADF view objects, MDX, XML over HTTP, web service, or other data sources
- Creating RTF, Microsoft Excel, and Adobe PDF templates
- Creating style templates and subtemplates for use with RTF templates
- Programmatically accessing BI Publisher web services
- Bursting reports, producing letters, and producing other print-style outputs

Before we cover the former list of topics, let's look at accessing BI Publisher from your web browser and performing some initial administration tasks.

Performing Oracle BI Publisher Administration Tasks

Although you can use BI Publisher immediately after installing Oracle Business Intelligence, you will probably want to set up some additional data sources, define printers for report output, and perform some other administration tasks before you get too involved in report definition. Even before that, though, you are probably wondering where BI Publisher is on the Oracle Business Intelligence Home page, as it's not mentioned anywhere by name.

Accessing Oracle BI Publisher for the First Time

Oracle BI Publisher is in fact referred to as "Published Reports" on the Oracle Business Intelligence Home page. Individual elements of BI Publisher functionality are listed as tasks on the Home page on the left-hand side, and are also available on the application menu that is shown in the common header area of the Home page.

To start using BI Publisher functionality, open a web browser and log into the Oracle Business Intelligence Home page (http://[*server_name*]:9704/analytics, for example). The first place to look for links to BI Publisher functionality is in the Create section on the left-hand side. Under the Published Reporting heading, there are three links, Report, Report Job, and More. Clicking More provides three additional links, Data Model, Style Template, and Sub Template.

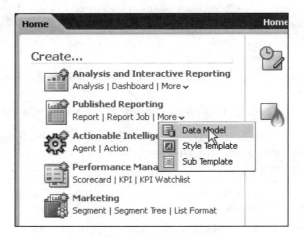

Below the Create section is the Browse/Manage section, where you will see a link to browse My Reports. BI Publisher reports, when BI Publisher is integrated with Oracle Business Intelligence, are stored in the same Oracle BI Presentation catalog in which analyses and other regular BI content are stored, and you can assign permissions to them, archive them, and unarchive them in the same way as any other BI object.

NOTE
For stand-alone installations of BI Publisher, report definitions are stored in a separate Oracle BI Publisher Repository, though you can import these into the Oracle BI Presentation catalog later on, if you want to.

Similar to the Create links, you can also access BI Publisher functionality from the New menu at the top of each screen. When you click the New menu, you will see the same five options as menu items, grouped under the Published Reporting heading.

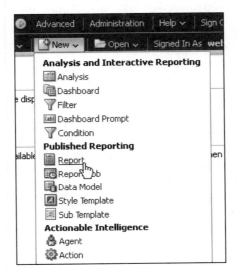

Administration of BI Publisher is performed using a separate web page on the Oracle Business Intelligence web site. To access this web page, first click the Administration link at the top of the Home page in the common header area, and then click Manage BI Publisher in the list of links on the main Presentation Services Administration screen.

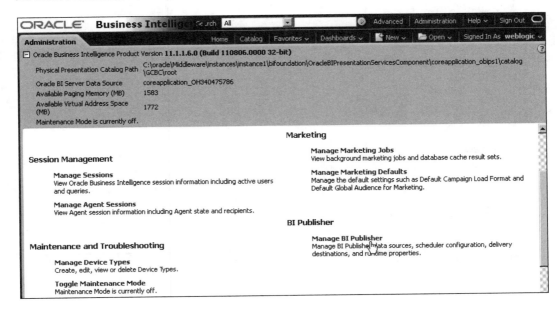

These are the main ways in which you can access BI Publisher functionality from within the Oracle Business Intelligence web site. But BI Publisher also has its own dedicated Home page, which is usually used when running BI Publisher as a stand-alone tool but can also be useful when you are working primarily with BI Publisher reports that you do not intend to integrate in dashboards.

Accessing the Oracle BI Publisher Stand-alone Home Page

The BI Publisher Home page can be accessed through its own URL, which is typically http://[server_name]:9704/xmlpserver. When you navigate to this web page, type in the administrator username and password (which are set during installation and, when installed alongside Oracle Business Intelligence, are the same administration credentials you have been using previously). Once logged in, you will see the BI Publisher Enterprise Home page, as shown in Figure 9-2.

If you are using BI Publisher integrated with Oracle Business Intelligence, you do not usually need to access this Home page, as all the functionality it provides is already available to you within Oracle Business Intelligence. However, if your organization has licensed only BI Publisher and you have installed it as a stand-alone tool, this web page provides you with the subset of functionality that is provided by BI Publisher. It is similar to the Oracle Business Intelligence Home page insofar as you can create new reports, data models, and report jobs and access your reports from the catalog (or BI Publisher Repository if installed stand-alone).

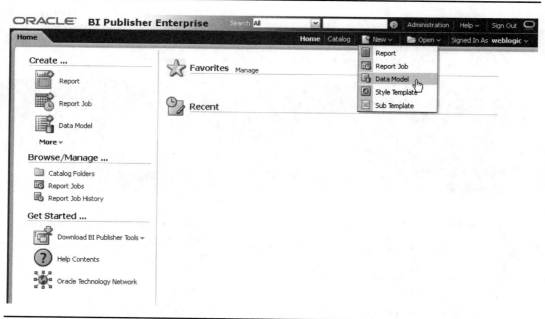

FIGURE 9-2. *BI Publisher Enterprise Home page*

Setting Up Data Sources

Out of the box, Oracle BI Publisher can access two data sources when integrated with Oracle Business Intelligence:

- The Oracle BI Repository, through a JDBC connection that is automatically set up to the Oracle BI Server.
- The logical SQL from an Oracle BI analysis held in your Presentation Services catalog. This then is passed through the above JDBC connection to the BI Server, giving you the ability to reuse queries contained in existing analyses as your data model definition.

As a primary reason to use BI Publisher is to access data sources in addition to the preceding two predefined sources, you are typically going to need to define these data sources using the BI Publisher Administration screen before you create any data models.

Example: Defining SQL Data Sources

To give you an example of defining data sources, consider a situation where you want to create an SQL data source that connects to the GCBC_SALES schema in an Oracle Database, as provided with the sample data set that accompanies this book. After you define this data source, you can then create data sets that use this data source either by typing SQL queries in directly or by creating SQL queries using the graphical Query Builder (which we will look at later in this chapter).

To define an SQL data source against a relational database such as Oracle Database, follow these steps:

1. Log into the Oracle Business Intelligence web site using a user account with administration privileges.

2. At the top of the Oracle Business Intelligence Home page, click the Administration link. When the Administration screen is displayed, click the Manage BI Publisher link.

3. The BI Publisher Administration screen will then be displayed, shown next. Under the Data Sources heading in the top left of the screen, you will see links to create data sources of various types. To create the new SQL data source using a JDBC connection, click the JDBC Connection link.

4. A new screen that initially shows preconfigured C data sources will then be displayed. With the JDBC tab selected, click the Add Data Source button to start creating your new data source.

5. On the Add Data Source screen, shown next, enter the following details to create a JDBC data source that connects to the GCBC_SALES schema on an Oracle Database 11*g* database:

   Data Source Name: GCBC Sales
   Driver Type: Oracle 11g
   Database Driver Class: oracle.jdbc.OracleDriver
   Connection String: jdbc:oracle:thin:@localhost:1521:orcl
   Username: gcbc_sales
   Password: *password*

   Adjust these values to connect to other databases. Once complete, click the Test Connection button to test the connection, and then click Apply to save your data source definition.

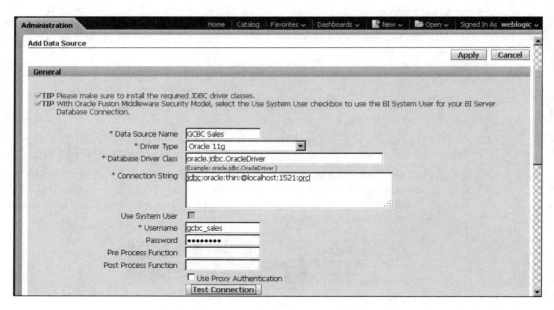

6. You can also define for this connection a backup data source that is used when the primary connection is unavailable. To do this, on the same screen, scroll down until you see the Backup Data Source section. Select the Use Backup Data Source check box to enable this feature, and then enter the connection string, username, and password for the

same database type and driver class. Test the connection as before and once confirmed as working correctly, press the Apply button to save the backup data source connection. BI Publisher will then attempt to use these connection details if the primary data source is not available.

Defining File Data Sources

Creating data sources that connect to Microsoft Excel spreadsheets is often useful to allow report developers to include reference data, or other departmental data that is not held in a database. To enable access to data sources such as these, you need to set up a file data source that points to the file system directory in which the spreadsheets are held; later, when you create a data model for your report, you connect to this directory and then select the spreadsheet that you need.

To create a file data source, follow these steps:

1. As with an SQL data source, log into the Oracle Business Intelligence web site, click the Administration link at the top of the Home page, and then click Manage BI Publisher to open the BI Publisher Administration screen.

2. In the top-left corner of the screen, select File under the Data Sources heading.

3. On the Data Sources screen, click the File tab and then click the Add Data Source button to start defining the new data source.

4. On the Add Data Source screen, type in the details of the data source; for example:

   Data Source Name: GCBC Files
   Full Path of Top-Level Directory: c:\Files

   The top-level directory you specify should be the one that contains the Microsoft Excel spreadsheet you wish to access when creating your report. Later on, when you create the report data model, you will specify this data source and then select the actual file that you wish to use as the provider of data for your report.

5. Click Apply and then click Return to save your data source definition and return to the Data Source Administration screen.

Setting Up Roles and Permissions

You may have noticed, when defining your data sources, that each data source definition has a section underneath it for definition permissions to use the data source. By default, any new data source that you create cannot be accessed by anyone until you grant access to application roles through the BI Publisher Administration screen.

You can grant access to data sources either when defining the data source, or through a separate link on the administration page for managing roles and permissions.

For example, when creating the GCBC Files file data source in the previous example, at the bottom of the data source definition page is a section headed Security. To grant access to this data source to all roles, select all roles from the Available Roles list and click the Move All button to move them to the Allowed Roles area.

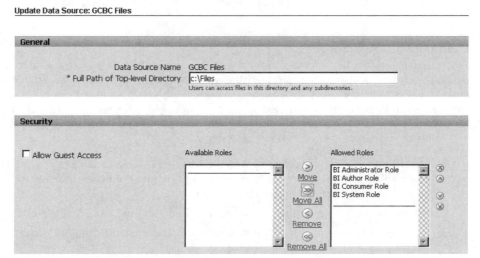

Selecting Roles that can Access a Data Source

Note that application roles and which users and LDAP groups they have been granted to are defined in Fusion Middleware Control rather than in the BI Publisher Administration screen, if you are using BI Publisher in the default Oracle Fusion Middleware security mode.

In addition to defining data source permissions within the data source definition, you can also configure these permissions using the Roles and Permissions link under the Security Center heading on the BI Publisher Administration screen. Using this approach allows you to select a particular application role and then assign data source access to it, rather than starting with the data source and then defining which roles can access it.

To use this method, follow these steps:

1. On the Oracle BI Publisher Administration screen, click the Roles And Permissions link under the Security Center heading.

2. On the Security Center screen, with the Roles and Permissions tab selected, locate the application role that you wish to grant data source access to, and click the Add Data Sources icon next to the role name.

3. A screen is displayed that groups data sources already defined in the system by type (for example, Database Connections, File Directories, and so on). Using the Move and Move All buttons, select those data sources to which you wish to grant access to the role, and then click Apply to save your selection.

Setting Up Printers, E-mail Servers, and Other Delivery Options

If you want to distribute BI Publisher reports to printers, e-mail accounts, fax machines, or other delivery channels, you can use the BI Publisher Administration screen to define these settings.

Example: Defining Print Servers for Oracle BI Publisher

Printers that are accessed by BI Publisher are accessed through the Internet Printing Protocol (IPP), which defines a connection to a print server that provides access to one or more printers. This means that for BI Publisher to access a printer on a Unix server, you need to install and configure Common Unix Printing Services (CUPS), while on a Microsoft Windows–based server, you need to configure Internet Information Services (IIS) and Windows Print Server for IPP. To perform these configurations, consult the *Oracle Fusion Middleware Administrator's Guide for Oracle Business Intelligence Publisher* manual on the Oracle Technology Network web site (http://otn.oracle.com).

Once you have set up IPP for your server, to define a print server for BI Publisher output to be sent to, follow these steps:

1. On the BI Publisher Administration screen, click the Printer link under the Delivery heading.

2. On the Delivery screen, with the Printer tab selected, click the Add Server button.

3. In the Add Server dialog box, enter the server name, the URI (the IPP address of the print server), the filter, and any other connection details (such as username and password) required to access the print server.

Later on, when you choose to use this print server as a delivery destination, you can specify settings such as the particular printer that will be used, the printer output tray, and any other settings that are provided by the particular print server.

Example: Defining E-mail Servers for Oracle BI Publisher

Similar to the procedure for defining printers and print servers for BI Publisher, if you want to distribute BI Publisher report output to e-mail addresses, you have to first define an e-mail server within the BI Publisher Administration screen options, which it then uses to send out the e-mails.

To define an e-mail server for use with BI Publisher, follow these steps:

1. On the BI Publisher Administration screen, click the Email link under the Delivery heading.

2. On the Delivery screen, with the Email tab selected, click the Add Server button.

3. On the Add Server screen, enter the details of the server name, host, port, username, and password, and select whether or not the e-mail server needs a secure connection.

Later on, when you want to schedule a report for delivery via e-mail, you will be able to specify the actual e-mail addresses to which the reports are delivered, or you can use the bursting feature to derive these details through a database query.

Now that you have looked at basic administration tasks for BI Publisher, let's get on with creating a report, starting with defining the report's data model.

Creating the Data Model

Reports in Oracle BI Publisher are made up of two main components: the data model that defines the data set used by the report, and the report template that specifies how the report is laid out. In this section, we will look at how data models are put together. We will use data sourced from an Oracle database and from a Microsoft Excel spreadsheet, to show how data can be integrated from multiple sources.

Understanding the Data Model and the Data Model Editor

Every BI Publisher report requires an associated data model, which you select when first defining the report. The data model defines the data sources that provide data for the report and is used by BI Publisher to create a single XML document containing the report's data, which is then combined with a template to produce the report output.

Data models are made up of one or more data sets, along with other details such as parameters and bursting details. A data set is a query to a data source type, such as an SQL query to a database or an MDX query to an OLAP server. When the report is run, each of these data sets is queried to return the data used by the report.

A data model can actually contain more than one data set, and you can either concatenate these data sets or join them together using a common field or element. Figure 9-3 shows a typical data model for a report that uses several data sets, allowing you to create a report that brings together data from disparate sources, not just ones mapped into the Oracle BI Repository.

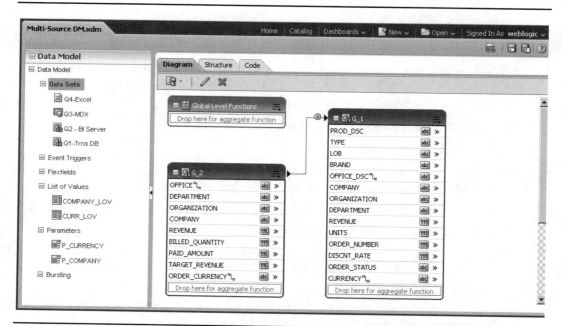

FIGURE 9-3. *A sample BI Publisher data model*

As shown on the left-hand side in Figure 9-3, BI Publisher data models are actually made up of several elements:

- **Data sets** There can be one or more data sets, with results either concatenated or joined together.

- **Event triggers** These are used to run PL/SQL code either before or after the report runs, to populate, for example, a table of data required for the report.

- **Flexfields** These are used when querying Oracle E-Business Suite application data.

- **Parameters** These are used in combination with data sets to return, for example, only data for a particular region or product. Parameters can be linked to presentation variables when embedding BI Publisher reports in dashboards.

- **Lists of values** These are used with parameters to provide menus of products or departments (for example, when users run reports onscreen).

- **Bursting** This is used when splitting a single report into separate elements, which are then sent to different delivery destinations but are based off of a single report execution.

Data models are defined to be reusable across different reports. They are stored alongside template definitions in the Presentation Services catalog when you use BI Publisher integrated with Oracle Business Intelligence.

Creating a Data Model Using a Single Data Source

Consider a situation where you wish to create a report against tables in the GCBC_SALES schema that is included as part of the sample data for this book. Using BI Publisher, you could create the data model for this report in one of three ways:

- You could create an analysis using data in this schema, and then use the analysis as a data source for a BI Publisher data model data set.

- You could create a data set using a logical SQL query against the Oracle BI Repository data model.

- You could connect to the schema directly.

We will use the last of these three options, which involves more steps but illustrates for you more of the process required to create a data model. Creating a data set against the Oracle BI Repository is a very similar process in that you create an SQL query to retrieve your data, instead using the Oracle BI Repository as your database source; however queries to this data source can be considerably simplified as you do not need to include aggregation functions (SUM, AVG, etc.) or grouping or ordering (GROUP BY, ORDER BY) clauses as the Oracle BI Server automatically adds these for you based on column definitions in the Oracle BI Repository's semantic model.

Example: Defining a Data Model Data Set Using an SQL Query Data Source

To create a data model that contains a single data set based on an Oracle Database data source, follow these steps:

1. Log into the Oracle Business Intelligence Home Page using the credentials of a user who has access to the Oracle BI EE data source (see the previous sections on data sources, and Roles and Permissions for details on how to create a data source and then assign permissions to use it to application roles).

2. From the application menu, select New | Data Model. The Data Model Editor will then be displayed, providing an overview of the data model definition.

3. The Properties panel for the data model allows you to define, among other data model–wide settings, a default data source that becomes the initial setting for all subsequent data sets in this data model. This default data source should also be used if you wish to use event triggers, as it defines the database schema that the triggers will look to when importing functions for the events.

   Set the default data source, in this instance, to GCBC Sales, and leave the rest of the settings at their default value.

4. To create a data set using data from this data source, click the Data Sets item in the navigation tree menu on the left-hand side of the page to display a set of three tabs on the right-hand side. With the Diagram tab selected, click the New Data Set button and select SQL Query from the list of data source types.

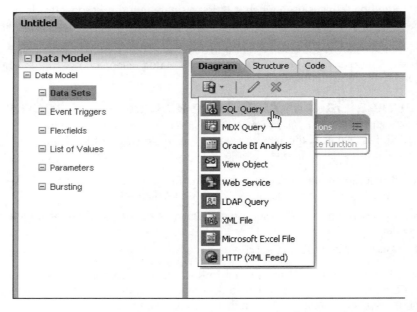

5. In the Create Data Set – SQL dialog box, type in a name for the data set (for example, Regional Sales Data), ensure that GCBC Sales is the selected data source, and then click the Query Builder button.

6. In the Query Builder dialog box, to construct the data set for your query, first ensure that the correct schema is selected from the Schema drop-down menu on the left-hand side, with catalogs corresponding to subject areas in the Oracle BI Repository.

7. Click the tables on the left-hand side of the Query Builder dialog box that you wish to add to the data set, and then, once they appear in the main dialog box canvas, select the check boxes next to individual columns to include them in the data set.

For example, to report on store and region sales, by month, measured by sale amount and sale amount target, select the following tables and columns for your data set:

STORES_RAGGED.REGION_NAME
STORES_RAGGED.STORE_NAME
TIMES.MONTH_DESC
SALES.FCAST_SAL_AMT
SALES.TARGET_SAL_AMT

8. If you are creating a data set using data sourced from a regular relational database (as opposed to the Oracle Business Intelligence repository), you have to define joins between the tables in your data set. To do this, you first click the white box to the right of the dimension table key column, and then click the corresponding fact table column to create the join. Later on, you can refine this join to make it an outer join, for example.

   Therefore, to create joins between the STORES_RAGGED and TIMES dimension tables and the SALES fact table, click the empty box to the right of the following dimension columns in the diagram, and then click the corresponding fact table columns, to create joins between the columns:

   STORES_RAGGED.STORE_PK = SALES.STORE_ID
   TIMES.MONTH_YYYYMM = SALES.MONTH_YYYYMM

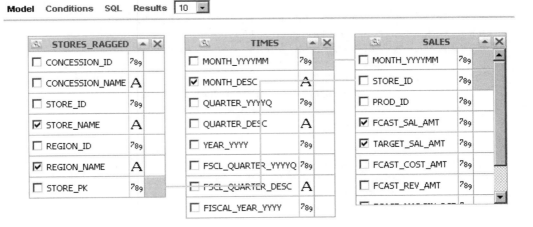

If you create your data set with data from Oracle Business Intelligence, you do not need to create these joins, as the BI Server, using join metadata in the repository, will join the tables for you when you run your query.

9. Similarly, if you source your data set from a relational database other than Oracle Business Intelligence, you will need to add GROUP BY clauses and aggregation functions to your query, as appropriate. This is not necessary if an Oracle BI Repository is your data source, as the BI Server will automatically apply GROUP BY clauses to dimension attribute columns and apply the default aggregation type to measure columns.

To add these items, click the Conditions link at the top of the right-hand panel, and then use the Function drop-down lists to select SUM for the measure columns—in this case, FCAST_SAL_AMT and TARGET_SAL_AMT.

Then, select the Group By check box for the MONTH_DESC, STORE_NAME, and REGION_NAME columns so that each column in the list has either an aggregation function or a GROUP BY applied.

	Column	Alias	Object	Condition	Sort Type	Sort Order	Show	Function	Group By	Delete
ⓐ ⓥ	MONTH_DESC	MONTH_DESC	TIMES		ASC ▾		☑	▾	☑	🗑
ⓐ ⓥ	STORE_NAME	STORE_NAME	STORES_RAGGED		ASC ▾		☑	▾	☑	🗑
ⓐ ⓥ	REGION_NAME	REGION_NAME	STORES_RAGGED		ASC ▾		☑	▾	☑	🗑
ⓐ ⓥ	FCAST_SAL_AMT	FCAST_SAL_AMT	SALES		ASC ▾		☑	SUM ▾	☐	🗑
ⓐ ⓥ	TARGET_SAL_AMT	TARGET_SAL_AMT	SALES		ASC ▾		☑	SUM ▾	☐	🗑

Model Conditions SQL Results 10 ▾ ... Save Cancel

10. Once you have made your column and table selection, click the Results link at the top of the Query Builder dialog box to view the results of the selection.

11. Click the Save button in the top-right corner of the Query Builder dialog box to save the query and return to the Create Data Set – SQL dialog box. Click OK to close this dialog box and return to the Data Model page.

Example: Adding Parameters and Lists of Values to a Data Model   You can also define parameters within a data model, which are then referenced in the data set queries to restrict the data sent back to BI Publisher when you run a report. To make it easier for users to select a parameter value to use with a report, you can also define lists of values that use separate queries to return values for a particular column, which are then used to provide drop-down lists for use with parameters when displaying a report on the screen.

In the following example, we will extend the data model definition created in the previous steps to add a parameter and associated list of values.

1. Within the Data Model Editor, locate and then select the data set that you just created, and make sure the Diagram tab on the panel on the left-hand side has been selected. A diagram of the data sets in your data model will be displayed, with the data set you created in the previous example normally named "G_1." With this data set selected, , hover your mouse cursor over the View Actions menu button and select the Edit Data Set menu item.

2. In the Edit Data Set dialog box that is then displayed, click the Query Builder button.

3. In the Query Builder dialog box that is displayed next, with the Model tab selected, click the Conditions tab, and enter the following condition into the Condition field for the table row that contains the Month column.

   = :MONTH_YEAR

   Click Save to close the Query Builder dialog, then press OK to close the Create Data Set dialog. As you have just saved a data set definition that uses a condition (in SQL terms, a "bind parameter") you will then be prompted to take this bind parameter and use it to create a parameter for your data model. Click OK to automatically create this parameter;

if you choose not to do it now, or you wish to create additional parameters; you can do so later on using the Data Model Editor.

To add a default value for this parameter or change any other of its settings, locate the Parameters folder in the left-hand side menu in the Data Model Editor, expand the folder and then click on the parameter that you just created to show the Parameter details on the right-hand side of the editor. Type a default value into the Default Value field (for example, OCT-2010), and make any other configuration changes that you require at this stage.

4. You can also define a list of values to accompany the parameter, which makes it easier for users to select parameter values when viewing the report online.

To create a list of values to associate with this parameter, locate the List Of Values folder in the same left-hand menu in the Data Model Editor and click on it. The Data Model Editor will then display a two-part list of values editor on the right-hand side of the page, which lists existing lists of values for this data model on the top half of the page and details of each selected one underneath.

To create a new list of values, press the Create New List Of Values button in the List Of Values panel in the top half of the screen and then configure its details, using, for example, the following settings suitable for use with the Month parameter created previously:

Name: Months_Year_LOV
Type: SQL Query
Data Source: GCBC Sales

Then, in the bottom section (you may need to move up the dividing bar to make more of this section visible), type in the following SQL query (or use the Query Builder to create the same query):

```
select      "TIMES"."MONTH_DESC" as "MONTH_DESC"
from        "GCBC_SALES"."TIMES" "TIMES"
group by "TIMES"."MONTH_DESC"
```

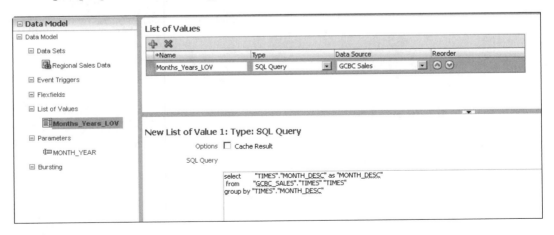

5. Lists of values are only displayed for a parameter when the parameter's "Parameter Type" setting is set to "Menu." To configure this setting for the parameter you created a moment ago, using the Data Model Editor, click back to the Parameter folder in the left-hand menu and locate your parameter within it; click on it to open it for editing, and then within the parameter settings that are then displayed for it on the right-hand side of the screen, change its Parameter Type to Menu. Then, using the bottom section of the page under the main parameter definition, locate the List of Values drop-down menu and select the list of values that you just created.

The data set that you created earlier typically inherits its column names from the SQL query used to define the data set, for example STORE_NAME. Report users will typically prefer these column names to be more readable and business-friendly, and you can define these for each column (referred to as "Display Names") using the Data Model Editor. To do so, navigate to the Data Sets folder in the menu on the left-hand side of the Data Model Editor, expand it to locate your data set, and click on it so that it is then displayed on the right-hand side along with the other data sets in your data model. With the data sets displayed, click on the Structure tab and then use the Display Name field for each column to provide more meaningful names; for example, Store Name instead of STORE_NAME, and Amount Sold instead of FCAST_SAL_AMT.

6. Finally, click Save, give the data model a name (for example, "Regional Data Model"), and then click OK to return to the main Data Model screen.

Example: Adding Calculations   You can also use the Data Model Editor to add additional columns to your data set, based on simple expressions. For example, you can create a column called VARIANCE that is based on the expression TARGET_SAL_AMT – FCAST_SAL_AMT, and BI Publisher will add this additional column to your data set when retrieving your data.

To create a calculation like this, follow these steps:

1. With the data set displayed in the Data Model Editor, hover your mouse pointer over the View Actions button on the data set and select Add Element By Expression.

2. In the Add Element by Expression – G_1 dialog box, enter the following details to define the expression:

   Name: VARIANCE
   Alias: VARIANCE
   Display Name: Variance
   Data Type: Integer
   Expression: G_1.TARGET_SAL_AMT - G_1.FCAST_SAL_AMT

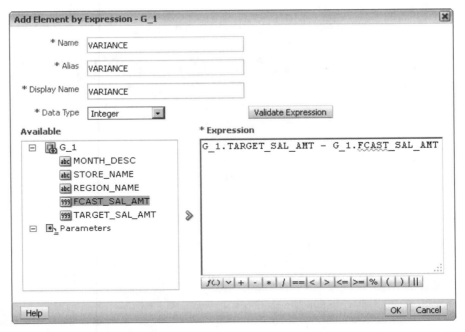

3. Once complete, click OK to close the dialog box. You will then see the new data element in the data set, with an icon to indicate that it is based on an expression (formula).

Example: Creating the XML Sample Data Set   The Online Layout Editor that you will use to design your report layout uses a subset of your source data to help you lay out the tables, charts, gauges, and other objects in your report. To obtain this sample set of data, you need to create an XML sample data set before you finish work on your data model.

Before you can create this sample data set, make sure you have first saved your data model. Then, follow these steps to create the sample XML data:

1. With the data model open for editing, click the Get XML Output button in the top right-hand side of the screen.

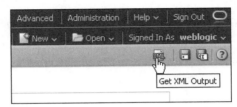

2. The Data Model Editor will then replace the existing page with one for showing details of your data set. At the top of the page are settings for the number of rows of sample XML data to generate, and if you have defined a parameter for the data set, fields to enter or select parameter values before generating the data. As this data set uses a month parameter, enter a value for it into the parameter field (for example, OCT-2010) and then click the Run button to create a sample set of XML data.

Check that all of the columns that you expected to be in the sample are present, and when you are finished, select Save As Sample Data from the menu to the right of the Return button.

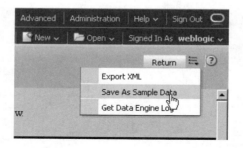

3. Save the data model to the catalog again, to now include the sample XML data in the data model definition.

Defining Data Sets Using Oracle BI Analyses Sources

In addition to defining data sets against relational database data sources or the Oracle BI Repository, you can also define data models that source their data from an Oracle BI analysis. When you run a report using an analysis as a data source, the analysis is executed first, and then it passes its results back to BI Publisher, which then renders it internally as XML and uses it to provide data for a template.

For example, suppose you have an analysis that displays product, date, and store data in a number of formats, but you want to take this same data set and use it to produce a formatted store report that is sent by e-mail to store managers. To create a data set against such a data source, follow these steps:

1. Log into the Oracle Business Intelligence web site and create a new data model as normal (New | Data Model).

2. Click the Data Sets item on the left-hand side of the page, and then select New Data Set | Oracle BI Analysis on the right-hand side.

3. In the Create Data Set – Oracle BI Analysis dialog box, enter a name for the data set (for example, Store Sales Analysis), enter a time-out value for the data retrieval (for example, 30 seconds), and then click the search button to the right of the Oracle BI Analysis field and select the analysis from the catalog.

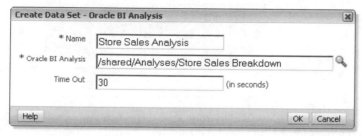

4. Save the data model, and then, as with a data set sourced from a database SQL query, click the Get XML Output button, generate some sample XML data, and then select Save As Sample Data from the drop-down menu to the right of the Return button.

5. Save the data model again, and it is now ready for use with a template.

Defining Data Sets Using Microsoft Excel Data Sources

Data for your data model can be sourced from a number of different data types, including web services, LDAP queries, MDX queries, and other sources. One of the most common non-database data sources you may want to report on, though, is Microsoft Excel.

When you create a data set based on Excel data, you can either create the data source in advance, as you did with the relational data source used previously, or upload the Excel spreadsheet at the time of creating the data set. We will use the latter approach to create a data set containing product category data.

To create a Microsoft Excel–based data set in this way, follow these steps:

1. With the Data Model Editor open, click the Data Sets menu item on the left, click the New Data Set button on the Diagram tab, and select Microsoft Excel File.

2. In the Create Data Set – Excel dialog box, enter a name for the data set (for example, Product Categories XLS).

3. The Workbook section provides two options for accessing the Excel spreadsheet. If you plan to use this Excel file across many data sets and data models, you should exit this dialog box and create a separate file data source for the file, and then return to this dialog box and select the Shared option to access it.

   If, however, you are using this spreadsheet only for this particular data set, then you can select the Local option and click the File Name link to browse, select, and then upload the spreadsheet to the BI Publisher server.

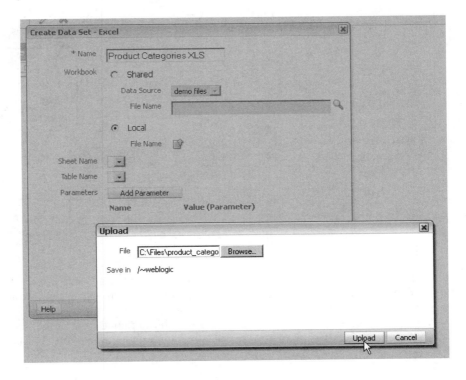

4. The Microsoft Excel file will then be uploaded to the BI Server or accessed through the data source, depending on the option you chose. Once complete, you can create your data model in the same way as you would for data sourced from a relational database.

Creating Data Models Using Multiple Data Sets

In the previous examples, each data model we created contained a single data set. You can, however, create data models with more than one data set, so that report developers can create reports that use each data set either individually or, if they wish, combined together.

Example: Concatenating Data Sets in a Single Data Model

Consider a situation where a single data model contains the following two data sets:

-   **Store Sales**   A data set, sourced from an Oracle database, that contains data on sales by product and store (for example, the GCBC_SALES database schema that comes with the sample data for this book)

-   **Customer Satisfaction**   A data set that contains data on customer satisfaction scores by store and month (taken, for example, from the GCBC_SURVEYS database schema that also comes with the sample data)

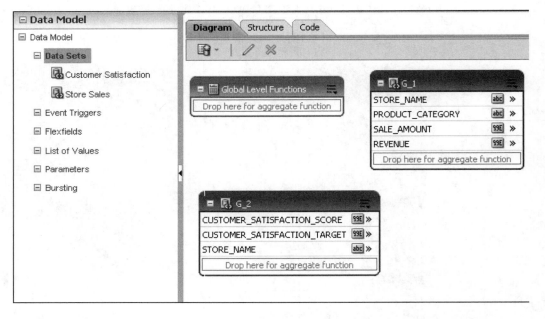

Adding the second data set just involves creating the first one, as previously detailed, and then clicking the Data Sets menu item on the left-hand side of the Data Model page and creating the second data set in the same way as the first one.

When you create a data model in this way, BI Publisher concatenates the results of the two data set queries together so that they are contained within the same internal XML document, but the results are kept separate from each other. You can see this when creating the sample XML data set for your data model. To do this, follow these steps:

1. With the Data Model Editor open and with two or more data sets added to the data model, first ensure that the data model is saved and then click the Get XML Output button.

2. On the XML output screen, click the Run button to generate the sample XML output. You will then see XML data for the first data set (typically called G_1), followed by XML data for the second data set (typically called G_2).

    In this instance, BI Publisher has queried the first data set, then the second, and concatenated the results together into a single XML document.

Now select Save as Sample Data from the drop-down menu to the right of the Return button, and then when you return to the main Data Model Editor page, save the model definition once more so that it includes this set of sample data. If you were now to use this data model to create a report definition, you would see the two data sets listed together in the Online Template Editor, like this:

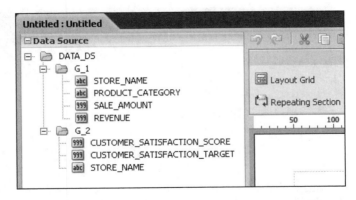

A data model configured like this can be used to create report templates that use either one or the other data set in each individual report component. If you want to include columns from both data sets in the same template component, you'll need to join the two data sets together, which we will look at next.

Example: Joining Data Sets

To reference two different data sets in the same template component, you have to join them together on a common column, or data element, in the data model. This is similar to joins between database tables, except the join takes place within BI Publisher after retrieving both sets of data from their respective source systems.

For example, you may have sales data in the GCBC_SALES Oracle database schema that we used in the previous examples, which has a table column called PRODUCTS.PROD_CAT_ID that contains IDs for product categories referenced in the data set. Descriptions of these product categories may, however, be in an Excel spreadsheet, such as the products.csv file that also comes with the sample dat. If you therefore wish to create reports that include layout components that use both data sets joined together, in this case on the product category ID that they both share, you would follow a set of steps like this:

1. In this example, the first data set is sourced from an Oracle database. To create it, select New | Data Model from the Oracle Business Intelligence web site menu, then click the Data Sets item on the left of the screen and select New Data Set | SQL Query. Create the data set using the GCBC_SALES schema and make sure that it contains a column that corresponds to the key value in the second data set (for example, PRODUCTS.PROD_CAT_ID).

2. Create the second data set (for example, from the products.csv spreadsheet). Make sure that the second data set contains the key value that is referenced in the first data set. In this example, the second data set contains a list of product category IDs and descriptions.

3. To join the two data sets together, starting with the master (less detailed) data set—in this case, the product categories data set sourced from Excel—click the double-arrow icon next to the data element name and select Create Link.

4. In the Create Link dialog box, select the corresponding element in the other data set that this element should join to; in this case, it would be the corresponding PROD_CAT_ID data element.

5. Click the OK button, and then save the data set.

6. Click the Get XML Output button and then click Run to create the sample output. You will notice that the detail-level source (in this case, sales data at the product level) is now nested inside the master data (product categories from the Excel spreadsheet). Similarly,

when you choose to create a template based on this data, you will see that the two data sets are joined and nested, and you can now create data tables, for example, that reference both data sets in the same component.

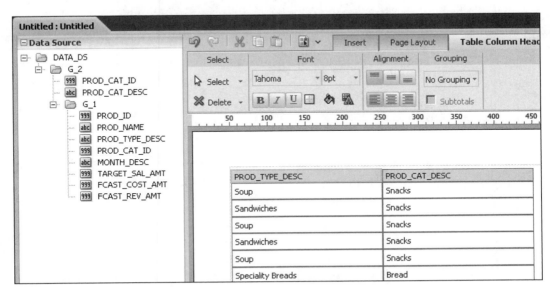

Example: Defining Data Set-Level Aggregates   In the previous example, we created a data model that contains master-level detail (product categories) from an Excel spreadsheet, and detail-level data (product sales data) from an Oracle database. The sales data contains measures for revenue, cost, and amount sold, which you can include in a data table to report on sales activity.

But what happens if we try to report on sales by product category? The next screenshot of the Online Layout Editor shows the data model and data sets that were used in the previous example ("Joining Data Sets"). When displayed in the Data Source panel of the Online Layout Editor, Sales measures from this data model are sourced from the detail-level source, and categories come from the master-level Excel spreadsheet, rather than being completely separate as with the example just before the last one ("Concatenating Data Sets in a Single Data Model").

Can you see though that metrics from the detail-level source are not being grouped (aggregated) by the data element in the master-level source, as you might normally expect them to be. Why is this?

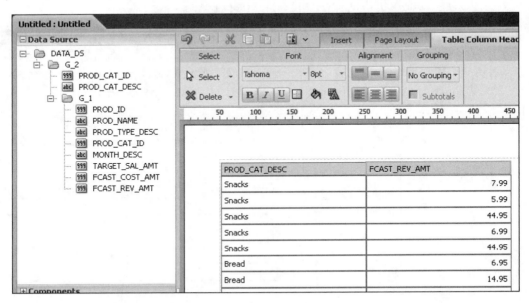

The reason for this behavior is because, in the underlying XML document created from the data model, the metrics are only grouped by the detail-level data. To group data by the detail of the master-level source, you need to create aggregates in that data set too.

To create an aggregate in a master-level data set based on one from a detail-level data set, follow these steps:

1. In this example, we have one data set that contains detail-level sales data for products, and another data set that provides a description for the product category IDs that are listed in the detail-level data set. The detail-level data set contains target sale amount, cost, and revenue metrics that we now wish to aggregate for the master-level data set.

    To aggregate these measures for the master-level data set, drag-and-drop the detail-level measure onto the Drop Here For Aggregate Function area at the bottom of the master-level data set.

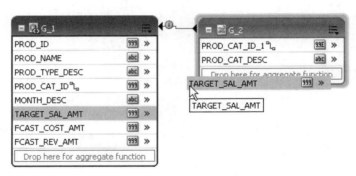

2. When you drop the measure into this area, a new measure will be added to the data set, with a system-generated name such as CS_1. Use the drop-down menu to the left of the measure to set the aggregation method (for example, Summary, for summing the measure).

3. You can also click the double-arrow icon to the right of the new measure to bring up a menu, and then select Properties to edit the properties of the new measure. Using this dialog box, you can rename the alias and display name for the new measure, change the data type, and define what happens if the measure returns a NULL value.

After saving the data model, regenerating the sample XML, and then saving it again, you can create a layout using the updated data model. Note that the master-level data set now has the aggregated measures within it, and when you add these to the layout along with the master-level data elements, your data is aggregated correctly.

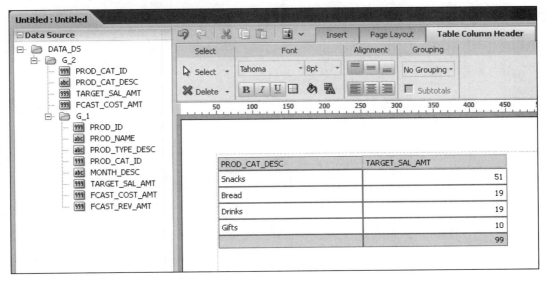

So now that we have looked at creating data models for reports, let's take a look at how layouts are created, using the Online Layout Editor.

Creating Report Layouts

Report layouts, or templates, define how data elements from the data model are arranged into a printed, electronically distributed, or onscreen report. Each layout uses a single data model, and any one report can contain one or more layouts.

BI Publisher gives you a number of ways to create layouts, including creating them using RTF (Rich Text Format) documents, Microsoft Excel spreadsheets, or Adobe PDF documents. If, however, you are creating layouts that contain BI objects such as charts, pivot tables, and gauges, the best way to create layouts is to use the Online Layout Editor, a new BI Publisher feature introduced with the 11*g* release that provides a visual layout editor in your browser with drag-and-drop functionality.

Before we look in detail at how to create dashboard-style reports and printed reports using BI Publisher and how to add new layout templates, let's take a few moments to look at the Online Layout Editor itself, and where the various features are that you can then use to create a report layout.

Introduction to the Online Layout Editor

The Online Layout Editor has three main components:

- ■ The toolbar ribbon at the top of the screen, for adding components to the template and configuring individual components
- ■ The layout canvas, below the toolbar ribbon
- ■ The "concertina" panel, on the left, that can be used to display menus for adding columns to the template, adding components such as graphs and tables in the same way as the toolbar ribbon, or configuring properties for the template such as margins and page size.

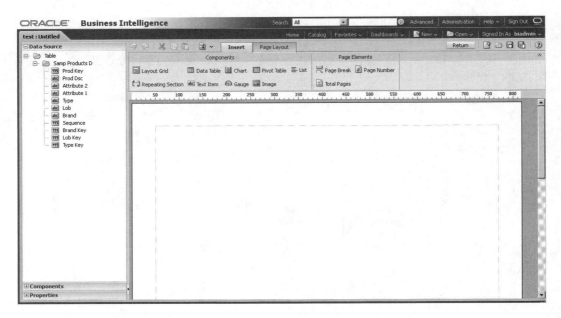

Using these components, you drag-and-drop layout components such as pivot tables, gauges, data tables, and charts onto the layout canvas from either the Components menu in the concertina panel or from the toolbar ribbon, and then drag-and-drop data elements from the Data Source panel onto them, to create your report layout. Layouts are then saved to either the Oracle BI Presentation catalog (if you are running BI Publisher integrated with Oracle Business Intelligence) or the BI Publisher Repository (if you are running BI Publisher stand-alone) as part of a report definition.

Toolbar Ribbon

The toolbar ribbon at the top of the page will be familiar to anyone who has worked with tools such as Microsoft Office 2007. It provides an expanded toolbar menu containing visual representations of report components, and context-sensitive tabs containing additional settings.

When you first start the Online Layout Editor, the toolbar ribbon displays the Insert tab, which has two categories: Components, which shows the available layout components, and Page Elements, which shows elements such as page number and page break.

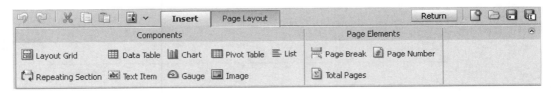

The toolbar ribbon includes a second tab, Page Layout, for working with the page layout. Clicking the Page Layout tab gives you a number of buttons and components that you can use to alter the orientation of the page, add footers and headers, and otherwise fine-tune the layout of the page.

When you select, for example, the Data Table component from the Insert tab and drop it onto the layout canvas, an additional tab (Table in this case) is added to the toolbar ribbon, giving you options and settings for this layout component. As you add and work with other layout components on your layout canvas, this additional tab changes to reflect the options and settings for the particular component that you have selected.

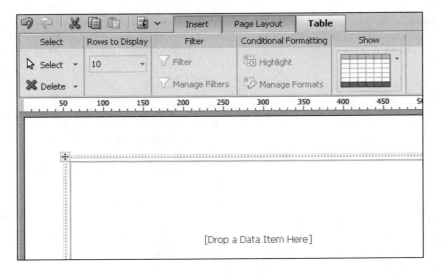

The "Concertina" Menu

Complementary to the toolbar ribbon, and repeating some of its functionality, is a "concertina"-style menu on the left-hand side of the Online Layout Editor screen that contains three panels for working with Data Sources, Components, and Properties. Using this menu you can select and add data elements to the layout components, drag-and-drop other layout components on the layout canvas, and edit the properties of selected components.

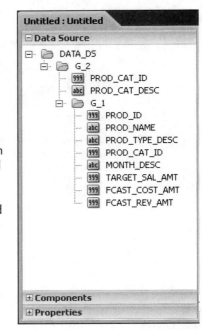

Data Source Panel   The Data Source panel allows you to select individual data elements and either add them directly to the layout canvas or drop them onto layout components such as data tables.

At the top of this panel is a folder called DATA_DS, which represents the data model that you selected for the report and the templates that are contained within the report. This top-level folder contains one or more data sets (typically named G_1, G_2, etc.) that are either listed in order or nested within each other, depending on whether you have concatenated, or joined, your data sets.

The icon next to each data element name shows you the data type (number, character, etc.), and you add these data elements to the layout canvas by dragging them from the panel and dropping them on the layout canvas.

Components Panel The Components panel repeats the features of the Insert tab in the toolbar ribbon and lists the various layout components that you can add to a layout canvas.

Properties Panel The Properties panel plays a very important role in designing your report layout. When you add, for example, a Chart component to your layout, selecting the Properties panel allows you to fine-tune settings such as the chart name, the height and width of the chart, the chart legend, and other settings.

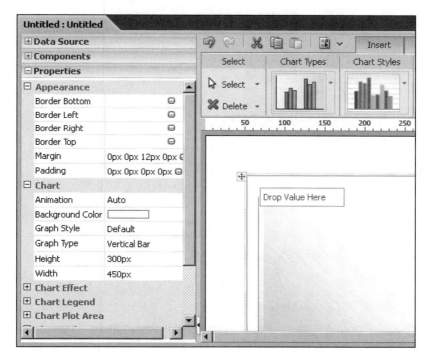

Creating a Dashboard-Style BI Report Layout

Now that you know your way around the Online Layout Editor, let's look at the process involved in creating a dashboard-style BI report using BI Publisher and the Online Layout Editor.

In this first example, we will look at how you can use BI Publisher to create a dashboard-style report that includes a data table, a pivot table, a chart, a gauge, and a list item, as shown in Figure 9-4.

As you will see, the report we are going to create can be deployed as a stand-alone report in BI Publisher Enterprise, can be run in a web browser on the Oracle Business Intelligence web site, or can be embedded in a BI dashboard page and parameter values passed to it. To create a report like this, the high-level steps you would need to perform would be as follows:

1. If required, create a data model made up of one or more data sets from your data sources.

2. Create the report definition, first selecting the data source and the basic template to define the page orientation, page size, and so on.

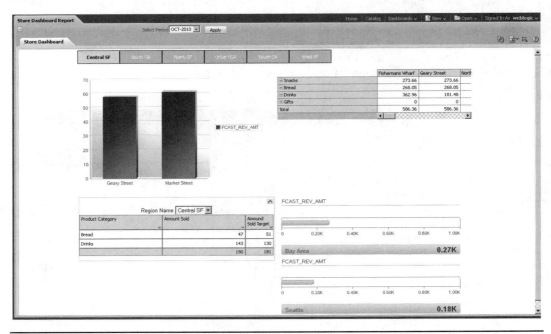

FIGURE 9-4. *The final dashboard-style BI Publisher report*

3. Then for this report definition, create a layout that the report can use that uses data objects and layout components to create a dashboard-style view of your data.

4. Once you've completed the template, save it, and then the report definition that it is included in, to the catalog so that it can then be run.

5. View the report, either stand-alone in BI Publisher Enterprise or you can add it as a dashboard object into a BI dashboard to display alongside other BI content.

For this example, we will use a new data model that is sourced from the same Oracle database schema (GCBC_SALES) and spreadsheet (products.csv) in the previous example, but this time including more columns from more tables in the SQL Query data set so that it provides a wider range of measures and attributes columns. To create the data model that we'll use in a moment to demonstrate the Online Layout Editor, using a new data model first create a data set using an SQL Query against the GCBC_SALES Oracle database schema, and include the following columns in the data set.

- PRODUCT_ATTRIBS.MANUFACTURER
- PRODUCT_ATTRIBS.REGIONAL_ORIGIN

- PRODUCTS.PROD_NAME
- PRODUCTS.PROD_TYPE_DESC
- PRODUCTS.PROD_CAT_ID
- SALES.FCAST_SAL_AMT
- SALES. FCAST_COST_AMT
- SALES.TARGET_SAL_AMT
- STORES_RAGGED.CONCESSION_NAME
- STORES_RAGGED.STORE_NAME
- STORES_RAGGED.REGION_NAME
- TIMES.MONTH_DESC
- TIMES.QUARTER_DESC
- TIMES.YEAR_YYYY

If you use the Query Builder to create the column selection, make sure you select the GROUP BY option for all of the columns except for the measures coming from the SALES fact table; for those, you should select the SUM aggregate function. Join the SALES, PRODUCTS, PRODUCT_ATTRIBS, STORES_RAGGED and TIMES tables together, so that the final SQL query for this data set looks like this:

```
select      "PRODUCT_ATTRIBS"."MANUFACTURER"
as "MANUFACTURER",
    "PRODUCT_ATTRIBS"."REGIONAL_ORIGIN"
as "REGIONAL_ORIGIN",

    "PRODUCTS"."PROD_NAME" as "PROD_NAME",
    "PRODUCTS"."PROD_TYPE_DESC" as "PROD_TYPE_DESC",
    "PRODUCTS"."PROD_CAT_ID" as "PROD_CAT_ID",

    sum("SALES"."FCAST_SAL_AMT") as "FCAST_SAL_AMT",

    sum("SALES"."FCAST_COST_AMT") as "FCAST_COST_AMT",

    sum("SALES"."TARGET_SAL_AMT") as "TARGET_SAL_AMT",

    "STORES_RAGGED"."CONCESSION_NAME" as "CONCESSION_NAME",

    "STORES_RAGGED"."STORE_NAME" as "STORE_NAME",

    "STORES_RAGGED"."REGION_NAME" as "REGION_NAME",

    "TIMES"."MONTH_DESC" as "MONTH_DESC",

    "TIMES"."QUARTER_DESC" as "QUARTER_DESC",

    "TIMES"."YEAR_YYYY" as "YEAR_YYYY"
```

```
from      "GCBC_SALES"."TIMES" "TIMES",

  "GCBC_SALES"."STORES_RAGGED" "STORES_RAGGED",
  "GCBC_SALES"."SALES" "SALES",

  "GCBC_SALES"."PRODUCT_ATTRIBS" "PRODUCT_ATTRIBS",

  "GCBC_SALES"."PRODUCTS" "PRODUCTS"

where     "PRODUCTS"."PROD_ID"="PRODUCT_ATTRIBS"."PROD_ID"

and       "SALES"."STORE_ID"="STORES_RAGGED"."STORE_PK"

and       "TIMES"."MONTH_YYYYMM"="SALES"."MONTH_YYYYMM"

and       "PRODUCTS"."PROD_ID"="SALES"."PROD_ID"

group by "PRODUCT_ATTRIBS"."MANUFACTURER",
"PRODUCT_ATTRIBS"."REGIONAL_ORIGIN",
"PRODUCTS"."PROD_NAME",
"PRODUCTS"."PROD_TYPE_DESC",
"PRODUCTS"."PROD_CAT_ID",
"STORES_RAGGED"."CONCESSION_NAME",
"STORES_RAGGED"."STORE_NAME",
"STORES_RAGGED"."REGION_NAME",
"TIMES"."MONTH_DESC",
"TIMES"."QUARTER_DESC",
"TIMES"."YEAR_YYYY"
```

NOTE
*Rather than use the Query Builder within the Data Model Editor to
visually create your SQL query, you can just type the SQL directly into
the Create Data Set–SQL dialog box if you have already written it.*

Create a bind variable in your SQL query to filter the "TIMES"."MONTH_DESC" column
against, so that the addition filter clause in your query looks like this:

```
"TIMES"."MONTH_YYYYMM"=:MONTH
```

then create a new parameter in the data model that maps to this filter clause. Once you've created
the first SQL query data set, create another using a Microsoft Excel datasource and then once it is
part of the data model, link it to the SQL query dataset, in this case via their common PROD_
CAT_ID columns. The dataset that you will then work with to create the report example coming
next will look like the next screenshot.

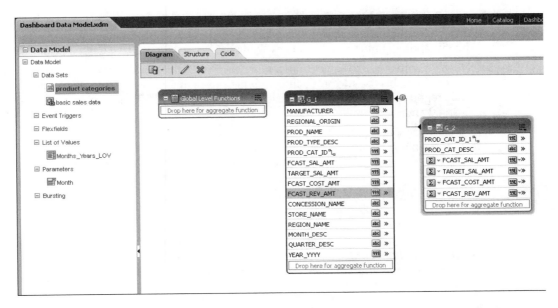

Finally, use the Structure tab in the Data Model Editor to provide Display Names for the various dataset columns, create your sample XML data set, and then save the data model in the catalog ready for the start of the example below.

So now that we have a suitable data model, let's start by creating the report.

Example: Creating a New Report Definition

A report in BI Publisher is a container for one or more layouts, referencing a single data model and with its own properties and settings. To create a report for our reporting dashboard using the 11.1.1.6 release of BI Publisher and Oracle Business Intelligence and the data model detailed in the previous sections, follow these steps:

1. Log into the Oracle Business Intelligence web site and select New | Report.

2. You will initially be prompted to either use an existing data model, upload a spreadsheet, or create a new data model for your report. As you have already created a data model for this report, select Use Existing Data Model.

3. Selecting the option to use an existing data model then displays the Create Report wizard, a three-stage dialog that guides you though the initial steps to create a report. The first step in the wizard is titled "Step 1 of 3 : Select Data Model," so use the catalog browser within the dialog to navigate to the data model that you just created, and select it for use with the report.

4. The second page of the Create Report wizard is titled "Step 2 of 4 : Guide or Create," and at this step you can choose to either have the wizard guide you in the creation of a basic report layout, or use can use the Report Editor option to leave the wizard dialog and create the layout yourself.

   Choosing the option to use the Guide Me feature is useful for end-users who want to put a simple report together with minimal work on their part, and the report and layout that it creates can subsequently be extended and amended using the Report Editor. For now though, select the Use Report Editor function, press the Finish button, and then save the initial report definition to the catalog using the Save As dialog that will be displayed next.

5. Now, you are asked to select from a number of predefined basic templates (you can add your own to this list, the procedure for which we will look at later on). For a dashboard-style report, you should select a basic template that is wider rather than taller, so click the Blank (Landscape) option to select it.

6. You are now presented with a blank, empty layout, to which we will add layout components to create our report in the next example.

NOTE
For releases of BI Publisher prior to 11.1.1.6, the initial report creation process is slightly different, and does not feature the multipage dialog box referenced in steps 2 and 3 that gives you the option of selecting columns and creating a default layout. Instead, you are asked to select a data model and then proceed to step 4. Beyond these steps, though, earlier 11g releases feature the same user interface as the 11.1.1.6 release.

Example: Creating the Dashboard Layout

Now that you have created the report that will contain your layout and have selected a screen size and data model, you can start to create your layout. In this layout, you are going to add the following layout components:

- A bar chart showing sales broken down by product category, located in the top left-hand corner
- A pivot table showing sales by product and store, located in the top right-hand corner
- A data table, with Region Name as a drop-down selector above it, showing sales by product category, located in the bottom left-hand corner
- A set of gauges showing sales by region of origin, located in the bottom right-hand corner
- A horizontal list of regions that can be clicked to filter by a particular region, located above the bar chart and pivot table
- A parameter list of values allowing you to select a particular month, located at the top of the report

BI Publisher also comes with a built-in filtering feature with online layouts. If you click, for example, a bar in a bar chart that represents a particular region, all of the other layout components then filter by that region. Similarly, if you click a pie chart segment in another layout component, the value that you click will get passed to the other components and added to the list of filters. This behavior is automatic (but can be selectively disabled if required), and we will use it to add point-and-click interactivity to our report dashboard.

To create a dashboard in this style, follow these steps:

1. Having followed the previous steps to define the report, select the data model and select the Blank (Landscape) basic layout. Once selected, the Online Layout Editor will then be displayed, with your empty layout ready for editing.

2. Let's start by adding a List component to the layout, which will allow the user to click a region and filter all other components based on it. To do this, select List on the Insert tab on the toolbar ribbon menu and drag-and-drop it onto the layout canvas. Then, drag the data element, in this case Region Name, from the Data Source panel on the left and drop it on the List component on the canvas.

3. By default, List components list their data elements vertically. To display the list horizontally, navigate to the Properties panel on the left, and set the Orientation property to Horizontal. Finally, resize the List component on the layout canvas so that it stretches across the top of the layout canvas.

4. Lay out the basic two row by two column structure of your dashboard. To do so, navigate back to the Insert tab in the toolbar ribbon and drag-and-drop a Layout Grid component so that it is placed underneath the List component on the layout canvas, and select a two row by 2 column grid when prompted.

   Your layout should now look as follows:

5. Now you can start adding components to the layout. Start by dragging a Chart component from the Insert tab on the toolbar ribbon and dropping it onto the top-left corner. Then set the X axis choice (the bars) by first selecting the Data Source panel in the concertina menu on the left-hand side of the Online Layout Editor, and then from the list of available columns dragging and dropping the Store Name data element onto the chart component's Drop Label Here area, then repeat this step again to drop the $ Revenue data element also into the chart's Drop Value Here area.

   Now, if you want to break down each store's measure values by, for example, product type, you could do so by dragging and dropping the Product Type data element onto the chart's Drop Series Here area, which would split each bar in the bar chart into individual values for each product category sold by each store.

Finally, by default the label for the Y axis is the XML element name for the measure (in this case, FCAST_REV_AMT); however, you can change this to something more meaningful by selecting the chart with your mouse pointer and then clicking the Properties panel to display the component's properties, one of which is the label value for the chart's legend. Locate the Label 1 value under the Chart Legend property, and set the property value to $ Revenue.

Once complete, your chart should look like this:

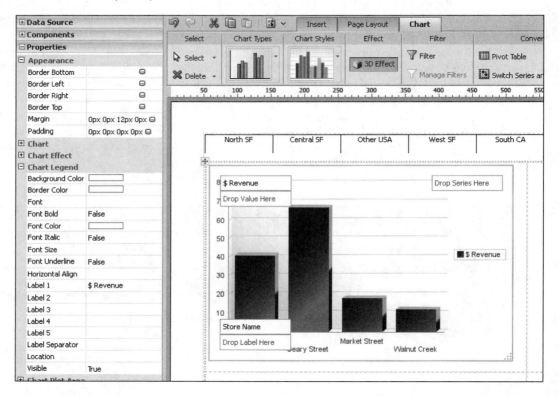

6. Next you will create the pivot table that you will place in the top right-hand corner of the layout. To do so, select the Insert tab on the ribbon menu and then drag-and-drop the Pivot Table component into this section, to display an empty pivot table for adding rows, columns, and data.

In this example, the rows will consist of product types grouped by product categories. First drag-and-drop the Product Category data element from the Data Source panel onto the Drop Rows Here area, and then drag-and-drop the Product Type data element into the same area, but to the right of the previous element.

Then drag-and-drop the data element that will be used for columns, in this case Store Name, into the Drop Columns Here area. Finally, drag-and-drop the $ Revenue data element into the Drop Data Here area. You will then see an initial view of the pivot table, but without the ability to drill down into the data that you will see later when viewing the report online.

7. Now add a data table component to the bottom left-hand corner. Before you do this, though, add a Repeating Section component to the area, and when prompted, select the Region Name Element to repeat/group by. This will place a drop-down menu listing regions above the data table, which will also be filtered by the list selection at the top of the page. To add the data table, drag-and-drop a Data Table component from the Insert tab into the space between the Start Grouping and End Grouping borders. Then drop the data elements (for example, Amount Sold and Amount Sold Target) onto the table so that it looks like this:

▼ Start Grouping - Region Name 🖉		
Product Category	Amount Sold	Amound Sold Target
Snacks	16	16
Bread	17	15
Drinks	13	13
Gifts	6	3
	52	47

End Grouping - Region Name

8. With the data table selected, you can use the toolbar ribbon at the top of the screen to set the font for the cells, the data format, conditional formatting, or other settings for the table. Similarly, you can use the Properties panel on the left-hand side to fine-tune the colors, border styles, and other properties of the table or individual table cells.

9. Add the gauge to the bottom right-hand corner of the layout. To do this, drag-and-drop the Gauge component from the Insert tab onto the layout. Drag data elements onto the Drop Value Here, Drop Label Here, and Drop Series Here areas, and then use the Properties panel to select between Dial, Status Meter, and Vertical Status Meter.

10. Your layout is almost ready to use. First, though, you can fine-tune how each component interacts with each other component when you click a bar chart bar or a list component item. To view and change these behavior (or "event") settings, click the Page Layout tab in the toolbar ribbon, and click the Configure Events button in the Interactivity area.

This displays the Configure Events dialog box. By default, all events are sent to all components, but if you want to, for example, stop the List component from sending filter events to the Pivot Table component, you can deselect that option here.

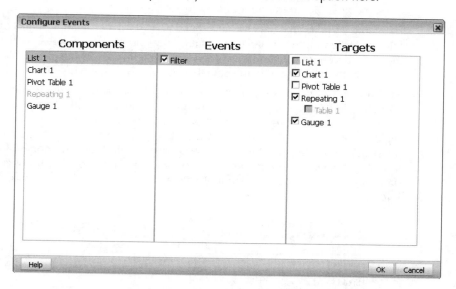

NOTE
Event filters only work when you use the Interactive option when viewing the report.

11. Click OK to close the Configure Events dialog box, and then click the Save button to save the layout within the report definition, selecting a locale as you do so. Different layouts for different locales can be defined within a report and automatically selected for users based on their user profile.

Saving and Viewing the Report

So now you have created a layout for your report. To return to the report definition, click the Return button at the top of the Layout Editor to display the Report editing screen. Using this screen, you can view and modify labels and default values for parameters, and set other report-level properties (which we will look at in more detail in the next section).

For now, though, click the Save button on this screen to save the report definition to the catalog, and then click the View Report button to view the report. Note that when you click, for example, the North CA region in the list at the top of the page, all the other components, except for the pivot table that you deselected for this event, will change their filter values on each click. Similarly, when you change the parameter value at the top of the report and then click Apply, the filter value is applied to all components.

Now that you have this report defined, you can access it stand-alone using BI Publisher Enterprise, which you can navigate to using the URL http://[*machine_name*]:port/xmlpserver (for example, http://obisrv1:7001/xmlpserver). You initially are presented with a Home page very similar to the Oracle Business Intelligence Home page, as shown next, from which you can navigate to and then run your report. Click the various chart items, the list item, and other objects and note how the other components on the page are automatically filtered by the values that you click.

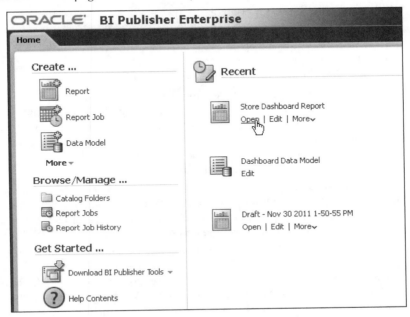

BI Publisher Enterprise is the dedicated home page for BI Publisher reports, and is typically used by customers who have licensed only BI Publisher rather than Oracle Business Intelligence in its entirety. But what if you want to run your report from Oracle Business Intelligence and, ideally, embed it in a dashboard, passing it parameter values from dashboard prompts on the page? Read on to find out how.

Embedding the Report in a BI Dashboard

You can run BI Publisher reports, such as the one you just created in the previous section, from the Catalog page on the Oracle Business Intelligence web site, just like you would run analyses, dashboards, or other BI objects. Alternatively, you can select the My Reports heading in the Browse/Manage section on the Home page to list just your reports, and run them from there.

You can, however, also embed BI Publisher reports into BI dashboard pages, with each template forming its own tab within the report area of the dashboard. If you want to pass parameter values to the report, you need to create dashboard prompts that set a presentation variable of the same name as the parameter, and the parameter value will be passed through to the report.

Let's do this now with the report we just created. To do so, follow these steps:

1. Navigate to the Oracle Business Intelligence web site at http://[*machine_name*]:port/ analytics (for example, http://obisrv1:7001/analytrics). Log in as a user with permission to create reports and other BI objects, and then either open an existing dashboard or create a new dashboard using New | Dashboard from the application menu.

2. Give the dashboard a name (for example, Stores Dashboard) and be sure to save it in the /Shared Folders/ area rather than in your personal folders, to ensure that it can be used by other users and seen in the Dashboards menu.

3. With the dashboard editor open, go to the Catalog pane in the bottom left of the screen, and then navigate through the catalog folder structure until you find your report. Then, drag-and-drop it onto the dashboard layout canvas.

4. To see the report in the dashboard page, first save the dashboard using the Save button, and then click the Run button to see it in your browser.

5. Set up a dashboard prompt that provides values for the report parameter (which, in this example, is called MONTHS) in the accompanying BI Publisher data model. To do so, first set up a dashboard prompt by selecting New | Dashboard Prompt. When prompted for the subject area, select one that corresponds to the data source used for the data model parameter—that is, points to the same underlying data source or can provide parameter values to match those used in the data model.

6. When the dashboard prompt screen is displayed, click the New button to create a new prompt. Select Column Prompt as the type, and then use the Select Column dialog box to select a subject area column for the prompt; in this example, we will select Dim Times.Month. Click OK to select the column.

7. To pass this dashboard prompt value to the report parameter, you need to have the prompt set a presentation variable of the same name as the parameter. To do so, with the New Prompt dialog box open, expand the Options area at the bottom of the dialog box and select Presentation Variable for the Set A Variable setting. In the text box that then opens for the presentation variable name, enter the same name as the BI Publisher parameter (Month, in this example). Click OK to close the dialog box.

8. Save the dashboard prompt to the shared folders area of the catalog, and then edit the dashboard you just created to add the prompt above the report. Now, when you change the dashboard prompt values on the dashboard page, the BI Publisher report contained within it will receive the filter values as well.

Creating a Print-Style Report Layout

In the previous example, we looked at creating a dashboard-style report that includes interactive charts, pivot tables, and gauges. BI Publisher can be useful for this type of output when you want to access data sources that are not mapped into your Oracle BI Repository, or when you want to deploy a lightweight dashboard outside of Oracle Business Intelligence but want it to share the same look and feel and be capable of being embedded inside a regular BI dashboard when needed.

A more common use of BI Publisher, though, is to produce print-style reports in formats such as Adobe PDF that can include graphics, text, and other items and can be distributed to users via methods such as e-mail, FTP, and a physical printer. In this way, BI Publisher complements the capabilities of Oracle Business Intelligence and allows you to produce report output with "pixel-perfect" control over the layout.

In this second example, therefore, we will look at producing a report that is designed for PDF output, includes text and graphics, and is split into separate documents and made available to individual users in a process called *bursting*.

The data model for this report is similar to the one in the previous example in that it sources data from the GCBC_SALES schema and includes information on sales, stores, and time, with a parameter defined for the month and year column. We will use this report to create a report, split and distributed by region, that shows sales for each branch in the region against target sales.

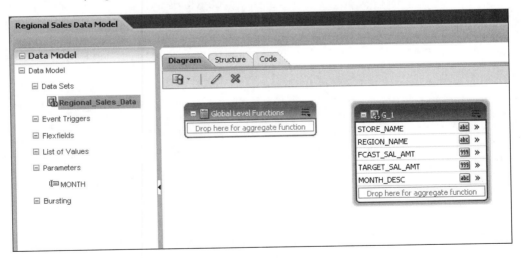

As before, there are a number of steps that we need take to create this style of report:

1. First we need to either create, or locate in the catalog, a data model to use with the report; in the example that follows, we'll use the data model that you created for the previous example in the "Creating a Data Model from a Single Source" section earlier in this chapter.

2. Then start creating the report definition, first selecting the data model and then selecting a template to use for the layout.

3. Define the template, adding layout components such as text and images as well as data tables and charts, and header and footer sections if required.

4. Test the report by viewing it initially online using the Interactive Viewer, and then choosing PDF as the output format to see how it might look in its final form.

5. Define bursting instructions for the report so that the single report is split by region and distributed, in this case, via e-mail to regional managers.

6. Test the final report by scheduling it and selecting the option to burst it using our bursting definition.

Example: Creating the Report Definition

As mentioned in the previous example, reports in BI Publisher are containers for one or more layouts, referencing a single data model and having their own properties and settings. To create a report for our print-style report, follow these steps:

1. Log into the Oracle Business Intelligence web site and select New | Report.

2. You are prompted to select an existing data model. Select Use Existing Data Model. In the Choose Existing Data Model dialog box, navigate through the catalog to select a data model to use with the report, for example, the Regional Sales Data Model that is defined in the "Creating a Data Model from a Single Source" example mentioned earlier. When prompted on the following dialog page in the Create a Report wizard, select the Use Report Editor option and press Finish, as you will define the report layout manually.

3. Save your report definition when prompted, and next you will be asked to select from a number of predefined basic templates. For a print-style report, you want to select a basic template that is in portrait orientation (taller rather than wider), and with headers and footers, so click the Header and Footer (Portrait) option to select it.

4. Once the report template has been selected, as before you will be presented with an empty layout within the Online Layout Editor, ready for you to design your report.

Example: Creating the Report Layout for a Print-Style Report

Creating the report layout for a print-style report is very similar to creating it for a dashboard-style report, except that we will now use layout components such as text items and images, and we need to consider items such as headers and footers, page breaks, and the like. As such, our layout will include the following:

- A header area, with the report title and a company logo
- A footer, showing the page number and total number of pages

- A separate page for each region's stores, with a page break to split each page up
- Some text to indicate the period and region for each section
- A data table and chart in the main body of the layout to show store performance within each region

To create a report layout like this, follow these steps:

1. To create the header, ensure the Insert tab is selected in the main area of the template, and then drag-and-drop a Layout Grid component into the header area. When prompted, select one row and two columns, and click OK.

   Next, switch back to the Insert tab and then drag-and-drop a Text Item component into the left-hand area in the layout grid area. When you drag-and-drop the text item onto the header area of the template, the tab switches from Insert to Text. With the Text tab still selected, type **Regional Sales Report : Company Confidential** into the text box, change the font size to 11, and make the font bold.

2. Add the company logo to the section just to the right of the Text Item component you just added. To do this, ensure the Insert tab is selected and then drag-and-drop an Image component onto the rightmost section in the layout grid. When prompted, use the dialog box to select the image file from your local file system, or provide its URL details if it needs to be accessed from a web server.

   Click the Insert button to close the dialog box and return to the template. The image is left-justified within the layout grid cell. To right-justify it, using the Select button above the layout grid, choose Select | Layout Grid Cell. Then, using the Properties panel on the left-hand side of the Layout Editor, locate the Text Alignment property and change it to Right.

   Check that the image is now right-justified. Finally, select the left-hand layout grid cell in the same way as before, and this time change the Vertical Alignment property value to Middle. Once these changes are made, your template header should now look as shown here:

Regional Sales Report : Company Confidential   Gourmet Coffee & Bakery Co.

3. Create the main body of the template. This consists of a repeating section that then contains details on sales for each region.

   To start creating the main body, ensure the Insert tab is selected and then drag-and-drop a Repeating Section component into the main body of the template. When the Insert A Repeating Section dialog box is shown, select REGION NAME as the element.

Click OK to save the selection, and your template should now contain the Repeating Section component, and look like this:

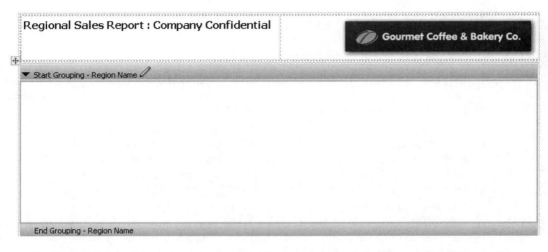

4. Start defining objects to go in the repeating section by dragging and dropping another Layout Grid component into the repeating section area, and select one row and two columns as before.

5. Add two items of text into this grid, a label for the region in the left-hand cell, and a label for the month and year in the right-hand cell (in step 7).

   To add the left-hand item, with the Insert tab selected, drag-and-drop another Text Item component into the layout grid cell, and enter the text **Region :** into the text item.

   In a moment, you will add the Region Name data item to the layout grid cell, alongside the Text Item component you just added. To ensure that it is displayed alongside the Text Item component, rather than in a new paragraph (the default), select the Text Item component and then, using the Properties panel on the left-hand side, set the Display property to Inline.

   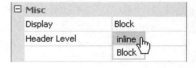

   The Text Item component should now be truncated in width, and when another Text Item component or data element is dropped next to it, the new item will be displayed inline next to the existing item, not in a new paragraph block.

6. Add the data item to go alongside the text item label. To do this, expand the Data Source panel and then drag-and-drop the G_1 Region Name data source element onto your template, just to the right of the label text item you just added. Once done, that section of the template should look as shown at right.

   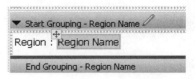

7. Repeat the preceding two steps for the right-hand layout grid cell, adding a Text Item component containing the text **Period :** and then dragging and dropping the G_1 Month data source element so that it is next to the label. Remember to set the Display property for the new Text Item component to Inline so that the Month element displays next to the label, not under it.

8. Add a chart to the template body, just under these labels. To do this, ensure the Insert tab is selected and then drag-and-drop a Chart component under the labels but in front of the End Grouping : Region Name divider.

    Then, with the Data Source panel open on the left, drag-and-drop the G_1 Sale Amount data source element onto the Drop Value Here area, and drag-and-drop the G_1 Store Name data source element onto the Drop Label Here area; your chart should now look as follows:

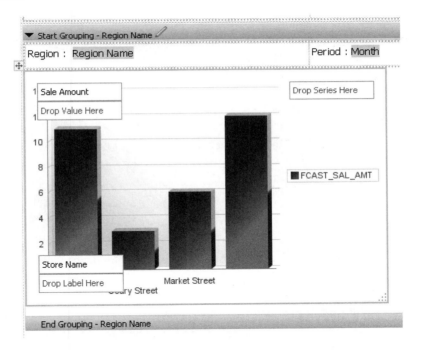

9. Add a data table to the template. To do this, ensure the Insert tab is selected again, and this time drag-and-drop a Data Table component to just under the chart.

    Now, within the Data Table component, using the Data Source panel, drag-and-drop the data elements onto the table; for example, under G_1:

    Store Name
    Sale Amount
    Sale Amount Target

    Then, set the formatting options for the two numeric columns. To do this, click any of the number cells within the Sale Amount column (not the column header) to display the

Column tab. Then, using the Data Formatting drop-down menu, select –$1,234.57 as the data format, like this:

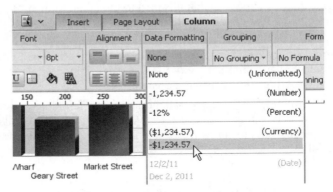

Then repeat this step for the other numeric cells, and apply any other data formatting that you would like to use for the data table.

10. In this example, there are some null entries in the Store Name column that relate to entries in this table for concessions not directly associated with a store. To ensure that this row is not included in reports, you can set a filter on the data table. To do this, select the whole data table (click anywhere in it and then choose Select | Table).

Then, with the Table tab selected, click the Filter button below it, like this:

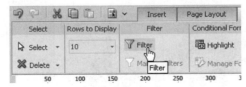

When the Filter dialog box is shown, select the following values:

Data Field: Store Name
Operator: is not equal to
Value: (*leave blank, to represent NULL*)

Click OK to close the dialog box and save the filter definition.

11. Define how page breaks will work. To ensure that each region appears on its own PDF page, select the whole repeating section (Select | Repeating Section) and then set the Page Break property value to Page, as shown at right.

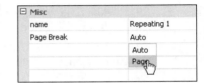

12. Define the footer contents for the template, in this case adding page number and total page count information to the left-hand side.

With the Insert tab selected, scroll down to the bottom of the template to locate the footer section. Then, drag a Text Item component into the footer area, and set the text to **Page :**. As before, edit the Text Item component properties so that the Display property value is set to Inline.

Select the Insert tab again, and then drag-and-drop the Page Number component within the Page Elements section so that it is next to the Text Item component that you just added.

Repeat these steps, adding a Text Item component containing the text **of :** next to the Page Number component (remember to set the Display property to Inline), and add the Total Pages component after it so that your footer looks as shown at right.

Saving and Viewing the Report

Your template is now ready for testing. First we will save it and the report definition, then we will view it in the default Interactive format, and then we will view it in its intended format, PDF.

1. Click the Save button, and in the Save Layout dialog box, call it **Regional Report Template**. Click the Save button on the dialog box, and when it closes, click Return to return to the report definition page.

2. Click the Save button to save the report definition itself. Call it **Regional Sales Report** and click OK to save it.

3. Click the View Report button in the top right-hand corner of the page. The report will now run, using your template, and display in the Interactive Viewer.

4. To view the report in PDF format, choose Run Report | PDF in the top right-hand part of the Interactive Viewer; the report should now open in your PDF viewer, with one page per region, as shown here:

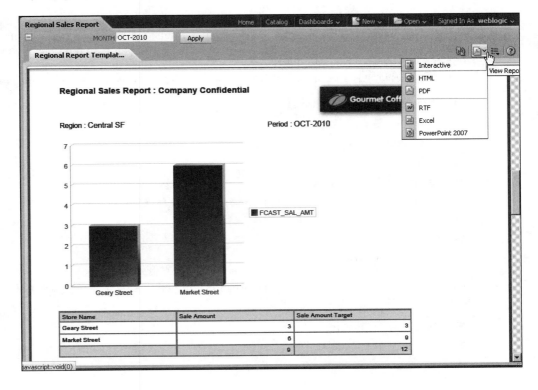

Example: Adding Bursting Instructions

The report layout that you have just created, in its current form, creates a single document with one region listed per page. In a moment, you will see how the report that uses this layout can be scheduled and e-mailed to an e-mail distribution list. But what if you want to split, or "burst," the report into a separate page per region, and then have that page sent individually to each regional manager? To do this, you have to set up bursting instructions for the report.

There are a number of delivery channels that you can use to distribute BI Publisher reports, including e-mail, printer, FTP, and the other delivery options that you can configure from the BI Publisher Administration screen. When bursting reports by any delivery channel, you have to provide, typically via an SQL query, the following pieces of information per burst document:

- **Key value**   Matches the Deliver By setting you will specify in a moment
- **Template name**   Has to match the name of a template in the report you burst
- **Locale**   Can vary per burst document if you want to provide labels in French, German, or another language
- **Output format**   For example, XLS, PDF, or RTF
- **Delivery channel**   For example, e-mail, fax, file, or FTP
- **Output name**   The name of the output in the job history display

Other optional parameters are detailed in the *Oracle Fusion Middleware Data Modeling Guide for Oracle Business Intelligence Publisher* document, available on the Oracle Technology Network web site (http://otn.oracle.com).

In addition to these standard parameter settings, each delivery channel has its own particular settings that you provide using Parameters 1 to 10 in the bursting instructions. Full details for all delivery channels are available in the previously referenced document on the OTN web site, but we'll take a look at two examples here.

First, the following is an example of what these parameters would be when bursting via e-mail:

- Parameter 1: Email Address
- Parameter 2: cc:
- Parameter 3: From
- Parameter 4: Subject
- Parameter 5: Message Body
- Parameter 6: Attachment value (true or false, used for PDF output)
- Parameter 7: Reply-to address
- Parameter 8: Bcc
- Parameters 9, 10: not used

For distributing files by copying them onto a local or network file system, the list of parameters is smaller:

- Parameter 1: Directory
- Parameter 2: File Name
- Parameters 3–10: not used

In the next example, we will use bursting to split the report that we just created into separate pages, with the pages being placed onto a network directory, ready to be accessed by individual regional managers. Each type of delivery channel uses its own set of parameters for which you will need to provide values, the full set of which are detailed in the *Oracle® Fusion Middleware Data Modeling Guide for Oracle Business Intelligence Publisher 11g Release 1*.

To set up bursting instructions in this way, follow these steps:

1. To set up bursting, you first need to edit the data model used for the report. To do this, from the common header menu, select Open and then navigate to your data model (for example, Regional Stores Data Model.xdm) to open the data model for editing.

    Then, with the data model open for editing, navigate to and click the Bursting item in the left-hand menu, click the Create New Bursting button in the right-hand panel, and then enter the following values:

    Name: Burst to Files
    Type: SQL Query
    Data Source: GCBC_SALES

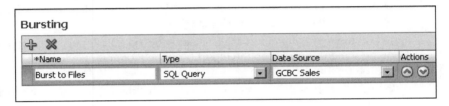

2. In the Burst To Files section below the bursting settings (you may need to move the dividing line up to see the area completely), select the column on which the report is split and delivered, and also the SQL query that returns the parameters required by the bursting process.

    For example, for the splitting and delivery choices, you could select the following values:

    Split by: /DATA_DS/G_1/REGION_NAME
    Deliver by: /DATA_DS/G_1/REGION_NAME

    For the SQL query, type in the following SQL statement to provide the parameter values that the FILE delivery channel requires:

```
select      "STORES_RAGGED"."REGION_NAME" as "KEY",
            'Regional Report Template' TEMPLATE,
                'en-US' LOCALE,
                'PDF' OUTPUT_FORMAT,
                'FILE' DEL_CHANNEL,
                'C:/TEMP' PARAMETER1,
                "STORES_RAGGED"."REGION_NAME" ||
                '_Sales_Report.pdf' PARAMETER2
from        "GCBC_SALES"."STORES_RAGGED" "STORES_RAGGED"
```

The Burst To Files detail section should now look like this:

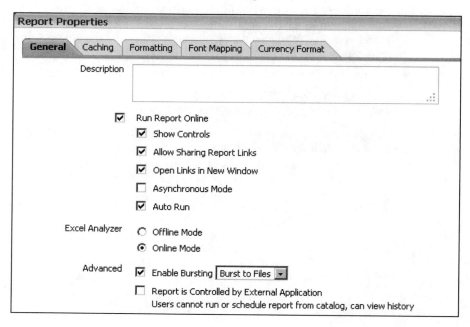

```
Bursting 1
                  Split By   /DATA_DS/G_1/REGION_NAME       ▼
                Deliver By   /DATA_DS/G_1/REGION_NAME       ▼
                SQL Query

select      "STORES_RAGGED"."REGION_NAME" as "KEY"
,           'Regional Report Template' TEMPLATE
,           'en-US' LOCALE
,           'PDF' OUTPUT_FORMAT
```

Save the updated data model by clicking the Save button.

3. Check that you have a folder called TEMP at the root of your C: drive (C:\TEMP). If you do not, create it before proceeding to the next step.

4. Associate the report you created previously with these bursting instructions. To do this, select Open | Open | My Folders | BIP101 | Regional Sales Report.xdo. This opens the report using the template you designed earlier.

    To edit the report definition itself, select Actions | Edit Report in the top right-hand corner of the screen. Then, when the report is opened for editing, click the Properties button in the top right-hand corner.

    In the Report Properties dialog box, ensure that the Enable Bursting check box is selected, and that Burst To Files is selected as the bursting definition.

```
Report Properties

  General    Caching   Formatting   Font Mapping   Currency Format

        Description   [                                              ]
                      [                                              ]

                  ☑  Run Report Online
                     ☑  Show Controls
                     ☑  Allow Sharing Report Links
                     ☑  Open Links in New Window
                     ☐  Asynchronous Mode
                     ☑  Auto Run

    Excel Analyzer    ○  Offline Mode
                      ◉  Online Mode

        Advanced   ☑  Enable Bursting  [Burst to Files ▼]

                   ☐  Report is Controlled by External Application
                      Users cannot run or schedule report from catalog, can view history
```

Click OK to save the report properties, and then click Save on the report definition screen to save the changes to the definition.

5. Schedule a test run of the report, with bursting enabled. To do this, select New | Report Job. The report job definition screen will then be displayed.

With the General tab selected, click the Choose button to open the Open dialog box, and then select your report, in this case called Regional Sales Report.

Click the Output tab and check the Use Bursting Definition To Determine Output & Delivery Destination check box, as shown here:

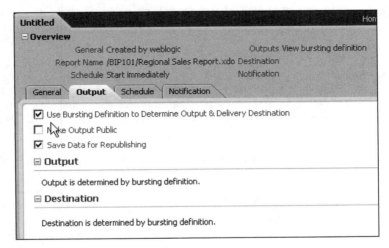

Click the Submit button, located in the top right-hand corner of the page, to submit the report job. In the Submit Job dialog box, type in some text as the Report Job Name and then click the Submit button. You should then see a message saying "Job successfully submitted." Click OK, and then click the Return button to complete the process.

6. To see the outcome of the scheduled job, navigate to the Report Job History link under Browse/Manage in the BI Publisher Enterprise screen that is then displayed.

Click the link to display the job history. When the Report Job History page is displayed, your job should be displayed with a status of Success. If not, check your bursting definition and repeat the process.

Using Windows Explorer, open the C:\TEMP directory, which should now have a report for each region that had sales in the selected month.

Adding New Layout Templates

Before we finish looking at BI Publisher and, in particular, the Online Layout Editor, you might be asking yourself how you can create your own basic templates so that report developers can, for example, start their layout definition using a template that already has your company logo at the top of the page and page numbers at the bottom.

To create your own custom, shared basic templates, you need to create a special report called Boilerplates and store it in a special directory called Components in the shared area of the catalog. Any layout template that you add to this report is then automatically made available to all other users when creating their reports, and other developers can add to this set of shared basic templates by adding layouts to this special report.

To create a shared layout template for others to later use, follow these steps:

1. From the Oracle Business Intelligence web site menu, select New | Report. When you are prompted to select a data model, click Cancel to close the dialog box.

2. A number of basic templates, and any shared templates if any are available, are presented to you. Click the one that you wish to base your new layout template on, such as Header and Footer (Portrait).

3. You are presented with a blank layout canvas, but with no data elements listed in the Data Source panel. Add layout components to your layout; for example, follow the design used in the previous example in this chapter to add a confidential notice, company logo, and page footers and headers.

4. Register this layout as a shared layout template. Save the layout with a name (for example, GCBC Portrait with Headers and Footers), click the Return button, and then save the report. When naming the report, call it **Boilerplates**, and save it into a new directory called **/Shared Folders/Components**. You can save other layout templates into this report as well, if you want others to be made available for users.

Now when you go to create a new report, your shared template will be visible in the list of available layout templates.

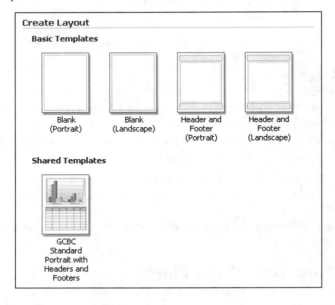

NOTE
Only templates saved in this special report and directory will be visible as shared layout templates to other users.

CHAPTER
10

Systems Management

ystems management refers to the tasks and processes required to manage an Oracle Business Intelligence domain. A typical Oracle Business Intelligence domain may span several physical servers and locations, and administrators may need to stop, start, or restart individual components, monitor performance, or make changes to system-wide parameters.

These tasks are typically carried out using Oracle Enterprise Manager Fusion Middleware Control, but alternatively they can be scripted using the WebLogic Scripting Tool and the Oracle BI Systems Management API. In this chapter, we will look at various aspects of Oracle Business Intelligence systems management and see how to use these tools to perform key tasks in this area.

Overview of Oracle Business Intelligence Systems Management

Systems management, as opposed to metadata management, is concerned with managing your Oracle Business Intelligence system as a whole and is typically carried out by a dedicated systems management person who may also look after other Oracle Fusion Middleware–based products. In Chapter 5, we looked in detail at administration tasks that you may need to carry out with the Oracle BI Server system component; this chapter deals with tasks such as starting and stopping components, gathering and analyzing metrics, managing repositories and catalogs, and other tasks that typically are carried out using Oracle Enterprise Manager Fusion Middleware Control but can instead be scripted using the WebLogic Scripting Tool together with the Oracle BI Systems Management API.

Systems Management Tasks

Chapter 1 described the architecture of Oracle Business Intelligence and referred to the system as an *Oracle BI Domain*. An Oracle BI Domain contains a single Oracle WebLogic domain, which in turn contains Java components and applications, and an Oracle BI instance, which contains legacy Java and non-Java system components such as the Oracle BI Server and Oracle BI Presentation Server. As a quick reminder and to define some other Oracle Business Intelligence architecture terms that we'll be using throughout this chapter, here's a quick glossary of BI component terms you'll need to understand when performing systems management tasks:

- **Oracle BI Domain** refers to the overall container for all Java components, non-Java components, configuration files, metadata repositories and infrastructure; this is the top-level container for an individual Oracle Business Intelligence system.

- **Oracle WebLogic Server Domain** (or "WebLogic Domain") refers to the complete set of Java components used by your system across all nodes in the cluster, is managed by an Administration Server, and is itself contained within the overall Oracle BI Domain.

- **Administration Server** is a type of WebLogic Server instance (a Java Virtual Machine server configured for a certain task and then deployed for use) that contains functionality for managing an Oracle WebLogic Server Domain; within the context of Oracle Business Intelligence, the Administration Server hosts Oracle Enterprise Manager Fusion Middleware Control, WebLogic Server Administration Console, and the Java JMX MBeans that both of these two applications use to perform systems management tasks. For Simple Installation types as detailed in Chapter 2, the Administration Server also hosts all of the Java components used by Oracle Business Intelligence.

- **Managed Servers** are another type of WebLogic Server instance that are clustered when used with Oracle Business Intelligence (other applications may deploy them outside of a cluster), and host the Java components that across all Managed Servers are contained within the Oracle BI Domain.

- **Oracle BI Instance** similarly refers to the collection of system (non-Java) components across all nodes in your cluster, and again is contained within the overall Oracle BI Domain.

- An **Oracle Instance** is a set of system components within a single node in a cluster, and when you first install Oracle Business Intelligence you start with just a single Oracle Instance. As you scale-out your installation over additional nodes in a cluster, the new set of system components on the new node form their own Oracle Instance, which together with the original Oracle Instance form an overall Oracle BI instance.

- **Oracle WebLogic Server** is a Java application server provided by Oracle Corporation that is a host to **Oracle Fusion Middleware**, Oracle Corporation's suite of identity management, integration, business intelligence, and other infrastructure products.

- **Fusion Middleware Control** is a part of the Oracle Fusion Middleware Control product family, and provides management and administration functionality for Oracle Fusion Middleware, in particular the BI Instance within our Oracle BI Domain.

- **coreapplication** is the name of the node within the Fusion Middleware Control's Business Intelligence folder, which provides the web-based administration interface for the Oracle BI instance within your overall Oracle BI Domain.

- **WebLogic Scripting Tool (WLST)** is a command-line scripting interface that you can use to administer directly, and indirectly, the components within your Oracle BI Domain through the use of Java JMX MBeans, which are also the means by which Fusion Middleware Control also provides systems management capabilities for your BI system.

- **JMX MBeans**, or Java Management Extensions Managed Beans, are Java objects that represent a resource that you can set properties for, and invoke to perform management functionality such as set performance options, upload a new repository file or restart your system. WLST scripts against JMX MBeans and uses the Jython scripting language to provide process control, looping, and other programmatic features.

Systems management tasks carried out using Fusion Middleware Control and WebLogic Scripting Tool can be categorized into the following areas:

- Starting, stopping, and restarting either the whole Oracle BI Domain or individual components within it

- Monitoring metrics and throughput, gathered using JMX MBeans

- Viewing and managing log files, including those produced by the Oracle BI Server, Oracle BI Presentation Server, and Oracle BI Scheduler system components

- Managing performance options, such as the query cache and various settings used by the Oracle BI Presentation Server system component

- Deploying repositories and catalogs, including configuring shared repositories and caches for clustered environments

Other areas of what might be considered systems management are covered in other chapters in this book. Configuring security, which is a topic area in itself, is covered in Chapter 8, but many of the tasks associated with it are also scriptable using WLST. Managing promotions of metadata and configuration settings between environments, cloning servers, and versioning metadata are covered in Chapter 11, while the topics of clustering and high availability are detailed in Chapter 2. Finally, as mentioned previously, there are also a number of tasks and settings particular to the Oracle BI Server, and these are covered in detail in Chapter 5.

This chapter instead focuses on those tasks that you carry out using Fusion Middleware Control and WLST. It is especially recommended reading for anyone who is considering an upgrade from version 10*g* of Oracle Business Intelligence to version 11*g*, as much of the functionality in this area is new with this release.

Systems Management Tools

The two main tools that you use to perform systems management tasks with Oracle Business Intelligence are Fusion Middleware Control and Oracle WebLogic Scripting Tool, which, as stated earlier, both in the background use JMX MBeans to perform the actual management tasks.

In addition, but outside the scope of this chapter, systems administrators typically also use the Oracle WebLogic Server Administration Console to perform WebLogic-related administration tasks, such as stopping, starting, and restarting Managed Servers, deploying and starting Java applications, and managing the embedded WebLogic Server LDAP Server, again all through calls to various JMX MBeans.

Overview of Fusion Middleware Control

Fusion Middleware Control is a web-based console that provides management and administration functionality for your Oracle Business Intelligence system. It has a component-based architecture that supports the use of plug-ins for specific products within Oracle Fusion Middleware, and is shown in Figure 10-1.

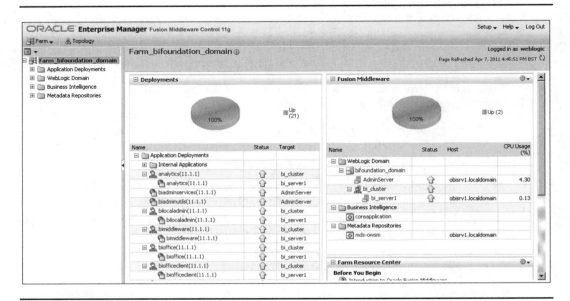

FIGURE 10-1. *Fusion Middleware Control*

One such plug-in is for Oracle Business Intelligence, and you can access its functionality through the navigation tree menu on the left-hand side of the Fusion Middleware Control screen by clicking the coreapplication node within the Business Intelligence folder. Clicking on coreapplication brings up a set of tabbed administration screens for Oracle Business Intelligence, and, as stated earlier, is mainly concerned with administering the system components within your Oracle BI Domain's BI instance.

Within the coreapplication screens, administration functionality is organized into the following six main tabs, as shown in Figure 10-2:

- **Overview**   For an overall view of the status and throughput of the Oracle instance
- **Availability**   For stopping, starting, and restarting system components, viewing the status, and managing failover settings
- **Capacity Management**   For viewing metrics, provisioning and removing system components, and managing performance parameters
- **Diagnostics**   For managing log settings and viewing and searching log files
- **Security**   For some system-wide security settings and for links to application roles and policies
- **Deployment**   For deploying repositories and catalogs, and for managing connection details for the scheduler, marketing, and e-mail

Each Fusion Middleware Control installation manages a single Oracle BI instance within a single Oracle BI Domain; however, system components within this Oracle BI instance may be spread over several physical servers, with each set of components within a particular server organized into their own Oracle Instances. Fusion Middleware Control also contains more general

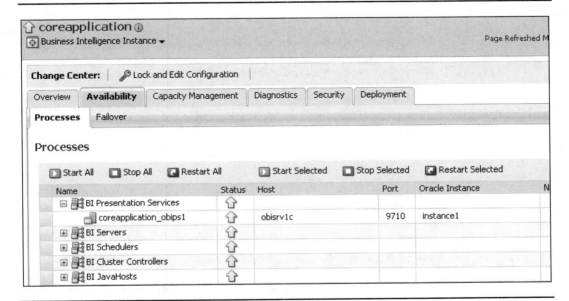

FIGURE 10-2.   *Fusion Middleware Control tabs and subtabs*

functionality for managing Fusion Middleware security and managing the Java components within the WebLogic domain that accompanies the Oracle instance. You will see in this chapter how these various administration functions are used to manage your system.

Overview of WebLogic Scripting Tool

WLST is a scripting environment for managing Oracle WebLogic Server domains. It gives you an interface into the JMX MBeans that provide configuration, management, and administration functionality for the WebLogic domain and the Oracle BI instance.

You can use WLST either in interactive mode, where you connect to a command-line environment and type in commands that work with the JMX MBeans, or in scripting mode, where you create scripts in Jython, a Java implementation of the Python language, that work with the JMX MBeans. WLST, as shipped with Oracle Fusion Middleware, also contains extensions to, for example, access the metrics provided by the Oracle Dynamic Monitoring Service (DMS).

To access the WLST command-line tool, open a command-line terminal on the server hosting Oracle Business Intelligence, navigate to the directory [*middleware_home*/Oracle_BI1/common/bin], and then invoke the WLST executable in the manner shown below, which calls the executable from a Microsoft Windows-based environment:

```
C:\>cd c:\Middleware\Oracle_BI1\common\bin
C:\Middleware\Oracle_BI1\common\bin>wlst
```

The environment will then initialize, and shortly afterward you will see the WSLT prompt. Make sure that you use this particular WLST executable in this path, rather than other WLST executables that may also be within the installation. This ensures that all JAR files that are specific to Oracle Fusion Middleware will be loaded as part of the initialization.

At this point, you are currently working offline (that is, you are not connected to a WebLogic Administration Server) and are in interactive mode. To connect to a WebLogic Administration Server and thereafter work online, use the command connect, like this:

```
connect ("weblogic","welcome1","localhost:7001")
```

where weblogic and welcome1 are the username and password of a WebLogic administration user, and localhost:7001 is the hostname and port number of the WebLogic Administration Server.

After WLST connects successfully to your Administration Server, it will report the connection and place you in online mode, with a command-line output like this:

```
Connecting to t3://localhost:7001 with userid weblogic ...
Successfully connected to Admin Server 'AdminServer' that belongs to

domain
'bifoundation_domain'.
Warning: An insecure protocol was used to connect to the
server. To ensure on-the-wire security, the SSL port or
Admin port should be used instead.
wls:/bifoundation_domain/serverConfig>
```

In online mode, your command-prompt will reflect your position in the JMX MBean tree hierarchy, defaulting initially to place you in a location suitable for configuring the overall WebLogic domain. As you navigate up and down the MBean tree hierarchy the prompt will change to reflect your location in the tree hierarchy, in the same way that it would do using a terminal command-line prompt when navigating through your filesystem directory. To disconnect from WSLT, use the exit() command, like this:

```
wls:/bifoundation_domain/serverConfig> exit()
Exiting WebLogic Scripting Tool.
C:\Middleware\Oracle_BI1\common\bin>
```

Note that, as with exit() in the preceding command, all WLST commands have to include open and close brackets at the end, even if no parameters are passed with the command.

To run a WLST script (in what is called scripting mode), call the WLST executable as you did previously, and add the script name, plus any parameters, after it, like this:

```
wlst UpdateEmailConfiguration.py weblogic welcome1 localhost 7001 mark@exam-
ple.com
```

You would generally use WLST in conjunction with JMX MBeans and the Oracle BI Systems Management API to perform systems management tasks in a scripting environment. In this chapter, where we discuss administration tasks that you would normally carry out using the GUI provided by Fusion Middleware Control, we will therefore also examine how the task can be performed using WLST and JMX MBeans so that you can script your administration tasks and reduce the amount of manual configuration that you need to perform.

Overview of JMX MBeans and the Systems Management API

Both Fusion Middleware Control and WLST perform their actual administrative functions by reading attribute values and calling methods provided by JMX MBeans. JMX MBeans are Java objects, organized into a hierarchical tree structure, that provide methods to, for example, add new system components to an Oracle Instance, turn caching on and off, stop and start system components, and create new Managed Servers. Some JMX MBeans that you will want to access are part of standard WebLogic Server functionality, while others are provided specifically by Oracle Corporation to help administer Oracle Business Intelligence.

Fusion Middleware Control and the WLST scripts you use to automate business intelligence systems administration use a variety of JMX MBeans provided as part of the Oracle Business Intelligence installation. Some of these beans are grouped together into what is called the Oracle BI Systems Management API, a set of JMX MBeans for performing tasks specific to business intelligence such as enabling and disabling caching or uploading a new repository. Other JMX MBeans are provided as part of core Oracle Fusion Middleware functionality and are used for distributing configuration files, stopping and starting components, or making changes to security settings. We will see some of these MBeans in action in scripting examples later in this chapter.

You can also, as shown in Figure 10-3, use the System MBean Browser within Fusion Middleware Control to view the JMX MBeans tree hierarchy, view the current values for MBeans attributes, and to invoke JMX MBean methods.

To view the System MBean Browser, log into Fusion Middleware Control using a WebLogic Server administration account (for example, weblogic/welcome1), expand Farm_bifoundation_ domain in the navigation tree menu and then expand WebLogic Domain and bifoundation_ domain. Right-click AdminServer and select System MBean Browser. You will see that the available MBeans are organized into three folders:

- Configuration MBeans
- Runtime MBeans
- Application Defined MBeans

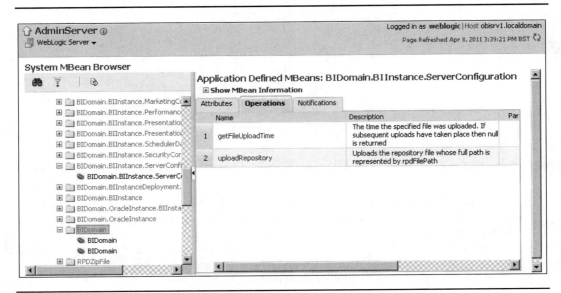

FIGURE 10-3. *System MBean Browser*

Generally, the JMX MBeans that you are interested in are within the Application Defined MBeans folder. Within this folder is a subfolder called oracle.biee.admin, and the JMX MBeans within it provide the functionality for the Oracle BI Systems Management API. The following are some key JMX MBeans within this list (the names in parentheses are the subfolder names in the MBean Browser tree):

- **ServerConfigurationMBean (BIDomain.BIInstance.ServerConfiguration)**   Contains methods for uploading new repositories and checking their status

- **BIDomainMBean (BIDomain)**   Contains methods for locking, releasing, and committing changes to system components (equivalent to the Lock and Edit Configuration, Release Configuration, and Activate Changes buttons in Fusion Middleware Control)

- **BIInstanceMBean (BIDomain.BIInstance)**   Contains MBeans for stopping and starting the whole Oracle BI instance or individual Java components, and is one of the MBeans called when you start and stop the Oracle Business Intelligence system using the Windows Start menu StartBIServices.bat and StopBIServices.bat batch files

- **BILogConfigurationMBean, EmailConfigurationMBean, and other configuration-setting MBeans within this tree**   Used for viewing and amending the various settings managed through Fusion Middleware Control

Other folders within the System MBean Browser navigation tree menu that you might want to investigate include oracle.as.management.mbeans.opmn, which contains MBeans for stopping, starting, restarting, and monitoring the system components via Oracle Process Management and Notification Server; and oracle.biee.local, which contains internal Oracle BI Domain information such as the sequence number for the current Oracle BI Repository file. We will see various administration examples that use these JMX MBeans and the Oracle BI Systems Management API later in this chapter.

Parameters and Settings Outside of the Oracle BI Systems Management API

While Oracle's long-term aim is to move as many configuration settings and processes as possible into the Oracle BI Systems Management API so that they can then be administered using Fusion Middleware Control and WLST, at the time of this writing, not all configuration tasks and settings are covered by this API. Therefore, for certain administration tasks and settings, you will need to manually edit configuration files such as NQSConfig.INI and instanceconfig.xml yourself, using a text editor such as Windows Notepad or vi/emacs on Unix/Linux.

You can see which configuration settings have to be manually managed in this way by opening a configuration file such as NQSConfig.INI (normally found under [*middleware_home*]/instances/instance1/config/OracleBIServerComponent/coreapplication_obis1) and reading each configuration setting. The settings that have the comment

```
# This Configuration setting is managed by Oracle Business Intelligence Enter-
prise Manager
```

after them are managed through the Oracle BI Systems Management API, and you should not manually alter them yourself by editing this file. The settings that do not have this comment after them have to be manually managed, and you will also need to ensure that all such manual changes are propagated to all copies of the configuration file across all nodes in the cluster. Any changes that you make to parameters that are managed by Fusion Middleware Control will in turn be overwritten when you next restart Oracle Business Intelligence.

Some tasks, also, have yet to be made available in Fusion Middleware Control and therefore need to be performed manually. For example, to set up usage tracking (detailed in Chapter 5), you have to make manual amendments to the NQSConfig.INI file and also add entries to your Oracle BI Repository. Other tasks (such as, in releases up to 11.1.1.6 of Oracle Business Intelligence, configuring Secure Sockets Layer [SSL] communications across the Oracle BI Domain) may have to be carried out using MBeans and WLST because Fusion Middleware Control does not yet provide corresponding graphical tools to perform them. This situation will change from release to release of Oracle Business Intelligence, so be sure to check the product documentation before embarking on manual configuration of your system.

Oracle Business Intelligence File System Structure

If you are upgrading from earlier versions of Oracle Business Intelligence or are not familiar with Oracle Fusion Middleware software deployments, the file system structure used by Oracle Business Intelligence may initially seem a bit confusing.

At a high level, the file system structure for Oracle Business Intelligence installed to the C:\ Middleware directory on a Microsoft Windows–based server appears as shown in Figure 10-4 (the same basic file system layout will be found on Unix- and Linux-based installations as well).

Key subdirectories within this structure include

- **\instances\instance1**   This is where you will find the logs, configuration files, and other "dynamic" files for the system components.
- **\Oracle_BI1\bifoundation**   This is where the system component binaries are located.

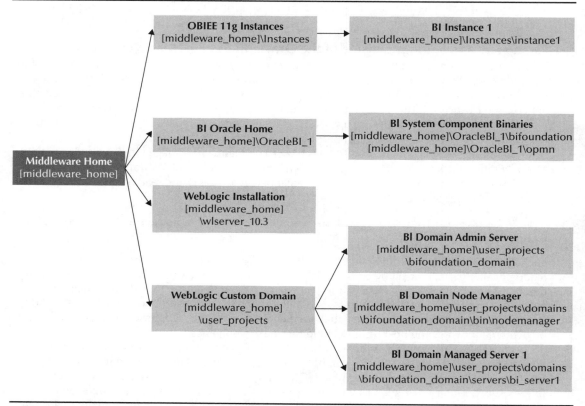

FIGURE 10-4. *File system structure for Oracle Business Intelligence on Windows*

- **\user_projects\domains\bifoundation_domain**   This is the location of the WebLogic domain created for Oracle Business Intelligence by the WebLogic configuration utility during installation.
- **\wlserver_10.3**   This is where the WebLogic Server binaries are kept.

Now that you have an overview of systems management and the tools that you use to perform it, let's take a look at some systems management tasks that you may wish to carry out on your Oracle Business Intelligence system.

Common Systems Management Tasks

In this section we examine some common systems management tasks that you will need to perform for an Oracle Business Intelligence system. We will look at how you perform these tasks both on a Microsoft Windows platform and on Unix/Linux platforms. You will see how you can perform these tasks using Fusion Middleware or with WLST scripts that you can use to automate some of your administration tasks.

The systems management tasks covered in this chapter are as follows:

- Starting and stopping the Oracle BI Domain
- Starting and stopping individual Java and system components within the Oracle BI Domain
- Monitoring metrics and system throughput
- Viewing and managing log files
- Managing performance options
- Managing repositories and catalogs

Starting and Stopping the Oracle BI Domain

Starting or stopping your entire Oracle BI Domain requires that you start or stop components in a particular sequence. When working with an installation of Oracle Business Intelligence on a Microsoft Windows platform, entries in the Start menu automate the process and will start and stop all components for you in the correct order. If you are working on a Unix or Linux system, though, or if you are starting or stopping a remote Microsoft Windows system, you will need scripts instead.

An alternative to manually stopping and starting the Oracle BI Domain yourself is to create auto-starting and auto-stopping services for the various servers and components. First, though, let's take a look at the simplest way to start and stop an Oracle BI instance: using the Windows Start menu.

Example: Starting and Stopping the Oracle BI Domain using Microsoft Windows

When you first install Oracle Business Intelligence on a Microsoft Windows–based server, the installer starts the various services and components for you as part of the configuration process. After you have rebooted the server, though, you will need to manually start the Oracle BI Domain yourself before you can use it again, using an entry in the Windows Start menu.

Before you begin this manual start, ensure that the database holding the Fusion Middleware repository schemas is online and available, and that you can connect to the repository schema that was installed by the Repository Creation Utility. Then, to start Oracle Business Intelligence, select Start | Programs | Oracle Business Intelligence | Start BI Services.

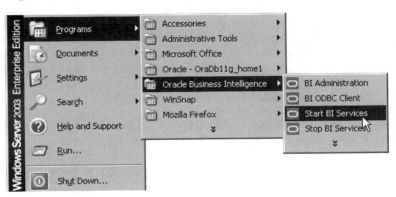

When you select this Windows Start menu item, it runs a script called StartStopServices.cmd with the option start_all, stored in the following location:

[*middleware_home*]\instances\instance1\bifoundation\OracleBIApplication\coreapplication\ startStopServices.cmd

This script sets a number of environment variables required by the startup process, and then calls an Apache Ant script that performs the following actions:

1. The first time the script runs, it asks for WebLogic Server administration user credentials, which it remembers for future starts of your system.

2. It starts the Administration Server via a WSLT script.

3. It waits until the Administration Server reports that it is running correctly.

4. It starts the default, single Managed Server via a WSLT script.

5. It waits until the Managed Server reports that it is running correctly.

6. It uses the Oracle Process Manager and Notification Server (OPMN) command-line utility to start all system components within the Oracle instance.

7. It opens your default web browser to the login screen for Oracle Business Intelligence.

For Simple Installation-type installations as described in Chapter 2, the steps to start and monitor the Manager Server are removed automatically from this script, as these types of installation do not include a Managed Server, instead installing all Java components in the Administration Server to conserve resources.

For Microsoft Windows-based installations, you may have noticed two services automatically added to your system to start up processes used by Oracle Business Intelligence:

■ Oracle Process Manager (instance1), used for automatically starting Oracle Process Manager & Notification Server (OPMN)

■ Oracle WebLogic NodeManager, which starts the Node Manager Weblogic utility that is used by Fusion Middleware Control and WebLogic Server Administration Console to stop and start Managed Servers

Note that, however, apart from the repository database being available, neither of the two services actually needs to be running for this script to execute successfully, as the script starts OPMN and the Oracle Process Manager service itself as part of the startup steps, then starting the Managed Server directly using a WLST script rather than using Node Manager to do so. It is good practice though to still have these services start automatically as part of your server startup, as having the Oracle Process Manager service already running will reduce the time that the script takes to run, and you may need the Node Manager later on if you decide to stop and start the Managed Server through Oracle WebLogic Server Administration Console.

To stop the Oracle BI Domain under Microsoft Windows, follow a similar process by selecting Start | Programs | Oracle Business Intelligence | Stop BI Services. This Windows Start menu entry runs the same script as for startup, but it always prompts you for the WebLogic administrator username and password, and then passes the stop_all parameter to the ant script, causing the shutdown sequence to be executed instead.

Example: Starting and Stopping the Oracle BI Domain Using Unix/Linux

There is no equivalent to the Start BI Services and Stop BI Services Start menu entries when you work with a Unix or Linux system, so you have to run the WLST and OPMN scripts yourself that these Start menu entries would otherwise run for you. Again, as with the Windows startup sequence, Node Manager does not necessarily need to be running before you start the Managed Server, but it is good practice to start it along with the other WebLogic servers in case you need it later on.

The four scripts and commands that you need to run that in sequence, start your WebLogic Server Administration Server, Node Manager, Managed Server, and system components are as follows:

1. [*middleware_home*]/user_projects/domains/bifoundation_domain/bin/StartWebLogic.sh

2. [*middleware_home*]/wlserver_10.3/server/bin/startNodeManager.sh

3. [*middleware_home*]/user_projects/domains/bifoundation_domain/bin/
   StartManagedWebLogic.sh <managed_server_name>

4. [*middleware_home*]/instances/instance1/bin/opmnctl startall

To run these scripts, create a Unix/Linux shell script that runs the scripts in order. An example of such a script follows:

```
#variables
export ORACLE_USER=oracle
export FMW_HOME=/u01/app/middleware
export MANAGED_SERVERNAME=bi_server1
export HOSTNAME=obisrv1
export WEBLOGIC_PORT=7001
#-----------------------------------------------
#Start OBI EE 11g
echo -e "Starting Weblogic Server..."
$FMW_HOME/user_projects/domains/bifoundation_domain/bin/startWebLogic.sh >
logs/start_weblogic_server.log    2>&1 &
sleep 30
echo -e "Starting Node Manager..."
$FMW_HOME/wlserver_10.3/server/bin/startNodeManager.sh > logs/start_nodeman-
ager.log 2>&1 &
sleep 30
echo -e "Starting Managed Server: $MANAGED_SERVERNAME..."
$FMW_HOME/user_projects/domains/bifoundation_domain/bin/startManagedWebLogic.
sh $MANAGED_SERVERNAME      "http://$HOSTNAME:$WEBLOGIC_PORT" > logs/start_
managed_server.log 2>&1 &
sleep 30
echo -e "Starting System Components..."
$FMW_HOME/instances/instance1/bin/opmnctl startall > logs/start_opmnctl.log
2>&1 &
sleep 30
```

A variation on this script would also work on a Microsoft Windows environment, and you may wish to use such a script instead of the supplied StartStopServices.cmd script if you have more than one Managed Server to start (for example, after a horizontal scale-out has taken place), or if you wish to take advantage of the boot.properties credentials file detailed in the next section.

Note that this script assumes a wait time of 30 seconds between the start of each service, which should be long enough but may need to be changed for your particular system.

Embedding Credentials in the boot.properties File   When you run the preceding Unix-specific scripts to start and stop the Administration Server and Managed Server, the scripts will by default prompt you for the username and password of the WebLogic Server administration account. To pass these credentials automatically to the scripts, you can create a file called boot .properties, which can hold, in an encrypted (and therefore secure) way, these credentials, and the StartWebLogic.sh and StartManagedWebLogic.sh scripts will use these credentials automatically during startup and shutdown.

NOTE
On Microsoft Windows–based systems, the StartBIServices.cmd script prompts you once for administrator credentials and then automatically sets up the boot.properties file for you; therefore, you do not need to follow the next set of steps unless you change the password and need to re-create the file.

Follow these steps to create the boot.properties file on Unix-based systems:

1.   Using a text editor, create a file called **boot.properties** in the following two locations:

[*middleware_home*]/user_projects/domains/bifoundation_domain/servers/AdminServer/security
[*middleware_home*]/user_projects/domains/bifoundation_domain/servers/bi_server1/security

NOTE
If you have installed Oracle Business Intelligence using the Simple Install type, then only the first location, for the Administration Server, will be present on your system. Similarly, if you have scaled out your system to additional servers (as described in Chapter 2), and therefore have more than one Managed Server in your WebLogic Domain, you need to create boot.properties files in their corresponding file system locations as well.

2.   Within each file, add two entries in the format

username=<*name of WebLogic administration user*>
password=<*password of WebLogic administration user*>

so that the file reads, for example:

```
username=weblogic
password=welcome1
```

When you next stop or start the Administration Server and Managed Server, the username and password within the file will be encrypted to read, for example:

```
password={AES}tHlEh4tOcNcrYSOeaStahQnn2MLDs98VX6MJOaikxWY\=
username={AES}hm15n+mOTdqBhnkXrhXsJ4yuOzE35i4bYxnh8uuSH24\=
```

Example: Creating Windows Services That Automatically Start and Stop on System Boot and System Shutdown

If you are used to using the earlier, 10g release of Oracle Business Intelligence, you may remember that key servers such as the Oracle BI Server, Oracle BI Presentation Server, and Oracle BI Scheduler ran from Windows services that could be configured to automatically start after the server booted. While as detailed earlier on Oracle Business Intelligence 11g has services for Oracle Process Manager and Node Manager that can be set to automatically start, there are no such services defined by default for the Administration Server and, in the case of enterprise installations, Managed Server(s).

Oracle WebLogic Server installations do , however, come with a utility that can create Windows services for the Administration and Managed Server(s). To run this utility and create services that start automatically when your servers, follow these steps:

1. Stop any WebLogic Administration Servers or Managed Servers that are currently running, either through the Windows Start menu (Start | Programs | Oracle Business Intelligence | Stop BI Services) or through the supplied scripts.

2. Using the steps outlined in the previous section, create boot.properties files for the Administration Server and Managed Server in the correct locations so that the two servers can automatically start with the correct credentials.

3. Create the command file that will be used to create the Administration Server Windows services. Use a text editor to create a file called **installAdminServerService.cmd** and enter the following commands into it, replacing the items in bold with the correct details for your environment:

```
SETLOCAL
set DOMAIN_NAME=bifoundation_domain
set USERDOMAIN_HOME=c:\middleware\user_projects\domains\bifoundation_
domain
set SERVER_NAME=AdminServer
set PRODUCTION_MODE=true
cd %USERDOMAIN_HOME%
call %USERDOMAIN_HOME%\bin\setDomainEnv.cmd
call "c:\middleware\wlserver_10.3\server\bin\installSvc.cmd"
ENDLOCAL
```

4. Create the Managed Server command file that will be used to create the Managed Server Windows services (do not create this file for Simple Install–type systems). To do this, use a text editor to create a file called **installManagedServerService.cmd** and enter the following commands into it (again, adjusting for your environment):

```
SETLOCAL
set DOMAIN_NAME=bifoundation_domain
set USERDOMAIN_HOME=c:\middleware\user_projects\domains\bifoundation_
domain
set SERVER_NAME=bi_server1
set PRODUCTION_MODE=true
set ADMIN_URL=http://localhost:7001
cd %USERDOMAIN_HOME%
call %USERDOMAIN_HOME%\bin\setDomainEnv.cmd
call "c:\middleware\wlserver_10.3\server\bin\installSvc.cmd"
ENDLOCAL
```

5. Using your Windows desktop, right-click the Computer icon, and select Properties. In the menu on the left, click Advanced System Settings and then click the Environment Variables button. In the Environment Variables dialog box, click the New button in the System Variables section and create a new system variable called **BI_ORACLE_HOME** and set it to your [*middleware_home*]\Oracle_BI1\ path (for example, C:\Middleware\ Oracle_BI1\).

6. Run the two command scripts you just created, to create and install the two Windows services. Check the list of services that are now available for your Windows installation (Start | Control Panel | Administrative Tools | Services), and you will see two new services:

   beasvc bifoundation_domain_AdminServer
   beasvc bifoundation_domain_bi_server1

   Start these services to test that they are working correctly, and check the status of each server through the log files at

   [*middleware_home*]\user_projects\user_projects\domains\bifoundation_domain\ servers\AdminServer\logs\AdminServer.log

   and

   [*middleware_home*]\user_projects\domains\bifoundation_domain\servers\bi_server1\ logs\bi_server1.log

7. Repeat step 4 for any additional Managed Servers that you create after initial deployment.

Starting and Stopping the Oracle BI Domain Using Oracle WebLogic Administration Console and Fusion Middleware Control

Although you will probably want to start and stop your Oracle BI Domain from the Windows Start menu, or from WLST and OPMN scripts when in a Unix/Linux environment, you may sometimes wish to start and stop the system using the graphical environments provided by Oracle WebLogic Server Administration Console and Fusion Middleware Control. You might also find this startup method useful if you are having problems starting the system and want to step through each stage in the process manually. Or, you may simply prefer to do as much in a graphical environment as possible and minimize use of the command line. Before you attempt to start the various WebLogic servers, if you are using a Microsoft Windows–based environment, ensure that the Oracle WebLogic NodeManager (C_Middleware_wlserver_10.3) and Oracle Process Manager (instance1) services are running and available as Oracle WebLogic Administration Console and Fusion Middleware Control both use them to start components in the domain.

Example: Starting the WebLogic Server Administration Server   Before you can start the rest of the parts of Oracle Business Intelligence using the graphical tools provided, you do, however, need to start from the command line the Administration Server itself and, on Unix/Linux, Node Manager.

   To start the Administration Server, run the following script:

```
[middleware_home]/user_projects/domains/bifoundation_domain/bin/StartWebLogic.
sh
```

Depending on whether you have created a boot.properties file, either the Administration Server will automatically start or you will be prompted to enter the credentials for a WebLogic Server administration user.

If you then need to start Node Manager (usually only if you are running under Unix/Linux, as it will have started as a service under Windows), run the following script:

```
[middleware_home]/wlserver_10.3/server/bin/startNodeManager.sh
```

Once this script has run successfully, you can use the WebLogic Server Administration Console, and then Fusion Middleware Control, to start the rest of the components and servers.

Example: Starting the Managed Server Using the Weblogic Server Administration Console

To start your Managed Servers, and therefore the Java components within Oracle Business Intelligence, using the Oracle WebLogic Server Administration Console, do the following:

1. Using your web browser, navigate to the Oracle WebLogic Server Administration Console login screen at http://<*machine_name*>:7001/console (for example, http://obisrv1:7001/console). When prompted, enter the username and password for your WebLogic administration user (for example, weblogic/welcome1).

2. In the Domain Structure navigation tree menu on the left-hand side of the Administration Console, expand the Environment link and click the Servers entry, as shown next.

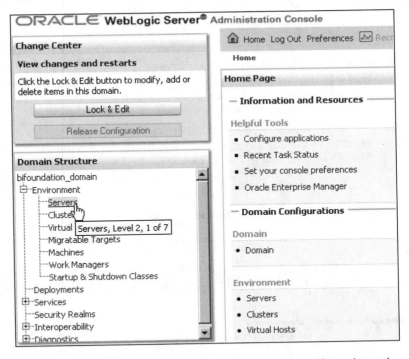

3. On the Summary of Servers screen, locate the table of servers halfway down the screen. It should show the Administration Server (AdminServer (admin)) State as RUNNING and the Managed Server (bi_server1) State as SHUTDOWN.

4. To start the Managed Server, click the Control tab just under the Summary of Servers heading, which initially has the Configuration tab selected instead.

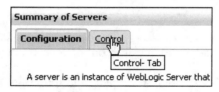

5. Select the check box to the left of the bi_server1 Managed Server and then click the Start button under it.

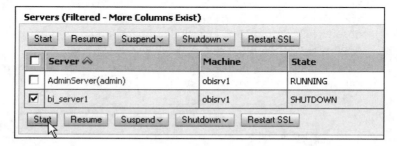

6. On the Server Life Cycle Assistant screen, at the Start Servers prompt, click the Yes button to begin the startup process. Note that this step will fail if the Node Manager is not running at this time, as the Node Manager is used by the Administration Console to instruct the Managed Server to start.

7. The Administration Console, through the Node Manager, starts the selected Managed Server. To automatically refresh the screen and see the updated status of the Managed Server, click the refresh button just above the table of servers.

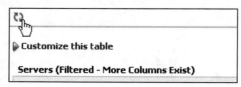

8. Once the startup process has completed successfully, the table of servers will show the Managed Server (bi_server1) State as RUNNING, and the Status of Last Action as TASK COMPLETED.

Servers (Filtered - More Columns Exist)

Server ⌃	Machine	State	Status of Last Action
AdminServer(admin)	obisrv1	RUNNING	None
bi_server1	obisrv1	RUNNING	TASK COMPLETED

If you later wish to stop your Managed Servers, follow the same process, but this time click the Shutdown button, choosing either the When Work Completes option, to allow all WebLogic transactions to complete, or the Force Shutdown Now option, to stop the server immediately at the expense of a recovery operation the next time the Managed Server starts.

Example: Starting the Managed Server Using Fusion Middleware Control   Once you have started the Administration Server for your Oracle BI Domain, you can also start the Managed Server through Fusion Middleware Control. To do so, follow these steps:

1. Using your Web browser, navigate to the Fusion Middleware login screen at http://<machine_name>:7001/em (for example, http://obisrv1:7001/em). When prompted, enter the username and password for your WebLogic administration user (for example, weblogic/welcome1).

2. Using the navigation tree menu on the left-hand side of the screen, expand Farm_ bifoundation_domain, WebLogic Domain, bifoundation_domain, bi_cluster, and select bi_server1 (or whichever Managed Server you wish to stop, start, or restart).

3. Right-click the Managed Server entry (for example, bi_server1) and select Control | Start Up or Control | Shut Down.

Fusion Middleware Control will then start up or shut down your Managed Server.

NOTE
Ensure that Node Manager is running on the server that hosts your initial Administration and Managed Servers, and also on any additional servers that have Managed Servers hosted on them if you have scaled-out your installation.

Example: Starting System Components Using Fusion Middleware Control   Starting the Managed Server only starts the Java components within the Oracle BI Domain. To start the system components within your Oracle BI instance such as the Oracle BI Server and Oracle BI Presentation Server, you can again use Fusion Middleware Control, which in turn uses OPMN to start them.

To use Fusion Middleware Control to start the system component within your Oracle BI instance, follow these steps:

1. Using your web browser, navigate to the Fusion Middleware Control login screen at http://<machine_ name>:7001/em (for example, http://obisrv1:7001/em). When prompted, enter the username and password for a WebLogic administration user (for example, weblogic/welcome1).

2. When the Fusion Middleware Control home page is displayed, use the navigation tree menu on the left-hand side to expand the Business Intelligence folder and select the coreapplication node.

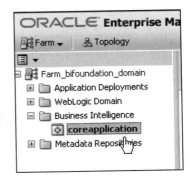

3. On the right-hand side of the screen, select the Overview tab to show the overall status of the system components. If you are running Oracle Business Intelligence on a Microsoft Windows–based server and have set the Oracle Process Manager Windows service to automatically start on system start, you will notice that all of the system components have the status of Up. If this is the case, you do not need to take any further action, and you can log out of Fusion Middleware Control and close your web browser.

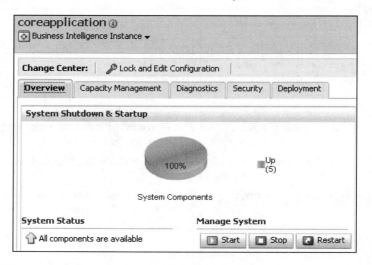

4. If this service is not running, or if you are starting system components on a Unix- or Linux-based system, the status of the system components will probably be shown as Down.

   To start all of the components, click the Start button under the Manage System heading, as shown next. In the Confirmation dialog box, click Yes to confirm. Fusion Middleware Control (through OPMN) will then start the system components.

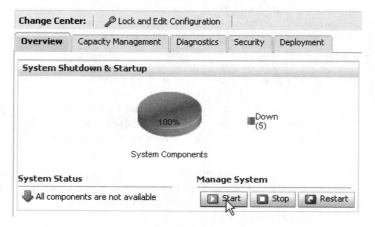

5. To subsequently stop or restart the system components, use the Stop and Restart buttons on the same page.

If you would now like to check that the system components within your Oracle BI instance are now available, use your web browser to navigate to the Oracle Business Intelligence Home page at http://<*machine_name*>:9704/analytics (for example, http://obisrv1:9704/analytics) and you will be presented with the Oracle Business Intelligence login screen. Enter the WebLogic administrator username and password (for example, weblogic/welcome1) and check that the Oracle Business Intelligence Home page shown here is then displayed.

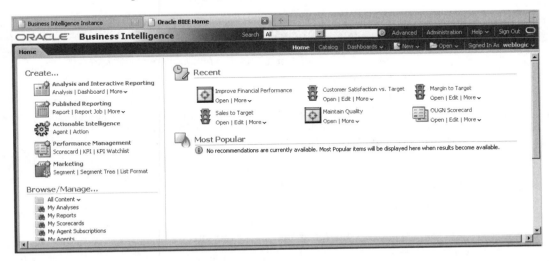

Starting and Stopping Individual Java and System Components

In addition to stopping, starting, and restarting the entire Oracle BI Domain, you may also want to stop, start, or restart individual system or Java components within the BI domain. This may be the case if a component has stopped responding to requests, or if you wish to restart a component to pick up changes to its configuration.

You can stop, start, and restart components either through Fusion Middleware Control, through command-line tools such as opmnctl, or through WLST scripts that make use of the Oracle BI Systems Management API. The most common component restart scenario, though, is where you have to restart one of the system components to start using a changed configuration setting, and the easiest way to do this is through the graphical environment provided by Fusion Middleware Control.

Starting, Stopping, and Restarting System Components

System Components, such as the Oracle BI Server and Oracle BI Presentation Server components, only start using new configuration settings when you restart them. For example, if you configure query caching to be enabled for a particular BI Server component, you will need to restart it before this new setting becomes active.

As previously mentioned, the three primary ways that you can stop, start, and restart system components are through Fusion Middleware Control, through the opmnctl command-line utility, and through WLST scripting.

Example: Starting, Stopping, and Restarting System Components Using Fusion Middleware Control Using Fusion Middleware Control, you can start, stop, and restart individual system components, groups of components of the same type, or all components in your Oracle BI instance across any cluster node.

To stop, start, or restart all of the system components within an Oracle BI instance, do the following:

1. Use your web browser to navigate to the Fusion Middleware Control web site, typically at http://<*machine_name*>:7001/em (for example, http://obisrv1:7001/em). When prompted, enter the credentials for a WebLogic Server administration user (for example, weblogic/ welcome1) and then expand the Business Intelligence folder on the left-hand side of the screen and select the coreapplication node.

2. Make sure that the Overview tab is selected on the right-hand side of the page. Then, within the System Shutdown & Startup area, under the Manage System heading, click either the Start, Stop, or Restart button, and then click Yes when prompted to start, stop, or restart all of the system components within the Oracle instance.

If you want to stop, start, or restart all system components of a particular type, or just an individual system component, do the following:

1. With the Fusion Middleware Control web site open, ensure that coreapplication is selected in the Business Intelligence folder, and then select the Availability tab and its Processes subtab on the right-hand side of the screen.

2. Under the Processes heading, there are six buttons for stopping, starting, or restarting either all components or individual components. The first three buttons do the same as the corresponding buttons on the Overview tab, but the second three buttons are used for stopping, starting, or restarting groups of components or individual components.

   To stop, start, or restart all BI Server components within the Oracle BI instance (because, for example, you have enabled or disabled query caching), select the box to the left of the BI Servers folder heading and then click either the Start Selected, Stop Selected, or Restart Selected buttons.

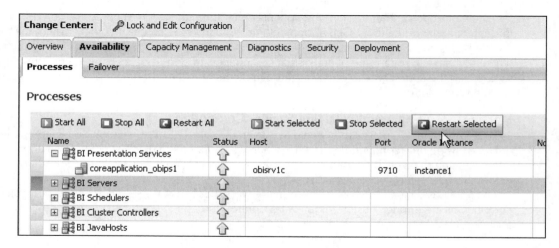

3. To stop, start, or restart an individual system component (for example, to start a newly provisioned BI Server component after vertical scale-out), within the same screen, expand the component folder and click the individual component you wish to start. Again, with the component selected, click either the Start Selected, Stop Selected, or Restart Selected button to perform the required action.

Change Center:	Lock and Edit Configuration					
Overview	**Availability**	Capacity Management	Diagnostics	Security	Deployment	

Processes   Failover

Processes

Start All   Stop All   Restart All   Start Selected   Stop Selected   **Restart Selected**

Name	Status	Host	Port	Oracle Instance	Note
⊟ BI Presentation Services	⇧				
coreapplication_obips1	⇧	obisrv1c	9710	instance1	
⊟ BI Servers	⇧				
coreapplication_obis1	⇧	obisrv1c	9703	instance1	
⊞ BI Schedulers	⇧				
⊞ BI Cluster Controllers	⇧				
⊞ BI JavaHosts	⇧				

Example: Starting, Stopping, and Restarting System Components Using opmnctl   When Fusion Middleware Control requests that a system component stop, start, or restart, the actual part of the Oracle BI Domain that performs the action is the Oracle Process Manager and Notification Server (OPMN) component, which runs as a service under Microsoft Windows and has a command-line interface for both Windows and Unix/Linux. The command-line interface is called opmnctl.bat (Windows) or opmnctl.sh (Unix/Linux) and can generally be found under /instances/instance1/bin.

Each Oracle instance within your overall Oracle BI instance will have its own copy of opmnctl, with normally only one Oracle instance per server. Each server's Oracle instance needs to be administered using its own local copy of opmnctl, which is by default configured to manage just that instance's system components. It is possible to configure individual opmnctl utilities to manage more than one Oracle instance's components, but that is not the configured behavior for Oracle Business Intelligence and is outside the scope of this book.

To use this command-line interface to OPMN, open a command-line session and, for example, using a Microsoft Windows-based environment, navigate to the utility using these commands:

```
C:\>cd c:\Middleware\instances\instance1\bin

C:\Middleware\instances\instance1\bin>opmnctl
```

Running opmnctl without any parameters in this way outputs help instructions and a listing of all allowed commands and parameters. You only need to know a small subset of these commands to perform stop, start, and restart actions on components, though, and the following are some key examples of what you might want to use.

To stop all system components within an Oracle instance, use the command

```
opmnctl stopall
```

To start all or restart all components within an Oracle instance, use startall or restartall instead. To start just OPMN for an Oracle instance, use the command

```
opmnctl start
```

To check the status of the system components being managed by OPMN within an Oracle instance, use the command

```
opmnctl status
```

If you have just run the status command after the start command, you will notice that all of the system components within that Oracle instance start when OPMN starts, as this is how Oracle has configured them to work within Oracle Business Intelligence 11g:

```
C:\Middleware\instances\instance1\bin>opmnctl status
Processes in Instance: instance1
---------------------------------+--------------------+---------+---------
ias-component                    | process-type       |     pid | status
---------------------------------+--------------------+---------+---------
coreapplication_obiccs1          | OracleBIClusterCo~ |    5956 | Alive
coreapplication_obisch1          | OracleBIScheduler~ |    5896 | Alive
coreapplication_obijh1           | OracleBIJavaHostC~ |    5860 | Alive
coreapplication_obips1           | OracleBIPresentat~ |    5840 | Alive
coreapplication_obis1            | OracleBIServerCom~ |    5788 | Alive
```

To stop an individual system component within a particular Oracle instance—for example, the initially configured Oracle BI Server in the default Oracle instance—use the command

```
opmnctl stopproc ias-component = coreapplication_obis1
```

To restart a Oracle BI Presentation Server component, use the command

```
opmnctl restartproc ias-component = coreapplication_obips1
```

Use the status command to see the names of other ias-components that you can start, stop, and restart in this way. Note that if you have added additional Oracle BI Servers, Oracle Presentation Servers, or other system components, different, sequential numbers will be used after the component name, so you may end up with a list of components such as this:

- coreapplication_obis1 (the default Oracle BI Server component)
- coreapplication_obijh1 (the default Oracle BI Java Host component)
- coreapplication_obis2 (a second Oracle BI Server component, added through vertical scale-out)
- coreapplication_obips2 (a second Oracle BI Presentation Server component, similarly added)

To start all components of the same class (known as *process types*) within an Oracle instance, for example, all Oracle BI Servers, use the process-type parameter instead of ias-component, like this:

```
opmnctl startproc process-type = OracleBIServerComponent
```

Other process types that you can use with this parameter are

- OracleBIPresentationServerComponent
- OracleBIClusterControllerComponent
- OracleBISchedulerComponent
- OracleBIJavaHostComponent

Note that when you use opmnctl to start, stop, or restart components or process types, you may need to log out of and then log back in to Fusion Middleware Control to see the updated status of the affected components.

Example: Starting, Stopping, and Restarting System Components Using WLST Scripting and the Oracle BI Systems Management API In addition to scripting the stop, start, or restart of system components through the opmnctl command-line tool, you can also script them using WLST and the Java JMX MBeans. When you invoke the MBean methods, they actually call the opmnctl command-line tool in the background, but using them in this way may better integrate with other command-line scripts that you use.

To create a WLST script that stops, starts, or restarts the entire Oracle BI instance (that is, all system components of all types) using a Microsoft Windows-based environment, follow these steps:

1. Using a text editor, create a script that includes the following commands:

```
# Example to stopping, starting, or restarting all system components
within an instance
#
# This scripts expects the following arguments:
#
# 1. wls.host (localhost)
# 2. wls.port (7001)
# 3. wls.user  (user1)
# 4. wls.password  (password1)
# 5. componentstatus (start, stop, or restart)
# ================================================================
import sys
import os
# Check the arguments to this script are as expected.
# argv[0] is script name.
argLen = len(sys.argv)
if argLen -1 != 5:
    print "ERROR: got ", argLen -1, " args."
    print "USAGE: wlst StopStartRestartInstance.py  WLS_HOST WLS_PORT
WLS_USER WLS_PASSWORD componentstatus"
    print "  eg: wlst StopStartRestartInstance.py localhost 7001 web-
```

```
logic welcome1 restart"
    exit()
WLS_HOST = sys.argv[1]
WLS_PORT = sys.argv[2]
WLS_USER = sys.argv[3]
WLS_PW = sys.argv[4]
componentstatus = sys.argv[5]
print 'Connecting to '+ WLS_HOST+ ':' + WLS_PORT + ' as user: ' + WLS_
USER + ' ...'
# Connect to WLS
connect(WLS_USER, WLS_PW, WLS_HOST+ ':' + WLS_PORT);
print 'Connecting to Domain ...'
domainCustom()
cd ('oracle.biee.admin')
print 'Connecting to BIDomain MBean ...'
cd ('oracle.biee.admin:type=BIDomain,group=Service')
biinstances = get('BIInstances')
biinstance = biinstances[0]
print 'Connecting to BIInstance MBean ...'
cd ('..')
cd (biinstance.toString())
if (componentstatus == "restart"):
    servicestatus=get('ServiceStatus')
    print 'BIInstance MBean; ServiceStatus: ' + servicestatus
    print 'Calling stop ...'
    objs = jarray.array([], java.lang.Object)
    strs = jarray.array([], java.lang.String)
    invoke('stop', objs, strs)
    servicestatus=get('ServiceStatus')
    print 'BIInstance MBean; ServiceStatus: ' + servicestatus
    print 'Calling start ...'
    objs = jarray.array([], java.lang.Object)
    strs = jarray.array([], java.lang.String)
    invoke('start', objs, strs)
    servicestatus=get('ServiceStatus')
    print 'BIInstance MBean; ServiceStatus: ' + servicestatus
elif componentstatus == "start":
    servicestatus=get('ServiceStatus')
    print 'BIInstance MBean; ServiceStatus: ' + servicestatus
    print 'Calling start ...'
    objs = jarray.array([], java.lang.Object)
    strs = jarray.array([], java.lang.String)
    invoke('start', objs, strs)
    servicestatus=get('ServiceStatus')
    print 'BIInstance MBean; ServiceStatus: ' + servicestatus
else :
    servicestatus=get('ServiceStatus')
    print 'BIInstance MBean; ServiceStatus: ' + servicestatus
    print 'Calling stop ...'
    objs = jarray.array([], java.lang.Object)
    strs = jarray.array([], java.lang.String)
```

```
        invoke('stop', objs, strs)
        servicestatus=get('ServiceStatus')
        print 'BIInstance MBean; ServiceStatus: ' + servicestatus
    exit()
```

2. Save the script file as **StopStartRestartInstance.py**, and then call it using the WLST executable at [*middleware_home*]\Oracle_BI1\common\bin, like this:

```
wlst stopStartRestartInstance.py localhost 7001 weblogic welcome1 re-
start
```

To create a script to start, for example, an individual system component within the default Oracle instance created during the installation process (for example, coreapplication_obis1, the default Oracle BI Server component in an instance) or a whole category of components (for example, coreapplication_obis), follow these steps based on a Microsoft Windows-based environment :

1. Using a text editor, type in the following WLST script:

```
import sys
import os
import java.lang
import string

# Check the arguments to this script are as expected.
# argv[0] is script name.
argLen = len(sys.argv)
if argLen -1 != 6:
    print "ERROR: got ", argLen -1, " args."
    print "USAGE: wlst.cmd startStopRestartSysComp.py WLS_HOST WLS_PORT
WLS_USER  WLS_PASSWORD componentstatus componentname"
    print "   eg: wlst.cmd startStopRestartSysComp.py localhost 7001
user1 password1 restart coreapplication_obis1"
    exit()
# Sample Usage
# 1. wlst.cmd localhost 7001 weblogic welcome1 restart coreapplication_
obips1
# 2. wlst.cmd localhost 7001 weblogic welcome1 start coreapplication_
obis (restarts all of specified type)

WLS_HOST = sys.argv[1]
WLS_PORT = sys.argv[2]
WLS_USER = sys.argv[3]
WLS_PW = sys.argv[4]
# componentstatus valid values: start, stop, restart
componentstatus = sys.argv[5]
# componentname valid values: coreapplication_obisn, coreapplication_
obis (similarly for other component# s)
componentname = sys.argv[6]
connect(WLS_USER, WLS_PW, WLS_HOST+ ':' + WLS_PORT);
# connect("weblogic","welcome1","localhost:7001")
domainCustom()
cd ('oracle.biee.admin')
```

```
cd ('oracle.biee.admin:type=BIDomain,group=Service')
# Get the Oracle Instance
oracleinstances = get('OracleInstances')
oracleinstance = oracleinstances[0]
cd('..')
cd(oracleinstance.toString())
# Get the BI Instance Deployment MBean under the Oracle Instance MBean.
biinstancedeployments = get('BIInstanceDeployments')
biinstancedeployment = biinstancedeployments[0]
cd('..')
cd(biinstancedeployment.toString())
# Get the Deployed OPMN Components under the BI Instance MBean.
components = get('Components')
# List down the total number of OPMN Components deployed
numbiservers=get('NumBIServers')
numclustercontrollers=get('NumClusterControllers')
numjavahosts=get('NumJavahosts')
numpresentationservers=get('NumPresentationServers')
numschedulers=get('NumSchedulers')

objs = jarray.array([],java.lang.Object)
strs = jarray.array([],java.lang.String)
cd('..')
itr=0
ptr=1
enteredcomponentname=componentname
# Iterate through all the components and check for the existence
# of the component specified in the Parameter, using a fuzzy match.
while (itr < len(components)):
    check=-1
    comstr=""
# Get the Process Component Name directly from the MBean for validation
    comstr=String(components[itr].toString()).split(",")
    print comstr[3]
    print componentname
# Check specific for BI Server alone.
# If coreapplication_obis is given as parameter,
# it is checked against each component to see whether
# the component name contains the coreapplication_obis
# string. This logic will work for all components
# except the BI Server as coreapplication_obis is
# contained within the scheduler component names as
# well; for example, coreapplication_obisch1.
# To bypass the error, one more check is added.
    if (componentname == "coreapplication_obis"):
        componentname=componentname+str(ptr)
    check=string.find(comstr[3],componentname)
    print check
    if (check != -1):
        cd(components[itr].toString())
# Check for start, stop, or restart.
```

```
          if (componentstatus == "restart"):
                invoke('stop',objs,strs)
                invoke('start',objs,strs)
                print comstr[3]+": Restarted"
          elif (componentstatus == "start"):
                invoke('start',objs,strs)
                print comstr[3]+": Started"
          else:
                invoke('stop',objs,strs)
                print comstr[3]+": Stopped"
          cd('..')
    else:
          print "No Match Yet"

    ptr=ptr+1
      itr=itr+1
exit()
```

2. Save the file to your file system as **startStopRestartSysComp.py**, and then call it using the WLST executable at [*middleware_home*]\Oracle_BI1\common\bin, like this:

```
wlst startStopRestartSysComp.py localhost 7001 weblogic welcome1 re-
start coreapplication_obis1
```

3. To restart an entire category of components within this Oracle instance such as all Oracle BI Presentation Server components, omit the component number from the component name parameter, like this:

```
wlst startStopRestartSysComp.py localhost 7001 weblogic welcome1 re-
start coreapplication_obips
```

Starting, Stopping, and Restarting Java Components

In addition to the system components within the Oracle BI instance, Oracle Business Intelligence also makes use of Java components such as Oracle BI Publisher and Oracle BI Office. While you will probably not need to stop, start, or restart these Java components as often as the system ones (as they generally do not need to be restarted after a configuration change), when you do, you can do so either through Fusion Middleware Control or through WLST and the Oracle BI Systems Management API.

Starting and Stopping Java Components Using Fusion Middleware Control   To stop or start an individual Java component using Fusion Middleware Control, follow these steps:

1. Using your web browser, navigate to the Fusion Middleware Control login screen at http://<*machine_name*>:7001/em (for example, http://obisrv1:7001/em). When prompted, enter the username and password for your WebLogic administration user (for example, weblogic/welcome1).

2. Using the navigation tree menu on the left-hand side of the screen, expand Farm_ bifoundation_domain and select Application Deployments.

3. Within the Application Deployments folder, navigate to the (optional) application cluster folder (for example, bipublisher(11.1.1)(bi_cluster)) and then the application entry (for example, bipublisher(11.1.1)(bi_server1)).

4. Right-click the application entry in the menu and select Control | Start Up or Control | Shut Down.

5. Fusion Middleware Control will then start up or shut down your Java component.

Starting, Stopping, and Restarting Java Components Using WLST You can also start up or shut down individual Java components across your Oracle BI domain using WLST and the JMX MBean-based Oracle BI Systems Management API. The following example WLST script shows the steps to stop, and then start, the BI Publisher Java component:

```
# Example to demonstrate restarting the BI Publisher Java component
#
# This script expects the following arguments:
#
# 1. wls.host (localhost)
# 2. wls.port (7001)
# 3. wls.user  (user1)
# 4. wls.password  (password1)
# =====================================================================

import sys
import os
 # Check the arguments to this script are as expected.
# argv[0] is script name.
argLen = len(sys.argv)
if argLen -1 != 4:
    print "ERROR: got ", argLen -1, " args."
    print "USAGE: wlst.cmd restartBIP.py WLS_HOST WLS_PORT WLS_USER WLS_PASS-
WORD"
    print "   eg: wlst.cmd restartBIP.py localhost 7001 weblogic welcome1"
    exit()

WLS_HOST = sys.argv[1]
WLS_PORT = sys.argv[2]
WLS_USER = sys.argv[3]
WLS_PW = sys.argv[4]

print 'Connecting to '+ WLS_HOST+ ':' + WLS_PORT + ' as user: ' + WLS_USER + '
...'

# Connect to WLS
connect(WLS_USER, WLS_PW, WLS_HOST+ ':' + WLS_PORT);

print 'Connecting to the Servers Configuration MBean ...'
cd('Servers')
ls()
## Stop BI Publisher
print 'Stopping BI Publisher Java component ...'
progress=stopApplication('bipublisher#11.1.1')
```

```
## Start BI Publisher
print 'Starting BI Publisher Java component ...'
progress=startApplication('bipublisher#11.1.1')
exit()
```

Substitute other application names if you wish to stop or start other Java applications; you can use Fusion Middleware Control to determine the names to use in the script by looking at the list of applications in the Application Deployments folder in the navigation tree menu.

Monitoring Metrics and Throughput

Systems administrators working with Oracle Business Intelligence need to be aware of the load and throughput of the system at particular points in time. Being aware of such information is useful in diagnosing system slowdowns, and can also help in planning capacity and the topology of your system.

Helpfully, Oracle Business Intelligence, through the Oracle Dynamic Monitoring Service (DMS), provides a number of metrics grouped into metric tables that you can use to monitor your system. You can access these metrics either through Fusion Middleware Control or through the WLST scripting tool, which comes with extensions for working with DMS.

In addition to accessing system-level metrics through these methods, it is also possible, through a feature called usage tracking, to access metrics and other data on the analyses that users run through the dashboard. This information is often used in conjunction with system-level metrics, and is explained in more detail in Chapter 5.

Fusion Middleware Control provides two main views of system metrics: a high-level view on the Overview tab, and more-detailed metrics on the Metrics subtab of the Capacity Management tab. Both of these sets of metrics are for the system components, and it is also possible elsewhere in Fusion Middleware Control to access metrics on the Java components and the WebLogic Server.

Using Fusion Middleware Control to Access High-Level Metrics

To access the high-level system component metrics, log into Fusion Middleware Control at http://<*machine_name*>:7001/em (for example, http://obisrv1:7001/em) and connect using the WebLogic Server administration user account and password (for example, weblogic/welcome1). Expand the Business Intelligence folder and select coreapplication. Select the Overview tab to view the Capacity Management panel, as shown in Figure 10-5.

This panel shows metrics broken down by Responsiveness and Load categories and covers the following metrics:

- Request Processing Time (ms)
- Average Query Time (seconds)
- Active Sessions
- Requests (per minute)
- Server Queries (per second)

These metrics will automatically refresh if you leave your browser window open. If you want to see new values before the auto-refresh takes place, either refresh your browser display or click the double-arrow refresh icon in the top right-hand side of the web page.

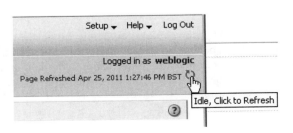

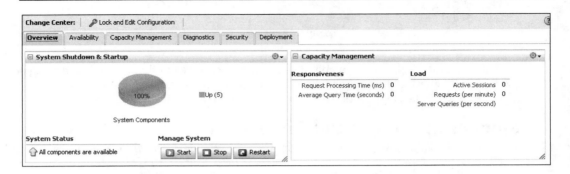

FIGURE 10-5. *System component metrics overview*

In addition to these high-level metrics concerning the system components, similar metrics on the WebLogic Server and the Java components can be found elsewhere within Fusion Middleware Control. To view CPU usage for the Administration and Managed Servers, click the Farm_bifoundation_domain top-level entry in the left-hand navigation tree menu, and Fusion Middleware Control will then display these metrics within the Fusion Middleware area, underneath the pie chart showing the status of the WebLogic servers.

Name	Status	Host	CPU Usage (%)
☐ 📁 WebLogic Domain			
☐ 📄 bifoundation_domain			
📄 AdminServer	⬆	obisrv1.localdomain	25.75
☐ 📄 bi_cluster	⬆		
📄 bi_server1	⬆	obisrv1.localdomain	0.49
☐ 📁 Business Intelligence			
◈ coreapplication			
☐ 📁 Metadata Repositories			
◈ mds-owsm		obisrv1.localdomain	

(Fusion Middleware — 100% — Up (2))

High-level metrics can also be displayed for individual Java components, for example, Oracle BI Publisher. To display metrics for these Java components, expand the Application Deployments folder under Farm_bifoundation_domain and click the component you are interested in. Fusion Middleware Control then displays usage and response time metrics, including a live chart, for that component, as shown in Figure 10-6.

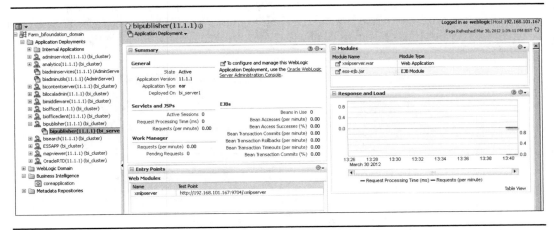

FIGURE 10-6. *Displaying high-level metrics for a Java component*

Similar metrics, including those for the whole WebLogic domain or for just the Administration Server or Managed Servers, can be accessed through the WebLogic Domain folder entry in the left-hand menu.

Using Fusion Middleware Control to Access Detail-Level Metrics

In addition to showing these high-level metrics, Fusion Middleware Control can also provide access to hundreds of detail-level counters that are provided via the Oracle BI Systems Management API. You can see an overview of the most commonly used counters, or create your own metrics display by selecting counters from a palette.

To access these detail-level metrics, from the coreapplication module in Fusion Middleware Control, select the Capacity Management tab and its Metrics subtab. At first, a selection of metrics is displayed under the Responsiveness, Load, and Reliability headings, as shown in Figure 10-7.

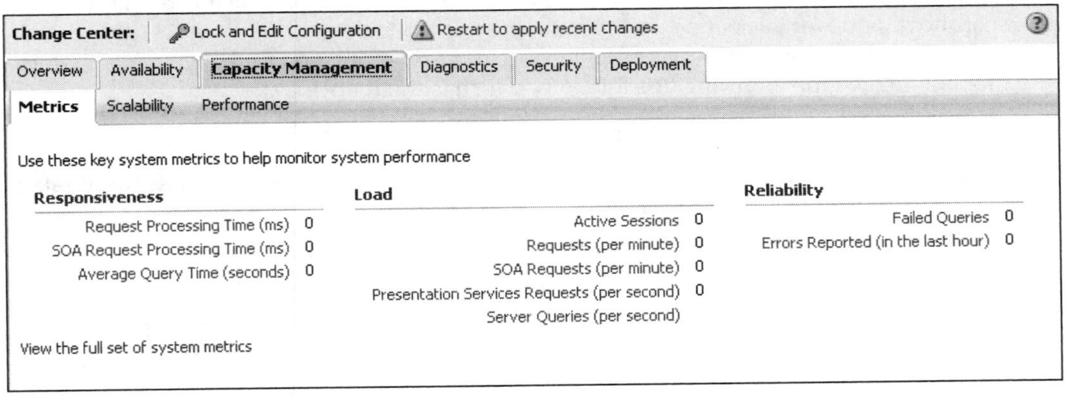

FIGURE 10-7. *Viewing the Metrics subtab in Fusion Middleware Control*

To access the full set of metrics, click the "View the full set of system metrics" link in the lower left-hand corner of the tab. Alternatively, from the Business Intelligence Instance drop-down menu under the coreapplication label above the tabs, select Monitoring | Performance to open the same screen.

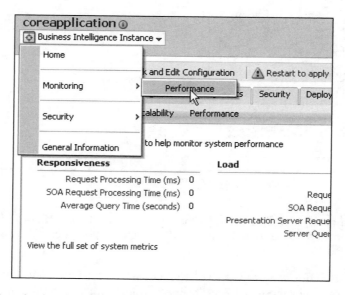

Both approaches display the Performance Summary screen, initially showing Active Sessions, Request Processing Time (ms), and Requests (per minute) in graph form for the previous 15 minutes.

To select your own set of metrics to include on this screen, click the Show Metric Palette button. When you click this button, a palette of available metric folders slides into view. The metric folders contain individual metrics with check boxes beside them, with those that are checked appearing in the updating graph view to the left, as shown in Figure 10-8. Use the Slider control, and the calendar control next to it, to lengthen, shorten, or otherwise adjust the time period displayed on the graph, or click the Table View link to display metric counts at various snapshot times over this period, in the form of a pop-up table.

Within the list of metrics available for selection, some key metrics that you may wish to monitor include the following (the folder for which is listed first):

- Oracle BI Data Cache: Hit Ratio as %
- Oracle BI DB Connection Pool: Avg. Requests/sec, Average Queued Requests, and Average Queued Time (ms)
- Oracle BI General: Active Logins and Queries/sec
- Oracle BI PS Request Processor: Completed Requests/sec and Failed Requests
- Weblogic BI Analytics Metrics: Active Sessions, Request Processing Time (ms), and Requests (per minute)

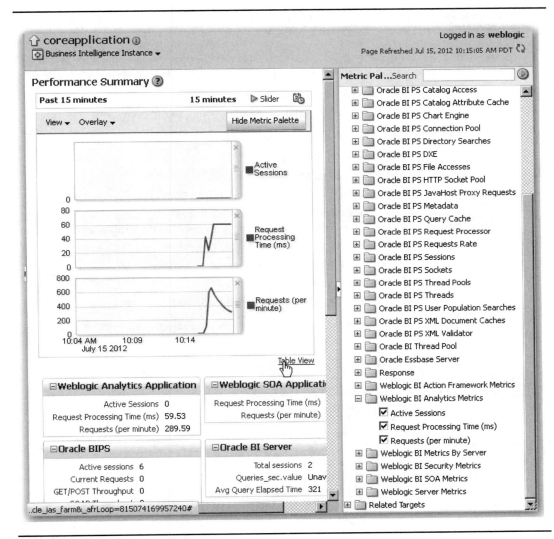

FIGURE 10-8.   *The Metric Palette*

Using WLST Scripting to Access and Store Detail-Level Metrics

In addition to accessing metrics through the Fusion Middleware Control GUI, you can also access them from the WLST scripting environment. Extensions to WLST shipped as part of Oracle Fusion Middleware allow you to interactively query a number of metric tables (equivalent to the metric folders that are displayed when you click the Show Metric Palette button in Fusion Middleware Control); or you can extract individual metrics from these tables and store them in files or database tables.

Interactively Querying Metric Tables Using WLST   To use WLST to interactively query DMS metrics, follow these steps, based on a Microsoft Windows environment:

1. On the server hosting Oracle Business Intelligence, open a command-line terminal and navigate to the directory [*middleware_home*]\Oracle_BI1\common\bin, like this:

   ```
   cd C:\Middleware\Oracle_BI1\common\bin
   ```

2. Start the WLST command-line environment by typing in the command **wlst**, like this:

   ```
   C:\Middleware\Oracle_BI1\common\bin>wlst
   ```

   Your environment will then initialize.

3. Connect to your WebLogic Administration Server, like this:

   ```
   connect ("weblogic","welcome1","localhost:7001")
   ```

   where weblogic is your WebLogic Server administration user, welcome1 is that user's password, and localhost:7001 is the hostname and port of the Administration Server.

4. To query a particular metric table (for example, Oracle_BI_General), use the displayMetricTables() command, like this:

   ```
   displayMetricTables('Oracle_BI_General')
   ```

   All of the metrics within the table will then be displayed:

   ```
   wls:/bifoundation_domain/serverConfig> displayMetricTables('Oracle_BI_
   General')
   -----------------
   Oracle_BI_General
   -----------------
   Active_Execute_Requests.value:  0
   Active_Fetch_Requests.value:    0
   Active_File_Handles.value:      1
   Active_Initblock_Executions.value:      0
   Active_Logins.value:    0
   Active_Prepare_Requests.value:  0
   Avg._Failed_Logins_Elapsed_Time.value:  0
   Avg._Initblock_Executions_Elapsed_Time.value:   0
   Avg._Succeeded_Logins_Elapsed_Time.value:       0
   Avg._query_elapsed_time.value:  0
   Busy_File_Handles.value:        0
   File_Handle_Waiters.value:      0
   Free_File_Handles.value:        502
   Host:   obisrv1
   Max._Initblock_Execution_Elapsed_Time.value:    0
   Max_File_Handles.value: 503
   Name:   Oracle BI General
   New_Execute_Requests.value:     1
   New_Fetch_Requests.value:       2
   New_Initblock_Executions.value: 0
   New_Logins.value:       1
   New_Prepare_Requests.value:     1
   New_Requests.value:     13
   ```

```
OBPERF_***.value:          1
Oracle_BI_Applications: Oracle BI Server
Parent: /Oracle BI Server
Process:        Oracle BI Server:2252:/instance1/coreapplication_obis1
Queries/sec.value:        0
ServerName:     /instance1/coreapplication_obis1
Succeeded_Initblock_Execution_Ratio_as_%.value: 0
Succeeded_Logins_Ratio_as_%.value:       1
Total_sessions.value:    0
wls:/bifoundation_domain/serverConfig>
```

5. To display a list of the available metric tables, use the command DisplayMetricTableNames(), and cross-reference the list with the metric folders in the Fusion Middleware Control Metric Palette in order to determine the ones you wish to investigate further.

Using WLST to Sample and Extract Metrics to a File   In addition to dumping all of the metrics within a metric table to the screen, you can also use WLST scripting to extract individual metrics to, for example, a file or database table. This approach is particularly useful as there is no easy way to print just a single metric to the screen from a metric table, and this approach allows you to parse the metric table and copy particular metrics into a more usable format.

The following Jython script accepts parameters for the metric table, metric of interest, and number of times to be sampled, and then outputs the metric to a file for later use. You can adapt this script to persist the output values to database tables instead, or you can adapt it to handle "two-dimensional" metrics such as Oracle_BI_Thread_Pool that store metrics across multiple areas.

To create the script, follow these steps:

1. Using a text editor, type in the following WLST script:

```
# Example for sampling a DMS metric to a text file
#
# Important : Run WSLT from [middleware_home]/Oracle_BI1/common/bin/
WLST to ensure DMS JARs are in path
#
# This script expects the following arguments:
#
# 1. wls.host (localhost)
# 2. wls.port (7001)
# 3. wls.user  (user1)
# 4. wls.password  (password1)
# 5. metric_table (Oracle_BI_General)
# 6. metric_of_interest (Avg._query_elapsed_time.value)
# 7. sample_length (100)
# ======================================================================
import sys
import os
from java.util import Date
from java.text import SimpleDateFormat
# Check the arguments to this script are as expected.
# argv[0] is script name.
argLen = len(sys.argv)
```

```
if argLen -1 != 7:
    print "ERROR: got ", argLen -1, " args."
    print "USAGE: wlst SampleDMSMetric.py WLS_HOST WLS_PORT WLS_USER
WLS_PASSWORD metric_table metric_of_interest"
    print "  eg: wlst SampleDMSMetric.py localhost 7001 weblogic Ora-
cle_BI_General Avg._query_elapsed_time.value"
    exit()
WLS_HOST = sys.argv[1]
WLS_PORT = sys.argv[2]
WLS_USER = sys.argv[3]
WLS_PW = sys.argv[4]
metric_table = sys.argv[5]
metric_of_interest = sys.argv[6]
sample_length = int(sys.argv[7])
print 'Connecting to '+ WLS_HOST+ ':' + WLS_PORT + ' as user: ' + WLS_
USER + ' ...'
# Connect to WLS
connect(WLS_USER, WLS_PW, WLS_HOST+ ':' + WLS_PORT);
# This section defines the output file name with unique time
start_time = str(SimpleDateFormat("dd-MMM-yyyy_HH-mm-ss").
format(Date()))
output_filename = start_time + "_" + metric_of_interest + "_dump.txt"
# Open the file and write summary of metric to be dumped
file = open(output_filename,'w')
print >>file, "Start Metric Dump of: " + str(metric_table) + " : " +
str(metric_of_interest) + " at " + str(SimpleDateFormat("dd-MMM-yyyy
HH-mm-ss").format(Date()))
# The following section forms a loop according to the sample length
defined earlier. The 'displayMetricTables()' command returns the metric
table in the
# form of a JMX composite data array. The code following this com-
mand accesses the metric data from this array. In this case, a particu-
lar metric of
# interest is tested for and only the value of that metric is output to
file.
#
counter = 0
while counter <= sample_length:
        results = displayMetricTables(metric_table)
        for table in results:
                name = table.get('Table')
                rows = table.get('Rows')
            rowCollection = rows.values()
            iter = rowCollection.iterator()
            while iter.hasNext():
                    row = iter.next()
            rowType = row.getCompositeType()
            keys = rowType.keySet()
            keyIter = keys.iterator()
            while keyIter.hasNext():
```

```
                             columnName = keyIter.next()
                             value = row.get(columnName)
                             if (columnName == metric_of_interest):
                                     print >>file, str(SimpleDateFormat("dd-
MMM-yyyy HH-mm-ss-SSS").format(Date())) + "," + str(value)
                                     counter = counter + 1
        file.close()
        disconnect()
```

   2. Save the script as **SampleDMSMetric.py,** and then run it from the [*middleware_home*]\
      Oracle_BI1\common\bin directory, like this:

```
   wlst SampleDMSMetric.py localhost 7001 weblogic welcome1 Oracle_BI_Gen-
   eral Active_Logins.value 1
```

   3. Navigate to the folder where the WLST executable is located, and locate the dump file
      containing the metric output.

Viewing and Managing Diagnostic Log Files

Most of the components within Oracle Business Intelligence generate diagnostic log file entries,
either by default or when configured to do so. The main logs that you will be interested in from a
business intelligence administration perspective are those generated by the various system
components, including the query log created by the Oracle BI Server system component. To help
you search entries that could potentially be stored in log files across distributed physical servers,
Oracle Business Intelligence makes use of Oracle Diagnostic Logging (ODL) and a web-based log
file view that comes as part of Fusion Middleware Control.

Oracle Diagnostic Logging

Oracle Diagnostic Logging is an Oracle Fusion Middleware feature that ensures log files are
written in a common format, and in a way that they can be aggregated and searched by an
application such as Fusion Middleware Control. Logs managed using ODL can be either in plain-
text format (such as the Oracle BI Server logs) or in XML format (for example, the Oracle BI
Presentation Server log), but all such logs have certain elements of metadata included, such as the
Execution Context ID, that allow them to be combined together and searched using tools such as
Fusion Middleware Control.

Execution Content ID

An additional metadata item added to log files by ODL is the Execution Context ID (ECID). ECIDs
are used to link together entries across log files that correspond to a single user action, so that an
error or other event associated with such an action can be traced across all the components that
participated in it. When viewing log files using the Fusion Middleware Control log viewer, ECIDs
can be useful in tracing the progress of a user transaction and thereby identifying the root cause
of an issue.

Key Diagnostic Log Files and Their Default Locations

There are a number of key diagnostic log files that you will want to be aware of when working
with an Oracle Business Intelligence system. Primarily, these log files are associated with the
system components within your Oracle BI instance and can be found in the [*middleware_home*]/

instances/instance1/diagnostics/logs directory and the equivalent ones for additional Oracle instances, with subdirectories for each component type.

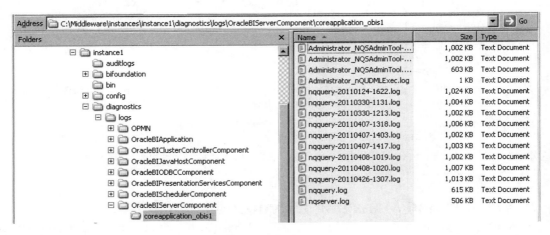

Key log files within this directory structure include the following:

- **The Oracle BI Server log:**

  ```
  /diagnostics/logs/OracleBIServerComponent/coreapplication_obis1/nqserv-
  er.log
  ```

  The BI Server log file contains entries for system startup, shutdown, aborting, and other Oracle BI Server events. It is particularly useful when diagnosing, for example, whether usage tracking has started successfully, whether initialization blocks have executed successfully, and why the BI Server cannot start (typically, because it cannot load a valid repository).

- **The Oracle BI Server query log:**

  ```
  /diagnostics/logs/OracleBIServerComponent/coreapplication_obis1/nqque-
  ry.log
  ```

  The Oracle BI Server query log file contains, depending on the log level set for a user, varying degrees of information about queries that the BI Server executes. The Oracle BI Server query log file does not get written to by default (because otherwise it could become a bottleneck as many parallel query processes try to write to it simultaneously), but if it is used sparingly, it can be invaluable in diagnosing issues with queries and, in particular, the logical and physical SQL statements that are associated with them. See Chapter 5 for more information on enabling query logging, and the various log levels that you can set for a user.

- **The Oracle BI Presentation Server log:**

  ```
  /diagnostics/logs/OracleBIPresentationServicesComponent/coreapplica-
  tion_obips1/saw0log.log
  ```

  If you are having issues with the Presentation Server (for example, if it crashes or behaves unexpectedly), the Presentation Server log should contain information to help you diagnose the problem.

■   The Oracle BI Cluster Controller log, and the Oracle BI Scheduler log:

```
/diagnostics/logs/OracleBIClusterControllerComponent/coreapplication_
obiccs1/nqcluster.log
```

```
/diagnostics/logs/OracleBISchedulerComponent/coreapplication_obisch1/
nqscheduler.log
```

The Oracle BI Scheduler and Cluster Controller components are less likely to encounter errors once you have initially set them up, but if you are having issues post-installation, connectivity problems for the Oracle BI Scheduler component, or network issues affecting the Oracle BI Cluster Controller compomnent, these are the log files to consult.

In addition, there are various log files generated during the installation process, and by other system and Java components. However, the preceding log files are the main ones that you should concern yourself with when managing a typical Oracle Business Intelligence system.

On single-node, Simple Install-type Oracle Business Intelligence systems, when you are working directly with the installation (for example, on a laptop or demo system), you can open these log files with a text editor such as Windows Notepad to see their content. However, when you are working remotely (away from the server) or, more typically, when you have system components distributed over several physical servers in a cluster, you should use the log viewer feature in Fusion Middleware Control to access the various log files.

Viewing and Managing Log Files Using Fusion Middleware Control

To manage and view the contents of log files using Fusion Middleware Control, log in and then, when prompted, enter the username and password of a WebLogic administrator (for example, weblogic/welcome1). Using the navigation tree menu on the left-hand side of the screen, select the Business Intelligence folder and then select the coreapplication node. Then, select the Diagnostics tab. Two subtabs appear under it, Log Messages and Log Configuration, as shown in Figure 10-9.

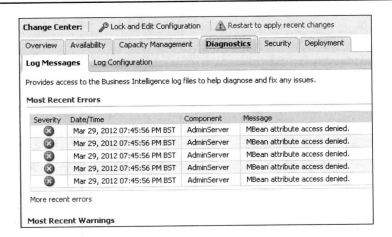

FIGURE 10-9.   *The Diagnostics tab in Fusion Middleware Control*

The Log Messages subtab is divided into several sections. First, the most recent errors and warnings across all components are displayed, with links under each table of warnings or errors to display more of the same. Under these tables, though, are links to each of the log files that are accessible to the log viewer, as well as a link to search all logs in combination.

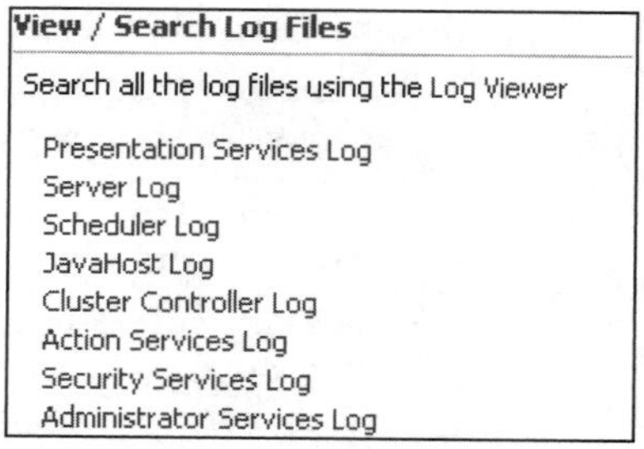

Clicking any of these links opens the Log Messages screen. Using this screen, you can search log files by date range, by content, by message type, or by other fields you add to the search, as shown in Figure 10-10.

You can expand the Selected Targets category on the Log Messages screen to add log files to or remove log files from the display.

The Log Configuration subtab of the Diagnostics tab is used for setting the maximum size of log files and for configuring log rotation policies. Use this tab to set the maximum size a log file can reach, to specify how long a log file can be written to before it is rotated, and to specify the log levels for diagnostic logs.

View / Search Log Files

Search all the log files using the Log Viewer

Presentation Services Log
Server Log
Scheduler Log
JavaHost Log
Cluster Controller Log
Action Services Log
Security Services Log
Administrator Services Log

Managing Performance Options

Oracle Business Intelligence provides a number of systems parameters that can be adjusted to change aspects of overall performance. Some of these parameters are managed through Fusion Middleware Control, and can also be managed through WLST scripting and the Oracle BI Systems Management API. Others that are not yet managed through Fusion Middleware Control can be altered by editing underlying configuration files.

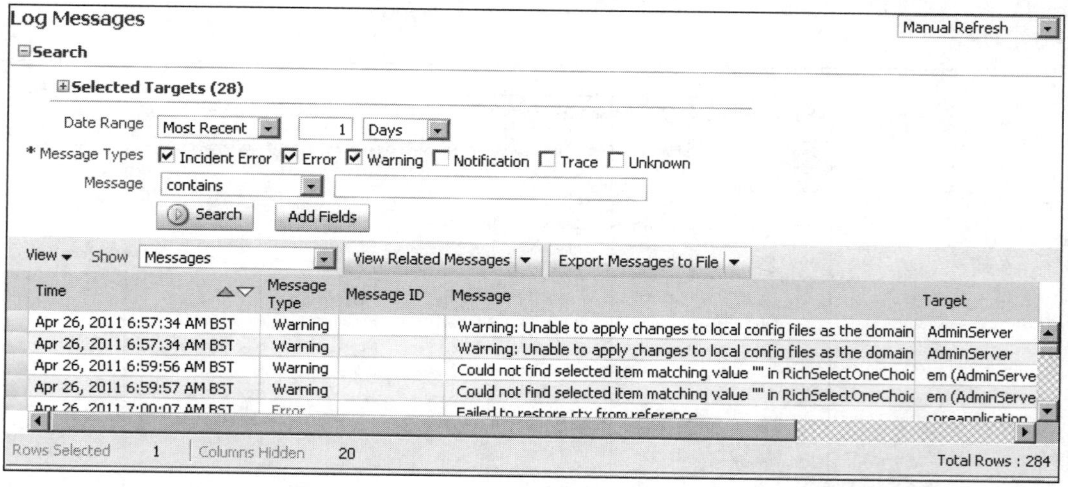

FIGURE 10-10. *The Log Messages screen*

Managing Performance Options Using Fusion Middleware Control

Fusion Middleware Control provides a graphical environment for managing the most commonly used performance configuration settings for Oracle Business Intelligence. These settings include

- Whether query caching is enabled or disabled
- If query caching is enabled, the maximum size of the cache and the maximum number of cache entries
- The expiry time for user sessions
- The maximum number of rows that can be processed in an analysis
- The global cache path and, if enabled, the maximum size of the global cache
- The maximum number of rows that can be downloaded by a user into Microsoft Excel
- The maximum number of rows to include in a page in an e-mail
- Whether online updates are allowed for the repository

To view or change these performance parameters, log into the Fusion Middleware Control web site at http://<machine_name>:7001/em (for example, http://obisrv1:7001/em) and, when prompted, enter the username and password of a WebLogic administrator user (for example, weblogic/ welcome1). Using the navigation tree menu on the left-hand side of the screen, expand the Business Intelligence folder and select the coreapplication node. When the main coreapplication screen is then displayed, select the Capacity Management tab and its Performance subtab.

To change any of these parameters, click the Lock And Edit Configuration button, confirm the action, and the parameters will then be available for editing, as shown in Figure 10-11.

Query caching is described in detail in Chapter 5. It is enabled by default on all new installations of Oracle Business Intelligence, but you will probably want to disable it for development systems if

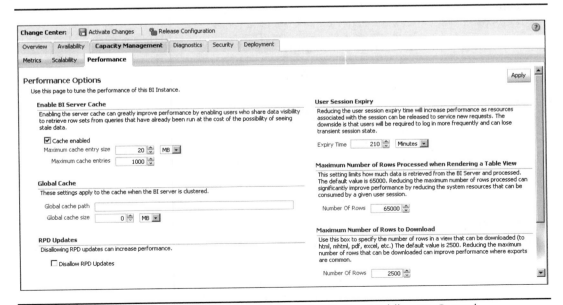

FIGURE 10-11. *Altering performance parameters using Fusion Middleware Control*

you plan to refresh data, or if you wish to see the physical or logical SQL for a query in the query log file. Global cache settings only apply if you have more than one BI Server system component within the Oracle BI instance, and the global cache, in turn, is only populated when you specifically choose to seed it using an agent.

You may wish to disable online updates to the RPD (the Oracle BI Server repository file described in detail in Chapters 3 and 4), as these can cause contention for other users or developers working with the repository at the time of the update. If you choose to disable this feature, though, be aware that you will not be able to make online changes to your repository until it is re-enabled.

Once you have made the changes to your parameters, either click the Apply button and then the Activate button to make the change, or click the Release Configuration button to revert back and unlock the domain. If you choose to activate the changes, use the Processes subtab of the Availability tab to restart the system component associated with the parameter, or click the Restart All button on that tab to stop and start all of the system components.

Managing Performance Options Using WLST and the Oracle BI Systems Management API

In addition to manually managing these performance parameters through Fusion Middleware Control, you can also script changes to them using WLST and the JMX MBeans–based Oracle BI Systems Management API. The following example scripts enable and disable the query cache and manage the maximum number of cache entries for the query cache; for full details of all the possible configuration options manageable through WLST scripting, see the PerformanceConfigurationMBean documentation available at:

[*middleware_home*]/Oracle_BI1/doc/javadoc/bifoundation/jmxapi/oracle/bi/management/adminservices/mbeans/PerformanceConfigurationMBean.html

Example: Enabling and Disabling Query Caching Using WLST   The following WSLT script either enables (newCacheStatus = 1) or disables (newCacheStatus=0) query caching and demonstrates the use of the PerformanceConfigurationMBean:

```
# Example for enabling or disabling cache
#
# This scripts expects the following arguments:
#
# 1. wls.host (localhost)
# 2. wls.port (7001)
# 3. wls.user  (user1)
# 4. wls.password  (password1)
# 5. newCacheStatus (0=disabled, 1=enabled)
# ================================================================import
sys
import os

# Check the arguments to this script are as expected.
# argv[0] is script name.
argLen = len(sys.argv)
if argLen -1 != 5:
    print "ERROR: got ", argLen -1, " args."
    print "USAGE: wlst.cmd enableDisableCache.py WLS_HOST WLS_PORT WLS_USER
```

```
WLS_PASSWORD newCacheStatus"
    print "   eg: wlst.cmd enableDisableCache.py localhost 7001 weblogic wel-
come1 1"
    exit()

WLS_HOST = sys.argv[1]
WLS_PORT = sys.argv[2]
WLS_USER = sys.argv[3]
WLS_PW = sys.argv[4]
newCacheStatus = sys.argv[5]

print 'Connecting to '+ WLS_HOST+ ':' + WLS_PORT + ' as user: ' + WLS_USER + '
...'

# Connect to WLS
connect(WLS_USER, WLS_PW, WLS_HOST+ ':' + WLS_PORT);

print 'Connecting to Domain ...'
domainCustom()
cd ('oracle.biee.admin')
print 'Connecting to BIDomain MBean ...'
cd ('oracle.biee.admin:type=BIDomain,group=Service')

print 'Calling lock ...'
objs = jarray.array([], java.lang.Object)
strs = jarray.array([], java.lang.String)
invoke('lock', objs, strs)

biinstances = get('BIInstances')
biinstance = biinstances[0]

print 'Connecting to BIInstance MBean ...'
cd ('..')
cd (biinstance.toString())

perfconfigbean = get('PerformanceConfiguration')
print 'Connecting to BIInstance Performance Config MBean ...'
cd ('..')
cd (perfconfigbean.toString())
currentCacheStatus=get('BIServerCacheEnabled')
print 'Current Cache Status = ' + str(currentCacheStatus)
print 'Now updating to new setting...'
set('BIServerCacheEnabled',int(newCacheStatus))
currentCacheStatus=get('BIServerCacheEnabled')
print 'New Cache Status = ' + str(currentCacheStatus)

print 'Calling commit ...'
cd ('..')
cd ('oracle.biee.admin:type=BIDomain,group=Service')
objs = jarray.array([], java.lang.Object)
strs = jarray.array([], java.lang.String)
invoke('commit', objs, strs)
```

```
print 'Committed OK'

exit()
```

After the script has run, your changes won't become active until you restart your Oracle BI Server component(s) using either Fusion Middleware Control, the opmnctl command-line utility, or a WLST script.

Example: Setting MaxCacheEntries Using WLST   You can create a similar script to manage other performance parameters, such as MaxCacheEntries. As with the previous script, you will need to restart your Oracle BI Server system component(s) before the change will become active.

```
# Example for setting the MaxCacheEntries Performance Parameter
#
# This scripts expects the following arguments:
#
# 1. wls.host (localhost)
# 2. wls.port (7001)
# 3. wls.user  (weblogic)
# 4. wls.password  (welcome1)
# 5. newMaxCacheEntries (1000)
# ================================================================import
sys
import os

# Check the arguments to this script are as expected.
# argv[0] is script name.
argLen = len(sys.argv)
if argLen -1 != 5:
    print "ERROR: got ", argLen -1, " args."
    print "USAGE: wlst.cmd setMaxCacheEntries.py WLS_HOST WLS_PORT WLS_USER
WLS_PASSWORD newMaxCacheEntries"
    print "   eg: wlst.cmd setMaxCacheEntries.py localhost 7001 weblogic wel-
come1 1000"
    exit()

WLS_HOST = sys.argv[1]
WLS_PORT = sys.argv[2]
WLS_USER = sys.argv[3]
WLS_PW = sys.argv[4]
newMaxCacheEntries = sys.argv[5]

print 'Connecting to '+ WLS_HOST+ ':' + WLS_PORT + ' as user: ' + WLS_USER + '
...'

# Connect to WLS
connect(WLS_USER, WLS_PW, WLS_HOST+ ':' + WLS_PORT);

print 'Connecting to Domain ...'
domainCustom()
cd ('oracle.biee.admin')
```

```
print 'Connecting to BIDomain MBean ...'
cd ('oracle.biee.admin:type=BIDomain,group=Service')

print 'Calling lock ...'
objs = jarray.array([], java.lang.Object)
strs = jarray.array([], java.lang.String)
invoke('lock', objs, strs)

biinstances = get('BIInstances')
biinstance = biinstances[0]

print 'Connecting to BIInstance MBean ...'
cd ('..')
cd (biinstance.toString())

perfconfigbean = get('PerformanceConfiguration')
print 'Connecting to BIInstance Performance Config MBean ...'
cd ('..')
cd (perfconfigbean.toString())
currentMaxCacheEntries=get('MaxCacheEntries')
print 'Current MaxCacheEntries = ' + str(currentMaxCacheEntries)
print 'Now updating to new setting...'
set('MaxCacheEntries',int(newMaxCacheEntries))
currentMaxCacheEntries=get('MaxCacheEntries')
print 'Current MaxCacheEntries = ' + str(currentMaxCacheEntries)

print 'Calling commit ...'
cd ('..')
cd ('oracle.biee.admin:type=BIDomain,group=Service')
objs = jarray.array([], java.lang.Object)
strs = jarray.array([], java.lang.String)
invoke('commit', objs, strs)

print 'Committed OK'

exit()
```

Managing Unmanaged Parameters Using Configuration Files

Not every possible performance parameter is managed through Fusion Middleware Control and the Oracle BI Systems Management API. For those types of parameters, you will need to manually edit, using a tool such as Windows Notepad, the configuration file used by the component within the filesystem used by its Oracle instance; for example, the configuration file subdirectories found within the [*middleware_home*]/instances/instance1/config directory. Examples of these configuration files include

■ **/OracleBIServerComponent/coreapplication_obis1/NQSConfig.INI** This file contains configuration settings for the Oracle BI Server system component, including additional settings for the query cache and global cache, memory settings, various server settings, and settings used for usage tracking.

- **/OracleBIPresentationServicesComponent/coreapplication_obips1/instanceconfig.xml**
  This file contains configuration settings for the Oracle BI Presentation Server component, including settings regarding map integration, the marketing server, and catalog upgrade. You normally should not need to edit this file, as all ongoing performance settings are in fact managed through Fusion Middleware Control.
- **/OracleBIJavaHostComponent/coreapplication_obijh1/config.xml**   This file contains settings for the Java host, most of which do not relate to performance. Again, you should not need to edit this file in the context of performance optimization.

The preceding locations assume that you have only a single BI Server, Presentation Server, and Java Host system component within a single Oracle instance. If you have added additional components or additional Oracle instances on new servers, you will need to locate their corresponding configuration files within the same directory structure and apply changes consistently across all files for the particular system component.

Note that settings within these files should not be changed if they have the comment "This Configuration setting is managed by Oracle Business Intelligence Fusion Middleware Control" next to them; those that do should only be changed through Fusion Middleware Control or WLST and the Oracle BI Systems Management API. Those that do not have this comment next to them can be edited within the file, after which the relevant system component should be restarted to register the change.

Managing Repositories and Presentation Server Catalogs

The repository used by the Oracle BI Server and the catalog used by the Oracle BI Presentation Server can be swapped in and out by an administrator as new systems are brought online. Only one repository and one catalog can be online and available for query by users at any one time (though these can be held in replicated files across the cluster), and management of these objects is performed either through Fusion Middleware Control or through WLST scripting and the Oracle BI Systems Management API.

Managing Repositories and Catalogs Using Fusion Middleware Control

Oracle BI Repositories (or "RPD files") are created and administered using the Oracle BI Administration tool. Repositories can be edited either online or offline, where online access involves the BI Administration tool connecting to the repository over the network to the Oracle BI Server, while offline access involves the BI Administration tool directly connecting to the repository file. When an administrator wishes to take online a repository that was developed offline, this task is generally performed using Fusion Middleware Control.

Example: Uploading a New Repository File and Taking It Online   To take an offline repository file and make it the default, online repository for an Oracle BI instance, log into the Fusion Middleware Control web site at http://<*machine_name*>:7001/em (for example, http://obisrv1:7001:/em) and enter the username and password for a WebLogic Server administrator account (for example, weblogic/welcome1). After you have successfully logged on, use the navigation tree menu on the left of the screen to open the Business Intelligence folder and select the coreapplication entry. Then, when the coreapplication screen is displayed, click the Deployment tab and its Repository subtab.

To upload a new repository, follow these steps:

1. Before you can make any changes to repository settings, you must first lock the domain. To do this, click the Lock And Edit Configuration button, and confirm your action.

2. To upload a new repository file, navigate to the Upload BI Server Repository section of the Repository subtab and click the Choose File button to navigate to the repository file.

3. Once selected, enter the repository password twice so that your screen looks as shown in Figure 10-12.

4. Once you have selected your repository and entered the repository password, to activate the change, first click the Apply button, and then click the Activate Changes button. If at any time before you activate the new repository you wish to cancel the process, just click the Release Configuration button to revert to the original choice of repository.

5. Once you have activated the new repository, navigate to the Availability tab and its Processes subtab and restart all BI Server components.

If, when restarting the Oracle BI Server component, Fusion Middleware Control reports an error, the issue is most likely either an invalid repository file or that you have entered the repository password incorrectly. Use the log viewer (the Log Messages subtab of the Diagnostics tab within Fusion Middleware Control) to view the server log and diagnose the issue.

Example: Specifying a New Presentation Server Catalog   Unlike repositories, you do not upload new catalogs to the Oracle BI instance; instead, you copy the catalog directory to the correct location and then use Fusion Middleware Control to register the catalog location with the BI instance, which in turn registers it with the Oracle BI Presentation Servers that it manages.

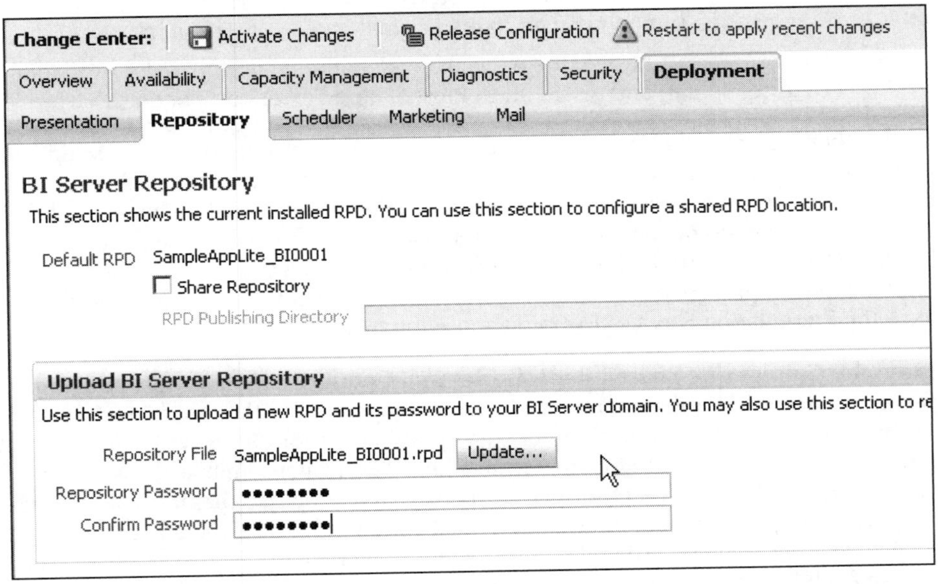

FIGURE 10-12.   *Selecting a new repository for upload*

To specify a new catalog location for your Oracle BI instance and Oracle BI Presentation Server components, follow these steps:

1. Using a file-system copy, or the Archive/Unarchive feature within the Catalog Manager application, copy the catalog and all of its contents directory to the following location:

   [*middleware_home*]/instances/instance1/bifoundation/
   OracleBIPresentationServicesComponent/coreapplication_obips1/catalog

NOTE
If you have more than one Presentation Server component configured for your instance, you should use the shared catalog approach (detailed after this section) instead of copying catalog files to subdirectories for each component.

2. Select the Deployment tab and its Repository subtab in Fusion Middleware Control, click the Lock And Edit Configuration button, and confirm your action.

3. Within the Repository screen, navigate to the Presentation Service Repository section, and type in the file system location of the new repository. Ensure that this location is accessible to the Oracle BI Presentation Server (that is, it is not on your workstation PC).

4. Once you have entered the location of your catalog, to activate the change, first click the Apply button, and then click the Activate Changes button. If at any time before you activate the new catalog location you wish to cancel the process, just click the Release Configuration button to revert to the original choice of repository.

5. Once you have activated the new catalog location, navigate to the Availability tab and its Processes subtab and restart all BI Presentation Server components.

If, when restarting the Oracle BI Presentation Server components, Fusion Middleware Control reports an error, the issue is most likely an invalid path or an inaccessible file location. If the directory that you specify is empty, or if it has not already been created but is a valid directory path that can be written to by the Oracle BI Presentation Server process, it will create a new, empty catalog when you restart the Presentation Server (this is in fact how you create a new catalog).

If the restart process errors, however, use the log viewer within Fusion Middleware Control to view the Presentation Services log to diagnose the issue.

Example: Configuring Shared Repositories and Catalogs   If you create additional Oracle BI Server or Oracle BI Presentation Server system components within your Oracle BI instance, each one will need access to a repository or catalog. While Fusion Middleware Control, or WLST scripting and the Oracle BI Systems Management API, will ensure that repository files are copied to each Oracle BI Server's repository directory when you upload them, it is recommended that you also configure a shared repository for use by the individual Oracle BI Server components.

When you configure a shared repository for use by multiple Oracle BI Server components in a cluster, each BI Server component still maintains its own repository file in its own local filesystem. When developers connect online using the Oracle BI Administration tool to the default, online repository the changes they make are recorded in the particular repository file used by the Oracle BI Server component that the Oracle BI Cluster Controller component connected the developer to.

To update all of the other repository files used by the remaining Oracle BI Server components in the Oracle BI domain, you then restart these components using, for example, Fusion Middleware Control and they obtain details of these changes from the shared repository. These changes are then copied to their own local repository files to ensure that they are synchronized with each other, and the repository that the developer originally edited through the online connection.

If you don't configure a shared repository when working with multiple Oracle BI Server components in a cluster, you will need to disable online editing of the repository and instead only allow offline edits, making sure you then upload any changed repositories back to the Oracle BI instance using Fusion Middleware Control to distribute the changes to each Oracle BI Server component. This approach is not recommended, and you should configure a shared repository instead.

To define a shared Oracle BI Repository, all you have to do is specify a network share that can be accessed by all of the BI Server components (which may potentially be provisioned on more than one physical server). Fusion Middleware Control or the Systems Management API will take care of copying the current, default repository to this new location, and amending the configuration of each BI Server component to use the new shared repository. To share a catalog, however, you will need to move the catalog files to the network share, while Fusion Middleware Control will take care of registering the new location with the various Presentation Server components.

To configure a shared repository using Fusion Middleware Control, follow these steps:

1. Create a shared directory on your file system, accessible to all physical servers that are part of your clustered Oracle BI instance, and make a note of the location.

2. Log into the Fusion Middleware Control web site using a WebLogic administrator username and password, and expand Business Intelligence in the navigation tree menu on the left-hand side of the screen and select coreapplication.

3. On the coreapplication screen, select the Deployment tab and its Repository subtab.

4. Click the Lock And Edit Configuration button, and confirm the action when prompted.

5. Within the BI Server Repository section, select the Share Repository check box. Within the Shared Location text box, enter the location of the shared directory that will host your repository files (for example, \\obisrv1\files).

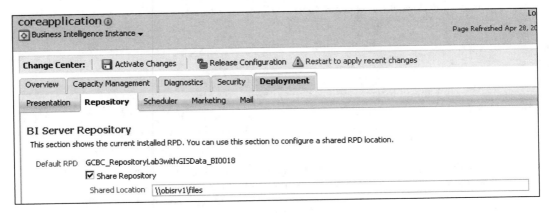

6. To save your changes, click Apply and then click Activate Changes. (To cancel the change, click the Release Configuration button.) Fusion Middleware Control then copies the default online repository file to the shared location. Repository files are still stored in the individual repository directories for each BI Server component, and you should leave them there because they are still required by the Oracle BI instance.

7. Switch to the Processes subtab of the Availability tab, highlight the BI Servers row under the System Component Availability heading, and click the Restart All button to pick up the configuration changes and start making use of the shared repository file.

Defining a shared Oracle BI Presentation Services catalog is a similar process, though Fusion Middleware Control does not copy the catalog files to the new location for you. Instead, you need to create the shared location and copy the files prior to the change, and the Oracle BI instance will then start using the new shared catalog after you have restarted the Presentation Server.

To define a shared catalog, follow these steps:

1. Create a shared directory on your file system, accessible to all physical servers that are part of your clustered Oracle BI instance, and make a note of the location.

2. Copy the catalog file system from the current location (typically, [*middleware_ home*]/instances/instance1/bifoundation/OracleBIPresentationServicesComponent/ coreapplication_obips1/catalog) to the new location, using a file system copy.

3. Log into the Fusion Middleware Control web site using a WebLogic administrator username and password, expand the Business Intelligence folder, and select coreapplication.

4. On the coreapplication screen, select the Deployment tab and its Repository subtab.

5. Click the Lock And Edit Configuration button, and confirm the action when prompted.

6. Within the Repository screen, locate the Presentation Service Repository section, and overwrite the existing Catalog Location entry with the network share location where the new shared catalog will be located (for example, \\obisrv1\files\GCBC_Catalog).

Presentation Service Repository

This section shows the current location of presentation repository for the presentation services. You can use this section to change the rep point to shared location to achieve shared catalog.

Catalog Location | \\obisrv1\files\GCBC_Catalog

7. To save your changes, click Apply and then click Activate Changes. To cancel the change, click the Release Configuration button.

8. Switch to the Processes subtab of the Availability tab, highlight the BI Presentation Servers row under the System Component Availability heading, and click the Restart All button to pick up the configuration changes and start making use of the shared catalog.

When specifying the location of the shared catalog, ensure that you reference it using a network share reference, not a drive letter (for Microsoft Windows). Also, as the catalog can contain many hundreds or thousands of files, make sure that whichever server or network file system you use will allow that many files to be stored on it.

Managing Repositories and Catalogs Using WLST and the Oracle BI Systems Management API

You can also upload new repositories and catalogs using WLST scripting and JMX MBeans. As with other configuration changes, you should restart the Oracle BI Server or Oracle Presentation Server components after you upload a new repository or define a new catalog. The first example script in this section performs this restart as part of the script.

Example: Uploading a New Oracle BI Repository Using WLST   The following example script first uploads a new repository file to the Oracle BI instance, and then performs a restart of the default Oracle instance after the upload has completed to enable the new repository:

```
# Example to demonstrate uploading a new repository and restarting the in-
stance
#
# This scripts expects the following arguments:
#
# 1. wls.host (localhost)
# 2. wls.port (7001)
# 3. wls.user  (weblogic)
# 4. wls.password  (welcome1)
# 5. repository filename and location
# 6. repository password
# =====================================================================

import sys
import os

# Check the arguments to this script are as expected.
# argv[0] is script name.
argLen = len(sys.argv)
if argLen -1 != 6:
    print "ERROR: got ", argLen -1, " args."
    print "USAGE: wlst.cmd RPDUpload.py WLS_HOST WLS_PORT WLS_USER WLS_PASS-
WORD repository_location repository_password"
    print "   eg: wlst.cmd RPDUpload.py localhost 7001 weblogic welcome1 c:\
SampleAppLite.rpd Admin123"
    exit()

WLS_HOST = sys.argv[1]
WLS_PORT = sys.argv[2]
WLS_USER = sys.argv[3]
WLS_PW = sys.argv[4]
rpdlocation = sys.argv[5]
rpdpassword = sys.argv[6]

print 'Connecting to '+ WLS_HOST+ ':' + WLS_PORT + ' as user: ' + WLS_USER + '
...'

connect(WLS_USER, WLS_PW, WLS_HOST+ ':' + WLS_PORT);
print 'Connecting to Domain ...'
domainCustom()
```

```
cd ('oracle.biee.admin')
print 'Connecting to BIDomain MBean ...'
cd ('oracle.biee.admin:type=BIDomain,group=Service')

objs = jarray.array([],java.lang.Object)
strs = jarray.array([],java.lang.String)
print 'Locking the domain ...'
invoke('lock',objs,strs)
biinstances = get('BIInstances')
biinstance = biinstances[0]
print ('Connecting to BIInstance MBean')
cd ('..')
cd (biinstance.toString())
print ('Retrieve the name of the MBean for managing the BI Server configura-
tion...')
biserver = get('ServerConfiguration')
print ('Connecting to the ServerConfigurationMBean ...')
cd ('..')
cd (biserver.toString())
print ('Uploading repository ...')
argtypes = jarray.array(['java.lang.String','java.lang.String'],java.lang.
String)
argvalues = jarray.array([rpdlocation,rpdpassword],java.lang.Object)
invoke('uploadRepository',argvalues,argtypes)
print ('Committing the update ...')
cd('..')
cd('oracle.biee.admin:type=BIDomain,group=Service')
objs = jarray.array([],java.lang.Object)
strs = jarray.array([],java.lang.String)
invoke('commit',objs,strs)
print 'Connecting to BIInstance MBean ...'
cd ('..')
cd (biinstance.toString())
print 'Getting instance status ...'
servicestatus=get('ServiceStatus')
print 'BIInstance MBean; ServiceStatus: ' + servicestatus
print 'Calling stop ...'
objs = jarray.array([], java.lang.Object)
strs = jarray.array([], java.lang.String)
invoke('stop', objs, strs)
servicestatus=get('ServiceStatus')
print 'BIInstance MBean; ServiceStatus: ' + servicestatus
print 'Calling start ...'
objs = jarray.array([], java.lang.Object)
strs = jarray.array([], java.lang.String)
invoke('start', objs, strs)
servicestatus=get('ServiceStatus')
print 'BIInstance MBean; ServiceStatus: ' + servicestatus
print 'RPD Upload now complete!'
exit()
```

Specifying a New Presentation Services Catalog Using WLST To specify a new location for the Oracle BI Presentation Services catalog (and if an empty or nonexistent directory is specified, create a new catalog), you can use a WLST script such as this:

```
# Example for setting the Catalog Path
#
# This scripts expects the following arguments:
#
# 1. wls.host (localhost)
# 2. wls.port (7001)
# 3. wls.user  (weblogic)
# 4. wls.password  (welcome1)
# 5. newWebCatpath (c:\temp\webcat)
# ================================================================

import sys
import os

# Check the arguments to this script are as expected.
# argv[0] is script name.
argLen = len(sys.argv)
if argLen -1 != 5:
    print "ERROR: got ", argLen -1, " args."
    print "USAGE: wlst.cmd updatecatalogPath.py WLS_HOST WLS_PORT WLS_USER
WLS_PASSWORD newWebCatPath"
    print "   eg: wlst.cmd updatecatalogPath.py localhost 7001 weblogic wel-
come1 c:\temp\webcat"
    exit()

WLS_HOST = sys.argv[1]
WLS_PORT = sys.argv[2]
WLS_USER = sys.argv[3]
WLS_PW = sys.argv[4]
newWebCatpath = sys.argv[5]

print 'Connecting to '+ WLS_HOST+ ':' + WLS_PORT + ' as user: ' + WLS_USER + '
...'

# Connect to WLS
connect(WLS_USER, WLS_PW, WLS_HOST+ ':' + WLS_PORT);

print 'Connecting to Domain ...'
domainCustom()
cd ('oracle.biee.admin')
print 'Connecting to BIDomain MBean ...'
cd ('oracle.biee.admin:type=BIDomain,group=Service')

print 'Calling lock ...'
objs = jarray.array([], java.lang.Object)
strs = jarray.array([], java.lang.String)
```

```
invoke('lock', objs, strs)

biinstances = get('BIInstances')
biinstance = biinstances[0]

print 'Connecting to BIInstance MBean ...'
cd ('..')
cd (biinstance.toString())

servicestatus=get('ServiceStatus')
print 'BIInstance MBean; ServiceStatus: ' + servicestatus

presserverbean = get('PresentationServerConfiguration')
print 'Connecting to BIInstance Presentation Server Config MBean ...'
cd ('..')
cd (presserverbean.toString())
currentwebcat=get('WebCatalogSharedLocation')
print 'Current Catalog Path = ' + currentwebcat
set('WebCatalogSharedLocation',newWebCatpath)
currentwebcat=get('WebCatalogSharedLocation')
print 'New Catalog Path = ' + currentwebcat
print 'Calling commit ...'
cd ('..')
cd ('oracle.biee.admin:type=BIDomain,group=Service')
objs = jarray.array([], java.lang.Object)
strs = jarray.array([], java.lang.String)
invoke('commit', objs, strs)

print 'Committed OK'

exit()
```

As with all configuration changes such as this, you will need to restart either the whole Oracle BI domain or your Oracle BI Presentation Server components before the new catalog will become active and available for queries.

CHAPTER
11

Managing Change

hen you are first developing your Oracle Business Intelligence system, you are typically developing just for yourself and on a workstation or laptop owned by yourself. When you finish your first system, typically it's only you that uses it and you don't have to worry about making it available for others to use as part of their work. This all changes, though, when your new system starts to become successful and other people want to start making use of it.

How you manage change in your Oracle Business Intelligence system is an important topic, and if you look through the product documentation, it's also one of the most complicated, with at least three chapters devoted to the topic. Historically, the Oracle Business Intelligence product set has been built up out of a number of different tools created by Oracle and other vendors, each of which has its own metadata stores, change management procedures, and technology foundations. This means that when you want to coordinate development between repository, catalog, and middleware teams, each team will hold its application data in different ways and will use different tools to manage its projects.

Managing change, in this context, is all about working with teams of often multiple developers promoting their projects from development all the way to test and production environments in such a way that you can develop parts of the project concurrently and in a way that corresponds with best practices in software development. In this chapter, we will look at different models of Oracle Business Intelligence project development, from a single developer creating all parts of the project to teams of developers working at different locations on individual parts of the project. We will look at how projects such as these are promoted among development, test, and production environments, and how you use tools such as Oracle Enterprise Manager Fusion Middleware Control, the Oracle BI Administration tool, and third-party products such as Apache Subversion to create a robust development environment that allows you to manage change in a controlled, predictable way.

Overview of Managing Change

What do we mean when we talk about managing change in an Oracle Business Intelligence system? Let us start off by considering why we might want to manage change on a business intelligence system and by looking at the types of project teams you might encounter when working on such a system. Then we will take a high-level look at the types of project elements you might want to manage, as well as security and working with clustered systems that become important as business intelligence is deployed across the enterprise.

Why Should Developers Be Concerned with Managing Change?

When you first start working with Oracle Business Intelligence, you are often developing just for yourself, learning as you develop your first system. When others start relying on the repositories, dashboards, and analyses you create, you need to find a way to keep their systems stable while giving yourself the freedom to keep developing and learning how the product works. This is a dilemma that all developers encounter and is why most organizations create separate development, test, and production environments for developers to work with. When working with Oracle Business Intelligence, the challenge for you is to work out how to move project artifacts such as the repository, catalog, and security settings between these environments, ideally in a way that does not involve lots of manual work by yourself.

In addition, once you move beyond your first experiments with the product and start developing a real system, you will probably want to start creating snapshots or checkpoints in your project so that you can refer back to these if your development takes a wrong turn and pass particular snapshots and project stages to your production team to deploy as a particular release of your project. This topic is known as *version,* or *source control,* and the Oracle BI Administration tool, since the 11.1.1.6 release of the product, now features source control integration along with a new repository storage format designed for source-controlling project artifacts called MDS XML Documents.

Team Development Compared to Single-User Development

Things get more complicated once it is more than just you working on a particular project. Your organization might feel that a particular project is so important that it is worth assigning several developers to it, each of whom needs to develop using the Oracle BI Repository and may be located in different countries and time zones. Ideally, you need to find a way to separate your repository into separate branches, each of which can be developed independently and then merged back into the main branch, and you need to find a way to manage any conflicts this may introduce without excessive manual intervention on your part.

Managing Change in the Oracle BI Repository

The Oracle BI Repository is probably where most of the work involved in managing change is concerned, partly because it is so central to the Oracle Business Intelligence system and has the greatest opportunity for conflicts, and partly because for historical reasons it is stored in a single, monolithic binary file that can't easily be written to by more than one developer at a time.

Because of this, much of the process around managing change in an Oracle Business Intelligence system is concerned with providing a way for more than one developer to work on any one repository at a time. In particular, the Multiuser Development Environment (MUDE), covered later in this chapter, is something you may wish to consider if you are working with a reasonable-sized team of developers. MUDE attempts to work around this restriction by breaking the repository file into separate *projects,* which are then worked with in separate developer "sandbox environments" before being merged back into the main repository file. MUDE is a complex topic, and this book will aim to provide you with a sound understanding of the principles, but developing using MUDE is a big topic in itself and you should read this chapter in combination with its product documentation.

Managing Change in the Oracle BI Presentation Catalog

Managing change in the Oracle BI Presentation catalog, where the analyses, dashboards, agents, and other objects users interact with are stored, is an interesting topic in itself and one that is quite different to managing change in the repository. Unlike the repository, which is generally created by developers and then promoted into a production environment, only to be changed there for bug fixes and tactical changes, most catalogs are developed by users within the production environment and only sometimes are taken through a formal release-management process. Managing change within the catalog is therefore concerned in a small way with what dashboards and analyses get promoted among development, test, and production environments (typically, "gold-standard" dashboards that are developed by IT as part of the delivery schedule for a project), but mostly it is concerned with governance and making sure that there is some structure and control over what reports are created, making sure there is a "single version of the truth."

Managing Change for Security and Application Roles

The 11g release of Oracle Business Intelligence introduced a number of features aimed at customers deploying BI within the enterprise, including support for the security layer within Oracle Fusion Middleware. Now, when you create an Oracle Business Intelligence system, you need to manage application roles and application policies that define access rights to your system, as well as mappings between these application roles and the users and groups that are provided by your corporate directory.

Managing these roles and policies becomes important when you promote systems you develop among development, test, and production environments and when you branch and then recombine systems together that were developed independently. In addition, new security features within the repository have to be considered when moving and merging security systems, and you ideally want to manage this in such a way that minimizes the amount of manual work and rekeying that you have to perform.

Propagation of Configuration Changes Across a Clustered, Highly Available System

Another complication that you have to consider when managing change is when your Oracle Business Intelligence system is deployed across multiple clustered servers, typically to leverage cheap commodity hardware and provide a highly available system to your users. When you work with such a system, you have to ensure that all changes you introduce are applied to all nodes in the cluster and that you minimize any downtime that users have to experience while you make the changes. Tools such as Fusion Middleware Control and the Oracle BI Systems Management API help with this task, but you need to understand certain techniques to ensure things run smoothly.

Tools and Utilities to Manage Change Within Oracle Business Intelligence Systems

Partly for historical reasons and partly because of the large number of components within the Oracle Business Intelligence platform, there are a number of tools and utilities you need to be aware of when managing change in an Oracle Business Intelligence system. Some of these are web based, some of them are Microsoft Windows–only client tools, and some are accessible only via the command line or via API calls. Your organization may also have corporate standards for what is termed "software configuration management," and you may wish to use some of these tools either to control the release management process or to provide functionality, such as using a source control server to integrate with the source control features introduced with the 11.1.1.6 release.

Oracle Enterprise Manager Fusion Middleware Control and the Oracle BI Systems Management API

Oracle Enterprise Manager Fusion Middleware Control is typically used in this context to propagate system configuration changes across the Oracle BI domain and to upload and distribute new repositories that you wish to deploy into a particular environment. Under the covers, Fusion Middleware Control uses the Java JMX MBean–based Oracle BI Systems Management API, as detailed in Chapter 10, to perform its administration tasks; and its scope also extends to such areas as deploying new Java applications, scaling out your business intelligence system over additional servers, and managing the security roles that control access to your system.

The Fusion Middleware Control BI Plug-In

Chapter 10 describes in detail the systems administration tasks you can perform using Fusion Middleware Control, the web-based administration console for your Oracle Business Intelligence infrastructure. Fusion Middleware Control is based around the concept of plug-ins, and one such plug-in provides administrative functions for the system components within your Oracle BI domain, such as the Oracle BI Server, Oracle BI Presentation Server, and the Oracle BI Scheduler. The advantage of using Fusion Middleware Control over the manual editing of configuration files that earlier releases of Oracle Business Intelligence used is that it provides a centralized way to manage the configuration of all of the nodes in your Oracle Business Intelligence cluster. When you make a configuration change using Fusion Middleware Control, that change is then propagated across all of the Oracle BI Server components, all of the Oracle BI Presentation Server components and any other affected parts of your system, ensuring all components are in-sync and with their status displayed clearly in Fusion Middleware Control's web-based console.

Figure 11-1 shows Fusion Middleware Control about to upload a new repository file, which will then be automatically distributed to all Oracle BI Server system components in the cluster, ready for you to restart them one at a time so that at least one BI Server is available to service user queries at any one time.

Fusion Middleware Management Screens

In addition to managing the system components within Oracle Business Intelligence, Fusion Middleware Control can manage most other aspects of your Oracle Business Intelligence

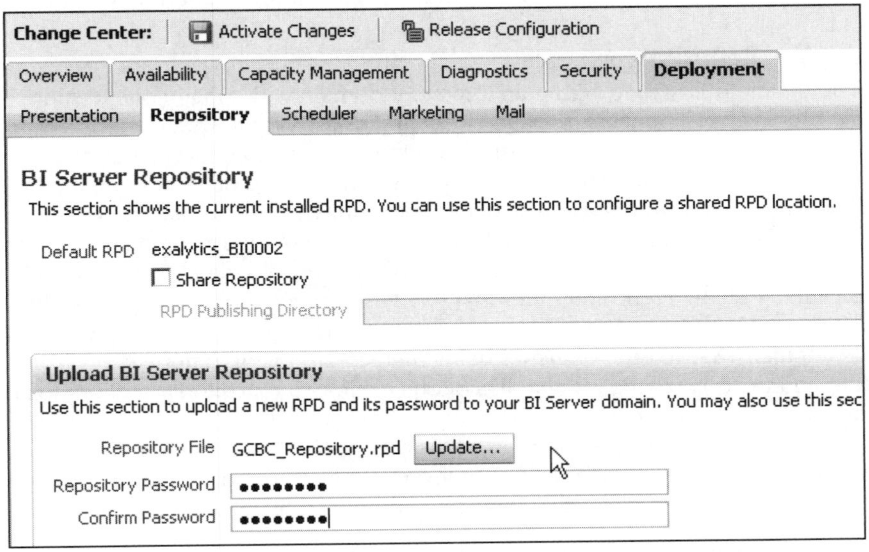

FIGURE 11-1.   *Uploading a new Oracle BI Repository using Fusion Middleware Control*

deployment. This includes such tasks as creating and managing application roles and policies, mapping these polices to LDAP groups and users, and deploying and managing Java applications and web services that run alongside your business intelligence system.

Your involvement with this part of Fusion Middleware Control typically begins when you need to manage changes and environment promotions for your security arrangements, and you may be lucky enough to be in a situation where a dedicated Fusion Middleware systems administrator takes care of this for you, but we'll cover the basics of this in this chapter so you know at least where to start with this part of Fusion Middleware Control.

Oracle BI Systems Management API

Chapter 10 also covers in some detail the Oracle BI Systems Management API, a set of Java JMX MBeans that you can use to automate the administration of your BI system in conjunction with the WebLogic Scripting Tool and a scripting language called Jython. We won't repeat what's in that chapter here, but there are some change management tasks that are particularly suited to scripting using this systems management API, and these will be covered later in this chapter.

The Oracle BI Administration Tool

The Oracle BI Administration tool, which was covered extensively in earlier chapters of this book, is primarily used for managing the Oracle BI Repository that maps your organization's overall logical dimensional model onto the databases and other data sources that you wish to report on. In the context of managing change, the BI Administration tool performs two main roles:

- It is used for manually merging repositories together using full or patch merges, and for working with the Multiuser Development Environment (MUDE), which is based on this feature.

- It supports integration with source control systems, in conjunction with a source control server and client and a new repository storage format called MDS XML.

Three-Way Repository Merges

A single Oracle BI instance within an Oracle BI domain will contain one or more clustered Oracle BI Server components managed through Fusion Middleware Control. This Oracle BI instance can only have a single repository online and available for queries at any one time, and because of this restriction you will need to have some means of combining multiple repository files into one, ideally with some way of dealing with what are termed *merge conflicts*.

The Oracle BI Administration tool has the ability therefore to combine multiple repository files into a single, combined file using a standard software development technique called a *three-way merge*. Taking the two repository files that you wish to merge plus an optional (but recommended) repository that both were originally derived from, this merge facility provides features to handle merge conflicts (where both branches being merged are trying to update the same repository object), and to equalize the internal IDs of objects in two repositories that are logically the same but over time have for whatever reason got out of sync.

Figure 11-2 shows the Oracle BI Administrator tool about to perform a three-way merge between a project's original "baseline" repository, the current "production" repository, and an updated repository containing changes since introduced by the development team.

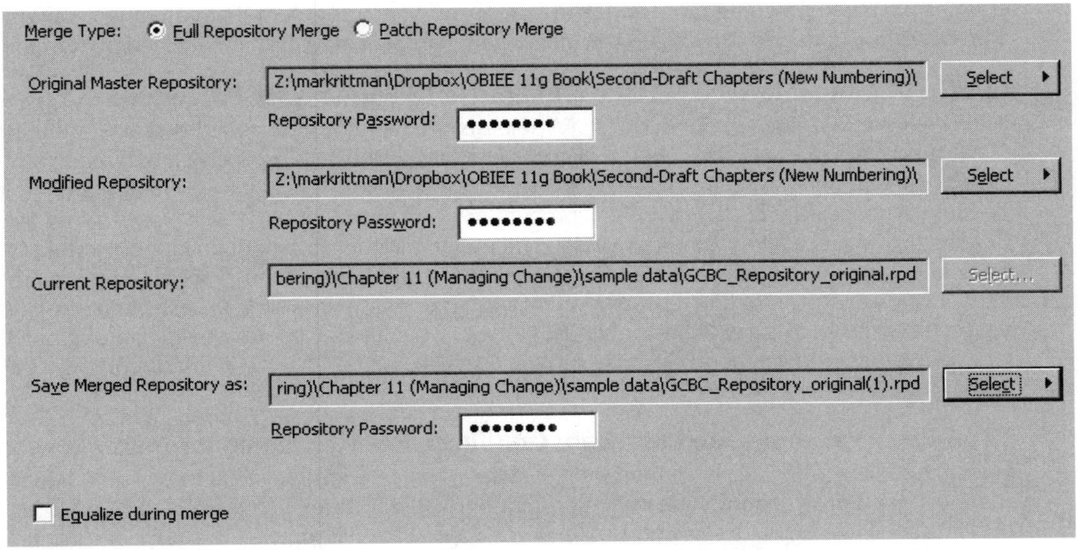

FIGURE 11-2. *Configuring settings for a three-way merge*

Merging repositories in this way, using the three-way merge facility in the BI Administration tool, is the recommended way to combine multiple repositories into one, even if you do not have a copy of the original repository that was the source for them both, as it allows you to resolve merge conflicts and ensures all internal IDs and references are maintained correctly. We will look in detail at the three-way merge process later in this chapter.

The Multiuser Development Environment

One step on from the merge facility within the Oracle BI Administration tool is the Multiuser Development Environment (MUDE). MUDE provides a framework for defining *projects,* subsets of the main repository file that a developer can work with that can then automatically be merged back into the main development branch when work is complete. MUDE automatically handles the merge process, and keeps track of what projects have been checked out, when they were checked back in, and who is holding locks on repository objects at any one time.

MUDE is quite a complex topic and requires careful planning before it is used. A considerable part of this chapter is devoted to working with MUDE, and this is a useful skill to master if you plan to work with large, distributed teams of repository developers.

RPD Command-Line Utilities and APIs

In addition to graphical tools such as Fusion Middleware Control and the Oracle BI Administration tool, a number of command-line tools exist, either as substitutes for graphical tools (for use in scripting, for example) or to provide functionality not present in the graphical tools.

For example, patching repository files can be carried out using two command-line utilities for creating and then patching repositories from a scripting environment. For patching catalogs, a command-line option for the Catalog Manager utility allows catalogs to be patched in a similar way.

Oracle BI Metadata Web Service and Oracle BI Server XML Procedures

A new feature introduced with the 11.1.1.5 release of Oracle Business Intelligence was the Oracle BI Metadata Web Service. This feature allows online repositories to be updated and manipulated, for example, to add new joins or tables to a business model or to alter a data type for a column.

Similarly, the Oracle BI Server XML procedures introduced with the same version of Oracle Business Intelligence allow administrators to amend the metadata for an online repository via ODBC calls, giving you the possibility to apply hotfixes to an online repository through a programmatic interface or develop an online repository using a programming API. While these features are outside the scope of this book, they are documented in the *Oracle Fusion Middleware Integrator's Guide for Oracle Business Intelligence Enterprise Edition 11g Release 1 (11.1.1)*, available on the Oracle Technology Network web site.

Third-Party Versioning and Software Configuration Management Tools

Finally, most organizations have their own software configuration tools that they would like to use, some of which provide functionality not present in Oracle Business Intelligence. For example, most organizations like to place snapshots of their development environments in source control systems like Subversion, or have release management tools that they use to distribute files or configuration changes to their systems. While the full details of these tools are outside the scope of this chapter, we will look at how tools such as Apache Subversion, together with the Windows desktop-integration tool TortoiseSVN, can be integrated into your change management process using the new source control integration features introduced with the 11.1.1.6 release of Oracle Business Intelligence.

Types of Oracle Business Intelligence Development Environments

Before we get into the details of how you manage change as well as development environments with Oracle Business Intelligence, let's take a moment to look at what types of development environments organizations use when working with Oracle BI projects.

The Single-Developer Environment

The simplest approach to developing Oracle Business Intelligence systems is to have a single developer create all required project metadata, and then promote it through test and then production environment themselves. This indeed describes a large number of organizations, as business intelligence might only be a relatively small part of a wider project involving deploying an ERP application and an associated data warehouse, and there may be only one person who is assigned to the BI part of the project. In reality, there may be more than one person assigned to this role, but only one of them is working on the project at any one time, and there is therefore no real need to put in place a formal process for managing concurrent development of the BI system's repository, catalog, and other metadata.

Typical Single-Developer Project Life Cycle

For development environments that only have a single developer, who is also responsible for promoting changes into test and then production environments, the typical project life cycle would look like this:

1. The developer creates the repository (RPD) file typically online, along with catalog objects, application roles, agent schedules, and other project artifacts.

2. Optionally, the repository is, at key stages in the project, saved into MDS XML format and checked into an external version control system such as Subversion.

3. The development system is regularly unit-tested by the developer.

4. When ready to be tested, the various objects are copied into a test environment, and testing takes place by a user acceptance testing team.

5. Once testing is complete, the objects in the test environment are copied into the production environment as a formal "release."

6. Users then create additional catalog objects in the production environment that are kept separate from objects created by the IT team, and they are not overwritten when the next release takes place.

Figure 11-3 shows a diagram of this process, with the flow of repository files between development, test, and production.

Benefits and Drawbacks of the Single-Developer Environment

The main benefit of the single-developer environment is simplicity. Apart from managing separate development, test, and production environments, there is no need to worry about concurrent development, merging development branches, or understanding the Multiuser Development Environment.

The main drawback of single-user development is the inability to scale development effort. Typically, when organizations sign off on a business intelligence project, they want to see the

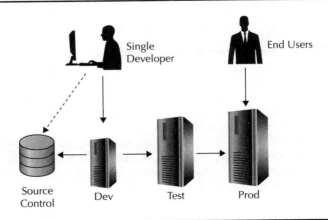

FIGURE 11-3. *The single-developer environment*

benefits immediately, and having only a single developer on your project can create a bottleneck. This can be addressed partly by adding more developers that are assigned to separate areas of project development, such as having a single repository developer, a single catalog developer, a single middleware administrator, and so on. For most organizations, this is about as far as they will want to resource the project, and if you can keep your project as simple as this, you should do so.

Shared Online Development

A variation on the single-developer environment that is now possible with the 11*g* release of Oracle Business Intelligence is the shared online development environment. In this environment, a single repository is developed and then migrated through testing and production environments, but in this instance the repository is hosted online, and up to five developers can make changes to it simultaneously. While online concurrent development of the repository was possible in earlier releases of Oracle Business Intelligence, those releases were certified to provide access only to a single online developer at a time, whereas Oracle has certified up to five with the 11*g* release.

In this type of environment, therefore, the typical project life cycle would look like this:

1. Up to five developers create the repository file concurrently, with the repository file hosted online by the development server. Each developer also creates catalog objects and other BI objects as necessary, and the Oracle BI Server manages locking between repository objects through a system of checking-out, and checking-in, repository objects.

2. Optionally, these objects at various stages are copied into a version control system such as Apache Subversion, using the MDS XML Documents repository storage format.

3. The development system is regularly unit-tested by the developer.

4. When ready to be tested, the various objects are copied into the test environment, and testing takes place by a user acceptance testing team.

5. Once testing is complete, the objects in the test environment are copied into the production environment as a formal "release."

6. Users then create additional catalog objects in the production environment that are kept separate from objects created by the IT team, and they are not overwritten when the next release takes place.

Figure 11-4 shows the typical flow of this type of environment.

Online vs. Offline Development of the Repository

Chapter 3 outlined the differences between online and offline development of the repository. To recap, a repository can either be opened offline, where the Oracle BI Repository tool opens the repository file or files directly, and only you will then have write access to these files (though other developers could also open and edit copies of these files, with their changes needing to be merged into yours at some later date).

As you have sole write access to the repository, you do not have to worry about other developers also editing, and thereby locking, parts of the repository at the same time. Therefore, there is no check-in/checkout process you need to follow when editing objects. You will, however, need to use Fusion Middleware Control to upload a copy of the repository in the binary RPD format to your

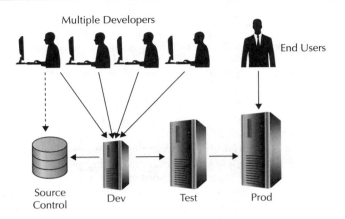

Multiple Developers

End Users

Source
Control

Dev   Test   Prod

FIGURE 11-4. *The shared online development environment*

Oracle BI instance before you, or other users or developers, can run queries against it or edit it in online mode.

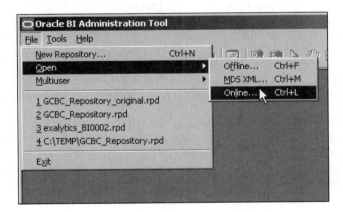

Online development, by contrast, connects the Oracle BI Administrator tool to the repository file through the Oracle BI Cluster Controller and Oracle BI Server system components, with the connection actually taking place via ODBC. Because the repository file is actually running "online" at that moment, any changes you make will be (more or less) immediately visible to users, making it an unsuitable approach for anything other than hotfixes when running in production. As you are accessing the repository file via a server process, though, this does give you the ability to provide concurrent access to more than one developer; and the BI Server manages any conflicts by checking out and locking objects as they are edited by developers, and then checking them back in again afterward.

While, in theory, an unlimited number of developers could connect to an online repository to edit it, past versions of Oracle Business Intelligence have certified only a single developer. The 11g version now certifies a total of five. You can add more concurrent developers than this if you wish, but Oracle Support probably will not help you if you go beyond this limit.

Benefits and Drawbacks of Shared Online Development
The main benefit of shared online development again is simplicity. Compared to the Multiuser Development Environment, which we will discuss in a moment, this single repository file environment is easy to administer, with the BI Server component handling locking of repository objects to prevent conflicts.

The disadvantages become more apparent the more developers you try to add to this environment. The checking-in, checking-out, and locking process can be slow, and it may be impractical to use this approach for a large repository that has many objects and dependencies. In addition, at the time of this writing, the 11.1.1.5 and earlier releases of Oracle Business Intelligence 11g had a known issue where "Transaction Update Failed" error messages would often be shown when developing online, usually due to stricter repository consistency checking rules compared to the 10g and earlier releases, but often this was due to unexplained issues that would stop you from saving changes to the repository. If you use this approach, therefore, make sure you are using the latest patch release of Oracle Business Intelligence for your version, and be sure to thoroughly "road-test" this approach before committing to it as your development environment.

Multiuser Development Environment, Single Semantic Model
While having just a single developer work on developing an Oracle Business Intelligence repository may have the benefit of simplicity, in reality it may be necessary to have more than just a single developer developing elements of the repository. The overall repository may in fact be made up of several subject areas that can realistically be developed in parallel, and it may be that your development teams are spread geographically and in different time zones, making it important that you have a formal process for managing concurrent development and addressing potential project conflicts.

The Multiuser Development Environment (MUDE), which comes with the Oracle BI Administration tool, is a development framework that is concerned with concurrent development of the Oracle BI Repository. It allows teams of repository developers to extract subsets of the repository, known as *projects,* and then work on these projects separately, merging their updated subsets back into the main repository when they are ready to commit their changes, as shown in Figure 11-5.

Alongside this repository work, the same or other developers can also concurrently develop catalog content and other project artifacts such as application roles, agents, actions, and scorecards. As the Multiuser Development Environment was primarily created to manage concurrent write access to the repository file (RPD), and the other project artifacts do not have this restriction over multiple developers trying to write to the catalog or the equivalent Fusion Middleware Repository, there is no special arrangement for their development in this type of environment.

Multiuser Development Environment, Multiple Semantic Models
A final variation on the Multiuser Development Environment is where completely independent teams develop their own repositories, containing independent semantic models, but then because of the limitation of the BI Server only being able to host a single repository file online, these repositories are

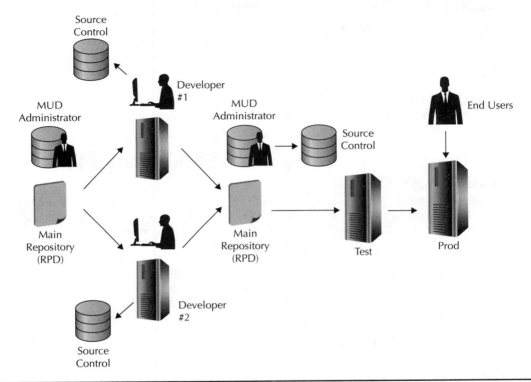

FIGURE 11-5.   *Multiuser development with a single semantic model*

brought together just before being promoted to test and production environments using the three-way merge feature within the Oracle BI Administration tool.

In this example, each development team may either develop their repositories using the single-developer approach, the shared online development approach, or may use their own full Multiuser Development Environment, but as an extra stage at the end their final repositories and catalogs are merged together using the BI Administrator tool's merge feature, or through a similar feature in the Catalog Manager application. Manual steps normally will need to be performed to merge Fusion Middleware artifacts such as application roles, and you should also expect work coordinating release schedules between the two teams.

As you have seen, there are various models for Oracle Business Intelligence development that you can follow, each of which gets more complex the more developers and separate semantic models you need to create. Before we get into the complexities of managing projects such as these, though, let's take a moment to think about how you manage system configuration changes to your Oracle Business Intelligence system, which is an area that, thankfully, does not get much more complex the more developers or repositories you add to the system.

Managing System Configuration Changes

Chapter 10 covered systems management for Oracle Business Intelligence and discussed topics such as changing performance configuration settings, stopping and starting your system, accessing metrics, and using the Oracle BI Systems Management API for scripting management tasks for your environment. In this chapter, we will take a brief look at this area again but will focus on the tasks involving change management. In particular, how do you introduce changes to your environment when you are running multiple, clustered servers that all need to have these changes applied to them, and how do you manage changes to the repository and catalog while minimizing downtime for your users?

Managing System Configuration Changes Using Fusion Middleware Control

When managing an enterprise deployment of Oracle Business Intelligence, you should always make system configuration changes using Fusion Middleware Control or script them using the WebLogic Scripting Tool along with the JMX MBean–based Oracle BI Systems Management API. You should not edit configuration files yourself unless the parameters you wish to change are not currently managed by Fusion Middleware Control or the Systems Management API. If you do try to manually alter parameters that are normally managed by Fusion Middleware Control, you will find that the changes you make will be automatically overwritten when you restart your system. If you are working in a clustered environment, you may find that you have applied the changes only to some nodes and not all.

Promoting Repositories Between Environments

Regardless of the development team environment your organization uses, at some point you will end up with a repository file that needs to be uploaded into your test, production, or other environment. Similarly, you may have catalog objects that you need to promote into a test or production environment, typically created by your development team for testing purposes or as standard analyses and dashboards that your team has agreed to produce for your users.

To take a development repository and promote it to your test environment, you would normally use Fusion Middleware Control to upload the file, unless you wanted to script the file movement using WLST and the Systems Management API. When you promote your repository file in this way, Fusion Middleware Control takes a copy of the file, typically held on your development workstation, and uploads it to the server hosting your Oracle Business Intelligence deployment. As part of this upload, the file is renamed to add a sequence number to the end of the filename, ensuring that you have separate copies on the Business Intelligence server of all the historical repositories you have uploaded.

To take a development or test repository and upload it to your test or production server, follow these steps:

1. Ensure that the repository file is available to you from your workstation, that all changes have been checked into it, that the repository validates correctly, and that it has been suitably tested by your developers.

2. Using your web browser, navigate to the Fusion Middleware Control web site (http://[*machine_name*]:7001/em) and enter the login credentials for an administrator account.

3. When the Fusion Middleware Control web site successfully starts, use the navigation tree menu on the left-hand side to select Business Intelligence | coreapplication.

4. When the coreapplication page is displayed, using the tabs and subtabs displayed across the screen, select Deployment | Repository.

5. Click Lock And Edit Configuration to lock the domain and allow only you to make configuration changes from this point onward.

6. Locate the Upload BI Server Repository section of the page, and click the Browse button to locate the repository file. Type in the repository password, and click Apply to save the changes.

7. To activate these changes, click the Activate Changes button at the top of the screen. Alternatively, if you wish to cancel the upload, click the Release Configuration button.

CAUTION
Make sure you either activate the changes or release the configuration; otherwise, the system will stay locked and no other administrator will be able to make configuration changes.

8. Once you have activated the changes, switch to the Availability tab and then the Processes subtab, highlight the BI Servers row, and click the Restart Selected button to restart the BI Server component and start making use of your new repository.

9. For an Oracle Business Intelligence deployment that has not been either horizontally or vertically clustered (see the next section for more details on what this means), the repository file that you have just uploaded can now be found on the Business Intelligence file system, at [*middleware_home*]\instances\instance1\bifoundation\ OracleBIServerComponent\coreapplication_obis1\repository. The file will have a sequence number appended to it to ensure that when it was uploaded it did not overwrite other, older repository files.

Name	Size	Type ▲
aw_BI0002.rpd	29 KB	Oracle BI Repositor...
coreapplication_OH505112991_BI0008.rpd	29 KB	Oracle BI Repositor...
essbase_BI0006.rpd	58 KB	Oracle BI Repositor...
GCBC_Repository_BI0007.rpd	51 KB	Oracle BI Repositor...
mclass_repository_BI0003.rpd	17 KB	Oracle BI Repositor...
mclass_repository_with_staff_fixed_BI0004.rpd	17 KB	Oracle BI Repositor...
SampleAppLite_BI0001.rpd	37 KB	Oracle BI Repositor...
wlst_rpd_example_BI0005.rpd	45 KB	Oracle BI Repositor...

Clustering and High-Availability Considerations   The preceding example showed how you might upload a repository to an Oracle Business Intelligence environment where there was just a single Oracle BI Server system component in the domain. The advantages of Fusion Middleware Control are more apparent, though, when you consider how you might promote a new repository to a test or production environment where there are, for example, multiple BI Server components spread over multiple physical servers.

When you "scale out" your Oracle Business Intelligence installation to add more Oracle BI Server components to either the initial cluster node, or additional nodes that you add to the cluster, you then need to ensure that any new repository files that you upload to the Oracle BI domain are copied to all BI Server components in the cluster, even if you take the recommended approach of also configuring a shared repository for the cluster. Fusion Middleware Control, and the Oracle BI Systems Management API on which it is based, takes care of this requirement for you automatically, distributing copies of the repository file to each component in the cluster and automatically updating their configuration when you upload a new repository to the domain.

When you then come to restart the BI Server system components in your cluster, you may wish to perform these restarts in a rolling fashion to avoid downtime for your users. If you followed the instructions given previously and you click the Restart Selected button to restart all BI Server components, Fusion Middleware Control will instruct all BI Servers (through the Systems Management API) to shut down at the same time and then restart, leaving potentially no BI Servers available within the cluster to service user requests. You can see this for yourself by repeatedly running the opmnctl status command ([*middleware_home*]\instances\instance1\bin\opmnctl status) after the Restart Selected button is clicked and checking the status value for each BI Server component during the restart.

If you wish to keep your system available during such a repository change, you will need to perform a manual rolling restart of your system. To do this, follow these steps:

1. Upload your new repository as before, and Fusion Middleware Control will upload the repository file and distribute it to all BI Server components in the cluster. Ensure that you click the Activate Changes button at the end of the process so that the changes are applied correctly to each component.

2. To perform the rolling restart of the BI Server components, switch to the Availability tab and then the Processes subtab within the Fusion Middleware Control screen, but this time highlight just one of the BI Server components rather than the whole BI Servers category. Then click the Restart Selected button to restart just this BI Server component. This technique also applies to rolling restarts of the Oracle BI Presentation Services components after a catalog directory location change, and the illustration below shows such as BI Presentation Server component restart about to take place.

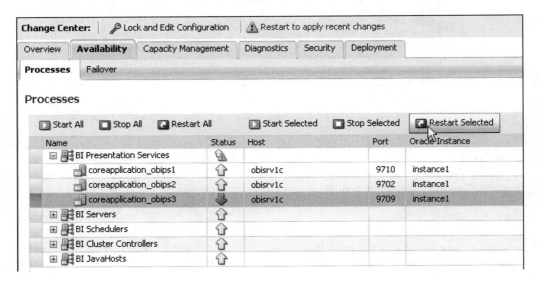

3. Follow any onscreen instructions to restart the component and, once complete, highlight the next BI Server component in the list and repeat these steps. Do this for each BI Server component until you have reached the end of the list; in this way you will deploy the new repository with no downtime for your users.

Promoting Catalogs Between Environments

Typically, in development you may create a number of analyses, dashboards, and other catalog objects that you wish to move into test and then production environments. These objects may be there for testing purposes, to help end users verify that the numbers being displayed onscreen are correct, or they may be objects that you have agreed to deliver, as "base" reports and dashboards.

In this part of the chapter, we are concerned only with promoting whole repositories and catalogs between environments. Later on, we will look at how you promote incremental changes between environments, or how you can merge environments together to protect, for example, any changes made by end users to the catalog from any new content that you upload. As such, promoting a catalog between environments when we do not need to consider whether we overwrite existing content is reasonably straightforward, although it differs from repository migrations in that Fusion Middleware Control does not upload the files to the new server environment for us, and we have to perform this step manually.

To upload a new catalog from, for example, a development environment to a test environment that has a single Oracle BI Presentation Server system component within the Oracle BI instance, follow these steps:

1. Using an archiving tool, create an archive file for your catalog, being sure to include all files across all directories in the catalog. Note that WinZip should not be used for this purpose if the catalog is either being transferred to or from a Unix or Linux environment, as it does not always handle Unix file permissions correctly. 7zip (http://www.7-zip.org/) is a good alternative that is often used for this purpose.

CAUTION
Ensure that your new environment has the same application roles
defined for it as the environment you are migrating from; otherwise,
permissions on objects may be lost or made unusable.

2. Copy this archive file to the [*middleware_home*]\instances\instance1\bifoundation\ OracleBIPresentationServerComponent\coreapplication_obips1\catalog directory, and unarchive the file there, creating a subdirectory under the \catalog directory.

3. Now, using your web browser, navigate to the Fusion Middleware Control web site (http://[*machine_name*]:7001/em) and enter the login credentials for an administrator account.

4. When the Fusion Middleware Control web site successfully starts, use the navigation tree menu on the left-hand side to select Business Intelligence | coreapplication.

5. When the coreapplication page is displayed, using the tabs and subtabs displayed across the screen, select Deployment | Repository.

6. Within the BI Presentation Catalog area, locate the Catalog Location text box and amend the existing folder name at the end of the path to reference your new folder instead.

BI Presentation Catalog

This section shows the current location of the catalog used by Presentation Services. Use this section to change the location of the catalog, or to share the catalog by pointing to a shared location.

Catalog Location `INSTANCE/bifoundation/OracleBIPresentationServicesComponent/$COMPONENT_NAME/catalog/SampleApp`

For example, if the current path shown in this text box reads:

```
$ORACLE_INSTANCE/bifoundation/OracleBIPresentationServicesComponent/$CO
MPONENT_NAME/catalog/Sales
```

and your new catalog folder is called SampleAppLite, then change this path to the following one:

```
$ORACLE_INSTANCE/bifoundation/OracleBIPresentationServicesComponent/$CO
MPONENT_NAME/catalog/SampleAppLite
```

7. Then, as with repository changes, switch to the Availability tab and then the Processes subtab, and then restart the BI Presentation Server component to pick up the configuration change.

Going forward, the new catalog will be available for use in the new environment.

Clustering and High-Availability Considerations   Unlike when working with the repository, where the BI Server will replicate changes made to one clustered repository to the other repositories in the cluster, after each BI Server is restarted there is no automatic replication feature that works between clustered BI Presentation Servers. Therefore, it is strongly recommended that when you provision additional BI Presentation Servers beyond the initial one that comes as part of the standard instance within the Oracle BI Domain, you use a shared catalog that is used by all Presentation Servers in the instance. Details on how to create a shared catalog can be found in the "Configuring Shared Locations for the Repository and Catalog" section at the end of Chapter 2 in this book.

If you do not enable a shared catalog, you will need to manually copy the catalog archive file to all directories within the Oracle Business Intelligence file system on each server that hosts the BI Presentation Server system component and manually synchronize each one to pick up any new, changed, or deleted catalog objects that users create. Then, to ensure that each Presentation Server knows where to find its current catalog directory, ensure that you specify the catalog path in the following format so that each Presentation Server substitutes its own $ORACLE_INSTANCE and $COMPONENT_NAME value in this path name:

**$ORACLE_INSTANCE**/bifoundation/OracleBIPresentationServicesComponent/**$COMPONEN
T_NAME**/[catalog_name]

This is the default setup for the catalog path in Fusion Middleware Control, but you should still avoid this route if at all possible, using the recommended shared catalog approach instead.

Managing Configuration Changes

Configuration changes, such as enabling or disabling query caching, changing the size of the cache, or changing the maximum number of rows returned by a query, should always be performed using Fusion Middleware Control or through the WebLogic Scripting Tool and the Oracle BI Systems Management API. When you make configuration changes using this method, all of the required configuration files that contain the required settings are updated, including the configuration files used directly by system components such as the BI Server and BI Presentation Server, and those used by Fusion Middleware Control and the WebLogic Administration Server.

For example, this is how you enable or disable query caching using Fusion Middleware Control:

1. Using your web browser, log into the Fusion Middleware Control web site at http://[*machine_name*]:7001/em, using the login credentials of a WebLogic administrator user.

2. When the Fusion Middleware Control home page opens, using the navigation tree menu on the left-hand side, select Business Intelligence | coreapplication.

3. When the coreapplication page is displayed, select the Capacity Management tab and then the Performance subtab.

4. Click the Lock And Edit Configuration button to lock the domain for administrative editing. From this point, until you activate the changes or roll back the configuration, no other user will be able to perform systems administration tasks.

5. Using the Performance subtab, select or deselect the Cache Enabled check box to enable or disable query caching. At this point, no changes have been made.

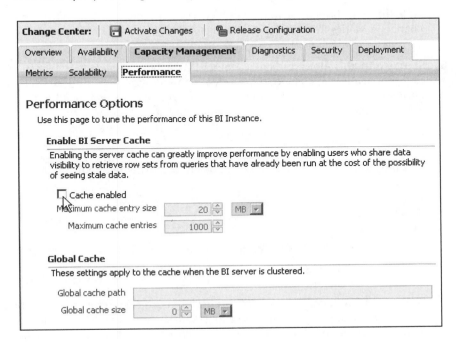

6. To register the change, click the Apply button in the top right-hand side of the screen. At this point no changes have been made, but the Java JMX MBean that controls management of this feature has now been called with a request to enable or disable query caching. No configuration files have yet been updated, nor has query caching been enabled or disabled.

7. To process this change, click the Activate Changes button at the top of the screen. When you click this button, another Java JMX MBean method is called that commits this change, and updates the configuration file below which contains a central record of all of the settings managed by Fusion Middleware Control and the Oracle BI Systems Management API:

   [*middleware_home*]\user_projects\domains]bifoundation_domain\config\fmwconfig\ biee-domain.xml

   If you open this file with a text editor, you will see two XML tags that define the start and end-point of your system's configuration record:

   ```
   <BIInstance name="coreapplication"></BIInstance>
   ```

   Between these tags are other XML elements that contain the setting for your Oracle Business Intelligence "instance," the collection of system components within your instance. One of these settings is

   ```
   <PerformanceOptions bIServerCacheEnabled="true|false" />
   ```

   which contains the value that you just set using Fusion Middleware Control (together with other settings also having to do with performance options).

   Note that you should not edit the contents of this file yourself directly, but should only change its values through Fusion Middleware Control or a WLST script using the Oracle BI Systems Management API.

8. Shortly after this file is updated, another JMX MBean detects that the file has changed and propagates the change to the actual configuration files used by each Oracle BI Server component, which in the case of an Oracle BI instance with just a single BI Server component would normally be located at:

   [*middleware_home*]\instances\instance1\config\OracleBIServerComponent\ coreapplication_obis1

   This file in-turn contains a setting that determines whether the BI Server component uses query caching or not:

   ```
   [CACHE]
   ENABLE = YES;  # This Configuration setting is managed by Oracle Business
   Intelligence Enterprise Manager
   ```

   For any values in this configuration file that have the following comment against the setting:

   ```
   # This Configuration setting is managed by Oracle Business Intelligence
   Enterprise Manager
   ```

   you should not update these values yourself but use Fusion Middleware Control or WLST to make the changes for you. For settings that do not have this comment against them, as we will see in the next section, you will have to make the changes manually.

9. For the BI Server system component to start making use of this new setting, you will need to restart it using the Availability tab and then the Processes subtab.

    Once the restart has taken place, the new query caching setting will apply to new queries.

Clustered-Environment Considerations   The advantage of using Fusion Middleware Control to make these configuration changes is that they are applied across all system components in the Oracle instance, automatically. For example, if you enable or disable query caching as per the previous example, all Oracle BI Server components within the instance will have this configuration change made to them, without further intervention on your part.

As with the earlier example in this chapter where a new repository was uploaded to the Oracle BI domain, if you have a clustered environment and wish to ensure that there is always at least one BI Server component available to service user queries when you restart them, make sure that you perform a rolling restart of each component in turn, rather than just highlighting the BI Servers catalog on the Processes subtab (under the Availability main tab) and clicking the Restart Selected button.

Managing System Configuration Changes Using Manual Configuration File Changes

Over time, Oracle's strategy is for all configuration settings to be exposed either through Fusion Middleware Control or at least through the Oracle BI Systems Management API that provides Fusion Middleware Control's functionality. Until this target is reached, though, there will still be settings in the configuration files used by the Oracle BI system components that you will need to manage by hand.

For a simple Oracle BI installation that has not been scaled-out to add additional BI Server, BI Presentation Server, or other system components to the cluster, the files that contain these configuration settings can be found in the following locations:

[*middleware_home*]\instances\instance1\config\OracleBIServerComponent\
coreapplication_obis1\
[*middleware_home*]\instances\instance1\config\OracleBIPresentationServerComponent\
coreapplication_obips1\
[*middleware_home*]\instances\instance1\config\OracleBISchedulerComponent\
coreapplication_obisch1\
[*middleware_home*]\instances\instance1\config\OracleBIClusterControllerComponent\
coreapplication_obiccs1\
[*middleware_home*]\instances\instance1\config\OracleBIJavaHostComponent\
coreapplication_obijh1\

Within these files, parameters that require manual management are those that do not have the following comment next to their entry:

```
# This Configuration setting is managed by Oracle Business Intelligence
Enterprise Manager
```

For example, the POPULATE_AGGREGATE_ROLLUP_HITS setting in the [*middleware_home*]\
instances\instance1\config\OracleBIServerComponent\coreapplication_obis1\NQSConfig.INI
file does not have this comment added, whereas the MAX_CACHE_ENTRIES setting does.

```
MAX_CACHE_ENTRIES = 1000;  # This Configuration setting is managed by Oracle
Business Intelligence Enterprise Manager
POPULATE_AGGREGATE_ROLLUP_HITS = NO;
```

For these settings, you will need to manually update the file contents yourself and then restart
the relevant system component to pick up the change. These manually managed settings will not
be automatically overwritten by the Administration Server after a reboot and are not available for
viewing or management through Fusion Middleware Control.

Clustered-Environment Considerations   If you add more system components either to the existing
server or to a new server, you will need to ensure that you make any configuration changes of this
type to all of the configuration files used by the new components. For example, if you have added
two more BI Server components to your existing server, you will need to ensure that any manual
changes you make to these types of parameters are applied also to the configuration files used by the
new components.

Similarly, if you use Fusion Middleware Control to provision new system components within
an instance, you will need to apply any changes of this type to the configuration files that are
created for the instance, as only configuration file settings managed by Fusion Middleware Control
will be applied to the newly created component's configuration files. Therefore, you should make
these configuration file changes only where absolutely necessary, particularly when working within
a vertically or horizontally scaled-out environment, as keeping all of the configuration files in sync
can be a laborious and error-prone task.

Managing System Configuration Changes Using WLST and the Oracle BI Systems Management API

When managing system configuration changes for your Oracle Business Intelligence installation,
it is often preferable to script those changes, particularly if you want to include the changes in any
promotion of a release between environments, such as between development and production.
These scripts can then be tested and included in a source control system, rather than having to
rely on a systems administrator manually making the changes each time using Fusion Middleware
Control.

If you want to script changes in this way, there are two recommended methods based on the
parameters you are changing:

- For configuration settings managed through Fusion Middleware Control and the Oracle
  BI Systems Management API, you should script the changes using the WebLogic Scripting
  Tool (WSLT).

- For settings that are not managed in this way, you will need to use a scripting
  environment (for example, Window Scripting Host) that can read from and write to text
  files. In this situation, it may be easier to just include a full configuration file containing
  your changes in your release process, deploy this file to your new environment, and then
  use WLST to apply the "managed" configuration file changes to this file after the new
  environment is deployed.

Use of the WebLogic Scripting Tool is described in detail in Chapter 10, including examples of WLST scripts for managing various configuration settings.

Clustered-Environment Considerations   As with the use of Fusion Middleware Control, the advantage of using WLST scripts and the Oracle BI Systems Management API is that any configuration changes you make are automatically applied across all components in the instance. Fusion Middleware Control "under the covers" uses the Systems Management API to make its changes, and the process it follows is the same as for changes you initiate through WLST scripts. See Chapter 10 for more details on how the Systems Management API is used to perform systems management tasks in your environment.

As detailed in the previous section, though, any changes that you script to parameters not managed by the Oracle BI Systems Management API will need to be applied equally to all system components in the instance, across all servers in your domain.

Incremental Releases of Repositories Using Merging and Patching

For development team environments other than those involving just a single developer or a team of developers working with a shared, online environment, at some point you may want to merge together two or more repositories to create a single one that can be hosted in your Oracle BI domain. In addition, any development team moving beyond the initial release of their project will at some point want to release a set of updates to the repository that need to be applied to the production system. To enable this, the Oracle BI Administrator tool has a set of features for merging repositories together and for creating "patch files" containing sets of changes that are then applied to a target repository.

These features can be used in several scenarios:

- Two or more development teams may have developed, separately, their own repository files, and these need to be merged into a single repository file before deploying to the production server.

- A developer may wish to incorporate a repository supplied by a vendor or by Oracle (for example, the Usage Tracking repository) into their main repository.

- A team may wish to deploy just the new and changed objects that have been created in their development environment as a patch file into their production repository. Together with past patch files, this file constitutes a set of updates that can be applied to the original repository file and stored in a version control system to allow any past version of the repository to be re-created.

When merging repositories, there are two types of merge that can take place:

- A *full merge,* in which the Oracle BI Administration tool gives you the ability to merge two repositories based off of a common, third baseline repository

- A *patch merge,* in which an updated repository is compared to an original one, and the differences are used to create an XML patch file that is then applied to a third repository

A similar feature for the catalog also exists and will be detailed in the section "Incremental Releases of Catalogs Using Merging and Patching," later in this chapter. Before we take a look at merging and patching repositories, though, let us take a look for a moment at something you may wish to do before merging repositories: comparing repository files against each other and performing a task called *equalization*.

If you wish to try out some of the techniques and features detailed in the rest of this chapter, the repository RPD files that are referred to in the text are within the /RPDs for Chapter 11 folder within the Sample Data folder provided with this book.

Comparing and Equalizing Repositories

Before merging two repositories together, or just to work out the differences between two repository files, you can compare them using the compare repositories feature in the Oracle BI Administration tool. Comparing repositories produces an onscreen report that lists the differences between the two files, and you can also use this as a starting point to create a repository patch file, described in more detail later in this chapter.

Internally within each repository file, Oracle Business Intelligence uses an *upgrade ID* to provide a unique identifier for each repository object. Because these IDs can get out of sync between two repositories as developers make edits, you often need to *equalize* your repositories to make sure these IDs are the same for logically equivalent objects.

Comparing Repositories Using the Oracle BI Administration Tool

Consider a situation in which a repository, for example, the GCBC_Repository.rpd file in the sample data set, has been taken by a developer and edited to make the following changes:

1. A new logical column called Staff Position has been added to the Dim Staff logical table.
2. The logical column Dim Times.Quarter has had its sort order column unset.
3. The Sales – Store Quality.Dim Survey Organization logical table has been deleted and then re-created identically.
4. A presentation table has been accidentally deleted and then re-created so that the definition of the objects is the same but internally the objects now have different upgrade IDs.
5. The updated repository is then saved to the file system and named GCBC_Repository_updated.rpd.

These two repository files, GCBC_Repository.rpd and GCBC_Repository_Updated.rpd, will now be compared and the equalization feature used later on, if needed. To compare them using the Oracle BI Administration tool, follow these steps:

1. Open the Oracle BI Administration tool from the Windows Start menu.
2. With the Oracle BI Administration tool open, select File | Open | Offline, and select the most recent repository file (in this instance, GCBC_Repository_updated.rpd). Enter the repository password when prompted (in this case, **welcome1**).
3. To compare this repository with the other one, select File | Compare from the application menu. Choose Select | Repository to browse to the other repository file, and enter the repository password when prompted (again, in this case, **welcome1**).

4. The Compare Repositories dialog box will then be shown.

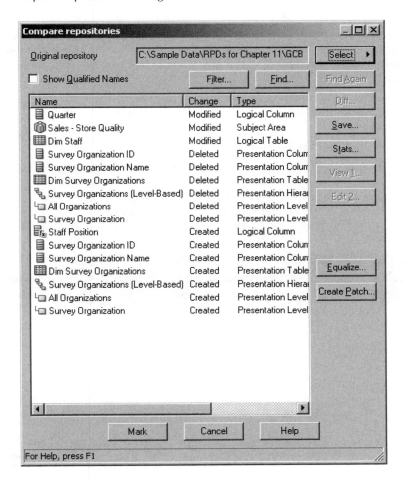

5. You can see the list of modified, updated, and created repository objects in your current repository compared to the one that you just selected. To view the number of created, modified, and deleted repository objects, click the Stats button. To create a patch file, details of which are described later in this chapter, click the Create Patch button.

Equalizing Repositories In the example of the two repositories that we have used here, there are a large number of deleted and created objects listed in this dialog box, due to the presentation table that had been deleted and then re-created identically between the two repositories. You may wish to continue to record this fact, or you may want to *equalize* the two repositories, giving both presentation tables the same upgrade ID and recognizing that they are in fact logically the same.

To equalize the two repositories used in the preceding example, you need to perform following additional tasks:

1. With the Oracle BI Administration tool and the Compare Repositories dialog box still open, click the Stats button to note the number of creations, modifications, and deletions between the two repositories. In the example that we have used, these figures are as follows:

   Deleted: 6
   Created: 7
   Modified: 3

2. Now click the Equalize button to equalize the two repositories.

3. In the Equalize Objects dialog box, shown in the illustration below, use the drop-down menu at the top of the dialog box to switch between repository object types that can potentially be equalized. In this example, there are presentation tables, presentation columns, a presentation hierarchy, and a presentation level that can be equalized, due to a whole presentation table being deleted and then re-created in one of the repositories.

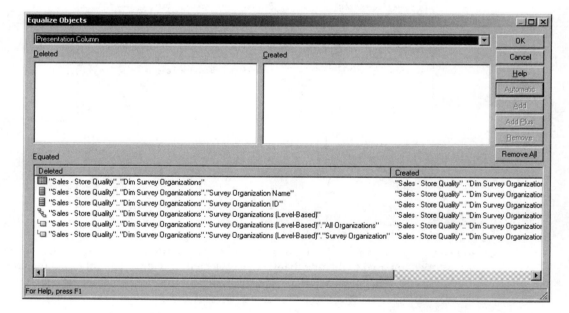

4. To automatically equalize objects that are logically the same, click the Automatic button. Clicking this button works across all object types listed in the dialog box and attempts to equalize them automatically. Alternatively, click the Add and Add Plus buttons to combine and equalize objects yourself.

5. To mark (highlight) objects in the repository that were equalized, click the Mark button. Otherwise, click OK, and then return to the Compare Repositories dialog box to see the effect of the equalization. The number of objects listed in the comparison dialog box should now reduce, and if you click the Stats button again, in this example the number of objects affected falls to the numbers listed here:

   Deleted: 0
   Created: 1
   Modified: 3

NOTE
To save repository files with their updated, equalized upgrade IDs, save the files and then continue to use them going forward. (For these sample repositories, make sure you save the equalized versions either in a separate folder or named differently so that the files are in their original state when we do other exercises.)

Equalization in this way reduces the number of "false positive" comparison differences between repositories and can be performed before, or as part of, a repository merge operation.

Merging Repositories

When you have two repository files that you want to combine into a single, combined one, you can use the merge feature within the Oracle BI Administration tool to perform this task. When you merge repositories in this way, you either create a combined repository file in the case of a full merge or a patch file that can be applied later on to another repository file, either through the Oracle BI Administration tool or through a command-line utility.

Repository merging is typically carried out in organizations where separate development teams have produced their own, department-specific repositories that need to be combined into a single repository file before being uploaded to the live production environment. For teams of developers that are all working on fragments of a single development branch, merging of their final repositories is handled for you automatically through the Multiuser Development Environment, which uses the same merge feature in the background.

Repository merging, like merging any software development source elements that make use of shared resources, can be a complex task due to the need to apply rules to the merge and deal with any potential conflicts. Let's start off by looking at the theory behind repository merging and understand some of the concepts between three-way merges, and three-way merge with no parent.

Overview of Three-Way and Three-Way with No Parent Merges

The Oracle BI Administration tool merges repositories using a standard software development technique called the "three-way merge." This merge technique uses three files as input and produces a single, merged file as the output. These three input files are given distinct roles and have different rules applied to them when it comes to the merge:

- There is an *original* file, from which the two other files were branched, which is used to confirm common parentage of objects in these two files.

- There's also a *current* file, the "development" version that has the most up-to-date changes.

- A *modified* file, again based on the original file, contains what was placed into "production" and may typically have one or two production system hotfixes applied to it.

Within the context of an Oracle Business Intelligence project and two repository files that were branched off of a common repository file, which we now wish to combine back into a single, merged repository, our files would typically be assigned like this:

- The *original* file would be the original base repository that the two repository branches were then derived from.

- The *modified* repository, one of the two repositories to be merged, in this case would be the "equal" of the other branched repository.

- The *current* repository would be the other repository to be merged and the "equal" of the modified repository.

Figure 11-6 shows these three repository files, together with the fourth repository, which contains the integrated repository objects.

This describes well the situation in which a single repository, for example, has been created as a starting point that is then branched and worked on independently by two development teams. Having this initial, baseline repository available to the merge process makes the merging more accurate, as it can trace back the parentage of objects in each repository and avoid making "guesses" as to which objects relate to which.

In situations where, instead of repositories being branched, you wish to merge changes into a production repository that may itself have had "hotfixes" applied to it, the three-way merge process also works well. In this case, our three repository files would be as follows:

- The *original* repository file typically would be the repository that represents the baseline repository before the current phase of development began.

- The *modified* repository file would be the production repository that may have had hotfixes applied to it or online changes made directly in production.

- The *current* repository file would be the development repository you now wish to add or merge the changes from into the production repository.

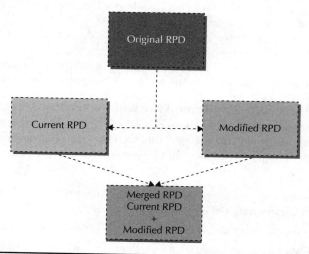

FIGURE 11-6. *The three-way merge*

Figure 11-7 shows this type of scenario, where the development repository is merged with the production one, referencing both back to the original repository from which they were derived, to create the new, merged production repository.

Three-way merges, while seeming more complicated because of the need to have a copy of the original repository that your development team then branched off, are usually less error prone than two-way merges and require less manual intervention, as this original repository provides a common point of reference for the two repositories being merged, making it easy to identify where objects that are being merged are logically equivalent.

However, in some situations there may be no common baseline repository, such as when two completely separate repositories need to be merged into one. In this case, though, you still need to use the three-way merge feature in the Oracle BI Administration tool to bring the files together. The original repository file is replaced with a blank, empty repository in what is termed a "three-way merge with no parent" so that:

- The *original* repository file is an empty repository that you create for the purpose of this two-way merge.
- The *modified* repository file is the first repository to be included in the merge.
- The *current* repository file is the other repository to be included in the merge.

Figure 11-8 shows a three-way merge with no parent using this approach.

Because they do not have a common, original parent repository that can be used as a reference point to confirm that similarly named objects are in fact logically the same, three-way merges with no parent have the potential to be more error prone and may require more manual intervention to resolve conflicts.

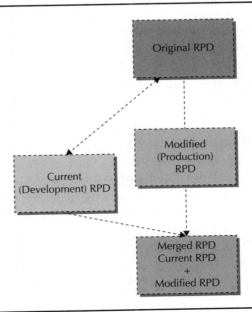

FIGURE 11-7. *Three-way merge development and production repository files*

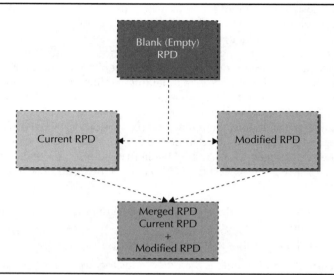

FIGURE 11-8. *The three-way merge with no parent*

Therefore, wherever possible, if you do in fact have access to the original repository file that formed the basis for the files you wish to bring together, ensure that you use it in the three-way merge rather than just substituting a blank RPD.

Merge Rules and Resolving Merge Conflicts   Regardless of whether you are performing a full or a patch merge, certain rules and assumptions are used by the merge feature when bringing your repositories together. It is important that you understand these rules so that you know what automatic decisions will be made during the merge and which ones will require you to make an explicit choice.

- It is assumed that you want to preserve any changes that you have introduced into the *modified* repository, such as production database usernames and passwords in connection pool settings. You might also have added hotfixes to the production repository or added new objects directly into production to support a new dashboard; therefore, objects you have added to this modified repository, or deleted from it, will automatically be added or deleted from the merged results.

- If, however, objects have been added or deleted from the *current* repository (in the example earlier, the development repository), you will be asked to confirm whether you wish to keep these changes in the merged results.

- If an object was added identically to both the *current* and *modified* repositories, or deleted from both repositories, it will be added to or deleted from the merged results automatically.

- If you have added the same object to both *current* and *modified* repositories, but there are small differences between the two additions, you will be prompted to select which version you want to put into the merged results. This could happen, for example, if you add the same logical table to both repositories but the column or table source definitions differ slightly between the two objects.

■ If you modify an existing object in either the *current* repository or in the *modified* repository (but not both at the same time), the change is kept and copied into the merged results. If you modify the object in both the current and modified repositories, though, this will cause a *merge conflict* and you will be prompted to select only one of them to include in the merged results.

■ Decisions that you make about individual objects (for example, logical tables) can determine a whole number of other decisions, such as about logical columns contained with the table. In addition, objects may be interconnected through dependencies, for example, leading to decisions being made about custom authenticators being taken because of a change you have made to a connection pool on which it is dependent.

Understanding these rules is important, as they can help to explain some of the questions you are asked when performing the merge, as well as which repository should be selected as the "modified" repository and which as the "current" repository when merging branches or independent repositories together. Other rules apply in special situations and for some particular types of repository objects, and you should consult the "Merge Rules" section of the *Oracle Fusion Middleware Metadata Repository Builder's Guide for Oracle Business Intelligence Enterprise Edition 11g Release 1 (11.1.1)* for full details.

Performing a Three-Way Repository Merge

In the following example, we will use the two repository files (GCBC_Repository.rpd and GCBC_Repository_updated.rpd) used in the previous example on comparing repositories, and a third repository file, GCBC_Repository_original.rpd, to perform a three-way merge. These files will play the following roles:

■ GCBC_Repository_original.rpd will be the original repository, from which the other two repositories were derived. This is the *original* repository created during the first development iteration of the project.

■ GCBC_Repository.rpd will be the *modified* repository used in production. Since being put into production, it has also been developed online, adding a new subject area and corresponding logical tables.

■ GCBC_Repository_updated.rpd will be the *current* repository that represents our most up-to-date development repository and has had the additional logical column, amended logical column, and deleted/re-created presentation table as described in the comparing repositories section earlier.

Figure 11-9 shows these repositories as part of the three-way merge process.

You can, if you choose, compare and equalize your repository files before starting the merge process. However, as equalization is offered as an option during the merge, we will perform this task as part of the merge process.

To perform a three-way merge of these repositories, follow these steps:

1. Open the Oracle BI Administration tool from the Windows Start menu.

2. With the Oracle BI Administration tool open, select File | Open | Offline, and select the current, development repository file (in this example, GCBC_Repository_updated.rpd). Enter the repository password when prompted, and the repository contents will be displayed on screen.

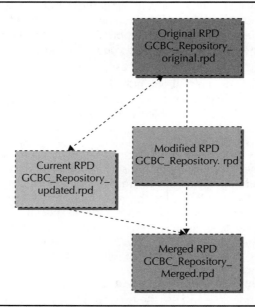

FIGURE 11-9. *The three repositories as part of the three-way merge process*

3. From the menu, select File | Merge to display the Merge Repository Wizard dialog box.

4. In this dialog box, ensure that the Full Merge radio button is selected, and then click the Select button next to the Modified Repository text box to select the modified (development, most recent) repository whose contents you wish to merge into this repository. In this example, the repository file we wish to merge into this one is called GCBC_Repository.rpd. Enter the repository password for the modified repository into the Password text box.

5. Now repeat this step for the original repository, clicking the Select button to select the original repository from which these two repositories were derived; in this case, the GCBC_Repository_original.rpd file. Enter the password for this repository into the corresponding Password text box.

6. To perform automatic equalization of the repositories, as described earlier in this chapter, select the Equalize During Merge check box. Selecting this box is recommended, as it synchronizes upgrade IDs for objects that may have been edited by different developers and been given new upgrade IDs as part of the process but that are logically the same as each other.

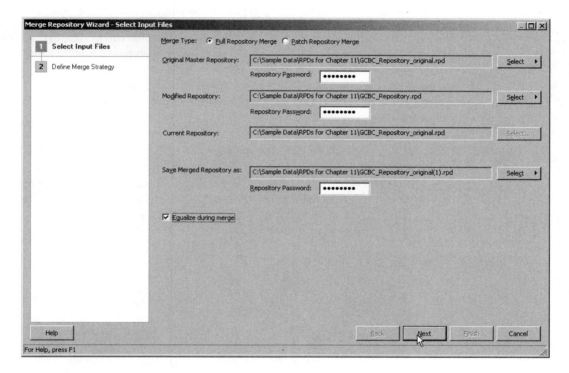

7. If there are no conflicts as part of this merge, the new merged repository file will then be opened for editing in the Administration tool, and you can then save this and upload it to your Oracle BI Domain for use by users.

In the preceding example, there were no merge conflicts between the two files being merged. If, however, we had another repository file, GCBC_Repository_with_hotfix.rpd, that had been modified online by a developer who inadvertently had modified a column that was also modified in the development (modified) repository, you would need to resolve the conflict before completing the merge using these steps:

1. Using the Oracle BI Administration tool, open the GCBC_Repository_updated.rpd repository and then select File | Merge.

2. Using the Merge Repository wizard, select GCBC_Repository_original.rpd as the original repository and GCBC_Repository_with_hotfix.rpd as the modified repository. Ensure that Full Merge is selected using the radio buttons at the top of the dialog box, and select the Equalize During Merge check box if you want to equalize the two repositories' upgrade IDs during the merge.

3. The Merge Repository Wizard – Define Merge Strategy dialog box will then be displayed. In this instance, a conflict has been listed due to two logical columns having been modified in both repositories. Clicking the column in the Conflict list shows what the issue is. In this case, the logical column "Sales"."Dim Times"."Quarter" had its sort order property modified in both repositories.

4. Because it is an individual property of a repository object that has the conflict, you must select By Property as the Choice value by the object in the Conflict list. This displays the list of properties, with the current and modified values listed for you to choose from. In this instance, we select the Modified value as the one we wish to keep in the merged repository, as it is the correct one for this column.

5. Repeat these steps for any other conflicts the merge creates, and click the "Check consistency of the merged RPD" check box to ensure that the merged repository is still logically consistent (that is, valid).

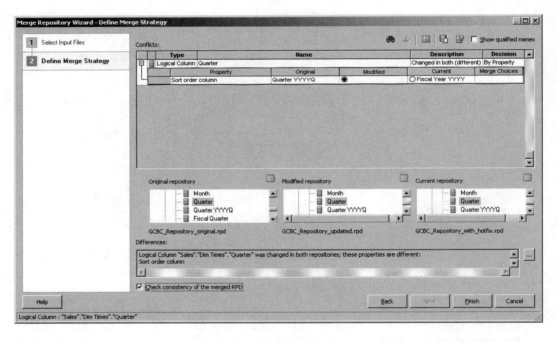

6. Click Finish to close the dialog box, and then save and close the resulting merged repository as before.

Performing a Three-Way Merge Without Parent Repository

Performing a three-way merge without parent repository is similar to a regular three-way merge in that you use the same merge process, except you use a blank, empty repository as the original repository.

Three-way merges without a parent are typically used to bring together repositories that have been developed independently, with no shared common parentage, and therefore you should expect more manual intervention and duplicated objects using this type of merge. In particular, you should try to ensure that both repositories being merged have, as far as possible, common names for business models, logical tables, columns and dimensions, and presentation layer contents so that the merge process can match them and try to avoid creating duplicated entries in the merged repository. Your organization should, therefore, implement naming standards even when creating repositories independently, in case you wish to merge the repositories at a later date.

For example, let's say our organization has two repositories that they wish to merge in this way:

■ GCBC_Repository_Sales_Only.rpd, which contains a single business model (GCBC Model) and fact and dimension tables based around a sales data mart. This will be the *current* repository in the three-way merge process.

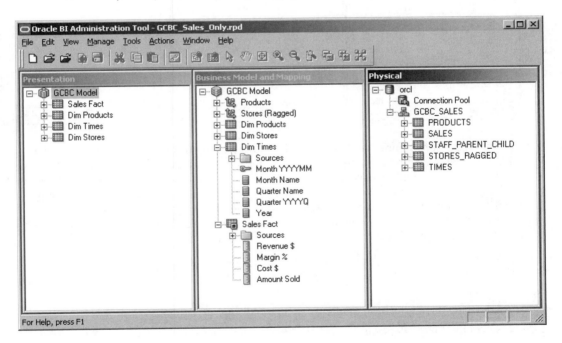

■ GCBC_Repository_Surveys_Only_(Naming_Stds).rpd, which contains a business model of the same name (GCBC Model), but its fact and dimension tables support survey analysis. This will be the *modified* repository in the three-way merge process.

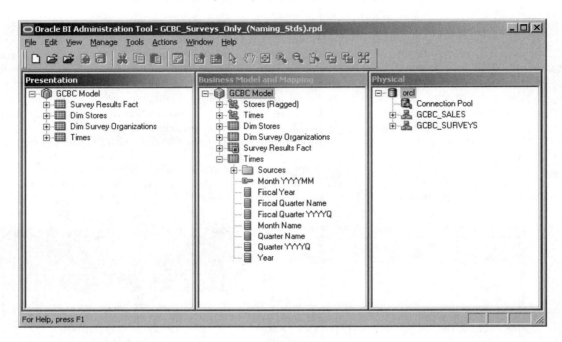

Both repositories implement Store and Time logical dimension tables, but the time logical table is named Dim Times in one model and Times in the other. Our objective in this exercise is to create a single, merged repository that contains a single business model and the combined table set from both repositories. We also have a third repository, GCBC_Blank.rpd, that contains no repository objects and that we will use as the *original* repository in this exercise.

To perform a two-way merge of these repositories using the Oracle BI Administrator merge process, follow these steps:

1. Using the Oracle BI Administrator tool, open the current repository (in this example, GCBC_Sales_Only.rpd) offline, and enter **welcome1** as the repository password when prompted.

2. Using the application menu, select File | Merge.

3. In the Merge Repository Wizard – Select Input Files dialog box, select the second repository (in this case, GCBC_Repository_Surveys_Only_(Naming_Stds).rpd) as the modified repository, and enter **welcome1** as the repository password. For the original repository, select a blank repository (in this case, GCBC_Blank.rpd) and enter its password (for the sample file, **welcome1**). Ensure that the Full Repository Merge radio button is selected as the merge type at the top of the dialog box.

4. Select the Equalize During Merge check box. Selecting this box will ensure that the merge process will attempt to merge objects based on their name, rather than their object IDs, which will benefit us if we have followed consistent naming standards for our repository objects.

5. Assuming that you selected the Equalize During Merge check box and that (as in this case) there is consistency over object naming in the two repositories, you will then be asked to resolve the merge conflicts between your models using the Define Merge Strategy dialog box.

   In this example, the merge process has matched the two business models in the repositories based on their common name and is now asking you to confirm for each of the matching columns which repositories' details to use (in this case, the choice of database account to connect to the source data with, because one repository connection pool connects through the GCBC_SALES database account, while the other connects through SYSTEM).

   You should now go through each of the merge conflicts listed, selecting the most appropriate attribute value from the options presented by the two repositories being merged, and then select the "Check consistency of the merged RPD" check box at the end to ensure that the resulting merged repository is valid.

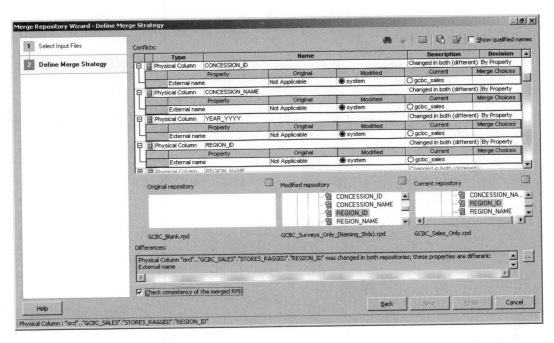

6. As the merging of two repositories with no common parentage can often raise high numbers of individual merge conflicts that have to be manually resolved, you can save a file of the decisions you make, and it can be recalled when performing similar merges in the future. To do this, click the Save Decisions To File (*.cvs) button at the top right-hand

corner of the dialog box and click the Load Decision File (*.cvs) button to load previously saved decision files in the future.

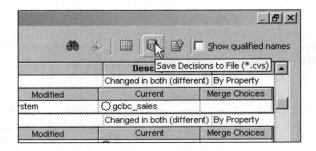

7. Once you have entered all the merge conflict decisions, click the Finish button to complete the merge, and the newly merged repository will then be opened in the Administration tool.

In this example, through use of naming standards, all objects including the business model had names that were common across both repositories, such that when the Equalize During Merge option was chosen, the two repositories' objects were largely matched up; the only object that was effectively duplicated in the new repository was the Dim Times/Times logical tables, which were both created in the new repository because their names could not be matched.

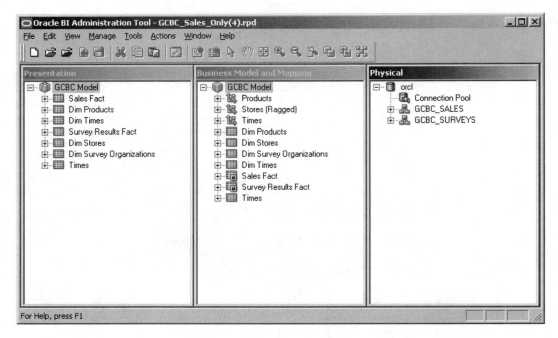

If, instead of naming standards being used, a third repository, GCBC_Survey_Only_(No_Naming_Stds).rpd, was used for the merge and this repository had its business model named GCBC Surveys instead of GCBC Model, the merge process even with equalization would have more problems in merging the two sets of objects.

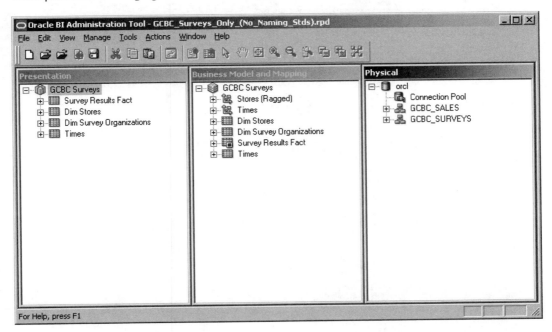

In this instance, regardless of the choices made in the Define Merge Strategy screen, the merge process will end up creating a separate business model, and subsequent subject area, for the objects coming from the second repository, as it would not be able to match up the two business models as their names were different and there was no common, original repository file to link the objects together through a shared, common object ID. This may be what you want (particularly in the case of independent semantic models that just need to share the same repository file), but if you want to combine models, be sure to implement naming standards in your organization.

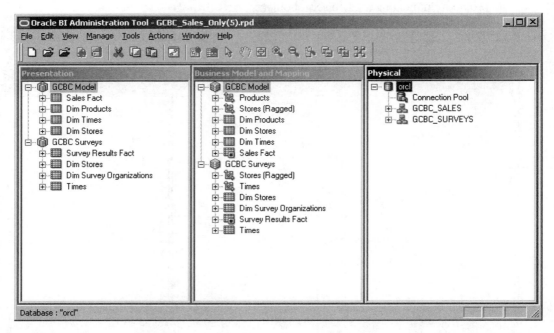

Patching Repositories

In the previous examples involving merging repositories, each of the merge operations involved what are termed *full merges*. A full merge, as you have seen in the previous examples, involves taking a *current* and *modified* repository, together with an *original* repository that was the parent of these two repository branches, and creates a fourth repository that contains their merged contents. This merging usually takes place interactively using the Oracle BI Administration tool and results in a new, merged repository at the end of the process.

Repository *patching* is a similar process, in that it involves current, modified, and original repositories, but instead of creating a new, merged repository straightaway, it instead creates a patch file that can be applied later on to bring, for example, a production repository up-to-date with new changes in development. As such, this approach can often be preferable for organizations that wish to carefully control the introduction of changes into their production environment, because the generating and applying of processes can be scripted, and the XML-based patched files can easily be stored in a release management or source control system.

Overview of Repository Patching

Repository patching is a two-stage process:

1. First, you create the patch file based on comparing the *current* (development) repository file to the *original* (baseline) repository file.

2. Then you apply this patch file to the *modified* (production) repository, bringing it up to date with the changes made in the *current* (development) repository file.

The second stage in this process, like the first, can be performed using the Oracle BI Administration tool; or you can use a command-line utility, as described in the upcoming section "Patching Repositories Using Command-Line Utilities" to perform the patching from a batch file or shell script.

Repository patching, at least in the current (11.1.1.6) version of Oracle Business Intelligence, does have the limitation that the patch contains *all* differences between the two repositories, rather than just a subset that you select for the patch. Because the patch file is, however, stored in XML format, in theory you can edit this file to retain only those object changes that you require; however, you need to be careful that the file is still valid after your editing.

What Is in an XML Repository Patch File? Repository patch files store their details in an XML format called XUDML, an XML markup language used by Oracle Business Intelligence components to exchange repository metadata. When you generate a patch file using the process described in a moment, the patch file contains XML definitions of objects in your repository, which are then used later on by the repository merge process to create them in the target repository.

For example, the XUDML to create a logical table might look like this:

```
<LogicalTable name="Dim Products" parentName="&quot;GCBC
    Model&quot;" parentId="2000:60" parentUid="90"
    id="2035:63" uid="123">
<Description></Description>
<Columns>
    <RefLogicalColumn id="2006:73" uid="137"
    qualifiedName="&quot;GCBC Model&quot;.&quot;Dim
Products&quot;.&quot;PROD_ID&quot;"/>
    <RefLogicalColumn id="2006:79" uid="143"
    qualifiedName="&quot;GCBC Model&quot;.&quot;Dim
Products&quot;.&quot;Product Category&quot;"/>
    <RefLogicalColumn id="2006:83" uid="147"
    qualifiedName="&quot;GCBC Model&quot;.&quot;Dim
Products&quot;.&quot;Product Type&quot;"/>
    <RefLogicalColumn id="2006:87" uid="151"
    qualifiedName="&quot;GCBC Model&quot;.&quot;Dim
Products&quot;.&quot;Product Name&quot;"/>
</Columns>
<TableSources>
    <RefLogicalTableSource id="2037:76" uid="140"
    qualifiedName="&quot;GCBC Model&quot;.&quot;Dim
Products&quot;.&quot;PRODUCTS&quot;"/>
</TableSources>
</LogicalTable>
```

NOTE
The syntax and format for XUDML is not documented in the online documentation for Oracle Business Intelligence, but its use is supported, and if you wish, you can generate your own XUDML documents or edit the ones generated by the Oracle BI Administration tool. Be careful, though, to ensure that any such documents are valid; otherwise, you may get unexpected results when processing them later on.

Patching Repositories Using the Oracle BI Administration Tool

Creating patch files and then applying them is a two-stage process. First you generate the patch file, comparing the current repository to the original repository, and then you apply the patch file to the modified repository using either the Oracle BI Administration tool or a command-line utility, should you instead wish to script the process.

In the following example, based on the repository merge example created earlier, we have three repository files that we wish to include in this process:

- A repository file called GCBC_Repository_updated.rpd that represents the development repository for the organization and that, in terms of the patch/merge process, is the *current* repository.

- Another repository file called GCBC_Repository.rpd that represents the production repository and that is the *modified* repository in this process.

- A third repository called GCBC_Repository_original.rpd that is the original version of the repository on which the production repository is based and is the development branch. This is the *original* repository in the patch/merge process.

In this process, we will first take the *current* repository, compare it to the *original* repository, and create a patch file of the differences. Then we will take this patch file and, along with the modified and original repository, apply the patch file to the *modified* (production) repository, as shown in Figure 11-10.

As such, the patch file plays the same role as the *current* repository when you perform a three-way merge to update the production (*modified*) repository, except that the patch file contains only the changes between the *current* and *original* repository, and it is in a format that you could potentially edit (carefully) and store in a source control system. When you then apply this patch file to the *modified* repository, because it is merged into this repository, normal merge rules apply and typically only new objects from the patch file are added to the *modified* repository.

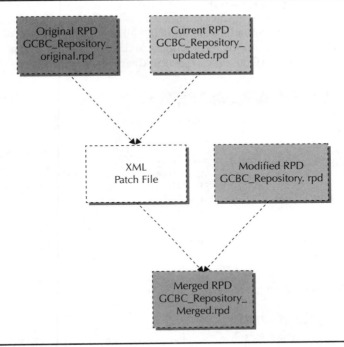

FIGURE 11-10. *The repository patching process*

To create such a patch file using the Oracle BI Administration tool, follow these steps:

1. Using the Oracle BI Administrator tool, open the current repository (in this example, GCBC_Repository_updated.rpd) offline, and enter the repository password welcome1 when prompted.

2. Using the application menu, select File | Compare.

3. When the Select Original Repository dialog box is shown, browse and select the original repository (in this instance, GCBC_Repository_original.rpd), and enter welcome1 as the repository password when prompted.

4. The Compare Repositories dialog box will then be shown. In this example, the current repository has a new business model and subject area within it, compared to the original repository. Be sure to click the Equalize button to remove any differences caused by logically identical objects having upgrade IDs out of sync, typically caused by developers deleting and then re-creating objects in the repository (detailed earlier in this chapter).

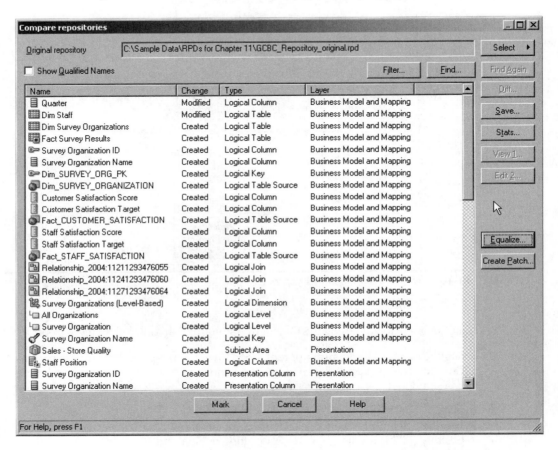

5. To create the patch file, click the Create Patch button. In the Create Patch dialog box, name the patch file (for example, GCBC_Prod_Patch.xml) and save it to the file system.

Now that you have created the patch file, you can apply it to the *modified* (in this case, GCBC_Repository.rpd) production repository, again using the Oracle BI Administration tool, but this time using the merge feature.

To apply a patch file using the Oracle BI Administration tool, follow these steps:

1. Open the Oracle BI Administration tool from the Windows Start menu.

2. With the Oracle BI Administration tool open, select File | Open | Offline, and select the current, production repository file (in this example, GCBC_Repository.rpd). Enter the repository password when prompted, and then the repository contents will be displayed onscreen.

3. From the application menu, select File | Merge.

4. In the Merge Repository Wizard – Select Input Files dialog box, select Patch Repository Merge as the merge type. Then select the original repository (GCBC_Repository_original .rpd) and the patch file that you just created as the patch file. When you are ready to process the patch file, click Next to proceed.

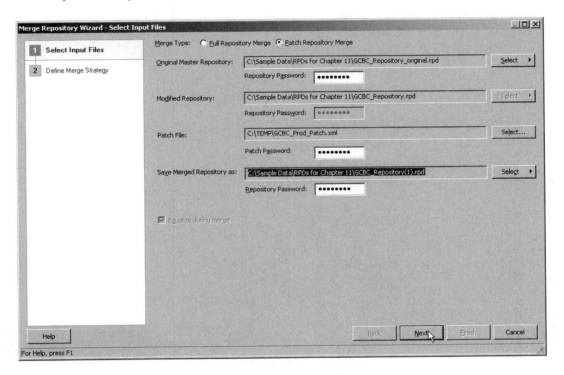

5. If there are no conflicts when the patch is applied (meaning none of the changes introduced with the patch file conflict with changes made to the modified repository) then the patch is applied immediately, and the repository file that is left open in the Oracle BI Administration tool is the modified repository with any new items from the current repository merged into it. See the earlier section "Performing a Three-Way Repository Merge" for more details on how this merge process works.

If, however, there is a merge conflict when the Oracle BI Administrator tries to apply the patch, as with full merges, you will then have to resolve the conflict. For example, as with the three-way merge example earlier in this chapter, the repository file GCBC_Repository_with_hotfix .rpd represents a production (*modified*) repository that has had online hotfixes applied to it, typically to address an issue in production that requires immediate resolution. Unfortunately, a column that was hotfixed in this way was also modified in the *current,* development repository (GCBC_Repository_updated.rpd) that was used to create the patch file.

To resolve such patch merge conflicts, follow these steps:

1. In this example, the hotfixed production repository GCBC_Repository_with_hotfix.rpd was opened offline at the start of this process. Then, as before, File | Merge was selected from the application menu, Patch Merge selected as the merge type, and the original repository and patch file selected as before.

2. This time, the Merge Repository Wizard – Define Merge Strategy dialog box is shown. Use this dialog box to select, at an object or property level, whether the value in the *original* repository, the *modified* repository (the production repository with the hotfix applied), or the *current* repository (the contents of the patch file) is applied. Once you select your choices, click Finish to apply the patch and leave the patched, merged repository open in the Administration tool.

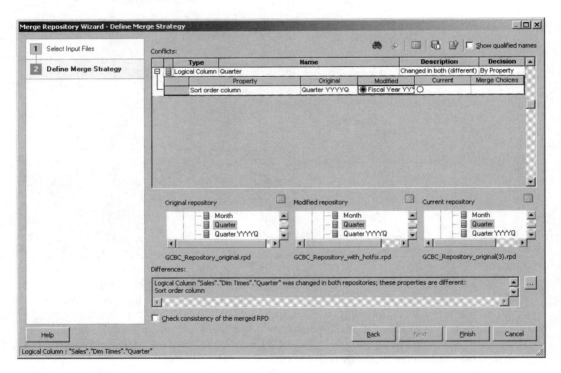

Patching Repositories Using Command-Line Utilities

Sometimes organizations may wish to generate and then apply patch files through an automated, scripted process so that the patching process can be performed "hands off" without the opportunity for operator error. To make this possible, two command-line tools are provided that, on the one hand, create the patch file, and on the other, apply it. Either of these two utilities can be used in conjunction with the interactive environment provided by the Oracle BI Administration tool.

To create repository patch files, you use the comparerpd utility normally found at [*middleware_home*]\Oracle_BI1\bifoundation\server\bin\comparerpd, which uses the following parameters:

comparerpd –P [*current repository password*] –C [*current repository path and name*] – W [*original repository password*] –G [*original repository path and name*] –D [*patch file path and name*]

For example:

```
comparerpd -P welcome1 -C c:\GCBC_Repository_updated.rpd -W welcome1 -G
c:\GCBC_Repository_original.rpd -D c:\patch.xml
```

Similarly, the patchrpd utility normally found at [*middleware_home*]\Oracle_BI1\bifoundation\ server\bin\comparerpd takes a number of parameters including the original repository name, the modified repository name, and the name of the patch file, and then applies a three-way merge between the objects to create a patched, modified repository. The parameters for patchrpd are as follows:

patchrpd -P [*modified repository password*] -C [*modified repository path and name*] -Q [*original repository password*] -G [*original repository path and name*] -I [*patch file path and name*] -O [*new repository path and name*]

For example:

```
patchrpd -P welcome1 -C c:\GCBC_Repository.rpd -Q welcome1 -G
c:\GCBC_Repository_original.rpd -I c:\patch.xml -O c:\GCBC_Repository2.rpd
```

Note that this utility can take several patch files in its list of parameters (in the format –I [*patch file path and name*]) to apply multiple patches in one operation.

Two additional patchrpd options introduced with the 11.1.1.6 release give you the ability to deal with any merge conflicts that might occur during the patching process:

- **-U**   This option automatically deals with any merge conflicts by using the default decisions for conflicts and allows the patching to then complete.

- **-V**   This option writes the default decisions that would have been made by the –U option into a decision file, which can then either be loaded into the Define Merge Strategy screen of the Merge Wizard to view, and potentially alter, these decisions. Alternatively, the decision file can be manually edited, and regardless of which of these two routes are chosen, the decision file can then be passed to the patchrpd utility using the –D option to have these decisions automatically applied next time.

As an example, to create a patch file and then apply it using these command-line tools for the original, current, and modified repositories used in the preceding examples and in the patching example for the Oracle BI Administration tool, follow these steps:

1. Using the Windows Start menu, select Start | Run and type **cmd.exe** at the Run prompt to start the command-line environment. If you are using a Unix or Linux server or workstation, start your command-line tool environment in the normal way.

2. In this example, we will use a Windows environment with all repository files stored in the C:\ folder. To create the patch file, type in the following commands, amending paths as necessary:

```
cd c:\middleware\Oracle_BI1\bifoundation\server\bin

comparerpd -P welcome1 -C c:\GCBC_Repository_updated.rpd -W welcome1 -G
c:\GCBC_Repository_original.rpd -D c:\patch.xml
```

3. If the command executes correctly, you should see the following message at the command-prompt console:

```
The following repository is opened: c:\GCBC_Repository_original.rpd
```

If you receive an error message (because, for example, the utility cannot find or open your repository file), resolve the issue and repeat this last step to create the patch file.

4. To apply the patch file, with the command-line open again, run the following command:

```
patchrpd -P welcome1 -C c:\GCBC_Repository.rpd -Q welcome1 -G
c:\GCBC_Repository_original.rpd -I c:\patch.xml -O c:\GCBC_Repository2.rpd
```

If the patching process completes successfully, you should see the message:

```
--------------Complete Success!!--------------
Complete Success of patch application on original repository!!
The following repository is opened: c:\GCBC_Repository.rpd
Repository equalized successfully.
[94017] Complete success of patch application on customer repository.
```

Again, if you receive an error message (because, for example, the utility cannot find or open your repository file or the patch file), resolve the issue and repeat this last step to apply the patch file.

5. If, however, you did not use the –U, -V, or –D options and the patching process cannot complete because there is a conflict that needs to be resolved (for example, because we are applying the patch to the GCBC_Repository_with_hotfix.rpd repository that features a modification to a column also modified in the patch file), you will receive an error message such as this:

```
--------------Complete Success!!--------------
Complete Success of patch application on original repository!!
The following repository is opened: c:\GCBC_Repository_with_hotfix.rpd
Repository equalized successfully.
[94036] Conflicts are found. Patch cannot be applied onto customer
repository. Admin tool can be used to resolve conflicts. Conflicts list:
Logical Column, "Sales"."Dim Times"."Quarter", Changed in both (different)
```

In this instance, you can either rerun the patchrpd command using the –U or –V options described a moment ago or use the Oracle BI Administration tool to resolve the merge issues manually using the graphical user interface.

Incremental Releases of Catalogs Using Merging and Patching

In a similar way to repositories, catalogs can be incrementally updated with content from other catalogs, such as to update a production catalog with changes from a development environment.
Typically, an organization will develop and roll out catalog content in this way:

1. The first release of the catalog is usually created in the development environment and then promoted, along with the repository, through testing and into production. This initial catalog typically contains standard analyses, dashboards, and other content developed by the IT department, along with content used for testing and auditing purposes, stored one or more sub-folders under the Shared Folders top-level catalog folder.

2. From this point, end users then typically develop their own content in the production catalog, using their own governance guidelines to ensure that content is organized effectively, storing shared BI content in sub-folders under the Shared Folders top-level catalog folder, and content private to them in their respective My Folders area (stored physically in the actual catalog file system structure as folders for each user under the \users top-level folder).

3. At a later date, the IT development team may release an updated repository using the techniques outlined earlier in this chapter. This new repository may then necessitate changes to the standard analyses and other content provided centrally by the IT department, which need to be incrementally moved into the test and then production environments.

4. Developers may also branch the repository, again using techniques outlined in this chapter, and develop catalog content to go with their development branch. When they then come to merge this development repository back into the main branch and promote it into production, they will want to perform a similar task for any catalog content they develop within IT-managed sub-folders under the Shared Folders catalog area.

This need to update production catalogs with new content from development, while preserving any existing user-generated content either in the Shared Folders or My Folders areas, means that we need a process to merge catalog content together from two or more sources and deal with any potential merge conflicts.
To achieve this, there are several techniques that you could use, listed below:

1. You can manually copy and paste catalog content between environments using the Catalog Manager utility.

2. You can use the Catalog page within the Oracle Business Intelligence web site to archive and then un-archive content between environments or perform a similar task using the Catalog Manager.

3. You can use a command-line interface for the Catalog Manager utility to create patch files, similar to the patch files created earlier in this chapter for the Oracle BI Repository, to patch catalogs with incremental content.

In the examples within this section, in a similar way to the repository migration examples, there are three catalogs that we will be using, and you can find them in the Catalogs_for_ Chapter11 folder within the Sample Data provided with this book:

- GCBC_Original, the original catalog as initially developed by the IT team and put into production with the initial repository. This is the *original* catalog.

- GCBC_Production, based on the original catalog but now in production and with some new objects created by end-users in this instance within their My Folders area. This is the *modified* repository.

- GCBC_Development, again based off of the original repository but with additional and modified objects within the shared folder but without the end user–generated objects in the My Folders area. This is the *current* repository.

The objective for the following catalog migration examples is to introduce the changes provided by the GCBC_Development catalog into the GCBC_Production catalog, while preserving the content of the My Folders area added by the end users since the catalog went into production. Let's look now at three techniques you can use to meet this objective.

Manually Migrating Catalog Content Using the Catalog Manager

If you have developed catalog content in one environment and wish to promote it into another, for example, from a development environment to a production environment, one of the simplest ways to do this is via the Catalog Manager utility.

The Catalog Manager utility is a Java-based graphical tool that is installed along with the BI Administration tool with full installations of Oracle Business Intelligence, and can also be installed on workstations using the Client Tools installer. Catalog Manager allows an administrator to connect online or offline to a catalog and then move, inspect, delete, or migrate content either within a single catalog or across separate catalogs. It is typically used in this scenario to copy content between catalogs, either directly by cutting and pasting between two separately opened instances of the utility or through archive files.

In the following example, content from the development catalog (GCBC_Development) will be manually migrated through the Catalog Manager to the production catalog (GCBC_Production). First, the content will be cut and pasted between two open instances of the Catalog Manager, and later on, a single Catalog Manager instance will be used to perform the migration through archive/de-archive steps:

1. Using the Windows Start menu, open the Catalog Manager application by selecting Start | Programs | Oracle Business Intelligence | Catalog Manager.

2. In the Open Catalog dialog box, select the following values, which assume that the catalog is available for access offline:

   Type: Offline
   URL: [*path to development/current catalog; for example,*
        C:\Sample Data\GCBC_Development]

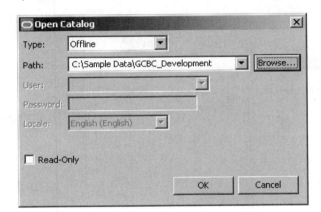

3. When the Catalog Manager workspace opens, use the tree navigation menu on the left-hand side of the screen to expand the catalog folders, and check that the content you expected to see is present. In this example, the /shared/Testing and Audit Reports folder has a new analysis (QA Scores) and a modified dashboard (IT Audit Dashboard) that we wish to move into the production catalog.

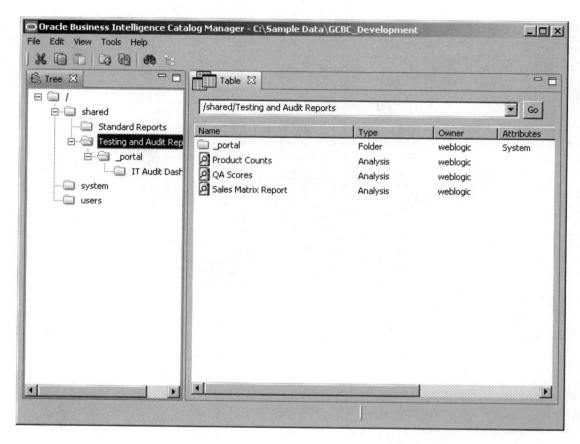

4. Now use the Windows Start menu to open a new, separate instance of the Catalog Manager application, and this time open the production catalog for offline access:

Type: Offline

URL: [*path to production/modified repository; for example:*
          C:\Sample Data\GCBC_Production]

5. You now have two instances of the Catalog Manager open, one displaying the development, current catalog and the other with the production, modified catalog. To copy an analysis (for example, /shared/Testing and Audit Reports/QA Scores) from the development to the production catalog, right-click the analysis in the development repository and select Copy.

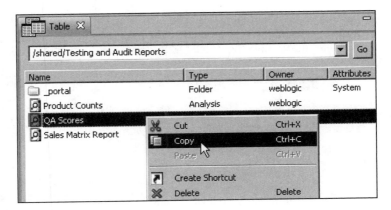

6. Now move over to the Catalog Manager instance that has the production, modified repository open, use the tree menu on the left-hand side to navigate to the correct folder, right-click within it, and click Paste.

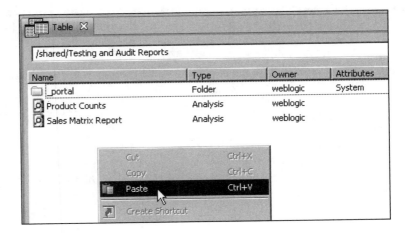

After pasting the new analysis in to the folder, it will then be available for use after the catalog is made available through Fusion Middleware Control, or immediately if the catalog is accessed online.

7. An alternative to having two separate instances of the Catalog Manager open is to use the Archive/Unarchive feature within Catalog Manager. To use this feature to migrate, for example, the updated /shared/Testing and Audit Reports/_portal/IT Audit Dashboard dashboard and all the objects under it, with the development catalog open, click the object or folder you wish to archive, and then select File | Archive from the application menu.

8. In the Archive Catalog dialog box, check that the catalog object is the one that you meant to archive, and then type in an archive file path to represent the file system location and filename for the archive file. Click OK to create the archive file.

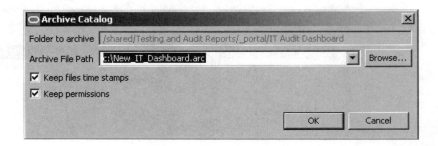

9. Now, with the same instance of Catalog Manager, close the current catalog (File | Close), and then open the catalog that you wish to migrate the object to (in this example, the production repository).

10. With the new catalog open, use the tree menu to navigate to the parent folder of the object that you archived, click it, and then select File | Unarchive. In the Unarchive Catalog dialog box, click the Browse button to locate your archive file, select it, and click OK to unarchive it.

Your content from the other catalog will now be present in this catalog.

TIP
Although you can connect to a catalog either online or offline, you will find that access to catalog objects is faster when connecting offline. Also, connecting offline to a catalog directory avoids permissions on user folders (where each user's My Folders areas are located), which will not usually be inaccessible if you connect online as the WebLogic administration user.

Manually Migrating Catalog Content Using the Catalog Web Page

As an alternative to the Catalog Manager that doesn't require a tool to be installed on a workstation, it is also possible to archive and unarchive BI objects using the Oracle Business Intelligence web site, as well as cut and paste objects between different folders in the same catalog.

The Oracle Business Intelligence web site has a common header area at the top of every page, with a Catalog link in the set of links on the right-hand side of the page.

Clicking this link displays the Catalog page, with a tree menu on the left-hand side displaying the folders within the catalog and a listing of objects within these folders on the right-hand side, as well as an optional Preview pane at the bottom. See Chapter 6 for more details on the Catalog page.

If a user has the Archive Catalog and Unarchive Catalog privileges, menu items appear next to objects in the Catalog view, allowing them to archive content, or unarchive content to the current location. This process works the same as archiving and unarchiving using the Catalog Manager and has the benefit of not requiring a client tool to be installed, but it does require each catalog to be available online at the time the feature is used.

For example, consider a situation where an organization has two instances of Oracle Business Intelligence, one for development purposes and one for production. The Presentation Server URLs for the two installations are as follows:

- Development instance: http://dev-server:9704/analytics
- Production instance: http://prod-server:9704/analytics

The development instance has a catalog currently online containing the objects for our development (current) environment, while the production has the production (modified) catalog also open online. As with the previous example, we have an analysis and a dashboard that we wish to manually migrate from development to production using this feature.

To perform this migration using the Catalog web page, follow these steps:

1. Log into the Oracle Business Intelligence web site for the server that has the catalog objects that you wish to migrate. The catalog should be currently running online, and you should have permissions to access the objects that you wish to migrate.

2. Using the common header area, locate the Catalog link and click it to display the Catalog page. Then, using the Folders view on the left-hand side and the details view on the right-hand side, locate the object or folder that you wish to archive; right-click it, and select Archive.

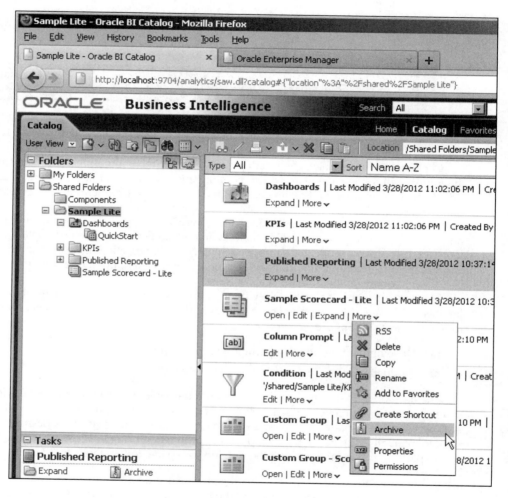

3. In the Archive dialog box, select the Keep Permissions and Keep Timestamps check boxes if required (recommended), and click OK. A dialog box will then be displayed where you can save the resulting archive file to your local file system.

4. To unarchive this file, log on to the other, in this case the production server, and click the Catalog link again. This time, though, using the Folders view and the detail-level view, locate a folder in the catalog to which you wish to unarchive the object or folder, right-click it, and select Unarchive.

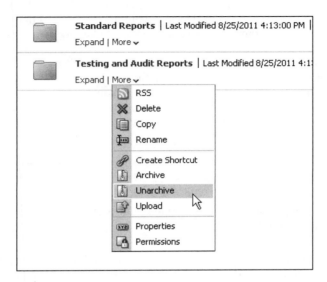

5. In the Unarchive dialog box, click the Browse button to select the archive file, and then select the Replace mode using one of the following options:

- ■ **All**   Replaces objects or folders with the same name as those contained in the archive file
- ■ **Old**   Replaces older objects
- ■ **None**   Adds new content but leaves old content untouched
- ■ **Force**   Adds and replaces all folders or objects, ignoring any "read-only" permissions that the All option would normally honor

Then select the ACL mode, using one of the following options:

- ■ **Inherit**   Inherits the permissions of the parent folder
- ■ **Preserve**   Keeps the permissions of the archived object, mapping accounts as necessary
- ■ **Create**   Keeps permissions but will also create, as well as map, accounts in the catalog

The archive file will then be applied to your catalog, migrating the object or folder from the other catalog.

Patching Catalogs Using the Catalog Manager Command-Line Interface

While both of the previous two approaches to migrating catalog content are workable, they do involve manual steps and would become complicated if migrating or merging large numbers of objects from two catalogs. Also, software development best practices require that promoting objects into production from test, for example, should largely be a hands-off process and, ideally, scripted.

Similar to the way in which repositories can be patched, it is also possible to generate a patch file for catalog objects that you can generate from the command line and include in a script. Using this approach has the benefit of automating the merge process and reduces the opportunity for human error, but it is a more complex procedure because it is only available from the command line.

In the following example, we have three catalogs that we wish to involve in such a patching scenario:

- GCBC_Production, the production catalog that contains items in both the shared and user folders. As far as the patching process is concerned, this is called the *modified* catalog.

- GCBC_Development, the development catalog that contains new and updated objects in the shared folder, but none of the objects in the user folders. This is called the *current* catalog.

- GCBC_Original, the original catalog from which production and development were originally derived. This is the *original* catalog.

As with repositories, patching is a variant of the three-way merge process, which requires access to the original (parent) catalog of the development and production repositories so that the patch and merge process can correctly link objects in both catalogs through their shared parentage.

If you do not have access to the original catalog, as with repository merges it is possible to substitute a blank catalog and perform a two-way merge, but this approach is more prone to error and may require additional manual intervention or may create additional duplicate items in the merged results where common parentage cannot be established.

When you use the catalog patching feature in Oracle Business Intelligence, creating and applying the patch is a three-step process:

1. First you create a diff (difference) file between the current (development) and the original catalog.

2. Then this diff file is combined with the modified (production) catalog to create the patch file.

3. Finally, this patch file is then applied to the modified (production) catalog.

To perform these tasks, the Catalog Manager application has a command-line interface that can accept diff, createPatch, and applyPatch commands, along with associated parameters.

The runcat executable can usually be found at [*middleware_home*]\instances\instance1\ bifoundation\OracleBIPresentationServicesComponent\coreapplication_obips1\catalogmanager\ runcat.cmd|.sh.

To create a difference (diff) file, in this instance using the Microsoft Windows version of the Catalog Manager, run the following command:

```
runcat.cmd -cmd diff -baseline [path to original catalog] -latest [path to
current catalog] -outputFile [path and filename for diff file] -folder
[subfolder to diff] -verbosity [all|conflict|change|details|same]
-winsConflict [latest|production|blendThenLatest|blendThenProduction]
```

To create the patch file from the diff file, run this command:

```
runcat.cmd -cmd createPatch -inputFile [path and filename for diff file]
-outputfile [path and filename for patch file] -production [path to modified
catalog] -winsConflict [latest|production|blendThenLatest|blendThenProduction]
```

Finally, to apply the patch file and update the production (modified) catalog, run this command:

```
runcat.cmd -cmd applyPatch -inputFile [path and filename for patch file]
-outputFiile [path and filename for patch results file]
```

NOTE
*For the apply patch step, you do not specify the path of the modified
(production) catalog, as its details are actually included in the patch file.*

Using the three catalogs detailed above, the steps to create and then patch the production catalog based on new and changed objects in the development catalog would go like this:

1. Copy the development (current), production (modified), and original (original) catalogs to an accessible location (for example, c:\catalogs).

2. Using the command prompt, change the directory to the location of the runcat.cmd or runcat.sh directory; for example:

   ```
   cd c:\middleware\instances\instance1\bifoundation\
   OracleBIPresentationServicesComponent\coreapplication_obips1\catalogmanager
   ```

3. Now run the command to create the diff file:

   ```
   runcat.cmd -cmd diff -baseline c:\catalogs\GCBC_Original -latest
   c:\catalogs\GCBC_Development -outputFile c:\catalogs\gcbc_diff.txt -folder
   /shared -verbosity detail -winsConflict latest
   ```

   You should then receive a message back indicating that the diff was performed successfully:

   ```
   Diffing c:\catalogs\GCBC_Original..2..1..Done!
   Diffing c:\catalogs\GCBC_Development..2..1..Done!
   ```

4. Next, you create the patch file using this diff file and a reference to the catalog you wish to patch (in this case, the production, modified catalog):

   ```
   runcat.cmd -cmd createPatch -inputFile c:\catalogs\gcbc_diff.txt -outputFile
   c:\catalogs\gcbc_patch.txt -production  c:\catalogs\GCBC_Production
   -winsConflict latest -folder /shared
   ```

The console will then show the output, which in this case notes the items that are in the diff file but not in the production (modified) repository:

```
Path not found (/shared/Testing and Audit Reports/_portal/IT Audit
Dashboard/QAAudit)
Path not found (/shared/Testing and Audit Reports/_portal/IT Audit
Dashboard/QAAudit)
Path not found (/shared/Testing and Audit Reports/_portal/IT Audit
Dashboard/Sales Audit)
Path not found (/shared/Testing and Audit Reports/_portal/IT Audit
Dashboard/Sales Audit)
Path not found (/shared/Testing and Audit Reports/QA Scores)
Path not found (/shared/Testing and Audit Reports/QA Scores)
```

5. Finally, the patch file is then applied to the production catalog:

```
C:\Middleware\instances\instance1\bifoundation\
OracleBIPresentationServicesComponent\coreapplication_obips1\
catalogmanager>runcat.cmd -cmd applyPatch -inputFile
c:\catalogs\gcbc_patch.txt -outputFile c:\catalogs\patch_results.txt
-folder /shared
```

The console then shows the (verbose) output:

```
Could not load catalog .  Either it does not exist or insufficient
permissions.
Could not load catalog .  Either it does not exist or insufficient
permissions.
Could not load catalog .  Either it does not exist or insufficient
permissions.
Could not load catalog .  Either it does not exist or insufficient
permissions.
Could not load catalog .  Either it does not exist or insufficient
permissions.
Could not load catalog .  Either it does not exist or insufficient
permissions.
Merging..5
..4
..3
..2
..1..Done!
```

If you check the contents of the output file, you will see what has been changed in the production repository:

```
Modified /shared/Testing and Audit Reports/_portal/IT Audit Dashboard/
dashboard layout
Added /shared/Testing and Audit Reports/_portal/IT Audit Dashboard/QA Audit
Added /shared/Testing and Audit Reports/_portal/IT Audit Dashboard/
Sales Audit
Added /shared/Testing and Audit Reports/QA Scores
Deleted /shared/Testing and Audit Reports/_portal/IT Audit Dashboard/page 1
```

If you then either open the patched catalog using Catalog Manager or use Fusion Middleware Control to view the catalog online, you will see the new items that have been added by the patching process.

Source-Controlling Business Intelligence Metadata

For projects that are anything other than prototypes or learning examples, most developers will want to store versions of their key project metadata objects in a version or source control system. By doing this, it is possible to retrieve previous versions of repositories, catalogs, and other metadata items and either retrieve objects from them or use them to restore a previous version of the system.

When considering source control for an Oracle Business Intelligence project, there are a number of project artifacts that you would want to include in such an initiative, such as:

- The Oracle BI Repository
- The Oracle BI Presentation Catalog
- Various configuration files
- UI customization elements

Storing project artifacts in a source control system also gives you a way to link together the parts of a project that relate to a particular release or deployment environment, ensuring that versions of the repository are matched with database table structures, ETL routines, and associated catalog objects.

Oracle Business Intelligence, and Oracle Fusion Middleware on which it is built, does not come with a built-in source control system, but instead relies on customers to use one of the many available third-party source control systems such as Apache Subversion, IBM Rational ClearCase, or Concurrent Versions System (CVS). Using these servers and their corresponding client tools, it is possible to take the various project artifacts, manually assemble them into a "working copy" of the project, and then check in and check out these files from the source control server as required.

In addition, the 11.1.1.6 release of Oracle Business Intelligence introduced two new features designed to aid integration with source control systems:

- A new offline repository storage format called MDS XML that stores first-class repository objects such as logical tables, logical dimensions, and physical databases as individual XML files, a more suitable format for loading into source control systems than the binary RPD format traditionally used for storing repositories
- Integration of new functions into the Oracle BI Administration tool that work in conjunction with third-party source control servers and client tools to maintain a repository under source control

Let's take a look now at how source control works with Oracle Business Intelligence by first looking at what project artifacts you would typically want to place under source control.

What Metadata Objects Should You Source-Control?

For source-controlling an Oracle Business Intelligence project (as opposed to performing backup and recovery, which is more concerned with taking snapshots of whole systems including binaries and configuration files), you would typically want to keep a source history of the following objects:

- The repository, either as a binary RPD file or in the new MDS XML format
- Repository subsets (projects) as created through the Multiuser Development Environment, again in either RPD or MDS XML format
- The catalog

You may also wish to version control other files, such as

■ Configuration files

■ Files used to create database schemas

■ JavaScript files, CSS files, or other user interface or actions elements

The purpose of version control is not to back up your entire system into the version control system, but instead to store together all elements that make up a project so that you can access the project as it was at a certain time or create defined snapshots, or "releases," that you can pass to a testing or production support team to make available to end users.

A key point to bear in mind with Oracle Business Intelligence projects is that any merging, splitting, branching, or manipulation of subsets of a metadata type (for example, the repository) should be performed using only the relevant Oracle tool. If, therefore, you wish to combine two projects together that have their own repository files and catalogs, you should check out the relevant metadata items from the version control system, perform the merge, split, or branch using the Oracle BI Administrator tool or Catalog Manager, and then check the results back into the version control system.

This makes working with version control systems somewhat easier (as you upload and download only whole metadata objects or folder archives), but it does limit you in what you can do with the version control system, compared to a software project that stores all its metadata in text files, for example.

Selecting a Third-Party Source Control System

Most developers have to adopt whatever version control system their organization mandates and then upload and download business intelligence metadata into that system. Within organizations, typical third-party version control tools that you might encounter include

Apache Subversion
CVS
PVCS
IBM Rational ClearCase
Mercurial
Microsoft Visual SourceSafe
Microsoft Team Foundation Server (TFS)
Perforce

Oracle Business Intelligence does not mandate the use of any particular source control system, and the new source control integration features in the 11.1.1.6 release of Oracle Business Intelligence are designed to integrate with any source control system with a command-line client interface. However, this version of the Administration tool comes with precreated configuration files for the Apache Subversion source control system, and because this is free software we will use it for the examples in this book.

For the Microsoft Windows platform, there are also two free tools that you might want to consider when setting up source control using Subversion (similar tools exist for Unix and Linux platforms):

- VisualSVN Server, which packages up the Apache web server, Apache Subversion, and a management interface, and has a "Standard Edition" that is free to use (http://www .visualsvn.com/server/)

- TortoiseSVN, a Subversion client that integrates with the Windows shell and is free-to-use open-source software (http://tortoisesvn.net/)

Of course, other source control servers and clients are available for you to use, should you wish.

Before we go through an example of setting up source control for your Oracle Business Intelligence project, let's take a look at how the Oracle BI Repository, in particular, is source-controlled, and how the new MDS XML repository storage format introduced with the 11.1.1.6 release makes this more practical.

Source Control of Oracle BI Repositories

Probably the most important project artifact that you will need to place under source control is the Oracle BI Repository, which contains the semantic model that describes your business. Until the 11.1.1.6 release of Oracle Business Intelligence, the only way that you could source-control the repository was to take the entire repository, in the binary RPD format, and upload it to the source control server as a binary file.

Taking this approach had the benefit of you being able to store versions of the repository file in your source control system, but it had a number of limitations, the most important of which was that it was impossible to track changes to individual repository objects such as logical tables, connection pools, and measure definitions. To address this limitation, the 11.1.1.6 release of Oracle Business Intelligence introduced a new, offline repository storage format called MDS XML. This new type of repository storage represents each high-level repository object as an individual XML document and also adds functionality to the Oracle BI Administration tool to provide integration with source control clients.

MDS XML Repository Storage Format

The traditional RPD file format for the Oracle BI Repository stores all of your repository objects in a single, monolithic binary file. In contrast, the new MDS XML format stores the repository as a set of XML documents in a hierarchical folder structure.

Let's take a look at this new format by taking an existing repository, GCBC_Repository – Final .rpd, which comes with your sample data, and convert it to the new MDS XML format. To do so, follow these steps:

1. Using the Oracle BI Administration tool, select File | Open | Offline, and then use the Open dialog box to navigate to, and then select, the GCBC Repository – Final.rpd repository file. When prompted, enter the repository password (in this case **welcome1**).

2. To now save it in the new MDS XML format, select File | Save As | MDS XML Documents from the application menu. When prompted by the Browse For Folder dialog box, select or create a new file system folder (for example, C:\GCBC_XML_MDS), and click OK to close the dialog box.

From this point on, the repository you are working with will be stored in this new MDS XML format. (You could have selected File | Copy As instead, and created a copy if you wished.) To view the structure and format of this new storage type, use Windows Explorer to navigate to the folder where the repository is stored and view the contents, which should look similar to the following illustration.

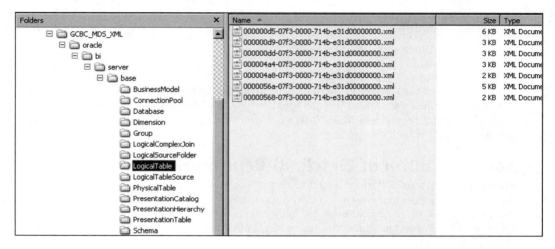

When your repository is stored in this format, you can perform all of your normal editing tasks and also perform operations such as three-way merges, comparing repositories, and altering the repository password. If you wish to place this repository online using Fusion Middleware Control to upload the repository to the Oracle BI instance, though, you will need to resave it in the binary RPD format before doing this.

Within this folder structure will be individual folders for object types, the set of which in your folder structure will change as you add and remove object types from your repository. Each high-level object such as a logical table is stored in its own XML file, which can be separately versioned to allow fine-grain tracking of changes to these objects.

Source Control Features in the Oracle BI Administration Tool

The reason the new MDS XML format for repository storage was introduced with the 11.1.1.6 release was to better support storage and retrieval of repository objects in a source control system. Now that each object is stored in its own XML file, source control systems can track and archive different versions of these files, giving you the ability to track metadata changes at a more fine-grained level.

When you store project artifacts in a source control system, the typical workflow for editing a part of the project, in this case the repository, is as follows:

1. The developer connects to the source control server and checks out a "working copy" of the project or project artifact to their local workstation.

2. That developer then uses a developer tool to edit the object, which may add, delete, or amend certain files in the working copy. Ideally, the developer tool will work closely with the client software for the source control server to update that system's record of what files have been added, removed, or amended in the working set.

3. Once the developer has finished making changes, he or she will then use the source control client software to commit the changes back to the source control server, creating new copies of those files that are new or changed, and recording who made the changes, why, and when.

The 11.1.1.6 release of the Oracle BI Administration tool supports this process by allowing you to designate a particular MDS XML format repository as being under source control. When you then come to save changes to that repository back to the set of XML documents that hold the repository definition, the Oracle BI Administration tool will issue commands to the source control client software to update its record of the working set so that when you come to commit your updated repository back to the source control server, the client software already knows what files have been added, deleted, or amended.

NOTE
The primary purpose of this new storage format and the source control extensions in the Oracle BI Administration tool is to permit fine-grained tracking and recording of changes to objects in a single repository. It is not a replacement for the Multiuser Development Environment, as it does not have any features for merge conflict resolution, which instead would need to be performed using the source control client tools. Also, it should not be used to combine or merge repositories held in separate source control systems, as only the Oracle BI Administration tool should be used for this task to avoid getting consistency check errors.

Source Control for Prior Releases of Oracle Business Intelligence   If you are using a release of Oracle Business Intelligence prior to the 11.1.1.6 release, you will not have access to this new repository storage format, nor will your version of the Oracle BI Administration tool come with source control integration features.

In this case, you will need to upload the whole binary RPD file into your source control server, and in general you will not have the ability to track, at an object level, changes to individual objects in the repository. Therefore, if you plan to use source control with your Oracle Business Intelligence project, it would make sense to upgrade to the 11.1.1.6 release before putting this in place.

Source Control for Other Project Artifacts   Other project artifacts, such as archived copies of the catalog and the various configuration files, will need to be manually managed by you within the checked-out set of working files by adding them to the working set directory structure and then including them in the working set as required. We will look at this manual process when we work through the source control example in a moment.

Example: Using Apache Subversion to Provide Basic Source Control for a Project

In this example, we will set up a source control system for your project artifacts using Oracle Business Intelligence 11.1.1.6, the third-party VisualSVN Server Standard Edition, and the TortoiseSVN Subversion client. The purpose of this source control system is detailed here:

- Store historical versions of your project artifacts and metadata
- Track changes to these objects over time
- Give you the ability to refer back to previous versions of repositories and catalogs
- Give you the ability to create "releases" that you can make available to your testing and production support team

We will be using the following products to create our source control system:

- **Apache Subversion**   A free and open-source version control system that can be downloaded, for most platforms, from http:// http://subversion.apache.org/
- **TortoiseSVN**   A free and open-source Subversion client for Microsoft Windows implemented as a Windows shell extension, downloadable from http://tortoisesvn.tigris.org/
- **VisualSVN Server Standard Edition**   A commercial tool available for free download that makes administering a Windows installation of Subversion more user-friendly, includes Subversion as part of the download, and is available from http://www.visualsvn.com/server/download/

VisualSVN Server Standard Edition, which includes Apache Subversion, will be installed on a workstation or server that all developers can connect to. TortoiseSVN, the client for Subversion, will be installed on each developer workstation and also on workstations used by the testing and production support teams. Figure 11-11 shows the topology of the version control system.

Installing Software for the Version Control System

The software required for this environment will be installed as follows:

1. VisualSVN Server will be installed (along with Subversion and the Apache web server, with which it is bundled) on a workstation or server running Microsoft Windows and accessible to all users.

2. TortoiseSVN and the Oracle Business Intelligence 11.1.1.6 (or higher) client tools will be installed on developer workstations.

3. TortoiseSVN and the Oracle Business Intelligence 11.1.1.6 (or higher) client tools, along with the testing tools used by the testing team, will be installed on the test workstation

4. TortoiseSVN and the Oracle Business Intelligence 11.1.1.6 (or higher) client tools, along with the release management tools used by the production support team, will be installed on the production support workstation.

With this client tools setup, there will also be a development server instance of Oracle Business Intelligence available for developers to use should they wish to place their repositories

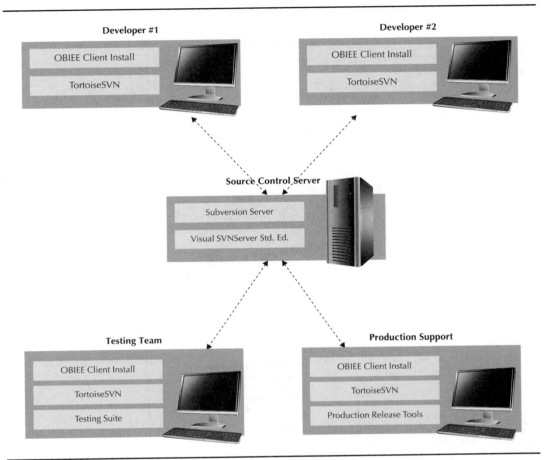

FIGURE 11-11. *Version control topology*

online for testing, along with test and production servers for use by the testing and production support teams.

To install VisualSVN Server, follow these steps:

1. Download VisualSVN Server from the web site download page at http://www.visualsvn. com/server/download/.

2. When the installer has successfully downloaded, double-click it to start.

3. Click Next to start the wizard, select the box to accept the product terms and conditions, and click Next again.

4. In the Select Components dialog box, select the VisualSVN Server And Management Console radio button, and then click Next.

5. In the Custom Setup dialog box, either leave the options at the default or use the options to customize the Subversion port number, file locations, or security mode.

6. Click Next, and then click Install to start the installation. Click Finish to close the installer once the installation completes successfully.

Once the installer completes, the VisualSVN Server management console will open, showing you your initial, unconfigured system.

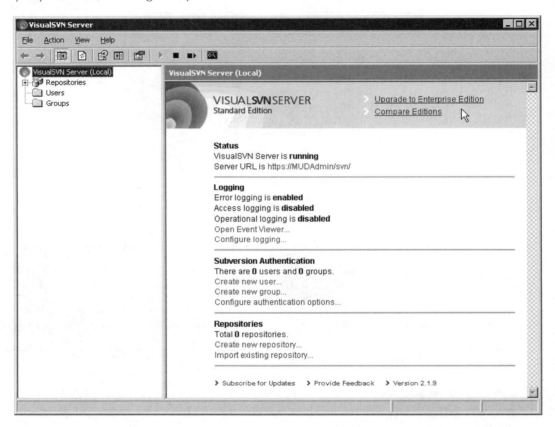

To install TortoiseSVN on each workstation, follow these steps (ensuring that you have administrator rights on the workstation):

1. Download TortoiseSVN from the web site download page at http://tortoisesvn.net/downloads.html.

2. When the installer has successfully downloaded, double-click it to start.

3. Click Next to start the wizard, select the radio button to accept the product terms and conditions, and click Next again.

4.   When the list of product options are displayed, ensure that you select the "command line client tools" option that is deselected by default, click Next, and then click Next again to start the installation. Click Finish to close the installer once the installation completes successfully.

5.   Because TortoiseSVN is a shell extension for Windows Explorer, you will have to restart the workstation for the new installation to become active. Do this, and then repeat it for any other workstations that will need to access the source control system.

Once you have restarted each workstation, right-click the desktop to check that the shell extension has installed correctly. If everything is in order, you should see SVN Checkout and TortoiseSVN menus in the right-click contextual menu.

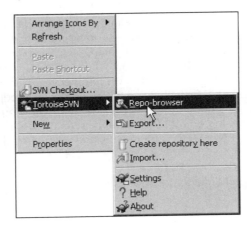

Now that you have set up the software on the various workstations and servers, you can create the Subversion repository using VisualSVN Server.

Creating and Configuring the Subversion Repository

When you work with a version control system such as Subversion, objects that you wish to version are typically stored in a database or repository. The Subversion repository is held in a file system and accessed, via HTTP/HTTPS, through the WebDAV file access protocol.

Typically, Subversion repositories have the following folder structure:

```
Repository Name
+--- Project Name
+------ Trunk
+------ Branches
+------ Tags
```

- The *Project Name* folder allows you to group the other folders by project and then branch and tag whole projects based on this project name.

- The *Trunk* folder is the mainline, standard version of your system, from which all branches are derived and, in time, merged back into.

- The *Branches* folder is for when you take a complete system and then customize it for a particular use. For example, you might develop a baseline Oracle Business Intelligence system and then create branches for particular countries, or you might have a main development branch and other branches for a rewrite of the repository, and another for an upgrade from version 11.1.1.5 of Oracle Business Intelligence to 11.1.1.6. In time, you might merge these branches back into the mainline version of your system stored in the Trunk folder.

- The *Tags* folder is used for marking particular versions as a specific release, and it can create a static "snapshot" of your project that you can make available for testing or production support teams.

Note that different organizations and developers can interpret these folders differently and might, for example, use the Trunk folder for your production release code, while using the Branches folder for development versions. For the Apache Subversion examples that we will use in this section of the chapter though, we will use the preceding definitions for these folders.

An important concept to understand is that when you store objects in the Branches folder or create tags, Subversion merely creates pointers to objects already stored in the repository; no additional objects are created. Each object in the repository is stored logically once, with different versions of it being maintained in the system. Note that you should not use the features of Subversion or other version control tools to merge separate branches together; you should do this with the merge tools provided with the Oracle BI Administration tool and with the Catalog Manager.

Within the Trunk folder for your project, you should create subfolders for the various types of metadata that you would like to store; for example, your folder structure for a project called GCBC could look like this:

```
GCBC
+--- GCBC_OBIEE
+------- Trunk
+----------- Repository
+----------- Catalog
+----------- Config
+------- Branches
+------- Tags
```

To create a repository folder structure to this format, you would use VisualSVN Server in the following way (or manually create the folders yourself, if using Subversion directly):

1. Start the VisualSVN Server management console using the Windows Start menu (Start | Programs | VisualSVN | VisualSVN Server Manager).

2. Before you can create the project and its folders, you first have to create the repository. Each organization generally would have its own repository, with folders for each project, which would then contain the folder structure just outlined.

To create the repository, locate the Repositories entry within the tree menu on the left-hand side of the VisualSVN Server management console, right-click it, and select Create New Repository.

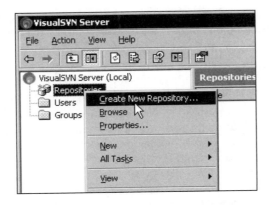

3. In the Create New Repository dialog box, give the repository a name (for example, GCBC), but do not select the check box to create the default Subversion folders, as you will create these yourself under the project you create in a moment. Click OK to create the repository.

4. To create your project, right-click the new repository and select New | Folder. Enter the project name (for example, GCBC_OBIEE), and then repeat this to create the Trunk, Branches, and Tags folders within it.

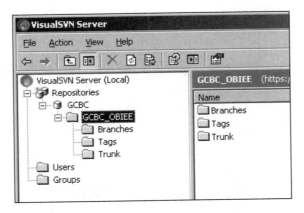

5. Now, if you expand the tree menu under the repository you have just created, you will see the folders that you created along with the repository. Next, you should create the subfolders for the Oracle BI Repository file, the catalog archive, and so on.

   To do this, right-click the Trunk folder within the repository tree structure and select New | Folder. Name the folder, and repeat this for the other subfolders until you have all of the folders that you need.

6. Now, you can create some user accounts so that your developers and other team members can access the source control repository. When you installed VisualSVN Server, there was an option to integrate with Windows logins, but if you did not do this, you can create user accounts within the product itself.

   To create users (for example, asmith and bjones), who we will use later on when looking at multiuser development, right-click the Users entry in the tree menu and select Create User.

7. In the Create New User dialog box, enter the details for the new user and click OK to create it. Repeat this step for any other users you wish to create, and then create groups for your users (for example, a group called "developers" for your BI development users) so that you can assign permissions to the groups, rather than to individual users.

8. Finally, you can grant access to your users, or preferably groups, to the repository that you just created. To do this, right-click the repository that you selected earlier and select Properties. In the Properties dialog box, click the Add button to add your group to the list, and then click the Remove button to remove the default read/write privilege from the Everyone group.

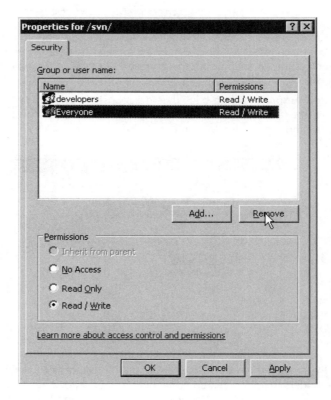

Your repository is now ready for use.

Configuring Developer and Other Workstations for Subversion Client Access

Now that you have configured your Subversion repository, you can check that your workstations can access it. To do this, go to one of the workstations that has had TortoiseSVN installed on it, and follow these steps:

1. With the Windows desktop visible, right-click it and select TortoiseSVN | Repo-browser.

2. In the URL dialog box, enter the URL for your Subversion repository, making sure to use a secure HTTP connection, in the following format:

   http://[*server_name*]/svn/[*repository_name*] (for example, https://obisrv1c/svn/GCBC)

3. The Authentication dialog box will then show, if you have enabled users and groups for your Subversion repository. Enter the username and password for a user that can access the repository, and then click OK to log in.

4. Once you have connected successfully the Repository Browser window will open, and you will see the repository that users will have access to. Pass the URL and login details to your developers, and have them follow the same process to check connectivity to the Subversion repository.

Configuring the Oracle BI Administration Tool for Source Control Integration

The final part of the configuration process is to install the Oracle BI client tools if you have not done so before and configure them to work with your source control client software.

When you place an MDS XML format repository under source control, the Administration tool sends commands to your source control system via the source control client software installed on your workstation to add, remove, or mark as amended the XML documents that make up your repository. To do this, it uses configuration files that provide the appropriate source control client command-line entries for each of these actions.

To access these configuration files, with the Oracle BI Administration tool open, select Tools | Options | Source Control. Select Use Source Control from the MDS XML Repository section, and then click either the Browse button to select an existing configuration file or click New to create a new one from scratch. For now, click New and, when prompted, name the file subversion.xml so you can see what's involved in creating one.

The SCM Configuration Editor Dialog Box   When you select the option to create a new
SCM (Software Configuration Management) configuration file, you are presented with the SCM
Configuration Editor dialog box, as shown in the following illustration.

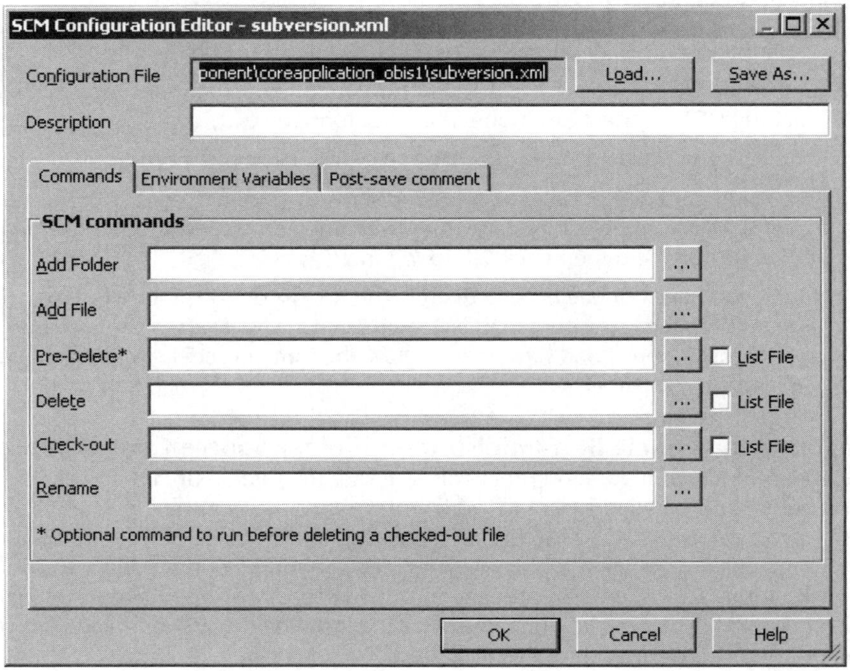

   Using this dialog box, you can enter the source control client's command-line instructions to
perform the following SCM client tasks:

- Add a new folder to the working set
- Add a file to the working set
- Delete a file from the working set
- Check out a file from the working set
- Rename a file in the working set
- Optionally issue a pre-delete command

When entering these commands, you can use the following substitution variables to include XML document filenames, or lists of filenames, in the command:

- **${file}**   Required for the Add Folder and Add File commands, passes across a single XML document filename and runs each command sequentially.

- **${filelist}**   With the List File check box selected (and only supported on certain source control systems), creates a temporary list of filenames which is then passed to the source control client for faster loading of large numbers of individual files. (If the source control system does not support this feature, the Administration tool will try to batch up as many filenames as possible on the command line and use that approach instead.)

- **${from} and ${to}**   Used to specify original and new filenames when a file rename happens

Not all source control servers support all commands, and you may therefore find that only a subset of these commands is applicable to your system. For example, the commands that would be configured for Subversion on a Microsoft Windows–based workstation would be as follows:

- Add Folder:

```
svn.exe add ${file}
```

- Add File:

```
svn.exe add ${file}
```

- Delete:

```
svn.exe delete --force ${file}
```

- Rename:

```
svn.exe move ${from} ${to}
```

You can also use the other tabs in this dialog box to set any required environment variables and type in any comments (for example, your name as a developer) that will be added as post-save comments to your source control system. These features, along with the checkout and commit functions in TortoiseSVN (the source control client), will be used to manage your source-controlled MDS XML Documents repository. Once you have finished configuring the file, click OK to close the dialog box.

Preconfigured SCM Configuration Templates   To save you from having to create configuration files for some source control systems, Oracle (as of the 11.1.1.6 release) has shipped two precreated SCM configuration files that you can use rather than creating your own one from scratch. These configuration files can be found in the [*middleware_home*]\instances\instance1\ config\OracleBIServerComponent\coreapplication_obis1\ directory on the server installation, and they provide the required details for Apache Subversion and also ADE, a source control client interface to a number of source control systems, including Oracle's (legacy) Software Configuration Manager server.

If you are working with just a client tools installation of Oracle Business Intelligence, you will need to copy these files to your workstation installation and place them in the following location:

[*client_install_home*]\oraclebi\orainst\config\OracleBIServerComponent\coreapplication\

To view the contents of one of these files, select Tools | Options | Source Control and click the Browse button to select either the scm-conf-svn.template.xml file for Subversion or the scm-conf-ade.template.xml file for ADE. Then click the Edit button to see the commands that it contains.

Development Life Cycle Using Version Control

Now that we have all of the components configured to support source control of your project, let's work through the typical development life cycle to see how the various tools are used.

First you will need to create an initial version of the project, including the repository in MDS XML format, and upload it to the source control server.

Creating the Initial Project and Repository in the Source Control Repository   The initial project that you'll store in your source control server's repository will typically consist of just the current version of the repository (or perhaps a blank, empty repository), with other directories such as Config or Catalog to be filled later. To create this initial repository using TortoiseSVN and the Subversion repository created previously so that it can be checked out and worked on by your developers, follow these steps:

1. On the developer workstation, right-click on your Windows desktop and select SVN Checkout (or right-click within any file system folder if you wish to store your project files somewhere other than on your Windows desktop).

2. If you have previously used the TortoiseSVN Repository Browser, the URL for the Subversion repository will already be populated, and all you have to do as append the [*project_name*]/trunk to the URL. If not, enter the details, click the ellipsis (...) button to choose the directory to check the repository contents out to, and leave the Revision selection as HEAD, in order to select the most recent version of these objects.

3. Once you perform the checkout, folders will appear on your workstation with a green check mark on them to denote that they are folders managed by TortoiseSVN. At the moment, all of these folders are empty, but now you will take your repository, convert it into the MDS XML format, and put those XML files in the Repository directory within your checked-out working set.

4. To do this, open the Oracle BI Administration tool and select either File | Open | Online or File | Select | Offline to open your repository in the binary RPD format. For example, you could open the GCBC Repository – Final.rpd file that comes with the sample data for this book.

5. Convert this repository to the MDS XML format. If your repository is small, you should select File | Source Control | Link To Source Control Files, which will first prompt you to select the directory to store the XML documents in. Select the Repository directory within the checked-out source control folders and click OK to select it. Next, you will be prompted to select an SCM configuration file to use with the process. Since you are using Subversion, you can select the predefined scm-conf-svn.template.xml file, which contains the required settings.

6.   To complete the process using this method, select File | Save and select the option to
check the repository for consistency errors. Then, after your repository has saved to the
file system, an additional dialog box will be displayed showing the individual XML files
that are about to be added to the source control working set.

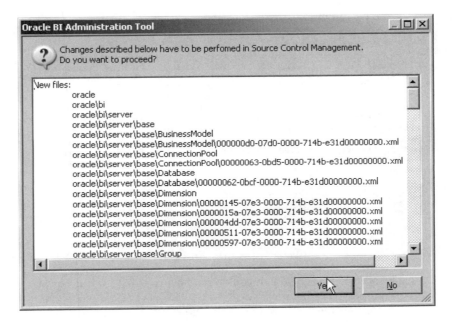

7.   Click Yes to confirm the operation, and the Source Control Log dialog box will be shown,
displaying the individual source control operations performed through the Administration
tool. Scroll through the log in the display window to check that all of the operations
completed successfully, and then click Close to close the dialog box.

Alternatively, while the approach you just used to create the MDS XML Documents
repository is useful for relatively small repositories, it becomes impractical when you
have hundreds of objects because each corresponding XML file gets added, one by one,
to the working set.

Instead, to create larger MDS XML format repositories and add them to the source control
working set, just select File | Save As | MDS XML Documents, and when the Browse For
Folder dialog box is shown, select the repository directory that you downloaded as part of
the source control working set.

To manually add these files to the working set, in this case using TortoiseSVN's more-
efficient handling of large sets of files, locate the Repositories folder in the checked-out
working set, right-click it, and select TortoiseSVN | Add. In the Add dialog box, ensure
that the Select / Deselect All check box is selected, and click OK to add these files to the
working set.

8. Now save these sets of folders back to the source control repository by committing the changes: right-click the top-level checked-out folder and select SVN Commit. You will see a dialog box that displays the progress of the commit, or upload, of the files into the Subversion repository, and at the end you should get a successful Commit Finished! dialog box.

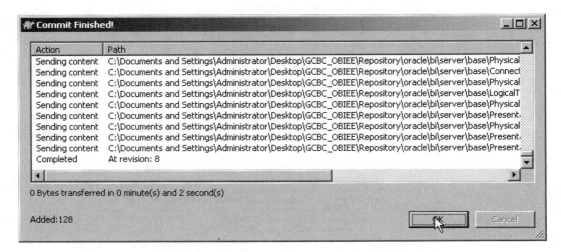

9. If your project is new and you do not have a repository file, or catalog, proceed to create your project as before; if you have previously checked project items into the Subversion repository, then retrieve them from these folders and upload them to your environment.

You now have your initial repository stored in the source control system, ready for developers to check it out, work on it, and then check their changes back into source control, with each XML file being separately tracked and all of its versions stored.

Making Changes to Projects   When working with a project stored in a source control system such as Subversion, the process you go through to make changes to the project is as follows:

1. Check out all or part of the project from the Subversion repository to a directory and subdirectories on your workstation or server.

2. Assuming that your checked-out working set includes a repository in MDS XML format, open the repository under source control using the Oracle BI Administration tool.

3. Make whatever changes, additions, and deletions you require from the project, adding, for example, logical tables to a repository or analyses to the catalog.

4. When you have finished, save the repository and allow the Administration tool to issue the required source control client commands to update the details of the working copy.

5. Make any required changes to any other configuration files, and then copy these into the working set directory.

6. Commit the updated files within these checkout directories back to the Subversion server to create new versions within the source control system.

Checking Out, Editing, and Committing Changes to Source Control   When developers subsequently wish to download, or check out, the repository and other files from the source control repository, the process is almost the same as with the steps for creating the initial project and repository, except that you will not have to re-create the repository in MDS XML format, as it is already stored that way.

Ensure that your developers have accounts on the source control server and that they set up their client software to use individual logins; then use the following approach to make some edits and commit the changes back to source control:

1. On the developer workstation, right-click on your Windows desktop and select SVN Checkout. When the Checkout dialog box is displayed, ensure that the correct URL for the Subversion repository is entered and click OK to download the most recent version of the project files from the repository.

   Alternatively, if you wish to download a specific revision number for the project (that is, previous versions of the files), select the Revision radio button and click the Show Log button to display a dialog box that lists all revisions. Select the revision you require and click OK to return to the previous dialog box. Once you are ready, click OK to check out a working copy of the files to your developer workstation.

   If, instead of checking out a working set of project files for the first time, you want to refresh your existing working set files with whatever changes other developers have made, select SVN Update (rather than SVN Checkout), which by default will download the latest revision of the project files and overwrite your existing copies.

2. Now open the MDS XML Documents–stored repository under source control so that the Oracle BI Administration tool will issue the required commands to maintain the working set's list of files under source control. To do this, using the Oracle BI Administration tool, select File | Open | MDS XML, and then use the Browse For Folder dialog box to select the checked-out repository directory. Click OK once you have selected the repository, and enter the password for the repository when prompted.

   When you open a repository stored in MDS XML format, you are prompted to choose whether to open the repository under source control or stand-alone. If you select the Standalone option, no source control client commands will be executed when you come to save the repository, and this option should therefore be used only if you are not source-controlling this repository.

   If instead you select the Use Source Control option, you will be prompted to select your SCM configuration file or create a new one. In this instance, select the SCM configuration file for Subversion, and then click OK to start editing the repository.

3. You can now make whatever changes you require to the checked-out repository and also perform tasks such as three-way merges, equalizations, and other metadata changes. In this example, create a new subject area in the presentation layer of the repository by right-clicking the Sales business model and selecting Create Subject Areas For Logical Stars And Snowflakes.

4. When you have finished working on your changes, click Save and run the consistency check when prompted. Then, as with the original process to create the MDS XML format repository, a dialog box will be displayed listing the XML files that will be added, amended, or removed from the working set. Click Yes to proceed with these changes, and then click Close to complete the save of your repository under source control.

5. If you have any other files that you need to manually add to these source control folders, such as new or amended configuration files or an archived copy of the catalog, copy those to the working set folders now.

6. Once you are ready to commit your changes back to the project, right-click the folders and select SVN Commit.

7. In the Commit dialog box, check through the list of files in the Changes Made panel, and if any of your manually included files need to be added into the working set, select their check boxes to add them in.

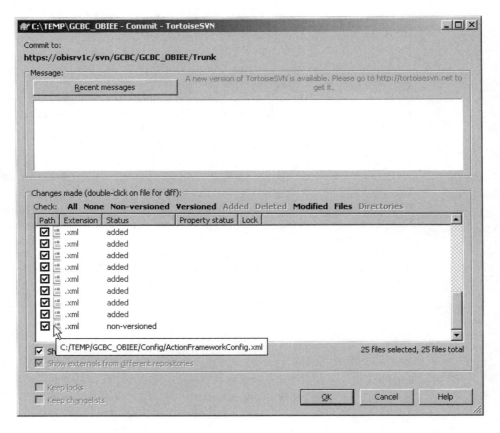

8. When you are ready to commit your changes to the Subversion repository, click OK, and a new dialog box will be displayed that shows the results of the commit process.

Creating Branches Using Subversion

Sometimes an organization will want to create additional development streams for a project to run in parallel with the main development stream, for example, to implement a BI system for an additional country or department. In this additional development stream, it is important that any changes introduced are isolated to this particular stream but that, at some point in the future, changes introduced there can be merged back into the main development stream. In version control terminology, this is called a "branch" and is supported by Subversion and most other source version control tools.

You would use Subversion branching in situations such as these:

- You have developed a "baseline" implementation of Oracle Business Intelligence, and you now want to create country-specific implementations with local customizations.

- You are currently implementing the 11*g* Release 1 version of Oracle Business Intelligence, and you now wish to try out an upgrade to a later release but any changes you make as part of this should not affect the main branch, which is still being developed on 11*g* Release 1.

- You are about to embark on a project to streamline and rationalize the Oracle BI Repository or the Oracle BI Presentation Catalog but do not want these changes to affect the main development stream until you are completely satisfied that they work correctly.

Figure 11-12 shows a main development stream being branched in these ways.

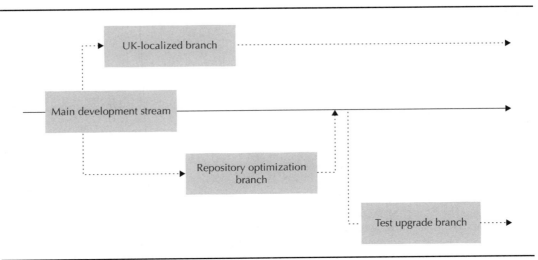

FIGURE 11-12. *A main development stream and development branches*

TIP
Although you can use Subversion's branching capability to create development branches such as those shown in Figure 11-12, you cannot subsequently use Subversion's ability to patch and merge development branches to bring them back together again. Instead, you should use the repository and catalog merging and patching features within the Oracle BI Administration tool and the Catalog Manager to ensure that your metadata stays consistent and is not corrupted, even if you are using the new MDS XML repository storage format, as Subversion's tools would not maintain and check the internal IDs and references that are used to check repository consistency.

In the following example, we will take an Oracle Business Intelligence project held in the main, Trunk folder within the Subversion repository and create a branch of it within the Branches folder. Then, after development on the branch has finished, we will look at how changes introduced into the branch can be merged back into the main, Trunk development stream.

1. Using TortoiseSVN, right-click within a folder on your workstation and select SVN Checkout.

2. When the Checkout dialog box is shown, type in the URL to the main folder for your project; for example, if your folder structure in the Subversion repository is

```
GCBC
+--- GCBC_OBIEE
+------- Trunk
+----------- Repository
+----------- Catalog
+----------- Config
+------- Branches
+------- Tags
```

then, for example, your URL should be

https://obisrv1c/svn/GCBC/GCBC_OBIEE

This ensures that your checked-out folders include one for the Trunk directory, which you will then branch in the next step.

Select either the HEAD revision (recommended) or a particular revision number if you wish to branch an earlier version of the project, and then click OK to start the checkout process.

3. The branch you are going to create will be for a UK-localized version of your system. In this localized version, you will add some new dashboards and add some objects to the Oracle BI Repository that you do not initially want to add to the main repository used in your organization.

To create the new branch, right-click the Trunk folder within the checked-out folders in your file system and select TortoiseSVN | Branch/tag.

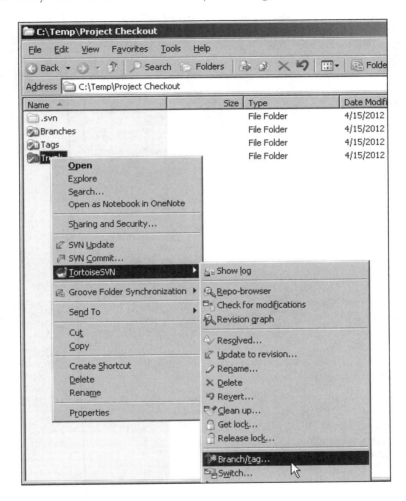

4. At the Copy(Branch / Tag) dialog box, within the To URL field, which currently reads (for example):

https://obisrv1c/svn/GCBC/GCBC_OBIEE/Trunk

change this URL to reference the new branch folder, which will automatically be created for you as part of the branching operation:

https://obisrv1c/svn/GCBC/GCBC_OBIEE/Branch/UK-Localized

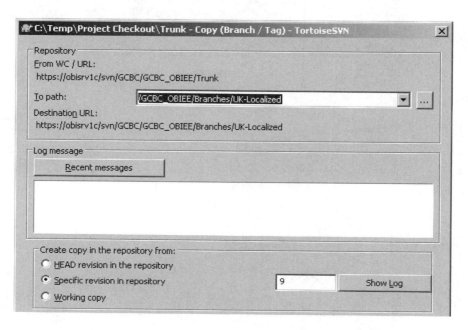

5. Click OK to create the branch, and check that the output shows that the branch was created successfully.

6. Right-click anywhere on the desktop now and select TortoiseSVN | Repo-browser. Ensure that the URL for your repository is entered into the URL text box (for example, https://obisrv1c/svn/GCBC/GCBC_OBIEE) and then use the Repository Browser to view your Subversion repository contents. If you expand the Branch folder, you will see the new branch that you have just created.

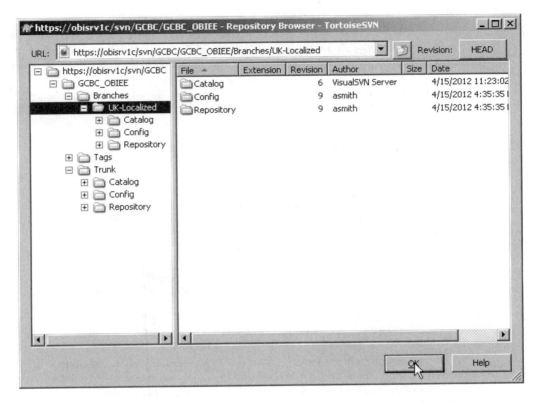

7. If a developer wishes to work on this new branch rather than the main development stream in the Trunk folder, all he or she has to do is specify its URL when checking out files to their desktop; for example:

https://obisrv1c/svn/GCBC/GCBC_OBIEE/Branch/UK-Localized

If the developer who created the branch now wishes to switch their locally checked-out files to this branch, they have to "switch" their checked-out files to use the branch as their "working copy." To do this, right-click the Trunk folder within your checked-out files, select TortoiseSVN | Switch, and then select the branch URL from the drop-down list.

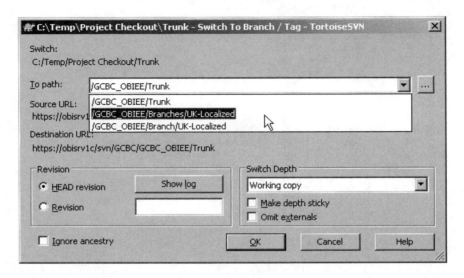

When the new branch is selected, TortoiseSVN will replace the local copies of files with those from the branch, and any subsequent check-ins from this folder will be to the branch, not the main development stream. Repeat this process, selecting the Trunk folder, if you wish to subsequently switch back to the main development stream.

8. If, at a later date, you wish to merge changes made in this stream back into the main development stream, use TortoiseSVN to check out first the branched repository file, for example, and then switch to the Trunk folder and do the same with the main repository file. Then use the three-way merge feature within the Oracle BI Administration tool, along with a copy of the repository file from the revision before the branch was made, to perform a three-way merge. Once complete, upload this new, merged repository back into the main, Trunk development stream's folders and continue development in this stream.

For the catalog, use the Catalog Manager patching facility to do the same for the catalog, following the steps outlined earlier in this chapter.

Tagging Releases Using Subversion

Subversion, and similar version control tools, has the concept of "tagged" releases of code. For example, you may have developed your main, Trunk version of your business intelligence project over several weeks, with many revisions of the repository, catalog archive, and other objects committed to the Subversion repository. You are now, for example, at revision 150, and you wish to mark this revision as "Version 1.0" so that your production support and testing teams can easily identify which revision to pull from the repository and promote into test and production.

The Subversion repository you created earlier had the following folder structure, now with an extra set of folders under the Branch folder, for the UK-Localized version created as a branch in the previous example:

```
GCBC
+--- GCBC_OBIEE
+------- Trunk
+----------- Repository
+----------- Catalog
+----------- Config
+------- Branches
+---------- UK-Localized
+-------------- Repository
+-------------- Catalog
+-------------- Config
+------- Tags
```

To create a tagged release of your project, you would therefore follow the same procedure as for creating a branch, but you would select a new subdirectory within the Tags folder instead of the Branch folder. Internally, when you copy files into new folders in this way, Subversion starts off by copying only a pointer, or shortcut, to your existing files, pointing to a particular revision of your main Trunk or Branch files. Then, when a user or administrator checks out a particular tagged version of your project, they will actually download a particular revision number of your project, which you have specified as your version "X."

This initial copying of file pointers into new Subversion folders is actually also how the branching process works. When you create a new branch, the new files that you see in the branch folders are initially just pointers back to the files in the main Trunk folders. If you subsequently make changes to those files in the Branch folder, for text and XML files Subversion will either store just the difference between the two files (which is how it then creates patch files for text file–based sources) or for repositories stored in binary, RPD format, catalog archives, and so on, it will store the whole new binary file.

For more information on Subversion, check out the product home page at http://subversion .apache.org/, or feel free to use any other version or source control system in a similar way.

Concurrent Online Editing of the Repository

When you start working with the Oracle BI Administration tool and open a repository, you can either open it offline or online. When you open a repository offline, you are opening the file directly using the Oracle BI Administrator tool, and only you have write access to it. When you connect to a repository online, though, other developers can connect online to the same repository, and they can write to the repository as well.

This multiuser write access gives you a simple way to provide a shared repository development environment for small teams of users. Up to five developers concurrently editing the repository is supported by Oracle, though in practice there are no restrictions on more than this number. To manage potential conflicts in this process, the Oracle BI Server and the Oracle BI Administration tool together effectively "serialize" edits to the repository file by checking out and then checking in changes that individual developers make.

For example, consider a situation where two developers, Adam Smith and Bill Jones, both want to access and edit the same online repository to develop metadata objects for their users. Both users have their own workstations with Oracle Business Intelligence installed, but the repository they want to edit is on a third, development server. The repository has a single business model, with two logical fact tables that share a set of logical dimensions, as well as dimensions that are specific to just their own fact tables. Figure 11-13 shows the Oracle BI Repository that both developers wish to edit online.

Setting Up Concurrent Online Editing of the Repository

When you install the full Oracle Business Intelligence technology stack, an ODBC data source name (DSN) is created for you that points to the Oracle Business Intelligence installation on the same server. If you install just the client tools, though, you will need to create this connection yourself, to point to the development server that you wish to connect to when you are connecting online.

Similarly, if several developers are going to connect online to the same Oracle Business Intelligence domain so that they can all edit the same repository online, you will need to create additional ODBC DSNs for them to do this.

To create an ODBC DSN that connects to a remote server, follow the instructions in Chapter 2 for setting up client-only installations of Oracle Business Intelligence. Then, when all developers have suitable ODBC DSNs for connecting to the remote server, you can start concurrent editing of the repository.

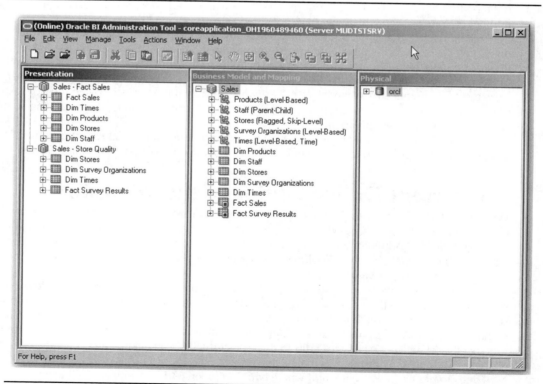

FIGURE 11-13. *The repository that will be edited online*

Checking Out and Checking In Repository Objects

In this scenario, we have two developers wishing to concurrently edit the same online repository:

■ Andrew Smith is responsible for the Fact Sales logical fact table, and he needs to edit the Dim Staff, Dim Products, Dim Stores, and Dim Times logical dimension tables that join to it. He also wishes to edit the Sales – Fact Sales subject area, which is based on these logical tables.

■ Bill Jones is responsible for the Fact Survey Results logical table and is also interested in the Stores and Times logical dimension tables, as well as the Dim Survey Organizations logical dimension table that only joins to this fact table. As with Andrew Smith, he also has a dedicated subject area, Sales – Store Quality, that is based on these logical tables.

Both developers have set up ODBC DSNs on their workstations to connect to the server that has this repository online, and on the first day they both start developing:

1. To open the online repository, Andrew Smith starts the Oracle BI Administrator tool and selects File | Open | Online from the application menu. To connect to the online repository, he selects the ODBC DSN for it, and enters the repository password and a username and password for the system. He now has the repository open online.

2. Bill Jones then does the same, and also now has the same online repository open for editing.

3. Andrew Smith now double-clicks on the Fact Sales logical table to open it for editing. At this point, the Check Out Objects dialog box is shown, and Andrew is given the choice of either checking out the object, making it unavailable for editing by anyone else until he checks it back in again, or clicking Cancel, which opens the object in read-only mode.

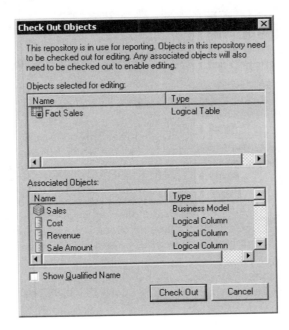

4. Andrew clicks the Check Out button to check out the objects, and then does the same for the Dim Times logical dimension table. At this point, his view of the repository shows check marks against those tables to show that they are checked out, and shows the business model that they are both contained in.

5. Andrew now adds a new column to the Fact Sales logical table, but then goes away to lunch without saving any of his changes.

6. In the meantime, Bill Jones has two tasks to perform. He logs into the same repository, double-clicks one of the physical databases in the physical layer of the repository, and is also shown the Check Out Objects dialog box. This object now shows a check mark against it in his view of the repository, but the other objects currently checked out by Andrew Smith do not have any indicators next to them to show their checked-out state.

7. Bill Jones then goes to the business model and mapping layer of the repository and double-clicks the Fact Survey Results logical fact table to edit it. He is again shown the Check Out Objects dialog box, but when he clicks the Check Out button, he is then presented with an error message indicating that an error occurred while trying to check out objects.

This is because, even though the other user only edited one other logical fact table and dimension in the business model, in fact the whole business model gets checked out, and Bill cannot edit it until Andrew checks in his changes or closes the repository without checking in his changes (that is, discards his changes).

This issue would also occur if Bill were to try to edit the subject area that is based on his tables, as this depends on the shared business model and would therefore be blocked from checkout. The only way that both developers could work simultaneously in this way is if both had completely separate business models to work on.

8. Andrew Smith then returns from lunch and checks in his changes, either by selecting File | Save from the application menu (which then prompts you to check in changes) or by clicking the Check In Changes button on the toolbar.

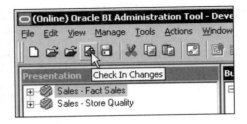

After prompting to check global consistency for the repository, the changes are checked in.

Bill Jones can now check out his own objects, and until he checks in his changes, Andrew Smith will have to wait to be able to check out his objects.

Refreshing Oracle BI Server Metadata in Presentation Services

When you develop repositories online, whether on your own or as part of a concurrent development team, you will need to refresh the Oracle BI Presentation Server's cached copy of the repository before your changes will be available to end users, or to you if you want to unit-test your changes. To do this, follow these steps:

1. Using your web browser, navigate to the Oracle Business Intelligence web site, at http://[*machine_name*]:9704/analytics.

2. Log in using an administrator username and password and then, using the common header area at the top of the screen, click the Administration link.

3. On the Administration page, locate the Maintenance and Troubleshooting section, and then click the Reload Files and Metadata link within that section.

4. The metadata refresh will then take place, and you can log out and close your browser window.

Similarly, if you have scaled out or scaled up your Oracle Business Intelligence domain to add additional BI Servers to your Oracle Business Intelligence instance, then you will need to restart all of these BI Server system components to pick up the online changes you have just made. This is because when you connect online to the repository, you are actually connecting to just one of the Oracle BI Server components, and the changes you make will be made only to its local copy of the repository.

To propagate these changes across all repositories, you will have to use the Availability | Processes tab in Fusion Middleware Control to restart all of your BI Server components.

Online Development Considerations

The previous examples in this section have probably highlighted for you the benefits and limitations of working concurrently on an online Oracle BI Repository. The primary benefit of this approach is that it takes very little setting up, and if you only occasionally need to have more than one developer access a repository, this is a convenient way to make this possible without the complexity of the full Multiuser Development Environment described in the next section. Online editing of the repository is also useful in situations where you need to make minor "hotfix" changes to a production repository without the associated server downtime from deploying a new repository using Fusion Middleware Control.

However, for development teams with multiple repository developers, all of which need constant access to the same repository, online development can quickly become unworkable for the following reasons:

- One developer checking out a business model could inadvertently stop other developers from working on logical tables and columns within that model, as well as from working on subject areas that are dependent on this model.

- Large repositories with many objects can become very slow to access when checking in and out large numbers of objects.

- For developers, there is little indication that objects are already checked out until such time as you try to open them for editing.

- There is no control over who can access what parts of the model, and therefore there is no formal process for dealing with merging sets of changes or controlling who has access to what components.

For these reasons, concurrent online editing of the repository is really only suitable for low-intensity development by developers who are able to wait until other developers have checked in their changes before applying their own. As an approach, it has the virtue of simplicity, but it quickly becomes unworkable for large development teams making lots of changes to shared areas of the repository.

The Multiuser Development Environment

So far in this chapter, we have looked at how teams consisting of a single developer, or a small team of developers who rarely do concurrent work, can create repositories and catalogs and move them between development, test, and production. While this approach can work well and has the virtue of simplicity, it does suffer from the following limitations:

- You are always working with a single, monolithic repository, and there is no way to separate it out into separate sections for developers to work on separately.

- Concurrent online access to repositories effectively "serializes" development, allowing only a single developer to make changes at any one time.

- Connecting online to a shared repository may not be practical or fast when developers are distributed around the world.

- There is no process for dealing with controlled merging of changes from different development teams.

- Overall, this is not a particularly "scalable" approach, and something else may need to be done to make it possible for large teams of developers to work on a common repository.

That "something else" is the Multiuser Development Environment (MUDE). MUDE is a set of features and a process to follow that allow teams of developers to take subsets of a repository (known in MUDE terms as *projects*), work on them separately, and then automatically merge their subsets back into the main, or *master*, repository. At the same time, these developers can also create other business intelligence content such as analyses, dashboards, and agents, which can be merged into the main catalog using the same three-way merge process we saw earlier.

MUDE can be a complex feature to master, however, and if you only need to provide access to a small number of repository developers making occasional changes to the repository, then shared online development or even sending the repository file via e-mail among developers may be more appropriate. But if you find yourself in a situation where this approach becomes unworkable and you are looking for some way to manage distributed groups of developers who need sole access to their own subset of the repository, then MUDE may be worth investigating.

Multiuser Development Concepts

Before we take a look at a typical MUDE development process, it is worth taking some time to understand some of the concepts behind MUDE. Once we have gone through these design principles, we will look at a typical project life cycle using MUDE and think about how its management of the repository also links in with the catalog and other elements of your business intelligence metadata.

What Is the Multiuser Development Environment (MUDE)?

The Multiuser Development Environment (MUDE) is a set of features within the Oracle BI Administration tool that permit distributed development of a main, master repository. When you enable MUDE for your developers, an administrator can define for a master repository a number of projects that can be checked out by developers and worked on separately. The developers' changes can then be published back in to the master repository.

When developers work on these projects, they work with a local repository file and have sole write access to it, avoiding the concurrency limitations of shared online access. When they have finished making their changes and their work is published back to the main repository, others can see their changes and they can then check out another project to work on.

How Does MUDE Work?

MUDE works using the existing repository files and repository merging features that you have seen previously in this chapter, together with a new feature called *projects* that let you extract consistent subsets of a repository and work on them as separate files.

In a MUDE environment, an administrator first defines one or more projects within your main repository, with each project representing a logical fact table together with supporting logical dimension tables, logical hierarchies, subject areas, variables, and other repository objects. This repository in then placed in a shared network directory, accessible to all developers, and becomes the "master" repository.

As shown in Figure 11-14, developers working on their own workstations or laptops then configure their installation of the Oracle BI Administrator tool to connect to this shared repository. From that point on, they can select and check out these projects from the master repository, and when they have finished they can check the changes back into the master repository. When they check out their project from the master repository, their Oracle BI Administrator tool creates a local repository file on their workstation that contains just the repository objects defined by the project, and they can either work with this file offline or upload it into their own local Oracle BI Domain so that they can access it online.

When the time comes to merge a developer's changes back into the master repository, those changes are first checked against subsequent changes that have happened to the master repository since the projects were checked out, and any merge conflicts that thereby arise are resolved. Once this is done, their confirmed changes are published back to the master repository, which is held in a shared directory on the network.

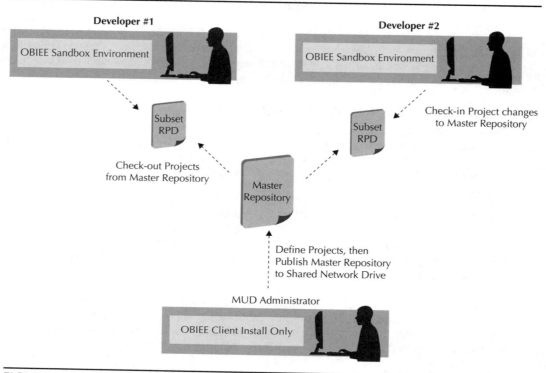

FIGURE 11-14. *Checking MUDE projects in and out*

The MUDE Administration System

In a MUDE environment, one workstation is generally designated as being the MUDE "administration system." This workstation will have a copy of the Oracle BI Administration tool installed (generally through the Client installation of Oracle Business Intelligence) and will be used to initially define projects against the main repository used by the organization, define access rights for these projects, and then copy the repository file into the shared network directory.

As this workstation does not need to run the full installation of Oracle Business Intelligence, it does not need to have too much memory or disk space assigned to it. (A workstation with 2GB of RAM, for example, would be sufficient.) Because of the way the MUDE process copies files to predefined directories on your workstation, though, it is best if you can separate this task onto its own workstation, rather than having one of the developers also use their workstation for this task.

Developer Sandboxes

In addition to the MUDE administration system that manages the definition of projects for your master repository, each individual developer ideally will have his or her own workstation or laptop running a full installation of the Oracle Business Intelligence technology stack.

These are termed "developer sandboxes," as any changes developers make to their repositories are isolated from the main environment your users use; but because they include the full technology stack, they can run their subset repositories online if they wish, and unit-test their work before merging their changes back into the master repository.

NOTE
It is not mandatory to have these full developer installations, and it is possible to use MUDE just with stand-alone client tools installations, though any development work carried out with their repositories will have to be carried out offline only.

Licensing Considerations

MUDE in itself does not incur any additional license costs for organizations, as long as you only install the client tools on each developer workstation; however, if you set up individual sandbox environments for each of your developers (a full installation of both the server and client parts of Oracle Business Intelligence), they will have to be licensed in the same way as the server environments that your users connect to.

If you do full installations of Oracle Business Intelligence on each developer workstation, you will therefore probably want to license your development environment using the Named User Plus licensing metric (currently with a 25-user minimum) and your production environment using the processor metric to allow unlimited users to connect to the production server. If you have test, preproduction, or other environments that you use to stage releases before making them available to users, you will either choose one or the other metric for these servers depending on the number of developers or users that will connect to them.

Oracle license terms can change at any time, though, and you should therefore check with your Oracle representative to confirm the best licensing approach for your organization. Remember, that development and test environments are not free, and you will need to ensure that they are licensed in some way before putting your project into production.

What Happens During the MUDE Project Life Cycle?

Earlier in this chapter, we looked at how you could merge two repositories together using the three-way merge feature in the Oracle BI Administration tool. MUDE builds on this feature, automatically adding the original repository into the merge process and handling merge conflicts for you through an interactive dialog box that lets you pick which changes to merge either into the developer's local copy of the project or into the master copy at the time of publishing back their changes. In addition, MUDE automates the process of extracting subsets of the repository into separate repository files for users to edit and wraps the whole process into a workflow built into the tool.

For example, a typical MUDE project life cycle could look like the following. Note that the MUDE workflow changes from release to release, and these steps are based on the 11.1.1.6 release of the product:

1. The MUDE administrator obtains a copy of the repository file that developers want to work with, opens it for editing, and creates projects within the repository to define how the repository should be subdivided for team development purposes.

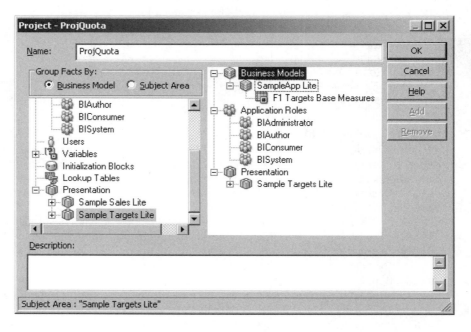

2. The repository file that has just had the projects added to it is then copied to a network directory share accessible to all developers (for example, a directory known universally as Y:\ and from here on referred to as the *master repository*). This directory, at that point, contains only this master repository file and no other files.

3. When a developer then wishes to check out a project from this master repository, he or she opens the Oracle BI Administration tool, registers the location of the shared directory, and selects File | Multiuser | Checkout.

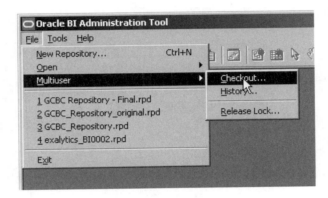

The developer is then asked to select the master repository to work with within this shared directory, enters the password for the repository, selects the project(s) to check out, and imports it into their environment.

On selecting the projects to check out, two repository files are then copied to the developer's default repository directory, and they can usually be found at [*middleware_home*]\ instances\instance1\bifoundation\OracleBIServerComponent\coreapplication_obis1\ repository directory. These repository files are

■ The subset repository file, based on the project selection made by the developer, with a filename chosen during the checkout process (for example, projSales.rpd)

■ A copy of this file, with "original" as the prefix (for example, originalprojSales.rpd)

Back on the shared network drive, additional files have been added to the directory after the project checkout took place that are used to keep track of who has checked out which projects, as well as keep track of other aspects of the MUDE process.

4. The developer will then either open the subset repository offline and edit it directly, or upload it to their online environment and edit it online. As normal, as changes are made, the repository should be saved regularly and checked for consistency.

5. Once a certain point has been reached with development, the developer may want to compare the changes they have made to the local copy of the subset repository. To do this, the BI Administration tool uses the compare repositories feature described earlier in this chapter and compares the edited subset repository with the copy that was also made at the time of checkout.

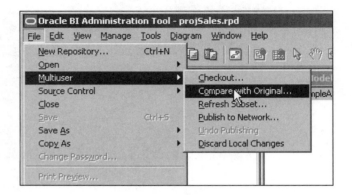

If satisfied with these changes, the developer can then publish them to the master repository, as shown in the following illustration.

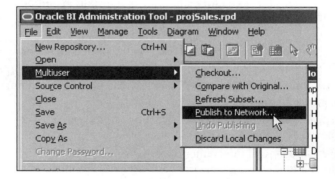

6. If desired, the developer can choose to refresh the local copy of the subset repository with any changes made subsequently to the master repository, or discard the local changes and return to their original repository subset. When refreshing the local copy, any merge conflicts introduced by changes subsequently made to the master repository can be dealt with using the Define Merge Strategy dialog box, which lets the developer choose either to keep the local change or the one introduced by the repository refresh.

7. If, however, the developer chooses to publish the changes to the master repository, the master repository is locked before this merge takes place.

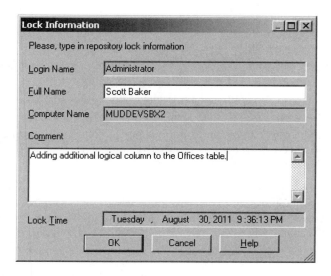

This lock is placed so that no more than one developer's Oracle BI Administration tool can be attempting to merge into the master repository file at the same time; once the lock is placed, if there are no merge conflicts, the changes are published immediately and the lock is released. If merge conflicts do arise, however, the developer resolves these using the same Define Merge Strategy dialog box as used when refreshing the local repository subset copy, with the changes then being published and the lock released.

8. At any time, developers can view the history of a master repository to show who has checked out projects, as well as show conflicts that were resolved when the project was merged back into the master repository and any comments that were added during the merge.

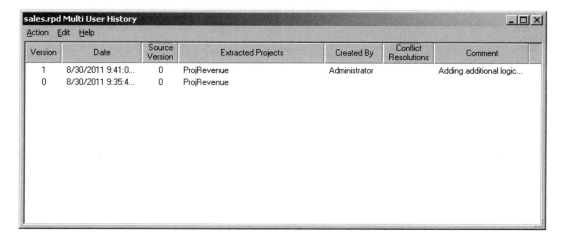

MUDE Merges vs. Regular Merges

While the merge process used within MUDE projects is mostly the same as the merge process you use for regular merges, when you choose to do a three-way merge between repositories, slightly different merge rules apply when using MUDE:

- Inserts of repository objects are applied automatically.

- Conflicts that are not associated with inserts but are resolved because of the automatic inserts are applied in favor of the subset repository.

- The database and connection pool details in the shared, master repository take precedence over ones that you may have used in your subset repository.

- Any changes you made to security settings and filters in your subset repository are discarded, and you need to make these changes to the master repository directly, removing it from the MUDE environment while you do so.

These changes generally make merging projects using MUDE more straightforward than manual three-way merges, but you may still have conflicts to resolve during this process; the example in the section "Step 6: Publishing Local Changes to the Network," later in this chapter, will outline a scenario where this may happen and how you might resolve it.

What Can I Include in a Project?

Now that you know more about how repository files are handled during the MUDE process, it is worth taking a moment to look in more detail at what makes up a MUDE project.

Projects are defined within repository files by selecting Manage | Projects from the application menu. If this is the first time that you have defined a project, you will then be presented with the Project Manager dialog box and an empty project list; otherwise, a list of projects already defined will be presented to you.

To create a new project, select Action | New Project from the dialog box, or right-click anywhere in the listing of projects and select New Project. When you do so, the Project dialog box will be shown, and you can name your project and start adding repository objects to it.

The following objects, as shown in the illustration, can be included in a project: business models (or individual logical fact tables from the business model and mapping layer), application roles, users, variables, initialization blocks, lookup tables, and presentation layer subject areas or individual presentation layer tables.

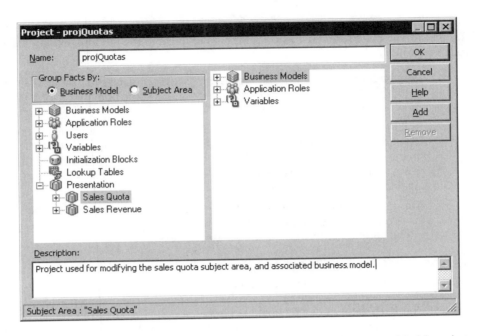

While physical layer objects are not displayed in the dialog box, they are added for whatever business model objects you include in the project.

When you add objects to the project, you typically select those presentation layer and business model objects that are required for developing a consistent area of the repository. Individual repository objects can be included in many separate project definitions, and when you check out a project, other developers can check out the same project or other projects that contain objects also within your selected project, which is why the final merge process back into the master repository has to be able to deal with merge conflicts that may occur.

Promoting MUDE Environments Through Development, Testing, and Production

Typically, MUDE is used only within the development stage of a project, and all changes (for a particular release) will be merged back into the master repository before it is given to the testing and then production support teams ready for release to users.

As such, MUDE generally applies only during the development phase, and the process for promoting MUDE-enabled repositories through testing and then production is the same as for any other repository:

1. The master repository is developed using MUDE; projects are extracted, changes are published back into the master repository, and at some point work for a particular release is considered to be complete.

2. The master repository file is then copied to the test environment, along with any catalog content and other artifacts that constitute the release. Optionally, the project definitions in the master repository can be removed, but there is no need to do this, and you can leave them there if you wish, even if you do not intend to use MUDE with this repository again.

3. This master repository file is then tested in the test environment, and once it is confirmed as acceptable, it is promoted into production, along with any other catalog content or project artifacts.

MUDE and Version Control

MUDE can be combined with version control systems, such as Subversion, by storing the subset repositories created by developers in subfolders underneath the main repository/RPD folder in the project. These repositories can be uploaded in their original binary RPD format, or they can be resaved in the new MDS XML format to permit fine-grained tracking and versioning of individual project elements.

For example, if your project directory structure in Subversion is currently this:

```
GCBC
+--- GCBC_OBIEE
+------- Trunk
+---------- RPD
+---------- Catalog
+---------- Config
+------- Branches
+------- Tags
```

you could accommodate the subset repositories created using MUDE by storing them in subdirectories, like this:

```
GCBC
+--- GCBC_OBIEE
+------- Trunk
+---------- RPD
+-------------- MUDE Master Repository
+-------------- Quotas Project
+-------------- Revenue Project
+---------- Catalog
+---------- Config
+------- Branches
+------- Tags
```

Developers could then check their subset repositories into these folders at regular intervals, in addition to holding the MUDE Master Repository as a separate object to the main repository that the MUDE administrator created it from.

If you already store your main project repository in MDS XML format and wish to start using MUDE, you can define projects in the repository in the same way as if you had your repository stored as a single, binary RPD file. However, when developers come to extract projects out of this master repository, the subset repositories will initially be created in the binary RPD format, though they can be resaved in MDS XML format if required, which still permits all of the standard repository compare, merge, and publish operations.

Why You Can Choose Not to Use MUDE

While MUDE is a powerful environment for team development of the repository, it is not always appropriate for all organizations. Management of the various subset and master repositories takes effort, and the MUDE process requires all involved to understand how project fragments are merged and how conflicts can still arise.

General good advice for most projects is to use the simplest development environment that is possible for your project. If you can work with just a single, shared repository with online access or have a single repository file that is shared by developers via e-mail, go with that. If, however, it is clear that you need a way to divide up your project and formally manage the integration process afterward, MUDE is a good solution that covers most scenarios.

Example: MUDE Use in an Enterprise Development Team

Now that you know the principals and concepts behind MUDE, let's take a look at a step-by-step example that shows how it works in practice using the 11.1.1.6 release of Oracle Business Intelligence.

In this example, we have a repository with a single business model, two fact tables, and two subject areas. Figure 11-15 shows the repository before any changes are made and any projects are defined.

There are three developers who wish to work with this repository:

- Andrew Smith, who wishes to work on the Sales – Fact Sales subject area and its corresponding logical fact table in the business model and mapping layer

- Bill Jones, who wishes to work on the Sales – Store Quality subject area and the corresponding logical fact table that it uses

- Chris Bailey, who also wants to work on the same Sales – Fact Sales subject area and its corresponding logical fact table

Each of these developers has a powerful workstation or laptop, with the full installation of Oracle Business Intelligence on it, to create developer sandboxes capable of working with their subset repositories either online or offline.

In addition to these three developers, there is also an administrator responsible for the MUDE environment:

- David Armstrong, who does not do any development but is responsible for creating the initial MUDE projects and managing the shared network directory.

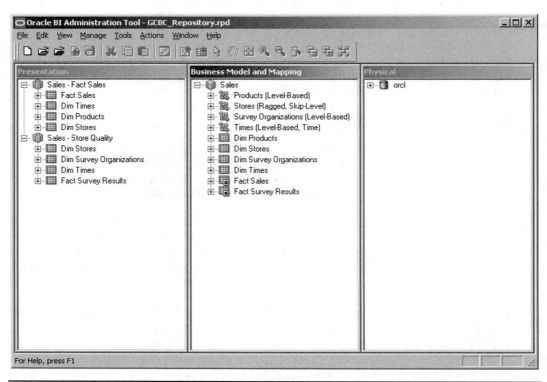

FIGURE 11-15. *The example repository, as used by MUDE*

In addition to this development environment, there are also test and production servers that have full installations of Oracle Business Intelligence installed on them, and a Subversion source control repository installed on the workstation also used for MUDE administration. Figure 11-16 shows the development environment used in the example, and the test and production servers to which changes are eventually deployed.

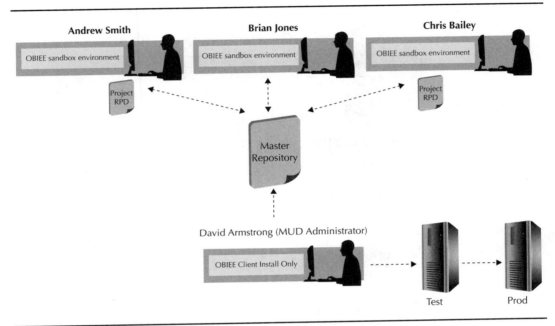

FIGURE 11-16.   *The example development environment*

Step 1: Defining the Projects

To create the projects within the development repository, David Armstrong, the MUDE administrator, would follow these steps:

1. Using the Oracle BI Administrator tool on the MUDE Administrator workstation, select File | Open | Offline to open the repository offline that you wish to create projects for.

2. From the application menu, select Manage | Projects to display the Project Manager dialog box.

3. To define the first project, based on the Sales – Fact Sales subject area, select Action | New Project from the dialog box menu.

4. Name the project Sales – Fact Sales, and select the Subject Area radio button for the Group Facts By option.

5. Expand the Subject Areas folder on the left-hand side, and select the Sales – Fact Sales subject area.

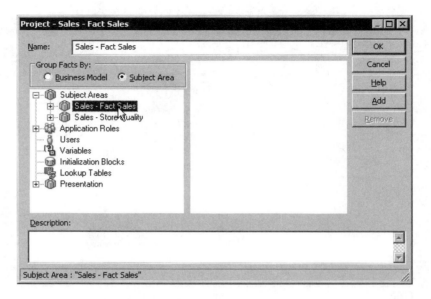

Click the Add button to add it to the right-hand panel. Then expand the Presentation folder on the right-hand side, and select the Sales – Fact Sales presentation layer objects so that the right-hand panel now shows the Sales business model, the Fact Sales logical fact table, and the Sales – Fact Sales subject area and presentation tables.

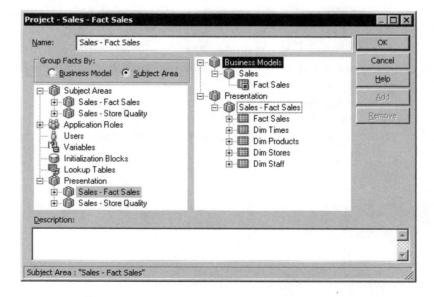

This constitutes the subset of the main repository that will comprise this project. Click OK to return to the Project Manager dialog box.

6. Now create any additional projects using the same steps, selecting repository objects to add to the project definition. Objects you select can also be featured in other projects, and by selecting a logical fact table or business model, you automatically select the logical dimension tables that join to the logical fact table, their logical dimensions and hierarchies, and the physical layer objects that are linked to them through logical table sources.

Step 2: Creating the Shared Network Folder and Copying the Repository to Create the Master Repository

After projects have been defined in the repository, they can be copied to a shared network drive and designated the "master repository." To do this, follow these steps:

1. In this example, a directory on the MUDE Administration system workstation will become the shared directory for the MUDE master repository. To create and share such a folder using Windows Explorer, open the directory into which you will place this shared directory (for example, C:\) and then select File | New | Folder.

2. Name the folder (for example, RPD_MUD), right-click and select Sharing And Security (or the equivalent for the version of Microsoft Windows that you are using). In the Properties dialog box, select the Share This Folder option. Click the Permissions button (or equivalent) to set access rights for the share, either giving all users full control over the files in the directory or restricting these rights to particular users or groups. Note that, for MUDE to work, users will need at least read and write access to this folder. Once done, press OK to close the dialog box.

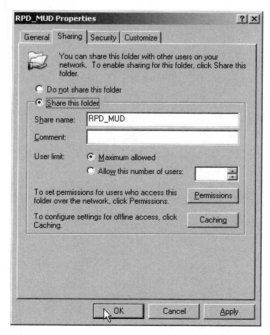

3. Now copy the repository file containing the projects to this shared folder.

Step 3: Configuring Developer Workstations to Access the MUDE Shared Folder

Each developer workstation now needs to be configured to access this shared directory. To do so, follow these steps:

1. Starting with the first developer workstation, use Windows Explorer to create a new mapped drive to the network share (Tools | Map Network Drive) and make a note of the drive letter that is assigned (for example, Y:\).

2. Open the Oracle BI Administration tool, but do not connect to a repository. Instead, select Tools | Options from the application menu, and in the Options dialog box select the Multiuser tab. Click the Browse button to select the mapped network drive that you created a moment ago, and enter the name of the developer (for example, Andrew Smith) into the Full Name text box.

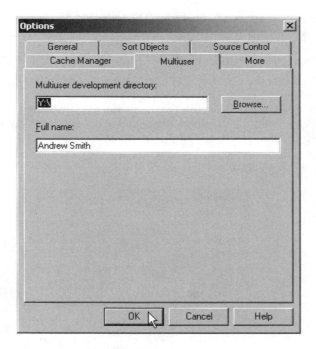

3. Repeat step 2 for all other workstations that will be accessing the MUDE environment. Once this is complete, your developers are ready to start using the MUDE environment.

Step 4: Checking Projects Out of the Master Repository

The three developers looking to make use of MUDE and the master repository can now check out their individual projects:

1. The first developer, Andrew Smith, wants to check out the Sales – Fact Sales project. To do this, with the Oracle BI Administration tool open, select File | Multiuser | Checkout.

    If there is just a single repository file in the network share directory, you will be prompted to enter the password for this repository. If there are several repository files in this directory, you will be prompted to pick the file first and then enter the password for it.

2. The Browse prompt will then be displayed. Select one or more projects to check out, and click OK. In this initial instance, Andrew Smith checks out the Sales – Fact Sales project.

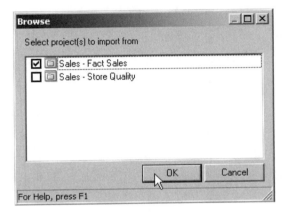

3. You will then be prompted to save the subset repository to your local workstation. Enter a name (for example, projFact_Sales.rpd) and click Save to save the file. At the same time, the Oracle BI Administration tool will save a second copy of this file, which can be used later to compare your changes with the project that you originally extracted.

4. The second developer, Bill Jones, repeats this process, this time selecting the Sales – Store Quality project and saving the subset repository to his file system with the name projFact_ Store_Quality.rpd.

5. The third developer, Chris Bailey, completes this task by also checking out the Sales – Fact Sales project, saving the extracted subset repository file to his file system using the filename projFact_Sales_CB.rpd.

Chris Bailey, like the other developers, now has a repository open within the Oracle BI Administration tool, which contains the subset of the master repository's objects as defined by the projects selected during the checkout.

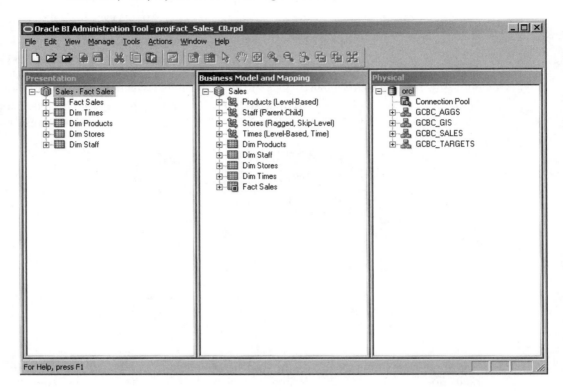

Step 5: Editing and Enhancing of Subset Repositories

Each developer can now edit their subset repository, either offline or online:

1. Andrew Smith, the first developer, makes the following changes to his subset repository, based on the Sales – Fact Sales project:

   ■ Adds a new logical column to the Dim Products logical table, called Product Size

   ■ Sets the Default Aggregation rule for the "Fact Sales".Cost logical column to Avg

   ■ Fixes an issue where the logical table source for the Dim Staff logical table has been previously deleted and now needs to be created

2. Once these changes are complete, he saves his repository by selecting File | Save, and checks the repository consistency as part of this process. If he should wish, Andrew can also check his subset repository into a Subversion or similar source control system, either in its existing binary RPD format or by selecting File | Save As | MDS XML Documents and using it in conjunction with the source control integration included from the 11.1.1.6 release onward.

3. Bill Jones, the second developer, makes the following changes to his subset repository, based on the Sales – Store Quality project:
   - Alters the Dim Stores.Concession logical column to append "(Concession)" to the concession name
   - Adds a new logical column to the Fact Survey Results table, called Score Standard

4. Finally, Chris Bailey, the third developer, opens his repository and makes the following changes:
   - Fixes the same issue where the logical table source for the Dim Staff table is missing, and needs to be re-created
   - Sets the Default Aggregation rule for the "Fact Sales".Cost logical column to Min
   - Deletes the Dim Times presentation table
   - Alters the Dim Stores.Concession logical column to append "(In Store Concession)" to the concession name

5. All three developers view the changes they have made to their subset repositories, compared to the ones they extracted earlier on, by selecting File | Multiuser | Compare With Original. Andrew Jones, for example, can now see that his changes have modified one logical table and column, created a new logical table source, and created one more logical column, whereas Chris Bailey will see a whole list of deletions that correspond with his deletion of a presentation table.

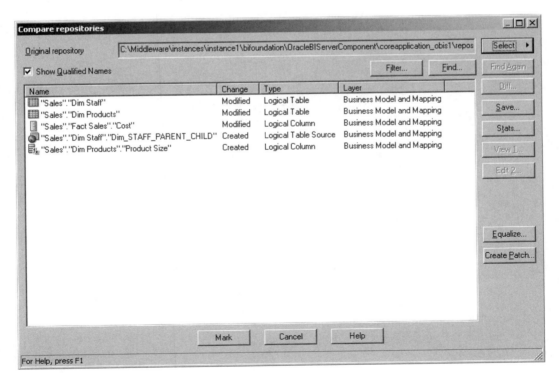

Step 6: Publishing Local Changes to the Network

Once each developer has made their changes, they will want to check in their work and then publish their changes so that others can work with the updated repository. This publishing process involves three steps, in the background:

1. The developer selects the option to publish their local changes, which then causes the BI Administration tool to take a lock on the master repository.

2. If any merge conflicts then arise, they are dealt with using the Define Merge Strategy dialog box, or the developer can choose to cancel the publish process by selecting the Undo Publishing option, optionally thereafter rolling back their changes using the Discard Local Changes option.

3. Once any issues are resolved, the changes are then published to the master repository on the network and the lock released so that other developers who subsequently access the master repository will see the updated repository objects.

When the lock is taken out on the master repository file, no other developer can publish changes at that time. Therefore, it is important that you complete this process as soon as possible or release the lock using the Undo Publishing option if you no longer wish to promote your changes.

In this example, the third developer, Chris Bailey, finishes his changes first and decides to check in his changes. To do this, he follows these steps:

1. With the Oracle BI Administration tool open and the subset repository open offline, he selects File | Multiuser | Publish to Network.

2. The Lock Information dialog box is then displayed, as shown in the illustration below.

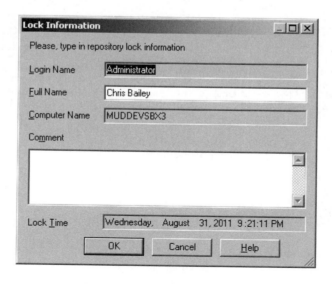

Comments to provide background information for the changes can be added here if required. Because no other developers have checked in changes that might conflict with Chris' changes, the publish and merge back into the master repository completes without issue, and the master repository lock is removed.

3. Andrew Smith now wishes to check in his changes and publish back to the master repository. Before he does this, though, because he works near Chris Bailey, who he knows is working on a similar project, he checks whether any merge conflicts are likely to happen by selecting File | Multiuser | Refresh Subset. As he suspects, the new updated master repository now has had changes applied to it that conflict with his, and these are displayed in the Merge Repository Wizard – Define Merge Strategy dialog box.

In this instance there are two conflicts to resolve; one where the previous developer, Chris Bailey, has deleted the Dim Times presentation table but it is still present in the subset repository belonging to Andrew, and the other where both developers have modified the properties of the Cost logical column.

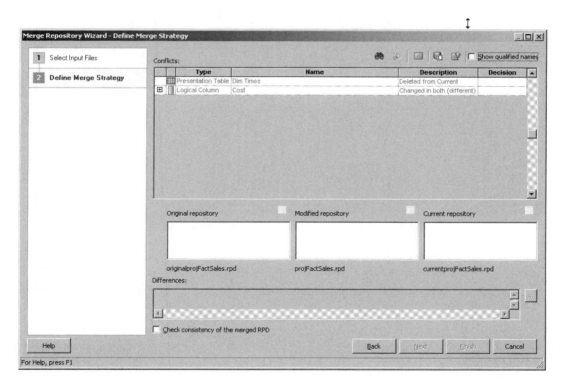

These merge conflict issues can either be dealt with here using this dialog box or later on when Andrew comes to publish his changes to the master repository.

In this instance, Andrew knows that Bill has deleted the Dim Times presentation table in error, so he chooses Modified as the decision for this conflict; he also knows that the change Bill made to the Cost logical column should be kept, and so he chooses Current as the decision for this conflict.

4. Now that the merge conflicts have been resolved, Andrew selects File | Multiuser | Publish to Network, which locks the master repository, merges the changes, and then unlocks it, but without any delay while Andrew sorts out any merge issues, as these have been resolved in the previous step.

5. At this point, to see the history of changes to the master repository, Andrew selects File | Multiuser | History from the Oracle BI Administration menu. In this scenario, the history now shows three checkouts and one conflict resolution.

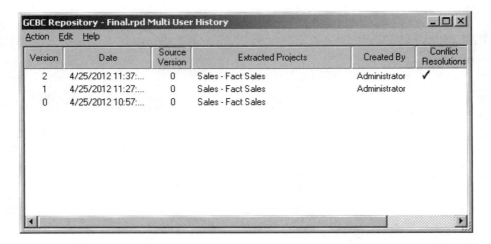

6. Bill Jones, the second developer, completes the process by publishing his local changes to the master repository.

7. Once all development on the master repository is complete, David Armstrong then moves the repository file, plus other metadata items such as application roles and catalog objects, through the test and production environments, as outlined earlier in this chapter.

That concludes the multiuser development process and our look at managing change in your Oracle Business Intelligence system. To conclude our study of the product, let's take a look in the final chapter of the book at the ultimate configuration for Oracle Business Intelligence: Oracle Exalytics In-Memory Machine.

CHAPTER
12

Oracle Exalytics
In-Memory Machine

o conclude this book, we will take a look at the newest member of Oracle's business intelligence product family: Oracle Exalytics In-Memory Machine. Similar to the other "engineered systems" products from Oracle Corporation, Oracle Exadata Database Machine and Oracle Exalogic, Oracle Exalytics In-Memory Machine is a combination of hardware and software designed to create a preintegrated platform for business intelligence.

In addition to this preintegration, Oracle Exalytics also provides new in-memory capabilities to significantly improve the performance of queries, and a new user interface that takes advantage of this improved query performance to provide "speed-of-thought" analytics.

Overview of Oracle Exalytics In-Memory Machine

Oracle Exalytics In-Memory Machine is a product sold by Oracle Corporation that combines hardware and a number of software components, some of which are only available when licensed as part of Oracle Exalytics. Exalytics is primarily marketed as a high-performance query system that works alongside your existing data warehouse and other data sources to provide dashboards, analyses, and other forms of business intelligence.

By using preconfigured and preintegrated hardware and software, the work that a customer has to do in choosing the correct hardware and installing and configuring the components is minimized, and the additional "engineering" elements in the product provide a level of query performance that would be hard to match with off-the-shelf components.

Oracle Exalytics Product Architecture

Oracle Exalytics In-Memory Machine is a product line from Oracle that will adapt and evolve over time, with additional software components and upgraded hardware being introduced from release to release. At the time of this writing, Oracle Exalytics consists of the hardware and software components listed here and shown in Figure 12-1:

- An optimized version of Oracle Business Intelligence Foundation, which at the time of writing is version 11.1.1.6

- In-memory analytics software, including a version of the Oracle TimesTen in-memory database with optimizations for analytic queries, a version of the Oracle Essbase OLAP server with in-memory capabilities, and cache and summary management tools

- In-memory analytics hardware

Hardware Element

As of May, 2012, Oracle Exalytics In-Memory Machine X2-4 is delivered on a Sun Fire X4470 M2 server, which is a 3RU rack-mountable server containing CPUs and storage, with, at the time of writing, the following hardware specification:

- Four Intel Xeon E7-4800 series processors, each with ten cores, for a total of forty cores

- 1TB of RAM

- 3.6TB of raw disk capacity with a high-performance RAID HBA

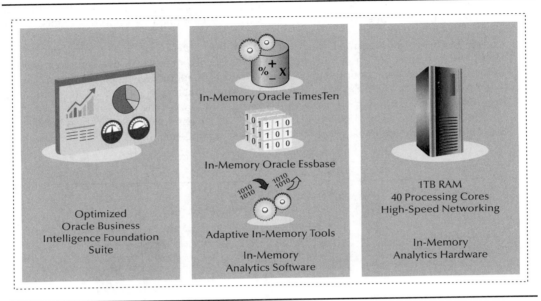

FIGURE 12-1. *Oracle Exalytics high-level product architecture*

- Two quad-data rate (QDR) 40GB/sec InfiniBand ports for connecting to other Exalytics machines in a cluster or Oracle Exadata database servers
- Two 10GB Ethernet ports, typically used to connect to enterprise data sources
- Four 1GB Ethernet ports for client access
- Integrated Lights Out Manager, for connecting to and managing Exalytics even when the machine is powered off

As with other Exa-family products from Oracle Corporation, this hardware specification will probably change over time as more powerful components become available for a similar price.

Software Element

In addition to the hardware element, Exalytics contains several software components that are based on standard shipping versions of Oracle products but including features, when enabled and used in conjunction with Exalytics, that will be only available on that platform.

These components are listed here:

- Oracle BI Foundation, made up of Oracle Business Intelligence Enterprise Edition with Exalytics extensions, Oracle Scorecard and Strategy Management, Oracle Mobile Business Intelligence, and Oracle Essbase
- Oracle TimesTen for Exalytics, an in-memory database with special extensions for performing analytic-style queries
- A set of tools for creating and managing aggregates and caching them in Oracle TimesTen and Oracle Essbase

Figure 12-2 shows the detailed product architecture for Oracle Exalytics, with components allocated to the developer workstation, the Exalytics server, and the supporting database schema.

Oracle Business Intelligence Enterprise Edition Plus Over time, the Oracle Business Intelligence element of Oracle Exalytics will make use of features only available to customers implementing it in conjunction with Exalytics. These may include visualizations available (and suitable for use) only with Exalytics and server features that are predicated on the BI Server and Presentation Server running on hardware with large amounts of memory and CPU.

For the initial release of Exalytics and the 11.1.1.6 release of Oracle Business Intelligence that accompanies it, the only feature of Oracle Business Intelligence that is specific to Exalytics is a

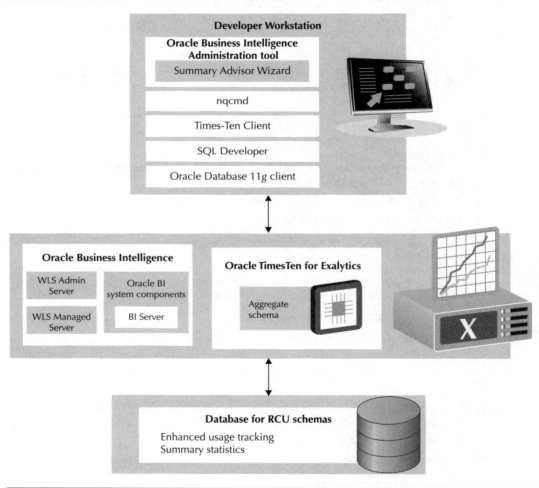

FIGURE 12-2. *Oracle Exalytics detailed product architecture*

new Summary Advisor utility within the BI Administration tool. Other features provided by the BI Presentation Server that are designed for use with Exalytics are also available for use with non-Exalytics installations, such as:

- Auto-complete and auto-suggest prompts
- "Go-less" prompts

With Exalytics installations, these visualizations are automatically enabled as part of the configuration process, while for non-Exalytics installations, they are disabled by default but can be enabled if required. Over time, it is expected that additional visualization features will be added for the Presentation Server that can only be used, from a licensing perspective, with Exalytics, such as:

- High-density, "trellis" and "sparkline"-style charts
- A view suggestion engine

However, these have not been confirmed by Oracle as being in the product as of the time of this writing, and they may appear in other forms, or not appear, as future releases are delivered.

The version of Oracle Business Intelligence Enterprise Edition that accompanies the Exalytics release has a number of extensions available only to Exalytics installations. This is partly due to the fact that their use is practical only on hardware platforms that are as powerful as Exalytics, and partly to Oracle differentiating Exalytics-based Oracle Business Intelligence systems from regular installations.

Oracle TimesTen for Exalytics   The key to the in-memory capabilities of Oracle Exalytics is the Oracle TimesTen for Exalytics in-memory database that it includes.

Oracle TimesTen is a product based on an acquisition Oracle Corporation made several years ago, and it was originally designed to handle very high-frequency inserts and updates to a relational data store, aimed typically at financial trading houses who needed to record and access very large numbers of financial trades. As such, TimesTen was a very powerful in-memory database but mainly aimed at online transaction processing (OLTP) applications.

Oracle TimesTen for Exalytics, which ships as part of the Oracle Exalytics In-Memory machine, however, is aimed at decision-support applications that need to aggregate, and then query, large sets of data. To make this possible, TimesTen was enhanced to create TimesTen for Exalytics, which in turn provides the following analytics-related features:

- Column-based compression, to make queries that scan individual dimension attribute columns much faster, for example, and to enable 5x compression compared to uncompressed data
- Enhancements to TimesTen's SQL aggregation functions, to support the GROUPING SETS, CUBE, and ROLLUP functions commonly used by the Oracle BI Server
- Various query optimization and query process management optimizations to better suit TimesTen to working with the Oracle BI Server

In addition, TimesTen was enhanced with an index advisor that makes recommendations based on a given workload and makes recommendations for indexes that can speed up single table, join, and ORDER BY operations.

As with the Exalytics-specific features provided as part of Oracle Business Intelligence, the features specific to TimesTen for Exalytics are available for use only as part of this product package and when installed on Exalytics hardware. However, unlike the Oracle Business Intelligence features, no special configuration is needed for TimesTen to enable these features, and it is up to the customer to ensure that they use these Exalytics features only on the Exalytics platform.

Oracle Essbase Server   Oracle Essbase Server, part of Oracle BI Foundation and also available stand-alone, is included in the Exalytics platform as well. Essbase in this release has also been enhanced to include in-memory features, including:

- Improvements to overall storage-layer performance
- Enhancements to parallel operations
- An enhanced MDX syntax
- An enhanced, high-performance MDX engine

These in-memory enhancements are general to Essbase and are available to all customers, regardless of whether they license the Exalytics platform or now; however, they were designed to be used with Exalytics-class hardware and may not provide the same degree of performance benefit on non-Exalytics hardware. Essbase on Exalytics does also provide some features exclusive to the platform that permit greater concurrency matching capabilities in the hardware platform, but their details are outside the scope of this book.

How Does Oracle Exalytics Work?

Now that you understand the fundamentals behind Oracle Exalytics In-Memory Machine, in practice how does it work? Much of how Exalytics works is the same as with generic Oracle Business Intelligence systems, except that it is hosted on a high-performance, multicore system with larger-than-usual amounts of memory available. However, features such as in-memory storage of aggregates and the new, high-density low–response time user interface require you to use additional product components not normally available in non-Exalytics systems.

Connectivity to Source Databases, Including Oracle Exadata

As with regular Oracle Business Intelligence systems, Exalytics-based systems generate physical source system queries in response to analyses included in interactive dashboards. These physical queries are generated in query languages such as SQL and MDX, and are sent to the underlying source systems, which in turn return data to Oracle Business Intelligence. Oracle BI then displays the results to the user in their web browser, mobile device, or other channel.

However, in addition to this detail-level access, Exalytics also has access to a cache of in-memory aggregates stored in either Oracle TimesTen or Oracle Essbase, as shown in Figure 12-3.

When processing a query, the Oracle BI Server component within Oracle Business Intelligence uses these in-memory aggregates to speed up the response times of queries that require this type of aggregation.

The additional memory and processing cores in Exalytics will also benefit queries that use detail-level data but need to combine data sources or perform post-retrieval processing of data using the Oracle BI Server and other components.

In addition, the InfiniBand connections available with the Exalytics hardware make it possible to retrieve detail-level data from Exadata systems very quickly, giving you the ability to combine

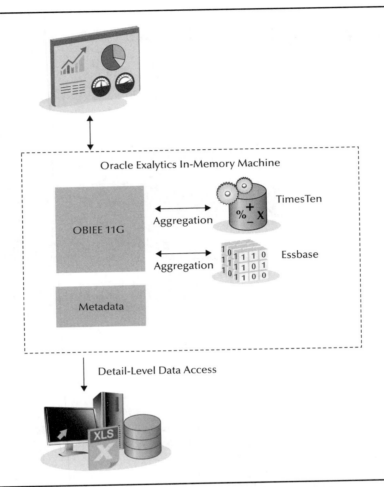

FIGURE 12-3. *Oracle Exalytics data flow*

the ability of Exadata to sort through and filter large volumes of detail-level data with Exalytics'
ability to handle aggregated data in-memory.

Using the Summary Advisor to Create In-Memory Aggregates

A feature in the Oracle BI Administrator tool only available for Exalytics-enabled installations of
Oracle Business Intelligence is the Summary Advisor. The Summary Advisor uses a record of
previous query executions to generate recommendations for aggregates, which are then created in
the TimesTen in-memory database to make similar queries run faster in the future.

Figure 12-4 shows the Summary Advisor recommending a set of aggregates based on a historic
workload, which can then be used to speed up the response time of queries that later on use the
same aggregation.

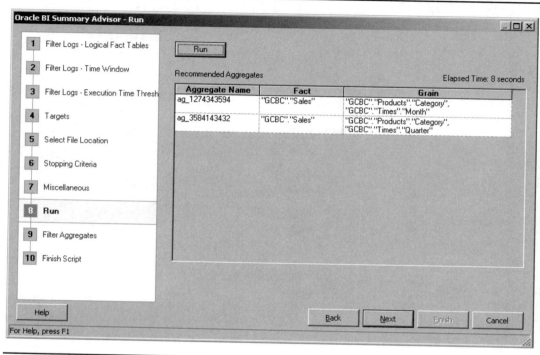

FIGURE 12-4.   *The Oracle BI Summary Advisor*

To enable the Summary Advisor, you first need to configure usage tracking for your system (detailed in Chapter 6), which in the 11.1.1.6 release of Oracle Business Intelligence populates two database tables, one of which now records the physical SQL for a given query and additional information about the granularity (level of detail) of the query. Once this is enabled, you then need to configure the Oracle BI Server to make use of these tables, along with an additional table used to store the recommendations generated by the Summary Advisor.

Once the Summary Advisor is configured, you then use it interactively to first recommend and then generate scripts for aggregates for your system. After this initial recommendation, you can run the scripts to generate the aggregates and run other scripts, either to refresh these aggregates or generate a fresh set of recommendations based on queries subsequently run on your system.

We will look in more detail at how the Oracle BI Summary Advisor is used later in this chapter.

Analyzing Data Using the Exalytics User Interface
In addition to the "back-end" features in Exalytics, there are two features involving prompts that were introduced with the 11.1.1.6 release that are enabled by default with Exalytics installations, and they can be enabled for non-Exalytics installations as well.

For releases prior to 11.1.1.6 and by default with non-Exalytics installations, prompts have two buttons associated with them labeled Apply and Reset. When you select a new value with these types of prompt, the value does not get applied until you click the Apply button. These buttons are removed for Exalytics installations so that the value is applied as soon as you change it, providing a much faster interface for users exploring the dashboard. Figure 12-5 shows a typical dashboard using this type of prompt.

In addition, auto-suggest and auto-complete features are enabled for prompts when used as part of Oracle Exalytics, displaying for users a list of suggested values for a prompt setting as soon as they start typing the prompt value into the prompt's text box. This feature is disabled by default for non-Exalytics installations, but it can be enabled through settings in the BI Presentation Server's configuration file. The following illustration shows the auto-suggest prompt feature in action.

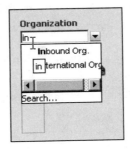

See Chapter 6 for details on prompts that have had the Apply and Reset buttons disabled and how they are used in dashboards, and see the *Oracle Fusion Middleware System Administrator's Guide for Oracle Business Intelligence Enterprise Edition 11g Release 1 (11.1.1)* for details on how to enable auto-suggest and auto-complete prompts for non-Exalytics systems.

FIGURE 12-5. *A prompt with the Apply and Reset buttons removed*

Installing and Initially Configuring Exalytics

As an engineered system sold and supported by Oracle Corporation, Oracle Advanced Customer Support (ACS) Services will have carried out for you the initial installation of your Exalytics system, including the installation of the software element of the package.

Typically, either they or the customer will have downloaded the latest versions of Oracle Business Intelligence, Oracle TimesTen, and Oracle Essbase and installed them to a standard file system location using a script that will also enable the Exalytics-specific features such as the Summary Advisor and changes to prompt behavior.

The specifics of this installation process will no doubt change from release to release, but at a high level the process carried out by Oracle ACS Services will include

- Physically installing the Exalytics hardware and connecting it to your network

- Creating the BIPLATFORM and MDS schemas in your database using the Repository Creation Utility

- Installing the Oracle WebLogic, Oracle Business Intelligence, Oracle TimesTen, and Oracle Essbase software

- Enabling the Oracle Business Intelligence software for Exalytics features

- Creating an initial TimesTen database and configuring its connectivity to the Oracle BI Server component

- Setting up the Integrated Lights Out Management server so that you can remotely administer and reboot the server

Exalytics Post-Installation Tasks

After this initial installation process, you will still need to carry out a number of tasks that are specific to your particular use of the server. These include

- Downloading and installing the Oracle BI client tools to your workstation, together with the TimesTen client software and Oracle SQL*Developer

- Importing the Usage Tracking and Summary Statistics tables into your repository, and then enabling the BI instance for usage tracking

- Creating a connection in your repository to the TimesTen database

We will now take a look at the tasks that you will need to perform post-installation from Oracle ACS Services, starting with downloading and installing the Oracle BI Administration tool.

Example: Downloading and Installing the Oracle BI Administration Tool

Oracle Exalytics is always installed on a Linux operating system, but to make use of the Oracle BI Administration tool you will also need access to a Microsoft Windows–based environment. This may take the form of a virtual machine environment on your Exalytics server (created using, for example, Oracle VirtualBox), or you might install the client tools on a workstation or other Microsoft Windows–based environment.

The client installer for the Oracle BI Administration tool can be accessed from the Oracle Business Intelligence dashboard, where it can be downloaded to a Windows-based environment and then installed. To access the installer file, log into Oracle Business Intelligence and then, from the Home page, navigate to the bottom of the page. Within the Get Started section, click the drop-down menu next to the Download BI Desktop Tools link.

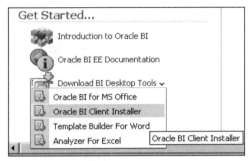

When the list of download links are displayed, select Oracle BI Client Installer and then download and install the software into your Microsoft Windows environment. Selecting the client installer in this way ensures that the version of the Oracle BI Administration tool that you install is matched with the version of Exalytics that you are working with.

See Chapter 2 for more details on the client tools installation for Oracle Business Intelligence.

Example: Configuring the Repository to Add Physical Metadata for Usage Tracking and Summary Advisor, and Creating a Repository Connection to the TimesTen Server

Now that your Oracle Business Intelligence is configured to connect to your Oracle TimesTen database and you have enabled the Exalytics features in the Oracle BI Server and Oracle BI Presentation Server, you can now configure your Oracle BI Repository so that you can make use of the Summary Advisor in order to start creating some in-memory aggregates.

As repository settings are specific to each individual Oracle BI Repository, you will need to do this for every repository (RPD file) that you wish to use with these in-memory features. Performing this configuration involves importing two sets of physical database metadata items into the repository:

- Metadata for the usage tracking and summary management tables in the BIPLATFORM schema

- Metadata, or at least a defined physical database and accompanying connection pool, for the Oracle TimesTen in-memory database so that you can reference it when creating aggregates using the Summary Advisor

To configure the repository to reference the Usage Tracking and Summary Advisor tables used by the Oracle BI Summary Advisor, follow these steps:

1. From your Microsoft Windows environment, start the Oracle BI Administration tool and connect to your repository either online or offline.

2. With the Oracle BI Repository open, select File | Import | Metadata.

3. When the Import Metadata dialog box is open, enter the connection details to your BIPLATFORM schema.

4. When the list of tables whose metadata is available for import is shown, select the S_NQ_ ACCT and S_NQ_SUMMARY_ADVISOR tables and click Finish to complete the metadata import and close the Import Metadata dialog box.

5.   Navigate to the physical layer of the Oracle BI Repository and check that these two tables are now listed as physical objects. Make a note, for the next step in the configuration process, of the physical database, schema and table names, and the name of the connection pool used to connect to the BIPLATFORM schema.

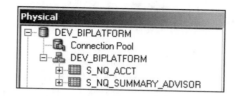

6.   Close the repository file.

The next step is to create a connection in your repository to the TimesTen in-memory database that you configured earlier. Unfortunately, you cannot import metadata for ODBC connections defined only through the Oracle Business Intelligence odbc.ini file, and therefore you will have to use a more roundabout route to set up the connection:

1.   Open the Oracle BI Repository again, either online or offline, and this time navigate to the physical layer of the repository.

2.   Right-click in the physical layer and select New | Database.

3.   In the Database dialog box, enter **TT_AGGR_STORE** as the name, and select TimesTen V11 as the database type.

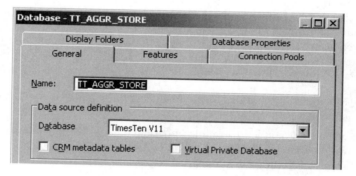

4.   Now right-click the new database entry in the physical layer and select New Object | Connection Pool. When the Connection Pool dialog box is shown, call the connection pool **TT_AGGR_STORE**, select TimesTen ODBC 3.5 as the call interface, and enter the username and password you defined earlier (for example, aima/aima) for the shared logon.

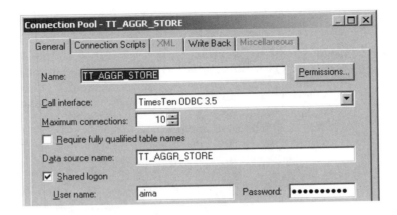

Example: Testing the Connection to the TimesTen Database   To test this connection to the TimesTen database and to help you view and work with the contents of it, you will need to configure your Windows environment so that it also can connect to the TimesTen database. This involves installing the TimesTen client software onto your Windows environment, creating an ODBC data source to the TimesTen database, and then using a tool such as Oracle SQL*Developer to test the connection and optionally view and create tables in TimesTen.

To perform these tasks, follow these steps:

1. Obtain and then install the Oracle TimesTen client software on your Windows environment.

2. Select Start | Settings | Control Panel from the Windows Start menu, and then select Administrative Tools | Data Sources (ODBC). Using the ODBC Data Source Administrator dialog box, create a new system data source name (DSN) using the TimesTen Client driver.

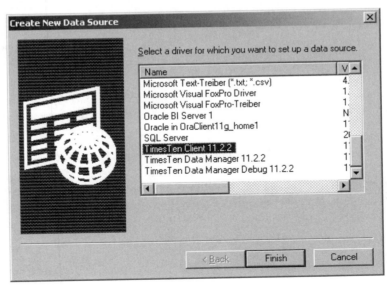

3. When the Oracle TimesTen Client DSN Setup dialog box is displayed, enter the following details:

Client DSN: TT_AGGR_STORE
Description: DSN for connecting to Exalytics in-memory database
Server Name: [*server name for your Exalytics server*]
Server DSN: TT_AGGR_STORE [*select by clicking the Refresh button*]
User ID: aima
Password: aima [*amend as appropriate*]

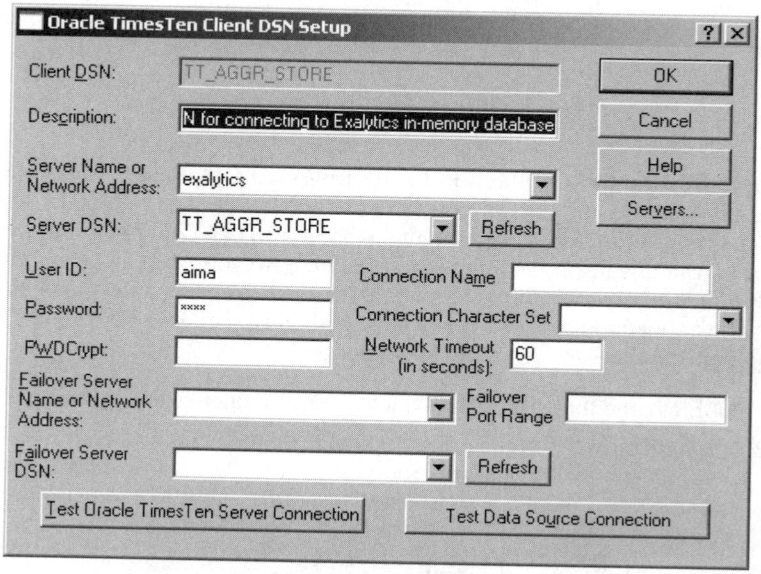

4. To test this connection, click the Test Oracle TimesTen Server Connection button, followed by the Test Data Source Connection button, and ensure that all tests are shown as having succeeded.

Now that the TimesTen client DSN on the Windows environment is configured correctly, you can use Oracle SQL*Developer to connect to the TimesTen database and view the current contents. To do this, follow these steps:

1. Install a recent build of Oracle SQL*Developer that has the ability to connect to TimesTen databases.

2. Start SQL*Developer and, within the Connections pane, click the New Connection button. In the New / Select Database Connection dialog box, enter the connection details for your TimesTen database; for example:

Connection Name: TT_AGGR_STORE
Username: aima
Password: aima

Select the TimesTen tab, and then select or enter the following values:

DSN: User specified
Connection type: Client/server
Connection string: DSN=TT_AGGR_STORE;

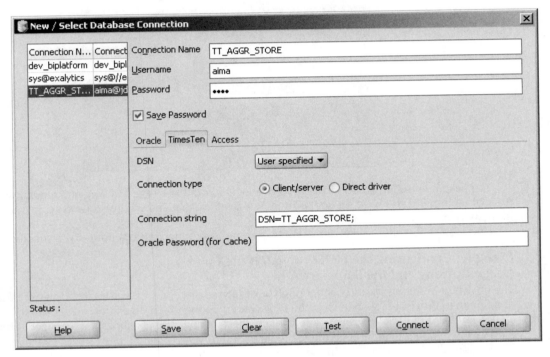

3. Click Save to save the connection.

You can now use this connection to view the tables in the TimesTen database. To do this, with the connection now defined, click the plus (+) icon next to this connection in the list of connections. This will allow you to view the list of tables, indexes, views, and other items in the database.

Initially, this database will be empty; to test connectivity from the Oracle BI Repository, create a new, dummy table called TABLE1 with one column called COLUMN1 within the TimesTen database. Add one row of data to it so that you have some sample data in the TimesTen database.

Finally, go back to the Oracle BI Administration tool, and add this table to the TT_AGGR_STORE physical database using these steps:

1. Right-click the TT_AGGR_STORE physical database, and select New Object | Physical Schema.

2. When prompted, call the physical schema **AIMA**.

3. Now right-click the new AIMA physical schema and select New Physical Table.

4. In the Physical Table dialog box, create the physical table with the same name and column definition as the dummy table you created in the TimesTen database a moment ago using Oracle SQL*Developer.

5. Right-click this new table and select View Data. If the connectivity is set up correctly, you should see a data grid with the one row of data you previously entered into the dummy TimesTen table.

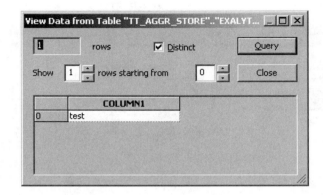

You have now set up your repository to connect to both the Usage Tracking and Summary Advisor tables, and you have set up the TimesTen database that you will use later on to create in-memory aggregates.

Click Test to test your connection, and check that the connection is reported as a success.

Example: Configuring the NQSConfig.INI file for Usage Tracking and the Summary Advisor

The final step in setting up and configuring your Exalytics system is to register the Usage Tracking and Summary Advisor table names in the BI Server component's configuration files. From the 11.1.1.6 release of Oracle Business Intelligence, these configuration settings are managed through a JMX MBean rather than through manual editing of the NQSConfig.INI file, and for Exalytics installations the process involves providing details of the Summary Statistics table as well as the usual Usage Tracking table used when configuring "standard" usage tracking.

To enable usage tracking and summary statistics for an Exalytics installation of Oracle Business Intelligence, follow these steps:

1. Using your web browser, log into Fusion Middleware Control using the credentials of an administrative user.

2. When the Fusion Middleware Control home page opens, expand the WebLogic Domain folder in the left-hand navigation tree menu, and then drill down until you see an entry for AdminServer under the bifoundation_domain heading. Right-click this entry and select System MBean Browser.

3. With the System MBean Browser displayed, select Application Defined MBeans | oracle .biee.admin | Domain: bifoundation_domain.

4. Lock the domain so that other administrators cannot make configuration changes while you perform these steps. To do this, expand the BIDomain folder, select the BIDomain MBean (where *group*=Service), and then select the Operations tab. To lock the domain, click the "lock" link, and then click the Invoke and Return buttons when prompted.

5. Now, expand the BIDomain.BIInstance.ServerConfiguration folder, and then select the BIDomain.BIInstance.ServerConfiguration MBean. Ensure that the Attributes tab is selected, and you will see a number of attributes names, descriptions, and values displayed in a table. Check that the UsageTrackingCentrallyManaged parameter's value is set to true. If it is set to false, then usage tracking needs to be configured as described previously (by manually editing the NQSConfig.INI file) or by setting it to true and managing as described in the next few steps.

6. Using this table, set the following parameters using the values appropriate for your system; for example:

> SummaryAdvisorTableName: "20 - RCU"."BIRCU_BIPLATFORM".
> "S_NQ_SUMMARY_ADVISOR"
> SummaryStatisticsLogging: YES
> UsageTrackingConnectionPool: "20-RCU"."RCU CP"
> UsageTrackingDirectInsert: true
> UsageTrackingEnabled: true
> UsageTrackingPhysicalTableName: "20 -RCU"."BIRCU_BIPLATFORM".
> "S_NQ_ACCT"

System MBean Browser

Application Defined MBeans: BIDomain.BIInstance.ServerConfiguration   [Apply] [Revert]

⊞ **Show MBean Information**

Attributes	Operations	Notifications

	Name	Description	Access	Value
12	stateManageable	If true, it indicates that this MBean provides State Management capabilities as defined by JSR-77.	R	false
13	statisticsProvider	If true, it indicates that this MBean is a statistic provider as defined by JSR-77.	R	false
14	SummaryAdvisorTableName	Physical Summary Advisor Statistics table in RPD	RW	"20 - RCU"."BIRCU_BIPLATFORM"."S_NQ_SUMMARY_
15	SummaryStatisticsLogging	Enable Summary Statistics Logging (YES, NO, or LOG_OUTER_JOINT_QUERIES_ONLY)	RW	YES
16	SystemMBean	If true, it indicates that this MBean is a System MBean.	R	false
17	UsageTrackingCentrallyManaged	Centrally manage Usage Tracking attributes	RW	true
18	UsageTrackingConnectionPool	Connection Pool for Usage Tracking Table	RW	"20 - RCU"."RCU CP"
19	UsageTrackingDirectInsert	Direct Inserts on the Usage Tracking table	RW	true
20	UsageTrackingEnabled	Enable Usage Tracking	RW	true
21	UsageTrackingPhysicalTableName	Physical Usage Tracking table in RPD	RW	"20 - RCU"."BIRCU_BIPLATFORM"."S_NQ_ACCT"

7. Once done, click Apply to save your changes.

8. Now, to commit your changes and release the lock on the domain, return to the BIDomain MBean where *group*=Service under oracle.biee.admin, Domain:bifoundation_domain, and BIDomain. Select the Operations tab and click the topmost "commit" link. Once done, click Invoke and then Return.

9. You have now finished with the System MBean browser. To restart your Oracle BI instance and start using the new configuration settings, including summary statistics, click the Business Intelligence | coreapplication menu item in the left-hand menu tree, select the Overview tab, and then click the Restart All button.

Using the Oracle BI Summary Advisor to Create Aggregates in the Oracle TimesTen In-Memory Database

One of the major features of the Exalytics platform is the ability to create and store aggregates in the TimesTen in-memory database, and the tool that you use to create and maintain these aggregates is the Oracle BI Summary Advisor, part of the Oracle BI Administration tool. This utility uses an extended set of usage tracking data to determine which aggregates should be created, and then allows you to select from them and create scripts that, when executed, create and refresh them.

To use the Summary Advisor, you must have set up usage tracking on your system and generated some usage tracking data by running some analyses and dashboards.

Example: Running the Summary Advisor for the First Time

Now that usage tracking is set up and you have some data in the Usage Tracking tables, let's run through the creation of our first in-memory aggregates using the Oracle BI Summary Advisor.

When you run the Oracle BI Summary Advisor, you use a series of steps to specify a scope that the utility uses when considering what aggregates to recommend to improve the performance of your system. It uses this scope to recommend a set of aggregates that are then implemented by running a script in a similar way to the Aggregate Persistence Wizard. In the future, you can either run this script again to refresh the aggregates or you can rerun the Summary Advisor to generate a fresh set of recommendations.

In this example, we will use the GCBC Repository – Simple for Summary Advisor.rpd repository within your sample data that contains a single business model and subject area based around the GCBC Repository used earlier in the book. To ensure compatibility with the Summary Advisor, the following logical dimensions have been removed, as they cannot be used with the Oracle BI Summary Advisor or the Aggregate Persistence Wizard (detailed in Chapter 5):

- Level-based logical dimensions with ragged or skip-level hierarchies (the "Stores" dimension)
- Value (parent-child)–based logical dimensions (the "Staff" dimension)

In addition to this business model and subject area, and their corresponding physical layer objects, there are also physical layer objects for the TimesTen in-memory database schema and the Usage Tracking and Summary Advisor tables used by the Summary Advisor tool. Figure 12-6 shows the repository prior to running the Oracle BI Summary Advisor.

To generate in-memory aggregates using the Oracle BI Summary Advisor, follow these steps:

1. Open the Oracle BI Administrator tool and connect to your repository online. Ensure that there are no unsaved or unselected objects in the repository, and that you are the only developer working online with the repository for the duration of this task.

2. From the menu, select Tools | Utilities | Oracle BI Summary Advisor | Execute.

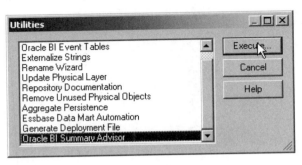

3. When the Oracle BI Summary Advisor – Filter Logs – Logical Fact Tables dialog box is shown, select the fact table(s) that you would like to include in the summary generation process.

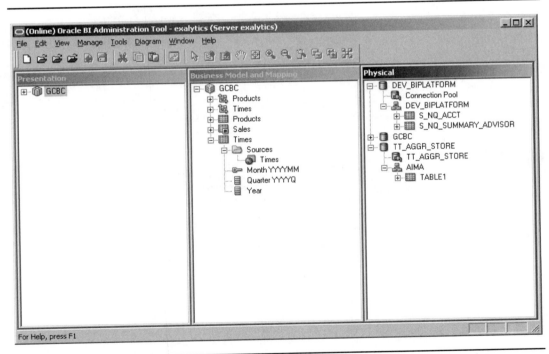

FIGURE 12-6. *The Oracle BI Repository prior to running the Oracle BI Summary Advisor*

4.   Click Next to proceed.

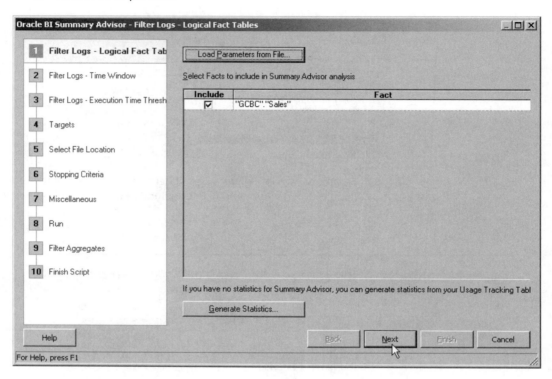

NOTE
*If you have recently upgraded to the release of Oracle Business
Intelligence required for Exalytics but have usage tracking data
available from earlier releases, then the Generate Statistics button at
the bottom of this dialog box can take this data and enhance it so
that it can be used with the Oracle BI Summary Advisor. To do this,
though, the Summary Advisor will need to execute queries using the
Impersonate feature, and you will therefore have to ensure that the
user credentials you use have the Impersonate User privilege granted
to them.*

5. The Oracle BI Summary Advisor – Filter Logs – Time Window dialog box will then be shown. If required, enter start and end dates for the advisor to consider when recommending aggregates, and then click Next to proceed.

6. In the Oracle BI Summary Advisor – Filter Logs – Execution Time Threshold dialog box, you can specify the minimum elapsed time for queries that should be considered when recommending your aggregates. By default this setting is set to zero, which means that all queries will be included in the analysis leading up to the aggregate recommendation.

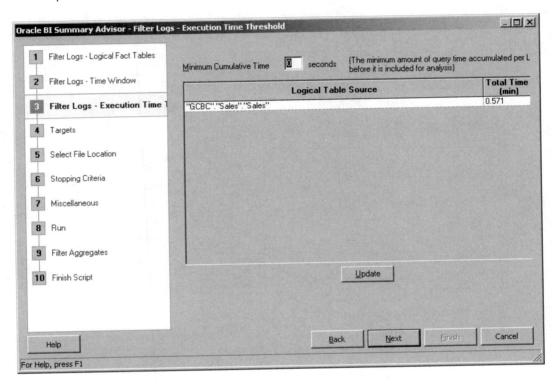

7. In the Oracle BI Summary Advisor – Targets dialog box, use the Database Schema and Connection Pool drop-down lists to select the Oracle TimesTen schema for which you imported metadata into the repository. Use the Capacity (MB) setting to indicate how much disk space is available in this database for the aggregates you wish to create.

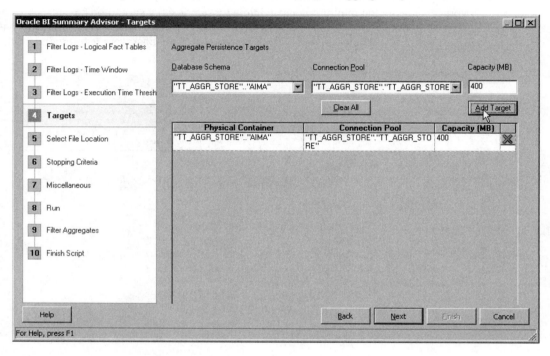

8. Click Add Target and then click Next to proceed.

9. The Oracle BI Summary Advisor – Select File Location dialog box will then be displayed. Use the Browse button to navigate to a directory on your workstation (for example, c:\ summary_advisor_scripts) and enter the filename that the advisor should use when creating the aggregate creation script (for example, agg_wiz.sql), then press Next to proceed.

10. In the Oracle BI Summary Advisor – Stopping Criteria dialog box screen, enter a maximum run time for the advisor to consider which aggregates to recommend, or leave the value at 0 to give it unlimited time.

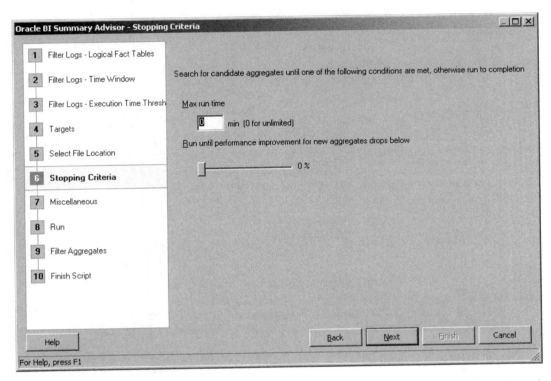

Similarly, use the slider to determine how long the advisor should run before the projected performance improvement for aggregates drops below a certain percentage. Again, leave this figure at 0 to place no restrictions on this process, and click Next.

11. The final choice you have to make is on the Oracle BI Summary Advisor – Miscellaneous dialog box. Use this to select the maximum size of any single aggregate, and optionally click the Browse button to create an XML file containing these settings, which you can make use of if you run the Summary Advisor again at a later date.

12.   Click Next.

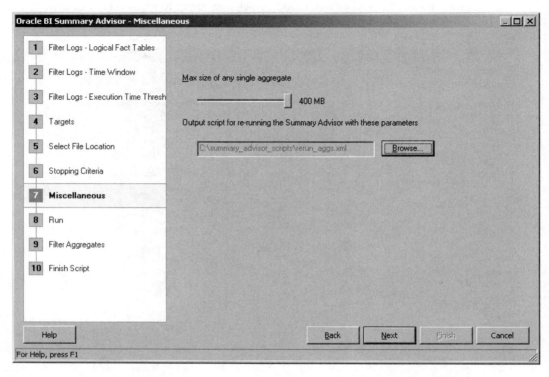

13.   In the Oracle BI Summary Advisor – Run dialog box, click the Run button, and the Summary Advisor will begin generating your list of aggregate recommendations.

In this instance, the Oracle BI Summary Advisor has recommended three aggregates, based on the history of queries found in the Usage Tracking tables and the choices made earlier in the process.

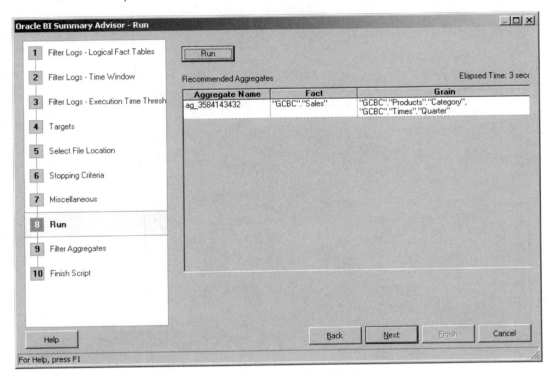

14. Click Next.

15. In the Oracle BI Summary Advisor – Filter Aggregates dialog box, you can remove selected aggregates from the recommendation list or leave them as they are.

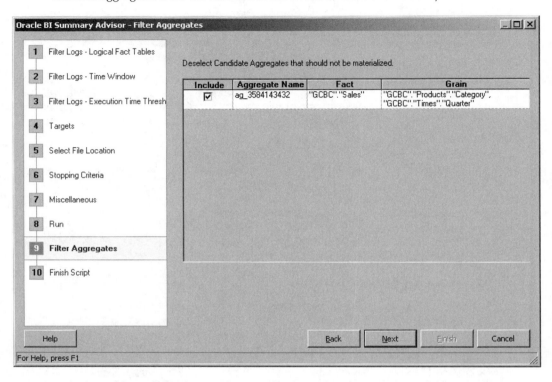

16. Click Next to move to the final dialog box, and then click Finish to close the Summary Advisor once you are done.

At this point, you have generated the script that will create the in-memory aggregates, but you have not run it. To do so, you will use the nqcmd.exe utility that provides a command-line interface to the Oracle BI Server.

To run the script generated by the Oracle BI Summary Advisor, follow these steps:

1. Start a command-line session on either the workstation or on the Exalytics server (after first copying the script to the server), and change the directory to the one hosting the nqcmd.exe utility, like this:

```
cd "c:\Program Files\Oracle Business Intelligence Enterprise Edition Plus
Client\oraclebi\orahome\bifoundation\server\bin"
```

2. Run the nqcmd.exe utility using the following parameters:

nqcmd.exe –d [*ODBC data source name*] –u [*administration username*] –p
[*administration password*] –s [*script name*]

For example:

```
nqcmd.exe -d exalytics -u biadmin -p welcome1 -s
c:\summary_advisor_scripts\agg_wiz.sql
```

3. The script will then execute and may take several minutes to complete successfully. After completion, you will see a report similar to the following one, which details the aggregates that were created and whether any errors were incurred during the process:

```
C:\Program Files\Oracle Business Intelligence Enterprise
Edition Plus Client\oraclebi\orahome\bifoundation\server\bin>
nqcmd.exe -d exalytics -u biadmin
-p welcome1 -s c:\summary_advisor_scripts\agg_wiz.sql
-------------------------------------------
            Oracle BI ODBC Client
            Copyright (c) 1997-2011 Oracle Corporation, All rights re-
served
-------------------------------------------
delete aggregate
"TT_AGGR_STORE".."AIMA"."ag_3584143432"
delete aggregates
"TT_AGGR_STORE".."AIMA"."ag_3584143432"
Statement execute succeeded

create aggregates

"ag_3584143432"
  for "GCBC"."Sales"("Cost","Margin","Revenue",
"Amount Sold","Target Amount Sold"
)
  at levels ("GCBC"."Products"."Category", "GCBC"."Times"."Quarter")
  using connection pool "TT_AGGR_STORE"."TT_AGGR_STORE"
  in "TT_AGGR_STORE".."AIMA"
create aggregates
"ag_3584143432"
  for "GCBC"."Sales"("Cost","Margin","Revenue"
,"Amount Sold","Target Amount Sold"
)
  at levels ("GCBC"."Products"."Category", "GCBC"."Times"."Quarter")
  using connection pool "TT_AGGR_STORE"."TT_AGGR_STORE"
  in "TT_AGGR_STORE".."AIMA"
Statement execute succeeded
Processed: 2 queries
```

If any errors are reported during the execution of the script, check the NQQuery.log and NQServer.log log files to determine the cause of the error, and then either rerun the Oracle BI Summary Advisor to create a new script or just rerun the script if this is sufficient.

Verifying the Use of the In-Memory Aggregate Cache

Assuming that you have run the script created by the Oracle BI Summary Advisor with no errors, you can now check that the aggregate tables were created correctly. You can verify the process in three ways:

- You can use Oracle SQL*Developer to check that the aggregate tables in the TimesTen database have been created correctly.

- You can use the Oracle BI Administrator tool to check that aggregate physical layer objects and business model logical table sources have been created as expected.

- You can run some test analyses, with query logging enabled to level 2 or above, to check that the Oracle BI Server makes use of the aggregates when appropriate.

Example: Verifying the Creation of Aggregates in the TimesTen Database

Running the script generated by the Oracle BI Summary Advisor should lead to aggregate tables being created in the TimesTen in-memory database. To check that these tables have been created, and then populated as expected, you can use Oracle SQL*Developer to connect to and then verify these tables.

To verify the tables in the Oracle TimesTen in-memory database, follow these steps:

1. On the workstation that you used to create the aggregates, start Oracle SQL*Developer.

2. If you have not done so already, create a new connection to the Oracle TimesTen database that holds your aggregates.

3. Connect to the TimesTen database, and then click the Tables entry in the tree menu to view the list of tables within the database. You should see a number of tables with SA_ prefixes (for dimension tables) and AG_ prefixes (for fact tables).

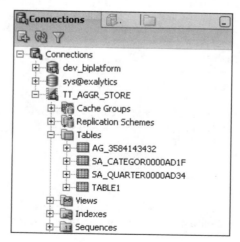

If you do not have at least one AG_ table, check the logs and rerun the process again, as this indicates that the process has not completed successfully. To check that these tables have been correctly populated, click one of the tables and select the Data tab to view the aggregated data in the table.

	PRODUCT_CA0000ACD3	COST0000ACE7	MARGIN0000ACE8	REVENUE0000ACE9
1	Bread	204	1039.5	435.8
2	Bread	38	256.04	84.7
3	Drinks	68.25	1894.6	130.12
4	Drinks	43.5	1218.29	72.29
5	Gifts	69	320.59	100.94
6	Gifts	25	125.43	30.98
7	Snacks	12	194.12	23.96
8	Snacks	70	876.47	145.82

dev_biplatform   TT_AGGR_STORE   **AG_3584143432**

Columns | Data | Indexes | Aging attributes | SQL

Sort... | Filter: ___ | Actions...

Example: Verifying the Addition of Aggregates to the Oracle BI Repository

In addition to creating and populating tables in the TimesTen database, the script that creates your in-memory aggregates also adds entries to the Oracle BI Repository for the physical aggregate tables and the logical table sources that reference them. To check that these have been created as expected, do the following:

1. Using the Oracle BI Administration tool, open your repository online. (This should be the repository that was referenced by the Oracle BI Summary Advisor, and the script it generated is the one you ran in the previous examples.)

2. Navigate to the physical layer of the repository and locate the physical database that represents your TimesTen database. Open the schema that was specified earlier as the target for your aggregates (for example, AIMA), and check that there are new physical objects within the schema that correspond to the TimesTen tables that you verified in the previous steps.

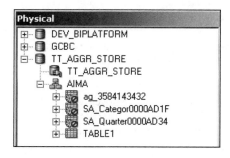

3. Move to the business model and mapping layer of the repository, and check that logical tables within the business model now have new logical table sources that correspond to these new physical layer objects.

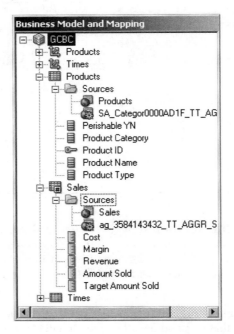

Over time, as you create more aggregates using the Oracle BI Summary Advisor, you will see more physical layer objects being added to the repository along with accompanying logical table sources, and you will see old ones being removed when they are no longer appropriate.

Example: Checking the Query Log for Appropriate Use of Aggregate Sources

Once you are happy that the aggregates recommended by the Oracle BI Summary Advisor have been created and registered as expected, you can run a test analysis to check that they are being used correctly.

To do this, you will first enable query logging (if this is not already in place) and then rerun the analyses that were used previously to generate usage tracking data so that you can subsequently check the query log and verify that the new in-memory aggregates are being used as expected:

1. If you have not done so already, use the Oracle BI Administration tool to enable level 2 query logging. To do this, start the Oracle BI Administration tool and open your repository online; then select Manage | Identity from the menu.

2. When the Identity Manager dialog box is shown, select Action | Set Online User Filter, and enter a wildcard, an asterisk (*), as the filter.

3. Double-click the user that you will use to check the aggregates and click the Check Out button when requested. When the User dialog box is then shown, set the logging level

to 2 or higher so that the physical SQL generated by the BI Server is added to the NQQuery.log file when analyses are executed.

4. Once complete, save your repository so future sessions initiated by this user account have query logging enabled.

5. Now log into the Oracle Business Intelligence web site as this user. Either create a new analysis using the subject area columns selected when creating usage tracking data, or select Open from the menu to open a previously created analysis.

6. Execute the analysis so that entries are added to the NQQuery.log file.

7. Using a text editor on the server running Exalytics, open the NQQuery.log file, usually found at:

```
[middleware_home]\instances\instance1\diagnostics\
logs]OracleBIServerComponent\coreapplication_obis1\nqquery.log
```

Look for entries at the end that reference the TimesTen database; for example:

```
[2011-11-06T07:48:07.000+00:00] [OracleBIServerComponent]
[TRACE:2] [USER-18] []
[ecid: b701e4484f1c0f05:-2aae2eed:133776339a5:-8000-0000000000000170]
[tid: 40498940] [requestid: 2f1c0001]
[sessionid: 2f1c0000] [username: biadmin]
--------------------
Sending query to database named TT_AGGR_STORE (id: <<4080>>)
, connection pool named TT_AGGR_STORE,
logical request hash fc11066b, physical request hash 664fe62c: [[
select distinct T44718.Revenue0000ACE9 as c1,
     T44705.Product_Ca0000ACD3 as c2,
     T44710.Quarter_YY0000AD05 as c3
from
     SA_Quarter0000AD34 T44710,
     SA_Categor0000AD1F T44705,
     ag_3584143432 T44718
where
  ( T44705.Product_Ca0000ACD3 = T44718.Product_Ca0000ACD3
and T44710.Quarter_YY0000AD05 = T44718.Quarter_YY0000AD05 )
```

If you do not see entries in the log file that reference the TimesTen database, check that query caching is not enabled, and repeat the previous two steps to ensure that aggregate tables were referenced in the physical SQL query as expected.

Refreshing and Adapting the In-Memory Aggregates

After you have created your initial aggregates, you can refresh them in one of two ways:

- You can rerun the same script that you ran previously to refresh the same aggregates with updated source data.
- You can rerun the Oracle BI Summary Advisor to create fresh recommendations, optionally making use of the XML configuration file you saved earlier that contains the settings you previously chose when running the Summary Advisor.

To rerun the same aggregate creation script as created previously, use the nqcmd.exe command-line utility and specify the same aggregate creation script as before; for example:

```
nqcmd.exe -d exalytics -u biadmin -p welcome1 -s
c:\summary_advisor_scripts\agg_wiz.sql
```

The script will then delete the existing aggregate tables specified by this script and re-create them using data in the source system, which may potentially have been updated since you ran the script originally.

To generate a fresh set of recommendations based on the same criteria you originally provided the Oracle BI Summary Advisor, run the Summary Advisor again. When the initial dialog box is shown, you can click the Load Parameters From File button on the first page to read the settings you previously specified when running the Summary Advisor, adjusting them afterward as appropriate.

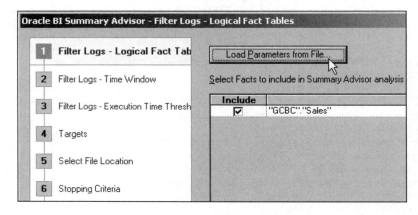

Finally, now that you have generated your in-memory aggregate tables, you can test them out using your dashboard and analyses.

So, that ends our look at Exalytics and the Oracle Business Intelligence platform as a whole. I hope you've enjoyed our journey through the architecture, data layer, dashboards, and administration of the Oracle BI platform, and you're now ready to create your own system, practicing the techniques you've learned in this book.

Index

D

F

GET YOUR FREE SUBSCRIPTION
TO *ORACLE MAGAZINE*

Oracle Magazine is essential gear for today's information technology professionals. Stay informed and increase your productivity with every issue of *Oracle Magazine*. Inside each free bimonthly issue you'll get:

- Up-to-date information on Oracle Database, Oracle Application Server, Web development, enterprise grid computing, database technology, and business trends
- Third-party news and announcements
- Technical articles on Oracle and partner products, technologies, and operating environments
- Development and administration tips
- Real-world customer stories

If there are other Oracle users at your location who would like to receive their own subscription to *Oracle Magazine*, please photocopy this form and pass it along.

Three easy ways to subscribe:

① **Web**
Visit our Web site at **oracle.com/oraclemagazine**
You'll find a subscription form there, plus much more

② **Fax**
Complete the questionnaire on the back of this card and fax the questionnaire side only to **+1.847.763.9638**

③ **Mail**
Complete the questionnaire on the back of this card and mail it to **P.O. Box 1263, Skokie, IL 60076-8263**

ORACLE

Want your own FREE subscription?

To receive a free subscription to *Oracle Magazine*, you must fill out the entire card, sign it, and date it (incomplete cards cannot be processed or acknowledged). You can also fax your application to +1.847.763.9638. **Or subscribe at our Web site at oracle.com/oraclemagazine**

O **Yes, please send me a FREE subscription** *Oracle Magazine*.   O No.

O From time to time, Oracle Publishing allows our partners exclusive access to our e-mail addresses for special promotions and announcements. To be included in this program, please check this circle. If you do not wish to be included, you will only receive notices about your subscription via e-mail.

O Oracle Publishing allows sharing of our postal mailing list with selected third parties. If you prefer your mailing address not to be included in this program, please check this circle.

If at any time you would like to be removed from either mailing list, please contact Customer Service at +1.847.763.9635 or send an e-mail to oracle@halldata.com. If you opt in to the sharing of information, Oracle may also provide you with e-mail related to Oracle products, services, and events. If you want to completely unsubscribe from any e-mail communication from Oracle, please send an e-mail to: unsubscribe@oracle-mail.com with the following in the subject line: REMOVE [your e-mail address]. For complete information on Oracle Publishing's privacy practices, please visit oracle.com/html/privacy/html

X	
signature (required)	date

name   title

company   e-mail address

street/p.o. box

city/state/zip or postal code   telephone

country   fax

Would you like to receive your free subscription in digital format instead of print if it becomes available? O Yes   O No

YOU MUST ANSWER ALL 10 QUESTIONS BELOW.

① WHAT IS THE PRIMARY BUSINESS ACTIVITY OF YOUR FIRM AT THIS LOCATION? (check one only)
- □ 01 Aerospace and Defense Manufacturing
- □ 02 Application Service Provider
- □ 03 Automotive Manufacturing
- □ 04 Chemicals
- □ 05 Media and Entertainment
- □ 06 Construction/Engineering
- □ 07 Consumer Sector/Consumer Packaged Goods
- □ 08 Education
- □ 09 Financial Services/Insurance
- □ 10 Health Care
- □ 11 High Technology Manufacturing, OEM
- □ 12 Industrial Manufacturing
- □ 13 Independent Software Vendor
- □ 14 Life Sciences (biotech, pharmaceuticals)
- □ 15 Natural Resources
- □ 16 Oil and Gas
- □ 17 Professional Services
- □ 18 Public Sector (government)
- □ 19 Research
- □ 20 Retail/Wholesale/Distribution
- □ 21 Systems Integrator, VAR/VAD
- □ 22 Telecommunications
- □ 23 Travel and Transportation
- □ 24 Utilities (electric, gas, sanitation, water)
- □ 98 Other Business and Services _____

② WHICH OF THE FOLLOWING BEST DESCRIBES YOUR PRIMARY JOB FUNCTION? (check one only)

CORPORATE MANAGEMENT/STAFF
- □ 01 Executive Management (President, Chair, CEO, CFO, Owner, Partner, Principal)
- □ 02 Finance/Administrative Management (VP/Director/ Manager/Controller, Purchasing, Administration)
- □ 03 Sales/Marketing Management (VP/Director/Manager)
- □ 04 Computer Systems/Operations Management (CIO/VP/Director/Manager MIS/IS/IT, Ops)

IS/IT STAFF
- □ 05 Application Development/Programming Management
- □ 06 Application Development/Programming Staff
- □ 07 Consulting
- □ 08 DBA/Systems Administrator
- □ 09 Education/Training
- □ 10 Technical Support Director/Manager
- □ 11 Other Technical Management/Staff
- □ 98 Other

③ WHAT IS YOUR CURRENT PRIMARY OPERATING PLATFORM (check all that apply)
- □ 01 Digital Equipment Corp UNIX/VAX/VMS
- □ 02 HP UNIX
- □ 03 IBM AIX
- □ 04 IBM UNIX
- □ 05 Linux (Red Hat)
- □ 06 Linux (SUSE)
- □ 07 Linux (Oracle Enterprise)
- □ 08 Linux (other)
- □ 09 Macintosh
- □ 10 MVS
- □ 11 Netware
- □ 12 Network Computing
- □ 13 SCO UNIX
- □ 14 Sun Solaris/SunOS
- □ 15 Windows
- □ 16 Other UNIX
- □ 98 Other
- 99 □ None of the Above

④ DO YOU EVALUATE, SPECIFY, RECOMMEND, OR AUTHORIZE THE PURCHASE OF ANY OF THE FOLLOWING? (check all that apply)
- □ 01 Hardware
- □ 02 Business Applications (ERP, CRM, etc.)
- □ 03 Application Development Tools
- □ 04 Database Products
- □ 05 Internet or Intranet Products
- □ 06 Other Software
- □ 07 Middleware Products
- 99 □ None of the Above

⑤ IN YOUR JOB, DO YOU USE OR PLAN TO PURCHASE ANY OF THE FOLLOWING PRODUCTS? (check all that apply)

SOFTWARE
- □ 01 CAD/CAE/CAM
- □ 02 Collaboration Software
- □ 03 Communications
- □ 04 Database Management
- □ 05 File Management
- □ 06 Finance
- □ 07 Java
- □ 08 Multimedia Authoring
- □ 09 Networking
- □ 10 Programming
- □ 11 Project Management
- □ 12 Scientific and Engineering
- □ 13 Systems Management
- □ 14 Workflow

HARDWARE
- □ 15 Macintosh
- □ 16 Mainframe
- □ 17 Massively Parallel Processing
- □ 18 Minicomputer
- □ 19 Intel x86(32)
- □ 20 Intel x86(64)
- □ 21 Network Computer
- □ 22 Symmetric Multiprocessing
- □ 23 Workstation Services

SERVICES
- □ 24 Consulting
- □ 25 Education/Training
- □ 26 Maintenance
- □ 27 Online Database
- □ 28 Support
- □ 29 Technology-Based Training
- □ 30 Other
- 99 □ None of the Above

⑥ WHAT IS YOUR COMPANY'S SIZE? (check one only)
- □ 01 More than 25,000 Employees
- □ 02 10,001 to 25,000 Employees
- □ 03 5,001 to 10,000 Employees
- □ 04 1,001 to 5,000 Employees
- □ 05 101 to 1,000 Employees
- □ 06 Fewer than 100 Employees

⑦ DURING THE NEXT 12 MONTHS, HOW MUCH DO YOU ANTICIPATE YOUR ORGANIZATION WILL SPEND ON COMPUTER HARDWARE, SOFTWARE, PERIPHERALS, AND SERVICES FOR YOUR LOCATION? (check one only)
- □ 01 Less than $10,000
- □ 02 $10,000 to $49,999
- □ 03 $50,000 to $99,999
- □ 04 $100,000 to $499,999
- □ 05 $500,000 to $999,999
- □ 06 $1,000,000 and Over

⑧ WHAT IS YOUR COMPANY'S YEARLY SALES REVENUE? (check one only)
- □ 01 $500, 000, 000 and above
- □ 02 $100, 000, 000 to $500, 000, 000
- □ 03 $50, 000, 000 to $100, 000, 000
- □ 04 $5, 000, 000 to $50, 000, 000
- □ 05 $1, 000, 000 to $5, 000, 000

⑨ WHAT LANGUAGES AND FRAMEWORKS DO YOU USE? (check all that apply)
- □ 01 Ajax
- □ 02 C
- □ 03 C++
- □ 04 C#
- □ 13 Python
- □ 14 Ruby/Rails
- □ 15 Spring
- □ 16 Struts
- □ 05 Hibernate
- □ 06 J++/J#
- □ 07 Java
- □ 08 JSP
- □ 09 .NET
- □ 10 Perl
- □ 11 PHP
- □ 12 PL/SQL
- □ 17 SQL
- □ 18 Visual Basic
- □ 98 Other

⑩ WHAT ORACLE PRODUCTS ARE IN USE AT YOUR SITE? (check all that apply)

ORACLE DATABASE
- □ 01 Oracle Database 11*g*
- □ 02 Oracle Database 10*g*
- □ 03 Oracle9*i* Database
- □ 04 Oracle Embedded Database (Oracle Lite, Times Ten, Berkeley DB)
- □ 05 Other Oracle Database Release

ORACLE FUSION MIDDLEWARE
- □ 06 Oracle Application Server
- □ 07 Oracle Portal
- □ 08 Oracle Enterprise Manager
- □ 09 Oracle BPEL Process Manager
- □ 10 Oracle Identity Management
- □ 11 Oracle SOA Suite
- □ 12 Oracle Data Hubs

ORACLE DEVELOPMENT TOOLS
- □ 13 Oracle JDeveloper
- □ 14 Oracle Forms
- □ 15 Oracle Reports
- □ 16 Oracle Designer
- □ 17 Oracle Discoverer
- □ 18 Oracle BI Beans
- □ 19 Oracle Warehouse Builder
- □ 20 Oracle WebCenter
- □ 21 Oracle Application Express

ORACLE APPLICATIONS
- □ 22 Oracle E-Business Suite
- □ 23 PeopleSoft Enterprise
- □ 24 JD Edwards EnterpriseOne
- □ 25 JD Edwards World
- □ 26 Oracle Fusion
- □ 27 Hyperion
- □ 28 Siebel CRM

ORACLE SERVICES
- □ 28 Oracle E-Business Suite On Demand
- □ 29 Oracle Technology On Demand
- □ 30 Siebel CRM On Demand
- □ 31 Oracle Consulting
- □ 32 Oracle Education
- □ 33 Oracle Support
- □ 98 Other
- 99 □ None of the Above

08014004